Government and Not-for-Profit Accounting

Concepts and Practices

Government and Not-for-Profit Accounting

EIGHTH EDITION

Concepts and Practices

Michael H. Granof
University of Texas, Austin

Saleha B. Khumawala
University of Houston

Thad D. Calabrese
New York University

Daniel L. Smith
New York University

EDITORIAL DIRECTOR Michael McDonald
EXECUTIVE EDITOR Lise Johnson
EDITORIAL MANAGER Judy Howarth
CONTENT MANAGEMENT DIRECTOR Lisa Wojcik
CONTENT MANAGER Nichole Urban
SENIOR CONTENT SPECIALIST Nicole Repasky
PRODUCTION EDITOR Indirakumari S.
COVER PHOTO CREDIT © Dima Sobko / Shutterstock

This book was set in 10/12 TimesLTStd-Roman by SPi Global and printed and bound by Quad Graphics

Founded in 1807, John Wiley & Sons, Inc. has been a valued source of knowledge and understanding for more than 200 years, helping people around the world meet their needs and fulfill their aspirations. Our company is built on a foundation of principles that include responsibility to the communities we serve and where we live and work. In 2008, we launched a Corporate Citizenship Initiative, a global effort to address the environmental, social, economic, and ethical challenges we face in our business. Among the issues we are addressing are carbon impact, paper specifications and procurement, ethical conduct within our business and among our vendors, and community and charitable support. For more information, please visit our website: www.wiley.com/go/citizenship.

ISBN: 978-1-119-49583-3 (PBK)
ISBN: 978-1-119-49584-0 (EVALC)

Library of Congress Cataloging-in-Publication Data

Names: Granof, Michael H., author. | Khumawala, Saleha B., author. | Calabrese, Thad D., author. | Smith, Daniel L., 1980- author.
Title: Government and not-for-profit accounting : concepts and practices / Michael H. Granof, Saleha B. Khumawala, Thad D. Calabrese, Daniel L. Smith.
Description: Eighth edition. | Hoboken, NJ : John Wiley & Sons, 2018. | Includes index. |
Identifiers: LCCN 2018038961 (print) | LCCN 2018041784 (ebook) | ISBN 9781119495789 (Adobe PDF) | ISBN 9781119495819 (ePub) | ISBN 9781119495833 (pbk.)
Subjects: LCSH: Finance, Public—United States—Accounting. | Finance, Public—Accounting—Standards—United States. | Nonprofit organizations—United States—Accounting. | Nonprofit organizations—Accounting—Standards—United States.
Classification: LCC HJ9801 (ebook) | LCC HJ9801 .G7 2018 (print) | DDC 657/.835—dc23
LC record available at https://lccn.loc.gov/2018038961

SKY10031935_121021

Michael H. Granof

In Memory of

My mother, Diana S. Granof (a teacher)

My father, David H. Granof (a CPA)

Saleha B. Khumawala

To my husband Basheer and

children Naaz and Mubeen

Thad D. Calabrese

To my wife Abby and children

Benjamin, Noah, and Ethan

Daniel L. Smith

To my wife Tara and

daughter Madison

Preface

The objectives of this, the eighth edition of Government and Not-for-Profit Accounting: Concepts and Practices, remain unchanged from those of the previous editions. Above all, the text aims to make students aware of the dynamism of government and not-for-profit accounting and of the intellectual challenges that it presents.

Government and not-for-profit accounting has changed dramatically in the past few decades. For certain, the nature of governments and not-for-profit organizations and the transactions in which they engage will continue to evolve further in the future. Therefore, so too must the corresponding accounting.

For the most part, the accounting issues faced by governments and not-for-profit organizations are far less tractable than those encountered by businesses. Businesses have the luxury of directing attention to profits—a metric that is relatively easy to define—inasmuch as the overriding objective of businesses is to earn a profit. Governments and not-for-profit entities, by contrast, have broader, much less clear-cut goals. They must determine not only how to measure their performance but also what to measure. Hence, the accounting profession is almost certain to be dealing with fundamental questions throughout the professional careers of today's students, and the pace of rapid change will continue unabated.

Obviously, we intend for this text to inform students of current accounting and reporting standards and practices—those with which they might need to be familiar in their first jobs. More important, however, we want to ensure that they are aware of the reasons behind them, their strengths and limitations and possible alternatives. We are more concerned that students are prepared for their last jobs rather than their first. The text aspires to lay the intellectual foundation so that the students of today can become the leaders of tomorrow—the members of the standard-setting boards, the partners of CPA firms, the executives of government and not-for-profit organizations, and the members of legislative and governing boards.

Courses in government and not-for-profit accounting are just one element of an accounting program and, indeed, of a college education. Therefore, we expect that this text will lead not only to an awareness of the issues of government and not-for-profit accounting, but also to a greater understanding of those in other areas of accounting. Almost all issues addressed in this text—for example, revenue and expense recognition, asset and liability valuation, the scope of the reporting entity, reporting cash flows—have counterparts in business accounting. By emphasizing concepts rather than rules and procedures, we hope that students will gain insight into how and why the issues may have been resolved either similarly or differently in the business sector.

Moreover, we trust that this text will contribute to students' ability to read, write, and "think critically." To that end we have made a special point of designing end-of-chapter problems that challenge students not only to apply concepts that are presented in the text, but also to justify the approach they have taken and to consider other possible methodologies.

Needless to say, many students will use this text to prepare for the CPA exam. We have endeavored to cover all topics that are likely to be tested on the exam—an admittedly difficult goal, however, now that the American Institute of Certified Public Accountants (AICPA) does not publish past exams. We have also included approximately 20 multiple-choice questions in most chapters as well as several other "CPA-type" questions. In addition, this text will be useful to students preparing for the Certified Government Financial Manager exam (CGFM) and other professional certification exams in which matters relating to government and not-for-profits are tested.

The need to update this text was made especially compelling by Governmental Accounting Standards Board (GASB) and Financial Accounting Standards Board (FASB) pronouncements that were either issued or had to be implemented since publication of the seventh edition. GASB issued Statement No. 77, Tax Abatement Disclosures, which are a common policy tool used by state and local governments to encourage certain economic activities. This new statement requires governments disclose their own tax abatement programs as well as those of other governments that affect their tax revenue capacity, and is discussed in Chapter 11. Chapter 9 discusses the new Statement No. 83, Certain Asset Retirement Obligations, which focuses on the retirement of tangible capital assets. Importantly, Statement No. 84, Fiduciary Activities, changed agency and trust funds reporting significantly. Notably, fiduciary funds are now reported in four types of funds, and is discussed in depth in Chapter 10. Further, Statement No. 87, Leases, altered how long-term leases were accounted for on governments' balance sheets. In addition, whereas in previous editions we indicated that in accounting for inventories governments had a choice between a purchases/acquisition basis and a consumption basis, in this edition we show why consistent with GAAP only the consumption method is permissible. Finally, the Government Accountability Office released the 2018 Generally Accepted Government Auditing Standards in July 2018, and Chapter 16 is updated to reflect changes to these audit standards.

Not-for-profit accounting and reporting underwent significant changes since the seventh edition. The FASB implemented a change in recognizing revenues, in *Accounting Standards Codification (ASC) 606, Revenue from Contracts with Customers*. This changes the manner in which exchange transactions are accounted for, although it leaves unchanged the accounting for contributions. Changes to revenue recognition are included in all relevant examples and problems throughout Chapters 12 through 14. FASB Accounting Standards Update (ASU) No. 2016-14 changed the number of donor-restricted categories from three (unrestricted, temporarily restricted, and permanently restricted) to two (without donor restrictions and with donor restrictions) for not-for-profit organizations. These changes are included and explained in Chapter 12. In this same chapter, the new liquidity disclosure requirements are discussed, and a sample illustration is included because financial reports using the new requirement were not available at the time this book was prepared. The standards updates also require all not-for-profit organizations, not just voluntary health and welfare organizations, to report an analysis of their functional expenses and are further discussed in Chapter 12. We also moved all discussions about endowment (including problems) to Chapter 12 from Chapter 10, because the material seemed more germane to not-for-profit entities. In addition to the existing material (which was updated), we added material on accounting for investment gains and losses in endowments; we also specifically added discussion of underwater endowments to the chapter, a topic of special importance following the economic volatility of 2007–2008. Finally, Chapter 12 also discusses the new placed-in-service approach to depreciating donated fixed assets. The health-care sector continues to undergo significant changes, and Chapter 14 updates many of the salient issues and data. It also discusses new community benefit and charity care standards explicitly.

This edition, like previous editions, includes illustrations of actual financial statements, primarily from Charlotte, North Carolina, so that students can observe how information discussed in the text is actually presented to financial statement users. We also continue in this edition to include three or four "Questions for Research, Analysis, and Discussion" to most of the chapters pertaining to state and local governments. Many of these questions were drawn from technical inquiries submitted to the Governmental Accounting Standards Board or the Government Finance Officers Association. These are intended to enrich the typical government and not-for-profit accounting course. Students are, in effect, called on to address the types of issues that are commonly faced by government accountants and their auditors. For most of these questions, students will have to look beyond the text to the standards themselves and to the various interpretative pronouncements and implementation guides published by the GASB. For others, they will have to exercise their own good judgment. For many of the questions, there are no single correct answers. Instructors with whom we spoke found these questions to serve as the basis for spirited class discussions. Hence, we have retained them for this edition.

OTHER SPECIAL FEATURES

CONTINUING PROBLEM

Each chapter dealing with state and local accounting principles includes a "continuing problem," which asks students to select a city, county, or state with a population over 100,000, review its comprehensive annual financial report (CAFR), and answer questions about it. The questions are applicable to the reports of any major municipal government. However, recognizing the advantages of having all students in a class work from the same report, instructors may want to require their students to download the 2017.pdf CAFR of City of Austin either from the website of the text or that of Austin comptroller's office (https://assets.austintexas.gov/financeonline/downloads/cafr/cafr2017.pdf). The solutions manual contains the "answers" to the continuing problem based on the Austin CAFR for fiscal year.

ONLINE CHAPTER

The Chapter "MANAGING FOR RESULTS" is available ONLINE from the text book's website for an in depth coverage of this topic.

COMPUTERIZED ACCOUNTING PRACTICE SETS—KEY FEATURE OF THIS EDITION

PRACTICE SETS

To provide an opportunity for students to get a taste of how accounting is practiced in the "real world," this edition of the text is supplemented by two "practice sets," one dealing with governments, the other with not-for-profit organizations. Each, however, is much more than a conventional bookkeeping exercise. They are built using Excel, so that students can not only learn the nuances of Governmental and nonprofit accounting but also sharpen their skills set with Excel as it is also a basic skill required by employers today and a tool set that they need for the CPA exam.

The practice sets enable students to form a new government or not-for-profit organization from scratch, enter, and post a relatively few summary transactions and prepare complete sets of financial statements (both fund and government-wide for governments and for not-for-profit entity under the new FASB standards). The main goal of the practice sets is to show students how the accounting and recording process fits together and to give the students a sense of accomplishment as they see their individual journal entries leading to a complete set of financial statements.

We have tried to make the recording process as blunder-proof as possible, thereby minimizing the sense of frustration that results when students inevitably make careless recording errors and have to spend an inordinate amount of time locating and correcting them. Accordingly, we give the students a comprehensive set of detailed instructions, including numerous check figures of total balances at the end of several projects and the deliverables required for each project. These instructions and chapter assignments related to the practice sets can be found at the textbook's companion website.

OTHER ACKNOWLEDGMENTS

We are especially grateful for the helpful comments of Professor Terri King, University of Houston, Penelope S. Wardlow, coauthor of *Core Concepts of Government and Not-for-Profit Accounting*, and our very own students, whose insights and ideas have found their way into this edition and have unquestionably improved it. We appreciate the help of Michael Andrada and Tracy Nguyen, who helped us with the computerized practice set and to prepare several tables in the text.

Additional thanks go to the following faculty who offered their helpful feedback and comments during the eight edition review process: Alice Upshaw (West Texas A & M University); Ann Selk (University of Wisconsin–Green Bay); David Jordan (Loyola University, Chicago); David P. Mest (Seton Hall University); John Lord (San Francisco State University); Karen Andrea Shastri (University of Pittsburg); Larita J. Killian (Indiana University at Columbus); Patricia Galetta (College of Staten Island); Patricia A. Johnson (Canisius College). We are also appreciative of Judy Howarth, project manager, Nichole Urban, content management manager, Nicole Repasky, content specialist, and Indirakumari Siva, production editor for their major support in bringing the text book to fruition. Finally, we are deeply indebted to our families for their substantial contribution through love, encouragement, and unwavering support without which this book would not be possible.

S.B.K.
Houston, Texas

M.H.G.
Austin, Texas

T.D.C.
New York, New York

D.L.S.
Newark, DE

Contents

8 Long-Term Obligations 325

9 Business-Type Activities 368

12 Not-for-Profit Organizations 519

CHAPTER 1

The Government and Not-for-Profit Environment

LEARNING OBJECTIVES

After studying this chapter, you should understand:

- The characteristics that distinguish governments and not-for-profit organizations from businesses and the accounting and reporting implications of these characteristics
- Why other characteristics of governments and not-for-profit entities may affect accounting and reporting practices
- The overall purpose of financial reporting in the government and not-for-profit sectors
- The information requirements of the primary users of the financial reports of governments and not-for-profit entities
- The specific objectives of financial reporting, as established by the Governmental Accounting Standards Board (for state and local governments), the Financial Accounting Standards Board (for not-for-profits), and the Federal Accounting Standards Advisory Board (for the federal government), and the obstacles to achieving these objectives within a set of financial statements prepared on a single basis of accounting
- How differences in accounting principles affect financial reporting and thus can have economic consequences
- The institutional arrangements for establishing accounting standards for these entities

Governments and **not-for-profit** organizations have much in common with businesses. However, the differences between the two environments are sufficiently pronounced that business schools have established a separate course in governmental and not-for-profit accounting apart from the usual accounting courses—financial accounting, managerial accounting, auditing, and information systems.

Every accounting issue or problem that affects governments and not-for-profit entities has a counterpart in the business sector. But the distinctions between accounting for governments and not-for-profits and accounting for businesses are so marked that the two disciplines warrant specialized textbooks, separate statements of concepts, and separate accounting principles and practices. As we shall see in this text, some of these differences may be justified by substantive distinctions in the two operating environments. Others are the result of long-standing differences in the traditions, composition, and perspectives of the standard-setting boards—the **Governmental Accounting Standards Board (GASB)**, for

state and local governments; the Federal Accounting Standards Advisory Board (FASAB), for the federal government; and the Financial Accounting Standards Board (FASB), for the private sector, including private (nongovernmental) not-for-profits.

This chapter is divided into eight sections. The first examines the ways in which governments and not-for-profits differ from businesses, and why they require unique accounting principles and practices. The second points out the characteristics of governments and not-for-profits that might *not* distinguish them from businesses, but nevertheless do have significant implications for accounting and reporting. The third contrasts governments and not-for-profits, emphasizing that although they have much in common, they also differ significantly. The next four sections provide an overview of financial reporting for governments and not-for-profits—highlighting key user groups, their information needs, and the resultant objectives of financial reporting—and address the question of whether differences in accounting practices really matter. The last section spotlights the GASB, the FASB, and the FASAB.

In this book, we use the term *not-for-profit* rather than the equally acceptable term *nonprofit*. Not-for-profit differentiates entities that don't intend to earn a profit from those that simply fail to do so.

HOW DO GOVERNMENTS AND NOT-FOR-PROFITS COMPARE WITH BUSINESSES?

Governments and not-for-profits differ from businesses in ways that have significant implications for financial reporting. For the most part, governments and not-for-profits provide services targeted at groups of constituents either advocating a political or social cause or carrying out research or other activities for the betterment of society. The objectives of governments and not-for-profits cannot generally be expressed in dollars and cents, are often ambiguous, and are not easily quantifiable. Moreover, governments and not-for-profits have relationships with the parties providing their resources that are unlike those of businesses.

DIFFERENT MISSIONS

As implied by the designation not-for-profits, the goal of governments and similar organizations is something other than earning profit. A key objective of financial reporting is to provide information about an entity's financial performance during a specified period. The main objective of a typical business is to earn a profit—to ensure that over the life of the enterprise, its owners get a return greater than the amount invested. Accordingly, financial statements that focus on net income are consistent with the entity's main objective. Specifically, an income statement is a report on how well the entity achieved its goals. To be sure, businesses may have objectives that go beyond "the bottom line." They may seek to promote the welfare of their executives and employees, improve the communities in which they are located, and produce goods that will enhance the quality of life. Financial accounting and reporting, however, are concerned almost exclusively with the goal of maximizing either profits or some variant of it, such as cash flows.

The financial reports of governments and not-for-profits can provide information about an organization's inflows (**revenues**) and outflows (**expenditures**) of cash and other resources. As a general rule, an excess of expenditures over revenues, particularly for an extended period of time, signals financial distress or poor managerial performance. However, an excess of revenues over expenditures is not necessarily commendable. An excess of revenues over expenditures may be achieved, for example, merely by reducing the services provided to constituents, which may be at odds with the entity's objectives.

If the financial statements of a government or not-for-profit incorporate only monetary measures, such as dollars and cents, they cannot possibly provide the information necessary to assess the organization's performance. For an organization to report properly on its accomplishments, it must augment its financial statements to include nonfinancial data that relate to its objectives. A school, for example, might include statistics on student achievement, such as test scores or graduation rates. A center for the homeless might present data on the number of people fed or adequately housed.

BUDGETS, NOT THE MARKETPLACE, GOVERN

Governments and not-for-profits are governed mainly by their budgets, not by the marketplace. These organizations control or strongly influence both their revenues and expenditures through the budgetary process. The revenues of a government may be determined by legislative action, and if they are, the government may not be subject to the forces of competition faced by businesses. Those of the not-for-profits, although they cannot be established by legal mandate, may be obtained from contributions, dues, tuition, or user charges—none of which are comparable to the sales revenue of a business.[1]

EXPENDITURES MAY DRIVE REVENUES

Governments and many not-for-profits establish the level of services that they will provide, calculate their cost, and then set tax rates and other fees to generate the revenues required to pay for them. Colleges and universities, unlike businesses, do not set tuition charges at the highest level that the market will bear. Instead, they calculate operating costs; estimate contributions, endowment revenues, and other sources of funds; and then set tuition charges at the rate necessary to cover the shortfall. Similarly, fraternities and sororities calculate their expenditures for housing, food, and social activities, and then set dues and other fees accordingly. In sum, expenditures drive revenues.

Although governments and not-for-profits do not participate in competitive markets, they cannot simply raise revenues without regard to their services or increase taxes without limit. Governments may be constrained by political forces. Universities may have to restrict tuition rates to approximately those of peer schools. Further, some not-for-profits, such as the United Way or organizations that fund medical research, base their expenditures exclusively on their revenues. The more funds they raise, the more they spend.

THE BUDGET, NOT THE ANNUAL REPORT, IS THE MOST SIGNIFICANT FINANCIAL DOCUMENT

For businesses, the annual report is the most significant financial document. A major company's announcement of annual earnings (the preview of the annual report) makes front-page news. By contrast, its annual budget is nothing more than an internal document, seldom made available to investors or the general public.

A government or not-for-profit's release of its annual report is customarily ignored by both organizational insiders and outsiders. Seldom does the report contain surprises, for if revenues and expenditures were markedly different from what were initially budgeted, the entity probably was required to amend the **budget** during the year.

For governments and not-for-profits, the budget takes center stage—properly so, because the budget is the culmination of the political process. It encapsulates almost all the decisions of consequence made by the organization. It determines which constituents give to the entity and which receive; which activities are supported, and which are assessed.

[1] Although market mechanisms are widely thought of as providing a more efficient distribution of goods and services, they can operate only when there can be no "free riders"—parties who are able to obtain the goods or services without paying for them. Many government services, such as police protection, cannot practically be provided only to paying customers. Hence, we must resort to nonmarket mechanisms to allocate resources. See Richard A. Musgrave and Peggy B. Musgrave, *Public Finance in Theory and Practice*, 5th ed. (New York: McGraw-Hill, 1989), Chapter 3, "The Theory of Social Goods," for a discussion of this concept from the perspective of economists.

Because it is so important, the budget, unlike the annual report, is a source of constituent concern and controversy. Government budget hearings often draw standing-room-only crowds to the legislative chambers. The budget debates of religious organizations such as churches and synagogues are frequently marked by fervor more intense than that found in the congregants' worship services.

A government's budget may be backed by the force of law. State and local government officials are ordinarily prohibited from spending more than what was budgeted. Indeed, they can go to jail for severe violations of budgetary mandates. The budget is not a document to be taken casually. In light of the significance of the budget relative to the annual report, it is ironic that the standard-setting agencies focus exclusively on the annual report. Except insofar as governments—such as states—establish rules for cities or other governments within their jurisdiction, or parent not-for-profits—such as national fraternities—set guidelines for local affiliates, budgetary practices are within the discretion of the individual entity. Neither the GASB nor the FASB or FASAB has been granted the kind of statutory authority over budgets that it has over annual reports. As a consequence—which shall be made evident in discussions to follow—annual reports are in fact better than budgets at capturing the economic substance of the transactions and are far less subject to preparer efforts to artificially boost revenues or reduce expenditures.

BUDGETS DRIVE ACCOUNTING AND FINANCIAL REPORTING

Constituents of an organization want information on the extent of adherence to the budget. They want assurance that the organization has not spent more than what was authorized. They want to know whether revenue and expenditure estimates were reliable. The accounting system and the resultant financial reports must be designed to provide that information.

In addition, managers need an accounting system that provides them with ongoing data about whether they are on target to meet budget projections. Even more critically, they need a system that either prevents them from overspending or sets off warning signals when they are about to do so. The budget is a control device, but it requires the support of a complementary accounting and reporting system. Finally, auditors and other parties concerned with the organization's performance require a basis on which to evaluate accomplishments. As will be discussed in subsequent chapters, state-of-the-art budgets establish that basis by indicating not only how much will be spent on a particular activity but also what the activity will achieve.

A postperiod assessment can then focus not only on whether the entity met its revenue and expenditure projections but also, equally important, on whether it attained what was expected of it. Evaluators can then assess organizational efficiency by comparing inputs (such as dollar expenditures) with outcomes (results). The accounting system should be fashioned to facilitate this comparison, ensuring that the organization reports and categorizes both revenues and expenditures in a way that is consistent with the budget. Currently, few governments and not-for-profits have established budgetary and accounting systems to measure and report adequately on the nonmonetary aspects of their performance. However, accounting standard-setting authorities have recognized the importance of performance measures and have taken steps to encourage the entities under their purview to provide them.[2]

NEED TO ENSURE INTERPERIOD EQUITY

Most governments are required by law, and most not-for-profits are expected by policy, to balance their operating budgets. Balanced operating budgets ensure that, in any particular period, revenues cover expenditures and that, as a group, the entity's constituents pay for what they receive. If organizations fail to balance their budgets—and borrow to cover operating deficits—then the cost of benefits enjoyed by the citizens of today must be borne by those of tomorrow.

---

[2] GASB issued Suggested Guidelines for Voluntary Reporting, SEA Performance Information (June 2010). The federal government passed the *Government Performance and Results Act of 1993*.

The concept that constituents pay for the services that they receive and do not shift the burdens to their children has traditionally been labeled as **intergenerational equity**. In recent years, to emphasize that entities should not transfer the costs even to future years, to say nothing of future generations, the term **interperiod equity** has been accepted as more appropriate.

To maintain interperiod equity, the accounting systems of governments and not-for-profits must provide information about whether this objective is being attained. Table 1-1 compares fiscal practices that promote interperiod equity with those that do not.

The concept of interperiod equity does not suggest that governments should never borrow. The prohibition against debt applies only to operating, not capital, expenditures. A government-constructed highway or university-purchased lab equipment will produce benefits over more than one year. It is only fair, therefore, that they be paid for by incorporating debt service costs into the taxes or tuition charges of the citizens or students who will benefit from them.

IN PRACTICE WHY IS STATE AND LOCAL GOVERNMENT ACCOUNTING IMPORTANT?

- There are over 90,000 state and local governments in the United States.
- State and local governments received $1.35 trillion in tax revenues in 2016.*
- Expenditures for state and local governments increased 28.4% to $2.58 trillion from 2006 to 2016. Consumption expenditures were the largest expenditures for state and local governments in 2016 at $1.69 trillion followed by government social benefit payments and Medicaid of $692.6 billion and $574.5 billion respectively.
- Total debt outstanding for state and local governments increased 6.4 percent, from $2.9 trillion in 2012 to $3.1 trillion in 2016.
- Education, the single largest functional category for all governments, employed 11.1 million people, or 57.0 percent of the total number of federal, state, and local government employees.

*Source: *2016 Quarterly Summary of State & Local Tax Revenue Tables*, U.S. Census Bureau.* ***https://www.census.gov/data/tables/2016/econ/qtax/historical.Q4.html***

TABLE 1-1 Fiscal Practices that Promote or Undermine Interperiod Equity

Promote	Undermine
1. Setting aside resources for employee pensions during the years in which the employees provide their services.	1. Paying the pensions of retired employees out of current operating funds.
2. Issuing conventional 30-year bonds to finance the purchase of a new building that is expected to have a useful life of 30 years; repaying the bonds, along with appropriate amounts of interest, over the 30-year period.	2. Financing the purchase of the new building with 30-year zero-coupon bonds that permit the entire amount of principal and interest to be paid upon maturity of the bonds; making no provision to set aside resources for payment of principal and interest on the bonds until the year they mature.
3. Paying the current-year costs of an administrative staff out of current operating funds.	3. Issuing 30-year bonds to finance the current-year operating costs of an administrative staff.
4. Charging payments of wages and salaries made in the first week of the current fiscal year to the previous fiscal year, that in which the employees actually provided their services.	4. Charging wages and salaries applicable to services provided in the last week of the current fiscal year to the following fiscal year, that in which the payments were made.
5. Charging the cost of supplies as expenditures in the year in which they were used rather than when they were purchased.	5. Charging the cost of supplies as expenditures in the year they were purchased, irrespective of the year in which they were used.
6. Recognizing interest on investments in the year in which it is earned, irrespective of when it is received.	6. Recognizing interest in the year in which it is received, irrespective of when it is earned.
7. Setting aside funds each year to pay for an anticipated 20-year renovation of a college dormitory.	7. Paying for an anticipated 20-year renovation of a college dormitory out of current funds in the year the work is performed.

REVENUE NOT INDICATIVE OF DEMAND FOR GOODS OR SERVICES

For competitive businesses, revenues signal customer demand for goods and services. Holding prices constant, the greater the revenues, the greater the demand—an indication that the entity is satisfying a societal need.

In a government or not-for-profit, revenues may not be linked to constituent demand or satisfaction. An increase in tax revenues, for example, tells nothing about the amount or quality of service provided. Therefore, a conventional statement of revenues and expenditures cannot supply information on demand for services. Supplementary information is required.

NO DIRECT LINK BETWEEN REVENUES AND EXPENSES

Just as the revenues of governments and not-for-profits may not be directly linked to customer demand, they may also be unrelated to expenditures. The revenues from donations of a not-for-profit entity may increase from one year to the next, but the change may be unaccompanied by a corresponding increase in the quantity, quality, or cost of services provided. Thus, the *matching concept*—financial accounting's central notion that expenditures must be paired with corresponding revenues—may have a different meaning for governments and not-for-profits than for businesses. Businesses attempt to match the costs of specific goods or services with the revenues that they generate. Governments and not-for-profits, however, can sometimes do no more than associate overall revenues with the broad categories of expenditures they are intended to cover.

CAPITAL ASSETS MAY NEITHER PRODUCE REVENUES NOR SAVE COSTS

Unlike businesses, both governments and not-for-profits make significant investments in assets that neither produce revenues nor reduce expenditures. Therefore, the conventional business practices used to value assets may not be applicable.

According to financial theory, the economic value of an asset is the present or discounted value of the cash inflows that it will generate or the cash outflows that it will enable the entity to avoid. Hence, conventional capital budgeting models specify that in evaluating a potential asset acquisition, the business should compare the present value of the asset's expected cash outflows with its inflows.

Many capital assets of governments and not-for-profits cannot be associated with revenues or savings. The highway or bridge being considered by a state or local government will not yield cash benefits—at least not directly to the government. The proposed college library may enrich the intellectual life of the community, but not the college's coffers. In fact, some governments and not-for-profit "assets," such as historical monuments and heritage sites, may be more properly interpreted as liabilities. Inasmuch as they have to be maintained and serviced, they will consume, rather than provide, resources.

RESOURCES MAY BE RESTRICTED

In contrast to the resources of businesses, many of the assets of government and not-for-profit entities are restricted to particular activities or purposes. As shown in Figure 1-1, for example, a sizable share of one government's revenues may be from other governments and, more than likely, restricted for specific purposes. The federal government may give a state or local government a grant for construction of low-income housing, in which case the award can be used only for low-income housing and not for any other purposes, irrespective of how worthy they might be.

Taxes and membership dues may also be restricted. A city's hotel tax may be dedicated to financing a local convention center or to promoting tourism. A state's gasoline tax may be targeted by law at highway construction and maintenance. A portion of a not-for-profit cemetery association's fees may have to be set aside for the acquisition of new land.

Both governments and not-for-profits need to assure the parties providing the restricted funds that the money is used properly. At the same time, they must show in their financial reports

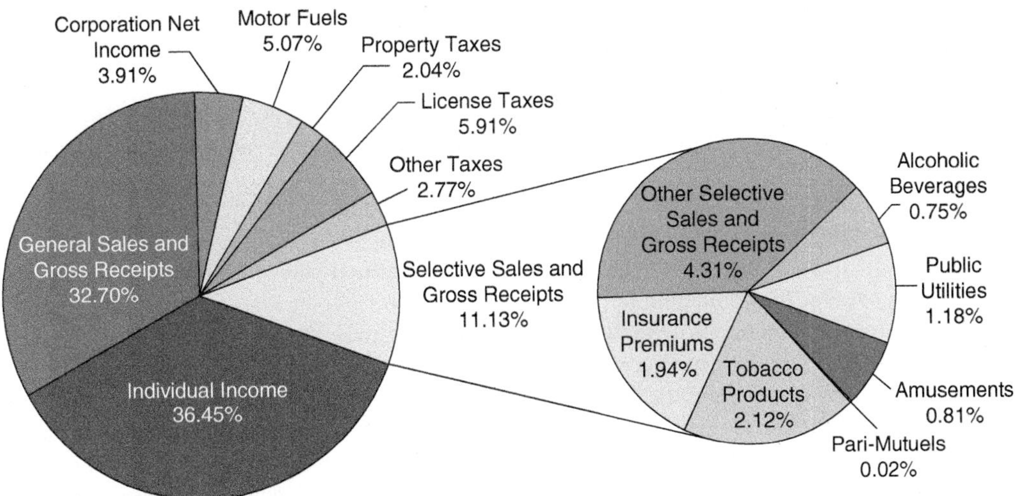

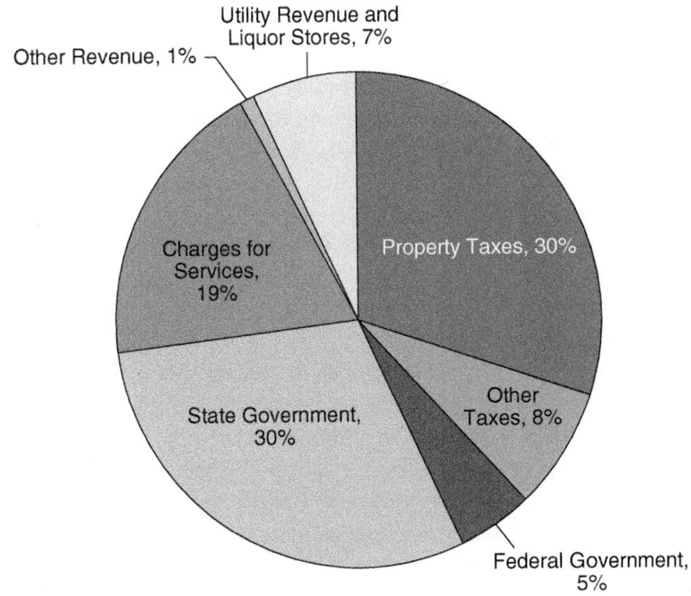

FIGURE 1-1 State and Local Government Revenues by Sources
Source: U.S. Census Bureau. Total State and Local Tax Revenues by Type – Fourth Quarter 2016.

that the restricted resources are unavailable for purposes other than those specified. Therefore, the financial statements must either segregate the restricted from the unrestricted resources or disclose by some other means that some resources can be used only for specific purposes.

As with budgetary mandates, slipups regarding restrictions carry serious consequences. At the very least, they may cause the organization to forfeit past and future awards. Therefore, as with budgets, the organization must design its accounting system so that management is prevented from inadvertently misspending restricted resources. To this end, governments and not-for-profits employ a system of accounting known as **fund accounting**, which is discussed in Chapter 2.

NO DISTINCT OWNERSHIP INTERESTS

Neither governments nor not-for-profits have defined ownership interests like those of businesses. Typically, these entities cannot be sold or transferred. Should they be dissolved, they involve no stockholders or bondholders who are entitled to receive residual resources.

The most obvious financial reporting implication of this distinction is that the mathematical difference between assets and liabilities cannot sensibly be termed *owners' equity*. Some other term is required.

More substantively, however, the distinction suggests that the financial statements of governments and not-for-profits must be prepared from the perspective of parties other than stockholders. (The main groups of statement users will be identified later in this chapter.) Similarly, for certain entities, the distinction implies that there may be less interest in the market values of their resources. Governments do not typically sell their highways and sewers, and few statement users are interested in their market values. Libraries and museums may be able to sell their collections, but may have to use the funds to acquire similar assets. The market values may be of concern only if the entire institution were to be closed and its assets liquidated. Yet, at the same time, market values may be relevant indicators of whether assets are being put to their optimum use. For example, a city might be better off selling an office building located downtown and using the proceeds to acquire property in outlying neighborhoods.

LESS DISTINCTION BETWEEN INTERNAL AND EXTERNAL ACCOUNTING AND REPORTING

In the government and not-for-profit arena, the line between external and internal accounting and reporting is less clear-cut than in the business sector. First, in the business sector, external reports focus on profits. Nevertheless, even in businesses, few organizational units are profit centers in which management controls all the key factors that affect profits. Therefore, internal reports present data on other measures of performance, such as total fixed costs or per-unit variable costs.

In the government and not-for-profit arenas, profit is no more an appropriate measure of performance for external parties than it is for internal departments. The relevant performance measures must be drawn from the organizations' unique goals and objectives and are unlikely to be the same for all user groups.

Second, in business, the budget is an internal document, seldom made available to external parties. In governments and not-for-profits, it stands as the key fiscal document that is as important to taxpayers, bondholders, and other constituencies as it is to managers.

Third, the distinction between internal and external parties in governments and not-for-profits is more ambiguous than it is in business. Taxpayers and organizational members, for example, cannot be categorized neatly as either insiders or outsiders. Although they are not paid employees (and thus, not traditional "insiders"), they may nevertheless have the ultimate say (through either direct vote or elected officers) on organizational policies.

WHAT OTHER CHARACTERISTICS OF GOVERNMENTS AND NOT-FOR-PROFITS HAVE ACCOUNTING IMPLICATIONS?

Governments and not-for-profits have additional characteristics that do not necessarily distinguish them from businesses but have significant accounting and reporting implications.

MANY DIFFERENT TYPES OF GOVERNMENTS AND NOT-FOR PROFITS

Approximately 90,000 local governments currently exist in the United States (Figure 1-2). In common usage, a **municipality** is a village, town, or city. Government specialists, however, use the term to refer also to any other nonfederal government, including school districts, public authorities, and even states.

The number of municipalities may be surprisingly large but consider how many separate governments have jurisdiction over a typical neighborhood. The neighborhood may be part of

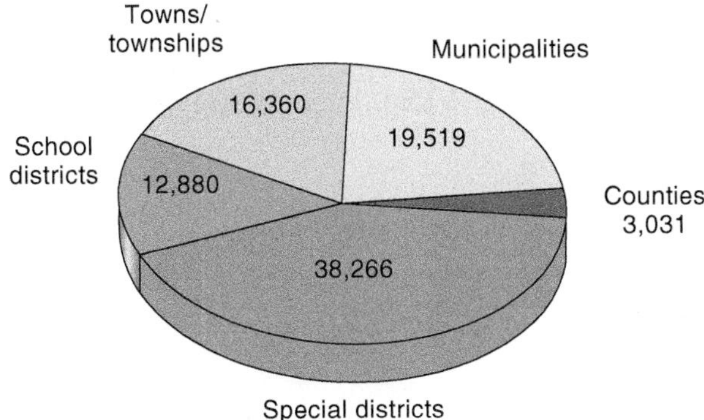

Total = 90,056

- The average number of local government units per state is 1,801, but Illinois has 6,963, whereas Hawaii has only 21.
- Nine states account for slightly less than half of all local government units in the nation.

FIGURE 1-2 Composition of the Local U.S. Government Units
Source: U.S. Census Bureau. 2012. *Census of Governments: Organization components. There are 90,056 Local Governments in the United States.* http://www2.census.gov/govs/cog/g12_org.pdf

a town, several of which constitute a township. The township may be part of a county, which, in turn, may be a subdivision of a state. Further, the neighborhood school may be administered by an independent school district. The local hospital may be governed by a hospital district, the water and sewage system by a utility authority, and the bus system by a transportation authority. The community college may be financed by a community college district, and the nearby airport may be managed by an independent airport authority.

Each category of government will likely differ from others in the services it provides, the type of assets it controls, its taxing and borrowing authority, and the parties to which it is accountable. Moreover, even governments in the same category may vary in the services they provide. New York and Dallas are among the nation's ten largest cities. But New York operates its own school system, whereas Dallas's schools are under the control of an independent school district. San Antonio—Texas's third-largest city—provides electric service to its residents, whereas in Houston—the state's largest city—the citizens receive their power from a privately owned utility.

As shown in Table 1-2, not-for-profits are also many in number: over one million in the United States. These entities constitute what is sometimes referred to as the **independent, or third, sector**. Their diversity limits the suitability of a common accounting model (i.e., set of accounting and reporting principles) for any single, or even for any particular type of, government or not-for-profit entity. Assuming that comparability among entities is a desirable characteristic of financial reporting, standard-setting authorities face a policy question. To what extent should they adopt common standards for all governments and not-for-profits, as opposed to common standards only for entities of the same type? When entities are similar, common standards may promote comparability. When the entities are not, common standards may, like ill-fitting clothes, distort reality. As will be discussed in succeeding chapters, rule-making authorities have issued one set of common principles for all not-for-profits and a separate set for all state and local governments.

SHORT-TERM FOCUS OF MANAGERS AND ELECTED OFFICIALS

U.S. managers of both corporations and public enterprises have been accused of sacrificing the long-term welfare of their organizations for short-term benefits—sometimes for their organizations and other times only for themselves. This failing is said to be especially pronounced in governments.

TABLE 1-2 Dimensions of the Not-for-Profit ("Independent") Sector

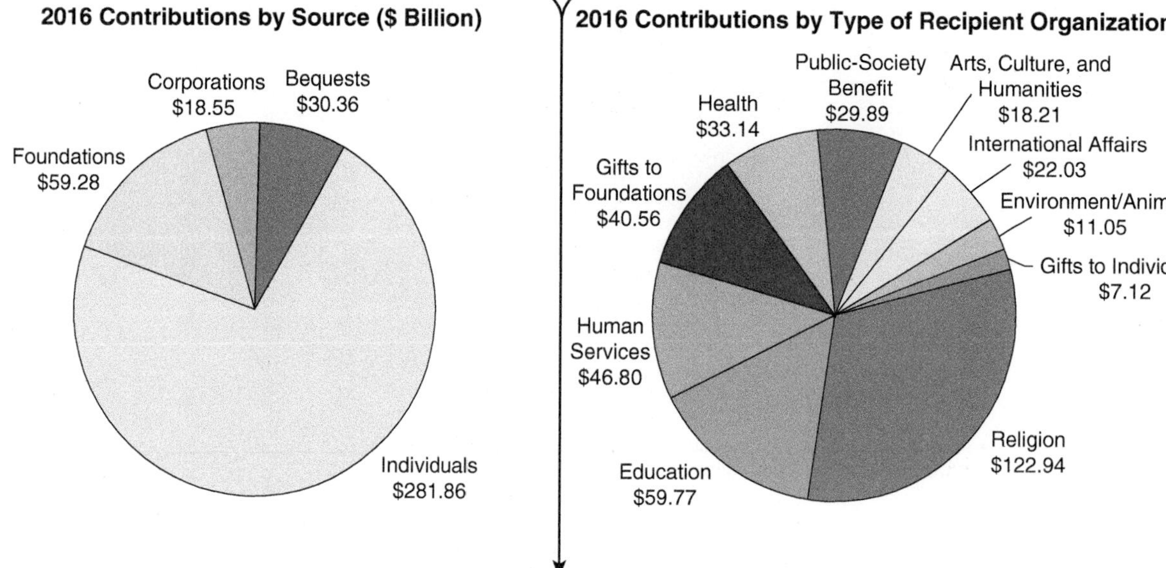

All figures are rounded. Total may not be 100%.
*Foundation Center and *Giving USA* estimate.

Total contributions for 2016: $391.5 billion

Current Highlights

The nonprofit sector in America includes hospitals, museums, schools, homeless shelters, houses of worship, symphony orchestras, research centers, youth groups, and many other organizations in every community across the nation. These charitable groups are sometimes collectively referred to as the "independent sector" to emphasize their unique role in society, distinct from business and government.

Size and Scope[a]	
Number of not-for-profit organizations registered with IRS (2016)	1.21 million
Total nonprofit sector revenues (2013)	$1.74 trillion
Percentage of wages and salaries paid in the United States by NFP (2013)	8.9%
Giving 2016	
Annual contributions from private sources[b]	$391 billion
Giving as a percentage of GDP[c]	2%
Volunteering 2016[d]	
Percentage of Americans who volunteered	24.9%
Number of Americans who volunteered	62.6 million
Number of hours volunteered on average annually per person	52
Value of volunteered time	$1.5 trillion

[a] https://www.councilofnonprofits.org/sites/default/files/documents/2017-Fast-Facts-About-the-Nonprofit-Sector.pdf
[b] https://www.nptrust.org/philanthropic-resources/charitable-giving-statistics/
[c] https://www.bea.gov/newsreleases/national/gdp/gdpnewsrelease.htm
[d] https://www.nationalservice.gov/vcla

Government officials typically face election (at the national level) every even-numbered year. In the periods preceding an election, they have powerful incentives both to avoid unpopular measures, such as tax increases and to make their government look fiscally sound. They can use budgetary and accounting techniques to make cosmetic improvements to their entity's budget or annual report. Many of these activities will be described throughout the text.

Standard-setting authorities, the accountants and auditors of individual organizations, and statement users need to be aware that budgets and financial statements can be intended to mislead. They must resist and adjust for any biases. The difficulty they face, however, is that the motives for slanting budgets and statements in a particular direction vary from situation to situation. In some circumstances, government officials may artificially overestimate revenues (or underestimate expenditures) to avoid cuts in services or increases in taxes. In others, however, they may do the opposite so they can take credit at year-end for managerial effectiveness by presenting better-than-anticipated results.

GOVERNMENTS AND NOT-FOR-PROFITS ENGAGED IN BUSINESS-TYPE ACTIVITIES

Many governments and not-for-profit organizations engage in business-type activities. Cities, for example, operate electric utilities, trash collection services, and golf courses. Colleges and universities operate bookstores, cafeterias, and computer repair services. Environmental organizations publish and sell magazines.

Even if profit maximization is not their overriding objective, these enterprises may, and perhaps should, be managed as if it were. Therefore, both their managers and the parties to whom they are accountable need the same type of financial information that the owners and operators of businesses do. The accounting and reporting practices that are appropriate for the business-type activities of governments and not-for-profits may differ from those that are most suitable for their nonbusiness activities. Thus, the challenge of developing accounting and reporting principles for governments and not-for-profits is made even more formidable by the potential need for more than one set of standards—even for a single organization.

HOW DO GOVERNMENTS COMPARE WITH NOT-FOR-PROFITS?

As explained earlier, governments and not-for-profits share characteristics that distinguish them from businesses. But there are also important differences between governments and not-for-profits. Governments, unlike not-for-profits, have the authority to command resources. They have the power to tax, collect license and other fees, and impose charges. Should a government lack funds to satisfy its obligations or enhance services, it can obtain them by legislative action. From the perspective of accountants or financial analysts, this ability suggests that the actual assets reported on a government's balance sheet may not represent all the assets under its control. To obtain a comprehensive picture of a government's fiscal health, one must consider not only the resources actually owned by the government but also those that it has the power to summon.

Suppose that two towns each report an operating deficit and a high ratio of debt to financial assets. One is a wealthy community with high property values, prosperous industries, little unemployment, and a low tax rate. The other has low property values, little industry, high unemployment, and high tax rates. Clearly, the fiscal capacity of the first town exceeds that of the second. With greater fiscal effort—that is, by increasing tax rates—the first town can readily improve its economic circumstances, whereas the second cannot. This point is further addressed in Chapter 11.

Governments are currently required to include in their annual reports substantial amounts of demographic and economic data about the jurisdictions they serve. An ongoing issue, however, is how much disclosure is enough: what types of data are needed by statement users and to what extent are such disclosures within the purview of accounting and financial reporting?

Surprisingly, whether an entity should be categorized as a government or as a not-for-profit is not always obvious, and no definitive criteria exist to distinguish the two. The homeowners' association of a residential development, for example, may carry out activities similar to those of a government—constructing and maintaining roads and providing utility and security services. Moreover, it may have the right to assess the residents' annual fees. The following characteristics, in addition to the power to tax, are indicative of a government:

- ***It may issue tax-exempt debt.*** Section 103(a) of the Internal Revenue Code exempts the interest on the debt of states, territories, and their political subdivisions from federal taxation. This privilege is a substantial economic benefit to governments because it reduces their borrowing costs. Virtually all local governments qualify as subdivisions of states and territories. Not-for-profits, such as colleges, universities, and hospitals, do not have this opportunity. However, they may be the beneficiaries of it, as governments may be permitted, on a limited basis, to issue tax-exempt debt on their behalf.
- ***Its governing bodies are either popularly elected or appointed by another government.*** The governing body of a typical government is elected by the citizens within its jurisdiction. The governing boards of other governments, particularly public authorities, may be appointed by the legislature or by public officials of another government.
- ***Another government can unilaterally dissolve it and assume its assets without compensation.*** Under our legal system, a government can arbitrarily seize the assets only of other governments within its jurisdiction—not those of not-for-profits or businesses.[3]

WHAT ARE THE OVERALL PURPOSES OF FINANCIAL REPORTING?

Financial statements have value only to the extent that they serve the needs of users. Having considered the characteristics of government and not-for-profit entities, we now consider the general purposes of financial statements and the groups most likely to use them. We can then address the need for specific objectives of financial reporting and can review the objectives developed by both the GASB and the FASB. The purposes for which external financial statements—those included in an annual report—are employed vary from user to user and facilitate a combination of functions.[4] For the most part, they should allow users to:

- ***Assess financial condition.*** Users need to analyze past results and current financial conditions to determine the ability of the entity to meet its obligations and to continue to provide expected services. By establishing trends, users are better able to predict future fiscal developments and to foresee the need for changes in revenue sources, resource allocations, and capital requirements.
- ***Compare actual results with the budget.*** In light of the importance of the adopted budget, users want assurance that the entity adhered to it. Significant variations from the budget may signify either poor management or unforeseen circumstances that require an explanation.
- ***Determine compliance with appropriate laws, regulations, and restrictions on the use of the funds.*** Users want evidence that the organization has complied with legal and contractual requirements, such as bond covenants, donor and grantor restrictions, taxing and debt limitations, and applicable laws. Violations not only can have serious financial repercussions but can also jeopardize the entity's viability.
- ***Evaluate efficiency and effectiveness.*** Users want to know whether the entity is achieving its objectives and, if so, whether it is doing so efficiently and effectively. Hence, they need to compare accomplishments (outcomes) with service efforts and costs (resource inputs).

[3] These characteristics have been drawn from Martin Ives, "What Is a Government?" *The Government Accountants Journal* 43 (Spring 1994): 25–33. They are similar to those that have been agreed upon by the American Institute of Certified Public Accountants (AICPA) and the Governmental Accounting Standards Board (GASB). See *State and Local Governments,* AICPA Audit and Accounting Guide (New York: AICPA, 2013), para. 1.12.

[4] These purposes are drawn from GASB Concepts Statement No. 1, *Objectives of Financial Reporting* (May 1987).

WHO ARE THE USERS, AND WHAT ARE THE USES OF FINANCIAL REPORTS?

The main users of the financial statements of governments and not-for-profits—like those of the financial statements of businesses—are the parties to whom the organizations are accountable. They include

- Governing boards
- Investors and creditors
- Taxpayers and citizens and organizational members
- Donors and grantors
- Regulatory and oversight agencies
- Employees and other constituents

General-purpose financial statements are targeted mainly at parties external to the organization. As is the case in corporate accounting, reports intended for external groups are inappropriate for many types of managerial decisions. Executives, agency heads, and other managers can, and should, rely on their organization's internal reporting system for the financial information they require. Nevertheless, the information needs of internal and external parties may overlap. Therefore, internal parties, though not intended to be principal users of general-purpose financial statements, may in fact rely on them for a considerable amount of necessary data.

This text focuses primarily on the information needs of external users and hence is concerned largely with general-purpose financial statements. However, special attention is also given to the interests of managers and other internal parties.

GOVERNING BOARDS

Just as the auditors' reports on the financial statements of corporations are generally addressed to their boards of directors, those of governments and not-for-profits are directed to their governing boards. That the governing boards are the prime recipients of the audit reports strongly implies that they are among the principal users of both the auditors' reports themselves and the accompanying financial statements.

A government's governing body is typically an elected or appointed legislature, such as a city council or a board of commissioners. A not-for-profit's governing body is usually a board of trustees or a board of directors.

Governing boards cannot neatly be categorized as either internal or external users. Customarily, they are composed of members from outside the management team. However, in almost all organizations they approve budgets, major purchases, contracts, employment agreements with key executives, and significant operating policies—thereby not only overseeing managers but also getting involved, sometimes directly, in the decisions that managers make.

INVESTORS AND CREDITORS

As noted earlier, neither governments nor not-for-profits have owners, and therefore they do not issue shares of stock. Nevertheless, they look to the same financial markets as do corporations to satisfy their capital requirements.

As shown in Figure 1-3, in the third quarter of 2016 state and local governments had an estimated $3.8 trillion of bonds outstanding. This compares with $8.4 trillion outstanding for U.S. corporations. The amounts highlight the economic significance of the municipal bond sector. The main purchasers of this debt are households (e.g., individual investors), money market funds, mutual funds, and insurance companies.

FIGURE 1-3 Outstanding U.S. Bond Market Debt as of 4Q 2016
Source: SIFMA. 2018. February 9. Accessed February 28, 2018. http://www.sifma.org/resources/research/us-bond-market-issuance-and-outstanding/

Both governments and not-for-profits issue bonds primarily to finance long-term assets. For governments, these include buildings, parking garages, office buildings, roads, highways, and utility systems. For not-for-profits, they include buildings, other facilities, and equipment.

Investors commonly acquire the bonds of governments and not-for-profits as part of an investment portfolio that also includes corporate securities. Their investment requirements are essentially the same as those for similar corporate bonds. They want assurance that the issuing entity will meet its obligations to make scheduled interest and principal payments. In a sense, therefore, the same group of investors constitutes the major users of business, government, and not-for-profit financial statements.

Many—probably most—bondholders do not themselves evaluate the bonds they acquire. Instead, they rely on the assessments of bond-rating services and are thereby only indirect users of financial reports. The three best-known rating services are Standard & Poor's, Moody's, and Fitch Ratings. These services assign a rating (e.g., AAA, AA, A, BBB) to publicly traded bonds reflective of the security's risk of default.

Governments and not-for-profits also borrow routinely from banks and other financial institutions. The loans may either finance new facilities or cover short-term imbalances between cash receipts and cash disbursements. The lenders and potential lenders use the financial statements of the governments and not-for-profits just as they would those of corporations—to help assess the creditworthiness of the borrowers.

CITIZENS AND ORGANIZATIONAL MEMBERS

Citizens (or taxpayers) are invariably placed near the top of any list of government financial statement users. In reality, few citizens ever see the annual reports of the governments that have jurisdiction over them. Moreover, a government's release of its annual report is seldom newsworthy. The reports are ordinarily issued at least three months after the close of the government's fiscal year, and current reporting practices are anything but user friendly. The majority of the governmental entities make their financial statements available on the Internet in either the HTML form or as a PDF document and thus do not routinely have to send their reports to the local newspaper. In fact, few local newspapers have reporters who can understand and interpret these reports.

Nevertheless, the significance of citizens as a primary user group should not be underestimated. Citizens obtain financial data through a variety of "filters," including civic associations such as the League of Women Voters, political action groups, and newspapers, TV, and radio. Even if they don't pay attention to the annual report, they most definitely take notice, at any time of the year, of instances of fiscal mismanagement or other unforeseen circumstances that will cause unexpected revenue shortfalls or cost overruns.

The extent to which members of not-for-profit organizations are interested in either the statements themselves or the data derived from them depends largely on the size of the organization and their involvement in it. A larger percentage of a country club's members can be expected to pay attention to their organization's fiscal affairs—mainly because it has a direct impact on their dues and fees—than members of broad-based organizations such as the National Geographic Society or the American Automobile Association.

DONORS AND GRANTORS

Few individuals—including accountants—request financial statements each time they drop their coins into Salvation Army kettles or Muscular Dystrophy Association canisters. But major donors and grantors—such as the United Way; the Ford Foundation; and federal, state, and local governments—are more discriminating in how they part with their resources. They not only will request financial reports and other relevant fiscal information from supplicant associations but will also examine and analyze them with the same care as a banker making a loan.

In addition, individual donors can, and should, obtain financial information about a charity prior to contributing to it. They can inquire as to the organization's allocation of resources, the proportion of its resources directed to substantive programs as opposed to fundraising, and the salaries of the most highly paid executives. Such data will likely be available from the organization itself, from state or local regulatory authorities, and from independent watchdog agencies such as Charity Navigator, GuideStar, and the Better Business Bureau's Wise Giving Alliance (and are generally accessible on their websites).

REGULATORY AGENCIES

Local governments are normally obligated to file financial reports with state agencies; charitable organizations may have to file IRS Form 990 with the federal government as well as similar financial forms with either state or local authorities, and religious and fraternal associations may have to file financial reports with their umbrella organizations. The recipients of these reports use them to ensure that the entities are spending and receiving resources in accordance with laws, regulations, or policies; to help assess management's performance; to allocate resources; and to exercise general oversight responsibility.

EMPLOYEES AND OTHER CONSTITUENTS

Few employees of governments or not-for-profits spend their off-hours poring over their organization's financial statements. Still, officers of their unions or employee associations may examine them, looking for ways to free up resources for salary increases or projects in which they have a special interest.

Other constituent or interest groups also use financial reports on an ad hoc basis. Almost certainly, few readers of this text have ever seen the financial statements of the college or university they attend. However, students have been known to use budgets and annual reports to support claims that their college or university need not raise tuition, that it can afford a new student activities center, or that it should privatize a money-losing cafeteria or bookstore.

WHAT ARE THE SPECIFIC OBJECTIVES OF FINANCIAL REPORTING AS SET FORTH BY THE GASB AND THE FASB?

As noted previously, the overall objective of financial reporting is to meet the information needs of statement users. But financial reports cannot possibly satisfy all the requirements of all users. Therefore, both the GASB and the FASB have established objectives that circumscribe the functions of financial reports. These objectives provide the foundation for their standards. Having agreed on objectives at the outset, the standard-setters should not have to determine the overall purpose of a proposed new standard each time they consider a specific accounting issue.

GASB OBJECTIVES

Taking into account the unique characteristics of governments and their environment, the Governmental Accounting Standards Board has established **accountability** as the cornerstone of financial reporting. "Accountability," the GASB says, "requires governments to answer to the citizenry—to justify the raising of public resources and the purposes for which they are used." It "is based on the belief that the citizenry has a 'right to know,' a right to receive openly declared facts that may lead to public debate by the citizens and their elected representatives." The GASB has divided the objective of accountability into three subobjectives:

- ***Interperiod equity.*** "Financial reporting should provide information to determine whether current-year revenues were sufficient to pay for current-year services." It should show whether current-year citizens shifted part of the cost of services they received to future-year taxpayers.
- ***Budgetary and fiscal compliance.*** "Financial reporting should demonstrate whether resources were obtained and used in accordance with the entity's legally adopted budget; it should also demonstrate compliance with other finance-related legal or contractual requirements."

TABLE 1-3 Governmental Accounting Standards Board's Additional Objectives of Financial Reporting

Financial reporting should assist users in evaluating the operating results of the governmental entity for the year.

a. Financial reporting should provide information about sources and uses of financial resources. Financial reporting should account for all outflows by function and purpose, all inflows by source and type, and the extent to which inflows meet outflows. Financial reporting should identify material nonrecurring financial transactions.

b. Financial reporting should provide information about how the government entity financed its activities and met its cash requirements.

c. Financial reporting should provide information necessary to determine whether the entity's financial position improved or deteriorated as a result of the year's operations.

Financial reporting should assist users in assessing the level of services that can be provided by the governmental entity and its ability to meet its obligations as they become due.

a. Financial reporting should provide information about the financial position and condition of a governmental entity. It should provide information about resources and obligations, both actual and contingent, current and noncurrent. The major financial resources of most governmental entities are derived from the ability to tax and issue debt. As a result, financial reporting should provide information about tax sources, tax limitations, tax burdens, and debt limitations.

b. Financial reporting should provide information about a governmental entity's physical and other nonfinancial resources having useful lives that extend beyond the current year, including information that can be used to assess the service potential of those resources. This information should be presented to help users assess long- and short-term capital needs.

c. Financial reporting should disclose legal or contractual restrictions on resources and risks of potential loss of resources.

Source: GASB Concepts Statement 1, *Objectives of Financial Reporting* (1987).

- ***Service efforts costs and accomplishments.*** "Financial reporting should provide information to assist users in assessing the service efforts costs and accomplishments of the governmental entity." This information helps users assess the government's "economy, efficiency, and effectiveness" and "may help form a basis for voting or funding decisions."[5]

The GASB established two additional objectives, each also having three subobjectives. These are set forth in Table 1-3.

The GASB objectives, taken independently, are unquestionably reasonable. But taken together, do they establish the basis for resolving specific issues and establishing specific standards? Consider the simplified example, "Clash Among Reporting Objectives."

Example

Clash Among Reporting Objectives

Voters approved the establishment of a county sanitation district, and the county provided the new district with $10 million in start-up funds. During its first year of operations, the district prepared a cash-based budget and engaged in the following summary transactions, all of which occurred without variance from the budget.

- It purchased sanitation vehicles and other equipment for $10 million cash. The anticipated economic lives of the assets were 10 years.
- It billed residents for $9 million, but because bills for the last month of the year were not mailed until early the following year (as planned), it collected only $8.2 million.
- It incurred operating costs, all paid in cash, of $6 million.

Let us prepare a statement of revenues and expenditures that would embody accounting standards consistent with the GASB objectives. The distinction between expenses and expenditures, a term commonly used in government accounting, is drawn in a subsequent chapter. For now, consider them to be the same.

Two problems are readily apparent:

- How should the district report the expense related to the equipment? Should it use the $10 million paid to purchase the equipment or $1 million, an amount representative of the one-tenth of the assets consumed during the period? The broader question is whether governments should be required to depreciate their assets.
- How much revenue should the district recognize? Should it be the $9 million billed or the $8.2 million collected? More generally, should revenues be recognized on a cash or an accrual basis?

Inasmuch as the district prepared its budget on a cash basis, a statement of revenues and expenditures that would fulfill the GASB's subobjective of reporting whether resources were obtained and used in accordance with the entity's legally adopted budget would also have to be on a cash basis. The district would recognize the revenue as the cash is collected; it would record the vehicle-related expense in the period in which the vehicles are acquired and paid for. Thus (in millions):

Revenues from customers		$ 8.2
Operating expenditures	$ 6.0	
Vehicle-related costs	10.0	16.0
Excess of revenues over expenditures		$ (7.8)

As a consequence of preparing statements on a cash basis—the same basis on which the budget was prepared—the entire cost of acquiring the long-term assets would fall on the taxpayers in the year of purchase. In the following nine years, the district would report no further expenses

[5] GASB Concepts Statement No. 1, *Objectives of Financial Reporting* (May 1987).

related to the purchase or "consumption" of these particular vehicles. The financial statements would thereby allow management to appear far more efficient in those years than in the first year. In addition, if tax rates were set so that revenues would cover expenses, taxpayers would enjoy a rate decrease. However, because the taxpayers of all 10 years will benefit from the assets, the reporting objective of interperiod equity would not be served. On the other hand, the government would be credited with only $8.2 million in revenues, even though it provided $9.0 million in services—another, though reverse, violation of the interperiod equity concept.

By contrast, a statement that would fulfill the interperiod equity subobjective would recognize the $10 million in vehicle costs over the 10 years in which they would be used and the $9.0 million in revenues in the years in which the services were provided. Thus:

Revenues from customers		$9.0
Operating expenses	$6.0	
Vehicle-related costs	1.0	7.0
Excess of revenues over expenses		$2.0

But the statement, prepared on a full accrual basis, cannot readily be compared with the adopted budget and therefore cannot, without adjustment, be used to demonstrate budgetary compliance.

As will be apparent throughout this text, the conflict between the two objectives of interperiod equity and budgetary compliance characterizes many of the issues that government accountants, and the GASB in particular, have to face in ensuring that financial statements are informative and useful to the parties that rely on them. In particular, the conflict casts doubt on whether the objectives can be fulfilled within a single set of financial statements or whether, as an alternative, two sets—one on a full accrual basis, the other on a budget or near-budget basis—might be necessary.

GASB STATEMENT NO. 34: TWO SETS OF FINANCIAL STATEMENTS

Upon its establishment in 1984, the GASB undertook to develop a new model for state and local government reporting. However, owing to numerous controversial issues, it did not issue its final pronouncement (Statement No. 34, *Basic Financial Statements—and Management's Discussion and Analysis—for State and Local Governments*) until June 1999. Statement No. 34 required the most significant changes to the reporting model in 60 years and, in fact, does require that governments prepare the two sets of financial statements cited in the previous paragraph.

FASB OBJECTIVES

Financial Accounting Standards Board objectives for not-for-profit entities are, for the most part, seemingly similar to those of the GASB for governments. They are presented, in summary form in Table 1-4. However, a careful reading reveals significant differences in emphasis. These disparities have resulted in accounting and reporting standards that give decidedly different looks to the financial reports of the two types of entities. For example, FASB objectives refer only obliquely to budgetary compliance. They provide that information should be useful in "assessing how managers of a nonbusiness organization have discharged their stewardship responsibilities." In elaborating on this objective, the FASB stresses that external financial statements can "best meet that need by disclosing failure to comply with spending mandates (which presumably are expressed in budgets) that may impinge on an organization's financial performance or on its ability to provide a satisfactory level of services." By contrast, the GASB makes budgetary and

TABLE 1-4 Financial Accounting Standards Board's Objectives of Financial Reporting

- Financial reporting by nonbusiness organizations should provide information that is useful to present and potential resource providers and other users in making rational decisions about the allocation of resources to those organizations.
- Financial reporting should provide information to help present and potential resource providers and other users in assessing the services that a nonbusiness organization provides and its ability to continue to provide those services.
- Financial reporting should provide information that is useful to present and potential resource providers and other users in assessing how managers of a nonbusiness organization have discharged their stewardship responsibilities and about other aspects of their performance.
- Financial reporting should provide information about the economic resources, obligations, and net resources of an organization, and the effects of transactions, events, and circumstances that change resources and interests in those resources.
- Financial reporting should provide information about the performance of an organization during a period, periodic measurement of the changes in the amount and nature of the net resources of a nonbusiness organization, and information about the service efforts and accomplishments of an organization.
- Financial reporting should provide information about how an organization obtains and spends cash or other liquid resources, about its borrowing and repayment of borrowing, and about other factors that may affect an organization's liquidity.
- Financial reporting should include explanations and interpretations to help users understand financial information provided.

Source: FASB Statement of Financial Accounting Concepts 4, *Objectives of Financial Reporting by Nonbusiness Organizations* (1980).

fiscal compliance a central concern of financial reporting. As a consequence, government financial statements incorporate numerous mechanisms to demonstrate that the entity has acted in accord with budgetary mandates, has adhered to the provisions of grants and contracts, and has complied with all applicable laws and regulations. These include reporting by fund, accounting for encumbrances (goods and services on order), and required actual-to-budget comparisons. Moreover, although the FASB statement of objectives, like that of the GASB, lists a wide range of potential users, in practice the FASB standards aim at a far narrower group of users—mainly donors and other contributors of resources.

SERVICE EFFORTS AND ACCOMPLISHMENTS

GASB and FASB objectives both endorsed the notion that financial reporting encompasses information on service efforts and accomplishments (SEA). This information cannot easily be expressed in monetary units and is still only rarely included in the financial statements of either state and local government or not-for-profit organizations. Yet, the reporting of SEA performance information is important in assisting both governments and not-for-profits to demonstrate accountability to citizens and other resource providers. SEA reporting provides decision-useful information about an entity's efficiency and effectiveness in providing services to its citizens and other constituents that is not included in traditional financial statements. In 1994, the GASB stressed the importance of SEA information by issuing Concepts Statement No. 2, *Service Efforts and Accomplishments Reporting*. Fourteen years later, after conducting research and constituent outreach, it reaffirmed the importance of SEA information by issuing Concepts Statement No. 5, *Service Efforts and Accomplishments Reporting (An Amendment of GASB Concepts Statement No. 2)*. This statement reflected developments in SEA accounting and reporting that occurred in the years since Concept Statement No. 2 was issued. Then, in July 2010, the GASB further promoted SEA reporting by issuing *Suggested Guidelines for Voluntary Reporting, SEA*

Performance Information. Nevertheless, the GASB has so far been unable to convince key constituents (mainly preparer groups) that SEA information should be an integral part of external financial reports. Consequently, it continues to encourage, but does not mandate, SEA reporting.

DO DIFFERENCES IN ACCOUNTING PRINCIPLES REALLY MATTER?

Financial statements demonstrate what happened to an entity in the past. But they present the evidence from the perspective of the accountant who prepared them. Other accountants may describe the events differently. The underlying accounting principles dictate how the evidence is presented. In this section, we address the issue of whether differences in accounting principles really affect the decisions made on the basis of financial statements.

Just as a witness's explanation of an accident cannot change what actually occurred, neither can an accountant's report on an entity's past transactions change what actually transpired. In the sanitation district example, the district paid $10 million in cash for vehicles, billed its customers $9 million for services, and paid $6 million in operating expenses. Whether the district's financial statements report revenues over expenditures of $2 million, expenditures over revenues of $7.8 million, or any amount in between is irrelevant to the actual event. Moreover, financial statements, no matter how they are prepared, do not directly affect the economic worth of an entity. At year-end, the district's customers owed it $0.2 million, irrespective of whether the district reports a receivable of that amount (as it would under an accrual basis of accounting) or of zero (as it would under a cash basis of accounting).

USER ADJUSTMENTS

Users of financial statements can be indifferent to how an entity's fiscal story is told, as long as they are given adequate information to reconfigure the statements to a preferred form. Research in the corporate sector provides compelling evidence that stockholders are able to see through certain differences in accounting practices and adjust financial statements to take the differences into account. Thus, if one firm reports higher earnings than another solely because it employs more liberal accounting principles, the total market value of its shares may be no greater.

The "efficiency" of the municipal bond market—the extent to which it incorporates all public information in pricing securities—has been investigated much less than that of the corporate stock market. Nevertheless, the available evidence, albeit inconclusive, suggests that investors in tax-exempt bonds, like their stock market counterparts, understand the impact of differences in accounting practices.

ECONOMIC CONSEQUENCES

Accounting principles can—and frequently do—have economic consequences. Important decisions and determinations are made on the basis of financial data as presented and without adjustment.

As stated earlier, budgets are governments' paramount financial documents. Most jurisdictions must present balanced budgets (expenditures cannot exceed revenues) in accord with accounting principles either that they select themselves or that are imposed on them by higher-order governments. The choice of accounting principles is critical. Whereas one set of accounting principles may result in a balanced budget, another set with identical revenue and expenditure proposals may not. Most governments budget on a cash or near-cash basis. If they were required to budget on a full accrual basis, their balanced budgets might quickly become unbalanced.

Governments may face restrictions on the amount of debt they can incur. The use of one set of accounting principles in defining and measuring debt (e.g., not recording a lease obligation as a liability) might enable them to satisfy the legal limits and thereby be permitted to issue additional bonds. The use of a different set (e.g., counting the lease obligation as a liability), might cause them to exceed the limits and be barred from further borrowing.

Other examples abound of how specific reporting practices have economic consequences. Many of these will be discussed again later in the book cite three:

- An alumnus makes a generous monetary gift to a university. He stipulates that the funds may be invested in stocks, bonds, and real estate, but only the income from the investment may be used to support university activities. If trading gains from the purchase and sale of the investments were accounted for as income, then the amount available to the university for expenditure would be significantly greater than if the gains were treated as an increase in the original capital.
- A government agrees to keep its pension plan fully funded—that is, to make sufficient annual contributions to ensure that the plan's assets equal or exceed the plan's actuarial liabilities. The way in which asset and liability values are established will determine its required annual payments.
- A city establishes a policy whereby it will contract out for any services that private vendors can provide for less than the city's own departments can. The principles used to establish the cost of internal services will affect the decision to use internal departments or outside vendors.

IN PRACTICE WILL ACCOUNTING CHANGES MAKE A DIFFERENCE?

In 2004, the Governmental Accounting Standards Board adopted new rules pertaining to how governments must account for certain of their employees' postretirement benefits. The rules were effective for large governments for periods beginning after December 15, 2006, and for smaller governments one or two years later. Prior to the pronouncement, most governments accounted on a "pay as you go" basis for health insurance to be provided to retirees; that is, they recognized an insurance expense only as they paid the premiums for the retirees. The rules require that they recognize an expense during the working years in which employees provide their services and thereby earn the benefits. To the extent that they don't "fund" (put aside the necessary cash) the benefits as the employees earn them, they will have to report a liability.

Before the new rules were established, most governments did not fund their postretirement benefits. The new rules do not require that they now do so—only that they report a liability if they fail to do so.

Have the new rules encouraged governments either to fund their postretirement benefits or to modify the plans? The evidence is that some governments, started to fund the benefits and that many others reassessed whether they can still afford the benefits they have been granting.

Moreover, in 2015, the GASB modified the rules in a way that, for most governments, would significantly increase both their reported health care liability and annual expenses. Several public-sector employee labor unions spoke out strongly against the rule changes when they were proposed, fearing that they would inevitably cause their employer governments to cut back on their benefits.

WHO ESTABLISHES GENERALLY ACCEPTED ACCOUNTING PRINCIPLES?

Generally accepted accounting principles (GAAP) embrace the rules and conventions that guide the form and content of general-purpose financial statements. These principles are expressed mainly in pronouncements of officially designated rule-making authorities and should be consistent with the objectives that they established. However, in the absence of pronouncements by those authorities, GAAP may also be derived from historical convention and widespread practice.

THE FUNCTION OF THE GASB, THE FASAB, THE FASB, AND THE AICPA

Each of the primary standard-setting authorities—the Governmental Accounting Standards Board (GASB) for state and local governments, the Federal Accounting Standards Advisory Board (FASAB) for the federal government, and the Financial Accounting Standards Board (FASB) for nongovernmental not-for-profits—has been sanctioned by the **American Institute of Certified Public Accountants (AICPA)** to establish accounting principles pursuant to Rule 203 of its Code of Professional Conduct.

IN PRACTICE ASSESSING THE PROFITABILITY OF AN ATHELETIC PROGRAM

The president and other officials of a major university assert that their school's athletic program is "extremely profitable." As evidence, they cite the program's budget and other financial reports that show impressive positive cash flows. But would they be equally supportive of the program if "profitability" were calculated differently? For example, how much was the program charged for:

- Wages and salaries of campus police who work overtime on game days
- Costs of players' medical exams and care of injuries
- The marching band
- University overhead (it is a safe assumption that the university president devotes more time to the athletic department than to the particular academic department)
- Interest on the debt incurred to build or modernize the sports arena
- The "opportunity" cost of using the prime land on which the stadium is located for sports rather than for an alternative purpose

On the other side of the journal, how much credit does the athletic program receive for the contributions of alumni and others attributable to the goodwill and publicity generated by the athletic team?

The program's "profitability," and hence all policies that affect it, may be no more objective than the team's ranking in the weekly polls.

Rule 203 provides that an auditor should not express an unqualified opinion on financial statements that are in violation of the standards established by the designated authorities. In addition, the AICPA provides accounting guidance on issues not yet addressed by either the GASB or the FASB. This guidance is now incorporated in the FASB's Accounting Standards Codification.

Both the GASB and the FASB are supported by advisory councils composed of representatives of constituent groups—the Governmental Accounting Standards Advisory Council (GASAC) for the GASB and the Financial Accounting Standards Advisory Council (FASAC) for the FASB. The boards share facilities in Norwalk, Connecticut. The GASB currently has a full-time chair, a half-time vice chair, and five part-time members; the FASB has seven full-time members, including its chair.

Established in 1984, the GASB succeeded the National Council on Governmental Accounting (NCGA) as the standard-setting body for state and local governments. The NCGA, which was sponsored by the Government Finance Officers Association (GFOA), was thought to be too unwieldy (21 volunteer members) and inadequately staffed to deal with the complexities of modern government finance.

The FASB, created in 1973, has directed its attention mainly to business enterprises rather than not-for-profits. However, in 1979, it assumed responsibility for the not-for-profit and other specialized-industry accounting principles that had previously been addressed in the AICPA industry audit guides and Statements of Position. In 1980, the FASB issued its statement of objectives and standards dealing with the form and content of financial statements, depreciation, revenue recognition from contributions, and valuation of investments, as discussed previously and summarized in Table 1-4.

In 2002, in response to financial scandals involving Enron Corporation and the CPA firm of Arthur Andersen, Congress passed the Sarbanes–Oxley Act (Public Law 107-204). In an effort to enhance the independence of the FASB, it provided that the Board should no longer have to rely for funding on contributions from its constituents. Instead, it would be supported by fees from SEC registrants. Then, in 2010, as a consequence of the financial crisis of 2008, Congress passed the Dodd–Frank Wall Street Reform Act (Public Law 111-203). This bill provided that the GASB, like the FASB, will be funded mainly from an independent source—in this case fees from financial firms that engage in secondary trading of municipal securities.

IN PRACTICE

GOVERNMENTS AND NOT-FOR-PROFITS MAY ALSO BE AGGRESSIVE IN THEIR ACCOUNTING

Public corporations are notorious for taking aggressive accounting measures to boost their earnings. But don't think for a moment that governments and not-for-profits are immune to the temptation to bias their financial statements.

- Elected or appointed officials and managers, like business executives, may attempt to mask operating deficits to make their own performance look better and thereby enhance their prospects for reelection or promotion.
- Members of legislative bodies and governing boards may benefit from revenue and expenditure management so that they can avoid having to raise revenues or make difficult choices on which programs to cut.
- Citizens may condone aggressive accounting and budgeting because they too wish to avoid (at least in the short run) tax and dues increases or spending cuts.
- Investment bankers—those who underwrite the bonds of not-for-profits and governments—may turn a blind eye to aggressive accounting because an entity that is seemingly healthy is more likely to undertake, and issue debt to support, major capital construction projects.
- "Independent" auditors—those who are most responsible for ensuring the integrity of financial statements—may avoid tough confrontations with officials of a not-for-profit or government client to retain the engagement and accompanying audit fees or sell the client various consulting services.

Sound professional judgment and integrity are no less important in government and not-for-profits than in business. (See Chapter 16 for a discussion and examples of ethical issues facing government and not-for-profit organizations.)

ENTITIES COMMON TO GOVERNMENT AND NOT-FOR-PROFIT SECTORS

Soon after the GASB was established, it, the FASB, and its constituents faced a politically sensitive and potentially divisive issue: Which of the two should set standards for entities, such as colleges and universities that are common to the government and the not-for-profit sector? Some constituents of the two boards asserted that there are too few conceptual or operational differences between same-type entities in the two sectors to justify different accounting standards and hence separate standard-setting authorities. Others, however, contended that governmental hospitals, utilities, and universities differ fundamentally from their not-for-profit counterparts in that they have different rights, responsibilities, and obligations. For example, governmental entities may have the ability to impose taxes and to issue tax-exempt debt and may be accountable to the citizenry at large rather than to a board of trustees.

The jurisdiction issue was made more complex by concerns over sovereignty. Some managers of the not-for-profit entities maintained that they had little in common with state and local governments and did not want to be within the authority of the GASB. Similarly, state and local government officials refused to yield standard-setting control over any of their component units to the FASB, a board mainly concerned with the private sector.

In 1989, the Financial Accounting Foundation and the constituents of the two boards agreed on a jurisdictional formula that, in essence, reaffirmed the status quo: The GASB would have authority over all state and local government entities, and the FASB would have authority over all other entities. Thus, government colleges and universities (such as the State University of New York, University of California) are now within the purview of the GASB, and private colleges and universities (such as New York University, Rice University) are within the purview of the FASB.

If the GASB or the FASB has not issued a pronouncement on a particular issue, then the organizations under each of their jurisdictions can look to other sources for guidance. These other sources are set forth in two "hierarchies" that are now incorporated in GASB Statement

No. 76, *The Hierarchy of Generally Accepted Accounting Principles for State and Local Governments*,[6] and FASB Statement No. 168. The requirements in this GASB Statement improve financial reporting by (1) raising the category of implementation guidance in the GAAP hierarchy; (2) emphasizing the importance of analogies to authoritative literature when the accounting treatment for an event is not specified in authoritative GAAP; and (3) requiring the consideration of consistency with the GASB Concepts Statements when evaluating accounting treatments specified in nonauthoritative literature. As shown in Table 1-5, the GAAP hierarchy sets forth what constitutes authoritative GAAP[7] for all state and local governmental entities. It establishes the order of priority of pronouncements and other sources of accounting and financial reporting guidance that a governmental entity should apply. In June 2009, the FASB issued Statement No. 168, *The FASB Accounting Standards Codification and the Hierarchy of Generally Accepted Accounting Principles*, which became the single official source of authoritative, nongovernmental U.S. GAAP. Thus, the FASB GAAP hierarchy includes only two levels of GAAP—authoritative (and in the Codification, Level 1 items in Table 1-5) and nonauthoritative (not in the Codification, Level 2 items in Table 1-5).

TABLE 1-5 A Summary of the "Hierarchy" of Generally Accepted Accounting Principles

Governmental Entities (GASB)	Nongovernmental Entities (FASB)
Level	Level
1. Officially established accounting principles—GASB Statements[a] 2. GASB Technical Bulletins[b]; GASB Implementation Guides[c]; and literature of the American Institute of Certified Public Accountants (AICPA) cleared by the GASB.[d]	1. Authoritative: FASB Statements and Interpretations; AICPA Accounting Research Bulletins; Accounting Principles Board Opinions; FASB Technical Bulletins; and AICPA Industry Audit and Accounting Guides, Statements of Position, and Practice Bulletins if cleared (not, objected to) by the FASB; consensus positions of the FASB Emerging Issues Task Force; Implementation guides published by the FASB staff; AICPA accounting interpretations and implementation guides 2. Nonauthoritative: Practices widely recognized and FASB concepts statements, guidance from and prevalent generally or in professional and regulatory organizations, the industry; other accounting textbooks, handbooks, etc.

[a]Category (a) standards, including GASB Interpretations heretofore issued and in effect as of June 2015.
[b]Authoritative material from GASB Implementation Guides is incorporated periodically into the *Comprehensive Implementation Guide*, and when presented in the *Comprehensive Implementation Guide,* retains its authoritative status.
[c]AICPA literature, such as AICPA Industry Audit and Accounting Guides, cleared by the GASB is subject to the *Memorandum of Understanding* between the GASB and the AICPA.
[d]Such literature specifically made applicable to state and local governmental entities contains a statement that indicates that it has been cleared by the GASB (that is, the majority of the GASB members did not object to its issuance).

[6] This Statement supersedes Statement No. 55, *The Hierarchy of Generally Accepted Accounting Principles for State and Local Governments*. It also amends Statement No. 62, *Codification of Accounting and Financial Reporting Guidance Contained in Pre-November 30, 1989 FASB and AICPA Pronouncements,* paragraphs 64, 74, and 82. The requirements of this Statement are effective for financial statements for periods beginning after June 15, 2015, and should be applied retroactively.
[7] Authoritative GAAP is incorporated periodically into the *Codification of Governmental Accounting and Financial Reporting Standards* (Codification) and, when presented in the Codification, retains its authoritative status.

If the accounting treatment for a transaction or other event is not specified within a source of authoritative GAAP described in category a (Table 1-5), a governmental entity should consider whether the accounting treatment is specified by a source in category b (Table 1-5) and then may consider nonauthoritative accounting literature from other sources that does not conflict with or contradict authoritative GAAP.

Sources of nonauthoritative accounting literature include GASB Concepts Statements; pronouncements and other literature of the Financial Accounting Standards Board, Federal Accounting Standards Advisory Board, International Public Sector Accounting Standards Board, and International Accounting Standards Board and AICPA literature cleared by the GASB; practices that are widely recognized and prevalent in state and local government; literature of other professional associations or regulatory agencies; and accounting textbooks, handbooks, and articles.

Even though FASB standards are classified as nonauthoritative accounting literature, the influence of the FASB on the accounting practices of governments is greater than might appear from the hierarchies because governments engage in many business-type activities, such as operating utilities, parking garages, and hospitals. Per standards issued by the GASB, governments are required to account for these activities similar to their private-sector counterparts.

FASAB FOR THE FEDERAL GOVERNMENT

Although the U.S. government was constitutionally established in 1789, it was not until the republic was more than two centuries old that Congress enacted the Chief Financial Officers Act of 1990. The act acknowledged that the federal government was losing billions of dollars each year through financial mismanagement and that its accounting system was incapable of issuing comprehensive financial statements that could earn the government an unqualified audit opinion. The measure took the first steps toward elevating the federal government to a level of fiscal proficiency taken for granted by businesses and other governments. The act:

- Established a chief financial officer (CFO) for fiscal management, a new position housed within the Office of Management and Budget
- Created corresponding CFO positions in each of the federal departments and agencies
- Mandated that the federal government develop accounting systems capable of providing complete, accurate, and timely financial information
- Required that selected federal agencies prepare annual financial statements and make them subject to audits

The act also led the federal government's "big three" agencies concerned with financial reporting—the Department of the Treasury, the Government Accountability Office (GAO),[8] and the Office of Management and Budget (OMB)—to join forces to create the Federal Accounting Standards Advisory Board (FASAB). This board establishes accounting standards for both the federal government at large and the individual federal agencies.

The FASAB, like the GASB and the FASB, has issued a statement of objectives and a series of accounting standards and related pronouncements. As a result, there is now a reasonable degree of consistency among the reporting practices of federal agencies. Today, owing largely to the CFO act and the standards of the FASAB, federal accounting, although no means perfect, is tremendously improved over what it was prior to the act and the establishment of the board.

---

[8] Until 2004, the Government Accountability Office was known as the General Accounting Office. The new designation is intended to better encapsulate the agency's main mission, which is to make the operations of the federal government more efficient and effective. GAO officials hope that it will dispel the common, but ill-conceived, image of the agency staff as the nation's official bean counters.

Because of the unique features of the federal government, federal accounting is addressed in Chapter 17, apart from that pertaining to other governments.

SUMMARY

Governments and not-for-profits need accounting principles and reporting mechanisms that differ from those of businesses. They have objectives other than profit maximization. Therefore, their performance cannot be assessed by the conventional "bottom line" of businesses. Moreover, they are governed by their budgets rather than by the competitive marketplace.

Other characteristics of governments and not-for-profits also have significant accounting and reporting implications. Governments and not-for-profits are extremely diverse, and therefore one set of principles may not fit all entities. Managers tend to have a short-term focus and may strive to delay recognition of expenditures and advance recognition of revenues. Business-type activities may be part of the organization and have to be accounted for differently compared with governmental activities. The distinction between internal accounting and external accounting is often blurred.

Governments, unlike not-for-profits, have the authority to command resources through taxes and other fees. Therefore, a government's financial wherewithal cannot necessarily be assessed by examining only the resources directly tied to the government itself. Those of its constituents may also have to be taken into account.

The main users of government and not-for-profit financial reports include governing boards, investors and creditors, citizens and organizational members, donors and grantors, regulatory and oversight agencies, and other constituents. Each group may have different information needs.

The GASB and the FASB have established objectives of financial reporting that stress the importance of providing information that enables users to assess interperiod equity and compliance with budgetary (or spending) mandates. Sometimes these objectives are in conflict in that a basis of accounting that satisfies one objective may not satisfy the other.

Choice of accounting principles has no direct effect on an entity's fiscal history or current status. It might, however, have significant economic consequences if decisions are based on the data as presented.

KEY TERMS IN THIS CHAPTER

accountability 16
American Institute of Certified Public Accountants (AICPA) 21
budget 3
expenditures 2
Federal Accounting Standards Advisory Board (FASAB) 2
Financial Accounting Standards Board (FASB) 2
fiscal compliance 19
fund accounting 7
generally accepted accounting principles (GAAP) 21
Governmental Accounting Standards Board (GASB) 1
independent, or third, sector 9
intergenerational equity 5
interperiod equity 5
municipality 8
not-for-profit 1
revenues 2

QUESTIONS FOR REVIEW AND DISCUSSION

1. What is the defining distinction between for-profit businesses and not-for-profit entities, including governments? What are the implications of this distinction for financial reporting?
2. Why is the budget a far more important document for both governments and not-for-profits than for businesses?
3. How and why might the importance of the budget affect generally accepted accounting principles for *external* (general-purpose) reports?
4. What is meant by "interperiod equity," and what is its consequence for financial reporting?
5. Why may the "matching concept" be less relevant for governments and not-for-profits than for businesses?

6. What is the significance for financial reporting of the many restrictions that are placed on a government's resources?
7. Why is it difficult to develop accounting principles that are appropriate for governments within the same category (e.g., cities, counties) and even more difficult to develop them for governments within different categories?
8. What is the significance for financial reporting of a government's power to levy a tax? How does it affect the government's overall fiscal strength?
9. Why has it proven especially difficult to establish accounting principles to satisfy all three elements of GASB's first objective of financial reporting in a single statement of revenue and expenditures or a balance sheet?
10. Why are measures of "service efforts and accomplishments" of more concern for government and not-for-profits than for businesses?
11. In what key ways does the FASB influence generally accepted accounting principles for governments?
12. Why is it more difficult to distinguish between internal and external users in governments than in businesses?

EXERCISES

EX. 1-1

Select the *best* answer.

1. The traditional business model of accounting is inadequate for governments and not-for-profit organizations primarily because businesses differ from governments and not-for-profit organizations in that
   - **a.** They have different missions
   - **b.** They have fewer assets
   - **c.** Their assets are intangible
   - **d.** Taxes are a major expenditure of businesses
2. If businesses are "governed by the marketplace," governments are governed by
   - **a.** Legislative bodies
   - **b.** Taxes
   - **c.** Budgets
   - **d.** State constitutions
3. The primary objective of a not-for-profit organization or a government is to
   - **a.** Maximize revenues
   - **b.** Minimize expenditures
   - **c.** Provide services to constituents
   - **d.** All of the above
4. In governments, in contrast to businesses,
   - **a.** Expenditures are driven mainly by the ability of the entity to raise revenues
   - **b.** The amount of revenues collected is a signal of the demand for services
   - **c.** There may not be a direct relationship between revenues raised and the demand for the entity's services
   - **d.** The amount of expenditures is independent of the amount of revenues collected
5. The organization responsible for setting accounting standards for state and local governments is the
   - **a.** FASB
   - **b.** GASB
   - **c.** FASAB
   - **d.** AICPA

6. The number of governmental units in the United States is approximately
   a. 900
   b. 9,000
   c. 90,056
   d. 900,000

7. Governments differ from businesses in that they
   a. Do not raise capital in the financial markets
   b. Do not necessarily engage in transactions in which they "sell" goods or services
   c. Are not required to prepare annual financial reports
   d. Do not issue common stock

8. Interperiod equity refers to a condition whereby
   a. Total tax revenues are approximately the same from year to year
   b. Taxes are distributed fairly among all taxpayers, regardless of income level
   c. Current-year revenues are sufficient to pay for current-year services
   d. Current-year revenues cover both operating and capital expenditures

9. Which of the following is *not* one of the GASB's financial reporting objectives?
   a. Providing information on the extent to which interperiod equity is achieved
   b. Ensuring that budgeted revenues are equal to or exceed budgeted expenses
   c. Reporting on budgetary compliance
   d. Providing information on service efforts and accomplishments

10. Which of the following is *not* one of the FASB's financial reporting objectives?
    a. Providing information about economic resources, obligations, and net resources
    b. Providing information to help resource providers make rational decisions
    c. Reporting on budgetary compliance
    d. Providing information on service efforts and accomplishments

EX. 1–2

Select the *best* answer.

1. Rule 203 of the AICPA's Code of Professional Conduct pertains to
   a. CPAs' independence
   b. Authorities designated to establish accounting standards
   c. Standards of competency
   d. Solicitation of new clients by a CPA

2. Which of the following rule-making authorities would establish accounting standards for Stanford University (a private university)?
   a. The AICPA
   b. The FASB
   c. The FASAB
   d. The GASB

3. Which of the following rule-making authorities would establish accounting standards for the University of Wisconsin (a public university)?
   a. The AICPA
   b. The FASB
   c. The FASAB
   d. The GASB

4. If the GASB has not issued a pronouncement on a specific issue, which of the following is true with respect to FASB pronouncements?
   a. They would automatically govern
   b. They could be taken into account but would have no higher standing than other accounting literature

c. They are irrelevant
d. They could be taken into account by the reporting entity but only if disclosure is made in notes to the financial statements

5. The FASB is to the GASB as
   a. A brother is to a sister
   b. A father is to a son
   c. A son is to a father
   d. An aunt is to a niece

6. Standards promulgated by the FASB are most likely to be adhered to by which of the following governmental units?
   a. A police department
   b. A public school
   c. An electric utility
   d. A department of highways

7. Which of the following practices is most likely to undermine interperiod equity?
   a. Paying for a new school building out of current operating funds
   b. Paying the administrative staff of a school out of current operating funds
   c. Issuing 20-year bonds to finance construction of a new highway
   d. Recognizing gains and losses on marketable securities as prices increase and decrease

8. The term "independent sector" refers to
   a. States that have opted not to receive federal funds
   b. Not-for-profit organizations
   c. Churches that are unaffiliated with a particular denomination
   d. Universities that are not affiliated with a particular athletic conference

9. Which of the following is not an objective of external financial reporting by either the GASB or the FASB?
   a. To enable the statement user to detect fraud
   b. To disclose legal or contractual restrictions on the use of resources
   c. To provide information about how the organizations meet their cash requirements
   d. To provide information that would enable a user to assess the service potential of long-lived assets

10. Which of the following is the least appropriate use of the external financial statements of a government?
    a. To assess the entity's financial condition
    b. To assess whether the compensation of management is reasonable in relation to that of comparable entities
    c. To compare actual results with the budget
    d. To evaluate the efficiency and effectiveness of the entity in achieving its objectives

EX. 1–3 Internet-based exercise

Go to the following websites and answer the questions.

a. Visit the GASB website (www.gasb.org)
   1. What is the GASB?
   2. What is the mission of GASB?
   3. Based on GASB's White Paper, *Why Governmental Accounting and Financial Reporting Is and Should Be Different,* describe the key environmental differences between governments and for-profit business enterprises.
b. Visit the GFOA website (www.gfoa.org)
   1. What is the GFOA, and what role does it play?
   2. Describe briefly the *Certificate of Achievement for Excellence in Financial Reporting Program* (CAFR Program).
   3. Determine the number of state and local governmental entities that was awarded the CAFR Certificate for the last fiscal year.

CONTINUING PROBLEM

Accompanying this text, on its website, is a Comprehensive Annual Financial Report (CAFR) of the city of Austin, Texas. A CAFR includes an entity's year-end financial statements; it is not the same as its budget. Austin's CAFR forms the basis of the "continuing problems" of these chapters. Download the CAFR, either from the website of the text or directly from that of the City of Austin (https://assets.austintexas.gov/financeonline/downloads/cafr/cafr2017.pdf) to your computer and practice navigating through it. Alternatively, with the consent of your instructor, you may obtain the CAFR of a different city, town, or county with a population of 100,000 or more.

A CAFR can generally be accessed from the city's website or by writing to the governmental entity's controller or finance director. Most institutions will provide the reports at no charge.

This continuing problem, unlike those in other chapters of the text, requires no written responses.

PROBLEMS

P. 1–1

Budgeting practices that satisfy cash requirements may not promote interperiod equity.

The Burnet County Road Authority was established as a separate government to maintain county highways. The road authority was granted statutory power to impose property taxes on county residents to cover its costs, but it is required to balance its budget, which must be prepared on a cash basis. In its first year of operations, it engaged in the following transactions, all of which were consistent with its legally adopted cash-based budget:

1. Purchased $10 million of equipment, all of which had an anticipated useful life of 10 years. To finance the acquisition, the authority issued $10 million in 10-year term bonds (i.e., bonds that mature in 10 years)
2. Incurred wages, salaries, and other operating costs, all paid in cash, of $6 million
3. Paid interest of $0.5 million on the bonds
4. Purchased $0.9 million of additional equipment, paying for it in cash; this equipment had a useful life of only three years
   - **a.** The authority's governing board levies property taxes at rates that will be just sufficient to balance the authority's budget. What amount of tax revenue will it be required to collect?
   - **b.** Assume that in the authority's second year of operations, it incurs the same costs, except that it purchases no new equipment. What amount of tax revenue will it be required to collect?
   - **c.** Make the same assumption as to the tenth year, when it will have to repay the bonds. What amount of tax revenue will it be required to collect?
   - **d.** Comment on the extent to which the authority's budgeting and taxing policies promote interperiod equity. What changes would you recommend?

P. 1–2

Financial statements of a government or not-for-profit organization may not provide sufficient information on which to make a loan decision.

Assume that you are a loan officer of a bank. A local church is seeking a $4 million, 20-year loan to construct a new classroom building. Church officers submit a comprehensive financial report that was audited by a reputable CPA firm. In the summary form (the actual statement showed details), the church's statement of revenues and expenditures indicated the following (in millions):

Revenues from dues and contributions	$1.8
Revenues from other sources	0.2
Total revenues	$2.0
Less: total expenditures	2.0
Excess of revenues over expenditures	$0.0

The church prepared its financial statements on a near-cash basis, accounting for all capital asset acquisitions as expenditures when acquired.

The church's balance sheet reported assets, mainly cash and investments (at market value), of $0.2 million. In addition, a note to the financial statements indicated that equipment is approximately $3 million. The church has no outstanding debt.

1. Is there any information in the financial statements that would make you reluctant to approve the loan? If so, indicate and explain.
2. Is there any other financial information of the type likely to be reported in a conventional annual report that you would like to review prior to making a loan decision? If so, indicate and explain.
3. Is there any other information, of any type, that you would like to review prior to making a loan decision? If so, indicate and explain.
4. Comment on the inherent limitations of the financial statements of this church, or any comparable not-for-profit organization, as a basis for making loan decisions.

P. 1–3

The dual objectives of assessing interperiod equity and ensuring budgetary compliance may necessitate different accounting practices.

A city engages in the transactions that follow. For each transaction, indicate the amount of revenue or expenditure that it should report in 2020. Assume first that the main objective of the financial statements is to enable users to assess budgetary compliance. Then calculate the amounts, assuming that the main objective is to assess interperiod equity. The city prepares its budget on a "modified" cash basis (that is, it expands the definition of cash to include short-term marketable securities), and its fiscal year ends on December 31.

1. Employees earned $128,000 in salaries and wages for the last five days in December 2020. They were paid on January 5, 2021.
2. A consulting actuary calculated that per an accepted actuarial cost method, the city should contribute $225,000 to its firefighters' pension fund for benefits earned in 2020. However, the city contributed only $170,000, the amount budgeted at the start of the year.
3. The city acquired three police cars for $35,000 cash each. The vehicles are expected to last for three years.
4. On December 1, 2020, the city invested $99,000 in short-term commercial paper (promissory notes). The notes matured on January 1, 2021. The city received $100,000. The $1,000 difference between the two amounts represents the city's return (interest) on the investment.
5. On January 3, 2020, the city acquired a new $10 million office building, financing it with 25-year serial bonds. The bonds are to be repaid evenly over the period they are outstanding—that is, $400,000 per year. The useful life of the building is 25 years.
6. On January 4, 2020, the city acquired another $10 million office building, financing this facility with 25-year term bonds. These bonds will be repaid entirely when they mature on January 1, 2042. The useful life of this building is also 25 years.
7. City restaurants are required to pay a $1,200 annual license fee, the proceeds of which the city uses to fund its restaurant inspection program. The license covers the period July 1 through June 30. In 2020, the city collected $120,000 in fees for the license period beginning July 1, 2020.
8. The city borrowed $300,000 in November 2020 to cover a temporary shortage of cash. It expects to repay the loan in February 2021.

P. 1–4

Do conventional financial statements satisfy the objectives of financial reporting?

The financial statements that follow were adapted from those of the University of Arizona. Both the statement of changes in fund balances and the notes to the statements have been omitted. Moreover, the statements show only the combined "totals" columns, whereas the actual statements are multicolumned, indicating the various restrictions placed on the university's resources. Also, a few of the line items have been aggregated, and the dates have been changed.

The University of Arizona Balance Sheet, as of June 30 (in millions)

	2021	2020
Assets		
Cash and investments	$ 145	$ 145
Donated land	3	3
Notes and accounts receivable	52	47
(net of allowances for uncollectibles)		
Inventories and supplies	8	8
Physical properties	995	945
Total assets	$1,203	$1,148
Liabilities and net assets		
Accounts payable	$ 16	$ 17
Accrued payroll	12	10
Deferred revenue and deposits	9	8
Funds held for others	11	8
Capitalized lease obligations	36	33
Bonds payable	241	243
Total liabilities	$ 325	$ 319
Net assets	$ 878	$ 829

The University of Arizona Statement of Revenues, Expenses, and Changes in Net Assets for Year Ending June 30 (in millions)

	2021	2020
Operating revenues		
Tuition and fees	$ 112	$ 111
Grants and contracts	208	194
Sales and services of educational departments	8	6
Sales and services of auxiliary enterprises	69	66
Others	8	8
Total operating revenues	$ 405	$ 383

1. Based on the information included in the financial statements, respond as best you can to the following questions. If you believe the data in the financial statements are inadequate to answer the questions, then tell what additional information you would like and where you would most likely find it.
   a. Were the accomplishments of the university greater or less in 2021 than in 2020?
   b. Did the university achieve its goals more efficiently in 2021 than 2020?
   c. Are the university's physical facilities adequate for the next two years? Ten years?
   d. Did the university's long-term financial position improve or deteriorate between year-end 2020 and year-end 2021, taking account of the fiscal demands that will be placed on it in the future?
   e. Will the university be able to satisfy its short-term demands for cash?

2. Review the GASB and FASB objectives of financial reporting. Are any of the preceding questions inconsistent with those objectives? Comment on the extent to which conventional financial statements

satisfy the GASB and FASB objectives and what additional types of information they will likely have to incorporate to satisfy these objectives.

P. 1–5

The jurisdictional overlap among governments may have significant implications for financial reporting.

Suppose that you live on a street adjoining the college in which you are taking this course.

1. List all the governments (e.g., state, county, city) that have jurisdiction over the residents or property of that street.
2. Indicate why it may be difficult to assess the financial wherewithal of one of those governments without taking into account the others. What are the implications for financial reporting of this jurisdictional overlap?

P. 1–6

Choice of accounting principles may have significant economic consequences.

In preparing its budget proposals, a city's budget committee initially estimated that total revenues would be $120 million and total expenditures would be $123 million.

In light of the balanced budget requirements that the city has to meet, the committee proposed several measures to either increase revenues or decrease expenditures. They included the following:

1. Delay the payment of $0.4 million of city bills from the last week of the fiscal year covered by the budget to the first week of the next fiscal year.
2. Change the way property taxes are accounted for in the budget. Currently, property taxes are counted as revenues only if they are expected to be collected during the budget year. New budgetary principles would permit the city to include as revenues all taxes expected to be collected within 60 days of the following fiscal year in addition to those collected during the year. The committee estimates that the change would have a net impact of $1.2 million.
3. Change the way that supplies are accounted for in the budget. Currently, supplies are recognized as expenditures at the time they are *ordered*. The proposal would delay recognition of the expenditures until they are actually *received*. The committee estimates a net effect of $0.8 million.
4. Defer indefinitely $1.5 million of maintenance on city roads. Except as just noted with respect to supplies, the city currently prepares its budget on a near-cash basis, even though other bases are also legally permissible. It prepares its year-end financial statements, however, on an accrual basis.
   - **a.** Indicate the impact that each of the proposals would have on the city's (1) budget, (2) annual year-end financial statements, and (3) "substantive" economic well-being. Be sure to distinguish between direct and indirect consequences.
   - **b.** It is sometimes said that choice of accounting principles doesn't matter in that they affect only the way the entity's fiscal "story" is told; they have no impact on the entity's actual fiscal history or current status. Do you agree? Explain.

P. 1–7

Should there be differences in the accounting and reporting systems between governments and businesses that provide the same services?

A town privatized its sanitation department, selling all its plant and equipment to a private corporation. The corporation agreed to hire most of the department's managers and other employees and was given an exclusive franchise, for a limited number of years, to offer the same service as previously provided by the town. When it operated the department, the town charged local residents fees based on the amount of trash collected. It set the scale of fees at a level intended to enable it to break even—to cover all its operating and capital costs, including interest on capital assets.

1. Do you believe that the objectives of financial accounting and *external* reporting of the private sanitation company should be any different from those of the town? Explain.

2. Do you see any differences in the information requirements of the *internal* managers now that they are employed by a private corporation rather than a government? If so, what are they?

P. 1–8

Capital acquisition decisions may be far more complex in not-for-profit organizations than in businesses.

The Chicago Youth Association (CYA) and the Palmer Athletic Club (PAC) are each considering purchasing a van.

The CYA is a not-for-profit organization serving at-risk inner-city youth. It operates a center that provides after-school tutoring, counseling, and supervised athletic activities. It would use the van mainly to drive students from their schools to the center and from the center back to their homes. The CYA estimates that the van would enable it to increase by 20 the number of students it serves at any one time. The CYA is supported entirely by contributions from the United Way and other private sources.

The PAC is a private, for-profit, athletic facility serving the youth of a suburban community. It provides access to athletic facilities and instruction in several sports, including swimming, tennis, and gymnastics. It would use the van for the same purpose as the CYA—to transport students to and from the facility. The PAC estimates that the van would enable it to increase center capacity by 20 customers, each of whom pays weekly fees of $65.

Each organization estimates that the incremental cost of serving the additional 20 clients (including the operating costs of the van) would be $50 per client per week. Each operates 50 weeks per year.

The two vans would each cost $30,000 and have estimated useful lives of three years. Each organization estimates that its cost of capital is 10 percent.

1. Should the PAC acquire the van? Explain and show all computations.

2. Should the CYA acquire the van? Explain and show all computations.

3. Comment on any critical differences between capital budgeting in a business and a not-for-profit organization.

P. 1–9

In a government, financial information that is appropriate for some purposes may be inappropriate for others—just as in business.

A city operates a computer service department. The department maintains and repairs the computers of all other city departments, billing them for each job performed. The billing rates are established to cover the repair service's full cost of carrying out its function.

For the latest year available, the department reported the following (all amounts in millions):

Revenues from billing other departments		$8.9
Less: Expenditures		
Wages and salaries	$4.0	
Supplies	2.6	
Other cash expenditures	1.3	
Overhead allocated from other departments	1.0	$8.9
Excess of revenues over expenditures		$0.0

The allocated overhead consists mainly of city administrative costs, most of which would remain the same even if the department were to cease operations. However, it also includes $0.3 million in rent. Were the department to be eliminated, the city could move its legal department into the space now occupied by the computer repair service department. The move would save the city $0.2 million, the amount currently paid in rent by the legal department.

A private corporation has offered to provide the same repair service as the computer department for $8.5 million.

1. Based on the limited data provided, should the city accept the offer from the private corporation? Comment on the relevance to this decision of the $8.9 million in total cost—the measure used to establish billing rates.

2. Suppose, instead, that the city did not allocate overhead costs, and hence total costs (and billing revenues) were only $7.9 million. Should the city accept the offer? Is the $7.9 million in unallocated costs any more relevant to this decision than the $8.9 million per the allocated statement?

P. 1–10

Year-end financial accounting and reporting can reveal the economic substance of government actions taken mainly to balance the budget.

Public officials, it is often charged, promote measures intended to make the government "look good" in the short term but that may be deleterious in the long term. Assume that the following actions, designed to increase a reported surplus, were approved by a city council:

1. It reduced the city's contributions to the employee "defined benefit" pension plan from the $10 million recommended by the city's actuary to $5 million to finance benefits earned in the current period. Under a defined benefit plan, the employer promises employees specified benefits on their retirement, and the level of benefits is independent of when and how much the employer contributes to the plan over the employees' years of service.

2. It reduced by $1 million the city's cash transfer to a "rainy day" reserve maintained to cover possible future reductions in tax collections attributable to a downturn in the region's economy.

3. It sold securities that had been held as an investment. The securities had been purchased five years earlier at a cost of $2 million. Market value at the time of sale was $5 million.

4. It delayed until the following year $10 million of maintenance on city highways.

Assume that the city's budget is on a cash or near-cash basis. Accordingly, each of these measures would, as the council intended, reduce budgetary expenditures or increase budgetary revenues.

a. Suppose you were asked to propose accounting principles for external reporting that would capture the true economic nature of these measures—actions that, in substance, did not improve the city's fiscal performance or condition. For each measure, indicate how you would require that it be accounted for and reported.

b. Can you see any disadvantages to the principles that you propose?

P. 1–11

Changes in how amounts are reported must be distinguished from those that affect their economic substance.

The statement of net position (i.e., a balance sheet) of a midsized city reports outstanding debt of $1,200,000,000. The city has a population of 800,000. The city is about to adopt the provisions of a new GASB pronouncement that changes the way defined benefit pension plans are accounted for and reported. A defined benefit pension plan promises employees a certain amount of income after they retire. The payments to the retirees are dependent on their last years' salary and the number of years that they have been employed.

Per the new rules the city will have to report on its balance sheet an additional $600,000,000 of pension liabilities. Such an amount was previously reported in the notes to the financial statements but was not accorded accounting recognition on the balance sheet itself. The new accounting rules affect only the way the pension obligation is reported; they have no effect on the actual promises made to current employees or those already retired.

1. Compute the city's per capita debt (as reported on the statement of net position) prior to the adoption of the new accounting rules.

2. Compute the city's per capita debt after the city adopts the new accounting rules.

3. In an editorial, the local newspaper wrote, "By increasing per capita debt by more 50 percent, the new rules put the city in a precarious fiscal position. Almost certainly the bond rating agencies will take notice and lower the city's bond rating, thereby causing interest rates on any new debt that the city issues to increase significantly."
   a. Do you agree with the newspaper editorial that the change in accounting principles will cause the city's fiscal position to deteriorate? Explain.
   b. If you were an analyst with the agency that rated the city's bonds, would the change in accounting principle cause you to lower the city's credit rating? Explain.

QUESTIONS FOR RESEARCH, ANALYSIS, AND DISCUSSION

1. This chapter has set forth several distinguishing features of state and local governments, the federal government, not-for-profit organizations, and businesses. Presently, there are separate standard-setting boards for state and local governments (the Governmental Accounting Standards Board) and the federal government (the Federal Accounting Standards Advisory Board). Yet, businesses and nongovernmental not-for-profit organizations are both within the purview of a single board (the Financial Accounting Standards Board). How can you justify such a standard-setting arrangement? Aren't the characteristics of state and local governments and the federal government at least as similar to one another as those of not-for-profit organizations and businesses? Aren't the characteristics of not-for-profits more similar to those of governments than to those of businesses?

2. Unquestionably, constituents of both governments and not-for-profits are no less interested in what the organization has accomplished than they are in financial data, such as revenues and expenses. How can you justify an accounting model and the resultant financial statements that fail not only to measure and report accomplishments but also to relate them to an entity's revenues and expenses?

CHAPTER 2

Fund Accounting

LEARNING OBJECTIVES

After studying this chapter, you should understand:

- The nature of funds, including why they are used and the interrelationship among them
- The elements of financial statements
- The hierarchy classification of fund balances
- The basic fund types used by governments—governmental funds, proprietary funds, and fiduciary funds
- The main components of a government's comprehensive annual financial report
- The primary financial statements—both government-wide and fund—issued by governments
- How the fund structures and financial reports of not-for-profits differ from those of governments

In Chapter 1, we set forth some of the key characteristics that distinguish governments and not-for-profit entities from businesses. We also discussed their implications for accounting and financial reporting. In particular, we noted that governments and not-for-profits use fund accounting. In this chapter, we explain the rationale for fund accounting, describe the main types of funds maintained, and examine the relationships among funds.

As noted in Chapter 1, in June 1999, the Governmental Accounting Standards Board (GASB) established the current reporting model for state and local governments. In this chapter, we highlight the key features of this current model. We begin by defining and explaining some common elements of fund and government-wide financial statements and also focus on more recent concepts, statements, and standards that enhance the reporting model. In addition, we present the main attributes of the Financial Accounting Standards Board (FASB)'s model for not-for-profit entities and show how it differs from the government model. A key purpose of our discussion is to emphasize that funds can be combined and reported in a variety of ways for purposes of external reporting.

WHAT IS A FUND?

Government and not-for-profit organizations establish their accounting systems on a fund basis. In governmental and not-for-profit accounting, the term *fund* has a different meaning than it does in business accounting. In business accounting, funds typically refer either to working capital (current assets less current liabilities) or to selected elements of working capital (such as cash and investments), and only a single consolidated accounting entity is used to account for all the activities of a business. The crux of nonbusiness accounting is fund accounting, and it forms the basic building block of governmental accounting and financial reporting. It is an accounting device that an entity uses to keep track of specific sources and uses of funds. In governmental and not-for-profit accounting, a fund is a fiscal and an accounting entity. Each fund has its own self-balancing set of accounts from which financial statements can be prepared.

Thus, governmental and not-for-profit entities customarily use several funds—that is, several fiscal and accounting entities—to account for their resources and activities. A government's fund structure rarely mirrors its organizational structure. The number and types of funds that a governmental entity uses is not dependent upon its size but rather upon how the government is organized, its sources of revenue, and the services it provides. For example, New York City has three major governmental funds (the General, Capital Projects, and General Debt Service funds), and Santa Ana, CA, has seven major governmental funds (the General, Special Revenue, Special Revenue Housing Authority, Special Revenue Gas Tax, Capital Projects Housing, Capital Projects Streets, and Debt Service funds). Funds divide a government or not-for-profit into classifications of resource restriction, not functional departments or operations. A nonprofit organization—for example, a church—may use one fund to account for its general operating revenues and expenses, another to account for resources set aside to construct a new building, and a third to account for its religious school.

WHAT ARE THE KEY ELEMENTS OF GOVERNMENT FINANCIAL STATEMENTS?

In a June 2007 Concepts Statement, the GASB took another step toward enhancing the government reporting model.[1] In that statement, the GASB provided definitions and explanations of seven key elements that comprise basic financial statements—five relating to financial positions and two relating to resource flows.[2]

The GASB defines the elements relating to financial position as follows:

- *"**Assets** are resources with present service capacity that the government presently controls."* Present service capacity of an asset is the characteristic that enables the government to provide services. Control is the ability of the government to use a resource's present service capacity and to determine the nature and manner of its use. Examples of assets include cash, receivables, investments, buildings and equipment, and intangibles such as the right to use intellectual property.

- *"**Liabilities** are present obligations to sacrifice resources that the government has little or no discretion to avoid."* They can result from legally enforceable obligations as well as from social, moral, or economic expectations. Thus, a promise to provide vacation benefits to employees may be a liability, even if it is not legally enforceable.

- *"A **deferred outflow of resources** is the consumption of net assets by the government that is applicable to a future reporting period."* Governments may use net assets in one period to provide benefits clearly applicable to future periods. For example, a government may give cash to a grantee to provide services in a future year. The cash payment reduces the cash of the government but does not increase any other asset or decrease any liability. Moreover, because the services must be provided in a future, rather than a current year, it makes sense that the government delay recognizing a grant expense until the future year. Hence, the decrease in cash (a credit) would be offset by a deferred outflow of resources (a debit)—an item that, such as assets, would be reported on a balance sheet or comparable statement that reports financial position.

[1] GASB Concepts Statement No. 4, *Elements of Financial Statements* (*June* 2007).

[2] Per GASB Statement No. 34, the equivalent of what is familiarly called a "balance sheet" (i.e., a statement showing the assets and liabilities and the residual difference between them) is referred to as a "balance sheet" in governmental fund financial statements, and as a "statement of net assets" in statements prepared on a full accrual basis (e.g., government-wide and proprietary fund financial statements). However, per Statement No. 63, *Financial Reporting of Deferred Outflows of Resources, Deferred Inflows of Resources, and Net Position* (June 2011), "statement of net assets" has been replaced by "statement of net position." Correspondingly, a statement that describes the flows of resources is called a "statement of revenues, expenditures and changes in fund balances" in governmental fund statements, and as a "statement of activities" in statements prepared on a full accrual basis.

- *"A **deferred inflow of resources** is the acquisition of net assets by the government that is applicable to a future reporting period."* Suppose that a government receives property taxes in the year prior to which they are due and in which they are intended to be spent. The net assets of the government increase inasmuch as the cash is received, but are not offset by a decrease in any other asset or an increase in a liability. Although the government is expected to use the cash to provide future services, no liability is created because an obligation to carry out the broad mission of government is not considered a liability. Further, it would be premature to recognize revenue in a year prior to that in which the taxes are budgeted. Hence, the increase in cash (a debit) would be offset by a deferred inflow of resources (a credit).
- *"**Net position** is the residual of all other elements presented in a statement of financial position; that is the assets and deferred outflows less the liabilities and deferred inflows."* In a balance sheet (the statement that shows the financial position of governmental funds—those prepared on a modified accrual basis), the residual difference is presented under the heading "fund balance."

The GASB defines the elements of financial reporting relating to resources flows as follows:

- *"An **outflow of resources** is a consumption of net assets by the government that is applicable to the reporting period."* This element embraces familiar items such as expenses and expenditures but may also include others such as losses and "other financing uses." It can result from a decrease in assets, an increase in liabilities, or a decrease in a previously recognized deferred outflow of resources.
- *"An **inflow of resources** is an acquisition of net assets by the government that is applicable to the reporting period."* Inflows of resources include revenues as well as other items such as gains and "other financing sources." An inflow of resources can result from an increase in assets, a decrease in liabilities, or a decrease in a previously recognized deferred inflow of resources.

Deferred inflows and outflows of resources are not unique to governmental accounting. Businesses also report items such as deferred revenues and deferred costs. They report the deferred inflows among the liabilities and the deferred outflows among the assets. GASB Statement No. 63, *Financial Reporting of Deferred Outflows of Resources, Deferred Inflows of Resources, and Net Position*, requires that governments, unlike businesses, report the deferred items in a separate category.[3] Thus, a statement of net position might be in a format comparable to the following:

Assets	$100
+ Deferred outflow of resources	50
– Liabilities	75
– Deferred inflows of resources	60
= *Net position*	$ 15

WHAT CHARACTERIZES FUNDS?

Each fund of a governmental entity can be represented by a variation of the accounting equation that describes a business entity. Instead of

$$\text{Assets} = \text{liabilities} + \text{owners' equity}$$

[3] GASB Statement No. 65, *Items Previously Reported as Assets and Liabilities* (March 2012), specifies the items that may be classified as deferred outflows and inflows of resources. Only those items explicitly indicated by GASB statements may be so classified.

fund accounting uses the following equation

$$\text{Assets} + \text{deferred outflows} = \text{liabilities} + \text{deferred inflows} + \text{fund balance}^4$$

In slightly different form

$$\text{Assets} + \text{deferred outflows} - \text{liabilities} - \text{deferred inflows} = \text{fund balance}$$

This form recognizes that governmental accounting, but not business accounting, distinguishes between assets and deferred outflows and between liabilities and deferred inflows. It also rearranges the elements to focus on fund balance. Funds of a not-for-profit entity would use the equation

$$\text{Assets} - \text{liabilities} = \text{fund balance}$$

Governments and not-for-profits do not have owners, so the term *owners' equity* is replaced by the terms **fund balance** or **net position**. Both fund balance and net position, like owners' equity, are residuals—the difference between assets (and deferred outflows in the case of governments) and the claims against those assets (liabilities and deferred inflows). According to GASB Statement No. 54, *Fund Balance Reporting and Governmental Fund Type Definitions*, the fund balance (the residual in modified accrual-based governmental funds) is reported in a hierarchy of classifications based primarily on the extent to which the government is bound to observe restrictions on how the amounts in those funds can be spent. Fund balance is the amount left to the parties with rights to the assets after all other claims have been liquidated.

Because funds can be represented by the basic accounting equation (with the slight modification for governments to distinguish between the assets and liabilities and the deferrals) that is used by businesses, they can also be accounted for by the same double-entry system of bookkeeping. Their current status and past performance can be summarized by financial statements similar to those of businesses. For example, the balance sheet of a fund can detail the specific assets, liabilities, deferrals, and elements of fund balance that underlie the accounting equation as of any point in time. A statement of revenues, expenditures, and other changes in fund balance can explain the reasons for changes in fund balance during a specified period of time.[5] A statement of cash flows can reconcile the changes in cash between the end and the beginning of a period. Fund balance information is important in identifying the available liquid resources to repay long-term debt, reduce property taxes, add new governmental programs, expand existing ones, or enhance the financial position of the government. GASB Statement No. 54 affects only the fund balance reported on the balance sheet of governmental-type funds. It does not affect the reporting of net position by proprietary or fiduciary funds. It also does not affect the reporting of net position of governmental activities in the government-wide financial statements.

Under GASB Statement No. 54, governmental fund balance information is reported in five different classifications, which provide a hierarchy indicating the extent to which the government is bound to honor constraints on the specific purposes for which amounts in the fund can be spent. Certain items are classified as nonspendable because the money has already been spent (e.g., inventory, prepaid insurance) or because it cannot be spent (e.g., endowment gifts, bequests to be held in perpetuity). For the spendable amounts, the constraints become tighter as the designation increases from unassigned to assigned, committed, or restricted (in that order).

- ***Nonspendable*** fund balance includes amounts that are not in spendable form or are legally or contractually required to be maintained intact.
- ***Restricted*** fund balance includes amounts constrained for specific purposes by external parties, through constitutional provisions or by enabling legislation.

[4] As noted earlier, in financial statements that are prepared on a full accrual basis, the residual amount is referred to as "net position"; in statements that are prepared on a modified accrual basis it is referred to as "fund balance."

[5] As will be addressed later in the text, in government accounting "expenditures" are distinguished from "expenses." For now, it is sufficient to note that the term *expenditures* is used in connection with funds that are accounted for on a modified accrual basis, whereas expenses is used in connection with those accounted for on a full accrual basis.

- ***Committed*** fund balance includes amounts constrained for specific purposes determined and adopted by a formal action by the highest decision-making authority of the government itself.
- ***Assigned*** fund balance includes amounts a government explicitly intends to use for specific purposes.
- ***Unassigned*** fund balance is the residual classification for the general fund and comprises all amounts not included in the other classifications.

Nonspendable Fund Balance

The **nonspendable fund balance** includes amounts that cannot be spent because they are either not in spendable form or are legally or contractually required to remain intact. "Not in spendable form" items include those that are *not expected to be converted to cash*, such as inventory, prepaid amounts, **deferred outflows of resources**, the long-term portion of loans and notes receivable, and property acquired for resale. However, if the use of proceeds collected from any receivables or sales is restricted, committed, or assigned, then they should be included in the appropriate fund balance classification rather than the nonspendable fund balance. An example of an amount that is legally or contractually required to be maintained intact is the principal of an endowment fund (an investment fund in which only investment income, not the principal, can be spent).

Restricted Fund Balance

The **restricted fund balance** includes amounts constrained to specific purposes by their providers, through constitutional provisions, or by enabling legislation. Constraints can be externally imposed by creditors, bondholders, grant providers, contributors, or laws and regulations of other governments. Enabling legislation authorizes the government to assess, levy, charge, or mandate payments of resources and includes a legally enforceable requirement that those resources be used only for the specific purpose stipulated in the legislation. Restrictions placed on resources may be changed or lifted only with the consent of the providers. Thus, the level of constraint on a restricted fund balance is equivalent to the level of constraint on the use of net assets in proprietary funds and the government-wide statements.

Committed Fund Balance

The **committed fund balance** includes amounts that can only be used for specific purposes pursuant to constraints imposed by formal action of the government's highest level of decision-making authority. Commitments cannot be lifted unless the government removes or changes the specified use by taking the same formal action that originally imposed the constraint. Committed funds include contractual obligations for which existing resources in the fund have been specifically committed for use. The funds may also include "rainy day" or "stabilization funds."

Assigned Fund Balance

The **assigned fund balance** includes amounts that are neither restricted nor committed but which the government intends to use for specific purposes. Intent can be expressed by either a governing body or an official, such as from a finance committee, which has been delegated the authority to assign amounts to be used for specific purposes. Unlike the committed fund balance, the authority for making an assignment does not have to be made by the government's highest level of decision-making authority. Thus, constraints imposed on assigned amounts can be more easily removed or modified than those that are imposed on committed amounts.

Unassigned Fund Balance

The **unassigned fund balance** is the residual classification for the **general fund** and includes amounts that have not been assigned to other funds and have not been restricted, committed, or assigned to specific purposes within the general fund. Thus, positive unassigned balances should be reported only in the general fund. For the other **governmental-type funds**, the only unassigned fund balance would be negative, which would indicate expenditures were greater than the resources available for specific purposes.

Fund Balance Disclosures

Fund balance classification policies and procedures should be reported in the notes to the financial statements. The government's highest level of decision-making authority and the formal action that is required to establish a fund balance commitment should be indicated. For the assigned fund balance, the government should disclose the body or official authorized to assign amounts to a specific purpose and what policy is established. The government should also report the order in which restricted, committed, assigned, and unassigned amounts are spent when amounts in more than one classification are available for a particular purpose. Finally, the government should disclose the purpose of each major special revenue fund.

USE OF MULTIPLE FUNDS TO ACCOUNT FOR AN ENTITY

Governments and not-for-profits separate resources into funds for reasons that differ considerably from those for which businesses establish subsidiaries. Businesses generally establish subsidiaries to account for their activities by product or region, to isolate certain business risks, and to minimize their tax obligations. Governments and not-for-profits, on the other hand, most commonly separate resources into funds to ensure that they adhere to restrictions placed on them by legislators, grantors, **donors**, or other outside parties. For example, if a university were to receive a donation that may be used only for scholarships, it would account for the resources received in a special scholarship fund. Fund accounting promotes both control and accountability over restricted resources. To a lesser extent, governments and not-for-profits establish funds to account for certain activities—often those of a business type—that are different in nature from their usual activities. For example, a government might account for its golf course, which operates similarly to a privately owned course, in a fund separate from that used to account for its general operations. By accounting for these types of activities in their own accounting and fiscal entities, the entities are better able to control the activities' revenues and expenditures and to assess their overall financial performance.

To appreciate the relationship between the two or more funds used to account for a single entity, one must remember that each fund is a separate accounting entity. Thus, every transaction that affects a fund must be recorded by at least one debit and one credit. Any transaction that affects two or more funds must be accounted for as if it affected two or more independent businesses and must be recorded individually in each fund. Suppose that a city maintains two funds: a general fund accounts for its unassigned resources and general operations, and a utility fund accounts for its electric utility, which sells electricity to city residents and other government departments. The electric utility bills the other city departments, all of which are accounted for in the general operating fund, for $10,000. The following entries would be appropriate:

Utility fund		
Accounts receivable (from general fund)	$10,000	
Revenue from sale of electricity		$10,000
To record the sale of electricity to general fund		

General fund		
Electricity expenditure	$10,000	
Accounts payable (to utility fund)		$10,000
To record the use of electricity		

BASIS OF ACCOUNTING AND MEASUREMENT FOCUS

The **basis of accounting** determines *when* transactions and events are recognized. For instance, if an entity adopts the full accrual basis of accounting, a transaction is recognized when it has its substantive economic impact. If, on the other hand, it adopts the cash basis, the transaction is recognized only when cash related to the transaction is received or paid. The **measurement focus** of an entity determines *what* is being reported on—which assets and liabilities will be given accounting recognition and reported on the balance sheet. The two concepts obviously are closely related; the selection of one implies the selection of the other. For example, if an entity adopts a cash basis of accounting, then its measurement focus will necessarily be on cash. Only cash will be reported on its balance sheet. Correspondingly, measurement focus also determines whether net profit (the net increase in all economic resources) or merely the net change in selected resource flows (such as the net increase in current financial resources) is being reported.

If an entity adopts a **full accrual basis** of accounting, which is required of businesses, then its measurement focus will automatically be on all economic resources, and its balance sheet will report on all assets and liabilities, both current and noncurrent. Increases or decreases in net capital assets and long-term obligations are recognized as revenues or expenses. Capital assets are a government's long-lived assets such as land, buildings, equipment, vehicles, roads, bridges, and streetlights. Suppose that an organization purchases a vehicle for $25,000 by issuing a note for the entire amount. The following entry (quite familiar to anyone who has studied conventional business accounting) would be appropriate:

Vehicles	$25,000	
Notes payable		$25,000
To record the acquisition of a vehicle		

Inasmuch as governments may be primarily concerned with the assets needed to satisfy current year obligations, they may adopt a **modified accrual basis** of accounting and a measurement focus on mainly short-term financial assets and liabilities.[6] Therefore, capital assets and long-term liabilities would be excluded from the balance sheet, and net changes in short-term financial assets and liabilities would be recognized as revenues or expenditures (as opposed to expenses). For example, if a government borrows $25,000 (issuing a long-term note) and uses the proceeds to purchase a vehicle, the following entries would be proper:

Cash	$25,000	
Proceeds from borrowing[7]		$25,000
To record the issuance of a long-term note		
Expenditure for vehicles	$25,000	
Cash		$25,000
To record the purchase of the vehicle		

The government would report neither the vehicle nor the long-term note on its fund balance sheet. Instead, it would record both the increase and subsequent decrease in a financial asset (cash) on the fund's statement of revenues and expenditures or a comparable statement that explains the changes in net financial resources. From an accounting standpoint, neither the vehicle nor the related liability would be recognized. The vehicle, in effect, would be written-off (expensed) at the time acquired. The proceeds from the note would be recorded as proceeds from borrowing, an increase in a fund balance account that, like a revenue, would be closed into fund balance at the end of the year.

---

[6] Although not-for-profits may adopt a modified accrual basis of accounting for purposes of internal management and control, FASB standards require that they prepare their general-purpose external reports on a full accrual basis.

[7] Proceeds from borrowing are reported as an "other financing source." Other financing sources, while not technically revenues, have key characteristics of revenues. That is, at year-end, like revenues, they are closed into (added to) fund balance.

In the remaining sections of this chapter, we study the financial reports of governments and not-for-profit organizations to observe how they use multiple funds to report their activities. To reinforce the purposes of fund accounting and the relationships among funds, we present a simple, highly stylized example, "Fund Accounting in a School District." We use as our illustration a public school district, which accounts for its funds on a modified accrual basis, and hence its measurement focus is on current financial resources. In particular, the illustration is intended to emphasize that

- Each fund is, in essence, a separate accounting and fiscal entity.
- Because the funds are not on a full accrual basis, some economic resources and obligations are not recognized on the balance sheet as assets and liabilities (and, hence, must be accounted for only in government-wide (full accrual) statements or in off-the-balance-sheet records).

Example

Fund Accounting in a School District

A newly formed public school district accounts for its operations on a modified accrual basis. It maintains four funds:

- ***A general fund.*** This fund accounts for taxes and other unassigned resources.
- ***A capital projects fund.*** This fund accounts for financial resources that are restricted, committed, or assigned to expenditures for capital outlays.
- ***A debt service fund.*** This fund accounts for financial resources that are restricted, committed, or assigned to expenditures for principal and interest on its long-term debt. It may be viewed as a savings account (or sinking fund) for resources restricted either by the debt covenants (agreements) or by policies of the district itself.
- ***A special revenue fund.*** This fund accounts for state grants that are restricted for specific purposes.

The following is a highly aggregated summary of the district's first year of operations:

1. The district levied $9.0 million of general property taxes, of which it actually collected $8.8 million. It expects to collect the balance shortly after year-end. These taxes are unassigned; they can be used for any legitimate educational purpose. Therefore, the district should record them in its general fund.

General fund		
Cash	$8.8	
Property taxes receivable	0.2	
Property tax revenue		$9.0
To record property taxes		

2. The district received a state grant of $0.2 million to purchase computers. This grant is restricted for a specific purpose and therefore must be recorded in a restricted fund, the special revenue fund.

Special revenue fund		
Cash	$0.2	
Grant revenue		$0.2
To record a state grant restricted for the acquisition of computers		

3. The district issued $12.0 million in long-term bonds to construct a school building. The proceeds must be used for the intended purpose and therefore must be recorded in the capital

projects fund. Because the capital project fund is on a modified accrual basis of accounting, which excludes the recognition of both long-term assets and long-term liabilities, the proceeds are recognized in a revenue-type account—one that will cause fund balance, rather than a liability, to increase. Of course, the district must maintain a record of both its long-lived assets and obligations in capital asset and long-term obligation ledgers or in other off-the-balance-sheet lists. They will also be recorded in the district's government-wide statements, as we will discuss shortly.

Capital projects fund		
Cash	$12.0	
Other financing source: Proceeds from borrowing		$12.0
To record the issuance of bonds		

4. The district constructed the school building for $11.0 million. The construction of the school building must be accounted for as an expenditure rather than a capital asset. The asset must be recorded in a supplementary ledger or list as well as on the district's government-wide statements.

Capital projects fund		
Construction of building (expenditure)	$11.0	
Cash		$11.0
To record the costs of constructing the school building		

5. The district incurred $6.0 million in general operating expenditures, of which it actually paid $5.5 million.

General fund		
General operating expenditures	$6.0	
Cash		$5.5
Accounts payable		0.5
To record general operating expenditures		

6. Using its state grant, the district purchased computers for $0.1 million. As with the construction of the building, the district would recognize the acquisition as an expenditure, but record the asset in a supplementary ledger or list as well as the government-wide statements.

Special revenue fund		
Acquisition of computers (expenditures)	$0.1	
Cash		$0.1
To record the acquisition of computers		

7. The district transferred $1.1 million from the general fund to the debt service fund to make the first payments of both principal and interest that are due in the following year. Broken down into its components, this transaction is straightforward, involving simple entries to each of the two funds:

General fund		
Other financing use: Nonreciprocal transfer-out to debt service fund	$1.1	
Cash		$1.1
To record transfer to the debt service fund		
Debt service fund		
Cash	$1.1	
Other financing source: Nonreciprocal transfer-in from general fund		$1.1
To record transfer from the general fund		

Tables 2-1 and 2-2 summarize the transactions into balance sheets and statements of revenues and expenditures for the four funds. To emphasize that each fund is a separate accounting and reporting entity, and hence their resources are not interchangeable, combined totals are deliberately omitted.

TABLE 2-1 School District's Balance Sheet (in millions)

	General	Special Revenue	Capital Projects	Debt Service
Assets				
Cash	$2.2	$0.1	$1.0	$1.1
Property taxes receivable	0.2			
Totals	$2.4	$0.1	$1.0	$1.1
Liabilities and fund balances				
Accounts payable	$0.5			
Fund balances (net assets)	1.9	$0.1	$1.0	$1.1
Totals	$2.4	$0.1	$1.0	$1.1

TABLE 2-2 School District's Statement of Revenues, Expenditures, and Other Changes in Fund Balances (in millions)

	General	Special Revenue	Capital Projects	Debt Service
Property tax revenue	$9.0			
Revenue from state grant		$0.2		
Total revenues	9.0	0.2	–	–
Operating expenditures	6.0			
Construction of building			$11.0	
Acquisition of computers		0.1		
Total expenditures	6.0	0.1	11.0	–
Excess of revenues over expenditures	3.0	0.1	(11.0)	–
Other financing sources (uses)				
Transfers in/(out)	(1.1)			$1.1
Proceeds from borrowing			12.0	
Increase in fund balance	$1.9	$0.1	$1.0	$1.1

HOW CAN FUNDS BE COMBINED AND CONSOLIDATED?

As noted in Chapter 1, GASB Statement No. 34 model mandates that governments prepare two separate, albeit related, sets of financial statements. The first set, the *government-wide statements*, concentrates on the government as a whole. It *consolidates* all of a government's operations and includes within its measurement focus all of the government's economic resources, including capital assets. The statements are presented on a full accrual basis. Tables 2-3 and 2-4 (which will be discussed later in the chapter) illustrate the government-wide statements of Charlotte, North Carolina.

The second set, the *fund financial statements*, views the government as a collection of separate funds. Governmental- and business-type funds are reported on separate schedules. The schedule that reports governmental funds includes one column for the general fund, one for each of the other major funds, and one that combines all the nonmajor funds. Although these statements contain "totals" columns, they merely *combine* rather than consolidate the funds. Hence, interfund items (such as receivables and payables or transfers from one fund to another) are not eliminated. These statements focus only on current financial resources and, accordingly, are prepared on a modified accrual basis. Tables 2-5, 2-6, and 2-7 present Charlotte's fund financial statements (including a reconciliation schedule, to be discussed later in the chapter) for governmental (as opposed to business) activities. It should be noted that the fund balance in the fund financial statements is presented based on the hierarchy under the five-fund classification per GASB Statement No. 54, *Fund Balance Reporting and Governmental Fund Type Definitions*, discussed earlier. Whereas the government-wide financial statements better serve the GASB's objective of reporting on the extent to which the government achieved interperiod equity, the fund financial statements focus on short-term fiscal accountability and thus are more closely tied to the objective of reporting on budgetary compliance.

Except for funds used to account for **business-type activities**, governments maintain their funds on a modified accrual basis. Thus, to prepare their government-wide statements, they must adjust the individual fund statements so that they are on a full accrual basis. They do not, of course, have to maintain two separate sets of books.

In prescribing how not-for-profit entities should report to external parties, the FASB takes a considerably different approach from that of the GASB. The FASB permits not-for-profits to consolidate the assets and liabilities of funds into a single balance sheet. However, the **net assets** (assets less liabilities) of the entity must be reported in two categories: *net assets without donor restrictions and net assets with donor restrictions* (the characteristics of each will be set forth later in this chapter and discussed in detail in Chapter 12). The FASB also requires that on its statement of activities (similar to a business's income statement) the entity display separately those revenues that are restricted by donors and those that are not. Assets are considered restricted when donors (as opposed to management, boards of governors, trustees, or creditors) place constraints on when or how they may be used.

The sections that follow present an overview of the main funds maintained by both governments and not-for-profits and how they are reported. Bear in mind that each fund, like a subsidiary of a corporation, is a separate accounting and fiscal entity for which separate financial statements can be prepared. Just as the financial statements of a corporation can be prepared on different bases (e.g., full accrual, cash, tax, regulatory), so can those of individual funds (e.g., modified accrual, full accrual). And just as the financial statements of a company's subsidiaries can be combined in different ways (e.g., by region, by product line, by size), so too can those of a government or not-for-profit (e.g., by type, by dollar value, by nature of restrictions).

TABLE 2-3 City of Charlotte, North Carolina

Statement of Net Position June 30, 2016 (in thousands)				
	Primary Government			Component Unit
	Governmental Activities	Business-type Activities	Total	Charlotte Regional Visitors Authority
Assets				
Cash and cash equivalents	$ 868,186	$ 998,518	$ 1,866,704	$21,323
Receivables, net	19,417	94,233	113,650	1,777
Due from other governmental agencies	88,995	157,507	246,502	663
Due from component unit	3,118	—	3,118	—
Due from primary government	—	—	—	954
Internal balances	(6,082)	6,082	—	—
Inventories	1,426	8,669	10,095	463
Other	90	—	90	395
Restricted assets:				
Temporarily restricted				
Cash and cash equivalents	6,394	400,052	406,446	—
Investments	127,076	59,866	186,942	—
Permanently restricted				
Cash and cash equivalents	3,111	—	3,111	—
Notes receivable	87,511	—	87,511	—
Other postemployment benefit assets (Note 5.f.)	—	26,133	26,133	—
Capital assets (Note 4.f.)				
Land	3,240,220	406,565	3,646,785	—
Buildings, improvements, infrastructure, intangibles, and machinery and equipment, net	2,487,510	4,389,783	6,877,293	—
Construction in progress	257,521	1,627,389	1,884,910	—
Total assets	7,184,493	8,174,797	15,359,290	25,575
Deferred Outflow of Resources				
Pension deferrals (Note 5)	1,634	53	1,687	60
Contributions to pension plan in current fiscal year (Note 5)	26,530	6,123	32,653	932
Accumulated decreases in fair value of hedging derivatives	67,220	50,781	118,001	—
Unamortized bond refunding charges	5,829	18,000	23,829	—
Total deferred outflow of resources	101,213	74,957	176,170	992

(Continues)

TABLE 2-3 **City of Charlotte, North Carolina** *(Continued)*

Statement of Net Position June 30, 2016 (in thousands)

	Primary Government			Component Unit
	Governmental Activities	Business-type Activities	Total	Charlotte Regional Visitors Authority
Liabilities				
Accounts payable/claims payable	100,880	105,008	205,888	4,949
Deposits and retainage payable	11,649	25,171	36,820	5,418
Accrued interest payable	12,590	35,330	47,920	—
Due to component unit	894	60	954	—
Due to primary government	—	—	—	3,118
Unearned revenues	859	—	859	29
Liabilities payable from restricted assets	5,407	62,020	67,427	—
Net pension liability (Note 5)	39,076	7,291	46,367	983
Noncurrent liabilities (Note 4.j.):				
Due within one year	267,748	106,990	374,738	—
Due after one year	1,473,582	2,827,519	4,301,101	6,993
Total liabilities	1,912,685	3,169,389	5,082,074	21,490
Deferred Inflow of Resources				
Prepaid taxes	316	—	316	—
Pension deferrals (Note 5)	23,672	2,668	26,340	511
Total deferred inflows of resources	23,988	2,668	26,656	511
Net Position				
Net investment in capital assets	4,563,879	3,676,609	8,240,488	—
Restricted for:				
State statute	68,699	—	68,699	—
Debt service	6,215	60,397	66,612	—
Perpetual care—nonexpendable	90,622	—	90,622	—
Other purposes (Note 1.d.(8))	188,989	—	188,989	—
Passenger facility charges	—	317,283	317,283	—
Contract facility charges	—	30,116	30,116	—
Airport working capital	—	35,588	35,588	—
Unrestricted	430,629	957,704	1,388,333	4,566
Total net position	$5,349,033	$5,077,697	$10,426,730	$ 4,566

TABLE 2-4 City of Charlotte, North Carolina

Statement of Activities for the Year Ended June 30, 2016 (in thousands)								
		Program Revenues			Net (Expense) Revenue and Changes in Net Position			
					Primary Government			Component Unit
	Expenses	Fees, Fines, and Charges for Services	Operating Grants and Contributions	Capital Grants and Contributions	Governmental Activities	Business-type Activities	Total	Charlotte Regional Visitors Authority
Activities								
Primary Government:								
Governmental-Public safety	$ 374,328	$ 38,772	$ 8,985	$ 3,339	$ (323,232)	$ —	$ (323,232)	$ —
Sanitation	55,717	8,824	509	500	(45,884)	—	(45,884)	—
General administration	58,256	2,913	—	—	(55,343)	—	(55,343)	—
Support services	31,210	35,828	16	21	4,655	—	4,655	—
Engineering and property management	52,044	11,224	—	222	(40,598)	—	(40,598)	—
Streets and highways	174,912	9,080	20,460	14,008	(131,364)	—	(131,364)	—
Culture and recreation	45,158	3,629	2,948	1,038	(37,543)	—	(37,543)	—
Community planning and development	75,889	4,859	18,274	1,682	(51,074)	—	(51,074)	—
Interest and other charges	57,498	—	—	—	(57,498)	—	(57,498)	—
Total governmental	925,012	115,129	51,192	20,810	(737,881)	—	(737,881)	—
Business-type								
Water	143,992	166,043	—	11,032	—	33,083	33,083	—
Sewer	163,565	211,084	—	15,238	—	62,757	62,757	—
Storm water	16,614	70,042	—	—	—	53,428	53,428	—
Airport	205,860	277,891	—	20,706	—	92,737	92,737	—
Public transit	173,243	32,404	10,945	194,994	—	65,100	65,100	—
Total business-type	703,274	757,464	10,945	241,970	—	307,105	307,105	—
Total primary government	$ 1,628,286	$ 872,593	$ 62,137	$ 262,780	$ (737,881)	$ 307,105	$ (430,776)	—

(Continues)

TABLE 2-4 **City of Charlotte, North Carolina** *(Continued)*

Statement of Activities for the Year Ended June 30, 2016 (in thousands)								
		Program Revenues			Net (Expense) Revenue and Changes in Net Position			
					Primary Government			Component Unit
	Expenses	Fees, Fines, and Charges for Services	Operating Grants and Contributions	Capital Grants and Contributions	Governmental Activities	Business-type Activities	Total	Charlotte Regional Visitors Authority
Component Unit:								
Charlotte Regional Visitors Authority	$ 59,699	$ 36,100	—	—	—	—	—	(23,599)
General revenues:								
Taxes								
Property					452,209	—	452,209	—
Sales					114,192	—	114,192	
Sales, levied for public transit					—	89,617	89,617	—
Utility franchise					53,545	—	53,545	—
Occupancy					49,079	—	49,079	—
Prepared foods					30,026	—	30,026	—
Business privilege					283	—	283	—
Municipal vehicle					17,068	—	17,068	—
Payment from City of Charlotte					—	—	—	25,260
Grants and contributions not restricted to specific programs					23,383	—	23,383	—
Investment earnings					4,670	7,065	11,735	55
Miscellaneous					7,012	(7,091)	(79)	160
Transfers					(21,609)	21,609	—	—
Total general revenues and transfers					729,858	111,200	841,058	25,475
Change in net position					(8,023)	418,305	410,282	1,876
Net position—beginning					5,357,056	4,659,392	10,016,448	2,690
Net position—ending					$ 5,349,033	$ 5,077,697	$ 10,426,730	$ 4,566

The notes to the financial statements are an integral part of this statement.

TABLE 2-5 **City of Charlotte, North Carolina**

	Balance Sheet Governmental Funds June 30, 2016 (in thousands)				
	General	**Debt Service**	**Capital Projects**	**Other Governmental Funds**	**Total Governmental Funds**
Assets					
Cash and cash equivalents	$ 184,036	$ 276,235	$ 107,465	$ 181,998	$ 749,734
Receivables, net:					
Property taxes	9,316	2,059	316	107	11,798
Accounts	5,546	—	120	191	5,857
Other	—	—	—	282	282
Total receivables	14,862	2,059	436	580	17,937
Due from other governmental agencies	46,894	5,732	19,563	16,798	88,987
Due from other funds	190	4,400	—	—	4,590
Due from component unit	—	2,820	298	—	3,118
Inventories	1,426	—	—	—	1,426
Prepaid expenditures	—	—	—	90	90
Restricted assets:					
Cash and cash equivalents	—	79	6,315	—	6,394
Investments	—	36	127,040	—	127,076
Total restricted assets	—	115	133,355	—	133,470
Notes receivable	13	—	50,261	37,237	87,511
Total assets	$ 247,421	$ 291,361	$ 311,378	$ 236,703	$ 1,086,863
Liabilities, Deferred Inflows of Resources, and Fund Balances					
Liabilities:					
Accounts payable	$ 34,281	$ 344	$ 9,861	$ 4,979	$ 49,465
Deposits and retainage payable	8,926	—	2,378	345	11,649
Due to other funds	—	—	4,400	190	4,590
Due to component unit	—	—	296	598	894
Unearned revenues	—	—	—	859	859
Liabilities payable from restricted assets	—	—	5,407	—	5,407
Total liabilities	43,207	344	22,342	6,971	72,864

(Continues)

TABLE 2-5 City of Charlotte, North Carolina *(Continued)*

	Balance Sheet Governmental Funds June 30, 2016 (in thousands)				
	General	**Debt Service**	**Capital Projects**	**Other Governmental Funds**	**Total Governmental Funds**
Deferred inflows of resources:					
Prepaid taxes	316	—	—	—	316
Unavailable revenues	12,892	4,879	734	395	18,900
Total deferred inflows of resources	13,208	4,879	734	395	19,216
Fund balances:					
Nonspendable:					
Inventories	1,426	—	—	—	1,426
Perpetual care	—	—	—	3,111	3,111
Long-term notes receivable	13	—	50,261	37,237	87,511
Restricted:					
State statute	62,967	5,732	—	—	68,699
Special obligation debt service	—	6,215	—	—	6,215
Other purposes (Note 1.d.(8))	—	—	—	188,989	188,989
Committed:					
Capital projects	21,795	—	238,041	—	259,836
Other purposes (Note 1.d.(8))	3,215	34,510	—	—	37,725
Assigned:					
Debt service	—	239,681	—	—	239,681
Unassigned (Note 3)	101,590	—	—	—	101,590
Total fund balances	191,006	286,138	288,302	229,337	994,783
Total liabilities, deferred inflows of resources, and fund balances	$ 247,421	$ 291,361	$ 311,378	$ 236,703	$ 1,086,863

The notes to the financial statements are an integral part of this statement.

TABLE 2-6 City of Charlotte, North Carolina

Reconciliation of the Governmental Funds Balance Sheet to the Statement of Net Position June 30, 2016 (In Thousands)	
Total fund balances for governmental funds	$ 994,783
Total net position reported for governmental activities in the statement of net position is different because:	
Capital assets used in governmental activities are not financial resources and, therefore, are not reported in the funds.	5,985,233
Contributions to pension plans in the current fiscal year are deferred outflows of resources.	26,415
Other long-term assets are not available to pay for current-period expenditures and, therefore, are deferred in the funds.	93,143
Internal service funds are used to charge the costs of insured and uninsured risks of loss as well as employee health and life claims to individual funds. The assets and liabilities of the internal service funds are included in governmental activities in the statement of net position.	52,369
Long-term liabilities are not due and payable in the current period and therefore are not reported in the funds (Note 2.a.).	(1,741,987)
Net pension liability	(38,944)
Pension-related deferrals	(21,979)
Total net position of governmental activities	$ 5,349,033

The notes to the financial statements are an integral part of this statement.

WHAT ARE THE MAIN TYPES OF A GOVERNMENT'S FUNDS?

In this section, we introduce the specific funds governments use to summarize and report on their activities. First, we present a brief overview of the funds structure, then we examine each type of fund in greater detail.

Most general-purpose governments engage in three broad categories of activities:

- ***Governmental activities*** are those financed predominantly through taxes and intergovernmental grants.
- ***Business-type activities*** are those financed predominantly through user charges.
- ***Fiduciary activities*** are those for which the government acts as a trustee or custodian for individuals, external organizations, or other governments.

Corresponding roughly to these three kinds of activities, governments classify funds into three broad categories: governmental funds, proprietary funds, and fiduciary funds.

GOVERNMENTAL FUNDS

Governmental-type funds are maintained to account for governments' operating and financing activities. A unique feature of governmental funds is that their expenditures are controlled by legally adopted annual budgets that are cash oriented and short run in nature. There are five primary and most common types of governmental funds.

- ***General fund.*** This fund accounts for all resources that are not required to be accounted for in other funds; in essence, it accounts for all unassigned resources.

TABLE 2-7 City of Charlotte, North Carolina

Statement of Revenues, Expenditures, and Changes in Fund Balances Governmental Funds for the Year Ended June 30, 2016 (in thousands)

	General	Debt Service	Capital Projects	Other Governmental Funds	Total Governmental Funds
Revenues:					
Property taxes	$ 348,988	$ 86,539	$ 11,153	$ 4,883	$ 451,563
Other taxes	101,993	18,131	11,003	77,386	208,513
Intergovernmental	99,938	1,158	9,425	55,942	166,463
Licenses, fees, and fines	27,973	58	14,504	828	43,363
Investment earnings	943	1,275	585	942	3,745
Private contributions	—	—	4,039	—	4,039
Administrative charges	34,793	—	—	—	34,793
Charges for current services	7,234	—	—	—	7,234
Miscellaneous	2,267	160	560	7,064	10,051
Total revenues	624,129	107,321	51,269	147,045	929,764
Expenditures:					
Current					
Public safety	347,184	—	—	12,003	359,187
Sanitation	52,265	—	—	—	52,265
General administration	38,475	—	—	1,819	40,294
Support services	29,707	—	—	21	29,728
Engineering and property management	20,973	—	—	—	20,973
Streets and highways	32,859	—	—	30,065	62,924
Culture and recreation	4,721	—	—	22,591	27,312
Community planning and development	26,765	—	(3,803)	26,851	49,813
Debt service					
Principal	—	112,033	—	—	112,033
Interest and other charges	—	66,557	—	—	66,557
Capital outlay	—	—	154,320	—	154,320
Total expenditures	552,949	178,590	150,517	93,350	975,406
Excess (deficiency) of revenues over (under) expenditures	71,180	(71,269)	(99,248)	53,695	(45,642)
***Other Financing Sources (Uses)*:**					
Sales of capital assets	934	—	33,043	50	34,027
Commercial paper issued	—	—	66,213	—	66,213
Installment purchases issued	—	185	23,500	—	23,685
Refunding debt issued	—	33,010	—	—	33,010
Premium on debt issuance	—	5,906	—	—	5,906
Payment to refunded bond escrow agent	—	(38,650)	—	—	(38,650)
Transfers in	3,268	93,173	75,984	14,572	186,997
Transfers out	(61,206)	(31,341)	(51,436)	(64,623)	(208,606)
Total other financing sources (uses)	(57,004)	62,283	147,304	(50,001)	102,582
Net change in fund balances	14,176	(8,986)	48,056	3,694	56,940
Fund balances—beginning	176,830	295,124	240,246	225,643	937,843
Fund balances—ending	$ 191,006	$ 286,138	$ 288,302	$ 229,337	$ 994,783

The notes to the financial statements are an integral part of this statement.

- ***Special revenue funds.*** These funds account for revenues that are restricted or committed to expenditure for specific purposes other than debt service or capital projects.
- ***Debt service funds.*** These funds are used to account for resources that are restricted, committed, or assigned for the payment of interest and principal on long-term debt.
- ***Capital projects funds.*** These funds are used to account for resources that are restricted, committed, or assigned for capital outlays.
- ***Permanent funds.*** These funds are used to report resources that are legally restricted so that only earnings, not principal, may be used to support the government's programs.

PROPRIETARY FUNDS

Proprietary-type funds are used to account for the ongoing business-type activities of a government—those that are operated in a manner similar to private business enterprises and in which a government's intent is to recover costs primarily through user charges. There are two types of proprietary funds:

- ***Enterprise funds.*** These funds are used to account for business-type activities in which the government sells goods or services to the general public at large (users external to the governmental unit).
- ***Internal service funds.*** These funds are used to account for business-type activities in which the customers are other funds, departments, or agencies within the same governmental unit, or occasionally to other governmental units.

Governmental-type funds may be characterized as **expendable funds**, in that their resources are received from taxes, fees, or other sources, and then spent. There is no expectation that the funds will be reimbursed for services rendered to constituents or other departments. In contrast, proprietary-type funds are said to be **nonexpendable** (or **revolving**) **funds**. The government may make an initial contribution to establish a proprietary fund but, thereafter, the fund is expected to "pay its own way" (at least in part) through customer charges.

FIDUCIARY FUNDS

Fiduciary-type funds are used to account for resources held by the government in a capacity that are intended to benefit parties other than the government itself. There are four types of fiduciary funds:

- ***Pension and other employee benefit trust funds.*** Many governments administer and control pension plans and retiree health care benefits, requiring the government to account for these plans through a fiduciary fund. The fund reports assets accumulated to fund liabilities owed to current employees and retirees. These assets, however, can only be spent by the government on employee benefits.
- ***Investment trust funds.*** Many states and counties sponsor investment pools for local governments. These local governments are able to invest available cash into these pools and earn a return on their assets, and then they can withdraw the funds when needed. As such, the assets, while under the control of the sponsor, do not belong to the sponsor but rather to the participants.
- ***Private purpose trust funds.*** These funds represent activities not covered by pension, other employee benefit, or **investment trust funds**. These funds might include endowments, certain scholarship funds, funds held for estates not yet settled in court, or funds in which a government has not found the owner.

- ***Custodial funds.*** These funds are used to account for resources not held in trust by governments, but instead are held temporarily by one government for another. While trust funds are held for a long period of time, **custodial funds** are typically held for a short time period, and the agent has limited responsibility for the management of the resources.

Unlike the other types of funds, fiduciary funds are neither consolidated with nor even incorporated into government-wide statements. That is because they benefit only outsiders, and a government cannot expect to have use of their resources.

Whereas a government should have only one general fund, it may have any number of the other types of funds. For example, a city may maintain a separate special revenue fund for each revenue source that is restricted. Similarly, it may maintain a separate **capital projects fund** for each of its major capital projects and a separate debt service fund for each issue of outstanding bonds.

Having provided an overview of the funds structure, we now take a more comprehensive look at each of the main types of funds.

THE GENERAL FUND

WHAT'S NOTABLE ABOUT EACH TYPE OF GOVERNMENTAL FUND?

The general fund is the most significant single fund maintained by all state and local governmental entities. It is used to account for all resources that are not legally or contractually restricted or arbitrarily set aside for specific activities. Accordingly, the general fund accounts for all the *unassigned* resources so the bulk of its fund balance will generally be classified as unassigned, and it will be the only fund that reports a *positive* unassigned fund balance, which may serve as a useful measure of a government's net resources available for spending at the end of the fiscal year. All governments with general **governmental activities** will have *one* general fund, and by default it is a major fund. All funds are not created equal; the general fund is more equal than the others. Ultimately, the general fund accounts for financial resources not reported in any other funds. In a city or other general-purpose government, it embraces most major governmental functions—police, fire, street maintenance, sanitation, and general administration.

Why does one single fund cover so many functions? Recall the rationale for fund accounting. Funds are established mainly to ensure that governments adhere to resource restrictions. As noted previously, a government's fund structure almost always differs from its organizational structure. Funds divide a government into categories of resource restriction, not functional departments or operations. To keep their accounting systems as simple as possible, governments should establish the minimum number of funds to ensure legal compliance or efficient administration. Governments finance their general operations mainly with unrestricted resources, such as property, sales, and personal and corporate income tax. Therefore, they can legally intermingle these resources and can properly account for all activities financed with unassigned resources in a single fund. The budgetary process controls or strongly influences both the revenues and expenditures. As a rule, most of the financial resources are expended and replenished on an annual basis.

Although the resources of the general fund are not subject to the types of restrictions that characterize other funds, they are not necessarily available for spending. Portions of fund balance may be considered nonspendable (e.g., offset by inventories, prepaid expenses, and deferred outflows of resources), and restricted, committed, or assigned for specific purposes. In other words, the general fund balance may be divided among all five fund balance classifications.

By noting the assets and liabilities reported in a fund, a statement user can draw meaningful inferences as to the fund's measurement focus and basis of accounting. The balance sheet of the general fund in Table 2-5 includes assets other than cash. Were the general fund accounted for on a cash basis, its only asset would be cash. Therefore, the general fund is accounted for on a basis broader than simply cash.

At the same time, however, the balance sheet in Table 2-5 shows neither capital assets nor long-term debt. Obviously, the city owns police cars, firefighting equipment, computers, and buildings. Moreover, it probably financed some of its capital assets with long-term debt. If the general fund were accounted for on a full accrual basis (full economic resources measurement focus), these assets and liabilities would be reported on the balance sheet. Instead, they have apparently been written off as acquired (and presumably listed in off-the-balance-sheet ledgers or other records). Therefore, the general fund is accounted for on a basis between cash and full accrual (i.e., a modified accrual basis) and has a measurement focus between cash and all economic resources (i.e., current financial resources). This basis and measurement focus is discussed in depth beginning in Chapter 4.

SPECIAL REVENUE FUNDS

Special revenue funds are established to account for specific revenue streams that are legally restricted or committed for specified purposes and are expected to comprise a substantial portion of the inflows reported in the fund. Examples of typical restrictions include the following:

- Gasoline tax revenues that must be used for highway maintenance
- Hotel occupancy taxes earmarked for specific purposes (such as supporting a convention and visitors bureau)
- Lottery fund proceeds that must be used for education
- A state law-enforcement grant that must be used to train police officers
- A state and federal grant used to promote public health and mental health programs
- Private donations that must be used to repair and maintain parks and other recreational facilities
- State and federal aid for elementary and secondary education

Thus, a governmental entity can have several special revenue funds, and each of these funds is treated as a separate accounting entity for record-keeping purposes. The City of Boulder, Colorado, for example, has 14 nonmajor special revenue funds. On the other hand, New York City has eight nonmajor special revenue funds. Because the focus of the fund financial statements is on major funds, financial information of only the major special revenue funds is presented in the governmental fund financial statements. Information on all the nonmajor special revenue funds is presented in a combining balance sheet of nonmajor governmental funds.

Inasmuch as special revenue funds are, by nature, used to account for restricted resources, no portion of fund balance would be classified as "unassigned." However, because special revenue fund might report inventories, prepayments, or similar assets that will not generate cash, portions of fund balance may be classified as nonspendable. Other portions of fund balance may be classified as committed, assigned, and, of course, restricted. In the event that the fund has an overall deficit, such deficit should be reported as a *negative* unassigned fund balance.

Special revenue funds—like the general fund and, indeed, like all governmental funds—use the same basis of accounting. Accordingly, almost all the guidelines pertaining to the general fund set forth in this text can be extended to special revenue funds and other governmental funds.

DEBT SERVICE FUNDS

Debt service funds are a particular type of special revenue fund in that they are maintained to account for resources restricted, committed, or assigned for a specific purpose: the payment of principal and interest on all general long-term obligation debt. Debt service funds have much in common with sinking funds (resources set aside to retire debt) maintained by businesses. The debt covenants often require that the borrowing government set aside financial resources intended for servicing the debt.

Debt service funds derive their resources from other funds (e.g., transfers from the general fund) or from taxes or fees dedicated for debt service. Fund resources are expended to pay principal and interest. When governments accumulate resources to service their long-term obligations, they commonly invest them in commercial paper, treasury bills, and other financial instruments that, although secure, still provide a reasonable return. Typically, therefore, many debt service fund transactions relate to the purchase and sale of marketable securities and the recognition of investment earnings and related costs.

Conspicuously missing from the balance sheet of a debt service fund is the obligation for the debt being serviced. This should come as no surprise. First, the purpose of the debt service fund is to account for the resources being accumulated to service the debt—not the debt itself. Second, as previously noted, the debt service fund is categorized as a governmental fund, like the general fund and special revenue funds, and no governmental fund gives recognition to long-term obligations. The long-term debt, for which resources are being accumulated in a debt service fund, is reported only in the government-wide (full accrual) statements and supplementary schedules.

The one exception to this general rule, that the debt being serviced is excluded from the debt service funds, applies to interest and principal that have matured and are therefore current obligations. They would be reported as matured interest payable or matured bonds payable. But this exception is of only minor practical importance. On the day, the interest or principal matures, it is due, it should be paid, and the obligation should be satisfied. Therefore, on year-end financial statements the liability for interest or principal should be reported only if payment is due but for some reason has been delayed.

CAPITAL PROJECTS FUNDS

Capital projects funds, like debt service funds, are categorized as governmental funds and are a form of special revenue funds. They must be used whenever they are legally and contractually required. They are maintained to account for, and report, financial resources that are restricted, committed, or assigned to be used for capital outlays, including the acquisition or construction of major capital facilities and other capital assets. Even when there is no legal or contractual requirement, most governmental entities still use the capital projects fund to enhance accountability over the resources related to each project. Governments often issue bonds to finance a specific project. The resources received are restricted, committed, or assigned to that project and must be placed in the proper fund. Capital projects funds typically derive their resources from the proceeds of bonds. However, they may also receive resources that were initially received by other funds and subsequently earmarked for the acquisition of capital assets.

Just as debt service funds are used to account for the resources accumulated to service a debt, but not the debt itself, so too are capital projects funds used to account for the resources set aside to purchase or construct capital assets, but not the assets themselves. The assets, whether in the form of construction in progress or of completed projects, are reported only in the government-wide statements and in supplementary schedules.

Moreover, as with the resources accumulated to service their debts, governments must invest any excess cash awaiting expenditure for capital projects. Therefore, many transactions of typical capital projects funds, such as those of debt service funds, relate to investment activities.

PERMANENT FUNDS

Permanent funds are a relatively new type of governmental fund, a creation of the GASB Statement No. 34 reporting model. Permanent funds are a type of trust fund, and although fiduciary in nature, they are not classified and accounted as fiduciary-type funds because they are public, rather than private purpose funds. Permanent funds and **private purpose trust funds** are similar in that usually only the income they generate, not the principal, may be spent. They differ, though, in that permanent funds benefit the citizens at large or the government itself, whereas private purpose trust funds (addressed in the section pertaining to fiduciary funds that follows) benefit individuals, private organizations, or other governments. Per GASB Statement No. 54, the principal of the permanent fund is reported in the nonspendable category of fund balance.

Suppose that a government received a donation to support one of its parks. The resources received were to be invested and only the income, not the principal, could be expended. The government would establish a permanent fund to account for and maintain the donation (the principal). As income is earned, the government would transfer it to a special revenue fund, from which it could be used for the intended purpose. By contrast, if it received a similar gift to provide scholarships to the children of its employees, then it would report it in a private purpose trust fund (a fiduciary fund). Not all governmental entities have permanent funds, and these funds may be major or nonmajor funds. For example, the City of Boston has three nonmajor permanent funds, and the City of San Francisco has only one nonmajor permanent fund (a bequest fund), whereas many other cities (e.g., Chicago, New York, Orlando) have no permanent funds. Accounting and financial reporting for permanent funds is the same as that for other governmental-type funds.

WHAT'S NOTABLE ABOUT EACH TYPE OF PROPRIETARY FUND?

ENTERPRISE FUNDS

Enterprise funds are used to account for business-type activities in which the government provides goods or services on a user-charge basis to the general public at large (users external to the governmental unit). The following are examples of the types of activities that governments may account for in enterprise funds:

- Utilities, such as electric, gas, water, and sewer
- Golf courses
- Hospitals
- Mass transportation
- Toll roads
- Landfill facilities
- Convention and entertainment facilities
- Parking lots and garages
- Airport and harbor facilities
- Housing authorities

Many government enterprises are financed similarly to businesses. Although a government enterprise does not sell stock to the general public, it may issue revenue bonds. The principal and interest of the bonds are payable exclusively out of the revenues of the fund itself—not out of the general revenues of the government at large. Therefore, the resources of the fund must be kept intact and cannot be commingled with those of the government's other funds. Normally a separate fund is established for each type of activity, and each of these funds may be a major or nonmajor fund.

INTERNAL SERVICE FUNDS

These funds, such as enterprise funds, are used to account for business-type activities, but they provide goods or services to other funds, departments, or agencies within the same governmental unit (or occasionally to other governments). They bill the receiving departments at rates intended to cover the cost of the goods or services. Although there are no specific guidelines on which intragovernment activities should be accounted for in **internal service funds**, the following are common examples:

- A vehicle repair service that maintains and services the cars and trucks of the police department, fire department, sanitation department, and so forth
- A motor pool that acts as an intragovernment rental car agency
- An electronic data processing department that maintains records and performs computer services for all other departments
- A store that sells office supplies to the other government departments
- A print shop that provides government-wide printing services

Internal service funds are typically established with contributions of resources from the general or other fund. Thereafter, they are expected to be self-sustaining.

Because internal service funds sell their goods and services mainly to other departments within a governmental entity, most of their transactions are with other funds. However, internal service fund accounting is relatively straightforward as long as each fund is seen as a separate accounting entity. When an internal service fund bills another department, it would recognize both a revenue and a receivable. Simultaneously, the fund that accounts for the other department would record both an expenditure and a payable. Most of the other departments to which an internal service fund sells its goods or services are likely to be accounted for in the government's general fund or one of its other enterprise funds. This is primarily because most governmental operations (as opposed to accumulations of resources for specific purposes) are accounted for in those funds. Accordingly, they are shown apart from the enterprise funds and under the caption "Governmental Activities—Internal Service Funds."[8]

[8] To better appreciate the connection between the fund statements and the government-wide statements, note how the various cash balances of the internal service funds (Table 2-8) and the governmental funds (Table 2-5) tie into those reported on the government-wide statements (Table 2-3):

Governmental Fund Statements—Table 2-5 (Total Governmental Funds)	
Cash and cash equivalents—unrestricted	$749,734
Cash and cash equivalents—restricted	6,394
Proprietary Fund Statements—Table 2-8	
Cash and cash equivalents—internal service funds	121,653
Total	$877,781
Government-Wide Statements—Table 2-3 (Primary Government—Governmental Activities)	
Cash and cash equivalents—unrestricted	$868,186
Cash and cash equivalents—temporarily restricted	6,394
Cash and cash equivalents—permanently restricted	3,111
Other	90
Total	$877,781

TABLE 2-8 City of Charlotte, North Carolina

Statement of Net Position Proprietary Funds June 30, 2016 (in thousands)

	Business-type Activities Enterprise Funds					Governmental Activities
	Water and Sewer	**Storm Water**	**Airport**	**Public Transit**	**Total**	**Internal Service Funds**
Assets						
Current assets:						
Cash and cash equivalents	$ 321,893	$ 75,706	$ 523,696	$ 77,223	$ 998,518	$ 121,563
Receivables, net-Accounts	47,083	10,604	32,941	1,303	91,931	—
Other	499	81	1,460	262	2,302	286
Total receivables	47,582	10,685	34,401	1,565	94,233	286
Due from other governmental agencies	1,697	478	20,835	134,497	157,507	8
Inventories	1,556	—	—	7,113	8,669	—
Restricted assets						
Cash and cash equivalents	4	6,752	392,492	804	400,052	—
Investments	5	14,029	32,575	13,257	59,866	—
Total restricted assets	9	20,781	425,067	14,061	459,918	—
Total current assets	372,737	107,650	1,003,999	234,459	1,718,845	121,857
Noncurrent assets:						
Other postemployment benefit assets	17,478	1,190	6,892	573	26,133	—
Capital assets						
Land	43,600	—	306,101	56,864	406,565	—
Buildings	27,770	—	910,665	121,602	1,060,037	—
Improvements other than buildings:						
Water and sewer systems	4,149,870	—	—	—	4,149,870	—
Storm water systems	—	460,735	—	—	460,735	—
Runways	—	—	415,382	—	415,382	—
Transit corridors	—	—	—	337,014	337,014	—
Other	—	—	148,865	36,584	185,449	—
Total improvements other than buildings	4,149,870	460,735	564,247	373,598	5,548,450	—
Intangibles	18,610	3,359	3,317	8,605	33,891	—
Machinery and equipment	39,143	69	114,134	221,678	375,024	181
Construction in progress	491,342	191,540	104,147	840,360	1,627,389	—
Total capital assets	4,770,335	655,703	2,002,611	1,622,707	9,051,356	181
Less accumulated depreciation	1,504,222	61,622	699,746	362,029	2,627,619	163
Total capital assets, net	3,266,113	594,081	1,302,865	1,260,678	6,423,737	18
Total noncurrent assets	3,283,591	595,271	1,309,757	1,261,251	6,449,870	18
Total assets	3,656,328	702,921	2,313,756	1,495,710	8,168,715	121,875

(Continues)

TABLE 2-8 **City of Charlotte, North Carolina** *(Continued)*

Statement of Net Position Proprietary Funds June 30, 2016 (in thousands)						
	Business-type Activities Enterprise Funds					Governmental Activities
	Water and Sewer	Storm Water	Airport	Public Transit	Total	Internal Service Funds
Deferred Outflows of Resources						
Pension deferrals	25	4	11	13	53	1
Contributions to pension plan in current fiscal year	2,757	474	1,501	1,391	6,123	115
Accumulated decreases in fair value of hedging derivatives	50,781	—	—	—	50,781	—
Unamortized bond refunding charges	15,421	1,406	1,070	103	18,000	—
Total deferred outflows of resources	68,984	1,884	2,582	1,507	74,957	116
Liabilities						
Current liabilities:						
Accounts payable	$ 20,746	$ 1,872	$ 28,388	$ 54,002	$ 105,008	$ 986
Claims payable	—	—	—	—	—	50,429
Deposits and retainage payable	4,914	1,509	4,672	14,076	25,171	—
Accrued interest payable	33,816	535	—	979	35,330	—
Due to component unit	—	—	60	—	60	—
Current maturities of long-term liabilities	91,391	7,737	1,166	6,696	106,990	115
Current liabilities payable from restricted assets:						
Accounts payable	—	7,181	275	14,061	21,517	—
Deposits and retainage payable	—	1,030	575	—	1,605	—
Accrued interest payable	—	—	12,992	—	12,992	—
Revenue bonds payable	—	—	25,906	—	25,906	—
Total current liabilities payable from restricted assets	—	8,211	39,748	14,061	62,020	—
Total current liabilities	150,867	19,864	74,034	89,814	334,579	51,530
Noncurrent liabilities:						
General obligation bonds payable—net of unamortized premium	108,233	6,180	—	—	114,413	—
Revenue bonds payable—net of unamortized premium	1,457,662	163,696	589,765	—	2,211,123	—
Revenue bond anticipation notes payable	—	—	65,621	—	65,621	—
Commercial paper notes payable	18,118	—	—	—	18,118	—
Other financing agreements—net of unamortized premium	10,576	—	—	256,562	267,138	—
TIFIA loan agreement	—	—	—	88,353	88,353	—

(Continues)

TABLE 2-8 **City of Charlotte, North Carolina** *(Continued)*

Statement of Net Position Proprietary Funds June 30, 2016 (in thousands)

	Business-type Activities Enterprise Funds					Governmental Activities
	Water and Sewer	Storm Water	Airport	Public Transit	Total	Internal Service Funds
Derivative instrument liability	50,781	—	—	—	50,781	—
Federal revolving loan payable	—	977	—	—	977	—
Refundable water and sewer construction deposits	4,539	—	—	—	4,539	—
Due to participants	—	—	—	—	—	11,596
Compensated absences payable	2,233	221	1,499	2,503	6,456	40
Net pension liability	3,189	572	1,944	1,586	7,291	—
Net OPEB liability	—	—	—	—	—	182
Total noncurrent liabilities	1,655,331	171,646	658,829	349,004	2,834,810	11,818
Total liabilities	1,806,198	191,510	732,863	438,818	3,169,389	63,348
Deferred Inflows of Resources						
Pension deferrals	1,385	192	347	744	2,668	60
Net Position						
Net investment in capital assets	1,583,337	436,668	732,366	924,238	3,676,609	18
Restricted for:						
Debt service	—	—	60,397	—	60,397	—
Passenger facility charges	—	—	317,283	—	317,283	—
Contract facility charges	—	—	30,116	—	30,116	—
Working capital	—	—	35,588	—	35,588	—
Unrestricted	334,392	76,435	407,378	133,417	951,622	58,433
Total net position	$ 1,917,729	$ 513,103	$ 1,583,128	$ 1,057,655	5,071,615	$ 58,451
Adjustment to reflect the consolidation of internal service fund activities related to enterprise funds					6,082	
Net position of business-type activities					$ 5,077,697	

The notes to the financial statements are an integral part of this statement.

The financial statements of the two types of proprietary funds—the enterprise funds and the internal service funds—are strikingly different from those of the governmental funds. As shown in Tables 2-8 and 2-9, the statement of net position (balance sheet) and the statement of revenues, expenses, and changes in net position (income statement) look decidedly like those of businesses. There are, however, a few exceptions. Thus, in this example, the net position (equity) section of the balance sheet takes the form Assets – Liabilities = Net Position (as opposed to the conventional Assets = Liabilities + Net Position). Further, the net position section highlights the amount of net investment in capital assets (capital assets less related debt) instead of showing contributed capital and retained earnings. Most significant, however, is that like the statements of businesses (and unlike the corresponding statements of governmental funds) the statement of net position reports capital assets and long-term debt, and the statement of revenues and expenses includes depreciation.

TABLE 2-9 City of Charlotte, North Carolina

Statement of Revenues, Expenses, and Changes in Fund Net Position Proprietary Funds for the Year Ended June 30, 2016 (in thousands)

	Business-type Activities Enterprise Funds					Governmental Activities
	Water and Sewer	Storm Water	Airport	Public Transit	Total	Internal Service Funds
Operating Revenues:						
Charges for services	$ 313,781	$ 70,042	$ 195,410	$ 32,404	$ 611,637	$ 124,755
Availability fees	37,113	—	—	—	37,113	—
Capacity fees	19,157	—	—	—	19,157	—
Miscellaneous	7,076	—	11,037	—	18,113	—
Total operating revenues	377,127	70,042	206,447	32,404	686,020	124,755
Operating Expenses:						
Administration	28,728	2,099	27,432	8,262	66,521	10,090
Operations and maintenance	91,487	7,482	77,417	120,369	296,755	—
Claims and insurance premiums	—	—	—	—	—	110,274
Other	1,929	—	13,166	—	15,095	—
Depreciation	103,772	7,731	50,681	37,659	199,843	5
Total operating expenses	225,916	17,312	168,696	166,290	578,214	120,369
Operating income (loss)	151,211	52,730	37,751	(133,886)	107,806	4,386
Nonoperating Revenues (Expenses):						
Sales tax	—	—	—	89,617	89,617	—
Grant contributions	—	—	—	10,945	10,945	—
Passenger facility charges	—	—	59,171	—	59,171	—
Contract facility charges	—	—	12,273	—	12,273	—
Investment earnings	1,768	304	4,595	398	7,065	512
Interest expense and other charges	(82,368)	643	(18,898)	(7,874)	(108,497)	—
Nonairline terminal revenue distribution	—	—	(18,525)	—	(18,525)	—
Miscellaneous	4,404	37	(11,973)	441	(7,091)	—
Total nonoperating revenues (expenses)	(76,196)	984	26,643	93,527	44,958	512
Income (loss) before contributions and transfers	75,015	53,714	64,394	(40,359)	152,764	4,898
Capital Contributions	26,270	—	20,706	194,994	241,970	—
Transfers In	—	—	—	21,609	21,609	—
Transfers Out	—	—	—	—	—	—
Change in net position	101,285	53,714	85,100	176,244	416,343	4,898
Total net position—beginning	1,816,444	459,389	1,498,028	881,411		53,553
Total net position—ending	$ 1,917,729	$ 513,103	$ 1,583,128	$ 1,057,655		$ 58,451
Adjustments to reflect the consolidation of internal service fund activities related to enterprise funds					1,962	
Change in net position of business-type activities					$ 418,305	

The notes to the financial statements are an integral part of this statement.

Because one of a government's typical objectives in providing the service may be to at least break even, the government officials responsible for the activity require the same types of financial information as their counterparts in industry. For example, they need data on the full cost (including depreciation) of the services provided so that they are able to establish prices. Outsiders, such as the tax or rate payers, concerned with the activity's performance or fiscal condition, need the same general information as would corporate shareholders. For this reason, proprietary funds are accounted for in essentially the same manner as private businesses. As suggested by their balance sheets, they employ the full accrual basis of accounting, and their measurement focus is on all economic resources. This text addresses the issue of which activities should properly be accounted for in proprietary funds but devotes little attention to specific principles and procedures. Most students, though unaware of it, have been studying proprietary funds since they first matriculated in their accounting principles courses.

WHAT'S NOTABLE ABOUT EACH TYPE OF FIDUCIARY FUND?

Fiduciary funds, unlike governmental and proprietary funds, benefit parties other than the government itself. These funds are used to account for assets held by a government in a trust or custodial capacity for others, which include employees, other governments, and specific individuals, corporations, or not-for-profit organizations. Accordingly, their activities do not result in revenues or expenses to support the government's programs—only in additions or deductions to the fund's net position. Although the financial statements of fiduciary funds are included in a government's comprehensive annual financial report, they are not included in the government-wide financial statements.

TRUST FUNDS

Kohler's Dictionary for Accountants defines a trust fund as a "fund held by one person (trustee) for the benefit of another, pursuant to the provisions of a formal trust agreement."[9] Most notably, as indicated by the definition, the resources of trust funds (as well as custodial funds) are intended to benefit parties other than the government itself. There are three types of trust funds:

- **Pension and other employee benefit trust funds** benefit the government's employees by providing income, disability income, health care insurance, and related forms of remuneration to retirees and their beneficiaries.
- **Investment trust funds**, which are similar to mutual funds, benefit the parties, usually other governments, which have entrusted their resources to the fund.
- **Private purpose trust funds** encompass all trust funds other than pension and investment trust funds, and unlike the other trust funds, these funds may be expendable or nonexpendable. They benefit specific individuals, private organizations, governments, or businesses. One type of private purpose trust fund is an *escheat* trust fund. Escheat property is the name given to property that reverts to a state when a person dies in the absence of heirs or other legal claimants. It also includes abandoned and unclaimed property, such as balances in bank accounts in which there has been no activity for a specified period of time. Private purpose trust funds may also be used to account for resources held for parties other than the government itself, such as a local not-for-profit historical society or museum.

[9] W. W. Cooper and Yuji Ijiri, eds., *Kohler's Dictionary for Accountants*, 6th ed. (Englewood Cliffs, NJ: Prentice-Hall, 1983), 516.

The resources of trust funds are generally held in financial instruments—such as stocks and bonds—and how well they perform in terms of investment earnings is of key concern to beneficiaries and fund managers. Therefore, they are accounted for on a full accrual basis, and the measurement focus is on economic resources.

CUSTODIAL FUNDS

Custodial funds are used to account for assets held, usually for a short period, on behalf of other governments, funds, not-for-profit entities, or individuals. Most commonly they are established to maintain control over:

- Taxes collected by one government for the benefit of another
- Special assessments collected to repay debt that the government services but for which it is not responsible
- Refundable deposits
- Pass-through grants—those requiring a government (such as a state) to distribute funds to other parties (such as school districts or individuals) but for which the government has no financial involvement and for which it performs no significant administrative functions such as selecting recipients or monitoring performance
- Amounts held for other governments in investment pools that do not meet certain GASB specified criteria (e.g., are not considered trusts)

In summary, governments maintain three main types of funds: governmental, proprietary, and fiduciary. The governmental funds, all of which are accounted for on a modified accrual basis, consist of the general fund, special revenue funds, debt service funds, capital project funds, and permanent funds. The proprietary funds, which are used to account for business-type activities and thus are on a full accrual basis, consist of enterprise funds and internal service funds. The fiduciary funds consist of trust funds and custodial funds. Like proprietary funds they are accounted for on a full accrual basis.

So far, we have discussed the basic funds maintained by a government. This section and the one that follows are directed to how governments report on these funds.

WHAT IS INCLUDED IN A GOVERNMENT'S COMPREHENSIVE ANNUAL FINANCIAL REPORT (CAFR)?

The complete annual report, known as a **Comprehensive Annual Financial Report (CAFR)**, consists of more than just the basic statements (some of which are illustrated in this chapter). Indeed, the annual reports of states, cities, counties, and other general-purpose governments are notable for their bulk. The reports of medium to large cities may exceed 200 pages, few of which contain pictures or other touches of frivolity. Government accountants are not typically compensated by the page. Why then are the reports so lengthy?

Annual reports are directed to different groups of users, each of which needs different types of information. As previously noted, some users, for example, focus on whether the government's current taxpayers are paying for the cost of services they are receiving. They want to view the government as a whole and want to take into account all the resources received and expended. Others are more concerned with budgetary compliance. They need data that focus on individual funds and are directed to flows of cash and other short-term financial resources. Further, as pointed out in Chapter 1, the fiscal wherewithal of a government cannot be assessed in isolation of the community to which it must provide services and from which it must draw its resources. As a consequence, the CAFR includes statements that combine and report on the government's activities from both a government-wide and a fund perspective. It also includes the statements of individual funds and an array of statistical data on both the government itself and its jurisdiction.

The CAFR is divided into three main sections:

- ***Introductory section.*** This includes a letter of transmittal and general information on how the government is organized and who are its key elected and administrative officials. The letter of transmittal (usually from the chief executive or finance officer) presents an overview of financial and economic conditions faced by the government and summarizes recent key financial developments. The introductory section may also include a "Certificate of Achievement for Excellence in Financial Reporting" if the CAFR of the previous year satisfied the reporting standards of the Government Finance Officers Association, an independent professional organization.
- ***Financial section.*** This is the main body of the CAFR. It contains
  - **Management's discussion and analysis (MD&A)**; similar in nature to the MD&A that is part of the financial statements of businesses, this narrative presents a brief, nontechnical overview of the government's financial performance during the year and its financial position at year-end
  - The basic financial statements (to be discussed in the following paragraphs)
  - Notes to the statements
  - Required supplementary information
  - Combining and individual fund financial statements (if required)

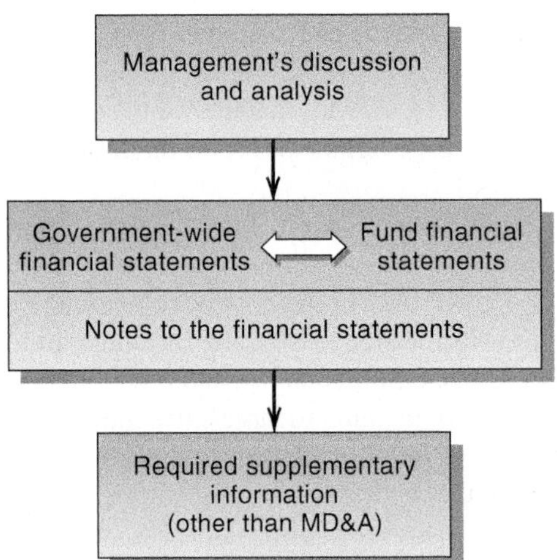

FIGURE 2-1 Minimum Requirements for General-Purpose Financial Statements
Source: GASB Statement No. 34, *Basic Financial Statements—and Management's Discussion and Analysis—for State and Local Governments.*

Figure 2-1 illustrates the key elements of this section.

- ***Statistical section.*** This contains current and historical data as to the jurisdiction's demographics, economy, tax rates, outstanding debt, and other information that supplements the basic financial statements. The specific data provided will, of course, differ among different types of governments.

THE FINANCIAL SECTION: AN OVERVIEW

Basic financial statements present information from both a government-wide and a fund perspective. As a consequence, they include up to ten primary statements and a dozen supplementary statements and schedules (depending on the government's fund structure) that are incorporated into notes and supplementary sections. The government-wide statements are on a full accrual basis. The fund statements are on the basis of accounting required for the specific category of fund—modified accrual basis for governmental funds and full accrual basis for proprietary funds.

Government-Wide Statements

The objective of the entity-wide (popularly known as government-wide) financial statements is to present a fairly broad condensed consolidated view of the financial position of the governmental entity. According to GAAP,[10] there are just two required government-wide statements:

- Statement of net position (balance sheet)
- Statement of activities (statement of revenues and expenses)

These statements provide a longer-term perspective and demonstrate operational accountability. The relative strengths of these statements are their comprehensiveness and comparability. The data for the statements are derived from the financial statements of governmental funds and proprietary funds. As illustrated in Table 2-3, the statement of net position is similar to the balance sheet of a business. Unlike that of a business, it has separate columns for governmental- and business-type activities, but the totals column consolidates the two types of activities. An additional column presents information on nonfiduciary "component units"—entities that are economically intertwined with the government albeit legally separate (and that are discussed in Chapter 11). Moreover, the difference between the government's assets and liabilities is shown as "net position," rather than "owner's equity" as it would be on the balance sheet of a business.

By contrast, the statement of activities in Table 2-4 bears no resemblance, at least at first glance, to the income statement of a business. Unlike the income statement of a business, the aim of this statement is to show the net cost of each of the government's main functions and programs—the cost that must be covered by taxes and other general revenues. Accordingly, the first column reports total expenses. The next three columns indicate revenues, such as those from charges for services and program-specific grants that help defray the expenses. The next columns (one for government activities, the other for business-type activities) show the differences between the expenses and the revenues, that is, the net cost of the functions and programs. The lower portion of the statement summarizes the taxes and other general revenues of the government at large—those that cannot be associated directly with specific functions and programs and that

[10] GASB Statement No. 34, para 12.

can be used to cover the net cost of the government's programs. The difference between the net expenses and general revenues is the change in net position.

The government-wide statements are prepared on a full accrual basis. Therefore, the statement of net position includes both capital (long-lived) assets and long-term debt. Correspondingly, program and function expenses include charges for depreciation, even though they are not broken out separately. The example "Government-Wide Statement of Activities" illustrates the form and content of a government-wide statement of activities.

Example

Government-Wide Statement of Activities

The government of Charier City performs only two functions: public safety and recreation. Expenses of the public safety function total $100 million. It offsets these expenses, in part, through miscellaneous revenues (e.g., fees for funeral escorts and fun-run patrols) of $4 million and receives a state grant of $6 million. Thus, it must cover the remaining balance of $90 million with taxes and other unassigned revenues. The recreation function incurs $30 million in expenses but collects user fees (for swimming pools, tennis courts, and golf courses) of $8 million and receives a state grant of $9 million. It must cover $13 million with unassigned revenues. Hence, the city as a whole must cover a total of $103 million with unassigned revenues. In fact, however, the city's general (unassigned) revenues total $105 million, and thus the city's net position increases during the period by $2 million.

The city's government-wide statement of activities is presented in Table 2-10. Although this format may require some getting used to, its virtue is that it highlights more clearly than the conventional statement of revenues and expenditures the net cost to the taxpayers of each of the government's functions.

TABLE 2-10 Charier City Government-wide Statement of Activities (in millions)

		Program-Specific Revenues		
	Expenses	Charges for Services	Operating Grants and Contributions	Net Expenses to Be Covered by General Revenues
Programs				
Public safety	$100	$ 4	$ 6	$ 90
Recreation	30	8	9	13
Total expenses	$130	$12	$15	$103
General revenues				
Property taxes				$ 60
Sales taxes				45
Total general revenues				105
Increase in net position				$ 2

Fund Statements

The three main categories of funds necessitate three sets of statements, one for each type of fund, with each containing a slightly different blend of statements. The following are the basic statements for each fund category:

- ***Governmental funds***—Balance sheet; statement of revenues, expenditures, and changes in fund balances (Tables 2-5 and 2-6)

- ***Proprietary funds***—Balance sheet; statement of revenues, expenses, and changes in net position (Tables 2-8 and 2-9); statement of cash flows (not illustrated)
- ***Fiduciary funds***—Statement of fiduciary net position; statement of changes in fiduciary net position (to be illustrated in Chapter 10)

As shown in Tables 2-5 and 2-6, which illustrate governmental fund statements, separate columns are presented for the general fund and each of Charlotte's "major" funds. Major funds are those in which total assets plus deferred outflows of resources, liabilities plus **deferred inflows of resources**, revenues, or expenditures/expenses are at least

- 10 percent of the relevant fund category (governmental or enterprise) *and*
- 5 percent of the corresponding total for all governmental and enterprise funds combined

The remaining "nonmajor" funds are combined into the column "other governmental funds." Note that the governmental fund balance sheet includes a reconciliation of total governmental fund balances ($994,783) with the net governmental assets ($7,184,493) per the government-wide statement of net position. A similar reconciliation (Table 2-7) ties the changes in fund balances per the fund statements ($56,940) with the changes in governmental net position per the government-wide statements (–$8,023).

Notes to the financial statements include schedules of changes in capital assets and changes in long-term liabilities. Supplementary information may include *combining statements* for the nonmajor funds. The combining statements present each of the nonmajor funds in a separate column. A totals column ties to the "other funds" column of the funds statements.

Supplementary information also includes actual-to-budget comparisons for the general fund as well as other major funds.

The statements of proprietary and fiduciary funds as well as the key required schedules and additional statements are discussed in more detail in subsequent chapters.

HOW DO THE FUNDS AND ANNUAL REPORTS OF NOT-FOR-PROFITS DIFFER FROM THOSE OF GOVERNMENTS?

The FASB, the rule-making authority for nongovernment entities, has established standards for how not-for-profits must aggregate and display their financial information in general-purpose, external financial reports. These standards are substantially different from those of the GASB.

FUND ACCOUNTING AS A CONVENIENCE, NOT A MANDATE

Although the GASB mandates fund-based reporting for governments, the FASB imposes no similar requirement on not-for-profits. As stressed earlier, fund accounting is an expedient means of control that helps ensure that governments or other organizations use resources only for the purposes for which they have been dedicated. But it is not the only means. After all, private businesses also must account for resources that are restricted (e.g., income taxes withheld from employees, sales taxes collected from customers, advance payments on government contracts, and proceeds from bond issues that must be spent on specific projects). Yet, they do not employ fund accounting.

Unless mandated by law, not-for-profit organizations need not employ fund accounting for purposes of internal accounting and administration. They must, however, comply with FASB requirements for external reporting. But they need only distinguish between resources that are restricted by donors and those that are not restricted by donors—they do not have to report on separate funds.

Nevertheless, for purposes of internal accounting and control, many not-for-profits do employ fund accounting, and they maintain funds that are comparable to those of governments. All not-for-profits maintain a *current* fund, which is like a government's general fund. Similarly, most maintain one or more *current restricted* funds, which are, in essence, special revenue funds. They may also maintain, as needed, funds to account for resources set aside for the acquisition of long-lived assets and for the repayment of debt. Many colleges and universities categorize all funds having to do with the capital assets and the related debt as **plant funds**. These include an *unexpended* plant fund (similar to a capital projects fund), a *retirement of indebtedness* fund (analogous to a debt service fund), and an *investment in plant* fund (which accounts for both capital assets and related long-term debts).

WHAT IS INCLUDED IN THE FINANCIAL REPORT OF A NOT-FOR-PROFIT ENTITY?

The financial reports of not-for-profit entities more closely resemble those of businesses than of governments. The reports need consist of only three primary statements—a statement of position (balance sheet), a statement of activities (statement of revenues and expenses), and a statement of cash flows. Unlike governments, not-for-profits need not present separate data on each of their major funds or even fund types. Although the FASB imposes some accounting and reporting requirements that are unique to not-for-profits, not-for-profits are generally subject to business standards.

The FASB requires that not-for-profits classify their net assets into two categories based on the restrictions of *donors*:

- Not restricted
- Restricted

Restricted resources include those that must be used for a specific purpose (e.g., to support donor-designated programs or activities) or cannot be spent until sometime in the future (e.g., when a donor makes good on a pledge). In addition, restricted resources also include endowments, only the income from which can be spent.

The FASB permits not-for-profits considerable flexibility as to the form of the primary statements. Tables 2-11 and 2-12 illustrate the statements of activities and financial position of a private college, adjusted for changes to financial statement presentation since they were issued. In Chapter 12, we consider in detail the form and content of these statements, but we also make occasional comparisons between government and not-for-profit practices in other chapters as well.

TABLE 2-11 **Hamilton College**

Statement of Activities Year ended June 30, 2017 (with summarized information for the year ended June 30, 2016) (Dollars in thousands)

	2017			
	Without donor restrictions	With donor restrictions	Total	2016 Total
Operating revenues:				
Tuition and fees	$ 97,963	–	$ 97,963	$ 94,784
Room and board	23,601	–	23,601	22,819
Scholarship aid	(37,545)	–	(37,545)	(36,050)
Net student fees	84,019	–	84,019	81,553
Investment return designated for operations	4,964	$ 33,265	38,229	35,456
Other investment income	6,634	–	6,634	4,121
Private gifts and grants	6,821	2,033	8,854	8,989
Other sources	2,778	979	3,757	3,715
Net assets released from restrictions	33,311	(33,311)	–	–
Total operating revenues	138,527	2,966	141,493	133,834
Operating expenses:				
Instruction	61,710	–	61,710	61,239
Research	927	–	927	966
Academic support	19,442	–	19,442	18,794
Student services	16,887	–	16,887	15,941
Institutional support	18,568	–	18,568	18,798
Auxiliary enterprises	21,787	–	21,787	21,565
Total operating expenses	139,321	–	139,321	137,303
Increase (decrease) in net assets from operations	(794)	2,966	2,172	(3,469)
Nonoperating activities:				
Private gifts	923	13,224	14,147	32,488
Investment return, net of amounts designated for operations	12,549	70,191	82,740	(80,090)
Changes in annuity and life income obligations	–	(2,208)	(2,208)	3,064
Net assets released from restriction and changed restrictions	4,835	(4,835)	–	–
Other	(88)	(17)	(105)	1,855
Increase (decrease) in net assets from nonoperating activities	18,219	76,355	94,574	(42,683)
Increase (decrease) in net assets	17,425	79,321	96,746	(46,152)
Net assets, beginning of year	249,027	771,712	1,020,739	1,066,891
Net assets, end of year	$ 266,452	$ 851,033	$ 1,117,485	$ 1,020,739

See accompanying notes to financial statements.

TABLE 2-12 **Hamilton College**

Statements of Financial Position June 30, 2017 and 2016 (Dollars in thousands)

Assets	**2017**	**2016**
Cash and cash equivalents	$ 32,449	$ 21,464
Short-term investments	16,916	16,846
Student and other accounts receivable including loans, net	2,877	3,381
Contributions receivable, net	12,686	19,669
Beneficial interest trusts	2,729	6,897
Deposits with trustees of debt obligations	74,865	1,326
Collateral received for securities lending	4,494	4,500
Medium-term investments	30,862	98,764
Investments	954,714	861,749
Other assets	3,724	3,122
Property, plant and equipment, net	257,200	262,575
Total assets	$ 1,393,516	$ 1,300,293
Liabilities and Net Assets		
Accounts payable and accrued liabilities	$ 9,838	9,742
Deposits and advances	3,409	3,360
Liability under securities lending transactions	4,494	4,500
Annuity and life income obligations	17,367	16,724
Accumulated postretirement benefit obligation	2,187	2,029
Other long-term obligations	3,333	3,647
Long-term debt	235,403	239,552
Total liabilities	276,031	279,554
Net assets:		
Without donor restrictions	266,452	249,027
With donor restrictions	851,033	771,712
Total net assets	1,117,485	1,020,739
Total liabilities and net assets	$ 1,393,516	$ 1,300,293

See accompanying notes to financial statements.

SUMMARY

Governments and not-for-profits organize their accounting systems on the basis of funds. Funds are independent fiscal and accounting entities, each with a self-balancing set of accounts. Fund accounting is an effective means of establishing control and accountability over restricted resources.

The fund structure of a government or not-for-profit is typically based on the nature of restrictions, not on the entity's organization chart. Governments classify funds into three broad categories: governmental funds, proprietary funds, and fiduciary funds.

Governments normally maintain five types of governmental funds to account for their operating and financing activities:

- The general fund to account for resources that are not accounted for and reported in another fund
- Special revenue funds to account for resources that are restricted or committed for specific purposes

- Capital projects funds to account for resources restricted, committed, or assigned for the construction, acquisition, or improvement of capital assets and facilities
- Debt service funds to account for restricted, committed, or assigned resources set aside for the payment of interest and the retirement of debt
- Permanent funds to report resources that are legally restricted in that only earnings, not principal, may be used to support the government's programs

Governments maintain two types of proprietary funds to account for their business-type activities:

- Enterprise funds to account for activities in which the government sells goods or services to the general public
- Internal service funds to account for activities in which the customers are other government departments or agencies

Governments maintain four types of fiduciary funds to account for resources that they hold for the benefit of parties other than themselves:

- Pension and other employee benefit trust funds to account for retirement contributions and investments, as well as health insurance benefits for retirees
- Investment trust funds for investment pools
- Private purpose trust funds that cover other purposes, such as escheat property
- Custodial funds to account for resources that they hold for other governments, such as taxes, deposits, and pass-through grants

In 1999, the GASB established the current reporting model that views an entity from both a government-wide and a funds perspective. The GASB enhanced this reporting model in 2007 in Concepts Statement No. 4, *Elements of Financial Statements*. In that statement, the GASB provided definitions and explanations of seven key elements that comprise basic financial statements—five relating to financial position (assets, liabilities, deferred outflow of resources, deferred inflow of resources, and net position) and two relating to resource flows. Statement No. 63, *Financial Reporting of Deferred Outflows of Resources, Deferred Inflows of Resources, and Net Position*, issued in 2011, operationalized this concept statement by showing how the deferred inflows and outflows of resources should be incorporated into the financial statements. In addition in 2009, the GASB issued Statement No. 54, *Fund Balance Reporting and Governmental Fund Type Definitions*, that established a hierarchy of fund balance classifications to show the constraints imposed on the use of the resources reported in governmental funds.

The government-wide statements consolidate the entity's governmental funds and proprietary funds into governmental activities and business-type activities, respectively, and report both kinds of activities on a full accrual basis. Hence, the statement of net position includes both capital assets and long-term debt. Correspondingly, the statement of activities incorporates charges for depreciation. The model's fund statements are presented either on a modified accrual basis or on a full accrual basis, depending on whether they are governmental, proprietary, or fiduciary. Fiduciary funds are reported only in the funds statements, not the government-wide statements, since they benefit parties outside of the governments and not the government itself. Table 2-13 presents the basic financial statements by fund category.

The complete annual report of a government—its Comprehensive Annual Financial Report (CAFR)—contains far more than basic financial statements. It also includes a letter of transmittal, a management's discussion and analysis (MD&A) that highlights the government's financial performance during the year and its financial position at year-end, and a wealth of statistical data.

Although the GASB requires that entities within its purview include fund financial statements within their basic financial statements, the FASB does not. Not-for-profits, therefore, employ fund accounting because it enhances internal control, not because it is required for financial reporting. The unique characteristics of the entity and the information needs of its managers, governing board, and constituents dictate its fund structures. For purposes of external reporting, not-for-profits aggregate and present their fund data quite differently than governments. The FASB requires that not-for-profits classify their net assets into three categories: donor unrestricted, donor temporarily restricted, and donor permanently restricted.

TABLE 2-13 **Basic Financial Statements by Fund Category**

Fund Category	Measurement Focus and Basis of Accounting	Basic Financial Statements
Governmental	Current financial resources; modified accrual	Balance sheet Statement of revenues, expenditures, and changes in fund balances
Proprietary	Economic resources; accrual	Statement of net position/balance sheet Statement of revenues, expenses, and changes in fund net position/fund equity Statement of cash flows
Fiduciary	Economic resources; accrual	Statement of fiduciary net position Statement of changes in fiduciary net position

Source: GASB Statement No.34, *Basic Financial Statements—and Management's Discussion and Analysis—for State and Local Governments* (1999), as modified by GASB Statement No. 63, *Financial Reporting of Deferred Outflows of Resources, Deferred Inflows of Resources, and Net Position* (2011).

KEY TERMS IN THIS CHAPTER

EXERCISE FOR REVIEW AND SELF-STUDY

The newly created State Recreation District established the following funds, each of which is a separate fiscal and accounting entity:

- A general fund to account for general operating resources that are unassigned
- A capital projects fund to account for the proceeds of bonds issued to finance the construction of recreational facilities
- A debt service fund to account for resources set aside to pay principal and interest on the bonds
- An internal service fund to account for the operations of an equipment repair department that will provide services to several departments that are accounted for within the general fund

A summary of the district's first-year transactions follows (all dollar amounts in millions).

1. It levies taxes of $300, of which it collects $250. It expects to collect the remaining $50 shortly after year-end. The taxes are unassigned as to how they may be used.
2. It incurs $240 in general operating expenditures, of which it pays $170.
3. It issues long-term bonds of $500. The bonds must be used to finance the acquisition of recreational facilities. Accordingly, they are recorded in a restricted fund—the capital projects fund. The capital

projects fund is a governmental fund. As such, it is not accounted for on a full accrual basis. It does not recognize long-term debt as an obligation. Therefore, the inflow of resources is accounted for as "bond proceeds," an account that, like a revenue, increases fund balance. The account is classified as "other financing sources" in a statement of revenues, expenditures, and changes in fund balances to distinguish it from operating revenues.

4. The district acquires $400 of recreational facilities using the resources available in the capital projects fund. Just as the capital projects fund recognizes the bond proceeds similarly to a revenue, so too it records the acquisition of the equipment as an expenditure.

5. The bond indenture (agreement) requires that the district periodically commit funds to repay the principal of the debt. The district transfers $40 from the general fund to the fund specially created to account for resources restricted for debt service. This transaction must be recorded in the two affected independent accounting entities, the general fund and the debt service fund.

6. The repair service, which is accounted for in an internal service fund, acquires $10 of equipment, giving a long-term note in exchange. Internal service funds are proprietary funds and as such are accounted for as if they were businesses. They are accounted for on a full accrual basis; they focus on all economic resources. Hence, they recognize both long-term assets and long-term obligations.

7. The repair service bills the district's other departments $15 and collects the full amount in cash. The other departments are all accounted for in the general fund. The service incurs cash operating expenses of $12 and recognizes $2 of depreciation.
   a. Prepare appropriate journal entries to record the transactions in individual funds. Governmental funds are accounted for on a modified accrual basis; proprietary funds on a full accrual basis.
   b. Based on the entries, prepare for the governmental funds a balance sheet and a statement of revenues, expenditures, and changes in fund balances.
   c. Prepare for the one proprietary fund (the internal service fund), a statement of net position (a balance sheet), and a statement of revenues, expenses, and changes in fund net position.
   d. Prepare a government-wide statement of net position (balance sheet) and a government-wide statement of activities (statement of revenues and expenses). These statements should consolidate all funds, including the internal service fund, and should be on a full accrual basis. Assume that the district charged depreciation of $40 on recreational facilities (in addition to the amount charged in the internal service fund). Although internal service funds are categorized as proprietary funds, they typically provide most of their services to governmental activities. Hence, in the government-wide statements, they are generally consolidated with the governmental funds rather than with enterprise funds.

QUESTIONS FOR REVIEW AND DISCUSSION

1. Distinguish between funds as the term is used in governmental as contrasted with business accounting.

2. In what way, if any, does the accounting equation as applied in governmental and not-for-profit accounting differ from that as applied in business accounting?

3. Distinguish between nonspendable, restricted, committed, and assigned fund balance.

4. Define the seven key elements that comprise the financial statements.

5. Upon examining the balance sheet of a large city, you notice that the total assets of the general fund far exceed those of the combined total of the city's ten separate special revenue funds. Moreover, you observe that there are no funds for public safety, sanitation, health and welfare, and general administration—all important functions of the government. Why do you suppose the city hasn't attempted to "even out" the assets in the funds? Why does it not maintain funds for each of its major functional areas?

6. Why are there generally no capital projects (work in progress or other long-lived assets) in governments' capital projects funds? Why are there generally no long-term debts in debt service funds?

7. The balance sheets of both enterprise funds and internal service funds report capital assets and long-term debt. What does that tell you about the funds' measurement focus and basis of accounting? Explain.

8. As will be emphasized later in this text, depreciation is recorded in proprietary funds but not in governmental funds. What is the rationale for recording depreciation in proprietary funds?

9. What are fiduciary funds? What are the four main types, and what are the distinctions between them?

10. What is permanent about a permanent fund?

11. From what two perspectives must the financial statements under the GASB No. 34 reporting model be prepared? How do the two differ from each other?

12. What is a custodial fund? For what types of transactions is it used to account?

13. What is a CAFR? What are its main components?

14. Distinguish among the two categories of restrictiveness into which the net assets of not-for-profit organizations must be separated for purposes of external reporting. By whom must these restrictions be imposed for resources to be considered restricted?

EXERCISES

EX. 2-1

The following relate to the town of Coupland (dollar amounts in thousands):

Equipment used in a vehicle repair service that provides service to other departments on a cost-reimbursement basis; the equipment has a 10-year life with no salvage value	$1,400
Property taxes levied and collected	$6,300
Hotel taxes (restricted to promotion of tourism) collected	$1,200
Proceeds of bonds to build a parking garage that must be repaid from user charges	$4,000
Proceeds of general obligation bonds to finance construction of a new city hall; the building, which was completed during the year, has a useful life of 30 years with no salvage value	$9,000
Proceeds of a federal grant to hire additional police officers	$1,000
Fees charged to, and collected from, customers by the electric utility	$8,000

Refer to the two lists below. Select the appropriate amounts from the lettered list for each item in the numbered list. An amount may be selected once, more than once, or not at all.

1. Revenue to be recognized in an enterprise fund
2. Revenue to be recognized in special revenue funds
3. Bonds payable to be recognized in the general fund
4. Bonds payable to be recognized in enterprise funds
5. Depreciation expenditure to be recognized in the general fund
6. Depreciation expense to be recognized in internal service funds
7. Revenue to be recognized in an internal service fund
8. Revenue to be recognized in the general fund
9. Long-lived assets to be recognized in the general fund

10. Long-lived assets to be recognized in internal service funds

a. $0	**g.** $2,200
b. $140	**h.** $4,000
c. $900	**i.** $6,300
d. $1,260	**j.** $8,000
e. $1,040	**k.** $8,500
f. $1,400	**l.** $10,400

EX. 2-2

Select the *best* answer.

1. Oak Township issued the following bonds during the year:

Bonds to acquire equipment for a vehicle repair service that is accounted for in an internal service fund	$3,000,000
Bonds to construct a new city hall	$8,000,000
Bond to improve its water utility, which is accounted for in an enterprise fund	$9,000,000

The amount of debt to be reported in the general fund is

a. $0
b. $3,000,000
c. $8,000,000
d. $20,000,000

2. Oak Township should report depreciation in which of the following funds:

a. General fund
b. Special revenue fund
c. Internal service fund
d. Capital projects fund

3. Assuming that Bravo County receives all of its revenues from unassigned property taxes, it is most likely to account for the activities of its police department in its

a. Police department fund
b. Police enterprise fund
c. Property tax fund
d. General fund

4. The city of Alpine incurred the following costs during the year in its property tax collection department:

Purchase of computer equipment	$10,000
Salaries and wages	$400,000
Purchase of electricity from the city-owned electric utility	$40,000
Purchase of supplies, all of which were used during the year	$10,000

As a consequence of these transactions, the amount that Alpine should report as expenditures in its general fund is

a. $400,000
b. $410,000
c. $450,000
d. $460,000

5. Grove City received the following resources during the year:

Property taxes	$50,000,000
A federal grant to acquire police cars	$400,000
Hotel taxes, which must be used to promote tourism	$3,000,000
Proceeds of bonds issued to improve the city's electric utility	$12,000,000

The amount that the city should most likely report as revenues in its special revenue funds is

a. $400,000
b. $3,000,000
c. $3,400,000
d. $15,400,000
e. $65,400,000

6. A city issues $20 million of general obligation bonds to improve its streets and roads. In accordance with the bond covenants, it committed $1 million to help ensure that it is able to meet its first payment of principal and $100,000 for its first payment of interest. The amount of liability that the city should report in its debt service fund is

a. $0
b. $18.9 million
c. $19 million
d. $20 million

7. During the year, Brian County collects $12 million of property taxes on behalf of Urton Township. Of this amount, it remits $10 million to the township, expecting to remit the balance shortly after the end of its fiscal year. The amount that the county should report as its year end net position is

a. $0
b. $2 million
c. $10 million
d. $12 million

8. The City of Round Lake receives a contribution of $20 million. The donor stipulates that the money is to be invested. The principal is to remain intact, and the investment proceeds are to be used to support a city-owned nature center. The city should report the contribution in a

a. Special revenue fund
b. Permanent fund
c. Fiduciary fund
d. Custodial fund

9. A city receives a $30 million contribution. The donor stipulates that the money is to be invested. The principal is to remain intact and the investment proceeds are to be used to provide scholarships for the children of city employees. The contribution should be reported as revenue of a

a. Special revenue fund
b. Permanent fund
c. Fiduciary fund
d. Custodial fund

10. The Summerville Preparatory School (a private not-for-profit school) receives a donation of $14 million. The donor stipulates that the entire amount must be used to construct a new athletic field house. The school should classify the donation as

a. Not restricted by donor
b. Restricted by donor
c. Semi-restricted
d. No transaction should be recorded

11. Who may impose constraints for the use of a committed fund balance?

a. The government's highest level of decision-making authority
b. Creditors or bondholders
c. A majority vote of the finance committee
d. Any government official

12. Under GASB Statement No. 54, what is the hierarchy classification of fund balances?

a. Spendable, unrestricted, committed, assigned, unassigned
b. Nonspendable, restricted, committed, assigned, unassigned
c. Nonspendable, unrestricted, committed, assigned, unassigned
d. Spendable, restricted, uncommitted, assigned, unassigned

EX. 2-3

Measurement focus is closely tied to basis of accounting.

A newly established not-for-profit organization engaged in the following transactions.

1. A donor pledged $1,000,000, giving the organization a legally enforceable 90-day note for the full amount.
2. The donor paid $300,000 of the amount pledged.
3. The organization purchased a building for $600,000, paying $120,000 and giving a 30-year mortgage note for the balance. The building has a 30-year useful life. When appropriate, the organization charges a full-year's depreciation in the period of acquisition.
4. It hired employees. By the end of the period, they had earned $4,000 in wages but had not yet been paid.

The organization accounts for its activities in a single fund.

a. Prepare journal entries to record the transactions, making the following alternative assumptions as to the organization's measurement focus:
   - Cash only
   - Cash plus other current financial resources (i.e., cash plus short-term receivables less short-term payables)
   - All economic resources

b. Based on your entries, prepare appropriate statements of revenues and expenses and balance sheets.

EX. 2-4

A special district's balance sheet may not capture its economic resources and obligations.

A special district accounts for its general fund (its only fund) on a modified accrual basis. In a particular period, it engaged in the following transactions:

- It issued $20 million in long-term bonds.
- It acquired several tracts of land at a total cost of $4 million, paying the entire amount in cash.
- It sold a portion of the land for $1 million, receiving cash for the entire amount. The tract sold had cost $0.8 million.
- It repaid $2 million of the bonds.
- It lost a lawsuit and was ordered to pay $9 million over three years. It made its first cash payment of $3 million.

1. Prepare journal entries to record the transactions in the general fund.
2. Based on your journal entries, prepare a balance sheet and a statement of revenues, expenditures, and other changes in fund balance.
3. Comment on the extent to which the balance sheet captures the district's economic resources and obligations. How can you justify such a balance sheet?
4. Comment on the extent to which the statement of revenues, expenditures, and other financing sources captures the district's cost of services. How can you justify such a statement of revenues, expenditures, and other changes in fund balance?

EX. 2-5

Funds are separate fiscal and accounting entities, each with its own self-balancing set of accounts.

The newly established Society for Ethical Teachings, a not-for-profit organization, maintains two funds—a general fund for operations and a building fund to accumulate resources for a new building. In its first year, it engaged in the following transactions:

1. It received cash contributions of $200,000, of which $40,000 were restricted to the acquisition of the new building.
2. It incurred operating costs of $130,000, of which it paid $120,000 in cash.
3. It earned $3,000 of interest (the entire amount received in cash) on resources restricted to the acquisition of the new building.

4. It transferred $17,000 from the operating fund to the new building fund.

5. It paid $12,000 in fees (accounted for as expenses) to an architect to draw up plans for the new building.
   a. Prepare journal entries to record the transactions. Be certain to indicate the fund in which these entries would be made.
   b. Prepare a statement of revenues, expenses, and other changes in fund balance and a balance sheet. Use a two-column format, one column for each of the funds. Note that for purposes of external reporting not-for-profits would not generally prepare statements on a fund basis. Instead, consistent with the requirements of the FASB, they would consolidate their funds into two categories of restrictiveness: without donor restrictions and with donor restrictions.

EX. 2-6

Typical transactions can often be identified with specific types of funds.

A city maintains the following funds:

1. General
2. Special revenue
3. Capital projects
4. Debt service
5. Enterprise
6. Internal service
7. Permanent (trust)
8. Custodial

For each of the following transactions, indicate the fund in which each transaction would most likely be recorded:

a. The city collects $3 million of taxes on behalf of the county in which it is located.
b. It spends $4 million to pave city streets, using the proceeds of a city gasoline tax dedicated for road and highway improvements.
c. It receives a contribution of $5 million. Per the stipulation of the donor, the money is to be invested in marketable securities, and the interest from the securities is to be used to maintain a city park.
d. It collects $800,000 in landing fees at the city-owned airport.
e. It earns $200,000 on investments set aside to make principal payments on the city's outstanding bonds. The bonds were issued to finance improvements to the city's tunnels and bridges.
f. It pays $4 million to a contractor for work on one of these bridges.
g. It pays $80,000 in wages and salaries to police officers.
h. It purchases from an outside supplier $40,000 of stationery that it will "sell" to its various operating departments.

CONTINUING PROBLEM

Review the Comprehensive Annual Financial Report (CAFR) that you obtained.

1. What are three main sections of the report?

2. Review the introductory section of the CAFR.
   a. Was the entity's annual report of the previous year awarded a "certificate of achievement for excellence in financial reporting" by the Government Finance Officers Association? What is the significance of this award?
   b. What are the key issues addressed in the letter of transmittal?

3. Review the financial section.
   a. Which, if any, independent audit firm performed an audit of the CAFR?
   b. Did the entity receive an "unqualified" audit opinion? If not, why not?
   c. Does the report contain management's discussion and analysis (MD&A)? If so, what are the key issues addressed?

d. Does the report provide a reconciliation between total governmental net position per the government-wide statement of net position and total governmental fund balances per the governmental funds balance sheet? If so, what are the main reconciling items?
e. What are the major governmental funds maintained by the entity? Does the entity's fund structure conform to its organizational structure?
f. Does the report include "required supplementary information"? If so, what are the main areas addressed?
g. Does the report include "combining statements"? If so, what is the nature of these statements?
h. Does the report include other supplemental information? If so, what types of information are in this section of the report?

4. Review the statistical section.
a. What is the population of the entity being reported on?
b. Who is the entity's major employer?
c. What types of information are included in the statistical section?

PROBLEMS

P. 2-1

Government-wide statements report on assets and liabilities that are denied recognition on funds statements.

Entrepreneurs Consultants, a state agency, was established to provide consulting services to small businesses. It maintains only a single general fund and accounts for its activities on a modified accrual basis.

During its first month of operations, the association engaged in, or was affected by, the following transactions and events:

1. It received an unassigned grant of $100,000.

2. It purchased five computers at $2,000 each.

3. It paid wages and salaries of $6,000.

4. It borrowed $24,000 from a bank to enable it to purchase an automobile. It gave the bank a long-term note.

5. It purchased the automobile for $24,000.

6. It made its first payment on the note—interest of $200.

7. It destroyed one of its computers in an accident. The computer was not insured.
a. Prepare journal entries in the general fund to record each of the transactions or other events.
b. Prepare a balance sheet and a statement of revenues and expenditures for the general fund.
c. Prepare a government-wide statement of net position (balance sheet) and statement of activities. These should be on a full accrual basis. Assume that the capital assets have a useful life of five years and that no depreciation is to be charged on the computer that was destroyed.

P. 2-2

Journal entries can be reconstructed from a balance sheet.

The Sherill Utility District was recently established. Its balance sheet, after one year, is presented below. Note the following additional information:

- The general fund received all of its revenue, $150 million, from taxes. It had operating expenditures, excluding transfers to other funds, of $100 million.

- The general fund transferred $20 million to the debt service fund. Of this, $15 million was to repay the principal on bonds outstanding; $5 million was for interest.

- The district issued $130 million in bonds to finance construction of a plant and equipment. Of this, it expended $40 million.

1. Prepare journal entries to summarize all transactions in which the district engaged. You need not make closing entries. Do not be concerned as to the specific titles of accounts to be debited or credited (e.g., whether a transfer from one fund to another should be called a "transfer," an "expense," or an "expenditure," or whether proceeds from bonds should be called "bond proceeds" or "revenues").

2. Comment on how the district's government-wide (full accrual) statement of net position would differ from the balance sheet presented.

Sherill Utility District Balance Sheet as of End of Year 1 (in millions)

	General Fund	Capital Projects Fund	Debt Service Fund	Totals
Assets				
Cash	$30			$ 30
Investments	—	$90	$20	110
Total assets	$30	$90	$20	$140
Liabilities and fund balances				
Net position	$30	$90	$20	$140

P. 2-3

Funds can be "consolidated," but only at the risk of lost or misleading information.

The following balance sheet was adapted from the financial statements of the Williamsburg Regional Sewage Treatment Authority (dates have been changed).

Fund Types

The transactions of the authority are accounted for in the following governmental fund types:

- General fund—To account for all revenues and expenditures not required to be accounted for in other funds.
- Capital projects fund—To account for and report financial resources that are restricted, committed, or assigned to expenditure for capital outlays. Such resources are derived principally from other municipal utility districts to which the Williamsburg Regional Sewage Treatment Authority provides certain services.

1. Recast the balance sheets of the two funds into a single *consolidated* balance sheet (statement of net position). Show separately, however, the restricted and the unrestricted portions of the consolidated net position (not each individual asset and liability). Be sure to eliminate interfund payables and receivables.
2. Which presentation, the unconsolidated or the consolidated, provides more complete information? Explain. Which presentation might be seen as misleading? Why? What, if any, advantages do you see in this presentation even though it might be less complete and more misleading?

Williamsburg Regional Sewage Treatment Authority Balance Sheet, October 31, 2021

	General	Capital Projects
Assets		
Cash	$ 751	$ 5,021
Time deposits	16,398	
Due on insurance claim	9,499	
Due from general fund	9,000	
Due from participants	66,475	4,414
Total assets	$76,725	$34,833
Liabilities and fund equity		
Accounts payable	$17,725	
Due to capital projects fund	9,000	
	$26,725	
Fund balance	50,000	34,833
Total liabilities and fund equity	$76,725	$34,833

P. 2-4

The more complete presentation is not always the easiest to understand.

Bertram County maintains a fund accounting system. Nevertheless, its comptroller (who recently retired from a position in private industry) prepared the following balance sheet (in millions):

Assets		
Cash		$ 600
Investments		1,800
Construction in progress		500
Capital assets		1,200
Total assets		$4,100
Liabilities and fund balance		
Bonds payable		$1,700
Fund balance		
Restricted for capital projects	$ 600	
Restricted for debt service	200	
Unassigned	1,600	2,400
Total liabilities and fund balance		$4,100

The fund balance restricted for debt service represents entirely *principal* (not interest) on the bonds payable.

1. Recast the balance sheet, as best you can, into separate balance sheets for each of the funds that are apparently maintained by the county. Assume that the county uses a modified accrual basis of accounting that excludes recognition in its funds of both capital assets and long-term debt. Assume also that cash and investments are divided among the funds in proportion to fund balances.

Town of Paris Balance Sheet Governmental Funds (in millions)

	General Fund	Hotel Tax (Special Revenue) Fund	Bridge (Capital Projects) Fund	Bond (Debt Service) Fund	Endowment (Permanent) Fund	Totals
Assets						
Cash	$ 38	$ 20	$ 35	$340	$ 10	$ 443
Investments	105	60	480	136	960	1,741
Due from other funds	—	—	—	—	—	—
Total assets	$143	$200	$561	$515	$970	$2,389
Liabilities and fund balances						
Accounts payable	$ 8					$ 8
Due to other funds	205					205
Fund balances	(70)	200	561	515	970	2,176
Total liabilities and fund balances	$143	$200	$561	$515	$970	$2,389

2. In your opinion, which of the two presentations gives the reader a more complete picture of the county's financial status? Why? Which presentation is easier to understand?

P. 2-5

Consolidated balances are not substitutes for individual fund balance sheets.

See the following balance sheet for the town of Paris governmental funds. In addition, you learn from other records that the town has capital assets with a book value (net of depreciation) of $1,450 million and has outstanding long-term bonds of $1,315 million.

1. Recast the balance sheets (taking into account the information on capital assets and long-term debt) in the form of a single consolidated, full accrual, government-wide statement of net position.
2. Put yourself in the place of an analyst. The town mayor presents you with the government-wide statement of net position similar to the one you just prepared. She asserts that the town is in excellent fiscal condition as measured by the exceedingly "healthy" balance of net position. Based on your having seen the combined balance sheet that shows the individual funds, why might you be skeptical of her claim?
3. Comment on why a government-wide consolidated statement of net position is no substitute for a combined balance sheet that reports upon major funds.

P. 2-6

The nature of a transaction gives a clue as to the type of fund in which it should be recorded.

Kendal County engaged in the following transactions. For each, prepare an appropriate journal entry and indicate the type of fund in which it would most likely be recorded:

1. It levied and collected $1million in taxes and dedicated to the repayment of outstanding general obligation bonds.
2. It billed sponsors of a charity bicycle ride $5,000 for providing police patrols during the ride.
3. It recognized $60,000 of cash dividends on investments dedicated to the support of a county arts center.
4. It recognized $70,000 of cash dividends on investments dedicated to scholarships for needy county residents.
5. It incurred $6 million in construction costs to complete a new county jail. The new jail was funded entirely with the proceeds of long-term bonds.
6. It transferred $400,000 of unrestricted funds to an appropriate fund to be invested and eventually used to repay the principal on the long-term jail bonds (entries in two funds required).
7. It recognized depreciation of $100,000 on equipment in a vehicle repair center that services all county departments that have motor vehicles.
8. It collected $30,000 in parking fees at the county-owned garage.
9. It issued $8 million in bonds to improve the city-owned electric utility.
10. It distributed $3 million in taxes collected on behalf of school districts located within the country.

P. 2-7

Is fund accounting less appropriate for businesses than for not-for-profits?

A newly formed not-for-profit advocacy organization, the Center for Participatory Democracy, requests your advice on setting up its financial accounting and reporting system. Meeting with the director, you learn the following:

- Member dues can be expected to account for approximately 80 percent of the organization's revenues.
- The organization plans to seek grants from private foundations to carry out research projects pertaining to various political causes.
- The center has already received a gift of $100,000. The donor specified that the funds are to be placed in investment-grade securities and that only the income is to be used to support center activities.
- The center leases office space but owns its furniture, fixtures, and office equipment.
- The center has taken out a five-year term loan of $100,000. Although the loan is not due until its term expires, the organization intends to set aside $17,740 each year with the prospect that, properly invested, these payments will provide the necessary $100,000.

1. Do you believe that the center should establish its accounting system on a fund basis? If so, why?

2. Assume you answered "yes" to question 1. What specific fund types do you think the center should set up? Explain.

3. Alternatively, suppose the center was a privately owned, profit-oriented consulting firm that provided political advice to its clients. The firm would charge its clients a fixed fee each month in return for which they would receive periodic newsletters and the opportunity to meet with the firm's partners. In addition, the firm expects to enter into contracts to carry out specific research projects for its clients. Would you now recommend that the firm establish its accounting system on a fund basis (assuming, of course, that it would prepare its external financial reports in accordance with generally accepted accounting principles applicable to businesses)? Explain.

P. 2-8

Business-type financial statements may be appropriate for some, but not all, not-for-profits.

The balance sheet of the Hillcrest Home Care Service, a not-for-profit organization providing assistance to the elderly, is presented here:

Hillcrest Home Care Service Balance Sheet as of December 31 (in thousands)

Assets	
Current assets	
Cash and cash equivalents	$ 115
Investments	232
Accounts receivable (net of estimated uncollectibles of $60,000)	652
Total current assets	$ 999
Equipment	
Medical and office equipment	75
Vehicles	60
	$ 135
Less accumulated depreciation	(52)
Net equipment	$ 83
Other assets	
Deferred finance charges	15
Total assets	$1,097
Liabilities and fund balances	
Liabilities	
Current maturities of long-term note	$18
Accounts payable	50
Accrued vacation costs	346
Estimated third-party payer settlements	35
Total current liabilities	$ 449
Long-term debt less current maturities	110
Total liabilities	$ 559
Fund balances	
Without donor restrictions	160
With donor restrictions	378
Total fund balances	$ 538
Total liabilities and fund balances	$1,097

1. As best as you can tell from the balance sheet, what are Hillcrest's measurement focus and basis of accounting? Explain.

2. Suppose that you are the independent CPA who audited the financial statements of Hillcrest. The comptroller of a town, also one of your clients, reviews the financial statements of Hillcrest and observes that they look remarkably like those of private businesses. He wonders why:
   a. The statements of his town are so seemingly complex, consisting of not one, but several, separate fund balance sheets and statements of operations.
   b. The financial report consists of two separate sets of statements, each from a different perspective on a different basis of accounting.
   c. The statements of his town can't be more like those of Hillcrest. What would be your most likely response?

P. 2-9

A hospital's balance sheet tells much about its basis of accounting.

See the balance sheet of a not-for-profit hospital presented on page 89. It is intended to display the hospital's fund structure. Inasmuch as it does not conform to FASB standards, it is inappropriate for external reporting.

1. On what basis of accounting is the general fund maintained? How can you tell?
2. Are the plant replacement and expansion funds on a cash basis of accounting? How can you tell?
3. Why do you suppose that the fund assets "whose use is limited [designated] by board for capital improvements" are reported in the general fund and not in a restricted fund?
4. Suppose the hospital was to present its balance sheet in two columns, one for resources without donor restrictions and one for with donor restrictions. Which of the funds would most likely be reported in each of the columns?
5. What funds in a government are likely to be most comparable to the specific purpose funds?

P. 2-10

Each fund must account for interfund activity as if it were a separate accounting entity.

The newly formed Buffalo School District engaged in the following transactions and other events during the year:

1. It levied and collected property taxes of $110 million.
2. It issued $30 million in long-term bonds to construct a building. It placed the cash received in a special fund set aside to account for the bond proceeds.
3. During the year, it constructed the building at a cost of $25 million. It expects to spend the $5 million balance in the following year. The building has an estimated useful life of 25 years.
4. It incurred $70 million in general operating costs, of which it paid $63 million. It expects to pay the balance early the following year.
5. It transferred $12 million from its general fund to a fund established to account for resources set aside to service the debt. Of this, $10 million was for repayment of the debt; $2 million was for interest.
6. From the special fund established to service the debt, it paid $2 million in interest and $6 million in principal.
7. It collected $4 million in hotel taxes restricted to promoting tourism. Since the resources were restricted, they were accounted for in a special restricted fund. During the year, the district spent $3 million on promoting tourism.
8. The district established a supplies store to provide supplies to the district's various departments by transferring $4 million from the general fund. It accounted for the store in an internal service (proprietary) fund. During the year, the store purchased (and paid for) $2 million in supplies. Of these, it "sold" $1 million, at cost (for cash), to departments accounted for in the general fund. During the year, these departments used all of the supplies that they had purchased.

a. Prepare journal entries to record the transactions and other events in appropriate funds. Assume that governmental funds are accounted for on a modified accrual basis and focus only on current financial resources (and thus do not give balance sheet recognition either to capital assets or long-term debts). Proprietary funds are accounted for on a full accrual basis.

b. Prepare a combined balance sheet—one that has a separate column for each of the governmental funds you established.

c. Prepare a combined statement of revenues, expenditures, and changes in fund balances for all governmental funds. Prepare a separate statement of revenues, expenses, and changes in fund net position for any proprietary funds you established.

d. Prepare a government-wide statement of net position and a government-wide statement of activities in which all funds are consolidated and are accounted for on a full accrual basis. Be sure to include both long-term assets and liabilities on the statement of net position and to depreciate the long-term assets. Also, be sure to adjust for any interfund activity. You may find it helpful to redo the journal entries you made in Part (a), this time recording the transactions (and not the interfund activity) as if the district accounted for its activities in a single entity and on the full accrual basis.

Central States Rehabilitation Hospital Balance Sheet as of December 31 (in thousands)

Assets		*Liabilities and Fund Balances*	
	General Fund		
Current assets		***Current liabilities***	
Cash and equivalents	$ 3,103	Accounts payable	$ 3,200
Patients accounts receivable	15,700	Accrued expenses	3,400
Supplies	1,817	Estimated third-party settlements	2,408
Other current assets	404	Other current liabilities	2,700
Total current assets	$21,024	Total current liabilities	$11,708
Noncurrent assets		***Noncurrent liabilities***	
Assets whose use is limited (designated) by board for capital improvements	$21,000	Estimated cost of malpractice	$4,760
		Long-term debt	34,000
Property, plant, and equipment (net of allowance for depreciation)	42,500		
Other assets	7,300	Fund balance	41,356
Total noncurrent assets	70,800		
Total assets	$91,824	Total liabilities and fund balance	$91,824
	Donor Restricted Funds		
	Specific Purpose Funds		
Cash	$ 389	Accounts payable	$ 205
Investments	250	Deferred grant revenue	80
Grants receivable	613	Fund balance	967
Total assets	$ 1,252	Total liabilities and fund balance	$ 1,252
	Plant Replacement and Expansion Funds		
Cash	$ 25		
Investments	250		
Pledges receivable	110		
Total assets	$ 385	Fund balance	$ 385
	Endowment Funds		
Cash	$ 1,600		
Investments	4,200		
Total assets	$ 5,800	Fund balance	$ 5,800

P. 2-11

Per GASB Statement No. 54, fund balances have to be presented based on a hierarchical classification.

As the auditor of Clearwater County, you learn that various assets are subject to spending constraints. Indicate how each of the following constraints would affect the county's reported fund balance (i.e., in which category of fund balance it would be reported):

1. Per a bond agreement, the county must maintain a cash balance equal to six months' interest—$300,000.
2. The county council voted to set aside in a special bank account $30,000 per year to pay for the county's centennial anniversary celebration, which will take place in five years. The current balance in the bank account is $120,000.
3. Legislation imposed by the state in which the county is located requires all counties to maintain a cash reserve equal to 5 percent of the prior year's expenditures. The required amount for the current year is $60,000.
4. The county has goods on order of $80,000, for which it will have to make payment early in the following fiscal year.
5. The county maintains an inventory of supplies of $70,000.

P. 2-12

Fund balances are classified according to degree of restrictiveness.

The following is from the governmental funds balance sheet section of the Town of Libertyville's Comprehensive Annual Financial Report.

	General Fund	Special Revenue Fund	Capital Projects Fund	Debt Service Fund	Total
Fund Balances					
Nonspendable					
Inventory	$ 125,000	$ 111,000			$ 236,000
Restricted for:					
Parks and recreation	95,000				95,000
Road repair		46,000			46,000
Debt service				$ 189,000	189,000
Highways			$ 560,000		560,000
Committed to:					
Economic stabilization	212,000				212,000
Education	54,000				54,000
City Hall renovation			110,000		110,000
Assigned to:					
Library acquisitions	46,000				46,000
Parks and recreation	24,000				24,000
Debt service				50,000	50,000
Other purposes	67,000				67,000
Unassigned	611,000				
Total fund balances	$ 1,234,000	$ 157,000	$ 670,000	$ 239,000	$ 2,300,000

1. What is the most likely reason that there are no unassigned balances in any of the funds other than the general fund?
2. Of the balance in the debt service fund, a portion is classified as "restricted," and a portion is classified as "assigned." What parties or entities likely "restricted" and "assigned" the resources, respectively?

3. Of the balance in the capital projects fund, a portion is classified as "restricted," and a portion is classified as "committed." What parties or entities likely "restricted" and "committed" the resources, respectively?

4. Why is inventory classified as "nonspendable"?

5. If Libertyville were to establish a Permanent Fund, how would the town classify *most* of its fund balance?

QUESTIONS FOR RESEARCH, ANALYSIS, AND DISCUSSION

1. This chapter has described the fund structure in governments. Do you think that it is necessary to display individual funds in a government's annual report? If so, then do you think it is any less necessary to display individual funds in a not-for-profit's annual report? On what basis can you justify displaying funds in the annual report of a government but not in that of a not-for-profit entity?

2. A school district receives a grant from the federal government to support programs directed at special needs students. The grant is a matching grant in which each dollar spent by the school district on teacher salaries for special needs education will be matched up to $1 million by the federal government. The federal government agrees that it will advance monies to the school district so that the school district will be able to pay a portion each month of teachers' salaries from federal funds. The grant's contractual terms stipulate that the school district must not commingle the federal monies that it has been advanced with other monies of the school district. The school district also is required to file quarterly and annual reports showing the amounts that the school district has spent on special needs education and the resultant amount that is either a receivable from or payable to the federal government.

   As a new comptroller, you must decide which funds should be used to account for the federal grant and the school district match. After some research, you believe that the school district has some options as to the governmental funds that it will use for financial reporting purposes. What are the options? In which funds would you report the transactions associated with the federal grant and school district match? Should they be accounted for in the same fund? What factors influenced your decision?

3. GASB Statement No. 34 has been widely criticized for mandating the preparation and presentation of government-wide statements. Mainly, the critics contend that the benefits of the statements are not commensurate with the costs of preparing them. They argue that the statements provide little information that is "decision-useful." Do you agree? For what types of decisions are statement users most likely to use the government-wide statements? If you have difficulty identifying such decisions, then is the GASB requirement defensible?

SOLUTION TO EXERCISE FOR REVIEW AND SELF-STUDY

a. Journal entries

1. **General fund**

Cash	$250	
Taxes receivable	50	
Tax revenues		$300
To record the levy and collection of taxes		

2. **General fund**

Operating expenditures	$240	
Cash		$170
Accounts payable		70
To record operating expenditures		

3. Capital projects fund

Cash	$500	
Bond proceeds		$500
To record proceeds of the bond issue		

Although the district does not report the obligation in a fund, it still needs to maintain accounting control over it. Therefore, it must record the obligation in a separate, off-the-balance-sheet ledger, or other "list" of long-term obligations.

4. Capital projects fund

Expenditure—acquisition of facilities	$400	
Cash		$400
To record the acquisition of facilities		

From an accounting perspective, the facilities are written off when acquired. As with the bonds, the district must maintain a separate, off-the-balance-sheet record of the assets.

5. General fund

Transfer to debt service fund	$40	
Cash		$40
To record the transfer of cash to the debt service fund (the transfer account is similar to an expenditure account)		

Debt service fund

Cash	$40	
Transfer from general fund		$40
To record transfer of cash from the general fund		

6. Internal service fund

Equipment	$10	
Long-term note		$10
To record acquisition of plant and equipment.		

Because this is a proprietary fund and accounted for on a full accrual basis, both the equipment and the note are recognized within the internal service fund itself.

7. Internal service fund

Cash	$15	
Operating revenues		$15
To record operating revenues		
Operating expenses	$12	
Cash		$12
To record cash operating expenses		
Depreciation expense	$2	
Equipment		$2
To record depreciation (alternatively, the credit could have been made to a contra account, "accumulated depreciation")		

The revenues of the internal service fund are expenditures to the general fund. Thus,

Operating expenditures	$15	
Cash		$15
To record operating expenditures in the general fund		

b. Governmental fund statements

State Recreation District Statement of Revenues, Expenditures, and Changes in Fund Balances—Governmental Funds, First Year (in millions)

	General Fund	Capital Projects Fund	Debt Service Fund	Total Governmental Funds
Revenues				
Tax revenues	$ 300			$ 300
Expenditures				
Operating expenditures	255			255
Acquisition of facilities	–	$ 400	–	400
Total expenditures	$ 255	$ 400	–	$ 655
Excess of revenues over expenditures	$ 45	$ (400)	–	$ (355)
Other financing sources (uses):				
Bond proceeds		500		500
Transfer to debt service fund	(40)			(40)
Transfer from general fund	–	–	40	40
Total other financing Sources and uses	$ (40)	$ 500	$40	$ 500
Net increase in fund balance	$ 5	$ 100	$40	$ 145

State Recreation District Balance Sheet—Governmental Funds End of First Year (in millions)

	General Fund	Capital Projects Fund	Debt Service Fund	Total Governmental Funds
Assets				
Cash	$25	$100	$40	$165
Taxes receivable	50	–	–	50
Total assets	$75	$100	$40	$215
Liabilities and fund balances				
Accounts payable	$70			$ 70
Fund balances	5	100	40	145
Total liabilities and fund balances	$75	$100	$40	$215

c. Proprietary fund statements

State Recreation District Statement of Net Position—Proprietary (Internal Service) Fund End of First Year (in millions)

Assets		
Cash		$ 3
Equipment	$10	
Less: accumulated depreciation	(2)	8
Total assets		$11
Liabilities and net position		
Long-term note		$10
Net position		1
Total liabilities and net position		$11

State Recreation District Statement of Revenues, Expenses, and Changes in Fund Net Position—Proprietary (Internal Service) Fund First Year (in millions)

Operating revenues		$15
Less: operating expenses	$12	
Depreciation expense	2	(14)
Change in net position		$ 1
Total net position—beginning of year		0
Total net position—end of year		$ 1

d. Government-wide financial statements

State Recreation District Statement of Net Position End of First Year (in millions)

Assets		
Cash		$168
Taxes receivable		50
Capital assets	$410	
Less: accumulated depreciation	(42)	368
Total assets		$586
Liabilities		
Accounts payable		$ 70
Long-term notes		10
Bonds payable		500
Total liabilities		$580
Net position		
Restricted to repayment of debt	$ 40	
Restricted to acquisition of capital assets	100	
Unrestricted	(134)	6
Total liabilities and net position		$586

State Recreation District Statement of Activities First Year (in millions)

Expenses	
Operating	$252
Depreciation	42
Total expenses	$294
General revenues	
Taxes	300
Increase in net assets	$ 6
Net position—beginning of year	0
Net position—end of year	$ 6

Explanation of government-wide statements:

- ***Capital assets:*** The capital assets are acquired with resources from both the capital projects fund and the internal service fund
- ***Depreciation and accumulated depreciation:*** Depreciation of $2 million on internal service fund assets and $40 million on recreational facility assets
- ***Restricted to payment of debt:*** Balance in the debt service fund
- ***Restricted to acquisition of capital assets:*** Balance in the capital projects fund
- ***Operating expenses:*** Operating expenditures of $255 million as reported in the governmental fund statement of revenues and expenditures less the $15 million billings from the internal service fund (in effect an intragovernment transfer) plus the $12 million of expenses incurred by the internal service fund

CHAPTER 3

Issues of Budgeting and Control

LEARNING OBJECTIVES

After studying this chapter, you should understand:

- The key purposes of budgets
- The need for more than one type of budget
- The various ways of classifying expenditures
- The benefits of performance budgets
- The key phases of the budget cycle
- Why budgets are generally prepared on a cash basis
- The limitations of budget-to-actual comparisons
- How budgets enhance control
- The means by which governments incorporate budgets into their accounting systems
- How an encumbrance system prevents overspending
- The circumstances under which budgetary and encumbrance entries are most beneficial

Budgets are to governments and not-for-profits what the sun is to the solar system. Trying to understand government and not-for-profit accounting without recognizing the centricity of the budget would be like trying to comprehend the earth's seasons while ignoring the sun. As emphasized in Chapter 1, and incorporated into generally accepted accounting principles, **budgets** are the key financial instruments.

Budgeting is an essential element of the financial planning, control, and evaluation processes of governments. Every governmental unit should prepare a comprehensive budget covering all governmental, proprietary, and fiduciary funds for each annual (or, in some states, biennial) fiscal period.[1]

Governments and not-for-profits are disciplined mainly by their budgets, not by the competitive marketplace. With few exceptions, governments reflect all significant decisions—whether political or managerial—in their budgets. As also pointed out in Chapter 1, a key objective of financial accounting and reporting is ensuring that an entity obtains and uses its resources in accordance with its budget. Budgeting exerts a major influence on accounting and financial reporting principles and practices.

The main purpose of this chapter is to provide an overview of budgets and the budgeting process and thereby establish a basis for appreciating the relationship between budgeting and

[1] NCGA Statement 1, *Governmental Accounting and Financial Reporting Principles* (1979), para. 77.

accounting. The first part of this chapter discusses functions of budgets, the different types of budgets, schemes of account classification, budgeting cycles, budgetary bases, and the significance of budget-to-actual comparisons. The second part shows how governments (and, to a lesser extent, not-for-profits) promote budgetary compliance by integrating the budget into their accounting systems. They do this primarily by preparing journal entries to record both the budget and the goods and services that have been ordered but not yet received.

Although this chapter will describe budgetary procedures and related accounting practices mainly in the context of governments, most of the points can properly be extended to not-for-profits. For example, whereas the legislatures of governments *appropriate* (a term reserved for governments) funds for expenditure, the boards of directors or trustees of private-sector not-for-profits *authorize* or *approve* outlays—performing essentially the same function. However, the budgets of governments have the force of law, and officials may be subject to severe penalties for violating them. To prevent overspending, governments are required to institute certain accounting controls—such as integrating both the budget and purchase orders into their accounting systems—that are optional for not-for-profits.

WHAT ARE THE KEY PURPOSES OF BUDGETS?

Budgets are intended to carry out at least three broad functions:

- ***Planning.*** In a broad sense, planning comprises *programming* (determining the activities that the entity will undertake), resource *acquisition*, and resource *allocation*. Planning is concerned with specifying the type, quantity, and quality of services that will be provided to constituents, estimating service costs, and determining how to pay for the services.
- ***Controlling and administering.*** Budgets help ensure that resources are obtained and expended as planned. Managers use budgets to monitor resource flows and point to the need for operational adjustments. Legislative bodies—such as city councils or boards of trustees—use budgets to impose spending authority over executives (such as city managers or executive directors), who in turn use them to impose authority over their subordinates (such as department heads).
- ***Reporting and evaluating.*** Budgets lay the foundation for end-of-period reports and evaluations. Budget-to-actual comparisons reveal whether revenue and spending mandates were carried out. More important, when tied to an organization's objectives, budgets can facilitate assessments of efficiency and effectiveness.

WHY IS MORE THAN ONE TYPE OF BUDGET NECESSARY?

The benefits of the budgetary process cannot be fully achieved by a single budget or type of budget. A well-managed government or not-for-profit—just like a well-managed business—should prepare budgets for varying periods of time from multiple perspectives. These include

- ***Appropriation budgets***, which are concerned mainly with current operating revenues and expenditures
- ***Capital budgets***, which focus on the acquisition and construction of long-term assets
- ***Flexible budgets***, which relate costs to outputs and are thereby intended to help control costs, especially those of business-type activities

In addition, many governments and not-for-profits prepare **performance budgets** (discussed later in this chapter).

APPROPRIATION BUDGETS

A government's *current* or *operating* budget covers its general fund. The operating budget is almost always an **appropriation budget**—one incorporating the legislatively granted expenditure authority, along with the related estimates of revenue. In most state and local jurisdictions, the operating budget must, by law, be balanced. Public attention focuses on the appropriation budget because it determines the amount of taxes, other revenues that must be generated to cover expenditures. Owing to the importance of appropriation budgets and the influence, they have had upon the establishment of accounting principles and practices, this chapter directs attention mainly to this type of budget.

Governments may require that appropriation budgets also be developed and approved for special revenue, debt service, or capital project funds, in addition to the general fund. However, such budgets may be unnecessary if a government has established adequate controls over spending by other means. For example, by accepting a federal grant and creating a special revenue fund to account for it, the government may implicitly approve expenditure of the grant resources. Similarly, by issuing bonds, it may authorize spending for specified capital projects. Still, principles of sound management dictate that a nonappropriation budget—a financial plan not subject to appropriation—be prepared each year for such funds and organizational units. Budgets of some type are almost always necessary if activities are to be effectively planned, controlled, and evaluated.

CAPITAL BUDGETS

Although the accounting cycle is traditionally one year, the budgeting process commonly extends for a considerably longer period. The needs of an organization's constituents must be forecast and planned for years in advance.

A **capital budget**, in contrast to an appropriation budget, typically covers multiple years, often as many as five. It concentrates on the construction and acquisition of long-lived assets such as land, buildings, roads, bridges, and major items of equipment. These assets can be expected to last for many years. Therefore, in the interest of interperiod equity, they generally are financed with long-term debt rather than taxes of a single year. The capital budget is, in essence, a plan setting forth when specific capital assets will be acquired and how they will be financed.

Capital budgets are closely tied to operating budgets. Each year a government must include current-year capital spending in its operating budget. If the capital projects are financed with debt, however, the capital expenditures will be offset with bond proceeds and will not affect the operating budget's surplus or deficit.

Legislators often spend more extravagantly on capital assets than on operating resources. Capital projects, they reason, can be financed with debt rather than taxes and thus will not affect the surplus or deficit of the general fund, the budget of which must be balanced. Their error is in failing to take into account the additional operating costs associated with new long-term assets. Roads must be repaired, buildings maintained, and equipment tuned up. Further, in future years the debt must be serviced with interest and principal payments made from operating resources. As of 2017, the American Society of Civil Engineers assigned America's infrastructure an overall grade of D+ for "poor" condition, one grade above "failing."

FLEXIBLE BUDGETS

These are budgets that focus on expected revenues, expenses, and net income under different assumptions of volume. Governments use **flexible budgets** for enterprise funds, which account for business-type activities, even though enterprise funds are generally not subject to the same statutory budget requirements as governmental funds. Nevertheless, budgets are as important to enterprise funds as they are to businesses and governmental funds. As a rule, governments should prepare the same types of budgets for enterprise funds as would a private enterprise carrying out similar activities. For certain, they should prepare a series of flexible budgets, each of which contains alternative budget estimates based on varying levels of output. Unlike **fixed budgets**, flexible budgets capture the behavior of costs, distinguishing fixed and variable amounts. A flexible budget is a form of "what-if?" analysis. Fixed budgets may be appropriate for governmental funds in which the expenditures and level of activity are preestablished by legislative authorization. Flexible budgets are especially suited to enterprise funds in which the level of activity depends on customer demand.

HOW ARE EXPENDITURES AND REVENUES CLASSIFIED?

How financial data are presented affects how they are used. Therefore, accountants, public administrators, political scientists, and economists have directed considerable attention to the form and content of budgets. They are aware that the way the budget is prepared and presented can significantly affect the allocation of resources among organizations, programs, and activities.

EXPENDITURES

The Governmental Accounting Standards Board (GASB) advises that "multiple classification of governmental expenditure data is important from both internal and external management control and accountability standpoints" as it "facilitates the aggregation and analysis of data in different ways for different purposes and in manners that cross fund and organizational lines." Suggested classifications include

- By *fund*—such as the general fund, special revenue funds, and debt service funds
- By *organizational unit*—such as the police department, the fire department, the city council, and the finance office
- By *function* or *program* (a group of activities carried out with the same objective)—such as general government, public safety, sanitation, and recreation
- By *activity* (line of work contributing to a function or program)—such as highway patrol, burglary investigations, and vice patrol
- By *character* (the fiscal period they are presumed to benefit)—such as "current expenditures," which benefit the current period; "capital outlays," which benefit the current and future periods; and "debt service," which benefits prior, current, and future periods
- By *object classification* (the types of items purchased or the services obtained)—such as salaries, fringe benefits, travel, and repairs[2]

REVENUES

In contrast to expenditures, revenues present less significant issues of classification. Most revenues are not designated for specific purposes (or, if they are, they are reported in separate funds); therefore, their classification is relatively straightforward. The GASB recommends that, in fund statements, revenues be classified first by fund (i.e., the columns on a statement of revenues and

[2] NCGA Statement 1, *Governmental Accounting and Financial Reporting Principles* (1979), para. 111.

expenditures) and then by source (i.e., the rows). Suggested major revenue source classifications include

- Taxes
- Licenses and permits
- Intergovernmental revenues
- Charges for services
- Fines and forfeits[3]

Most governments divide these classifications into numerous subclassifications—such as property taxes, sales taxes, and hotel taxes.

WHY ARE PERFORMANCE BUDGETS NECESSARY?

The traditional, and most commonly prepared, budget is referred to as an **object classification budget** because it is characterized by the expenditure classification that categorizes objects—such as the type of goods or services to be acquired. The primary virtue of an object classification budget is that it facilitates control. The managers who prepare the budget, and the legislators who pass it, establish rigid spending mandates and thereby direct, in detail, how every dollar should be spent. But this strength may also be a shortcoming:

- By expediting control, an object classification budget discourages planning. It encourages top-level decision makers to focus on specific line items rather than on overall entity objectives, strategies, and measurable performance targets. Thus, the officials of a school district may focus on the need for increased appropriations for salaries, fuel, supplies, and food while failing to consider how the additional outlays will affect the school's primary educational mission.
- It promotes bottom-up rather than top-down budgeting, with each unit presenting its fiscal requirements for approval in the absence of coordinated sets of goals and strategies.
- It overwhelms top-level decision makers with details. As a consequence, the decision makers are induced to take budgetary shortcuts—such as increasing all expenditures by a fixed percentage.
- By failing to relate specific *inputs* (factors used to provide goods and services) to *outputs* (units of service) or *outcomes* (accomplishments in terms of organizational objectives), it limits post-budget evaluation to whether spending mandates were observed.

Owing to these deficiencies, many governments and not-for-profits have adopted performance budgets in place of, or as a supplement to, object classification budgets. Performance budgets focus on measurable units of efforts, services, and accomplishments. They are formulated so that dollar expenditures are directly associated with anticipated units of outputs or outcomes. They enable managers to define goals, plan their resource needs, and measure the achievement of their various objectives. Table 3-1 illustrates an example of a government's performance metrics in its annual budget.

Comprehensive performance budgeting systems require managers to specify objectives, consider alternative means of achieving them, establish workload indicators, and perform cost–benefit analyses.

To be sure, other sound managerial approaches can overcome the limitations of object classification budgeting. Performance budgets, however, institutionalize effective decision processes and help ensure that they are carried out.

[3] NCGA Statement 1, *Governmental Accounting and Financial Reporting Principles* (1979), para. 110.

TABLE 3-1 City of Houston Citywide Performance Measures—Excerpt from FY 2018 Adopted Budget

Citywide Performance Measures

Citywide performance measures provide decision makers and the public with a better understanding of the overall financial and operational health of the City. These measures show the results of the City's work and set targets aimed at making tangible improvements toward the Mayor's Priorities. The measures are categorized by Priority-area as follows:

Public Safety	FY2016 Actual	FY2017 Budget	FY2017 Estimate	FY2018 Budget
911 Emergency Calls Answered within 10 Seconds	97%	90%	97%	90%
Dangerous Buildings Demolished	542	425	425	425
Fear of Crime Index[a]	25%	25%	18%	18%
Fire First Unit Response Time (Minutes)	7.4	7.3	7.3	7.4
Percent of Buildings Inspected by Fire in 5 Years	N/A**	N/A	30%	45%
Police Priority 1 Calls Responded to within 6 Minutes	56.6%	65.5%	68.3%	68.3%
Police UCR Part 1 Crime Clearance Rate	14.9%	17.3%	13.4%	13.9%
Police UCR Part 1 Crime Rate (Per 100,000)	5,505	5,945	5,397	5,734
Traffic Fatalities	240	210	255	224

Services & Infrastructure	FY2016 Actual	FY2017 Budget	FY2017 Estimate	FY2018 Budget
Average Age of Fleet	8.6	7.0	8.6	7.0
Citizen Satisfaction Rating of Flood Prevention (1–4)	N/A	N/A	1.9	2.5
Citizen Satisfaction Rating of Traffic Signals (1–4)	N/A	N/A	2.6	2.6
Citywide 311 Service Request On-Time Performance	N/A	N/A	65%	90%
Commercial Plan Reviews Completed within 15 Days	44%	90%	98%	90%
Overall City Customer Satisfaction Rating (1–4)	N/A	N/A	2.4	3.0
Pavement Condition Index—City Streets Average (1–100)	73	73	72	73
Potholes Repaired within Next Business Day	65%	95%	95%	95%
Sanitary Sewer Outflows (Per 100 Miles of Pipe)	25	25	21	18

**Please note that several of the measures have "N/A" or "TBD" values, as they are new City performance measures.

[a]Fear of Crime Index is based on the percentage of respondents who were "very worried" about becoming a victim of a crime. Houston Area Survey, Rice Kinder Institute, May 2017.

Citywide Performance Measures

Complete Communities *(Measures still in development)*	FY2016 Actual	FY2017 Budget	FY2017 Estimate	FY2018 Budget
Citywide Average School Rating[b] (1–100)	43	NIA	TBD	TBD
Harris County Unemployment Rate	4.7%	4.5%	5.9%	5.0%
Residents Living within a Quarter Mile of Transit	N/A	N/A	TBD	TBD
Residents Who Spend 45% or Less of Income on Housing and Transportation[c]	82%	N/A	TBD	TBD
Residents within a 10-Minute or Half-Mile Walk to a Park[d]	48%	48%	48%	48%
Residents without Adequate Food Access Nearby[e]	34%	NIA	TBD	TBD

(Continues)

TABLE 3-1 **City of Houston Citywide Performance Measures—Excerpt from FY 2018 Adopted Budget** (*Continued*)

Sound Financial Management	FY2016 Actual	FY2017 Budget	FY2017 Estimate	FY2018 Budget
General Fund Balance % of Expenditures	11.8%	9.39%	11.02%	8.94%
General Fund Surplus or (Deficit)	($47M)	($10M)	($12M)	($46M)
General Fund Expenditures Budget *vs* Actual Utilization	98%	98%	101%	98%
General Fund Revenues Budget *vs* Actual Utilization	100%	100%	101%	100%
General Fund Expenditures Per Capita	$872	$889	$887	$870
General Fund Revenues Per Capita	$1,002	$998	$1,009	$1,010
Pension Payments as a % of Expenditures	9.0%	8.6%	9.0%	8.0%
Pension Payments Per Capita	$163	$167	$169	$157

See Appendix section page XV - 17 - for Definitions of Performance Measures.
[b]*Source*: Children at Risk: Annual School Rankings, 2017 (released in June for prior calendar year).
[c]*Source*: Center for Neighborhood Technology, Housing & Transportation Index.
[d]*Source*: Trust for Public Land, Parkscore Index 2018.
[e]*Source*: USDA Food Access Research Atlas.

Performance budgets are closely related to **program budgets**, whereby resources and results are identified with programs rather than traditional organizational units, and expenditures are typically categorized by activity rather than by object. Program budgets often report performance metrics by objective and may be couched in broader thematic budget areas. For example in Table 3-2, the City of Alexandria's Department of Community and Human Services' programs are reported in the "Healthy & Thriving Residents" budget area. Program budgeting is discussed in detail in Chapter 15.

WHAT ARE THE KEY PHASES FOR THE BUDGET CYCLE?

Budgeting practices in governments and not-for-profits are not standardized; they differ from entity to entity. However, irrespective of whether the budget is of object classification or performance type, in most organizations budgeting is a continuous, four-phase process:

- Preparation
- Legislative adoption and executive approval
- Execution
- Reporting and auditing

PREPARATION

Budgets are most commonly prepared by an organization's executive branch (e.g., the office of the mayor or executive director) and submitted to the legislative branch (e.g., a city council or board of trustees) for approval. In some jurisdictions, particularly states, the legislature may either prepare its own budget or join with the executive branch in developing a common budget.

Budgeting generally necessitates flows of policies and information to and from all parties involved in the budgetary process. Legislators, for example, will apprise the executive branch as to what they think is politically feasible for revenue measures. Department heads will inform the legislative or executive budget committees as to what they see as their requirements. The

TABLE 3-2 City of Alexandria's Department of Community and Human Services Program Budget Excerpt

Program		FY 2016 Actual	FY 2017 Approved	FY 2018 Proposed	$ Change 2017–2018	% Change 2017–2018
Leadership and General Management						
This program provides support to Facilities Management, Human Resources, Leadership & General Management, Finance, Quality Assurance and Program Evaluation, and Technology Services.						
	Program Expenditures (All Funds)	$8,324,421	$7,852,468	$8,122,376	$269,908	3.4%
	Program FTEs	61.03	57.03	56.03	(1.00)	–1.8%
Adult Leadership & General Management						
This program provides leadership and management services to the Adult Services Center.						
	Program Expenditures (All Funds)	$1,621,944	$1,728,917	$1,791,944	$63,027	3.6%
	Program FTEs	16.10	16.10	16.10	0.00	0.0%
Children Leadership & Management						
This program provides leadership and management services to the Children and Family Center.						
	Program Expenditures (All Funds)	$787,854	$964,091	$776,599	($187,492)	–19.4%
	Program FTEs	5.43	5.43	5.43	0.00	0.0%
Economic Leadership & Management						
This program provides leadership and management services to the Economic Support Center.						
	Program Expenditures (All Funds)	$485,199	$488,632	$579,079	$90,446	18.5%
	Program FTEs	4.28	4.68	4.68	0.00	0.0%
Acute & Emergency Services						
This program provides Mental Health (MH) Outpatient Services, Substance Abuse (SA) Outpatient Services, MH and SA Support Groups, Opioid Treatment, 24-Hour Detox Services, and New Lease of Life.						
	Program Expenditures (All Funds)	$9,248,314	$10,011,621	$10,047,284	$35,663	0.4%
	Program FTEs	78.84	81.84	81.84	0.00	0.0%
Aging & Adult Services						
This program provides Adult Day Services, Adult Protective Services, and Older Adult Clinical Services.						
	Program Expenditures (All Funds)	$5,585,282	$5,933,349	$6,104,213	$170,864	2.9%
	Program FTEs	33.20	33.20	33.20	0.00	0.0%
Alexandria Fund for Human Services						
The Alexandria Fund for Human Services allows the City to support human service programs vital to meeting the needs of the community with broadly defined service priorities for young children, youth, immigrants, the elderly and the disabled.						
	Program Expenditures (All Funds)	$2,000,483	$1,996,430	$1,996,430	$0	0.0%
	Program FTEs	0.00	0.00	0.00	0.00	0.0%
Benefit Programs						
This program provides assistance for CommonHelp, and determines eligibility for Supplemental Nutrition Assistance (SNAP), Family Access to Medical Insurance Security Plan (FAMIS), Refugee Assistance, Medicaid, Temporary Assistance for Needy Families (TANF), and Auxiliary Grant Program.						
	Program Expenditures (All Funds)	$4,884,678	$5,339,357	$5,441,969	$102,613	1.9%
	Program FTEs	53.50	53.50	53.50	0.00	0.0%

City of Alexandria FY 2018 Proposed Budget 11.12

(Continues)

TABLE 3-2 City of Alexandria's Department of Community and Human Services Program Budget Excerpt *(Continued)*

Program [Continued from previous page]	FY 2016 Actual	FY 2017 Approved	FY 2018 Proposed	$ Change 2017–2018	% Change 2017–2018
Child & Family Treatment					
This program provides Mental Health and Substance Abuse Outpatient Services for children, youth and families; Community Wraparound services to support youth with serious mental health needs and their families; and Family Partners who support families accessing services.					
Program Expenditures (All Funds)	$2,777,414	$2,927,107	$3,159,434	$232,326	7.9%
Program FTEs	29.57	29.57	29.57	0.00	0.0%
Child Welfare					
The Child Welfare Program provides Child Protective Services; Foster Care and Adoption, Prevention Services, and comprehensive and specialty care through Child Assessment and Treatment Center for Health (CATCH).					
Program Expenditures (All Funds)	$11,588,351	$10,937,596	$11,084,432	$146,836	1.3%
Program FTEs	53.75	53.00	53.00	0.00	0.0%
Community Services					
This program provides several community safety-net services including Prescription and Burial Assistance, Rental Assistance, Utility and Cooling Assistance, and Homeless Services (Emergency Shelter & Eviction Services) and information and/or referral for food, clothing and furniture.					
Program Expenditures (All Funds)	$3,806,536	$4,307,504	$4,529,909	$222,405	5.2%
Program FTEs	17.76	17.76	17.76	0.00	0.0%
Children's Services Act					
This program provides Children's Services Act funding to support the complex needs of high risk youth and their families.					
Program Expenditures (All Funds)	$8,228,485	$8,369,987	$8,834,987	$464,999	5.6%
Program FTEs	3.00	3.00	3.00	0.00	0.0%
Domestic Violence & Sexual Assault					
This program provides intervention, support, shelter and hotline services for victims of domestic violence and crisis intervention, advocacy, counseling and hotline services for victims of sexual assault.					
Program Expenditures (All Funds)	$1,656,657	$1,659,174	$1,931,625	$272,451	16.4%
Program FTEs	17.50	17.50	17.50	0.00	0.0%
Early Childhood					
This program provides child care regulation, information and training for providers, developmental services for children 0–3 via Parent Infant Education (PIE), and mental health support in preschools through Preschool Prevention Programs.					
Program Expenditures (All Funds)	$7,830,094	$7,720,068	$7,768,857	$48,789	0.6%
Program FTEs	23.23	22.23	21.23	(1.00)	–4.5%
ID Services for Adults					
This program provides assistance to families and individuals with intellectual disabilities and their families, including in-home training, respite care and day programs including placement in jobs, work crews, sheltered workshops and prevocational programs.					
Program Expenditures (All Funds)	$6,756,741	$6,765,814	$6,736,468	($29,346)	–0.4%
Program FTEs	61.45	61.45	61.45	0.00	0.0%

City of Alexandria FY 2018 Proposed Budget 11.13

(Continues)

TABLE 3-2 City of Alexandria's Department of Community and Human Services Program Budget Excerpt *(Continued)*

Program [Continued from previous page]	FY 2016 Actual	FY 2017 Approved	FY 2018 Proposed	$ Change 2017–2018	% Change 2017–2018
Workforce Development Center					
This program provides employment services and training for both adults and youth and offers staffing solutions to businesses by providing employees who are skilled and ready to work.					
Program Expenditures (All Funds)	$3,657,626	$3,558,317	$3,547,978	($10,339)	–0.3%
Program FTEs	29.17	28.17	28.17	0.00	0.0%
Residential & Community Support					
This program provides Mental Health (MH) and Substance Abuse (SA) Residential Services, MH/SA Case Management Services, Psychosocial Rehab and MH Vocational Services.					
Program Expenditures (All Funds)	$7,768,775	$7,607,149	$8,830,930	$1,223,781	16.1%
Program FTEs	82.13	83.65	83.65	0.00	0.0%
Youth Development					
This program plans and coordinates services to promote positive development among Alexandria's youth by providing Office of Youth Services, School-Age Youth Development, Substance Abuse Prevention Coalition of Alexandria, Alexandria Campaign on Adolescent Pregnancy, and Project Discovery.					
Program Expenditures (All Funds)	$1,673,480	$2,150,671	$2,222,815	$72,144	3.4%
Program FTEs	15.54	16.54	16.54	0.00	0.0%

**The FY 2016 & FY 2017 FTE count varies from the FY 2017 Approved Book due to FTE reconciliation that occurred in FY 2017. The above reflects the correct FTEs. Additionally, the FY 2017 Approved number reflects 6.3 additional FTEs due to the PACT grant received mid-year, a decrease of 3.78 FTEs due to the FY 2017 Mental Health Residential Redesign, and a mid-year 0.4 FTE transfer of a SNAP/EBT Coordinator from the Department of General Services for a net impact of mid-year adjustments of 2.92 FTEs.*

City of Alexandria FY 2018 Proposed Budget 11.14

committees, in turn, will develop guidelines for funding priorities and establish ranges of funding increases and cuts.

The preparation of a budget requires both forecasts and estimates. Relatively few types of revenues can be determined accurately in advance of the budget period. These types are limited mainly to those that are contractually established (e.g., from lease agreements), have been previously promised (e.g., grants from other governments), or are set by law and affect a known number of parties (e.g., property taxes and special assessments). Most, however, depend on factors that are largely outside the government's control. Most types of tax revenues, for example, are influenced by economic conditions; revenues from fines and fees are affected by the predilections of the citizenry.

Some expenditures are fixed by legislative action or can be determined accurately. Examples of these types of expenditures include salaries of key officials (assuming no turnover), grants to other organizations, acquisitions of equipment, payments of interest, and repayments of debt. Others, however, are affected by unforeseen circumstances. Snow removal, parades for championship sports teams, repair of equipment, and purchases of fuel are some examples of unpredictable expenditures.

The public budgeting literature is replete with descriptions of forecasting models and techniques. However, these models or techniques are no better than the underlying assumptions and the legislative constraints faced by the officials, who have tried to balance their current budgets through various means (see "In Practice: Budgeting and Legislative Constraints"). In addition, as might be expected, the differences between actual results and budgetary estimates can be substantial.

IN PRACTICE BUDGETING AND LEGISLATIVE CONSTRAINTS

As reported by *National Public Radio* (February 8, 2018), the State of Oklahoma faces budgetary gridlock and cuts to essential services as a result of a large structural budget deficit. Policy makers cut taxes amid an oil boom in the late 2000s, and they expected economic activity to keep pace such that revenues would be sufficient to maintain public services. The state faces a hard budget constraint in the form of a legislative supermajority: Due to a voter referendum in the 1990s, a tax increase requires the support of 75 percent of the legislature. While there is bipartisan support among Oklahoma policy makers for tax increases, the source of the stalemate is that Democratic and Republican state legislators disagree on how the burdens of those increases should be distributed.

Significant errors in budget estimates, irrespective of direction or cause, thwart the political process and may lead to a distribution of resources that misrepresent what was expressed by voters through their elected representatives. At the very least, as suggested by "In Practice: Budgeting and Legislative Constraints," they can make for colorful political contretemps. Insofar as budgets are used by investors or creditors, they may contribute to misguided fiscal decisions and misallocation of resources.

LEGISLATIVE ADOPTION AND EXECUTIVE APPROVAL

When the budget is presented to a legislature for consideration, it is typically turned over to one or more committees for review. In some legislatures—such as the U.S. Congress—the committees that act on revenues are separate from those that recommend expenditures. Moreover, the committees authorizing new programs may be different from those determining the amount to be spent on them. The committees typically make recommendations to the legislature as a whole; the legislature may revise their proposals as it deems appropriate.

Upon agreeing to the budget, a legislature officially adopts it by enacting an **appropriation** measure authorizing expenditures. Legislatures differ in the degree of control that they exert over the details of appropriations. Some appropriate lump sums to departments or programs, giving the executive branch the flexibility to allocate the resources among the various object classifications. Others go further, specifying not only the departments or programs but also the object classifications on which authorized funds can be expended. Then, any subsequent shifts from one classification to another require legislative approval.

Property taxes are commonly *levied* (authorized by the legislature) annually. Most other revenues—such as income and sales taxes—are not authorized each year unless there is to be a change in rates or other provisions.

EXECUTION

The budget is executed (carried out) by an organization's executive branch. In some jurisdictions, expenditures are assigned in particular months or quarters by **allotments** or **apportionments**. Both allotments and apportionments are periodic allocations of funds to departments or agencies, usually made by the chief executive's office, to ensure that an entire year's appropriation is not dissipated early in the period covered by the budget. They also prevent a department or agency from spending resources that may not be available in the event that actual revenues fall short of budgeted revenues.

As discussed later in this chapter, governments integrate their budgets into their accounting systems. In that way, they are able to monitor continually how revenues and expenditures to date compare with the amounts that have been estimated or authorized. Moreover, to enhance control and facilitate end-of-period, budget-to-actual comparisons, they use the same account structure for their budgets as for their actual revenues and expenditures.

Governments, like businesses, should issue interim financial statements to report on their progress in executing their budgets. Per GASB standards:

> *Appropriate interim budgetary reports should be prepared during the fiscal period to facilitate management control and legislative oversight of governmental fund financial operations. Such reports are important to both revenue and expenditure control processes and to facilitate timely planning and budgetary revisions.*[4]

REPORTING AND AUDITING

To complete the budget cycle, information on how the budget was executed must be provided to the analysts and governing officials, who must prepare and adopt the subsequent budget. At a minimum, both governments and not-for-profits should include in their annual financial statements or supplementary reports budget-to-actual comparisons for each of the funds for which they have adopted budgets. These comparisons will be discussed later in this chapter.

Performance budgets, unlike traditional object classification budgets, create the basis for evaluating and auditing organizational efficiency and effectiveness. These budgets specify anticipated outputs or outcomes in a quantifiable, measureable form. They thereby provide auditors (both internal and independent) with objective benchmarks by which to gauge organizational accomplishments and to compare them with budgetary expectations. By assessing performance, instead of mere compliance with budgetary spending mandates, auditors can transform the audit from what administrators may perceive as an annoyance into an essential element of the management process. Performance audits are addressed in Chapter 16.

ON WHAT BASIS OF ACCOUNTING ARE BUDGETS PREPARED?

Despite the importance of budgets and the influence of budgeting on financial reporting, both the GASB and the Financial Accounting Standards Board (FASB) establish generally accepted principles only for financial reporting, not for budgeting. Budgetary principles are established either by individual governments or organizations or by the governments or organizations that supervise them (e.g., states may establish the principles for their cities, towns, and districts; national associations may establish principles for their local chapters).

Although it lacks the authority to establish standards for budgeting, the GASB nevertheless recommends that governments prepare their annual budgets for governmental funds on the modified accrual basis—the same basis they are required to use for reporting on the governmental funds in their external financial statements.[5]

The modified accrual basis does not allow for balance sheet recognition of long-term assets and debts. However, it does permit a wide array of transactions and events to be recognized when they have their substantive economic impact, not merely when they result in cash inflows and outflows.

Many governments, however, reject the GASB's advice. They opt to prepare budgets on a cash basis or a slightly modified cash basis.

[4] NCGA Statement 1, *Governmental Accounting and Financial Reporting Principles* (1979), para. 93.
[5] NCGA Statement 1, *Governmental Accounting and Financial Reporting Principles* (1979), para. 87.

Governments that budget on a cash basis assign revenues and expenditures to the period in which the government is expected to receive or disburse cash. Some governments modify the cash basis by requiring that **encumbrances** (commitments to purchase goods or services) be accounted for as if they were the equivalent of actual purchases. Others permit certain taxes or other revenues to be recognized in the year in which they are due rather than expected to be collected, as long as they are expected to be collected within a reasonable period of time.

RATIONALE FOR BUDGETING ON THE CASH BASIS

Governments have valid reasons for budgeting on a cash basis. After all, bills must be paid with cash, not receivables or other assets; therefore, the required cash must be on hand in the year the payments have to be made. And goods or services must be paid for in the year of acquisition (or in the periods set forth in a borrowing agreement), not necessarily in the year or years in which the benefits will be received.

Correspondingly, when a government is able to defer payments, it need not have the cash on hand until disbursements are required. Taxpayers are understandably reluctant to part with their dollars so that the government can retain the cash as "savings" until the year needed. Suppose that government employees are permitted to defer until future years vacations that are earned in a current year. Although the services of the employees unquestionably benefit the period in which the vacations are earned, the government does not need—and the taxpayers might object to providing—the cash for the vacation payments until the employees actually take the vacations. Thus, in the face of a balanced budget requirement, the cash basis of accounting ensures that the government receives in taxes and other revenues only what it is required to disburse.

IN PRACTICE STATES BALANCE THEIR BUDGETS THE PAINLESS WAY

In an article appropriately headlined, "When Budgets Get Rough, States Get Gimmicky," the Associated Press reports on how several states are resolving their budget problems (at least in part). Here is an abbreviated list.

California moved up the collection dates on income tax withholding. Correspondingly it moved back, by one day, the date on which state employees receive their paychecks. It thereby moved the payroll costs into the following fiscal year.

Washington changed the mortality assumptions used to calculate its pension expense, now figuring that employees will retire later but die sooner.

Alabama stopped paying for school supplies, thus transferring the cost to local school districts (which were having their own fiscal difficulties).

Kansas refinanced some bonds, temporarily lowering principal and interest payments.

Illinois authorized its governor to make over $2 billion in budget cuts but did not specify the costs to be reduced. Nevertheless, the full amount of the cuts was assumed to be real savings. Other states did the same.

Several states simply moved dollars from various special revenue or rainy-day funds into a general fund (i.e., from one pocket into another) and claimed the transfers as savings.

Source: Based on a report by Curt Woodward, July 30, 2009.

ADVERSE CONSEQUENCES OF THE CASH BASIS

The adverse consequences of the cash basis should not be overlooked. The cash basis may distort the economic impact of a government's planned fiscal activities. A budget that is balanced on a cash basis may be decidedly unbalanced as to economic costs and revenues. It may give the appearance of a budget that has achieved interperiod equity when it really has not.

The cash basis permits a government to balance its budget by taking any number of steps that artificially delay cash disbursements and advance cash receipts, which is very well illustrated in "In Practice: States Balance Their Budgets the Painless Way." Consider the quintessential budget-balancing tactic employed by a number of states and local governments: changing the date on which employees are paid from the last day of the month to the first of the next month. In the year of the change the government is able to pay its employees for one fewer payroll period than it would otherwise.

On the revenue side, a comparable scheme works equally well: advancing the due date of taxes or fees from early in the following budget year to late in the current year, thereby picking up an extra tax or fee payment in the year of the change. This tactic, like that of delaying the payday, can be employed only once for each revenue or expenditure. New devices must continually be developed.

IN PRACTICE THE COST OF GAAP

Despite the adverse consequences of cash budgeting, budgeting on a full accrual basis is not without its costs. According to a column by Paul Choiniere in *The Day* (June 30, 2013), Governor Dannel Malloy of Connecticut ran on a platform of converting the state's budget from a cash basis to a full accrual basis. The reform was lauded, even cheered, by legislators. In practice, however, policy makers found that the conversion to a full accrual basis would result in a $1.2 billion budget deficit. As Choiniere writes, "There was no mood in Hartford to cut programs and services to meet a seemingly arbitrary accounting goal." Ultimately, the state decided to cover $750 million of the gap by issuing 15-year bonds, and $450 million through general expenditure cuts over approximately a decade. The estimated interest cost at the time of Choiniere's column was $186 million.

Source: http://www.theday.com/article/20130630/OP04/306309962

The deleterious consequences of cash basis budgeting are exacerbated by the use of fund accounting. Because each fund is a separate accounting entity, governments can readily transfer resources from a fund that has a budget surplus or that does not require a balanced budget to one that needs extra resources. Some governments budget interfund "loans" for the last day of one fiscal year and repayments for the first day of the next. Others delay, for one day, required payments from the general fund to other funds or sell assets, sometimes to entities that they themselves created and control, and lease them back. Still others reduce expenditures in ways that may balance the budget in the short term but will unquestionably have deleterious consequences in the long term (as illustrated in "In Practice: Balancing the Budget by Selling Assets to Yourself").

The "one-shot" budget balancing techniques would generally not affect revenues and expenditures as reported in the annual financial statements. Governments must prepare the external financial reports of their governmental funds on a modified accrual basis. As defined by the GASB, the modified accrual basis requires that short-term loan proceeds, whether from another fund or from an outside source, be accounted for as liabilities rather than revenues. Similarly, most required outlays are reported as expenditures in the period to which they apply, irrespective of when they are actually paid.

Cash basis budgeting complicates financial accounting and reporting. Governments must maintain their accounts to facilitate preparation of two sets of reports—one that demonstrates compliance with the budgetary provisions and one in accordance with GAAP.

IN PRACTICE BALANCING THE BUDGET BY SELLING ASSETS TO YOURSELF

On April 1, 1991—April Fools' Day—New York's Governor Mario Cuomo announced the sale of Attica prison *to the state itself* for over $200 million—all of which was counted as general revenues. The buyer was a state agency that financed the purchase by floating bonds. The bonds were backed by the state and were, therefore, economic obligations of the state. The purchaser immediately leased the prison back to the state under terms specifying that the "rent" payments would be exactly equal to the debt service on the bonds. In essence, the state balanced its operating budget with a loan in the amount of the prison's sale price. The benefits of the loan were reaped by the taxpayers of the year of the transaction; principal and interest will be paid by the taxpayers of the future.

In the previous year, the state sold its Cross Westchester Expressway to the New York Thruway Authority—also to itself—but that transaction was only for $20 million. Following the lead of its neighbor, New Jersey sold a portion of its highway system to a state-owned agency, the New Jersey Turnpike Authority.

Unfortunately, this example is not merely of historical interest. It is a variation of a sale–lease back technique that is especially popular in California. In 2007, Oxnard, California, (population approximately 200,000) sold its streets to a newly created finance authority (which consists of the city council and the mayor). The aim, according to the *Los Angeles Times* (December 31, 2008), was to pay for part of a $150 million street-paving project by issuing bonds to be repaid from the city's share of a state gasoline tax. The state constitution, however, forbids local governments from issuing bonds against that revenue. Instead, the new finance authority issued the bonds with the intent of repaying them by eventually selling the streets back to the city. Where would the city get the money to buy back the streets? From its share of the state's gasoline tax, of course.

Sleight-of-fiscal-hand transactions of this type are not cost-free. Because the bonds issued by the finance authorities are more risky than conventional general obligation securities, they require the payment of substantially higher interest rates.

WHAT CAUTIONS MUST BE TAKEN IN BUDGET-TO-ACTUAL COMPARISONS?

As emphasized in Chapter 1, a primary objective of government financial reporting is to "demonstrate whether resources were obtained and used in accordance with the entities' legally adopted budget." Accordingly, generally accepted accounting principles (GAAP) dictate that governments include in their annual reports, as required supplementary information, a comparison of actual results with the budget for each governmental fund for which an annual budget has been adopted.[6]

DIFFERENCES IN HOW ACTUAL RESULTS ARE DETERMINED

Whereas the GASB specifies the principles of accounting to which governments must adhere in reporting on their governmental funds, it is silent on those they can use in preparing their budgets. Unless a government reports its actual results using budgetary principles or its budget using GAAP, a comparison between the budget and actual results would not be meaningful. Therefore, per Statement No. 34, the GASB requires that governments present their budget-to-actual comparisons on a *budgetary* basis and include a schedule that reconciles the budgetary and the GAAP amounts.

The differences between legally adopted budgets and the GAAP-based financial statements can be attributed to several factors. Among them are

- ***Differences in basis of accounting.*** As previously noted, governments often prepare their budgets on a cash or near-cash basis, whereas their financial statements must be prepared on a modified accrual basis.

- ***Differences in timing.*** As shown in its budget, a government may appropriate resources for a particular project rather than for a particular period. For example, in approving resources for a construction project, the government will typically establish the total amount that can be spent. It will not allocate resources to specific years. By contrast, the annual report of the fund in which the project is accounted would have to present the expenditures year by year. Moreover,

[6] GASB Concepts Statement 1, Objectives of Financial Reporting (1987), para. 77b.

governments may permit departments to carry over to subsequent years resources not spent in the year for which they were budgeted. Thus, expenditures in a particular year may not have been budgeted in that year.

- ***Differences in perspective.*** Governments may structure their budgets differently from their financial reports. For example, a government may budget on the basis of programs. The programs, however, may be financed by resources accounted for in more than one fund. Thus, the amounts expended in each of the funds cannot be compared to any particular line item in the budget.
- ***Difference in the reporting entity.*** As you will learn in Chapter 11, GAAP requires that a government's reporting entity include organizations that are legally independent of the government, yet, in political or economic reality, an integral part of it. For example, a city may create a financing authority—a separate legal entity—to issue bonds on behalf of the city. If the city has political control over the authority (e.g., the mayor appoints the majority of the governing board) or is responsible for its financial affairs (e.g., approves its budget), then GAAP dictates that the authority be reported upon in the city's financial statements. Yet because the authority is a separate legal entity, the city may exclude it from its legally adopted budget.

GOVERNMENTS MUST REPORT BOTH ORIGINAL AND FINAL BUDGETS

Budget-to-actual comparisons may demonstrate either legal compliance or managerial effectiveness in adhering to budget estimates. The current GASB model requires governments to report their actual results and both their original and final appropriated budgets. For some governments, their final budget incorporates changes they authorized only after they were aware of the actual revenues and expenditures of the year.

The GASB encourages, but does not require, governments to present in a separate column the variances (i.e., differences) between actual results and the budget. It recommends that, if presented, the variances be based on the final rather than the original budget. However, inasmuch as governments must include columns that show both the original budget and the final budget, statement users can readily calculate the differences between actual results and the original budget as well as the changes in the budget that were authorized during the year.[7]

Table 3-3 presents the budget-to-actual comparison of Charlotte's general fund.

TABLE 3-3 Charlotte, North Carolina

General Fund

Statement of Budgetary Comparison for the Year Ended June 30, 2017 (in thousands)

	Budgeted Amounts		Actual (Budgetary Basis)	Variance with Final Budget Positive (Negative)
	Original	Final		
Revenues:				
Property taxes	$ 351,235	$ 351,235	$ 353,050	$ 1,815
Sales tax	96,462	96,462	99,299	2,837
Other taxes	5,643	5,643	6,197	554
Utilities sales tax	53,096	53,096	52,628	(468)
CATV franchises	7,960	7,960	7,763	(197)

(Continues)

[7] GASB Statement No. 34, *Basic Financial Statements—and Management's Discussion and Analysis—for State and Local Governments* (June 1999), para. 130; see also GASB Statement No. 41, *Budgetary Comparison Schedules—Perspective Differences* (May 2003).

TABLE 3-3 Charlotte, North Carolina *(Continued)*

General Fund				
Statement of Budgetary Comparison for the Year Ended June 30, 2017 (in thousands)				
	Budgeted Amounts		Actual (Budgetary Basis)	Variance with Final Budget Positive (Negative)
	Original	Final		
Other intergovernmental	38,766	39,648	39,054	(594)
Refuse fees	10,953	10,953	11,019	66
Other licenses, fees, and fines	17,046	17,046	19,160	2,114
Investment earnings	637	637	707	70
Administrative charges	36,646	36,646	37,031	385
Charges for current services	8,608	8,608	8,670	62
Miscellaneous	2,775	2,932	2,450	(482)
Sales of capital assets	1,430	1,430	1,130	(300)
Transfers in				
Debt service	112	1,215	1,215	—
Capital projects	—	379	379	—
Special revenue—convention center tax	3,475	3,697	3,697	—
Cemetery trust	96	96	18	(78)
Total transfers in	3,683	5,387	5,309	(78)
Resources available for appropriation	634,940	637,683	643,467	$5,784
Fund balance appropriated (contributed)	—	44,537	27,513	
Total amounts available for appropriation	$634,940	$682,220	$670,980	
Expenditures:				
Public safety	$365,368	$372,811	$372,793	$ 18
Sanitation	57,233	61,013	58,984	2,029
General administration	41,593	42,739	42,292	447
Support services	34,864	38,765	35,971	2,794
Engineering and property management	24,134	25,048	23,808	1,240
Streets and highways	36,407	37,757	35,646	2,111
Culture and recreation	5,243	5,278	5,278	—
Community planning and development	28,721	29,986	27,385	2,601
Transfers out				
Debt service	17,256	17,567	17,567	—
Capital projects	18,224	44,852	44,852	—
Special revenue:				
State street aid	4,261	4,261	4,261	—
Tourism	1,291	1,291	1,291	—
Public safety and other grants	345	852	852	—
Total transfers out	41,377	68,823	68,823	—
Total charges to appropriations	$634,940	$682,220	$670,980	$11,240

(Continues)

TABLE 3-3 **Charlotte, North Carolina** (*Continued*)

Reconciliation of the Statement of Budgetary Comparison to the Statement of Revenues, Expenditures and Changes in Fund Balances General Fund for the Year Ended June 30, 2017 (in thousands)	
Actual amounts (budgetary basis) "available for appropriation" from the statement of budgetary comparison	$670,980
Differences—budget to GAAP:	
Contributed fund balance is a budgetary resource available for appropriation but is not a current-year revenue for financial reporting purposes.	(27,513)
Transfers from other funds are inflows of budgetary resources but are not revenues for financial reporting purposes.	(5,309)
Proceeds from the sale of salvage and land are budgetary resources but are regarded as other financing resources, rather than revenue, for financial reporting purposes.	(1,130)
Total revenues as reported on the statement of revenues, expenditures, and changes in fund balances—governmental funds	$637,028
Uses (outflows) of resources:	
Actual amounts (budgetary basis) "total charges to appropriations" from the statement of budgetary comparison	$670,980
Differences—budget to GAAP:	
Encumbrances for supplies and equipment ordered but not received are reported in the year the order is placed for budgetary purposes, but in the year the supplies are received for financial reporting purposes.	(16,921)
Transfers to other funds are outflows of budgetary resources but are not expenditures for financial reporting purposes.	(68,823)
Total expenditures as reported on the statement of revenues, expenditures, and changes in fund balances—governmental funds	$585,236

The notes to the financial statements are an integral part of this statement.

HOW DOES BUDGETING IN NOT-FOR-PROFIT ORGANIZATIONS COMPARE WITH THAT IN GOVERNMENTS?

As discussed in Chapter 1, the not-for-profit sector covers organizations that range from those that depend entirely, or almost entirely, on donor contributions (e.g., certain social service organizations) to those that are run much like business (e.g., a university "co-op" bookstore). Accordingly, the budgeting process must be custom designed to suit each particular type of entity.

Not-for-profits differ from governments in at least one critical respect: they lack the authority to tax. Governments can first determine the level of services they wish to provide and then impose the taxes and fees sufficient to provide those services. Nonbusiness types of not-for-profits, by contrast, are limited in their ability to generate revenues and hence must adjust the level of services they provide to the corresponding level of revenues raised.

The general approach to budgeting suggested in this chapter for governments is relevant, with some obvious modifications, to not-for-profits. The budget process is the same four-phase process: preparation, adoption (although by a board of directors or trustees rather than a legislature), execution, and reporting and auditing.

Not-for-profits, of course, are not subject to the same types of penalties for violating budgetary mandates as governments are. Nevertheless, reliable estimates of revenues and expenditures are no less important. The consequences of underestimating costs or overestimating revenues are obvious. Not-for-profits, like businesses, are not guaranteed continued existence. The consequences of overestimating costs or underestimating revenues, while not as potentially devastating as the reverse, can also be severe—especially to the organization's intended beneficiaries. A homeless shelter may unnecessarily reduce the number of people that it serves;

a church or synagogue can cut back programs that it otherwise could have provided; a private college may defer maintenance only to have to incur greater costs to play catch-up in the future.

HOW DO BUDGETS ENHANCE CONTROL?

Owing to the adverse consequences of violating budgetary mandates, both governments and not-for-profits can build safeguards into their accounting systems that help ensure budgetary compliance. These include preparing journal entries both to record the budget and to give recognition to goods and services that have been ordered but not yet received. We begin the discussion by describing the basic books of account maintained by governments and not-for-profits and showing how they accommodate these safeguards.

THE BASIC BOOKS OF ACCOUNT

The basic books of account of both governments and not-for-profits correspond to those of businesses. They consist, either in manual or in electronic form, of:

- ***Journals,*** in which journal entries are recorded. Most transactions are entered initially in a special journal—such as a property tax cash receipts journal, a parking fines cash receipts journal, a purchases journal, or a cash disbursements journal. Both nonroutine transactions and account totals from special journals are recorded in a general journal.
- ***Ledgers,*** in which all balance sheet and operating accounts are maintained. The general ledger consists of control accounts that summarize the balances of the detailed subsidiary accounts that are maintained in subsidiary ledgers.

A city or other general-purpose government is likely to maintain hundreds of accounts. For example, the control account, general property taxes, may be subdivided as follows:

General property taxes
- Real property (e.g., land and buildings)
- Personal property
  - Tangible personal (e.g., business inventories, machinery, household furnishings, and vehicles)
  - Intangible personal (e.g., stocks, bonds, and bank deposits)

In addition, these accounts would be further divided into accounts for each individual taxpayer.

Similarly, one branch of the expenditure tree for police might be structured as follows (with only a small number of the object classification accounts displayed):

Police
- Crime control and investigation
- Crime laboratory
  - Salaries
    - Regular
    - Overtime
  - Social Security contributions
  - Rentals
    - Land and buildings
    - Equipment and vehicles
  - Supplies
    - Custodial
    - Fuel
    - Office

BUDGETARY CONTROL FEATURES

As in a ledger for a business, each account consists of columns for debits, for credits, and for the balance (the difference between the two). However, the ledger accounts of governments (and some not-for-profits) incorporate budgetary control features not conventionally found in those of businesses.

The ledger accounts for revenues incorporate an additional debit column: estimated revenues. In this column, the government posts the revenue side of an entry (to be described and illustrated in the next section) to record the budget. The difference between the estimated revenues (a debit), actual revenues recognized to date (credits), and any unusual adjustments (debits or credits) equals the amount of budgeted revenues still to be recognized. Thus, the subledger account "Real Property Taxes" might appear as follows (dates and references omitted):

Revenues—Real Property Taxes

Estimated Revenues (Dr.)	Actual Revenues (Cr.)	Adjustments (Dr. or Cr.)	Balance (Dr. or Cr.)
15,000,000			15,000,000
	2,300,000		12,700,000
	1,100,000		11,600,000
	500,000		11,100,000

Based on the data shown, the government budgeted real property tax revenue of $15 million and has recognized $3.9 million to date. Therefore, $11.1 million remains to be recognized.

Similarly, the ledger accounts for expenditures incorporate two extra columns. In one column—appropriations—the government posts a credit for the amount appropriated per the budget. In the second extra column the government posts, as debits, encumbrances—*commitments* to purchase goods or services. The difference between the appropriation (a credit), resources encumbered (debits), actual expenditures to date (also debits), and any unusual adjustments equals the amount of the appropriation that is still uncommitted and is therefore available to be spent (the unencumbered balance). Thus, crime laboratory expenditures might appear as follows:

Expenditures—Crime Laboratory

Appropriations (Cr.)	Encumbrances (Dr.)	Expenditures (Dr.)	Adjustments (Dr. or Cr.)	Unencumbered Balance
300,000				300,000
		50,000		250,000
		30,000		220,000
	15,000	40,000		165,000

This account indicates that the government appropriated $300,000 for the crime laboratory. To date it has spent $120,000 and has outstanding commitments for goods and services of $15,000. Therefore, it has $165,000 available for future spending.

WHAT ARE THE DISTINCTIVE WAYS GOVERNMENTS RECORD THEIR BUDGETS?

By recording its budget, a government builds into its accounting system a gauge that warns of excesses in spending and deficiencies in collections. This gauge serves only as an *internal* control function. The budgetary entries are reversed at year end and have no impact on year-end financial statements. To external report users, budgetary entries are irrelevant. Nevertheless, because of their significance in controlling both revenues and costs, students need to be aware of how they affect the accounts.

CREDITING OR DEBITING THE BUDGETED DEFICIT OR SURPLUS DIRECTLY TO FUND BALANCE

Most students initially find budgetary entries counterintuitive and confusing. Mainly, that's because when a government records its budget, it *debits* estimated revenues and *credits* appropriations (in effect, estimated expenditures). Most students, of course, are used to crediting revenues and debiting expenditures. The practice of debiting estimated revenues and crediting appropriations makes sense, however, when you understand that each estimated revenue and appropriation account will be tied directly to its related *actual* revenue and *actual* expenditure account (see "Example: Budgetary Entries" for a case in point). The resulting differences equal the revenues yet to be recognized and the appropriations still available to be spent. Thus (ignoring encumbrances):

$$\text{Estimated revenues (Dr.)} - \text{Actual revenues (Cr.)} = \text{Revenues still to be recognized}$$

and

$$\text{Appropriations (Cr.)} - \text{Actual expenditures (Dr.)} = \text{Balance available for expenditure}$$

In a sense, the estimated revenue and appropriations accounts can be thought of as contra accounts to the actual revenue and expenditure accounts.

Moreover, the entries appear to put the cart before the horse. The difference between the debit to estimated revenues and the credit to appropriations is offset by fund balance. Thus, the entity's fund balance may be increased or decreased upon merely *adopting* the budget—that is, wishes and whims—rather than actual transactions. Fortunately, as with other widely used bookkeeping procedures that allow accounts to be temporarily in error (e.g., periodic inventory methods), the entries cause no harm as long as appropriate adjustments are made prior to the preparation of financial statements.

Example

Budgetary Entries

A school district adopts a budget calling for total revenues of $400 million and total expenditures of $390 million. The following entries would record the budget:

	(b1)		
Estimated revenues		$400	
Fund balance			$400
To record estimated revenues			
	(b2)		
Fund balance		$390	
Appropriations			$390
To record appropriations (estimated amount to be spent)			

The entries illustrated in this chapter will be made only to control accounts. In reality, corresponding entries would be made to the estimated revenue and appropriation subaccounts that support the control accounts. The sum of the debits and credits to the subaccounts should, of course, equal the entries to the respective control accounts.

Suppose that during the year both revenues and expenditures were as estimated and that all transactions were for cash. The transactions would be recorded with standard revenue and expenditure entries (with appropriate entries to the subaccounts as well):

	(1)		
Cash		$400	
Revenues			$400
To record revenues			
	(2)		
Expenditures		$390	
Cash			$390
To record expenditures			

At year-end, each of the budgeted and actual revenue and expenditure accounts would be *closed* (i.e., reversed) to fund balance. Thus:

	(cl 1)		
Appropriations		$390	
Fund balance		10	
Estimated revenues			$400
To close budgetary accounts			
	(cl 2)		
Revenues		$400	
Expenditures			$390
Fund balance			10
To close revenues and expenditures			

The net effect of the entries is to increase fund balance by the difference between the actual revenues and expenditures—the same increase as would have been recorded had the budgetary entries not been made.

Suppose alternatively that actual revenues and expenditures differed from what were budgeted—for example, that actual revenues were $420 and actual expenditures were $415. Actual revenues and expenditures would have been recorded as follows:

	(1a)		
Cash		$420	
Revenues			$420
To record revenues			
	(2a)		
Expenditures		$415	
Cash			$415
To record expenditures			

Closing entries would take the same form as illustrated previously:

	(cl 1a)		
Appropriations		$390	
Fund balance		10	
Estimated revenues			$400
To close budgetary accounts			
	(cl 2a)		
Revenues		$420	
Expenditures			$415
Fund balance			5
To close revenues and expenditures			

In this situation, as shown in the T-accounts presented in Figure 3-1, the year-end fund balance would again be the difference between *actual* revenues and *actual* expenditures. Actual revenues were $420, and actual expenditures were $415. Ending fund balance, after the closing entries have been posted, is thus $5—the same as if the budgetary entries had not been made.

The components of both the budgetary and the closing entries could, of course, have been combined differently. For example, appropriations and expenditures (rather than appropriations and estimated revenues) and revenues and estimated revenues (rather than revenues and expenditures) could have been closed in the same entry. The net impact on fund balance would have been the same.

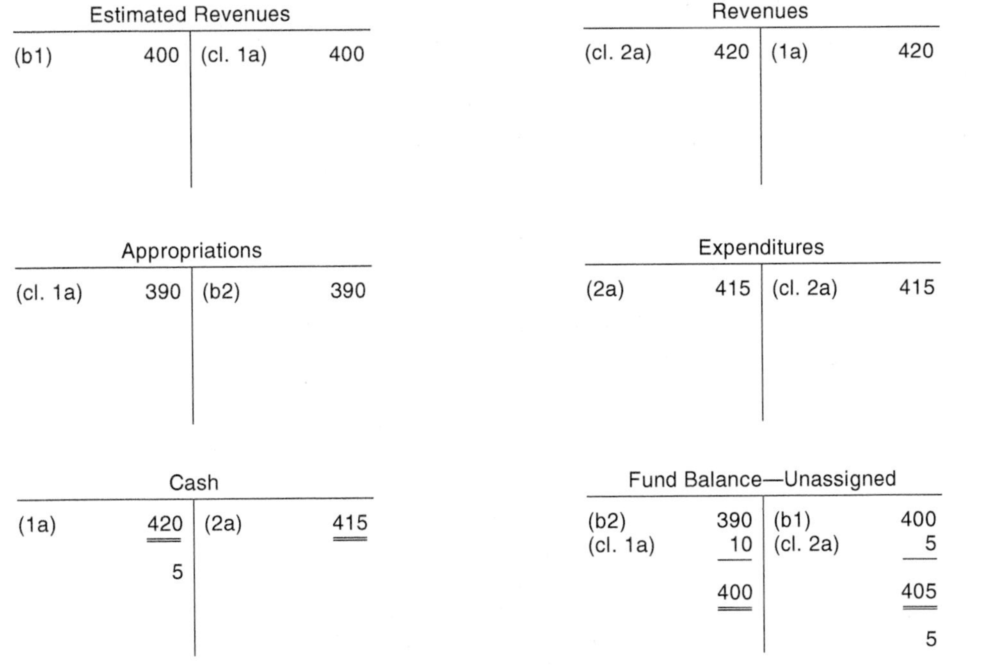

FIGURE 3-1 Illustration of Budgetary Entries (Assuming Differences between Budgeted and Actual Amounts)

AN ALTERNATIVE METHOD: CREDITING OR DEBITING THE DIFFERENCE BETWEEN REVENUES AND EXPENDITURES TO "BUDGETARY CONTROL"

Some governments maintain an account called **budgetary control**. In recording the budget they debit or credit this account instead of fund balance. Budgetary control is a temporary account. At year-end, the appropriations and estimated revenues are closed to this account, so that after the closing entries are made, its balance is always zero.

Governments prefer (or in some cases, must take) this approach to avoid contaminating the actual fund balance with appropriations and estimated revenues. The actual fund balance is affected only by authentic revenues and expenditures, which, as in the "Budgetary Entries" example, are closed at year-end, to fund balance. The account reflects only genuine transactions, not forecasts (and in some cases mere hopes) of what will occur during the year.

Thus, when the government adopts the budget, it would make the following entry:

Estimated revenues	$400	
Appropriations		$390
Budgetary control		10
To record estimated revenues and appropriations (estimated expenditures)		

At year-end, irrespective of actual revenues and expenditures, the budgetary entry would be reversed:

Budgetary control	$ 10	
Appropriations	390	
Estimated revenues		$400
To close estimated revenues and appropriations		

During the year, actual revenues and expenditures would be recorded in the normal manner, and at year-end they would be closed to the ordinary fund balance account.

HOW DOES ENCUMBRANCE ACCOUNTING PREVENT OVER-SPENDING?

Governments and some not-for-profits record encumbrances to help prevent overspending the budget. The entry to record an encumbrance is usually prepared when a purchase order is issued, a contract is signed, or a commitment is made (e.g., when a university makes faculty and staff appointments for a semester or year). Most organizations do not encumber all anticipated expenditures. Many, for example, do not encumber salaries and wages because it is a routine recurring expenditure, other expenditures below a specified amount, and expenditures that are adequately controlled by other means.

THE BASIC ENTRIES

The entry to record an encumbrance reduces the budgeted amount available for expenditure (as if the amount had already been spent) and concurrently designates a portion of what would otherwise be *unassigned* fund balance as *committed* or *assigned* for encumbrances (i.e., for expenditures to which the organization is obligated). The entry is reversed as the goods or services are received and expenditures are recorded, as shown in "Example: The Encumbrance Cycle—Year 1."

Whereas both budgetary entries and encumbrances are mainly internal control devices, encumbrances are of slightly greater concern to external parties because they have a minor impact on the basic financial statements. Outstanding obligations at year-end are to be reported under GASB Statement No. 54, *Fund Balance Reporting and Governmental Fund Type Definitions*, on the entity's fund (not government-wide) *balance sheet* as a *committed* or *assigned* fund balance, and, accordingly, they reduce the unassigned portion of fund balance.

Example

The Encumbrance Cycle—Year 1

A state university contracts for repair services that it estimates will cost $5,000. The following entry will commit the funds to meet the anticipated expenditure:

Encumbrances	$5,000	
Reserve for encumbrances (committed or assigned)		$5,000
To encumber $5,000 for repair services		

In addition to these control account entries, corresponding entries would be made in the repair-related subaccounts (e.g., encumbrances—electrical contractors).

The reserve for encumbrances account is a balance sheet account—a commitment of fund balance. The encumbrance account, although most definitely *not* an expenditure, is similar to an expenditure in that at year-end any remaining balance is closed to unassigned fund balance. The encumbrance account indicates the net amount that was transferred during the period from unassigned fund balance to fund balance that is assigned or committed.

The repairs are completed and, as anticipated, the university is billed for $5,000. The repair expenditure must be recorded with the usual entry:

Expenditures	$5,000	
Accounts payable		$5,000
To record repair expenditures		

In addition, the reserve for encumbrance is no longer required. The services have been received and the expenditure has been charged. The reserve must be eliminated by reversing the entry establishing it:

Reserve for encumbrances (committed or assigned)	$5,000	
Encumbrances		$5,000
To reverse the encumbrance entry upon receipt of services		

At year-end, the expenditures would be closed out in standard fashion, thereby reducing fund balance.

Consider two alternative possibilities. Assume first that the contractor *completes* the repairs but bills the university for only $4,800, not the encumbered $5,000. The university must now record an expenditure for the actual amount to be paid:

Expenditure	$4,800	
Accounts payable		$4,800
To record repair expenditures		

As before, it must eliminate the entire reserve. With regard to the repairs, the university has no further commitment; it therefore needs no reserve:

Reserve for encumbrances (committed or assigned)	$5,000	
Encumbrances		$5,000
To reverse the encumbrance entry upon receipt of services		

If the contractor's bill were for more than the encumbered amount, the same approach would be taken. The expenditure would be charged for the amount to be paid; the full amount of the reserve would be eliminated. The university's error in encumbering less than its actual commitment would have no consequences for financial reporting. At worst, it temporarily increased the university's risk of overspending its budget.

As the second possibility, assume that in the current period the contractor completes only 40 percent of the repairs and accordingly bills the university for only $2,000. It expects to fulfill the remainder of its contract in the following period. In this situation, only a part of the encumbrance entry can be reversed; the university still has an outstanding commitment for $3,000. Thus:

Expenditures	$2,000	
Accounts payable		$2,000
To record repair expenditures		
Reserve for encumbrances (committed or assigned)	$2,000	
Encumbrances		$2,000
To reverse the encumbrance entry upon the contractor's completion of $2,000 of the $5,000 in anticipated services		

At year-end, the expenditures and the encumbrances would be closed to fund balance. The reserve for encumbrances need not be closed because it is a balance sheet account. Continuing with the last set of assumptions (expenditures of $2,000; balance in the encumbrances account of $3,000), the following closing entry would be in order:

Fund balance—unassigned	$5,000	
Expenditures		$2,000
Encumbrances		$3,000
To close expenditures and encumbrances		

As a consequence of these entries, $3,000 of the university's fund balance—the amount committed for completion of the repairs—remains assigned or committed for outstanding commitments for repairs. Hence, the reserve for encumbrance will be reported on the balance sheet as either "assigned fund balance" or "committed fund balance."

ACCOUNTING FOR COMMITMENTS OUTSTANDING AT THE START OF A YEAR

Governments differ in how they budget—and therefore how they account—for contractual obligations (commitments made) outstanding (left over from the prior year). Many governments require that the cost of goods or services be charged against budgeted appropriations of the year in which they are received. In other words, all appropriations lapse at year-end. To satisfy its outstanding obligations (commitments), a government must reappropriate the funds for the following year or meet them out of whatever resources are budgeted for the following year within an applicable expenditure classification. Other governments, for either all or only selected types of commitments (particularly long-term projects), allow appropriations to continue into future years. When the goods or services are received, they are charged against the budget of the year of appropriation.

In the circumstances in which appropriations lapse and the government charges the cost of goods or services against appropriations of the year in which they are received, the accounting for commitments made in a previous year is relatively simple, as is shown in "Example: The Encumbrance Cycle—Year 2." At the start of the new year, the government need only restore the encumbrances that were closed at the end of the previous year. This can be accomplished by reversing the closing entry (i.e., debiting encumbrances and crediting fund balance unassigned). By restoring the encumbrances, both the reserve for encumbrances (which, as a balance sheet account, was never closed and under GASB Statement No. 54 is presented on the balance sheet as fund balance committed or assigned) and the encumbrances would have the same balances as if the closing entries had not been made. Thereafter, the entries to record the fulfillment of the commitments would be the same as if the goods or services were received in the year the encumbrances and the reserve were initially established.

Example

The Encumbrance Cycle—Year 2

At the end of the first year—the start of the second—the university had $3,000 of outstanding commitments for repairs. The following entry would restore the $3,000 of encumbrances for repairs:

Encumbrances	$3,000	
Fund balance—unassigned		$3,000
To restore encumbrances at the start of the new year		

When the contractor completes the repairs, the university will charge expenditures for the amount billed and reverse the encumbrances and the reserve for encumbrances.

Expenditures	$3,000	
Accounts payable		$3,000
To record repair expenditures		
Reserve for encumbrances (committed or assigned)	$3,000	
Encumbrances		$3,000
To reverse the encumbrances entry upon the contractor's completion of the remaining $3,000 of repairs[8]		

[8] If the appropriation does not lapse and the government charges the cost of goods or services against appropriations of the year in which the commitment was made, then the encumbrance should *not* be restored. Instead, when the commitment is fulfilled, the expenditure should be "dated" to indicate that it is applicable to the previous year. Thus:

Expenditures—Year 1 (prior year)	$3,000	
Accounts payable		$3,000
To record repair expenditures		

These expenditures would then be closed to the previously established reserve for encumbrances (which would have been reported on the balance sheet as fund balance committed or assigned):

Reserve for encumbrances (committed or assigned)	$3,000	
Expenditures—Year 1 (prior year)		$3,000
To close expenditures for the previous year and eliminate the applicable reserve for encumbrances		

Per GASB Statement No. 54, reserves for encumbrances should not be reported on the balance sheet, but significant amounts should be disclosed in the notes. Thus, in the example, the accounts "reserve for encumbrances (committed or assigned)" would not be shown explicitly on the balance sheet. Instead, they would be aggregated with other fund balance amounts that were either committed or assigned. The decision as to whether they should be committed or assigned would depend on the specific characteristics of the amounts—whether they better fit the description of one category or the other.

The next example, "Impact of Encumbrances on Fund Balance," highlights the impact of the encumbrance procedures on fund balance by focusing on a single purchase commitment. Note that over the two-year period the total reduction in fund balance equals the total expenditures.

Example

Impact of Encumbrances on Fund Balance

Year 1

As of January 1, a government's general fund balance sheet shows the following:

Cash	$1,000
Fund balance—unassigned	$1,000

During the year, the government orders $1,000 of supplies (which are to be charged as expenditures when received):

(a)

Encumbrances	$1,000	
Reserve for encumbrances (assigned)		$1,000

To encumber $1,000 for supplies on order (It is assumed in this example that the reserve for encumbrances will be classified as "assigned" fund balance.)

Part of the supplies order costing $800 is received and paid for in cash:

(b)

Supplies expenditures	$800	
Cash		$800

To record the receipt of, and payment for, supplies

(2)

Reserve for encumbrances (assigned)	$800	
Encumbrances		$800

To reverse the encumbrance entry for the portion of the supplies order received

The government prepares the following year-end closing entries:

(cl. 1)

Fund balance—unassigned	$1,000	
Encumbrances		$200
Supplies expenditures		800

To close encumbrances and expenditures

Table 3-4 presents the year-end balance sheet and a schedule of changes in unassigned fund balance.

Year 2

The government expects to honor its commitment for the supplies on order, and its budgeting policies dictate that the cost of the supplies on order be charged as expenditures of the year in which they are received. Therefore, at the start of the new year, it restores the encumbrances that had been closed at the end of the prior year:

	(d)	
Encumbrances	$200	
Fund balance—unassigned		$200
To restore encumbrances		

It receives, and pays for, the remainder of the supplies. However, the additional charges are only $150, not $200 as encumbered:

	(e)	
Supplies expenditures	$150	
Cash		$150
To record the receipt of, and payment for, supplies		
	(f)	
Reserve for encumbrances (assigned)	$200	
Encumbrances		$200
To reverse the encumbrance entry for the remainder of the supplies		

It prepares appropriate year-end closing entries:

	(cl. 2)	
Fund balance—unassigned	$150	
Supplies expenditures		$150
To close expenditures (Note: The balance in the encumbrances account is zero; it need not be closed.)		

Figure 3-2 summarizes the entries to the accounts. The government began the two-year period with an unassigned fund balance of $1,000. During the two years, it incurred expenditures of

Encumbrances

	Debit		Credit
(a)	1,000	(c)	800
		(cl. 1)	200
(d)	200	(f)	200

Supplies Expenditures

	Debit		Credit
(b)	800	(cl. 1)	800
(e)	150	(cl. 2)	150

Cash

	Debit		Credit
Beg. Bal.	1,000	(b)	800
Yr. 1 Bal.	200		
		(e)	150
Yr. 2 Bal.	50		

Reserve for Encumbrances—Unassigned

	Debit		Credit
(c)	800	(a)	1,000
		Yr. 1 Bal.	200
(f)	200		
Yr. 2 Bal.	0		

Fund Balance—Unassigned

	Debit		Credit
(cl. 1)	1,000	Beg. Bal.	1,000
		Yr. 1 Bal.	0
(cl. 2)	150	(d)	200
		Yr. 2 Bal.	50

FIGURE 3-2 Summary of Budget Entries

$950. As shown in the T-account, its unassigned fund balance at the end of the second year is $50—the same as if an encumbrance system were not being employed. The assigned fund balance in this example is simply the reserve for encumbrances. If there were other amounts of fund balance that had been assigned for purposes other than the encumbrances, then the reserve for encumbrances would have been added to those amounts. The fund's balance sheet at the end of each of the two years and a schedule explaining the change in unassigned fund balance are shown in Table 3-4.

TABLE 3-4 Encumbrance Example

Balance Sheet

	Year 1	Year 2
Cash	$200	$50
Fund balance		
Assigned	$200	$0
Unassigned	0	50
Total fund balance	$200	$50

Schedule of Changes in Unassigned Fund Balance

	Year 1	Year 2	Total
Revenues	$ 0	$ 0	$ 0
Expenditures	800	150	950
Excess of revenues over expenditures	(800)	(150)	(950)
Less: Increase/(decrease) in reserve for encumbrances	200	(200)	0
Net change in unassigned fund balance during the year [increase/(decrease)]	(1,000)	50	$(950)
Add: Beginning of year balance	1,000	0	
End of year balance	$ 0	$ 50	

Note: If the appropriations did not lapse, then the entry to restore the encumbrances would *not* have been made. Instead, when the goods were received, the following entries would be necessary:

Supplies expenditures—Year 1	$150	
Cash		$150
To record the receipt of, and payment for, supplies		
Reserve for encumbrances (assigned)	$200	
Supplies expenditures—Year 1		$150
Fund balance		50
To close the supplies expenditures for Year 1 and eliminate the reserve for encumbrances		

ARE BUDGETARY AND ENCUMBRANCE ENTRIES REALLY NEEDED?

Some governments and most not-for-profits do not integrate their budgets into their accounting systems or encumber the cost of goods or services for which they are committed. Under what circumstances should they do so? The general answer is that they should do so when the benefits of added control are worth the costs (in both dollars and inconvenience).

Consistent with this answer, governments are more likely to establish these controls than are not-for-profits because the penalties for overspending government budgets are likely to be more severe. Similarly, governments are more likely to implement these mechanisms in their general fund than in some other governmental funds—such as their capital projects funds or their debt service funds—because adequate controls may already be in place in those funds. For example, sufficient controls over the cost of a capital project may be established simply by ensuring that the agreed-upon price with the contractor is within the amount of bond proceeds. The expenditures of a debt service fund may be set by the payments of principal and interest spelled out in the bond indentures.

Modern computer systems make it possible for the controls provided by both budgetary entries and encumbrances to be achieved by means other than formal journal entries. For example, a government can simply "load" the budget into its computer. The computer can be programmed to issue a warning whenever actual expenditures and commitments exceed a specified percentage of budgeted expenditures.

SUMMARY

Almost all aspects of management in government and not-for-profit organizations revolve around the entities' budgets. The budget is at the center of planning, controlling, administering, evaluating, and reporting functions.

Budgets can take many forms. Appropriation budgets indicate governments' estimated revenues and authorized expenditures. Capital budgets concentrate on long-lived assets. Flexible budgets, which governments use for enterprise funds, contain alternative budget estimates based on different levels of output. Performance budgets focus on measured units of effort and accomplishment and relate costs to objectives.

Most governments follow a four-phase cycle for budgeting: preparation, legislative adoption and executive approval, execution, and reporting and auditing.

For legislative purposes, most governments prepare cash or near-cash budgets. But these may fail to capture the economic cost of carrying out government activities and are not an adequate basis for planning and assessing results.

To demonstrate that they complied with their budgets, governments are required to include in their annual reports a budget-to-actual comparison on a budget basis (i.e., the same basis on which they prepare their budget, usually cash or near-cash). However, the revenues and expenditures from the budget may not be readily comparable to those in GAAP-based statements. Differences may be attributable to the basis of accounting (e.g., cash versus modified accrual), timing (e.g., period over which a project will be completed versus a single year), perspective (e.g., program versus object classification), and reporting entity (legal versus economic). Therefore, governments must both explain and reconcile the differences between budgeted and actual amounts on a GAAP basis.

The accounting systems of governments are similar to businesses in that they use comparable journals and ledgers. However, they differ in that governments include corporate budgetary control features to ensure adherence to spending mandates. In addition, they encumber goods and services in order to prevent themselves from overcommitting available resources.

KEY TERMS IN THIS CHAPTER

allotments 105
apportionments 105
appropriation 105
appropriation budget 97
budgetary control 117
budgets 95
capital budget 97
encumbrances 107
fixed budgets 98
flexible budgets 97
object classification budget 99
performance budgets 96
program budgets 101

EXERCISE FOR REVIEW AND SELF-STUDY

To enhance control over both revenues and expenditures, a government health-care district incorporates its budget in its accounting system and encumbers all commitments. You have been asked to assist the district in making the entries to record the following transactions:

1. Prior to the start of the year, the governing board adopted a budget in which agency revenues were estimated at $5,600 (all dollar amounts in this exercise are expressed in thousands) and expenditures

of $5,550 were appropriated (authorized). Record the budget using only the control (summary) accounts.

2. During the year, the district engaged in the following transactions. Prepare appropriate journal entries.
   a. It collected $5,800 in fees, grants, taxes, and other revenues.
   b. It ordered goods and services for $3,000. Except in special circumstances it classifies reserves for encumbrances as "assigned" fund balance.
   c. During the year, it received and paid for $2,800 worth of goods and services that had been previously encumbered. It expects to receive the remaining $200 in the following year.
   d. It incurred $2,500 in other expenditures for goods and services that had not been encumbered.
3. Prepare appropriate year-end closing entries.
4. Prepare a balance sheet showing the status of year-end asset and fund balance accounts.
5. Per the policy of the district's board, the cost of all goods and services is to be charged against the budget of the year in which they are received, even if they had been ordered (and encumbered) in a previous year. The next year, to simplify the accounting for the commitments made in the prior year, the district reinstated the encumbrances outstanding at year-end. Prepare the appropriate entry.
6. During the year, the district received the remaining encumbered goods and services. However, the total cost was only $150, rather than $200 as estimated. Prepare the appropriate entries.

QUESTIONS FOR REVIEW AND DISCUSSION

1. Why is it important that governments and not-for-profits coordinate their processes for developing *appropriations* budgets with those for developing *capital* budgets?
2. Why may *flexible* budgets be more important to a government's business-type activities than to its governmental activities?
3. What is the main advantage of an *object classification* budget? What are its limitations? How do *performance* budgets overcome these limitations?
4. Why do most governments and not-for-profits budget on a cash or near-cash basis even though the cash basis does not capture the full economic costs of the activities in which they engage?
5. A political official boasts that the year-end excess of revenues over expenditures was significantly greater than was budgeted. Are "favorable" budget variances necessarily a sign of efficient and effective governmental management? Explain.
6. What are *allotments?* What purpose do they serve?
7. Why may a government's year-end results, reported in accordance with generally accepted accounting principles, not be readily comparable with its legally adopted budget?
8. The variances reported in the "final" budget-to-actual comparisons incorporated in the financial statements of many governments may be of no value in revealing the reliability of budget estimates made at the start of the year. Why? How can you rationalize this limitation of the budget-to-actual comparisons?
9. In what way will budgetary entries and encumbrances affect amounts reported on year-end balance sheets or operating statements?
10. How is reserve for encumbrances reported on a year-end balance sheet?
11. What is the purpose and effect of reinstating year-end encumbrances on the books at the beginning of the following year?
12. Why do many governments consider it unnecessary to prepare appropriation budgets for, and incorporate budgetary entries into the accounts of, their capital project funds?

EXERCISES

EX. 3-1

Select the *best* answer.

1. Appropriation budgets are typically concerned with
   a. The details of appropriated expenditures
   b. Long-term revenues and expenditures
   c. Current operating revenues and expenditures
   d. Capital outlays
2. Which of the following types of budgets would be most likely to include a line-item "purchase of supplies"?
   a. Object classification
   b. Performance
   c. Capital
   d. Program
3. Per GASB Statement No. 34, a budget-to-actual comparison must include columns for the actual results and
   a. The original budget only
   b. The final budget only
   c. Both the original and the final budget
   d. Both the amended and the final budget
4. Apportionments are made during which phase of the budget cycle?
   a. Preparation
   b. Legislative adoption and executive approval
   c. Execution
   d. Reporting and auditing
5. In adopting and recording the budget, a government should
   a. Debit estimated revenues and credit revenues
   b. Credit estimated revenues and debit fund balance
   c. Debit revenues and credit fund balance
   d. Debit estimated revenues and credit fund balance
6. In closing budgetary and expenditure accounts at year-end, a government should
   a. Debit appropriations and credit expenditures
   b. Credit appropriations and debit expenditures
   c. Debit expenditures and credit fund balance
   d. Credit appropriations and debit fund balance
7. The prime function of budgetary entries is to
   a. Apportion appropriated expenditures to specific accounts
   b. Help the government monitor revenues and expenditures
   c. Amend the budget during the year
   d. Facilitate the year-end budget-to-actual comparisons
8. A government should debit an expenditure account upon
   a. Recording the budget
   b. Approving an apportionment
   c. Ordering supplies
   d. Recording the receipt of an invoice from its telephone service provider
9. If a government records the budget, and actual revenues exceed budgeted revenues, what would be the impact on the year-end financial statements?
   a. The difference between actual and budgeted revenues would be reported on neither the balance sheet nor the statement of revenues and expenditures

b. The difference between actual and budgeted revenues would be recorded as a budgetary reserve on the balance sheet

c. The difference between actual and budgeted revenues would be shown as a revenue contra account on the statement of revenues and expenditures

d. The actual revenues would be shown on the statement of revenues and expenditures as a deduction from estimated revenues

10. A "cash basis" budget relative to a "modified accrual basis" budget

a. Better facilitates the preparation of year-end financial statements in accordance with generally accepted accounting principles

b. Better facilitates the day-to-day management of an organization's cash flows

c. Limits the opportunities of an entity to balance its budget by arbitrarily delaying cash payments from one period to the next

d. Better ensures that a government will achieve interperiod equity

EX. 3-2

Select the *best* answer.

1. Upon ordering supplies a government should

a. Debit encumbrances and credit reserve for encumbrances

b. Debit reserve for encumbrances and credit encumbrances

c. Debit expenditures and credit encumbrances

d. Debit expenditures and credit vouchers payable

2. Upon receiving supplies that had previously been encumbered a government should

a. Debit reserve for encumbrances and credit encumbrances

b. Debit fund balance and credit reserve for encumbrances

c. Debit fund balance and credit expenditures

d. Debit reserve for encumbrances and credit expenditures

3. Upon closing the books at year-end, a government should

a. Debit fund balance and credit reserve for encumbrances

b. Debit encumbrances and credit reserve for encumbrances

c. Debit fund balance and credit encumbrances

d. Debit reserve for encumbrances and credit encumbrances

4. A government requires that all appropriations lapse at the end of a year. At the end of Year 1, that government has $100,000 of goods and services on order. At the start of Year 2, the government should

a. Debit fund balance and credit encumbrances

b. Debit reserve for encumbrances and credit encumbrances

c. Debit encumbrances and credit reserve for encumbrances

d. Debit encumbrances and credit fund balance

5. Which of the following accounts would a government be most likely to debit as part of its year-end closing process?

a. Appropriations, encumbrances, and estimated revenues

b. Estimated revenues, appropriations, and reserve for encumbrances

c. Revenues, appropriations, and encumbrances

d. Revenues, appropriations, and fund balance

6. A government places an order for a particular item of equipment and encumbers $5,500. The item arrives accompanied by an invoice for $5,200. The entries that the government should make should include (but are not necessarily be limited to):

a. A debit to expenditures for $5,200, a debit to fund balance for $300, and a credit to reserve for encumbrances for $5,500

b. A debit to expenditures for $5,200, a credit to encumbrances for $5,200, and a credit to accounts payable for $5,200

c. A debit to expenditures for $5,200, a credit to encumbrances for $5,500, and a credit to accounts payable for $5,200
d. A debit to expenditures for $5,200, a credit to reserve for encumbrances for $5,200, and a credit to accounts payable for $5,200

7. A primary virtue of an object classification budget is that it
   a. Covers a period of more than one year
   b. Facilitates control by establishing detailed spending mandates
   c. Shows the impact on the budget of various possible levels of output
   d. Relates inputs to measurable outcomes

8. Per GASB Statement No. 34, governments must
   a. Prepare a general fund budget on a cash basis
   b. Prepare a general fund budget on a modified accrual basis
   c. Prepare a schedule that reconciles any differences between amounts reported on a GAAP basis and a budgetary basis
   d. Prepare a schedule that reconciles any differences between the original budget and the amended budget

9. The amount that a government has available to spend for a particular purpose in a particular year would be indicated by
   a. Encumbrances minus the sum of appropriations, expenditures, and net adjustments
   b. Reserve for encumbrances plus appropriations minus the sum of expenditures and net adjustments
   c. Appropriations plus encumbrances minus the sum of expenditures and net adjustments
   d. Appropriations minus the sum of expenditures, encumbrances, and net adjustments

10. For which of the following funds, would a government be least likely to record its annual budget and thereby integrate it into its accounting system?
   a. General fund
   b. Special revenue fund
   c. Capital project fund
   d. Enterprise fund

EX. 3-3

A county engages in basic transactions.

Kilbourne County engaged in the following transactions in summary form during its fiscal year. All amounts are in millions. You need not be concerned with the category of funds balances to which reserves for encumbrances are classified on the fund balance sheet.

1. Its commissioners approved a budget for the current fiscal year. It included total revenues of $860 and total appropriations of $850.
2. It ordered office supplies for $20.
3. It incurred the following costs, paying in cash:

Salaries	$610
Repairs	$ 40
Rent	$ 25
Utilities	$ 41
Other operating costs	$119

4. It ordered equipment costing $9.
5. It received the equipment and was billed for $10, rather than $9 as anticipated.

6. It received the previously ordered supplies and was billed for the amount originally estimated. The county reports the receipt of supplies as expenditures; it does not maintain an inventory account for supplies.

7. It earned and collected revenues of $865.
   a. Prepare journal entries as appropriate.
   b. Prepare closing entries as appropriate.
   c. What would have been the difference in the year-end financial statements, if any, had the county not made the budgetary entries?

EX. 3-4

Encumbrances are recorded in a capital projects fund similar to a general fund.

Wickliffe County authorized the issuance of bonds and contracted with the USA Construction Company (UCC) to build a new sports complex. During 2017, 2018, and 2019, the county engaged in the transactions that follow. All were recorded in a capital projects fund.

1. In 2017, the county issued $310 million in bonds (and recorded them as "bond proceeds," an account comparable to a revenue account).

2. It approved the sports complex contract for $310 million and encumbered the entire amount.

3. It received from UCC an invoice for construction to date for $114 million, an amount that the county recognized as an expenditure.

4. It paid UCC the amount owed.

5. In 2018, it received from UCC an invoice for an additional $190 million.

6. It paid the amount in full.

7. In 2019, UCC completed the sports facility and billed the county an additional $7 million. The county approved the additional costs, even though the total cost was now $311 million, $1 million more than initially estimated.

8. The county transferred $1 million from the general fund to the capital projects fund.

9. The county paid the $7 million.
   a. Prepare the journal entries, including closing entries, to record the transactions in the capital projects fund. Assume that expenditures do not have to be appropriated each year. Hence, the county need not reestablish encumbrances at each year subsequent to the first. Instead, it can close the expenditures of the second and third years to reserve for encumbrances rather than fund balance.
   b. What other funds, other than the capital projects fund, statements, or schedules would be affected by the transactions?

EX. 3-5

Both budgeted and actual revenues and expenditures are closed to the fund balance.

The budgeted and actual revenues and expenditures of Seaside Township for a recent year (in millions) were as presented in the schedule that follows.

1. Prepare journal entries to record the budget.

2. Prepare journal entries to record the actual revenues and expenditures. Assume all transactions resulted in increases or decreases in cash.

3. Prepare journal entries to close the accounts.

4. Determine the net change in fund balance. Does it equal the net change in actual revenues and expenditures?

	Budget	Actual
Revenues		
Property taxes	$ 7.5	$ 7.6
Sales taxes	2.1	2.4
Other revenues	1.6	1.5
Total revenues	$11.2	$11.5
Expenditures		
Wages and salaries	$ 6.2	$ 6.1
Supplies	3.1	3.0
Other expenditures	1.3	1.2
Total expenditures	$10.6	$10.3
Increase in fund balance	$ 0.6	$ 1.2

EX. 3-6

Encumbrance accounting has no lasting impact on fund balance.

London Township began Year 1 with a balance of $10 million in its bridge repair fund, a capital projects fund. The fund balance is classified as restricted.

At the start of the year, the governing council appropriated $6 million for the repair of two bridges. Shortly thereafter, the town signed contracts with a construction company to perform the repairs at a cost of $3 million per bridge.

During the year, the town received and paid bills from the construction company as follows:

- $3.2 million for the repairs on Bridge 1. The company completed the repairs, but owing to design changes approved by the town, the cost was $0.2 million greater than anticipated. The town did not encumber the additional $0.2 million.
- $2.0 million for the repairs, which were not completed, on Bridge 2.

At the start of the following year, the governing council reappropriated the $1 million to complete the repairs on Bridge 2. During that year, the town received and paid bills totaling $0.7 million. The construction company completed the repairs, but the final cost was less than anticipated—a total of only $2.7 million.

1. Prepare journal entries to record the events and transactions over the two-year period. Include entries to appropriate, reappropriate, encumber, and reencumber the required funds; to record the payment of the bills; and to close the accounts at the end of each year.
2. Determine the restricted fund balance at the end of the second year. Is it equal to the initial fund balance less the total cost of the repairs?

EX. 3-7

Encumbrances have an impact on unassigned fund balance, but do not affect total fund balance.

At the start of its fiscal year on October 1, Fox County reported the following (all dollar amounts in thousands):

Fund balance:	
Committed for encumbrances	$200
Unassigned	400
Total fund balance	$600

During the year, the county (all dollar amounts in thousands):

- Estimated that revenues for the year would be $6,300.
- Appropriated $6,500 for operations.
- Ordered goods and services estimated to cost $6,000. Of these, the county received (and used) goods and services that it had estimated would cost $5,000. Actual cost, however, was $5,200.
- Received (and used) all goods that it ordered in the previous year. Actual cost was only $180.
- Recognized actual revenues of $6,400.

1. Prepare a schedule, similar to that illustrated in the text, of changes in unassigned fund balance.
2. Show how the total fund balance (including the unassigned and committed portions) would be displayed at year-end.
3. Does the total fund balance at the beginning of the year, plus the actual revenues, minus the actual expenditures, equal the total fund balance at the end of the year?

EX. 3-8

The following schedule shows the amounts related to general purpose supplies that a city debited and credited to the indicated accounts during a year (not necessarily the year-end balances), excluding closing entries. The organization records its budget, encumbers all its expenditures, and initially vouchers all payments. It accounts for supplies on a *purchases* basis.

1. Some information is missing. By reconstructing the entries that the organization made during the year, you are to determine the missing data. You need not show the entries; simply fill in the blanks. The city began the year with $5,000 of supplies in inventory and ended the year with $7,000. Assume that the reserve for encumbrances will be properly reported in the appropriate classification of fund balance.

	(in thousands)	
	Debits	*Credits*
Cash	$ 0	$ 70
Vouchers payable	?	?
Appropriations	0	115
Encumbrances	?	?
Expenditures	58	0
Reserve for encumbrances	58	93
Fund balance—unassigned	?	0

2. In which classification of fund balance would the reserve for encumbrances most likely be incorporated?
3. Assume instead that the city accounts for supplies on a consumption basis. Which of the preceding amounts (assuming that appropriations remained unchanged) would be different and what additional accounts would have to be added? What would be the new debits and credits in those accounts?
4. The mayor of the city requests your advice about whether it is actually necessary to (1) incorporate the budget into the accounting system and (2) use fund accounting. What would be your response?

CONTINUING PROBLEM

1. In which section of the Comprehensive Annual Financial Report (CAFR) are the budget-to-actual comparisons of the major funds?
   a. Which accounting basis did the City follow to prepare its annual operating budget?
   b. Are the actual amounts on a GAAP or a budgetary basis? Do the statements include a reconciliation of any differences between GAAP and budgetary amounts? If so, what are the largest reconciled items?
   c. Are the reported variances based on the original budget or the year-end amended budget?
2. Does the CAFR include budget-to-actual comparisons of nonmajor funds? If so, in what section?
3. Does the government encumber goods or services that have been ordered but have not yet been received? How, if at all, are encumbrances reflected on the governmental fund balance sheet? How, if at all, are they reflected on the government-wide statement of net position?
4. Do encumbrances that remain outstanding at year-end lapse? That is, do the amounts that will be expended in the following year, when the goods or services are received, have to be rebudgeted in the following year? How can you tell?

PROBLEMS

P. 3-1

Is accrual-based budgeting preferable to cash-based budgeting?

The Disability Research Institute receives its funding mainly from government grants and private contributions. In turn, it supports research and related projects carried out by universities and other not-for-profits. Most of its government grants are reimbursement (expenditure-driven) awards. That is, the government will reimburse the institute for the funds that it disburses to others.

The institute estimates that the following will occur in the forthcoming year:

- It will be awarded $5 million in government grants, all of which will be paid out to subrecipients during the year. Of this amount, only $4.5 million will be reimbursed by the government during the year. The balance will be reimbursed in the first six months of the next year. The institute will also receive $200,000 in grant funds that were due from the previous year.
- It will receive $600,000 in pledges from private donors. It expects to collect $450,000 during the year and the balance in the following year. It also expects to collect $80,000 in pledges made the prior year.
- It will purchase new furniture and office equipment at a cost of $80,000. It currently owns its building, which it had purchased for $800,000, and additional furniture and equipment, which it acquired for $250,000. The building has a useful life of 25 years; the furniture and equipment have a useful life of five years.
- Employees will earn wages and salaries of $340,000, of which they will be paid $320,000 during the forthcoming year and the balance in the next year.
- It will incur other operating costs of $90,000, of which it will pay $70,000 in the forthcoming year and $20,000 in the next year. It will also pay another $10,000 in costs incurred in the previous year.

1. Prepare two budgets, one on a cash basis and the other on a *full* accrual basis. For convenience, show both on the same schedule, with the cash budget in one column and the accrual in the other column.
2. Comment on which budget better shows whether the institute is covering the economic cost of the services that it provides.
3. Which is likely to be more useful to
   a. Institute managers?
   b. Members of the institute's board of trustees?
   c. Bankers from whom the institute seeks a loan?

P. 3-2

Missing data can be derived, and journal entries constructed, from information in the accounts.

The following schedule shows the amounts (in thousands) related to expenditures that a city welfare department debited and credited to the indicated accounts during a year (not necessarily the year-end balances), *excluding* closing entries. The department records its budget, encumbers all its expenditures, and initially vouchers all payments. Some information is missing. You are to determine the missing data and construct all entries (in summary form), excluding closing entries, that the department made during the year.

	(in thousands)	
	Debit	*Credit*
Cash	$ 0	$28
Vouchers payable	?	?
Estimated expenditures (appropriations)	0	55
Encumbrances	?	?
Expenditures	30	0
Reserve for encumbrances	32	50
Fund balance—unassigned	?	0

P. 3-3

Missing data can be derived, and journal entries constructed, from information in the accounts.

The following schedule shows the amounts related to supplies that a city debited and credited to the indicated accounts during a year (not necessarily the year-end balances), excluding closing entries. The city records its budget, encumbers all its expenditures, and initially vouchers all payments. All revenue was collected in cash. Some information is missing. By reconstructing the entries that the city made during the year, you are to determine the missing data and construct the journal entries (in summary form), excluding closing entries.

	(in thousands)	
	Debits	*Credits*
Cash	$117	$?
Estimated revenues	?	0
Revenues	0	?
Vouchers payable	70	54
Appropriations	0	?
Encumbrances	?	58
Expenditures	?	0
Reserved for encumbrances	?	93
Fund balance—unassigned	115	120

P. 3-4

A city imposes an overhead charge on one of its departments to alleviate its fiscal problems.

A city's visitors' bureau, which promotes tourism and conventions, is funded by an 8 percent local hotel occupancy tax (a tax on the cost of a stay in a hotel). Because the visitors' bureau is supported entirely by the occupancy tax, it is accounted for in a restricted fund.

You recently received a call from the director of the visitors' bureau. She complained that the city manager is about to impose an overhead charge of a specified dollar amount on her department. Yet the statute creating the hotel occupancy tax specifies that the revenues can be used only to satisfy "direct expenditures" incurred to promote tourism and bookings at the city's convention center. The manager says that she understands that the city is having difficulty balancing its budget, but she fails to see how the charge to her department will do much to alleviate the city's fiscal problems.

1. In light of the city's fiscal problems, what is the most likely motivation for the new charge? Will the new overhead charge achieve its objective?
2. What would be the impact of the new charge on the city's annual fund financial statements, prepared in accordance with GAAP (which requires that the city account for its governmental funds on a modified accrual basis)? Would the impact be the same if the city accounted for its governmental funds on a cash basis?
3. What would be the impact of the new charge on the city's government-wide statements, in which all governmental funds are consolidated? Would it have an impact on reported net position?
4. In what way might the charge have a substantive impact on the city's economic condition?
5. Assuming that the city provided accounting, legal, and purchasing services to the visitors' bureau, do you think the charge would be consistent with the statutory requirement that the hotel occupancy tax be used to meet only "direct expenditures" related to tourism and use of the convention center (an issue not addressed in this text)?

P. 3-5

Government activities may be less "profitable" than they appear.

A city prepares its budget in traditional format, classifying expenditures by fund and object. In 2010, amid considerable controversy, the city authorized the sale of $20 million in bonds to finance construction of a new sports and special events arena. Critics charged that, contrary to the predictions of arena proponents, the arena could not be fiscally self-sustaining.

Five years later, the arena was completed and began to be used. After its first year of operations, its general managers submitted the following condensed statement of revenues and expenses (in millions):

Revenues from ticket sales	$5.7	
Revenues from concessions	2.4	$8.1
Operating expenses	6.6	
Interest on debt	1.2	7.8
Excess of revenues over expenses		$0.3

At the city council meeting, when the report was submitted, the council member who had championed the center glowingly boasted that his prophecy was proving correct; the arena was "profitable."

Assume that the following information came to your attention:

- The arena is accounted for in a separate enterprise fund.
- The arena increased the number of overnight visitors to the city. City administrators and economists calculated that the additional visitors generated approximately $0.1 million in hotel occupancy tax revenues. These taxes are dedicated to promoting tourism in the city. In addition, they estimated that the ticket and concession sales, plus the economic activity generated by the arena, increased general sales tax revenues by $0.4 million.
- The city had to improve roads, highways, and utilities in the area surrounding the arena. These improvements, which cost $6 million, were financed with general obligation debt (not reported in the enterprise fund). Principal and interest on the debt, paid out of general funds, were $0.5 million. The cost of maintaining the facilities was approximately $0.1 million.
- On evenings when events were held in the arena, the city had to increase police protection in the arena's neighborhood. Whereas the arena compensated the police department for police officers who served

within the arena itself, those who patrolled outside were paid out of police department funds. The police department estimated its additional costs at $0.1 million.

- The city provided various administrative services (including legal, accounting, and personnel) to the arena at no charge at an estimated cost of $0.1 million.
- The city estimates the cost of additional sanitation, fire, and medical services due to events at the center to be approximately $0.2 million.

1. Would you agree with the council member that the arena was fiscally self-sustaining?
2. In which funds would the additional revenues and expenditures be budgeted and accounted for?
3. Comment on the limitations of both the traditional object classification budget and fund accounting system in assessing the economic costs and benefits of a project—such as the sports and special events arena.
4. What changes in the city's budgeting and accounting structure would overcome these limitations? What additional problems might these changes cause?

P. 3-6

To what extent do the unique features of government accounting make a difference on the financial statements?

The transactions that follow relate to the Danville County Comptroller's Department over a two-year period.

Year 1

- The county appropriated $12,000 for employee education and training.
- The department signed contracts with outside consultants to conduct accounting and auditing workshops. Total cost was $10,000.
- The consultants conducted the workshops and were paid $10,000.
- The department ordered books and training materials, which it estimated would cost $1,800. As of year-end, the materials had not been received.

Year 2

- The county appropriated $13,500 for employee education and training.
- The department received and paid for the books and training materials that it ordered the previous year. Actual cost was only $1,700. The county's accounting policies require that the books and training materials be charged as an expenditure when they are received (as opposed to being recorded as inventory and charged as an expenditure when used).
- It authorized employees to attend various conferences and training sessions. Estimated cost was $10,500.
- Employees submitted $10,800 in reimbursement requests for the conferences and training sessions they attended. The department paid them the requested amounts and at year-end did not expect to receive any additional reimbursement requests.

1. Prepare all required journal entries that would affect the expenditure subaccount "education and training," including budgetary and closing entries. Assume that all appropriations lapse at year-end (thus, all expenditures in Year 2 would be charged against that year's appropriation of $13,500, even if the goods and services were ordered in Year 1).
2. Indicate (specifying accounts and dollar amounts) how the transactions would be reported in the county's general fund:
   a. Balance sheet
   b. Statement of revenues and expenditures

3. Alternatively, suppose that the county did not record its budget and did not encumber its commitments. What would be the difference in the year-end financial statements?

4. Assume instead that appropriations for goods on order at year-end do not lapse. When the goods are received, they are charged as expenditures against the budget of the year in which they were encumbered. How would this change affect your entries and the year-end financial statements? How would it affect the amount that the department had available to spend in Year 2 on goods or services not previously ordered?

P. 3-7

Different budget-to-actual comparisons serve different purposes.

The following information was drawn from a county's general fund budgets and accounts for a particular year (in millions):

	Amended Budget	Original Budget	Actual Results (Budget Basis)
Revenues			
Property taxes	$46.6	$42.5	$53.0
Sales taxes	16.3	13.6	15.1
Licenses and permits	1.1	1.0	1.0
Other	3.2	2.9	3.4
Total revenues	$67.2	$60.0	$72.5
Expenditures			
General government	$18.2	$16.2	$18.1
Public safety	29.2	25.1	28.5
Sanitation	9.7	9.4	9.6
Culture and recreation	8.1	7.8	8.1
Interest	1.4	1.4	1.4
Total expenditures	$66.6	$59.9	$65.7
Excess of revenues over expenditures	$ 0.6	$ 0.1	$ 6.8

You also learn the following:

	Beginning of Year	End of Year
Encumbrances (commitments) outstanding	$2.7	$1.1
Supplies inventories on hand	1.8	1.0
Wages and salaries payable	0.5	0.7
Property taxes expected to be collected within 60 days	1.7	2.5

- For purposes of budgeting, the county recognizes encumbrances as the equivalent of expenditures in the year established; for financial reporting, it recognizes expenditures when the goods or services are received, as required by GAAP.
- For purposes of budgeting, it recognizes supplies expenditures when the supplies are acquired; for financial reporting, it recognizes the expenditure when the supplies are consumed.

- For purposes of budgeting, it recognizes wages and salaries when paid; for financial reporting, it recognizes the expenditures when the employees perform their services.
- For purposes of budgeting, it recognizes as revenues only taxes actually collected during the year; for financial reporting, it recognizes taxes expected to be collected within the first 60 days of the following year.

1. Prepare the following four separate schedules in which you compare the budget-to-actual results and compute the budget variance. You need to present only the *total* revenues, *total* expenditures, and excess of revenues over expenditures.
   a. Actual results on a budget basis to the amended budget
   b. Actual results on a budget basis to the original budget
   c. Actual results as would be reflected in the financial statements to the amended budget restated so that it is on a financial reporting basis
   d. Actual results as would be reflected in the financial statements to the original budget restated so that it is on a financial reporting basis

Village of Denaville

			Amounts Received		
	Estimated/ Appropriated	**Amounts Encumbered**	**Estimated Cost**	**Actual Cost**	**Actual Revenues**
Revenues					
Property taxes	$ 7,900				$ 7,800
Sales taxes	3,900				3,600
Licenses	300				200
Other	700				400
	12,800				$12,000
Expenditures/Appropriations					
General government	3,000	$ 2,600	$ 2,400	$ 2,800	
Public safety	6,000	5,900	5,000	4,900	
Recreation	1,200	1,200	800	900	
Health and sanitation	2,300	2,200	2,200	2,100	
	$12,500	$11,900	$10,400	$10,700	
Excess of estimated revenues over appropriations	300				
Beginning unassigned fund balance	1,200				
Estimated unassigned ending fund balance	$ 1,500				

2. The county executive has boasted that the "better than anticipated results" (based on the comparison of the schedule that appears in the financial statements) are evidence of "sound fiscal management and effective cost controls" on the part of the county administration. Do you agree?
3. Which of the three schedules best demonstrates legal compliance? Explain.
4. Which schedule best demonstrates effective management? Explain.

P. 3-8

Budget variances have to be interpreted with caution.

The data presented below were taken from the books and records of the village of Denaville. All amounts are in millions. The village encumbers all outlays. As is evident from the data, some goods or services that were ordered and encumbered have not yet been received. City regulations require that all appropriations lapse at year-end.

1. Prepare summary entries to record
a. The budget
b. The encumbrance of the goods and services
c. The receipt of the goods and services. All invoices were paid in cash.
d. The actual revenues (all cash receipts)

2. Prepare summary entries to close the accounts.

3. What would be the year-end
a. fund balance (unassigned)?
b. reserve for encumbrance balance (irrespective of how classified)?

4. Prepare a schedule in which you compare budgeted to actual revenues and expenditures.

5. A citizen reviews the budget to actual schedule that you have prepared. She comments on the rather substantial favorable variance between budgeted and actual expenditures and questions why the government did not spend the full amount of money that it appropriated. Briefly explain to her the nature of the variance.

P. 3-9

A city's note to its financial statements provides considerable insight into its budget practices.

Shown below is an excerpt from a note, headed *Budgets*, from the Smith City, annual report for the fiscal year ended June 30.

1. The note distinguishes between the "budget ordinance" and the "more detailed line-item budgets."
a. Provide examples of expenditures that you would expect to see in the budget ordinance.
b. Provide examples of expenditures that you would expect to see in the line-item budgets.

2. Why do you suspect that budgetary control is not exercised in trust and custodial funds?

3. Generally accepted accounting principles require that governments reconcile differences between the entity's budget practices and GAAP either in the financial statements themselves or in accompanying notes. Smith City's budget-to-actual comparison contained no such reconciliation. Why do you think a reconciliation was also omitted from the notes?

4. Explain how Smith City's appropriation process for its general fund would differ from that for its capital projects fund. How would this difference most likely affect the city's budgetary entries?

5. The schedule included in the notes shows the original budget, total amendments, and the final budget. Where would a reader look to compare actual general fund expenditures with budgeted expenditures?

Note from Smith City Annual Report

Budgetary control is exercised in all funds except for the trust and custodial funds. The budget shown in the financial statements is the budget ordinance as amended at the close of the day of June 30. The city is required by the General Statutes of the state to adopt an annual balanced budget by July 1 of each year. The General Statutes also provide for balanced project ordinances for the life of projects, including both capital and grant activities, that are expected to extend beyond the end of the fiscal year. The city council officially adopts the annual budget ordinance and all project ordinances and has the authority to amend such ordinances as necessary to recognize new resources or reallocations of budget. As of June 30, the effect of such amendments, less eliminating transfers, is shown below.

	Original Budget	Total Amendments	Budget June 30
General fund	$145,259,996	$2,965,856	$148,225,852
Special revenue funds	49,087,784	5,034,632	54,122,416
General capital projects funds	135,304,688	4,038,509	139,343,197
Proprietary funds	145,984,461	2,557,523	148,541,984
Internal service funds	845,657	16,640	862,297

All budgets are prepared on the modified accrual basis of accounting, as is required by state law. Appropriations for funds that adopt annual budgets lapse at the end of the budget year. Project budgeted appropriations do not lapse until the completion of the project.

Budget control on expenditures is limited to departmental totals and project totals as specified in the budget ordinances. Administrative control is maintained through the establishment of more detailed line-item budgets, which correspond to the specific object of the expenditure. All budget transfers, at both the ordinance and the line-item levels, are approved by the city council. The city manager is authorized to transfer line-item budgeted amounts up to $1,000 within a fund prior to their formal approval by the city council.

Encumbrances represent commitments related to unperformed contracts for goods or services. Encumbrance accounting—under which purchase orders, contracts, and other commitments for the expenditure of resources are recorded to reserve that portion of the applicable appropriation—is utilized in all funds. Outstanding encumbrances at year-end for which goods or services are received are reclassified to expenditures and accounts payable. All other encumbrances in the annual budgeted funds are reversed at year-end and are either canceled or included as reappropriations of fund balance for the subsequent year. Outstanding encumbrances at year-end in funds that are budgeted on a project basis automatically carry forward along with their related appropriations and are not subject to an annual cancellation and reappropriation.

P. 3-10

Different types of funds justify different practices as to budgets and commitments.

Review the budget note to the Smith City's financial statements presented in the previous problem. Assume that the city engaged in the following transactions in 2020 and 2021:

- In 2020, it signed a service contract with a private security company. The company agreed to provide security services to the city's for one year at a cost of $72,000 ($6,000 per month). By year-end the company provided, and the city paid for, services for three months.
- In 2021, the company performed, and the city paid for, the remaining nine months of the contract. However, because of agreed-upon changes in the services provided by the company, the total charges for 2021 were reduced from $54,000 to $50,000.

1. The city properly budgeted for the services and appropriated the funds consistent with policies set forth in the note. Prepare all budgetary, encumbrance, and expenditure entries relating to the service contract that would be required in 2020 and 2021. In 2020, when the city signed the contract, it appropriated the entire $72,000. Then, at the start of 2021, inasmuch as the city expended only $18,000 in 2020, it reappropriated $54,000.

a. Assume first that the contract was accounted for in Smith City's *general fund*.

b. Assume next that it was accounted for in a *capital projects fund* established for the construction of its Walnut Creek Amphitheatre. The city prepares annual financial statements for capital projects funds, but it does not close out its accounts. Moreover, it prepares budgets for the entire project, not for particular periods. The project was started in 2020 and completed in 2021.

2. Justify the city's practice of accounting differently for commitments in the two types of funds.

Fund: General government
Account: Consulting fees

Date	Encumbrances Dr. (Cr.)	Expenditures Dr. (Cr.)	Appropriations Cr. (Dr.)	Available Balance
1/1			$78,000	$78,000
1/1	$7,900			70,100
1/5	(4,000)	$3,000		71,100
1/14		4,500		66,600
2/5	6,000			60,600
2/15	(3,200)	3,400		60,400

P. 3-11

Journal entries can be derived from a city's ledger.

Shown below is an excerpt from a city's subsidiary ledger for the first two months of its fiscal year. Missing is the column that explains or references each of the entries.

1. Prepare the journal entries that were most likely made in the account, adding to each a brief note of explanation. Each line of the account records a single transaction (e.g., the receipt of an invoice); however, the entries on January 1 were made before the city engaged in any actual transactions (i.e., with outside parties).

2. The appropriation for consulting fees was intended to last for the entire year. Apparently, the city is spending or committing funds at a faster pace than planned. Can you propose an additional control mechanism to help ensure that the funds are spent evenly throughout the year?

P. 3-12

Speeding up tax collections helps balance a state's appropriations budget.

The following is an excerpt (with dates changed) from *Against the Grain*, a series of recommendations by the State Comptroller of Texas on how to "save" $4.5 billion and thereby balance the state's budget:

> *Require an Annual August Remittance of One-Half of August's Sales Tax Collections by Monthly Taxpayers. The Legislature should require sales taxpayers to remit half of August's collections during that month.*

Background

Currently, sales tax payments are remitted monthly, quarterly, or annually. They also may be prepaid either on a quarterly or on a monthly basis.

Monthly taxpayers, including those who collect taxes on their own purchase or use of taxable items, are required by law to remit to the state all tax collections—less any applicable discounts—by the 20th day of the month following the end of each calendar month. The state's fiscal year ends on August 31.

Recommendation

The Legislature should require all monthly taxpayers to remit one-half of each August's sales tax collections during that month.

Specifically, sales taxes collected between August 1 and August 15 would be due with their regular August 20th payment. Monthly taxpayers would remit tax in the usual manner during all other months.

This is not a prepayment plan, but a speeding up of the remittance of actual taxes collected and owed to the state. This would impose an additional burden and would reduce taxpayer cash flow, but should be considered as preferable to a tax increase.

Implications

An annual payment by monthly filers of taxes actually collected during the first 15 days of August would increase August's collections and decrease September's collections. Although the initial imposition of this proposal might temporarily inconvenience some taxpayers, the prompt payment to the state of some of its sales tax revenues—collected, but not yet remitted—will enhance the revenue stream at a critical time each fiscal year. During the first year of implementation, all months would have normal collection patterns except August, which would be larger than usual, thereby producing a fiscal gain.

Each following year would see smaller-than-normal (current) collections in September and larger collections in August. These differences would essentially offset each other. It is important to stress that failure to speed up collections each year after implementation would cause a fiscal loss. The gain to the general fund in the year of implementation would be $215 million.

Fiscal Year	Gain to the General Revenue Fund
2019	$215,113,000
2020	$ 0
2021	$ 0
2022	$ 0
2023	$ 0

1. On what basis does the state probably prepare its appropriation budget? Explain.
2. Do you believe the state will be better off, in economic substance, as a result of the proposed change?
3. According to the comptroller (last paragraph), the change would have no impact on revenues in future fiscal years as long as collections are also pushed forward in those years. Do you agree? If so, is there any reason not to adopt the proposal?

P. 3-13

Multiple funds provide multiple sources of revenue.

The following is a recommendation from *Against the Grain*, a series of proposals by the State Comptroller of Texas on how the state could enhance revenues and decrease expenditures:

Amend the Lottery Act to Abolish the Lottery Stabilization Fund

The state should amend the Lottery Act to abolish the Lottery Stabilization Fund requirement and use the income to fund critical services.

Background

The State Lottery Act requires the establishment of a Lottery Stabilization Fund. The fund will contain lottery revenue in excess of the Comptroller's Biennial Revenue Estimate. The Lottery Stabilization Fund is then to provide revenue to the General Revenue Fund if the lottery fails to generate monthly revenue as estimated.

In months that lottery revenue exceeds one-twelfth of the annual estimate, the Comptroller is required to deposit $10 million plus the amount of net lottery revenue in excess of the estimate to the Lottery Stabilization Fund. The Act provides only two circumstances under which revenue could be transferred from the Lottery Stabilization Fund to the General Revenue Fund. In months that lottery revenue is less than 90 percent of one-twelfth of the annual estimate, the difference is to be transferred from the Lottery Stabilization Fund to general revenue. The Act also provides for the transfer of one-half of the balance of the Lottery Stabilization Fund to the General Revenue Fund on the first day of every biennium.

In view of the seriousness of the state's fiscal situation, the Legislature should set aside the stabilization fund requirement. The state already maintains a significant rainy-day fund, and effective revenue forecasting should be adequate to avoid problems with potential future revenue stream instability.

Recommendation

The state should repeal the provision in the State Lottery Act that establishes the Lottery Stabilization Fund. This action would provide additional revenue to the General Revenue Fund to be used for state programs at the Legislature's discretion.

Implications

Releasing Lottery Stabilization Funds would increase the available revenue for state programs without increasing taxes. General revenue is reduced by at least $10 million in months when lottery revenue exceeds one-twelfth of the annual lottery estimate. In effect, the state is penalized for correctly estimating lottery revenue and operating the lottery efficiently. Repealing the provision that establishes this fund would remove this penalty.

This action would increase general revenue about $65 million per year in the next biennium.

1. Explain briefly how the comptroller's recommendation would increase general revenue by $65 million per year. In what way would the proposal affect the fiscal well-being of the state?
2. What impact would the comptroller's recommendation have on the state's budget if the state were to prepare a "consolidated" budget—one in which all funds are combined?
3. With reference to this recommendation, what are the advantages and disadvantages of budgeting on the basis of individual funds as opposed to combining all funds?

QUESTIONS FOR RESEARCH, ANALYSIS, AND DISCUSSION

1. Generally accepted accounting principles require governments to include in their annual reports a comparison of actual results with the budget for each governmental fund for which an annual budget has been adopted. This information is generally presented as "required supplementary information" and as such is not subject to the same degree of auditor scrutiny as is data included in the basic financial statements or accompanying notes. Do you think the budget-to-actual comparison is sufficiently important to be included as part of the basic financial statements? Are governments permitted to include their budget-to-actual comparisons as part of the basic financial statements?
2. The GASB requires a government to prepare budgetary comparisons for its general fund and major special revenue funds that have a legally adopted annual budget. The city for which you work does not have a legally adopted budget prepared specifically for its general fund and major special revenue funds. Instead, the city prepares a legally adopted master budget for the entire government and divides it into functions and programs. With the functional and program information provided in the budget, the accounting department can specifically assign the budgetary amounts to governmental funds for budgetary control purposes. The government has a general fund and two special revenue funds. What budgetary comparison schedules should the government prepare, if any?
3. In your government, appropriations for goods and services that remain encumbered at year-end are automatically carried forward to the next year. Thus, the budget for the following year must include the amounts required to pay for the goods that were encumbered at year-end. The budget, however, must be adopted prior to the start of the following year, and, therefore, the amount of year-end encumbrances is not known when the budget is adopted. In presenting the original budget in an actual-to-budget comparison, should the amounts of encumbrances be included even though they were not included when the budget was first adopted?
4. Your government is permitted to amend the budget even after the end of the year. When presenting the final actual-to-budget comparisons, is it permitted to include the amendments that were adopted after the year-end?

SOLUTION TO EXERCISE FOR REVIEW AND SELF-STUDY

1.	Estimated revenues	$5,600	
	Appropriations		$5,550
	Fund balance—unassigned		50
	To record the budget		

The budget would specify in detail the revenues anticipated and expenditures appropriated. Hence, the corresponding subledger accounts should be debited and credited for amounts estimated or authorized.

2.

a. Cash	$5,800	
Revenues		$5,800
To record revenues		
b. Encumbrances	$3,000	
Reserve for encumbrances (assigned fund balance)		$3,000
To encumber resources assigned to fulfill commitments for goods and services on order		
c. Expenditures	$2,800	
Cash		$2,800
To record expenditures		
Reserve for encumbrances (assigned Fund balance)	$2,800	
Encumbrances		$2,800
To unencumber funds for goods and services already received that have been charged as expenditures		
d. Expenditures	$2,500	
Cash		$2,500
To record other expenditures		

3.	Revenues	$5,800	
	Estimated revenues		$5,600
	Fund balance		200
	To close revenue and estimated revenue accounts		
	Appropriations	$5,550	
	Expenditures		$5,300
	Encumbrances		200
	Fund balance—unassigned		50
	To close expenditures, encumbrances, and appropriations		

The district's closing entries deviate slightly from those illustrated earlier in the text, in which the budget accounts were closed in one entry and the actual accounts in another. The end result is the same regardless of the grouping used for the closing entries.

4. The following schedule summarizes the impact of the transactions on fund balance:

Revenues	$5,800
Expenditures	5,300
Increase in total fund balance	500
Less: Encumbrances (transfer from unassigned to assigned fund balance)	200
Net increase in unassigned fund balance	$ 300

The following balance sheet shows the status of year-end asset and fund balance accounts:

Cash	$500
Fund balance	
Assigned	$200
Unassigned	300
Total fund balance	$500

5.	Encumbrances	$200	
	Fund balance—unassigned		$200
	To restore encumbrances of the previous year		
6.	Expenditures	$150	
	Cash		$150
	To record expenditures		
	Reserve for encumbrances (assigned fund balance)	$200	
	Encumbrances		$200

To unencumber funds for goods and services already received and charged as expenditures (the entire $200 is reversed, inasmuch as the entire order has been fulfilled; no additional amount need be assigned)

CHAPTER 4

Recognizing Revenues in Governmental Funds

LEARNING OBJECTIVES

After studying this chapter, you should understand:

- Why governments focus on current financial resources and use the modified accrual basis to account for their governmental funds
- Why governments focus on all economic resources and use the full accrual basis in their government-wide financial statements
- The key distinctions between the modified and full accrual bases of accounting
- The distinction between exchange and nonexchange transactions
- The main types of nonexchange transactions
- The impact of the "available" criterion on revenue recognition
- How each of the following types of revenues are accounted for:
  - Property taxes
  - Sales taxes
  - Income taxes
  - Licenses and permits
  - Fines
  - Grants and donations
  - Sales of capital assets
  - On-behalf payments

We now turn to what are among the most intriguing questions of government and not-for-profit accounting: when should revenues and expenditures or expenses be recognized, and how should the related assets, liabilities, and deferred inflows and outflows of resources be measured?

In **Chapters 4** and **5**, we consider revenue and expenditure recognition in governments, and in **Chapters 12, 13**, and **14** we address revenue and expense recognition in not-for-profit entities. Most of the examples in this and the next chapter will implicitly be directed toward governments' general funds. However, the discussion is equally applicable to all *governmental* funds, including special revenues funds, capital projects funds, debt service funds, and *permanent* funds. In **Chapter 9**, we examine the same issues as they apply to proprietary funds (those that account for business-type activities).

WHY AND HOW DO GOVERNMENTS USE THE MODIFIED ACCRUAL BASIS?

RATIONALE FOR THE MODIFIED ACCRUAL BASIS

The foundation for our discussion of revenue and expenditure recognition was laid out in Chapter 1. In that chapter, we pointed to two key objectives of financial reporting:

- Indicating the extent to which the entity achieved interperiod equity (i.e., whether current-year revenues were sufficient to pay for current-year services)
- Demonstrating whether the entity obtained and used its resources in accordance with its legally adopted budget

As suggested in Chapter 1, no set of financial statements prepared on a single basis of revenue and expenditure recognition can adequately fulfill both objectives. Therefore, standard setters must choose among three courses of action:

- Adopt principles that fulfill one of the objectives, but not the other
- Adopt principles that compromise between the two objectives, fulfilling both to some extent, but neither one adequately
- Develop a reporting model that incorporates more than one basis of revenue and expenditure recognition—either statements that embrace more than one basis of accounting or statements that incorporate two or more sets of statements within the same report

Generally accepted accounting principles as incorporated in the current Governmental Accounting Standards Board (GASB) model reflect the third approach. The government-wide statements consolidate all funds on a full accrual basis (except for fiduciary funds, which are not consolidated because the beneficiaries of their resources are parties other than the government). They thereby demonstrate whether the entity's current-year revenues were sufficient to pay for the current year's services. The fund statements, by contrast, present governmental funds on a modified accrual basis (and, for reasons to be explained in Chapter 9, proprietary funds statements are presented on a full accrual basis).

The modified accrual basis is far more budget-oriented than the full accrual basis in that the budgets of most governments focus on either cash or cash plus selected short-term financial resources. However, the budgetary principles of any individual government are determined by applicable state or local laws. Except for governments that elect or are required to budget on a modified accrual basis as defined by GAAP, the revenue and expenditure principles that underlie their fund statements would not necessarily be identical to those of their legally adopted budgets. Hence, as discussed in Chapter 3, schedules that show the variances between budgetary estimates and actual results may have to include a reconciliation that indicates the portion of the variances attributable to the differences in accounting principles.

In developing its current model, the GASB opted to retain the modified accrual basis of the previous model—rather than a budget basis—for governmental funds statements. This approach ensures that all governments report on the same basis and thereby facilitates comparisons among entities. Comparisons would have been difficult if each entity reported on its own particular budget basis.

RELATIONSHIP BETWEEN MEASUREMENT FOCUS AND BASIS OF ACCOUNTING

The criteria by which an entity determines when to recognize revenues and expenditures necessarily stems from its measurement focus and its basis of accounting. As pointed out in Chapter 2, *measurement focus* refers to *what* is being reported on—that is, to which assets, liabilities, and deferrals are being measured. *Basis of accounting* refers to *when* transactions and other events are recognized. The two concepts obviously are closely linked. If an entity opts to focus on cash,

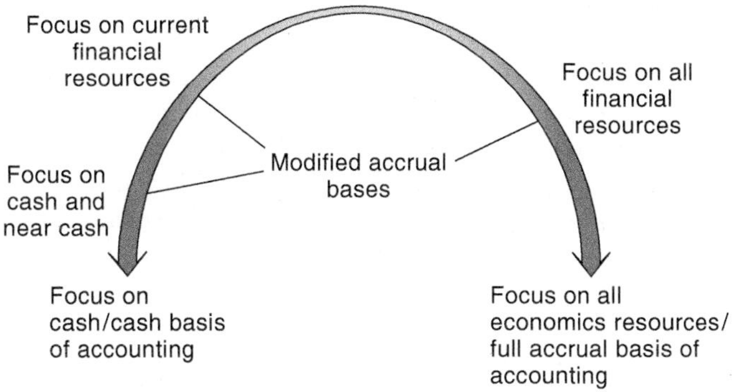

FIGURE 4-1 Measurement Focus and Basis of Accounting

then it will necessarily adopt a *cash basis of accounting*. Correspondingly, if it elects to focus on *all economic resources* (both current and long-term assets and liabilities), then it will adopt a *full accrual basis of accounting*.

Measurement focus and basis of accounting can be viewed as a continuum. As depicted in Figure 4-1, on one end of the continuum is a cash focus, and correspondingly the cash basis of accounting. On the other end is a focus on all economic resources, and thus the full accrual basis. Between the two ends of the continuum are any number of "modified accrual" (or "modified cash") bases of accounting in which the focus is on resources in addition to cash but not on the full array of economic resources.

If a government's budget is on a cash or near-cash basis, as is common, then a basis of accounting near the cash end of the continuum best satisfies the reporting objective of demonstrating that resources were obtained in accordance with the legally adopted budget. A basis of accounting on the full accrual end of the continuum best fulfills the interperiod equity objective. Any basis between the extremes would compromise the two objectives, satisfying both objectives to some extent, but neither one completely.

OVERVIEW OF THE MODIFIED ACCRUAL BASIS

Per today's generally accepted practices, governmental funds are accounted for on a modified accrual basis. The measurement focus is on **current financial resources**. "Current financial resources" has been interpreted to mean "expendable financial resources"—cash and other items that can be expected to be transformed into cash in the normal course of operations (less current liabilities). The "other items" include investments and receivables but *not* capital assets.

As discussed in Chapter 4, inventories and prepaid items are also reported on the balance sheet, even though they do not fall within the conventional view of a financial resource. A frequently cited justification for this apparent inconsistency is that these assets will not ordinarily be transformed into cash (i.e., inventories will be consumed, not sold for cash), but they generally will result in short-term cash savings in that the entity will not have to expend additional cash to acquire them.

The current claims against financial resources include wages and salaries payable, accounts payable, and deferred inflows. They exclude long-term obligations such as the noncurrent portions of bonds payable and the liabilities for vacation pay, sick leave pay, and legal judgments. Consistent with conventional relationships between the balance sheet and operating statement accounts, revenues and expenditures are accompanied by an increase or decrease in net financial resources (as opposed to increases or decreases in net economic resources, as would be true under the full accrual basis).

RECOGNITION OF REVENUE

Accepting the accrual basis of accounting (even if modified) still leaves unresolved the thorny issue of when revenues should be recognized. What key economic event in the revenue generation process should trigger the recognition of revenue and the corresponding increase in net position? In business accounting, revenues are ordinarily recognized when a firm has fulfilled contractual performance obligations. But standard setters as well as individual firms still have to grapple with the problem of when the various types of revenue transactions satisfy these criteria. To enhance consistency of practice, standard setters have established specific guidelines for the recognition of such diverse revenues as those from ordinary sales, from sales that bundle both goods and services, licensing agreements, and construction contracts.

The revenue-recognition issues facing governments are less amenable than those of businesses. Businesses derive their revenues mainly from exchange transactions—those in which each party gives and receives consideration of equivalent value. Governments (except those that engage primarily in business-type activities) derive their revenues mainly from nonexchange transactions—those in which one party gives or receives value without directly receiving or giving equivalent value in exchange.

GASB Statement No. 33, *Accounting and Financial Reporting for Nonexchange Transactions* (1998), governs the recognition of revenue under both the modified accrual basis (for governmental funds) and the full accrual basis (for proprietary and fiduciary funds and the government-wide statements). The recognition guidelines discussed in the next sections are the same for both bases. However, when accounted for under the modified accrual basis, revenues are subject to an additional, extremely significant, stipulation. They cannot be recognized until they are both *measurable and available to finance expenditures of the fiscal period.*

MEANING OF AND RATIONALE FOR "AVAILABLE TO FINANCE EXPENDITURES OF THE CURRENT PERIOD"

The nonexchange revenues of governments are intrinsically associated with expenditures; they are generated solely to meet expenditures. Budgets are formulated so that each period's estimated revenues are sufficient to cover appropriated expenditures. Expenditures of a current period may either require cash outlays during the period or create liabilities that must be satisfied shortly after the end of the period. For example, goods or services that a government receives toward the end of one year would ordinarily not be required to be paid for until early the next year. *Available* therefore means "collected" within the current period or "expected to be collected soon enough thereafter to be used to pay liabilities of the current period."[1]

Business accounting principles dictate that the collection of cash must be probable before revenue can be recognized. The "available" stipulation ensures that, in addition, the cash has been collected or will be collected soon enough to pay the liabilities they are intended to cover.

The liabilities that the revenues may be used to pay are only *current liabilities*. Recall that long-term liabilities are outside the measurement focus of governmental funds and hence are not recorded by them. As discussed in the following chapter, under the modified accrual basis of accounting, transactions that result in long-term liabilities are not recorded as expenditures.

How many days after the close of the year must revenues be received to satisfy the criteria of having been received soon enough to pay the liabilities of the current period? With respect to *property taxes*—and only property taxes—existing standards provide that, in the absence of unusual circumstances, revenues should be recognized only if cash is expected to be collected within *60 days* of year-end.[2]

[1] GASB Statement No. 33, *Accounting and Reporting for Nonexchange Transactions* (December 1998), n. 16.

[2] GASB Interpretation No. 5, *Property Tax Revenue Recognition in Governmental Funds* (November 1997).

Because existing standards provide no specific guidance as to time periods for recognition of other revenues, this "60-day rule" has become a widely used benchmark for all types of revenues, not just property taxes. However, many governments have established other time periods—30 days, 90 days, or even one year—for revenues other than property taxes.

WHAT ARE THE MAIN TYPES OF NONEXCHANGE REVENUES AND THE LIMITATIONS ON HOW AND WHEN THEY CAN BE USED?

GASB Statement No. 33, *Accounting and Financial Reporting for Nonexchange Transactions*, defines nonexchange transactions as those in which the government receives value without directly giving equal value in return. There are four types of nonexchange transactions.

1. ***Imposed nonexchange revenues.*** These are assessments imposed on individuals and business entities. The most prominent of these are property taxes and fines and are recognized in the year for which they are levied.

2. ***Derived tax revenues.*** These are taxes derived (i.e., that result) from assessments on exchange transactions carried on by taxpayers. They include sales taxes (derived from sales transactions) and income and other taxes on earnings or assets (derived from various income-producing commercial transactions) and are recognized in the period in which the income is earned.

3. ***Government-mandated nonexchange transactions.*** These occur when a government at one level (e.g., the federal or a state government) provides resources to a government at another level (e.g., a local government or school district) and requires the recipient to use the resources for a specific purpose. For example, a state may grant funds to a county stipulating that the resources be used for road improvements. Acceptance and use of the resources are mandatory and are recognized when all eligibility requirements are met.

4. ***Voluntary nonexchange transactions.*** These result from legislative or contractual agreements entered into willingly by two or more parties. They include grants given by one government to another and contributions from individuals (e.g., gifts to public universities). Often the provider imposes eligibility requirements or restrictions as to how the funds may be used. These types of transactions are similar to the government-mandated nonexchange transactions but differ in that the recipient government is not required to accept the awards. However, if the government accepts the awards it must observe the accompanying requirements on how they may be spent. Like the government-mandated nonexchange transactions, they too are recognized when all eligibility requirements are met.

Statement No. 33 establishes standards, discussed in the next sections, for each of the four types of transactions. The standards for government-mandated and voluntary nonexchange transactions apply to both revenues and expenditures. Thus, payments from one government to another are expected to be accounted for symmetrically.

Statement No. 33 also identifies two types of limitations that constrain when and how a government may use the resources it receives in nonexchange transactions:

1. ***Time requirements.*** These specify the period during which resources must be used or when use may begin. For example, local governments typically levy property taxes designated for a particular fiscal year. Similarly, state governments that grant funds to local school districts may require that the funds be used during the state's fiscal year.

2. ***Purpose restrictions.*** These specify the purpose for which the resources must be used. For example, certain sales taxes must be used for road improvements, certain property taxes must be used to repay debt, and certain grants or private donations must be used to acquire specific goods or services.

As noted in the discussions of the various types of revenues, governments should not recognize revenue or expenditures on nonexchange transactions until time requirements have been met (e.g., until the start of the specific time period during which resources may be used). By contrast, however, they need not delay recognition of revenue until they have satisfied the purpose restrictions. Nevertheless, they must specifically identify resources that are subject to purpose restrictions by appropriately classifying a portion of the fund balance in the general fund financial statements as restricted or by reporting the revenues in a special revenue fund. In government-wide statements they would identify restricted resources by denoting a portion of net position as "restricted." These requirements continue in force until the restricted amounts are spent for the purposes specified.

HOW SHOULD PROPERTY TAXES AND OTHER IMPOSED NONEXCHANGE REVENUES BE ACCOUNTED FOR?

Property taxes are the bread and butter of local governments. Although gradually being supplemented by other taxes and fees, they still account for approximately 27 percent of local government revenues (see Figure in Chapter 1).

Classified as *ad valorem taxes* (based on value), property taxes are most typically levied against real property (land and buildings). However, some jurisdictions also include within the tax base personal property—such as automobiles, boats, and business inventories—and intangible assets, such as securities and bank deposits.

Property taxes are levied against the assessed value of taxable assets. Most jurisdictions are required to assess (i.e., assign a taxable value to) property at 100 percent of its appraised fair market value. Many, however, assess property as a fraction of appraised value (perhaps in the hope of discouraging taxpayer protests) and then adjust the tax rate upward to offset the reduction in tax base.

IN PRACTICE — NATURAL DISASTERS RAISE NEW PROBLEMS FOR ACCOUNTANTS AND AUDITORS

Hurricane Harvey, which battered the Texas coast in 2017, continues to affect the finances of both state and local governments, creating challenges not only for government officials charged with maintaining essential services but also for their accountants and auditors. The $65 billion in housing and commercial damage caused property values, and hence property tax revenues, to plummet. In Texas, property taxes are the top source of revenue for local governments and especially for school districts. For accountants and auditors, this means that previous guidelines for preparing budgets and estimating the allowances for uncollectible taxes were, in effect, carried out with the winds of the storm.

The issues faced by accountants and auditors in Texas are nothing new to their counterparts in Florida and other states in which local governments rely heavily on property taxes and have been hit by major storms. For example, following Hurricane Katrina in 2005, property tax collections in New Orleans dropped 17 percent and did not rebound until five years later. The storm forced the city to dismiss thousands of teachers and other city workers and resulted in increased borrowing costs following a downgrade in the city's credit rating.

Governments establish the property tax rate by dividing the amount of revenue that it needs to collect from the tax by the assessed value of the property subject to tax. For example, if a government needs $400 million in tax revenue and its jurisdiction has $22 billion in taxable property, then the tax rate would be the $400 million in needed revenue divided by the $22 billion in taxable property—1.818 percent, or 18.18 *mils* (dollars per thousand).

In reality, the computation is somewhat more complex, as allowances must be made for discounts, exemptions, and taxes that will be delinquent or uncollectible. Most jurisdictions experience a relatively low rate of bad debts on property taxes because they are able to impose a **lien** (right to seize and sell) on the taxed property. However, it may take several years before the government is actually able either to collect from a property owner or to seize and sell the property.

Many jurisdictions grant discounts for early payment. For example, taxpayers may be given discounts of 3 percent, 2 percent, or 1 percent for paying, respectively, three months, two months, or one month prior to the due date. If they pay after the due date, taxpayers are generally subject to both interest and penalties.

Not all properties within a jurisdiction is subject to tax. Property held by other governments and by religious institutions is ordinarily exempt. In addition, many jurisdictions grant *homestead* exemptions to homeowners on their primary residences. These exemptions include both basic allowances—often of a fixed dollar amount (e.g., $5,000)—that are available to all taxpayers, and supplementary amounts granted to senior citizens and members of other designated classes. Thus, if a residence was assessed at $200,000 and the homeowner was granted a $5,000 exemption, the property's net assessed value would be $195,000. If the tax rate were 18.18 mils, the tax would be $195,000 multiplied by 0.01818, or $3,545.

SIGNIFICANT EVENTS IN THE REVENUE GENERATION PROCESS

Several events in the property tax timeline have potential accounting significance:

- The legislative body levies the tax, establishing the tax rate and estimating the total amount to be collected.
- Administrative departments determine the amount due from the individual property owners, enter the amounts on the *tax roll* (a subsidiary ledger that supports the taxes receivable control account), and send tax notices (bills) to property owners.
- The taxes are collected—most prior to the due date, some afterward.
- The taxes are due, and the government has the right to impose a lien on that property for which taxes have not been paid.

The *stated* due date must be distinguished from the *substantive* due date. Some jurisdictions establish a due date but do not impose interest, penalties, or a lien until a later date. The substantive due date is that date on which interest and penalties begin to accrue or a lien is imposed.

The question facing governments concerns which of the events is sufficiently significant to warrant revenue recognition, subject (on the fund statements) to the "available" constraint.

In this and subsequent chapters, we spotlight accounting issues by placing them within the context of short examples. We prepare journal entries to emphasize the impact of the possible options on both the statement of operations and the balance sheet. In many of the examples, a single entry may be used to summarize what would be in practice many individual entries. The illustrated entry is intended to show the impact of the described events on the year-end financial statements. In most of the examples, we assume, for convenience that the entity's fiscal year ends on December 31, even though the fiscal year of most governments ends on the last day of June, July, August, September, or October.

Example

Property Taxes

In October 2019, a city levies property taxes of $515 million for the year beginning January 1, 2020. During 2020, it collects $410 million. It collects $30 million of the remaining 2020 taxes during each of the first three months of 2021 and estimates that the $15 million balance will be uncollectible.

In addition, in 2020, it collects $20 million in taxes applicable to 2021. Taxes are due on January 31 of each year, and the government has the right to impose a lien on the taxed property if it has not received payment by that date.

GASB STANDARDS

Governments should recognize *assets* from property taxes and other imposed nonexchange transactions in the period during which they first have an enforceable claim to the assets or when they first receive the assets, whichever comes first. For property taxes, the date when they have an enforceable claim is specified in the legislation authorizing or imposing the tax and is frequently referred to as the lien date.

Governments should recognize *revenues* from property taxes *in the period for which the taxes are levied.* As a consequence of this provision, governments must delay recognition of taxes collected in advance until the period for which they have been budgeted, thereby satisfying the relevant time requirement. In addition, in their fund statements, the taxes must be "available"—that is, "collected within the current period or expected to be collected soon enough thereafter to be used to pay liabilities of the current period. Such time thereafter shall not exceed sixty days."[3]

GASB Statement No. 65, *Reporting Items Previously Recognized as Assets and Liabilities* (2012), requires that when an asset is recorded in governmental fund financial statements, but the revenue is not available, the government should report a deferred inflow of resources until such time as the revenue becomes available. Thus, if property taxes satisfy the criteria for asset recognition before they satisfy those for revenue recognition (e.g., if they are collected prior to the period for which they are budgeted or they will not be collected in time to pay liabilities of the current period), then the government should debit an asset (e.g., "cash" or "property taxes receivable") and offset it with a credit to a deferred inflow of resources account (e.g., "taxes collected in advance" or "deferred property taxes [a deferred inflow of resources]").[4]

[3] GASB Interpretation No. 5, *Property Tax Revenue Recognition in Governmental Funds*, paras. 1 and 4, 1997.

[4] Per GASB Statement No. 65, *the use of the term deferred* should be limited to deferred outflows of resources or deferred inflows of resources.

In the property taxes example, therefore, the total amount of revenue to be recognized in 2020 on a modified accrual basis would be $470 million—the $410 million due and collected during the year and applicable to it, plus the $60 million collected in the first 60 days of the next year. The $30 million to be collected after 60 days would be recognized as a deferred inflow. These transactions would be summarized in the following entries for 2020:

Property taxes receivable (2020)	$515	
Property taxes (deferred inflow of resources)		$500
Allowance for uncollectible property taxes		15
To record the property tax levy for 2020		
Cash	$410	
Property taxes receivable (2020)		$410
To record the collection of property taxes in 2020		
Property taxes (deferred inflow of resources)	$410	
Property tax revenue		$410
To recognize revenue on the taxes collected		
Property taxes (deferred inflow of resources)	$60	
Property tax revenue		$60
To recognize revenue on the taxes to be received in the first 60 days of 2021		

(Because this entry would be made as of the year-end, it may appear to recognize only an estimate of the tax receipts collectible for the first 60 days of 2021. In reality, the government would record its actual collections. Few governments are able to close their books and prepare financial statements within 60 days of year-end. Therefore, by the time they close their books and prepare financial statements, they are able to determine exactly how much revenue from collections subsequent to year-end must be recognized.)[5]

Cash	$20	
Property taxes (deferred inflow of resources)		$20
To record collection of property taxes received in advance of the year to which they are applicable		

The taxes collected in advance are intended to cover 2021 expenditures. Hence, they should be recognized as revenue in 2021 and thereby matched with the expenditures.

At year-end, overdue taxes receivable should be reclassified as delinquent so they are not intermingled with the current receivables of the following year:

Property taxes receivable—delinquent (2021)	$105	
Property taxes receivable (2020)		$105
To reclassify uncollected taxes as delinquent		

This entry has no impact on revenues, expenditures, or governmental fund balances. It provides statement readers with additional information as to the status of property taxes receivable. An increase in delinquent property taxes relative to property tax revenues should serve as a warning of a possible economic downturn in the government's jurisdiction or of ineffective tax collection practices on the part of the government.

As the delinquent property taxes are collected, they would be recorded as follows:

Cash	$60	
Property taxes receivable—delinquent (2021)		$60
To record the tax collections of the first two months of 2021, which had been recognized as revenue of 2020		
Cash	$30	
Property taxes (deferred inflow of resources)	0	
Property taxes receivable—delinquent (2021)		$30
Property tax revenue (2021)		0
To record the tax collections of the third month of 2021, which had not been recognized as revenue of 2020		

Despite their powers to enforce their claims against recalcitrant taxpayers, governments are not always able to collect the full amount of tax levies. In some instances, seized property cannot be sold at prices sufficient to cover outstanding balances. In others, the costs of recovery would be inadequate to cover the expected yield, so the governments elect not to exercise all available legal options.

[5] In practice, governments may, at the start of the year to which the taxes are applicable, recognize as revenue (rather than a deferred inflow of resources) the full amount of taxes levied (less the amount estimated to be uncollectible). Then, at year-end they would debit revenues for the portion of the taxes estimated to be collected after the first 60 days of the following year, crediting the deferred inflow.

As a government writes off uncollectible taxes, it should offset the reduction in taxes receivable with a corresponding reduction in the allowance for uncollectibles. Thus, if the $15 million of taxes (now classified as delinquent) were written off:

Allowance for uncollectible property taxes (2021)	$15	
Property taxes receivable—delinquent (2021)		$15
To write off delinquent taxes		

This entry has no impact on revenues, expenditures, or governmental fund balance. The government gave substantive accounting recognition to the potential uncollectible taxes in the period in which it established the allowance for uncollectible taxes.

Governments may accrue interest charges and penalties on delinquent taxes as they impose them. However, on their fund statements they should recognize revenue only when it is measurable and available. Until those criteria are satisfied, they should offset interest and penalties receivable with a deferred inflow rather than revenue.

DIFFERENCES IN GOVERNMENT-WIDE STATEMENTS

The same general rules of revenue recognition apply to government-wide statements as they apply to fund statements, with the exception that the "available" criterion does not have to be satisfied. Thus, a government can recognize revenue from property taxes as soon as it has either (1) an enforceable claim to the property taxes or (2) collected the taxes (whichever comes first)—subject, of course, to the time requirement that the taxes not be recognized prior to the period for which they were budgeted.

In the example, the city could recognize $500 million in revenue—the $410 million actually collected during the year plus the entire $90 million that it expects to collect. The taxes to be recognized as revenue no longer have to be collected within 60 days of year-end. The following entry summarizes the 2020 activity pertaining to the 2020 taxes:

Cash	$410	
Property taxes receivable—delinquent (2020)	105	
Property tax revenue		$500
Allowance for uncollectible property taxes		15
To summarize 2020 property tax activity pertaining to 2020 taxes		

For most governments, the difference between the amount of property taxes recognized as revenues on the fund statements and the amount on the government-wide statements is relatively small. As long as the ratio of property taxes levied to property taxes collected remains fairly constant, the government-wide gains owing to the year-end accruals of taxes to be collected beyond the 60-day window will be offset by the losses attributable to the taxes collected in the current year but recognized as revenues in the previous year. However, the differences in the balance sheets will be more pronounced because the balance sheets will incorporate the full amount of the deferred inflows and thereby reduce fund balances.

It must be emphasized that the government-wide entries in this example and similar examples throughout the text are not ones that a government would actually make. Governments need not maintain two sets of books, one for fund statements and one for government-wide statements. Instead, governments typically maintain the accounts on a modified accrual basis, appropriate for the funds statements. Then, at year-end, they make the required adjusting entries using a multicolumn worksheet (or its electronic equivalent). Thus, because $470 million of revenue would be recognized under the modified accrual basis and $500 million would be recognized under the full accrual basis, the following entry would be appropriate:

Property taxes (deferred inflow)	$30	
Property tax revenue		$30
To convert from fund to government-wide statements		

Some governments opt to "sell" their delinquent tax receivables to a third party, such as a collection agency. Similarly, they may sell other anticipated cash receipts, such as those from tobacco settlements, mortgages, or student loans. The supposed sale may enable the governments to have access to the cash immediately and avoid the hassles of collection. An accounting issue may arise in circumstances when the supposed sale is, in economic substance, not a sale at all but rather a collateralized borrowing arrangement. Assume that a city places a lien on a building owing to the failure of its owner to pay property taxes. The city "sells" the lien to a third party in exchange for cash. Per agreement between the two parties, the government will assist in collecting the delinquent taxes and retains the right to substitute different liens for the one transferred to the third party. Further, the lien is transferred "with recourse"—that is, if the third party is unable to collect on the lien, then it can "sell" it back to the government. In this instance, the arrangement is less a sale than a loan. GASB Statement No. 48, *Sales and Pledges of Receivables and Future Revenues and Intra-Entity Transfers of Assets and Future Revenues*, sets forth criteria for distinguishing between sales and borrowing arrangements. The key criterion is that in a sale, the government will have no continuing involvement with the receivable or with future revenues.

FINES: KEY DATES AND EVENTS

The other main type of imposed nonexchange revenues is fines. Although the question of when a government should recognize its revenues from fines is not typically important in terms of dollar amount, it is nevertheless provocative. Consider the several dates and events relating to parking tickets and other traffic violations:

- Tickets are issued; from historical experience, the government can estimate the percentage of tickets that will actually be paid.
- Violators must either pay or protest the fines by specified dates; if they do not protest, the government has a legal claim to the basic fines plus penalties for late payment.
- For ticketed parties who opt to protest, hearings are scheduled and held; if a party is found guilty, the government has a legal claim to the basic fine plus penalties for late payment.

Example

Fines

In November 2020, police issued $200,000 in parking tickets. Of the fines assessed, $130,000 are paid without protest by the due date of December 31, 2020. Of the balance, $4,000 have been protested and are subject to hearings. The government estimates that an additional $18,000 will trickle in but will not be available for expenditure in 2020. The balance of $48,000 will be uncollectible.

The government should record the $18,000 of fines—those that have been included among the assets—as a deferred inflow of resources because, as noted previously in the discussion of property taxes, GASB Statement No. 65, *Items Previously Reported as Assets and Liabilities*, requires that when a government recognizes an asset, but the revenue is not yet available, such asset should be offset by a deferred inflow of resources account.

GASB STANDARDS

The GASB standards direct that both the assets and the revenues from fines, penalties, and most other imposed nonexchange transactions be recognized when the government has an enforceable legal claim to the assets to be received or has collected the cash. Most commonly, a government has a legal claim to a fine only after the protest period expires (typically, on the payment due date) or if a court imposes a penalty. However, in the fund statements, revenue recognition is, of course, also subject to the "measurable and available" stipulation.

Hence, in its fund statements, the government should recognize as revenue only the $130,000 actually received during the year—the only amount on which the government has a legal claim and which will be collected in time to satisfy liabilities of the current period. The government can recognize neither an asset nor revenue on the $4,000 in tickets under protest because it has no enforceable claim on the alleged violators unless and until the courts eventually rule in its favor. The following entry would be appropriate:

Cash	$130,000	
Parking tickets receivable (not protested)	66,000	
Revenue from parking fines		$130,000
Parking fines (deferred inflow of resources)		18,000
Allowance for uncollectible parking tickets		48,000

To summarize 2020 activity related to November tickets

DIFFERENCES IN GOVERNMENT-WIDE STATEMENTS

In the government-wide statements, revenue recognition is not subject to the "available" test. Therefore, both the fines that have been collected and those expected to be collected, for which the government has an enforceable legal claim, may be recognized as revenue:

Cash	$130,000	
Parking tickets receivable (not protested)	66,000	
Revenue from parking fines		$148,000
Allowance for uncollectible parking tickets		48,000

To summarize 2020 activity related to November tickets

HOW SHOULD SALES TAXES AND OTHER DERIVED TAX REVENUES BE ACCOUNTED FOR?

Sales taxes, along with income taxes, are categorized as *derived tax revenues*. They are derived from exchange transactions, such as the sale of goods or services, or other income-producing commercial transactions.

Sales taxes are imposed on customers who purchase goods or services. The merchant providing the goods or services is responsible for collecting, reporting, and transmitting the taxes. Unlike property taxes, which are government assessed, sales taxes are taxpayer assessed; the tax base is determined by parties other than the beneficiary government. Thus, the government must wait for, and rely on, merchant tax returns to become aware of the proceeds to which it is legally entitled.

SIGNIFICANT EVENTS IN THE "EARNINGS PROCESS"

Three significant dates underlie sales tax transactions:

- The date of the sales transaction and the collection of the tax by the merchant

- The date the merchant is required to file the tax return and transmit the taxes (generally the same)
- The date the merchant actually files the return and transmits the taxes

The date of the sale is arguably the most significant of the three dates because the transaction producing the tax takes place then, the amount of the tax is established, and the liability of the merchant to transmit the tax is created. However, the government is not entitled to the tax until the date the return is to be filed and the tax paid. Moreover, except for unusual circumstances, such as when a merchant files a return but fails to make timely payment, the government does not know what the amount will be until it actually receives the tax.

Example

Sales Taxes

In December 2020, merchants collect $20 million in sales taxes. Of these, $12 million is collected prior to December 15 and must be remitted by February 15, 2021; the remaining $8 million must be remitted by March 15, 2021.

GASB STANDARDS

Current standards, as set forth in GASB Statement No. 33, require that revenues from sales taxes and other derived nonexchange revenues be recognized at the time the underlying exchange transaction takes place. For sales taxes, this would be the date of the sale.

In the fund statements, the sales taxes must also satisfy the "available" test to be recognized as revenue. Neither GASB Statement No. 33 nor other official pronouncements provide guidance as to the length of the period after the close of the fiscal year in which resources must be received to be considered available. As noted previously, the "60-day rule" applies only to property taxes, not to other revenues. Hence, governments must exercise their own judgment as to what constitutes "available." At the very least, they must ensure consistency of practice from one year to the next.

The standards also stipulate that governments should recognize assets from derived nonexchange transactions in the period in which the underlying transaction takes place. Thus, a government should recognize an asset—sales taxes receivable—on taxes derived from sales of the current year even if the taxes will not be collected in time to be available to meet the current liabilities of that year.

Assuming that the government adopts 60 days as the "available" criterion, then it could recognize as revenue of 2020 only the $12 million in taxes that it expects to collect within 60 days of year-end. The $8 million balance must be deferred until 2021:

Sales taxes receivable	$20	
Sales tax revenue		$12
Sales taxes (deferred inflow of resources)		8
To summarize December sales tax activity		

Suppose instead that the sales taxes were imposed only on motor fuels and had to be used to construct and maintain roads. Would this purpose restriction affect the recognition of revenue?

Inasmuch as the revenues were now restricted, they should properly be reported in a special revenue fund rather than in the general fund. Special revenue funds, like the general fund, are governmental funds. The GASB rules (and the discussion in this and the following chapter on expenditures) apply uniformly to all governmental funds. Per GASB Statement No. 33, purpose restrictions should not affect the timing of revenue recognition. If the underlying transaction has taken place and the resources are measurable and available, then the government has benefited from an increase in net assets and, according to the GASB, it should recognize this increase.

DIFFERENCES IN GOVERNMENT-WIDE STATEMENTS

The same general principles of revenue recognition apply to both the fund and the government-wide statements, with the exception that under the government-wide (full accrual) statements, the "available" criterion is inapplicable. Hence, in the example, the government should recognize the entire $20 million of taxes derived from the sales of December:

Sales taxes receivable	$20	
Sales tax revenue		$20

To summarize December sales tax activity

The government-wide statements consolidate the governmental funds, so that if the taxes were subject to a purpose restriction, they would not automatically be shown separately from unrestricted resources. To make the distinction between restricted and unrestricted resources, the GASB directs that until the resources are expended for the designated purpose, the resultant net position should be shown on the government-wide balance sheet as restricted.

SALES TAXES COLLECTED BY ANOTHER GOVERNMENT

Sales taxes are levied by both state and local governments. However, to avoid duplication of effort, most states collect and administer the sales taxes imposed by their local governments. For example, a state may impose a 5 percent sales tax, allowing local governments to add an additional 2 percent tax on sales within their jurisdictions. The state will collect the entire 7 percent tax, acting as an agent for the local governments with respect to their 2 percent.

The issue facing local governments is whether they can properly recognize revenue as soon as the state satisfies the recognition criteria or whether they must delay recognition until a later date—either when the state notifies them of the amount collected on their behalf or when it actually transmits the tax to them.

Example

Sales Taxes Collected by State

Assume a slight variation of the previous example. In November and December 2020, merchants collect $20 million in sales taxes. Of these, $5 million is remitted to the state as due by December 15, 2020; the remaining $15 million is due on January 15, 2021. The state remits the taxes to the city 30 days after it receives them.

GASB STANDARDS

The GASB standards do not differentiate between taxes collected by the government itself and those collected by another government on its behalf. The critical date remains the same—that of the underlying sales transaction. Thus, the city should recognize revenue as if it had received the taxes directly, as long as they will be received in time to meet the "available" criterion.

In this example, the city should recognize as revenue for 2020 the entire $20 million in taxes collected by the state in both December 2020 and January 2021, all of which will be received by the city in time to satisfy 2020 obligations:

Sales taxes receivable	$20	
Sales tax revenue		$20

To summarize December sales tax activity

However, if it were the practice of the state to remit the taxes to the city 90 days after receipt—subsequent to when the city could use them to meet 2020 liabilities—then the city could recognize none of the taxes as 2020 revenue. It would have to report all as a deferred inflow of resources.

DIFFERENCES IN GOVERNMENT-WIDE STATEMENTS

Because the GASB standards do not distinguish between taxes collected by the government itself and those collected on its behalf by another government, the city should recognize the entire amount of December taxes, just as if it had collected them itself. The "available" criterion is inapplicable to the government-wide statements, so the date of anticipated collection is irrelevant.

Situations in which a state collects sales tax revenues on behalf of a local government must be distinguished from those in which the state imposes the tax but opts to share a designated portion of the tax revenues with local governments within its jurisdiction. In such situations, the local government should consider the amount it receives from the state as a grant and should recognize revenue as it would any comparable grants.

INCOME TAXES: THE COLLECTION PROCESS

Almost all states and a few major cities—such as New York, Philadelphia, and Detroit—impose taxes that are based on personal or corporate revenues or income. Some of these states impose what they call a "franchise" tax on businesses, but the tax is nevertheless based, at least in part, on gross revenues or net income.

Income taxes present especially vexatious issues of revenue recognition, owing to their multistage administrative processes. Consider the following:

- The tax is based on income of either a calendar year or a fiscal year elected by the taxpayer, but such year might not coincide with the government's fiscal year.
- Taxpayers are required to remit tax payments throughout the tax year, either through payroll withholdings or periodic payments of estimated amounts. Within three or four months after the close of the year, they are required to file a tax return in which they inform the government of the actual amount of tax owed. At that time, they are expected to make a final settlement with the government, by either paying additional taxes due or requesting a refund of overpayments. Thus, the taxes received by the government during the year may be more or less than the amount to which it is entitled.
- Governments review all tax returns for reasonableness and select a sample for audit. Moreover, some taxpayers are delinquent on their payments. Thus, taxes continue to trickle in for several years after the due date. Although governments can reliably estimate the amount of late collections based on historical experience, they may not have a legal claim to the taxes until taxpayers either file their returns or agree to the adjustments resulting from an audit.

Example

Income Taxes

A state is on a June 30 fiscal year. However, income taxes are based on taxpayer income during the calendar year ending December 31. Employers are required to withhold taxes from employees and remit the withheld taxes monthly, and individuals with significant nonsalary earnings are required to make quarterly estimated tax payments. By April 15 of the year following the end of the calendar year, taxpayers must file a tax return on which they either request a refund of overpayment or pay any remaining tax owed.

In its fiscal year ending June 30, 2020, the state collects $95 billion in income taxes for the calendar years 2019 and 2020. It refunds $15 billion of taxes based on the returns filed by April

15, 2020. As the result of audits of prior-year returns, the state bills taxpayers $10 billion for earlier calendar years; it collects $7 billion of this before its fiscal year-end and expects to eventually collect the entire remaining $3 billion.

GASB STANDARDS

Income taxes are derived from the transactions that produce the income. Therefore, in concept at least, governments should recognize the taxes as revenue during the period in which the income is earned. In practice, however, determining the amount of revenue attributable to income of a particular year is exceedingly difficult inasmuch as the government learns of actual earnings only when a taxpayer files a return or the government conducts its own audit. Moreover, the returns themselves cover a calendar year and therefore do not separate out income earned in each of the fiscal years. Therefore, in an illustration of how income taxes should be accounted for, the GASB suggests that governments base the amount of income to be recognized on the amount of withholding and estimated tax payments received during the year (adjusted for settlements and refunds when tax returns are actually filed)—in essence that they recognize revenue on a cash basis.

In the example, the state collects $102 billion in taxes ($95 billion for 2019 and 2020 and $7 billion for prior-year audits) and refunds $15 billion—a net collection of $87 billion. Hence on a cash basis (the pragmatic basis suggested by the GASB), the state would recognize $87 billion in revenue. The GASB does not specifically address how the amounts billed—here, the $3 billion still due from audited returns—should be accounted for, but there seems no reason why the state should not recognize them as assets. Thus:

Cash	$87	
Taxes billed but not collected (a receivable)	3	
Revenue from income taxes		$87
Income taxes (deferred inflow)		3

To recognize income taxes for the fiscal year ending June 30

In practice, several states recognize income tax revenue, not on a strict cash basis, but rather on one in which they adjust actual cash collections during the year for collections applicable to the current year but received within a specified period after the end of the year.

DIFFERENCES IN GOVERNMENT-WIDE STATEMENTS

The general standards for the government-wide full accrual statements are the same, with the exception that all taxes receivable can be recognized as revenue regardless of whether they will be available to meet current-year obligations. Thus, consistent with the general standards (although not specifically addressed by the GASB), the state could recognize as revenue both taxes actually collected and those expected to be collected. Thus (assuming that the collections based on prior-year audits had not yet been recognized as revenue):

Cash	$87	
Taxes billed but not collected (a receivable)	3	
Revenue from income taxes		$90

To recognize income taxes for the fiscal year ending June 30

WHAT ARE TAX ABATEMENTS AND WHY AND HOW MUST THEY BE DISCLOSED?

Tax abatements are reductions in taxes that result from an agreement between a government and a taxpayer, typically a corporation. The taxes reduced are usually property taxes, but they could be sales taxes or income taxes as well. Abatements are almost always granted by a government to stimulate economic development. They are commonly given to entice companies to locate a plant, store, or office within the government's jurisdiction, but are also granted to companies already within the jurisdiction as an incentive to expand their operations. Almost always, the abatements are accompanied by specific demands upon the recipient, such as to create a specific number of jobs. The abatements can be for all, or only a portion, of taxes owed; they can be for an unlimited period of time or for a specified number of years.

In granting an abatement, the government expects that the direct and immediate loss in taxes will, at least over time, increase revenues. This may be the result of an overall increase in economic activity (e.g., more jobs and thus more taxpayers in the community) or by other new businesses being attracted to the area. For example, a town may abate taxes of a shopping center, anticipating that other stores, restaurants, and even hotels will likely be enticed to locate nearby.

In economic substance tax abatements are a form of expenditures. Not requiring a company to pay taxes is economically the same as collecting its taxes and then issuing it a refund check. If a government followed this course, the collected amount would be reported as revenue and the refunded amount as an expenditure. By simply not collecting the tax, the government recognizes neither a revenue nor an expenditure but the impact on "the bottom line" is identical.

In Statement No. 77, *Tax Abatement Disclosures* (August 2015), the GASB does not require that government recognize both a revenue and expenditure for taxes abated. It does, however, mandate that governments make significant disclosures about the tax abatements. These include, but are not limited to:

- a brief description of tax abatement programs,
- the specific taxes being abated,
- the gross amount of the taxes that were reduced during the reporting period,
- the commitments made by recipients,
- the criteria that made the recipients eligible for the abatements,
- provisions for recapturing taxes if the recipient fails to meet its commitments.

Notably, the taxes of a government may be reduced by abatements entered into by other governments and over which it has no control. Thus, for example, a state may agree to abate all taxes of a company, including those that would be levied by counties, towns, and school districts within the state. Governments affected by abatements imposed upon them by other governments must also disclose those abatements, but can provide substantially less detail about them.

Tax abatements must be distinguished from **tax expenditures.** Tax expenditures, unlike tax abatements, do not result from a deal with a particular taxpayer. Rather, they are special provisions of the tax code that reduce the taxes any taxpayer than satisfies certain eligibility conditions. Thus, for example, many jurisdictions have provisions that cap the property taxes of senior citizens. Others tax agricultural land at rates lower than other forms of real property. Most states, exempt sales or selected goods or services from sales taxes. Tax expenditures, such as tax abatements, reduce governmental revenues and have the same impact on fund balances as direct expenditures. As will be noted in Chapter 17, the federal government is required to disclose in its annual report, the impact of tax expenditures on its tax collections. The GASB, however, places no such obligation on state and local governments.

HOW SHOULD GRANTS AND SIMILAR GOVERNMENT-MANDATED AND VOLUNTARY NONEXCHANGE REVENUES BE ACCOUNTED FOR?

State and local governments receive grants and similar forms of financial assistance from both other governments and private sources. Some grants are mandated by a higher-level government; the lower-level government has no choice but to accept them (as when the federal government requires states to undertake specified environmental cleanup efforts and provides the necessary resources for them to do so). Most, however, are voluntary; the government can choose not to accept the funds if it is unwilling to accept the attached conditions or to carry out the specific programs the grant is intended to finance.

Typical intergovernmental grants and similar nonexchange revenues include the following:

- ***Restricted grants***—These are payments intended for designated purposes, projects, or activities. The most common form of grants, they are usually made to reimburse specific types of expenditures. They may be either mandated or voluntary.
- ***Unrestricted grants***—These are payments that are unrestricted as to purpose, project, or activity.
- ***Contingent grants***—These are grants contingent upon a specified occurrence or action on the part of the recipient (e.g., the ability of the recipient to raise resources from other parties).
- ***Entitlements***—These are payments, usually from a higher-level government, to which a state or local government is automatically entitled in an amount determined by a specified formula. Entitlements are often designated for a broad functional activity, such as education.
- ***Shared revenues***—These are revenues raised by one government, such as a state, but shared on a predetermined basis with other governments, such as with cities.
- ***Payments in lieu of taxes***—These are amounts paid by one government to another in place of property taxes that it would otherwise be required to pay were it not a government and thereby tax-exempt. Such payments constitute an important source of revenue for governments that have within their jurisdiction a substantial amount of facilities of other governments. For example, the federal government, whose property is tax-exempt, may make payments to school districts in which military bases are located, to compensate for the cost of educating military dependents. Some large not-for-profits with significant property holdings make similar payments to governments.

Examples of voluntary nonexchange revenues from private (i.e., from nongovernment) sources include donations to school districts and universities, contributions of land from developers (often tied, at least indirectly, to a project they are undertaking), and gifts of collectible items to museums or cultural centers. Sometimes they take the form of endowments. Endowments are gifts that stipulate that the contribution must be invested, and only the income from the investments can be spent.

GASB STANDARDS

Recipients of grants, irrespective of whether the grants are mandatory or voluntary, should recognize both revenue and related receivables only when all eligibility requirements have been met (subject, of course, in the fund statements to the "availability" criterion). Resources received before the eligibility requirements have been met should be reported as deferred inflows of resources.

Reimbursement grants are generally considered to have an inherent eligibility requirement—the recipient is eligible for the grant only if and when it incurs allowable costs. Hence, recipients typically must recognize revenue from reimbursement grants during the period in which they make the expenditures for which they will be reimbursed.

Endowment contributions that stipulate that only the income from investing the contributions can be spent are subject to infinite time requirements. Does this mean that the recipients can never recognize revenue from the gift? No. The GASB makes an exception to the general rule that revenue from contributions cannot be recognized until all time requirements have been satisfied. Per GASB Statement No. 33, governments can recognize revenue from endowments and similar gifts in which the main benefit to the recipient is from the derived income, not the gift itself, as soon as they receive the gift. These revenues would most likely be recorded in a permanent fund. Similar rules apply to gifts of historical treasures and artworks that the recipient agrees it will hold rather than sell.

Example

Unrestricted Grant with Time Requirement

In October 2020, a school district is notified that, per legislatively approved formulas, the state awarded it $15 million in assistance. The funds, transmitted to the district in December 2020, may be used to supplement teachers' salaries, acquire equipment, and support educational enrichment programs. The funds can be used only in the year ending December 31, 2021.

The grant is unrestricted. The stipulation that the funds must be used to supplement teachers' salaries, acquire equipment, and support educational enrichment programs is not a purpose restriction. It is a requirement only in form, not in substance; the state demands nothing of the district that it would not otherwise do. However, the grant is subject to a time requirement—the resources must be used in 2021. Hence, the school district must defer recognizing grant revenue until 2021:

Cash	$15	
State grant (deferred inflow of resources)		$15
To record the receipt of state funds in 2020		
State grant (deferred inflow of resources)	$15	
Grant revenue		$15
To recognize grant revenue in 2021		

Example

Grant with Purpose Restriction

In October 2020, a school district is notified that, per legislatively approved formulas, the state granted it $15 million to enhance its technological capabilities. The funds, transmitted by the state in December 2020, must be used to acquire computers but may be spent at any time.

This grant is subject only to a purpose restriction. Purpose restrictions do not affect the timing of revenue recognition; the district should recognize the revenue as soon as the grant is announced. Nevertheless, owing to the purpose restriction, the district should record the grant in a special revenue fund, and in its government-wide statements it should report $15 million of its net position as "restricted to purchase of computers."

Cash	$15	
Grant revenue		$15
To recognize grant revenue (in a special revenue fund) in 2020		

Example

Reimbursement (Eligibility Requirement) Grant

In December 2020, a city is awarded a grant of $400,000 to train social workers. During December 2020, it spends $300,000 in allowable costs, for which it is reimbursed $250,000. It expects to be reimbursed for the $50,000 balance in January 2021 and to expend and be reimbursed for the remaining $100,000 of its grant throughout 2021. The city is subject to an eligibility requirement in that to be eligible for the grant it must first incur allowable costs.

In this example, the government can recognize the grant only as it incurs allowable costs. Thus, in 2020, it can recognize $300,000 in both revenue and increases in assets:

Expenditures to train social workers	$300,000	
Cash (or payables)		$300,000
To record allowable costs		
Cash	$250,000	
Grants receivable	50,000	
Grant revenue		$300,000
To recognize grant revenue		

Example

Unrestricted Grant with Contingency Eligibility Requirement

In January 2020, a private foundation agrees to match all private cash contributions up to $20 million received by a state-owned museum during its 2020–2021 fund drive. In 2020, the museum receives $14 million in private cash contributions.

The museum is eligible for the foundation's matching contribution only insofar as it receives funds from other sources. Thus, in 2020, it can recognize only $14 million of matching foundation revenue (in addition, of course, to the $14 million in private donations):

Grant receivable (foundation)	$14	
Grant revenue (foundation)		$14
To recognize $14 million of a foundation grant		

If the foundation will not actually make its contribution in time for the resources to be available to meet its 2020 current liabilities, then on its modified accrual fund statements the museum should recognize the grant as a deferred inflow of resources, rather than realized revenue.

Example

Endowment Gift

A private citizen donates $1 million to a city to maintain and repair historical monuments. He stipulates that the principal remain intact permanently and that only the income be used for the intended purpose.

Endowments that are intended to support a government's activities and thereby benefit the public are accounted for in a permanent fund, a type of governmental fund. Inasmuch as the gift is intended to provide an ongoing source of income, the city should recognize the $1 million as revenue upon receipt. In its government-wide statements, however, it should show $1 million of its assets as restricted and thereby unavailable for general expenditure.

Example

Pledges

A private citizen pledges $10,000 to a county-operated zoo. The government is confident that the promised donation will actually be made.

Governments should recognize revenue from pledges on the same basis as other grants—that is, as soon as they meet all eligibility requirements. Thus, if a government has to do nothing further to receive a donation (and the resources are probable of collection), it can recognize revenue at the time the pledge is made. However, in its fund statements, consistent with the "available" criterion, it must delay revenue recognition until the resources will be available to meet the current liabilities of the period. In effect, therefore, it would recognize a receivable (offset by a deferred inflow of resources) but must wait to recognize the revenue until the period in which the cash is to be received (or will be received within an appropriate number of days—perhaps 60—60 days thereafter).

Example

Payments in Lieu of Taxes

The federal government has an agreement with a local government to pay a $5 million annual PILOT. The federal government makes the payment at the start of fiscal year 2021, resulting in the local government recording in both the governmental funds and the government-wide financial statements:

Cash	$5	
PILOT (revenue)		$5
To recognize PILOT payment from federal government		

If the PILOT was not derived from an external entity, the treatment would be different. Suppose a local government received $5 million PILOT from a local enterprise fund, and this amount is based on the assessed valuation of the property owned (and, therefore, exempted) by the enterprise fund:

Cash	$5	
Interfund transfer (other financing sources)		$5
To recognize PILOT payment from enterprise fund		

Paragraph 112b of GASB Statement 34 requires that such internal PILOTs be reported as transfers rather than interfund services provided and used. Even though the PILOT is calculated similarly to a tax, it still is not an exchange and, hence, not a revenue.

DIFFERENCES IN GOVERNMENT-WIDE STATEMENTS

The general standards for recognition of grant revenues are the same for full accrual government-wide statements as for modified accrual fund statements. As emphasized with respect to other revenues, however, recognition under the modified accrual basis is subject to the "available" test, whereas under the full accrual basis it is not.

ACCOUNTING FOR GIFTS OF CAPITAL ASSETS

Gifts of capital assets present an especially intriguing accounting issue, mainly because capital assets are not typically reported in governmental funds. Donated capital assets, current standards make clear, should be recorded in either the fund to which they relate if such fund is a proprietary fund or in the schedule of capital assets if such fund is a governmental fund. Are there instances, however, in which donated capital assets can properly be recorded in a governmental fund?

Example

Donations of Land for Differing Purposes

A builder donates two parcels of land to a city. Each has a fair value of $4 million. The city intends to use one as a park and to sell the other.

In current practice, capital assets intended for use cannot be recorded in a governmental fund as assets; correspondingly, donations of capital assets cannot be recognized as revenue. The donated assets should be recorded in the schedule of capital assets. Thus, the land intended as a park would not be recorded in either the general fund or any other governmental fund. It would be recorded only in the schedule of capital assets and in the government-wide statement of net position.

By contrast, capital assets held for sale are unlike capital assets held for use. From the perspective of the recipient government, they are the equivalent of marketable securities or other short-term investments. They are expected to be transformed soon into cash. Arguably, therefore, capital assets intended to be sold should be recorded in governmental funds (such as the general fund or a capital projects fund), and donations of these assets should be recognized as revenues. Nevertheless, the Government Finance Officers Association (GFOA) recommends that for governmental funds such as the general fund, the government should report the asset on year-end financial statements only if it has actually succeeded in selling the asset by the time it issues those statements. If the government sells the asset after year-end but within the availability period (e.g., within 60 days), then it would recognize revenue from the gift. Thus, it would make the following entry:

Land held for sale	$4	
Revenue from donations		$4
To record a gift of land that the city sold within the availability period		

If, however, the city sold the land after the availability period but before it issued the financial statements, then it would recognize the land as an asset but defer the recognition of revenue. Thus:

Land held for sale	$4	
Donated land (deferred inflow of assets)		$4
To record a gift of land that the city sold after the availability period but prior to the issuance of financial statements		

If, by contrast, the city failed to sell the land by the time it issued the financial statements, then in a government fund it would not recognize the asset and not recognize either revenue or a deferred inflow of resources. The rationale for this position is that there is no arm's-length transaction with a third party to provide objective evidence of the land's value.[6]

Governments may report capital assets in their governmental funds for other reasons as well. For example, they may foreclose on properties because the owners failed to meet tax obligations. Almost always the governments intend to sell, rather than keep, these properties. Normally they would value them at the lower of the properties' liens or the anticipated net realizable values.

DIFFERENCES IN GOVERNMENT-WIDE STATEMENTS

The GFOA takes a different (some may contend inconsistent) position with respect to government-wide statements. In government-wide, full accrual statements, it recommends that the government should account for the donation of capital assets just as it would a donation of any other type of asset. The government should recognize both the revenue and the property received, irrespective of whether and when the land was sold. If the land is not sold by the time the financial statements are issued, then the government should estimate its value. Presumably, inasmuch as the government-wide statement of net position, but not a governmental fund balance sheet, already includes other capital assets, the impact of any error in the estimated value of the donated asset would be relatively small.

ACCOUNTING FOR PASS-THROUGH GRANTS

Some types of grants—those for which the recipient is required to distribute the resources to other parties or for which payment is made directly to a third party for the benefit of the recipient—raise

[6] This recommendation is based on Stephen J. Gautier, *Governmental Accounting, Auditing, and Financial Reporting* (Chicago: Government Finance Officers Association, 2012), 174. This position is consistent with guidance provided by the GASB in Statement No. 11, *Measurement Focus and Basis of Accounting—Government Fund Operating Statements*, para. 11. We say "consistent with" rather than "per" Statement No. 11 because Statement No. 11 was never implemented and hence is not authoritative.

the additional question of whether the grant should even be recognized by the recipient government. Suppose that a state receives federal funds earmarked for each of its local school districts. Should the state record the receipt of the funds as revenues and the disbursement as expenditures? Or alternatively, should it omit the grant from both its budget and its accounts on the grounds that, with regard to these funds, it is nothing more than an agent of the federal government?

Grants that a government must transfer to, or spend on behalf of, a secondary recipient, are referred to as **pass-through grants**. Pass-through grants vary in the extent of responsibility they impose on the primary recipient. For example, a state may receive federal funds over which it has no discretion in determining how, or in what amounts, they can be disbursed. Once it distributes the funds, it may have no responsibility for monitoring how they are spent. At the other extreme, a state may be permitted to distribute federal funds within broad guidelines, and it may be held accountable for ensuring that the funds are used in accordance with federal specifications.

In the past, some governments opted to exclude pass-through funds from both their revenues and their expenditures. Perhaps wanting to show that they held the line on spending, they accounted for the funds "off the budget"—often in agency funds in which only assets and liabilities are reported.

To reduce diversity of practice, in 1994, the GASB stated that "as a general rule, cash pass-through grants should be recognized as revenue and expenditures or expenses in governmental, proprietary, or trust funds."[7] Only in those "infrequent cases" in which the government serves as a "cash conduit" may pass-through grants be reported in an agency fund. A government serves as a "cash conduit," the GASB explains, if it "merely transmits grantor-supplied moneys without having 'administrative involvement.'" *Administrative involvement* would be indicated if the government selected the secondary recipients of the funds (even based on grant or established criteria) or monitored compliance with grant requirements.

ACCOUNTING FOR FOOD STAMPS

The Supplemental Nutrition Assistance Program (SNAP), formerly known as the federal food stamp program, is a form of pass-through assistance. The federal government gives the "stamps" to the states, which distribute them in accord with specified guidelines. Most commonly, the stamps are nothing more than a credit to an account maintained for each state. Until 1994, many governments gave no accounting recognition to food stamps. Then, in its pronouncement on pass-through grants, the GASB asserted that food stamps received and distributed should be recognized as both a revenue and an expenditure.[8]

Today, food stamps are most commonly distributed to recipients electronically, usually in the form of a debit card or equivalent. When a recipient presents the card to a merchant, the state automatically recognizes both an expenditure (the disbursement of the funds to the merchant) and an offsetting revenue (the receipt of the funds from the federal government). Correspondingly, the federal government debits the account of the state.

ACCOUNTING FOR ON-BEHALF PAYMENTS

In the multigovernment system of the United States, one government may make payments for employee fringe benefits "on behalf" of (i.e., for the direct benefit of) another. For example, a state may contribute to a pension plan for schoolteachers on behalf of the independent school districts that employ the teachers.

The key issue concerning **on-behalf payments** is whether and in what circumstances the recipient government should recognize the payments as if it had received and then spent a cash

---

[7] GASB Statement No. 24, *Accounting and Financial Reporting for Certain Grants and Other Financial Assistance* (1994), para. 5.

[8] Ibid., para. 6.

grant—that is, whether it should recognize a revenue and an offsetting expenditure, or give no recognition at all to the transactions.

As with so many other accounting issues, the challenges of standard setting are compounded by the variety of forms that a transaction can take. Some state on-behalf payments, for example, are made in lieu of health insurance or other compensation that the recipient local government would otherwise have been required by state law to provide on its own. Other payments are made by the state to cover programs or activities in which the local government would otherwise not engage. Some accountants believe that recipient governments should recognize only the on-behalf payments that cover costs for which they are legally responsible.

Example

On-Behalf Payments

In a particular year, a state government elects to subsidize teachers' health insurance benefits. It contributes $3 million to the state's health insurance plan on behalf of an independent school district.

GASB STANDARDS

The GASB ruled, as another part of its grants project, that the recipient government should recognize both revenue and corresponding expenditures for *all* on-behalf payments of fringe benefits and salaries. Despite the objections of two of its five members, it required recognition irrespective of whether or not the beneficiary government was legally responsible for the payments.[9]

The school district would make the following entry:

Health insurance expenditures	$3	
State aid—insurance premiums (revenue)		$3
To record the on-behalf insurance premiums paid by the state		

Correspondingly, the state would also record an expenditure:

State aid to school districts (expenditure)	$3	
Cash		$3
To record the insurance premiums paid on behalf of an independent school district		

A paying government should classify its on-behalf payments in the same manner as similar cash grants to other entities. For example, if it classifies other educational grants as educational expenditures, then it should classify the payments for health insurance premiums as educational expenditures, not insurance expenditures.

HOW SHOULD SALES OF CAPITAL ASSETS BE ACCOUNTED FOR?

Governments sell capital assets for the same reasons businesses do—the services the assets impart can be provided more economically by another means or by replacement assets. The unique accounting problem faced by governments when they sell general capital assets is that the financial resources received are accounted for in a governmental fund, but the assets that are sold are not.

[9] Ibid., paras. 7–13.

Example

Sales of Capital Assets

On December 31, 2020, a city purchases a new police car for $40,000. On January 2, 2021, the vehicle is damaged in an accident. The vehicle is uninsured; the city is able to sell the nearly demolished vehicle for $5,000.

Current practice requires the following seemingly odd entry:

Cash	$5,000	
Other financing sources—sale of vehicle		$5,000
To record the sale of general capital assets		

The entry is "seemingly odd" because "other financing sources" are reported on a statement of revenues, expenditures, and other changes in fund balance (below the revenues and expenditures). Although not exactly revenue, it is similar to revenue in that it may be budgeted as revenue, and it results in an increase in fund balance.

From an accounting perspective, therefore, the accident that destroyed a $40,000 vehicle left the government $5,000 better off; that is, the governmental fund's assets and fund balance increased by $5,000. This outcome, while bizarre—and not suggestive of appropriate means by which governments should reduce their deficits—is inevitable when the measurement focus of governmental funds excludes capital assets. As indicated in Chapter 2, when governmental fund resources are used to acquire an asset, its cost is written off (i.e., charged as an expenditure) as it is paid for. Consequently, the police vehicle, which is clearly evident to most citizens, is invisible to the governmental fund's accountant.

Although this accounting outcome may seem bizarre, business accounting may produce a similar result. The capital assets of businesses are carried at historical cost less depreciation—amounts that may be considerably less than fair market values. Suppose that a vehicle owned by a business was destroyed in an accident and that the vehicle was insured for more than its book value. That accident, too, would cause the business to report a gain owing to the mishap.

Both businesses and governmental funds state their capital assets at amounts bearing little relationship to their economic worth. Whereas businesses carry them at historical cost less depreciation, governmental funds report them at zero.

DIFFERENCES IN GOVERNMENT-WIDE STATEMENTS

In their government-wide, full accrual statements, governments would report their capital assets just as businesses would. They would state them at historical cost less accumulated depreciation. Upon sale of an asset, they would recognize a gain or loss in the amount of the difference between sale proceeds and book value. Hence, in the example, assuming that no depreciation had yet been charged, the government would recognize a loss of $35,000—the difference between cost of $40,000 and the sale price of $5,000.

Like businesses, governments can take advantage of capital asset accounting to improve the look of their financial statements even in the absence of substantive fiscal improvement. Thus, in its government-wide statements a government can recognize a gain and a corresponding increase in net position by selling a capital asset having a market value greater than its book value. In its governmental fund statements it can report both "other financing sources" and a corresponding increase in fund balance by selling any capital asset, irrespective of the relationship between its book and market values.

HOW SHOULD LICENSES, PERMITS, AND OTHER EXCHANGE TRANSACTIONS BE ACCOUNTED FOR?

Governments issue licenses (or permits) that allow citizens and businesses to carry out regulated activities over a specified period of time. However, the license period may not coincide with the government's fiscal year.

The primary concern relating to licenses is whether the revenue should be recognized when a license is issued and cash is received (usually concurrently), or whether it should be spread out over the period covered by the license. In other words, is the significant economic event the collection of cash or is it the passage of time?

The issue is by no means clear-cut in light of the following characteristics of licenses:

- Some license fees are intended to cover the cost of services provided to the licensee or related to the activity in which the licensee engages. These license fees have the characteristics of exchange transactions. The licensee pays cash and receives value in exchange. For example, the funds generated from restaurant licenses may be used to inspect restaurants, thereby ensuring customers that the restaurants meet minimum standards of cleanliness. Similarly, bicycle registration fees may support bicycle safety programs. Other fees, however, may bear little relation to the cost of services provided and may be imposed mainly as a source of general revenue. They are more in the nature of nonexchange revenues.
- Generally, license fees are not refundable. Therefore, unless a license fee is tied to specific services, once the government receives the fee it has no further obligation—actual or contingent—to the licensee.

Example

License Fees

In June 2020, a city imposed license fees on barber and beauty shops for the first time. It collected $360,000. The fees are intended to cover the cost of health inspections. The licenses cover the one-year period from July 1 to June 30.

GASB STANDARDS

In Statement No. 33, the GASB acknowledged that license fees and permits are not always pure exchange transactions. They may not be paid voluntarily, and rarely is the amount paid reflective of the fair value of benefits received by the licensee. Still, the GASB maintains that they should be accounted for as if they were true exchange transactions. With respect to miscellaneous exchange transactions, the GASB standards state simply: "*Miscellaneous Revenues.* Golf and swimming fees, inspection charges, parking fees and parking meter receipts, and the vast multitude of miscellaneous exchange revenues are best recognized when cash is received." The following entry would therefore summarize the 2020 activity.[10]

Cash	$360,000	
Revenue from license fees		$360,000

To summarize 2020 license fee activity

This current standard was developed prior to the issuance of Statement No. 33 and (in that it recognizes miscellaneous revenues on a cash basis) is inconsistent with the accrual basis of accounting. The accrual basis would require that the fees be recognized over the period covered by the license (as when a business grants a licensee permission to use a patent or trademark). The current standard was developed as a pragmatic approach to recognizing revenues that for most governments are not of major consequence.

The spirit of Statement No. 34 suggests that in government-wide statements exchange revenues should be accounted for on an accrual basis, as they are in businesses. However, mainly because these miscellaneous types of revenue are not of great significance, the GASB has not definitively stated whether in their government-wide statements governments must accrue these revenues (the conceptually sound approach) or may account for them on a cash basis as they do in their fund statements (the pragmatic approach).

[10] NCGA Statement No. 1, *Governmental Accounting and Financial Reporting Principles* (1979), para. 67.

HOW SHOULD GOVERNMENTS REPORT REVENUES IN THEIR GOVERNMENT-WIDE STATEMENTS?

A primary objective of the government-wide statement of activities is to show the relative financial burden to the taxpayers of each function—the amount that has to be financed out of general revenues. As indicated in Chapter 2, the government-wide statement of activities reports the net expenses of each of the government's main functions. The net expenses of a function are its expenses less any revenues that can be directly attributable to it. As a consequence, governments must determine which revenues should be classified as program (function) revenues and which as general revenues. "General revenues" is the default classification; all revenues that cannot be classified as program revenues are considered general revenues.

As a rule, revenues from charges or fees imposed upon parties that benefit from specific activities are classified as program revenues; so are grants from other governments or outside parties that must be used for specific purposes. By contrast, taxes that are imposed upon the reporting government's citizens are considered general revenues, even if they are restricted to specific programs. Thus, a general sales tax would be classified as general revenue, even though it might be dedicated to education or road construction. Interest and other earnings from investments, as well as other nontax revenues, such as grants and contributions, would be counted as general revenues unless explicitly restricted for specific programs.

As illustrated in Chapter 2, Table 2-4, the government-wide statement of activities reports program-specific revenues in three separate columns and in as many rows as there are functions. The three columns are for:

- ***Charges for services***—These would include fees for services such as garbage collection, licenses and permits, and special assessments for roads or other capital projects.
- ***Program-specific operating grants and contributions***—These would include federal or state grants for specific operating purposes, such as law enforcement, education, and recreation.
- ***Program-specific capital grants***—These would include grants for the purchase and construction of long-term assets, such as for buses, jails, and roads.

Some government grants are for multiple purposes. If the amounts can be identified with specific programs (through either the grant application or the grant notification), they should be apportioned appropriately. If they cannot, they should be reported as general revenues.

SUMMARY

To better achieve two primary objectives of financial reporting—to provide information relating to interperiod equity and to demonstrate budgetary compliance—governments prepare two types of financial statements: fund and government-wide. The fund statements of governmental funds are on a modified accrual basis; the government-wide statements are on a full accrual basis.

Because the modified accrual statements focus on expendable financial resources, revenues must be available to pay liabilities of the current period before they can be recognized. The GASB has specified that property taxes can be considered "available" if they are collected during the year for which they are intended or within 60 days thereafter. Although the GASB leaves it to the judgment of individual governments to determine an appropriate number of days for other types of revenues, the "60-day rule" has become a widely accepted benchmark.

GASB Statement No. 33, *Accounting and Financial Reporting for Nonexchange Transactions*, provides guidance as to which events are most significant in the process of revenue generation and should therefore dictate the timing of revenue recognition. Nonexchange transactions are those in which one party gives or receives value without directly receiving or giving equivalent value in return.

Statement No. 33 is applicable to financial statements prepared on either the full accrual or the modified accrual basis. However, when reporting on the modified accrual basis, governments should recognize revenues only to the extent that they satisfy the "available" criterion. There is no difference between accrual and modified accrual accounting in the timing of recognition of assets, liabilities, or expenditures.

The revenue recognition guidelines set forth by the GASB in Statement No. 33, as well as other pronouncements, include the following:

- Property taxes, which are *imposed* revenues, should be recognized as revenues in the period for which they are levied. If they are collected in advance of the period for which they are intended, they should be accounted for as deferred inflows of resources. Governments should recognize revenues from fines and penalties—the other major type of imposed revenues—as soon as they either receive the assets or have an enforceable legal claim to them.
- Revenues that are *derived* from underlying exchange transactions should be recognized when the underlying transactions take place. Thus, sales taxes should be recognized in the period of sale. Income taxes should be recognized during the period in which the income is earned. However, if practical difficulties prevent them from determining when the income has been earned, governments may recognize income tax revenues in the period in which the taxes are collected (taking into account refunds and other adjustments).
- Tax abatements are reductions in taxes that result from an agreement between a government and a taxpayer, typically a corporation. The taxes reduced are usually property taxes, but they could be sales taxes or income taxes as well. Abatements are almost always granted by a government to stimulate economic development. Almost always, the abatements are accompanied by specific demands upon the recipient, such as to create a specific number of jobs. In granting an abatement, the government expects that the direct and immediate loss in taxes will, at least over time, increase revenues.
- Grants should be recognized when the government has satisfied all eligibility requirements. Grants that cannot be spent until a specific date are considered to be subject to time requirements and therefore should not be recognized until that date. To be eligible for reimbursement grants, governments must first incur the costs for which they are to be reimbursed. Hence, they should recognize receivables and revenues only as they make the related expenditures.
- Revenues from the sale of capital assets and from other exchange transactions are recognized during the period of the exchange. Because governments do not report capital assets in their governmental funds, the book value of the assets is zero. Therefore, in the fund statements, the gain from the sale of a capital asset is equal to the sale proceeds. In the government-wide statements, by contrast, governments account for their capital assets as do businesses. The gain or loss is equal to the difference between the sales proceeds and the adjusted book value (i.e., cost less accumulated depreciation).
- Revenues from most licenses and similar exchange transactions (even if not "pure" exchange transactions in that they may not involve exchanges of equal value) are generally recognized as cash is received (even if the benefits will be provided over more than one period), primarily for practical reasons.

Table 4-1 summarizes the principles of revenue and asset recognition as they apply to the main types of revenue-producing transactions in governmental funds.

TABLE 4-1 Summary of Asset and Revenue Recognition in Governmental Funds

Imposed nonexchange transactions (Examples: property taxes and fines)	*Revenue:* In the period in which the revenue is intended to be used *Asset:* When the government has an enforceable legal claim or when resources are received, whichever comes first
Derived taxes (Examples: sales taxes, income taxes, hotel taxes, and fuel taxes)	*Revenue:* In the period of the underlying transaction *Asset:* In the period of the underlying transaction or when resources are received, whichever comes first
Government-mandated nonexchange transactions (Example: a federal grant to pay for a required drug prevention program)	*Revenue:* When all eligibility requirements, including time requirements, have been met *Asset:* When all eligibility requirements have been met, or when resources are received, whichever comes first

(*Continues*)

TABLE 4-1 Summary of Asset and Revenue Recognition in Governmental Funds *(Continued)*

Voluntary nonexchange transactions (Examples: entitlements, federal grants for general education)	Same as for government-mandated nonexchange transactions
Exchange and "exchange-like" transactions (Examples: license fees, permits, and inspection charges)	*Revenue:* When cash is received *Asset:* When cash is received

Note: The above guidelines apply to both the government-wide (full accrual) and governmental fund (modified accrual) statements. However, in the fund (modified accrual) statements, revenues should be recognized no sooner than the period in which the resources to be received are measurable and available to satisfy liabilities of the current period.

KEY TERMS IN THIS CHAPTER

current financial resources 147
lien 150
on-behalf payments 167
pass-through grants 167
tax abatements 161

EXERCISE FOR REVIEW AND SELF-STUDY

The town of Malvern engages in the following transactions during its fiscal year ending September 30, 2021. All dollar amounts are in thousands. Prepare summary journal entries to reflect their impact on year-end fund financial statements prepared on a modified accrual basis. Base your entries on generally accepted accounting principles now in effect. In addition, indicate how your entries would differ if the statements were government-wide and prepared on a full accrual basis.

1. During fiscal 2021, the town levied property taxes of $154,000, of which it collected $120,000 prior to September 30, 2021, and $5,000 over each of the next six months. It estimated that $4,000 will be uncollectible.
2. On November 20, 2021, it received $12,000 from the state for sales taxes collected on its behalf. The payment was for sales made in September that merchants were required to remit to the state by October 15.
3. In April, the town was awarded a state training grant of $400 for the period June 1, 2021, through May 31, 2022. In fiscal 2021, the town received the entire $400 but spent only $320. Although the funds were received in advance, the city would have to return to the state any amounts that were not used to cover allowable training costs.
4. The town requires each vendor who sells at its farmers' market to obtain an annual permit. The funds generated by the sale of these permits are used to maintain the market. The permits, which cover the period from June 1 through May 31, are not refundable. In May 2021, the town issued $36 worth in permits.
5. Several years earlier the town received a donation of a parcel of land, upon which it expected to build. During fiscal 2021, it opted to sell the land for $135. When acquired by the town, the land had a market value of $119.

QUESTIONS FOR REVIEW AND DISCUSSION

1. Why is a choice of *basis of accounting* unavoidably linked to *measurement focus*?
2. What are the measurement focuses and basis of accounting of governmental funds? What is the traditional rationale for this basis of accounting (used in governmental fund statements)—as opposed to, for example, either a full accrual basis or a budgetary basis?
3. What is the difference between an *exchange* and a *nonexchange* transaction?

4. What are the main categories of revenues per GASB Statement No. 33, *Accounting and Financial Reporting for Nonexchange Transactions*?

5. What criteria must be met before revenues can be recognized on a modified accrual basis? What is the rationale for these criteria?

6. What is the general rule for recognizing property taxes as revenues? How would property taxes be accounted for differently in the fund statements, as opposed to in the government-wide statements?

7. What is meant by "deferred inflow of resources"? Provide an example of when a government might credit such an account.

8. What is the earliest point in the sales tax collection process that revenue may be recognized? How can you justify recognizing revenue on the basis of this event?

9. What special problems do governments face in measuring the income taxes associated with a particular year?

10. Explain tax abatements and how are they different from tax expenditures?

11. Explain the distinction between reimbursement grants and entitlements. How does this distinction affect the way each type of grant is accounted for?

12. A private citizen makes an unrestricted pledge of $5 million to a city's museum. The city is confident that the donor will fulfill her pledge. However, the cash will not be received for at least two years. How will the amount of revenue recognized differ between the fund statements and the government-wide statements? Explain.

13. What are pass-through grants? Under what circumstances must a recipient government report them as both a revenue and an expenditure?

14. A student comments: "A government destroys a recently acquired car, sells the remains for scrap, and its general fund surplus for the year increases. That's ridiculous. Government accounting makes so much less sense than private-sector accounting." Explain why the situation described by the student arises. Does government accounting in fact differ so much from business accounting?

EXERCISES

EX. 4-1

Select the *best* answer.

1. Under the modified accrual basis of accounting, revenues cannot be recognized
   - **a.** Until cash has been collected
   - **b.** Unless they will be collected within 60 days of year-end
   - **c.** Until they are subject to accrual
   - **d.** Until they are measurable and available

2. "Available" (as in "measurable and available") means
   - **a.** Available to finance expenditures of the current period
   - **b.** Subject to accrual
   - **c.** Collectible
   - **d.** Available for appropriation

3. Property taxes are an example of
   - **a.** An imposed exchange transaction
   - **b.** An imposed nonexchange transaction
   - **c.** A derived transaction
   - **d.** A government-mandated nonexchange transaction

4. To be considered "available," property taxes must have been collected either during the government's fiscal year or within
   a. The time it takes for the government to liquidate its obligations from the prior year
   b. Thirty days of year-end
   c. Sixty days of year-end
   d. The following fiscal year

5. For its fiscal year ending September 30, 2020, Twin City levied $500 million in property taxes. It collected taxes applicable to fiscal 2020 as follows (in millions):

June 1, 2019, through September 30, 2019	$20
October 1, 2019, through September 30, 2020	$440
October 1, 2020, through November 30, 2020	$15
December 2020	$4

   The city estimates that $10 million of the outstanding balance will be uncollectible. For the fiscal year ending September 30, 2020, how much should Twin City recognize in property tax revenue (in millions) in its general fund?
   a. $440
   b. $460
   c. $475
   d. $490

6. Assume the same facts as in the previous example. How much should Twin City recognize in property tax revenue (in millions) in its government-wide statement of activities?
   a. $440
   b. $460
   c. $475
   d. $490

7. A school district received property taxes in advance of the year in which they were due and for which they were budgeted. Such taxes should be recognized as
   a. Revenue
   b. A liability
   c. Deferred revenue
   d. A deferred inflow of resources

8. Central City was awarded two state grants during its fiscal year ending September 30, 2020: a $2 million block grant that can be used to cover any operating expenses incurred during fiscal 2021, and a $1 million grant that can be used any time to acquire equipment for its police department. For the year ending September 30, 2020, Central City should recognize in grant revenue in its fund financial statements (in millions):
   a. $0
   b. $1
   c. $2
   d. $3

9. Assume the same facts as in the previous example. How much should the city recognize in grant revenue in its government-wide statements?
   a. $0
   b. $1
   c. $2
   d. $3

10. Assuming that a government will collect its sales taxes in sufficient time to satisfy the "available" criterion, it would ordinarily recognize revenue from sales taxes in its governmental fund statements
    a. When the underlying sales transaction takes place
    b. On the date the merchant must remit the taxes to the government
    c. On the date the merchant must file a tax return
    d. When the taxes are received by the government

11. Assuming that a government will collect its sales taxes in sufficient time to satisfy the "available" criterion, it would ordinarily recognize revenue from sales taxes in its government-wide statements
    a. When the underlying sales transaction takes place
    b. On the date the merchant must remit the taxes to the government
    c. On the date the merchant must file a tax return
    d. When the taxes are received by the government

EX. 4-2

The following information relates to Hudson City for its fiscal year ended December 31, 2020.

- During the year, retailers in the city collected $1,700,000 in sales taxes owed to the city. As of December 31, retailers have remitted $1,100,000. $200,000 is expected in January 2021, and the remaining $400,000 is expected in April 2021.
- On December 31, 2019, the Foundation for the Arts pledged to donate $1, up to a maximum of $1 million, for each $3 that the museum is able to collect from other private contributors. The funds are to finance construction of the city-owned art museum. During 2020, the city collected $600,000 and received the matching money from the Foundation. In January and February 2021, it collected an additional $2,400,000 and also received the matching money.
- During the year, the city imposed license fees on street vendors. All vendors were required to purchase the licenses by September 30, 2020. The licenses cover the one-year period from October 1, 2020, through September 30, 2021. During 2020, the city collected $240,000 in license fees.
- The city sold a fire truck for $40,000 that it had acquired five years earlier for $250,000. At the time of sale, the city had charged $225,000 in depreciation.
- The city received a grant of $2 million to partially reimburse costs of training police officers. During the year, the city incurred $1,500,000 of allowable costs and received $1,200,000. It expects to incur an additional $500,000 in allowable costs in January 2021 and to be reimbursed for all allowable costs by the end of February 2021.

Refer to the two lists that follow. Select the appropriate amounts from the lettered list for each item in the numbered list. An amount may be selected once, more than once, or not at all.

1. Amount of sales tax revenue that the city should recognize in its funds statements
2. Amount of sales tax revenue the city should recognize as revenue in government-wide statements
3. Increase in deferred inflows in funds statements from sales tax revenues not yet received
4. Contribution revenue from Foundation for the Arts to be recognized in funds statements
5. Contribution revenue from Foundation for the Arts to be recognized in government-wide statements
6. Revenue from license fees to be recognized in funds statements
7. Increase in general fund balance owing to sale of fire engine
8. Increase in net position (government-wide statements) owing to sale of fire engine
9. Revenue in fund statements from police training grant

10. Revenue in government-wide statements from police training grant

a. $0	g. $200,000	m. $1,000,000
b. $1,500	h. $225,000	n. $1,200,000
c. $15,000	i. $240,000	o. $1,300,000
d. $30,000	j. $400,000	p. $1,500,000
e. $40,000	k. $600,000	q. $1,700,000
f. $60,000	l. $998,000	r. $2,000,000

EX. 4-3

Property taxes are not necessarily recognized as revenue in the year collected.

The fiscal year of Duchess County ends on December 31. Property taxes are due on March 31 of the year in which they are levied.

1. Prepare journal entries (excluding budgetary and closing entries) to record the following property tax-related transactions in which the county engaged in 2020 and 2021.
   a. On January 15, 2020, the county council levied property taxes of $170 million for the year ending December 31, 2020. Officials estimated that 1 percent would be uncollectible.
   b. During 2020, it collected $120 million.
   c. In January and February 2021, prior to preparing its 2020 financial statements, it collected an additional $45 million in 2020 taxes. It reclassified as delinquent the $5 million of 2020 taxes not yet collected.
   d. In January 2021, the county levied property taxes of $190 million, of which officials estimated 1.1 percent would be uncollectible.
   e. During the remainder of 2021, the county collected $2.5 million more in taxes relating to 2020, $160 million relating to 2021, and $1.9 million (in advance) applicable to 2022.
   f. In December 2021, it wrote off $1 million of 2020 taxes that it determined would be uncollectible.
2. Suppose the county were to prepare government-wide statements and account for property taxes on a full accrual basis of accounting rather than the modified accrual basis. How would your entries differ? Explain.

EX. 4-4

Grants are not necessarily recognized as revenue when they are awarded.

Columbus City was awarded a state reimbursement grant of $150,000 to assist its adult literacy program. The following were significant events relating to the grant:

- The city, which is on a calendar year, was notified of the award in November 2020.
- During 2021, it expended $30,000 on the literacy program and was reimbursed for $20,000. It expected to receive the balance in January 2022.
- In 2022, it expended the remaining $120,000 and was reimbursed by the state for the $10,000 owing from 2021 and the amount spent in 2022.

1. Prepare journal entries to record the events in a governmental fund.
2. Suppose instead that the city received the entire $150,000 in cash at the time the award was announced in 2020. How much revenue should the city recognize in its governmental fund statements in each of the three years? Explain.
3. Suppose alternatively that the state awarded the city an unrestricted grant of $150,000, which the city elected to use to support the adult literacy program. The city received the entire $150,000 in cash at the time the award was announced in 2020. How much revenue should the city recognize in its governmental fund statements in each of the three years? Explain.

EX. 4-5

Transactions affect fund statements differently than they do government-wide statements.

Preston Village engaged in the following transactions:

1. It issued $20 million in bonds to purchase a new municipal office building. The proceeds were recorded in a capital projects fund.
2. It acquired the building for $20 million.
3. It recognized, as appropriate, $300,000 of depreciation on municipal vehicles.
4. It transferred $2,060,000 from the general fund to a debt service fund.
5. It paid $60,000 in interest on long-term debt and repaid $2 million of principal on the same long-term debt.
6. It sold for $5 million village land that had been acquired for $4 million. The proceeds were recorded in the general fund.
    - **a.** For each of the transactions, prepare journal entries to record them in appropriate governmental funds (which are accounted for on a modified accrual basis).
    - **b.** Prepare journal entries to reflect how the transactions would be reflected in government-wide statements (which are prepared on a full accrual basis).
    - **c.** How can governments justify preparing two sets of financial statements, each on a different basis?

EX. 4-6

The accounting for contributions may depend on how they will be used.

Green Hills County received the following two contributions during a year:

- A developer (in exchange for exemptions to zoning restrictions) donated several acres of land that the county intended to convert to a park. The land had cost the developer $1.7 million. At the time of the contribution, its fair market value was $3.2 million.
- A local resident donated several acres of land to the county with the understanding that the county would sell the land and use the proceeds to fund construction of a county health center. The land had cost the resident $2.5 million. The county sold the land intended for the health center for $3 million 30 days after the end of its fiscal year.

1. Prepare journal entries to record the contributions. Be sure to specify the appropriate fund in which they would likely be made.
2. Comment on and justify any differences in the way you accounted for the two contributions.
3. Comment on how each of the contributions would be reported on the county's government-wide statements.
4. How would your answers differ if the land intended for the health center were not sold by the time year-end financial statements were issued?

EX. 4-7

Sales taxes should be recognized when the underlying event takes place.

A state requires "large" merchants (i.e., those with sales over a specified dollar amount) to report and remit their sales taxes within 15 days of the end of each month. It requires "small" merchants to report and remit their taxes within 15 days of the end of each quarter.

In January 2021, large merchants remitted sales taxes of $400 million owing to sales of December 2020. In February 2021, they remitted $280 million of sales taxes owing to sales of January 2021. In January, small merchants remitted sales taxes of $150 million owing to sales of the fourth quarter of 2021.

1. Prepare an appropriate journal entry to indicate the impact of the transactions on the state's fund financial statements for the year ending December 31, 2020.

2. Suppose, instead, that 10 percent of the taxes received by the state were collected on behalf of a city within the state. It is the policy of the state to remit the taxes to the city 30 days after it receives them. Prepare an appropriate journal entry to indicate the impact of the transactions on the city's fund financial statements for the year ending December 31, 2020.

3. Suppose instead that it was the policy of the state to remit the taxes to the city 90 days after it receives them. How would your response to Part (2) differ? Explain. Would your response be the same with respect to the city's government-wide statements?

EX. 4-8

The recognition of revenue from fines does not necessarily reflect the amount "earned" by merely issuing tickets.

In August 2021, the last month of its fiscal year, Goldwaithe Township issued $88,000 worth of tickets for parking and traffic violations. Of these, the township collected $45,000. It expects to collect an additional $20,000 within 60 days of the close of the fiscal year and to collect $3,000 subsequent to that. It will have to write off the balance. The tickets are due and the protest period expires on September 15.

1. How much revenue should the township recognize from the tickets issued in August 2021? Explain.

2. How might your answer change with respect to the township's government-wide statements?

EX. 4-9

The amount of revenue to be recognized from grants depends on the type of grant.

The following relate to three grants that the town of College Hills received from the state during its fiscal year ending December 31, 2021.

Prepare journal entries to record the three grants.

1. A cash grant of $200,000 that must be used to repair roads

2. $150,000 in cash of a total grant of $200,000 to reimburse the town for actual expenditures incurred in repairing roads; during the year the town incurred $150,000 in allowable repair costs

3. A cash entitlement grant of $200,000 that is intended to supplement the town's 2022 budget and must be expended in that year

EX. 4-10

Tax abatements are reductions in taxes that result from an agreement between a government and a taxpayer, typically a corporation.

In 2018, Lionsgate Logistics struck a deal with the city of Des Moines to move their headquarters to a property within the city to create jobs. Part of the incentive for the company to move its headquarters is a 5-year tax abatement deal that would require the company to pay only 20% of the property tax in 2019 after the headquarters completes, 30% in 2020, 40% in 2021, 50% in 2022, and 60% in 2023. Afterward, the company must pay 100% of the property tax in subsequent years. The gross property tax for each year is as follows:

2019: $100,000

2020: $120,000

2021: $96,000

2022: $114,000

2023: $114,000

2024: $120,000

Determine the property tax that Lionsgate Logistics will pay for the years 2019–2024.

CONTINUING PROBLEM

Review the Comprehensive Annual Financial Report (CAFR) that you obtained.

1. What are the main sources of the government's revenues, including those from both governmental and business-type activities?
2. How are revenues from property taxes accounted for, i.e., as a single amount, or in multiple categories? Identify the various categories and indicate the percentage breakdown (e.g., residential property taxes are 50 percent of the total property tax revenues).
3. Which of the entity's governmental functions or activities had the greatest amount of directly identifiable revenues?
4. Does the report discuss the accounting basis for recognizing revenues?
5. Does the government's government-wide statement of net position or governmental-fund balance sheet report "deferred revenue" (or deferred inflows of resources)? If so, what is the most likely reason this amount has been deferred?
6. What is the government's property tax rate?
7. At what percentage of fair market value is real property assessed?
8. When are property taxes due? When do interest and penalties begin to accrue?
9. By what percentage did each of the three largest sources of tax revenue increase over the last ten years?
10. Did the government generate revenue from traffic fines? As best you can tell, are these revenues reported in the government-wide statements as program revenues (e.g., associated with police or public safety) or as general revenues?
11. What is the total fund balance in the general fund? Can this amount be appropriated and spent for any purpose? Explain.
12. Were there any tax abatements disclosed for the year? If so, provide a brief description and the gross amount of taxes that were reduced during the reporting period.

PROBLEMS

P. 4-1

The general principles of revenue recognition are the same for both governmental and government-wide statements.

For each of the following situations, indicate the amount of revenue that the government should recognize in an appropriate governmental fund as well as in its government-wide statement of activities in its fiscal year ending December 31, 2021. Briefly justify your response, making certain that, as appropriate, you identify the key issue of concern.

1. In October 2020, a state received a federal grant of $300 million (in cash) to assist local law enforcement efforts. The federal government has established specific criteria governing how the funds should be distributed and will monitor the funds to ensure that they are used in accordance with grant provisions. The grant is intended to cover any allowable expenditure incurred in the calendar years 2021 through 2022. In 2021, the state incurred $160 million of allowable expenditures.
2. In December 2020, a city levied property taxes of $500 million for the calendar year 2021. The taxes are due on June 30, 2021. The city collects the taxes as follows:

December 2020	$30 million
January 1, 2021, to December 31, 2021	$440 million
January 1, 2022, through March 31, 2022 ($8 million per month)	$24 million
Total	$494 million

3. It estimates the balance will be uncollectible.

4. In January 2021, a city received a cash gift of $1 million to support its museum of city history. Per the wishes of the donor the funds are to be invested and only the income may be expended. In 2021, the endowment generated $50,000 in income, none of which was spent during the year.

5. For the year 2021, the teachers of the Nuvorich School District earned $26 million in pension benefits. In January 2022, the state in which the district is located paid the entire amount into the State Teachers Retirement Fund.

P. 4-2

For each of the following indicate the amount of revenue that Beanville should recognize in its 2020 (1) government-wide statements and (2) governmental fund statements. Provide a brief justification or explanation for your responses.

1. The state in which Beanville is located collects sales taxes for its cities and other local governments. The state permits small merchants to remit sales taxes quarterly. The state sales tax rate is 6 percent. In December 2019, city merchants collected $50 million in sales taxes that they remitted to the state on January 15, 2020. The state, in turn, transferred the taxes to the city on February 15, 2020.

2. In December 2019, the federal government awarded Beanville a reimbursement grant of $500,000 to train law-enforcement agents. The city had applied for the grant in January of that year. The city may incur allowable costs any time after receiving notification of the award. In 2020, the city incurred $400,000 in allowable costs and was reimbursed for $350,000. It was reimbursed for the $50,000 balance in February 2021. In January and February 2021, it incurred the remaining $100,000 in allowable costs and was reimbursed for them in April 2021.

3. In December 2019, the city levied property taxes of $1 billion for the calendar year 2020. The taxes are due on June 30, 2020. The city collected these taxes as follows:

December 2019	$56 million
January 1, 2019, to December 31, 2019	$858 million
January 1, 2020, through March 31, 2020 ($18 million per month)	$54 million
Total	$968 million

4. It estimates the balance of $32 million would be uncollectible. In addition, in the period from January 1 through February 28, 2020, the city collected $16 million in taxes that were delinquent as of December 31, 2019. In the period March 1 through June 30 2020, the city collected $8 million of taxes that were also delinquent as of December 31, 2019.

5. In December 2020 Beanville sold a city-owned warehouse to a private developer. Sales price was $4.2 million. The warehouse had cost $4 million when it was acquired 10 years earlier. It had an estimated useful life of 40 years (with no salvage value).

6. In December 2020, Beanville's city-owned radio station held its annual fund drive. A local business offered to match all pledges made on December 2, 2020, up to $50,000, assuming that the amount pledged was actually collected. Based on past experience the city estimates that 90 percent of the pledges will actually be collected. By year-end 2020, the city had collected $25,000 of the pledges, and in January and February it collected an additional $15,000. It received $25,000 of the matching funds on February 15, 2021. ***Respond with respect only to the $50,000 in matching funds.***

P. 4-3

Nonexchange revenues can be of four types.

The GASB has identified four classes of nonexchange revenues:

- Derived tax
- Imposed
- Government mandated
- Voluntary

For each of the following revenue transactions affecting a city, identify the class in which the revenue falls and prepare an appropriate fund journal entry for the current year (2021) as necessary. Provide a brief explanation of, or justification for, your entry.

1. In December, the state in which the city is located announced that it would grant the city $20 million to bring certain public facilities into compliance with the state's recently enacted disability/accessibility laws. As of year-end, the city had not yet received the funds, and it had not yet expended any funds on the state-mandated facility improvements.
2. The city imposes a $100 tax on each sale of real estate. The tax is collected by the title companies that process the sales and must be forwarded to the city within 30 days of the transaction. In December, there were 600 sales of real estate. As of year-end, the city had collected $40,000 of the $60,000 that it was owed.
3. In December, the state announced that the city's share of state assistance for the calendar year 2022 would be $120 million.
4. The city imposes a tax on all boats owned by residents. The tax is equal to 1 percent of the assessed value of a boat (determined by the city, taking into account the boat's original cost and age). The tax is payable on the last day of the year prior to the year for which the tax is applicable. In 2021, the city levied $640,000 of 2022 boat taxes, of which it collected $450,000.
5. A local resident sends to the city a copy of her will in which she bequeaths $3 million to the city museum upon her death.
6. The U.S. Department of Justice announces that it will reimburse the city up to $400,000 for the purchase of telecommunications equipment. As of year-end, the city had incurred only $200,000 in allowable expenditures.
7. A resident donates $10 million in securities to the city to support a cultural center. Only the income from the securities, not the principal, can be spent.

P. 4-4

Disproportionate assessments lead to inequities.

The town of Blair determines that it requires $22.5 million in property tax revenues to balance its budget. According to the town's property tax assessor, the town contains taxable property that it assessed at $900 million. However, the town permits discounts for early payment, which generally average about 2 percent of the amount levied. Further, the town grants homestead and similar exemptions equal to 3 percent of the property's assessed value.

1. Calculate the required tax rate, expressed in mils.
2. A resident's home is assessed at $300,000. He is permitted a homestead exemption of $10,000 and a senior citizen's exemption of $5,000. What is the resident's required tax payment prior to allowable discounts for early payment?
3. Blair assesses property at 100 percent of its fair market value. Sussex, a nearby town in the same county, assesses property at only 80 percent of fair market value. The county bases its own tax assessments on the assessments of the individual towns. However, the county grants no exemptions or discounts. Its tax rate is 8 mils.
   a. A taxpayer in Sussex owns a home with a market value of $300,000—the same as that of the Blair resident. Compute and compare the amount of county tax that would be paid by each resident.
   b. Comment on why governments find it necessary to "equalize" tax assessments based on assessments of other governments.

P. 4-5

A change to the full accrual basis may have little impact upon reported revenues.

A city levies property taxes of $4 billion in June 2021 for its fiscal year beginning July 1, 2021. The taxes are due by January 31, 2022. The following (in millions) indicates actual and anticipated cash collections relating to the levy:

June 2021	$100
July 2021 through June 2022	$3,600
July 2022 through August 2022	$80
September 2022 through June 2023	$150

The city estimates that $30 million will eventually have to be refunded, owing to taxpayer appeals of the assessed valuation of their property, and that $70 million will be uncollectible.

1. Prepare a journal entry that summarizes the city's property tax activity for the fiscal year ending June 30, 2022, based on:
   a. The modified accrual basis (i.e., for fund statements)
   b. The full accrual basis (i.e., for government-wide statements)

2. Indicate the differences in amounts that would be reported on both the statement of net position and the statement of activities on a full accrual basis.

3. Suppose that in the following year the tax levy and pattern of collections were identical to those of the previous year. What would now be the difference in amounts reported on the statement of net position and the statement of activities on a full accrual basis?

P. 4-6

Derived taxes are derived from underlying transactions.

A state imposes a sales tax of 6 percent. The state's counties are permitted to levy an additional tax of 2 percent. The state administers the tax for the counties, forwarding the proceeds to the counties 15 days after it receives the proceeds from the merchants.

The state requires merchants to file a return and transmit collections either monthly, quarterly, or annually, depending on the amount of taxable sales made by the merchant. This problem pertains only to taxes that must be paid quarterly.

Merchants must file their returns and transmit their taxes within one month after the end of a quarter. The quarters are based on the calendar year. Thus, taxes for the quarter ending March 31 are due by April 30; those for the quarter ending June 30 are due by July 31.

The fiscal year of both the state and its counties ends on September 30.

For the quarter ending September 30, 2021, merchants collected and paid (in October) $300 million in taxes. Of these, 80 percent ($240 million) are applicable to the state; 2 percent ($6 million) are applicable to Cayoga County.

1. Prepare journal entries to summarize the state's sales tax activity for its share of taxes for the quarter ending September 30, 2021:
   a. On a modified accrual basis
   b. On a full accrual basis

2. Prepare journal entries to summarize the county's sales tax activity for the quarter ending September 30, 2021:
   a. On a modified accrual basis
   b. On a full accrual basis

   Be concerned only with any entries that would affect the fiscal year ending September 30, 2021.

3. Some critics have charged that current standards (i.e., those of Statement No. 33) allow for premature recognition of sales tax revenue. What do you think is the basis for their position? What arguments can be made in defense of the Statement No. 33 standards?

P. 4-7

The "60-day rule" may not be applicable to all types of revenues.

Manor County was awarded a state grant to establish evening athletic programs for at-risk youth. The $3.6 million award, to cover the calendar year 2021, was announced on November 15, 2020.

According to the terms of the grant, the county will be reimbursed for all qualifying costs within 30 days of its filing an appropriate request-for-reimbursement form (a "voucher").

During 2021, the county incurred $300,000 of costs each month. It filed a reimbursement claim shortly after the end of each month and received a reimbursement check approximately 45 days after the end of the month in which it incurred the costs. Hence, it received 12 checks, the first on March 15, 2021, and the last on February 15, 2022.

The county operates on a fiscal year beginning October 1.

1. Prepare journal entries to summarize the county's grant-related activity for its fiscal year ending September 30, 2021, on a modified accrual basis.
2. Suppose alternatively that the state would reimburse the county for its costs in four installments, the first on June 30, 2021, and the last on March 31, 2022. Do you think that the county, in its fund financial statements, should recognize the reimbursement of December 31, 2021, as revenue of the county's fiscal year ending September 30, 2021? Justify your answer.

P. 4-8

License fees present challenging, although not necessarily consequential, issues of revenue recognition.

Kyle Township charges residents $100 per year to license household pets. As specified in a statute enacted in 2021, residents are required to purchase a license by October 1 of each year; the license covers the period October 1 through September 30.

The license fees are not refundable. The statute authorizing the fees specifically states that the revenues are to be used to support the township's animal control program. The program, which will be carried out throughout the year, is not expected to receive financial support from any other sources.

During the calendar year 2021 (which corresponds to the township's fiscal year), the township collected $36,000 in license fees for the 2021–2022 licensing period.

1. Prepare a journal entry to record the township's receipt of the license fees.
2. Would you consider the license fees to be exchange or nonexchange revenue? Explain.
3. How do you justify the accounting standard on which your entry is based (especially because the license period overlaps two fiscal years)?

P. 4-9

The distinction between an entitlement and a reimbursement grant is not always obvious.

A city received two state grants in fiscal 2021. The first was an award for a maximum of $800,000, over a two-year period, to reimburse the city for 40 percent of specified costs incurred to operate a job opportunity program. During 2021, the city incurred allowable costs of $1.4 million (paid in cash) on the program. It was reimbursed for $500,000 and anticipates that it will receive the balance of what it is owed for 2021 early in fiscal 2022.

The second was an award of $600,000, also to cover a two-year period, to assist the city in administering a day care program. Granted only to selected cities, the award was based on several criteria, including the quality of the program and need for assistance. The amount was calculated as a percentage of the funds incurred by the city on the program in the prior year. Although the award must be spent on the day care program, there are no specific matching requirements. During the year, the city received the entire $600,000. It spent $550,000 (in cash) on the program.

1. Prepare entries to summarize the grant activity during 2021.
2. In a few sentences, justify any differences in your approach to the two grants.

P. 4-10

It's not always obvious whether governments should recognize the revenues or expenditures associated with grants and awards.

For each of the following grants and awards, indicate whether the recipient government should recognize revenues and expenditures. In a sentence or two, justify your response.

1. As the result of damaging floods, the state of New York receives disaster assistance relief that it must distribute in predetermined amounts to specified cities and towns. The governor had appealed to the president to declare the affected areas as being in a "state of emergency," but the state has no responsibility for monitoring how the funds are spent by the localities.
2. Cleveland receives money from the state to distribute to private health and welfare organizations within the city. The organizations applied for the funds directly to the state, but Cleveland is responsible for ensuring that the approved programs are audited by independent CPAs.
3. Santa Fe serves as a representative of the state in administering the federal food stamp program. State governments, which participate in the program, receive stamps from the federal government in the form of a credit to their account. The federal government establishes eligibility requirements and the scale of benefits. The states, however, are responsible for selecting the recipients and distributing the stamps.

   Some states involve both local governments and private institutions, such as banks and check-cashing outlets, in the administrative process. Under a contract with the state, Santa Fe, for example, checks the eligibility of food stamp applicants. It serves all stamp applicants and recipients who come to its offices, irrespective of whether they are residents of the city. It receives an annual fee for its administrative services. Food stamp recipients are provided with a debit-like card, which they present to the merchant, from whom they purchase their food. When they do so, their remaining food stamp balance is decreased and simultaneously so is the state's balance with the federal government.
4. Arlington Township is responsible for all costs of operating its volunteer fire department, with one exception. Its volunteer firefighters receive medical insurance through a state program. The state pays 80 percent of their insurance premiums, and the firefighters themselves pay the rest. The township has no legal responsibility for providing insurance benefits to its firefighters. The insurance program was adopted by the state mainly to encourage citizens to join the volunteer departments.

P. 4-11

Seemingly minor changes in the terms of a grant can affect the timing of revenue recognition.

The Foundation for Educational Excellence has decided to support the Tri-County School District's series of teacher training workshops intended to improve instruction in mathematics. The foundation is considering four ways of wording the grant agreement, which would be dated December 1, 2021:

1. The foundation agrees to reimburse the district for all workshop costs up to $200,000.
2. The foundation is pleased to enclose a check for $200,000 to be used exclusively to support a series of teacher training workshops intended to improve instruction in mathematics.
3. The foundation will donate $200,000 to the school district as soon as the district conducts its planned series of teacher training workshops, intended to improve instruction in mathematics.
4. The foundation is pleased to enclose a check for $200,000 to be used exclusively to support a series of teacher training workshops intended to improve instruction in mathematics. The workshops are to be conducted between January 1 and December 31, 2022.

The school district expects to conduct the workshops in 2022.

Explain how the wording of the grant agreement would affect the year in which the school district recognized revenue. Indicate the relevant restriction, contingency, or eligibility requirement (e.g., time requirement; purpose restriction) to which each grant is subject and explain how it bears on the issue of revenue recognition.

P. 4-12

Policy changes and other measures will have varying effects on reported revenues.

1. The board of trustees of an independent school district is contemplating several policy changes and other measures, all of which it intends to implement within the fiscal year that ends August 31, 2021. It requests your advice on how the changes would affect the reported general fund revenues. For each of the proposals, indicate the impact on revenues (or accounts comparable to revenues, such as proceeds from sale of capital assets) and provide a brief explanation. Address the impact on both the fund and the government-wide financial statements.

2. Allow a three-month grace period for the payment of property taxes. District property taxes for the fiscal year ending August 31 are currently payable in 10 installments. The final installment is due on August 31. The proposed change would give taxpayers a three-month grace period before interest and penalties are assessed. The district estimates that the change would affect $2 million in receipts.

3. Sell a parcel of land that the district purchased three years earlier for $450,000. Current market value is $500,000.

4. Request that a donation be advanced from December 2021 to August 2021. An alumnus of a district high school has indicated a willingness to donate to the district laboratory equipment having a fair market value of $400,000, along with real estate having a fair market value of $300,000. The district intends to use the equipment in student labs. It plans to sell the real estate as soon as possible and, in fact, has an acceptable offer from a buyer.

5. Sell parking permits to students in the semester prior to that for which they are applicable. The district now sells parking permits to students at the beginning of the fall semester. The permits cover the period from September 1 through June 30. To reduce the start-of-year administrative burden upon staff, the district proposes to begin sale of the permits the previous spring. It estimates that in spring 2021 it will sell $6,000 worth of permits that would otherwise be sold the following September.

P. 4-13

In some types of transactions, assets are recognized concurrently with revenues; in others they are not.

In October 2021, the Village of Mason levied $80 million of property taxes for its 2022 fiscal year (which is the same as the calendar year). The taxes are payable 50 percent by December 31, 2021, and 50 percent by June 30, 2022. The village collected $55 million of the 2022 taxes by year-end 2021 and the $25 million balance by the end of 2022. The government has a legally enforceable claim on the taxed property on the first due date—that is, December 31, 2021.

In December 2021, the state announced that the village would receive $3 million in state assistance. The funds were paid in January 2022 and could have been used (per terms of the state legislation) to cover any legitimate village expenditures incurred in 2022.

1. Prepare fund journal entries to summarize the property tax and grant activity for the fiscal years ending December 31, 2021, and 2022.

2. How would you justify any apparent inconsistencies as to if and when you recognized the taxes receivable as opposed to the grants receivable?

P. 4-14

The reporting of on-behalf payments may have political consequences.

In 2021, the Bakersville Independent School District incurred $12 million in expenditures for teachers' salary and benefits. In that year, the legislature of the state in which the district is located voted to enhance the pension benefits of all teachers in the state by making a one-time supplementary contribution to the teachers' retirement fund of each independent school district in an amount equal to 2 percent of teachers' salaries. This amount would be in addition to the contributions currently made by the school districts themselves.

As a result of this measure, the state contributed $240,000 on behalf of teachers in the Bakersville district.

1. How would the state's contribution to the pension fund be accounted for on the books of Bakersville? Prepare a summary journal entry (if required).

2. In the 2022 election for school board, one of the candidates charged that the incumbent board had promised to hold the line on school district spending. Yet, despite its promises, the board increased expenditures on teachers' compensation by 2 percent. Do you think the school district should be required to report the state's contribution as an expenditure, even though the district did not make the payment and had no say on whether it should be made? Would your response be different if the state had given the district a cash grant of $240,000 with the requirement that the money be used to increase the district's contribution to the Teachers' Retirement Fund?

3. Suppose instead that the state made a contribution of $240,000 to the Teachers' Retirement Fund on behalf of the school district. This contribution enabled the district to reduce its payment from what it had previously been and for which the school district is legally responsible. Do you think that the district should be required to report the state's contribution as an expenditure?

P. 4-15

The distinction between exchange and nonexchange revenues is not always obvious.

You are the independent auditor of various governments. You have been asked for your advice on how the following transactions should be accounted for and reported. Characteristic of each transaction is ambiguity as to whether it is an exchange or a nonexchange transaction.

For each transaction indicate whether you think it is an exchange or a nonexchange transaction and make a recommendation as to how it should be accounted for (i.e., the amount and timing of revenue recognition). Justify your response. Note: The GASB has not explicitly distinguished between exchange and nonexchange transactions. Hence, in this problem, you should consider how you think the transaction should be accounted for; you need not be limited by current GASB standards.

1. A government receives from a developer a donation of 1,000 acres of land valued at $4 million. In return, the government grants the developer zoning variances on nearby property.

2. A college of pharmacy receives a grant of $2 million from a drug company to carry out research on a new formulation. The college agrees to submit the results to the company and to publish them only with the company's approval.

3. A city charges a developer an "impact fee" of $15,000 to compensate, in part, for improvements to the infrastructure in the area in which the developer plans to build residential homes. The city will make the improvements when construction on the new homes gets under way.

4. A city charges restaurants a license fee of $2,500. The license covers a period of two years. The fees must be used for health department inspections.

5. The city issues permits for residents to use city tennis courts. The fee is $100 per year—a small fraction of what it would cost to play on comparable private courts and an amount that covers only a small portion of the cost of constructing, maintaining, and operating the courts.

P. 4-16

"One-shots" have a greater impact on cash-based budgets than on accrual-based financial statements.

A city recently proposed the following "one-shot" measures to help balance its 2020 ***general*** fund budget (the only budget that is required by law to be balanced). For each of the measures, indicate how it would affect revenues (or their equivalent, such as gains) on its 2020 budget as well as its fund and government-wide December 31, 2020, financial statements. That is, indicate the amount, if any by which revenues will increase. The city's budget is prepared on a cash basis; its financial statements are prepared in accordance with generally accepted accounting principles.

Briefly explain and justify your answer.

1. The city will sell bonds (accounted for in the general fund) that it planned to hold to maturity as an investment. The bonds currently have a market value of $1,030,000 and could be sold for that amount. They were acquired for $1,000,000.

2. The city will reduce the protest period on traffic fines by 15 days, thereby increasing the amounts due in 2020 by $45,000. Of this amount, $20,000 will be paid without protest, and $10,000 will be protested (hearings to be held in 2021). Of the $10,000 that will be protested, only $2,000 will actually have to be paid (all by February 2021). The balance will be voided as the result of successful protests. Of the remaining $15,000 that was neither paid nor protested in 2020, $6,000 will eventually be paid—evenly over the first six months of 2021 (i.e., $1,000 per month). The $9,000 balance will be uncollectible.

3. The city will sell an office building for $45 million. At the time of sale, the building had a book value of $18 million (cost of $30 million less $12 million accumulated depreciation).

4. It will advance the date on which sales taxes are due. Currently, small merchants must remit by January 15 taxes on sales made in October and November. They will now have to remit them by December 31. The change will affect $4 million in taxes.

5. The city has been awarded a grant of $2 million from the county. The grant specifies that the funds are to be used by the city in 2022 to cover certain costs of a low-income housing program. Although the city expects to receive the funds from the county in January 2021, the county has agreed to the city's request that it advance payment of the funds to December 2020.

6. The city will increase interest and penalties on delinquent property taxes. As a consequence, the city expects to collect in December 2020 approximately $5 million in 2020 taxes that it otherwise would have collected in each of the first three months of 2021.

QUESTIONS FOR RESEARCH, ANALYSIS, AND DISCUSSION

1. The GASB has established a "60-day" rule for the recognition of property taxes in governmental funds. On what basis can you justify such a rule for property taxes but not for other revenues? Do you think the 60-day rule should be extended to all revenues?

2. The Hensley School District was notified by the state education department that it has been awarded a $2 million grant to implement a unique elementary school reading program. The district has met all eligibility requirements for the grant. As of the end of the district's fiscal year, however, the state legislature had not yet appropriated the resources for the grant. Do you think that the district should recognize revenue in the period in which it was notified of the grant, or delay recognition until the state officially appropriates the resources?

3. The Lewiston School District receives a $200,000 grant from the Bates Foundation to upgrade its high school computer labs. Total cost of the upgrade is estimated at $450,000. Because the grant is restricted, it accounts for the grant in a special revenue fund. During the year, the district incurs $225,000 in upgrade costs, paying for them out of general revenues. Can the district continue to report the $200,000 received from the foundation as restricted resources?

4. Going 70 mph in a 60-mph zone, you've just been caught in the infamous Goldwaithe Township speed trap. You pay your fine of $150. In the government-wide statement of activities, revenues must be associated with the specific programs (e.g., public safety) that generate them. However, state law applicable to Goldwaithe specifically requires that all fines be considered general revenues; they cannot be restricted to specific programs, activities, or departments. How would you recommend your fine be accounted for in Goldwaithe's statement of activities?

5. A school district is awarded a cash grant to conduct a teacher-training program. As part of the grant, the district is given, rent-free, both office space and training facilities in the building of the state education department. How, if at all, should the district account for and report the value of the office space and the training facilities?

SOLUTION TO EXERCISE FOR REVIEW AND SELF-STUDY

1. **Modified accrual basis:**

Cash	$120.000	
Property taxes receivable	34,000	
Property tax revenue		$130,000
Property taxes (deferred inflow of resources)		20,000
Allowance for uncollectibles		4,000
To record property tax revenue		

Revenue would be recognized on actual collections plus those of the 60 days following the end of the period—hence, $120,000 plus $10,000. The $20,000 of taxes expected to be collected in the following four months would be reported as a deferred inflow.

Full accrual basis:

Cash	$120.000	
Property taxes receivable	34,000	
Allowance for uncollectibles		$ 4,000
Property tax revenue		150,000
To record property tax revenue		

Revenue would be recognized on all actual and anticipated collections.

2. **Modified accrual basis:**

Sales taxes receivable	$12.000	
Sales tax revenue		$12,000
To record sales taxes		

Sales taxes are derived from sales transactions. The sales transactions took place in September. Therefore, as long as the city received the taxes in time for them to satisfy the "available" criterion it should recognize them as September revenues. It is assumed that when it received the cash in November (and thus first became aware of the amount of the revenue), it had not yet closed its books for the year ending September 30, 2021.

Full accrual basis

The taxes should be recognized in the period of sale irrespective of when they will be received by the city. In this case, the entry would be the same.

3. **Modified accrual basis**

Cash	$ 80	
Expenditures	320	
Grant revenues		$320
Training grant (deferred inflow of resources)		80
To record grant expenditures and revenues		

The revenue from this reimbursement grant would be recognized as the related costs are incurred. Hence, only the funds that were expended can be recognized as revenue; the difference between the cash receipts ($400) and the expenditures ($320) must be reported as a deferred inflow of resources.

Full accrual basis

The government is eligible for the grant only as it makes the required expenditures. Therefore, under the modified accrual basis, it would only recognize revenue to the extent of the $320 actually expended.

4. Modified accrual basis

Cash	$36	
Revenue from permits		$36
To recognize revenue from permits		

According to current standards, miscellaneous exchange revenues, such as those from permits, are best recognized as cash is received.

Full accrual basis

The revenue recognition standards—and hence the entry—are the same.

5. Modified accrual basis

Cash	$135	
Proceeds from sale of land		$135
To record the sale of land		

When the land was acquired, the city would not have recorded it as a general fund asset because capital assets are not recognized in governmental funds. Therefore, when the city sells the land it would recognize the entire proceeds as "proceeds from the sale of land"—an "other financing source."

Full accrual basis

Cash	$135	
Donated land		$119
Gain on sale of land (revenue)		16
To record the sale of land		

Under the full accrual basis, the donation of land would have been recognized as revenue when the land was received. The increase in market value would be recognized as a gain at time of sale.

CHAPTER 5

Recognizing Expenditures in Governmental Funds

LEARNING OBJECTIVES

After studying this chapter, you should understand:

- The modified accrual basis of accounting for expenditures and the rationale for differences between that basis and the full accrual basis
- How each of the following expenditures are accounted for:
  - Wages and salaries
  - Compensated absences
  - Pensions
  - Claims and judgments
  - Acquisition and use of materials and supplies
  - Prepayments
  - Acquisition and use of capital assets
  - Interest and principal on long-term debt
  - Grants
- The different types of interfund activity and how they are reported
- What constitutes other financing sources and uses
- The overall rationale for, and limitations of, the fund statements

In the previous chapter, we addressed the question of when revenue should be recognized in governmental funds. We turn now to the other side of the ledger and consider how expenditures should be accounted for.

Like revenues, expenditures can be of two types: exchange and nonexchange. Our discussion of revenues centered mainly on nonexchange revenues, as most governmental fund revenues are of that type. By contrast, our discussion of expenditures focuses primarily on exchange expenditures. Most governmental fund expenditures result from exchanges—the acquisition of goods and services for cash or other assets. This is not to say that governments do not engage also in nonexchange transactions. Just as governments receive grants from other governments, they also provide them—to other governments, to private (mainly not-for-profit) organizations, and to individuals (e.g., assistance payments). GASB Statement No. 33, Accounting and Financial Reporting for Nonexchange Transactions, applies to both nonexchange revenues and nonexchange expenditures. Nonexchange expenditures, per the statement, should be accounted for as the mirror image of nonexchange revenues. Therefore, we need direct only minimal attention to nonexchange expenditures.

Governmental fund expenditures, like revenues, are accounted for on a modified accrual basis on the fund statements. For the most part, although there are several exceptions, exchange transactions are accounted for on a full accrual basis, and the GASB has adopted most of the relevant standards of the FASB. This chapter, therefore, is devoted

mainly to accounting for and reporting expenditures on a modified accrual basis—the area in which governmental accounting is unique. As we did in the previous chapter with respect to revenues, however, we also note how the various expenditures would be accounted for differently on the full accrual basis.

HOW IS THE ACCRUAL CONCEPT MODIFIED FOR EXPENDITURES?

THE DISTINCTION BETWEEN EXPENDITURES AND EXPENSES

Under the modified accrual basis of accounting, governmental funds are concerned with **expenditures**. By contrast, proprietary funds, like businesses, focus on **expenses**. Expenditures are narrower in scope than expenses. Whereas expenditures are decreases in net current financial resources, expenses are decreases in net economic resources. An expenditure is generally recognized when an asset is acquired, whereas an expense is generally recognized when an asset is consumed. Thus, funds that are accounted for on a modified accrual basis would report equipment costs as "capital outlays"—expenditures to be recognized at the time of acquisition. By contrast, those that are accounted for on a full accrual basis would report the equipment costs initially as an asset and then depreciate (expense) them over the life of the equipment.

THE VIRTUES OF ACCRUAL ACCOUNTING AND THE RATIONALE FOR MODIFICATION

As pointed out in the previous chapter, the accrual basis of accounting is generally considered the superior method of accounting for organizations because it captures the substance of events and transactions, not merely the inflows and outflows of cash or near-cash.

We have seen that the accrual concept is applied differently in governmental funds than in businesses or in proprietary funds, which are accounted for as if they were businesses, as well as in government-wide statements. Governmental fund accounting is heavily influenced by governmental budgeting. Owing to the importance of the budget, expenditures are closely tied to cash flows and near-cash flows rather than to flows of economic resources. In addition, governmental funds report only current, not long-term, liabilities. They focus on obligations that must be funded by current, not future, taxpayers.

Although the general principles of accrual accounting apply to governmental funds, there are key differences between how they are applied in governmental funds and how they are applied in businesses. In this chapter, we will discuss *seven* key differences in how expenditures are accrued in governments versus businesses. They are compensated absences, pension and other postemployment benefits, claims and judgments, inventories, prepayments, capital assets, and principal and interest payment on debt. The differences are consistent with the concept that under the modified accrual basis of accounting, expenditures are decreases in net current financial resources—current assets less current liabilities. But unlike a business's current liabilities, defined as those that must be paid within a year, a government's liabilities are considered current only when they must be liquidated with expendable available financial resources.

In the context of governmental funds, "**financial resources**" refers to current financial resources—cash and other assets that are expected to be transformed into cash in the normal course of operations. "*Net* financial resources" refers then to financial resources less claims against them.

A government should recognize an expenditure when its net expendable available financial resources are reduced—that is, when it either pays cash for goods or services received or accrues a liability. But when should it *accrue* (i.e., give accounting recognition to) a liability? Under the modified accrual basis, a government should, as a general rule, accrue a liability in the period in which it *incurs* (i.e., becomes obligated for) the liability. This general rule, however, does not by itself distinguish the modified accrual basis from the full accrual basis. What does distinguish the two bases are the several exceptions to this general rule set forth by the

GASB.[1] These exceptions permit governments to delay recording both a governmental fund liability and its associated expenditure until the period in which the liability must be paid—that is, when payment will reduce expendable available financial resources. Until that period, the government need report the liability only in its government-wide statements (as well as in its schedule of long-term obligations).

HOW SHOULD WAGES AND SALARIES BE ACCOUNTED FOR?

Wages and salaries may be earned in one fiscal year but paid in the next. Most governments pay their employees periodically—on a specified day of a week or month. Whenever the end of a pay period or the pay date does not coincide with the end of the fiscal year, then the government must carry over wages earned in one year until the next. Therefore, the question arises of whether the wages and salaries should be reported as expenditures in the period earned or in the period paid.

IN PRACTICE TAX EXPENDITURES THAT ARE ACTUALLY REDUCTIONS IN REVENUE

Some "expenditures" are never recorded at all in the financial statements of governments (local and state as well as federal). Typically called "tax expenditures," they are actually reductions in revenue. They result from tax benefits that are targeted at either a single taxpayer, a narrow group of taxpayers, or specified transactions engaged in by taxpayers.

Suppose that to lure a major employer to its jurisdiction, a city grants a company property tax abatement. A tax abatement is a particular type of tax expenditure. It is a reduction in revenues that results from an agreement with a *specific* entity, usually in return for promises on the part of that entity to locate or remain in the jurisdiction or to create a certain number of new jobs. Obviously, by waiving the taxes the city incurs a cost. However, the lost taxes would be recorded neither as an expenditure (inasmuch as the city would not make an actual payment to the company) nor as a reduction of revenue.

Far better, according to some accountants, the government should be required to record the lost taxes as revenue, offset by a corresponding expenditure. The GASB has compensated in part for this deficiency by issuing a new statement on tax abatement disclosures that requires that governments disclose in the notes to their financial statements: information about the taxes abated, including eligibility criteria, provisions for recapturing abated taxes, and the types of commitments made by tax abatement projects; the number of tax abatement agreements entered into in the reporting period, and the total number in effect as of the end of the period; the dollar amount of taxes abated in the reporting period; and commitments made by government, other than to abate taxes, as part of its tax abatement agreements.

For example, Berkshire Hathaway Inc. is an American multinational conglomerate holding company that is headquartered in Omaha, Nebraska. The owner and CEO is Warren Buffet. Subsidiaries include, but are not limited to: Geico, HomeServices of America, Dairy Queen, BNSF Railway, NetJets, See's Candies, Acme Brick, and Orange Julius. With all these subsidiaries, Berkshire Hathaway is one of the largest, if not the world's largest financial services company by revenue. The conglomerate is also awarded billions of dollars of subsidies. Below is a summary of the subsidy value and number of awards of Berkshire Hathaway:

Subsidy Summary	Subsidy Value	Number of Awards
State/Local	$1,491,867,623	460
Federal (grants and allocated tax credits)	$ 183,346,280	16
Total	$1,675,213,903	476

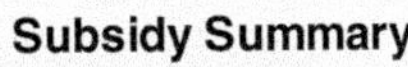

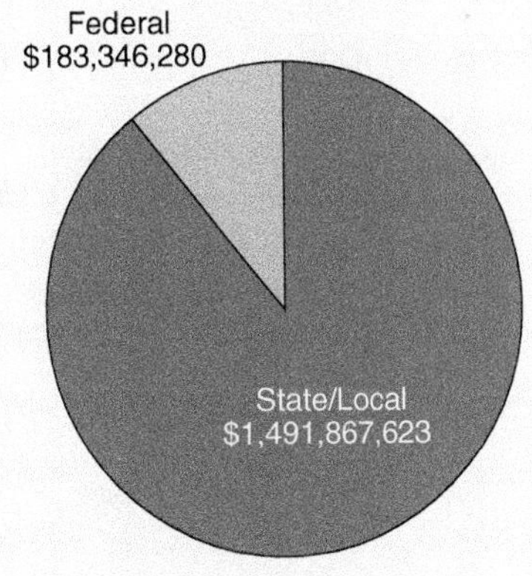

[1] See discussion in GASB Interpretation No. 6, *Recognition and Measurement of Certain Liabilities and Expenditures in Governmental Fund Financial Statements* (March 2000).

The conglomerate receives subsidies in 40 states, although some of those amounts are not disclosed. The Top 5 States for State/Local Awards are summarized below:

Top 5 States for State/ Local Awards	Total Subsidy	Number of Awards
Texas	$802,720,000	2
New York	$390,579,788	160
Ohio	$ 76,184,403	19
Louisiana	$ 71,015,033	12
Oregon	$ 42,209,746	32
All Others	$109,158,653	235

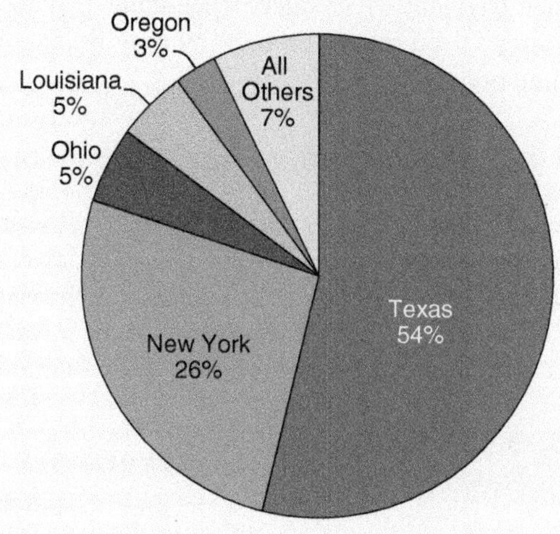

In regard to property tax abatement subsidies, however, it is worth noting that Berkshire Hathaway only has property tax abatement agreements in eight states (Indiana, Louisiana, Maine, Michigan, Ohio, Oregon, Tennessee, and Texas).

Source: https://subsidytracker.goodjobsfirst.org/prog.php?parent=berkshire-hathaway

Example

Wages and Salaries

A city pays its employees for the two-week period ending January 8, 2022, on January 11, 2022. The portion of the payroll applicable to December 2021 is $40 million, an amount included in the city's 2021 budget.

GASB STANDARDS

The GASB *Codification* does not specifically address wages and salaries. Hence, the general principles of modified accrual accounting apply. Wages and salaries should be recognized in the period in which the employees earn their wages and salaries, as long as the government's obligation will be liquidated with expendable available financial resources.

In this example, the employees will be paid within days of year-end and with resources budgeted for 2021 expenditures—resources that would generally be assumed to be available and expendable. Thus (ignoring the usual payroll-related taxes, withholdings, and benefits):

Payroll expenditures	$40	
Accrued wages and salaries		$40

To record the December payroll (in 2021)

In the following year, when the employees are paid, the entry to record the 2021 portion of the payroll would be:

Accrued wages and salaries	$40	
Cash		$40

To record the payment of wages and salaries recognized as 2021 expenditures (in 2022)

The entries in this chapter designate an **object** classification (such as payroll, insurance, and supplies). Alternatively, they could designate an *organizational unit* (such as police department, fire department, and sanitation department) or a *function or program* (such as public safety, general government, culture, and recreation). Although the financial statements of most governments report expenditures by organizational unit, function, or program, the expenditures are typically charged initially to an object account.

DIFFERENCES IN GOVERNMENT-WIDE STATEMENTS

Wages and salaries are already recognized on an accrual basis; no change would be required by a shift to a full accrual basis.

HOW SHOULD COMPENSATED ABSENCES BE ACCOUNTED FOR?

Governments compensate employees for time not worked for a variety of reasons: vacations, holidays, sick leave, sabbatical leave, jury duty, or military reserve. In concept, the accounting issues are similar to those of wages and salaries earned in one period but paid in another. But there are differences as well. Most significantly, compensated absences are earned in one period, but they are often not paid until several periods later. Hence, the liability cannot be considered current. In addition, the amount of compensation to be paid is not always certain. First, some employees may leave the organization before they take all the time off to which they are entitled. Second, the amount of compensation is almost always based on the employee's wage or salary rate in effect when the time off is taken, not when it is earned.

ACCOUNTING FOR VACATIONS

As in the private sector, government employees are almost always granted paid vacation after completing a specified period of service. The number of vacation days generally varies with years of employment. While on vacation, employees are paid at their current wage rate, irrespective of when they earned their vacation. From their perspective, the paycheck they receive for vacation days is usually indistinguishable from that received for working days. Employers, however, usually charge the expenditure to a vacation pay account instead of their standard wages or salary account.

IN PRACTICE — CHANGING THE PAY DATE BY ONE DAY

In Texas, as in many cities and states, state government employees receive their monthly paycheck on the first day of the month following that to which it is applicable. They used to receive it a day earlier, on the last of the month. Why the change? In one year, the state needed additional funds to balance its budget. What better way than to move the pay date forward by one day, thereby shifting one complete payroll from the current fiscal year to the next? This scheme worked, of course, for budgeting purposes only, because the state budgets on what is essentially a cash basis. For reporting purposes, however, most of the payroll is accounted for in governmental funds, which are on a modified accrual basis. Therefore, the expenditure must be reported in the fiscal year in which the employees earn their wages and salaries, irrespective of the date that the state issues and distributes their checks.

Example — Vacation Leave

City employees earn $8 million in vacation leave. Of this amount, they are paid $6 million in 2021 and postpone the balance until future years. The leave vests (i.e., employees are legally entitled to it, even if they resign or are discharged) and can be taken any time up to retirement or as additional compensation at the time of retirement.

GASB STANDARDS

GASB standards state that vacation leave and comparable compensated absences should be accrued as a liability as the benefits are earned by the employees if both of the following conditions are met:

- The employees' rights to receive compensation are attributable to services already rendered.
- It is probable that the employer will compensate the employees for the benefits through paid time off or some other means, such as cash payments at termination or retirement.

The compensation should be based on the wage or salary rates in effect at the balance sheet date, and employers should adjust for benefits that are expected to lapse.[2] Although this guidance may appear to sanction accrual of vacation pay, there is a catch. GASB standards explain that compensated absence liabilities are normally liquidated with expendable available resources in the periods in which the payments to employees are made. Therefore, both the vacation pay expenditures and the related fund liabilities should be recognized in the periods in which the payments are due. Until those periods, the liabilities should be reported only on the government-wide statement of net position and a schedule of long-term obligations, not on a governmental fund balance sheet.

[2] GASB Statement No. 16, *Accounting for Compensated Absences* (November 1992), para. 7.

The following entry, in the general fund or other appropriate governmental fund, would give effect to the GASB standards:

Vacation pay expenditures	$6	
Cash (or wages payable)		$6
To record vacation pay		

The $2 million postponed until future periods should not be recognized as either an expenditure or a liability in the governmental fund. Instead, it should be reported only on the government-wide statement of net position and a schedule of long-term obligations.

The postponed amount should, of course, be recognized in the general fund as an expenditure in the years the vacations are taken and paid for.

DIFFERENCES IN GOVERNMENT-WIDE STATEMENTS

Consistent with the accrual concept as applied in the FASB business model, the government-wide statements provide for balance sheet recognition of long-term liabilities. Accordingly, the "standard" accrual entry would be appropriate:

Vacation pay expense	$8	
Cash (or wages payable)		$6
Accrued vacation pay		2
To record vacation pay		

Each year the accrued vacation pay account would be adjusted to reflect not only the vacation days taken by the employees, but also any changes in wage rates.

ACCOUNTING FOR SICK LEAVE

It might appear as if sick leave is a compensated absence with characteristics similar to those of vacation leave and should, therefore, be accounted for in the same way. However, there is at least one critical distinction between the two types of leave. Vacation leave, along with most other types of paid time off, is within the control of the employee or the employer. Separately or together they decide when the employee will take a vacation or a paid holiday. Sick leave, by contrast, is beyond the control of both the employer and the employee.

In the public sector, sick leave most commonly accumulates, but either only a portion or none of it vests. That is, employees can store sick days that they don't take in a particular year until they need it. However, if they resign or are terminated, they are not entitled to compensation for all of their unused leave.

Example

Sick Leave

A city allows employees one day of sick leave a month and permits them to accumulate any sick leave that they do not take. If they terminate after at least 10 years of service, they will be paid for unused sick leave up to 30 days. In 2021, employees earned $12 million of sick leave that they did not take during the year. The city estimates that of this amount $8 million will be paid to employees in future years as sick leave, $1 million will be paid to 10-year employees on their termination, and $3 million will not be paid.

GASB STANDARDS

GASB standards state that sick leave should be recognized as a liability only insofar as "it is probable that the employer will compensate the employees for the benefits through cash payments *conditioned on the employees' termination or retirement ('termination benefits')*" (emphasis added). In other words, sick leave should be recorded only to the extent that it will *not be paid to employees who are sick*. Instead, it should be recorded only when expected to be paid to employees on their discharge, resignation, or retirement.[3] The standards are grounded in the rationale that sick leave, other than the portion that vests, is contingent on an employee getting sick. The key economic event, therefore, is not the employee's service, but rather his or her illness.[4]

[3] GASB Statement No. 16, *Accounting for Compensated Absences* (November 1992), para. 8.

[4] FASB Statement No. 43, *Accounting for Compensated Absences* (November 1980), draws a similar distinction between sick leave and other types of compensated absences. Whereas employers are required to accrue the costs of other types of compensated absences, they are not required to accrue a liability for nonvesting sick leave; also FASB ASC 710–10.

In the example, therefore, the city would recognize a liability only for the $1 million to be paid in termination benefits.[5] However, as with vacation pay, only the portion of the liability expected to be liquidated with expendable available financial resources may be recorded in a governmental fund. Assuming, therefore, that none of the termination benefits will be paid with funds budgeted for the current year, no entry is required in the general or other governmental fund. The obligation would be recognized only in the government-wide statement of net position and a schedule of long-term obligations.

DIFFERENCES IN GOVERNMENT-WIDE STATEMENTS

Recognition of sick leave on a full accrual basis would not affect the measurement of the obligation, only where and when it is reported. As with vacation pay, both the expense and the obligation would be reported in the government-wide financial statements in the period the sick leave is earned. Thus,

Sick leave termination benefit expense	$1	
Accrued sick leave		$1

To record sick leave termination benefits

As with vacation pay, the accrued sick leave must be adjusted each year to take into account both, the sick days taken during the year and changes in the wage rates.

[5] GASB Statement No. 16, *Accounting for Compensated Absences* (November 1992), provides detailed guidance as to how government entities should estimate the amounts to be paid on termination.

ACCOUNTING FOR SABBATICAL LEAVE

Government entities, mainly colleges, universities, and public schools, may offer employees sabbatical leaves. After a specified term of service, commonly seven years, employees (usually teachers) may be granted a paid leave of either a semester or an academic year.

As with sick leave, sabbatical leaves may appear to be similar to vacations and accounted for as such. Few teachers, however, perceive them as a time for rest and relaxation. Vacations are provided as a fringe benefit in lieu of salaries and wages. They are compensation for service already rendered. Sabbaticals, by comparison, are typically offered to benefit both the employee and the employer in the future, not the past. Employees are commonly required to perform research or public service, to take courses, or to engage in other activities that will enhance their job-related abilities. The accounting issue relating to sabbaticals is when the employer should first recognize the sabbatical costs. There are three possibilities:

- As they are earned by the employee in the period leading up to the leave
- Over the course of the leave
- Over the years to be benefited from the leave (e.g., from the end of one leave until the start of the next)

Example

Sabbatical Leave

A school district grants faculty members a one-year leave after each seven years of service to engage in research, further study, or other authorized activities. In a particular year, it paid $2 million to faculty on leave. In addition, it estimated that faculty "earned" $2.4 million toward leaves they are likely to take in the future.

In the example, the sabbatical leaves are restricted to approved activities. Therefore, they should be accounted for during the period of the leave; the school district need not accrue amounts expected to be paid in the future. Only the amount actually paid to employees on leave should be recorded as an expenditure:

Sabbatical leave expenditure	$2	
Cash (or salaries payable)		$2
To record the salaries of faculty on sabbatical		

GASB STANDARDS

GASB standards prescribe that the accounting for sabbatical leave depends on the purpose of the leave. If the leave is to provide employees with relief from their normal duties so they can perform research, obtain additional training, or engage in other activities that would "enhance the reputation of or otherwise benefit the employer," then the sabbatical should be accounted for in the period the leave is taken. No liability should be accrued in advance of the leave. If, however, the leave is for "compensated unrestricted time off," then the government should accrue a liability during the period that the leave is earned.[6]

[6] GASB Statement No. 16, *Accounting for Compensated Absences* (November 1992), para. 9.

If, by contrast, the leave were unrestricted as to purpose, then a liability must be accrued in advance, and, as with other compensated absences, only the portion expected to be liquidated with expendable available resources would be reported in a governmental fund. The balance of the liability would be recorded on the government-wide statement of net position and in a schedule of long-term obligations.

The accounting for compensated absences, including vacation pay, sick leave, and miscellaneous leave, represents the *first* major difference between how the accrual basis is applied in governmental funds and how it is applied in businesses.

DIFFERENCES IN GOVERNMENT-WIDE STATEMENTS

The switch to the full accrual basis would not affect the criteria of whether the sabbatical costs should first be recognized prior to, or during, the leave. Assuming, therefore, that the sabbatical leave is for approved activities, and not for unrestricted time off (the usual case), then both the expenditure and the related liability need not be recognized until the period in which the leave is taken. The entry at that time would be the same as that for the fund statements.

HOW SHOULD PENSIONS AND OTHER POSTEMPLOYMENT BENEFITS BE ACCOUNTED FOR?

Pensions are sums of money paid to retired or disabled employees owing to their years of employment. Under a typical plan, an employer makes a series of contributions to a special fund (referred to as a "plan") over the working lives of its employees. Under some plans the employees also contribute.

Calculating the employer contributions to the plan is necessarily complex and is based on a number of estimates, including employee life expectancy, employee turnover, and anticipated earnings of fund investments. The issue of how to compute an employer's annual pension expense and the related question of how to measure and report its actuarial liability are addressed in Chapter 10, which deals with fiduciary funds.

In this chapter, we address the relatively straightforward concern of how a governmental fund should report the expenditure and related liability for amounts to be liquidated with expendable available resources.

Example

Pension Expenditure

A city is informed by the administrator of its pension plan that per its contractual arrangement its required contribution for the current year is $55 million. It expects to make the contribution shortly after year-end.

The required entry to recognize the contractually obligated payment would be:

Pension expenditure	$55	
Pension liability		$55
To record the pension expenditure for the year		

GASB Statement No. 75, *Accounting and Financial Reporting for Postemployment Benefits Other Than Pensions* (2015), directed that other postemployment benefits (commonly referred to as OPEB and consisting most prominently of retiree health benefits) be accounted for similarly to pensions. Accordingly, as it would do with pensions, a government should report as an expenditure in its governmental funds only the amount that will be liquidated with expendable available financial resources. By contrast, on its government-wide statements a government would report an actuarially calculated amount. Pension and postemployment benefit accounting represents the *second* difference between how the accrual concept is applied in governmental funds and in businesses.

DIFFERENCES IN GOVERNMENT-WIDE STATEMENTS

In their government-wide statements, governments and proprietary funds should report as their pension and postemployment benefit expenses and liabilities amounts representative of the economic cost of the benefits. Thus, they will base them on actuarial determinations, not merely the amounts contributed to the plans during the year or expected to be contributed shortly after year-end. (This will be detailed in Chapter 10.)

HOW SHOULD CLAIMS AND JUDGMENTS BE ACCOUNTED FOR?

Governments face many types of claims and judgments. Common examples include those arising from:

- Injuries to employees (e.g., workers' compensation)
- Negligence of government employees (e.g., medical malpractice in city hospitals, failure to properly repair streets, auto accidents, wrongful arrests)
- Contractual disputes with suppliers
- Employment practices (e.g., civil rights violations, sexual harassment, wrongful discharge)

As in the private sector, the key accounting questions relating to claims and judgments are when and in what amounts expenditures and liabilities should be reported. These questions arise, first, because of the considerable length of time between when an alleged wrong takes place and when the claim is ultimately resolved and, second, because of the uncertainties as to the likelihood and dollar amount of a required payment.

In governmental funds, the major constraint in accounting for claims and judgments is identical to that faced in accounting for compensated absences. The event causing the claim or judgment usually precedes by one or more years the actual disbursement of financial resources. Yet, the governmental fund balance sheet has no place for long-term obligations.

Example

Claims and Judgments

A county is sued for personal injuries resulting from negligence on the part of a road maintenance crew. The case is settled for $400,000, to be paid in four annual installments of $100,000 beginning immediately. Inasmuch as the county uses a discount rate of 10 percent to evaluate all long-term projects, officials determine the "present value" of the eventual payment to be $348,685.

GASB STANDARDS

GASB standards for recognizing the liability for claims and judgments are drawn from FASB Statement No. 5, *Accounting for Contingencies*.[7] They are set forth in GASB Statement No. 10, *Accounting and Financial Reporting for Risk Financing and Related Insurance Issues*. A liability for claims and judgments should be recognized when information available before the issuance of financial statements indicates

- It is probable that an asset has been impaired, or a liability has been incurred at the date of the financial statements, *and*

[7] FASB ASC 958-450-25.

- The amount of the loss can be reasonably estimated.[8]

However, as with compensated absences, only the portion of the total liability that would be paid with available financial resources would be reported in the governmental fund. The balance would be reported on the government-wide statement of net position and a schedule of long-term obligations. Thus, the expenditure would be reported in the period that the liability is liquidated, not when the offending incident took place or a settlement was agreed on or imposed.

[8] GASB Statement No. 10, *Accounting and Financial Reporting for Risk Financing and Related Insurance Issues* (November 1989), para. 53.

In the example, the county estimates the present value of its liability to be $348,685, only $100,000 of which is expected to be liquidated with available financial resources. Thus, it would make the following entry in the current year (assuming that it makes its required payment):

Claims and judgments (expenditures)	$100,000	
Cash		$100,000

To record the first payment of settling claims and judgments

It would make similar entries in each of the next three years. The accounting for claims and judgments is the *third* difference between governments and businesses in the application of the accrual concept.

DIFFERENCES IN GOVERNMENT-WIDE STATEMENTS

As with compensated absences and pensions, the full accrual basis would require that the expense be recognized at the time the loss liability first satisfies the criteria of FASB Statement No. 5. Per GASB Statement No. 10, "The practice of presenting claims liabilities at the discounted present value of estimated future cash payments (discounting) is neither mandated nor prohibited. However, claims liabilities associated with structured settlements should be discounted if they represent contractual obligations to pay money on fixed or determinable dates." The statement defines a structured settlement as "a means of satisfying a claim liability, consisting of an initial cash payment to meet specific present financial needs combined with a stream of future payments designed to meet future financial needs, generally funded by annuity contracts."[9]

[9] GASB Statement No. 10, *Accounting and Financial Reporting for Risk Financing and Related Insurance Issues* (November 1989), para. 24.

In the example at hand, the settlement is clearly structured, so the county would make the following entry in the current year:

Claims and judgments (expense)	$348,685	
Cash		$100,000
Liability for claims and judgments		248,685

To record the cost of settling the lawsuit and the first cash payment

Then, in each subsequent year, two entries would be necessary—one to adjust the liability to its new present value (i.e., to add interest to the balance) and the other to account for the payment. Thus, in the year in which the second payment is made:

Interest expense	$24,869	
Liability for claims and judgments		$24,869
To adjust the liability to its new present value (10 percent of $248,685)		
Liability for claims and judgments	$100,000	
Cash		$100,000
To record the second cash payment		

In the following two years, of course, the interest expense would be different; it would be calculated as 10 percent of the existing liability for claims and judgments.

HOW SHOULD THE ACQUISITION AND USE OF MATERIALS AND SUPPLIES BE ACCOUNTED FOR?

The acquisition and use of materials and supplies (and the related issue of prepaid expenditures, to be discussed in the next section) present unique accounting problems in governmental funds. Materials and supplies and prepaid items are not strictly *expendable available financial resources*, in that they will neither be transformed into cash nor be used to satisfy governmental fund obligations. Nevertheless, having supplies on hand obviates the government from needing to purchase the items in the future.

Unlike businesses, governments do not generally acquire inventories with the intention of either reselling them or using them in manufacturing processes. They do, however, maintain inventories of office supplies, road maintenance and construction materials, spare parts, and other materials needed to carry out day-to-day operations.

Among the primary issues pertaining to governmental fund materials and supplies are

- The timing of the expenditure; specifically, should governmental funds recognize an expenditure when they *acquire*, *pay for*, or *use* the materials and supplies?
- The reporting of the asset; specifically, should inventory be reported as an asset, even though it is not strictly an expendable available financial resource?

Example

Supplies

During the year a city purchases supplies that cost $3.5 million, pays for $3.0 million of the supplies, and uses $3.3 million of them. At the start of the year it had no inventory on hand. Hence, at year-end it has $0.2 million of supplies available for future use.

GASB STANDARDS

GASB standards permit a choice. Governments may recognize inventory items either when purchased (the *purchases* method) or when consumed (the **consumption method**). However, irrespective of which method is used, significant amounts of inventory should be reported on the balance sheet.[10] Governments may *not* account for inventories on a payment (cash) basis.

[10] NCGA Statement No. 1, *Governmental Accounting and Financial Reporting Principles* (March 1979), para. 73.

The Purchases Method

Using the purchases method, a government would record the *purchase* of the inventory as an expenditure. Thus, in the example:

Supplies expenditure	$3.5	
Accounts payable		$3.5

To record the acquisition of supplies

Although the accounting is seemingly unambiguous, there's a complexity. Current standards state that significant amounts of inventory must be reported on the balance sheet. Metaphorically, they prescribe that governments may eat their cake yet have it too. By writing off the inventory on acquisition, governments implicitly deny its existence. How, then, can governments account for the full amount of the inventory acquired as an expenditure, yet still report the unused inventory as an asset? Simple, according to current standards! Show the inventory as an asset, offset by a fund balance—nonspendable. The following entry would do the trick:

Supplies inventory	$0.2	
Fund balance—nonspendable		$0.2

To record the inventory on hand at year-end

The year-end entry increases reported assets and increases the nonspendable fund balance. It has no impact on either expenditures or unassigned fund balance.

In subsequent years, the supplies inventory and the nonspendable fund balance would be adjusted to reflect the change in inventory during the year. If, at the conclusion of the following year, inventory on hand were only $150,000, then both supplies inventory and the nonspendable balance would be reduced by $50,000 (the difference between the $200,000 on hand at the end of the previous year and the $150,000 on hand at the end of the current year):

Fund balance—nonspendable	$0.05	
Supplies inventory		$0.05

To adjust the supplies inventory and related fund balance designation to reflect inventory on hand (following year)

The Purchases Method—Qualification

Few governments today account for inventories using the purchases method as described and illustrated above. This method is consistent with GASB Codification, Section 1600.127. However, it is inconsistent with Codification Section 2200.165 (drawn from GASB Statement 34, paragraph 86). That section specifies the form and content of the statement of revenues, expenditures, and changes in fund balances. It states that the statement should present the following information in the format and sequence indicated:

Revenues (detailed)
Expenditures (detailed)
  Excess (deficiency of revenues over expenditures)
Other financing sources and uses, including transfers (detailed)
Special and extraordinary items (detailed)
  Net change in fund balances
Fund balances—beginning of period
Fund balances—end of period

This "all inclusive" format provides no means to adjust the fund balance for an item that does not fit into one of the specified classifications. Hence, there is no way that governments can make the year-end adjustment to the fund balance, and thus to inventory required of the purchases method.

Some governments continue to use the purchase method despite the apparent conflict in GASB standards. They expense inventory as purchased, but do not make the year-end adjustment, noting that Section 1600.127 requires that only "significant amounts of inventory" need be reported on the balance sheet and that their inventory balances do not satisfy this criterion.

The Consumption Method

Using the **consumption method**, a government would account for inventory the same as would a business, with one additional feature—the designation of an amount equal to the inventory balance as nonspendable, as opposed to spendable. As it acquires inventory, the government would record it as an asset:

Supplies inventory	$3.5	
Accounts payable		$3.5
To record the acquisition of supplies		

Then, as it uses the inventory, it would record an expenditure and reduce the balance in the inventory account:

Supplies expenditure	$3.3	
Supplies inventory		$3.3
To record the consumption of inventory		

The reported expenditure for the year would be $3.3 million—the amount of supplies consumed. At year-end, the inventory balance would be $0.2 million—the amount of supplies on hand. Hence, a portion of fund balance equal to this amount would now have to be designated as nonspendable:

Fund balance—unassigned	$0.2	
Fund balance—nonspendable		$0.2
To reclassify fund balance to reflect year-end inventory		

In the example, irrespective of whether it uses the purchases or the consumption method, the government would record the payment for the goods purchased with the conventional entry:

Accounts payable	$3.0	
Cash		$3.0
To record payment of amounts owed to suppliers		

Inventory accounting, specifically the option to use the purchases method, is the *fourth* difference in how expenditures are accrued in governments and businesses.

DIFFERENCES IN GOVERNMENT-WIDE STATEMENTS

The purchases method is inconsistent with full accrual accounting. Hence, inventory should be reported on a consumption basis. Thus, the entries would be similar to those illustrated earlier for the consumption method, with the exception that as the supplies are used supplies *expense* rather than supplies *expenditure* would be debited. There would be no need for any reclassification of net position (the government-wide equivalent of fund balance).

HOW SHOULD PREPAYMENTS BE ACCOUNTED FOR?

Prepaid expenditures are economically comparable to inventories. For example, a government purchases an insurance policy. As with materials and supplies, it will consume a portion in one period and the balance in the following periods. Or, by paying rent in one period, it acquires the right to use property in a subsequent period.

Example

Prepayments

On September 1, 2021, a town purchases a two-year insurance policy for $60,000 (a cost of $2,500 per month).

GASB STANDARDS

"Expenditures for insurance and similar services extending over more than one accounting period need not be allocated between or among accounting periods," the standards state. Instead, they "may be accounted for as expenditures of the period of acquisition."[11]

[11] NCGA Statement No. 1, *Governmental Accounting and Financial Reporting Principles* (March 1979), para. 73.

If the town were to use the *consumption* method, then it would make the following entry upon purchasing the insurance policy:

Prepaid insurance	$60,000	
Cash (or accounts payable)		$60,000
To record purchase of a two-year insurance policy		

Then, each month for the next two years (or at year-end by way of a summary entry) it would record both an expenditure and a reduction in the balance of prepaid insurance:

Insurance expenditure	$2,500	
Prepaid insurance		$2,500
To recognize insurance expenditure for one month		

The consumption method would recognize only $10,000, the economic cost of four months of insurance.

GASB STANDARDS

GASB standards do not distinguish between "current" and "long-term prepayments." Thus, the unused portion of an insurance policy for two or more years would be reported as an asset—the same as a one-year policy. Like inventories, prepayments are not spendable and therefore the offsetting fund balance has to be classified as nonspendable.

HOW SHOULD CAPITAL ASSETS BE ACCOUNTED FOR?

Capital (fixed) assets provide services in periods beyond those in which they are acquired. In that regard, the accounting issues pertaining to capital assets are comparable to those of each of the costs addressed so far in this chapter. A three-year insurance policy benefits a government over the period covered by the policy, irrespective of whether it is paid for before, during, or after the policy period. Similarly, a computer with a three-year useful life benefits the government over the same number of years regardless of the timing of payments.

In businesses, the cost of a capital asset is recorded on the balance sheet when the asset is acquired. This cost is allocated over the asset's productive life, through the process of depreciation, to the periods in which it provides its benefits. In that way, the cost of the asset is matched to the revenues that it helps to generate.

Governmental funds could, of course, account for capital assets in the same way as businesses. Many statement users and accountants have suggested that they should. As emphasized earlier, however, governmental accounting aims to provide information as to both the extent to which interperiod equity was achieved and whether resources were used in accordance with the entity's legally adopted budget. Governments must budget and appropriate the resources for capital assets in the periods when they are to be paid for, not those in which they will be used. Therefore, accounting practices in which capital asset expenditures are tied to services rather than to payments may not provide the sought-after budget-related information.

Example

Capital Assets

A village purchases road maintenance equipment for $90,000 and pays for it at the time of acquisition. The equipment is expected to have a useful life of three years.

GASB STANDARDS

"General capital assets" are the capital assets of a government that are not specifically related to activities that are reported in proprietary or fiduciary funds. Most often they result from the expenditure of governmental fund financial resources. As pointed out in previous chapters, GASB standards preclude governments from reporting general capital assets on governmental fund balance sheets or from depreciating them on governmental fund statements of revenues, expenditures, and changes in fund balance. Instead, governments report them in the period requiring the outflow of expendable available financial resources.

In the example, the following entry would be appropriate when the assets are acquired:

Capital assets—expenditure	$90,000	
Cash		$90,000
To record the acquisition of equipment		

ACQUISITION OF CAPITAL ASSETS FINANCED WITH DEBT

The main accounting issue presented by the acquisition of capital assets with debt arises because the purchase of the asset does not coincide with the repayment of the debt and, in effect, with the outflow of the cash or other expendable resources required to obtain the asset. Thus, it is not obvious when the expenditures associated with the acquisition of the asset and the repayment of the debt should be recorded. For example, should the cost of the asset be recognized at the time of purchase, even in the absence of a cash outflow, or only as the debt is repaid?

When governments issue bonds to acquire assets, they often account for the debt proceeds in a capital projects fund. However, governments may also account for debt proceeds in other governmental funds, such as the general fund or special revenue funds. The debt may take the form of conventional notes, installment notes, or capital leases. The accounting for capital projects funds is discussed in Chapter 6. At this time it should be noted, however, that because capital projects and special revenue funds are governmental funds, the same general principles of accounting apply to them as to the general fund.

Example

Installment Notes

As in the "Capital Assets" example, a village purchases road maintenance equipment for $90,000. This time, however, the equipment is acquired on an installment basis with three annual installments of $36,190—the amount required to liquidate a loan of $90,000 over three periods at an interest rate of 10 percent.

Inasmuch as long-term obligations are not reported in governmental funds, GASB standards require that the proceeds of long-term debt be reflected as "other financing sources" in the recipient fund's operating statement.[12] Thus, were the village to *borrow* $90,000 cash, the following entry would be appropriate in the governmental fund receiving the proceeds:

Cash	$90,000	
Other financing sources—installment note proceeds		$90,000
To record a loan		

Were the government to use the proceeds to acquire a capital asset, the governmental fund entry illustrated in the previous example would be appropriate:

Capital assets—expenditure	$90,000	
Cash		$90,000
To record the acquisition of equipment		

In the example at hand, the government borrowed the purchase price (through the installment note) and acquired the asset, but at the time of acquisition did not actually receive or pay cash. Hence, it could properly make the following combining entry that eliminates the debit and credit to cash:

Capital assets—expenditure	$90,000	
Other financing sources—installment note proceeds		$90,000
To record the acquisition of equipment		

The related accounting question is how the loan repayment should be recorded. Specifically, to what type of account should the payment be charged, because no long-term liability is reported on the governmental fund balance sheet?

Consistent with the current model in which expenditures are recognized when there is a decrease in current financial resources, the repayment must be charged as an expenditure. Thus, the following entry would recognize the first payment of principal and interest:

Debt service expenditure (note principal)	$27,190	
Debt service expenditure (interest)	9,000	
Cash		$36,190
To record the first payment of installment note interest (10 percent of $90,000) and principal		

On the government fund statement of revenues and expenditures, none of these revenues and expenditures would be shown along with ordinary operating amounts. The proceeds of the installment note would be reported in the section of the statement for other financing sources (uses); the capital asset expenditure would be reported in that for capital outlays; the repayment of the note principal and the payment of the interest would be reported in that for debt service. Subsequent payments would be recorded in the same way, with only the division of the payment between principal and interest changing from period to period. As a result of these entries, neither the equipment nor the related long-term debt would be shown on the fund balance sheet. They would, of course, be reported on the government-wide statement of net position as well as on any schedules of capital assets and long-term debt.

The series of entries may be disconcerting in that it results in the asset being recorded as an expenditure twice—once when acquired and again as the loan is repaid. Nonetheless, the double-counting does not cause fund balance to be misstated because the expenditure recorded upon acquisition of the asset is offset by "other financing sources"—a credit to fund balance that adds back the amount of the charge.

[12] NCGA Statement No. 1, *Governmental Accounting and Financial Reporting Principles* (March 1979), para. 108.

CAPITAL LEASES

A capital lease is the equivalent of a purchase–borrow transaction. In economic substance, the lessee (the party that will use the property) becomes the owner of the leased asset. The lessee treats the lease as a purchase of the asset. It makes periodic payments, each of which represents a partial repayment of the amount "borrowed" (the value of the property at the inception of the lease), plus interest.

Example

Capital Leases

Instead of purchasing the $90,000 of equipment, the village leases it under an arrangement that satisfies the criteria of a capital lease. The term of the lease is three years. The village agrees to make three annual payments of $36,190, an amount that reflects interest at an annual rate of 10 percent.

Current standards specify that capital leases should be accounted for similarly to other purchase/borrow acquisition of capital assets.[13] Thus, in the example, the village would record the lease in the same way as it did the installment purchase, varying only the account descriptions:

Capital assets—expenditure	$90,000	
Other financing sources—capital lease		$90,000
To record the acquisition of equipment under a capital lease		
Debt service expenditure (lease principal)	$27,190	
Debt service expenditure (lease interest)	9,000	
Cash		$36,190
To record the first lease payment consisting of interest (10 percent of $90,000) and principal		

As with the installment note, subsequent payments would necessitate a different division of the payment between principal and interest.

The accounting for capital assets, whether they are acquired for cash or paid for over time, is the *sixth* difference between expenditure accruals in businesses and governments.

DIFFERENCES IN GOVERNMENT-WIDE STATEMENTS

Capital assets, irrespective of whether acquired with cash, in an installment purchase or by capital lease, are reported on the government-wide statement of net position (balance sheet) at historical cost, net of accumulated depreciation. Correspondingly, the debt associated with the assets is also given balance sheet recognition. A charge for depreciation of the assets is included in the statement of activities (a statement of revenues and expenses). The accounting for capital assets, including special rules pertaining to infrastructure, is discussed in greater detail in Chapter 7.

[13] NCGA Statement No. 5, *Accounting and Financial Reporting Principles for Lease Agreements of State and Local Governments* (December 1982).

HOW SHOULD INTEREST AND PRINCIPAL ON LONG-TERM DEBT BE ACCOUNTED FOR?

Interest on long-term debt is a major expenditure for many governments. Most typically, government debt takes the form of bonds that pay interest twice per year. Many governments accumulate the resources to pay both the interest and principal on their debts in a debt service fund (a governmental fund). However, the original source of payments is likely to be either general revenues or revenues specially dedicated for debt service. As the scheduled payments from the debt service fund must be made, the government transfers the necessary cash from the general fund or a special revenue fund.

Long-term debts, as previously emphasized, are not recorded as liabilities in governmental funds; they are included only in the government-wide statements and listed in the schedule of long-term obligations. When bonds or other forms of debt are issued, the increase in (debit to) cash is offset by a credit to "bond proceeds," an operating statement account, rather than to "bonds payable," a balance sheet account. Therefore, when the bonds are repaid the offset to cash cannot be to a liability account. Instead, it must be to an expenditure or a comparable operating statement account.

The key accounting issues with regard to long-term debt interest and principal arise because debt service payments may extend beyond a fiscal year. A six-month interest payment may cover some months in one year and some in another. Similarly, a principal repayment may be due every six months, a period that extends over two fiscal years. Should the expenditures be allocated proportionately among the years (i.e., accrued), or should they be recognized entirely in the year of payment?

Given the virtues of the accrual basis of accounting in capturing the economic substance of events and transactions, the answer may appear obvious: allocate proportionately among the years. But bear in mind that debt service may involve large dollar amounts. Taxpayers obviously prefer to provide resources only as they are required to satisfy current obligations. Most governments budget (appropriate) resources for principal and interest only for the period in which they must make actual payments. They do not set aside resources for payments to be made in the future. Therefore, the goal of reporting on budgetary compliance, in contrast to that of reporting on interperiod equity, would suggest that the expenditures be recognized entirely in the year the payments are due.

Example

Long-term Debt

A state issues $100 million of 20-year bonds on August 1, 2020, at an annual rate of 6 percent. Interest of $3 million per semiannual period is payable on January 31 and July 31. The bonds are sold for $89.3 million, a price that reflects an annual yield of 7 percent (semiannual yield of 3.5 percent). The first payment of the interest is due on January 31, 2021.

GASB STANDARDS

GASB standards specify that in governmental funds neither interest nor principal on long-term debt should be accrued in advance of the year in which it is due. Both should be accrued only in the period in which they are due. Until then, they are not current liabilities; they will not require the liquidation of expendable available financial resources.

In the example, the government would make *no entry* in 2020 to accrue either interest or principal on the debt. It would not record an interest expenditure until January 31, 2021, when the first bond interest payment is due. The following entry would then be required in the fund out of which the payment was to be made:

Debt service, interest—expenditure	$3	
Matured bond interest payable		$3
To record obligation for bond interest due		

When the bonds mature in July 2037, the government would make a comparable entry to record the obligation for principal:

Debt service, principal—expenditure	$100	
Matured bonds payable		$100
To record obligation for matured bonds payable		

ADVERSE CONSEQUENCES OF FOCUS ON CASH PAYMENTS

Consistent with the standards that neither interest nor principal should be accrued until due, current standards for governmental funds make no provision for recognizing and amortizing bond discounts or premiums. As a result, the reported interest expenditure fails to capture the true economic cost of using borrowed funds. Instead, it indicates merely the required interest coupon payments. In the preceding example, the state borrowed only $89.3 million (the amount of the proceeds), not $100 million (the face value). Its true economic cost of using the borrowed funds in the six months ending January 31, 2021, was $3.1 million ($89.3 million times the effective interest, or yield, rate of 3.5 percent per period), not $3.0 million (the required payment). Nevertheless, as illustrated, the state would record an interest expenditure equal to the $3.0 million required payment.

The failure of current standards to recognize premiums and discounts may not be particularly serious when the difference is small between a bond's coupon rate and yield rate. But when the difference is large, it results in financial statements that seriously distort borrowing costs. Consider an extreme case. A government issues $100 million in 20-year **zero coupon bonds**. The bonds are sold for $25.26 million, a price that provides an annual yield of about 7 percent (3.5 percent per semiannual period). As implied by their name, these bonds pay zero interest each period. Instead, they are sold at a deep discount, in this case a discount of $74.74 million. Upon maturity, the investor, who loaned the government $25.26 million, would receive $100 million. Inasmuch as $25.26 million is the present value of $100 million discounted at a rate of 3.5 percent for 40 periods, the bonds provide a return of 3.5 percent (compounded) per semiannual period. The accompanying "In Practice" highlights the severity of this issue even further.

Under current standards for governmental funds, the government would record *no* interest or principal costs until the bonds mature. In the period of maturity, it would recognize the entire $100 million as a debt service expenditure. Fortunately, users are informed of the economic costs through the government-wide statements in which long-term debt is accounted for on a full accrual basis.

IN PRACTICE CALIFORNIA SCHOOL CHILDREN MAY PAY FOR THEIR OWN EDUCATION

Do zero coupon bonds make sense? They may if you are a California school district with a need to improve facilities and are unable to afford the interest payments on conventional bonds.

That's what motivated the Poway Unified School District, located in San Diego County, to issue $105 million in "capital appreciation" bonds. The bonds, issued in 2011, do not require the district to pay either interest or principal until 2033. As reported in the *Voice of San Diego* (a web-based news service), voters authorized the district to borrow money to modernize its schools, but the district promised not to increase taxes.* Therefore it could not afford to issue conventional bonds.

The capital appreciation bonds (in effect, zero coupon bonds) do not come cheap. The interest rate on the bonds was 6.8 percent compared to a going rate on conventional bonds of approximately 4.2 percent. That means that for the $105 million that the district borrowed, it will have to pay $877 million in interest by the time the bonds fully mature in 2051. This compares to less than $145 million if the district had issued bonds that were similar to a mortgage and thereby made annual interest payments and paid down the principle over time.

Children attending school in 2011 will be taxpayers in 2033 when the first bills are due. Hence, their parents are saddling them with the cost of their own education.

The Poway bonds are not unique. School districts in the United States sold almost $4 billion of similar bonds in 2011.

*Posted August 6, 2012. Available at http://www.voiceofsandiego.org/education/article_c83343e8-ddd5-11e1-bfca-001a4bcf887a.html. See also, Floyd Norris, "Schools Pass Debt to the Next Generation," New York Times (August 16, 2012).

ACCRUAL OF INTEREST AND PRINCIPAL WHEN RESOURCES ARE TRANSFERRED

GASB standards make one exception to the general rule that neither interest nor principal be accrued. If resources to service the debt are transferred to a debt service fund from another governmental fund in a current year for payment of principal and interest due early the next year (within no more than a month), then both the expenditure and related liability *may* be (but is not *required* to be) recognized in the recipient debt service fund.[14]

Suppose that in the example, in 2020, the general fund transferred to the debt service fund $2.5 million of the $3 million bond interest payment due on January 31, 2021. The debt service fund would, of course, recognize the cash received as an asset and would record an increase in fund balance. Per the standard, to avoid reporting a misleadingly high fund balance, the debt service fund would be permitted also to accrue the related bond interest expenditure. Thus:

Debt service, bond interest—expenditure	$2.5	
Accrued bond interest payable		$2.5

To accrue bond interest for five months in the amount of resources received from the general fund

The accounting for debt interest and principal is the *seventh* difference in the application of the accrual concept.

DIFFERENCES IN GOVERNMENT-WIDE STATEMENTS

Just as long-lived assets must be recorded at cost less accumulated depreciation in the government-wide statements, long-term debt must be reported at face value plus any unamortized premiums or less any unamortized discounts. Interest must be accrued; the timing of cash payments is irrelevant to the period in which the expense is recognized. Thus, the state would record the issuance of the bonds as follows:

Cash	$89.3	
Discount on bonds payable	10.7	
Bonds payable		$100.0

To record the issuance of operating debt

Then as it pays interest, it would record the payment ($3.0 million), the interest expense (the yield rate times the net carrying value of the bonds), and the amortization of the premium or discount (the difference between the two). As of December 31, 2020, the end of the first period, in which no interest was yet paid, the following entry would be appropriate to accrue five months' interest:

Interest expense	$2.6	
Accrued interest payable		$2.5
Discount on bond payable		0.1

To accrue five months' interest (interest expense = 5/6 of the effective interest rate of 3.5 percent times the effective liability of $89.3 million; accrued interest payable = 5/6 of the required payment of $3.0 million; discount on bond payable = the difference between the two, that is, 5/6 of the total amount of bond discount to be amortized at time of the first interest payment)

Long-term debt is addressed in detail in Chapter 8.

HOW SHOULD NONEXCHANGE EXPENDITURES BE ACCOUNTED FOR?

Chapter 4, "Recognizing Revenues in Governmental Funds," deals primarily with *nonexchange* revenues, as most governmental fund revenues are derived from nonexchange transactions. This chapter, however, is directed mainly to *exchange* expenditures, as relatively few types of government expenditures are associated with nonexchange transactions. Governments, for example, do not typically pay taxes or fines (nonexchange transactions), though they do make grants to other governments (also nonexchange transactions).

[14] GASB Interpretation No. 6, *Recognition and Measurement of Certain Liabilities and Expenditures in Governmental Fund Financial Statements* (March 2000).

GASB STANDARDS

Nonexchange expenditures should generally be recognized symmetrically with their revenue counterparts. Thus, providers of grants should recognize an expenditure when the recipient has satisfied all eligibility requirements, including time requirements.

Example

Unrestricted Grant with Time Requirement

In December 2021, a county's council approves a $300,000 grant to a not-for-profit health clinic. The funds are to be paid in 2022 out of funds budgeted for that year and are intended to support the clinic's activities in 2022.

Inasmuch as the funds are intended to be used in 2022, the grant is subject to a time requirement. Because the county disbursed no cash in 2021 and the time requirement has not yet been satisfied, it need not make any entry in that year. It should delay recognizing both a grant expenditure and an offsetting liability until the time requirement is satisfied.

Example

Grant with Purpose Restriction

In December 2021, a state department of transportation awards a county $400,000 for road improvements. Payment is made at the time the award is announced. The county is permitted to use the funds upon receipt but intends to use them in 2022.

Purpose restrictions have no impact on the timing of either expenditure or revenue recognition, nor does the county's intent to use them in a particular year. The state must recognize an expenditure as soon as it makes the award:

Grant expenditure	$400,000	
Cash		$400,000
To record grant expenditure (in 2021)		

Example

Reimbursement (Eligibility Requirement) Grant

In December 2021, a state awards a city $200,000 for the acquisition of an emergency telephone system. The grant is to be paid as the city incurs and documents allowable costs. In 2021, the city submits claims for $150,000, of which the state pays $125,000. The state expects to pay the $25,000 balance of submitted claims in January 2022 and the $50,000 balance of the grant by June 2022.

The city is eligible for the award only as it incurs and documents allowable costs. In 2021, the city became eligible for $150,000 of the grant—the amount that the state should recognize as an expenditure.

Grant expenditure	$150,000	
Cash		$125,000
Grants payable		25,000
To recognize a reimbursement grant expenditure (in 2021)		

DIFFERENCES IN GOVERNMENT-WIDE STATEMENTS

The standards of GASB Statement No. 33, *Accounting and Financial Reporting for Nonexchange Transactions*, are applicable to both modified and full accrual statements. On the modified, but not the full, accrual statements, revenues must be available for expenditure before they can be recognized. That requirement is not, of course, relevant to expenses. Hence, the grants would be recognized as expenses in the same period in the government-wide statements as in the fund statements.

ASSETS VERSUS DEFERRED OUTFLOWS

Now that the GASB has distinguished between assets and **deferred outflows**, it may not be obvious how specific items should be classified. Fortunately, individual governments do not have to make those judgments. Concepts Statement No. 4, Elements of Financial Statements, stipulates that recognition of both deferred outflows and deferred inflows should be limited to instances explicitly specified by the Board in its authoritative pronouncements.

Concepts Statement No. 4 defines assets as "resources with present service capacity that the government presently controls." By contrast, it defines deferred outflows as the "consumption of net assets by the government that is applicable to a future reporting period" (emphasis added).

In the view of the Board, prepayments, such as prepaid insurance and prepaid rent, should continue to be classified as assets because they have present service capacity that a government presently controls.[15] Thus, in the Prepayments example illustrated earlier in the chapter that involved prepaid insurance, the prepaid insurance would be reported as an asset, not a deferred outflow. Similarly, cash or other resources advanced to a grant recipient should continue to be classified as an asset until eligibility requirements, other than time requirements, have been met. Until then, the government has control over the resources that have been advanced to the grant recipient because it can demand repayment if the recipient fails to satisfy the eligibility requirements.

By contrast, once the recipient has satisfied the eligibility requirements, other than time requirements, it is no longer likely that the government can reacquire its resources. Hence, the government should classify the offset to the cash advanced with a deferred outflow rather than with an asset. Suppose in the example, Unrestricted Grant with Time Requirement, in 2021 the health clinic had satisfied all eligibility requirements for the grant and, as stated, the grant was intended to support the clinic's 2022 activities. However, contrary to the stated facts, if the government had made the cash payment to the clinic in 2021, then in that case, upon making the cash payment, the county should record a deferred outflow (e.g., "advance to grantee"); presumably it has surrendered the cash and is unlikely to be able to recover it.

Other than transactions involving grants, the GASB specified relatively few situations in which it would be appropriate to record deferred outflows. They deal with fees related to loans and leases.

HOW SHOULD INTERFUND TRANSACTIONS BE ACCOUNTED FOR?

As stressed in Chapter 2, each of a government's funds is an independent fiscal and accounting entity. When the focus is on individual funds, many types of activities between funds create revenues and expenditures. Yet, when the government is viewed as a whole, most of these activities are nothing more than intragovernmental transfers. If certain types of activities were classified as revenues of one fund and expenditures of another, then the revenues and the expenditures of the government as a whole would be overstated.

[15] Items to be reported as deferred inflows and outflows are specified mainly in Statement No. 65, *Items Previously Reported as Assets and Liabilities* (2012). See paragraphs 67 through 70 for the basis for conclusions pertaining to government-mandated nonexchange transactions and voluntary nonexchange transactions.

In Concepts Statement No. 4, *Elements of Financial Statements*, para. 59 the GASB explains why prepaid rent meets the definition of an asset: "It meets the definition of an asset because it is an item with present service capacity (use of the rented item) that is controlled by the government. It does not meet the definition of a deferred outflow of resources because the prepayment of rent did not result in a consumption of net assets. The asset, cash, decreased at the same time as the asset, prepaid rent, increased. Thus, net assets are unchanged."

Example

Interfund Transfer

A government transfers $3 million from its general fund to a debt service fund for payment of interest. When the debt service fund pays the interest, it will record the payment as an expenditure.

Should the general fund record the payment to the debt service fund as an expenditure and the debt service fund record the receipt as a revenue? As independent entities, both funds incur expenditures; the debt service fund also earns revenue. Yet, if each fund recognizes an expenditure, the government as a whole would recognize the interest cost as an expenditure twice (once in the general fund when the resources are transferred to the debt service fund and again when the interest is paid out of the debt service fund).

Example

Interfund Purchase/Sale

A government department, which is accounted for in the entity's general fund, acquires $30,000 of supplies from a supply center that is accounted for in an internal service fund.

The internal service fund will report the cost of the supplies "sold" as an expense. Should the general fund also report an expenditure? If it does not, then its reported expenditures—the measure of the cost of general government operations—would be less than if it had purchased the same supplies from outside vendors.

GASB STANDARDS

Statement No. 34 differentiates between two types of interfund activity:

1. ***Reciprocal interfund activity.*** This is the internal equivalent of exchange transactions (those in which the parties receive and surrender consideration of approximately equal value). They include
   - *Payments for the purchase of goods and services at a price that approximates their external fair value, such as when the general fund acquires goods from an internal service fund.* These transfers should be reported as revenues in the seller fund and expenditures (or expenses) in the purchasing fund.
   - *Loans and repayments of loans.* If the loans are expected to be repaid within a reasonable period of time, the lending fund should report the loan as a receivable and the borrowing fund should report it as a payable. This activity should not be reported as other financing sources or uses in the fund financial statements. If the loans are not expected to be repaid within a reasonable period of time (and hence are not bona fide loans), then the transaction should be accounted for by the disbursing fund as a nonreciprocal transfer-out and by the receiving fund as a nonreciprocal transfer-in.
2. ***Nonreciprocal interfund activity.*** This is the internal equivalent of nonexchange transactions. They include
   - *Transfers of cash for which goods or services of equivalent value have not been received, such as when the general fund transfers cash to a debt service fund for payment of principal or interest on long-term debt or when the general fund transfers cash to a newly established internal service fund for "start-up capital."* These transfers should be reported as other financing uses in the funds making the transfers and as other financing sources in the funds receiving transfers.
   - *Interfund reimbursements—repayments from a fund responsible for an expenditure to the fund that initially paid for them.* These should not be reported at all in the financial statements. Thus, if the general fund paid a bill for a cost that was the responsibility of a capital projects fund, the expenditure and the corresponding reduction in cash should be reported only in the capital projects fund—as if the capital projects fund had paid the bill itself. The capital projects fund should not report a transfer-out to the general fund; the general fund should report neither a payment to the vendor nor a transfer-in from the capital projects fund.

In the "Interfund Transfer" example, the payment of interest by the general fund to the debt service fund would be recorded by the general fund as nonreciprocal transfer-out and by the debt service fund as a nonreciprocal transfer-in:

Nonreciprocal transfer-out to debt service fund (other financing use)	$3	
Cash		$3
To record transfer to debt service fund (in general fund)		
Cash	$3	
Nonreciprocal transfer-in from general fund (other financing sources)		$3
To record transfer from general fund (in debt service fund)		

In the "Interfund Purchase/Sale" example, by contrast, the payment by the general fund to the internal service fund for supplies would be considered a reciprocal transaction and hence recorded as if it were an exchange transaction:

Supplies expenditure	$30,000	
Cash		$30,000
To record the purchase of supplies (in the general fund)		
Cash	$30,000	
Sales revenue		$30,000
To record the sale of supplies (in the internal service fund)		

DIFFERENCES IN GOVERNMENT-WIDE STATEMENTS

As implied by their title, government-wide statements present revenues and expenses from the perspective of the entity, not individual funds. Reported expenses are generally those of the entity as a whole (divided into columns for governmental and business-type activities), not of individual funds. To avoid double-counting, interfund revenues and expenditures must be eliminated.

Special provisions of GASB Statement No. 34 direct how interfund activity involving internal service funds should be eliminated. Internal service fund residual balances (those remaining after the interfund activity has been eliminated) are included in the governmental activities column because they provide services mainly to governmental funds. These provisions are addressed in Chapter 9 pertaining to business-type activities.

WHAT CONSTITUTES OTHER FINANCING SOURCES AND USES?

Governmental funds receive or use resources from transactions that, under a full accrual basis, would affect long-term assets or liability accounts. For example, if a business issues long-term debt, it would establish a long-term liability. However, the measurement focus of governmental funds excludes both capital assets and long-term liabilities. Therefore, resources received from the issuance of bonds cannot be recorded as liabilities. Although similar to revenues in that they increase fund balance, they lack the characteristics of conventional revenues in that they will need to be repaid. Similarly, the proceeds from the sale of equipment can neither reduce a reported asset nor be interpreted as revenue.

Generally accepted accounting and reporting standards direct that certain governmental resource flows that would otherwise affect long-term assets or liabilities be classified on statements of revenues, expenditures, and changes in fund balances as other financing sources and uses. The main types of other financing sources and uses are

Sources

- Proceeds of long-term debt
- Proceeds from the sale of capital assets
- Present value of liabilities created by capital leases
- Nonreciprocal transfers-in

Uses

- Payments to bond "escrow" agents who maintain accounts for the eventual repayment of long-term obligations
- Nonreciprocal transfers-out

HOW SHOULD REVENUES, EXPENDITURES, AND OTHER FINANCING SOURCES AND USES BE REPORTED?

In light of the variety of activities and transactions in which the multitude of entities engage, governments need flexibility as to the form and content of their financial statements. At the same time, though, a certain degree of uniformity is required if statement users are to make meaningful comparisons among governments. Therefore, the GASB has set forth only the general framework of the statement of revenues, expenditures, and changes in fund balances.

The governmental funds statements of revenues, expenditures, and changes in fund balances of Charlotte, North Carolina, were illustrated in Chapter 2, Table 2-6.

GASB STANDARDS

Revenues, expenditures, and changes in fund balances should be reported in governmental funds in a statement that takes the following form:

Revenues (detailed)	$100
Expenditures (detailed)	90
Excess of revenues over expenditures	10
Other financing sources and uses, including transfers (detailed)	(5)
Special items (detailed)	1
Extraordinary items (detailed)	7
Net change in fund balance	13
Fund balances beginning of period	11
Fund balances end of period	$ 24

Expenditures would generally be shown by function (e.g., public safety, recreation, administration) rather than by object (e.g., salaries, travel, rent).

Extraordinary items are transactions or other events that are both unusual in nature and infrequent in occurrence. These are transactions that are clearly incidental or unrelated to the ordinary activities of the entity. **Special items**, although similar to extraordinary items in that they are also unusual in nature and infrequent in occurrence, are significant transactions that are *within the control of management.*[16] Moreover, special items include transactions that meet one of the two criteria but not the other—that is, transactions which are either unusual in nature or infrequent in occurrence, but not both.[17]

[16] GASB Statement No. 34, *Basic Financial Statements—and Management's Discussion and Analysis—for State and Local Governments* (June 1999), paras. 55 and 56.

[17] Stephen J.Gautier, *Governmental Accounting, Auditing, and Financial Reporting* (Chicago: Government Finance Officers Association, 2012), 114.

WHAT IS THE SIGNIFICANCE OF THE CURRENT FINANCIAL GOVERNMENTAL FUND STATEMENTS? AN OVERVIEW

The ultimate question faced by governmental fund financial statement readers is, "What does it all mean?" A governmental fund balance sheet presents the fund's resources at a particular point in time; its operating statement accounts for the net change in those resources during a particular period of time. All measurements, however, are in accord with generally accepted accounting principles (GAAP).

As made apparent in this and the previous chapter, governmental fund revenues and expenditures are frequently determined on different bases for purposes of budgeting rather than for financial reporting. Assuming the budget is on a cash or near-cash basis, examples of significant differences include

- For purposes of budgeting, governments may recognize taxes as revenues only as collected; in accord with GAAP, they must recognize them as revenues only when they are both measurable and available to finance expenditures of the fiscal period.
- For purposes of budgeting, governments may account for wages and salaries on a cash basis; as required by GAAP, they must accrue compensation expenditures as long as the payments will be made with expendable available financial resources.
- For purposes of budgeting, governments may account for supplies and prepayments on a cash basis; as permitted by GAAP, they may use the consumption method.

Consequently, the reported revenues and expenditures, and the resultant surplus or deficit, may not be comparable with corresponding budgeted amounts.

Moreover, the balance sheet may not present a clear picture of either resources available for appropriation or the claims against those resources. It may not reflect taxes and other receivables that the government may be able to use to cover expenditures of the following and future years. Correspondingly, it may not show all of the claims against the fund's resources, such as those for deferred compensation, interest, and legal judgments.

The operating statement also cannot be counted on to reveal the true economic costs of government operations or the economic value of resources that it actually received or to which it became entitled during the year. Because they are based on modified rather than full accrual accounting, governmental fund operating statements fail to recognize the cost of using as opposed to purchasing supplies, of renting equipment or other property as opposed to making the rent payments, and of using as opposed to acquiring capital assets.

The GASB standards of revenue and expenditure recognition satisfy both the interperiod equity and the budgetary compliance objectives of financial reporting, but only to a limited extent. The government-wide statements provide greater information on the economic costs of operations and on the economic value of resources. However, in the absence of other changes in principles, the fund statements will continue to fall short of indicating budget-based revenues and expenditures and the resources that are legally available for appropriation.

The limitations of the fund statements do not, by themselves, imply criticisms of either the statements themselves or the rule-making authorities responsible for them. As suggested in Chapter 1, it is questionable whether a single set of financial statements can satisfy all the key accounting and reporting objectives. It is for that reason that the complete government reporting model encompasses two sets of financial statements—fund and government-wide.

SUMMARY

Rulemaking authorities recommend use of the accrual basis to the fullest extent practicable in the government environment. But they have substantially modified the accrual basis from the way it is applied in governmental funds as opposed to businesses, proprietary funds, and government-wide statements.

As pointed out in the previous chapter, for revenues to be recognized in governmental funds not only must a key underlying event take place but also the resources to be received must be *measurable and available to finance expenditures of the fiscal period.*

In this chapter, we stressed that governmental fund expenditures are defined as "decreases in *net financial resources*," in contrast to *expenses*, which represent outflows or consumption of *overall net assets*. As a consequence, we identified seven differences in how the accrual concept is applied in governments as opposed to businesses. These are accounting for compensated absences, pension and OPEB, claims and judgments, inventories, prepayments, capital assets, and principal and interest payment on debt.

We also noted that governmental fund nonexchange transactions (mainly grants) are accounted for symmetrically to nonexchange revenues. Hence, grants are recognized as expenditures when the recipient has met all eligibility requirements and the grantor thereby incurs an obligation. Table 5-1 summarizes the general principles of expenditure and expenses recognition. However, now that governments must distinguish between assets and deferred outflows, cash advances to grantees before eligibility requirements (excluding time requirements) have been met should be reported as deferred outflows. By contrast, prepayments should continue to be classified as assets.

TABLE 5-1 Summary of Expenditure/Expense Recognition Principles

I. Governmental statements in general are accounted for on an accrual basis.

A. However, the accrual basis is modified in the following ways for fund financial statements as to when *expenditures* are recognized.

1. Vacations, sick leave, and other compensated absences are not accrued unless they will be liquidated with current financial resources.
2. The reported pension expenditure includes only the governmental fund's actual contribution for the year, not, as in businesses or on government-wide statements, an actuarially determined contribution.
3. Claims and judgments are reported as expenditures only insofar as they will be paid out of current financial resources.
4. Inventory (and hence the cost of using supplies) must be accounted for using a consumption method.
5. Prepaid items must also be accounted for on a consumption basis.
6. The costs of capital assets are reported as expenditures when the assets are acquired; capital assets are not depreciated.
7. Repayment of long-term capital debt is reported as expenditure as payments are made; interest on the debt is ordinarily not accrued. However, interest and principal *may* be accrued in a debt service fund if resources have been transferred in from another fund to make payments that are due early the next year (within no more than a month).

B. Liabilities are recognized in governmental fund statements only to the extent that they will be liquidated with current financial resources.

C. Nonexchange transactions are recognized symmetrically to their revenue counterparts. (See Chapter 4.)

II. Government-wide statements are accounted for on a full accrual basis. Hence, *expenses* are generally recognized as they are in businesses and in governments' proprietary funds.

KEY TERMS IN THIS CHAPTER

consumption method 202
deferred outflows 213
expenditures 192
expenses 192
extraordinary items 216
financial resources 192
object 194
special items 216
zero coupon bonds 210

EXERCISE FOR REVIEW AND SELF-STUDY

For years beginning January 1, 2021, the City of Arbor Hills will finance its parks and recreation activities with a special property tax levy. Accordingly, it will account for resources related to parks and recreation in a special revenue fund. During 2021, it engaged in the following transactions:

1. The fund received $6 million from the city's special parks and recreation property tax levy.
2. During the year, the parks and recreation employees earned $4.5 million in wages and salaries. Of this amount, the city paid $4.1 million in 2021 and is to pay the balance early in 2022.
3. Parks and recreation employees earned $0.26 million in vacation leave and were paid for $0.20 million. The city estimates that it will pay the entire balance in the future.
4. The employees earned $0.17 million in sick leave but were paid for only $0.14 million. The leave accumulates but does not vest.
5. According to city actuaries, employees earned $0.37 million in pensions. However, the city had budgeted only $0.30 million. During the year, it contributed to its pension fund $0.25 million and plans to contribute an additional $0.05 million in early January 2022.
6. During 2021, the city received in parks and recreation supplies $0.70 million, used $0.55 million, and paid for $0.50 million. The city uses the *consumption* method to account for supplies inventory.
7. In January 2021, the city purchased $1 million in parks and recreation equipment. It paid $0.20 million in cash and gave an installment note for the balance. The first payment on the note ($0.30 million plus interest of $0.05 million) is due on January 12, 2022.
8. In December 2021, the City approved, and made payment on, a grant to the local food bank for $0.15 million. The grant could be applied to the food bank costs only in the calendar year 2022. At the time of payment, the food bank had met all eligibility requirements other than the time requirement.
   a. Prepare journal entries to summarize the transactions that affected the special revenue fund in 2021.
   b. Prepare a statement of revenues, expenditures, and changes in fund balance and a balance sheet for the Parks and Recreation Fund as of December 31, 2021.
   c. Indicate any assets, liabilities that would be reported in the city's schedules of capital assets, or long-term obligation as a consequence of the transactions engaged in by the Parks and Recreation Fund.
   d. Comment on how each of the transactions would be reported on the city's government-wide statements.

QUESTIONS FOR REVIEW AND DISCUSSION

1. What is the distinction between expenditures and expenses as the terms are used in governmental accounting?
2. A government expects to pay its electric bill relating to its current fiscal year sometime in the following year. An official of the government requests your advice as to whether the anticipated payment should be charged as an expenditure of the current or the following year. How would you respond?
3. Under pressure to balance their budgets, governments at all levels have resorted to fiscal gimmicks, such as delaying the wages and salaries of government employees from the last day of the month to the first day of the following month. In the year of the change they thereby had one fewer pay periods. How would the change affect the reported expenditures of a governmental fund under GAAP?
4. A government permits its employees to accumulate all unused vacation days and sick leave. Whereas (in accord with current standards) it may have to "book" a liability for the unused vacation days, it may not have to record an obligation for the unused sick leave. Explain and justify the applicable standards.
5. A school district grants teachers a sabbatical leave every seven years. Yet, consistent with GAAP, it fails to accrue a liability for such leave over the period in which the leave is earned—not even in its government-wide statements. How can you justify such accounting?

6. A government accounts for inventory on the consumption basis. Why do some accountants believe that it should offset the year-end inventory balance with a fund balance—nonspendable when no comparable fund balance is required for cash, taxes receivable, or most other assets?

7. Many accountants note that for most governments the reported "bottom line" of their financial statements (i.e., revenues less expenditures/expenses and other charges that affect fund balance/net position) will not greatly differ between their fund statements and their government-wide statements insofar as the expenditures/expenses relate to long-term assets and the long-term liabilities issued to finance those assets. That's because governments typically repay the debt evenly over a period which approximates the economic life of the related asset. Assuming the accountant's assumption as to means of financing to be correct, will the expenditures and related charges affecting fund balance of the governmental fund statements approximate the expenses of the government-wide statements?

8. Governments are not required to accrue interest on long-term debt in governmental funds even if the interest is applicable to a current period and will be due the first day of the following year. Explain and justify the standards that permit this practice.

9. A school district accounts for its pension costs in a governmental fund. In a particular year, the district's actuary recommends that it contributes $18 million for the year. The district, however, had only budgeted $15 million and chooses to contribute only what was budgeted. The district is not legally or contractually required to follow the actuary's recommendation. What should the district report as its pension expenditure for the year? Explain.

10. A city's electric utility transfers $40 million to its general fund. Of this amount, $30 million is a return of the general fund's initial contribution of "start-up capital." The balance is a payment in lieu of property taxes that a private utility operating in the city would have had to pay. Explain how each element of the transfer would be reported in the general fund's operating statement.

11. A government's unassigned fund balance in the general fund at year-end should be indicative of the amount that the government has available for appropriation in future years. Explain and provide an example to support your answer.

12. Per GASB standards if a government gives a cash advance to a grantee and the grantee has not yet satisfied all eligibility requirements, the government would offset its credit to cash with a debit to an asset. By contrast, if the grantee has satisfied all eligibility requirements then it would offset the credit to cash with a debit to a deferred outflow of resources. On what basis can this difference in accounting be justified?

EXERCISES

EX. 5-1

Select the *best* answer.

Assume that Nolanville's fiscal year ends on December 31.

1. Nolanville's payroll for one of its departments is $15,000 per week. It pays its employees on the Thursday of the week following that in which the wages and salaries are earned. In 2021, December 31 falls on a Friday. For the workweek beginning Monday, December 27, 2021, and ending Friday, December 31, 2021, employees were paid on Friday, January 7, 2022. For fiscal 2021, what amount should the city recognize as wage and salary expenditure/expense pertaining to the week ending Friday, December 31, 2021, in its fund statements and its government-wide statements?

Fund Statements	Government-Wide Statements
a. $ 0	$ 0
b. $15,000	$15,000
c. $ 0	$15,000
d. $15,000	$ 0

2. In its fund financial statements, the city would recognize the receipt of a new computer (to be used for general administrative purposes) that it had ordered the previous year as an
   a. Encumbrance
   b. Expense
   c. Expenditure
   d. Asset

3. In 2021, city employees earned $1.4 million in sick leave that they did not take during the year. The city estimates that of this amount, $0.8 million will actually be paid to employees who take sick leave. Of the balance, $0.1 million will be paid to employees upon their retirement or resignation and $0.5 million will not have to be paid (since employees are limited in the number of sick days that they can carry over from one year to the next). The amount that the city should add to a fund-statement liability account as of year-end 2021 is
   a. $0
   b. $0.1 million
   c. $0.8 million
   d. $0.9 million

4. Assume the same facts as in the previous question. The amount that the city should add to the liability account in the government-wide statement of net position as of year-end 2021 is
   a. $0
   b. $0.1 million
   c. $0.8 million
   d. $0.9 million

5. In 2021, city employees earned $3.6 million in vacation pay that they did not use during the year. The city estimates that of this amount $2.8 million will be paid in 2022 (out of amounts budgeted for that year), $0.6 million will be paid in subsequent years, and the balance of $0.2 million will not have to be paid. The amount that the city should add to a fund-statement liability account as of year-end 2021 is
   a. $0
   b. $2.8 million
   c. $3.4 million
   d. $3.6 million

6. Assume the same facts as in the previous question. The amount that the city should add to the liability account in the government-wide statement of net position as of year-end 2021 is
   a. $0
   b. $2.8 million
   c. $3.4 million
   d. $3.6 million

7. Nolanville starts fiscal 2021 with $25,000 in supplies. During the year, it orders $180,000 in supplies, receives $170,000, and uses $190,000. It accounts for inventories on the consumption basis. In its 2021 governmental fund financial statements it should report

Expenditure	Nonspendable Fund Balance
a. $180,000	$ 0
b. $170,000	$ 5,000
c. $190,000	$ 0
d. $190,000	$15,000

8. Assume the same facts as in the previous question. In its 2021 government-wide financial statements it should report

Expense	Inventory
a. $170,000	$ 0
b. $170,000	$15,000
c. $190,000	$ 5,000
d. $190,000	$15,000

9. On December 1, 2021, Nolanville issued $10 million of 30-year, 8 percent bonds for $9.78 million, a price that reflects a semiannual yield of 4.1 percent. Interest ($400,000 per semiannual period) is payable on May 31 and November 30, beginning May 31, 2022. In its 2021 fund and government-wide statements, Nolanville should report an interest expenditure/expense of

Fund Statements	Government-Wide Statements
a. $ 0	$ 0
b. $66,667	$66,667
c. $66,830	$66,830
d. $ 0	$66,830

10. In May 2023, Nolanville repaid $2 million of the bonds that it had issued in 2021. In its 2023 fund and government-wide statements, Nolanville should report an expenditure/expense relating to the repayment of the bonds of

Fund Statements	Government-Wide Statements
a. $ 0	$ 0
b. $2 million	$ 0
c. $ 0	$2 million
d. $2 million	$2 million

EX. 5-2

The Eaton School District engaged in the following transactions during its fiscal year ending August 31, 2021.

- It established a purchasing department, which would be accounted for in a new internal service fund, to purchase supplies and distribute them to operating units. To provide working capital for the new department, it transferred $1.7 million from its general fund to the internal service fund.
- During the year, operating departments that are accounted for in the general fund acquired supplies from the internal service fund for which they were billed $300,000. Of this amount, the government transferred $200,000 from the general fund to the internal service fund, expecting to transfer the balance in the following fiscal year. The supplies had cost the purchasing department $190,000. During 2021, the operating departments used only $220,000 of the supplies for which they were billed. They had no supplies on hand at the start of the year.
- The school district transferred $150,000 from its general fund to its debt service fund to make its required March 31, 2021 interest payment. This amount was paid from the debt service fund when due. It represented interest on $8 million of bonds that were issued, at par, on September 30, 2020. The next interest payment of $150,000 is due on September 30, 2021. The district also transferred $75,000 from the general fund to the debt service fund to provide for the eventual repayment of principal.
- The district transferred $4.5 million from the general fund to its pension fund (a fiduciary fund) in partial payment of its actuarially determined contribution of $5.0 million for the year.
- On August 31, the district acquired school buses at a cost of $900,000. The district gave the supplier installment notes that required the district to make three annual payments of $361,903. The first payment is due on August 2022. The buses have a useful life of 10 years, with no salvage value.
- On March 1, the district purchased and paid $150,000 for a one-year insurance policy.

Refer to the two lists below. Select the appropriate amounts from the lettered list for each item in the numbered list. An amount may be selected once, more than once, or not at all.

1. Amount that the general fund should recognize as supplies expenditure, assuming that inventory is accounted for on a consumption basis

2. Amount that the district should recognize as a pension expenditure in its general fund

3. Amount that the district should recognize as a pension expense in its government-wide statements

4. Amount that the general fund should recognize as nonreciprocal transfers-out

5. Amount that the district should recognize as total debt service expenditures in its governmental funds

6. Amount that the government should recognize as total debt service expense in its government-wide statements

7. Amount that the district should recognize as other financing sources in its general fund financial statements

8. Amount that the district should recognize as capital-related expenditures, including depreciation, pertaining to its buses in its governmental fund financial statements (the district recognizes a full year's depreciation on all capital assets in the year of acquisition)

9. Amount that the district should recognize as capital-related expenses, including depreciation, pertaining to its buses in its government-wide financial statements (the district recognizes a full year's depreciation on all capital assets in the year of acquisition)

10. Amount that the district should recognize as nonspendable fund balance in its governmental fund statements

11. Amount that the district should recognize as a deferred outflow of resources relating to its insurance policy.

a. $0
b. $75,000
c. $80,000
d. $90,000
e. $137,500
f. $150,000
g. $220,000
h. $275,000
i. $300,000
j. $900,000
k. $1,925,000
l. $4,500,000
m. $5,000,000
n. $8,000,000
o. $8,900,000

EX. 5-3

Transactions may have significantly different impacts on a government's budget, governmental fund statements, and government-wide statements.

A city prepares its budget on a cash basis. For each of the following, indicate the amount (if any) of an expenditure/expense that the city would be recognize in (1) its budget, (2) its fund statements, and (3) its government-wide statements. Provide a brief explanation of your response.

The city uses the consumption method to account for its inventory. It is the policy of the city to take a full year's depreciation in the year of acquisition and no depreciation in the year of sale or retirement. It recognizes depreciation on a straight-line basis.

1. As budgeted, the city ordered supplies that cost $8 million, received supplies (including those ordered in a prior year) that cost $9 million, paid for supplies that cost $7 million, and used supplies that cost $7.5 million. The city began the year with a supplies inventory that cost $1.5 million.

2. In the **prior** year, the city signed a five-year lease of telecommunications equipment. The equipment had a fair-market value of $5 million. In the **current** year, the city made its first required annual rent payment of $1,252,282. This amount reflected an implicit interest rate of 8 percent. The lease qualifies as a capital lease.

3. The government of the state in which the city is located is responsible for making 50 percent of the city's required contribution to a firefighters' life insurance fund. In the current year, the state and the city each contributed $4 million of the required $8 million.

4. In December, the city transferred $3 million from the general fund to a debt service fund to cover interest on 30-year bonds, which were issued 10 years earlier. Interest of $6 million on the bonds is due each September 30th and March 31st and the $3 million transfer is intended to cover the interest from October 1 through December 31st that will be due the following March 31st. With respect to the funds statement, consider only the effect on the debt service fund and assume that the city prepares an annual budget for the debt service fund.

5. During the year, city employees earned $4 million in sick leave that they did not take during the year. City policy dictates that employees may accumulate up to five years of sick leave and apply it to days lost to illness while they are employed. The city estimates that of the $4 million, $3.5 million will be taken. The remaining $0.5 will be forfeited.

EX. 5-4

A government would account for inventory the same as would a business, with one additional feature.

The Boyd School District began a recent fiscal year with $3,000 of supplies in stock. During its fiscal year, it engaged in the following transactions relating to supplies:

- It purchased supplies at a cost of $22,000.
- It paid for $19,000 of the supplies.
- It used $20,000 of the supplies and therefore had $5,000 in supplies inventory at year-end.

Record the transactions assuming that the district uses the consumption method.

EX. 5-5

Inventory transactions can be derived from a limited amount of data.

The following schedule shows the amounts related to supplies that a city debited and credited to the indicated accounts during a year (not necessarily the year-end balances), excluding closing entries. The organization records its budget, encumbers all its expenditures, and initially vouchers all payments. It accounts for supplies on a consumption basis.

	(in thousands)	
	Debits	**Credits**
Cash	$ 0	$ 70
Inventory	—	0
Vouchers payable	—	—
(Appropriations)	0	115
Encumbrances	—	—
Expenditures	57	0
Reserve for encumbrances	57	93
Unassigned fund balance	—	0
Nonspendable fund balance (supplies inventory)	0	—

Some information is missing. By reconstructing the entries that the organization made during the year, you are to determine the missing data. The city began the year with $5,000 of supplies in inventory and ended the year with $6,000.

EX 5-6

Fund balance, both nonspendable and unassigned, can be computed from a limited amount of information.

The schedule that follows reports the beginning balances and activity during the year in a town's supplies fund (a governmental fund). The government accounts for supplies on a consumption basis (in thousands).

Fund balance (unassigned), January 1		$400
Fund balance, assigned (encumbrances), January 1		240
Fund balance, nonspendable (inventory), January 1		170
Total fund balance, January 1		$810
Appropriations (for purchases of supplies)	$3,400	
Estimated revenues	3,200	
Actual revenues	3,300	
Supplies ordered	3,160	
Supplies received	3,360	
Supplies paid-for	2,800	
Supplies used	3,280	

Compute the following (and show your computations):

a. Fund balance, nonspendable (inventory), December 31
b. Fund balance, assigned (encumbrances), December 31
c. Fund balance (unassigned), December 31

EX. 5-7

Irrespective of how capital assets are acquired, they are recorded differently in governmental funds than in businesses.

In a recent year, Ives Township acquired six police cars at a total cost of $200,000. The vehicles are expected to have a useful life of four years.

1. Prepare the journal entries that the township would make in its general fund in the year of acquisition for each of the following assumptions:
   - It paid for the cars in cash at the time of acquisition.
   - It leased the cars and agreed to make, starting in the year of acquisition, four equal payments of $63,095, an amount that represents the annuity required to liquidate a loan of $200,000 at 10 percent interest. The lease would satisfy the criteria necessary to be accounted for as a capital lease.
   - It issued $200,000 in installment notes to the car dealer, agreeing to repay them in four annual payments of $63,095, starting in the year of acquisition.
2. Comment on how any "off the balance sheet" assets or obligations would be reported in supplementary schedules and the government-wide statements.

EX. 5-8

Expenditures for vacations do not necessarily reflect the amounts the employees have earned.

In 2021, employees of Pecos River County earned $5 million in vacation pay. They were paid for $4.2 million but deferred taking the balance of their earned vacations until subsequent years. Also, employees were paid $0.7 million for vacation earned in previous years.

1. Prepare the journal entry in the general fund to reflect the vacation pay earned in 2021.
2. Prepare the journal entry to reflect the payments for vacation days that had been earned in prior years.
3. Comment on how the schedule of long-term obligations would be affected by these transactions.
4. Comment on how the government-wide statements would be affected by these transactions. Specifically, what would be the reported vacation expenses for 2021, and what would be the year-end accrued liability for vacation pay assuming that the beginning of year liability was $0.7 million?

EX. 5-9

Obligations for sick leave should not be recognized as liabilities if they are to cover the wages of employees who actually become ill.

Lemon County permits employees to accumulate any sick leave that they do not take. If employees do not use accumulated sick leave, then they will be paid for those days upon retirement or termination (up to a maximum of 45 days). In 2021, employees earned $4.0 million in sick leave. Of this amount they were paid $3.1 million. The county expects that they will be paid $0.6 million as they take sick days in future years and $0.2 million upon retirement or termination. The balance of $0.1 million will not have to be paid.

1. Based on current standards, prepare journal entries in the general fund to reflect the sick leave earned and paid for in 2021. Indicate the amount to be reported in the schedule of long-term obligations and the government-wide statements.
2. What is the rationale for the standards that underlie your entries?

EX. 5-10

The manner in which a transfer is accounted for depends on its nature.

Prepare general fund journal entries to record the following cash transfers that a city made from its general fund to other funds. Be sure your entry reflects the nature of the transfer.

1. $4,000,000 to provide start-up capital to a newly established internal service fund that will account for the city's data processing activities
2. $50,000 to pay for data processing services provided by the data processing internal service fund
3. $38,000 to reimburse the capital projects fund for equipment rental costs that it incurred on behalf of activities accounted for in the general fund
4. $300,000 to pay the electric utility fund for four months of electric service
5. $600,000 to enable the debt service fund to make timely payments of principal and interest on outstanding general obligation debt

EX. 5-11

Prepayments need to *be accounted for on a consumption basis.*

During its fiscal year ending June 30, 2020, the Parkville Independent School District enters into a two-year lease for office space covering the period May 1, 2020, through April 30, 2022. Annual rent is $60,000. The lease specifies that the entire rent for each year is to be paid, in advance, on May 1.

Prepare journal entries to record the lease payments and the lease expenditures for fiscal years ending June 30, 2020, 2021, and 2022, assuming that the district uses the consumption method.

CONTINUING PROBLEM

Review the Comprehensive Annual Financial Report (CAFR) that you obtained.

1. How does the government classify its governmental expenditures, by function or by "object"? Are the classifications approximately the same in both the government-wide and the fund statements?
2. What was the city's largest expenditure for fiscal year 2017? By how much did this increase or decrease since FY 2016? Since FY 2012 (see statistical section)? Can you draw any inferences from this comparison as to the efficiency and effectiveness of the city in providing this service? If not, what other information would you need to make such a judgment?
3. What are the major differences in expenditures/expenses (i.e., reconciling items) as they are reported in the governmental fund and the government-wide statements?

4. On what basis does the government account for its inventories (purchases or consumption)? Does the City maintain a "fund balance-nonspendable" amount for inventories?
5. On what basis does it account for insurance or other prepaid items in its governmental funds? How can you tell?
6. To and from which funds or component units have there been general fund transfers?
7. Explain the nature of any governmental fund balance sheet classifications related to expenditures.
8. Does the entity report depreciation as an expense in its government-wide statements? If not, why not?
9. What types of other financing sources and uses does the governmental entity report in the general fund? What effect do these items have on the net change in fund balance for the year?

PROBLEMS

P. 5-1

Transactions may have significantly different impacts on a government's budget, governmental funds statements, and government-wide statements.

A school district prepares its budget on a cash basis. It is contemplating the changes or actions that follow. For each, indicate the impact that the change would have (1) on year-ending June 30 2020, general fund expenditures or transfers and (2) on year-ending June 30, 2020, government-wide expenses (e.g., "increase expenditures by $X" or "no impact"). Provide a brief explanation of your response, indicating that you are aware of the relevant financial reporting issue.

1. Owing to a special discount offered by a supplier, the district will purchase $100,000 of supplies in June 2020 that they otherwise would not have purchased until July 2020. They will not, however, have to pay for the supplies until July. The district accounts for supplies on a consumption basis.
2. In fiscal 2020, the district increases the number of vacation days to which employees are entitled to take, thereby increasing the cost of vacation leave that employees earned in 2020 but will take in subsequent fiscal years by $250,000. The vacation days vest; they can be taken as termination benefits.
3. The district increased the number of sick days to which employees are entitled to take, thereby increasing the cost of sick days that employees earned in 2020 but will take in future years by $150,000. The sick leave can be taken only as employees are sick; it cannot be paid for as a termination benefit.
4. In 2020, the district established a sabbatical leave program for certain categories of teachers. Teachers will be granted one year of leave after each seven years of service. Teachers granted the leave will have to spend it engaging in various specified activities, such as research, aimed at improving their teaching. Teachers will first be eligible to take the leave in 2027. The district estimates that one-seventh of the cost will be $1,500,000.
5. The district delayed from June to July the approval of a grant of $50,000 to a local health clinic that provides examinations to low-income students. The funds are to be paid out of resources budgeted for the fiscal year ending June 30, 2020, and are intended for use by the clinic in that same period.
6. The district delayed from June to July purchasing, and paying for, 10 school buses at a cost of $750,000. The buses are expected to last for 10 years and have no salvage value. The district charges depreciation on a straight-line basis and takes a full year's depreciation in the year of acquisition.
7. The district is required to transfer 50 percent of any annual surplus from the general fund to a "rainy day" fund (a special revenue fund). Usually the transfer based on the surplus of the fiscal previous year is made in December. The district proposes to delay the transfer that would ordinarily be made in December 2020 until July 2021, thereby decreasing its cash outlay for fiscal year 2020 by $3 million.

P. 5-2

All paid time off may not be the same.

A city has adopted the following plan for compensated time off:

- City employees are entitled to a specified number of days each year for holidays and vacation. The number depends on length of service (20 days for employees with fewer than 5 years of service, 25 days for employees with between 5 and 10 years, 30 days for employees with more than 10 years). Employees may accumulate up to 40 days, which they can either carry over to future years or be compensated for on termination.
- Employees are also entitled to 7 sick days per year. They may carry over to future years up to 60 sick days.

However, upon termination they can be paid for no more than 20 unused days.

During 2021, the city paid employees $4.2 million for holidays and vacations during the year. Of this amount, $0.4 million was for days carried over from previous years. In addition, employees earned $0.5 million in time off that they expect to use, and be paid for, in the future.

The city also paid $1.5 million in sick leave, none of which was paid to employees on termination. Of this amount, $0.3 million was carried forward from previous years. The city estimates that employees earned an additional $0.8 million in unused sick leave. Of this, $0.5 million will eventually be paid for as time off, $0.2 million will be paid on termination, and $0.1 million will lapse.

1. Prepare a general fund journal entry to record the holiday and vacation compensation. Indicate the amount of any other liability that would be recorded on both the government-wide statements and the schedule of long-term obligations.

2. Do the same for the sick leave.

3. Justify any differences between the two sets of entries.

4. Suppose additionally that for the first time in 2021 the city offered up to eight weeks of paid maternity leave to eligible employees. In 2021, the city paid $0.2 million to employees on leave. In addition, employees earned an estimated $0.3 million in leave to be taken in the future. Consistent with your previous entries and justifications, explain how (and why) you would account for this leave (which is not specifically addressed by current GASB pronouncements).

P. 5-3

The guidance on sabbatical programs leaves much to the judgment of school officials and their accountants.

The Allendale School District recently signed a contract with its teachers' union. The contract provides that all teachers will receive a one-semester sabbatical leave after seven continuous years of employment. The preamble to the contract provision stresses that the leave is intended for "renewal, additional education, and academic enrichment." It provides examples of the types of activities it is intended to promote: formal postbaccalaureate courses, service with public or not-for-profit organizations, and independent study and research.

The contract indicates that the leave is guaranteed to all teachers who satisfy the time in service and other specified criteria. Although teachers must apply for the leave, the district is required to approve it if the criteria are met. If a teacher opts not to take the leave after seven years, then he or she may accumulate it and either take it in the future or receive payment for it on retirement. Teachers do not have to report to the school officials either on what they plan to accomplish while on leave or on what they actually accomplished.

School officials' estimate that the new sabbatical provision will add to its annual compensation costs approximately $3,000 per currently employed teacher per year (after taking account of teachers who will never satisfy the leave criteria). The district currently employs 2,500 teachers. The program will be phased in gradually; the first teachers will be eligible to take their leaves in seven years.

Another school district, the Balcones West School District, which is not unionized, adopted a similar sabbatical program the same year. However, the Balcones West program does not guarantee teachers a leave.

Instead they must be granted the leave on the basis of an interview and lengthy application, which includes a schedule of planned activities. Teachers who win approval for the leave must agree to work for the district for at least one year subsequent to the leave. If they fail to return to the district, they will be required to reimburse the district for salary and benefits received while on leave. Moreover, they must submit a written report to the district on their accomplishments during the leave.

Balcones West officials estimate that the cost of its leave will be approximately $2,000 per currently employed teacher per year. The district currently employs 1,000 teachers. As with the Allendale district, the program will be phased in gradually, and the first teachers will be eligible for leaves in seven years.

Prepare any entries that you would recommend that (1) the Allendale District and (2) the Balcones West District prepare in the first year after adopting their sabbatical programs. Specify the fund in which your entries would be made. Explain and justify your answers, citing relevant accounting standards.

P. 5-4

Inventory transactions can be derived from year-end balances.

	December 31, 2021 (Preclosing)	December 31, 2020 (Preclosing)
Expenditures	$315,000	—
Supplies inventory	81,000	$54,000
Encumbrances	36,000	—
Reserve for encumbrances	45,000	9,000
Nonspendable fund balance (supplies)	54,000	54,000

All the amounts shown relate only to supplies. All purchases during the year were paid in cash.

Assume that the city uses the consumption method to account for supplies.

a. Reconstruct all journal entries relating to supplies that were made in 2021.

b. Make any additional entries that would be required at year-end 2021 to close the accounts.

P. 5-5

Generally accepted modified accrual accounting practices pertaining to inventories may not fulfill the objectives of financial reporting.

The following is an excerpt from a note to the financial statements of the city of Dallas (dates changed):

The city prepares its annual appropriated general fund, debt service fund, and proprietary operating funds budgets on a basis (budget basis) which differs from generally accepted accounting principles (GAAP basis) . . . The major differences between the budget and GAAP bases are that encumbrances are recorded as the equivalent of expenditures (budget) rather than a commitment of fund balance (GAAP) in the governmental funds.

The city accounts for inventories on the consumption basis. One of the city's departments, which is accounted for in the general fund, budgeted $199,000 in supplies expenditures for fiscal 2021. It began the 2021 fiscal year with $30,000 of supplies on hand. It also had $12,000 of supplies on order. During the year it ordered an additional $180,000 of supplies, received (and paid for in cash) $185,000 of supplies, and consumed $178,000 of supplies.

1. Prepare all journal entries, consistent with GAAP, including budgetary and encumbrance entries that the department should make in 2021.
2. Indicate the accounts and amounts related to supplies that the city would report on its year-end statement of revenues, expenditures, and changes in fund balance and balance sheet.
3. By how much did the department over or underspend its supplies budget (on a budget basis)?
4. Comment on the extent to which the city's statement provides a basis to:
   a. Assess the "true" economic costs associated with supplies
   b. Determine whether the city adhered to budgetary spending mandates

5. Suppose that in the last quarter of the year, department officials realized that the department was about to overspend its supplies budget. They therefore ceased placing new orders for supplies. However, they imposed no restrictions on the use of supplies and thereby allowed the supplies inventory to decline to near zero.

   What impact would these cost-cutting measures have on supplies expenditures as reported in an actual-to budget comparison (on a budget basis)?

P. 5-6

Can a government sell assets to itself to generate revenue?

A city is having fiscal problems in 2021. It expects to report a deficit in its general fund, the only fund that is statutorily required to be balanced.

To eliminate the anticipated deficit the city opts to "sell" its city hall—to itself—for $5 million. The city establishes a "capital asset financing agency." The agency is a separate legal entity but will have to be reported as a component unit (per standards to be discussed in Chapter 11). As such it will be accounted for in a fund other than the general fund. The city structures the transaction as follows:

- The financing agency pays the city $5 million in 2021 in exchange for "ownership" of city hall. The city hall has been carried as general capital asset.
- The agency acquires the necessary cash by issuing 20-year, 6 percent notes. The notes will be repaid in 20 annual installments of $435,920. The notes are guaranteed by the city at large. Hence, they are ultimately a liability payable from the general fund.
- The agency leases the city hall back to the city at large. Lease payments are to be paid out of general fund resources.

1. Prepare journal entries in the general fund to record the sale and concurrent lease-back of the city hall. The lease-back satisfies the criteria of a capital lease transaction.
2. Prepare journal entries in the general fund to record the first lease payment, which was made in 2021.
3. Will the transaction, in fact, reduce the 2021 anticipated fund deficit? Briefly justify the accounting principles that underlie this type of accounting.

P. 5-7

How an acquisition is financed may dictate the annual reported expenditure.

The Mainor School District is about to establish a 30-machine computer lab. It is considering six alternative means of acquiring and financing the machines:

1. Buy the machines outright; cost will be $60,000.
2. Buy the machines and finance them with a $60,000, three-year, 10 percent interest term note. The district will repay the note and pay the entire interest with a single payment of $79,860 when the note matures.
3. Buy the machines and finance them with a $60,000, three-year, 10 percent interest, installment note. The district will repay the note (plus interest) in three end-of-year installments of $24,127 each.
4. Lease the equipment but structure the lease so that it satisfies the criteria of a capital lease. The district will make three $24,127 end-of-year lease payments.
   a. The district estimates that the equipment has a useful life of three years.
   b. Determine the present value (using a discount rate of 10 percent) of the cash payments under each option.
   c. Comment on any incentives that district officials might have either to spread out the payments over the three-year period (either by a lease or borrowing arrangement) or to postpone the full payment until the third year, rather than to pay for the computers entirely in the year of acquisition.
   d. Comment on any significant differences in how the six options would be accounted for in government-wide statements instead of governmental fund statements. How would each year's reported expense be determined?

P. 5-8

Accounting practices for interest expenditures may neither reflect actual economic costs nor mirror those for interest revenues.

A town plans to borrow about $10 million and is considering three alternatives. A town official requests your guidance on the economic cost of each of the arrangements and advice as to how they would affect the town's reported expenditures.

1. For each of the town's three alternatives, determine (1) what the town's economic cost would be of using the funds in the year ending December 31, 2021, and (2) what amount of interest expenditure the town would be required to report for the year ending December 31, 2021, in its governmental funds.
   a. The town would issue $10 million of 20-year, 6 percent coupon bonds on July 1, 2021. The bonds would be issued at par. The town would be required to make its first interest payment of $300,000 on January 1, 2022.
   b. The town would issue $10 million of 20-year, 6 percent bonds on June 30, 2021. The bonds would be sold for $9,552,293, a price that reflects an annual yield (effective interest rate) of 6.4 percent. The town would be required to make its first interest payment of $300,000 on December 31, 2021.
   c. The town would issue $32,071,355 of 20-year zero coupon bonds on July 1, 2021. The bonds would be sold for $10 million, an amount that reflects an annual yield of 6 percent. The bonds require no payment of principal or interest until June 30, 2038.

2. Suppose that the town elects the first option and issues $10 million of 20-year, 6 percent coupon bonds at par on July 1, 2021. The town establishes a debt service fund to account for resources that it sets aside to pay principal and interest on the bonds. On December 31, 2021, the town transfers $300,000 from the general fund to the debt service fund to cover the first interest payment that is due on January 1, 2022.
   a. How would the transfer be reported in the general fund?
   b. How would the transfer be reported in the debt service fund? What options are available to the town to record 2021 interest in the debt service fund?

3. Suppose that the town borrowed $10 million on July 1, 2018, and temporarily invested the proceeds in two-year, 6 percent Treasury notes. The first payment of interest, $300,000, is payable on January 1, 2022.
   a. What would be the town's economic gain from investing the funds in the year ending December 31, 2021? Ignore borrowing costs.
   b. How much investment revenue should the town report for the year ending December 31, 2021? Assume there was no change in prevailing interest rates.

P. 5-9

Not all interfund activities are classified as "transfers."

The following information was abstracted from a note, headed "Interfund Transactions," to the financial statements of Independence, Missouri.

Interfund Charges for Support Services

Interfund charges for support services (which would otherwise be acquired from outsiders) and rent paid to the General Fund during the fiscal year were as follows:

	Interfund Charges	**Rent**
Tourism fund	—	$ 4,372
Power and light fund	$1,285,011	230,933
Water fund	522,244	36,883
Sanitary sewer fund	629,442	34,243
Central garage fund	152,330	3,411
	$2,589,027	$309,842

Rent charges, which consist of leased office space and computer charges, are included in other revenue of the general fund.

Payments in Lieu of Taxes

The payments of $5,161,609, $628,371, and $880,637 in the fiscal year by the power and light, sanitary sewer, and water (enterprise) funds, respectively, to the general fund in lieu of taxes represent franchise taxes and real estate taxes on plants in service. The franchise tax rate, established by city ordinance at 9.08 percent for the year, is applied to gross billed operating revenues less amounts written off to arrive at the franchise tax due the general fund. Real estate taxes are charged at a set amount.

Interfund Operating Transfers

Interfund operating transfers for the fiscal year were as follows:

	Transfer to	Transfer from
General	$ 173,617	$ 944,327
Special revenue		307,772
Debt service	930,000	
Capital projects	440,551	157,918
Enterprise		3,000
Internal service		140,604
Permanent	9,453	
Total operating transfers	$1,553,621	$1,553,621

1. Based on the information provided, prepare four journal entries (for support services, rent, payments in lieu of taxes, and interfund operating transfers) to record the transfers into the general fund. Be sure the account titles you use make clear the nature of the transaction (e.g., revenue, reciprocal transfer, nonreciprocal transfer).
2. Justify any differences in how you classified the interfund transactions.

P. 5-10

Analysts may (depending on account classification) be able to derive information on cash flows from a statement of revenues, expenditures, and changes in fund balance and balance sheets.

Highbridge County imposes a motor fuel tax to finance road maintenance. It therefore accounts for all road maintenance in a special revenue fund, the entire fund balance of which is legally restricted. The fund's statement of revenues, expenditures, and changes in fund balance and balance sheet are presented as follows.

Road Maintenance Special Revenue Fund Statement of Revenues, Expenditures, and Changes in Fund Balance for Year Ending December 31, 2021 (in thousands)

Motor fuel tax revenues		$710
Expenditures:		
Wage and salaries	$410	
Contribution to pension fund	35	
Supplies	190	
Acquisition of equipment	90	
Legal settlement	3	
Other expenditures	70	798
Excess of revenues over expenditures		(88)

Other financing sources:	
Proceeds of long-term debt	90
Increase in supplies inventory	8
Total other financing sources	98
Excess of revenue and other financing sources over expenditures	10
Fund balance, beginning of year	69
Fund balance, year-end	$ 79

Balance Sheet as of December 31 (in thousands)

	2021	2020
Assets:		
Cash	$26	$17
Motor fuel taxes receivable	15	11
Prepaid expenditures	18	22
Supplies inventory	40	32
Total assets	$99	$82
Liabilities and fund balances:		
Accounts payable (for supplies)	$ 6	$ 4
Accrued wages and salaries	7	9
Claims and judgments payable	3	0
Current obligation to pension fund	4	0
Total liabilities	20	13
Fund balance		
Total fund balance—restricted	79	69
Total liabilities and fund balance	$99	$82

1. The county prepares its budget for the road maintenance special revenue fund on a strict cash basis—no accruals whatsoever. Based on the information in the financial statements, prepare a schedule in which you account for all inflows and outflows of cash. The county reports inventories on a consumption basis. Be sure that your schedule accounts for the entire $7,000 increase in cash during the year.

2. Are you able to determine from the fund statements presented any of the following?
   a. The actual amount of any claims and judgments incurred during the year.
   b. The amount of pension benefits earned by employees during the year.
   c. The interest cost applicable to the long-term debt issued.
   If not, would this information be reported elsewhere in the financial statements? Explain.

3. Most governments do not classify their expenditures by object classification as in this example. Instead they report them by function, such as general government, public safety, recreation, and so on. However, they present their assets and liabilities in a fashion similar to that in the example. Is it possible, therefore, to derive information on cash flows from the statement of operations and balance sheets? Explain. Why do you think governments report expenditures by function rather than by object classification?

P. 5-11

It is not easy to distinguish assets from deferred outflows of resources.

As indicated in Chapter 2, the GASB defines assets as "resources with present service capacity that the government presently controls." It explains that present service capacity of an asset is its capability to enable the government to provide services and to determine the nature and manner of use of the present service capacity embodied in the resource.

The GASB defines a deferred outflow of resources as "the consumption of net assets by the government that is applicable to a future period." Net assets are consumed (although their consumption is not necessarily applicable to a future period) when there is a decrease in an asset or increase in liability without a corresponding increase in another asset or a decrease in another liability—as when, for example, employees provide services that will be paid for in a following period. In such case, there is an increase in a liability without a corresponding increase in an asset or decrease in another liability.

Consider the transactions described following. In your opinion, do they result in the creation of an asset or a deferred outflow. Be sure to assess whether the transaction will enable the government to provide current services or only future services and whether the government has control over the resource that the transaction generates.

1. The government purchased a new computer, giving the buyer a three-year note that requires payments of $10,000 per year.
2. It signed a three-year lease requiring the payment of $10,000 per year. As required, it made first payment prior to the commencement of the lease.
3. It approved a three-year $30,000 grant to a not-for-profit agency. The grant is intended to cover specified allowable costs. The government paid the agency $10,000 in advance of the agency incurring the allowable costs. Presumably, if the agency never fulfills its obligations per the grant terms—that is, never incurs the allowable costs—the government can demand repayment of the funds advanced.
4. It approved a one-year $30,000 grant to a different not-for-profit agency to conduct an employee training program that the agency was to conduct during the government's next fiscal year. The agency satisfied all requirements for the grant, and the government made its first payment of $10,000 in the year prior to that in which the program was to be conducted. Unlike the grant in item #3, this was not a reimbursement grant, and because the agency had already satisfied all eligibility requirements, it was highly unlikely that the $10,000 paid in advance of the start of the program would ever be returned to the government.

P. 5-12

Nonexchange expenditures are the mirror image of nonexchange revenues.

A state government provided several grants to school districts and local governments during its fiscal year ending August 31.

1. On August 1, 2021, it announced a $2 million grant to a local school district for the purchase of computers. The district can spend the funds upon receipt. On September 15, 2021, the state mailed a check for the full amount to the district. The district spent $1.5 million on computers during fiscal 2022 (i.e., the year ending August 31, 2022) and expects to spend the remaining $0.5 million in fiscal 2023.
2. On the same date, the state announced a $10 million grant to another school district for the acquisition of equipment. However, per the provisions of this grant the state will make payments only upon receiving documentation from the district that it has incurred allowable costs. In fiscal 2022, the district incurred and documented allowable costs of $8 million. Of this, the state paid only $7 million, expecting to reimburse the district for the balance early in fiscal 2023.
3. The state also announced a $5 million grant to a third school district, again for the acquisition of computers. The state will make annual five $1 million payments to the district, starting on September 15, 2022. The district is required to expend the funds in the fiscal year in which they are received.

4. Toward the end of fiscal 2022, it awarded a $500,000 contract to the accounting department of a local university to support a review of the state's cost accounting system. The department intends to carry out the review during 2023 and issue its final report to the state in early 2021. Upon announcing the award, the state made an advance payment of $100,000 to the department. It intends to pay the balance when the department completes the project to the satisfaction of the state.

5. In August 2022, the state announced, and paid, a $75,000 grant to a local health district to fund various prenatal services that were to be provided in fiscal 2023. At the time the grant was awarded, the health district has satisfied all eligibility requirements other than a time requirement.
   - **a.** Prepare the journal entries that the state would make in fiscal 2022 to record the awards in an appropriate governmental fund. Briefly justify the amount of expenditure that you recognized.
   - **b.** What, if any, adjustment to the amount of expenditure recognized would the state have to make in preparing its government-wide statements?
   - **c.** Describe briefly how the recipients would account, in both fund and government-wide statements, for the awards.

QUESTIONS FOR RESEARCH, ANALYSIS, AND DISCUSSION

1. Which of the following do you think a city should classify as "special" items:
   - **a.** The settlement of an age discrimination lawsuit
   - **b.** The sale, at a sizable gain, of city-owned land to a private developer
   - **c.** The unreimbursed cost of providing housing and other assistance to hurricane victims who have relocated from other areas
   - **d.** A major donation, which the city had actively solicited from a local corporation to support a city science center

2. A state's department of human resources is responsible for providing certain training courses for various agencies within the state. The department does not actually conduct the training itself. Instead it contracts with outside consultants. The department then bills the recipient agencies for the actual costs of the consultants. How should both the department and the agencies account for the payment by the agencies to the department?

3. A city acquires $1 million of public safety emergency communication equipment by entering into a capital lease. The city divides its first rent payment of $135,868 between lease interest and lease principal as follows:

Lease interest	$60,000
Lease principal	$75,868

   The city comptroller is not sure how to report the lease payment on the government-wide statement of activities—specifically whether all, none, or a portion of the lease payment should be reported as a public safety expense. What is your advice?

4. A city on the coast of Florida has incurred losses (including impairment of assets, clean-up costs, additional public safety costs, etc.) of $50 million owing to a recent hurricane. This was the third time in as many years in which the city was hit by major storms. Should the losses be classified as "extraordinary"?

SOLUTION TO EXERCISE FOR REVIEW AND SELF-STUDY

a. Journal entries (in millions)

1. Funds received from the City's special parks and recreation property tax levy.

	Debit	Credit
Cash	$6.00	
Property tax revenue		$6.00
To record property tax revenues		

2. The general rule is that revenues and expenditures are recognized in governmental funds, such as special revenue funds, on an accrual basis. There are exceptions, but wages and salaries are *not* among them.

Wages and salaries—expenditure	$4.50	
Cash		$4.10
Accrued wages and salaries		0.40
To record wages and salaries		

3. Vacation leave should be accrued as a liability as long as employees have earned the time off and the employer is expected to compensate employees for it in the future. However, only the portion of the liability expected to be liquidated with expendable available financial resources should be reported as a governmental fund obligation. The balance should be reported as a liability on the government-wide statement of net position.

Vacation pay expenditure	$0.20	
Cash		$0.20
To record vacation pay		

4. Unused sick leave should be accrued only insofar as employers expect to compensate employees for the leave as a termination benefit. In this case, the leave only accumulates; it does not vest. Thus, the city will not have to compensate employees for leave not taken as a termination benefit. It should charge as expenditure only the amount that was liquidated with expendable financial resources. It need not report a liability even on the government-wide statement of net position.

Sick leave expenditure	$0.14	
Cash		$0.14
To record sick-leave pay		

5. Pension costs should be reported as an expenditure only insofar as they were, or will be, liquidated with expendable financial resources (in this case, actual amounts paid plus amounts to be paid early in the following year).

Pension expenditure	$0.30	
Cash		$0.25
Current obligation to pension fund		0.05
To record pension contributions		

6. Because the city accounts for inventories on the consumption method, as it acquires inventory, the city would record it as an asset. Then, as it uses the inventory, it would record an expenditure and reduce the balance in the inventory account. At year-end, the inventory balance would be $0.15 million—the amount of supplies on hand. Hence, a portion of fund balance equal to this amount would now have to be designated as nonspendable.

Supplies inventory	$0.70	
Cash		$0.70
To record the acquisition of supplies		
Supplies expenditure	$0.55	
Supplies inventory		$0.55
To record the consumption of inventory		
Fund balance—unassigned	$0.15	
Fund balance—nonspendable		$0.15
To record the consumption of inventory		

7. Capital assets should be recognized as expenditures as acquired. The proceeds of noncurrent debt issued to finance them should be reported as "other financing sources." Interest and principal on long-term debt need not be recognized as expenditures until they are due.

Expenditures—capital assets	$1.00	
Other financing sources—installment note proceeds		$0.8
Cash		0.2
To record the acquisition of equipment		

8. The food bank had met all eligibility requirements other than time requirements. Hence, the cash payment should be offset by a deferred outflow of resources.

Grant paid in advance (deferred outflow of resources)	$0.15	
Cash		$0.15

b. Statements shown on the right.

c. The following assets or liabilities (in millions) would be reported in the city's schedules of capital assets or long-term obligations.

Capital assets	
Parks and recreation equipment	$1.00
Long-term obligations	
Obligation for vacation pay	$0.60
Obligation for pensions	$0.07
Installment note	$0.80

d. Impact on government-wide statements

1. No difference. The taxes would be recognized as revenue.

2. No difference. Wages and salaries would be accrued—same as on the fund statements.

Parks and Recreation Fund Statement of Revenues, Expenditures, and Changes in Fund Balance for Year Ending December 31, 2021

Property tax revenue		$6.00
Expenditures:		
Wages and salaries	$4.50	
Vacation pay	0.20	
Sick leave	0.14	
Pensions	0.30	
Supplies	0.55	
Acquisition of capital assets	1.00	6.69
Excess of revenues over expenditures		(0.69)
Other financing sources:		
Proceeds of installment notes		0.80
Increase in supplies inventory		0.15
Total other financing sources		0.95
Excess of revenues and other financing sources over expenditures		0.26
Fund balance, beginning of year		0.00
Fund balance, year-end		$0.26

Balance Sheet Parks and Recreation Fund as of December 31, 2021

Assets	
Cash	$0.26
Supplies inventory	0.15
Total assets	$0.41
Deferred outflows of resources	
Grant paid in advance	$0.15
Total assets and deferred outflows of resources	$0.56
Liabilities and fund balances	
Accrued wages and salaries	0.40
Current obligation to pension fund	0.05
Total liabilities	0.45
Fund balance—restricted	0.11
Total liabilities and fund balance	$0.56

3. The entire $0.26 million of vacation pay would be accrued and charged as an expense.
4. The same measurement rules apply to sick leave on both the full and modified accrual basis. In this case, because the leave would not be paid as a termination benefit (it does not vest), only the $0.14 million paid need be charged as an expense.
5. Per current standards, the entire $0.37 million earned by employees would be charged as an expense.
6. No difference, the $0.55 million of supplies used would be charged as an expense.
7. Capital assets would be capitalized and depreciated. The $0.05 million (approximately) of interest for the period must be accrued and charged as an expense.
8. The grant paid in advance would be recorded as a deferred outflow of resources.

CHAPTER 6

Accounting for Capital Projects and Debt Service

LEARNING OBJECTIVES

After studying this chapter, you should understand:

- Why and how governments use capital projects funds to account for resources accumulated to acquire capital assets
- Why and how governments use debt service funds to account for resources accumulated to repay debt principal and interest
- How governments account for special assessments
- What arbitrage is, and why it concerns governments
- The nature of debt refundings, the circumstances in which governments can benefit from them, and the manner in which governments account for them

As indicated in previous chapters, both governments and not-for-profits maintain separate funds (accounting and reporting entities) for resources to be used to acquire long-lived assets and to service debt. Governments classify these funds as *governmental*, as opposed to proprietary. In not-for-profits, the resources in these funds are categorized as either *without donor restrictions* or *with donor restrictions*, depending on their source. For the most part, the principles of revenue and expenditure recognition presented in earlier chapters are applicable to these funds. Nevertheless, because these funds are used to account for transactions having unique features and involving sizable amounts of resources, they warrant special consideration.

Our concern in this chapter is with the *resources* to acquire assets and to service debts, not with the assets or debts themselves. In governments, the resources to acquire capital assets, especially those that are financed with debt, are generally accounted for in **capital projects funds.** However, the costs of capital assets may also be accounted for in the general fund or even special revenue funds, particularly if they are relatively low. Because the general and special revenue funds, like the capital projects funds, are governmental funds, the accounting entries and issues are similar. The resources to service debts are typically accounted for in **debt service funds.** Accounting for the assets and liabilities themselves is addressed in Chapters 7 and 8.

Our focus is on each of the funds as independent fiscal and accounting entities. Both funds are governmental and accordingly are accounted for on a modified accrual basis. However, like other governmental funds, when they are consolidated with other funds in government-wide statements, their accounts are adjusted so that they are on a full accrual basis.

First we discuss capital projects and debt service funds. Then we address the related issues of special assessments, arbitrage, and debt refunding.

HOW DO GOVERNMENTS ACCOUNT FOR CAPITAL PROJECTS FUNDS?

Governments establish capital projects funds to account for and report financial resources that are restricted, committed, or assigned to expenditure for capital outlays. This includes the acquisition or construction of capital facilities (other than those to be financed by proprietary funds and trust funds for individuals, private organizations, or other governments) and other capital assets. They may maintain a separate fund for each major project or combine two or more projects in a single fund. Capital facilities include buildings, infrastructure projects (such as roads, bridges, airports, and sewer systems), and plants and equipment. However, this fund is not used to account for capital assets that are purchased directly with current revenues of the general fund or a special revenue fund.

REASONS FOR MAINTAINING CAPITAL PROJECTS FUNDS

Governments *must* maintain capital projects funds for resources that are *legally restricted and contractually required* for the acquisition of capital assets. The primary purpose of this fund is to ensure and demonstrate the expenditure of the dedicated financial resource is both legally and contractually compliant. Some governments also maintain capital projects funds for resources that they have assigned for capital purposes at their own discretion. Although this practice is permitted, it may mislead statement users into assuming that the resources are legally or contractually restricted when they are not.

Major capital projects are most commonly financed with general obligation bonds or other forms of long-term debt, but they may also be funded by intergovernmental grants, special tax levies, or assessments. Restrictions on capital project resources usually stem from debt covenants or from legislation authorizing the taxes or assessments. Generally, the restrictions are exceedingly specific about how the resources may be used. For example, the funds may be used only for the construction of a particular bridge or the purchase of a narrowly defined type of equipment.

BASIS OF ACCOUNTING

Capital projects funds are similar to special revenue funds in that their revenues are restricted for special purposes. Accordingly, the principles of revenue and expenditure spelled out in Chapters 4 and 5, which are applicable to all governmental funds, are also appropriate for capital projects funds. Capital projects funds are accounted for on the **modified accrual basis**. In government-wide statements the funds are accounted for on a full accrual basis (as discussed in previous chapters with respect to governmental funds in general) and consolidated with the government's other governmental funds.

BUDGETARY ENTRIES

As pointed out previously, budgetary entries give formal accounting recognition to the budget and enhance control. They help ensure that expenditures do not exceed authorizations.

Governments generally budget capital expenditures on the basis of projects rather than periods. Therefore, they may not find it necessary to prepare an annual budget, to make annual budgetary entries, or to include comparisons of budget-to-actual expenditures for the year in their financial statements.

Nevertheless, budgetary accounts are as useful in maximizing control over project expenditures as they are over period expenditures. Therefore, the GASB requires budgetary account integration in circumstances in which control cannot readily be established by means other than a budget. Integration is essential, for example, "where numerous construction projects are being financed through a capital projects fund or where such projects are being constructed by the government's labor force."[1] On the other hand, when a government can establish control by entering into a fixed-price contract with a single vendor or construction company, then budgetary entries are not necessary.

The budgetary entries for capital projects would follow the pattern illustrated in Chapter 3 for other governmental funds, and the same set of financial statements is prepared. Budgetary entries are strictly an internal control mechanism; they do not affect year-end financial statements. A unique feature of capital projects funds is that the financial statements prepared at the end of the fiscal year may be considered interim financial statements because the capital projects funds exist only for the term (life) of the project under construction.

REPORTING BOND PROCEEDS AND ISSUE COSTS

Government long-term obligations can take many forms—the most common of which is **bonds**. Bonds are formal certificates of indebtedness, most frequently issued by governments for the long term. The discussion in this section can be generalized to other forms of debt—such as long-term leases and certificates of participation—which often differ from bonds more in legal form than in economic substance.

Governmental funds, including capital projects funds, do not report long-term obligations. Therefore, when the proceeds of bonds or other long-term obligations are received by a capital projects fund, they must be accounted for as "other financing sources."

When governments issue bonds, they seldom receive in cash an amount exactly equal to the bonds' face value. There are at least two sources of the difference between face value and cash received:

- ***Issue costs.*** The bond underwriters (the brokers and dealers who will distribute the securities to other brokers and dealers or sell them directly to investors) charge for their services and will withhold a portion of the gross proceeds as their fees.
- ***Premiums and discounts.*** The bond **coupon rate** (the stated interest rate) is rarely exactly equal to the market rate at the time of sale. Market rates fluctuate constantly, and the market rate that will prevail at the time of issue cannot be determined accurately in advance. The exact rate that the bonds will yield is established by issuing the bonds at a price greater or less than face value. A bond sold to yield an interest rate *greater* than the coupon rate will be sold at a *discount*. Because the prevailing rate is greater than the coupon rate, the bond is of less value to an investor than a bond with a comparable face value paying the prevailing rate; hence, the investor will pay less than the face value for it. Conversely, a bond sold to yield an interest rate *less* than the coupon rate will be sold at a *premium*. Because the prevailing rate is less than the coupon rate, the bond is of greater value than a bond with a comparable face value paying the prevailing rate. Historically, bonds were printed with a coupon rate days or weeks prior to the issue date, and hence there could be a significant difference between the coupon rate and the prevailing market rate at the date of sale. Today most bonds are issued in electronic rather than paper form. Moreover, U.S. tax laws discourage investors from acquiring bonds at a discount. Accordingly, premiums and discounts tend to be much smaller than in the past.

Governments should report the underwriting and other **issue costs** as expenditures. If the issue costs are not set out separately from premiums and discounts, then the government should estimate them.

---

[1] NCGA Statement No. 1, *Governmental Accounting and Financial Reporting Principles* (March 1979), para. 90.

Example

Bond Issue Costs

A city issues $10.0 million of bonds at a premium of $0.2 million. It incurs $0.6 million in issue costs, and thereby nets $9.6 million.

The following entry would be appropriate:

Cash	$9.6	
Expenditure—bond issue costs	0.6	
Other financing source—bond proceeds (face value)		$10.0
Other financing source—bond proceeds (bond premium)		0.2
To record the issuance of bonds and related issue costs		

ACCOUNTING FOR BOND PREMIUMS AND DISCOUNTS

Bond premiums and discounts become an accounting issue only insofar as there is uncertainty about how the "excess" cash will be disposed of and the manner of compensating for any cash deficiency.

Example

Bond Premiums and Discounts

A government authorizes two highway construction projects—Project 1 and Project 2—each to cost no more than $50 million. To finance the projects, it issues two series of bonds—Series 1 and Series 2—each with a face value of $50 million. Both mature in 30 years (60 semiannual periods) and pay interest at an annual rate of 6 percent (semiannual rate of 3 percent). Owing to prevailing interest rates of 5.9 percent on the issue date, Series 1 is issued for $50,699,000 (a premium of $699,000). However, as a consequence of subsequent increases in prevailing interest rates to 6.1 percent, Series 2 is issued for $49,315,000 (a discount of $685,000).

The initial entries to record both bond issues (ignoring issue costs) are straightforward:

Cash	$50,699,000	
Other financing sources—bond proceeds (face value)		$50,000,000
Other financing sources—bond proceeds (bond premium)		699,000
To record the issue of Series #1		
Cash	$49,315,000	
Other financing sources—bond proceeds (bond discount)	685,000	
Other financing sources—bond proceeds (face value)		$50,000,000
To record the issue of Series #2		

Both projects were authorized to cost no more than $50 million. Therefore, the $699,000 premium should not be used to add unauthorized frills to the planned highway. Instead, it should be applied to future interest payments. The bonds were issued with a coupon rate of 6 percent. Because of favorable market conditions, the government was able to borrow funds at only 5.9 percent. Still, its annual cash interest payments will be $3.0 million (6 percent of $50 million)—not $2,950,000 (5.9 percent of $50 million). The premium of $699,000 can be seen as interest that investors paid the government "up front" to receive "extra" interest of $0.1 million each year over the life of the bonds. Accordingly, the government should transfer the $699,000 to the debt service fund—the fund that will be used to accumulate the resources required to pay interest and principal on the bonds. The following entry would give effect to this policy:

Other financing use—nonreciprocal transfer of bond premium to debt service fund	$699,000	
Due to debt service fund		$699,000
To record the premium payable to the debt service fund		

Accounting for the discount is generally not the mirror image of that for the premium. A bond discount, like a bond premium, adjusts the bond issue price to align the coupon rate with the prevailing rate. Because of the unfavorable market conditions, the government had to pay interest at a rate greater than the bond coupon rate. Therefore, it received less than the face value of the bonds, and less than it apparently planned to spend on the capital project. When the bonds are issued at a premium, the capital projects fund can transfer resources to the debt service fund. However, when the bonds are issued at a discount, the debt service fund will not have resources available for transfer to the capital projects fund. Therefore, the government has a choice. It can either reduce the scale of the project or make up the deficiency by some other means. If it elects to reduce the scale of the project, then no further journal entries are required. If it opts to fund the shortfall by other means, then the source of the funds will dictate the additional accounting entries. For example, if the government were to appropriate $685,000 of general-fund resources, then the following capital projects fund entry would be necessary:

Due from general fund	$685,000	
Other financing sources—nonreciprocal transfer from general fund		$685,000
To record the anticipated transfer from the general fund to compensate for the bond discount		

Comprehensive Example

Main Types of Transactions Accounted for in Capital Projects Funds

The voters of New City authorize the issuance of $20 million in general obligation bonds to finance the construction of a new highway. The project is expected to cost $30 million (including bond issue costs), with the additional $10 million to be financed with a state grant. Although the grant may be paid in advance, it is intended to reimburse the city for actual costs incurred.

Authorizing the Project and Recording the Budget

The city is required to account for the resources in a fund dedicated exclusively to this project. It elects to adopt a budget and integrate it into its accounts:

Estimated bond proceeds	$20,000,000	
Estimated grant revenues	10,000,000	
Fund balance		$30,000,000
To record estimated revenues and other financing sources		
Fund balance	$30,000,000	
Appropriations		$30,000,000
To record appropriations (estimated expenditures)		

Issuing the Bonds

The city issues $20 million of bonds. Because of favorable market conditions, the bonds are sold for $20.2 million. After deducting issue costs of $0.15 million, the sale nets $20.05 million:

Cash	$20,050,000	
Issues costs (expenditures)	150,000	
Other financing sources—bond proceeds (face value)		$20,000,000
Other financing sources—bond proceeds (bond premium)		200,000
To record the issuance of bonds		

Transferring the Premium to the Debt Service Fund

The city transfers the premium, net of the issue costs, to the debt service fund:

Other financing use—nonreciprocal transfer of bond premium to debt service fund	$50,000	
Cash		$50,000
To transfer the bond premium, net of issue costs, to the debt service fund		

Encumbering Available Resources

The city signs several construction-related contracts for goods and services to cost $16 million. Capital projects funds, no less than the general fund, can avoid overspending by encumbering fund balance in the amount of purchase orders and similar commitments.

Encumbrances	$16,000,000	
Reserve for encumbrances		$16,000,000
To encumber $16 million for contracts signed		

Assuming that the fund balance is already legally restricted for construction of the new highway, the reserve for encumbrances is a temporary account maintained strictly to enhance internal control. For reporting purposes, insofar as there remains a year-end balance, it will be incorporated into "restricted fund balance."

Recording Grants

The city receives $8 million of its grant from the state. To be consistent with the approach taken in other governmental funds, the recognition of reimbursement grant revenue should be expenditure driven. Hence, the city should record the advance payment from the state as a liability until it is spent.

Cash	$8,000,000	
Grant received in advance (liability)		$8,000,000
To record the advance from the state		

Per GASB Statement No. 65, *Items Previously Reported as Assets and Liabilities*, resources transferred as grants before the recipient has satisfied eligibility requirements should be reported as an asset by the provider and a liability by the recipient. The rationale is that the recipient does not control the prepayment because in the event it does not meet the eligibility requirements it must return the advance payment to the provider. In this example, it is assumed that the city has not met the eligibility requirements until it has incurred the allowable construction costs. Hence, it must offset the cash received with a liability.

Recording Expenditures

The city receives and pays contractor invoices of $15 million for construction and related services.

Expenditures—construction related	$15,000,000	
Cash		$15,000,000
To record construction and related expenditures		

Capital projects funds are maintained to account for resources that will be expended on capital projects, not for the capital projects themselves. Therefore, construction outlays are charged as expenditures, not construction in process.

The current model, unlike the one it replaced, requires that infrastructure assets be accounted for similarly to other types of capital assets. As defined by the GASB, infrastructure assets are "long-lived capital assets that normally are stationary in nature and normally can be preserved for a significantly greater number of years than most capital assets." They include roads, bridges, tunnels, drainage systems, water and sewer systems, dams, and lighting systems. They do not, however, include buildings, except those that are an ancillary part of a network of infrastructure assets.[2] Hence the government should report the construction in process in its schedule of capital assets and its government-wide statements.

[2] GASB Statement No. 34, *Basic Financial Statements—and Management's Discussion and Analysis—for State and Local Governments* (June 1999), para. 19.

Upon recording the expenditures in the capital projects fund, the city must reverse the related encumbrance accounts and recognize the revenue that was previously deferred.

Reserve for encumbrances	$15,000,000	
Encumbrances		$15,000,000
To reverse the encumbrance entry upon receipt of services		
Grant received in advance (liability)	$8,000,000	
Grant receivable	2,000,000	
Revenue from grants		$10,000,000
To recognize grant revenue based upon incurring all $10,000,000 of allowable costs		

This entry is based on the assumption that the government recognizes grant revenue as soon as it has incurred any costs that the grant is permitted to cover. Hence, it does not divide its costs between those applicable to the bonds and those applicable to the grant.

Recognizing Investment Earnings

The city invests $5 million in U.S. Treasury notes to earn a return on temporarily available cash.

Marketable securities	$5,000,000	
Cash		$5,000,000
To record the purchase of Treasury bills		

As of year-end, it has earned $0.15 million in interest, but it does not expect to actually receive the interest until the notes mature. However, the accrued interest is reflected in the market price of the notes. As observed in Chapter 4, the GASB pronouncements require that appreciation in the fair value of investments be recognized as revenue.

Marketable securities	$150,000	
Investment revenue		$150,000
To recognize appreciation in investments		

Closing the Accounts

If a government needs to prepare an operating statement that shows revenues, expenditures, and similar accounts for the particular year (as it would for general-purpose external reporting), then it can readily close these accounts, along with the related budgetary accounts, in the manner illustrated in Chapter 3. Closing the accounts would reduce the balances in these accounts to zero and enable the government to record the revenues and expenditures of the following year. If the budget were for the entire project, not for a particular year, then the government would have to restore the budgetary accounts at the start of the next year in the amount of the balances not yet expended.

However, if the government intends to prepare reports that indicate only cumulative amounts of revenues and expenditures over the life of the project, then there is no need to close the accounts. They can remain open until the project is completed. Then, the accounts can be closed and remaining resources disposed of in accordance with the government's policy or applicable legal or contractual specifications. The transfer of unspent resources to another fund would be classified as a nonreciprocal transfer.

Table 6-1 presents an operating statement and balance sheet for the capital projects fund.

TABLE 6-1 Capital Projects Fund—Construction of Highway

Statement of Revenues, Expenditures, and Changes in Fund Balance for the City's Fiscal Year	
Revenues	
Grant from state	$10,000,000
Investment revenue	150,000
Total revenues	10,150,000
Expenditures	
Bond issue costs	150,000
Construction related	15,000,000
Total expenditures	15,150,000
Excess of revenues over expenditures	(5,000,000)
Other financing sources (uses)	
Proceeds of bonds (including premium)	20,200,000
Nonreciprocal transfer of premium to debt service fund	(50,000)
Total other financing sources (uses)	20,150,000
Excess of revenues and net financing sources over expenditures	15,150,000
Fund balance, beginning of year	0
Fund balance, end of year	$15,150,000

Balance Sheet as of the End of the City's Fiscal Year	
Assets	
Cash	$ 8,000,000
Marketable securities	5,150,000
Grant receivable	2,000,000
Total assets	$15,150,000
Fund Balance—Restricted	$15,150,000

HOW DO GOVERNMENTS ACCOUNT FOR RESOURCES DEDICATED TO DEBT SERVICE?

Debt service funds are maintained to account for and report financial resources that are restricted, committed, or assigned to expenditure for principal and interest on all general long-term debt. This does not include debt issued for and serviced by enterprise or internal service funds and some trust funds. Debt service funds do *not* account for the long-term debt itself. Indeed, the only circumstance in which the principal of debt is reported as an obligation is when it has matured but actual payment has been delayed.

REASONS FOR MAINTAINING DEBT SERVICE FUNDS

Generally accepted accounting principles direct that debt service funds be established when:

- Legally required, or
- Financial resources are being accumulated for principal and interest payments maturing in future years.[3]

Legal mandates to maintain debt service funds are commonly incorporated into agreements associated with the issuance of the debt. Lenders want assurance that the funds will be available

[3] NCGA Statement No. 1, *Governmental Accounting and Financial Reporting Principles* (1979), para. 30.

to make timely payments of interest and principal. Therefore, they may require that the borrower maintain a specified amount, perhaps one year's interest, in a "reserve" fund—similar to the way a landlord requires a tenant to provide a deposit of one month's rent.

Debt service funds may receive their resources from several sources:

- Transfers from the general fund
- Special taxes restricted to the payment of debt (e.g., to construct a new high school, a school district may dedicate a portion of its property tax to the repayment of high school bonds)
- Special assessments (charges to an identifiable group of residents who will receive a disproportionate share of the benefits of a project for which long-term debt was issued)
- As with capital projects funds, governments may be required to maintain several independent debt service funds or may be permitted to combine some or all into common funds.

BASIS OF ACCOUNTING

Like capital projects funds, debt service funds are *governmental* funds, which are accounted for on the modified accrual basis.

As discussed in Chapter 5, GASB standards stipulate that the major exception to the general rule of expenditure accrual relates to unmatured principal and interest on general long-term debt. Until the period in which they must be paid, interest and principal are not considered current liabilities of the debt service fund, as they do not require the expenditure of existing fund assets. Moreover, the resources required for payment are unlikely to be appropriated—and transferred to the debt service fund—until the period in which the interest and principal actually must be paid, not before. To accrue the debt service fund expenditure and liability in one period but record the transfer of financial resources for debt service purposes in a later period, it has been argued, would be confusing and would result in the overstatement of debt service fund expenditures and liabilities and the understatement of the fund balance. The standards make clear, however, that when the general fund appropriates resources for debt service in one year for payment early (within one month) in the next, then the government *may* (but is not required to) accrue the expenditure and related liability in the debt service fund.[4]

In contrast to the manner in which the expenditures for debt service are accounted for, the interest *revenue* on bonds held as investments is, in effect, accrued as earned, because investments must be stated at fair value, and interest earned but not yet paid affects fair value.

BUDGETARY ENTRIES

Both budgets and budgetary entries are less needed, and accordingly, less common in debt service funds than in other governmental funds. Insofar as debt service funds receive their resources from other funds, overall internal control is established by the budgets in those other funds. Moreover, the expenditures of debt service funds are typically limited to payments of principal and interest, the amount and timing of which are established by the terms of the outstanding debt.

However, if the resources of a debt service fund are derived mainly from special taxes or assessments, then an appropriations budget, and suitable accounting entries, may help enhance internal control and demonstrate legal compliance. In many circumstances, the decision of whether to adopt an appropriations budget is beyond the control of accountants; it is specified in the legislation authorizing the debt or establishing the fund.

[4] GASB Interpretation No. 6, *Recognition and Measurement of Certain Liabilities and Expenditures in Governmental Fund Financial Statements* (March 2000), para. 13.

Comprehensive Example

Main Types of Transactions Accounted for in Debt Service Funds

In January 2021, Carver City establishes a debt service fund to account for a serial issue of $100 million of 6 percent bonds sold at a premium of $0.2 million. Principal is to be repaid evenly over a period of 20 years beginning on December 31, 2021. Interest is payable semiannually, beginning June 30, 2021. Of the bond proceeds, $2 million is to be retained in the debt service fund as a reserve for payment of interest and principal.

The debt is to be repaid from a voter-approved addition to the property tax, plus earnings from debt service fund investments. However, any revenue shortage is to be made up by a general-fund appropriation. Although the revenues generated by the property tax are expected to increase over time, the city estimates that in 2021 it will collect only $8 million, far less than the required interest and principal payments.

Serial bonds are repaid in installments over the life of the issue, as distinguished from term bonds, which mature on a single specified date. The first installment may be delayed for several years after the serial bonds have been issued, and uniform payments may not be required. The amount of principal repaid with each installment, although established in advance, may vary from year to year. Serial bonds are, in essence, nothing more than a collection of term bonds, each of which matures at a different time.

Recording the Budget

The city estimates its revenues and expenditures as reflected in the entry that follows:

Estimated revenues—investments	$60,000	
Estimated revenues—property taxes	8,000,000	
Estimated transfer-in—capital projects fund	2,200,000	
Estimated transfer-in—general fund	2,940,000	
Appropriations—interest		$6,000,000
Appropriations—principal		5,000,000
Fund balance		2,200,000
To record the budget		

Transferring in the Bond Premium and the Amount to Be Held as a Reserve

The bonds are issued, and the proceeds are placed in a capital projects fund. The premium of $200,000 and the $2 million to be held in reserve are transferred from the capital projects fund to the debt service fund.

Cash	$2,200,000	
Other financing source—nonreciprocal transfer-in from the capital projects fund		$2,200,000
To record the transfer-in of the bond premium and the amount to be placed in reserve		

The debt itself would be recorded only in the government-wide statements and in off-the-balance sheet schedules, not in the debt service fund.

Recognizing Investment Earnings

The city purchases as an investment $1 million (face value) long-term U.S. Treasury notes. Acquired in the secondary market, the notes pay interest at a rate of 6 percent annually (3 percent each semiannual period) and mature in seven years. They are purchased for $894,369—a price that provides an effective yield of 8 percent annually (4 percent semiannually).

Investment in notes	$894,369	
Cash		$894,369
To record purchase of notes as an investment		

As discussed previously, investments will be carried at fair value. Therefore, the note discount need not be reported separately from the notes.

During the year, the city receives two semiannual interest payments of $30,000 (3 percent of $1 million). Meanwhile, the fair value of the notes increases by $5,775 in the first period and by $6,006 in the second period. In the absence of changes in prevailing interest rates, the fair value of the notes can be expected to increase each period by the amount by which the discount would otherwise be amortized. In that way, their fair value at maturity would be equal to their face value. In this instance, the increases in value can be attributed entirely to the amortization of the discount.

Cash	$30,000	
Investment in notes	5,775	
Investment revenue		$35,775
To record the first period's interest		
Cash	$30,000	
Investment in notes	6,006	
Investment revenue		$36,006
To record the second period's interest		

Recognizing Tax Revenue

During the year the city collects $7.5 million of the $8.0 million in dedicated property taxes due during the period. It expects to collect the balance within 60 days of year-end.

Cash	$7,500,000	
Property taxes receivable	500,000	
Property tax revenue		$8,000,000
To record property taxes		

Property taxes are recognized as revenue on the same basis as if recorded in the general fund or any other special revenue fund. Taxes restricted to a specific purpose may be recorded initially in the general fund, especially if, as in this situation, they are part of a larger tax levy. However, it is generally preferable that they be reported directly in the fund to which they are dedicated.

Recording the Transfer from the General Fund

During the year the city, as budgeted, transfers $2,940,000 from the general fund to the debt service fund.

Cash	$2,940,000	
Other financing source—nonreciprocal transfer from the general fund		$2,940,000
To record the transfer from the general fund		

Recording the Payment of Interest and Principal

The city makes its first payment of interest on the $100 million of bonds, as due, on June 30:

Expenditure—debt service, interest	$3,000,000	
Matured bond interest payable		$3,000,000
To record the obligation for the first bond interest payment		
Matured bond interest payable	$3,000,000	
Cash		$3,000,000
To record the first bond interest payment		

Many governments use a bank or other fiscal agent to distribute payments of interest and principal to bondholders. If they do, then any cash transferred to the fiscal agent should be reported as an asset "cash with fiscal agent." "Cash with fiscal agent," along with the liability "matured bond interest (or principal)," should be reduced as the fiscal agent reports that it has made the required payments to the bondholders.

Although the second payment of interest and the first payment of principal are due on December 31, 2021, the city does not actually mail the checks until January 2, 2022. Nevertheless, the expenditure and related obligation must be recognized when the payments are due:

Expenditure—debt service, interest	$3,000,000	
Expenditure—debt service, principal	5,000,000	
Matured bond interest payable		$3,000,000
Matured bonds payable		5,000,000
To record the obligation for the second payment of interest and the first payment of principal		

Closing the Accounts

At year-end, the city would have to close the nonbalance sheet accounts:

Appropriations—interest	$6,000,000	
Appropriations—principal	5,000,000	
Other financing source—nonreciprocal transfer from the general fund	2,940,000	
Other financing source—nonreciprocal transfer from the capital projects fund	2,200,000	
Property tax revenue	8,000,000	
Investment revenue	71,781	
Estimated revenues—investments		$ 60,000
Estimated revenues—property taxes		8,000,000
Expenditure—debt service, interest		6,000,000
Expenditure—debt service, principal		5,000,000
Estimated transfer-in—capital projects fund		2,200,000
Estimated transfers-in—general fund		2,940,000
Fund balance (restricted for debt service)		11,781
To close the accounts		

Table 6-2 presents a statement of revenues, expenditures, and changes in fund balance and a balance sheet for the debt service fund for the year 2021.

TABLE 6-2 Debt Service Fund

Statement of Revenues, Expenditures, and Changes in Fund Balance
For Year Ending December 31, 2021

Revenues	
Property taxes	$8,000,000
Investments	71,781
Total revenues	8,071,781
Expenditures	
Debt service, interest	6,000,000
Debt service, principal	5,000,000
Total expenditures	11,000,000
Excess (deficiency) of revenues over expenditures	(2,928,219)
Other financing sources	
Nonreciprocal transfer from the general fund	2,940,000
Nonreciprocal transfer from the capital projects fund	2,200,000
Total other financing sources	5,140,000

(Continues)

TABLE 6-2 **Debt Service Fund** (*Continued*)

Statement of Revenues, Expenditures, and Changes in Fund Balance
For Year Ending December 31, 2021

Excess of revenues and other financing sources over expenditures	2,211,781
Fund balance, beginning of year	0
Fund balance, end of year	$ 2,211,781

Balance Sheet as of December 31, 2021

Assets	
Cash	$ 8,805,631
Property taxes receivable	500,000
Investment in notes	906,150
Total assets	$10,211,781
Liabilities and fund balance	
Matured interest payable	$ 3,000,000
Matured bonds payable	5,000,000
Total liabilities	8,000,000
Fund balance—restricted for debt service	2,211,781
Total liabilities and fund balance	$10,211,781

HOW DO GOVERNMENTS HANDLE SPECIAL ASSESSMENTS?

Governments sometimes construct capital projects or provide services that primarily benefit a particular group of property owners rather than the general citizenry. To assign the costs to the beneficiaries, they assess (i.e., charge) those taxpayers the entire, or a substantial share, of the cost of the project or services. Generally, the majority of property owners within the area must vote their approval of the particular project or services and of the assessments. They can ordinarily pay the assessments in installments over several years, but they must pay interest on unpaid balances.

REASONS FOR SPECIAL ASSESSMENTS

Cities and towns often levy special assessments when taxpayers in areas beyond their jurisdiction either want to be annexed into the city or town or want to benefit from certain of the city or town's facilities and services. In some circumstances, the area to be assessed may be designated a special-purpose government district (such as a local improvement district) and may be authorized to levy and collect the assessments. In others, the assessments are levied and administered by the city or town itself.

Most often, special assessments are levied for infrastructure improvements—such as water and sewer lines, sidewalks, roads, and streetlights. They could also be used for discrete projects such as parks, tennis courts, swimming pools, and recreation centers.

Special assessments for services are often levied when a community wants greater services than the government would normally provide. For example, a community that would otherwise be protected by a volunteer fire department may request that it be serviced by a professional fire department. Or a neighborhood may petition the city to maintain and provide electricity for its streetlights (perhaps after the neighborhood installs the lights itself), to provide trash collection service, or to snowplow its roads. Assessments for services present few, if any, unique accounting and reporting problems. They should be accounted for in the fund that best reflects the nature of the assessment and the services to be provided—usually either the general fund, a special revenue fund, or an enterprise fund.

Inasmuch as the enhancements in either infrastructure or services may provide at least some benefits to the citizenry at large (e.g., improved roads are not for the exclusive use of the taxpayers who live along them), governments may share in the cost of the improvements. Therefore, the projects may be financed in part by direct government contributions, by general obligation debt, or by revenue debt (debt to be repaid from user fees—such as water and sewer charges).

Governments ensure collectability of the assessments by attaching liens against the affected properties. Thus, they can foreclose on delinquent property owners and can prevent the properties from being sold or transferred until the assessments are current.

Like other financing mechanisms, special assessments may be subject to misuse and are not always advantageous, relative to conventional taxes, to property owners. The accompanying "In Practice: Use and Abuse of Special Assessments" suggests why.

ACCOUNTING FOR SPECIAL ASSESSMENT PROJECTS AND THE RELATED DEBT

Capital improvement special assessments involve two distinct, albeit overlapping, phases: the construction and financing phase and the debt service phase.

In the first phase—the construction and financing phase—a project is authorized and the property owners are assessed. To finance the project, the government issues long-term debt. It then undertakes construction.

In the second phase, the property owners pay their assessments, and the debt is serviced. Whereas the first phase is usually fairly short—the time required to complete the construction—the second phase may extend over many years.

Until the late 1980s, special assessments were accounted for in a special type of fund called a *special assessment fund*. Today, however, special assessments are accounted for just as any other capital projects are. The construction phase is accounted for in a capital projects fund. The debt service phase is accounted for in a debt service fund.

When a government issues debt to finance a special assessment capital project, it should place the proceeds in a capital projects fund. It should account for issue costs, bond premiums and discounts, and construction costs no differently than those relating to other projects.

IN PRACTICE USE AND ABUSE OF SPECIAL ASSESSMENTS

Although special assessments are a reasonable means of paying for projects in which the benefits can be associated directly with specific property owners, they can be readily abused. For example, governments may opt to circumvent caps on property taxes by paying for routine services—such as sidewalk and road maintenance—with special assessments instead of with property taxes. Some governments have even established special districts to provide basic services—such as fire protection and ambulance transportation—financing them with assessments against local property owners.

The following are examples of some special assessments that might have been goals other than those publicly stated.

- In Mason County, Washington, a special assessment was imposed on nonforested land. However the funds were being directed to a general purpose fund for the benefit of all residents of Mason County (*The Tax Foundation*, January 28, 2011). A special benefit was clearly not being conferred, and as a consequence, a lawsuit was filed, calling the assessment unconstitutional for being a disguised tax.
- In Lake Worth, Florida, a $60-per-dwelling fire assessment was approved by the city commission to cover the cost of firefighter pensions (*The Palm Beach Post*, January 25, 2012). However, after much debate and campaign promises, the assessment was repealed.
- Finally, the state of Florida borrowed $1.8 billion from the federal government to pay unemployment benefits, so the Florida Department of Revenue imposed an assessment on all employers to cover the $61.4 million of interest on the loan. This resulted in an assessment of $9.52 per employee for the affected employers in the system (*Jacksonville.com*, February 1, 2011). Whatever their virtues, special assessments may also pose decided disadvantages relative to property taxes. First, they may not be based on the value of property but rather on some other measure, such as in the case of Lake Worth, Florida. And second, unlike property taxes, special assessments are not deductible for purposes of federal income taxes.

When the government levies the special assessments, it should recognize them in a debt service fund. Special assessments are imposed nonexchange transactions. They should be recorded as assets in the period in which the government has an enforceable legal claim to the resources that it will receive. In the debt service fund itself, which like other governmental funds is accounted for on a modified accrual basis, they can be recorded as revenues only when available for expenditure. Therefore, when a government levies the special assessments, it should offset the assessments receivable with a *deferred inflow of resources*. Only as it collects the assessments (or as the assessments become available to meet current year expenditures) should it recognize them as revenues. It should report contributions from the general fund or other sources just as if they were for other types of projects.

The government should account for interest and principal payable on special assessment debt in a debt service fund no differently from that on debt relating to other projects. Thus, it should recognize expenditures (and a corresponding liability) only when the payment is actually due. It should not accrue either interest or principal.

Accounting for special assessments is illustrated in the exercise for review and self-study at the end of this chapter.

GOVERNMENT OBLIGATIONS AS TO PROPERTY OWNERS' DEBT

The key accounting issue pertaining to special assessments is if, and under what circumstances, a government should report the special assessment debt as its own debt. Special assessment debt is the primary responsibility of the property owners on whom the assessments are levied. In economic substance, though not necessarily legal form, it is usually an obligation of the property owners, not the government. Arguably, therefore, the government need not report the debt on its own financial statements.

In most circumstances, however, the government is linked to the debt in some manner. These ties can be in a variety of arrangements:

- The government itself may issue the debt (as general obligation debt) with the expectation that the special assessments will be sufficient to cover the debt service.
- To help make the debt more marketable and lower the interest rate, the government may either back the debt with its full faith and credit or guarantee it with some other type of commitment.
- The government may have no legal commitment for the debt, but nevertheless may assume responsibility for it to protect its own credit standing.
- The government may agree to share in the cost of the project and thereby to be responsible for a specified proportion of the debt.

GASB STANDARDS

GASB standards require that a government account for the debt as its own as long as it is *obligated in some manner* to assume responsibility for the debt in the event of property owner default. Conditions that would indicate that a government is obligated in some manner for the debt include the following:

- The government is obligated to honor any special assessment deficiencies.
- The government establishes a fund to pay off the debt as it matures, to purchase or redeem it prior to maturity, or to satisfy any commitments or guarantees in the event of default.
- The government explicitly indicates by contract—such as the bond agreement or offering statement—that in the event of default it may cover delinquencies, even if it has no legal obligation to do so.

- Legal decisions within the state or previous actions by the government make it probable that the government will assume responsibility for the debt in the event of default.

Put more strongly, the government is *obligated in some manner* unless:

- It is *prohibited* (by constitution, charter, contract, or statute) from assuming the debt in the event of property owner default, *or*
- It is not legally liable for assuming the debt and makes no statement, or gives no indication that it will, or may, honor the debt in the event of default.

If the government is obligated in some manner for the special assessment debt, then it should account for the project as just described. It should record the construction phase in a capital projects fund and the debt service phase in a debt service fund. It should report the capital assets and the special assessment debt as if they were its own—that is, in schedules of capital assets and long-term obligations and in the government-wide statements.

If the government is *not* obligated for the debt but simply collects the assessments from property owners and forwards them to the bondholders, then it should

- Report the debt service transactions in an agency fund (reflecting the government's role as a mere agent).
- Report construction activities, like other capital improvements, in a capital projects fund.
- Report the capital assets in the schedule of capital assets and the government-wide statements.
- Disclose in notes to the financial statements the amount of debt and the government's role as an agent of the property owners; it should not report the debt in either its schedule of long-term obligations or its government-wide statements.[5]

[5] GASB Statement No. 6, *Accounting and Financial Reporting for Special Assessments* (January 1987), paras. 16–20.

ACCOUNTING FOR SPECIAL ASSESSMENTS IN PROPRIETARY FUNDS

Governments sometimes assess property owners for projects that they would ordinarily account for in proprietary funds. These projects typically involve infrastructure associated with utilities—such as water, sewer, and power lines and related facilities.

If special assessment debt is related to, and expected to be paid from, a proprietary fund, then all transactions related to both the debt and the improvements financed by the debt should be accounted for in a proprietary fund. The government should account for the special assessment revenues and receivables on a full accrual basis and should capitalize improvements financed with the assessments in the same manner as other capital improvements.

In some situations, the governmental entity is not responsible, in any manner, for special assessment debt issued to finance improvements that are accounted for in a proprietary fund. Instead, the debt is an obligation exclusively of developers, property owners, or other outside parties. If so, then the government should report a "capital contribution" (in a section of its statement of revenues, expenses, and changes in fund net position that follows "nonoperating revenue") equal to the amount of the property that it capitalized.[6]

DIFFERENCES IN GOVERNMENT-WIDE STATEMENTS

In their government-wide full accrual statements, governments display neither debt service nor capital projects funds in separate columns, irrespective of whether the funds satisfied the criteria of "major" funds. Instead, they would combine the funds with all other governmental funds in the governmental activities column and include the related general capital assets and long-term debt. However, inasmuch as the resources of both the capital projects and the debt service funds may be restricted by the bond indentures to asset acquisition or debt service, the nature of the restriction should be clearly conveyed. This can be accomplished by displaying the government's net position (i.e., its assets plus deferred outflows of resources minus

[6] GASB Statement No. 6, *Accounting and Financial Reporting for Special Assessments* (January 1987), paras. 16–20, as modified by GASB Statement No. 34, *Basic Financial Statements—and Management's Discussion and Analysis—for State and Local Governments* (June 1999), paras. 92 and 100.

liabilities and deferred inflows of resources) in three sections: net investment in capital assets; restricted; and unrestricted. The net investment-in-capital assets component of net position would include the government's general capital assets, net of accumulated depreciation less its capital-related debt. The restricted component would show the net assets set aside in capital projects, debt service, and other restricted funds. Thus:

Net position		
Net investment in capital assets		$200
Restricted to:		
Capital projects	$10	
Debt service	5	
Other purposes	3	18
Unrestricted		25
Total net position		$243

It might appear that the amount shown as restricted to capital projects would exactly equal the combined fund balances of the government's capital projects funds and that the amount shown as restricted to debt service would exactly equal the combined fund balances of its debt service funds. Such is not always the case. As was emphasized in Chapters 4 and 5, the government-wide statements are prepared on a full accrual basis, whereas the fund statements are prepared on a modified accrual basis. Thus, revenues of the government-wide statements would be subject to the same standards as applicable to the fund statements with the notable exception that the "available" test would not have to be met. Expenses would also be subject to the same standards, except that the several exceptions—those that transform the full accrual basis into the modified accrual basis—would not apply to the government-wide statements. Thus, in government-wide, but not in fund, statements:

- Interest on long-term debt would be accrued and charged as an expense as a function of time, irrespective of when payment is actually due.
- Discounts and premiums on bonds payable would be amortized over time—just as they currently are on the financial statements of businesses as well as the enterprise funds of governments.
- Property taxes that are dedicated to debt service would be recognized as revenues in the year for which they are levied, even if they wouldn't be collected within 60 days of year-end.
- The principal of (but not the interest on) special assessments would be recognized as both assets and revenues (as opposed to deferred inflows of resources) in the period in which the government has a legal claim against the resources to be received, irrespective of when the resources will actually be received. At the same time, however, the full amount of the debt incurred to construct the capital assets would be reported as a liability. Similarly, the construction costs would be capitalized as assets as they are incurred.

WHY IS ARBITRAGE A CONCERN OF GOVERNMENTS?

Arbitrage, as it applies to states and other municipalities, refers to the issuance of debt at relatively low, tax-exempt rates of interest and the investment of the proceeds in taxable securities yielding a higher return. Arbitrage is of major concern to governments and can have important financial and accounting consequences for both capital projects and debt service funds.

The interest paid on debt issued for *public* purposes by state and local governments is not subject to federal taxation. The federal government draws the distinction between public and private purposes so as to prevent governments from providing assistance to private corporations by substituting their own low-interest, tax-exempt debt for that of the companies.

State and local governments can issue bonds for public purposes at lower interest rates than either the federal government or private corporations because, taking into account the required taxes on the taxable bonds, the tax-exempt bonds can provide the investor a return equivalent to that on the taxable bonds. For example, a 6 percent tax-exempt bond provides a return to an investor in a 30 percent tax bracket equal to that of an 8.571 percent taxable bond [6.0% ÷ (1 – 0.30) = 8.571%].

Arbitrage subverts the federal government's rationale for exempting state and local debt from federal taxation—that of indirectly subsidizing state and local governments by enabling them to save on interest costs. At one time it was argued that the federal government did not have the constitutional right either to regulate the issuance of state and local debt or to tax the interest on it. Today the federal government does regulate the issuance of state and local debt, and it is widely believed that a tax on municipal bond interest could withstand constitutional challenges.

IN PRACTICE WHAT WE MIGHT LEARN FROM "NET INVESTMENT IN CAPITAL ASSETS"

The "Net investment in capital assets" section of the government-wide statement of net position can highlight bad policy decisions that might otherwise go undetected. Sound fiscal policy dictates that the maturity of debt should be no longer than the life of assets that it is used to finance. Suppose that a school district issues 30-year bonds to finance a new high school that has an estimated useful life of 40 years. So far, so good. But what if included in the cost of the school are payments for computers, equipment, and furniture and fixtures having a useful life of only five years? Not so good.

A yellow flag warning of such a situation would be a negative balance in "net investment in capital assets." It would suggest that the existing outstanding capital debt is not offset by matched assets—that is, that assets have depreciated more rapidly than the related debt is being repaid.

Were governments permitted to engage in arbitrage, they could generate virtually unlimited amounts of earnings simply by issuing their own bonds and investing the proceeds in higher-yielding, risk-free, federal government securities. Using the federal securities as collateral for their own bonds, they could also ensure that their own debt was risk-free.

To prevent municipalities from reaping the benefits of arbitrage, the federal government has added restrictions to the Internal Revenue Code and accompanying regulations.

COMPLEXITY OF FEDERAL REGULATIONS

As previously discussed, governments typically spend the proceeds of bonds over the period of project construction. Major projects may take several years to complete. Moreover, governments may transfer a portion of the proceeds from a capital projects fund to a debt service fund, either because the proceeds include a premium or because the debt covenants stipulate that they must maintain a reserve fund to guard against default. Sound fiscal management dictates that proceeds held for anticipated construction costs, for future debt service, or as bondholder-required reserves be invested in interest-earning securities, such as those issued by the U.S. government.

The tax provisions are complex because they must allow for legitimate temporary investment of funds, yet at the same time prevent arbitrage abuse. To achieve this objective, the federal government has produced a set of regulations so complex that few governments can administer them without assistance from outside experts. In essence, they are of two types:

- ***Arbitrage restrictions.*** Primarily developed in 1969, these provisions establish a general rule prohibiting arbitrage. But they set forth several exceptions. Issuers are permitted to invest both construction funds and reserve funds for limited periods of time (e.g., 85 percent of the proceeds must be spent within three years).

- ***Arbitrage rebates.*** Instituted as part of the Tax Reform Act of 1986, these regulations require that all arbitrage earnings, again with some exceptions (e.g., the proceeds are spent within six months or 75 percent of the proceeds are spent on construction within two years), be remitted to the federal government.

Thus, even if a government is permitted to earn arbitrage under the 1969 restrictions, it may nevertheless have to remit it to the federal government under the 1986 rebate requirements.

A government that fails to comply with these mandates can compromise the tax-exempt status of its bonds, thereby subjecting itself to bondholder litigation and political embarrassment.

ACCOUNTING PROBLEMS

The main accounting problems arise because the regulations permit issuers to calculate and remit their required rebates as infrequently as every five years. Moreover, the arbitrage earnings may be measured over multiyear, rather than annual, periods. At the conclusion of any one year the government may be unable to determine its expenditure and related liability for that year. Thus, although the GASB has not issued a pronouncement pertaining to arbitrage, it is clear that governments must estimate their rebate obligations and recognize an appropriate expenditure and liability.

Lacking explicit guidance from the GASB, governments take one of two approaches to accounting for the estimated rebates. Some report the rebates as a deduction from interest revenue (a debit) offset by a payable to the U.S. government. Others treat the obligation as if it were a claim or judgment. In the debt service fund or capital projects fund in which the arbitrage is earned, they recognize (as both an expenditure and a liability) only the portion of the obligation to be liquidated with currently available resources. They account for the balance of the obligation as they would other long-term obligations.

HOW CAN GOVERNMENTS BENEFIT FROM DEBT REFUNDINGS?

Governments, as well as not-for-profits, retire debt prior to maturity for a variety of reasons. For example, if revenues are greater than anticipated, they may be able to pay off bonds earlier than planned. Or they may elect to sell facilities financed by the debt and use the proceeds to liquidate the obligations.

In this section, however, we are concerned with **bond refundings**—the early retirement of existing debt so that it can be replaced with new debt. Governments refund—that is, **refinance**—their debt to take advantage of more favorable (lower) interest rates, to shorten or lengthen the debt payout period, or to rid themselves of restrictive bond covenants (such as those that prevent them from incurring new debt).

GENERAL RULE ON POTENTIAL FOR ECONOMIC GAINS

As a general rule, if a government had to retire outstanding debt by repurchasing it in the open market and paying a price reflective of current interest rates, then there would be no benefit to refunding—even in the face of prevailing interest rates that are substantially lower than those on the existing debt. There would be no economic gain because the premium to retire existing bonds would exactly offset the present value of the future interest savings. A simple example will demonstrate the point.

Example

Debt Refundings

A government has bonds outstanding that pay interest at an annual rate of 8 percent (4 percent per semiannual period). The bonds mature in 10 years (20 periods). In the years since the bonds were issued, annual interest rates on bonds with similar risk characteristics have decreased to 6 percent. Because of the decline in interest rates, each of the government's bonds ($1,000 face value) is selling in the secondary market for $1,148.78.

The **economic cost** to the government of the debt, assuming that it will remain outstanding until maturity in 10 years, is $1,148.78—the same as its market value.

Economic cost means the present value of all future payments, based on the prevailing interest rate of 6 percent (3 percent per period). Hence, the economic cost is the 20 semiannual interest payments of $40 each and a single principal payment of $1,000:

Present value, at 3 percent, of $1,000 principal (a single sum) to be paid at the end of 20 periods (present value of $1 = $0.55368)	$ 553.68
Present value, at 3 percent, of $40 interest (an annuity) to be paid at the end of each of 20 periods (present value of an annuity of $1 = $14.87747)	595.10
Total economic cost of existing bonds	$1,148.78

Were the government to retire the debt, it would have to pay the market value of $1,148.78. Assuming that it still needs the funds initially borrowed, it would have to issue new bonds to obtain the required $1,148.78. Inasmuch as current market rates have now fallen to 6 percent, it could reduce its semiannual interest payments from $40 to $34.46 (3 percent of $1,148.78). The present value of all future payments on the new debt (based on the prevailing annual interest rates of 6 percent—3 percent per period) would also be $1,148.78:

Present value, at 3 percent, of $1,148.78 principal (a single sum) to be paid at the end of 20 periods (present value of $1 = $0.55368)	$ 636.07
Present value, at 3 percent, of $34.46 interest (an annuity) to be paid at the end of each of 20 periods (present value of an annuity of $1 = $14.87747)	512.68
Total economic cost of new bonds	$1,148.75

The economic cost of the new bonds is the same as that of the existing bonds. Hence, there is no economic gain to refunding. The slight discrepancy of three cents is attributable to rounding. It is, of course, no coincidence that the economic cost of the new bonds is the same as their face value. The present value of bonds issued at par is always the same as their face value.

IN PRACTICE CURRENT AND ADVANCE REFUNDINGS

Prior to 2018, there were two types of municipal bond refundings that involved bond redemptions: current and advance. In a current refunding, outstanding bonds are redeemed within 90 days of issuing the refunding debt. In an advance refunding, the refunded bonds would remain outstanding for longer than 90 days. States and municipalities could do a tax-exempt advance refunding once per debt issue. The Tax Cut and Jobs Act of 2017, however, ceased tax-exempt advance refundings; the bonds issued as part of an advance refunding would no longer be considered tax exempt. The rationale behind this change is that the bonds issued in an advance refunding tend to have lower rates than taxable bonds. A municipality could therefore use an advance refunding to issue unlimited amounts of debt at low rates and invest the proceeds in higher earning securities. This would be counter to a key objective of exempting municipal bonds from taxation—that is to encourage municipalities to invest in infrastructure. Per a report in *The Bond Buyer* (December 18, 2017), the elimination of tax-exempt advance refundings involving redemptions will limit states' and municipalities' flexibility and raise their issuance costs.

REALIZING ECONOMIC GAINS: EXCEPTIONS TO THE GENERAL RULE

There are exceptions, however, to the general rule that there is no benefit to refunding. First, *yield curves* (the relationship between interest rates and time to maturity) may be such that by refunding the existing bonds with new bonds having a different maturity (and thus different prevailing interest rates and prices), the government can obtain true economic savings. Second, bonds are often issued with specified **call prices**. These give the issuer the opportunity to redeem (call) the bonds at a preestablished price, irrespective of the current market price. The call price places a ceiling on the bond's market price. After all, why would an investor pay more for a bond than its call price, knowing that the government could, at its discretion, buy back the bond at the call price? If a government can redeem a bond at a call price less than the economic value of the existing bonds (i.e., what the market price of the bonds would be in the absence of a call provision), then, of course, it could realize an economic saving.

Governments attach call provisions to their bonds to give themselves the opportunity to take advantage of falling interest rates. In the event that interest rates decline from what they were when the bonds were issued, the government can recall the outstanding high-interest bonds and replace them with lower-interest debt.

Suppose, in the example, that the bonds contained a call provision giving the government the opportunity to redeem the bonds at a price of $1,050. The government refunds the existing debt, issuing $1,050 of new bonds at the prevailing annual interest rate of 6 percent for

10 years—an obligation having a present economic value of $1,050. The government would thereby realize an economic gain of $98.78—the existing bonds' economic value of $1,148.78 less the new bonds' economic cost of $1,050.00.

Most call provisions do not become effective until a specified number of years after the bonds have been outstanding. By delaying the effective date, an issuer is able to assure investors that they will receive their agreed-upon return for the indicated period and thereby enhance the marketability of its bonds.

Even if a call provision is not yet effective, the government can still lock in the savings that would result from a decline in prevailing interest rates. It can do this through a process known as an **in-substance defeasance**—a kind of advance refunding that does not entail a bond redemption and in which the borrower *economically*, although not legally, satisfies its existing obligations. Issuing new debt, the government places in trust sufficient funds to make all required interest payments through the earliest call date and to redeem the debt on that date.

Example

In-Substance Defeasance

A government has outstanding the same 10-year, 8 percent bonds described in the previous example. The call provision permits the government to redeem the bonds at a price of $1,050 per bond, but the earliest call date is five years (10 semiannual periods) in the future. Prevailing interest rates are 6 percent (3 percent per period).

To defease the bonds in substance, the government would have to place $1,122.51 with a trustee. This amount, determined as follows, is based on an assumption that the bond proceeds will be invested in securities earning the prevailing annual interest rate of 6 percent (3 percent per period):

Present value, at 3 percent, of the $1,050 (a single sum) required to redeem the bonds after 10 periods (present value of $1 = $0.74409)	$ 781.30
Present value, at 3 percent, of the $40 interest to be paid at the end of each of 10 periods (present value of an annuity of $1 = $8.53020)	341.21
Total economic cost of redeeming the bonds in five years (10 periods)	$1,122.51

The government would borrow the required $1,122.51 at an annual rate of 6 percent, an obligation that would have an economic cost of $1,122.51. This amount, if invested in securities earning 6 percent, would be just sufficient to make the required 10 interest payments of $40 and the single principal payment of $1,050.

Most commonly (though not necessarily) the maturity date of the new bonds would be the same as those on the existing bonds. If so, the government would have the same amount of time to repay the debt as it had originally planned.

The total economic cost of taking no action is that of the existing bonds, determined previously to be $1,148.78. Therefore, the economic saving from defeasing the bond, in substance, is $26.27 per each $1,000 of existing bonds outstanding—$1,148.78 less $1,122.51.

Reporting the In-Substance Defeasance in Governmental Funds

The in-substance defeasance would generally be reported in the debt service fund. The accounting is straightforward:

Cash	$1,122.51	
Other financing source—proceeds of refunding bonds		$1,122.51
To record the issuance of refunding (the "new") bonds		
Other financing use—payment to trustee	$1,122.51	
Cash		$1,122.51
To record the transfer of cash to the trust responsible for servicing and redeeming the existing bonds		

GASB STANDARDS

Assuming that an in-substance defeasance transaction satisfies certain conditions intended to ensure that the government has, in economic substance, no further responsibility for the existing debt, then it may remove the existing bonds from its schedule of long-term obligations and replace them with the new bonds. Among the conditions are

- The debtor must irrevocably place cash or other assets with an escrow agent in a trust to be used solely for servicing and retiring the debt.
- The possibility of the debtor having to make future payments on the debt must be remote.
- The assets in the escrow fund must be essentially risk-free, such as U.S. government securities.
- In addition, the government must detail the transaction in notes to the financial statements, indicating the resultant economic gain or loss.[7]

[7] GASB Statement No. 7, *Advance Refundings Resulting in Defeasance of Debt* (March 1987). In 2017, the GASB issued Statement No. 86, Certain Debt Extinguishment Issues. This statement permits governments to account for in-substance defeasances in which they place their own resources in an irrevocable trust fund just as if they had placed borrowed resources in an irrevocable trust. Statement No. 7, by contrast, is directed exclusively to in-substance defeasances in which governments place borrowed resources in an irrevocable trust. Statement No. 86 also mandates certain additional disclosures when, in periods following the in-substance defeasance, governments are permitted to substitute assets that are not essentially risk-free for those that are.

The more controversial question involves how refundings should be accounted for on a full accrual basis—both in government-wide and proprietary fund statements. The issue arises because on a full accrual basis long-term liabilities are reported on the balance sheet. Hence, when a debt is refunded and must be removed from the balance sheet, a gain or loss may have to be recognized.

RECOGNIZING THE GAIN OR LOSS IN PROPRIETARY FUNDS AND IN GOVERNMENT-WIDE STATEMENTS

Suppose that the bonds described in the previous example were issued initially at par and are thereby reported in a proprietary fund at face value of $1,000. Were the bonds to be defeased by placing $1,122.51 in trust, the following entry would be in order to remove the existing debt from the books:

"Loss" (past, present, or future?)	$ 122.51	
Bonds payable	1,000.00	
Cash		$1,122.51

To record the in-substance defeasance of the existing bonds

As demonstrated previously, the government realizes an economic gain by defeasing the debt prior to maturity. Yet because the book value of debt is less than the reacquisition price, it is forced to recognize an "accounting" loss. As implied by the parenthetical question in the entry, the salient accounting issue relates to the disposition of the loss. There are at least three possibilities:

- ***Recognize the loss over the prior years in which the debt has been outstanding.*** The loss is attributable to declines in interest rates (and corresponding increases in bond prices) over those years. Given perfect foresight as to when, and at what amount, it would defease the debt, the issuer would have amortized the anticipated difference between issue price and reacquisition price over those years. The loss, therefore, should be charged against those past years. In reality, however, it is impractical to do that upon defeasance because several years of previous financial statements would need to be restated.
- ***Recognize the loss at the time of defeasance.*** Accepting that it is impractical to assign the loss to the periods the debt was actually outstanding, this policy would recognize it as soon as feasible. Immediate recognition may be objectionable, however, because the operating results of that period would be distorted. Not only would the government be required to report a loss

GASB STANDARDS

The GASB opted for the third method. It requires that the difference between the book value of the existing debt and the reacquisition price be deferred (recorded as a **deferred outflow of resources**) and amortized over the remaining life of the existing debt or the new debt, whichever is shorter.[8] This period of amortization is consistent with an interpretation that the new debt is merely a restructured version of the old. The GASB does not permit the amortization to extend past the maturity date of the existing debt because it sees any debt outstanding beyond that date as essentially a new borrowing for an additional period of time. This approach is arguably the least acceptable in concept in that it delays to the future recognition of a loss attributable to past events and decisions yet the most reasonable in practice in that it avoids either restatements of previously issued reports or the recognition of a loss that took place over multiple years in a single year. Moreover, it can be argued that the economic loss has been incurred strictly to reduce interest rates in the years following the defeasance and thereby benefit the future.

By contrast, in its Statement No. 140 (issued in 2000), the FASB ruled that for entities within its jurisdiction a debtor can "derecognize" a liability only if the debtor has either paid the obligation or been legally released from it.[9] Therefore, the debtor must report on its balance sheet both the debt that it in-substance defeased and the assets set aside to refund it. Correspondingly, it must include on its statement of revenues and expenses both the interest expense on the defeased debt and the investment revenue on the assets that it has set aside.

[8] GASB Statement No. 23, *Accounting and Financial Reporting for Refundings of Debt Reported by Proprietary Activities* (December 1993), para. 4.
[9] FASB Statement No. 140, *Accounting for Transfers and Servicing of Financial Assets and Extinguishments of Liabilities*—a replacement of FASB Statement No. 125 (September 2000). (FASB ASC 860–10).

when in economic substance it realized a gain, but, as if to compound the fiscal injury, it would be forced to recognize the entire amount in a single period.

- ***Defer the loss and amortize it over future years.*** This approach is grounded on the assumption that the defeasance is merely a substitution of new debt for existing debt with a corresponding adjustment in interest rates.

What needs to be emphasized is that the reported gain or loss from defeasance, whether amortized over several periods or recognized at once, may be counter to the economic gain or loss. Entities may be tempted, therefore, to defease debt at an economic loss just so they can report a gain.

SUMMARY

Both governments and not-for-profit organizations maintain special funds to account for resources set aside for the purchase and construction of long-lived assets and for the service of long-term debt. Governments both account for and report these resources in capital projects and debt service funds.

Governments account for capital projects and debt service funds on a modified accrual basis. The principles of revenue and expenditure recognition are the same for these funds as for the general fund and special revenue funds. Accordingly, these funds do not report either long-term assets or long-term liabilities, and interest on outstanding long-term debt need not be accrued. The long-term assets and liabilities are accounted for "off the balance sheet."

Special assessments are accounted for just as are any other capital projects. The construction phase is accounted for in a capital projects fund, and the debt service phase is accounted for in a debt service fund. Even though the debt issued to finance special assessment projects is often the responsibility of the property owners rather than the government, the government should nevertheless report it as its own if it is obligated for it in some manner (i.e., unless the government is prohibited from making payments on the debt or it gives no indication that it will, or may, honor the debt in the event of default). Governments may account for enterprise-related special assessments either in an enterprise fund or in the funds in which they account for other types of assessments.

In their government-wide statements, governments combine their capital projects and debt service funds with their other governmental funds and present the combined total in the governmental activities column. Both revenues and expenses are recognized on a full accrual basis. Accordingly, both capital assets and the related long-term debt are reported on the statement of net position. Interest is charged as an expense as a function of time irrespective of when it will be paid, and bond premiums and discounts are amortized.

Arbitrage, which refers to the issuance of debt at relatively low, tax-exempt interest rates and the investment of the proceeds in taxable securities yielding a higher return, subverts the federal government's rationale for exempting state and local debt from federal taxation. Consequently, the federal government has established complex regulations to deter municipalities from engaging in this practice. These regulations cause accounting problems, mainly because they require governments to rebate their arbitrage earnings and expose the governments to substantial penalties if they violate the regulations.

As a general rule, bond refundings do not bring economic gains to a government, unless the government is able to call the bonds at less than their market value. However, even if the call date is in the future, a government can lock in the economic gains from the future call through an in-substance defeasance—a transaction in which the government sets aside the resources necessary to make all required interest and principal payments on the bonds to be refunded.

In the next two chapters, we consider issues associated with long-lived assets and long-term obligations.

KEY TERMS IN THIS CHAPTER

Arbitrage 255
bond refundings 257
bonds 241
call prices 258
capital projects funds 239
coupon rate 241
debt service funds 239
economic cost 257
in-substance defeasance 259
issue costs 241
modified accrual basis 240
refinance 257

EXERCISE FOR REVIEW AND SELF-STUDY

With the approval of neighborhood property owners, the White City Council voted to construct sidewalks in a newly annexed neighborhood, assess the property owners for the cost, and issue debt to finance the project.

1. For the 2021 transactions that follow, prepare journal entries in White City's capital projects and debt service funds:
   a. On January 1, 2021, the city council assessed the property owners the estimated cost of $8,000,000. The assessments are payable over a five-year period ($1,600,000 per year) with interest at 6 percent annually (3 percent per semiannual period) on the unpaid balance. The first installment is due on December 31, 2021.
   b. The city issued $8,000,000 of five-year, 6 percent, serial bonds. The bonds were issued at a premium of $200,000, but the city incurred issuance costs of $150,000. It transferred the premium (net of the issuance costs) to the debt service fund.
   c. It constructed the sidewalks at the estimated cost of $8,000,000.
   d. It collected the first $1,600,000 installment of the assessments, along with $480,000 in interest.
   e. It made one payment of $240,000 interest on the bonds. The next payment of interest, along with the first payment of $1,600,000 in principal, is due in January 2022.

2. For the capital projects fund and the debt service fund prepare: (1) statements of revenues, expenditures, and changes in fund balance and (2) balance sheets.

3. Assume that the city engaged in no other transactions during the year and that the city amortized $36,000 of the bond premium. Prepare two schedules in which you present the revenues, expenses, assets, liabilities, and net position of the funds as they would affect the government-wide statement of activities and statement of net position.

4. The bond agreement permits the city to redeem the $1,600,000 of bonds that are due in January 2026 one year early (in January 2025), at par, without penalty. In January 2023 (with six semiannual periods until the January 2026 maturity date), interest rates decrease to an annual rate of 4 percent, and the city has the opportunity to defease the bonds "in substance."

a. What is the "economic cost" of the $1,600,000 of bonds outstanding as of January 2023, assuming that the city would have to make six additional interest payments of $48,000 (the semiannual coupon rate of 3 percent times $1,600,000) plus a principal payment of $1.6 million? Base your valuation on the prevailing interest rate of 4 percent (2 percent per period).

b. How much would the city have to place with a trustee in January 2023 so that it would have sufficient resources on hand to retire the bonds in January 2025—that is, the four required interest payments of $48,000 through January 2025 and the one payment of principal of $1,600,000? Assume that the funds placed with the trustee would earn interest at the annual rate of 4 percent (2 percent per period).

c. Assume that the city would borrow the funds to be placed with the trustee by issuing bonds yielding the prevailing rate of 4 percent. What would be the "economic cost" of this new debt? How does it compare with that of the old debt?

d. Suppose that with six semiannual periods until maturity, the city were to defease (in substance) the $1,600,000 of bonds. At the time, the book value of the bonds was $1,625,270. That is, the unamortized premium was $25,270. Prepare a journal entry to reflect the defeasance on the government-wide statements.

e. How do you explain the reported loss (in this case deferred) even though the transaction resulted in economic savings?

QUESTIONS FOR REVIEW AND DISCUSSION

1. Although many governments prepare budgets for both capital projects and debt service funds and integrate them into their accounts, budgetary control over these funds is not as essential as it is for other governmental funds. Do you agree? Explain. If budgets are prepared for capital projects funds, in what significant way may they differ from those prepared for other funds?

2. When bonds are issued for capital projects, premiums are generally not accounted for as the mirror image of discounts. Why not?

3. It is sometimes said that in debt service funds the accounting for interest revenue is inconsistent with that for interest expenditure. Explain. What is the rationale for this seeming inconsistency?

4. At one time governments maintained a unique type of fund to account for special assessments. This fund recorded the construction in process, the long-term debt, and the assessments receivable. Explain briefly how governments account for special assessments today.

5. Special assessment debt may be, in economic substance and/or legal form, an obligation of the assessed property owners rather than a government. Should the government, therefore, report it in its statements as if it were its own debt? What are the current standards for when a government should recognize special assessment debt as its own obligation?

6. How should governments report their capital projects and debt service activities in their government-wide statements?

7. A government issues bonds at a discount. Where would the government report the discount on its (a) fund statements and (b) government-wide statements?

8. What is *arbitrage*? Why does the Internal Revenue Service place strict limits on the amount of arbitrage that a municipality can earn?

9. Under what circumstances can a government refund outstanding debt and thereby take advantage of a decline in interest rates?

10. What is meant by an *in-substance defeasance*, and how can a government use it to lower its interest costs? How must it recognize a gain or loss on defeasance if it accounts for the debt in a proprietary fund? How do the GASB standards pertaining to in-substance defeasances differ from those of the FASB?

EXERCISES

EX. 6-1

Select the *best* answer.

1. A government opts to set aside $10 million of general-fund resources to finance a new city hall. Construction is expected to begin in several years, when the city has been able to accumulate additional resources.
   a. The government *must* account for the $10 million in a capital projects fund, and in its government-wide statements it *must* report the $10 million as "restricted."
   b. The government *may* account for the $10 million in a capital projects fund, and in its government-wide statements it *may* report the $10 million as "restricted."
   c. The government *may not* account for the $10 million in a capital projects fund, and in its government-wide statements it *may not* report the $10 million as "unrestricted."
   d. The government *may* account for the $10 million in a capital projects fund, but in its government-wide statements it *may not* report the $10 million as "restricted."

2. A government should distinguish underwriting and other issue costs from bond premiums and discounts and in a governmental fund should
   a. Report them as expenditures
   b. Add them to the face value of the bond
   c. Report them in a separate account and amortize them over the life of the bond
   d. Deduct them from the bond premiums or add them to the bond discount

3. When a government issues bonds at premiums or discounts and records the proceeds in a capital projects fund, it should
   a. Transfer an amount equal to the premiums from the capital projects fund to a debt service fund, and an amount equal to the discounts from a debt service fund to the capital projects fund
   b. Transfer an amount equal to the premiums from the capital projects fund to a debt service fund, but make no transfer of an amount equal to the discounts from a debt service fund to the capital projects fund
   c. Make no transfers between the capital projects fund and a debt service fund
   d. Transfer an amount equal to the discounts from a debt service fund to the capital projects fund, but make no transfer of an amount equal to the premiums from the capital projects fund to the debt service fund

4. A city holds U.S. Treasury notes as an investment in a capital projects fund. During the year, the market value of the notes increases by $50,000. Of this amount, $14,000 can be attributed to a decline in prevailing interest rates and $36,000 to interest that has been earned but not yet received. As of year-end, the city should recognize as revenue
   a. $0
   b. $14,000
   c. $36,000
   d. $50,000

5. Which of the following accounts is least likely to be shown on the balance sheet of a debt service fund?
   a. Bonds payable
   b. Investments (at fair value)
   c. Cash
   d. Special assessments receivable

6. Special assessment debt should be reported on the balance sheet of a city if the debt is to be paid from assessments on property owners and
   a. The city has guaranteed payment of the debt and the probability of the city having to make good on the guarantee is 50 percent or greater
   b. The city has guaranteed payment of the debt but the probability of the city having to make good on the guarantee is remote
   c. The city has no legal responsibility for the debt, but in the past has made up for any property owner defaults
   d. All of the above

7. In its governmental fund statements, a government should recognize revenue from special assessments
   a. Entirely in the year in which the assessment is imposed
   b. In the years in which the assessments are paid
   c. In the years in which the assessments are due
   d. In the years in which the assessments become available for expenditure

8. In the year it imposes a special assessment, a government should recognize in its government-wide statements
   a. The amount of the assessment, plus anticipated interest, as both revenue and an asset
   b. The amount of the assessment as both a deferred inflow of resources and an asset
   c. Only the amount of the assessment due in the current year as revenue but the full amount of the assessment as an asset
   d. Only the amount of the assessment due in the current year as both revenue and an asset

9. Under existing federal statutes, *arbitrage* as it applies to state and local governments
   a. Is illegal
   b. Is illegal unless the government can demonstrate a "just cause" for engaging in it
   c. Is legal in some circumstances, but the government may be required to remit arbitrage earnings to the federal government
   d. Is illegal unless there is no more than a 2 percent difference between interest earned and interest paid

10. Bond refundings are most likely to result in an economic gain when
   a. The bonds are subject to arbitrage
   b. There is an inverted yield curve
   c. The bonds were initially issued at a premium
   d. The bonds are subject to a call provision

EX. 6-2

Select the *best* answer.

1. Which of the following items is least likely to appear on the balance sheet of a capital projects fund?
   a. Cash
   b. Investments
   c. Construction in process
   d. Reserve for encumbrances

2. The fund balance of a debt service fund is most likely to be incorporated into the reporting entity's government-wide statement of net position as
   a. Net position, net investment in capital assets (net of related debt)
   b. Net position, restricted
   c. Net position, unrestricted
   d. Capital assets

3. The repayment of bond principal should be reported in the fund statements of a debt service fund as
   a. An expenditure
   b. An "other financing use"
   c. A reduction of bonds payable
   d. A direct charge to fund balance

4. A state issues bonds, at a premium, to finance road construction projects. The premium would affect
   a. "Interest expenditure" as reported in the state's debt service fund
   b. Nonreciprocal transfers-out as reported in the state's general fund
   c. "Capital assets" as reported in the state's government-wide statement of net position
   d. "Net position, net investment in capital assets (net of related debt)" in the state's government-wide statement of net position

5. If a government issues bonds at a discount, the discount should be reported as
   a. A reduction of fund balance in the balance sheet of a capital projects fund
   b. An amortization expenditure in the statement of revenues, expenditures, and changes in fund balance of a capital projects fund in the periods in which the bonds are outstanding
   c. An amortization expense in the government-wide statement of activities in the periods in which the bonds are outstanding
   d. A liability in the government-wide statement of net position

6. A city issued bonds on July 1. Interest of $600,000 is payable the following January 1. On December 31, the city transfers the required $600,000 from its general fund to its debt service fund. On its December 31 debt service fund statement of revenues, expenditures, and changes in fund balance, the city
   a. Must report interest expenditure of $0
   b. Must report interest expenditure of $600,000
   c. Must report interest expenditure of $500,000
   d. May report interest expenditure of either $0 or $600,000

7. A city issues $10 million of debt that it uses to acquire an office building. In the year that it issues the debt and acquires the building the city neither makes any interest payments nor repays any of the debt principal. Assume that the city accounts for all capital acquisitions in a capital projects fund and all payments of interest and principal in a debt service fund. The transaction would
   a. Increase expenditures of the capital projects fund
   b. Increase other financing sources of the debt service fund
   c. Increase fund balance of the capital projects fund
   d. Increase expenditures of the debt service fund

8. A city assesses property owners $50 million to extend sewer lines to their neighborhood. By year-end, however, it has not begun construction of the new lines and has not collected any of the assessments. It accounts for its wastewater services in an enterprise fund. In its year-end enterprise fund financial statements, the government should
   a. Recognize the assessments as assessments receivable and a deferred inflow of resources
   b. Recognize the assessments as assessments receivable and revenue
   c. Recognize the assessments as assessments receivable and a liability for future construction costs
   d. Not recognize the assessments until they will be available for expenditure

9. A county engages in an in-substance defeasance of its bonds. The transaction results in an economic gain but an accounting loss. In its government-wide statements the county should
   a. Recognize the loss entirely in the year of the defeasance
   b. Amortize the loss over the remaining life of either the existing debt or the new debt
   c. Report the loss as a direct charge to net position
   d. Not recognize the loss, but instead continue to report the defeased bonds (as well as the new bonds) as liabilities

10. A government issued, at par, $10 million of 20-year, 6 percent bonds that it accounts for in its electric utility fund. The bonds do not contain a call provision. Ten years later prevailing interest rates have fallen to 5 percent. The government is considering whether to purchase the outstanding bonds at their market price and retire them. It would acquire the necessary funds by issuing new ten-year, 5 percent bonds. The transaction would most likely result in
    a. An economic gain but an accounting loss
    b. An economic loss but an accounting gain
    c. An economic gain and an accounting loss
    d. Neither an economic gain or loss but an accounting loss

EX. 6-3

Construction and debt transactions can affect more than one fund.

During 2021 Luling Township engaged in the following transactions related to modernizing the bridge over the Luling River. The township accounts for long-term construction projects in a capital projects fund.

- On July 1 it issued 10-year, 4 percent bonds with a face value of $1 million. The bonds were sold for $1,016,510, an amount that provides an annual yield of 3.8 percent (semiannual rate of 1.9 percent). The city incurred $10,000 in issue costs.
- On August 1, it was awarded a state reimbursement grant of $800,000. During the year it incurred allowable costs of $600,000. Of these it paid $500,000 in cash to various contractors. It received $450,000 from the state, expecting to receive, early in 2022, the $150,000 difference between allowable costs incurred and cash received. Moreover, it expects to receive the balance of the grant later in 2022.
- It invested the bond proceeds in short-term federal securities. During the year it received $8,000 in interest, and at year-end the market value of the securities was $1,000 more than the township had paid for them.
- It transferred the bond premium (net of issue costs) to an appropriate fund.
- It transferred $20,000 from the general fund to an appropriate fund to cover the first payment of bond interest that was due, and paid, on December 31.
- On January 1, the township defeased in substance $400,000 of bonds that had been issued years earlier to construct the bridge. The bonds had been issued at par. To effect the transaction the township issued $405,000 of new bonds, at par, and placed the proceeds in a trust. The old bonds have a coupon rate of 5 percent; the new bonds have a coupon rate of 4 percent.

What amount should Luling report in its December 31, 2021, financial statements as:

1. Nonreciprocal transfers-in to its debt service fund
2. Interest expenditure in its debt service fund
3. Interest expense on its government-wide statements (after taking into account amortization of the bond premium)
4. Investment revenue in its capital projects fund
5. Bonds payable in its capital projects fund
6. Total expenditures in its capital projects fund
7. Bond proceeds in its capital projects fund
8. Bond proceeds in its debt service fund
9. Deferred outflow of resources (loss on defeasance) in its debt service fund
10. Grant revenue in its capital projects fund
11. Grants receivable in its capital projects fund
12. Carrying value of bonds payable (on issue of July 1 only) in its government-wide statements

Select each response from the amounts that follow. An amount may be selected once, more than once, or not at all.

a. $0
b. $8,000
c. $9,000
d. $16,510
e. $19,314
f. $20,000
g. $26,510
h. $38,627
i. $150,000
j. $200,000
k. $400,000
l. $405,000
m. $500,000
n. $600,000
o. $610,000
p. $1,000,000
q. $1,006,510
r. $1,016,510
s. $1,015,824

EX. 6-4

Capital projects funds account for construction expenditures, not for the assets that are being constructed.

The Wickliffe City Council authorizes the restoration of the city library. The project is to be funded by the issuance of bonds, a reimbursement grant from the state, and property taxes.

1. Prepare journal entries in the capital projects fund to reflect the following events and transactions:
   - **a.** The city approves (and gives accounting recognition to) the project's budget of $9,027,000, of which $6,000,000 is to be funded by general obligation bonds, $2,500,000 from the state, and the remaining $527,000 from the general fund. The city estimates that construction costs will be $8,907,000 and bond issue costs $120,000.
   - **b.** The city issues 9 percent, 15-year bonds that have a face value of $6,000,000. The bonds are sold for $6,120,000, an amount reflecting a price of $102. The city incurs $115,000 in issue costs; hence, the net proceeds are $6,005,000.
   - **c.** The city transfers the net premium of $5,000 to its debt service fund.
   - **d.** It receives the anticipated $2,500,000 from the state and transfers $527,000 from the general fund.
   - **e.** It signs an agreement with a contractor for $8,890,000.
   - **f.** It pays the contractor $8,890,000 upon completion of the project.
   - **g.** It transfers the remaining cash to the debt service fund.
2. Prepare appropriate closing entries.

EX. 6-5

The accounting for bond premiums is not the mirror image of that for bond discounts.

Pacific Independent School District issued $100 million of general obligation bonds to finance the construction of new schools. The bonds were issued at a premium of $0.6 million.

1. Prepare the capital projects fund journal entries to record the issue of the bonds and the transfer of the premium to an appropriate fund.
2. Suppose, instead, that the bonds were issued at a discount of $0.6 million but that the project will still cost $100 million. Prepare the appropriate entries.
   - **a.** Contrast the entries in this part with those in part 1.
   - **b.** Indicate the options available to the school district, and state how they would affect the entries required of the district.
   - **c.** Suppose that the government chose to finance the balance of the project with general revenues. Prepare the appropriate capital projects fund entry.

EX. 6-6

Governments can seldom realize an economic gain by refunding bonds in the absence of call provisions.

A government has outstanding $100 million of 20-year, 10 percent bonds. They were issued at par and have 16 years (32 semiannual periods) until they mature. They pay interest semiannually.

1. Suppose current prevailing interest rates had decreased to 8 percent (4 percent per period). At what amount would you estimate the bonds were trading in the open market?
2. Suppose the government elected to purchase the bonds in the market and retire them. To finance the purchase it issued 16-year (32-period) bonds at the prevailing rate of 8 percent (4 percent per period). What would be the "economic cost" (i.e., the present value of anticipated cash flows) of issuing these bonds? Would the government realize an economic gain by retiring the old bonds and issuing the new?

3. Suppose a call provision permitted the government to redeem the bonds at any time for a total of $101 million. Could the government realize an economic gain by recalling the bonds and financing the purchase by issuing $101 million in new, 8 percent, 16-year bonds?

EX. 6-7

Debt service funds account for resources accumulated to service debt, not the debt itself.

On July 1, a city issued, at par, $100 million in 6 percent, 20-year general obligation bonds. It established a debt service fund to account for resources set aside to pay interest and principal on the obligations.

In the year that it issued the debt, the city engaged in the following transactions involving the debt service fund:

1. It estimated that it would make interest payments of $3 million and have interest earnings of $30,000 from investments. It would transfer from the general fund to the debt service fund $2.97 million to pay interest and $500,000 to provide for the payment of principal when the bonds mature. Further, as required by the bond indentures, it would transfer $1 million of the bond proceeds from the capital projects fund to the debt service fund to be held in reserve until the debt matures.
2. Upon issuing the bonds, the city transferred $1 million of the bond proceeds from the capital projects fund. It invested $977,254 of the funds in 20-year, 6 percent Treasury bonds that had a face value of $1 million. The bond discount of $22,746 reflected an effective yield rate of 6.2 percent.
3. On December 31, the city received $30,000 interest on the Treasury bonds. This payment represented interest for six months. Correspondingly, the market value of the bonds increased by $294, reflecting the amortization of the discount.
4. On the same day the city transferred $2.97 million from the general fund to pay interest on the bonds that it had issued. It also transferred $500,000 for the eventual repayment of principal.
5. Also on December 31, it made its first interest payment of $3 million to bondholders.
   a. Prepare appropriate journal entries in the debt service fund, including budgetary and closing entries.
   b. The bonds issued by the city pay interest at the rate of 6 percent. The bonds in which the city invested its reserve have an effective yield of 6.2 percent. Why might the difference in rates create a potential liability for the city?

CONTINUING PROBLEM

Review the Comprehensive Annual Financial Report (CAFR) that you have obtained.

1. How many capital projects funds does the government maintain? How can you tell? Are any of these major funds? If so, for what purposes are they maintained?
2. How many debt service funds does the government maintain? How can you tell? Are any of these major funds? If so, for what types of obligations are they maintained?
3. How are the capital projects and debt service funds reported in the government-wide statement of net position?
4. Select one of the more recently established (and larger) capital projects funds (a major fund, if there is one).
5. From where did the fund receive most of its resources?
6. Did the city acquire or construct new capital assets using resources of this fund? If so, in what amount?

7. Does this fund have any long-term debts associated with it? If so, does the government maintain a debt service fund to account for the resources to service the debt?

8. Did the government issue additional long-term debt to support governmental activities during the year? Did it repay any long-term debt used to support governmental activities? Did it engage in any in-substance defeasances?

PROBLEMS

P. 6-1

The financial statements of an actual capital projects fund leave it to the report reader to draw inferences on key transactions.

The accompanying statements of the parks, recreations, and municipal capital improvement bond fund (a capital projects fund) were drawn from an annual report of Parkville. According to a note in the report (the only one pertaining to the fund), the fund is maintained "to account for bond proceeds to be utilized for the construction and refurbishment of parks and recreation facilities and the refurbishment of other municipal facilities."

1. The variances in expenditures between budget and actual are substantial. What is the most likely explanation?

2. A schedule of long-term debt payable (in the statistical section of the report) indicates that only $7 million, of parks, recreation, and municipal capital improvement bonds were authorized and issued. How do you reconcile that amount with the proceeds from bonds payable reported in the statement of revenues, expenditures, and changes in fund balance?

3. Another schedule of transfers between funds (in the same section) indicates that $131 thousand was transferred to the general fund. What conclusions can you draw about whether interest on fund investments must be used either to repay the capital improvement bonds or to construct and refurbish city facilities?

4. How much of fund resources did the government spend during the year on capital improvements?

5. How do you explain the absence in the balance sheet of "construction in process"?

6. Why is a major portion of the fund balance "restricted"?

Parks, Recreation, and Municipal Capital Improvement Bond Fund Balance Sheet
December 31, 2021 (in thousands)

Assets	
Receivables	$ 2
Investments	5,874
Total assets	$5,876
Liabilities and Fund Balance	
Liabilities	
Accrued wages and salaries	$ 4
Construction contracts payable	202
Due to other funds	220
Total liabilities	$ 426
Fund Balance	
Restricted for bond projects	$5,019
Committed	431
Total fund balance	$5,450
Total liabilities and fund balance	$5,876

Parks, Recreation, and Municipal Capital Improvement Bond Fund Statement of Revenues, Expenditures, and Changes in Fund Balance—Budget and Actual Year Ended December 31, 2021 (in thousands)

	Budget	Actual
Revenues		
Interest earnings	$ 75	$ 131
Expenditures		
Capital outlay		
General government—facility	1,552	425
Culture and recreation—facility	5,500	1,177
Total expenditures	$ 7,052	$ 1,602
Deficiency of revenues over expenditures	$ (6,977)	$ (1,471)
Other financing sources (uses)		
Proceeds from bonds payable	$ 7,052	$ 7,052
Nonreciprocal transfers out	(75)	(131)
Total other financing sources (uses)	$ 6,977	$ 6,921
Excess of revenues and other sources over expenditures and other uses	$ 0	5,450
Fund balance, beginning of year		0
Fund balance, end of year		$ 5,450

P. 6-2

The transactions of a capital projects fund can be derived from its basic financial statements.

Crystal City established a capital projects fund to account for the construction of a new bridge. During the year the fund was established, the city issued bonds, signed (and encumbered) $6 million in contracts with various suppliers and contractors, and incurred $4.3 million of construction costs. It temporarily invested a portion of the bond proceeds and earned $20,000 in interest, which was received in cash. The accompanying statement of revenues, expenditures, and changes in fund balance and balance sheet were taken from its year-end financial report. Based on the data in the two statements, as well as those provided in the previous paragraph, prepare journal entries to summarize the transactions in which the fund engaged. You should prepare budgetary entries, but need not prepare closing entries.

Crystal City, Capital Projects Fund Statement of Revenues, Expenditures, and Changes in Fund Balance—Actual and Budget Year Ended December 31 (in thousands)

	Actual	Budget
Revenues		
Cash grant from state	$ 2,000	$ 2,000
Interest	20	
Total revenues	$ 2,020	$ 2,000
Expenditures		
Bond issue costs	$ 50	
Construction costs	4,300	5,000
Total expenditures	$ 4,350	$ 5,000
Excess of revenues over expenditures	$ (2,330)	$ (3,000)
Other financing sources (uses)		
Proceeds of bonds	$ 10,000	$ 10,000
Proceeds of bonds (premium)	200	
Nonreciprocal cash transfer of bond premium (less issue costs) to debt service fund	(150)	
Increase in reserve for encumbrances	(1,700)	
Total other financing sources (uses)	$ 8,350	$ 10,000
Excess of revenues and net financing sources over expenditures	$ 6,020	$ 7,000
Fund balance, beginning of year	0	0
Fund balance, end of year	$ 6,020	$ 7,000

Crystal City, Capital Projects Fund Balance Sheet As of December 31 (in thousands)

Assets	
Cash	$ 5,320
Investments	5,000
Total assets	$10,320
Liabilities	
Accounts payable (to contractors)	$ 2,600
Fund balance	
Committed	$ 1,700
Assigned	6,020
Total fund balance	$ 7,720
Total liabilities and fund balance	$10,320

P. 6-3

The transactions of a debt service fund can be derived from its basic financial statements.

Durwin County issued $200 million in long-term debt to fund major improvements to the county's road and transportation systems. The debt is to be serviced from the proceeds of a specially dedicated property tax. The accompanying statement of revenues, expenditures, and changes in fund balance and balance sheet were taken from its year-end financial report.

Based on the data in the two statements, prepare journal entries to summarize the transactions in which the firm engaged. You should prepare budgetary entries, but need not prepare closing entries.

Durwin County, Debt Service Fund Statement of Revenues, Expenditures, and Changes in Fund Balance—Actual and Budget Year Ended December 31 (in thousands)

	Actual	Budget
Revenues		
Property taxes	$21,520	$20,000
Interest	50	—
Total revenues	$21,570	$20,000
Expenditures		
Principal retirement	$ 6,000	$ 6,000
Interest	12,500	12,500
Total expenditures	$18,500	$18,500
Excess of revenues over expenditures	$ 3,070	$ 1,500
Other financing sources (uses)		
Nonreciprocal transfer of bond premium from capital projects fund	150	—
Excess of revenues and net financing sources over expenditures	$ 3,220	$ 1,500
Fund balance, beginning of year	0	0
Fund balance, end of year	$ 3,220	$ 1,500

Durwin County, Debt Service Fund Balance Sheet as of December 31 (in thousands)

Assets	
Cash	$ 70
Investments	1,000
Property taxes receivable	2,150
Total assets	$3,220
Fund balance	$3,220

P. 6-4

The financial statements of a debt service fund may reveal less information than is apparent.

The balance sheet and a comparative statement (budget-to-actual) of revenues, expenditures, and changes in fund balance of Parkville's general obligation debt service fund (date changed) is presented as follows.

General Obligation Debt Service Fund Balance Sheet as of December 31, 2021 (in thousands)

Assets	
Equity in pooled cash and cash equivalents	$ 18
Cash with fiscal agent	21
Investments, at market value	1,527
Receivables—accrued interest	2
Due from other funds	44
Total assets	$1,612
Liabilities and fund balance	
Liabilities	
Vouchers and accounts payable	$ 1
Fund balance	
Restricted for special purposes	1
Assigned	1,610
Total fund balance	$1,611
Total liabilities and fund balance	$1,612

General Obligation Debt Service Fund Statement of Revenues, Expenditures, and Changes in Fund Balance Budget and Actual Year Ended December 31, 2021 (in thousands)

	Budget	Actual
Revenues		
Investment earnings	$ —	$ 151
Expenditures		
Administrative services	25	22
Debt service payments		
Principal	2,592	2,592
Interest	4,088	4,088
Total expenditures	$ 6,705	$ 6,702
Excess (deficiency) of revenues over expenditures	$(6,705)	$(6,551)
Other financing sources (uses)		
Nonreciprocal transfers-in	6,292	7,790
Nonreciprocal transfers-out	(10)	(10)
	6,282	7,780
Excess (deficiency) of revenues and other sources over expenditures and other uses	$ (423)	1,229
Fund balance, beginning of year		382
Fund balance, end of year		$ 1,611

1. Of what significance is the *deficiency* of revenues over expenditures? Is it an indication of poor management?
2. The fund reported a smaller deficit than was budgeted. Is this variance a sign of good management? Explain.

3. Can you assess whether the fund will have the fiscal wherewithal to satisfy its obligations of principal and interest as they come due? Explain.

4. Included among the nonreciprocal transfers-in is a transfer of $1,498 from a related capital projects fund. What is a likely explanation for the transfer?

5. A schedule of operating transfers indicates that the transfers-in were as follows:

From the general fund	$2,080
From the permanent parks and recreation fund	25
From the transportation fund	15
From the open space fund (to account for the acquisition of greenbelt land)	3,944
From the major maintenance and equipment replacement fund	228
Total	$6,292

The major maintenance and equipment replacement fund is a capital projects funds; each of the other funds, other than the general fund, is a special revenue fund. What are the most likely reasons for the transfers from the special revenue funds?

P. 6-5

The construction and financing phase of a special assessment project is accounted for in a capital projects fund, and the debt service phase is accounted for in a debt service fund (see the next problem).

Upon annexing a recently developed subdivision, a government undertakes to extend sewer lines to the area. The estimated cost is $10.0 million. The project is to be funded with $8.5 million in special assessment bonds and a $1.0 million reimbursement grant from the state.

The balance is to be paid by the government out of its general fund. Property owners are to be assessed an amount sufficient to pay both principal and interest on the debt.

During the year, the government engaged in the following transactions, all of which would be recorded in a capital projects fund.

It recorded the capital projects fund budget. It estimated that it would earn $0.20 million in interest on the temporary investment of bond proceeds, an amount that will reduce the required transfer from the general fund. It estimated that bond issue costs would be $0.18 million.

1. It issued $8.5 million in bonds at a premium of $0.30 million and incurred $0.18 million in issue costs. The premium, net of issue costs, is to be transferred to a newly established debt service fund.

2. It received the $1.0 million grant from the state, recognizing it as a liability until it incurred at least $1.0 million in construction costs.

3. It invested $7.62 million in short-term (less than one year) securities.

4. It issued purchase orders and signed construction contracts for $9.2 million.

5. It sold $5.0 million of its investments for $5.14 million, the excess of selling price over cost representing interest earned. By year-end the investments still on hand had increased in value by $0.06 million, an amount also attributable to interest earned.

6. It received invoices totaling $5.7 million. As permitted by its agreement with its prime contractor, it retained (and recorded as a payable) $0.4 million pending satisfactory completion of the project. It paid the balance of $5.3 million.

7. It transferred $0.12 million to the debt service fund.

8. It updated its accounts, but did not close them because the project is not completed and its budget is for the entire project, not for a single period.
   a. Prepare appropriate journal entries for the capital projects fund.
   b. Prepare a statement of revenues, expenditures, and changes in fund balance in which you compare actual and budgeted amounts.

c. Prepare a year-end (December 31) balance sheet.
d. Does your balance sheet report the construction in process? If not, where might the construction in process be recorded?

P. 6-6

The debt service phase special assessment bonds are accounted for in a debt service fund.

As stated in the previous problem, a government issued $8.5 million of special assessment bonds to finance a sewer-extension project. To service the debt, it assessed property owners $8.5 million. Their obligations are payable over a period of five years, with annual installments due on March 31 of each year. Interest at an annual rate of 8 percent is to be paid on the total balance outstanding as of that date.

The bonds require an annual principal payment of $1.57 million each year for five years, due on December 31. In addition, interest on the unpaid balance is payable twice each year, on June 30 and December 31 at an annual rate of 8 percent.

The government agreed to make up from its general fund the difference between required debt service payments and revenues.

At the start of the year, the government established a debt service fund. During the year it engaged in the following transactions, all of which would affect that fund.

1. It prepared, and recorded in its accounts, its annual budget. It estimated that it would collect from property owners $1.3 million in special assessments and $0.5 million of interest on the unpaid balance of the assessments. In addition, it expected to earn interest of $0.08 million on temporary investments. It would be required to pay interest of $0.68 million and make principal payments of $1.7 million on the outstanding debt. It anticipated transferring $0.5 million from the general fund to cover the revenue shortage.
2. It recorded the $8.5 million of assessments receivable, estimating that $0.2 million would be uncollectible.
3. The special assessments bonds were issued at a premium (net of issue costs) of $0.12 million. The government recognized the anticipated transfer of the premium to the debt service fund.
4. During the year the government collected $2.0 million in assessments and $0.4 million in interest (with a few property owners paying their entire assessment in the first year). During the first 60 days of the following year it collected an additional $0.1 million in assessments and $0.01 million in interest, both of which were due the previous year.
5. It transferred $0.12 million (the premium) from the capital projects fund.
6. It purchased $0.8 million of six-month treasury bills as a temporary investment.
7. It made its first interest payment of $0.34 million.
8. It sold the investments for $0.85 million, the difference between selling price and cost representing interest earned.
9. It recognized its year-end obligation for interest of $0.34 million and principal of $1.7 million, but did not actually make the required payments.
10. It prepared year-end closing entries.
    a. Prepare appropriate journal entries for the debt service fund.
    b. Prepare a statement of revenues, expenditures, and changes in fund balance in which you compare actual and budgeted amounts for the year ending December 31.
    c. Prepare a year-end balance sheet.
    d. Does your balance sheet report the balance of the bonds payable? If not, where might it be recorded?

P. 6-7

In a government, financial information that is appropriate for some purposes may be inappropriate for others—just as in business.The conversion from fund to government-wide statements involves more than summing the funds.

The accompanying combined statement of revenues, expenditures, and fund balance was drawn from the statements of Plant City, Florida, which, of course, included a general and other funds that are not shown. Suppose, however, that these were the only funds maintained by the city.

1. Prepare a government-wide statement of net position (balance sheet) and a statement of activities. Make the following assumptions:
   - At year-end the city had $4.39 million in cash and equivalents (its only assets) in its capital projects fund. It had accounts payable and other short-term liabilities in that fund of $0.71 million. It had neither assets nor liabilities in its debt service fund.
   - At year-end the city had $28.28 million in capital assets ("construction in process and other assets").
   - It charged depreciation of $2.1 million for the year. Accumulated depreciation at year-end was $10.4 million.
   - It had $3.12 million in general obligation long-term debt.
   - Interest paid for the year was equal to interest expense. You need not reconcile beginning and ending balances of net position, and the statement of activities can be in the "traditional" format (i.e., with the revenues and expenses shown in rows rather than columns).

2. Comment on the main differences in the revenues, expenditures/expenses, and other financing sources uses as reported on the fund statements and on the government-wide statements. Would you expect that over the life of the government the cumulative changes in fund balance (net position) as reported on the two types of statements would be different? Explain.

Plant City Statement of Revenues, Expenditures, and Changes in Fund Balance (in millions)

	Debt Service	Capital Projects
Revenues and other financing sources		
Intergovernmental revenues	$0.30	
Fees and miscellaneous revenues		$2.47
Total revenues and other financing sources	0.30	2.47
Expenditures		
Retirement of principal	$0.16	
Interest	0.14	
Construction costs		$2.17
Total expenditures	0.30	2.17
Excess of revenues and other financing sources over expenditures	$ 0	$0.30
Fund balance, beginning of year	0	3.38
Fund balance, end of year	$ 0	$3.68

P. 6-8

Governments may report substantially different amounts of interest on their government-wide and fund financial statements.

Charter City issued $100 million of 6 percent, 20-year general obligation bonds on January 1, 2020. The bonds were sold to yield 6.2 percent and hence were issued at a discount of $2.27 million (i.e., at a price of $97.73 million). Interest on the bonds is payable on July 1 and January 1 of each year. On July 1, 2020, and January 1, 2021, the city made its required interest payments of $3 million each.

1. How much interest expenditures should the city report in its debt service fund statement for its fiscal year ending December 31, 2020? During 2020, the city did not transfer resources to the debt service fund for the interest payment due on January 1, 2021.

2. How much interest expense should the city report on its government-wide statements for the year ending December 31, 2020? (It might be helpful to prepare appropriate journal entries.)

3. On January 1, 2037, the city repaid the bonds. How would the repayment be reflected on the city's (1) fund statements and (2) government-wide statements?

P. 6-9

Special assessment debt may take different forms.

A city agrees to extend water and sewer lines to an outlying community. To cover the cost, the affected property owners agree to *special* assessments of $12 million. The assessments are to be paid over five years, with interest at the rate of 6 percent per year. For each of the following situations describe how the city should account for the special assessment debt.

1. The city finances the project by issuing special assessment bonds. The bonds are to be repaid with the special assessment revenues, which the city will account for, as received from property owners, in a debt service fund. The newly constructed lines will be accounted for as general capital assets.

2. The project is financed by bonds issued by a specially created municipal utility district, which is not part of the city's financial reporting entity. Although the city is to construct and own the lines, the utility district is responsible for collecting the assessments and making all required principal and interest payments. The city has no explicit responsibility for the debt but has indicated to the bond underwriters in a letter that it accepts a "moral obligation" to assume the debt in the event the municipal utility district defaults.

3. The project is financed by bonds issued by a specially created municipal utility district, which is not part of the city's financial reporting entity. The city has agreed to collect the assessments and make all required principal and interest payments on behalf of the municipal utility district. The city is constitutionally prohibited from assuming responsibility for this type of debt.

4. The project is carried out, and the bonds are issued by the city's water and sewer utility, which is accounted for in an enterprise fund.

P. 6-10

A hospital's footnote distinguishes between the book value and the economic value of long-term debt.

The financial report of Montefiore Medical Center, which operates a major New York City hospital, included the following item in a summary of long-term debt outstanding (dates changed):

	December 31	
(in thousands)	2019	2018
Revenue bonds payable	$4,178	$4,303

An explanatory note indicated the following:

The proceeds from the 8.625 percent revenue bonds, dated November 1, 2002, issued by the Dormitory Authority of the State of New York, were used by the Medical Center to construct a parking garage. The fair value of these bonds was estimated to be approximately $5.1 million and $5.4 million on December 31, 2019, and December 31, 2018, respectively, using a discounted cash flow analysis based on the Medical Center's incremental borrowing rates for similar types of borrowing arrangements. The bonds are payable serially through June 30, 2033, at increasing annual amounts ranging from $130,000 in 2020 to $500,000 in 2033. Bonds may be redeemed before maturity, for which call premiums are 0.5 percent through June 30, 2020, after which call premiums cease. Under the terms of the revenue bond agreement, certain escrow funds are required to be maintained. On December 31, 2019, escrow assets aggregated approximately $1.2 million, which exceeded minimum escrow requirements.

1. Why would the *fair* value of the bonds, as calculated by the center, be so much greater than their *face* value?

2. The note states that the "bonds are payable *serially*." What does that mean?

3. Assuming that prevailing interest rates remain constant, why would the market price of the bonds be greater before June 30, 2020, than after?

4. Is it likely that the fair value of the bonds is as great as the fair value calculated by the center? Explain.

P. 6-11

Bond refundings may result in an economic gain but a book loss. When should the loss be recognized?

Colgate County issued $1 million of 30-year, 8 percent term bonds to finance improvements to its electric utility plant. The *bonds*, accounted for in an enterprise fund, were issued at par.

After the bonds were outstanding for 10 years, interest rates fell, and the county exercised a call provision to redeem the *bonds* for $1.1 million. The county obtained the necessary cash by issuing $1.1 million in new, 20-year, 6 percent bonds.

1. Prepare the entry that the county should have made in its enterprise fund to record the issuance of the original debt (the same entry as in business accounting).
2. Prepare the entry that the county should have made to record the interest expense and payment each semiannual period.
3. Prepare the entry that the county would make to record the redemption of the original debt. Be sure your entry is in accord with the GASB standards.
4. Did the county incur an *economic* gain or loss by refunding the debt? Of how much?
5. Suppose, instead, that the county could have predicted that it would redeem the debt after it had been outstanding for 10 years (20 periods) for $1.1 million.
   a. What entry should it have made to record the issuance of the bonds?
   b. Over how many periods should the county have amortized the bond discount?
   c. During the 10 years that the bonds were outstanding, what would have been the average reported interest expense each semiannual period, taking into account the amortization of the bond discount? (Assume that the county amortizes bond discounts on a straight-line basis. Although straight-line amortization is not conceptually sound, it provides a measure of the average amortization that would result if the more correct compound interest method were used.)
   d. Prepare the journal entry the county would have made to record interest expense each semiannual period.
6. What is the economic nature of the refunding loss that the county would have to report? In what sense is it really a loss? When did it occur?
7. Compare your response to part 6 with both the GASB and the FASB standards pertaining to recognizing refunding gains and losses. Why would it not be practical to recognize the loss in the periods in which it actually occurs?

P. 6-12

Debtors may be able to realize an economic gain by defeasing their debt "in substance."

A hospital has outstanding $100 million of bonds that mature in 20 years (40 periods). The debt was issued *at* par and pays interest at a rate of 6 percent (3 percent per period). Prevailing rates on comparable bonds are now 4 percent (2 percent per period).

1. What would you expect to be the market price of the bonds, assuming that they are freely traded? Would there be an economic benefit for the hospital to refund the existing debt by acquiring it at the market price and replacing it with new, "low-cost" debt?
2. Assume that the bonds contain a provision permitting the hospital to call the bonds in another five years (10 periods) at a price of $105 and that any invested funds could earn a return equal to the prevailing interest rate of 4 percent (2 percent per period). What would be the economic savings that the hospital could achieve by defeasing the bonds "in substance"?

P. 6-13

A debt service fund reports both routine principal and interest payments as well as an in-substance defeasance.

The revenue and expenditure statement that follows is from an annual report of the City of Fort Worth, Texas. It was accompanied by the notes that follow.

Defeasance of Prior Debt

During the year, the city issued $194,520 of general obligation bonds. The proceeds were used to refund debt obligations with a face value of $181,985. A portion of the proceeds from the issuance of the bonds was placed in an irrevocable escrow account and invested in U.S. obligations that, together with interest earned thereon, would provide an amount to call the bonds on the appropriate call dates. The advance refunding resulted in an economic gain of $4,816.

Arbitrage

The City of Fort Worth frequently issues bonds for capital construction projects. These bonds are subject to the arbitrage regulations. On September 30, the liability for rebate of arbitrage was $560 for general obligation bonds and $51 for enterprise bonds. These amounts are included in the "Payable to Federal Government" category of the debt service and enterprise funds.

City of Forth Worth Statement of Revenues, Expenditures, and Changes in Fund Balance Debt Service Fund Year Ended September 30 (000s omitted)

Revenues	
Revenues from use of money and property	$ 6,170
Expenditures	
Defeasance of certificates of obligation	$ 1,837
Principal retirement	39,842
Interest and service charges	26,659
Total expenditures	$ 68,338
Excess of revenues over (under) expenditures	$(62,168)
Other financing sources (uses)	
Proceeds from refunding bonds	190,009
Proceeds from general obligation bonds	9,617
Nonreciprocal transfers-in	55,565
Payment to refunded bond escrow account	(186,860)
Nonreciprocal transfer-out	(1,995)
Total other financing sources	$ 66,336
Excess of revenues and other financing sources over expenditures and other financing uses	$ 4,168
Fund balance, beginning of year	10,401
Fund balance, end of year	$ 14,569

1. Based on your knowledge of debt service funds, what is the most likely source of "revenue from use of money and property"?
2. Explain in your own words the significance of "proceeds from refunding bonds" and "payment to refunded bond escrow account." (Do not attempt to reconcile the amounts in the statement with those in the footnotes; a portion of the bonds refunded was accounted for in a proprietary fund.)
3. The note pertaining to the bond defeasance also indicates that the refunding resulted in an accounting loss of $536, which was reported in the water and sewer fund—an enterprise fund. How is it possible that the city had an economic gain but an accounting loss? Why is a loss reported in an enterprise fund but not this type of debt service fund?
4. What is the most likely source of the nonreciprocal transfer-in? What was its purpose?
5. What is the most likely reason that the city had an obligation to the federal government for arbitrage? Is the liability necessarily an indication of poor management?

QUESTIONS FOR RESEARCH, ANALYSIS, AND DISCUSSION

1. Do you think that capital projects funds should be limited to accounting for resources that are *externally* restricted? What about debt service funds?

2. Near the end of its fiscal year a school district issues $80 million of bonds to construct a new high school. By year-end the district has received the proceeds of the bonds and invested them in short-term securities. It has not yet incurred any construction costs. In which component of net position should the district include both the assets and the debt on its government-wide statement of net position? For example, should the cash and the related debt be included in "net investment in capital assets" or should the cash be reported along with other cash and the debt excluded from the computation of "invested in capital assets"?

3. A city levies a property tax that is restricted for future period payments of principal and interest on outstanding debt. The tax receipts are recorded in a debt service fund and are invested in interest-and-dividend-earning securities. Hence, the amount of the taxes levied is less than the ultimate amount to be paid. Should the taxes received in a current period be reported as deferred tax revenues and recognized as revenue only at the start of the future periods in which the payments of interest and principal are actually due?

4. A city engages in an in-substance defeasance of long-term bonds and accordingly invests in, and sets aside, the long-term securities necessary to make the required interest and principles payments on the debt to be retired. Should, and if so under what circumstances, the city report the securities on its financial statements?

5. The "In Practice" box on page 258 notes that tax-exempt advance refundings involving debt redemptions are no longer allowed under U.S. tax law and that, as a result, the cost of debt issuance may go up for state and local governments. What are two ways states and cities can mitigate the impact of this change in tax law?

SOLUTION TO EXERCISE FOR REVIEW AND SELF-STUDY

1. Journal Entries

a.

Assessments receivable—current	$1,600,000	
Assessments receivable	6,400,000	
Revenues		$1,600,000
Assessments not yet recognized as revenue (deferred inflow of resources)		6,400,000

To record the assessments (debt service fund, the fund that will account for resources used to service the debt)

The first-year assessments may be recognized as revenues because they will be available for current-year expenditure. The balance must be deferred in the funds statements inasmuch as it is not "available." Assuming that the government has a legal claim to the assessments, it can recognize the entire amount as revenue in the government-wide statements.

b.

Cash	$8,050,000	
Expenditures—bond issue costs	150,000	
Other financing sources—bond proceeds (face value)		$8,000,000
Other financing sources—bond proceeds (bond premium)		200,000

To record the issuance of the bonds (capital projects fund, the fund that will account for resources used to construct the project)

Other financing use—nonreciprocal transfer of bond premium to debt service fund	$50,000	
Cash		$50,000

To record transfer-out of the bond premium to the debt service fund (capital projects fund)		
Cash	$50,000	
Other financing sources—nonreciprocal transfer from capital projects fund		$50,000
To record transfer-in of the bond premium to the debt service fund (debt service fund)		

Inasmuch as the city issued the debt in its name (and is thereby obligated in some manner for repayment), the bonds would be recorded in the government-wide statements. Like other long-term debts, however, they would not be recognized in the funds statement balance sheet.

c.

Expenditures—construction	$8.000.000	
Cash		$8,000,000
To record construction of the sidewalls (capital projects fund)		

Infrastructure assets are accounted for in a manner similar to other capital assets. Therefore, the sidewalks should be recorded as an asset in the government-wide statements.

d.

Cash	$2,080,000	
Assessments receivable—current		$1,600,000
Interest revenue		480,000
To record collection of interest (6 percent of $8,000,000) plus the first assessment installment (debt service fund)		

e.

Expenditures—Bond interest	$240,000	
Cash		$240,000
To record bond interest payment (debt service fund)		

Because the debt service fund is a governmental fund and thereby accounted for on the modified accrual basis, neither the interest nor the principal due in 2022 needs to be accrued.

2. Fund Statements of Revenues, Expenditures, and Changes in Fund Balances (see statements below)

Fund Statements Statement of Revenues, Expenditures, and Changes in Fund Balances—for Year Ending December 31, 2021

	Capital Projects	Debt Service
Revenues		
Assessments	$1,600,000	
Interest	480,000	
Total revenues	2,080,000	
Expenditures		
Bond issue costs	150,000	
Construction	8,000,000	
Interest	240,000	
Total expenditures	8,150,000	$ 240,000
Excess of revenues over expenditures	(8,150,000)	1,840,000

(Continues)

Fund Statements Statement of Revenues, Expenditures, and Changes in Fund Balances—for Year Ending December 31, 2021 *(Continued)*

	Capital Projects	Debt Service
Other financing sources or uses		
Bond proceeds—face value	8,000,000	
Bond proceeds—bond premium	200,000	
Nonreciprocal transfer to/from other funds	(50,000)	50,000
Net other financing sources or uses	8,150,000	50,000
Increase in fund balance	$ 0	$ 1,890,000

Balance Sheets—as of December 31, 2021

	Debt Service
Assets	
Cash	$1,890,000
Assessments receivable	6,400,000
Total assets	8,290,000
Deferred inflows of resources	
Assessments not yet recognized as revenue	6,400,000
Fund balance	
Fund balance—restricted to debt service 1	1,890,000
Total deferred inflows of resources and fund balances	$8,290,000

3. Government-Wide Statement of Activities

Revenues	
Assessments	$ 8,000,000
Interest—assessments	480,000
Total revenues	$ 8,480,000
Expenses	
Bond issue costs	$ 150,000
Interest ($480,000 less 36,000 amortization of bond premium)	444,000
Total expenditures	$ 594,000
Excess of revenues over expenditures	$ 7,886,000

Government-Wide Statement of Net Position

Assets	
Cash	$ 1,890,000
Assessments receivable	6,400,000
Infrastructure assets (sidewalks)	8,000,000
Total assets	$16,290,000
Liabilities	
Interest payable	$ 240,000
Bonds payable (including unamortized premium of $185,000)	8,164,000
Total liabilities	$ 8,425,000
Net position	
Net investment in capital assets	$ (164,000)
Restricted to debt service	8,041,000(a)
Total net position	7,886,000
Total liabilities and net position	$16,413,000

(a) This amount is equal to the $1,890,000 balance in the debt service fund, less the $240,000 of interest recognized as an expense in the government-wide full accrual statements but not in the modified accrual fund statements, plus the $6,400,000 in assessments that were deferred in the fund statements but recognized as revenue in the government-wide statements.

Note that in the government-wide statements (1) the infrastructure assets are capitalized; (2) the long-term debt, including the bond premium, is reported as a liability; (3) interest, taking into account amortization of the bond premium, is reported on a full accrual basis; and (4) assessments are recognized as revenue as soon as the government has a legal claim to them.

4. Debt Defeasance

a.

Present value, at 2 percent, of $1,600,000 principal (a single sum) to be paid at the end of six periods (present value of $1 = $0.88797)	$1,420,754
Present value, at 2 percent of $48,000 interest (an annuity) to be paid at the end of each of six periods (present value of an annuity of $1 = $5.60143)	268,869
Total economic cost of "old" bonds	$1,689,623

b.

Present value, at 2 percent, of $1,600,000 principal (a single sum) to be paid at the end of four periods (present value of $1 = $0.92384)	$1,478,153
Present value, at 2 percent of $48,000 interest (an annuity) to be paid at the end of each of four periods (present value of an annuity of $1 = $3.80773)	182,771
Amount that would have to be placed with trustee	$1,660,924

c. The economic cost of the new bonds would be the same as the amount required to be borrowed. Hence, the economic savings is the difference between the old bonds and the new: $1,689,623 minus $1,660,924, or $28,699.

d.

Bonds payable	$1,600,000	
Premium on bonds payable	25,270	
Loss on defeasance (deferred outflow of resources)	35,654	
Cash		$1,660,924

To record the loss on the in-substance defeasance

e. The city must report a deferred loss even though it realized an economic gain because it carries the bonds on its books at historical cost (i.e., the amount received when it issued the bonds less the unamortized premium). This amount does not reflect changes in market value attributable to decreases in interest rates over the years in which the bonds were outstanding. In effect, the reported deferred loss represents the cumulative loss since the bonds were issued. If the bonds had been carried at market value, and other factors held equal, the defeasance transaction would not result in a reported gain or loss.

CHAPTER 7

Capital Assets and Investments in Marketable Securities

LEARNING OBJECTIVES

After studying this chapter you should understand:

- Why and how governments account for capital assets in both fund and government-wide statements
- Why and how governments account for transactions involving donated assets, trade-ins, and collectibles
- GASB's controversial provisions regarding infrastructure
- What special problems asset impairments create
- How investments should be reported
- Why investments in marketable securities may be of high risk and thereby present special problems of accounting and reporting

The accounting for both capital assets (sometimes referred to as "fixed" or "long-lived" assets) and investments, albeit for different reasons, should be of vital concern to statement users and preparers. Capital assets are a key component of many of the services provided by governments and not-for-profits. They include its police cars, administrative buildings, and utility lines and roads. If they are inadequate to meet the demands for services to be delivered in the future, then the organization will either have to reduce its services or come up with the financial resources to enhance the assets. At the same time, existing stocks of capital assets have to be either maintained or replaced, thereby necessitating an ongoing commitment of financial resources. In addition, the constituents of governments and not-for-profits generally want and are entitled to assurance that the organization is using its assets efficiently and effectively.

Whereas the previous chapter was concerned with the *resources* that are used to acquire "general" capital assets, this chapter is directed to the assets themselves.

The accounting issues relating to governments, not-for-profits, and businesses are similar. In fact, they are now being resolved in much the same way. Until the Financial Accounting Standards Board (FASB) issued Statement No. 93, *Recognition of Depreciation by Not-for-Profit Organizations*,[1] in 1987, not-for-profits could record their capital assets at cost; they did not have to recognize depreciation. Similarly, until 1999 when the Governmental Accounting Standards Board (GASB) issued Statement No. 34, *Basic Financial Statements—and Management's Discussion and Analysis— for State and Local Governments* (the statement that established the current reporting model), governments also were able to report their general capital assets at their undepreciated original cost.

[1] FASB ASC 958-360-35.

According to the current model, as emphasized in previous chapters, governments may not charge depreciation in their modified accrual fund statements but must do so in their full accrual government-wide statements (albeit with certain exceptions). Key constituents of the GASB strongly opposed the provisions of Statement No. 34 when they were first issued, objecting in particular to the requirement that infrastructure assets be reported on the balance sheet and depreciated. With the passage of time, the critics of the requirements (particularly statement preparers), seem to have adapted to them and have muted their criticisms. Many, in fact, resist any efforts to alter the key provisions of Statement No. 34. Nevertheless, among some the statement remains controversial.

The second part of the chapter addresses marketable securities held for investment. Investments are at the opposite end of the liquidity spectrum from capital assets and present contrasting issues of both disclosure and control. They are of critical concern to both governments and other not-for-profits. Unlike capital assets, they are subject to significant risks of declines in fair (i.e., market) values as well as of fraud and mismanagement on the part of both the financial institutions with which they deal and their own employees. The entity needs to inform statement users of these risks and to establish policies and procedures to manage and control them.

WHAT ACCOUNTING PRACTICES DO GOVERNMENTS FOLLOW FOR GENERAL CAPITAL ASSETS?

In Concepts Statement No. 1, *Objectives of Financial Reporting*, the GASB set forth the purpose of capital asset reporting and laid the foundation for the current provisions:

> *Financial reporting should provide information about a governmental entity's physical and other nonfinancial resources having useful lives that extend beyond the current year, including information that can be used to assess the service potential of these resources.*
>
> *This information should be presented to help users assess long- and short-term capital needs.*[2]

MAINTAINING ACCOUNTING CONTROL OVER CAPITAL ASSETS

General capital assets—capital assets that, by definition, are associated with the government as a whole, rather than with any specific fund— are distinguished from the assets of proprietary funds (enterprise funds and internal service funds) and of fiduciary funds (pension and other trust funds in which land, buildings, and other capital assets are, for the most part, held as investments).

Nonfinancial in character, general capital assets are excluded from governmental funds because the measurement focus of governmental funds is on financial resources. Therefore, in governmental funds, the costs of capital assets are reported as expenditures when the assets are acquired rather than capitalized as assets and subsequently written off as the assets are consumed.

To prepare their government-wide statements and a required schedule of capital asset activity, governments must maintain records of their capital assets (and the related accumulated depreciation) that are not recorded on the balance sheets of their governmental funds. They can be listed in a ledger; they need not be in double-entry format.

The most common classifications for general capital assets include

- Land
- Buildings

[2] GASB Concepts Statement 1, *Objectives of Financial Reporting* (May 1987), para. 78.

- Equipment
- Improvements to land and buildings
- Construction in progress
- Works of art
- Historical treasures
- Infrastructure (e.g., roads, bridges, tunnels, drainage systems)
- Intangible assets

The definition of capital assets (the threshold in terms of dollar amount and useful life) varies among governmental entities. For example, the City of Boulder, Colorado, defines capital assets as assets with an initial, individual cost of more than $5,000 ($50,000 for infrastructure) and an estimated useful life in excess of one year.[3]

GASB Statement No. 51, *Accounting and Financial Reporting for Intangible Assets*, requires that all intangible assets (not specifically excluded by its scope provisions) be classified as capital assets. Intangible assets that a government may own include library books and recordings, computer software (whether purchased or developed in-house), water rights, and easements. For example, Austin, in its proprietary funds, reports as an intangible asset the amortized cost of a $100 million contract between itself and the Lower Colorado River Authority (a major provider of electricity) for a 51-year assured water supply agreement, with an option to extend another 50 years.[4]

DIFFERENCES IN GOVERNMENT-WIDE (FULL ACCRUAL) STATEMENTS

Capital assets, including infrastructure, should be reported on the government-wide statement of net position at historical cost net of accumulated depreciation, if applicable. Accumulated depreciation may be reported on the face of the balance sheet or disclosed in notes. Most assets should be depreciated over their estimated useful lives in a manner that is "rational and systematic" (i.e., using one of the methods commonly used by businesses). However, governments, like businesses, do not have to depreciate inexhaustible assets, such as land, works of art, or historical treasures. Moreover, as is addressed in a section to follow, governments do not have to depreciate infrastructure assets if they can demonstrate that they are preserving the assets in a specified condition.

A government does not have to include a separate line item for depreciation on its government-wide statement of activity (statement of revenues and expenses). Inasmuch as the statement will typically report expenses by function (e.g., public safety, recreation, health), it may aggregate the depreciation charge applicable to each of the functions with other types of expenses.

A government must, however, include in its notes to the financial statements information on each of its major categories of capital assets. Usually presented in schedule format, this information would include: beginning and ending balances; acquisitions, sales, and retirements; and current period depreciation (including the amount charged to each of the functions reported on the statement of activities). The City of Charlotte's schedules relating to general capital assets for governmental activities are presented in Table 7-1.

The sections that follow address issues that apply to *proprietary* funds and the government-wide statements.

[3] City of Boulder, Co CAFR 2016

[4] City of Austin CAFR 2016

TABLE 7-1 **Charlotte, North Carolina Information about Capital Assets June 30, 2017 (dollar amounts in thousands)**

Capital asset activity for governmental activities for the year ended June 30, 2017, was as follows:

	Beginning Balance	Increases	Decreases	Ending Balance
Governmental activities				
Capital asset, not being depreciated:				
Land	$3,240,220	$69,231	$5,935	$3,303,516
Construction in progress	257,521	146,368	114,181	289,708
Total capital assets, not being depreciated	3,497,741	215,599	120,116	3,593,224
Capital assets, being depreciated:				
Buildings	1,169,786	20,324	-	1,190,110
Infrastructure	2,636,779	64,326	-	2,701,105
Intangibles	25,008	6,584	-	31,592
Machinery and equipment	206,234	23,596	11,122	218,708
Total capital assets being depreciated	4,037,807	114,830	11,122	4,141,515
Less accumulated depreciation for:				
Buildings	369,844	29,039	-	398,883
Infrastructure	1,007,763	66,640	-	1,074,403
Intangibles	16,237	3,004	-	19,241
Machinery and equipment	156,453	18,643	10,995	164,101
Total accumulated depreciation	1,550,297	117,326	10,995	1,656,628
Total capital assets, being depreciated, net	2,487,510	(2,496)	127	2,484,887
Governmental activities capital assets, net	$5,985,251	$213,103	$120,243	$6,078,111

Depreciation expense was charged to activities as follows:

Governmental activities:	
Public safety	$16,550
Sanitation	3,982
General administration	2,170
Support services	2,518
Engineering and property management	5,053
Streets and highways	62,224
Community planning and development	5,520
Culture and recreation	17,705
Economic development	1,604
Total depreciation expense–governmental activities	$117,326

ACQUIRING AND PLACING VALUE ON CAPITAL ASSETS

When a government acquires an asset by purchase, construction, or capital lease, it should follow the same general guidelines used by businesses to determine the costs to be capitalized. Thus, capitalized value should include all costs necessary to bring an asset to a serviceable condition.

For purchased assets, the capitalized cost should include purchase price (less any discounts, such as those for prompt payment or for favored customers), plus transportation and installation costs. For an asset such as land, it would include legal fees, title fees, appraisal costs, closing costs, and costs of demolishing existing structures that cannot be used (less recoveries from salvage).

For constructed assets, it would include direct labor and materials, overhead costs, architect fees, and insurance premiums during the construction phase. However, unlike businesses, governments should not capitalize interest on general capital assets that they construct themselves.[5] This is because, per Statement No. 34, interest expense on general long-term liabilities should be treated as an indirect expense, rather than being attributed to specific functions or programs, such as public works.

Just like businesses, governments also acquire their assets through capital leases, which are, in essence, financing arrangements where the lessee acquires an asset in exchange for a long-term note. Leases are discussed in Chapter 8.

Governments should report donated assets at their estimated acquisition value (replacement cost) at the time the gift is received. If the assets are exhaustible, then in their government-wide statements governments should depreciate the assets over their remaining useful lives.

ACCOUNTING FOR TRADE-INS

Example

Trade-Ins

A government trades in an old automobile for a new one. The old automobile had cost $30,000; its fair value at the time of the trade is $12,000. To date the government has charged $10,000 in depreciation. Therefore, the book value of the asset is $20,000. The fair value of the old automobile is $12,000, whereas that of the new one is $40,000. Hence, the government is required to pay an additional $28,000 in cash.

In its general or other governmental fund, only the cash aspects of the transaction need be recognized. The acquisition would be reported as an expenditure:

Expenditure—acquisition of equipment	$28,000	
Cash		$28,000
To record the trade-in transaction		

In its government-wide statements, the government would have to recognize a loss on the transaction—the difference between the amount for which the old automobile was, in effect, sold (its fair value of $12,000) and its book value ($20,000):

Equipment (new auto)	$40,000	
Loss on trade-in	8,000	
Accumulated depreciation (old auto)	10,000	
Equipment (old auto)		$30,000
Cash		28,000
To record the trade-in of an old automobile for a new one		

ACCOUNTING FOR COLLECTIBLES

Like their not-for-profit counterparts, government museums, universities, libraries, and history centers own works of art, rare books, and historical artifacts. These "collectibles" often have considerable monetary value and for some entities may be their most significant assets.

Governments and not-for-profits have generally opposed both capitalizing the collectibles they hold and recognizing as revenue the collectibles they receive as contributions. They contend

[5] GASB Statement No. 37, *Basic Financial Statements—and Management's Discussion and Analysis—for State and Local Governments: Omnibus* (June 2001), an amendment of GASB Statements No. 21 and No. 34, paras. 6 and 7.

that the value of such objects, like their beauty, is in the eye of the beholder, and only the most philistine of accountants would even consider placing a dollar sign beside a "priceless" work of art. Moreover, works of art are not assets that can be associated with future cash receipts or savings. Rather, when retained, they are a drain on resources because they require ongoing protection. They generate cash only on sale. To report them as assets, it can be argued, would result in financial statements that are as surrealistic as some of the art itself.

GASB STANDARDS

In its Statement No. 34, the GASB follows the lead of the FASB, which in Statement No. 116, *Accounting for Contributions Received and Contributions Made*,[6] addresses the same issues. Statement No. 34 does not require (but nevertheless encourages) governments to capitalize their art and similar assets as long as they meet the following conditions:

- They are held for public exhibition, education, or research in furtherance of public service, rather than for financial gain
- They are protected, kept unencumbered, cared for, and preserved
- They are subject to an organizational policy that requires the proceeds from sales of collection items to be used to acquire other items for collections

Works of art and other collectibles that do *not* meet these conditions (e.g., a work of art held purely as an investment or acquired for an administrator's office that is not accessible to the public or for research purposes) must be capitalized. The City of Atlanta, Georgia, in its CAFR, FY 2017, in the notes to the basic financial statements, stated:

The City has elected not to capitalize works of art and historical treasures based on its policy that these items are not held for financial gain. They will be preserved and any proceeds from the sale of the items will be used to acquire other collections.

If governments do capitalize their art or historical collections, then they should depreciate the assets that are exhaustible but not those that are not expected to decline in value with time.

Governments should recognize contributions of collectibles as revenue just as if they had received other assets (i.e., per the guidelines discussed in Chapter 4). However, if the items were to be added to noncapitalized collections, then the governments should offset the revenue with a charge to a program expense rather than to an asset. In contrast, per FASB Statement No. 116, nongovernmental not-for-profits are not allowed to recognize revenue for items contributed to noncapitalized collections.

[6] FASB ASC 958-360-25.

WHY AND HOW SHOULD GOVERNMENTS REPORT INFRASTRUCTURE?

A government's infrastructure is its capital assets that are immovable and can be preserved for a significantly longer period than most other assets. They are of value only to the government itself. They include roads, sidewalks, bridges, tunnels, highways (apart from those that are part of the interstate highway system), lighting systems, drainage systems, water and sewer facilities, and dams. Although many citizens take the nation's infrastructure for granted, public officials, investors, and economists are expressing serious concern over it. In the past 40 years, spectacular failures have called attention to the deteriorating condition of much of the country's public physical plant. The accompanying "In Practice" indicates the seriousness with which civil engineers view the problem. Other studies confirm that there is an increasing gap between the nation's infrastructure requirements and its ability to pay for them.

Infrastructure may be a national problem, but it must be solved mainly at the state and local levels. After all, most roads and highways (apart from those that are part of the interstate system), bridges, drainage, and water and public power systems are the responsibility of state and local governments.

Governments are accountable for infrastructure assets, and it is difficult to see how the objectives of financial reporting can be fulfilled without comprehensive information regarding not only expenditures for infrastructure but also the assets' status. For example, data on infrastructure are essential if government financial reports are to achieve the following general goals set forth in the GASB's *Objectives of Financial Reporting*:

- To help users assess the economy, efficiency, and effectiveness with which government used the resources within its command
- To determine whether the entity's financial position improved or deteriorated during the reporting period
- To provide information about a government's physical and other nonfinancial resources having useful lives that extend beyond the current year, including information that can be used to assess the service potential of those resources
- To help users assess long- and short-term capital needs

Until the GASB issued Statement No. 34, governments provided virtually no information as to their infrastructure. Except for those assets (such as sewer and power lines) accounted for in proprietary funds, governments charged infrastructure assets as fund expenditures as they constructed them. They neither reported them in a fund balance sheet nor described them in the notes to the financial statements.

IN PRACTICE NATION'S INFRASTRUCTURE EARNS A CUMULATIVE GRADE OF D+

The American Society of Civil Engineers indicated in its 2017 *Infrastructure Report Card* that the nation's infrastructure earned an overall grade of D+, which is not much above failing.

The association graded the infrastructure in the separate areas to follow. Here are the individual scores:

Aviation	D
Bridges	C+
Dams	D
Drinking water	D
Energy	D+
Hazardous waste	D+
Inland waterways	D
Levees	D
Parks and recreation	D+
Ports	C+
Rail	B
Roads	D
Schools	D+
Solid waste	C+
Transit	D-
Wastewater	D+

According to the association it will take an investment by 2025 of at least $4.6 trillion to bring the infrastructure to a state of reasonably good repair—that is to enable the country to earn at least a grade of B.

GASB STANDARDS

Statement No. 34 requires that, in general, governments account for infrastructure assets just as they do other capital assets. That is, they should report infrastructure costs as expenditures in their fund statements as they are incurred. In their government-wide statements they should capitalize the costs and depreciate the assets over their estimated useful lives.

Nevertheless, acknowledging the limitations of depreciation as a measure of the cost of using infrastructure assets, the statement permits governments to avoid charging depreciation if they can demonstrate that they incur the costs necessary to preserve the assets in a specified condition. If a government satisfies certain conditions, then it may elect to report as period expenses in its government-wide statements all infrastructure costs relating to eligible assets *except* those that result in additions or improvements. It need not charge depreciation and need not reduce the capitalized cost of the assets with accumulated depreciation.

To use this modified approach on all or some of its infrastructure assets, a government would have to assess periodically (at least every three years) the condition of its infrastructure assets and estimate the annual amount necessary to maintain and preserve the assets at the specified "condition level" (which would be established by the government itself). In addition, it would have to document that the assets are, in fact, being maintained at or above that level.

THE MODIFIED APPROACH COMPARED WITH STANDARD DEPRECIATION

Under the modified approach, the initial cost of the asset is capitalized but preservation costs (outlays that extend the useful life of an asset beyond the originally expected useful life) are expensed as incurred. No depreciation is charged on either the initial cost of acquiring the asset or the subsequent preservation costs. By contrast, under the standard approach both the initial cost and the subsequent preservation costs are capitalized and depreciated over their expected useful life. Suppose, that to preserve a road at a specified condition, a government must repave it every five years at a cost of $200,000. Under the modified approach, the government would report the $200,000 as an expense when incurred. Under the standard approach, it would capitalize the $200,000 and depreciate it over a period of five years. Thus, for this particular road, the modified approach would result in a charge of $200,000 every five years; the standard approach would result in a charge of $40,000 per year plus the depreciation on the initial cost of the road.

If a government elects the modified approach, then it must disclose (as "required supplementary information") the assessed condition of the assets and the basis on which it made that assessment. The basis would ordinarily be an engineering measurement scale, such as one that ranks pavements from zero (unsafe) to 100 (perfect). The government must also report, for the latest five years, the estimated cost of maintaining the assets at the specified condition as compared to the amounts actually expensed. Table 7-2 presents a note to the basic financial

TABLE 7-2 State of Minnesota Infrastructure Disclosures Pertaining to Its Roads (Modified Approach)

Measurement Scale

The Minnesota Department of Transportation (MnDOT) uses three pavement condition indices to determine the condition of the trunk highway system: Present Serviceability Rating (PSR), Surface Rating (SR), and Pavement Quality Index (PQI). The PSR is a measure of pavement smoothness, the SR measures pavement distress (cracking), and the PQI is a composite index equal to the square root of the PSR multiplied by the SR.

The five qualitative categories used to describe pavement condition are shown in the following table.

Description	PQI Range	PSR Range	SR Range
Very Good	3.7–4.5	4.1–5.0	3.3–4.0
Good	2.8–3.6	3.1–4.0	2.5–3.2
Fair	1.9–2.7	2.1–3.0	1.7–2.4
Poor	1.0–1.8	1.1–2.0	0.9–1.6
Very Poor	0.0–0.9	0.0–1.0	0.0–0.8

The PQI is used as the index for determining whether the pavement infrastructure is being maintained in a serviceable level. The PQI is an overall index, combining both pavement smoothness (PSR) and cracking (SR)

Established Condition Level

Principal arterial pavements will be maintained at 3.0 PQI (good) or higher and all other pavements will be maintained at 2.8 PQI (good) or higher.

Assessed Conditions

The state assesses condition on 100 percent of the pavement surfaces at least once every two years.

	Principal Arterial Average PQI	Non-Principal Arterial Average PQI
2016	3.46	3.31
2015	3.42	3.32
2014	3.41	3.35

statements on infrastructure assets reported under the modified approach for the State of Minnesota in its CAFR for FY 2017.

Knowledgeable sources estimate that only a small percentage (1 to 5 percent) of cities and other local governments have opted for the modified approach. Their reluctance to adopt the modified approach may be attributable to the high cost of the required engineering studies. This contrasts with a substantially larger percentage (30 percent) of states that have done so.

Although the modified approach may be at odds with conventional business practice, it is consistent with the theoretical underpinning of depreciation accounting. Properly maintained infrastructure assets may, like land, have infinite useful lives. They do not decline in economic value. Indeed, as evidenced by the aqueducts in Rome, the Great Wall in China, or the Taj Mahal in India, properly cared-for assets can last well beyond the number of years that are of concern to financial statement users.

A CONTROVERSIAL PRONOUNCEMENT

Critics of Statement No. 34 have presented several arguments on why its infrastructure provisions are flawed:

- Statement users have given no indication that they want or would use data on the historical cost of infrastructure. In fact, a research study presented a sample of statement users, including investors, managers, and legislators, with six types of information that governments could provide: historical cost, replacement cost, constant dollar cost, budget-to-actual data, financial plans, and engineering information. The users ranked engineering and financial plan information first and second as most useful. They ranked historical cost data dead last.[7] Not surprisingly, many of these users find the modified approach to be more informative than the standard approach.
- A key reason for maintaining control over assets is to prevent fraud or abuse. But infrastructure assets cannot be stolen or misused. Therefore, there is no reason to capitalize them.
- Another important reason for reporting assets is to enable statement users to assess whether the assets have been used efficiently. Governments are not expected to earn a monetary return on infrastructure. Therefore, a comparison between a measure of output (performance) and any monetary value that might be assigned to the assets in the financial statements is not likely to be meaningful.
- A further rationale for reporting assets is to enable statement users to consider alternative uses for them. Infrastructure assets, however, cannot be either sold or moved. They seldom have alternative uses.
- The cost of infrastructure assets constructed in the past is of no significance. Many of a government's infrastructure assets were probably not constructed as part of a single project. Instead, they evolved over time. For example, a government does not typically construct a four-lane highway through virgin fields or forests. More likely, the highway began as a footpath and metamorphosed over generations to an unpaved road, a paved road, and a two-line highway.

In brief, it is argued that the information that must be reported on the face of the government-wide statement of net position facilitates no decisions, and therefore, the cost of record keeping and reporting is not worth the benefits.

[7] Relmond P. Van Daniker and Vernon Kwiatkowski, *Infrastructure Assets: An Assessment of User Needs and Recommendations for Financial Reporting* (Norwalk, CT: Governmental Accounting Standards Board, 1986).

The GASB, of course, took note of these criticisms in its deliberations. Its position, however, is not that the historical cost of infrastructure is useful for purposes of decision making. Rather, it is that if the government-wide statements are to provide a long-term measure of the cost of services, and thereby to be on a full accrual basis, then the statements cannot ignore the costs associated with a class of assets as significant as infrastructure.

THE QUESTION OF DEFERRED MAINTENANCE

As pointed out earlier in the text, government assets, especially infrastructure, can be seen as liabilities as much as assets. **Infrastructure assets** must be maintained, and like an individual's car and home, they are a continuing drain on fiscal resources.

Governments can postpone asset upkeep costs, but they cannot avoid them. For some assets, engineers have developed sophisticated maintenance schedules that minimize long-term costs. For example, streets and highways should be resurfaced after a specified number of years. If governments delay beyond that period, then the costs to repair the further deterioration will outweigh the financial benefits of having put off the expenditures.

Deferred maintenance costs are defined as "delayed repair, or upkeep, measured by the outlay required to restore a plant or individual asset to full operating characteristics."[8] They could be measured as the amount necessary to bring the assets up to their expected operating condition. Deferred maintenance costs may be interpreted as a potential call on government resources—an obligation that is being passed on to taxpayers of the future. They are an indication that taxpayers of the past or present have not paid for the maintenance costs applicable to the services received.

In the GASB infrastructure study, at least 84 percent of the academic, investor, legislator, and citizen groups were in favor of including information on deferred maintenance in annual financial reports. Only managers (who would be responsible for providing the data) were less enthusiastic, with only 52 percent advocating inclusion.[9]

Statement No. 34 goes partway toward providing the information that users want. Governments that do not depreciate their assets must demonstrate that they are, in fact, maintaining their assets at, or above, a specified condition. In addition they must disclose, for a five-year period, their actual maintenance costs as compared to what would be necessary to maintain those assets at the specified condition (see Table 7-3 for an example). Governments that elect to depreciate their assets are not required to provide this information.

GASB Statement No. 34 elevated the level of governments' capital asset reporting and accountability to that of businesses. Most notably, it requires that governments capitalize their infrastructure and charge depreciation on exhaustible assets. Prior to the issuance of Statement No. 34, many governments maintained exceedingly lax accounting control over their capital assets. This is, in part, because once acquired, the assets were not reported on fund balance sheets or statements of revenue and expenditure; they had no impact on fund balances.

LIMITATIONS OF INFORMATION REPORTED ABOUT LONG-TERM ASSETS

Although GASB Statement No. 34 undoubtedly improved financial reporting, "improved" reporting should not be mistaken for "adequate" reporting. In reality, readers can still learn very little from financial statement data on long-term assets—no more than they could from the financial

[8] W. W. Cooper and Y. Ijiri (eds.), *Kohler's Dictionary for Accountants*, 6th edition (Englewood Cliffs, NJ: Prentice-Hall, 1993), 155.

[9] Van Daniker and Kwiatkowski, op. cit., 112.

TABLE 7-3 State of Minnesota: Comparison of Needed-to-Actual Maintenance Costs

Budgeted and Estimated Costs to Maintain

The following table presents the state's estimate of spending necessary to preserve and maintain the pavement and bridges at, or above, the Established Condition Levels cited above, and the actual amount spent (in thousands):

		Costs to be Capitalized			Maintenance of System			
		Bridges	**Payment**	**Total Cost**	**Bridges**	**Payment**	**Total Cost**	**Total Construction Program**
Budget	2017	$ 149,000	$ 376,000	$ 525,000	$ 100,000	$ 500,000	$ 600,000	$ 1,125,000
	2016	234,366	400,943	635,309	112,444	462,387	574,831	1,210,140
	2015	255,033	230,075	485,108	55,789	403,213	459,002	944,110
	2014	251,019	248,341	499,860	78,143	627,255	705,398	1,205,258
	2013	179,581	289,898	469,479	36,480	691,872	728,352	1,197,831
Actual	2017	$ 114,106	$ 337,294	$ 451,400	$ 84,046	$ 526,975	$ 611,021	$ 1,062,421
	2016	232,087	403,563	635,650	79,748	652,665	732,413	1,368,063
	2015	197,844	384,351	582,195	71,852	606,939	678,791	1,260,986
	2014	233,201	301,058	534,259	64,837	593,933	658,770	1,193,029
	2013	137,387	190,739	328,126	58,127	615,638	673,765	1,001,891

statements of a business. Even the new financial statements fail to facilitate the significant decisions or judgments that statement users are likely to make.

Consider typical questions relating to capital assets that either city officials or external parties might ask:

- ***Should the city sell an asset and replace it with another?*** For this decision, the recorded amount (indicative of the initial cost of the asset) is irrelevant. It is a "sunk cost" and has no bearing on cash flows of the future. By contrast, the current market price of the asset—that for which it could be sold or replaced—is of direct concern.
- ***Are assets being used efficiently?*** As with the previous question, the historical cost of the assets is irrelevant. Suppose that the city owns two parcels of land, which it uses as sports fields. Both have the same market value. It would make no sense to assert that one is being used more efficiently than the other merely because it was acquired earlier and at a lower price.
- ***Is the city replacing assets that it sells or retires?*** The comparison between additions and book value of retirements would shed little light on whether the city is maintaining its asset base because it would relate assets at current prices with those of the past.
- ***Are the city's assets adequately insured?*** The adequacy of insurance must be assessed by comparing the amount of coverage with the cost of replacing the assets.
- ***Is the city adequately maintaining its assets?*** Those cities that do not opt for the modified approach (and thereby elect to depreciate their assets) do not have to report on either the condition of their assets or on the extent that they have deferred needed maintenance.

Ironically, the true economic value of infrastructure is becoming of greater significance as governments look to close their budget gaps by selling their assets to private concerns.

IN PRACTICE FAIR VALUES MAY (OR MAY NOT) FACILITATE SALES DECISIONS

Facing budget gaps, cities and states are considering selling off office buildings, parks, prisons, power plants, and even zoos. Perhaps the most controversial proposed asset sale of recent years was that of the Detroit Institute of Art's collection that purportedly was worth somewhere between $1 billion and $4.6 billion.

Detroit was in bankruptcy in 2014. It was shutting off water to its some of its poorer citizens who were unable to pay its recently hiked water rates. It was forced to cut services to the bone, and thousands of retirees and current employees were facing drastic cuts in their pensions. Why not, some asked, shouldn't the city sell off some of its museum holdings so as to enable it to provide essential services to its residents?

Why not? Because, others argued, the benefits of art cannot be expressed monetarily, and the museum's paintings by Van Gogh, Picasso, Rembrandt, Degas, and the like should never be viewed through a prism of dollar signs. Selling art, they say, will cause irreparable damage to the city's sense of history and civic pride—intangible assets that are no less valuable than a triple A bond rating. Museum managers described the art as a public trust to be preserved rather than an asset to be sold.

In the end, the art was not sold. In a unique arrangement, a consortium of outsiders agreed to contribute $800 million to the city's underfunded pension fund in exchange for taking the art off the sale table.

INTANGIBLE ASSETS

In recent years, it has become widely acknowledged that the financial statements of businesses, especially those in high-tech industries, fail to capture a firm's **intangible assets** such as intellectual capital, internally developed software, marketing skills, and brand names. The most notable evidence of this deficiency is the wide disparity between the book and stock market values of many of our leading companies. For example, the stock market values of Google and Amazon are many times the book values.

Governments, too, have intangible assets that are becoming an increasingly large proportion of their total assets. Information technology in the public sector has been an ongoing focus of professional conferences and government-oriented journals for decades. Governments use both local and cloud-based computing not only to account for financial transactions, but also to regulate traffic flow, dispatch emergency personnel, and read utility meters. Although some of the software to manage these functions may be purchased off the shelf, much of it is internally generated by the government itself, or the government leases it from private sector firms.

GASB STANDARDS

GASB Statement No. 51, *Accounting and Financial Reporting for Intangible Assets*, mandates that intangible assets be accorded accounting recognition if:

- They are separable; that is, they are capable of being separated or divided from the government and sold, transferred, licensed, rented, or exchanged, either individually or together with a related contract, asset, or liability
- They arise from contractual or other legal rights

These assets should be accounted for like other long-lived assets—that is, reported on the government-wide balance sheet and amortized over their economic lives.

Outlays for internally generated intangible assets, mainly computer software, should be capitalized as an asset only when the resultant project reaches a fairly advanced stage of completion—that is, when it can be demonstrated that the project is technologically feasible and will provide the services expected of it. All outlays incurred prior to that point should be expensed as incurred. Moreover, once the project is substantially completed and ready for its intended use the capitalization of costs should cease. Thus, both training and maintenance costs should be expensed.

HOW SHOULD GOVERNMENTS ACCOUNT FOR ASSETS THAT ARE IMPAIRED?

A capital asset is considered impaired when both its service utility has declined significantly and the event or change in circumstances is outside the normal life cycle of the capital asset. Impairment can be a consequence of physical damage, technological obsolescence, changes in laws or regulations (e.g., those that impose new environmental standards), changes in manner or duration of use, or construction stoppage (e.g., where construction on a building is halted owing to a lack of funding). In business it is conceptually clear when the service utility of an asset has declined: It will no longer provide the cash flows or generate the cash savings expected of it. In governments and not-for-profit organizations, by contrast, capital assets are not associated with cash flows; they are expected to provide services, the value of which is typically not clear. Accordingly, GASB has had to develop an approach to measuring impairment losses that differs significantly from that taken by the FASB.

GASB STANDARDS

Per GASB Statement No. 42, *Accounting and Financial Reporting for Impairment of Capital Assets and for Insurance Recoveries*, governments should test a capital asset for impairment whenever a prominent change in circumstances indicates that its service utility has declined. If it determines that the reduction in service utility is both significant and unexpected, then a portion of the asset's historical cost representing the impairment should be written off. The amount of the impairment may be measured by one of three methods:

- ***Restoration cost approach.*** The amount of impairment is the estimated cost to restore the utility of the asset. However, the cost to restore must be converted to historical cost. This can be done either by deflating the restoration costs using an appropriate cost index or by applying a ratio of restoration cost over replacement value to the carrying value of the asset. This method (illustrated in the example that follows) would be most appropriate for impairments caused by physical damage.
- ***Service units approach.*** The dollar amount of the impairment is determined by first calculating the percentage decline in number of service units (e.g., number of years of expected service or number of units of output) owing to the impairment event or change in circumstances. This percentage is then applied to the carrying value of the asset. This method is appropriate for impairments caused by technological obsolescence, changes in environmental or legal factors, and changes in manner or duration or use.
- ***Deflated depreciated replacement cost approach.*** Under this approach the amount of impairment is determined by subtracting the carrying value of the asset from what would be the current cost of an asset that would provide the current (impaired) level of service. However, the current cost of the replacement asset must be adjusted to reflect the facts that: (1) the original asset was not new (and hence the replacement cost must be depreciated by the proportion of the original asset's life that has already been consumed), and (2) the replacement cost is stated in current rather than historical dollars (and hence must be deflated by a ratio of historical costs to current costs). This method is appropriate for impairments caused by changes in manner or duration of use.

Example

Restoration Approach

The carrying value of the Marlin School District's high school was $30 million (cost of $40 million less accumulated depreciation of $10 million). The school is 10 years old and has an estimated useful life of 40 years.

A fire damaged the school; estimated costs to restore the school to a usable condition are $5 million. The cost to replace the school today would be $55 million.

The impairment loss would be computed as follows:

Historical cost of school	$40,000,000
Less: Accumulated depreciation	10,000,000
Carrying value of school	$30,000,000

Restoration cost expressed in historical, rather than current, dollars

Restoration cost—current dollars	$ 5,000,000	
Deflation factor		
Original cost of school (historical dollars)	$40,000,000	
Current replacement cost (current dollars)	÷55,000,000	× .7273
Deflated restoration cost		$ 3,636,364

Proportion of asset's original historical cost impaired (deflated restoration cost as a percent of historical cost, i.e., $3,636,364/$40,000,000)	9.0909%
Impairment loss (proportion of asset's original historical value impaired times asset's carrying value (9.0909% of $30,000,000)	$ 2,727,273

The school district would reduce the carrying value of the school as follows:

Carrying value of school	$30,000,000
Less impairment loss	2,727,273
Adjusted carrying value	$27,272,727

The Board concluded that the impairment and the restoration should be viewed as separate events. Hence, should the school district in fact repair the building at the cost of $5,000,000 then it would add $5,000,000 to the adjusted value; the new carrying value after restoration would be $32,272,727.

Example

Service Units Approach

As in the restoration approach example, the carrying value of the Marlin School District's high school was $30 million (cost of $40 million less accumulated depreciation of $10 million). The school is 10 years old and has an estimated useful life of 40 years.

The school was built to accommodate 4,000 students. However, owing to a loss of population and changing demographics, enrollment is currently and is expected in the future to be only 1,000 students.

The loss would be computed as follows:

Historical cost of school		$40,000,000
Less: Accumulated depreciation		10,000,000
Carrying value of school		$30,000,000
Acquisition cost		$40,000,000
Original service units per year	4,000	
Estimated useful life in years	× 40	
Total number of originally expected service units		÷ 160,000
Original estimate of cost per service unit		$ 250
New estimate of service units per year	1,000	
Remaining useful life in years	× 30	
New estimate of total remaining service units		× 30,000
Remaining total service units times cost per unit		$ 7,500,000
Current carrying value of school		$30,000,000
Current value of school, based on remaining service units		7,500,000
Impairment loss		$22,500,000

The new carrying value of the school would be $7,500,000.

Example

Deflated Depreciated Replacement Cost Approach

As in the previous two examples, the carrying value of the Marlin School District's high school was $30 million (cost of $40 million less accumulated depreciation of $10 million). The school is 10 years old and has an estimated useful life of 40 years.

This time, however, owing to the declining enrollments, the district decides to close the school and transform the building into a warehouse. The current cost to construct a comparable warehouse would be $15 million. When the school was constructed, a commercial construction cost index value was 100. Currently that same index is 137.5.

The impairment loss would be computed as follows:

Historical cost of school		$40,000,000
Less: Accumulated depreciation		10,000,000
Carrying value of school		$30,000,000
Replacement cost of warehouse		$15,000,000
Percentage assumed to have been used to date (10 of 40 years)		× .25%
Assumed accumulated depreciation		$ 3,750,000
Depreciated replacement cost of warehouse ($15,000,000 less $3,750,000)		$11,250,000
Commercial construction index at date school was constructed	100.0	
Commercial construction index at date of impairment	÷137.5	
Factor to express depreciated replacement cost of warehouse at historical cost		× .7273
Deflated depreciated cost of warehouse		$ 8,181,818
Current carrying value of school		$30,000,000
Less: Deflated depreciated cost of warehouse		8,181,818
Impairment loss		$21,818,182

The carrying value of the warehouse would be $8,181,818.

WHAT ISSUES ARE THE CRITICAL ISSUES WITH RESPECT TO MARKETABLE SECURITIES AND OTHER INVESTMENTS?

REASONS FOR PURCHASING MARKETABLE SECURITIES

Both governments and not-for-profits may have large pools of cash available for investment. The following are among the major reasons:

- They periodically receive large amounts of cash—from donations, tax collections, tolls, fees for services, and so forth. A fundamental rule of cash management is the less cash on hand, the better. As long as the cash is not required to meet required expenditures of the same day, it should be placed in short-term—even overnight—securities.
- They are required by law or policy to maintain reserve funds to repay debts or to save, either for a particular purpose or for a "rainy day."
- They accumulate resources in pension funds.
- They maintain permanent endowments, which are established to generate investment revenues.
- They invest, for reasons similar to those of businesses, to earn a return, either through a steady stream of interest, dividends, or rents, or as gains on sale.

Many governments invest their funds directly in stocks, bonds, notes, and other financial instruments. Others, especially smaller units, participate in **investment pools** maintained by other governments. For example, most states operate investment pools for their cities, counties, and school districts. These pools enable these units to gain the benefits of increased portfolio size—lower trading costs, greater opportunity to diversify, and shared expenses for sophisticated investment advice.

INVESTMENTS SHOULD BE REPORTED AT FAIR VALUES

Both the FASB and the GASB require that *all* debt and equity securities held by not-for-profit entities and government as investments (with a few exceptions) be "marked-to-market"—that is, reported at fair value. The FASB approach to not-for-profits differs considerably from that to businesses. Per Statement No. 115, *Accounting for* Certain *Investments in Debt and Equity Securities*, the FASB requires businesses to divide their investment portfolios into three categories: trading securities (those that enterprises intend to hold for only a short period of time), held-to-maturity securities (mainly long-term bonds), and available-for-sale securities (other securities, such as stock held for the long term). They must carry their portfolios of both trading securities and available-for-sale securities at fair (i.e., market) values but their held-to-maturity portfolios at adjusted cost.[10] However, the FASB explicitly exempted not-for-profits from the purview of Statement No. 115, addressing them instead in Statement No. 124, *Accounting for Certain Investments in Debt and Equity Securities*.[11]

In Statement No. 124, the FASB mandated that not-for-profits also report investments at fair value. However, inasmuch as the requirement that investments be classified into the three categories was intended mainly to accommodate specialized industries, such as banks and insurance companies, it was omitted from the not-for-profit pronouncement. Instead, the statement requires that, with limited exceptions, all debt and equity securities, including held-to-maturity securities, be stated at fair value. Moreover, gains and losses on investments, both realized and unrealized, must be recognized as such and reported in the statement of activities.

GASB STANDARDS

Following the FASB's lead, in 1997 the GASB determined that governments, like businesses and not-for-profits, should state their investments (including bonds *and* other debt securities) at fair value. GASB Statement No. 31, *Accounting and Financial Reporting for Certain Investments and for External Investment Pools*, requires that investment income, including changes in fair value, be reported in the operating statement or other statement of activities of all entities and funds.

The GASB made a notable exception for short-term securities that are not subject to the same volatility as long-term instruments. Governments are permitted to report money market investments having a remaining maturity at time of purchase of one year or less at amortized cost rather than market value. These investments typically include mainly certificates of deposit, commercial paper, and U.S. Treasury obligations.

The reasons for reporting investments at fair value are as compelling for governments and not-for-profit organizations as for businesses. Those frequently advanced include the following:

- As the GASB made clear in Concepts Statement No.6, *Measurement of Elements of Financial Statements* (March 2014), "remeasured amounts are more appropriate for assets that will be converted to cash (financial assets)" because a remeasured amount "better reflects the current value of the cash flows that the assets are expected to produce."[12]
- For virtually all decisions involving investments, fair value is more relevant than historical cost.
- Investments are often held as cash substitutes. They can be liquidated with a phone call to the entity's broker or a quick ///computer entry.

[10] FASB Statement No. 115, *Accounting for Certain Investments in Debt and Equity Securities* (May 1993); also FASB ASC 320–10.

[11] FASB Statement No. 124, *Accounting for Certain Investments Held by Not-for-Profit Organizations* (November 1995); also FASB ASC 958-320-15.

[12] Summary and paragraph No. 18.

- Fair values are generally objective; up-to-the-minute prices of many types of investments are available from computer and telephone information services.
- The performance of investment managers, and their employer governments, is measured by total return—dividends, interest, and changes in fair values. Insofar as government and not-for-profit portfolio managers are expected to achieve specified investment goals, statement users are entitled to the information needed to assess how well the managers have done.
- To be sure, prices that go up can also come down. But financial statements report on performance within specified periods. An increase in the value of a security in a particular year is indicative of sound investment performance in the year it occurs. A subsequent decline in the following year reflects poor performance in that year. Statement users are entitled to this information.

The rationale for valuing held-to-maturity securities, such as long-term bonds, at fair values is somewhat more problematic. The fair value of held-to-maturity securities will vary from year to year as interest rates change. As interest rates rise, their value will decrease; as interest rates fall, their value will increase. Over time, however, the value will approach the redemption value of the security and indeed at the date of maturity will equal such value. Why, then, should a government or not-for-profit have to recognize period-to-period changes in value when, by definition, they intend to hold the securities to maturity and thereby receive their redemption value? There are, perhaps, several legitimate (if controversial reasons). The key ones are

- A held-to-maturity classification is based on intent. Intent, however, is a subjective criterion and is subject to change. Indeed, unexpected economic conditions may make it fiscally necessary or desirable for the entity to prematurely sell a security that it planned to hold to maturity.
- Recognizing changes in fair value provides users of financial statements with a means of assessing whether the entity made the correct decision to hold the security rather than to sell it.
- Even though an entity may eventually sell or redeem a held-to-maturity at redemption value, it may have incurred an "opportunity" cost or realized an "opportunity" gain by locking itself in to a fixed interest rate when prevailing rates either increased or decreased. Recognizing changes in fair value enables statement users to measure that opportunity cost or gain.

The GASB's approach to investments has been extremely controversial and unpopular among many government officials. It is easy to see why: It widens the gap between financial reporting and budgeting. The investment portfolios of many governments are dominated by notes and other securities having a fixed maturity date. If a government holds its securities to maturity, changes in market value have no impact on the cash that is available for expenditure. Yet increases in fair value must be reported as revenues (increases in fund balance), and decreases must be reported as expenditures (decreases in fund balance). Imagine the difficulty of having to explain to members of governing boards why an increase in fund balance is only a "paper gain" that cannot really be spent. Or try telling a TV reporter in 30 seconds why a decline in the value of a government's portfolio will have no impact on the amount for which the securities will eventually be sold.

DETERMINING FAIR VALUE

In its Statement No. 72, *Fair Value Measurement and Application* (February 2015), the GASB explicitly defined what is meant by fair value and provided guidance on how it should be measured. **Fair value**, it said, "is the price that would be received to sell an asset or paid to transfer a liability in an orderly transaction between market participants at the measurement date." That is, fair value is to be determined by the amount at which a security can be traded in the marketplace; it is not dependent on the value to any particular entity.

Statement No. 72 specified that fair value would be considered an *exit* price. An exit price is the amount for which an asset could be sold as opposed to the amount that would have to be paid to acquire it.

Most commonly, governments could determine the fair value of an investment by looking to prices that are quoted in active markets. Often such prices are readily available on the Internet. However, many types of securities are not traded in active markets. For such investments, governments must apply alternative valuation techniques. For example, suppose a government holds a bond that has not recently been traded in an active market. The government might look to the prices at which other bonds having similar risk characteristics and maturities have been traded. Or, suppose a government holds real estate as an investment and there are no similar properties to which the assets can be compared. In that circumstance, the government might have to resort to an "income" approach in which it computes the present value of anticipated cash flows.

Statement No. 72 establishes a hierarchy of the inputs used to establish fair values:

- Level 1 inputs are quoted prices in an active market for identical assets or liabilities.
- Level 2 inputs are quoted prices for similar assets or liabilities.
- Level 3 inputs are those that are not based on observable quoted prices, but rather are based on the best information available in the circumstances.

The Statement requires governments to disclose into which each level in their fair value hierarchy their investments fall. Table 7-4 provides an illustration of such disclosure and also suggests the variety of instruments in which governments might invest.

RECOGNIZING INCOME BASED ON FAIR VALUE MEASUREMENTS

Example

Investment Income

The following table summarizes the 2020 investment activity in a county's general fund (all amounts in thousands):

	Cost	Fair Value on Jan. 1	Purchases	Sales (proceeds)	Fair Value on Dec. 31
Security A	$120	$120			$140
Security B	520	540			540
Security C	200	200		$250	0
Security D	90		$90		75
	$930	$860	$90	$250	$755

Per GASB Statement No. 31, the investments should be reported on the county's December 31, 2020, statements at their fair value—$755. The gain or loss to be reported on the country's 2020 operating statements can be determined by subtracting investment inputs from outputs. The inputs are the securities on hand at the start of the year (stated at fair value as of the beginning of the year) plus the purchases during the year. The outputs are the securities on hand at year-end (stated at fair value as of year-end) plus the proceeds from the sale of securities during the year. Thus:

Outputs		
Fair value, December 31	$755	
Sales	250	$1,005
Inputs		
Fair value, January 1	$860	
Purchases	90	950
Increase (decrease) in fair of value of investments		$ 55

The following entry would therefore be appropriate:

Investments	$ 55	
Revenue—increase in fair value of investments		$ 55[13]
To record the increase in the fair value of the investments		

[13] Alternatively the city could have recognized a gain of $50 at the time Security C was sold (i.e., the difference between the selling price of $250 and the beginning-of-year market value of $200). Then, at year-end, only a $5 increase in the fair value of the investments would have been required to be recorded.

TABLE 7-4 Disclosure of Fair Value Measurements

($ in millions)		Fair Value Measurements Using		
	12/13/X1	Quoted Prices in Active Markets for Identical Assets (Level 1)	Significant Other Observable Inputs (Level 2)	Significant Unobservable Inputs (Level 3)
Investments				
Debt securities				
U S Treasury securities	$ 85	$ 85		
Commercial mortgage-backed securities	50			$ 50
Collateralized debt obligations	35			35
Residential mortgage-backed securities	149		$ 24	125
Corporate bonds	93	9	84	
Total debt securities	412	94	108	210
Equity securities				
Financial services industry	150	150		
Health-care industry	110	110		
Other	15	15		
Total equity securities	275	275		
Hedge fund investments				
Equity long/short	55		55	
Event-driven hedge funds	45		45	
Global opportunities	35		26	9
Multistrategy hedge funds	40		40	
Real estate funds	47			47
Private equity funds—international	43		43	
Total hedge Amd investments	265		209	56
Venture capital investments				
Direct vennire capital—health care	53			53
Direct venture capital—energy	32			32
Total venture capital investments	85			85
Total investments	$1,037	$ 369	$ 317	$ 351
Derivative instruments				
Interest rate swaps	$ 57		$ 57	
Foreign exchange contracts	43		43	
Total derivative instruments	$ 100		$ 100	

Source: GASB Statement No. 72, *Fair Value Measurement and Application*.

Many local governments invest what would otherwise be idle cash in investment pools maintained by their states or other governmental units. These investment pools are similar to mutual funds. Each participant purchases shares in the underlying portfolio. Statement No. 31 specifies that with certain exceptions relating to pools that invest exclusively in short-term investments (and addressed in Chapter 10), governments should state their investments in a pool at the fair value per share of the pool's underlying portfolio. Each period they should recognize the change in fair value as a gain or loss.

IN PRACTICE — SOME GOVERNMENTS MAY MAKE SUBOPTIMAL INVESTMENT DECISIONS IN ORDER TO AVOID FINANCIAL STATEMENT VOLATILITY

Statement No. 31 requires governments to recognize gains and losses from changes in all marketable securities, including held-to-maturity debt securities that have a maturity greater than one year. Typically the longer the maturity of a debt security (such as a U.S. Treasury note or bond), the higher its interest rate. Thus, a two-year note would almost always provide a greater return than a one-year note.

Investment advisors report that some governments are opting to invest in one-year securities rather than two-year securities even though sound investment strategies would suggest that the two-year securities would provide the higher yield and would be more appropriate for their portfolios. As a consequence, they are losing up to 30 basis points (that is, 0.3 percent annual return) on their investments.

Government officials are unwilling to assume the risks of having to report losses from the changes in market values of the two-year securities. In particular, they note that the political costs of having to report losses greatly outweigh the benefits of being able to report gains. They are, in effect, willing to sacrifice real dollars for the dubious virtues of cosmetically enhanced financial statements.

HOW SHOULD INTEREST AND DIVIDENDS BE ACCOUNTED FOR?

The GASB does not provide specific guidance on when governments should recognize interest and dividends on their investments. However, by recording the changes in fair value, governments will automatically accrue interest and dividends as they are earned.

Example

Interest Income

On December 1, a town purchased a $1,000, two-year discount note for $873, a price that reflects an annual yield of approximately 7 percent. As a discount note, the security provides no periodic payments of interest. However, assuming no change in prevailing interest rates or other factors that would also affect fair value, the note's fair value can be expected to increase by approximately $5 the first month. On December 31, if the fair value of the note were $878, the following entry would recognize the $5 of investment income attributable in economic substance to the interest earned:

Investments	$5	
Revenue—increase in fair value of investments		$5
To record the increase in the fair value of the investments		

If the security were a short-term Treasury note (one year or less), the government would not look to fair value to adjust the security. Instead, it would amortize the initial discount over the life of the note. If, for example, the initial discount on a six-month, 6 percent, $1,000 note were $30, the following entry would recognize one month's interest income:

Discount on note (or investments)	$5	
Revenue—interest income		$5
To record one-month's interest		

The impact of the two approaches on both net position and change in fund balance is the same. Both would give recognition to the interest earned and the resultant change in the value of the underlying security.

CAUSES FOR SPECIAL CONCERN

At one time the investment activities of governments and not-for-profits received relatively little attention from accounting standard-setting authorities. Generally, governments and not-for-profits were satisfied with "conservative securities" that provided steady, if relatively modest, returns. Accordingly, their risks of loss were low.

Now, however, treasurers and other officials responsible for their organizations' investments are under considerable pressure to increase their portfolio yields. In part, the demands can be attributed to the need for their organizations to maintain or enhance services in the face of increasing costs. Also, though, the treasury function has become more professional. No longer can treasurers simply divide their available resources among local banks or friendly brokerage houses. Today their performance and, consequently, their salary increases and opportunities for advancement are more likely to be tied to the yields on the portfolios they control. In the face of these incentives, it is easy for portfolio managers to ignore a fundamental concept of finance: The greater the returns, the greater the risk. At the same time, the range of investment "products" offered by Wall Street has increased dramatically. Succumbing to aggressive sales tactics from brokers and dealers, many treasurers purchase securities that they don't understand and that are clearly unsuited to their institutions' investment objectives.

When governments and not-for-profits restricted their portfolios to conventional financial instruments, the accounting issues of asset classification (e.g., current or noncurrent) and valuation (cost or market) and of revenue recognition (on change in value or only on sale) were far less complicated than they are today. The new financial instruments are often multifaceted and extremely difficult to value. In addition, identical types of financial instruments can be held for diametrically opposed purposes (e.g., to increase risk or to decrease risk).

SPECIAL RISKS OF DERIVATIVES

Over the last two decades many governments and not-for-profits have invested in derivatives. A **derivative** is defined as a security whose value depends on (is *derived* from) that of some underlying asset (such as a share of stock), a reference rate (such as a prevailing interest rate), or an index (such as the Standard & Poor's index of stock prices). Derivatives embrace many types of securities, ranging from the ordinary to the esoteric. For example, they include ordinary stock options (such as puts and calls), debt instruments that are backed by pools of mortgages, and interest-only or principal-only "strips" (bond-like securities in which the obligations to pay principal and interest are traded separately). Most derivatives are highly volatile instruments and can enable an investor to achieve gains, or cause it to incur losses, greatly out of proportion to the change in the value of the securities or assets to which they are linked.

Ironically, many types of derivatives were developed to *reduce* overall investment risks (as illustrated in the accompanying "In Practice"). Hence, they may have a legitimate place in the portfolios of even the most conservative organizations. However, they were widely misused by some governments and not-for-profits (and businesses) as a means of speculation.

In the last decade both government and not-for-profit organizations have lost millions of dollars on derivatives and other similar types of investments. Sometimes the losses could be attributable to calculated risks made by sophisticated investment managers. Other times, however, they are the result of flawed practices and deficient internal or administrative controls. The accompanying in-practice provides examples of both.

GASB STANDARDS

As set forth in GASB Statement No. 53, *Accounting and Financial Reporting for Derivative Instruments* (June 2008), derivatives should be reported at their fair values. As a general rule, changes in fair value should be reported as gains or losses on both fund and government-wide statements of changes in net position.

The major exception to the requirement that the gains and losses resulting from changes in market value be recognized in statements of changes in net position pertains to derivative instruments that represent effective hedges against other assets or liabilities. Such gains or losses should be deferred and reported on balance sheets as deferred inflows or outflows. A hedging instrument is one that significantly reduces financial risk by substantially offsetting the changes in cash flows or fair values of the item with which it is associated. Thus, for example, most interest rates swaps—those designed to protect a government against increases in interest rates on variable rate bond obligations—would fall into this category. Although Statement No. 53 is lengthy, much of it deals with determining the extent to which a derivative is truly an effective hedge.

The statement also mandates extensive disclosures. Governments must explain the nature of derivative transactions, indicate the reasons why they were entered into, and include a discussion of their exposure to credit risk (that of the other party defaulting), market risk (that of changes in interest rates or market prices), and legal risk (that of the transaction being determined to be prohibited by law, regulation, or contract). Moreover, they must disclose the significant terms of the transactions and must reveal any violations of legal, regulatory, or contractual provisions by investing in derivatives.

IN PRACTICE ONE COMMON-TYPE DERIVATIVE

Governments typically engage in derivative transactions not to speculate but, rather, to reduce risk. Here's an example. A government issues 20-year bonds that have variable interest rates. That is, the interest rates change periodically (such as every six months) based on a widely used index such as the LIBOR (London Interbank Offered Rate). The government issues the bonds with a variable rate rather than a fixed rate because market conditions are such that there is a strong demand by investors for securities with the variable rates. As a consequence, the government believes that it can lower its overall costs of borrowing by issuing the variable rate bonds.

To protect itself against increases in interest rates, the government enters into a floating to fixed rate "swap" with a "counterparty," such as a broker. The government exchanges its obligation to make variable rate payments for the counterparty's obligation (on some other security) to make fixed rate payments. Operationally, the government (although still legally bound to the bondholders for the variable payments) agrees to make fixed interest payments to the counterparty. The counterparty then makes the variable rate payments to the bondholders.

IN PRACTICE INVESTMENT DEBACLES

- The University of California gambled on investment-type strategies involving interest rate swaps. The university system issued bonds that carried variable interest rates. At the time variable rates were lower than fixed rates. Predicting that variable rates would rise, however, the system arranged with banks to swap their variable-rate obligations for fixed-rate obligations. Unfortunately for the university system, variable rates decreased rather than increased so that the system was either locked into paying the higher fixed rates or unwinding the swap contracts with the banks at a cost of tens of millions of dollars. ("UC Lost Millions on Interest-Rate Bets," *Orange County Register*, February 24, 2014).

- Five Wisconsin School Districts invested $200 million in highly speculative subprime-related securities called "**collateralized debt obligations**." Apparently school officials thought they were acquiring standard corporate bonds. Instead, they were, in effect, insuring against corporate defaults. Potentially they stand to lose almost all of their investment. ("Exotic Investments Trip Up Wisconsin Schools," *U.S. News*, March 25, 2010)
- Yeshiva University lost 28 percent of its endowment owing to investments in a fund managed by Bernard Madoff. Madoff was a trustee of the university and highly respected in financial circles, having served as Chairman of the Board of Directors of the National Association of Securities Dealers. Madoff eventually carried out one of the largest Ponzi schemes in U.S. history, one that engulfed scores of wealthy individuals as well as numerous not-for-profit organizations. Federal prosecutors estimated the size of the fraud to be over $60 billion, and Madoff was sentenced to 150 years in prison. (Various sources)

SUNSHINE AND COMMON SENSE AS THE BEST APPROACH TO SOUND INVESTMENTS

Disclosure of Risks

The GASB has no authority to set standards for the investment practices of governments. It can direct only how governments account for and report their investments in their general-purpose financial statements. Nevertheless, by requiring governments to make extensive disclosures on the securities that they hold, the GASB can induce them to invest only in instruments that are appropriately conservative. After all, few governments would want to reveal that they are taking Las Vegas-style risks with taxpayers' money.

GASB STANDARDS CURRENT DISCLOSURE REQUIREMENTS FOR GOVERNMENT INVESTMENTS

Current standards mandate extensive disclosures on investment risks. Per GASB Statement No. 40, *Deposit and Investment Risk Disclosures, an Amendment of GASB Statement No. 3* (March 2003), governments should organize these disclosures by investment type (e.g., U.S. Treasuries, corporate bonds, or commercial paper) and should make separate disclosures for governmental activities, business-type activities, major funds, nonmajor funds in the aggregate, and under certain circumstances, fiduciary funds. Most significantly, they should describe their deposit and investment policies related to the various types of risks they assume. Thus, if a government has a concentration of investments with a single party and there is a risk that the party will default on its obligations to the government, the government should disclose its policies regarding this type of credit risk. If it has investments denominated in foreign currencies, it should describe its policies on foreign investments. In addition, governments should make the following additional disclosures as to specific types of risks:

Credit risks. Governments should indicate the credit quality ratings of investments in debt securities as described by nationally recognized rating agencies. Further, they disclose the amount of balances that are subject to "custodial" credit risk. Custodial risk arises when securities are uninsured, uncollateralized, not in the name of the government itself, or not in the physical possession of the government.

Concentration of credit risks. Governments should disclose, by amount and issuer, investments in any one issuer that represent 5 percent or more of total investments of the particular fund or activity for which disclosures are required.

Interest rate risks. Governments should disclose information on how sensitive their investments are to changes in interest rates. They should do this by using one of several methods described and illustrated in the pronouncement and should disclose the terms of investments that are highly sensitive to changes in interest rates.

Foreign currency risks. Governments should disclose the U.S. dollar balances of investments subject to these risks organized by currency type and, if applicable, investment type.

COMMON SENSE

In the mid-1990s, as the result of misguided use of highly speculative investment practices, Orange County, one of the wealthiest counties in the United States, suffered losses so severe that it led to what up until then was the largest municipal bankruptcy in U.S. history. Several public universities in Texas also suffered major losses as a consequence of similar practices. As a consequence, the Texas State auditor's office issued a report in which it made several sound, commonsense, recommendations on how governments can avoid future fiscal fiascos. Summarized in the In Practice that follows, they are as relevant now as when they were made.

IN PRACTICE COMMON SENSE INVESTMENT PRACTICES

- Strengthen management controls by
  - Developing an investment policy with clearly defined goals and objectives.
  - Periodically reviewing the policy to take into account changes in the market.
  - Designing a system to ensure active monitoring of investments by senior management and governing board members.
- Establish an ethics policy that addresses conflicts of interest and implement a system whereby potential conflicts of interest are documented for governing board members and key employees involved in investment decisions.
- Ensure that personnel possess the necessary qualifications and expertise to make investment decisions consistent with investment policy. Investments should not be made if personnel and management do not fully understand the transactions and related risks. Internal auditors should also be specially trained to evaluate the investment function.
- Make certain that investments are properly analyzed. Use various pricing sources in purchasing securities, and have an independent evaluation of the portfolio to ensure that investments are consistent with established risk levels and expected rates of return.

Source: Based on *Derivative Instruments by Texas State Entities,* 1995, a report by the Texas State Auditor.

SUMMARY

In their governmental fund statements, which are accounted for on a modified accrual basis, governments report general capital assets as expenditures when they construct or acquire them. The assets are not reported on the balance sheet, and therefore governments must maintain "off the balance sheet" records of them.

The accounting model as described in GASB Statement No. 34 requires that in their government-wide statements, governments capitalize capital assets and depreciate them over their economic lives. In notes to the statements, they must include a schedule that shows the beginning and ending balances of their capital asset and accumulated depreciation accounts and the changes that took place during the year.

Statement No. 34 mandates that governments account for their infrastructure assets just as they do other capital assets. However, governments are not required to depreciate infrastructure assets if they preserve them at a specified "condition level." If they do so, they may report as expenditures the costs of maintaining the assets at that level, but must disclose the actual amounts spent on maintenance as compared with the amounts necessary to maintain the assets at the specified condition level.

The provisions of Statement No. 34 bring governments into line with other not-for-profits and businesses on how they report capital assets. They result in financial statements that give users more information than they previously received, but still leave them short of what is needed for many fixed-asset-related judgments and decisions.

Investments are of concern because of the substantial risk that investors can incur—losses through default, declines in value, and even fraud. In recent years, interest in investments has been heightened by major losses caused by purchases of overly speculative securities.

GASB standards require that with few exceptions all investments, including those, such as bonds, that governments intend to hold to maturity, should be reported at fair value. As a consequence, gains and losses in value must be recognized in a flows statement each period as changes in fair value occur.

Fair value is considered to be an exit price—"the price that would be received to sell an asset or paid to transfer a liability in an orderly transaction between market participants at the measurement date." The GASB has established a hierarchy of inputs to determine the fair value of the various types of investments. Thus:

- Level 1 inputs are quoted prices in active market for identical assets or liabilities.
- Level 2 inputs are quoted prices for similar assets or liabilities.
- Level 3 inputs are those that are not based on observable quoted prices, but rather are based on the best information available in the circumstances.

Governments today commonly invest in complex securities, such as derivatives, which may be especially risky. The major risk from a derivative is that the value of the underlying securities will decline, causing the value of the derivative to decline by a disproportionately greater amount. Through its standards, the GASB requires disclosure of a wide range of investment information, intended to inform statement users of the risk that the government has assumed.

KEY TERMS IN THIS CHAPTER

collateralized debt obligations 306
deferred maintenance costs 293
derivative 304
fair value 300
general capital assets 285
infrastructure assets 293
intangible assets 295
investment pools 298

EXERCISE FOR REVIEW AND SELF-STUDY

In 2020, Oneida County constructs 10 miles of a new highway at a cost of $10 million, all of which was raised through the issuance of general obligation bonds. Engineers estimate that the highway will have a 50-year useful life and that the county will have to incur $0.3 million in costs per year to keep it functioning at a specified level of condition.

1. Prepare an appropriate journal entry to record the initial construction costs in a governmental fund (such as a capital projects fund). Indicate the amount that the government would record in its government-wide financial statements.
2. Prepare a journal entry to reflect how the county would report the road's first-year depreciation in its government-wide statements.
3. Prepare the journal entry to record the $0.3 million in road preservation costs in a governmental fund. Prepare a second entry to reflect the costs in the government-wide statements.
4. Prepare the journal entry to reflect the annual depreciation of the road preservation costs in the government-wide statements. Is it necessary to record depreciation in the governmental fund?
5. Suppose instead that the county opts not to depreciate infrastructure, and it makes the requisite periodic condition assessments. It incurs the $0.3 million necessary to preserve the road at the specified condition. Prepare the entry (which would be essentially the same for both the fund and the government-wide statements) to record the costs incurred.
6. The county reported its courthouse at $4 million (initial cost of $6 million less accumulated depreciation of $2 million). The courthouse had been constructed 10 years earlier. Provide an example, if possible, of one decision or assessment to be made (e.g., whether the building should be insured, whether it should be sold, whether it should be renovated) for which this book value would be a relevant consideration for the county. Explain and justify your response, telling specifically how the information would be taken into account.

QUESTIONS FOR REVIEW AND DISCUSSION

1. Why are *general* capital assets not recorded in governmental funds?
2. A state incurs interest on funds used while a highway was under construction. How will this interest be accounted for on the state's (a) capital project's fund statements and (b) government-wide statements?
3. How should governments report their long-lived assets in their government-wide financial statements?
4. A city establishes an art museum. What options does it have in accounting for its collection of paintings?
5. Although Statement No. 34 requires that infrastructure assets be accounted for similar to other capital assets, it allows for a major exception with regard to depreciation. What is that exception?
6. Why have many government officials objected to Statement No. 34's requirement that infrastructure assets be accounted for similar to other capital assets?
7. What are *deferred maintenance* costs, and when and how must a government report them (as they relate to infrastructure) in its financial statements?
8. Per the provisions of Statement No. 34, governments must report their capital assets similar to businesses in their government-wide statements. Yet the information provided is still inadequate to facilitate the major types of decisions and judgments made by statement users. Do you agree? Explain.
9. What are the differences between market risk, credit risk, and legal risk? Suppose that a local government invests in 20-year U.S. government bonds. Assess each of the three risks, and discuss the disclosures required by a government on its financial statements.
10. What are *derivatives*? Why can they be especially high-risk securities?
11. How can governments use derivatives as a means of *reducing* investment or borrowing risks?
12. The GASB establishes a hierarchy of inputs to determine the fair values of investments. What are the three levels of the hierarchy?
13. Per the GASB, held-to-maturity securities, such as bonds, must be reported at fair value, even if they will be eventually redeemed at stated or face value. Thus gains and losses on changes in fair value must be periodically recognized, even if such losses will never be realized. How can such an approach be defended?

EXERCISES

EX. 7-1

Select the *best* answer.

1. Which of the following would be least likely to be classified as a city's *general* capital assets?
   - **a.** Roads and bridges
   - **b.** Electric utility lines
   - **c.** Computers used by the police department
   - **d.** Computers used by the department that collects the city's sale tax, which is dedicated to debt service on general obligation bonds
2. A city should not report on its general fund balance sheet an office building constructed over 100 years ago because
   - **a.** the building would likely be fully depreciated.
   - **b.** it would be too difficult to determine the historical cost of the building as measured in current dollars.
   - **c.** the measurement focus of the general fund is on current financial resources and the building is not a current financial resource.
   - **d.** the building would be considered an infrastructure asset, and infrastructure assets are excluded from governmental funds.

3. Which of the following costs should *not* be capitalized and reported on a city's government-wide statement of net position?
   a. Payments to a city artist to design a new city logo
   b. Computer software that the city purchased from outsiders
   c. Paintings purchased for display in the city's art museum
   d. Legal fees incurred in acquiring land to be used for a city park

4. Which of the following collectibles need *not* be capitalized and reported on a city's government-wide statement of net position?
   a. A statue donated to the city, which it intends to sell and use the proceeds from the sale to fund a children's art center
   b. A series of books that the city intends to place in its library's general circulation collection
   c. An abstract painting that the city purchased to decorate the mayor's office
   d. An early twentieth-century impressionist painting that the city's art museum purchased for its permanent collection

5. Per GASB Statement No. 34, roads and bridges should be capitalized and reported as assets on
   a. both a government-wide statement net of assets and a general fund balance sheet.
   b. neither a government-wide statement of net position nor a general fund balance sheet.
   c. a government-wide statement of net position but not a general fund balance sheet.
   d. a general fund balance sheet but not a government-wide statement of net position.

6. Which of the following conditions does a government *not* have to satisfy to use the modified approach to reporting infrastructure assets?
   a. It must assess the condition of its infrastructure at least once every three years.
   b. It must estimate the annual amount necessary to preserve the assets at a specified condition level.
   c. It must document that the assets are, in fact, being preserved at or above the specified condition level.
   d. It must use the modified approach for all its infrastructure assets.

7. Per the modified approach, a government need not
   a. capitalize infrastructure assets.
   b. depreciate infrastructure assets
   c. report in its fund statements expenditures to acquire or construct infrastructure assets.
   d. record maintenance costs as expenditures

8. A government constructed a bridge 20 years ago at a cost of $30 million. The replacement cost of the bridge today would be $90 million. The bridge has a useful life of 60 years. In its government-wide statements the government should record the bridge at a value, net of accumulated depreciation, of
   a. $20 million.
   b. $60 million.
   c. $90 million.
   d. $0.

9. Per GASB Statement No. 34, deferred maintenance costs
   a. must be estimated and reported in notes to the financial statements.
   b. must be reported in the government-wide statement of net position but not in fund statements.
   c. must be estimated and reported in the management's discussion and analysis.
   d. need not be explicitly measured or reported when capital assets are depreciated.

10. A city would probably not have to recognize an impairment loss on its hospital building if
    a. It were severely damaged in a fire
    b. It will likely be used to serve far fewer patients than expected when acquired
    c. Its market value declines significantly
    d. It will be transformed into a warehouse

EX. 7-2

Select the *best* answer.

1. A government repaves a section of highway every four years at a cost of $2 million to preserve it at a specific condition level. How much should it report in depreciation charges under the modified approach to accounting for infrastructure? The standard approach?

	Modified Approach	Standard Approach
a.	$ 0	$ 0
b.	$500,000	$500,000
c.	$500,000	$ 0
d.	$ 0	$500,000

2. States typically maintain investment pools for their towns and counties primarily to
   a. provide the participants with the benefits of increased portfolio size.
   b. ensure that the participants maximize their investment returns.
   c. enable the participants to engage in arbitrage.
   d. spread the risk of losses among the participants.

3. A government owns shares of common stock in a publicly owned company, the stock of which is widely traded. Such an investment would be categorized as
   a. a Level 1 investment.
   b. a Level 2 investment.
   c. a Level 3 investment.
   d. an investment that fits into none of the three categories.

4. A government acquires as an investment a 30-year U.S. Treasury bond having a face value of $10,000. At the end of year 20, with 10 years remaining until maturity, the bond had a fair value of $10,200. Taking into account the discount at which the government initially purchased the bond, its amortized cost was $9,760. Assuming that it held the bond in a governmental fund, the government should report the bond at a value of
   a. $0.
   b. $9,760.
   c. $10,000.
   d. $10,200.

5. Derivatives are
   a. variable interest rate bonds, the interest rate on which is derived from (based on) the prime rate of interest.
   b. shares of common stock, the value of which is derived from the market value of the underlying assets (typically investments in subsidiaries) of the issuing corporation.
   c. investments, the value of which is derived from some underlying asset or reference rate.
   d. investment pools, the value of which is derived from the pools' investments.

6. Which of the following statements is true with respect to derivatives?
   a. They are highly speculative instruments and therefore are suitable only for governments that are willing to accept a high degree of investment risk.
   b. Their market values are typically less volatile than those of the underlying assets.
   c. GASB standards require that governments explain in their annual reports the reasons why they invested in derivatives.
   d. They need not be reported on governments' financial statements; they need only be disclosed in notes to the financial statements.

7. The risk that a company will go bankrupt and thereby be unable to repay a bond that a government holds as an investment as required is known as
   a. credit risk.
   b. market value risk.

c. interest rate risk.
d. counterparty risk.

8. Investments would generally be considered subject to the least custodial risk if they are
   a. registered in the government's name but in the possession of a broker–dealer.
   b. registered in the government's name and in the physical possession of the government itself.
   c. registered in the broker–dealer's name and in the possession of the broker–dealer.
   d. registered in the broker–dealer's name but in the possession of the government itself.

9. A city needs to determine whether it should sell its downtown administrative facility and move to an outlying location. The value of the facility that is most relevant to this decision is
   a. historical cost.
   b. fair value.
   c. historical cost less accumulated depreciation.
   d. assessed value.

10. Which of the following costs should not be included in the cost of a highway that a county constructed itself?
    a. Insurance premiums paid while the project was under construction
    b. Interest incurred on debt used to finance the project while it was under construction
    c. Overhead costs of the construction department
    d. Fees paid to consultants to determine the highway's optimum route

EX. 7-3

General capital assets are accounted for differently in fund and government-wide financial statements.

A city engaged in the following transactions during a year:

1. It acquired computer equipment at a cost of $40,000.

2. It completed construction of a new jail, incurring $245,000 in new costs. In the previous year the city had incurred $2.5 million in construction costs. The project was accounted for in a capital projects fund.

3. It sold for $16,000 land that it had acquired three years earlier for $28,000.

4. It traded in a four-year-old sanitation department vehicle for a new model. The old vehicle had initially cost $27,000, its carrying value at the time of trade was $17,000, and its market value was $13,000. The city paid an additional $39,000 cash for the new model. The fair value of the new model was $52,000.
   a. Prepare journal entries to reflect the transactions in an appropriate governmental fund (e.g., a general fund or a capital projects fund).
   b. Prepare journal entries to reflect the transactions in the city's government-wide statements.

EX. 7-4

Capital assets are accounted for in government-wide statements on a full accrual basis.

The following summarizes the history of the Sharp City Recreation Center.

1. In 1993, the city constructed the building at a cost of $1,500,000. Of this amount, $1,000,000 was financed with bonds and the balance from unrestricted city funds.

2. In the 10 years from 1993 through 2002, the city recorded depreciation (as appropriate) based on an estimated useful life of 30 years.

3. In the same period, the city repaid $750,000 of the bonds.

4. In 2004, the city renovated the building at a cost of $3,000,000. The entire amount was financed with unrestricted city funds. The renovation was expected to extend the useful life of the building so that it would last a total of 25 more years—that is, until 2029.

5. In the 15 years from 2004 through 2018, the city recorded depreciation (as appropriate). Depreciation was calculated by dividing the undepreciated balance of the original cost, plus the costs of renovation, over the anticipated remaining life of 25 years.

6. In the same period, the city repaid the $250,000 balance of the debt.

7. In 2019, the city demolished the building so that the land on which it is situated could be converted into softball fields.

Prepare the journal entries to summarize the history of the building as it would be reported in the city's government-wide statements.

EX. 7-5

Capital assets are accounted for in governmental fund statements on a modified accrual basis.
Refer to the transactions in the previous exercise.

1. Prepare journal entries that the city would make in its governmental funds (e.g., its general fund or a capital projects fund).

2. How would you recommend that the city maintain accounting control over the capital assets themselves—those you did not record as assets in the governmental funds?

EX. 7-6

The initial value to be assigned to an asset is not always obvious.
A city acquired general capital assets as follows:

1. It purchased new construction equipment. List price was $400,000, but the city was granted a 10 percent "government discount." The city also incurred $12,000 in transportation costs and paid $4,000 to its own employees to customize the equipment.

2. It received a donation of land to be set aside for a nature preserve. The land had cost the donor $300,000. At the time of the contribution it was valued on the city's tax rolls at $1.7 million. However, independent appraisers estimated its fair value at $1.9 million.

3. It constructed a new maintenance facility at a cost of $2 million. During the period of construction the city incurred an additional $110,000 in interest on funds borrowed to finance the construction.

Indicate the value that the government should assign to these assets. Justify briefly the value you assigned and, as appropriate, indicate any other acceptable alternatives.

EX. 7-7

Government must classify investments into one of three categories of input to establish fair value.
A government holds the following investments. For each, indicate the category in which it should most likely be classified.

1. A 20-year, 4 percent corporate bond rated AA by a leading rating agency. The bond is not widely traded in a market.

2. Shares in a privately held high-tech "start-up" company.

3. Shares in a corporation listed on the New York Stock Exchange.

4. Interest rate swaps with a major bank as the counterparty.

CONTINUING PROBLEM

Review the comprehensive annual financial report (CAFR) you obtained.

1. What are the principal classes of capital assets associated with governmental activities that the city reports in its financial statements?

2. What was the total amount of capital assets used in governmental activities added during the year? What was the amount retired?

3. What is the city's threshold policy on capitalizing general capital assets and intangible assets?

4. How much depreciation did the government charge in its government-wide statements on capital assets used in governmental activities?

5. Did the government capitalize infrastructure assets acquired during the year? Did it account for infrastructure assets using the "standard" or the "modified" approach?

6. Did the government capitalize collections of art or historical treasures? Did it depreciate such collections?

7. Judging from the disclosures pertaining to investments, does the entity have any investments that appear to be especially risky? In your judgment, to which risk (e.g., credit risk, interest rate risk, foreign currency risk) is the exposure of the entity the greatest?

8. Does the government own any "unusual" securities such as derivatives? If so, does the report contain an explanation of these transactions?

PROBLEMS

P. 7-1

Entries to record capital assets can be derived from the schedule of changes in capital assets. Assets acquired with federal funds pose an interesting accounting issue (albeit one not addressed in the text).

	Balance June 30, 2020	Additions	Deletions	Balance June 30, 2021
Land	$100,298,761	$8,575,641	$2,318,535	$106,555,867
Buildings	173,307,375	11,241,166	3,672,542	180,875,999
Improvements and equipment	122,911,080	24,777,538	10,568,363	137,120,255
Construction work in process	44,449,433	6,209,591	11,769,183	38,889,841
Infrastructure	345,554,452	43,600,000	10,500,280	378,654,172
Total historical cost	$786,521,101	$85,828,295	$36,510,368	$842,096,134
Less accumulated depreciation for:				
Buildings and improvements	$ 26,893,189	$ 1,075,728	$ 2,530,000	$ 25,438,917
Improvements and equipment	49,164,432	12,690,135	4,380,320	57,474,247
Infrastructure	160,550,000	8,638,861	2,100,676	167,088,185
Total accumulated depreciation	$236,607,621	$22,404,724	$ 9,010,996	$250,001,349
Capital assets, net	$549,913,480	$63,423,571	$27,499,372	$592,094,785

A city included the schedule above in its financial statements.

1. Prepare entries to reflect the activity relating to improvements and equipment in both the general-fund and the government-wide statements, assuming, as appropriate, that all transactions were for cash. The deleted improvements and equipment were sold during the year for $12,000,000.

2. The schedule is based on numbers drawn from an actual city. What percentage of total assets, at historical cost (ignoring accumulated depreciation), represents infrastructure at year-end? Despite this sizable percentage, which is typical of most cities, what arguments have critics of GASB Statement No. 34 made in support of their contention that governments should not be required to give balance-sheet recognition to infrastructure assets?

3. A note to the schedule states that "the federal government funded a portion of the capital assets and thereby has an interest in them. This interest includes the right to approve the sale of such assets and to require the return to the federal government of a portion of any sales proceeds." Suppose that the government funded 50 percent of a law enforcement center that had a cost of $10 million and accumulated depreciation of $5 million, and thus had a book value of $5 million. During the year the

government sold the center for $4 million and per the agreement with the federal government was required to return 50 percent of the sales proceeds to the government. Prepare a government-wide statement entry to record the sale. What reservations might you have with regard to this entry? Do you have any suggestions for an alternative way to account for federally funded assets?

4. Assume that the land on which the city's administrative offices are constructed was acquired in 1900 for $500. At what value would that land be reported today? Of what significance is that value to statement users?

P. 7-2

Governments must now account for their capital assets, including infrastructure, and they must recognize in their accounts that the assets may not last forever (unless continually preserved).

In the year a road maintenance district was established, it engaged in the transactions that follow involving capital assets (all dollar amounts in thousands). The district maintains only a single governmental fund (a general fund).

1. Received authority over roads previously "owned" by the county. The estimated replacement cost of the roads was $60,000. On average they have a remaining useful life of 40 years.

2. Acquired machinery and equipment for $700, with general fund resources. They have a useful life of 10 years.

3. Incurred costs of $3,000 to construct a building. The construction was financed with general obligation bonds. The building has a useful life of 30 years.

4. Acquired equipment having a fair value of $60 in exchange for $20 cash (from general-fund resources) plus used equipment for which the district had paid $50. The used equipment had a fair value at the time of the trade of $40; depreciation of $25 had previously been recognized.

5. Sold land for $70 that had been acquired for $90.

6. Received a donation of land from one of the towns within the district. The land had cost the town $120, but at the time of the contribution had a fair market value of $500.

7. Incurred $1,200 in road resurfacing costs. The district estimates that its roads must be resurfaced every four years if they are to be preserved in the condition they were in when they were acquired.

8. Recognized depreciation of $100 on its building, $70 on its machinery and equipment, and $1,500 on its roads, in addition to any depreciation relating to the resurfacing costs.
   a. Prepare entries to record the transactions so that they could be reflected in the district's government-wide statements. The district has opted to depreciate its infrastructure assets.
   b. Suppose instead that the district has elected not to depreciate its roads but to record as an expense only the costs necessary to preserve the roads in the condition they were in when acquired. How would your entries differ?
   c. If, in fact, the roads have a useful life of 40 years, do you think it is sound accounting not to depreciate the roads? Explain.
   d. If, in fact, the preservation costs are sufficient to preserve the roads in the condition they were in when the district acquired them, do you think it is sound accounting to depreciate the roads? Explain.

P. 7-3

Which is the proper value to be assigned to certain donated assets? (This is a question for which answers cannot be found in either GASB pronouncements or in this text.)

A city's road maintenance department received "donations" of two types of assets:

1. From the county in which the city is located it received earthmoving equipment. The equipment had cost the county $800,000 when it was acquired five years earlier. Accounted for in a county proprietary

fund, its book value, net of accumulated depreciation at the time of donation, was $500,000. Its fair value was $530,000.

2. From the city's own utility fund (a proprietary fund) it received motor vehicles that had cost the city $400,000 when acquired three years earlier. At the time of transfer, the vehicles were recorded on the utility's books at $180,000, net of accumulated depreciation. Their fair value was $225,000.
   a. At what value should the city record in its government-wide financial statements: (1) the earth-moving equipment, and (2) the motor vehicles?
   b. Briefly justify your response, commenting on any apparent inconsistencies in the values assigned to each of the two types of assets.
   c. Comment on the significance of the resultant book values for decisions or assessments to be made by statement users.

P. 7-4

Governments sometimes add to, but do not delete, their capital assets.

The following totals were drawn from Independence City's "Schedule of Changes in Capital Assets by Function and Activity," included in the city's financial statements for the year ending June 30, 2021:

General capital assets, July 1, 2020	$33,276,151
Additions/transfers-in	459,430
Deletions/transfers-out	(265,795)
General capital assets, June 30, 2021	$33,469,786

The complete schedule disaggregates the data by function (e.g., general government, public safety, public works, health and welfare, culture, and recreation) and subfunction (e.g., park maintenance, recreation, tourism). Another schedule, "Schedule of General Capital Assets by Source," shows the beginning and ending balances of the specific types of assets:

	2021	2020
Land	$ 8,209,380	$ 8,209,380
Buildings	9,293,847	9,292,611
Improvements other than buildings	1,088,307	1,088,307
Office furniture and equipment	4,863,535	4,536,506
Mobile equipment	7,834,277	8,073,945
Other equipment	2,180,440	2,075,402
Total	$33,469,786	$33,276,151

1. Assume that the assets, excluding land, had an average useful life of 20 years. What percentage of the total assets, excluding land, would you expect to have been retired each year?

2. What percentage of the assets (beginning of year values), excluding land, were actually retired during 2021 (assuming that all deletions/transfers out represent retirements)?

3. What was the average useful life of the assets as implied by this percentage?

4. Assume that the entire $265,795 of the deletions and transfers-out applied to the mobile equipment. What would have been the useful life of the equipment as suggested by the percentage of the equipment retired?

5. Do you think it is likely that the city was conscientious about removing assets from its general capital assets account as they were taken out of service?

6. Is it true that under the provisions of Statement No. 34 a government's failure to remove from its accounting records assets that it has taken out of service after they exceeded their useful lives have relatively little significance on its government-wide statements? Explain.

P. 7-5

Favorable revenue-to-expenditure ratios may not always be as favorable as they appear.

In the management discussion and analysis accompanying its 2021 financial statements, Tiber County reported that "for the fifth consecutive year revenues exceeded expenditures." However, a note included in required supplementary information disclosed the following:

County Roads and Highways—Comparison of Needed to Actual Maintenance/Preservation Costs (in thousands)

	Actual	Needed
2021	$3,400	$4,200
2020	$3,000	$4,000
2019	$2,900	$3,000
2018	$3,100	$3,100
2017	$2,800	$2,700

The county has not been depreciating its infrastructure system but instead has been taking GASB Statement No. 34's modified approach.

1. What reservations might you have about the significance of the county's excess of revenues over expenditures in 2021?

2. Suppose that you were the county's independent auditor. What reservation might you have about the county's reporting practices?

3. Suppose that the county was required to switch from the modified approach to the standard approach. As of year-end 2021 the estimated initial cost of the roads was $100 million and their estimated useful life was 40 years.
   a. How would the change from the modified approach to the standard approach affect the county's general fund excess of revenues over expenditures?
   b. How would it affect the county's government-wide excess of revenues over expenses?

P. 7-6

The schedule of capital assets has a significant impact on the reconciliations between fund and government-wide statements.

The schedule that follows pertaining to governmental capital assets was excerpted from the annual report of Urbana, Illinois (with changed dates):

A related schedule indicates the following:

Capital outlays	$ 3,358,611
Depreciation	(2,268,579)
	$ 1,090,032

1. As required by GASB Statement No. 34, the annual report includes reconciliations between: (1) total fund balance, governmental funds (per the funds statements), and net position of governmental activities (per the government-wide statements); and (2) net change in fund balance, governmental funds (per the funds statements), and change in net position of governmental activities (per the government-wide statements). In what way would the data provided in the accompanying schedules be incorporated into the two reconciliations? Be specific.

2. The amount deleted from the equipment account ($452,194) exactly equals the amount deleted from the related accumulated depreciation account. Is this merely a coincidence? Would the amounts always be the same?

3. Based simply on the amount of equipment retired, what would you estimate to be the average useful life of the equipment? Is this reasonable?

	Balance June 30, 2020	Additions	Deletions	Balance June 30, 2021
Land (not depreciated)	$ 2,843,487	$ 128,528	—	$ 2,972,015
Capital assets being depreciated:				
Buildings and improvements	8,956,049	188,399	—	9,144,448
Accumulated depreciation	(1,991,173)	(159,402)	—	(2,150,575)
Buildings and improvements (net)	6,964,876	28,997	—	6,993,873
Equipment	7,760,379	1,123,568	$ 452,194	8,431,753
Accumulated depreciation	(3,775,555)	(904,509)	(452,194)	(4,227,870)
Equipment (net)	3,984,824	219,059	—	4,203,883
Infrastructure	39,983,947	1,918,116	—	41,902,063
Accumulated depreciation	(8,935,986)	(1,204,668)	—	(10,140,654)
Infrastructure (net)	31,047,961	713,448	—	31,761,409
Total, governmental activities	$44,841,148	$1,090,032	—	$45,931,180

P. 7-7

There may be legitimate reasons to borrow—even in times of plenty. Expenditures for amortizing debt principal may be a rough surrogate for depreciation, and hence the new depreciation rules may have less impact than is first apparent.

A school district constructs a new elementary school at a cost of $24 million. It finances the project by issuing 30-year general obligation serial bonds, payable evenly over the outstanding term ($800,000 per year). District officials estimate that the school will have a useful life of 30 years (with no residual value).

1. Prepare summary entries, in a capital projects fund, to record the issuance of the bonds and construction of the school.

2. Assume that the district repays the bonds out of current revenues. Prepare the entry that it would make each year in its general fund to record the bond principal payments.

3. Assume that the school district must balance its budget; all general-fund expenditures must be covered by general-fund tax and other revenues. A member of the district's board of trustees pointed out that, owing to an unanticipated increase in property values, the district enjoyed a budget surplus in the previous two years and consequently had accumulated $4 million in "savings." She argued that the district should have borrowed only $20 million and financed the balance out of savings. Further, she contended, because prosperous times were expected to continue for the next several years the district should have issued bonds repayable over 10 years rather than 30. Focusing exclusively on issues of "intergenerational equity," how would you defend the financing arrangement actually entered into by the district?

4. Compare the total amount that the school district would report as expenditures (repayment of principal or depreciation, as applicable) on its general-fund statements and its government-wide statements. Suppose that the district were required to balance its budget; expenditures could not exceed revenues. With respect to expenditures relating to the new building, would it matter whether the expenditures were measured on a full or a modified accrual basis? Would your response be the same if the repayment schedule on the bonds differed from the pattern of depreciation (e.g., the bonds were repaid over only 10 years or depreciation were charged on an accelerated basis)?

P. 7-8

If governments don't preserve their infrastructure assets they must depreciate them.

In 2020 Bantham County incurred $80 million in costs to construct a new highway. Engineers estimate that the useful life of the highway is 20 years.

1. Prepare the entry that the county should make to record annual depreciation (straight-line method) to facilitate preparation of its government-wide statements.

2. What reservations might you have as to the engineers' estimate of useful life? Why might any estimate of a highway's useful life be suspect?

3. The engineers have determined that in 2021 the county would have to incur $1 million in resurfacing costs every four years to preserve the highway in the same condition as it was when the road was completed. In 2021, the county spent the $1 million to resurface the highway.
   a. Prepare the entries, including the one for first-year depreciation, the county should make.
   b. Assume instead that as permitted by Statement No. 34, the county opts to report a road preservation charge in lieu of depreciation. Prepare the entry the county should make.

4. Suppose that in 2021 the county added a new lane to a portion of the highway. The cost was $1.5 million. Prepare an appropriate journal entry to facilitate preparation of the government-wide statements regardless of whether the county takes the depreciation or the modified approach.

P. 7-9

Similar collectibles may be accounted for quite differently.

The City of Allentown recently received a donation of two items:

1. A letter written in 1820 from James Allen, the town's founder, in which he sets forth his plan for the town's development. Independent appraisers have valued the letter at $24,000.

2. A 1920 painting of the town's city hall. Comparable paintings by the same artist have recently been purchased for $4,000.

The town intends to place the letter on public display in its city hall. It plans to sell the painting, using the proceeds to redecorate the city council's meeting chambers.

a. It is the town's policy to capitalize collectibles only when required by GASB standards to do so.

b. Prepare journal entries, as necessary, to reflect how each of the contributions should be reported on the city's government-wide financial statements. Briefly explain and justify any apparent inconsistencies in the entries.

c. Suppose that the city had purchased each of the items. Would that affect whether or not you capitalized each of the assets?

d. Suppose that when the city accepted the painting it agreed that if it sold the painting it would use the proceeds only to acquire other works of art. Would that affect how you accounted for the painting?

e. Suppose that the city operated a museum. The museum's building, furniture, and fixtures had cost $10 million and, on average, were now midway through their useful life. They had a replacement cost of $12 million. The art collection had a market value of $300 million. Consistent with your response to part (a), what value would you place on the art collection? What value would you place on the building, furniture, and fixtures? Briefly justify your response, commenting specifically on whether you think the resultant balance sheet would provide useful information to statement users.

P. 7-10

Unrealized investment gains and losses may be difficult to explain to legislators and constituents.

A government held the securities shown in the following table in one of its investment portfolios. All the securities are either stocks or bonds that mature in more than one year.

1. Ignoring dividends and interest, how much gain or loss should the government recognize during the year?

2. What was the government's "realized" gain or loss (i.e., sales proceeds less cost) for the year? Which gain or loss—the amount that would have to be reported on the financial statements as computed in part (1), or the realized gain or loss—would be more indicative of the change in resources available for future expenditure?

3. Suppose that Security B is a long-term bond that the government intends to hold to maturity. What is the most probable reason for the decline in fair value during the year? In what sense is the reported loss indicative of an economic loss?

	Beginning Balance		Transactions during the Year		Ending Balance	
	Cost	Fair Value	Purchases	Sales	Cost	Fair Value
A	$100	$100			$100	$120
B	520	540			520	510
C	200	240		$250		0
D			$330		330	315
	$820	$880	$330	$250	$950	$945

P. 7-11

Recording investments at fair value may provide a measure of income similar to that if investments were stated at amortized historical cost, but is it consistent with the "measurable and available" criteria?

On August 2, 30 days prior to the end of its August 31 fiscal year, a government issues $3 million of general obligation bonds. The proceeds are being accounted for in a capital projects fund (a governmental fund). To earn a return on the bond proceeds before they have to be spent, the government invests $1 million in each of three financial instruments:

- A 60-day discount note with a face value of $1,010,000. The note pays no interest. The purchase price of the note is $1 million (a price that provides an annual yield of 6 percent—0.5 percent per month).
- A two-year note that pays interest at an annual rate of 6 percent. Both interest and principal are payable upon the maturity of the note.
- Shares in an investment pool of government debt securities that provide a fixed return of 6 percent per year. The pool pays no dividends; the returns are reflected as an increase in the value of the shares.

1. Assuming no changes in prevailing interest rates between the date of purchase and year-end, what would you expect to be the fair (i.e., market) value of each of the three investments? Explain.
2. Prepare journal entries, as appropriate, to record investment income and changes in fair values as of the year ending August 31.
3. Why might it be said that your entry for the two-year note is inconsistent with the general rule for fund statements that revenues should be recognized only when they are "measurable" and "available?" Why might it also be argued that your entry is perfectly consistent with the rule?

P. 7-12

Investment notes enable the reader to assess both credit and interest rate risks.

	Fair Value (in thousands)	Weighted Average Maturity (days)
Local government investment pool	$ 6	1
Treasuries	27,600	790
Agencies	80,400	520
Total	$108,006	589

Credit risk. As of September 30, the U.S. Treasuries and the U.S. Agency Bonds were rated AAA by Standard & Poor's. The local government investment pool was rated AA.

Interest rate risk. As a means of minimizing risk of loss due to interest rate fluctuations, the investment policy requires that the dollar-weighted average maturity using final stated maturity dates shall not exceed seven years. The portfolio's weighted average maturity, however, may be substantially shorter if market conditions so dictate. As of September 30, the dollar-weighted average maturity was 589 days (1.61 years).

1. Why would the city limit the weighted average maturity of its portfolio to seven years rather than a greater number of years, even though investments with a longer maturity generally provide a greater investment yield?

2. Why might the city indicate that the average maturity of the local government investment pool is only one day when, in fact, the pool holds investments that have an average maturity of over 30 days?

3. What is meant by "credit risk?" How would you assess the credit risk of the U.S. Treasury and U.S. agency bonds? Explain.

P. 7-13

Fair values cannot always be determined by readily available quoted market prices.

A government holds as investments the assets set forth below and determines its fair value as described. For each, indicate the level (1, 2, or 3) within the hierarchy of inputs to valuation techniques in which the investment should be classified and how the fair value would likely be determined.

1. Shares of common stock in Johnson Controls, Inc. a company that is listed on the New York Stock Exchange.

2. A minority interest in a retail shopping mall. Although there are similar malls in other cities, the malls are seldom bought or sold.

3. A mutual fund, which each day publishes the price at which shares can be purchased or redeemed.

4. Corporate bonds for which there is no active market. However, the bonds are rated AA by Moody's Investor service, a leading bond rating agency.

5. An interest rate swap with a major bank that cannot be sold or traded to a third party. The value of the swap will depend on the prevailing London Interbank Offered Rate (LIBOR).

P. 7-14

Inspired by the bankruptcy of Orange County in the 1990s, this problem shows the risks of investing in seemingly safe securities.

Bear County maintains an investment pool for school districts and other governments within its jurisdiction. Participating governments contribute cash to the pool, which is operated like a mutual fund, and receive in return a proportionate share of all dividends, interest, and gains. They also, of course, must share in any losses.

The governments may withdraw part or all of their funds at any time, receiving their share of the pool's resources. As of year-end, the value of the Bear County investment pool was approximately \$1.2 billion.

Governments have been eager to place their funds in the Bear County pool because it has provided historically higher returns than they could earn independently. The individual governments must restrict their investments to short-term, highly liquid securities, inasmuch as they will likely have need for cash within days, weeks, or months. By contrast, the investment pool can invest a substantial portion of its resources in longer-term, higher-yielding securities because it is unlikely that all the participating governments will withdraw their funds at the same time.

The county pool places its funds only in U.S. government notes and bonds or securities guaranteed by the U.S. government. Hence, there is virtually no default risk; the county can be certain that it will receive timely payment of principal and interest.

1. Assume that the county invests \$1 billion of the \$1.2 billion of its pool portfolio in 10-year, 6 percent government bonds (retaining the balance in cash and short-term securities). Shortly after it purchases the bonds, prevailing interest rates on comparable securities increase to 8 percent. What would you

expect the fair value of the bonds to be after the increase in rates? [*Hint:* The bonds pay interest semiannually. Therefore, using a discount rate of 4 percent per period (one-half the prevailing rate of 8 percent) calculate the present value of $1 billion principal to be received in 20 periods. Then, using the same discount rate of 4 percent, determine the present value of the 20 interest payments of $30 million each (based on one-half the coupon rate of 6 percent).]

2. Suppose that the county invests $1 billion in the 10-year, 6 percent bonds just described. However, it also finances the purchase of an additional $1 billion of bonds with similar terms by entering into "reverse repurchase" agreements. That is, it borrows $1 billion promising to repay the loan in one year. It puts up the 10-year bonds as collateral. Inasmuch as the loan is short-term, the interest rates are only 4 percent—substantially lower than on the long-term bonds.

a. Determine the net percentage return for one year on the $1 billion in the portfolio, taking into account the total interest received on the entire $2 billion and the total interest paid on the amount borrowed. Exclude consideration of the $0.2 billion held in cash and short-term securities.

b. Suppose that long-term interest rates were to increase to 8 percent. What will be the total fair value of the portfolio, net of the amount borrowed (and excluding consideration of the $0.2 billion in cash and short-term securities)?

c. In the face of the sharp decline in the fair value of the investment portfolio, county officials assured participating governments that they have nothing to be concerned about because:

- The county intends to hold all bonds to maturity, and therefore the fluctuations in fair values are not relevant.
- Based on historical experience, the county will have sufficient funds on hand to meet all routine withdrawals. Assume also that short-term interest rates increased to 7 percent. If you were the treasurer of a participating government, would you be comforted by the statements of the county officials? Explain. Would it make sense for you to withdraw your funds from the pool?

d. Suppose you—and treasurers of other governments—were not comforted and did, in fact, withdraw funds from the pool. What would be the probable consequences to both the pool and the pool participants?

P. 7-15

The restoration approach is usually most appropriate for impairments caused by physical damage.

The Middleville School district has discovered mold in one of its schools. The school was constructed 10 years ago at a cost of $30 million. It had an expected useful life of 50 years and hence was 20 percent depreciated. The cost to replace the school today would be $40 million. The district estimates that the cost of eliminating the mold and making the associated repairs would be $4,000,000. The entire amount would be covered by insurance.

1. How much of an impairment loss, without taking into account the insurance recovery, should the district recognize?

2. What would be the new carrying value of the school after adjusting for the impairment?

3. How much of a net gain should the district recognize taking into account the insurance recovery?

P. 7-16

The service units approach is most appropriate for impairments caused by technological obsolescence.

Clarkstown State University acquired specialized laboratory equipment with the expectation that it would be used to perform approximately 3,000 tests per year over a 10-year period. The cost was $600,000. After the equipment had been used for only three years and was 30 percent depreciated, the university realized that the machine would likely be used to perform only 500 tests per year over the following seven years owing to the introduction of more efficient equipment.

1. How much of an impairment loss should the university recognize?

2. What should be the new carrying value of the equipment?

P. 7-17

The deflated depreciated replacement cost approach is most appropriate for impairments caused by changes in manner of use.

Northstate University had constructed a theater at a cost of $20 million. It anticipated a useful life of 30 years. After 18 years (with the building 60 percent depreciated), the university dropped its drama program; it no longer had need for a theater. It opted to transform the building into a study hall. A comparable study hall could be constructed today for $3 million. When the theater was constructed a construction cost index was at 40; today it is at 120.

1. How much of an impairment loss should the university recognize?
2. What should be the new carrying value of the study hall?

QUESTIONS FOR RESEARCH, ANALYSIS, AND DISCUSSION

1. Should parks be classified as ordinary capital assets or as infrastructure? Should the various elements that make up a park be classified separately? Parks include lighting, restrooms, sports fields, hiking and horse trails, roads, sewage systems, playground equipment, and concession stands.
2. A state acquired a large parcel of forest land, which at some time in the future, it expects to license to timber companies so that they can harvest and sell the trees. For now, however, the land is used primarily for recreation. The state maintains hiking trails and camping facilities. Should the forest land be considered an investment?
3. A city maintains botanical gardens that contain valuable plants. Should these plants be considered "collectibles," such as museum pieces, or infrastructure, such as parks?

SOLUTION TO EXERCISE FOR REVIEW AND SELF-STUDY

1. Governmental fund

Road construction expenditures	$10	
Cash		$10
To record construction expenditures		

The government would record the highway in its government-wide statements at its cost, $10 million.

2.

Depreciation expense	$0.2	
Accumulated depreciation (infrastructure)		$0.2
To record first-year depreciation ($10 million divided by 50 years)		

3.

Road preservation expenditures	$0.3	
Cash		$0.3
To record the road preservation costs in a governmental fund		
Road preservation costs (asset)	$0.3	
Cash		$0.3
To record road preservation costs (an asset) in the government-wide statements		

4.

Depreciation expense	$0.06	
Road preservation costs (asset)		$0.06

To record the depreciation of the road preservation costs in the government-wide statements

It would be unnecessary to depreciate the road preservation costs in the governmental fund. As with other long-lived assets, the costs would be recognized as expenditures as incurred.

5.

Road preservation expense/expenditure	$0.3	
Cash		$0.3

To record first-year preservation costs

6. There are few, if any, decisions or assessments for which an asset's historical cost—or even its historical cost less accumulated depreciation—is relevant (excluding, of course, decisions or assessments for which historical costs are specified, as when a bank demands that an organization maintain particular financial ratios that are defined in terms of historical cost book values). Relevant information would include the amount for which the asset could be sold, its replacement value, and the amount required to maintain it in its current condition.

CHAPTER 8

Long-Term Obligations

LEARNING OBJECTIVES

After studying this chapter you should understand:

- Why information on long-term debt is important to statement users
- The significance of bankruptcy in a governmental and not-for-profit context
- Why and how governments account for long-term obligations in both fund and government-wide statements
- The nature of demand bonds, bond anticipation notes, tax anticipation notes, and revenue anticipation notes, and how they should be accounted for and reported
- The reasons governments lease assets and how leases are accounted for and reported
- Why governments issue revenue bonds
- What is meant by overlapping debt and how it is computed
- What is meant by conduit debt and how it is accounted for and reported
- The significance of other types of information that users want about debt—including credit enhancements, debt margin, payout schedules, reserve funds, and key ratios
- The role of rating agencies

This chapter focuses on long-term obligations, including liabilities (such as bonds) that are accorded balance sheet recognition, and other commitments (such as loan guarantees) that may be disclosed only in notes. Liabilities may be interpreted as negative long-lived assets. They present comparable issues of valuation and reporting and, for the most part, are accounted for as mirror images of their asset counterparts, which were discussed in Chapter 7. Governments exclude long-term liabilities from governmental funds but report them in their government-wide statement, just as both businesses and not-for-profits do—that is, on a full accrual basis. Long-term liabilities are important to governments and not-for-profits for the same reasons they are to businesses. They represent claims on the entity's resources; failure to satisfy them can seriously jeopardize the entity's ability to provide the services expected of it.

The first major section of this chapter sets forth the goals of long-term debt reporting. The next section raises the intriguing question of whether governments and not-for-profits can, like businesses, go bankrupt if they fail to meet their obligations. The third section is

directed to the "debits and credits" of accounting for long-term debt by governments. The fourth section addresses the issue of what types of obligations should be included within the rubric long-term debt for reporting, legal, and analytical purposes. The fifth section discusses credit enhancements and other features of debt that are of concern to statement users. The concluding section pertains to bond ratings, a subject common to both governments and not-for-profits.

WHY IS INFORMATION ON LONG-TERM DEBT IMPORTANT TO STATEMENT USERS?

The issues addressed in this chapter are closely tied to a key objective of financial reporting. As stated by the GASB:

> Financial reporting should provide information about the financial position and condition of a government entity. *Financial reporting should provide information about resources and obligations, both actual and contingent, current and noncurrent. The major financial resources of most governmental entities are derived from the ability to tax and issue debt. As a result, financial reporting should provide information about tax sources, tax limitations, tax burdens and debt limitations.*[1]

The FASB has set forth similar objectives for not-for-profits, emphasizing the importance of information on liquidity and cash flows.

Information on long-term debt is especially important to statement users because an entity's failure to make timely payments of interest and principal can have profound repercussions, for both its creditors and itself. Creditors will obviously incur losses. But insofar as governments and not-for-profits rely on debt to fund acquisitions of infrastructure, buildings, and equipment, a loss of credit standing can seriously harm their ability to provide the services expected of them.

CAN GOVERNMENTS AND NOT-FOR-PROFITS GO BANKRUPT?

An entity's failure to satisfy claims against it can produce dire results, including bankruptcy. In such a situation both governments and not-for-profits can seek protection under the Federal Bankruptcy Code, just as individuals and businesses can. Not-for-profits are covered under the same chapter of the code as businesses—although creditors cannot force not-for-profits into bankruptcy as they can with businesses; a special section of the code—Chapter 9—covers governments.

Until recently bankruptcy filings by major governments have been rare, although several cities such as New York, Yonkers, Washington, DC, Pontiac and Benton Harbor (Michigan), and Bridgeport (Connecticut) avoided bankruptcy only by being brought under the authority of "financial control boards" by higher-level governments. Bankruptcies were confined mainly to smaller governments especially utility districts. The economic downturn that started in 2007 changed that. According to the National Association of State Budget Officers, only 239 municipalities declared bankruptcy between 1980 and 2010.[2] Since 2010 at least 61 municipalities declared bankruptcy.[3] The largest of them were Jefferson County (Alabama), Harrisburg (Pennsylvania), Boise County (Idaho), Detroit (Michigan), San Bernardino and Stockton (California), and Central Falls (Rhode Island). Although general-purpose governments such as these receive the bulk of the popular press on the subject, most municipal bankruptcies are special districts that are created for particular purposes. For example, about 12 sanitary districts in Omaha (Nebraska) have declared bankruptcy since 2010.

As suggested by the "In Practice: Not so Easy to Declare Municipal Bankruptcy," the concept of municipal bankruptcy is elusive. Governments have the power to tax and in return are

[1] GASB Concepts Statement No. 1, *Objectives of Financial Reporting* (May 1987), para. 79.

[2] "Municipal Bankruptcy and the Role of the States, August 21, 2012.

[3] Governing Magazine at http://www.governing.com/gov-data/municipal-cities-counties-bankruptcies-and-defaults.html (accessed March 2, 2018).

expected to provide certain essential services. In a sense, their access to resources is limited only by the wealth of their population. Correspondingly, their expenditures can be reduced to zero by cutting back on services. In reality, however, there are practical limits to both their taxing authority and the extent to which they can eliminate services. Raise taxes above a certain level, and both residents and businesses flee the jurisdiction, thereby reducing overall revenues. Reduce services below a certain point, and the safety and overall well-being of the community are impaired. In addition, state and federal laws narrowly define the conditions under which governments may declare bankruptcy. Moreover, many special districts do not have unlimited taxation power and are instead limited to charging fees that may be insufficient for their long-term financial health.

When a court does grant a government bankruptcy protection, it temporarily transfers control over the government's affairs to an independent trustee. The eventual outcome, with the court's approval, is that the government's debts are reduced, and as indicated in the accompanying In Practice, the government may be permitted to void both its contracts with its labor unions and its pension promises to retirees.

In 2009, the GASB issued Statement No. 58, *Accounting and Financial Reporting for* Chapter 9 *Bankruptcies*. The statement requires that when a bankruptcy plan is approved by the bankruptcy court, the government should revalue all liabilities that the court has permitted it to restructure. Correspondingly, it should report a gain on the restatement. Governments that are not expected to emerge from bankruptcy as going concerns should also remeasure and restate their assets to reflect the amount they would expect to receive on liquidation.

IN PRACTICE IT IS NOT SO EASY TO DECLARE MUNICIPAL BANKRUPTCY

In 1994 Orange County, California, filed what up until then involved the greatest amount of liabilities ($1.6 billion) in U.S. history. Orange County was one of the wealthiest counties in the country and owing to the strength of its underlying economy was quickly able to regain strong investment grade credit rating and issue new debt.

Ironically, in 1991, the U.S. Bankruptcy Court, in a precedent-setting decision, denied the petition of Bridgeport Connecticut, one of the poorest cities in the country, to declare bankruptcy and thereby reduce some of its debts. Bridgeport officials testified that the city already had fewer police officers than required to provide adequate services, that reduced garbage collections created a rodent and arson hazard, and that closure of senior citizen centers were adversely affecting a large portion of the city's most vulnerable population. Nevertheless the court held that the key test for bankruptcy is whether the city is, in fact, **insolvent**—that is, it has either failed, or is unable, to pay its debts as they come due. Bridgeport, the court declared had not yet failed to meet its required debt payments and, owing to a cash reserve, could likely meet its debts in the future.

Prichard, Alabama, is a sad story similar to Bridgeport. Like Bridgeport, Prichard (population approximately 27,600) has one of the lowest median household incomes in the nation. When, after years of fiscal mismanagement, it was forced, in 2010, to file for bankruptcy protection again (having done so initially in 1999), the court blocked its petition on the grounds that it failed to satisfy certain conditions set forth in Alabama law—specifically that bond debt (rather than unfunded pensions) was required for bankruptcy protection. A key consequence of the court's refusal to grant bankruptcy relief was that retired city employees had to absorb an approximately two-thirds reduction in their expected pensions; there was simply no money in the treasury to make the promised payments. In 2012, the Alabama Supreme Court permitted Prichard to move forward with bankruptcy protection.

In 2011, when Jefferson County, Alabama (which encompasses Birmingham) applied for bankruptcy, it surpassed Orange County as filing the largest bankruptcy petition in U.S. history at that time ($4 billion). Jefferson County's troubles stemmed from both internal corruption and the 2008 nationwide credit crunch that caused the unraveling of the complex transactions that the county had used to finance certain sewer bonds. Like Prichard, however, the bankruptcy court was initially unwilling to authorize bankruptcy as a means of reducing its debts, although it was permitted in 2012 as well. The courts retained oversight of the county's plan of adjustment to ensure compliance even as the county moved out of formal bankruptcy in 2013.

Harrisburg, Pennsylvania, is another high-profile city that has sought bankruptcy protection in 2011 but has faced state laws that limit the ability of municipalities to take that route to fiscal solvency. Harrisburg's financial difficulties could be attributed mainly to a misguided investment in an expensive, but decidedly environmentally unfriendly, trash incinerator.

In an earlier case, Vallejo, California, was permitted to declare bankruptcy. Notably in that case, the presiding bankruptcy judge permitted the city to void its union contracts. Over the objections of union attorneys, the judge ruled that various bankruptcy reforms that Congress passed in the 1990s did not provide public employees with the same protections that it granted private workers. Although the city initially planned to also cut workers' pensions, it backed off after the state's pension system, which administered Vallejo's plan, threatened long and costly litigation.

Central Falls, Rhode Island, on the other hand, in 2011 was not only permitted to declare bankruptcy but also, in contrast to Vallejo, was able to reduce its fiscally unsustainable pension obligations. In what was considered a groundbreaking settlement, the city's retired police and firefighters agreed to take sharp cuts in their pensions. The willingness of the retirees to grant the concessions was motivated by a new state law that put the claims of bondholders ahead of those of the retirees and a political environment in which pension benefits of government workers were considered overly generous.

The largest municipal bankruptcy to date occurred in 2013 when the city of Detroit filed for Chapter 9 bankruptcy. The city had long suffered a declining revenue base, shrinking population, oversized costs for retiree pensions and health care, corrupt elected officials, and borrowing to cover routine operating expenses. The initial application for bankruptcy was not accepted by the courts (as in the Alabama cases), but successful appeals followed, and Detroit was ruled eligible on nearly $19 billion in debt (made up of bonds and unfunded pension liabilities).

Opposition to bankruptcy can also come from actors other than the courts. San Bernardino, California, filed for bankruptcy in 2012, also straining under its labor and pension costs. The city halted its monthly payments to the California Public Employees' Retirement System (CalPERS) as part of its bankruptcy request. CalPERS, in turn, objected to the filing and asked the court to permit it to sue the city for the payments. The courts ruled in favor of the city's bankruptcy in 2013. However, the city and CalPERS arrived at a compromise in 2014 in which all missed city payments to CalPERS would be paid over time.

In August 2015 Puerto Rico defaulted on a $58 million bond payment. Although Puerto Rico is not covered by U.S. bankruptcy statutes, as of 2018 its debt is being restructured under the supervision of a special oversight board appointed by President Obama.

HOW DO GOVERNMENTS ACCOUNT FOR LONG-TERM OBLIGATIONS?

General long-term debt has been defined as:

> *Unmatured principal of bonds, warrants, notes, special assessment debt for which the government is obligated in some manner, or other forms of noncurrent or long-term general obligation debt that is not a specific liability of any proprietary fund or fiduciary fund. General long-term debt is not limited to liabilities arising from debt issuances per se, but may also include noncurrent liabilities on capital and operating leases, certificates of participation, compensated absences, claims and judgments, underfunded pension plan and underfunded OPEB contributions, special termination benefits, landfill closure and postclosure care, and other commitments that are not current liabilities properly recorded in governmental funds.*[4]

General long-term debt is the obligation of the government at large and is thereby backed by the government's general "full faith and credit" and revenue-raising powers. It is distinguished from *revenue* debt, which is secured only by designated revenue streams—such as from utility fees, highway tolls, rents, receipts from student loans, and patient billings.

The long-term debts of governments by no means include *all* their financial obligations, no more than do those of businesses. As a general rule, only debts resulting from past transactions for which the government *has already received a benefit* are recognized. Reported obligations thereby exclude commitments for payments of interest when the government has not yet enjoyed the use of the borrowed funds, the salary of a city manager that, although

[4] *GASB Codification, Section 1500.103.*

contractually guaranteed, has not been earned, and amounts owed under long-term service contracts when the promised services have not yet been provided. What cannot be stressed strongly enough is that in assessing the fiscal wherewithal of a government, these "unrecorded" obligations can be as significant as those that are recorded. After all, the contractual commitment of a government to make timely payments of interest on a bond or payroll payments to an employee is no less of a legal obligation than to pay the principal on the bond or the installments on a capital lease.

ACCOUNTING FOR LONG-TERM OBLIGATIONS IN GOVERNMENTAL FUNDS

As previously emphasized, **governmental funds** focus on financial resources. A long-term obligation does not require current-year appropriation or expenditure of governmental fund financial resources. Therefore, as noted by the National Council of Governmental Accounting (NCGA), "to include it as a governmental fund liability would be misleading and dysfunctional to the current period management control (e.g., budgeting) and accountability functions."[5]

When the proceeds of long-term debt are received by governmental funds, the debit to cash (or other assets) is offset with a credit to "other financing sources—bond proceeds," or some comparable account signifying an inflow of resources, not by crediting a liability. Just as the existence of buildings, vehicles, and other long-term assets is ignored in governmental funds, so also are long-term debts, including the portion of bonds, notes, claims and judgments, and obligations for sick leave and vacations for which payment is not required out of resources appropriated for the current year. As a consequence, long-term debt includes amounts arising out of operating as well as capital transactions. As emphasized in previous chapters, the expenditures relating to these operating transactions will be charged in the periods in which the resources are appropriated for payment—in effect, when the long-term debts are liquidated—not necessarily in those in which the government reaped the benefits.

DIFFERENCES IN GOVERNMENT-WIDE (FULL ACCRUAL) STATEMENTS

In their government-wide statements, governments should account for their general long-term obligations in the same manner as do businesses. They record debt either at face value or, if the debt is issued at a premium or discount, at the unamortized issue price. Debt costs (except for prepaid insurance costs) are reported as an outflow of resources in the period in which the debt is issued rather than as an asset. Each period they must amortize the premium or discount, offsetting the unamortized premium or discount with a decrease or increase respectively in interest expense.

A bond premium or discount represents the difference between the face value of a bond and the amount for which it is issued. A bond is sold at a premium whenever its specified interest rate (its coupon rate) is greater than interest rates prevailing at the time of issuance (the yield rate). It is sold at a discount whenever the specified rate is less than the prevailing rates. The greater the difference between the coupon rate and the yield rate and the greater the number of years to maturity, the greater is the premium or discount. Just as a government must include a schedule of changes in capital assets in notes to its financial statements, so must it also present a corresponding schedule of changes in long-term obligations. This schedule of changes should incorporate not only debts—such as bonds, notes, and leases—but also other liabilities—such as compensated absences and claims and judgments. It should show the beginning and ending balances and the increases and decreases during the year.

The portion of the schedule of Changes in Long-Term Liabilities for Charlotte, North Carolina, pertaining to governmental activities is presented in Table 8-1.

[5] NCGA Statement No. 1, *Governmental Accounting and Financial Reporting Principles* (March 1979), para. 44.

TABLE 8-1 Charlotte, North Carolina Schedule of Changes in Long-Term Liabilities Government Activities Only, June 30, 2017 (dollar amounts in thousands)

	Beginning Balance	Additions	Reductions	Ending Balance	Due Within One Year
Governmental Activities					
General obligation bonds	$ 570,993	$ 116,230	$ 39,846	$ 647,377	$ 45,631
Plus unamortized premiums	76,456	19,377	5,990	89,843	6,441
Total bonds payable	647,449	135,607	45,836	737,220	52,072
Special obligation bonds	6,215	—	1,115	5,100	1,175
Installment purchases	740,476	—	56,229	684,247	58,929
Plus unamortized premiums	28,100	—	3,452	24,648	3,147
Less unamortized discounts	(721)	—	(32)	(689)	(32)
Total installment purchases	767,855	—	59,649	708,206	62,044
General obligation bond anticipation notes	—	34,503	—	34,503	—
Commercial paper notes payable	133,323	1,677	135,000	—	—
Derivative instrument liability	67,220	—	21,728	45,492	—
Swaption borrowing payable	7,328	—	553	6,775	538
Compensated absences	51,964	37,214	32,888	56,290	26,039
Section 108 loan guarantee	5,780	—	—	5,780	—
Due to participants	11,596	1,019	—	12,615	—
Net pension liability (LGERS)	19,164	75,597	—	94,761	—
Total pension liability (LEO)	108,318	—	534	107,784	—
Unfunded OPEB liability	15,272	2,819	—	18,091	—
Total governmental activities	$1,841,484	$288,436	$297,303	$1,832,617	$141,868

Example

Accounting for Bonds in Government-Wide Statements

A city issues $10 million of 6 percent, 20-year term bonds at a price of $10,234,930 (i.e., at a premium of $234,930). The issue price provides an effective yield of 5.8 percent per year (2.9 percent per semiannual period).

The city would recognize the issuance of the bonds in its government-wide statements as follows:

Cash	$10,234,930	
Bonds payable		$10,000,000
Bond premium		234,930
To record the issuance of bonds		

Upon making its first semiannual interest payment of $300,000, the city would report an interest expense of $296,813, which represents the yield rate of 2.9 percent times $10,234,930, the book value of the liability (bonds payable plus bond premium). Thus,

Bond interest expense	$296,813	
Bond premium	3,187	
Cash		$300,000
To record the first semiannual payment of bond interest		

This entry would reduce the unamortized premium to $231,743, so the bond interest expense to be reported when the second payment is made would be only $296,721 (2.9 percent of $10,231,743):

Bond interest expense	$296,721	
Bond premium	3,279	
Cash		$300,000
To record the second semiannual payment of bond interest		

By contrast, in the city's capital projects fund (or whichever governmental fund received the proceeds of the bond issuance) no liability would be recognized; the cash received would be offset by "other financing sources—bond proceeds." The periodic interest expenditures in the debt service fund (or whichever governmental fund paid the interest) would be in the amount of the required cash payment, not the cash payment less the amortization of the premium.

IN PRACTICE VALUING A LOTTERY PRIZE

An accountant lucky enough to win the state lottery may have the opportunity to strike a blow for truth in government accounting as well as advertising. Lottery prizes are almost always paid out over an extended period of time, commonly 20 years. When presented with the first $3 million installment of a much publicized prize of $60 million, for example, the winner should graciously thank the government official presenting the check. But he or she should also point out that, contrary to the government's advertisements and publicity campaigns, the economic value of the prize (assuming a discount rate of 6 percent) is only $34,409,764—sufficient to provide a comfortable living, but nevertheless only 57 percent of the prize's stated value.

For many governments the issue of valuing the prize liability on their balance sheets never arises. Rather than appropriating funds over the payout period, they satisfy the obligation immediately by setting aside sufficient resources (in this example, $34,409,764) in a trust fund, or purchasing an "annuity" from a private financial institution, to ensure that the required payments are made.

WHAT CONSTITUTES A GOVERNMENT'S LONG-TERM DEBT?

The basic entries required to account for liabilities are, for the most part, unambiguous. However, when an obligation should be characterized as a liability and whether it should be classified as long term or short term is much less clear.

The issue of whether an obligation should be reported as a long term rather than a current liability is especially consequential in governments because it determines not just in which *section* of a balance sheet it should be reported, but even on *which* balance sheet. Governments account for short-term liabilities—those expected to be liquidated with currently available assets—within governmental funds. They report long-term liabilities (except for those relating to proprietary and fiduciary funds) only in government-wide statements. Thus, if assets are held constant, short-term debt reduces a government's general-fund (or other governmental fund) balance, whereas long-term debt does not.

TERM VERSUS SERIAL BONDS

Although for pedagogical purposes it is convenient to illustrate *term bonds*, in reality governments are more likely to issue *serial bonds*. An issue of term bonds will mature on a single date—perhaps 20 or 30 years in the future. An issue of serial bonds, by contrast, will mature in installments over a series of dates on a piecemeal basis—perhaps one-twentieth of the issue will mature each year over a period of 20 years. Serial bonds present no conceptual problems, for they can be interpreted as a series of term bonds, with the bonds maturing on each separate date being seen as an independent issue. In fact, it is almost certain that each set of bonds will bear a different rate of interest, most probably with the interest rates increasing as the maturity dates extend further into the future. Serial bonds make sense in that they ensure that each year's taxpayers pay their fair share of not only bond interest, but also of bond principal. Thus, serial bonds are consistent with the concept of interperiod equity—in which taxpayers of each period pay for the goods or services that they consume. In the case of the bonds, the taxpayers will, in effect, be paying for the use of the assets that those bonds financed.

DEMAND BONDS: CURRENT OR LONG-TERM LIABILITIES

Demand bonds are obligations that permit the holder (the lender) to demand redemption within a specified period of time, usually 1 to 30 days after giving notice. They are referred to as *put bonds* because the right of redemption is the equivalent of a put (or sell) option. Although demand bonds may have maturity periods of up to 30 years, their redemption date is not only uncertain but is beyond the issuers' control. Issuers cannot classify them with confidence as long-term (i.e., nonfundable) obligations because they may have to redeem them at any time. Yet they may be overly conservative in classifying them as short-term obligations, because they may not have to redeem them until maturity.

One apparent resolution to the classification dilemma is for the issuer to estimate the proportion of bonds likely to be called within the short term (similar to estimating the proportion of receivables that will be uncollectible). It would classify these as governmental fund obligations and the balance as nonfund liabilities. But this solution is specious in that it fails to consider the inherent characteristics of the bonds and the reasons for redemption.

Demand bonds are issued to permit the borrower to take advantage of the lower interest rates paid on short-term obligations. If prevailing short-term rates increase, then the bondholders will no longer find them attractive. They will demand redemption so that they can use the funds to purchase higher yielding bonds. Because the economic conditions motivating redemption are common to all bondholders, the issuer should expect that if some bonds are presented for redemption, they all will be. In substance, therefore, demand bonds, from the perspective of the lender, are short-term, not long-term, instruments because the lender has made no long-term commitments and has assumed no long-term risks.

Most issuers provide for the possibility of redemption by arranging with a financial institution to convert the bonds to long-term notes. In a contract called a **take-out agreement**, the financial institution promises to lend the issuer sufficient funds to repay the bonds. The payback period on the notes is usually long term, sometimes 10 years or more. Thus, if the borrower-issuer is assured that as a result of the take-out agreement it will not have to come up with the cash to redeem the demand bonds in the short term, the demand bondscan rightfully be viewed as a long-term instrument.

GASB STANDARDS

In a 1984 interpretation, the GASB tied the classification of demand bonds to the take-out agreement. Demand bonds that are exercisable within one year of the balance sheet date, it said, should be reported as *long-term* liabilities only in the government-wide statement of net position (not in the balance sheet of a governmental fund) as long as the entity has entered into a take-out agreement that satisfies the following criteria:

- It does not expire within one year.
- It is not cancelable by the lender or prospective lender during that year.
- The lender or prospective lender is financially capable of honoring the take-out agreement.[6]

If the demand bonds do not satisfy these criteria, then they should be reported as liabilities of the governmental fund receiving the proceeds. Usually this would be a capital projects fund.

[6] GASB Interpretation No. 1, *Demand Bonds Issued by State and Local Governmental Entities* (December 1984), para. 10. GASB Codification, para. D30.108.

The statement does not specify the interest rate to be paid by the borrower on loans resulting from the take-out agreement. Thus, in the event the bonds had to be redeemed, the issuer might have to pay a considerably higher interest rate on the new loan than on the old.

Example

Demand Bonds

A government issues $20 million of demand bonds and obtains an acceptable take-out agreement from a bank. In a governmental fund, it would record the bond proceeds like those from any other long-term obligation:

Cash	$20	
Proceeds from sale of demand bonds		$20

To record the proceeds of the demand bonds (in a capital projects or other fund receiving the bond proceeds)

If the demand bonds do not qualify as long-term debt because the government did not obtain an acceptable take-out agreement, then the government would record the bonds as a governmental fund liability as if they were current obligations:

Cash	$20	
Bonds payable		$20

To record the proceeds of the demand bonds (in a capital projects or other fund receiving the bond proceeds)

The government would report the demand bonds as a liability in its government-wide statement of net position irrespective of whether it reports them as a government fund liability. However, if it reports them as governmental fund liability, then it would classify them as it does its other short-term debts; otherwise, it would report them along with its other long-term obligations.

BOND ANTICIPATION NOTES

Bond anticipation notes (BANs) present an issue similar to that of demand bonds—should the debt be classified as current (and thereby reported as a governmental fund liability) or as long-term (and reported only in the government-wide statements)? BANs are short-term notes issued by the lender with the expectation that they will soon be replaced by long-term bonds. Governments can issue BANs only after obtaining the necessary voter approval and legislative authorization to issue long-term bonds. Their advantage is that BANs enable governments to postpone issuing the bonds in the hope of obtaining more favorable long-term interest rates or to begin work on construction projects without having to wait until they have cleared the lengthy administrative and legal hurdles to issue the bonds.

If a government can, as planned, refund the BANs with long-term bonds, then the notes are, in essence, long-term obligations; the government will not have to repay them with current financial resources. However, if it is unable to refund them, then it must repay them when due—and must have on hand the requisite cash.

The issue of whether to classify the BANs as short term or long term is not as intractable as that of demand bonds. Governments do not typically issue financial statements until at least three months after the close of the fiscal year. By then, they have usually either issued the long-term bonds or consummated an agreement to do so.

GASB STANDARDS

Generally accepted accounting principles provide that a government may recognize BANs as long-term obligations if, by the *date the financial statements are issued*, "all legal steps have been taken to refinance the bond anticipation notes and the intent is supported by an ability to consummate refinancing of the short-term on a long-term basis."[7] Evidence of this comes through meeting the conditions initially set forth by the FASB in Statement No. 6, *Classification of Short-Term Obligations Expected to Be Refinanced:*

The entity has already refinanced the BANs; or

1. It has entered into a financing agreement that

   a. Does not expire within one year of the balance sheet date and is noncancelable by the lender;

   b. Has not been violated as of the balance sheet date; and

   c. Is capable of being honored by the lender.

[7] NCGA Interpretation No. 9, *Certain Fund Classifications and Balance Sheet Accounts* (April 1984), para. 12; also FASB ASC 470-10-45[7] FASB ASC 840-10-15.

Example

Bond Anticipation Notes

A government issues $3 million of 90-day BANs. Because the government expects to roll them over into long-term bonds, it would record the proceeds in a governmental fund—such as a capital projects fund. It would not recognize a liability in that fund:

Cash	$3	
Proceeds from sale of bond anticipation notes		$3
To record the proceeds of the BANs		

If, however, by the time the financial statements were issued, it were unable to demonstrate the ability to refinance the BANs, then it would "correct" this entry so that the BANs were recorded as a liability rather than as a source of financial resources:

Proceeds from sale of bond anticipation notes	$3	
Bond anticipation notes payable		$3
To reclassify the BANs as a short-term fund obligation		

As with demand bonds, governments would report the obligations as liabilities in their government-wide statements, regardless of whether they must also report them as fund liabilities. They must, however, be sure to properly describe and classify them—for example, as BANs or bonds, and as short- or long-term obligations.

TAX ANTICIPATION AND REVENUE ANTICIPATION NOTES

Governments usually do not receive their taxes or other revenues evenly throughout the year. Property taxes, for example, may not be due until three or more months after the start of a fiscal year. To meet cash and other expenditure needs earlier in the year, governments can issue **tax anticipation notes (TANs)** and **revenue anticipation notes (RANs)** or a combination of both known as TRANs—short-term notes payable out of specified streams of revenues.

Like bond anticipation notes, TANs and RANs are a means of borrowing against expected cash proceeds. But unlike bond anticipation notes, they will not be converted into long-term instruments. Therefore, they must be accounted for in the funds in which the related revenues will be reported; they cannot be relegated to off-balance-sheet status.

Example

Tax Anticipation Notes

A government issues $5 million of TANs, backed by property taxes that will be recorded in the general fund. The appropriate general-fund entries to record both the issuance and subsequent repayment of the notes are as follows:

Cash	$5	
Tax anticipation notes payable		$5
To record the issuance of a TAN		
Tax anticipation notes payable	$5	
Cash		$5
To record the repayment of a TAN		

LEASES

In 2017, the GASB issued Statement No. 87, *Leases* (effective for years beginning after December 15, 2019) that significantly altered how governments must account for leases. Under the new standard, virtually all leases with terms of one-year or more must be accounted for as financing (also known as a capital) leases.[8]

In the past, leases could be accounted for as either operating leases or a financing leases, depending on whether they met certain specified criteria. An operating lease is accounted for as a "conventional" rental agreement— that is like a typical apartment or short-term car rental. The **lessee** recognizes an expense for the applicable rent as it makes use of the asset and correspondingly credits cash (or an increase in a liability if it delays payment, or a reduction in an asset if it had prepaid the rent in advance).

A **financing lease**, by contrast, is one that is accounted for, in essence, as a purchase/borrow arrangement. That is, the lessee accounts for the lease as if it had purchased the right to the asset for all or a portion of its useful life and borrowed the purchase price. Upon signing the lease it would report an asset equal to value of the rights and a corresponding liability to the lessor equal to the amount owed —that is the present value of the lease payments. Over the term of the lease it would amortize (i.e., depreciate) the right-to-use asset, just as it would any capital asset with a limited economic life. At the same time, it would amortize the liability and recognize an appropriate interest expense just as if it had borrowed the funds to acquire the asset.

The underlying rationale for the new rules that require that all leases other than very short-term leases be accounted for as financing leases is that the lessee receives the contractual right to use an underlying asset for a specified period of time and in exchange finances that right with an obligation to make specified payments (which include an element of interest) over time. Conversely, the **lessor** surrenders the right to use the asset for the specified period and in return receives a promise of future payments. Both the lessee and the lessor should recognize this economic reality of the arrangement and most notably should give the appropriate recognition to the assets and liabilities that the lease creates.

How Does the GASB Define a Lease?

The GASB defines a lease as "a contract that conveys control of the right to use another entity's nonfinancial asset (the underlying asset) as specified in the contract for a period of time in an exchange or exchange-like transaction." Statement No. 87 covers leases of capital assets such as buildings, land, and equipment. However, mainly because of their unique characteristics, it explicitly excludes leases of intangible assets such as computer software, mineral rights, motion picture rights as well as leases of inventory and timber lands.

How Is the Term of a Lease Determined?

Determining the term of a lease might seem straight-forward—the period specified in the lease contract. Regrettably, it is not so simple. Leases may contain options that allow either the lessee or the lessor to prematurely cancel the lease or to extend it for additional periods beyond the stated expiration date. In some circumstances the terms of the lease may be such that one of the parties will have compelling economic incentives either to extend or to prematurely terminate the lease. In others, the decisions of the parties to extend or prematurely terminate may depend on conditions that cannot be foreseen at the time the lease is signed. Accordingly, it may not be clear whether such extension or termination options are likely to be exercised. Statement No. 87 specifies that the lease term is the period during which the lessee has a noncancelable right to use

[8] An exception is made for certain "regulated" leases that are subject to external regulations and legal rulings. For example, the U.S. Department of Transportation and the Federal Aviation Administration establish rules governing airport facilities, such as gates.

the asset plus any periods for which it is "reasonably certain" the lease will be extended or terminated given the options available to either the lessee or lessor to extend or terminate the lease. Without this "reasonably certain" test, it should be noted, a government could sign a 364 day lease with numerous options to extend that they fully intended to exercise. In that way it could account for the arrangement as a short-term (i.e., operating) lease and thereby avoid having to report a long-term liability.

Government leases frequently contain **nonappropriation clauses** (sometimes called **fiscal funding clauses**). These provisions stipulate that a government's legislative body must explicitly appropriate each year's lease payments. If it fails to do so the government has the right to cancel the lease, typically on an annual basis. These clauses, however, are rarely exercised, if for no other reason that the lease may also include severe penalties if the government does so. Statement No. 87 explicitly indicates that these clauses should not affect the lease term unless it is reasonably certain that the government will exercise the clause.

Example

Lessee Accounting

A municipality signs a three-year lease for construction equipment agreeing to make annual payments of $200,000. Based on an interest rate of 4 percent that is implicit in the agreement, the present value of liability is $555,018 (i.e., the present value of an annuity of $200,000 for three years discounted at 4 percent).

Upon entering into the lease, the municipality would make the following entry in its government-wide statements (or any fund accounted for on a full accrual basis):

Government-wide statements

Equipment held under lease (a long-live asset)	$555,018	
Lease liability		$555,018

To record the right to use equipment under a lease and the corresponding obligations

As it makes its first lease payment of $200,000 it would allocate the payment between interest expense and a reduction in the liability:

Government-wide statements

Interest expense (lease interest)	$22,201	
Lease liability	177,799	
Cash		$200,000

To record the first lease payment (Interest expense equals 4 percent of $555,018)

At the same time, if would amortize (depreciate) the lease asset. Assuming that it opted to use the straight-line method (although any systematic and rational method would be appropriate):

Government-wide statements

Amortization of equipment held under lease	$185,006	
Equipment held under lease		$185,006

To record amortization of the lease asset ($555,018 divided by 3)

In years two and three, the cash payment of $200,000 would remain the same but as the liability is reduced, so also would the interest expense. Thus, the interest expense in years two and three would be $15,089 and $7,692, respectively (4 percent of each year's remaining balance of the liability) and the reduction in the liability in those years would be $184,911 and $192,308 (a total, of course, over the three-years of $555,018). The annual amortization, assuming the straight-line method would continue to be $185,006 per year.

In an appropriate governmental fund, the municipality would account for the lease similarly to how it would account for other borrowing arrangements:

Governmental fund		
Long-lived asset expenditure	$555,018	
Other financing sources—leases		$555,018
To record the right to use equipment under lease		

Governmental fund		
Debt service expenditure (lease interest)	$ 22,201	
Debt service expenditure (lease principal)	177,799	
Cash		$200,000
To record the first lease payment		

Example

Lessor Accounting

Assume now that a county, as a lessor, leases equipment to other governments. The county signs a three-year lease for construction equipment with a municipality. The municipality agrees to make annual payments of $200,000. As in the previous example, based on the interest rate of 4 percent that is implicit in the agreement, the present value of the county's lease receivable is $555,018. Assume, in addition, that the county had purchased the equipment at a cost of $800,000 and that the useful life of the equipment is 10 years. Thus, the county is leasing the equipment to the municipality for only three of its 10-year economic life. Presumably, therefore when the county returns the equipment to the municipality it will still provide seven more years of economic benefit.

Generally speaking, the lessor should account for the transaction as the mirror image of the lessee. That is, the lessor should account for it as a sale/lending transaction. Unfortunately, there may be—and in this example, there is—a complication. The lessor is not selling rights to the entire asset, only the right to use three years out of a total economic life of 10 years. In a conventional sale of a long-lived asset a seller would recognize a receivable equal to the present value of the consideration to be received and correspondingly would derecognize the adjusted historical cost of the asset sold (i.e., its "book" value). The difference between the two would be recognized as a gain on the sale. However, when the right to use asset for only a portion of the asset's total life is sold it may be impractical to determine the historical cost of such portion and the amount thereby to be derecognized. Consider, for example, the difficulty of determining the amount to be derecognized when a lessor leases a portion of a building (e.g., one floor of many) for only a few years of the building's useful life.

The GASB determined that upon signing a lease the lessor should not derecognize any portion of the underlying asset to be leased. Instead, it should offset the receivable from the lessee with a deferred inflow of resources of an equal amount. Then, as the receivable is reduced as the lessee makes its payments it should reduce the deferred inflow by the same amount. Hence, the deferred inflow of resources, with its credit balance would always be equal to the receivable, with its debit balance. The lessor would continue to recognize the underlying leased asset and depreciate over its anticipated full useful life as it would any other long-lived asset.

In our example, upon signing the lease, the lessor county would recognize a receivable, offset by a deferred inflow of resources, in the amount of the present value of the anticipated lease receipts:

Government-wide statements		
Lease receivable	$555,018	
Deferred inflow of resources (leases)		$555,018
To record the signing of the lease		

As it receives the lease payments, it would recognize interest on the receivable and reduce the balances of both the receivable and the offsetting deferred inflow of resources, recognizing revenue from both interest and the rental of the equipment.

Government-wide statements		
Cash	$200,000	
Interest revenue (leases)		$ 22,201
Lease receivable		177,799
To record collection of the first lease payment		

Government-wide statements		
Deferred inflow of resources (leases)	$177,799	
Lease revenue		$177,799
To recognize lease revenue		

At the same time, the lessor would depreciate the underlying asset that it had acquired for $800,000 (and that we presume had been previously recorded) over its remaining economic life of 10 years.

Government-wide statements		
Depreciation expense	$ 80,000	
Allowance for depreciation (construction equipment)		$ 80,000
To record depreciation on the construction equipment (straight-line method)		

In years two and three, in symmetry with the entries made by the lessee, the interest portion of the cash collected would decrease, while that of the receivable would decrease. At the conclusion of the lease the balances in both the receivable and the deferred inflow of resources would be reduced to zero. Total revenue (both interest on the receivable and from the right to use the equipment) would be $600,000 ($200,000 per year). The book value of the equipment would be $560,000, reflecting that 3/10th of its economic life had been consumed.

The lessor, in its governmental funds, would make entries to record both the initiation of the lease and the subsequent receipt of lease payments similar to those for its government-wide statements or its proprietary funds. These entries are not the mirror image of those made by the lessee mainly because the current financial resources measurement focus includes long-term receivables, but not long-term liabilities. The lessor, would not, of course, record either the underlying asset (the leased equipment) or depreciation on such an asset in its governmental funds.

Governmental fund		
Lease receivable	$ 555,018	
Deferred inflow of resources (leases)		$555,018
To record the signing of the lease		

Governmental fund		
Cash	$200,000	
Interest revenue (leases)		$ 22,201
Lease receivable		177,799
To record collection of the first lease payment		

Governmental fund		
Deferred inflow of resources (leases)	$177,799	
Lease revenue		$177,799
To recognize lease revenue		

Both lessees and lessors are required to make extensive disclosures about their lease activities. These include general descriptions of their leases, key terms, and amounts of inflows and outflows of resources.

Not surprisingly, the accounting for financing leases may be considerably more complex than might be inferred from the above entries. Other issues to be considered, and which are addressed in Statement No. 87 include the accounting for:

- mid-lease modifications to the lease terms
- leases with multiple components (e.g., a lease of a copy machine that includes not only the right to use the machine but also repair and maintenance services)
- sale and leaseback transactions and subleases
- leases with variable payments (e.g., a copy machine lease in which the payments are based on number of copies made).

How Should Short-Term Leases Be Accounted For

Short-term leases are accounted for as **operating leases**. The lessee would debit an outflow of resources (either expenditure or expense) during the period the asset is used. Corresponding, it would credit cash (or, as appropriate a prepaid rent or rent payable account). The lessor would do the opposite, crediting an inflow of resources (a revenue) and debiting as appropriate cash, rent receivable or rent received in advance accounts.

FASB LEASING STANDARDS

Not-for-profit organizations must adhere to the FASB leasing standards, which are far more complex than those of the GASB.[9] The FASB, like the GASB, requires that a *lessee* must recognize both assets and liabilities for the rights and obligations created by other than short-term leases. However, the FASB continues to distinguish between capital (financing) leases and operating leases, a distinction it bases on whether the lessee effectively obtains control of the underlying asset. For capital leases, the lessee will have to recognize and report separately the amortization of the right-to-use asset and the interest on the lease liability. For operating leases, however, it can recognize and report the lease payments as single lease expenses.

For *lessors*, the FASB distinguishes between three types of leases: sales type, direct financing and operating. Sales type and direct financing leases are similar to each other. In a sales-type lease the lessor, in effect, sells the entire asset to the lessee and hence expects to profit from both the sale of the asset (i.e., the difference between selling price and book value) and interest from financing the sale. Hence, in accounting for the lease, the lessor would recognize a portion of the revenue from the lease payment (in essence, the profit on the sale of the asset) at the inception of the lease and the balance (the interest) over the life of the lease. A direct financing lease is also a form of capital lease except that the lessor expects to profit only from the interest earned over the term of the lease, not from the sale. Accordingly, the lessor recognizes income as the interest is earned over time.

For operating leases, those that are not considered sales or direct financings, both the lessee and the lessor would recognize expenses or revenues over the term of the lease, generally on a straight-line basis.

[9] The FASB standards are incorporated in ASC 842.

Why Might Leasing Be a Costly Substitute for Conventional Financing?

Governments enter into some leases for the same reasons as individuals and businesses—they need an asset for only a small part of its useful life or they wish to avoid risks of ownership, such as declines in market value and technological obsolescence.

As suggested earlier, a government may also enter into leasing arrangement as a means of financing what is, in economic substance, an asset purchase. In fact, a lease may be structured like an ordinary mortgage note or a coupon bond. The lessor (the lender) may be a manufacturer, retailer, or financing institution. If it were a financing institution it would first purchase the property from the retailer or manufacturer on behalf of, and for lease to, the ultimate user (the purchaser/borrower). The financing institution may even sell shares in the lease (called **certificates of participation** or *COPs*) to investors for whom the shares would be an alternative to bonds or notes. If the lessee were a government, then the shares might be exempt from federal taxation, just as if they were the government's bonds.

Financing-type leases are almost always secured only by the leased assets, not by the issuer's full faith and credit. The leased assets, however, are often inadequate as collateral. First, if seized by the lessor, they may have only limited value. If a government were to abrogate its lease, it may do so for the very reason that the property is of less value than anticipated (e.g., it has become technologically obsolete). Second, seizing government property might be extremely costly in terms of bad publicity and public ill will. After all, which local bank or finance company would like to be shown on the six o'clock news repossessing a city's ambulance or emergency communications equipment? In addition, to the extent that the leases contain nonappropriation clauses, the government may have a ready-made opportunity to cancel the lease. Therefore, leases are decidedly less attractive to lenders than comparable full faith and credit instruments and the lenders demand greater returns.

Why then would a government opt to finance the acquisition of an asset with a lease rather than a conventional bond or bank loan? A primary answer is that leasing may be an effective means of circumventing debt limitations. Restrictions on the amount of debt that state and local governments are permitted to incur were first imposed in the 1840s. During a period of rapid growth between 1820 and 1837, many states financed public works—such as railroads and canals—with general obligation debt. The bond proceeds were invested in the stock of private rail and canal companies, with the expectation that dividends from these companies would be sufficient to service the debt. When the economy collapsed in 1837, many companies failed, and governments were forced to default on their bonds.

To ensure fiscal discipline in the future, state governments limited the amount of debt they or their subdivisions could incur. The original limitations were expressed as fixed dollar amounts. Today, however, they are generally set as a percentage of the assessed value of the jurisdiction's property. Alternatively, the limits can be established indirectly through restrictions on tax and/or expenditure increases, balanced budget mandates, or requirements that voters approve either all debt or debt above a specified amount.

The extent to which lease obligations are considered as debt, and thereby subject to debt limitations, has been the object of extensive litigation. The outcomes vary by state, but in at least 26 states the courts have upheld financing leases as being beyond the purview of debt restrictions. As might be expected, the court decisions have often run counter to prevailing accounting and financial wisdom. For example, in some states the courts have keyed their opinions to the nonappropriation clauses, asserting that because the lease payments are subject to annual authorization, the leases lack the characteristics of long-term debts.

Leasing is especially popular in municipalities in which the debt limitations take the form of voter approvals and in which financing leases are not considered to be debts. It is a convenient means of acquiring assets that public officials might consider more essential to the public welfare than the electorate does. However, it is almost always a costly alternative to conventional financing.

LINKS BETWEEN REVENUE BONDS AND GENERAL OBLIGATION BONDS

Revenue bonds, unlike general obligation (GO) bonds, are backed only by specific revenues, frequently from a government's business-type activities. They are generally reported in enterprise funds and are thereby accounted for as if they were issued by a business. Nevertheless, revenue bonds are integrally linked to GO bonds, and the government's debt burden cannot be assessed without taking both into account.

Even if a government is legally responsible for servicing its revenue debt only out of designated revenues, fiscal reality may dictate that it back the bonds with its full faith and credit. Were a government to default on the revenue debt of one of its component units (e.g., a utility, convention center, parking garage, or airport), the fiscal community is likely to view the failure as one of the government at large. Thus, the credit standing of the entire government would be severely diminished, and the government would either be denied access to the credit markets or would be admitted only by paying a substantial interest penalty.

Governments generally have a choice whether to finance revenue-generating activities with GO or revenue bonds. Because revenue bonds (like capital leases) are not backed by the government's full faith and credit, they almost always bear higher interest rates than comparable GO bonds. Why then would a government issue the more costly revenue bonds? At least two reasons can be cited, both of which point to the interrelationship between the two types of securities:

- Revenue bonds, because they are not obligations of the government at large, are usually not subject to voter approvals or other forms of voter oversight. Therefore, revenue bonds are another means of circumventing constitutional or legislative constraints on GO borrowing.

- By using revenue bonds, the government can readily incorporate costs of debt service into user fees. Thus, the facilities financed by the bonds will be paid for out of user charges, not taxes or other general revenues. The costs will be shared among the constituents of the government in proportion to benefits received rather than the factors on which other taxes or revenues are based. Revenue bond financing may be especially appropriate when parties residing outside the government's property tax jurisdiction are to be the major users of the facilities. These parties might otherwise escape paying for the assets.

In addition, it should be noted that whereas any single incremental issue of revenue bonds is likely to be more costly than a comparable issue of GO bonds, the choice between the two types of debt may not affect the issuer's total borrowing costs. A government's total revenues and other resources available to service its debt are not changed by the type of debt issued. Accordingly, its overall risk of default remains the same irrespective of whether it issues GO or revenue bonds. The mix of bonds affects only the distribution of the risk among the bondholders. By issuing revenue bonds, the government shifts a portion of the risk—and the attendant interest costs—to the revenue bondholders, who are in a less secured position than the GO bondholders. Were the government to issue only GO bonds, however, the same risk and interest costs would have to be assumed by the GO bondholders, and the interest rates on the GO bonds would then increase.

OVERLAPPING DEBT

Overlapping debt refers to the obligations of property owners within a particular government for their proportionate share of debts of other governments with overlapping geographic boundaries. Concern for overlapping debt arises because the property located in one government's jurisdiction may serve as the tax base for one or more other governments.

Suppose, for example, that a town is located within a surrounding county. The taxable property of the town is assessed at $600 million; that of the county (including the town) is assessed at $800 million. The town has outstanding debt of $30 million; the county has outstanding debt of $50 million.

Based on the ratio of the value of the property within the town to that within the entire county, the town supports 75 percent ($600 million/$800 million) of the county's debt. Thus, the town's overlapping debt would be 75 percent of the county's $50 million debt—$37.5 million. The taxable property of the town also supports 100 percent of the town's own direct debt of $30 million. The town's combined overlapping and direct debt would be $67.5 million—overlapping debt of $37.5 million plus direct debt of $30 million.

Insofar as property taxes are the mainstay revenue of local governments, financial analysts look to the ratio of assessed value of property to total debt outstanding as a primary measure of ability to sustain both existing and proposed liabilities. They obviously would run the risk of overstating the town's fiscal capacity if they took into account only the town's direct debt and ignored that of the county, which will be repaid from taxes on the same property as that of the town.

The computation of overlapping debt may be more complicated than suggested by the previous illustration because governments may be overlapped by not one, but several, taxing authorities. Moreover, the boundaries of the governments may not be concentric; instead, only a portion of one entity may lie within the geographical boundaries of another. The general principal of computing overlapping debt is the same as in the simple example, however. A government's share of each other entity's debt is determined by the percentage of the other entity's property that is within the government's boundaries.

Example

Overlapping Debt

The property of a city is located within a total of five governmental units as shown in the following schedule and in Figure 8-1.

	Outstanding Debt	Assessed Valuation of Taxable Property
	(in millions)	
County	$320	$2,000
School district	160	2,000
Library district	12	2,400
Hospital district	40	4,000
City	400	1,800

The city's *direct* debt is $400 million. The city's share of debt of the overlapping jurisdictions is based on the ratio of the assessed value of the city's own property to that of each of the other jurisdictions. Thus:

	Debt	Share of City Proportion	Percent	Amount
		(dollar amounts in millions)		
Direct debt				
City	$400	$1,800/$1,800	100%	$400
Overlapping debt				
County	320	$1,800/$2,000	90%	288
School district	160	$1,800/$2,000	90%	144
Library district	12	$1,800/$2,400	75%	9
Hospital district	40	$1,800/$4,000	45%	18
Total overlapping debt				$459
Total direct and overlapping debt				$859

The schedule indicates that the city's property (assessed at $1,800 million) supports not only $400 million of the city's own debt but also $459 million of the debt of other governments with overlapping geographic boundaries.

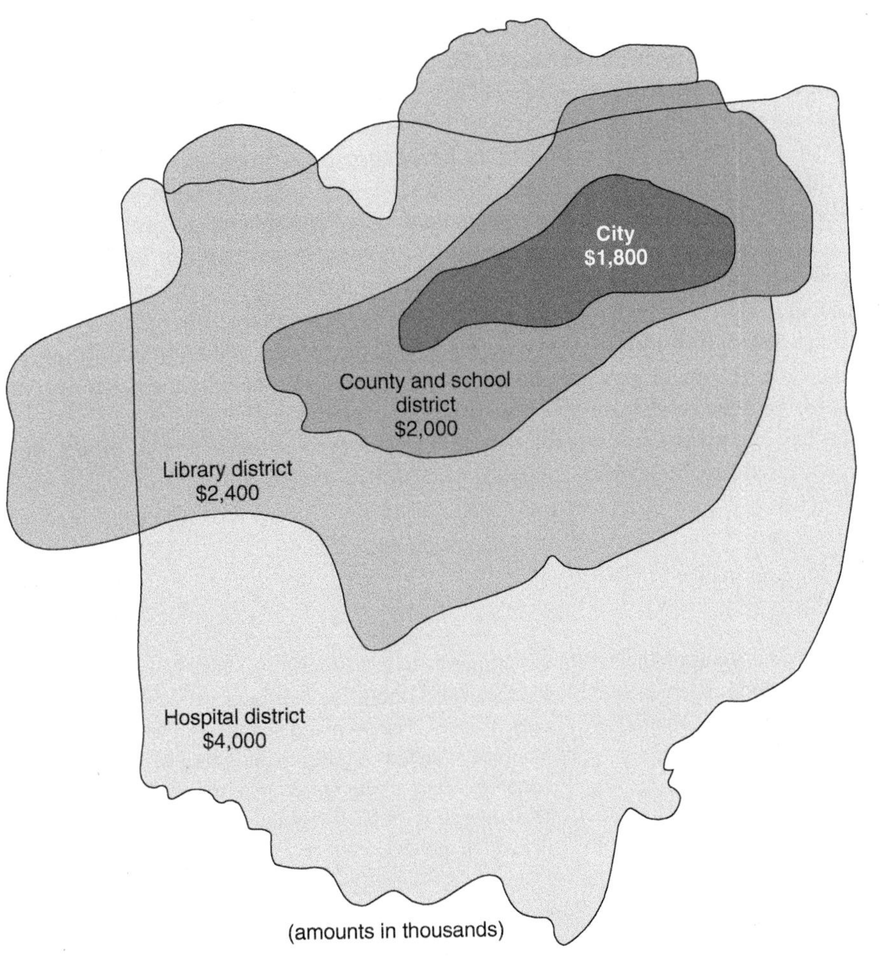

FIGURE 8-1 Diagram of Overlapping Jurisdictions and Assessed Value of Property

Because the overlapping debt is not an actual liability of the reporting entity, a government cannot report it on its own statement of net position or balance sheets. Owing to its analytical significance, however, a government should include a schedule of direct and overlapping debt as supplementary information in the statistical section of its annual report.

CONDUIT DEBT

Conduit debt refers to obligations issued in the name of a government on behalf of a specific third partymost commonly a private entity such as a business or a not-for-profit organization. These obligations might be issued directly through a government, or through an authority established specifically to assist these private entities. The debt is expected to be serviced entirely by the nongovernmental entity and usually takes the form of revenue bonds or certificates of participation. Often the government retains title to the property financed by the obligations and leases it back to the beneficiary. Other times, it simply loans the resources to the beneficiary. The lease or loan payments are typically established so as to match the payments on the debt. The bonds are payable exclusively from the debt payments. Generally the debt is secured by the property financed by the bonds, and in the event of default the bondholders have claims only on the property and the lease or loan payments. In economic substance, the government issuer has no responsibility for making either principal or interest payments on the debt. Therefore, conduit debt is also referred to as **noncommitment debt**.

Conduit debt is a form of government assistance to the beneficiary organizations in that it enables them to obtain financing at lower rates than if they issued the debt themselves. The lower rates can be obtained because interest on debt issued by a government is exempt from federal income taxes, whereas that on debt issued by the beneficiary may be taxable. Bonds that a government issues to attract a private corporation to its jurisdiction are known as **industrial development bonds**. Although the bonds benefit and will be repaid by the corporation, not the government, they nevertheless qualify as tax-exempt municipal debt. The federal government imposes strict limitations on the dollar amount of industrial development bonds that can be issued within each state. These limitations constrain municipalities from transferring to corporations the interest-rate subsidies that Congress intended for governments. Conduit debt issued on behalf of not-for-profits are known as **501(c)(3) bonds**, named after the applicable section of the Internal Revenue Code.

Like industrial development bonds, 501(c)(3) bonds are repaid by the not-for-profit organization and are not the responsibility of the conduit or government.[10]

The key reporting question relating to conduit debt is the extent to which the issuing government should account for the obligations as if they were its own.

GASB STANDARDS

Although governments may elect to report conduit obligations in their government-wide and proprietary fund statements, the GASB has ruled that note disclosure is sufficient.[11] The following information, it said, must be provided:

- A general description of the conduit debt transactions
- The aggregate amount of all conduit debt obligations outstanding
- A clear indication that the issuer has no obligation for the debt beyond the resources provided by related leases or loans[12]

In 2018 the GASB issued an exposure draft of a proposed standard that would make explicit the circumstances in which governments will, and will not, have to report on their own balance sheets both the debt and the related assets that the debt finances. The proposed standard provides that in the most common situations a government issuer will not have to report either the debt or the assets as its own unless for one reason or another it is "more likely than not" that the beneficiary will default on the obligation and the government will have to make required debt-related payments.

[11] Most states report conduits as discreetly presented component units in the financial statements.

[12] GASB Interpretation No. 2, *Disclosure of Conduit Debt Obligations* (August 1995). GASB Codification, para. C65.102.

IN PRACTICE 49ERS SCORE BIG IN THE FINANCIAL ARENA

In December 2011, the Santa Clara City Council voted unanimously for the funding of a new stadium for the San Francisco 49ers NFL football team (*San Francisco Chronicle*, Dec. 14, 2011). The 68,650-seat football stadium was completed for the 2014 NFL season. The Santa Clara Stadium Authority borrowed $850M for a loan syndicated by Goldman Sachs, Bank of America, and US Bank. This loan covered most of the construction costs for the total $1.3 billion stadium. The $850M loan plus interest will be repaid over 25 years from the new stadium's ticket sales, rent from the team ($30 million annually), and naming rights. Other funding for the stadium came from the city of Santa Clara which contributed $114 million, and the NFL, which approved a $200 million G-4 loan to the 49ers. The G-4 loan is the NFL's new funding program that supports teams building new stadiums. The NFL loan is expected to be repaid from premium seating revenue.

[10] Although not legally compelled to pay, governments may feel morally or politically compelled to intervene if a not-for-profit were unable to make debt payments. For example, not-for-profit hospitals are the largest issuers of 501(c)(3) bonds. If a locality had only a single hospital, a government might intervene to prevent the hospital's default and resultant interruptions to its delivery of services to the community.

TOBACCO BONDS

Since 1998 many states have issued "tobacco bonds," a special type of revenue bond. A 1998 settlement with the leading tobacco companies resulted in a commitment by the industry to pay $246 billion to states over 25 years as compensation related to smoking-related deaths and diseases. But instead of tackling the enormous health problems caused by past and continued use of tobacco products, at least 34 states are using proceeds from the settlements to plug their current budget deficits. They do this by establishing a separate authority, a "tobacco settlement authority," which issues revenue bonds secured by the anticipated payments from the tobacco companies. The tobacco settlement authorities then transfer the bond proceeds to the sponsoring state governments.

The issuance of tobacco bonds unquestionably violates the principle of interperiod equity in that the states are, in effect, trading the future revenues for a one-time infusion of cash to meet current operating costs. The tobacco funds to be received over the next 25 years will be used to pay off the bonds rather than for their intended purpose of providing public health services. The actual amount of cash to be received from the tobacco companies is subject to a formula, based in part on the volume of cigarettes shipped into the state by the manufacturers. Accordingly, the GASB has ruled that for purposes of external reporting, neither a tobacco settlement authority nor its sponsoring state may recognize revenue until the year in which the cigarettes are shipped.[13] Still, for purposes of budgeting, the bond proceeds are available for expenditure.

IN PRACTICE — TOBACCO BONDS ARE BOTH RISKY AND INCONSISTENT WITH GOVERNMENT POLICIES

In the 1990s nearly every state sued tobacco companies for misleading the public about the dangers of smoking and leaving the states, as they argued, to bear the cost of treating patients who developed health problems due to smoking. The tobacco companies settled in 1998 and agreed to provide annual compensating payments to the states (called the Master Settlement Agreement—or MSA). However, the settlement payments are not fixed, but linked to tobacco sales. Tobacco bonds are not only risky, but are also inconsistent with governments' public health goals. This is mainly because the amounts to be received by the states depend in large measure on both the amounts of cigarettes sold and the continued fiscal viability of the tobacco companies.

Rating agencies are taking a close look at the states that have relied on tobacco bonds. Major bond rating agencies and some municipal finance experts have warned for years that the number of smokers was decreasing more rapidly than expected, which could negatively impact state budgets. Tobacco companies made $6 billion in annual payments in 2012 and 2011, down from $6.3 billion in 2010 and $7.5 billion the year before. On average, annual payments have been more than 20 percent below estimated payouts when the original MSA was signed, with an average of $1 billion less going to U.S. states each year than anticipated.[14] If the bonds default, it wouldn't be bad just for investors. For example, the *Huffington Post* reports, California guaranteed a portion of its bonds with general fund revenue (*Huffington Post*, February 2012). If tobacco settlement money does not cover the debt, the state will have to pick up some of the tab. Rhode Island and New Jersey have reissued bonds to guarantee bond repayments (*New York Times*, October 6, 2014). A 2012 agreement reduced the amount of money tobacco companies had to pay because of reduced consumption of cigarettes by consumers. As of 2018 cigarette consumption continued to decline (although, owing to higher prices the profitability of cigarette manufacturers increased). Because the payments by the companies to the states are based on consumption and not on revenues, the risk that states would default on their tobacco bonds remained high. As a consequence, the prices at which the bonds traded fell and their effective yields increased.

[14] Data from Craig L. Johnson, Sharon N. Kioko, and Yulianti Abbas (2013). "Tobacco Securitization and Public Spending." *Albany Government Law Review* 6, 21–48.

[13] GASB Technical Bulletin No. 2004-1, *Tobacco Settlement Recognition and Financial Reporting Entity Issues* (June 2004). GASB Codification, para. T50.601.

WHAT OTHER INFORMATION DO USERS WANT TO KNOW ABOUT OUTSTANDING DEBT?

The magnitude and nature of an entity's obligations, each with its own unique characteristics and risks, are obviously of major concern to the entity's creditors as well as to other statement users. As might be expected, both governments and not-for-profits devote a substantial portion of their annual financial reports to long-term debt. The disclosures pertaining to long-term debt are far more comprehensive than those relating to long-term assets. They typically include not only technical features of the debt—such as interest rates, payout schedules, and collateral—but also selected financial ratios that incorporate debt.

The economic burden of long-term debt is dependent on the issuer's ability to pay. Ability to pay is tied to a wide range of financial, social, economic, political, and administrative factors, only some of which are reported in financial statements. This section will focus on some of these factors, but will be limited to those tied directly to the debt itself. Broader measures of ability to pay will be considered in Chapter 11, which is directed to financial analysis.

CREDIT ENHANCEMENTS

An issuer can enhance the security of its bonds by replacing its credit standing with that of a more fiscally sound entity. Two such means are by acquiring bond insurance and by obtaining the moral obligation of another issuer to back its debt.

Bond Insurance

Bond and other forms of debt insurance guarantee the timely payment of both interest and principal. Although it is purchased by the bond issuers, it is intended to protect the bondholders.

Premiums on bond insurance range from 0.1 to 2.0 percent of principal and interest, depending on the risk. However, bond insurance typically results in net savings to the issuer because the bond rating agencies assign the bond insurer's credit rating to the issuer. Obviously, the higher the bond rating, the lower the interest cost. The extent of any savings will depend mainly on the credit standing of the government issuing the bonds, the credit standing of the insurance company, and market conditions at the time of the bond sale.

Through 2007 bond insurance was written mainly by a small number of specialized companies, the two largest of which were American Municipal Bond Assurance Corporation (AMBAC) and Municipal Bond Insurance Association (MBIA), and between 50 and 60 percent of all new issues on average were insured. Large insurers carried AAA credit ratings—the highest available. Then came the financial crisis of 2008. The leading municipal bond insurance companies were hit especially hard, mainly as the result of losses in activities apart from their municipal bond business. Their own creditworthiness came into question, and as of 2009, the bonds of AMBAC and MBIA were rated at or near "junk" status. Thus, they were no longer in a position to write new insurance. In 2007, more than 80 percent of new money issues were insured; by 2014, this had fallen to around 22 percent—although this was a slight increase from 2010 when less than 20 percent of new issues were insured.[15] Worse, however, the hundreds of billions of dollars insurance that the major companies had written was now of questionable worth, thereby reducing the value of the bonds that they had backed. By 2012 AMBAC as well as other new companies (such as BAM) were again writing insurance contracts, but not to the extent that they were prior to the financial crisis.

Credit Guarantees

It is common for one government to guarantee the financial obligations of another government, a not-for-profit organization or even a private entity, without receiving any compensation or value in exchange (in other words, in a non-exchange or non-insurance transaction). For example, a

[15] Data calculated from Bond Buyer, "Annual Bond Sales."

state may guarantee certain bonds issued by its independent school districts. In the event that a district fails to make its required principal or interest payments the state will make them on its behalf.

GASB Statement No. 70, *Accounting and Financial Reporting for Nonexchange Financial Guarantees* addresses the accounting and reporting issues for these types of guarantees. It mandates that both the governments that extend financial guarantees and those that benefit from guarantees disclose specified details of the agreements. For guarantor governments the disclosures should include a description of the guarantees, the legal authority used to provide the guarantee, the relationship between the guarantor and the debt issuer, recovery arrangements, length of time of the guarantees, and the amount of guarantees outstanding as of the reporting date. Those required of the beneficiary government are similar, although somewhat less comprehensive.

In addition, Statement No. 70, prescribes that when it is "more likely than not," based on "qualitative factors and historical data," that a government will have to make good on a guarantee then it must recognize its expected payments as its own liability. If the amount of such payments is not known with certainty, the liability should be the discounted present value of the minimum amount of a possible range of payments.

Moral Obligation Debt

Bonds or notes issued by one entity (usually a state agency) but backed by the promise of another entity (usually the state itself) to make up any debt service deficiencies are referred to as **moral obligation debt**. The obligation is described as "moral" because it is not legally enforceable.

Moral obligation debt is motivated mainly by a state's intent to avoid voter approvals or to circumvent debt limitations. To issue debt that would otherwise be proscribed, a state, with legislative approval, borrows in the name of a state agency, sometimes one formed specifically to issue the debt. To enhance the creditworthiness of the agency, the state supports the bonds with a promise to cover debt service shortages.

The state does not typically place its full faith and credit behind its pledge. Rather, it promises only to seek future appropriation for any required debt service payments. This promise may be of only dubious value. When New York State issued moral obligation bonds, for example, the promise took the form of a so-called moral makeup clause, wherein the state budget director was required to ask for an appropriation to make up any shortfall in its debt service reserve fund. However, the legislature was not committed to honoring the budget director's request.

Moral obligation bonds obviously are not as secure as the state's general obligation bonds, and rating agencies typically assign them a rating at least one grade below that of the state's general obligation bonds. Still, the rating is likely to be significantly higher than if the bonds were issued by the state agency without the backing of the state.

DEBT MARGIN

As discussed earlier, governments may be limited in the amount of debt that they can incur. The difference between the amount of debt outstanding (computed according to applicable legal provisions, not necessarily as reported on the issuer's balance sheets) and the amount of debt allowed is described as **debt margin**.

Example

Debt Margin

A government's general obligation bond debt is legally limited to 6 percent of the assessed value of taxable property within its jurisdiction. The assessed value of the property is $10 billion, and therefore the government can issue a maximum of $600 million in debt. If the government currently has $450 million of debt outstanding, then its legal debt margin is $150 million (25 percent of its limit).

PAYOUT SCHEDULES

Payout schedules can take a variety of forms, ranging from those in which a substantial portion of the principal is repaid early in the bond's life to those in which the principal is paid entirely at the end. A typical payout schedule is one in which 50 percent of the debt is retired in 10 years. Often, but by no means always, this is accomplished through a 20- to 25-year serial bond issue with an equal proportion of the issue maturing each year. Usually lenders see a faster retirement schedule as positive, as long as it does not place too great a fiscal strain on the issuer. Schedules in which the payout is extended over 30 to 40 years, although not uncommon, are viewed as negative.

Consistent with the concept of interperiod equity addressed in Chapter 1, sound fiscal policy dictates that the payout schedule correspond to the useful life of the property being financed. Indeed, the very rationale for borrowing is that the burden of paying for long-lived assets should be borne by the parties who will use them. When the schedule is shorter than the useful life, then only the early-year users will pay for the assets. When it exceeds the useful life, then parties beyond the period of use will be required to pay for them, and in effect, a portion of the debt will be financing operations rather than capital assets.

RESERVE FUNDS

As discussed in Chapter 6 on debt service funds, lenders commonly stipulate that an issuer maintain a reserve fund to ensure that it keeps current on its principal and interest payments. Usually the amount to be set aside is based on principal and interest payments—for example, the highest year's debt service. A reserve fund can generally be dipped into only for the final year's debt service or in the event that the issuer is otherwise unable to make its required payments. From the perspective of a lender, the reserve fund provides a cushion against difficult fiscal times and thereby makes the bond a more attractive investment.

COMMON RATIOS AND PAST HISTORY

Investors and other statement users look to a variety of bond-related ratios and other data to assess ability to pay and risk of default. The most notable of these include the following:

- ***Debt service costs as a percentage of total general-fund and debt service fund expenditures.*** Similar to the times-interest-earned ratio that is widely used in business, this ratio is usually considered high if it exceeds 20 percent of total general and debt service fund expenditures.
- ***Debt per capita and debt as a percentage of taxable property.*** Both of these ratios are measures of *fiscal capacity*. They relate the bonded debt, not to resources or resource flows within the government, but to the ultimate sources of a government's revenues. As with most ratios involving long-term obligations, debt can be expressed with varying degrees of inclusiveness. For example, debt could be limited to GO debt or could also include revenue debt. Moreover, it could incorporate only the issuer's direct debt or both the direct and overlapping debt.
- ***History.*** As any banker will testify, character dominates all quantifiable measures in capturing a borrower's credit standing. Users want information as to whether past payments were made on time. Whereas the bond community may forgive borrowers for unintentionally missing or being late on payments, it may be less tolerant of an issuer who evades payments through bankruptcy or comparable legal maneuvers.

Ratios pertaining to revenue bonds are discussed in Chapter 9, dealing with business-type activities. The long-term debt of hospitals, universities, and other not-for-profits are often of this type. A more comprehensive discussion of the appropriate use, and limitations, of ratios in analyzing a government's fiscal condition is included in Chapter 11.

WHAT ARE BOND RATINGS, AND WHY ARE THEY IMPORTANT?

The leading bond rating agencies—Standard & Poor's (S&P), Moody's Investors Service, and Fitch Ratings—will assign a quality rating to the debt instruments of any issuer (government, not-for-profit, or business) that requests it. Their fees, paid by the issuers, generally range from $2,500 to $80,000. Issuers may purchase a rating from one or more rating agency for any debt issue.

The agencies base their ratings on a comprehensive review of all factors affecting the issuer's ability to pay. A review would include analysis of the debt instrument itself, the issuer's financial reports and budgets, key demographic data, and a range of economic statistics. It would also incorporate interviews with city officials and assessments of their competence.

The rating services continue to monitor an issuer even after they have assigned an initial rating, and they expect the issuer to update them continually with current information. A rating generally remains in effect until the issuer's next offering of comparable securities. Sometimes, however, as a result of new developments the agencies will change their initial classification.

The classification bond rating scheme of Moody's Investors Service is presented in Table 8-2.

Debt ratings are of critical concern to both issuers and investors because they affect the debt's marketability and hence its interest rate. In fact, many institutions are legally prohibited from investing in securities classified by a specified rating service as less than "investment grade." Investment grade bonds are those rated Baa3 or higher by Moody's or BBB—or higher by S&P.

A rating service downgrade, even though it generally does nothing more than spotlight information that was already widely known, can be a traumatic fiscal event for an issuer. Almost always it increases the issuer's future interest costs, thereby adding to its fiscal anguish.

Despite the significance attached to bond ratings, investors should no more rely solely on them than they should rely on a report from a stock brokerage firm. The rating agencies are

TABLE 8-2 Moody's Investors Service Bond Ratings Global Scale

Aaa	Obligations rated Aaa are judged to be of the highest quality, subject to the lowest level of credit risk.
Aa	Obligations rated Aa are judged to be of high quality and are subject to very low credit risk.
A	Obligations rated A are judged to be upper-medium grade and are subject to low credit risk.
Baa	Obligations rated Baa are judged to be medium-grade and subject to moderate credit risk and as such may possess certain speculative characteristics.
Ba	Obligations rated Ba are judged to be speculative and are subject to substantial credit risk.
B	Obligations rated B are considered speculative and are subject to high credit risk.
Caa	Obligations rated Caa are judged to be speculative of poor standing and are subject to very high credit risk.
Ca	Obligations rated Ca are highly speculative and are likely in, or very near, default, with some prospect of recovery of principal and interest.
C	Obligations rated C are the lowest rated and are typically in default, with little prospect for recovery of principal or interest.

Note: Moody's appends numerical modifiers 1, 2, and 3 to each generic rating classification from Aa through Caa. The modifier 1 indicates that the obligation ranks in the higher end of its generic rating category; the modifier 2 indicates a midrange ranking; and the modifier 3 indicates a ranking in the lower end of that generic rating category.

Source: Moody's Investors Service, *Rating Symbols and Definitions*, July 2017.

fallible, and they are neither prophets nor seers. Their ratings are merely opinions, not guarantees. The information on which they base their ratings—all of which is in the public domain—is subject to varying interpretation, and an independent analysis may provide insights in addition to, or at variance with, those of the agencies.

In recent years bond rating agencies have come under harsh criticism. Mainly, this owes to their alleged lack of independence. As noted previously, rating agencies are paid by the issuers—the very parties that stand to benefit from favorable ratings. Accordingly, even though the agencies may claim they are objective and above issuing biased ratings to win repeat business from a government, they are most definitely not independent in appearance.

SUMMARY

Long-term obligations represent claims on the entity's resources, and failure to satisfy them can seriously jeopardize the entity's ability to provide the services expected of it. Hence, an analyst interested in a government's fiscal condition must pay careful attention to them.

Whereas bankruptcy filings by major governments are rare, those of small units and especially special districts are more common. Although many governments have taxing authority and their access to resources may seem almost unlimited, there are practical limits to the extent of tax increases and service cutbacks. Governments account for their governmental funds on a modified accrual basis and focus on current financial resources. Therefore, they do not give balance sheet recognition either to long-term obligations or to the assets that the obligations finance. By contrast, in their government-wide statements, which are on a full accrual basis and focus on all economic resources, they report both their long-term obligations and capital assets. They record their long-term debts initially at issue price. Thereafter, they amortize any premiums or discounts. In essence, therefore, the book value of an obligation represents the present value of future cash obligations (based on a discount rate established when the bonds were issued). Indeed, in their government-wide statements, governments account for long-term obligations as do both businesses and not-for-profits.

Demand bonds may be reported as long-term debt only if the issuer has entered into a "take-out" agreement, ensuring that if the bonds are presented for redemption the debt can be refinanced. Similarly, bond anticipation notes may be reported as long-term debt only if the issuer has already refinanced the notes or has a binding refinancing agreement. In contrast, tax anticipation notes and revenue anticipation notes are not converted into long-term debts, so they cannot be accounted for as long-term obligations.

Leases longer than one year are accounted for as financing arrangements and hence are also reported as long-term debt. Some leasing arrangements are unquestionably motivated by an effort to avoid the debt limitations and voter approvals to which conventional general obligation bonds are subject. But whether, in fact, they can be used for that purpose is a matter of state law and judicial decisions.

Revenue bonds and overlapping debt, though not strictly full faith and credit liabilities of the reporting governments, impose financial obligations on their citizens and should be taken into account in assessing the capacity of the government to sustain new and existing debt. In contrast, conduit debt may bear the name of the government issuer, but it may not be an economic obligation because it is expected to be repaid by the beneficiary, not the issuer.

Although the ultimate ability of a government to repay its debt depends on fundamental financial, social, economic, political, and administrative factors, creditors must also be concerned with features of the debt itself: credit enhancements such as guarantees, moral obligations and bond insurance; debt margin (the difference between allowable debt and outstanding debt); debt payout schedule, reserve fund requirements, and debt rating.

Bond ratings are of critical concern to issuers and investors because they affect the debt instrument's marketability and hence its interest rate. Nevertheless, the ratings are opinions, not guarantees.

KEY TERMS IN THIS CHAPTER

501(c)(3) bonds 344
bond anticipation notes (BANs) 333
certificates of participation 340
conduit debt 343
debt margin 347
demand bonds 332
financing leases 335
fiscal funding clause 336
governmental funds 329
industrial development bonds 344

EXERCISE FOR REVIEW AND SELF-STUDY

A city agrees to lease an emergency communications system. The term of the lease, which is noncancelable, is 10 years. It provides for annual payments of $1,086,944, an amount reflective of an $8 million loan (the fair value of the asset) and interest at a rate of 6 percent.

1. Prepare entries to reflect the lease agreement in the city's (1) general-fund statements; and (2) government-wide statements.
2. Prepare entries to record the first year's lease payment and depreciation. Assume that the useful life of the equipment is 10 years (the same as the lease) and that depreciation will be recorded on a straight-line basis.
3. Suppose, instead, that the city financed the acquisition of the equipment with bonds that could be redeemed at any time at the option of the holder. The bonds pay interest at the rate of 6 percent. At year-end, prevailing rates of interest had decreased to 5 percent. The city does not have a take-out agreement providing for refinancing if the bonds are presented for payment. How should the city record the debt?
4. The city is permitted to issue a maximum of $30 million of general obligation bonds. It already has $19 million of qualifying debt outstanding. What would be the city's debt margin after issuing $8 million of new debt subject to the limits?
5. The city is served by an independent school district that includes the city as well as nearby towns. The assessed value of taxable property within the city is $600 million; that of the school district is $800 million. The school district has $48 million of debt outstanding. What is the city's overlapping debt with respect to the school district?

QUESTIONS FOR REVIEW AND DISCUSSION

1. What unique issues arise when a government, as opposed to a business, is declared bankrupt?
2. What is the distinction between *general obligation* debt and *revenue* debt? Which one is likely to bear higher interest rates?
3. At what value would a government report bonds payable on its government-wide statements? Why might this value differ from the bonds' face value? Why might it differ from their market value?
4. A government's interest expenditure, as reported in its debt service fund, differs significantly from its interest expense, as reported in its government-wide statements. What is the most likely explanation for the difference?
5. What are *demand* bonds? When can they be reported as long-term, rather than current, obligations?
6. If, under GAAP, leases for terms greater than one year are considered long-term obligations, why, in many jurisdictions, are they not subject to debt limitations?
7. What are *BANs*, *RANs,* and *TANs*? Why are they accounted for differently?
8. What is *overlapping debt,* and why is it of significance to financial analysts and other users of a government's financial statements?
9. What is *conduit debt*? Who issues debt through these conduits? Why are governments required to report it only in notes to their financial statements, not on their balance sheets?

10. What distinguishes *moral obligation* bonds from other types of debt? Why would one government assume a moral obligation for another government's bonds?

11. Why are bond ratings of vital concern to bond issuers?

EXERCISES

EX. 8-1

Select the *best* answer.

1. Which of the following is true with respect to bankruptcy?
   a. Per the federal bankruptcy code, a municipality can be declared bankrupt but not insolvent.
   b. Many major cities have avoided bankruptcy by being placed under the control of financial control boards by their state governments.
   c. The concept of bankruptcy does not apply to governments because they have the authority to increase taxes and reduce services.
   d. Municipalities that are declared bankrupt by a court are brought under the control of independent trustees whose primary objective is to ensure that obligations to bondholders are satisfied in full.

2. A government issues $1 million in 30-year, 6 percent coupon bonds at a discount of $27,092. The bonds were sold to yield 6.2 percent. At what amount would the bonds be reported (net) in the government-wide statement of net position and governmental fund balance sheet immediately upon issuance?

	Government-Wide	Fund
a.	$1,000,000	$1,000,000
b.	$ 972,908	$ 972,908
c.	$ 972,908	$ 0
d.	$ 972,908	$1,000,000

3. The government issues the bonds described in question 2. It makes its first semiannual interest payment of $30,000. How much interest expense/expenditure would it likely have to report in its government-wide and governmental fund statements?

	Government-Wide	Fund
a.	$30,000	$30,000
b.	$30,160	$30,160
c.	$30,160	$ 0
d.	$30,160	$30,000

4. The government makes subsequent interest payments. Reported interest expense/expenditure in the government-wide and governmental fund statements will:

	Government-Wide	Fund
a.	Increase	Remain the same
b.	Increase	Increase
c.	Remain the same	Remain the same
d.	Decrease	Remain the same

5. Suppose a government issues $1 million in bonds at a premium of $50,000. It temporarily invests the proceeds of $1,050,000 in U.S. Treasury bonds having a face value of $1 million (i.e., at a premium of $50,000). At what value would the government report the bonds payable and the investment in bonds in its government-wide statements subsequent to the date of the transactions?

	Bond Payable	Investment in Bonds
a.	Amortized cost	Market value
b.	Market value	Market value
c.	Amortized cost	Amortized cost
d.	Market value	Amortized cost

6. Which of the following is true of demand bonds?
   a. They give the issuer the right to call the bonds at a preestablished price.
   b. They give the issuer the right to demand that the bondholders purchase additional bonds at a preestablished price.
   c. They give the bondholder the right to demand repayment prior to maturity.
   d. They give the bondholder the right of first refusal with respect to any additional bonds sold by the issuer.

7. Demand bonds should be reported as governmental fund liabilities
   a. if the government has not entered into a take-out agreement.
   b. if prevailing interest rates are higher than the interest rate on the bonds.
   c. if prevailing interest rates are lower than the interest rate on the bonds.
   d. if the government, by the time it issues its financial statements, has neither refinanced the bonds nor entered into an agreement to do so.

8. A city issues bond anticipation notes on October 21, 2020. It refunds the notes with 30-year bonds in January 2021. In its financial statements for the fiscal year ending December 31, 2020, which are issued in April 2021, it should report the bond anticipation notes as obligations
   a. in both its government-wide statement of net position and a governmental fund balance sheet.
   b. in its government-wide statement of net position but not its governmental fund balance sheet.
   c. in its governmental fund balance sheet but not its government-wide statement of net position.
   d. in neither its governmental fund balance sheet nor its government-wide statement of net position.

9. A city issues revenue anticipation notes on October 21, 2020. It repays the notes in January 2021. In its financial statements for the fiscal year ending December 31, 2020, which are issued in April 2021, it should report the revenue anticipation notes as obligations
   a. in both the government-wide statement of net position and a governmental fund balance sheet.
   b. in the government-wide statement of net position but not a governmental fund balance sheet.
   c. in a governmental fund balance sheet but not the government-wide statement of net position.
   d. in neither a governmental fund balance sheet nor the government-wide statement of net position.

10. In which of the following lease arrangements would a county government lessor not recognize a lease receivable as a noncurrent asset: It signs
    a. a 10-year lease for one floor of a five-story office building.
    b. a two-year lease with another government for an automobile; lease payments will be determined in part by number of miles driven.
    c. a five-year lease on construction equipment with a town within its jurisdiction that includes a non-appropriation clause.
    d. a three-year lease on a copy machine that gives the lessee the option to terminate the lease at the end of either the first or second year of the contract.

EX. 8-2

Select the *best* answer.

1. A town signs a 10-year lease by which it acquires equipment with a market value of $1 million. The lease incorporates an implicit interest rate of 8 percent per year. Accordingly, annual lease payments are $149,029. When the town makes its *second* annual lease payment, it would report in its government-wide statements
   a. interest expense of $80,000.
   b. rent expense of $149,029.
   c. interest expense of $74,478.
   d. rent expense of $100,000.

2. State courts that have held that financing leases do not qualify as long-term debt subject to debt limitations commonly base their decision on the inclusion in the lease agreement of a
   a. nonsubstitution clause.
   b. nonappropriation clause.
   c. nonparticipation clause.
   d. forward funding clause.

3. Revenue bonds, compared with general obligation bonds, generally
   a. are paid out of property or sales tax revenues.
   b. bear lower interest rates.
   c. are subject to the same debt limitations.
   d. are not backed by the full faith and credit of the issuing government.

4. A town is located within both a school district and a county. The assessed property valuations and bonded debts of the three governments are as follows (in millions):

	Assessed Valuation	Bonded Debt
Town	$ 800	$40
School district	$1,600	$90
County	$2,400	$18

   The combined direct and overlapping debt of the town is
   a. $40 million
   b. $51 million
   c. $91 million
   d. $148 million

5. Clifford City has issued $10 million of revenue bonds to help finance a factory for Travis, Inc., a private manufacturing company. The city owns the factory and leases it to the company. The bonds are payable exclusively from the lease payments. In the event the company defaults on its lease payments, the bondholders have claims only on the factory. The city has no obligation for the bonds other than to transmit to the bondholders the lease payments that it receives from the company. In its annual financial statements the city should report the bonds
   a. on its government-wide statement of net position but not in any fund statements.
   b. only in notes.
   c. only as required supplementary information.
   d. both on its government-wide statement of net position and in its proprietary funds balance sheet.

6. Which of the following is *not* a common reason for issuing revenue bonds rather than general obligation bonds?
   a. To obtain lower interest rates
   b. To incorporate debt service costs into user fees
   c. To avoid debt limitations or voter approvals

d. To shift a portion of the burden of paying for the project to parties who reside outside the issuer's jurisdiction but nevertheless benefit from the project

7. On December 1, 2021, a city issued $20 million in BANs and $6 million in RANs. By April 15, 2022, the date the city issued its financial statements for the fiscal year ending December 31, 2021, the city had neither converted the BANs into long-term bonds nor entered into a refinancing agreement to do so. However, the city repaid the RANs on February 28, 2022. The amount the city should report as an obligation of its general fund in its December 31, 2021, financial statements is

a. $0

b. $6 million

c. $20 million

d. $26 million

8. A state authority (which is an independently legal entity) issues bonds back with a moral obligation of the state. This debt

a. is probably backed by the full faith and credit of the state

b. is probably subject to the same debt limitations as if it had been issued by the state itself

c. probably bears a lower interest rate than if there were no moral obligation associated with it

d. imposes greater pressure on the agency to repay the debt than if there were no moral obligation associated with it

9. Certificates of participation have the most in common with

a. revenue bonds.

b. pension annuities.

c. participating preferred stock

d. short-term leases.

10. A city issues the following bonds:

Revenue bonds to fund improvements to the town-owned electric utility $50 million

Conduit bonds issued to assist a fast-food franchisee to construct a restaurant for $7 million

The amount that the city should report as an obligation in its government-wide statement of net position and its proprietary funds balance sheet is

	Government-Wide	**Proprietary Fund**
a.	$57 million	$57 million
b.	$57 million	$ 0
c.	$50 million	$50 million
d.	$ 0	$ 0

EX. 8-3

Government debts may be reported differently in governmental and government-wide statements.

The Alpine school district engaged in the following transactions in its fiscal year ending August 31, 2021. By law, the district is required to establish a capital projects fund to account for school construction projects and a debt service fund to account for resources legally restricted to the payment of long-term principal and related interest.

- On March 1, it issued $40 million in general obligation bonds to finance the construction of a new junior high school. The bonds were to mature in 20 years (40 periods) and had a coupon rate of 4 percent per year (2 percent per semiannual period). They were sold for $38,924,728 (a discount of $1,075,272), a price that reflected an annual yield of 4.2 percent (2.1 percent per period).
- On August 31 the district made its first interest payment of $800,000.

- During the year the builder with whom the district contracted to construct the building completed approximately 10 percent of the building and billed the district for $4 million.
- On August 31, the district issued $10 million in bond anticipation notes to finance improvements to its athletic facilities. By the time the district issued its fiscal year-end 2021 financial statements in December 2021, it still had not refinanced these notes and had not yet started construction on the facilities.
- In June the district issued $2 million in tax anticipation notes. It repaid these notes in September. Interest applicable to the notes for the fiscal year ending August 31, 2021, was $25,000, all of which was paid in September when the notes matured.
- In August, the district settled a lawsuit with a group of former teachers. Per a structured settlement, the district agreed to make several payments totaling $1,600,000 to the teachers. The district has a policy of recording long-term obligations at present value whenever required or permitted by GAAP. It estimates the present value of this settlement to be $1,350,000.

What amount relating to these transactions should the district report in its August 31, 2021, financial statements as:

1. Interest expenditure in its debt service fund statement of revenues and expenditures?
2. Interest expense in its government-wide statement of activities?
3. Long-term debt in the capital projects fund balance sheet?
4. Current debt in the capital projects fund balance sheet?
5. Long-term debt in the debt service fund balance sheet?
6. Bonds payable (net of bond discount) in the government-wide statement of net position?
7. Other noncurrent debt in the government-wide statement of net position?
8. Invested in capital assets, in the government-wide statement of net position?
9. Current liabilities in the general-fund balance sheet?

   Select each response from one of the amounts that follow. An amount may be selected once, more than once, or not at all.

   a. $(34,942,147)
   b. $0
   c. $25,000
   d. $800,000
   e. $817,419
   f. $842,419
   g. $1,350,000
   h. $1,600,000
   i. $2,000,000
   j. $2,025,000
   k. $10,000,000
   l. $12,000,000
   m. $12,025,000
   n. $38,924,728
   o. $38,942,147

EX. 8-4

Both the reported value of long-term debt and periodic interest charges should be based on unamortized issue price (plus or minus unamortized premiums or discounts) and initial yield.

The City of Fairfield issued $100 million of 20-year, 6 percent coupon bonds (3 percent per semiannual period) for $89.32 million. The price reflected a yield of 7 percent (3.5 percent period semiannual period).

1. Prepare entries to reflect how the following would be reported in the city's government-wide statements:
   a. The issuance of the bond
   b. The first semiannual payment of interest
   c. The second semiannual payment of interest
2. Prepare entries to account for the same transactions in an appropriate governmental fund.

EX. 8-5

The accounting for BANs depends on events subsequent to year-end.

In anticipation of issuing of long-term bonds, a state issues on May 1, 2021, $200 million of 60-day BANs to finance highway construction. It expects to roll over the BANs into long-term bonds within 60 days. Its fiscal year ends on May 31. The state issues its financial statements approximately four months after the end of its fiscal year.

1. Prepare the appropriate journal entry in a governmental fund (such as a capital projects fund) to record the issuance of the $200 million, 60-day BANs on May 1, 2021.
2. Prepare the appropriate journal entry, if required, to record the conversion of the BANs to long-term bonds on June 18, 2021.
3. Prepare the appropriate journal entry, if required, to adjust the accounts as of year-end May 31, 2021, assuming that the state was unable to convert the BANs to long-term bonds by the time it issued its financial statements.
4. Comment on how the BANs would be reported on the government-wide statements as of May 31, 2021, assuming, first, that they were converted and, second, that they were not converted.

EX. 8-6

Debt is accounted for differently in fund and government-wide statements.

The following transactions affected a city's general fund. Prepare a table in which you indicate for each transaction the expenditure/expense and change in liabilities that the city would report in its (a) general fund and (b) government-wide statements.

1. City employees earned $7.7 million in vacation pay during the year, of which they took only $6.6 million. They may take the balance in the following three years.
2. The employees were paid $0.5 million for vacations that they had earned in previous years.
3. The city settled a claim brought against it during the year by a building contractor. The city agreed to pay $10 million immediately and $10 million at the end of the following year.
4. The city issued $100 million in general obligation bonds at par.
5. It paid $4 million in debt service. Of this, $3 million was for the first payment of interest, the balance for repayment of principal.

EX. 8-7

Leases create both assets and liabilities.

Pearl City leases an emergency communications system. The term of the lease is 10 years, approximately the useful life of the equipment. Based on a sales price of $800,000 and an interest rate of 6 percent, the city agrees to make annual payments of $108,694. Upon the expiration of the lease the equipment will revert to the city.

1. Prepare an appropriate entry in the city's government-wide statements to reflect the signing of the lease.
2. Prepare appropriate entries to record the first payment on the lease. The city charges depreciation using the straight-line method.
3. Will your entries to record the final payment on the lease be the same as the first? Explain.
4. Comment briefly on how the lease transactions would be recorded in the city's general fund or other appropriate governmental fund.

EX. 8-8

Not-for-profits account for bonds similar to businesses.

The Cleveland Historical Society issues $40 million of 6 percent, 15-year bonds at a price of $36,321,000 to finance the construction of a new museum. The price reflects an annual yield of 7.0 percent.

1. Prepare the journal entry to record the issuance of the bonds. Indicate the category of funds (e.g., restricted for unrestricted) in which the entry would be made.
2. Prepare the journal entry to record the first *semiannual* payment of bond interest.
3. Prepare the journal entry to record the second *semiannual* payment of bond interest.

CONTINUING PROBLEM

Review the comprehensive annual financial report (CAFR) you obtained.

1. Per the city's schedule of long-term obligations, what is the total long-term obligation for both governmental and business-type activities? Does this amount reconcile with the long-term liabilities as reported on the government wide statement of net position?
2. In addition to bonds payable, what other kinds of long-term debt for governmental activities did the city report in its statement of net position?
3. Did the city increase or decrease its long-term borrowings during the year? What was the effect on total long-term liabilities at year end? Explain.
4. What is the percentage of total net bonded debt to assessed value of property? What is the amount of net debt per capita?
5. What is the city's legal debt margin?
6. Does the city have any lease obligations outstanding? Are these accounted for as operating or financing leases? Can you determine if any of these leases were initiated during this year? What is the amount of payments related to financing leases?
7. Compute the total amount of the city's direct and overlapping debt?
8. Does the city have outstanding any conduit debt?

PROBLEMS

P. 8-1

Government-wide statements are on a full accrual basis; fund statements are on a modified accrual basis.

The East Eanes School District engaged in or was affected by the following events and transactions during its fiscal year ending June 30, 2021.

1. Teachers and other personnel earned $350,000 in vacations and other compensated absences that they did not take but for which they expect to be paid in the future.
2. The district settled a suit brought by a student, agreeing to pay $3 million by December 31, 2022.
3. The district issued $8 million in GO bonds to finance an addition to its high school. By year-end, it had expended $1 million in construction costs.
4. The district signed a one-year (i.e., short-term) lease for office space. Rent, which the county paid in its entirety, is $40,000 per year.

5. It acquired school buses and other vehicles, financing them with an eight-year lease. Annual lease payments are $140,000. Had the district purchased the equipment outright, the price would have been $869,371, reflecting an interest rate of 6 percent.

6. The district transferred $500,000, representing the final year's principal payment, to a reserve fund required by the bond indenture.

7. To smooth out cash flows, the district issued 90-day tax anticipation notes of $950,000.

8. The district paid teachers and other personnel $150,000 for compensated absences earned in previous years.
   a. For each event, prepare the entries (as required) to record the transactions in the general fund or whatever other governmental fund seems most appropriate.
   b. Prepare the entries that would be needed to reflect the transactions and events in the district's government-wide statements.

P. 8-2

Governments now report their effective liabilities and interest costs, but do not adjust for changes in market values or rates.

On January 1, a public school district issued $6 million of 6 percent, 15-year coupon bonds to finance a new building. The bonds, which require semiannual payments of interest, were issued for $6,627,909—a price that provides an annual yield of 5 percent (a semiannual yield of 2.5 percent).

1. Prepare the journal entry that the district would make to reflect the issuance of the bonds on its government-wide statements. Comment on why the net reported liability differs from the face value of the bonds.

2. Prepare the entry that the district would make to reflect the first payment of interest on its government-wide statements. Indicate the value at which the bonds would be reported immediately following the payment. Comment on why the reported interest expense is not equal to the amount paid.

3. Suppose that immediately following the first payment of interest, prevailing interest rates fell to 4 percent. For how much could the district liquidate its obligations by acquiring all outstanding bonds in the open market? [*Hint:* Determine the present value (based on the prevailing interest rate of 2 percent per period) of the remaining 29 coupon payments of $180,000 and the repayment of the $6 million of principal.] Comment on whether this amount would be reported in the district's financial statements (both fund and government-wide). Comment also on why and how this amount might be of interest to statement users.

4. Comment on how the district would report both the liability and interest costs in its fund statements.

P. 8-3

Demand bonds may provide the issuer with the disadvantages, but not the advantages, of long-term debt.

On June 1, 2021, a city issues $2 million in 7 percent demand bonds. Although the bonds have a term of 10 years, they contain a "put" option permitting the holder to present the bonds for redemption, at par, any time after May 31, 2022. The bonds pay interest semiannually.

1. Prepare journal entries to reflect how the bonds would be recorded in the city's general fund or other governmental fund for fiscal year December 31, 2021, financial statements assuming:
   a. The city has entered into a qualifying take-out agreement.
   b. The city has not entered into a qualifying take-out agreement.

2. Suppose that on January 1, 2023, prevailing interest rates for bonds of similar credit risk had fallen to 4 percent. A bondholder needed immediate cash for personal reasons. Assuming that the bonds were

publicly traded, do you think the bondholder would redeem his bonds? Do you think that any other bondholders would redeem their bonds? Explain.

3. Suppose, instead, that prevailing interest rates had increased to 9 percent. Do you think that the bondholder needing cash would redeem his bonds? Do you think that the other bondholders would redeem their bonds?

4. Suppose that, because it is not mandated by the applicable GASB pronouncement, the take-out agreement does not specify the interest rate at which the financing institution would provide the funds necessary for the city to redeem its bonds. If prevailing rates had increased to 9 percent, at approximately what rate is it likely that the financing institution would loan the city the required funds?

5. Comment on the extent to which the demand bonds provide the city with one of the primary benefits of issuing long-term debt—the guarantee of a fixed interest rate over the life of the bond. To what extent does it burden the city with the corresponding disadvantage—being required to pay no less than the stated rate over the life of the bond (or otherwise retire the bonds at market prices)?

P. 8-4

BANs, TANs, and RANs may sound alike, but they are not necessarily accounted for in the same way.

In August 2020, voters of Balcones, a medium-sized city, approved a $15 million general obligation bond issue to finance the construction of recreational facilities. In order to begin construction immediately, without waiting to complete the lengthy process of issuing long-term bonds, the city issued $4 million in bond anticipation notes (BANs). The notes matured in March 2021, but the city had the right to prepay them any time prior to maturity.

On February 15, 2021, the city issued $15 million of 6 percent, 20-year GO bonds. Upon receiving the proceeds it repaid the BANs, along with $80,000 in interest.

1. Prepare a journal entry to indicate how the city should report the BANs in its December 31, 2020, fund financial statements, assuming that it issued the statements after February 15, 2021.

2. Suppose that the city did not refinance the BANs prior to the date the financial statements were issued. What other evidence must the city present to justify reporting the BANs as long-term obligations? Prepare a journal entry to indicate how the city should report the BANs if it is unable to provide this evidence.

3. Assume, also, that the city experienced a cash flow shortage in November 2020. Anticipating tax collections in January 2021, it issued $2 million in tax anticipation notes (TANs) due February 2021. In February 2021, instead of repaying the notes, it "rolled them over" for an additional six months. In which fund or account group should the city report the TANs? Explain.

4. Assume further that in July 2020 the city was awarded a $1 million reimbursement grant. It expected to receive the grant funds in January 2021. Inasmuch as it expected to incur many of the expenditures covered by the grant in 2020, it issued $1 million in six-month revenue anticipation notes (RANs). As of December 31, the city had not repaid the notes but had secured the written agreement of the lender that they could be extended for an additional six months. How should the city report the RANs on its December 31, 2020, financial statements? Explain.

P. 8-5

For some types of debt, note disclosure is sufficient.

For each of the following items relating to the debt of Marfa City, indicate whether and how the debt would be reported on a balance sheet of one of the city's governmental funds. If it would not be reported on a balance sheet of one of the city's governmental funds, then state whether it would be reported instead on the government-wide statement of net position or in notes to the financial statements. Insofar as you would need additional information to determine how the debt should be reported, specify such information and tell how it would affect the determination. Briefly justify your response.

1. The city issues $10 million in 30-year, 6 percent revenue bonds to enable a local nursing home to construct new facilities. The facilities will be leased to the home for the term of the bonds, and the lease payments will be exactly equal to the debt service on the bonds. At the expiration of the lease, the property will revert to the home. The bonds are backed exclusively by the lease payments from the nursing home.

2. The city issues $20 million in 8 percent BANs, which it expects to refund approximately nine months after year-end, when, it hopes, long-term interest rates will drop. As part of an annexation agreement, the city constructs roads to an adjacent municipal utility district. The city funds the roads by issuing $15 million in bonds. The bonds are backed exclusively by assessments on the district's property owners. Although the city will collect the assessments and transmit the required payments to the bond trustee, the city is barred by both the state constitution and its own charter from assuming responsibility for the debt in the event of property owner defaults.

3. Ten years ago, the city issued, at par, $15 million in 6 percent, 20-year GO bonds. After the bonds have been outstanding for six years from the date of issue, they are redeemable at the option of the bondholders. The bonds are rated AAA and are fully insured by a highly reputable bond insurance company. Interest rates on comparable bonds are currently 5 percent.

4. A school district, the boundaries of which are the same as the city, has outstanding $120 million of GO bonds. The school district, which is governed by an independently elected board, is not a component unit of the city. However, both derive their revenues mainly from taxes on the same property, and the city serves as the district's property tax collection agent.

P. 8-6

Accountants and lawyers may have differing concepts of debt.

Officials of Danville, determining that the city needed additional administrative space, decided to acquire an available office building. Aware that city voters were unlikely to approve a bond issue to finance the purchase of the building, they decided instead to lease the property.

If the city had purchased the building outright, the acquisition price would have been $5 million. If it had issued general obligation bonds at the prevailing interest rate of 6 percent and elected to service the debt with equal payments over 20 years, then annual interest and principal payments (assuming annual compounding) would have been $435,923.

The city arranged for a financial institution to purchase the building and lease it to the city for 20 years. The lease specified annual payments of $435,923 and gave the city the option to purchase the building for $1 at the expiration of the agreement. The financial institution would sell shares in the lease to the public, just as if the city had issued bonds to acquire the building.

The lease also contained a nonappropriation clause stipulating that the city would make "good faith" efforts to adhere to its payment schedule, but that its obligation was limited to amounts that the city council appropriated annually.

1. Prepare a journal entry to reflect acquisition of the building by lease in the city's government-wide statements.

2. Prepare journal entries to record the first lease payment and the first year's depreciation (assuming a 20-year useful life). Indicate how the entries to record the second lease payment would differ from the first.

3. Suppose you were asked to represent the Danville Taxpayers Association, a group of citizens opposed to the acquisition of the building. The association contended that under the city's charter, the city was required to obtain voter approval for all general obligation debt over $1 million. The lease, it said, was the equivalent of general obligation debt. Therefore, it charged, the lease violated the city's charter and should be voided. What arguments would you make in support of the association's position?

4. Suppose, instead, that you were asked to represent the city. What arguments would you make to support the contention of city officials that the lease is not the equivalent of general obligation debt?

P. 8-7

Overlapping debt can significantly alter key measures of debt capacity.

The following information was taken from the City of Wyoming, Michigan's, schedule of direct and overlapping debt.

Name of Government Unit	Net Debt Outstanding	Percentage Applicable to City
City of Wyoming	$103.352.972	100.000%
Kent County	$123,225,000	9.350%
Grand Rapids Community College	$ 61,295,000	9.070%
Wyoming Public Schools	$ 36,910,000	99.700%
Godwin Heights Public Schools	$ 5,805,000	93.580%
Kelloggsville Public Schools	$ 3,510,000	63.000%
Grandville Public Schools	$ 17,430,000	29.080%
Kentwood Public Schools	$ 54,485,000	0.490%
Godfrey Lee Public Schools	$ 18,489,696	100.00%
Byron Center Public Schools	$ 84,329,655	1.370%

1. What is the most likely way the applicable percentages were derived?
2. Compute the total amount of the City of Wyoming's direct and overlapping debt.
3. The notes to the financial statements report that assessed value of property is $1,842,677,000 and that the population is 74,100. What would be the ratio of *direct debt* to assessed value? What would be the ratio of *total net direct debt and overlapping debt* to assessed value of property? What is the direct debt per capita? What would be the total net direct and overlapping debt per capita?
4. Why might a statement user be at least as concerned with the ratios that include overlapping debt as with those limited to direct general obligation debt?

P. 8-8

A lessor must report on its balance sheet both a receivable and the underlying asset.

Bean County recently acquired a commercial office building at a cost $20 million, paid in cash. It estimates that the economic life of the building is 40 years (with no salvage value).

Not requiring the entire building for its own use in the near-term, it leased-out four of its 10 floors to a private consulting firm. Annual rent was $800,000 per year and the term of the lease was 10 years. The county determined 6 percent was an appropriate discount rate to use in determining the present value of the anticipated rent receipts.

1. Prepare any journal entries that the county should make to reflect the acquisition of the building and the signing of the lease in its government-wide statements. Assume for convenience that all rent payments will be made at year-end.
2. Prepare any journal entries that it should make upon collection of the first-year's rent.
3. A key rationale for accounting for all leases as financing transactions is that the lessors, in economic substance "sells" the rights to use an asset for all or part of its useful life. How, therefore, can you justify not "derecognizing" that portion of the office building that will no longer be available for use by the county and correspondingly not recognizing an immediate gain (or loss) on the sale of such rights.

P. 8-9

Entries in both governmental funds and government-wide statements can be reconstructed from a city's schedule of changes in long-term debt.

The accompanying table was drawn from the City of Fort Leah's schedule of long-term liabilities (all amounts in thousands).

City of Ft. Leah Schedule of Long-Term Liabilities

	Beginning Balance	Additions	Reductions	Ending Balance
Governmental Activities				
Bonds and notes payable:				
General obligation debt	$503,341	$ 121	$ 30,179	$473,283
Leases	85,423	35		85,458
Special assessment bonds	1,200			1,200
Equipment note	370	156	27	499
Total bonds and notes payable	$590,334	$ 312	$ 30,206	$560,440
Other liabilities:				
Compensated absences	$125,600	$32,800	$ 29.700	$128,700
Net pension liability	62,000	47,000	53,500	55,500
Claims and judgments	11,360	4,340	2,000	13,700
Total other liabilities	$198,960	$84,140	$ 85,200	$197,900
Total long-term liabilities	$789,294	$84,452	$115,406	$758,340

1. Prepare the entry in the city's general fund to record the transactions affecting compensated absences during the year.
2. Prepare the entries to reflect the compensated absence transactions in the city's government-wide statements.
3. Prepare the entries in the capital projects and debt service funds to record the issuance and retirement of general obligation debt.
4. Prepare the entries to reflect the issuance and retirement of the general obligation debt in the government-wide statements.
5. Pension accounting is discussed in Chapter 10, which deals with fiduciary funds. However, based on what you know about expenditures and obligations in governmental funds, discuss the significance of the $47 million addition to, and $53.5 million reduction in, "net pension liability."
6. Suppose that the schedule above was taken from the government's 2018 financial statements, before it implemented GASB Statement No. 87, *Leases. During 2018* The city signed a five-year lease to rent space in an office building. The building had a 50-year estimated useful life. Annual rent was $100,000 per year. Where, if at all, on the schedule would the rent liability appear? Suppose instead that the government had already implemented Statement No. 87. How would your answer differ? Explain.

P. 8-10

Legal debt margins do not typically include all of a government's obligations.

The following was taken from the statistical section of the City of Wyoming, Michigan's annual report (see also Problem 8-7).

Computation of Legal Debt Margin for General Obligation Bonds as of June 30	
Assessed value, estimate	$1,934,971,000
Debt limit—10 percent of assessed value	193,497,110
Debt applicable to limit:	
City direct debt	103,352,972
Less: revenue bonds	(86,999,142)
Total net debt applicable to limits	$ 16,353,830
Legal debt margin	$ 177,143,280

Assume that in its fiscal year ending June 30, the city issued an additional (net of repayments) $30 million in general obligation bonds and $6 million in revenue bonds. Moreover, owing to both a recession and a change in valuing property, the assessed value of its property decreased by 5 percent.

1. What is the maximum the city could issue in general obligation bonds as of June 30? What would the city's net debt be?

2. Suppose the city:
   a. Signed a five-year agreement with a waste disposal firm. The firm agreed to provide services to the city for $50,000 per year. The city could not cancel the contract unless the firm failed to deliver the specified services.
   b. Signed a five-year lease to acquire equipment. The useful life of the equipment was also five years. Annual payments were $50,000, and the city had the option to purchase the equipment at the end of its useful life for $1. The lease agreement was based on an interest rate of 8 percent and contained a "nonappropriation clause," which local courts recognized as being decisive with respect to whether the debt was subject to the legal debt margin.

   How would each be reflected in the city's government-wide statement of net position? If you were writing the legislation establishing debt limits, would you make either leases or service contracts subject to the limits?

3. As indicated in the schedule, and as is typical of most debt limitations, the debt margin does not apply to revenue bonds. What do you think is the reason for this exemption? What argument could you make that revenue bonds should not be exempt?

P. 8-11

Key information as to long-term obligations may be found in a city's comprehensive annual financial report (CAFR) in sections other than the primary financial statements.

This problem is based on a recent annual report of the City of Tucson. Dates have been changed.

1. The MD&A reports that the city's general obligation bonds were rated AA—by Standard & Poor's. What is the significance of an AA—rating? (Standard & Poor's ratings are similar to those of Moody's.)

2. Another city of approximately the same size received the same bond rating as Tucson, even though its overall financial condition by all reasonable measures was substantially weaker than that of Tucson. What would be the most likely explanation of why the city received a higher relative rating than Tucson, even though Tucson is more financially sound?

3. A note to the financial statements indicates that the total required general obligation debt service payments over the life of the GO bonds were $266 million. Yet the total reported liability for GO bonds

was less than $215 million. What is the most likely explanation for the difference? How can you justify reporting the lower amount, when it is the higher amount that will have to be paid?

4. The city's list of bonds payable (Note 9) indicates that GO bonds were issued in 2003 with an interest rate of 5.75 percent. GO bonds issued in 2017 carried interest rates between 3 and 5 percent. Why do you suppose the city does not refund (redeem) the 2003 bonds and replace them with lower-interest obligations?

5. The Arizona Constitution limits the amount of debt that a city can have outstanding to 20 percent of the assessed value of its property if the debt is for water, sewer, parks, open space, and recreational facilities. The assessed valuation of property in Tucson in 2017 was $3,151,042,287 (Table XIII). What was the amount of the city's legal debt margin? How much of the city's debt limit is exhausted?

6. In 2011 the assessed value of the property in Tucson was $3,914,105,239, and the city had $222,360,610 in GO debt (and no balances in debt service funds). By 2017 the assessed value of property had decreased to $3,151,042,287, but bonded debt had also declined to $214,760,000. Taking into account the amount in the debt service funds, would you say that, other factors being equal, the city's debt burden was greater or less in 2017 than it was in 2011? Explain, making relevant computations.

P. 8-12

This example provides an overview of transactions addressed in this and previous chapters.

Zeff Township assessed property owners $1,000,000 to construct sidewalks. The assessments were payable over a period of 10 years in annual installments of $123,290, an amount that reflects interest at a rate of 4 percent.

To fund the improvements, the city issued $1,000,000 of 10-year, 4 percent bonds. The bonds were sold to yield interest of 3.8 percent (1.9 percent per period) and were thereby sold at a premium of $16,510 (i.e., at a total of $1,016,510). The township transferred the premium to an appropriate fund. Interest on the bonds is payable semiannually (i.e., $20,000 each six months).

In as much as the amounts to be received from the property owners are not coincident with the required payments to bondholders, the township will invest all available cash, and any assets that remain after the bonds have been repaid will be transferred to the general fund.

In the same year that the township assessed the property owners and issued the notes, it constructed the sidewalks at a cost of $1,000,000. During that year it made one payment of interest on the bonds and collected one installment from the property owners. It invested $119,800 in U.S. Treasury notes—the difference of $103,290 between the assessments received and the interest paid, plus the $16,510 bond premium. It earned $3,000 (cash) interest on these securities.

Assume that the township recognized one full year's interest on the assessments receivable and that it recorded one full year's depreciation (based on a useful life of 20 years) on the sidewalks.

1. Prepare summary journal entries in all appropriate funds.

2. Prepare alternative journal entries to reflect how the transactions would be recorded in the township's government-wide statements.

P. 8-13

Search online for the CAFR of the city of Charlotte, North Carolina. What is the total loan guarantees for the Community Development Block Grant (i.e.,Section 108 Loan Guarantee) disclosed in the notes? How does this compare to the city's outstanding general obligation bonds?

QUESTIONS FOR RESEARCH, ANALYSIS, AND DISCUSSION

1. As discussed in Chapter 4, governments must mark-to-market their investments (including held-to-maturity debt securities). Suppose that a city has in its portfolio debt securities that it intends to hold to maturity. Interest rates increase. Therefore the market value of the securities decreases, and accordingly the city, must recognize an investment loss. Correspondingly, the city also has issued debt. As interest rates increase, the market value of its outstanding bonds also decreases. Irrespective of current accounting standards, do you think that the city should recognize a gain from the decrease in value of its outstanding bonds? Explain.

2. A city funds the construction of a golf course by issuing $50 million in general obligation bonds. However, it accounts for the golf course in an enterprise fund, and it intends to repay the debt from green fees. Should the city, in its government-wide statement of net position, report the debt as a governmental activity and the golf course as a business-type activity? Alternatively, should it report both the debt and the golf course in the same category of activity? If so, then which one?

SOLUTION TO EXERCISE FOR REVIEW AND SELF-STUDY

1. In its general-fund statements, the entry would be:

Capital assets expenditures	$8.000.000	
Other financing sources—debt proceeds		$8,000,000

To record the expenditure and offsetting receipt of resources (in the general fund)

In its government-wide statements, it would record both the equipment and the lease obligation:

Equipment held under lease	$8.000.000	
Lease obligations		$8,000,000

To record the acquisition of equipment under a long-term lease

2. Of the first payment of rent, $480,000 (6 percent of $8 million) represents interest and $606,944 represents principal. The city must record the entire payment as expenditures in its general fund:

Lease expenditure— interest	$480.000	
Lease expenditure—Principal	606,944	
Cash		$1,086,944

To record the first lease payment (in the general fund)

In its government-wide statements it would recognize both interest expense and a reduction of the debt:

Lease obligations (lease principal)	$606.944	
Interest expense (lease interest)	480,000	
Cash		$1,086,944

To record the first lease payment

At the same time it would record annual depreciation:

Depreciation expense	$800.000	
Accumulated depreciation—equipment held under lease		$800,000

To record first year's depreciation ($8 million divided by 10 years)

3. Because the city does not have a take-out agreement, it cannot record the bonds as long-term obligations, irrespective of whether prevailing interest rates are higher or lower than those of the bonds. It must record the debt as a short-term obligation of the general (or some other governmental) fund. Thus,

Capital assets expenditures	$8.000.000	
Demand bonds payable		$8,000,000

To record the acquisition of the capital asset as financed with demand bonds that do not satisfy the criteria of long-term debt

Both the assets and the debt would be reported on the government-wide statement of net position. The debt would be classified as short term:

Equipment	$8.000.000	
Demand bonds payable		$8,000,000
To record equipment acquired with demand bonds		

4. After issuing the $8 million of new debt, the city would have total debt outstanding of $27 million. Its debt margin would be only $3 million—10 percent of its $30 million limit.

5. Of the taxable property in the school district, 75 percent ($600 million of $800 million) is located within the city. Therefore, the city is responsible for 75 percent of the school district's debt—$36 million.

CHAPTER 9

Business-Type Activities

LEARNING OBJECTIVES

After studying this chapter you should understand:

- What types of funds involve business-type activities
- Why governments and not-for-profits engage in business-type activities
- How governments distinguish between proprietary and governmental activities, and the reasons for and against different accounting practices
- The fundamental principles of proprietary fund accounting
- The unique accounting issues raised by the use of enterprise funds, including those pertaining to capital contributions, restricted assets, and landfills
- The special accounting issues relating to internal service funds
- How governments account for insurance activities
- The special problems of reporting proprietary funds in government-wide statements
- How investors assess revenue debt

Governments and not-for-profits engage in a variety of functions that are similar to those carried out by businesses. They range in size from the small gift shops of churches to multibillion-dollar regional power authorities.

Thus, in this chapter we will look at accounting principles applicable to business accounting. As shall soon be evident, the business-type activities of governments and not-for-profits are accounted for similar to corresponding enterprises in the private sector. Their financial statements are on a full rather than a modified accrual basis, and their measurement focus is on all economic resources, not on merely current financial resources.

We shall direct relatively little attention, therefore, to the general principles (such as those of revenue and expense recognition) of full accrual accounting. Because these are the same as those of businesses, they are covered in other courses dealing with financial accounting.

Instead, our objectives are more specific:

- To consider criteria for distinguishing between business and governmental activities and to raise pertinent questions as to whether and why these activities should be accounted for differently
- To address several selected accounting issues that are unique to government enterprises

- **To set forth the purposes and assess the consequences of using internal service funds to account for goods and services provided by one government department to another**
- **To show how business-type activities can be incorporated into government statements**
- **To present examples of the information needed to assess revenue bonds—the type of debt associated with both a government's business-type activities and not-for-profit organizations**

WHAT TYPES OF FUNDS INVOLVE BUSINESS-TYPE ACTIVITIES?

Governments segregate their business-type activities into *proprietary* funds, which are of two types: enterprise funds and internal service funds. These funds are said to be nonexpendable (or revolving) and thus focus on determining operating net income, changes in net position (or cost recovery), financial position, and cash flows.

- **Enterprise funds account** for operations in which goods or services are provided to the general public at large (users external to the governmental unit) on a user charge basis.
- **Internal service funds** account for operations in which goods or services are provided by one government department to other funds, departments, or agencies within the same governmental unit or occasionally to other governmental units on a user-charge or cost-reimbursement basis.

Some of the accounting and reporting issues pertaining to business-type activities are common to enterprise funds and internal service funds. However, each fund has unique features, so at the risk of repetition, we shall devote separate sections to each of the fund types.

Governments account for proprietary funds—both enterprise and internal service—on a full accrual basis. They recognize exchange revenues as earned and expenses (rather than expenditures) as incurred, irrespective of when cash is received or paid. They accord balance sheet recognition to both capital assets and long-term debt, depreciating the capital assets and amortizing any premiums or discounts on long-term debt.

Not-for-profits, in contrast to governments, account for their business-type activities—both internal and external—within their current operating funds. However, the current operating funds of not-for-profits, unlike those of governments, are on a full accrual rather than a modified accrual basis. Therefore, not-for-profits, like governments, also account for their business-type operations on a full accrual basis, giving balance sheet recognition to long-lived assets and long-term debt. The resources associated with these activities are generally donor-unrestricted and hence are so classified per the guidelines of Financial Accounting Standards Board (FASB) Accounting Standards Update (ASU) No. 2016-14, *Financial Statements of Not-for-Profit Organizations*.

WHY DO GOVERNMENTS AND NOT-FOR-PROFITS ENGAGE IN BUSINESS-TYPE ACTIVITIES?

Governments and not-for-profits engage in a wide variety of activities that are also carried out by for-profit businesses. For example:

- Governments provide waste removal; supply electric and other utility services; maintain hospitals (often in competition with stockholder-owned hospitals); and operate swimming pools, tennis courts, and golf courses.
- Universities sell computers, books, and clothing; sponsor professional-like sports teams; operate cafeterias and restaurants; and maintain dormitories.
- Churches, synagogues, hospitals, museums, and zoos sell religious artifacts, gifts, posters, and books.
- Girl Scouts sell cookies; Boy Scouts sell candy.

In the United States, prevailing political and economic doctrine dictates that goods and services be provided mainly by the private business sector. Why, then, do governments and not-for-profits engage in activities similar to those carried out by private enterprise? Several reasons can be cited:

- The activities provide resources that would otherwise have to be raised by taxes, contributions, tuition, or other means. Gift shops, for example, may be major sources of revenue for museums; government-owned utilities may generate cash as well as electricity, and are thereby a substitute for taxes and other forms of revenue.
- The activities complement and support the main mission of the entity. Thus, for example, college cafeterias, bookstores, and sports programs are an integral part of a university environment.
- The entity wants control over the activity. Thus, universities operate dormitories not necessarily because they can do so at lower cost than private contractors, but to maintain authority over them. Similarly, some cities and counties have rejected proposals to sell their hospitals to private firms so as to keep them entirely within their command.
- The entity can provide the services more cheaply or efficiently than a private firm can. This may be especially true if the government or not-for-profit is not subject to the income, property, or sales taxes that would be charged to private businesses. Public housing authorities, for example, have an inherent cost advantage over private landlords in providing apartments to low-income families in that their operations are not subject to state and federal income taxes.
- The entity wants either to subsidize the activity or to ensure that the goods or services are available at lower than market rates. Thus, a city might maintain a bus service or a public golf course even though it is unprofitable to do so.
- The activities, because of their nature, are believed to be inherently governmental rather than those of the private sector. Thus, police and fire services are almost always provided by governments even though there are examples of both being provided by businesses. In recent years, many governments have outsourced the operation of their prisons, but whether this is an appropriate function for **privatization** is open to controversy.

Both governments and not-for-profits have come under attack of late for operating programs and services that critics believe should be carried out in the private sector. Opponents of large government have urged the privatization of services, claiming that, lacking the profit motive, governments are inherently inefficient. Merchants have charged tax-exempt universities and museums with unfair competition in selling books, computers, and other items at lower than prevailing prices.

The issue of whether business-type activities should be carried out by governments and not-for-profits is beyond the scope of this text. But the reasons they carry them out are directly pertinent to questions of both how to distinguish business-type from governmental activities and how to account for them.

SHOULD BUSINESS-TYPE ACTIVITIES BE ACCOUNTED FOR DIFFERENTLY THAN GOVERNMENTAL ACTIVITIES?

A fundamental question pertaining to business-type activities is whether and why they should be accounted for differently than **governmental activities**—those that are financed predominantly through taxes and intergovernmental grants. The question that arises in particular is why business-type activities should be accounted for on a full rather than a modified accrual basis of accounting, even in fund statements.

Key reasons cited for using business-type accounting to account for proprietary-fund activities include:

- The full accrual basis of accounting (i.e., the measurement focus on all economic resources) captures all the resources and obligations, including capital assets and long-term obligations, associated with an activity. It thereby provides a more complete picture of the entity's fiscal status and operating results.

- The measurement focus on all economic resources is more consistent with the objectives of the Governmental Accounting Standards Board (GASB) that financial reporting should provide information to determine whether current-year revenues were sufficient to pay for current-year services and to assist users in assessing service efforts, costs, and accomplishments.
- Full accrual accounting provides information on depreciation, which is an essential cost of operations.
- Business-type accounting facilitates comparisons with similar private enterprises.

At the same time, there are cogent arguments against separate accounting principles for proprietary activities:

- Two separate measurement focuses and bases for accounting within the same set of financial statements are confusing and add complexity to the reporting process.
- As suggested earlier, there are no clear-cut distinctions between business and nonbusiness activities. Despite many similarities, governmental activities cannot—and should not—be compared to activities carried out in the private sector. A government should have sound political and economic reasons—other than merely earning a profit—for conducting a particular activity in the public sector. If it does not, then the activity should be privatized. These reasons by themselves should suggest that the activities be assessed by criteria other than profits—the *bottom line* of business-type financial reports.
- Surveys of statement users indicate that information on depreciation is not of high priority to governmental decision makers. They are concerned mainly with the ability of revenues to cover debt service and other obligations rather than with depreciation. This applies especially to users interested in toll roads, tunnels, and bridges.

Closely tied to the issue of whether proprietary activities should be accounted for using separate accounting principles is whether they should be accounted for and reported in separate funds. A key rationale for fund accounting and reporting in general is that legally restricted resources should be reported apart from those that are unrestricted. To be sure, the resources of some proprietary funds may be contractually dedicated to servicing revenue bonds. The resources of others, especially those accounted for in internal service funds, however, are often not legally restricted. They can be used for all purposes of government and are subject to the claims of general creditors. As discussed later in this chapter, governments must present restricted proprietary fund assets (usually owing to revenue bond covenants) separately from those that are unrestricted. Both, however, may be presented within the same fund.

Obviously, there are compelling reasons to account *internally* for each of a government's business-type activities in separate funds. Separate funds facilitate budgeting, planning, and control. However, when resources that are not legally restricted are reported on apart from unrestricted resources, statement users may have difficulty determining the total resources available for future appropriation or payment to creditors. They may be misled into thinking that unrestricted resources are, in fact, restricted.

In contrast to governments, not-for-profits prepare financial reports that are guided by the underlying principle that unrestricted resources, even if used to carry out business-type activities, should be reported on in a common fund. Not-for-profits have traditionally reported on their business-type activities within their current unrestricted funds, even though they may have maintained separate sets of books for each separate enterprise. This practice has been officially sanctioned since FASB Statement No. 117, *Financial Statements of Not-for-Profit Organizations*,[1] which required not-for-profits, for purposes of external reporting, to intermingle all resources, irrespective of whether they are associated with business or nonbusiness activities, unless they are *donor* restricted.

[1] FASB ASC 958-225-45.

Nevertheless, the arguments in favor of reporting on proprietary activities apart from governmental activities are also compelling. Up to the point of "information overload," more information is better than less. If managers need separate reports to assess the performance and fiscal status of business-type activities, so too do citizens, investors, and other statement users. Insofar as statement users are concerned with the total amount of unrestricted resources, they can readily add the resources in unrestricted proprietary funds together with those in the general and other unrestricted funds.

WHAT ARE THE THREE BASIC STATEMENTS OF PROPRIETARY FUND ACCOUNTING?

Similar to businesses, governments are required to prepare three basic proprietary fund statements:

- A statement of net position (balance sheet)
- A statement of revenues, expenses, and changes in net position (income statement)
- A statement of cash flows

Whereas the amounts reported in the individual fund statements of governmental funds are significantly different from those incorporated in the government-wide statements, those of proprietary funds are generally the same. As emphasized previously, the individual proprietary fund statements, like the government-wide statements, are on a full accrual basis of accounting.

THE STATEMENT OF NET POSITION (BALANCE SHEET)

In Statement No. 63, *Financial Reporting of Deferred Outflows of Resources, Deferred Inflows of Resources, and Net Position*, the GASB grants governments an option comparable to that regarding government-wide statements. Governments are encouraged to present the statement of net position in a format that displays assets, plus deferred outflows of resources, less liabilities, less deferred inflows of resources, equals net position. However, a more traditional balance sheet format (assets plus deferred outflows of resources equals liabilities plus deferred inflows of resources, plus net position) is also permitted. In either case, net position should be displayed in three broad components:

- Invested in capital assets (net of related debt, which is the total capital assets, less accumulated depreciation less the remaining debt used to acquire, construct, or improve these assets)
- Restricted net position
- Unrestricted net position

Governments should also segregate the restricted assets themselves (as opposed to the offsetting net position). Suppose that a government holds in a separate bank account cash that is restricted to debt service. To classify that cash as a current asset would suggest that it is available for general use. Therefore, the government should report that cash as a restricted asset, apart from its other current assets.

The distinctions between restricted and unrestricted assets, as well as other issues relating to restrictions, are addressed in a subsequent section. It should be noted that GASB Statement No. 54, *Fund Balance Reporting and Governmental Fund Type Definitions*, which requires the fund balances to be categorized as restricted, committed, assigned, and unassigned, applies only to the fund balances of governmental funds, not the net position of proprietary funds.

THE STATEMENT OF REVENUES, EXPENSES, AND CHANGES IN NET POSITION (INCOME STATEMENT)

The statement of revenues, expenses, and changes in net position is comparable to the income statement of a business. It differs, however, in that it is all-inclusive. That is, it reports not only operating revenues and expenses, but also capital contributions.

Further, it incorporates a reconciliation of beginning and ending net position. The following summarizes its key elements:

Operating revenues	
Fees and charges	$10,000
Others (detailed)	2,000
Total operating revenues	12,000
Operating expenses	
Wages and salaries	8,000
Others (detailed)	1,500
Total operating expenses	9,500
Operating income (loss)	2,500
Nonoperating revenues and expenses	
State operating grants	2,400
Others (detailed)	500
Total nonoperating revenues and expenses	2,900
Income before other revenues, expenses, gains, losses, and transfers	5,400
Capital contributions and other changes in net position	
Federal capital grant	800
Others (e.g., additions to permanent and term endowments, special and extraordinary items, and transfers)	300
Total capital contributions	1,100
Increase (decrease) in net position	6,500
Net position—beginning of period	20,000
Net position—end of period	$26,500

The distinction between operating and nonoperating revenues and expenses is not always clear and is subject to management discretion. In general the classification scheme should follow that adopted for the statement of cash flows (as shown in Table 9-1). Issues pertaining to capital contributions will be discussed in a section to follow.

The Statement of Revenues, Expenses, and Changes in Net Position, and the Statement of Net Position for the proprietary funds of Charlotte, North Carolina, were presented in Chapter 2 (Table 2-9).

THE STATEMENT OF CASH FLOWS

Governments are required to prepare a statement of cash flows for proprietary funds, but not for governmental funds. There is less need for a statement of cash flows for governmental funds because governmental funds are accounted for on a modified accrual basis. Therefore, the statement of revenues and expenditures of governmental funds focuses—if not on cash itself—then on resources that are near-cash and are currently available for disbursement.

The preparation of a statement of cash flows can be complex and tedious, but it presents few, if any conceptual problems. In essence, the statement is a summary of an entity's cash account. The issues that both the FASB and the GASB have had to address pertain mainly to transaction classification.

Different Standards for Governments and Businesses

The GASB and FASB standards for statements of cash flows establish differing classification schemes. FASB Statement No. 95 (*Statement of Cash Flows*), which does not apply to governments, requires that cash transactions be classified into three categories:

- ***Cash flows from operating activities***, such as receipts from sales of goods and services; interest; and dividends and disbursements for goods and materials, interest, and taxes.
- ***Cash flows from financing activities***, such as proceeds from issuing stocks and bonds, and payments for dividends and repayments of loans.
- ***Cash flows from investing activities***, such as receipts and disbursements from the sale and purchase of marketable securities and long-lived assets.[2]

These categories have obvious limitations if applied to governments. Governments typically characterize their activities as either operating or capital. Capital activities—those involving the acquisition and financing of long-lived assets—are often both budgeted and accounted for apart from operating activities. Yet the FASB classification scheme draws no distinction between the two.

To remedy this deficiency the GASB issued its Statement No. 9 (Reporting Cash Flows of Proprietary and Nonexpendable Trust Funds and Governmental Entities That Use Proprietary Fund Accounting), which provides for a classification scheme with four categories:

- Cash flows from operating activities
- Cash flows from noncapital financing activities
- Cash flows from capital and related financing activities
- Cash flows from investing activities

Table 9-1 sets forth the main transactions included in each category.

The GASB and FASB standards also differ in how interest should be reported. In a significant departure from the precedent of FASB Statement No. 95, the GASB pronouncement requires that government enterprises classify interest paid as financing activities and interest received as investing activities rather than operating activities. Whether interest paid is classified as a capital rather than a noncapital financing activity depends on how the underlying debt is classified. The GASB maintains that by classifying interest received and disbursed in the same categories as purchases and sales of the underlying securities, governments provide a more complete picture of the cash flows associated with financing and investing activities.

In another very significant departure from FASB Statement No. 95, GASB Statement No. 34 mandates that governments report their cash flows using only the direct method. The direct method explicitly reports the operating cash flows in a way that makes clear their source or use (e.g., cash receipts from customers; cash payments to employees). The indirect method, by contrast, reconciles operating cash flows to operating income. Thus, the reporting entity would add to or subtract from operating income any differences between cash flows (e.g., cash receipts from customers; cash payments to employees) and the related revenues or expenses (e.g., sales

[2] FASB ASC 230-10-05.

TABLE 9-1 Classification of Cash Receipts and Disbursements per GASB Statement No. 9, Reporting Cash Flows of Proprietary and Nonexpendable Trust Funds and Governmental Entities that Use Proprietary Fund Accounting

Cash Flows from Operating Activities

Inflows

- Sales of goods or services, including collections of receivables
- Grants for operating activities
- Receipts from interfund services provided by other funds or from interfund reimbursements
- All other cash receipts not defined as capital, financing, or investing transactions

Outflows

- Payments to acquire materials for providing services, including payments on accounts payable
- Payments to employees
- Grants to other governments for operating activities
- Payments for taxes, duties, fines, and other fees or penalties
- Payments for interfund services used by other funds, including certain payments in lieu of taxes
- All other cash payments not defined as capital, financing, or investing transactions

Cash Flows from Noncapital Financing Activities

Inflows

- Proceeds from bonds, notes, or other debt instruments not clearly attributable to the acquisition, construction, or improvement of capital assets
- Grants from other governments that are not specifically restricted for capital purposes or are not for specific activities considered to be operating activities of the grantor government (e.g., a grant to finance an operating deficit)
- Receipts from other funds except (1) amounts clearly attributable to acquisitions, construction, or improvement of capital assets; (2) interfund services provided; and (3) reimbursements for operating transactions
- Receipts from property and other taxes collected for the governmental enterprise that are not specifically restricted for capital purposes

Outflows

- Repayments of amounts borrowed for noncapital purposes
- Interest payment on amounts borrowed for noncapital purposes
- Grants to other governments except for those specific activities that are considered to be operating activities of the grantor government
- Cash paid to other funds, except for interfund services used

Cash Flows from Capital and Related Financing Activities

Inflows

- Proceeds from issuing bonds, notes, or other debt instruments for the acquisition, construction, or improvement of capital assets
- Capital grants
- Receipts from the sale of capital assets
- Contributions from other funds, governments, or other entities for acquiring, constructing, or improving capital assets
- Special assessments and property taxes to finance capital assets

(*Continues*)

TABLE 9-1 Classification of Cash Receipts and Disbursements per GASB Statement No. 9, Reporting Cash Flows of Proprietary and Nonexpendable Trust Funds and Governmental Entities that Use Proprietary Fund Accounting *(Continued)*

Outflows

- Payments to acquire, construct, or improve capital assets
- Repayments of capital debt
- Interest on capital debt

Cash Flows from Investing Activities

Inflows

- Receipts from sales of marketable securities
- Interest and dividends received from investments
- Withdrawals from investment pools
- Collections of loans made by the government (except for program loans)

Outflows

- Purchases of marketable securities
- Disbursement for loans (except for program loans)
- Deposits into investment pools

revenues; wage and salary expense). The FASB encourages businesses and not-for-profits to use the direct method but permits them to use the indirect method. But despite the FASB's expressed preference for the direct method, the overwhelming majority of businesses elect to use the indirect method. This may change now that, per ASU No. 2016-14, businesses and not-for-profits that report cash flows using the direct method no longer must also report a reconciliation that essentially amounts to the indirect method.

Charlotte, North Carolina's Statement of Cash Flows for its proprietary funds is presented in Table 9-2.

WHAT ACCOUNTING ISSUES ARE UNIQUE TO ENTERPRISE FUNDS OF GOVERNMENTS?

Although governments have adopted the business accounting model to account for their enterprise funds, they nevertheless face several unique issues. Two very basic questions pertain to when an activity should be accounted for in an enterprise fund and what principles should govern the accounting for an enterprise fund. Other more specific issues relate to budgetary reporting, capital contributions, restricted assets, and landfills.

CRITERIA FOR ESTABLISHING AN ENTERPRISE FUND

Almost all government departments engage in some form of entrepreneurial activity.

Accordingly, there is no obvious way to distinguish activities that should be accounted for in enterprise funds, and in the past there has been considerable diversity of practice. To reduce this diversity, the GASB established general criteria as to when a government may, and when it must, account for an activity in an enterprise fund.

The GASB standards, although much tighter than those that they replaced, still allow governments considerable discretion in determining which of their activities to account for in enterprise funds. Most notably, for example, they state that a government *may* use an enterprise fund to account for any activity for which it charges fees. Thus, governments have the option of using either an enterprise or a governmental fund to account for those activities for which they charge fees but which do not satisfy any of the three mandatory criteria.

TABLE 9-2 City of Charlotte, North Carolina, Statement of Cash Flows Proprietary Funds for Year Ended June 30, 2017 (in thousands)

	Business-type Activities-Enterprise Funds					Governmental Activities—Internal Service Funds
	Water and Sewer	Storm Water	Airport	Public Transit	Total	
Cash flows from operating activities:						
Receipts from customers	$ 403,325	$ 70,629	$ 231,989	$ 31,909	$ 737,852	$ —
Receipts from participants	—	—	—	—	—	42,264
Payments to suppliers	(75,586)	(262)	(77,536)	(53,041)	(206,425)	(10,563)
Internal activity—(payments to) receipts from other funds	(25,156)	(1,315)	(24,003)	(11,430)	(61,904)	74,171
Receipts from trust	—	—	—	—	—	24,838
Receipts from recovery of losses	—	—	—	—	—	180
Payments to employees	(45,329)	(8,456)	(28,607)	(70,239)	(152,631)	(1,624)
Payments to airlines for non—airline terminal revenue distribution	—	—	(17,776)	—	(17,776)	—
Payments for claims	—	—	—	—	—	(92,957)
Payments for premiums	—	—	—	—	—	(28,811)
Other receipts (payments)	21,139	20	(105,707)	367	(84,181)	934
Net cash provided (used) by operating activities	278,393	60,616	(21,640)	(102,434)	214,935	8,432
Cash flows from noncapital financing activities:						
Operating grants	—	—	—	12,053	12,053	—
Sales tax	—	—	—	94,373	94,373	—
Transfers	—	—	(222)	22,243	22,021	—
Net cash provided by noncapital financing activities	—	—	(222)	128,669	128,447	—
Cash flows from capital and related financing activities:						
Proceeds from capital debt	49,554	—	247,037	—	296,591	—
Passenger facility charges	—	—	59,015	—	59,015	—
Contract facility charges	—	—	12,820	—	12,820	—
Acquisition and construction of capital assets	(153,382)	(48,922)	(145,861)	(241,897)	(590,062)	—
Principal paid on capital debt	(83,247)	(6,082)	(46,218)	159,527	23,980	—
Interest and other charges paid on capital debt	(71,952)	(6,528)	(9,683)	(13,802)	(101,965)	—
Capital contributions	4,644		11,131	199,887	215,662	—
Net cash used by capital and related financing activities	(254,383)	(61,532)	128,241	103,715	(83,959)	—
Cash flows from investing activities:						
Purchase of investments	(1,500)	(36)	(255,281)	(35)	(256,852)	—
Proceeds from sale and maturities of investments	—	13,958	187,678	11,256	212,892	—
Interest received	1,312	462	4,321	274	6,369	687
Net cash provided by investing activities	(188)	14,384	(63,282)	11,495	(37,591)	687
Net increase (decrease) in cash and cash equivalents	23,822	13,468	43,097	141,445	221,832	9,119
Cash and cash equivalents—beginning of year	321,897	82,458	916,188	78,027	1,398,570	121,563
Cash and cash equivalents—end of year	$ 345,719	$ 95,926	$ 959,285	$ 219,472	$ 1,620,402	$ 130,682

GASB STANDARDS

In Statement No. 34, the GASB prescribes that governments *may* account for an activity in an enterprise fund as long as it charges fees to external users for goods and services. They *must* account for an activity in an enterprise fund if the activity satisfies one of the following criteria:

- The activity is financed solely with revenue debt, as opposed to general obligation debt. Whereas general obligation debt is backed by the full faith and credit of the entire government, revenue debt is secured merely by the revenues from a specific activity.
- Laws or regulations require that the activity's costs of providing services (including capital costs) be recovered by fees and charges rather than general purpose taxes or similar charges.
- The pricing policies of the activity establish fees and charges designed to recover its costs, including capital costs (such as depreciation or debt service).[3]

The criteria should be applied to an activity's principal source of revenue—not to insignificant sources. Thus, even if a police department charges fees for escorting funeral processions or for controlling traffic at charitable "fun runs," the activities need not be accounted for in an enterprise fund.

[3] GASB Statement No. 34, *Basic Financial Statements—and Management's Discussion and Analysis—for State and Local Governments* (June 1999), para. 67.

ACCOUNTING PRINCIPLES

In general, proprietary funds are accounted for similar to businesses; for the most part they must adhere to pronouncements that were initially issued by the FASB and, in some cases, the AICPA. Until 2011, governments actually looked to the specific pronouncements of those organization for accounting guidance. In 2010, however, the GASB issued Statement No. 62, *Codification of Accounting and Financial Reporting Guidance Contained in Pre-November 30 1989 FASB and AICPA Pronouncements*, in which it explicitly adopted all FASB and AICPA pronouncements that are relevant to governments as its own. These pronouncements are now incorporated into the GASB *Codification* as if the GASB itself had issued them.

THE NEED FOR BUDGETS AND BUDGET-TO-ACTUAL COMPARISONS

Government enterprises are disciplined by the marketplace rather than by their budgets. Both their revenues and expenses, unlike those of governmental funds, are determined mainly by "customer" demand, not by legislative action. Principles of sound management dictate that governments, like businesses, prepare annual budgets. However, the budgets of proprietary funds play a decidedly different role than those of governmental funds. Like those of businesses, they facilitate planning, control, and evaluation. They are not, however, the equivalent of either spending authorizations or tax levies. Accordingly, governments are not required to obtain formal legislative approval for their proprietary fund budgets or to incorporate them into their accounting systems. Moreover, in their annual reports they need not compare the budgeted amounts with actual results.

Governments, like businesses, should ordinarily prepare several different types of budgets. For example, they should formulate the following:

- A cash budget to facilitate cash management and help ensure that they will have adequate but not excessive cash on hand
- A capital budget to expedite the acquisition of capital assets
- A flexible budget, indicating anticipated fixed and variable costs at different levels of output, to help control costs

CAPITAL CONTRIBUTIONS

Enterprise funds receive capital contributions from both internal (i.e., other funds) and external (e.g., new customers, developers, and other governments) sources. The key accounting and reporting issues pertain to determining how capital contributions should be presented on the financial statements and distinguishing capital contributions from ordinary revenues. Consider several examples of different types of nonroutine receipts:

- ***Tap (system development) fees.*** A city charges new customers of an electric or water utility a tap fee to hook up to an existing system. The amount of the fee may exceed the cost of connecting the customer to the system; part may cover the customer's share of the capital cost of the system already in place.
- ***Impact fees.*** A municipal utility district charges developers a fee for anticipated improvements, such as new water and sewer lines, that will be required because of new development. Unlike tap fees, these fees cannot necessarily be associated with specific projects or improvements.
- ***External subsidies.*** A municipal transit authority receives a federal grant to both purchase new buses and defray operating costs.
- ***Internal subsidies.*** A county hospital receives an annual transfer from the county's general fund based on the number of indigent patients it serves. The transfer enables the hospital to cover both operating expenses and acquire new equipment.
- ***Debt forgiveness.*** A state provides a loan to its state-operated liquor stores. The stores have historically been unprofitable, and there is little possibility of the loan ever being repaid.

Insofar as tap fees and similar types of charges cover the actual costs of hooking a customer into a utility system, they should be considered exchange transactions and accounted for as operating revenues. To the extent, however, that they exceed the actual costs or are unrelated to them, they should then be interpreted as nonexchange transactions and be classified as capital contributions or nonoperating revenues.[4]

RESTRICTED ASSETS AND NET POSITION

Governmental proprietary units are, in key respects, reporting entities within reporting entities. Although accounted for in separate funds, they issue debt and are responsible for servicing it. Accordingly, some of their resources may be restricted. For example:

- Bond proceeds and grants from other governments may have to be used for the construction or acquisition of specific assets.
- Resources may have to be set aside for the repayment of bond principal or the payment of interest.
- Customer deposits may have to be segregated from other resources to ensure that they are available for return.

To indicate that assets are restricted, governments should report their restricted enterprise-fund assets apart from unrestricted assets. Correspondingly, they should also report any offsetting net position in a separate equity account.

Governments should include within the restricted category resources that are restricted by both outside parties (such as bondholders and other creditors, grantors, or the laws of higher-level governments) or themselves (through legislation that limits the use of assets to specified

---

[4] Government Finance Officers Association. *Governmental Accounting, Auditing, and Financial Reporting* (2012), 212–214.

purposes). Restricted resources must be distinguished from resources that are merely "designated" by a government's policy for an intended purpose. Thus, for example, if a government informally sets cash aside for a "rainy day," that cash should not be classified as restricted. To avoid confusion, governments should not report designations of net position on the face of the balance sheet.

The accounting for restrictions may get a bit complex because some restricted assets are offset not by net position, but instead by liabilities. Compare, for example, two types of restricted assets relating to debt.

- A government issues bonds and has temporarily invested the proceeds in marketable securities. The marketable securities are restricted assets in that they must be used for the purpose specified in the bond indenture. The securities are offset by a liability, "bonds payable." Hence, the securities and the related bonds have no impact on net position (assets less liabilities). Therefore, even though the securities are restricted (and should be so classified), it would be inappropriate to categorize any amount of net position as restricted.
- A government, as required by bond covenants, sets aside cash in a special account restricted to the payment of interest on long-term debt. The interest has not yet been recognized as either an expense or a liability. Accordingly, both the cash and an equal amount of net position should be classified as restricted.

Example

Revenue Bond Proceeds as Restricted Assets

A government issues $10 million in revenue bonds that are restricted to the construction of plant and equipment. The following entry would be appropriate:

Cash restricted for construction	$10	
Revenue bonds payable		$10
To record the issuance of revenue bonds and to designate the proceeds as restricted		

Inasmuch as the restricted cash is offset by a liability, there is no need to reclassify a portion of unrestricted net position as restricted. Subsequently, the government sets aside an additional $2 million cash to pay interest on the debt:

Cash restricted for debt service	$ 2	
Cash (unrestricted)		$ 2
To record the designation of cash as restricted		

At the same time, because unrestricted net position have now been reduced by $2 million, the government must reclassify that amount as restricted:

Net position—unrestricted	$ 2	
Cash (unrestricted)		$ 2
To reclassify a portion of net position to reflect resources restricted for debt service		

LANDFILL COSTS

One of the most pressing economic and political issues of the foreseeable future will be how to maintain—and pay for—a clean environment. Both governments and private industry will face billions of dollars of costs to dispose of wastes, prevent additional pollution, and mitigate already-existing hazards. Because the magnitude of the potential costs is so great, and the timing, specific amounts, and distribution of cash outlays are so uncertain, the associated accounting issues are necessarily complex. Prior to 2016, the GASB had issued official pronouncements on only two aspects of the issues—accounting for landfill costs and accounting for pollution remediation.[5] GASB Statement No. 83, issued November 2016, deals with decommissioning capital assets such as nuclear power plants and sewage treatment plants.

Governments account for landfills in either governmental or enterprise funds, depending mainly on whether they charge usage fees. Because most governments do charge usage fees, they generally account for them in enterprise funds. The GASB standards to be discussed are equally applicable to both enterprise and governmental funds with regard to the calculation of the *amount* of the landfill liability to be reported. But inasmuch as the two types of funds differ in their measurement focus and basis of accounting, they differ as to *where* the liability should be reported and *when* the related expenditure must be charged.

Landfills provide benefits over the period they accept waste, often 30 or 40 years. However, both state and federal regulations make landfill operators responsible for properly closing their landfills and subsequently caring for and monitoring them. Therefore, an operator must incur sizable costs when it closes the landfill and for an extended period, as long as 20 years, thereafter.

The accounting problems pertaining to closure and postclosure costs are comparable to those of employee pensions. The benefits are received over the years the landfill accepts waste (and in the case of pensions, benefits ARE received over the years employees provide their services). Although some costs may be incurred prior to the point of landfill closure (and prior to employees' retirement), most are incurred during the years of closure (and during retirement) and beyond. Moreover, the actual costs to be incurred are subject to unpredictable factors.

GASB STANDARDS

Consistent with the pension accounting principles in both industry and government, the GASB has directed that proprietary funds allocate closure and postclosure costs to the years in which the landfill accepts waste rather than to the years when these costs are paid. Therefore, in each year of a landfill's useful life, the government should recognize as both an expense and an increase in liability an appropriate portion of the estimated total costs for closure and postclosure care.

Total costs would include the following:

- Cost of equipment expected to be installed and facilities expected to be constructed near or after the date that the landfill stops accepting waste (e.g., gas monitoring and collection systems, storm water management systems, and groundwater monitoring wells)
- Cost of final cover
- Cost of monitoring and maintaining the landfill during the postclosure period

The amount to be added to a liability account at the end of each year would be based on the percentage of the landfill actually used up to that point. It would equal the percentage of the landfill used during the year times the total estimated costs. At any point during the life of the landfill, the balance in the liability account would equal the sum of the yearly amounts added to the account, less any costs incurred.

From a slightly different perspective, the amount to be added to a liability each year—and to be charged as the expense for that year—would be the total amount that should have been recognized as an expense (added to the liability) up to the date of computation, less the amount that has actually been recognized so far. Thus, the amount to be added each year (the current year expense) equals:

$$\frac{\text{Estimated total cost} \times \text{Landfill capacity used to date}}{\text{Total landfill capacity}} - \text{Amounts recognized in the past}$$

Both costs and capacity would be based on *current* conditions at the time of the computation. Each year the government would reestimate both total landfill capacity and total closure and postclosure costs, taking into account inflation, new regulatory requirements, and technological improvements since the previous computation.

[5] GASB Statement No. 18, *Accounting for Municipal Solid Waste Landfill Closure and Postclosure Care Costs* (August 1993), and GASB Statement No. 49, *Accounting and Financial Reporting for Pollution Remediation Obligations* (November 2006).

The GASB does *not* deal with the issue of when governments should *finance* closure and postclosure costs. Therefore, a government is not necessarily required to "fund" the costs during the landfill's useful life; it merely must report both an expense and a liability for them. Moreover, in contrast to the manner in which it would compute its pension liability, a government should not take into account the time value of money in making any of its calculations.

The example that follows illustrates how a government would account for a landfill in an enterprise fund (as well as in its government-wide, full accrual statements). If it accounted for the landfill in a governmental fund, only the journal entries, not the total liability or the amount to be added each year, would differ. Inasmuch as governmental funds do not report long-term obligations, the liability for the closure and postclosure costs would be reported only in the government-wide statements, not in the fund itself. Correspondingly, the governmental fund would not report an annual expenditure for the amount added to the liability account. As with other long-term obligations, a fund expenditure would be charged only in the period that the liability is to be liquidated with currently available financial resources. The result is that with respect to the expenditure, the government is therefore on a "pay-as-you-go" basis.

Example

Landfill Costs in an Enterprise Fund

At the start of Year 1, a government opens a landfill, which it elects to account for in an enterprise fund. It estimates that total capacity will be 4.5 million cubic feet, that the site will be used for 30 years, and that total closure costs will be $18 million.

Year 1

During Year 1, the government uses 90,000 cubic feet of the landfill. At year-end, it estimates that total capacity will still be 4.5 million cubic feet but that closure-related costs will now be $18,036,000. The required expense addition to the liability would be computed as follows:

Total estimated costs	$18,036,000
Proportion of landfill used (90,000/4,500,000)	× .02
Required expense (addition to liability)	$ 360,720

Journal Entry

Landfill expense	$360,720	
Liability for landfill costs		$ 360,720
To record the landfill liability and expense for Year 1		

The end-of-year balance in the liability account would be $360,720.

Year 2

In Year 2, the government uses 120,000 cubic feet of the landfill. At year-end, it estimates that total closure-related costs have increased to $18,526,600 and that landfill capacity has decreased to 4,275,000 cubic feet. Thus:

Total estimated costs	$18,526,600
Proportion of landfill used to date (90,000 + 120,000)/4,275,000	× .049122
Amount that should have been added to the liability to date (cumulative expense)	910,079
Less: amount recognized previously	360,720
Required expense (addition to liability)	$ 549,359

Journal Entry		
Landfill expense	$549,359	
Liability for landfill costs		$549,359
To record the landfill liability and expense for Year 2		

The end-of-year balance in the liability account would be $360,720 + $549,359 = $910,079.

Year 3

In Year 3, the government uses 135,000 cubic feet of the landfill. At year-end, it estimates that total closure-related costs have increased to $18,840,254 and that landfill capacity has remained at 4,275,000 cubic feet. During the year the government also spends $277,221 on closure-related costs.

Total estimated costs	$18,840,254
Proportion of landfill used to date (90,000 + 120,000 + 135,000)/4,275,000	× 0.080700
Amount that should have been added to the liability to date (cumulative expense)	1,520,442
Less: amount recognized previously	910,079
Required expense (addition to liability)	$ 610,363

Journal Entry		
Landfill expense	$610,363	
Liability for landfill costs		$610,363
To record the landfill liability and expense for Year 3		

Because the government actually incurs the closure-related costs of $277,221, it would record the payment as follows:

Liability for landfill costs	$277,221	
Cash		$277,221
To record the payment of closure or postclosure costs		

It would not matter if these costs were incurred for the acquisition of capital assets (e.g., earth-moving equipment) or for operating purposes (e.g., salaries). The government does *not* record as capital assets the equipment and facilities included in the estimate of closure-related costs. When the government acquires the capital assets, it simply credits cash and debits the previously established liability for landfill costs.

Capital assets to be used after the landfill has been closed (and which are thereby included in the estimate of postclosure costs) must be distinguished from capital assets used to operate the landfill while it is in operation. The capital assets spent to operate the landfill while it is in active use should be capitalized and depreciated over their useful lives. They should be fully depreciated by the time the landfill stops accepting waste. The end-of-year balance in the liability account would be $360,720 + $549,359 + $610,363—$277,221 = $1,243,221.

ASSET RETIREMENT OBLIGATIONS

Conceptually similar to landfills are **asset retirement obligations** (AROs). An asset retirement obligation is defined in GASB Statement No. 83, *Certain Asset Retirement Obligations* (November 2016) as "a legally enforceable liability associated with the retirement of a tangible capital asset (i.e., the tangible capital asset is permanently removed from service)." Just as landfills provide service over numerous years but require costly closure and postclosure activities, so also do various types of capital assets. Most notably, for example, nuclear reactors must be decommissioned and sewage treatment plants must be dismantled, typically at considerable expense. As with landfills, interperiod equity requires that the closure and post-closure expenses be recognized in the periods that the assets are in use, and provide their benefits, rather than those in which they are being retired. Moreover, since the obligations are unavoidable—they are defined as legally enforceable—they satisfy the GASB's definition of a liability: "present obligations to sacrifice resources that the government has little or no discretion to avoid."

GASB Statement No. 83 mandates that a government recognize a liability for an ARO when the liability is incurred and is reasonably estimable. For many assets, such as a nuclear power plant or a wind farm, the liability would normally be recognized when the facility is constructed or acquired. For others, such as a university's research laboratory, it might be recognized upon the occurrence of an event that results in chemical or biological contamination that will have to be remedied when the laboratory is shut down. For other assets it might be when new federal, state or local laws or regulations are approved that will cause the government to incur previously unexpected shut-down costs.

Per GASB Statement No. 83 a government should initially measure an ARO liability as the *current value* of retirement outlays expected to be incurred. This would include the cost of applicable equipment, facilities and services as if they were to be acquired as of the end of the current reporting period. Of course, many assets will not be retired for decades after the ARO liability must first be recognized. Therefore, each year subsequent to that in which it first recognizes the liability, the government should adjust the liability for changes in its current value. These changes might be a consequence of general inflation, ups or downs in prices of specific goods or services, technological modifications that increase or decrease costs, or new government regulations. Presumably, therefore, the book value of the liability in the year that the asset is retired will approach the actual costs to be incurred.

The government should offset the initial liability with a deferred outflow of resources. Then, each year, it should amortized the deferred outflow of resources on a systematic and rational manner over the estimated useful life of the asset. Moreover, as it adjusts the liability over time to reflect the changes in current value, it should correspondingly adjust the deferred outflow of resources by the same amount.

A government should provide in notes to the financial statements a general description of its AROs, describe the methods and assumptions used to measure the liabilities and indicate whether all legally required funding provisions, such as surety bonds and insurance policies, are being met. If the government does not recognize the liability for an ARO because it is not reasonably estimable, then it should disclose that fact and the reason why.

POLLUTION REMEDIATION COSTS

Government can be held accountable for pollution cleanup costs owing to a variety of circumstances. For example:

- A city's electric utility or its public works department permitted poisonous chemicals to be discharged into the ground
- A school district discovered mold or asbestos in one of its buildings
- Toxic substances from an abandoned county dump seeped into a nearby water supply
- A city purchased residential houses with the intention of remodeling them for sale to low-income citizens. As part of the remodeling process, city staff must remove any toxic substances

As with landfill costs, pollution remediation costs may be accounted for in either governmental or enterprise funds. If accounted for in a governmental fund, then consistent with the nature of such funds, only current outlays would be recognized as expenditures; no long-term liabilities would be recorded. If accounted for in enterprise funds, as well as in government-wide statements, then estimates of costs to be incurred in the future would be reported as both expenses and offsetting liabilities.

GASB STANDARDS

Per Statement No. 49, *Accounting and Financial Reporting for Pollution Remediation Obligations* (November 2006), the pollution remediation costs to be accounted for include those for:

- Precleanup activities such as site assessments, site investigations, corrective measures feasibility studies, and designs of remediation plans
- Cleanup activities such as removal and disposal of pollutants and site restoration
- Government oversight and enforcement-related activities such as work performed by an environmental regulatory authority dealing with the site and chargeable to the government
- Postremediation monitoring

These costs should be estimated and recognized as an expense and liability when the government knows or has reason to believe that a site is polluted, that it will be responsible for the cleanup, and it can make reasonable estimates of the ultimate cost. Thus, for example, a cost assessment would be required if there is an imminent danger to public health, the government has been identified as a responsible party, or the government has been named in a lawsuit. The estimate should be based on the expected current value of the cash outflows (net of any amounts to be recovered from other parties) that will eventually be required. The current value of the cash outflows is the amount that would be paid if all equipment, facilities, and services included in the estimate were acquired during the current period. When the government can do no better than determine a range of potential cash outflows, the cost estimate should be the sum of probability-weighted amounts within such range. Estimates should be reviewed periodically and adjusted as new and better information becomes available.

As a general rule, all costs, including those for plant and equipment, should be expensed rather than capitalized. The main exceptions are when the government is preparing the polluted property for an anticipated sale or when property is purchased for a specific purpose and the government knows in advance that it will have to remediate the site. Thus, for example, if a government buys a contaminated parcel of land with the intention of cleaning it up and building on it, the remediation costs should be added to the purchase price of the land.

Governments are required to disclose in notes the nature and source of pollution remediation obligations, methods, and assumptions underlying the cost estimates and any expected cost recoveries.

Example

Pollution Remediation Costs in an Enterprise Fund

A city-operated parking lot was on land that had once been adjacent to a manufacturing plant. During the year the city became aware of underground storage tanks that were leaking chemicals into a nearby stream. Owing to uncertainty as to the extent of pollution, engineers estimate that there was a 60 percent probability that the cost would be $200,000 and a 40 percent probability that it would be only $160,000.

Taking into account this limited information, the city would recognize an expense and corresponding liability of $184,000:

$200,000 × .60	$120,000
$160,000 × .40	$ 64,000
Total	$184,000

Suppose instead that the city had acquired the property with the intent of using it as a parking lot and knowing that it would cost $200,000 to remedy the chemical leaks. In that situation the $200,000 would be capitalized—that is, added to the purchase price of the property.

WHAT ARE INTERNAL SERVICE FUNDS, AND HOW ARE THEY ACCOUNTED FOR?

Internal service funds are used to account for governmental units or departments that provide goods or services to other funds, departments, or agencies or to other governments on a user charge or cost-reimbursement basis. Like other funds, they are *accounting*, rather than organizational, entities. Most commonly the accounting entities correspond to related organizational units, such as data processing or vehicle repair centers. Sometimes, however, an internal service fund may be established to account for an activity for which there is no parallel organizational unit. For example, an internal service fund may be used to account for "self-insurance," which may be administered by a finance or accounting department.

REASONS AND BASIS FOR ESTABLISHING

Internal service funds are intended to promote efficiency in the acquisition, distribution, and use of goods and services. The department providing the goods or services is, in effect, a profit center. Therefore, it is expected to keep its costs in line with its revenues and to satisfy the requirements of its "customers." At the same time, the customers are charged for the goods or services that they receive and thereby have incentives to demand only what they can optimally use. In addition, internal service funds are a means of allocating the costs of functions and activities to the departments that are the ultimate beneficiaries.

As with enterprise funds, governments have considerable discretion in establishing internal service funds. Statement No. 34 permits governments to establish internal service funds "to report any activity that provides goods or services to other funds, departments, or agencies of the primary government and its component units, or to other governments, on a cost-reimbursement basis." Only rarely are all the resources assigned to internal service funds legally restricted. Therefore, it would usually be as proper for a government to account for them in its general fund or some other governmental fund as to account for them in an internal service fund.

Present practice reflects the absence of specific standards for establishing internal service funds, and the range of activities that some governments account for in internal service funds is far-reaching. Examples include

- Supplies stores
- Motor pool
- Central parking garage
- Printing and reproduction services
- Legal, accounting, auditing, and personnel services
- Maintenance and janitorial services
- Insurance
- Capital asset leasing
- Telecommunications and information

A separate fund is used for each identifiable unit or activity of this fund. The city of San Francisco has four internal service funds (central shops fund, finance corporation fund, reproduction fund, and telecommunications and information fund), Baltimore has six internal service funds (risk management, reproduction and printing, municipal telephone exchange, energy conservation, building maintenance, and municipal post office), whereas the cities of Detroit and New York have no internal service funds.

ACCOUNTING PRINCIPLES

Internal service funds, like enterprise funds, use business-type accounting. Therefore, like enterprise funds, they follow the FASB model and are subject to standards similar to those of businesses to the extent they have been adopted by the GASB.

Internal service funds derive their revenues from other governmental or proprietary funds. Although they may provide services to a large number of different departments, most of their revenues are generally earned from a small number of funds—typically, the general fund and the enterprise funds. Nevertheless, some internal service funds, particularly those established to account for accounting or data processing activities, may provide services to capital projects, debt service, and other restricted governmental funds.

Per the principles of accrual accounting, the revenues of an internal service fund are recognized when earned, not necessarily when cash is received. Thus, internal service funds ordinarily recognize revenue as they deliver the goods or services. However, they might also recognize revenue uniformly over time—as would be appropriate for a fund that leases assets or underwrites insurance.

The expenses of internal service funds are the costs incurred to produce the goods and services. These, too, are recognized on a full accrual basis. They thereby include both depreciation on capital assets and amortization of bond premiums and discounts. Correspondingly, internal service funds account for, and report on their balance sheets, both capital assets and long-term debt.

Tables 9-3 and 9-4 present the statements of net position and of revenues, expenses, and changes in net position for two internal service funds for Charlotte, North Carolina. Note that except for some governmental-specific accounts, the statements could readily be those of a private service business.

The budgets of internal service funds, like those of enterprise funds, seldom require legislative approval and are almost never incorporated into the funds' accounting system. Like those of enterprise funds, the revenues and expenses are driven by customer demand rather than specific legislative action. Moreover, control over the demand may be established by the budgets of the funds receiving the internal service fund's goods or services. Governments should, of course, prepare the same types of budgets (cash, flexible, capital, etc.) as would be expected of any business that provides similar goods or services.

The example that follows highlights the key features of internal service fund accounting.

BASIS FOR ESTABLISHING RATES

Internal service funds are used to account for goods and services provided to other governmental units on a cost-reimbursement basis. This dictum implies that billing rates should be established so as to cover costs. As any student of management accounting can appreciate, however, *cost* can have several different meanings: full cost, incremental cost, opportunity cost, and direct cost.

In practice, *cost* has been interpreted to mean full cost. Internal service funds are not expected over time, either to earn profits or to incur losses. As a consequence, billing rates should reflect all operating costs, including depreciation, interest, and other indirect costs.

The accumulation of unrestricted net position surpluses may suggest that billing rates exceed actual costs. However, governments may intentionally establish rates that exceed cost.

TABLE 9-3 City of Charlotte, North Carolina Internal Service Funds Combining Statement of Net Position June 30, 2017 (in thousands)

	Risk Management	Employee Health and Life	Total
Assets			
Current assets:			
Cash, cash equivalents and investments	$89,415	$41,267	$ 130,682
Receivables—other	310	95	405
Due from other funds	—	620	620
Due from other governmental agencies	5	2	7
Total current assets	89,730	41,984	131,714
Capital assets:			
Machinery and equipment	181	—	181
Less accumulated depreciation	163	—	163
Total capital assets, net	18	—	18
Total assets	89,748	41,984	131,732
Deferred Outflows of Resources			
Pension deferrals	388	—	388
Contributions to pension plan in current fiscal year	135	—	135
	523	—	523
Liabilities			
Current liabilities:			
Accounts payable	93	749	842
Claims payable	43,690	10,666	54,356
Current maturities of noncurrent liabilities	101	—	101
Noncurrent liabilities:			
Due to participants	12,615	—	12,615
Compensated absences payable	76	—	76
Net pension liability	605	—	605
Net OPEB liability	191	—	191
Total noncurrent liabilities	13,487	—	13,487
Total liabilities	57,371	11,415	68,786
Deferred Inflows of Resources			
Pension deferrals	22	—	22
Net Position			
Net investment in capital assets	18	—	18
Unrestricted	32,860	30,569	63,429
Total net position	$32,878	$30,569	$ 63,447

TABLE 9-4 **City of Charlotte, North Carolina Internal Service Funds Combining Statement of Revenues, Expenses and Changes in Fund Net Position for the Year Ended June 30, 2017 (in thousands)**

	Risk Management	Employee Health and Life	Total
Operating Revenues:			
Charges for services-			
Risk management and safety fees	$ 3,288	$ 8,056	$ 11,344
Claims:			
Employer	13,381	46,127	59,508
Employee	-	11,162	11,162
Other	144	935	1,079
Total claims	13,525	58,224	71,749
Premiums	5,378	20,246	25,624
Reimbursement from trust	-	24,838	24,838
Total operating revenues	22,191	111,364	133,555
Operating Expenses:			
Administration	3,968	8,056	12,024
Claims	15,274	76,321	91,595
Insurance premiums	5,337	20,246	25,583
Total operating expenses	24,579	104,623	129,202
Operating income (loss)	(2,388)	6,741	4,353
Nonoperating Revenues:			
Investment earnings	330	313	643
Change in net position	(2,058)	7,054	4,996
Total net position - beginning	34,936	23,515	58,451
Total net position - ending	$32,878	$30,569	$ 63,447

Example

Internal Service Fund Accounting

Establishment of Fund

A government establishes an internal service fund to account for a new data processing department. It transfers $0.6 million from its general fund to the internal service fund as an initial contribution of capital.

Cash	$0.6	
Nonreciprocal transfer-in from general fund		$0.6
To record the capital contribution from the general fund		

The general fund would record a corresponding nonreciprocal interfund transfer-out.

Issuing Long-Term Debt

The government issues $1.0 million in general obligation bonds to support the new department. It intends to service the debt entirely from the revenues of the data processing fund.

Cash	$1.0	
Bonds payable		$1.0
To record the long-term debt		

Even though the bonds are general obligation bonds, they can be recorded as a fund liability as long as the government intends to repay them from the internal service fund.

Acquisition of Capital Assets

The department acquires long-lived assets (buildings, computers, furniture, etc.) for $1.4 million.

Capital assets (specified in detail)	$1.4	
Cash		$1.4
To record the acquisition of capital assets		

Billings to Other Departments

For services rendered during the year, the department bills the utility fund for $0.3 million and bills the police department, fire department, and all other departments accounted for in the general fund for $0.8 million.

Due from general fund	$0.8	
Due from utility fund	0.3	
Operating revenues		$1.1
To record billing to other departments		

Correspondingly, the general fund would report an expenditure, and the utility fund an expense, for the amounts billed. The two funds would recognize expenditures or expenses, rather than intragovernmental transfers because these transactions qualify as interfund services used—costs that would be characterized as expenditures or expenses if the services were provided by outside vendors.

Depreciation and Other Expenses

The data processing department incurred $0.2 million in depreciation and $0.7 million in other operating expenses. In addition, it acquired $0.1 million in supplies inventory that remained on hand at year-end.

Depreciation expense	$0.2	
Other operating expenses (specified in detail)	0.7	
Supplies inventory	0.1	
Accounts payable		$0.8
Accumulated depreciation		0.2
To record depreciation and other expenses		

Other transactions—such as those involving purchases of investments, use of materials and supplies, and accrual of interest—would be accounted for in the same manner they would be accounted for in a comparable business.

This enables them to accumulate the resources required either to replace existing assets or to expand the asset base to meet anticipated increases in demand.

Ironically, the practice of establishing billing rates at full cost may subvert a key objective of internal service funds—that the supplying department provides and the receiving department takes an optimal quantity of goods and services. As illustrated in the accompanying "In Practice: Full-Cost Pricing May Encourage Dysfunctional Decisions," full-cost prices do not reflect the cost of providing incremental amounts of goods or services. Therefore, they may encourage departments to purchase either more goods and services or fewer goods and services than are optimal from the perspective of the government as a whole.

IN PRACTICE FULL-COST PRICING MAY ENCOURAGE DYSFUNCTIONAL DECISIONS

A city accounts for a vehicle repair unit in an internal service fund and bills departments at full cost. The unit's fixed costs are $80,000 per month; its variable costs are $40 per hour. On average it provides 4,000 hours of service per month.

Accordingly, its billing rate is $60 per hour:

Fixed costs per month	$ 80,000
Variable costs (4,000 hours at $40)	160,000
Total costs per month	$240,000
Number of hours	÷ 4,000
Cost per hour	$ 60

The police department receives a bid of $3,000 from an outside garage to repair one of its vehicles. The city's repair service calculates that the job will take 60 hours, and therefore submits an estimate to the police department of $3,600 (60 hours at $60 per hour). Because the price is greater than $3,000, the police department accepts the outside bid.

Assuming that the repair service had the necessary capacity to carry out the repairs, its fixed costs would have been unaffected by the job for the police department. It would have incurred only the additional variable costs of $2,400 (60 hours at $40). From the perspective of the city as a whole, the police department's decision to use the outside garage was dysfunctional. The city passed up the opportunity to receive $3,000 of incremental benefits in exchange for incremental costs of $2,400.

RAMIFICATIONS FOR OTHER FUNDS

The accounting and operating practices of departments accounted for in internal service funds have critical implications for not only the internal service funds themselves, but also for the other funds with which they interact.

Duplicate Reported Expenses

Costs reported by internal service funds are reported twice within the same set of financial statements. They are reported once by the internal service fund providing the goods and services, and a second time by the fund that is billed for them. Correspondingly, revenues are also reported twice: once by the fund received from outside parties (as taxes or fees) and again when earned by the internal service fund.

Fortunately, however, as explained in a section that follows on proprietary fund reporting requirements, the duplications are largely eliminated in the consolidated government-wide financial statements.

Transfer of Depreciation to Governmental Funds

Governmental funds do not report capital assets; they do not charge depreciation.

However, insofar as an internal service fund incorporates depreciation expense into its billing rates, the depreciation charge is transferred, along with all other costs, to the funds that it bills.

The impact on reported expenditures of a governmental fund can be telling. Suppose one government accounts for a motor pool in an internal service fund and another in its general fund. The motor pool of each government serves only other departments that are accounted for in the government's general fund. The general fund of the government maintaining the internal service fund will record the cost of the motor pool vehicles over their useful lives (through the depreciation expense incorporated into the billing rates). That of the other government will record the cost as the vehicles are acquired or paid for.

Detract from Objectivity of Financial Statements

An internal service fund should establish its billing rates so as to cover its costs. Yet cost is an elusive concept. It depends on estimates (such as useful life of assets), choices among accounting methods (as to expense recognition, depreciation, inventory), and bases of overhead allocation. Although generally accepted accounting principles may establish broad guidelines for cost determination, they leave considerable latitude for individual companies or governments.

Owing to the leeway permitted to governments in establishing costs, neither the billing rates nor the total revenues of an internal service fund can be seen as being objective. And if its revenues are not objective, then neither are its changes in net position for the year, nor its total net position.

The inevitable subjectivity of individual internal service fund financial statements might be of only minor concern to statement users if the impact were limited to the internal service fund statements. But it is not. The revenues of an internal service fund are the expenditures and expenses of other funds. Thus, if the revenues of an internal service fund are subjective, then so too are the expenditures of the general fund, and all other funds to which the internal service fund provides goods or services. And if their expenditures are subjective, then so too are their annual excess of revenues over expenditures, their fund balances, and their assets or liabilities.

By controlling billing rates, government officials can fine-tune the reported excess of revenues over expenditures of the general fund—the fund most subject to balanced-budget requirements and public scrutiny. For example, faced with pressure to hold down general-fund expenditures, a government can delay imposing rate increases that would otherwise be warranted. Or, with an eye to maximizing cost recovery under a state or federal grant, it can increase the internal service fund charges to the programs whose costs are eligible for reimbursement.

Obscure Fund Balance Surpluses or Deficits

By adjusting billing rates, government officials can transfer surpluses or deficits (i.e., positive or negative fund balances) from the general fund to the internal service fund. These surpluses or deficits might be prohibited if they remained in the general fund. Suppose, for example, that government officials see a need to commit resources for the replacement of long-lived assets or for a "rainy day." They recognize, however, that if the general fund were to report a surplus, legislators would seek either to increase spending or to reduce taxes.

The officials could achieve their objective by increasing the billing rates of an internal service fund, thereby transferring resources from the general fund to the internal service fund. The reserve would be maintained in the internal service fund rather than the general fund. To be sure, the reserve would be reflected in the net position of the internal service fund. But the internal service fund may not be as carefully examined as the general fund. Because net position includes a conglomeration of cumulative earnings over many years and for many purposes, the reserve could be readily obscured.

WHAT SPECIAL PROBLEMS ARE CREATED WHEN AN INTERNAL SERVICE FUND OR THE GENERAL FUND ACCOUNTS FOR "SELF-INSURANCE"?

Many governments seeking ways to reduce costs elect to "self-insure" all or a portion of their risks, especially risks for less than catastrophic losses. Independent insurance companies set premiums at rates that allow them to cover anticipated claims, administrative costs, and capital costs. For the portion of its policy applicable to routine losses, such as from automobile accidents or worker injuries, an insured entity's premiums are almost always based on the entity's own claims history. **Self-insurance** may provide an opportunity for the government to reduce the portion of the premium that covers the administrative and capital costs.

The GASB permits governments to account for their self-insurance activities in either the general fund or an internal service fund.[6] Irrespective of which is used, the insurance "department" (which may be only an accounting entity, not an organizational unit) operates as if it were an independent insurance company. It periodically bills other departments for premiums, and it pays their claims as losses are incurred.

Self-insurance presents intriguing and controversial issues of accounting. The term self-insurance is an oxymoron. The essence of insurance is the transfer of risk to an outsider. When a government self-insures, it retains the risk itself, irrespective of whether it accounts for the activity in an internal service fund or the general fund. Therefore, self-insurance is no insurance.

ACCOUNTING FOR INSURANCE PREMIUMS

The key accounting issues pertain to when and in what amount the insured departments should recognize expenditures for premiums paid, and when and in what amount the insurance departments should recognize revenues for the insurance premiums received.

Suppose a government accounts for its insurance activities in an internal service fund and all the departments that it insures are accounted for in the general fund. The general fund, therefore, pays annual premiums to the internal service fund.

If the general fund paid these premiums to an outside insurance company, the premiums would be recorded as an expenditure. Consistent with the principles that interfund services be accounted for as expenditures, it might appear that premiums paid to the internal service fund should also be accounted for as an expenditure.

Payments for self-insurance premiums, however, are different from other types of charges from internal service funds. The general fund does not actually transfer risk to the internal service fund; any losses incurred are a general obligation of the government-at-large. Except for the portion of the premiums that covers losses actually incurred, it simply sets aside funds to provide for possible losses in the future. In that regard the transaction is comparable to a transfer of resources to a debt service fund for the future repayment of bonds. Therefore, it has been argued, only the portion of the premium that covers actual losses should be reported as an expenditure in the general fund. The excess should be accounted for as a nonreciprocal transfer. Correspondingly, only the portion of the premium that represents a reimbursement for actual losses should be recognized as revenue in the internal service fund.

---

[6] GASB Statement No. 10, *Accounting and Financial Reporting for Risk Financing and Related Insurance Losses*, para. 10 (November 1989); Codification, Section C50.124.

GASB STANDARDS

Rejecting arguments that premium payments are nothing more than nonreciprocal internal transfers, the GASB has held that as long as specified criteria are satisfied, an internal service insurance fund can recognize revenues, and the insured funds (departments) can recognize expenditures, for the full amount of the premiums billed.

The GASB ruled that an internal service insurance fund can use any basis to establish its premiums that the government considers appropriate as long as the premiums satisfy *either* of the following conditions:

- The total charge covers the actual losses incurred by the fund.
- The total charge is based on an actuarial method or historical cost method and is adjusted over time so that internal service fund revenues and expenses are approximately equal.

The premiums can also include a provision for expected catastrophic losses.

If the premiums satisfy either of these criteria, then the internal service insurance fund may recognize revenue on billing the insured funds. Correspondingly, the insured funds may recognize an expenditure. If, however, the premiums exceed the amount that satisfies these criteria, the excess should be reported as a nonreciprocal transfer from the insured funds to the internal service fund. If they are less, the resultant deficit in the internal service fund should be charged back to the insured funds and be reported as expenditures in those funds.

Consistent with FASB Statement No. 5, *Accounting for Contingencies*, the internal service insurance fund should recognize its expenses for claims expenses and liabilities when:

- It is probable that an asset has been impaired or a liability incurred.
- The amount of loss can be reasonably estimated.[7]

[7] Now incorporated into GASB Statement No. 62, *Codification of Accounting and Financial Reporting Guidance Contained in Pre-November 30, 1989 FASB and AICPA Pronouncements*, para. 96–113 and the GASB Codification, C50.151–168.

Example

Insurance Premiums

A government maintains an internal service fund to insure all government vehicles for loss and damage and for liability to third parties. It establishes premiums using actuarial techniques intended to ensure that over time the premiums will cover claims, administrative expenses, and catastrophic losses. In a particular year, the internal service fund bills the general fund $260,000 and the utility fund $130,000—a total of $390,000. Of this amount $25,000 is for potential catastrophes. During the year it incurs $360,000 in claims losses, none of which resulted from catastrophes.

The internal service fund would recognize as revenues the entire $390,000 in premiums:

Cash	$390,000	
Revenues—insurance premiums		$390,000
To record premium revenue		

At the same time, the general fund would recognize an expenditure of $260,000 and the utility fund an expense of $130,000.

The internal service fund would also recognize claims expenses for the actual $360,000 of losses:

Expenses—claims	$360,000	
Claims liability (or cash)		$360,000
To record losses incurred		

As a consequence of closing the revenue and expense accounts at year-end, net position will increase by $30,000. Of this sum, $25,000 is attributable to the premiums for the potential catastrophes. The GASB standards direct that this amount should be designated in the notes to the statements as intended for catastrophes.

ACCOUNTING FOR SELF-INSURANCE IN A GENERAL FUND

Although this chapter is directed toward proprietary funds, this section digresses to contrast how self-insurance activities would be accounted for in a general fund rather than an internal service fund.

GASB STANDARDS

The GASB stipulates that when self-insurance activities are accounted for in a general fund, the amount of premium revenue recognized by the general fund should be limited to actual claims expenditures (i.e., those losses that satisfy the criteria of FASB Statement No. 5).

Correspondingly, total expenditures and expenses recognized by the general fund and any other insured funds should be limited to the same amounts. Any amounts charged to the other funds (including the general fund itself) in excess of the actual claims should be accounted for as nonreciprocal transfers. The differences in accounting principles are justified, according to the GASB, because the general fund transfers neither risk nor actual resources to either an outside party or to a separate fund.

Example

Self-Insurance in a General Fund

Assume the same facts as in the previous example except that the insurance activities are accounted for in the general fund. The insurance "department" bills other general-fund departments for $260,000 in premiums and the utility fund for $130,000, a total of $390,000. As before, the government incurs only $360,000 in actual claims.

The general fund would recognize the claims, as would an internal service fund (except that the general fund would report the claims as an expenditure rather than an expense):

Expenditure—claims	$360,000	
Claims liability (or cash)		$360,000
To record losses incurred		

However, the maximum that the insurance department could recognize as premiums from the other departments would now be $360,000—the amount of the actual claims. Of this, one-third ($130,000/$390,000), or $120,000, would be attributable to the utility fund and two-thirds ($260,000/$390,000), or $240,000, to the other general fund departments. The premiums would be recognized as interfund reimbursements and reported as reductions in expenditures. The $10,000 that the utility fund paid above its share of the allowable premium revenue would be reported as an interfund transfer. Thus, the general fund would record the billings to the utility fund as follows:

Cash	$130,000	
Interfund reimbursements—insurance premiums		$120,000
Nonreciprocal transfer-in (from utility fund)		10,000
To record premiums collected from utility fund		

The utility fund would recognize a premium expense of $120,000 and a nonreciprocal transfer-out of $10,000.

Although the insurance department would also record the billings to the other departments accounted for in the general fund, the entries are not shown here. Because the insurance department is also accounted for in the general fund, there would be no impact on the financial statements. Intrafund revenues and expenditures would net out.

HOW ARE PROPRIETARY FUNDS REPORTED?

ENTERPRISE FUNDS

The reporting of enterprise funds is relatively straightforward compared with that of internal service.

Government-Wide Statements

The government-wide statement of net position (balance sheet) contains two columns under the heading "primary government." One is for governmental activities, and the other is for business-type activities. The balances of the various enterprise funds are consolidated and reported in the column for the business-type activities.

The government-wide statement of activities reports on revenues and expenses by functions. The rows listing the functions are divided into separate categories for governmental and business-type activities. As discussed and illustrated in Chapter 2, the statement has one column that indicates the expenses for each function and one or more columns for the revenues (such as fees for goods or services or restricted grants) that are directly associated with the functions. The net expenses (the differences between the expenses and revenues) are shown in one of two columns—one for governmental activities, the other for business-type activities. The net expenses of enterprise funds are, of course, shown in the column for the business-type activities.

The government-wide statements consolidate the government's funds and report on the government as a whole—not as a series of independent funds. Therefore, interfund revenues, expenses, receivables, and payables generally must be eliminated. Suppose, for example, that a city's electric utility sold electricity to departments accounted for in its general fund. At year-end the utility fund had a receivable of $100,000 from the general fund—and correspondingly the general fund had a payable of $100,000 to the utility fund. From the perspective of the government as a whole, both the receivable and the payable would have to be eliminated on the government-wide statement of net position. The government cannot owe money to itself. Nevertheless, the government-wide statements distinguish between business-type and governmental activities and report them in separate columns. The enterprise fund does have a receivable from the general fund, and the general fund does have a payable to the enterprise fund. These must be shown in the columns for each activity, yet they cannot be shown in the "total" column—that which presents the balances for the government as a whole. How can a government show the receivables and payables in the individual columns but not in the totals column?

GASB STANDARDS

Interfund receivables and payables may be reported either on a single line—with one a positive amount and the other a negative amount—or on separate lines with the amounts being excluded from the "total" column. Thus, for example, if shown on a single line the amounts might be reported among the assets as follows:

	Governmental Activities	Business-Type Activities	Total
Internal balances	$100,000	($100,000)	—

If shown on two lines (one in the asset section, the other in the liability section) they would be presented as:

	Governmental Activities	Business-Type Activities	Total
Interfund receivable	$100,000		—
Interfund payable		$100,000	—

In concept, the sales of a utility fund and purchases by a general fund should also be eliminated. However, the units accounted for in the general fund usually amount to only a few of the many customers of the utility department. These customers acquire electricity that they would otherwise have had to purchase from outside parties. Thus, to eliminate the sales and purchases would understate both the operating costs of the governmental activities and the revenues of the business-type activities. Per the GASB, therefore, interfund services provided and used between functions need not be eliminated.

Funds Statements

In the section of the basic financial statements containing the funds statements, the three required statements of proprietary funds (statement of net position; statement of revenues, expenses, and changes in fund net position; and statement of cash flows) are presented apart from the statements of governmental funds. The accounts of each major enterprise fund are reported in separate columns. In these statements, each fund is reported as if it were an independent entity. Hence, no eliminations are necessary. Correspondingly, in the statements of the funds that received the services, the interfund activities would be accounted for as if they were transactions with external parties.

INTERNAL SERVICE FUNDS

Government-Wide Statements

The government-wide statements present an overview of the government as a whole and, hence, consolidate the various individual funds. Inasmuch as internal service funds exist to service government units that are accounted for in other funds, interfund receivables, payables, and the related revenues and expenses must be eliminated in the consolidation process.

Example

Eliminating Interfund Balances and Transactions

Suppose that a data processing internal service fund provided service to other units, all of which were accounted for within the general fund or other governmental funds. The data processing fund billed the other funds for $10 million, an amount that reflected the "full" cost of providing its services. At year-end it had uncollected receivables of $2 million from the other funds. These transactions would have been reflected in the individual data processing fund and the various governmental funds as follows:

	Data Processing Internal Service Fund	Various Other Governmental Funds	Total
Sales revenues	$10		$10
Expenses	10	$10	20
Accounts receivable	2		2
Accounts payable		2	2

From the perspective of the government as a whole, the cost of providing the data processing services was only $10 million—not the total of $20 million that is reported as expenses in the "total" column above. Correspondingly, the government as a whole had zero revenue from the interfund "sales" and no receivables and payables from the amounts that one department owed to another. Therefore, both sales revenues and expenses must be reduced by $10 million, and both receivables and payables must be reduced by $2 million.

Internal service funds do not exist to earn a profit. As noted earlier, their billings to other departments should reflect actual costs. Accordingly, their revenues should equal their expenses, and both can be eliminated in their entirety in the consolidation process. In fact, even if the rates were not set to equalize revenues and expenses, they should be retroactively adjusted so that the internal service funds just break even. The end result will be that all the costs of operating the internal service funds can be charged back to, and reported as expenditures or expenses by, the funds that were the consumers of the internal service funds' goods and services.

By contrast, the assets and the liabilities, other than interfund receivables and payables, would not be eliminated in the consolidation process. These include cash, capital assets, and obligations to outsiders. A question arises, therefore, as to whether these assets and liabilities (and the resultant net position) should be classified as governmental or business-type activities. Internal service funds are, of course, proprietary funds. Nevertheless, they typically provide services mainly to government units that are accounted for in the general fund or in other governmental funds.

GASB STANDARDS

The GASB has prescribed that internal service fund balances that are not eliminated in the consolidation process should ordinarily be reported in the statement of net position (balance sheet) in the governmental activities column, unless the fund provides services predominantly to enterprise funds. If the internal service fund provides services mainly to enterprise funds, then the government should report the balances in the business-type activities column.[8]

[8] GASB Statement No. 34, *Basic Financial Statements—and Management Discussion and Analysis—for State and Local Governments*, para. 62 (June 1999).

The consequence of these standards is that in the government-wide statements the revenues of the internal service fund and the offsetting expenses of the service recipient funds are eliminated in the consolidation process. The expenses of the internal service fund are charged back to the service recipient funds and thereby aggregated with their applicable functional expenses. In the usual situation, that in which the internal service fund provides services mainly to departments accounted for in governmental funds, the internal service fund is considered a governmental fund. Therefore, any receivables from, and payables to, other governmental funds are eliminated in the consolidation process. By contrast, because business-type activities are reported in a separate column, receivables from and payables to enterprise funds are not eliminated in the consolidation process. They are included, as appropriate, in either the governmental or business activities column, but are excluded from the "total" column. Instead, they are reported in a manner similar to that in the earlier illustration, in which a utility fund had a receivable from the general fund. At the same time, internal service fund assets and liabilities such as capital assets and payables to outsiders that are not eliminated in the consolidation process are reported in the governmental activities column.

Funds Statements

In the funds (as opposed to the government-wide) statements, internal service funds are categorized as *proprietary* funds. In each of the three required proprietary funds statements (statement of net position; statement of revenues, expenses, and changes in net position; and statement of cash flows), data for all internal service funds are aggregated into a single column. This column is presented alongside those for each of the major enterprise funds. However, even though internal service funds are incorporated into the proprietary fund statements, they appear under the heading, "Governmental Activities—Internal Service Funds." Moreover, owing to their different characteristics, the balances in the internal service funds are not combined with those of the enterprise funds into a single "total" column. Financial statements for individual internal service funds may (but are not required to) be included in the comprehensive annual financial report (CAFR) as supplementary information.

ACCOUNTING FOR SEVICE CONCESSION ARRANGEMENTS

Service concession arrangements are basically a type of arrangement in which a government transfers to an independent operator (usually a private firm but sometimes another government) the right and related obligation to provide services through the use of infrastructure or some other public asset. In exchange, the government receives from the operator either an up-front payment or a series of payments over time. The operator then collects tolls or other fees from the facility users. The government, however, maintains certain controls over the transferred asset; it has the ability to specify the service that the operator must provide and can set the rates or prices that the operator may charge. Moreover, it will receive back the asset at the end of the arrangement. In some arrangements the government does not transfer an existing asset to the operator. Instead the operator constructs the asset itself.

Common service concession arrangements involve toll roads, hospitals, student housing, water treatment and supply facilities, motorways, car parks, tunnels, bridges, airports, and telecommunication networks. In one such transaction the city of Chicago transferred all 36,000 of its parking meters to a private company in exchange for a one-time lump sum payment of $1.2 billion. The term of the arrangement is 75 years.

Recognizing the prevalence of these service concession arrangements, the GASB issued Statement No. 60 *Accounting and Financial Reporting for Service Concession Arrangements* in 2010. The thrust of the GASB standard is that a government should recognize as an asset any up-front payments of cash or the present value of any promised installment payments from the operator. Correspondingly, if the contract calls for the government to incur any future costs (e.g., to improve to or maintain the asset), it should recognize the present value of those costs as a liability. Most notably, the government should not recognize any "gain" on the transaction—that is, the difference between the consideration received and the costs to be incurred—all at once. Rather, it should defer the gain—report it as a deferred inflow—and account for it as revenue in a "systematic and rational manner" over the term of the arrangement.

The GASB statement also specifies that the government should report on its own financial statements any new asset that the operator has constructed and should continue to report on its own financial statements the asset that it has transferred to the operator. It should depreciate those asset as it normally would similar assets.

Service concession arrangements are increasingly popular among governments as well as colleges and universities because, in a period of declining revenues and other fiscal constraints, they provide a quick and easy source of cash. Nevertheless, many of these arrangement should be seen for what they are—that is, the economic equivalent of borrowing transactions. In a borrowing arrangement, a government receives cash up front and then repays the loan, plus interest, over time. In a common service concession arrangement, the government also receives cash up front, but instead of making principal and interest payments over time, it sacrifices revenues to which it would otherwise would have been entitled (i.e., the tolls or other fees).

IN PRACTICE WANT TO OWN A BRIDGE?

"If you believe that, then I've got a bridge for sale," is a classic retort to an incredulous statement. The bridge referred to is New York's Brooklyn Bridge. Although the Brooklyn Bridge has not yet been considered for sale, others have been sold—or leased—along with airports, tunnels, and toll roads to private investors or management companies.

Indiana, for example, leased its toll road to an Australian and Spanish consortium for $3.85 billion cash up front. In addition, the consortium agreed to install an electronic toll collection system, make other improvement to the highway, and maintain the road at a specified level. To proponents of the transaction, it was a great deal for the state. Indiana accountants had projected the present value of the road, taking into account forecasted revenues and expenses, to be only $1.9 billion over the 75-year lease period. To critics, however, the transaction had the markings of a fancy borrowing arrangement. The state got an immediate infusion of cash but would be repaying the "loan" over the lease period by way of forgone toll revenues.

WHAT DO USERS WANT TO KNOW ABOUT REVENUE DEBT?

In the previous chapter we highlighted the main types of ratios and other data that investors and other statement users look to in assessing a government's ability to repay its general obligation debt. In this section we do the same with regards to revenue debt.

Revenue bonds encompass the debt that will be paid from a dedicated revenue stream produced by the assets that the debt financed. These assets typically include utilities, convention centers, stadiums, parking facilities, and similar fee-generating projects. Revenue bonds are also commonly issued by not-for-profit entities, including health care organizations, universities, and museums.

In light of the vast array of entities that issue revenue bonds, it is difficult to generalize as to the information needed by users. The salient fiscal characteristics of a government-operated hospital, for example, may differ considerably from those of a public university. Nevertheless, some types of information are central to the evaluation of any revenue-backed security. Among the types identified by Standard & Poor's are the following:[9]

- ***Security provisions.*** Revenue bonds are secured by specific fees or taxes. These may include user charges (such as highway tolls, college tuition, and hospital billings) or dedicated taxes (such as a sales tax restricted to debt service or a gasoline tax restricted to highway improvements).

- ***Competition.*** Revenue bonds, unlike general obligation bonds, are often used to support activities that are competitive. For example, hospitals, universities, airports, parking garages, and museums compete with other public and private institutions that provide similar services. Whereas the general obligation (GO) bonds are backed by the full faith and credit of the government—and thus by its power to tax—revenue bonds are backed only by specified revenues. Competition introduces a credit risk not normally associated with GO bonds.

- ***Service area.*** Projects financed by revenue bonds do not necessarily serve areas that are within predetermined geographic boundaries. For example, a university may attract students from throughout the world. A hospital may compete statewide for patients. The broader the geographic base of a revenue stream, the less likely it is to be affected by local economic downturns.

- ***Revenue-raising flexibility.*** Some user charges can be raised more easily than others. For example, a city may be constitutionally prohibited from increasing a restricted sales tax, whereas a hospital may have considerable flexibility in increasing patient charges. The greater the revenue-raising flexibility, the less the credit risk.

The specific information depends, of course, on the nature of the institution. Table 9-5 outlines the factors that Standard & Poor's deems important in evaluating the revenue debt of municipal parking facilities. The list is especially notable for the prominence of nonfinancial factors. It shows that even to assess the ability of the bond issuer to service its debt—the primary concern of a rating service—users must look beyond conventional financial statements.

---

[9] The information requirements presented in this section were drawn from U.S. Public Finance: "Methodology: Definitions and Related Analytic Practices for Covenant and Payment Provisions in U.S. Public Finance Revenue Obligations." *Principles of Credit Ratings* (New York: Standard & Poor's Rating Group, 2011).

TABLE 9-5 Factors Focused on (and Documents Required by) Standard & Poor's in Evaluating the Revenue Bonds of Municipal Parking Facilities

Basic documents

- Official statement
- Bonds resolution or trust indenture
- Five years financial audits
- Consultant's feasibility studies
- Capital programs
- Current budgets

Operational factors

- Description of existing facilities
- Service area
- Occupancy rates
- Description of type of use (monthly, daily, or hourly)
- History of rates and rate increases
- Proposed rate schedule
- Rate setting procedure
- Competing facilities (location, number of spaces, and rates)
- Collection and enforcement procedures

Economic factors

- Leading employers
- Employment and labor force trends
- Wealth and income indicators
- Retail sales activity
- Building activity

SUMMARY

Governments account for and report business-type activities in proprietary funds. Activities carried out with outside parties are accounted for in enterprise funds; those with other departments within the government or with other governments are accounted for in internal service funds. Governments (as well as not-for-profits) account for their business-type activities using business-type accounting. They apply a full accrual, all economic resources, model.

Governments and not-for-profits engage in business-type activities for many reasons. Most commonly, the activities provide resources that otherwise would have to be raised through taxes or contributions, or they complement and support the entity's main mission.

As a general rule, governments *may* account for an activity in an enterprise fund if it charges fees to external users for goods and services. However, they *must* account for it in an enterprise fund if it is financed with revenue debt, is required by law to cover its expenses with user charges, or is expected to be self-supporting.

The GASB has established specific guidelines on how to account for landfills. Landfills are often accounted for in enterprise funds, inasmuch as they typically charge user fees. Still, they are sometimes accounted for in governmental funds. Irrespective of fund, however, governments must report the obligation for the estimated costs of closing and monitoring a landfill when it will be taken out of service. The amount of the obligation should be based on the proportionate share of the landfill used to date. As with other long-term obligations, where and how the liability is reported depends on the type of fund with which it is associated. Thus, if the landfill is accounted for in an enterprise fund, the liability will be reported in the fund itself and, of course, in the government-wide statements. If it is accounted for in a governmental fund, it will be reported *only* in the government-wide statements and not in the fund itself.

GASB also has established a standard for decommissioning capital assets such as nuclear power plants and sewage treatment plants. The standard requires that the closure and postclosure expenses be recognized in the periods that the assets are in use, and provide their benefits, rather than those in which they are being retired. A government should initially measure an ARO liability as the current value of retirement outlays expected to be incurred. Each subsequent year, the government should adjust the liability for changes in its current value. The government should offset the initial liability with a deferred outflow of resources, and it should amortize the deferred outflow of resources over the estimated useful life of the asset. Moreover, as it adjusts the liability over time to reflect the changes in current value, it should correspondingly adjust the deferred outflow of resources by the same amount.

Like those for landfills, pollution remediation costs may be accounted for in either governmental or proprietary funds. GASB standards now require that in enterprise funds an estimate of pollution remediation costs be recognized as expense and offsetting liability as soon as the government becomes aware of its obligations. At that time, the government should estimate the costs. Such an estimate should be the current value of the future outlays, taking into account the probability of various amounts within a range. In governmental funds, only as the obligation is liquidated with current financial resources should an expenditure be recognized.

Internal service funds are established to promote efficiency in the acquisition, distribution, and use of goods and services. Like enterprise funds, they are accounted for on a full accrual basis. Internal service funds bill the funds to which they provide services at rates intended to cover their costs. However, in the absence of standards as to how the costs should be calculated, governments have considerable flexibility in establishing those rates.

By their very nature, internal service funds affect the other funds with which they interact. The consequences of accounting for activities in internal service funds rather than governmental funds are that revenues and costs are counted twice within the same set of financial statements, depreciation charges are incorporated in the expenditures of the funds billed, and surpluses and deficits can be transferred from the funds billed to the internal service funds. These limitations are substantially mitigated, however, in government-wide statements. Government-wide statements present the financial position and results of operations from the perspective of the government as a whole. These statements consolidate the individual funds, and interfund activities and balances are thereby eliminated.

Many governments maintain internal service funds to account for self-insurance. Self-insurance, however, does not result in a transfer of risk to outsiders. Therefore, the GASB has established standards as to the policies by which governments can determine the premium revenue to be recognized by self-insurance funds and the expenditures to be charged by the funds that they insure.

Governments also enter into service concession arrangements, which are long-term arrangements in which the government enters into a contract with a private-sector entity or another government to operate a major capital asset such as toll roads, hospitals, or student housing, in return for the right to collect fees from users of those capital assets.

Business-type activities of governments are often supported by revenue bonds, which are backed by specific revenue streams such as dedicated taxes or user charges. The ability of the issuer to maintain these streams can seldom be evaluated by focusing exclusively on factors reported in the financial statements. Users must look to the entire range of elements that affect the entity's operating environment.

KEY TERMS IN THIS CHAPTER

Asset retirement obligations 383
Debt forgiveness 379
Enterprise funds account 369
External subsidies 379
governmental activities 370
Impact fees 379
Internal service funds 369
Internal subsidies 379
privatization 370
self-insurance 393
Service concession arrangements 398
Tap (system development) fees 379

EXERCISE FOR REVIEW AND SELF-STUDY

The statement of net position and statement of revenues, expenses, and changes in fund net position for the City of Kingsland's proprietary funds are presented on pages 400 and 401.

1. On what basis of accounting (i.e., cash, accrual, or modified accrual) are the statements prepared? How can you tell?
2. Is it necessary for the city to adopt a budget comparable to that of a governmental fund for its enterprise funds and to incorporate it into its accounting system by making annual budgetary entries? Explain.
3. The electric utility reports $116.4 million as "invested in capital assets." Are you able to reconcile that amount with the reported assets and liabilities?
4. The golf course's restricted cash and investments of $2.389 million are not equal to its restricted net assets of $2.323 million. What might account for the difference?
5. Assume that one of the government's internal service funds was for data processing services, for which the golf course was billed $30,000, all of which was classified as "contractual services" in the golf course fund. How would that amount be reported in the column for internal service fund? How would it be reported in the government-wide financial statements?
6. The internal service fund reported $2.7 million in depreciation, an amount that the government takes into account in establishing the rates charged to other funds. How would this charge be reflected in the government-wide statements?
7. Suppose that the electric utility charged a customer a $200,000 tap fee to hook into its electric system. The actual cost of the hookup to the customer was only $80,000. How would the $200,000 be reported by the utility fund?
8. Suppose that the electric utility owed $50,000 to the internal service fund. How would this most likely be reported in the proprietary funds' statement of net position? How would it be reported in the government-wide statement of net position?
9. In which column on the government-wide statement of net position—that for governmental or business-type activities—is it most likely that the assets and liabilities of the internal service funds would be included? Explain.

QUESTIONS FOR REVIEW AND DISCUSSION

1. You are the independent CPA for a medium-sized city. The city manager asks your guidance as to whether, according to generally accepted accounting principles, the municipal golf course should be accounted for in an enterprise fund. What would be your response?
2. How would you compare the accounting for enterprise funds with that of (a) businesses and (b) governmental funds? Summarize the reasons both for and against accounting for enterprise funds differently than governmental funds.
3. Although proprietary fund accounting is similar to business accounting, there are considerable differences in standards pertaining to the statement of cash flows. What are the main differences?
4. A government accounts for a municipal landfill in an enterprise fund. How will it determine how much to charge as an expense (and add to a liability) each year that the landfill is in use? Suppose instead that it accounts for the landfill in a governmental fund. What will be the amount charged as an expenditure?
5. For what types of activities are internal service funds used to account? Provide several examples. Is a government required to account for the activities you cite in an internal service fund, or may it account for them instead in its general fund?
6. It is sometimes asserted that the absence of specific principles as to what constitutes "cost" detracts from the objectivity of the financial statements of not only internal service funds but also financial statements of the general fund. In what sense might this be true?
7. It is often said that "self-insurance" is an oxymoron. Why? If it is, what are the implications for a government that is permitted to recognize self-insurance premiums as a general fund expenditure when paid to an internal service fund?

8. What is a service concession arrangement? Why do governments enter in to these agreements?

9. In what way must a government account for premium revenue differently if it accounts for self-insurance in an internal service fund rather than in its general fund?

10. You have been given the responsibility of assigning a bond rating to a municipal parking garage. Indicate the type of information you would consider essential to your assessment, noting in particular information that is unlikely to be reported on in the facility's financial statements.

11. In government-wide statements, enterprise funds are reported differently than are internal service funds. Explain why and justify.

12. Enterprise funds are also reported differently than are internal service funds in the proprietary fund statements of net position, and in the statements of revenues, expenses, and changes in net position. Explain why.

13. The balance sheet of an enterprise fund reports an asset as "restricted cash and investments" and shows a portion of "net position" as restricted. Provide an example of the types of restrictions to which the assets of a proprietary fund might be subject. Why might the "restricted cash and investments" not be equal to the portion of "net position" that is restricted?

City of Kingsland Statement of Revenues, Expenses, and Changes in Net Position Proprietary Funds Year Ended December 31, 2021

	Business-type Activities			Governmental Activities—
	Electric Utility	Golf Course	Totals	Internal Service Funds
Operating revenues:				
Fees and charges	$ 18,127,813	$2,144,417	$ 20,272,230	$24,409,862
Miscellaneous	—	6,122	6,122	1,706,818
Total operating revenues	18,127,813	2,150,539	20,278,352	26,116,680
Operating expenses:				
Wages and salaries	5,440,894	1,219,757	6,660,651	6,651,450
Contractual services	551,075	153,651	704,726	935,034
Utilities	1,206,571	161,162	1,367,733	343,699
Repairs and maintenance	1,195,704	103,387	1,299,091	3,136,784
Supplies	797,141	27,390	824,531	375,112
Insurance claims and expenses				12,806,858
Depreciation	1,861,024	867,278	2,728,302	2,732,594
Total operating expenses	11,052,409	2,532,625	13,585,034	26,981,531
Operating income (loss)	7,075,404	(382,086)	6,693,318	(864,851)
Nonoperating revenues (expenses):				
Interest and dividends	727,668	234,490	962,158	215,573
Other revenues	167,880	167,880	33,368	
Interest expense	(2,561,328)	(1,866,474)	(4,427,802)	(66,586)
Miscellaneous expense	—	(74,954)	(74,954)	(281,605)
Total nonoperating revenue (expenses)	(1,833,660)	(1,539,058)	(3,372,718)	(99,250)
Net income (loss) before contributions and transfers	5,241,744	(1,921,144)	3,320,600	(964,101)
Capital contributions	2,633,470		2,633,470	30,061
Transfers-out	(464,000)	(338,254)	(802,254)	(280,053)
Change in net assets	7,411,214	(2,259,398)	5,151,816	(1,214,093)
Total net position—beginning	126,494,425	5,264,470	131,758,895	6,005,599
Total net position—ending	$133,905,639	$3,005,072	$136,910,711	$ 4,791,506

City of Kingsland Statement of Net Position Proprietary Funds December 31, 2021

	Business-type Activities			Governmental Activities—Internal Service Funds
	Electric Utility	Golf Course	Totals	
Assets				
Current assets				
Cash and cash equivalents	$ 13,466,645	$ 590,669	$ 14,057,314	$5,337,758
Investments	274,733			
Accounts and notes receivable	5,703,338	5,656	5,708,994	218,133
Due from other governments	66,390	66,390		
Inventories	202,678		202,678	222,925
Total current assets	19,439,051	596,325	20,035,376	6,053,549
Noncurrent assets				
Restricted cash and investments		2,389,315	2,389,315	
Capital assets				
Land	1,301,621	28,846,666	30,148,286	
Buildings and equipment	233,023,758	4,834,619	237,858,378	23,554,858
Less accumulated Depreciation	(24,526,257)	(1,258,405)	(25,784,662)	(9,250,775)
Capital assets, net	209,799,122	32,422,880	242,222,002	14,304,083
Total assets	229,238,173	35,408,520	264,646,693	20,357,632
Liabilities				
Current liabilities				
Accounts payable	715,883	486,405	1,202,288	1,248,912
Due to other funds	280,000	280,000	1,872,621	
Compensated absences	180,560	14,123	194,683	380,304
Claims and judgments				2,700,760
Bonds, notes, and loans payable	6,311,374	576,000	6,887,374	398,889
Total current liabilities	7,487,817	1,076,528	8,564,345	6,601,486
Noncurrent liabilities				
Compensated absences	722,238	56,490	778,728	
Claims and judgments				8,964,640
Bonds, notes, and loans payable	87,122,479	31,270,430	118,392,909	
Total noncurrent liabilities	87,844,717	31,326,920	119,171,637	8,964,640
Total liabilities	95,332,534	32,403,448	127,735,982	15,566,126
Net position				
Invested in capital assets, net of related debt	116,365,269	576,450	116,941,719	13,905,194
Restricted		2,323,194	2,323,194	
Unrestricted	17,540,370	105,428	17,645,798	(9,113,688)
Total net position	$133,905,639	$ 3,005,072	$136,910,711	$4,791,506

EXERCISES

EX. 9-1

Select the *best* answer.

1. What basis of accounting do enterprise and internal service funds use?

	Enterprise	Internal Service
a.	Modified accrual	Modified accrual
b.	Modified accrual	Full accrual
c.	Full accrual	Modified accrual
d.	Full accrual	Full accrual

2. Which of the following is *not* a GASB-required statement for proprietary funds?
   a. Statement of net position
   b. Statement of revenues, expenses, and changes in fund net position
   c. Statement of cash flows
   d. Statement of changes in fund net position

3. A government need not necessarily account for an activity in an enterprise fund even though it
   a. charges fees for the activity and those fees are material in amount.
   b. finances the activity solely with revenue debt.
   c. is required by law or policy to recover the cost of the activity by fees.
   d. opts to establish pricing policies to recover its costs, including capital costs.

4. Tap fees, to the extent that they do not exceed the cost of hooking customers into the utility, should be accounted for as
   a. capital contributions.
   b. ordinary revenues.
   c. a combination of capital contributions and ordinary revenues.
   d. extraordinary items.

5. Tap fees, a portion of which exceed the cost of hooking customers into the utility, should be accounted for as
   a. capital contributions.
   b. ordinary revenues.
   c. a combination of capital contributions and ordinary revenues.
   d. extraordinary items.

6. Landfill closure and postclosure costs should be recognized as expenses
   a. in the periods incurred.
   b. in the period that the landfill is closed.
   c. in the periods that the landfill is in operation.
   d. in the period in which the landfill is opened.

7. Which of the following would not be included in the computation of the amount to be recognized as a landfill closure expense?
   a. The total estimated closure costs
   b. The capacity of the landfill
   c. The proportion of capacity used in prior years
   d. An appropriate discount rate

8. A city maintains a staff of internal auditors. It may properly account for its internal audit costs in an internal service fund only if
   a. it is required to do so by state or city statutes or regulations.
   b. the internal audit activity is carried out in a discrete organizational unit.
   c. it charges a fee to the city departments for which it provides service.
   d. a GASB pronouncement specifies that internal audit activity is eligible for internal service fund accounting.

9. A government accounts for its self-insurance activities in an internal service fund. Per GASB guidelines, the premiums charged to other funds
   a. must, in total and over time, cover the actual losses incurred by the fund.
   b. cannot include a provision for catastrophic losses.
   c. must be competitive with what an independent insurer would charge.
   d. must be at least as great as the losses incurred each year.

10. If a government accounts for self-insurance activities in its general fund, then premiums charged in excess of actual claims should be accounted for as
   a. ordinary revenues.
   b. an offset against claims expenditures.
   c. an increase in claims reserves.
   d. a nonreciprocal transfer-in.

EX. 9-2

Select the *best* answer.

1. A city's general fund has an outstanding payable to its electric utility, which is accounted for in an enterprise fund. The utility has a corresponding receivable from the general fund. In the city's government-wide statement of net position, which would be correct?
   a. The payable and the corresponding receivable would be eliminated in the consolidation process and thus would not be reported.
   b. The payable may be aggregated with payables to an internal service fund and reported as "payables to proprietary funds."
   c. The payable should be reported in the governmental activities column and the receivable in the business-type activities column.
   d. The payable and the receivable would each be reported in the "totals" column, but would not be reported in either the governmental activities column or the business-type activities column.

2. A city's general fund has an outstanding payable to its vehicle repair internal service fund, which has a corresponding receivable from the general fund. In the city's government-wide statements, which would be correct?
   a. The payable and the corresponding receivable would be eliminated in the consolidation process and thus would not be reported.
   b. The payable may be aggregated with payables to an enterprise fund and be reported as "payables to proprietary funds."
   c. The payable would be reported in the "governmental activities" column and the receivable in the "business-type activities" column.
   d. The payable and the receivable would each be reported in the "totals" column, but would not be reported in either the "governmental activities" column or the "business-type activities" column.

3. Which of the following projects is a state university most likely to finance with revenue bonds rather than general obligation bonds?
   a. A football stadium
   b. An outdoor swimming pool
   c. An intramural field house
   d. A boathouse for its rowing team

4. In what way would the statement of cash flows of a government-owned electric utility differ from that of a privately owned counterpart?
   a. It would not include a category for operating activities.
   b. It would have separate categories for cash flows from noncapital financing activities and cash flows from capital and related financing activities.
   c. It would not include a category for cash flows from investing activities.
   d. It would include a category for cash flows from other nonoperating activities.

5. A government decided to account for a vehicle repair service in an internal service fund rather than its general fund. In a year in which the repair service acquired an unusually large amount of repair equipment, the amount recorded as an expense in the *internal service* fund would be
   a. the same as if the repair service were accounted for in the general fund.
   b. greater than if the repair service were accounted for in the general fund because the general fund would not charge depreciation on the newly acquired assets.
   c. greater than if the repair service were accounted for in the general fund because the internal service fund would charge depreciation on the assets but the general fund would not.
   d. less than if the repair service were accounted for in the general fund because the general fund would have recognized the entire cost of the equipment in the year acquired as an expenditure rather than the amount billed by the internal service fund.

6. A school district's internal service fund has cash on hand at year-end of $2 million. On its government-wide financial statements, this amount would be reported as an asset in the
   a. governmental activities and total columns.
   b. business-type activities and total columns.
   c. total column only.
   d. business-type activities column only.

7. In its first year of operations, a self-insurance internal service fund billed the general fund $500,000 for premiums. Of this amount, $75,000 was intended for catastrophes. During the year, the insurance fund paid out $380,000 in claims, none of which was for catastrophes. As a consequence of these transactions, the insurance fund would report on its statement of net position
   a. Net position of $120,000
   b. Net position of $45,000
   c. Reserve for catastrophes of $75,000
   d. Claims reserves of $120,000

8. A city makes an interest payment of $6 million on its utility fund revenue bonds that were issued to finance new sewer lines. In the utility fund statement of cash flows, the payment would be reflected as a cash flow from
   a. operating activities.
   b. noncapital financing activities.
   c. capital and related financing activities.
   d. investing activities.

9. A utility fund temporarily invests the proceeds from the issuance of revenue bonds in U.S. Treasury bills and receives interest of $300,000. In the utility fund statement of cash flows, the receipt would be reflected as a cash flow from
   a. operating activities.
   b. noncapital financing activities.
   c. capital and related financing activities.
   d. investing activities.

10. A city's transportation service, which is accounted for in an enterprise fund, has outstanding $10 million in revenue bonds. The bonds are also guaranteed by the city itself. These bonds should be reported as a liability in
    a. both the governmental fund statements and the proprietary fund statements, and in both the "business-type activities" column and the "governmental activities" column of the government-wide statements.
    b. only the proprietary fund statements and the "business-type activities" column of the government-wide statements.
    c. only the governmental fund statements and the "governmental activities" column of the government-wide statements.
    d. only the proprietary fund statements.

EX. 9-3

Internal service funds are accounted for similar to businesses.

William County opted to account for its duplication service center in an internal service fund. Previously the center had been accounted for in the county's general fund. During the first month in which it was accounted for as an internal service fund the center engaged in the following transactions:

1. Five copiers were transferred to the internal service fund from the government's general capital assets. At the time of transfer the copiers had a book value (net of accumulated depreciation) of $70,000.
2. The general fund made an initial cash contribution of $35,000 to the internal service fund.
3. The center borrowed $270,000 from a local bank to finance the purchase of additional equipment and renovation of its facilities. It issued a three-year note.
4. It purchased equipment for $160,000 and paid contractors $100,000 for improvements to its facilities.
5. It billed the county clerk's office $5,000 for printing services, of which the office remitted $2,500.
6. It incurred, and paid in cash, various operating expenses of $9,000.
7. The fund recognized depreciation of $1,500 on its equipment and $900 on the improvements to its facilities.
   - **a.** Prepare journal entries in the internal service fund to record the transactions.
   - **b.** Comment on the main differences resulting from the shift from the general fund to an internal service fund in how the center's assets and liabilities would be accounted for and reported.

EX. 9-4

Enterprise funds face unique problems in accounting for restricted assets.

The Louisville City bus system engaged in the following transactions:

1. It issued $10,000,000 in 8 percent revenue bonds. It used the proceeds to acquire new buses. The bonds were issued at par.
2. Consistent with a bond covenant, the system set aside 1 percent of the bonds' gross proceeds for repair contingencies. Correspondingly, it designated an equal dollar amount of net position as restricted to repairs.
3. The bus system accrued nine months' interest ($600,000) at year-end.
4. The bus system incurred $50,000 of repair costs, paying for them with the cash set aside for repair contingencies.
   - **a.** Prepare appropriate journal entries.
   - **b.** Comment on how assets set aside for repairs, as required by bond covenants, would be accounted for if the bus system were reported in the government's governmental funds.

EX. 9-5

Internal service fund activities conducted with departments accounted for in governmental funds are reported differently than are those conducted with departments accounted for in proprietary funds.

The following data relate to the City of Spicewood's data processing internal service fund:

Billings to police and fire departments	$ 800,000
Billings to water utility department	$ 200,000
Year-end receivable from police and fire departments	$ 80,000
Year-end receivable from water utility department	$ 12,000
Net position other than receivables from other departments	$1,300,000

The police and fire departments are accounted for in the general fund. Their activities are classified as "public safety." The water utility department is accounted for in a proprietary fund. The internal service fund establishes billing rates at amounts reflective of the actual costs of providing its services.

Explain how each of the indicated amounts (and the related expenses and payables of the funds receiving the services provided by the data processing department) would be reported in the city's government-wide statement of net position and statement of activities. Be specific.

EX. 9-6

Cash flows of a government must be presented in four categories, rather than the three used by businesses.

The following list of cash flows was taken from the statement of cash flows of Grand Junction's internal service fund (with all amounts expressed in thousands):

Cash on hand at beginning of year	$ 122
Interest from investments	45
Wages and salaries paid	(3,470)
Purchases of supplies	(1,650)
Collections (for services) from other funds	6,380
Interest on long-term debt	(150)
Repayment of loans to other funds	(880)
Purchase of capital assets	(900)
Proceeds of revenue bonds	800
Purchases of investments	(440)
Proceeds from sale of capital assets	23
Proceeds from sale of investments	33
Loans from other funds	600

Recast the list into a statement of cash flows, adding a line for cash on hand at the end of the year.

EX. 9-7

The insurance expense recognized by an enterprise fund depends on the type of carrier.

The water and wastewater utility (enterprise) funds of three cities each paid $1 million in casualty insurance premiums. City A is insured by a small independent insurance company. City B is self-insured and accounts for its insurance activities in an internal service fund. City C is self-insured and accounts for its insurance activities in its general fund. Each of the insurers collected a total of $10 million in premiums from all the parties that it insures, including the city utility funds. Of this amount, each paid out $8 million in actual claims. The balance was held in reserve for major catastrophes.

Prepare the journal entry that each of the three utility funds should make to record its insurance payment and expense for the year. Comment on any differences.

EX. 9-8

Landfill expenses depend on estimates that may change from year to year.

In 2020 Marquette County opened a landfill that was expected to accept waste for four years. The following table indicates the estimates county officials made at the end of each of the four years:

Year	Total Capacity (millions of cubic feet)	Capacity Used This Year (millions of cubic feet)	Expected Closure Costs (millions of dollars)
2020	10	4	$ 8
2021	10	2	$ 9
2022	12	2	$10
2023	12	4	$10

Determine the total expected closure costs ($10 million) that should be assigned to each of the years that the landfill accepts waste.

CONTINUING PROBLEM

Review the comprehensive annual financial report (CAFR) you obtained.

1. Indicate the activities accounted for in both internal service funds and major enterprise funds. Comment on whether any of these activities could also have been accounted for in a general or other governmental fund.
2. How are the internal service fund activities reported in the government-wide statement of net position? How are they reported in the proprietary funds statement of net position?
3. Did any of the internal service funds report significant operating surpluses or deficits for the year? Were any accumulated significant net asset balances over the years not invested in capital assets?
4. Were any of the government's enterprise funds "profitable" during the year? If so, what has the government done with the "earnings"? Has it transferred them to the general fund?
5. Does the government have revenue bonds outstanding that are related to business-type activities? If so, for what activities?
6. Do the financial statements include a statement of cash flows for proprietary funds? Is the statement on a direct or an indirect basis? In how many categories are the cash flows presented? Which of these categories resulted in net cash inflows? Which resulted in net cash outflows?
7. What was the total operating income? What was total net cash provided by operating activities? What accounts for the largest difference between these two amounts?
8. Has the city entered into any service concession arrangements? Which specific ones, and why?

PROBLEMS

P 9-1

Enterprise funds are accounted for like comparable businesses; nevertheless, they have their quirks.

The Green Hills Water District was established on January 1 to provide water service to a suburban development. It accounts for its operations in a single enterprise fund. During the year it engaged in the following transactions:

1. It issued $6,000,000 of revenue bonds.
2. For $4,500,000, it purchased the plant and equipment of the private water company that previously served the area.
3. It incurred $500,000 in costs to improve and expand its plant and equipment.
4. It billed customers for $1.8 million, of which it collected $1.5 million.
5. It billed and collected $200,000 in tap connection fees from developers. The actual cost of the hookups (paid in cash) was $140,000.
6. It incurred the following operating costs (all paid in cash):
   - Purchases of water, $850,000
   - Labor and contract services, $320,000
   - Interest, $80,00
   - Supplies and miscellaneous, $60,000
7. It recognized depreciation of $350,000 on its capital assets.
   a. Prepare journal entries to record the transactions.
   b. Prepare a year-end statement of revenues, expenses, and changes in net position.
   c. Prepare a year-end balance sheet.

d. In some jurisdictions, water districts may account for their operations entirely in an enterprise fund or in several funds, as if they were full-service governments. If a water district chose the latter, then it would report all revenues and operating expenditures in its general fund, and it would maintain other funds as appropriate. Describe briefly how the financial statements of the Green Hills Water District would differ if it chose to prepare its financial statements as if it were a full-service government. Be specific (note changes in capital assets, long-term debt, etc.).

P. 9-2

The premiums charged by self-insurance funds depend on whether they are accounted for in internal service or governmental funds.

Believing that it is more economical to manage its risks internally, a county elects not to purchase commercial insurance. Instead, it sets aside resources for potential claims in an internal service "self-insurance" fund. In a recent year, the fund recognized $1.5 million for claims filed during the year. Of these it paid $1.3 million. Based on the calculations of an independent actuary, the insurance fund billed, and collected, $2.0 million in premiums from the other county departments insured by the fund. Of this amount, $1.2 million was billed to departments accounted for in the general fund and $0.8 million was billed to the county utility fund. The total charge for premiums was based on historical experience and included a reasonable provision for future catastrophe losses.

1. Prepare the journal entries in the internal service fund to record:
a. The claims recognized and paid.
b. The premiums billed and collected.

2. Suppose instead that the county accounted for self-insurance within its general fund. As in part 1, of the $2.0 million in premiums charged, $1.2 million were billed to the other departments accounted for in the general fund and $0.8 million were billed to the utility department.
a. Prepare the general fund journal entry to record the claims recognized and paid.
b. Prepare the general fund entry to record the premiums billed and collected from the utility fund. (Those billed and collected from the other general fund departments would "net out" against their premium expenditures for purposes of external reporting.)

3. What would be the net expenses (i.e., expenditures less premium revenues) reported by the general fund if the self-insurance were accounted for: (1) in the internal service fund, and (2) in the general fund? What would be the total expenses charged by the utility fund if the self-insurance were accounted for: (1) in the internal service fund, and (2) in the general fund? Comment on the rationale for standards that permit such differences.

P. 9-3

The differences in accounting for an activity in an internal service fund rather than in the general fund may be striking.

A school district establishes a vehicle repair shop that provides service to other departments, all of which are accounted for in its general fund. During its first year of operations the shop engages in the following transactions:

- It purchases equipment at a cost of $24 million and issues long-term notes for the purchase price. The useful life of the equipment is eight years, with no residual value.
- It purchases supplies at a cost of $4 million. Of these it uses $3 million. In its *governmental* funds, the district accounts for supplies on a *purchases* basis.
- It incurs $13 million in other operating costs.
- It bills other departments for $19 million.

For purposes of *external* reporting, school district officials are considering two options:

- Account for the vehicle repair shop in an internal service fund.
- Account for the vehicle repair shop in the general fund.

1. For each of the following items indicate the amounts that would be reported in the year-end financial statements of: (1) the internal service fund, assuming that the school district selected the first option, and (2) the general fund, assuming that it selected the second option.
   a. Billings to other departments (revenues)
   b. Cost of supplies (expense or expenditure)
   c. Expenses or expenditures relating to acquisition or use of equipment
   d. Other operating costs
   e. Equipment (asset)
   f. Accumulated depreciation
   g. Inventory (asset)
   h. Notes payable
   i. Nonspendable fund balance (for inventory)

2. What would be the total expenses reported in the internal service fund, assuming that the school district selected the first option?

3. What would be the total amount of expenditures reported in the *general fund*, assuming that the school district: (1) selected the first option; (2) selected the second option?

4. What would be the reported revenue and expenses relating to the vehicle-repair shop in the district's government-wide statements? Would it matter whether the district accounted for the shop in an internal service fund or in the general fund?

P. 9-4

Internal service funds can be used to reduce general fund expenditures.

A city maintains an internal audit department and accounts for it in its general fund. In the coming year, the department will purchase $300,000 of computer and other office equipment, all of which will be paid for out of current resources (i.e., not with debt).

City officials have given top priority to reducing general fund expenditures. To that end, the city comptroller has proposed accounting for the internal audit department in an internal service fund rather than in the general fund. As envisioned by the comptroller, the audit department would bill each of the units (all of which are accounted for in the general fund) for each audit performed. Fees would be established so that they would cover all audit department costs. The fund would be established by a transfer of $300,000 from the general fund to cover the cost of the new equipment.

The city estimates that for the coming year the audit department's operating costs, excluding any costs relating to the new equipment, will be $1,600,000. The equipment is expected to have a useful life of five years.

1. Assume that the city accepts the comptroller's suggestion. Prepare journal entries in the internal service fund to record:
   a. The transfer-in of the $300,000
   b. The acquisition of the equipment
   c. The operating and other costs
   d. The billings to and collection of cash from the general fund

2. Prepare journal entries in the general fund to record:
   a. The transfer-out of the $300,000
   b. The billings from and payment of cash to the internal service fund

3. Would the establishment of the internal service fund result in a decrease in overall government costs (e.g., cash outflows)? Would it result in a reduction in reported general fund expenditures? Explain.

4. Suppose that in the following year, the city does not plan to acquire additional capital assets. Comment on whether reported general fund expenditures would be greater if the internal service fund were to be established than if it were not.

P. 9-5

A city's financial statements and related disclosures about one of its internal service funds raise intriguing questions.

The balance sheet and statement of revenues, expenses, and changes in fund net position of a medium-sized city's "Support Services" internal service fund are as follows:

Support Services Fund Statement of Net Position

Assets	
Pooled investments and cash	$ 546,463
Prepaid expenses	239,582
Total current assets	786,045
Property plant and equipment	3,587,524
Less accumulated depreciation	(2,007,684)
Net property, plant, and equipment	1,579,840
Total assets	$2,365,885
Liabilities	
Accounts payable	$ 39,034
Accrued payroll	854,956
Accrued compensated absences	291,470
Due to other funds	89,876
Total current liabilities	1,275,336
Bonds payable	1,049,902
Total liabilities	$2,325,238
Net position	
Invested in capital assets	529,938
Unrestricted	(489,291)
Total net position	$ 40,647

Statement of Revenues, Expenses, and Changes in Net Position

Billings to other departments	$ 20,340,426
Operating expenses	
Operating expenses before depreciation	32,228,281
Depreciation	122,544
Total expenses	32,350,825
Operating income (loss) before transfers	(12,010,399)
Transfers-in	9,083,006
Increase (decrease) in net position	(2,927,393)
Net position, beginning of year	2,968,040
Net position, end of year	$ 40,647

The financial statements provide a limited amount of additional information about the Support Services Fund:

- The Support Services Fund "includes the activities of the various support service departments."
- The Support Services Fund provides services exclusively to departments accounted for in the general fund.

- The transfer-in was from the general fund.

The city's general fund reported the following (in millions):

Revenues	$196
Expenditures	227
Excess (deficiency) of revenues over Expenditures	(31)
Transfers-in	43
Transfers-out	(9)
Net transfers-in	34
Net change in fund balance	3
Fund balance, beginning of year	25
Fund balance, end of year	$ 28

1. The financial statements do not provide additional information about what constitutes "support services." What are some likely activities that "support services" could include?
2. What is the significance of the internal service fund's balance sheet deficit in "unrestricted net position"? What concern might this raise as to the proper application of accounting principles?
3. What is the significance of the internal service fund's operating deficit as it relates to the general fund's excess of revenues over expenditures?
4. If you were the city's independent auditor, what changes in the billing practices of the internal service fund might you propose that the city consider?
5. In the city's government-wide statements, how would the revenues and expenses of the internal service fund be reported? Which of the revenues and expenses or which expenditures of the internal service fund and the general fund would be eliminated?
6. Suppose that the city accounted for the support services in its general fund, instead of in an internal service fund.
   a. Approximately how much more or less would the general fund's net change in fund balance have been?
   b. Which of the internal service fund's expenses would not be reported as general fund expenditures?
   c. Which of the internal service fund's assets and liabilities would not be reported as general fund assets or liabilities?

P. 9-6

The rates to be charged by internal service funds may not be obvious—and can have a significant impact on who pays the costs of government.

A city maintains an internal service fund to account for a maintenance department. The department provides services to all city departments, which—with one exception—are accounted for in the city's general fund. The exception is the department responsible for the city's golf course. It is accounted for in an enterprise fund.

The maintenance department estimates that it provides approximately 20,000 hours of service per year. However, the volume is seasonal. During the "slack season"—four summer months—it provides approximately 1,400 hours of service per month; during the eight other months it provides approximately 1,800 hours of service per month. The department has determined its fixed costs to be $33,333 per month ($400,000 per year) and its variable costs to be $30 per hour ($600,000 per year, if it provides 20,000 hours of service).

The departments accounted for in the general fund request 17,600 hours of service per year. The department in charge of the golf course requests the remaining 2,400 hours of service per year. However, all its service is requested during the summer months—600 hours per month. Were it not for the demands of the golf course department, the maintenance unit would otherwise have substantial excess capacity during the slack months, considering that no other department would require those 600 hours of service per month.

1. Suppose that the maintenance department determines its billing rates on an annual basis, based on total estimated costs for the year.
   a. What would be the cost per hour of service?
   b. How much of the total costs for the year would be billed to the golf course enterprise fund? How much would be billed to the general fund?

2. Suppose instead that the maintenance department determines its billing rates on a monthly basis, based on total costs for each month.
   a. What would be the cost per hour of service in the busy months (when it provides 1,800 hours of service)?
   b. What would be the cost per hour of service in the slack months (when it provides only 1,400 hours of service)?
   c. How much of the total annual costs would be billed to the golf course enterprise fund? How much of the total annual costs would be billed to the general fund?

3. If you were in charge of the golf course, why would you argue that both billing policies are unfair?

4. What difference might the choice of policies have on the distribution of costs among the city's payers of taxes and fees?

P. 9-7

Internal service fund revenues and expenses must be eliminated in the government-wide statements to avoid "doubling up."

The data in the accompanying table were extracted from a city's fund statements (in millions).

1. Prepare in summary form a government-wide statement of activities and a statement of net position. Although you need not prepare the statement in the format prescribed by the GASB, be sure to have separate columns for governmental and business-type activities and for "totals."

2. GASB Statement No. 34 states that "the effect of interfund services provided and used between functions—for example, the sale of water or electricity from a utility to the general government—should not be eliminated in the statement of activities." What would be the rationale for such a position?

	General Fund	Utility Fund	Internal Service Fund
Revenues (from outside sources)	$240	$ 64	—
Revenues (from other funds)	—	—	$16
Total revenues	240	64	16
Expenses/expenditures (to outsiders)	220	56	16
Expenses/expenditures (to internal service fund)	12	4	—
Total expenses/expenditures	232	60	16
Excess of revenues over expenses/expenditures	$ 8	$ 4	$ 0
Assets (excluding interfund receivables)	$340	$220	$ 9
Receivables (from other funds)	—	—	5
Total assets	340	220	14
Liabilities (to outsiders)	178	180	6
Payables (to internal service fund)	4	1	—
Total liabilities	182	181	6
Net position	$158	$ 39	$ 8

P. 9-8

Financial statements must be adjusted to ensure proper accounting of internal service fund activities.

Sun City accounts for its telecommunication services in an internal service fund. In a recent year its records indicated the following:

Billings to units accounted for in governmental funds	$400,000
Billings to units accounted for in proprietary funds	$100,000
Year-end accounts receivable from units accounted for in governmental funds	$ 25,000
Year-end accounts receivable from units accounted for in proprietary funds	$ 10,000

Per city policy, the telecommunications department bills other departments for the actual cost of providing its services.

1. Explain how each of the following would be reported in the city's government-wide statement of net position and statement of activities:
   a. The billings of the internal service fund (and offsetting purchases of services by other funds)
   b. The year-end accounts receivable and payable

2. Explain how each of the following would be reported in the balance sheets and statements of revenues and expenses/expenditures of the individual governmental and proprietary funds to which the internal service fund provided services and of the internal service fund itself:
   a. The billings from the internal service fund
   b. The year-end accounts payable and receivable

3. Internal service funds are classified as proprietary funds. Yet in the government-wide statements, their assets and liabilities that have not been eliminated in the consolidation process are reported in the "governmental activities" column. How can you justify this apparent inconsistency?

P. 9-9

A government's reported landfill closing expense may exceed its required cash payments.

A municipality expects to use a landfill evenly throughout the 25 years from January 1, 2020, to December 31, 2044. Upon closing the landfill it estimates that it will incur closing costs of $300,000. Thereafter, it anticipates it will have to monitor the site yearly for the following 30 years at an annual cost of $10,000.

The government intends to pay for the closure and monitoring costs evenly over the 25 years that the landfill is in use (2020 through 2044) by making annual cash contributions to a trust fund. The resources of the trust fund will be invested in government securities that can be expected to earn interest at a rate of 5 percent.

1. How much would the municipality need in the trust fund as of December 31, 2044, to satisfy its monitoring obligations for the next 30 years? [*Hint:* What is the present value of an annuity of $10,000 for 30 years?] How much would the government need in the fund to pay the closing costs?

2. How much would it have to contribute to the fund during each of the 25 years it brings waste to the landfill to have a sufficient amount in the fund at the end of 2044 to satisfy its obligations for *both* the closure and the monitoring costs? [*Hint:* The required sum, based on the calculations in part 1, is the equivalent of the future value of a 25-year annuity of unknown amount (x) compounded at a rate of 5 percent.]

3. Per the GASB reporting standards, what amount would the government have to report as its landfill closure and monitoring expenses during each of the 25 years (2020 through 2044), irrespective of how much it actually contributes to the trust fund? Assume that the costs were as estimated.

4. If the government were to make the contributions as you calculated in part 2, but charged the expenses that you calculated in part 3, would it be overstating its closure and monitoring expenses? Explain. What might be a factor that mitigates the overstatement of the expenses?

P. 9-10

Landfill costs must be reported as expenses during the periods of use—but only in enterprise funds.

In 2021, a city opens a municipal landfill, which it will account for in an enterprise fund. It estimates capacity to be 6 million cubic feet and usable life to be 20 years. To close the landfill, the municipality expects to incur labor, material, and equipment costs of $3 million. Thereafter, it expects to incur an additional $7 million of costs to monitor and maintain the site.

1. In 2021, the city uses 300,000 feet of the landfill. Prepare the journal entry to record the expense for closure and postclosure costs.
2. In 2022, it again uses 300,000 feet of the landfill. It revises its estimate of available volume to 5.8 million cubic feet, and reestimates closure and postclosure costs at $10.2 million. Prepare the journal entry to record the expense for closure and postclosure costs.
3. In 2040, the final year of operation, it uses 350,000 feet of the landfill. The actual capacity has proven to be only 5 million cubic feet, and closing costs are now estimated to be $15 million. Through the year 2036, the municipality had used 4,650,000 cubic feet and recorded $14.2 million in closure and postclosure costs. In 2037, it actually incurs $5 million in closure costs, the entire amount of which is paid in cash.
   a. Prepare the journal entry to record the expense for closure and postclosure cost.
   b. Prepare the journal entry to record the actual closure costs paid.
4. Suppose instead that the landfill was accounted for in the government's general fund. Indicate how the entries would differ from those in the enterprise fund.

P. 9-11

Decommissioning cost are often nontrivial and must be recognized years in advance

A city constructs a power plant at a cost of $600 million. The facility has an estimated useful life of 50 years. At the end of the year in which the plant goes on-line, city engineers determine that if the plant had to be decommissioned at the balance sheet date, then it would cost approximately $100 million to satisfy all federal and state regulatory requirements.

1. Prepare an appropriate entry to record the estimated decommissioning costs at year-end in the city's government-wide statements.
2. At the end of the following year, city engineers estimated that owing to increases in the prices of the equipment that would be needed to retire the plant, estimated costs had increased to $105 million. Prepare a journal entry to record the increase in the current value of the decommissioning costs.
3. After 35 years, the city concluded that the plant was not economically viable and decided to decommission the plant. Owing to inflation and various changes in technology, the balance in its ARO liability account at the time was $240 million. Engineers estimated that the decommissioning process would take at least three years. In the first year, the city incurred $155 in decommissioning costs. Prepare an entry to record the first year's decommissioning costs.
4. How, if at all, would these events and transactions be recorded in the city's enterprise fund that is used to account for the facility?

P. 9-12

Pollution remediation costs must be recognized as soon as a government is aware of them and can estimate them.

In Year 1, as a result of routine testing, a city discovers that local wells are polluted. Investigation reveals that the source of the contamination is an abandoned waste dump that the city owns. At a cost of $25,000, the county conducts a feasibility study, as a result of which engineers make the following estimates:

- Cost of acquiring and installing pumps and other equipment will range between $160,000 and $200,000 with the high and low amounts being considered equally likely.

- Cost of removing the waste will be between $100,000 and $140,000 with an 80 percent probability that it approximates the lower amount and a 20 percent probability that it will be near the higher amount.
- Cost of monitoring the site over a 10-year period will total between $180,000 and $220,000 with no amount being more likely than another.

In addition, the city estimates that it will be able to recover $50,000 of the costs from a previous owner of the property.

In Year 2, the city acquires and installs the pumps and other equipment at an actual cost of $190,000 and incurs actual waste removal costs of $105,000 (all paid in cash). It also reached a settlement with the previous owner for $45,000 and receives payment in cash.

1. Prepare the entries that the city should make in years 1 and 2 as they would serve as the basis for preparation of its government-wide statements.
2. Suppose instead that the city had acquired the land knowing that it was polluted but with the intention of turning it into a park. Indicate any differences in your entries.

P. 9-13

The operating cash flows of internal service funds can be reconciled with operating income.

What follows are the statement of revenues, expenses, and changes in net position, and the statement of cash flows for Tucson, Arizona's fleet services internal service fund.

1. How do you account for the difference between net operating income of $105 and cash from operating activities of $10,789? Prepare a reconciling schedule in which you account for the difference.
2. How would the revenues and expenses of the fund be reported on the city's government-wide statement of activity?
3. How would the revenues and expenses of the fund be reported on the city's statement of revenues, expenses, and changes in net position?
4. How would the difference between charges for services and cash received from customers be reflected on the city's government statement of net position?
5. How would the charges for services most likely be reflected on the city's general fund statement of revenues and expenditures and changes in fund balance?

Fleet Services Fund Statement of Revenues, Expenses, and Changes in Net Position Balance (in thousands)

Charges for services	$ 24,019
Operating expenses	
Wages and salaries	$ 4,609
Contractual services	1,765
Supplies	8,826
Depreciation	8,714
Total operating expenses	23,914
Net operating income	$ 105
Nonoperating revenues (expenses)	
Investment income	$ 498
Interest expense	(182)
Gain from sale of property	751
Capital grants	215
Total nonoperating revenues	$ 1,282
Net income	$ 1,387
Net position—Beginning of year	$ 3,880
Net position—End of year	$ 5,267

Fleet Services Fund Statement of Cash Flows (in thousands)

Cash flows for operating activities	
Cash received from customers	$ 24,530
Cash payments to suppliers for goods and services	(9,023)
Cash payments to employees	(4,718)
Net cash provided by operating activities	$ 10,789
Cash flows from noncapital financing activities	0
Cash flows from capital and related financing activities	
Acquisition or construction of capital assets	$ (9,219)
Proceeds from sale of property and equipment	1,914
Principal paid on capital debt	(1,168)
Interest paid on capital debt	(182)
Net cash flows from capital and related financing activities	$ (8,655)
Cash flow from investing activities	
Investment income	$ 467
Net cash flows from investing activities	$ 467
Net increase in cash and cash equivalents	$ 2,601
Cash and cash equivalents, beginning of year	5,253
Cash and cash equivalents, end of year	$ 7,854

P. 9-14

Based on actual circumstances, this minicase illustrates an issue faced by government-operated utilities (one that has not been addressed by standard setters and is not discussed in the text).

The City Electric Utility (CEU), which a city accounts for in its enterprise fund, provides cash rebates to customers who install insulation, storm windows, or energy-saving appliances. The payments are intended to reduce the demand for electricity and thereby enable the CEU to avoid having to add generating capacity.

Like many government-operated utilities, the CEU establishes rates based on a number of factors, of which cost is only one. It is the policy of the city, for example, to make substantial transfers each year from the CEU to its general fund. Utility fees are thereby a form of taxation, and the revenue requirements of the general fund are taken into account in setting the rates.

The CEU comptroller has raised the question of whether the rebates should be charged as an expense as paid, or be capitalized and charged as an expense over time (i.e., be amortized). Moreover, he then asks what the basis should be for determining the length of the amortization period.

Required: Write a brief memo in which you recommend to the CEU comptroller how the rebates should be accounted for. Be sure to support your position.

P. 9-15

A department's internal service charges may be affected by other departments' usage.

The city of Tribville recently centralized its mobile technology (phones, computers, and tablets) functions for the government in a single internal service fund. City officials want the fund to break even, so they need rates to be set appropriately. The combined data for the fund for the year are as follows (expressed in $000):

Salaries and wages	$191,600
Supplies:	17,400
Insurance (a two-year warranty coverage policy on equipment)	1,500
Depreciation on equipment:	7,000
Total annual costs	$217,500

The fund charges based on the number of mobile devices a department *uses*. The budget office estimates that there are a total of 15,000 mobile devices in operation across the government.

1. Based on the data present above, what amount would each user department be charged per phone.

2. The police department uses 5,000 of the phones, and the fire department uses 2,000 of the phones. How much would be the total annual charge to the fire department?

3. Suppose that of the $217,500 of annual costs, $45,000 are fixed and $172,500 are variable ($11.50 per phone). The police department decides that it needs only 3,000 phones.
   a. What would be the amount that the internal service fund now charges per phone?
   b. What would be the total amount now charged to the fire department, assuming that the fire department continues to use 2,000 phones?

QUESTIONS FOR RESEARCH, ANALYSIS, AND DISCUSSION

1. Do you think the current criteria for establishing enterprise funds are adequate? For example, are they too flexible in that governments *may* account for a wide range of activities in enterprise funds? Or are they too rigid in that governments *must* account for activities in enterprise funds if they satisfy specified criteria?

2. The City of Lewisville collected $600,000 in tap fees last year. Of this amount, $400,000 covered the direct costs of connecting customers to the city's water lines. The balance contributed to improvements in and maintenance of the overall water system. How should these fees be reported in the water utility fund's statement of revenues, expenses, and changes in fund net position (e.g., should they be reported as operating or nonoperating revenues)? How should these fees be reported on the utility's statement of cash flows (e.g., in which category of cash flows should they be reported)? How should the fees be reported on the city's government-wide statement of activities (e.g., as operating revenues or capital contributions)?

3. As noted in Chapter 7, interest incurred while assets to be used for governmental activities are being constructed should not be capitalized. Does the same rule apply to assets to be used for business-type activities? Suppose that the assets used for business-type activities were financed with general obligation bonds. Should the construction period interest be capitalized? What if assets used in an enterprise fund on which interest has been capitalized are transferred from that fund to be used for government activities? Should the capitalized interest be removed?

4. It unquestionably makes sense for governments to manage certain government-wide services, such as vehicle repair and computer services, in a separate organizational unit, and to control demand by beneficiary units by charging them usage fees. In the government-wide statements, internal service fund assets and liabilities are classified as governmental activities, and expenses, most of which are typically accounted for in the general fund, are charged back to the beneficiary units. Moreover, the resources of internal service funds are seldom legally restricted. Would it not make sense for purposes of external (albeit not internal) reporting to do away with internal service funds entirely, and to report all assets, liabilities, and expenses in the funds used to account for the beneficiary units?

SOLUTION TO EXERCISE FOR REVIEW AND SELF-STUDY

1. Capital assets (property, plant, and equipment, with accumulated depreciation) and long-term liabilities appear on the statement of net position; depreciation expense is shown on the statement of revenues, expenses, and changes in net position. Thus the statements are based on the full accrual basis of accounting.

2. Both the revenues and the expenses of the enterprise funds are determined by outside demand for the funds' goods and services. It is therefore not possible for the city to budget its revenues and expenses as if they could be determined by legislative fiat. Moreover, the revenues of the internal service funds (and hence the level of services to be provided by these funds) are already controlled through the budgets

of the departments to which they provide services. For purposes of planning, of course, the city should prepare budgets for its proprietary funds—just as any private business would. But in the absence of unusual circumstances, the city does not need to incorporate them into its accounting system.

3. Yes. The $116.4 million that is invested in capital assets (net of related debt) is equal to the capital assets, net ($209.8 million) less the bonds, notes, and loans payable (current of $6.3 million and non-current of $87.1 million). In many situations, such a reconciliation is not possible, either because the current portion of the bonds payable is aggregated with other current liabilities or because a portion of bond proceeds has not yet been spent and is therefore aggregated with other cash or short-term investments.

4. The difference between reported restricted assets and reported restricted net position would arise if the restricted cash and investments included unspent proceeds of long-term debt. These restricted assets would be offset by bonds payable, rather than by a restriction of net position.

5. In the fund statements the billings of the internal service fund to the golf course would be reported as revenue of the internal service funds and as an expense of the golf course. The related costs of providing the service would be reported as an expense of the internal service fund. In the government-wide statements the billings would be reported only as an expense of the golf course. The revenues and expenses of the internal service fund would be eliminated in the consolidation process.

6. The depreciation charges are incorporated into the amounts billed to the funds to which the internal service funds provide services. Therefore, in the government-wide statements they would be incorporated into the expenses of the functions accounted for in those funds.

7. The fees paid by the customers are in part a capital contribution to the utility fund. The $80,000 hookup cost would be reported as an operating revenue; the $120,000 excess as a capital contribution (a non-operating revenue).

8. In the funds statement of net position, the electric utility would report a payable; the internal service fund a receivable. In the government-wide statement of net position, the business-type activities would report a payable; the governmental activities would report a receivable.

9. Unless the internal service funds provide services mainly to units accounted for in proprietary funds, their assets and liabilities would be reported in the column for "governmental-type activities."

CHAPTER 10

Pensions and Other Fiduciary Activities

LEARNING OBJECTIVES

After studying this chapter you should understand:

- Why pensions are important
- The distinctions between defined contribution and defined benefit pension plans
- The relationships between an employer and its pension trust fund
- The main issues faced by government employers in accounting for pension plans and how the GASB has resolved them
- How pension plans are accounted for
- How postemployment health care benefits are accounted for
- What are fiduciary funds
- What is meant by control
- Who are parties other than the government itself
- What are own-source resources
- What are the four types of fiduciary funds
- How should governments account for and report fiduciary funds
- What are permanent funds and how are they accounted for

This chapter deals first with one of the most significant and controversial issues facing governments from both accounting and policy perspectives: how to deal with employee pensions and other postemployment benefits. It then addresses issues of fiduciary and related activities. Although it is natural to think of the assets of governments or not-for-profits as being mainly highways, buildings, police cars, research laboratories, and the like, in fact, governments and not-for-profits represent some of the nation's largest holders of stocks, bonds, and similar securities. These assets are often concentrated in pension and other fiduciary funds.

WHY IS PENSION ACCOUNTING SO IMPORTANT?

The accounting for pensions is, and no doubt will continue to be for many years to come, among the most important, yet controversial, issues of our era. The accounting for pensions would be important for no other reason than the magnitude of the assets and liabilities involved. The assets of state and local government pension funds are huge. For example, as of June 30, 2017 CalPERS, the California Public Employees' Retirement System, had over

$350 billion of assets; CalSTRS the California State Teachers' Retirement System, had over $236 billion. The liabilities are similarly huge, and they are a cause of major fiscal strain for many governments.

The significance of pension accounting goes beyond the numbers; it has a direct impact on public policy. Conservative political groups that favor decreased government spending and believe that the retirement plans of government employees are overly generous have forcefully promoted accounting standards that increase the reported liabilities of pension plans. They believe that if the plans were required to present their fiscal status in a more conservative light, the public would pressure their elected officials to modify the plans and reduce employee compensation. Understandably, liberals and, of course, employee unions take an opposite position, favoring accounting rules that minimize the reported liabilities and put the most favorable fiscal shine on the plans.

The road to governmental fiscal failure has long been paved with inadequately funded pensions. In the years following World War II, New York City substantially expanded its workforce. In exchange for smaller increases in direct wages and salaries, the city offered some groups of employees exceedingly generous retirement benefits. In the subsequent years, the city failed to contribute adequately to its pension funds, sometimes basing its contributions on outmoded actuarial tables. By the mid-1970s, when many of the employees hired after the war reached retirement age, the required pension outlays consumed such a large portion of the city's current budget that they were a major cause of its fiscal crisis and the city's resultant forced reorganization. In more recent years, the bankruptcies of Detroit, Stockton (California), and Central Falls (Rhode Island) can be tied directly to inadequately funded pension plans. So, too, can the current fiscal problems of New Jersey, Illinois, and Connecticut. But the problems of these governments are hardly uncommon. Government officials are far more willing to grant benefits that will have to be paid for many years in the future—when they will no longer be in office—than they are to offer current wage and salary increases.[1] As noted in the accompanying In Practice, the pension plans of many state and local governments continue to be severely underfunded and threaten the fiscal sustainability of numerous local and well as state governments.

A pension is a sum of money paid to retired or disabled employees based on their years of employment. Although employees earn their pensions—and their employers benefit from their services—during their years of employment, the actual cash payments do not have to be made to the employees until their years of retirement. Thus, the benefits received and the cash payments may be mismatched by many years. As will be evident from our discussion of pensions, the difficult accounting issues arise because, depending on the type of plan, (a) the amount of the eventual cash payments to the employees may depend on variables that are unknown at the time the employees provide their services, and (b) it is not obvious how the eventual costs of the benefits should be allocated to the particular years in which the employees provide their services.

The accounting issues pertaining to **Other Post-Employment Benefits (OPEB)**, mainly retiree health insurance, are closely tied to those of pensions. As will be discussed, these other types of benefits have economic characteristics similar to those of pensions and though less publicized may be no less of a threat to governments' fiscal well-being. These benefits will be addressed later in this chapter.

[1] This problem is not confined to governments. Many private companies, most notably those in the automobile industry, can trace their fiscal difficulties to compensation policies that favored benefits that would have to be paid for in the distant future over wages and salaries that would have to be paid for in the present.

IN PRACTICE FUNDED STATUS OF STATE DEFINED BENEFIT PLANS—TEN BEST AND TEN WORST

	Ten Worst	Funding Status in %		Ten Best	Funding Status in %
1	New Jersey	30.90	50	Wisconsin*	100.00
2	Kentucky	31.40	49	South Dakota	96.90
3	Illinois	35.60	48	Tennessee	95.90
4	Connecticut	44.10	47	New York	94.50
5	Colorado	46.00	46	Nebraska	88.80
6	Pennsylvania	52.60	45	North Carolina	88.30
7	Minnesota	53.20	44	Idaho	87.70
8	South Carolina	53.80	43	Utah	86.00
9	Hawaii*	54.70	42	Washington	84.00
10	Rhode Island	55.30	41	Iowa	81.60

The funded status is the ratio of the plans' total cash and investment holdings to its pension obligations.

*The data were drawn from the 2016 Comprehensive Annual Financial Reports of the Individual States, and were reported as required by GASB Statement No. 67. However, the percentages for Wisconsin and Tennessee are based on GASB Statement No. 25. Moreover, those for New York are from the state's 2017 CAFR rather than the 2016 CAFR.

Source: "Pension Fund Problems Worsen in 43 States," *Bloomberg (on-line),* August 29, 2017, https://www.bloomberg.com/graphics/2017-state-pension-funding-ratios/ (accessed November 20, 2017).

DEFINED CONTRIBUTION PLANS

HOW DO DEFINED CONTRIBUTION PLANS DIFFER FROM DEFINED BENEFIT PLANS?

Employers maintain two types of pension plans. The first, and by far the simpler to account for, is a **defined contribution plan**. Under a defined contribution plan, an employer agrees to make a series of **pension contributions** to a pension fund. Typically, the amount is expressed as a percentage of each employee's salary, and very often the pension fund is totally independent of the employer. For example, a college may contribute 8 percent of a faculty member's salary to TIAA (Teachers Insurance and Annuity Association), provided that the faculty member also contributes a corresponding percentage. TIAA invests the contributions, and upon retirement, the employee can begin to withdraw the funds, plus accumulated investment earnings. The actual benefits to be received by the employee depend on the fund's investment performance. The employee bears all the investment risks. If the investment portfolio does well, the employee reaps the benefits. If it does poorly, it is the employee who will have to cut back on his or her anticipated retirement lifestyle. As implied by the plan's name, the employer defines (specifies) the inputs—its contributions; it makes no guarantees as to the outputs—the payments to be made to its employees when they retire.

Defined contribution plans present few financial or accounting complexities. The employer reports an annual expense for the amount that it is obligated to contribute to the pension fund. As a result, the plan has no unfunded actuarial liabilities. Governmental Accounting Standards Board (GASB) standards require note disclosures that include a description of the plan and the benefits provided. In addition, to the extent that the employer makes the contributions to a fiduciary fund that it controls itself (as some employers do), it must also provide details about the investments that it holds. Although most municipalities maintain defined benefit plans, many also have established defined contribution plans for certain of their employees.

DEFINED BENEFIT PLANS

This chapter is concerned mainly with the type of plan that is more common in government—and more difficult to account for—the **defined benefit pension plan**. Under a defined benefit plan, the employer specifies the benefits—the actual pension payments—that the employee will receive. Usually the benefits will vary according to length of service and salary. For example, a college might promise to pay faculty members 2.5 percent of their average annual salaries during their last three years of service for each year of employment. Faculty members with 30 years of service who earned an average of $100,000 during the three years prior to retirement would be guaranteed an annual pension of $75,000 (2.5 percent × 30 years × $100,000). In contrast to the defined contribution plan, the employer guarantees the outputs (payments to the retirees), not the inputs (contributions to the pension fund). It is therefore up to the employer to ensure that it sets aside sufficient resources each year to make the required payments.

Both funding and accounting decisions relating to defined benefit plans are complex, mainly because of the uncertainties about the amounts that will have to be paid to the retirees and that will be earned on fund investments. Sound financial policy and the need to report on interperiod equity dictate that the costs of pensions be allocated to the periods in which employees perform their services and earn their pension benefits—not those in which they receive the cash benefits. However, the actual cost cannot be known for certain until the employees receive all the benefits that they have been promised. These will not be known until the employees (and sometimes their spouses, if they are also entitled to benefits) have died. The key uncertainties affecting the actual cost of a defined benefit pension plan include

- Employee life expectancy
- Employee turnover rates (employees usually must accumulate a specified number of work years before qualifying for even minimum benefits and must satisfy other conditions relating to length of employment and age to qualify for full benefits)
- Future wage and salary rates
- The investment returns on pension fund assets

The amount that an employer must provide each year to meet its future **pension obligations** can be calculated actuarially. Actuaries are statisticians who compute insurance risks and premiums.

In the private sector, almost all companies that launch new pension plans now establish defined contribution plans as opposed to defined benefit plans, and many firms that previously had defined benefit plans are converting them into defined contribution plans. The reasons are multiple. Defined contribution plans are more portable; that is, they permit employees to change jobs without losing any of the funds that their retirement account has accumulated. They are less subject to federal regulation, in particular the Employee Retirement Income Security Act of 1974 (ERISA). They present less risk to the employer; once it has made its contributions to the designated fund, it bears no investment or actuarial risks. Most saliently from an accounting perspective, once the employer has made its required contribution, it does not have to report any pension-related liabilities on its balance sheet.

IN PRACTICE — DEFINED BENEFIT PLANS ARE MORE EFFICIENT THAN DEFINED CONTRIBUTION PLANS

In state and local governments, defined benefit plans are still dominant, covering about 90 percent of current employees. However, because the pension plans of so many governments are severely underfunded—and are thereby a threat to the governments' fiscal sustainability—there is considerable pressure on them to convert to defined contribution plans. This pressure, however, is ironic. Most actuaries contend that defined benefit plans are more efficient than defined contribution plans. Dollar for dollar of contribution, they provide the greater benefit. In large part this is because in defined contribution plans resources are assigned to individual employees. Employees are entitled only to what has been accumulated in their individual accounts. Employees, therefore, bear not only investment risks but also that of their mortality. Thus, to be safe, employees must assume that they will have the good fortune to live for perhaps 30 or even 35 years beyond the customary retirement age of 65. That good fortune, however, may result in fiscal disaster if they outlive the resources in their plans. By contrast, in defined benefit plans, the risks are pooled and thereby spread among all members of the plan. Statistically, therefore, the average life expectancy of the employee pool may be no greater than 17 years beyond retirement. Hence, fewer dollars, in total, need to be put into a defined benefit plan than into a defined contribution plan.

In addition, because the resources of all employees are mingled in a single investment fund, investment yields of defined benefit plans may be greater than those of defined contribution plans. Sound retirement planning suggests that as employees age and approach their retirement, they should generally move to increasingly conservative investment portfolios (e.g., those with an increasing proportion of fixed income securities, such as bonds, as opposed to stocks). That is because if stock prices take a tumble, there is less time for them to recover. Typically, more conservative—less risky—investments provide lower returns. In a defined contribution plan as individual employees get older, they must move to more conservative, lower-yielding, investments. In a defined benefit plan, however, the population includes young employees as well as retirees and employees approaching retirement. New, young employees join the plan and replace older ones. Therefore, the average age of the members of the plan may remain relatively constant, and it need not move, over time, to the more conservative, lower-yielding, portfolio.

IN PRACTICE CAN DEFINED BENEFIT PLANS BE SAVED?

In light of the fiscal stress that underfunded pension plans are placing on state and local governments, the need for reform is widely acknowledged. As noted in the text, some critics of defined benefit plans contend that governments should convert these plans to defined contribution plans. But, if, as many actuaries maintain, defined benefit plans are more efficient than defined contribution plans, then any cost savings for government employers will result in reduced benefits for their employees. Are there other reforms that governments should consider short of shifting to defined contribution plans? Here are some possibilities:

- *Eliminate "spiking."* Many plans base benefits on compensation earned in the last year of employment. To increase their compensation and thereby enhance their benefits some employees work extra hours of overtime in their final year of employment. They thereby manage to earn more in retirement than in a typical year of employment. To eliminate spiking, pension benefits should be based on some long-term average (e.g., the final three years) of compensation and exclude overtime hours.
- *Reduce opportunities for "early" retirement.* Governments typically provide for full retirement benefits after as few as 20 years of service. Thus, employees who began their careers at age 25 are able to collect pensions at age 45. Although relatively early-age retirement may be appropriate for some city workers, such as police officers and firefighters, it is clearly inappropriate for others.
- *Increase the age at which benefits can be collected.* In some governments, pensions can be collected as soon as employees retire. Thus, if employees retire from government at age 50, but then take other jobs, they still collect their government pensions. Pension plans could be structured so that benefits do not begin until an employee reaches a "normal" retirement age, perhaps 65.

In arguing for pension reform, it is often pointed out that retirement benefits for government employees are more generous than for those in the private sector. Whereas that may be correct, it should also be noted that retirement benefits are only one form of compensation. In comparing compensation of government employees to those in the private sector, all forms of compensation must be taken into account. To be sure, some government employees, especially those in unskilled positions, earn more than their private-sector counterparts. Others, notably in high-level positions, do not. This was vividly illustrated in a class taught by one of the textbook's authors. He asked a student, who was serving in the army, how much the general who was in charge of the U.S. wars in Iraq and Afghanistan earned each year. His response was, "I'm not certain, but it is most definitely less than that of his translator, who is an employee of a private contractor."

WHAT ARE THE DISTINCTIONS AMONG SINGLE, AGENT MULTIPLE-EMPLOYER, AND COST-SHARING PLANS?

Assets that have been set aside for pensions per a defined benefit plan are generally legally restricted and are held for the benefit of employees. Therefore, they are accounted for in a pension trust (fiduciary) fund. Government pension trusts that are organizationally separate from their sponsoring governments are often referred to as **Public Employee Retirement Systems (PERS)**.

Some pension plans are established by a single employer and cover only the employer's own employees. These are referred to as **single (or sole) employer plans**. Others are established by a sponsoring organization, such as a state or a county for employees of governments within its jurisdiction. Under one type of multiple-employer plan (an **agent multiple-employer plan**), the invested assets are pooled. However, separate accounts are maintained, and actuarial computations are made, for each employer. In substance, therefore, each employer has its own plan; the sponsoring **agent** merely provides administrative and investment services. Thus, the accounting for agent multiple-employer plans is, in essence, the same as for single employer plans.

Under another type of multiple-employer plan, a **cost-sharing multiple-employer plan**, the employees of all participating governments are placed in a common pool. The employers share all risks and costs and make contributions at the same rate. Plan assets may be used to pay any employee's benefits, regardless of the participating government for which the employee worked. As discussed later in this section, each employer must account for its share of the overall plan's costs, assets, and actuarial obligations.

WHAT IS THE RELATIONSHIP BETWEEN AN EMPLOYER AND ITS PENSION PLAN?

A pension plan (also referred to as a pension *fund*) is an arrangement in which the pension investments are held and managed. Commonly, but not always, the pension plan takes the form of a trust fund in which the trust assets are legally separate from those of its sponsoring employer. However, whether maintained by the employer itself or an outside party, the plan is an independent financial and accounting entity. If maintained by the employer, then the employer must include the plan in its financial statements just as it does its other fiduciary funds. If the plan is maintained by an outside party, then the employer must disclose information about its financial condition in notes to its financial statements.

The assets of a pension plan consist mainly of cash, securities, and other income-producing assets. Its *economic* obligations (irrespective of whether and when they are given accounting recognition) are the pension benefits that have been earned by its plan members—both employees already retired and those currently in the workforce.

Even though pension plans are independent fiscal and accounting entities, they are inexorably linked to their sponsoring employers and the individual funds from which the pension contributions will be received. Under a defined benefit plan, an employer is ultimately liable for the benefits to be paid to retirees. Therefore, the obligations of the plan are, in economic substance, those of the employer. Similarly, if the plan assets increase or decrease in value, the ultimate benefits or costs revert to the employer in that its future contributions can be greater or less.

In this chapter, we first discuss how *employers* should account for and report pension costs, obligations, and assets. We then turn to issues relating to the pension *plan* (i.e., trust fund). Our focus will be on governments rather than other not-for-profits primarily because pensions tend to be of greater significance to governments than not-for-profits. Not-for-profits most commonly participate in defined contribution rather than defined benefit plans, and the plans are usually maintained by independent financial institutions.

For more than two decades, the accounting for pensions was governed by GASB Statement No. 25, *Financial Reporting for Defined Benefit Pension Plans and Note Disclosures for Defined Contribution Plans* (1994), and GASB Statement No. 27, *Accounting for Pensions by State and Local Governmental Employers* (1994). These statements, critics charged, allowed governments to greatly understate their reported pension obligations and expenses. In response to the criticism, the GASB in 2012 issued Statement No. 67, *Financial Reporting for Pension Plans,* and Statement No. 68, *Accounting and Financial Reporting for Pensions*. These two statements, which became effective, respectively, for years beginning after June 15, 2013, and 2014, dramatically altered the pension accounting landscape.

WHAT IS THE UNDERLYING RATIONALE FOR THE GASB APPROACH?

The GASB approach is grounded on the assumption that pensions are a form of compensation that is provided to employees in exchange for the services that they provide to the government. The government benefits from the services in the period that they are provided even though its employees may not receive the cash payments until many years later. Accordingly, the government must recognize an expense (at least in government-wide and other statements prepared on a full accrual basis) and corresponding obligation in the period in which the employees provide the services and the government benefits from them. Moreover, the government is the party that is primarily responsible for the obligation to the employees and should recognize a balance sheet liability to the extent that there are insufficient assets in a qualified trust (i.e., the pension plan) to satisfy that obligation. In other words, the government should recognize a balance sheet liability for the *unfunded* portion of the total obligation.

It is important to note that the GASB establishes standards for accounting and financial reporting. It does not establish standards for funding. Thus, the GASB directs how much governments must report as a pension expense; it does not tell governments how much they must contribute each year to their pension plans.

HOW SHOULD THE EMPLOYER MEASURE ITS PENSION OBLIGATION?

Per GASB Statement No. 68, the government employer is required to report as its pension liability the difference between the **total pension liability** and the **net plan position**. This difference is referred to as the **net pension liability**. The total pension liability is an actuarial determination – the present value of the benefits that will be paid to plan members The net plan position is the total assets (cash and investments) in the pension plan less any pension *plan* liabilities. As will be emphasized later in this chapter, the pension plan does not recognize as a liability the actuarial value of the amounts that will eventually have to be paid in retiree benefits. Rather, it recognizes only amounts that are currently due to plan members and various accrued investment and administrative expenses, all of which are almost always minor in relation to the accumulated assets.

The calculation of the total pension liability can be measured in three steps as indicated in Figure 10-1. For simplicity, this figure and the related discussion focus on a single hypothetical employee rather than an employee population at-large.

- *The actuary must first estimate the amount that will be required to make the cash payments to employees during their years of retirement.* In this example, taking into account life expectancy, anticipated years of service, and future salary increases, an actuary determines that the one employee, who is currently age 55, will retire at age 65, live for another 17 years thereafter, and be entitled to benefits of $100,000 per year.
- *The actuary must discount these payments to the valuation date (a current or near-current date).* The 55-year-old employee has already worked for the government for 20 years, since age 35. The actuary estimates that he will work for another 10 years. Assuming a discount rate of 6 percent, the pension plan will have to have accumulated $1,047,726 by the time the employee retires to make the necessary 17 payments of $100,000. The present value of that single sum, discounted for the 10 years remaining until the date of retirement, is $585,045.

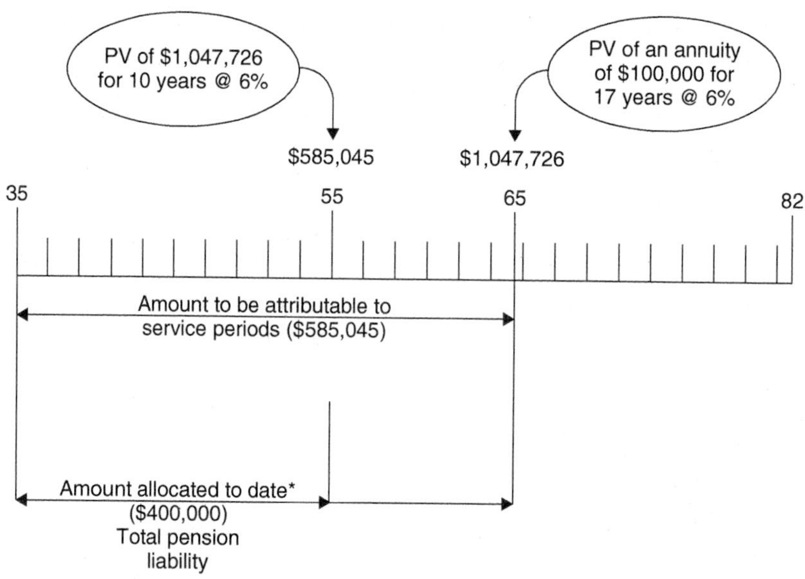

FIGURE 10-1 Calculation of Total Pension Liability

- *The actuary must allocate the $585,045 to the 30 total periods of past, present, and future service.* The means of allocating this cost is done by means of an **actuarial cost method**. The portion of the liability that has been assigned to the years of service up to the valuation date is the total actuarial liability—in this example, assume $400,000.

Actuarial cost methods have much in common with depreciation methods. Whereas a depreciation method allocates the cost of long-lived assets over the periods in which the assets are in use, an actuarial method allocates pension costs over the periods in which employees provide service. Just as depreciation can be allocated in many different patterns (e.g., straight line or double declining) so, too, can pension costs. The GASB specifies that for purposes of accounting and reporting, the allocation must be made using a method called the **entry age actuarial cost method**. This method allocates the present value of the projected benefits over the course of an employee's career as a level percentage of payroll. The total pension liability as of a specific date is that portion of the present value of projected benefits that has been allocated to the past years up through that date.

HOW IS THE DISCOUNT RATE DETERMINED?

The most controversial aspect of pension accounting is likely the selection of the discount rate. The lower the discount rate, the greater will be the total (and hence the net) pension liability. The higher the discount rate, the lower will be the total pension liability. Prior to the implementation of Statement No. 68, governments were required to use as a discount rate the expected long-term rate of return on pension plan assets. Sensitive to criticisms that such rate was conceptually inappropriate (and often too high), the GASB, in Statement No. 68, took a different tack. The new discount rate, it asserted, should be a "blended" rate. It should be the single rate that reflects

- The long-term expected rate of return on plan investments to the extent that plan's fiduciary net position (plan asset less plan liabilities) is projected to be sufficient to meet future benefit payments and satisfy administrative costs

- A yield or index rate on high-quality 20-year municipal bonds to the extent that plan's fiduciary net position is projected to be insufficient to meet future benefit payments.

The rationale for this approach is that the expected return on plan assets is relevant only so far as the government actually holds assets that can earn that return. If, and when, it will exhaust those assets, it will likely have to borrow the funds necessary to pay the benefits as well as to meet required administrative costs. Hence, the proper rate at beyond the point at which it runs out of resources is its likely borrowing rate. In effect (although the computation is complex), the blended rate is a weighted average of the two rates.

HOW SHOULD THE PENSION EXPENSE IN FULL ACCRUAL STATEMENTS BE DETERMINED?

Generally speaking, the pension expense for a particular year in government-wide statements and proprietary funds can be seen as the change during that year in the *net* pension liability—the difference between the total pension liability and the fiduciary net position of the pension plan. However, there are exceptions, the most notable of which will be addressed later. First, however, we shall identify the factors that affect the two components of the net pension liability—the total pension liability and the fiduciary net position of the pension plan.

CHANGES IN THE TOTAL PENSION LIABILITY

The change in the total pension liability in a particular year is affected by the factors that follow. The first three might be considered routine or ongoing.

- ***The amount allocated per the actuarial cost method.*** This amount is referred to as the service, (or normal, cost).
- ***Interest on the total pension liability.*** As indicated previously, the total pension liability represents the share of discounted future benefit payments that have been assigned to the years of service up through the valuation date. Each year, therefore, with the passage of time, the present value of those payments increases by an amount equal to the balance of the extant liability times the discount rate.
- ***Benefit payments to retirees.*** The benefits paid to the retirees decrease the amount owed to retirees and hence decrease the total pension liability. As will be noted later in the discussion of the factors that affect the plan, the benefits paid to retirees also reduce the assets of the plan and therefore have no impact on the *net* pension liability.

The next three factors involve either discretionary changes on the part of the government or differences between actuarial estimates and actual experience.

- ***Changes in pension benefits.*** If an employer changes pension benefits, by, for example, modifying the formula used to compute the benefits, then the total pension liability would also change.
- ***Changes in actuarial assumptions.*** As a result of needed changes in actuarial methods or actuarial assumptions, such as those pertaining to mortality, turnover, or salaries, the total pension liability may increase or decrease.
- ***Differences between expected and actual experience.*** In any particular year, the experience of the government may differ from what was incorporated into long-term actuarial assumptions. Thus, for example, more employees may have retired than was anticipated. These differences, like the changes in actuarial assumptions, have an immediate impact on the total pension liability.

Changes in the Plan Fiduciary Net Position

Changes in the fiduciary net position of the plan commonly result from the following:

- ***Contributions of the employer.*** Employer contributions (as well as those from outside parties, such as when a state government makes contributions to the pension plan of a school district) increase the assets of the plan.
- ***Investment earnings.*** These earnings—interest, dividends, as well as both realized and unrealized gains or losses—cause the plan assets to either increase or decrease.
- ***Benefit payments to retirees.*** Just as these payments reduce the total pension liability of the employer, they reduce the assets of the plan. As noted previously, however, the benefits paid to retirees have no impact on the net pension liability and hence on the pension expense. The reduction in plan assets is offset by the corresponding reduction in the total pension liability.
- ***Administrative and other miscellaneous costs.*** Administrative and similar costs, which are typically minor in amount, also reduce plan assets.

Exceptions to the General Rule That Pension Expense Is Equal to the Change in the Net Pension Liability

Several exceptions modify the general rule that pension expense is equal to the change in the net pension liability.

- This first is a required technical adjustment. The contributions of the employer must be excluded from the computation. That is, contributions to the pension plan that would otherwise reduce the net pension liability should not be taken into account. Instead, they should be added back to what would otherwise be the change in the net pension liability. The reported expense cannot include both the contributions of the employer and all the other factors taken into account in computing the change in the net pension liability. The contributions of the employer are determined by the other factors, so including them both would result in double-counting the same costs.

Each of the other exceptions relates to factors that would also cause the net pension liability to change and would thereby ultimately affect the pension expense. An issue arises, however, whether the full impact of these factors should be recognized in the reported pension expense entirely in a single year—that in which they occurred—or spread out over a number of years. Recognizing them in a single year might result in wide swings in the pension expense from year to year. On the one hand, it might be argued that if the events or transactions took place in a particular year, they should be recognized in that year; it is not the objective of accounting to provide smooth patterns of either revenue or expenses. On the other hand, it might be said that in light of the career-long, ongoing relationship between employer and employee, they should affect pension expense only over an extended period of time. Insofar as a key purpose of financial reporting is to facilitate predictions of future performance, a smoothed measure of pension expense might better facilitate the judgments and decisions of statement users.

After considerable deliberation, the GASB determined that three additional main exceptions should be made for factors that affect the net pension liability[2]:

- ***Changes in actuarial assumptions.*** Changes in actuarial assumptions are necessitated by factors beyond the direct control of the employer and arise because of the inherent inaccuracies underlying those assumptions. For example, over time life expectancies increase, and employee turnover may decrease owing to unexpectedly tight job markets. Accordingly, the Board determined that changes to actuarial assumptions should be recognized in the pension expense over an extended period of time. That period of time, the Board said, should be

[2] An additional exception, not addressed in this text, is that contributions from nonemployer entities that are not in a special funding situation (i.e., are not legally required to make contributions) should be recognized as revenues.

the average expected remaining service years of all employees who are plan members. This average should include both active employees and retirees. Because retirees, by definition, have an expected remaining service life of zero, they substantially reduce the average. Insofar as actuarial gains and losses are not immediately included in the pension expense, they would be debited or credited to "deferred inflows of resources" or "deferred outflows of resources," and the balances in those accounts would be recognized (that is amortized and incorporated into pension expense) over the average of the expected remaining service lives of plan members starting in the year of the gains or losses.

- ***Differences between expected and actual experience with regard to economic or demographic factors.*** These changes result when in a particular year actual experience differs significantly from what was assumed in the actuarial projections. They might, for example, be a consequence of a greater number of employees retiring than was incorporated into the actuarial assumptions. Inasmuch as these differences are similar in nature to changes in actuarial assumptions, the Board requires that they be accounted for similarly—that is, debited or credited initially to deferred inflow of resources or deferred outflow of resources and recognized (and incorporated into pension expense) over the expected remaining service lives of plan members.
- ***Differences between actual and projected investment earnings on plan assets.*** The GASB added one more exception to the general principle that the pension expense should equal the change in the net pension liability. Even though the net fiduciary position of the pension plan is affected by *actual* earnings on plan investments, the GASB requires that the pension expense incorporate *projected*, rather than actual, earnings. The difference between actual and projected earnings would initially be deferred (i.e., added to deferred inflow of resources or deferred outflow of resources) and subsequently recognized over a period of five years. In other words, the difference would be taken into pension expense over a period of five years rather than a single year. Five years was chosen because it represents a typical general market cycle, and hence gains and losses could be expected to even out over such time. This approach reflects the long-term nature of plan investments and ensures that pension expense is not overly influenced by wide year-to-year swings in the financial markets.

By contrast, it should be noted that changes in the terms of the pension plan, such as those in the formula used to compute retiree payments, is not among the exceptions. Such changes, the Board reasoned, are within the control of the employer and therefore should be recognized in full in the period of the change.

Example

The Pension Expense

The following data (dollar amounts in thousands) relate to an employer's pension liability and its related pension plan and indicate the various changes that occurred in a particular year. The net pension liability—the portion of the total pension liability that is unfunded—would be the amount reported on the employer's balance sheet.

	Total Pension Liability	Net Plan Position	Net Pension Liability
Balance at start of period	$2,000,000	$1,800,000	$200,000
Service cost	80,000		80,000
Interest	120,000		120,000
Earnings on plan assets		150,000	(150,000)
Employer contributions to plan		25,000	(25,000)
Benefits paid to retirees	(100,000)	(100,000)	-
Balance at end of period	$2,100,000	$1,875,000	$225,000

During the year when the net pension liability increased by $25,000, and the employer contributed $25,000 to the plan. Hence, the employer's expense for the year would be $50,000—the change in the net pension liability excluding the reduction in the liability owing to the employer's contribution.

Viewed from a different perspective the pension expense includes $80,000 in service cost and $120,000 interest on the total pension obligation—a total of $200,000. From this must be deducted the $150,000 earnings on plan assets—a net of $50,000.

The following journal entries would capture the impact of the events and transactions on the books of the employer:

Pension expense	$50,000	
Net pension liability		$50,000
To record the pension expense		
Net pension liability	$25,000	
Cash		$25,000
To record the contribution to the pension fund		

Now assume some additional facts.

First, the employer enhanced retiree benefits, resulting in what the actuary estimated was an addition of $90,000 to the total pension liability. Inasmuch as these changes are within the control of the employer, the entire $90,000 would be incorporated in the pension expense.

Second, the employer changed various economic and demographic assumptions, such as those relating to employee turnover and mortality. These actuarial changes, not previously recognized, would *reduce* both the total and net pension liabilities by $48,000. They would be credited initially to "deferred inflows of resources" and would reduce pension expense over a period equal to the average remaining service lives of pension plan members. If such an average were six years, then the impact would be only $8,000 in the period of the change.

Third, the employer determined that in the current year, actual experience resulted in a total pension liability $18,000 *greater* than would have been expected, given various actuarial assumptions. These discrepancies, like the need for changes in actuarial assumptions, resulted from inaccuracies in actuarial estimates and per the GASB should not immediately reduce the employer's expense. Instead, they should be debited initially to "deferred outflows of resources" and amortized over the six-year average remaining service lives of pension plan members. Thus, the impact on pension expense in the current year would be an increase of $3,000.

Fourth, owing to a good year in the bond and stock markets, the $150,000 in earnings on plan assets was $60,000 *greater* than projected. Unlike, in the prior three situations, in which the change or difference had not yet been incorporated into either the previous computation of pension expense or the net pension liability, in this case, it had been included in both (per the pension expense entry, in which the calculation of the $50,000 debit to pension expense incorporated the $150,000 in investment earnings). Because the net pension liability remains correctly stated, the adjustment must be made to the pension expense. Thus, pension expense should initially be increased by the $60,000 of the additional earnings and such amount credited to deferred inflow of resources. Then, in each of five years over which the GASB specifies the difference must be amortized, the pension expense would be reduced by $12,000.

To the extent that there were prior balances in deferred inflows or outflows accounts associated with either the changes in actuarial assumptions or the differences between actual and expected earnings, those balances would also have to be amortized and would thereby further affect the pension expense. We assume that there were none.

The following entries would reflect these additional events and transactions on the books of the employer:

Pension expense	$ 90,000	
Net pension liability		$ 90,000

To recognize the improvements in the pension benefits that increased the total pension liability

Net pension liability	$ 48,000	
Deferred inflow of resources		$48,000

To recognize the changes in actuarial assumptions that reduced the total pension liability

Deferred inflow of resources	$ 8,000	
Pension expense		$ 8,000

To record one year's amortization of the deferred inflow of resources relating to the changes in actuarial assumptions

Deferred outflow of resources	$18,000	
Net pension liability		$18,000

To recognize the differences between expected and actual experience that increased the total pension liability

Pension expense	$ 3,000	
Deferred outflow of resources		$ 3,000

To record one year's amortization of the deferred outflow of resources relating to the differences between expected and actual experience

Pension expense	$ 60,000	
Deferred inflow of resources		$60,000

To increase the pension expense by the full amount of the difference between actual and projected earnings

Deferred inflow of resources	$ 12,000	
Pension expense		$12,000

To recognize one-fifth of the excess of actual earnings over projected earnings in the current year

The net impact of these adjustments would be an increase in pension expense of $145,000, bringing the total pension expense when added to the previously calculated expense of $50,000 to $183,000.

In summary:

	Total Pension Liability	**Net Plan Position**	**Net Pension Liability**
Balance at start of period	$2,000,000	$1,800,000	$200,000
Service cost	80,000		80,000
Interest	120,000		120,000
Earnings		150,000	(150,000)
Contribution to plan		25,000	(25,000)
Benefit to retirees	(100,000)	(100,000)	–
Improvement to plan	90,000		90,000
Difference between expected and actual experience	18,000		18,000
Change in actuarial assumptions	(48,000)		(48,000)
Balance at end of period	$2,160,000	$1,875,000	$285,000

Change in net liability (ending less beginning balances)	$ 85,000
Exclude (add back) employer's contribution to plan	25,000
Adjusted change in net liability—preliminary expense	110,000
Other adjustments: Factors that affect the liability in their entirety but are amortized for purposes of calculating the pension expense	
Add the full amount by which the liability was reduced by changes in actuarial assumptions	48,000
Subtract the portion of such change that was amortized during the year	(8,000)
Subtract the full amount by which the liability was increased by the excess of current year actuarial experience over expected experience	(18,000)
Add the portion of such excess that will be amortized during the year	3,000
Add the full amount by which the liability was reduced by the excess of actual earnings over expected earnings	60,000
Subtract the portion of such excess that will be amortized during the current year	(12,000)
Adjusted expense	$183,000

HOW SHOULD THE PENSION EXPENDITURE IN GOVERNMENTAL FUNDS BE DETERMINED?

In government funds, which are accounted for on a modified accrual basis, the reported pension expenditure would be the contribution to be liquidated with expendable available financial resources—that is, the amount actually contributed plus contributions expected to be made with current-year resources shortly after the end of the current year. Thus, in the preceding example, the pension expenditure would be only the $25,000 that the employer contributed to the pension plan:

Pension expenditure	$25,000	
Cash		$25,000

To record the annual pension contribution and expenditure.

WHAT SPECIAL PROBLEMS DO MULTIPLE-EMPLOYER COST-SHARING PLANS POSE?

GASB Statement No. 68 adopts a new and exceedingly controversial approach toward multiple-employer cost-sharing plans—those in which participating employers pool or share their obligations to provide pensions to their employees, and in which plan assets can be used to pay the pensions of the employees of any member employer. Per the previous rules, a member employer recognized as an expense only the amount that it was required to pay into the plan. It recognized a liability only to the extent that it failed to make the required payment. Statement No. 68, by contrast, requires each member employer to report a pension liability equal to its proportionate share of the *collective* liability of all employers in the plan. Its share would be based on its proportion of overall employer contributions to the plan. Thus, for example, if a plan had an unfunded actuarial liability of $100 million, and a particular employer makes 10 percent of the contributions to the plan, then it would be required to report on its own financial statements a pension liability of $10 million. Correspondingly, it would also have to report as a pension expense 10 percent of what the expense would have been had it been computed for a single employer.

Multiple-employer cost-sharing plans are common in the United States; they are maintained by virtually all states for at least some of the employees of local governments within their jurisdiction. For example, most school districts do not maintain their own pension plans. Instead, the districts provide the pension benefits through a cost-sharing plan administered by the state in which they are located. Previously, as long as they paid their required contributions, the districts need not have reported a pension liability. Under the current rules, however, insofar as the plan in which they are members is underfunded—as in recent years almost all plans were—they now have to report a sizeable liability. For many districts, that results in government-wide negative net assets—total liabilities exceed total assets—thereby undoubtedly causing considerable consternation among school district officials as well as local citizens.

HOW SHOULD THE PENSION PLAN BE ACCOUNTED FOR?

In this section, we shift our attention from the employer that provides the pension contributions to the pension plan that receives them. Fortunately for both accounting students and practitioners, the accounting for pension plans, unlike that for the employer, is relatively straight forward. The accounting for the pension plan is based on the premise that the ultimate obligation to make the benefit payments to retirees is that of the employer, not the pension plan. Accordingly, the liabilities of the plan include only amounts to the beneficiaries that are currently due and payable; they exclude the total benefit liability—that which is the actuarially determined.

Per GASB Statement No. 67, *Financial Reporting for Pension Plans,* a pension plan should prepare two basic statements:

- ***A statement of fiduciary net position.*** Essentially a balance sheet, this statement reports on the plan's assets, liabilities, and deferred inflows and outflows of resources.
- ***A statement of changes in fiduciary net position.*** This statement provides information on the inflows and outflows of financial resources during the period.

Statement of Fiduciary Position

The main assets of a pension plan are its investments. Although plans typically invest primarily in "traditional" assets, such as stocks and bonds, many plans also maintain positions in real estate as well as private equity. Plan assets should be reported at fair value. Insofar as plans have receivables, they generally are short term and consist of contributions due from employers and other contributing entities and of interest and dividends earned but not yet received.

The chief liabilities of a plan are, as noted, the benefits to plan members that are currently due and payable as well as any investment and administrative fees that have not yet been paid.

The difference between the assets and liabilities (and deferred inflows and outflows of resources, if any)—the plan fiduciary net position—is reported as *net position restricted for pensions.*

Statement of Changes in Fiduciary Net Position

The statement of changes in fiduciary net position reports on the additions to, and deductions from, the plan's net position. The additions consist predominantly of investment income and contributions from employers and other contributing entities. The investment income is generally interest, dividends, and other returns from investments. Inasmuch as the investments are reported at fair value, it also includes gains and losses, both realized and unrealized, on those investments. The principal deductions from plan net position are the benefit payments to retirees. They generally also include various investment and administrative expenses. Table 10-1 illustrates the two basic pension plan statements.

TABLE 10-1 City of Charlotte, North Carolina Statement of Fiduciary Net Position Fiduciary Funds June 30, 2017 (in thousands)

	Firefighters' Retirement Pension Trust	Employee Benefit – Other Employee Benefit Trust	Total
Assets			
Cash, cash equivalents and investments	$ 4,633	$ 20,325	$ 24,958
Receivables:			
Employer contributions	171	–	171
Member contributions	171	–	171
Interest and dividends	530	68	598
Total receivables	872	68	940
Investments:			
Equity securities—stocks	136,440	–	136,440
Fixed income securities—bonds	100,176	–	100,176
Mutual funds	278,023	60,439	338,462
Total investments	514,639	60,439	575,078
Capital assets, at cost, net of accumulated depreciation of $422	145	–	145
Total assets	520,289	80,832	601,121
Liabilities			
Accounts payable	525	167	692
Net Position			
Restricted for pensions	$ 519,764		519,764
Held in trust for other postemployment benefits		$ 80,665	80,665
			$ 600,429

City of Charlotte, North Carolina Statement of Changes in Fiduciary Net Position Fiduciary Funds for the Year Ended June 30, 2017 (in thousands)

	Firefighters' Retirement Pension Trust	Employee Benefit – Other Employee Benefit Trust	Total
Additions:			
Contributions			
Member	$ 9,636	–	$ 9,636
Employer	9,106	16,361	25,467
Other	–	208	208
Total contributions	18,742	16,569	35,311
Investment income			
Net appreciation (depreciation) in fair value of investments	54,521	5,837	60,358

(Continues)

TABLE 10-1 City of Charlotte, North Carolina Statement of Changes in Fiduciary Net Position Fiduciary Funds for the Year Ended June 30, 2017 (in thousands) *(Continued)*

	Firefighters' Retirement Pension Trust	Employee Benefit – Other Employee Benefit Trust	Total
Interest	2,133	1,695	3,828
Dividends	3,762	–	3,762
	60,416	7,532	67,948
Investment expense	2,735	232	2,967
Net investment income	57,681	7,300	64,981
Total additions	76,423	23,869	100,292
Deductions:			
Benefits	31,075	6,207	37,282
Refunds	70	–	70
Insurance premiums	–	7,510	7,510
Administration	621	1,130	1,751
Depreciation	13	–	13
Total deductions	31,779	14,847	46,626
Change in net position	44,644	9,022	53,666
Net position—beginning	475,120	71,643	546,763
Net position—ending	$ 519,764	$ 80,665	$ 600,429

WHAT TYPES OF DISCLOSURES ARE REQUIRED?

Owing to the complexity of pensions, the numbers reported on the financial statements provide only a small portion of the information essential to an understanding of their impact on a government's fiscal status and prospects for the future. As might be expected, therefore, the GASB requires extensive disclosures in the financial statements of both the employer and the plan.[3] Some must be included in notes, others as "required supplementary information" (RSI). The required note disclosures include

- A description of the plan including benefit terms, the classes of employees covered, the number of active and inactive employees, and the contribution requirements
- Information about the net pension liability, including significant assumptions and details on how the discount rate was determined. In addition (in large part owing to the controversy surrounding how the discount rate should be determined), alternative measures of the net pension liability calculated using a discount rate one percent point higher and one percent point lower than was actually used.
- Particulars as to the pension plan's assets, liabilities, and deferred inflows and outflow of resources.
- Details as to the changes in the total and net pension liability, including beginning and ending balances, the service cost, interest, contributions, benefit payments, and investment earnings.

[3] Much of the information that must be disclosed by the pension plan is duplicative of that which must be reported by the employers. However, if the plan is maintained by the employer and is thereby reported within its own comprehensive annual financial report then the same information need not be reported twice.

The disclosures required as RSI reflect the importance of evaluating pensions over an extended period of time. Thus, extensive data for a 10-year period, including the following, must be provided:

- Changes in the total and net pension liabilities, including the details indicated above that are required in the notes for a single year.
- The net pension liability as a percentage of covered-employee payroll.
- The actuarially determined contribution, if calculated. An actuarially determined contribution is the amount that the government's actuary recommends that the government contribute to the plan to ensure that it is fiscally sound. Unfortunately, some governments either do not calculate such a number or simply fail to make the recommended contribution.

HOW SHOULD POST-EMPLOYMENT BENEFITS OTHER THAN PENSIONS (OPEB) BE ACCOUNTED FOR?

Employers commonly offer retirees benefits other than pensions. Primary among them are continued health care benefits (including medical, dental, vision, and hearing costs), but they may also include life insurance, disability insurance, and nursing-home care.

Postemployment benefits have characteristics similar to pensions. They are a form of compensation provided to employees by a government in exchange for the services that the employees provide. The government reaps the benefits of those services in the period provided, irrespective of when and how it compensates the employees for them. As with pensions, even if the government accumulates resources in a qualified trust fund, it is primarily responsible for the unfunded portion of the obligation to the employees.

Postemployment health-related benefits present all the issues associated with pension benefits—and then some. The ultimate net cost of providing health-related benefits to retirees is subject to the same uncertainties as pensions—mortality rates, investment rates, turnover rates, and so on. In addition, however, the cost will depend on the health of employees after they retire, medical technology, and the institutional and economic structure of health care—factors difficult to predict five years in the future, to say nothing of the potential 80 or so years between the start of an employee's career and the end of his or her life. Nevertheless, actuaries have established methods to address these uncertainties. Almost no governments pay for the services directly. Instead, they either insure them with an outside carrier or self-insure them. Hence, the costs to be estimated are mainly those of the insurance premiums, which are not necessarily any easier to estimate inasmuch as they are dependent on the cost of the services. Therefore, many government simply extrapolate from long-term trends in overall health care costs.

Although there is significant variation among governmental health care plans, most have certain common features. Usually they provide full benefits only between the date an employee retires and when he or she become eligible for federal government-sponsored Medicare. At that time, benefits are either discontinued or the employer becomes a secondary insurer covering only costs that are not covered by Medicare.

In light of the similarity between pensions and other postemployment benefits, the GASB has taken the same approach toward the two. In 2015, it issued Statement No. 74, *Financial Reporting for Postemployment Benefits Other than Pension Plans,* and Statement No. 75, *Accounting and Financial Reporting for Postemployment Benefits Other Than Pensions*. Both of these mirror their respective counterparts pertaining to pensions.

In these two pronouncements, as in those pertaining to pensions, the GASB distinguishes between reporting by the employer and reporting by the plan. As with pensions, the Board held that the employer should report on its balance sheet the total actuarial liability less the fiduciary net position of the plan. The annual OPEB expense, like the pension expense, should be the change during the year in the net liability, excluding the contributions to the plan by the employer and adjusted for items, such as changes in actuarial assumptions and differences between actual and projected earnings that require recognition over an extended period of time.

The requirements for disclosures in notes and supplementary schedules are also akin to those for pensions. They include, therefore, descriptions of the benefits, details as to the amounts reported on the balance sheet and statement of changes in fiduciary net position, explanations of assumptions, and various 10-year trends.

In a departure from its approach to pensions, the GASB allows small governments (those with fewer than 100 members in their benefit plans) to simplify their calculations of the annual required contribution and related measures. Instead of applying the actuarial assumptions that would satisfy the standards of the Actuarial Standards Board, they may use alternative assumptions that meet specified GASB criteria.

In terms of dollars, the total obligations for OPEB are almost always less than they are for pensions. However, whereas most governments have a long tradition of maintaining **pension trust funds**, until recently they have financed their health care benefits on a pay-as-you-go basis.[4] Consequently, they tend to have relatively few assets in their OPEB plans, and thus their net OPEB liabilities are often substantial—frequently far greater than their net pension liabilities. When they are required to report under the new standards (for years beginning June 15, 2016, for the statement dealing with OPEB plans and those beginning June 15, 2017, for those dealing with the employer), many governments are almost certain to have to report on their balance sheets liabilities for OPEB that far exceed those for pensions.

WHAT ARE FIDUCIARY FUNDS?

Fiduciary funds are maintained to account for assets that a government holds in a capacity of a *fiduciary*. A *fiduciary* is basically a person or organization that owes to another party duties of good faith and trust. In the case of governments, that typically means "controlling" (e.g., holding and managing) resources for the benefit of individuals, organizations, or other governments for a variety of purposes: pensions, taxes collected for other governments, certain student activity funds, investment funds maintained for other governments and pass-through grants, to name but a few.

In Statement No. 84, *Fiduciary Activities*, which is effective for periods beginning after December 15, 2018, the GASB significantly modified the manner in which fiduciary activities are accounted for and reported. In essence, the Board stipulated that a fiduciary fund should be used to account for resources that the government controls, that are for the benefit of parties other than the government itself and that are not solely derived from its own-source revenues. The financial statements of fiduciary funds, are considered to be "basic" financial statements and, hence are reported similarly to governmental and proprietary funds. Unlike those funds, however, they are excluded from the government-wide statements. That is because the resources in those funds are not available to finance the operations of the government itself; they are intended for beneficiaries that are not part of the government's reporting entity.

Even though the resources held in fiduciary funds do not benefit the government itself, they are of critical concern to both statement preparers and statement users not only because they may be substantial in amount, but also because they are likely to be liquid and thereby subject to risk of loss through both reduction in market value and fraud. Moreover, the resources may be relied upon as a main source of income by parties closely associated with the government itself, such as retired employees, endowment beneficiaries and related governments.

[4] It was not until 2004, when GASB issued Statement No. 43, *Financial Reporting for Postemployment Benefit Plans Other Than Pension Plans,* and Statement No. 45, *Accounting and Financial Reporting by Employers for Postemployment Benefits Other Than Pensions,* that governments were required to measure and report their unfunded liabilities for OPEB.

If an activity fails to satisfy the criteria to be reported in a fiduciary fund, then the resources associated with it must be reported in a governmental or proprietary fund. The distinction is important to many organizations in that the classification will signal statement users whether the resources are available for use by the government itself or only to beneficiaries.

WHAT IS MEANT BY CONTROL?

A government is said to control assets if it either (1) holds the assets or (2) has the ability the direct the use, exchange or employment of the assets. Often, but not always, the government will hold the assets in a **trust**—a generic term to describe a formal relationship in which one party (a trustee) holds assets for the benefit of another, the assets are dedicated to providing benefits to recipients in accordance with specified benefit terms and the assets are legally protected from the claims of the government's creditors.

Roughly speaking, the ability to "direct the use, exchange of the assets" implies that the government has the authority to invest the assets (e.g., stocks and bonds) as it deems appropriate and to buy and sell them at its discretion. However, fiduciary arrangements may place restrictions on how the assets may be invested—some broad, some narrow—so it is not always apparent as to whether a government satisfies this control criterion.

The concept of control does not imply that the government has the right to determine who should be the beneficiary of the resources or to what purpose the resources must be put. Almost always the donor or other party that provides the resources establishes those requirements. Moreover, GASB Statement No. 84, instructs that, in specified circumstances the government may not have *administrative involvement* with the assets. Thus, it cannot determine the specific individuals that are eligible to receive benefits and cannot monitor whether the beneficiaries complied with the terms of donor-established criteria. Suppose, for example, that a donor contributed resources to a university for student scholarships. It stipulated that it was the responsibility of the university to select the scholarship recipients. Under those circumstances, the university would consider the resources to be its own, accounting for them in its general fund or a special revenue fund. By contrast, if an outside agency awarded a scholarship to a specific student but gave the funds to the university with a request that it pass along funds to that student, then the university would account for resources in a fiduciary fund.

WHO ARE PARTIES OTHER THAN THE GOVERNMENT ITSELF?

Fiduciary funds are intended to benefit parties other than the government itself and that are not part of its reporting entity. Suppose for example, that citizens contributed to an **endowment**, to provide scholarships for the children of fallen police officers. That is, the sum was to be invested permanently. Only the income (e.g., the dividends and interest) from the investments was to be available for expenditure. Because the beneficiaries are not the city itself the endowment would be accounted for in a fiduciary fund. By contrast, assume instead that a donor contributed to a city a sum that was to be maintained as an endowment for the benefit of the city-operated nature center. Because the endowment was intended to support the activities of the city itself, it would have to be accounted for in a governmental fund, most likely a permanent fund.

For certain, there are many situations in which it is not obvious whether the beneficiary is the government itself or an "outside" party. Suppose a university requires certain student clubs and other student organizations to place their cash holdings in university-maintained accounts. Are the activities engaged in by the clubs and organizations integral to the university's provision of goods or services to its constituents, or is the university holding the resources merely as a convenience for the organizations? The key factor a university would have to consider, however, is the extent of the university's involvement with the clubs and organizations. Per the criteria of Statement No. 84, partially funding the clubs and organization, supervising their activities, and establishing rules to which they must adhere would all suggest that the beneficiaries are part of the university itself and should therefore be accounted for in a governmental rather than a fiduciary fund.

WHAT ARE OWN-SOURCE RESOURCES?

In keeping with the notion that funds related to the provisions of activities that are inherently governmental should be reported in governmental or proprietary funds rather than fiduciary funds, Statement No. 84 provides that to be reported in a fiduciary fund the assets cannot be derived solely from the government's own-source revenues. Own-source revenues would include taxes, investment earnings, and revenues from exchange transactions, such as water and sewer charges. A notable exception to this general rule are assets in pension funds. These assets are commonly contributed by the government from the same governmental and proprietary fund as are wages and other employee benefits.

WHAT ARE THE FOUR TYPES OF FIDUCIARY FUNDS?

There are four types of fiduciary funds:

- Pension and other employee benefit trust funds
- Investment trust funds
- Private purpose trust funds
- Custodial funds

Pension and other employee benefit trust funds

As discussed earlier in this chapter, pension and OPEB plans are typically separate legal entities (i.e., qualified trusts). Nevertheless, as indicated, the government employer and the trust are economically intertwined, and hence the government employer is required to report the unfunded liability of the plan on its own balance sheet and to disclose considerable details of the plan. Whether or not the government should account for and report the assets of the pension fund in a fiduciary fund of its own depends primarily on the extent of control over, and administrative responsibility for, the management of the pension or OPEB resources.

Some plans may be administered and controlled by parties independent of the government itself, for example by trustees elected by the government's employees. In these circumstances the government does not act in the capacity of a fiduciary and hence would not report the resources of the plan in a fiduciary (or any other fund)—only in notes.

By contrast, others plans may be administered and controlled by the government itself. In these situations the government would account for the plan in a fiduciary fund, specifically a pension or OPEB trust fund. Although, as discussed below, Statement No. 84 prescribes the form and content of fiduciary funds, it makes an exception for pension and other employee benefit trust funds. These funds must follow the guidance of the statements pertaining to pensions and other postemployment benefits; that is, Statement No. 67, *Financial Reporting for Pension Plans* and Statement No. 74, *Financial Reporting for Postemployment Benefits Plans Other Than Pension Plans.*

Investment Trust Funds

Investment trust fund are used to account for and report investment pools in which the assets are held in trust for the benefit of others. Governments, especially states and counties, may sponsor investment pools as a service to the other governments within their jurisdiction. They operate these pools like mutual funds. Governments are permitted to invest temporarily available cash in these pools and thereby earn a return on their assets without having to incur the costs and risks of either managing an investment portfolio themselves or giving their assets over to private money managers.

Sponsoring governments must account for their investment pools in accord with the provisions of GASB Statement No. 31, *Accounting and Financial Reporting for Certain Investments and for External Investment Pools*. With only a few exceptions, the statement requires governments to account for their investment pool assets just as they do for their own assets. Most notably, therefore, investment pool investments, both equity and debt securities, must be reported at fair value. Changes in fair values must be recognized as gains and losses as they occur.

The main exception pertains to "2a7-like" pools. These pools derive their description from the U.S. Securities and Exchange Commission's (SEC) Rule 2a7 of the Investment Company Act of 1940. This rule permits certain types of mutual funds to report their assets at amortized historical cost rather than market values. The funds to which the rule applies are "money market" funds. These funds invest in securities, such as Treasury bills, notes, and certificates of deposit, that are both safe and have short maturities—typically 60 days or less. Accordingly, they are not subject to major price swings. The GASB, like the SEC, permits 2a7-like external investment pools to report their investments at amortized cost provided they meet certain specified conditions.

As set forth in GASB Statement No. 79, *Certain External Investment Pools and Pool Participants,* the conditions are designed to ensure that it is highly unlikely that the pool will incur losses due to changes in interest rates or the credit quality of the securities held. Thus, for example, the statement requires that the portfolio should maintain an average maturity of 60 days or less, that all securities held should be highly rated by a nationally recognized rating agency, that the portfolio must be highly diversified, and that all securities must be highly liquid.

Many governments intermingle their own investments with those of other governments. In keeping with the notion that fiduciary funds are intended to account for resources held for the benefit of others, only the external portion of the pool should be reported in an investment trust fund. The portion representing the government's own investments should be reported in a fund other than a fiduciary fund. Also, investments held for the benefit of others that are not in a trust would ordinarily be reported in custodial fund.

Private Purpose Trust Funds

Private purpose trust funds are used to report fiduciary activities in which the resources are held in a trust and are *not* required to be reported in either pension (or other employee benefit) trust funds or **investment trust funds**. As with other types of fiduciary funds, the trust assets must be for the benefit of either individuals or organizations that are not part of the government itself, they cannot be solely from the government's own sources, the government cannot have administrative or direct financial involvement with them, and they must be within the control of the government.

Private purpose trust funds can take many forms and can be used for a variety of purposes. Examples include but are by no means limited to:

- an endowment held in trust to benefit needy employees or their families
- a trust fund used to account for **escheat property**—that is, assets, such as inactive bank accounts and property of deceased persons that are temporarily held by a government until they can be transferred to the rightful owner or they revert to the state. (It should be emphasized, however, that in keeping with the nature of fiduciary funds, amounts expected to revert to the government itself should ordinarily be accounted for in either a governmental fund or a proprietary fund.)
- a university scholarship trust fund in which the assets were received from donors, they are disbursed to student-beneficiaries in accordance with terms of the trust agreement and the university has no administrative control or direct involvement with the assets.

Custodial Funds

Custodial funds are used to report fiduciary activities that are not reported in any one of the other three funds. As noted, each of the other three funds are trust funds. Hence, custodial funds are used to account for all fiduciary assets that are not held in trust (or an equivalent arrangement). These assets typically include assets from "pass through" grants and similar resources that a government holds for a short period of time and over which it does not have administrative or direct financial involvement. Custodial funds capture many of the activities that, prior to the issuance of Statement No. 84, were accounted for in what were known as "agency" funds.

A classic example of when it would be appropriate to report activities in a custodial fund is when one government collects resources for another. Suppose, for example (as is common), a county government collects its own property taxes as well as those levied by the school districts and towns within its geographical domain. The county has no responsibility for the taxes collected on behalf of the other governments other than to safeguard and transmit them to the recipients within a reasonable period of time.

Other circumstances in which a custodial fund might be used include the following:

- A city that has issued conduit debt collects the interest or principal payment from the beneficiary of the debt; its only responsibility is to pass it on to the holders of the debt
- A county collects payments from property owners for debt service on special assessment debt for which the government is not obligated in any manner
- A state receives a federal grant which it is required to distribute to specific cities and for which it has no administrative or direct financial involvement.

IN PRACTICE **DIFFICULTY OF DETERMINING WHETHER AN ACTIVITY IS FIDUCIARY OR GOVERNMENTAL**

A county jail permits families of inmates to deposit in a fund small amounts of money that the inmates can use to pay for phone calls and make purchases in the jail canteen. An individual account is maintained for each inmate. Any funds not used when the prisoner is released are returned to the prisoner.

The jail also collects a commission on all outgoing calls from the company that provides inmate phone services. The amounts collected are placed in a trust fund and by county statute can be used only to provide various amenities that improve the quality of jail life, such as TVs, books, and special holiday meals.

Can either or both of the funds be classified as fiduciary activities?

Statement No. 84 does not, of course, address specific situations; it does, however, specify criteria that can guide the determination. In the first example, the resources are obtained from sources other than the government's own revenues, the use of the funds is determined by each individual inmate and the beneficiaries are the individual inmates, not the jail. Hence, the fund would qualify as a fiduciary activity and be reported in a custodial fund because the activities are not held in a trust.

In the second example, the benefits are more general; they are for the benefit of the entire jail population and arguably cover costs that might otherwise have to be paid for out of the county's own sources. Moreover, the decisions as to how the money is spent are apparently made by the jail officials, not by the inmate beneficiaries or the providers of the funds. Hence, the moneys should be accounted as a governmental activity and most likely reported in a special revenue fund.

HOW SHOULD GOVERNMENTS ACCOUNT FOR AND REPORT FIDUCIARY FUNDS

Governments should report their fiduciary funds in two basic statements: a *Statement of Fiduciary Net Position* and a *Statement of Changes in Fiduciary Net Position.* They should account for the funds using the economic resources measurement focus (i.e., on a full accrual basis). Hence, the statement of net position would include the usual array of assets, liabilities, deferred inflows and outflow of net resources and fiduciary net position. Each of the four fiduciary types should be reported in a separate column, but funds of each type may be aggregated.

Fiduciary funds should recognize liabilities (and corresponding distributions to beneficiaries) when an event has occurred that compels the government to disburse the fiduciary assets. That could be when the beneficiary has demanded the assets or when no further action, approval, or condition is required to be taken or met by the beneficiary for it to receive the assets. For example, in the case of an investment trust, that would ordinarily be when the participant has asked to redeem its shares. In that of a county that collects the taxes for other governments that would be when it collects the taxes, even if the governments have not yet explicitly demanded the taxes. Once the county has collected the taxes, the other governments are entitled to the taxes; they have satisfied all conditions to receive them.

The statement of changes in fiduciary net position should report all additions and deductions from the funds, disaggregating the additions by source and the deductions by type. Statement No. 84 stipulates that investment earnings, investment costs (including management and custodial fees), and net investment earnings (investment earnings less investment costs) should be displayed separately. So too should administrative costs.

There are two notable exceptions to these guidelines. First, pension and OPEB trust funds should report in accordance with the standards set forth in the relevant pension and OPEB plan GASB statements.

Second, custodial funds *may* report single aggregated totals for additions and for deductions if the fund resources would normally be held for three months or less. The GASB granted this exception as a practical expedient to reduce the costs of preparers and auditors in circumstances in which the added disclosure would probably be of little benefit to statement users. This exception is especially relevant to governments that collect taxes for other governments and quickly turn them over to the intended recipients. Table 10-2 illustrates the form and content of the two statements.[5]

TABLE 10-2 Sample City Statement of Fiduciary Net Position June 30, 2020 (in thousands)

			Private-Purpose	
	Pension Trust	Investment Trust	Trust	Custodial
Assets				
Cash and cash equivalents	$ 150,000	972,235	87,000	22,500
Receivables				
Employee	1,236			
Employer	55,607			
Interest and dividends	162,555	19,007		
Total receivables	219,448	19,007	–	–
Investments at fair value				
Short-term investments	3,500,666	259,000	43,000	
Bonds	22,443,111	809,000	122,222	
Common stocks	44,001,230		540,988	
Real estate	2,456,000			
Total investments	72,401,007	1,068,000	706,210	–
Total assets	$72,770,455	$2,059,242	$793,210	22,500
Liabilities				
Accounts payable	122,567	1,444	44,645	
Due to other governments				22,500
Other liabilities	1,007		7,890	
Total liabilities	$ 123,574	$ 1,444	$ 52,535	$22,500

(Continues)

[5] The statements of an actual government could not be illustrated because as the text went to press Statement No. 84 had not yet become effective.

TABLE 10-2 Sample City Statement of Fiduciary Net Position June 30, 2020 (in thousands *(Continued)*

	Pension Trust	Investment Trust	Private-Purpose Trust	Custodial
Net Position				
Restricted for				
Pensions	72,646,881			
Pool participants		2,057,798		
Trust beneficiaries			740,675	
Total net position	$72,646,881	$2,057,798	$740,675	–

Sample City Statement of Changes in Fiduciary Net Position For Year Ended June 30, 2020 (in thousands)

	Pension Trust	Investment Trust	Private-Purpose Trust	Custodial
Additions				
Contributions				
Members	187,660			
Employers	1,799,876			
Gifts and bequests			150,000	
Total contributions	$1,987,536	–	$150,000	–
Investment earnings				
Net increase in fair value	1,300,900	55,003	31,000	
Interest and dividends	1,200,777	45,000	23,000	
Investment costs	(45,000)	(3,400)	(1,209)	
Net investment earnings	2,456,677	96,603	52,791	
Tax collections for other governments				302,500
Total additions	4,444,213	96,603	202,791	302,500
Deductions				
Payments to retirees	1,456,099			
Administrative expenses	13,086		44	
Payments to beneficiaries			199,844	
Distributions to investees		54,056		
Payments to other governments				302,500
Total deductions	1,469,185	54,056	199,888	302,500
Net increase in fiduciary net position	2,975,028	42,547	2,903	–
Net position—beginning	69,671,853	2,015,251	737,772	–
Net position—ending	72,646,881	2,057,798	740,675	–

WHAT ARE PERMANENT FUNDS AND HOW ARE THEY ACCOUNTED FOR?

As emphasized previously, fiduciary funds are used to account for assets that are for the benefit of parties other than the government itself. Assets held to benefit the government itself are reported in either governmental or proprietary funds.

Endowments, as indicated earlier, are contributions for which the donor requires that the principal be invested and remain intact; only the income from the investments may be expended. Governments may receive endowments that support their own activities as well as those of outside parties. In colleges and universities endowments considered to support their own activities may provide funding for scholarships as well as specific programs and professorial chairs. In cities and towns they may help maintain museums, zoos, and nature centers. The nonexpendable assets of such endowments, assuming that they are not derived from business-type activities, are accounted for in **permanent funds**. Permanent funds are classified as governmental funds.

As discussed in Chapter 4, inflows of assets are recognized as revenue in governmental funds only when they are available to finance expenditures of the current period. That presents an obvious dilemma. If the resources contributed to a permanent fund are, by definition, permanently nonexpendable, and inflows can be recognized only when available for expenditure, then the donated assets could never be recognized as revenue. The GASB resolved this quandary by stating simply that "the recipient should recognize revenues when the resources are received, provided that all eligibility requirements have been met."[6]

Governments report their permanent funds as they do other governmental funds. In government-wide statements they are combined with other governmental funds. In fund statements that combine the various governmental funds they are shown in a separate column only if they are considered "major" funds; otherwise they are aggregated with other nonmajor funds. In fund statements that show all governmental funds (i.e., combining statements, which per GASB Statement No. 34 are optional), each permanent fund is displayed in a separate column under the general heading "permanent funds."

SHOULD INVESTMENT INCOME OF A PERMANENT FUND BE REPORTED IN THE PERMANENT FUND ITSELF OR THE BENEFICIARY FUND

The income from a government's permanent (nonexpendable trust) funds is intended to benefit other funds and must eventually be transferred to them. At issue, however, is whether investment earnings should first be recognized as revenue within the permanent funds and then transferred to the beneficiary funds or whether they should be recorded directly in the beneficiary funds.

The significance of the issue is mainly in whether the income should be reported in the recipient governmental fund as revenue or as a nonreciprocal transfer. If reported as revenue, then it would be incorporated into "excess of revenues over expenditures." If reported as a transfer, however, it would be shown "below the line" and included among "other financing sources." The impact on fund balance is the same; the difference is one of statement-user perception. When investment income is reported as revenue, an organization's ongoing operations may appear to be generating a larger surplus (or incurring a smaller deficit) than if shown as a transfer-in.

[6] GASB Statement No. 33, *Accounting and Financial Reporting for Nonexchange Transactions* (December 1993), para. 22.

GASB STANDARDS

Although the issue is not explicitly addressed in the GASB Codification, it has been common practice among governments to account for all nonexpendable endowment fund income within the permanent (i.e., nonexpendable) fund itself. Periodically (either at the discretion of government officials or as required by law, contract, or donor stipulation) the income (net of investment expenses, if applicable) is transferred to the beneficiary funds. As a consequence, neither all the resources nor the net assets of the nonexpendable fund may in fact be permanently restricted. Some may be available for immediate transfer to another fund.

GASB Statement No. 34 directs that governments should report permanent fund investment earnings as specific program revenues in their government-wide statements if they are restricted to a specific program. If not restricted to a specific program, they should be shown as "investment earnings" within the category of "general revenues" (those that are reported in the lower portion of the statement of activities). Per GASB Statement No. 54, *Fund Balance Reporting and Governmental Fund Type Definitions*, the fund balance of "funds required to be retained in perpetuity" should be classified as nonspendable.[7]

[7] GASB Statement No. 54, Para. 7.

Example

Expendable Investment Income

A city receives a gift of $1 million in securities, the income from which is restricted to the support of its botanical gardens. During its first year, the endowment earns $60,000, of which the city transfers $40,000 to a governmental fund restricted to supporting the gardens.

On its year-end permanent fund statement of revenues, expenditures, and changes in fund balances, the city would report investment revenues of $60,000 and transfers-out of $40,000. On its balance sheet, it would report a total fund balance of $1,020,000. Of this amount the $1 million would be classified as nonspendable because it must be retained in perpetuity; the $20,000 would be classified as restricted as it must be used to support the botanical gardens.

On its government-wide statement of activities, the city would report the entire $60,000 as revenues of the program "Parks and Recreation." On its statement of net position, in the column for governmental activities, it would categorize the entire $1,060,000 as "restricted."

SUMMARY

Because of their dollar magnitude, pensions are of vital concern to statement preparers and users. Defined contribution plans—which are becoming increasingly popular—are simple to account for because the employer defines the inputs (contributions) and makes no guarantees as to outputs (benefits paid to retirees). Therefore, the reported expenditures are generally the agreed-on contributions. Defined benefit plans are far more complex because the employer defines the outputs and is required to contribute a sufficient amount to pay the required benefits when its employees retire. But inasmuch as the benefits are subject to uncertainties, the funding and accounting determinations have to be based on estimates and allocations.

Although a government employer and its pension trust fund may each be independent legal and reporting entities, the two are inextricably linked. The government is responsible for ensuring that the trust fund has sufficient resources to pay retirees. Ultimately—albeit indirectly—the government benefits from investment and actuarial gains and incurs the cost of corresponding losses.

Per GASB standards, a government should report on its balance sheet its net pension liability—that is, its unfunded pension obligation. This amount is the difference between the total pension liability as actuarially determined and the net plan position as indicated on the balance sheet of the pension trust. The total pension liability should be determined based on the entry age actuarial cost method and a "blended" discount rate. Such a rate should be a single rate that reflects the long-term expected rate of return on plan assets to the extent that the plan's net position is projected to meet future benefits and a yield rate on high-quality, 20-year municipal bonds to the extent that the plan's net position is insufficient to meet future benefits.

As a general rule, a government should report as its pension expense the change in the net pension liability excluding the government's contributions to the plan. There are, however, exceptions. Changes in the liability owing to both changes in actuarial assumptions and differences between expected and actual experience with regard to economic or demographic factors should be deferred and amortized over the average expected remaining service lives of plan members. Differences between actual and projected investment earnings should be deferred and amortized over a period of five years.

Governments that participate in multiple-employer cost-sharing plans should report their share of the collective liability and expense of all employers in the plan.

Health care and other postemployment benefits present accounting challenges similar to those of pensions. Accordingly, per GASB pronouncements, they should be accounted for and reported in parallel fashion. However, up until now many governments have funded their postemployment health care benefits on a pay-as-you-go basis. Therefore, their unfunded obligation for these benefits may be substantial.

Fiduciary funds report assets that governments hold as trustees or agents for individuals, private organizations, or other governmental units. They should be used to account for resources that the government controls, that are for the benefit of parties other than the government itself and that are not solely derived from its own-source revenues.

A government controls assets if it either (1) holds the assets or (2) has the ability the direct the use, exchange or employment of the assets. Generally speaking "direct the use" of the assets means that it can invest the assets as it deems appropriate.

Parties other than the government itself implies that the funds are to be used to support either activities or individuals that are independent of the government—those for whom the government is acting as a fiduciary. If the activities or individuals are integral to the mission of the government, then they should be accounted for in either governmental or proprietary funds.

Own source resources are mainly taxes and resources derived from exchange-type transactions. The specification that fiduciary funds must be derived from own-source resources is in keeping with the notion that fiduciary funds should be used to account for assets for which the government holds in trust for others.

The four main types of fiduciary funds are:

- Pension and other employee benefit trust funds
- Investment trust funds
- Private purpose trust funds
- Custodial funds

Governments should report these funds in two basic statements: a *Statement of Fiduciary Net Position* and a *Statement of Changes in Fiduciary Net Position.*

Permanent funds are a form of governmental funds. They are used to account for endowments that benefit the government itself rather than outside parties. Even though the endowments that they receive are, by definition, never available for expenditure, still they can be recognized as revenue when received.

KEY TERMS IN THIS CHAPTER

actuarial cost method 430
agent 428
agent multiple-employer plan 428
cost-sharing multiple-employer plan 428
defined benefit pension plan 426
defined contribution plan 425
endowment 442
entry age actuarial cost method 430
escheat property 444
fiduciary funds 450
investment trust funds 444
net pension liability 429
net plan position 429
Other Post-Employment Benefits (OPEB) 424
pension contributions 425
pension obligations 426
pension trust funds 441
permanent funds 448
Public Employee Retirement Systems (PERS) 428
single (or sole) employer plans 428
total pension liability 429

EXERCISE FOR REVIEW AND SELF-STUDY

The following was drawn from the pension note and related required supplementary information of the Adam City CAFR.

The City maintains a single employer defined benefit pension plan, the Adam City Employees Pension Plan (ACEPP), that provides pensions for all permanent full-time general and public safety employees.

The ACEPP provides retirement benefits that are calculated as 2.5% of the employee's final four-year average salary times the employee's years of service. Employees with 10 continuous years of service are eligible to retire at age 60; those with 30 years of service may retire at any age.

The following information relates to a particular year.

Total pension liability (in thousands)	
Service cost	$ 150,200
Interest	531,400
Changes in benefit terms	48,000
Changes in actuarial assumptions	75,900
Impact of actual actuarial experience over what was assumed	15,000
Benefit payments	(230,000)
Net change in total pension liability	590,500
Total pension liability—beginning of year	4,750,000
Total pension liability—end of year	$5,340,500
Plan fiduciary net position	
Employer contributions	$ 180,000
Net investment income	210,000
Benefit payments	(230,000)
Administrative costs	(4,900)
Net change in fiduciary net position	155,100
Plan fiduciary net position, beginning of year	4,250,000
Plan fiduciary net position, end of year	$4,405,100
City's net pension liability	$ 935,400

The city's net pension liability at the start of the year was $500,000. Hence it increased during the year by $435,400.

The excess of actual over projected net investment income was $25,000.

1. What would be the amount that the city would report as a pension liability on its government-wide balance sheet?

2. Suppose that the reported pension expense was $555,863. Indicate how each of the following items would affect the calculation of the expense. Assume that there were no previous deferred inflows or outflows of resources associated with the pension plan. The average remaining service life of plan members, including retirees, is eight years.
   a. Service cost
   b. Interest
   c. Net investment income
   d. Difference between projected and actual earnings on investments
   e. Employer contributions
   f. Benefit payments
   g. Changes in actuarial assumptions
   h. Excess of actual costs over those that were expected
   i. Changes in benefit terms
   j. Administrative costs

3. What amount should the city report in its governmental funds as a pension expenditure?

4. Suppose that the city were to increase its discount rate. How would that affect the total plan liability?

5. In general terms, what would be the nature of assets and liabilities that the plan, as opposed to the employer, would report on its balance sheet?

6. Suppose instead that the city also maintains a defined contribution plan for certain of its employees. How would the accounting for such plan differ from that for its defined contribution plan?

QUESTIONS FOR REVIEW AND DISCUSSION

1. Distinguish between a defined benefit plan and a defined contribution plan. Why does a defined benefit plan present far more complex accounting issues than a defined contribution plan?
2. How should an employer determine the amount to report on its government-wide statements as its pension liability?
3. What should it use as its discount rate in determining its pension obligation?
4. How should it determine its expense in full accrual statements?
5. What is a cost-sharing plan? What does an employer who is a member of a cost-sharing plan have to report as a pension obligation?
6. Why are the problems of accounting for postemployment health care benefits similar to those of accounting for pensions? Why, however, are they even less tractable?
7. Why is it likely that unfunded actuarial liabilities for postemployment health benefits of many governments will be greater than the correspondingly unfunded actuarial liabilities for pensions, even though the annual required contributions for pensions are greater than for health benefits?
8. What are the key distinguishing characteristics of fiduciary funds?
9. What are the four types of fiduciary funds?
10. What is the rationale for the requirement that only resources held for the benefit of parties other than the government itself can be accounted for in a fiduciary fund?
11. As a general rule, when should a government recognize a fiduciary fund liability to the beneficiaries of the fund? More specifically when should a government that collects taxes on behalf of another government recognize the liability to the beneficiary government?
12. What are *permanent* funds used to account for? In light of the requirement that governmental funds can recognize revenues only when they are measurable and available, how can a permanent fund ever recognize revenue?
13. In what two basic financial statements should a government report its fiduciary funds? On what basis of accounting should they be prepared?
14. What are *investment* pools? Why might a government maintain an investment pool? On what basis are the assets measured and reported?

EXERCISES

EX. 10-1

Select the *best* answer. Items 1 through 5 refer to Riverview City.

1. Riverview City received a gift of $1 million. The sum is to be maintained as an endowment, with income used to preserve and improve the city's jogging trails. The $1 million should be reported in
   a. a governmental fund.
   b. an 2a7-like fund.
   c. a fiduciary fund.
   d. a proprietary fund.
2. Riverview City collected $80 million in property taxes on behalf of the Riverview Independent School District. The $80 million should be reported in
   a. a governmental fund.
   b. a custodial fund.
   c. a private purpose trust fund.
   d. a proprietary fund.

3. The $80 million collected by Riverview City would be reflected in its statement of fiduciary net position as cash and an offsetting
   a. liability.
   b. net position account.
   c. fund balance.
   d. custodial reserve.

4. In the city's government-wide statements, the $80 million would be reported as
   a. a liability.
   b. a reserve.
   c. net assets.
   d. none of the above.

5. The city maintains a $1-million endowment to provide financial assistance to needy retired employees and their families. In its government-wide statements, the $1 million would be reported as an asset in the column for
   a. governmental activities.
   b. business-type activities.
   c. totals, but not in the column for either governmental or business-type activities.
   d. none of the above.

6. As of year-end, a city's pension plan had $1.5 million in current obligations to retired employees. The city would report this amount as a liability on
   a. the pension plan statements only.
   b. the pension trust fund statements and the government-wide statements.
   c. the government-wide statements only.
   d. neither the pension trust fund statements nor the government-wide statements.

7. A commercial office building held as an investment in an investment pool should be reported at
   a. historical cost.
   b. present value of estimated cash flows.
   c. fair value.
   d. depreciated historical cost.

8. Which of the following would not be reported on a pension plan's statement of plan net position?
   a. Long-term investments at fair value
   b. Current liabilities to retirees
   c. Net assets held in trust for pension benefits
   d. Actuarial accrued liabilities to current and retired employees

9. A city received a donation of $10 million. The amount was to be set aside in an endowment fund with income only to be used to preserve and improve its parks. In the year it was received the $10 million should be
   a. recognized as revenue in a special revenue fund.
   b. recognized as a direct increase to fund balance in a permanent fund.
   c. recognized as revenue in a permanent fund.
   d. recognized as revenue in a fiduciary fund.

10. In a particular year, the Haynes Independent School District collects $100 million in property taxes. State law requires that property-rich school districts appropriate and contribute 2 percent of all property taxes that they collect to a state pool, which will be divided among property-poor districts. Upon receipt of the taxes, the Haynes district, which the state considers a property-rich district, should account for
    a. $100 million in a custodial fund.
    b. $98 million in a governmental fund and $2 million in a custodial fund.
    c. $100 million in a governmental fund.
    d. $98 million in a governmental fund and $2 million in a fiduciary fund other than a custodial fund.

EX. 10-2

Select the *best* answer.

1. A city's annual pension expense represents
   a. actual cash contributions to the pension trust fund.
   b. required payments to retired employees per the terms of the pension plan.
   c. normal cost, as determined by an appropriate actuarial method.
   d. change during that year in the city's net pension liability, subject to various adjustments.
2. The amount that a city should recognize as its pension *expenditure* in a governmental fund would be
   a. the contribution to the pension fund to be liquidated with expendable available financial resources.
   b. the change in the net pension liability.
   c. required payments to retired employees per the terms of the pension plan.
   d. normal cost, as determined by an appropriate actuarial method.
3. A government employer's net pension liability (the amount to be reported on its accrual-based balance sheets) refers to
   a. the difference between the benefit plan's net position and the total pension liability as computed by an appropriate actuarial method.
   b. the total amount expected to be paid to current and retired employees computed by an appropriate actuarial method.
   c. the share of the total amount to be paid to current and retired employees, computed by an appropriate actuarial method, that has been earned by those employees to date.
   d. the difference between the total amount to be paid to current and retired employees, computed by an appropriate actuarial method, and the amount that has actually been paid to them.
4. Which of the following would *not* be reported on a plan's statement of fiduciary net position?
   a. Obligations to retired employees that are past due
   b. Plan investments at fair value
   c. Actuarial accrued liabilities
   d. Contributions receivable from employers
5. A defined benefit plan is one in which
   a. the employer promises specified payments to employees on their retirement.
   b. the specific provisions are defined by the Internal Revenue Code.
   c. the specific provisions are defined by the Uniform Code of Retirement Plans.
   d. the employee can specify the mix of benefits (e.g., health, pension, insurance) that will be received on retirement.
6. A pension plan in which the employees of all participating governments are placed in a common pool and in which the employers share all risks and costs and make contributions at the same rate is known as a
   a. multiple-employer agent plan.
   b. multiple-employer cost sharing plan.
   c. multiple employer consolidated actuarial plan.
   d. single consolidated multiple-employer plan.
7. The rate used to discount future benefits should be based on
   a. the government's marginal borrowing rate.
   b. an index of tax-exempt bonds rated AA.
   c. an index of taxable bonds rated AA.
   d. a "blended" rate that takes into account, as appropriate, the government's expected rate of return on plan assets and the yield on high-quality municipal bonds.
8. The GASB requires that the difference between actual and expected earnings on plan investments be
   a. charged immediately to a revenue or expense account as appropriate.
   b. charged immediately to an asset or liability account as appropriate.
   c. amortized over a period of five years.
   d. amortized over the average remaining service lives of plan participants.

9. The means of allocating pension costs over years of participant service is known as
   a. an actuarial contribution allocation method.
   b. an actuarial cost method.
   c. a participant-cost assignment method.
   d. a pension distribution method.

10. Which of the following is not typically taken into account by actuaries in calculating pension expense?
   a. Mortality rates
   b. Employee turnover rates
   c. Projected salary increases
   d. Projected trends in costs of health care

EX. 10-3

Fiduciary funds are of four major types

For each of the following indicate the type of fiduciary fund in which it is most likely the fiduciary activity should be accounted for and reported.

1. Per a trust agreement a state maintains an investment pool in which governments within the state can temporarily invest the proceeds of tax exempt bonds that they have issued. The state will invest only in securities that would not violate IRS arbitrage provisions.

2. A county collects property taxes for towns and cities within its jurisdiction and distributes them to the governments shortly after it receives them.

3. A city solicits donations from its citizens to support a local food bank. Per a trust agreement all funds must be invested in investment grade securities and each year all earnings (except for a percentage equal to an inflation index) must be distributed to the food bank.

4. The state requires banks within its jurisdiction to turn over the balances in savings and checking accounts that have been inactive for a period of five years or more. Per a trust agreement, any amounts that are not claimed by the depositors within six years revert to the state's general fund.

5. A city makes annual contributions to a qualified OPEB trust fund.

6. Each school within a school district collects parent–teacher association dues and contributions and turns them over to the school district for safe-keeping. The district remits the funds to the associations upon request and makes no decisions, and places no restrictions, as to how they are used.

7. A state university receives cash from a not-for-profit child welfare agency that provides scholarships to students who have graduated out of the foster care system. The agency selects the students and stipulates that the scholarship is intended to cover miscellaneous expenses other than tuition and fees, such as for meals and recreation. The university dispenses the funds to the students upon their requests, usually within days after they have been received from the agency.

8. A state university maintains an endowment to provide one scholarship each year to a student who graduated from Llano County High School. As per the donor's stipulations in a trust agreement, each year the High School selects the scholarship recipient.

EX. 10-4

Who selects scholarship recipients matters

A wealthy alumnae donates $500,000 in marketable securities to her alma mater to establish a scholarship fund. Per the trust agreement only the interest and dividends (including any gains in fair value) from the securities can be distributed to scholarship recipients. In addition, she stipulates that the recipients must be graduates of her own high school and members of its honor society and are to be selected by a committee of teachers from that high school.

1. In what type of fund would the resources be accounted for and reported.

2. Prepare journal entries in that fund to record the following events and transactions.

a. The university accepted the marketable securities.
b. The securities increased in fair value by $20,000
c. The university received $14,000 in interest and dividends
d. The university transferred $6,000 to its general fund to cover the tuition of a student who was selected as a scholarship recipient.

3. In what way would your answer to the above questions differ if the university, rather than the high school, selected the scholarship recipient and there were no specific constraints on who could be selected.

EX. 10-5

Recorded pension expenditures are not always influenced by actuarial computations.

Hayward City maintains a defined benefit pension plan for its employees. In a recent year, the city contributed $5 million to its pension fund. However, its annual pension cost as calculated by its actuary was $7 million. The city accounts for the pension contributions in a governmental fund.

1. Record the pension expenditure in the appropriate fund.
2. Suppose in the following year the city contributed $6 million to its pension fund, but its annual pension cost per its actuary was only $5 million. Prepare the appropriate journal entries.
3. Briefly justify why you did, or did not, take into account the pension cost as calculated by the actuary.

CONTINUING PROBLEM

Review the comprehensive annual financial report (CAFR) you obtained.

1. Does the government maintain any permanent funds? If so, are they major or nonmajor funds and for what purposes?
2. Does the government maintain any fiduciary funds? If so, for what purposes?
3. Does the government contribute to one or more pension plans? Are they defined benefit or defined contribution plans? If they are defined benefit plans, are they single employer (maintained by the government itself) or multiple-employer plans?
4. Does the government report pension expenses or expenditures? If so, in which fund or funds?
5. Does the government report pension liabilities? If so, in which fund or funds?
6. Does the CAFR indicate the actuarial value of plan assets and liabilities? Are the plans over- or underfunded?
7. Does the CAFR include the financial statements of the pension plans? Does it indicate that the pension plans issue their own reports and that these are publicly available?
8. Did the pension fund investments have a "good year"?
9. Does the CAFR indicate that the government provides other postemployment benefits? If so, what is the nature of these benefits? How are they reported?
10. Does the government maintain any custodial funds? How many and for what purposes?

PROBLEMS

P. 10-1

The factors affecting pension expense are not always obvious.

As the accountant for Sunlight City, you determine the following with respect to the city's pensions in a particular year.

Service cost	$356,000
Interest on total pension liability	400,000
Actual earnings on pension plan investments	500,000
Projected earnings on pension plan investments	450,000
Employer contribution to the plan	180,000
Benefits paid to retirees	211,000

1. Based on the information provided, what should the city report as its pension expense for the year?
2. Suppose that the benefits paid to retirees were actually $251,000 rather than $211,000. How would that affect the pension expense? Explain.
3. Suppose also that the city failed to contribute anything to the pension plan.
   a. How would that affect the pension expense to be reported on the government-wide statements? Explain.
   b. How would it affect the pension expenditure to be reported on the statements of the general fund?

P. 10-2

Changes in the net pension liability affect amounts reported on both balance sheets and statements of resource flows.

The following was taken from a pension note of Geffen County.

	Total Pension Liability	Plan Net Position	Net Pension Liability
Balance, 1/1	$2,853,455	$2,052,589	$800,866
Changes for the year			
Service cost	75,864		75,864
Interest	216,515		216,515
Contributions—employer		79,713	(79,713)
Net investment income		196,154	(196,154)
Benefit payments to retirees	(119,434)	(119,434)	–
Administrative expense		(3,373)	3,373
Other changes		8	(8)
Net changes	172,945	153,068	19,877
Balance at 12/31	$3,026,400	$2,205,657	$820,743

During the year, there were no changes to employees' benefits, no changes in actuarial assumptions, no difference between expected and actual experience, and no differences between actual and projected earnings.

1. What is the amount that the county should report as a pension liability on its government-wide balance sheet?
2. What is the amount that it should report as a pension expense/expenditure on its
   a. Government-wide statement of activities
   b. Governmental-fund statement of revenues and expenditures and changes in fund balances.
3. Suppose instead that the county's actuary determined that owing to changes in estimates of future salaries, the total pension liability had increased by $50,000. The average expected service life of pension plan members, including retirees, is 10 years. What impact would the change have on the city's reported pension expense in the year of the change? Be as specific as possible.
4. The year-end, balance sheet of the pension *plan* reported total assets of $2,305,657 and total liabilities of $100,000 (and hence a net position of $2,205,657). How could the plan report liabilities of only $100,000 when the preceding schedule indicates that the present value of obligations to employees and retirees was over $3 million?

P. 10-3

A plan net position is directly tied to the employer's net pension liability.

The CAFR of North Orange included the statement of fiduciary net position for its employee pension plan presented here:

North Orange Employee Pension Plan Statement of Fiduciary Net Position June 3, 2021
(Dollar amounts in thousands)

Assets	
Cash and cash equivalents	$ 140,279
Receivables:	
Contributions	13,285
Investment income	8,100
Total receivables	21,385
Investments:	
Fixed income securities	1,111,088
Domestic equity securities	2,345,543
International equities	870,240
Real estate	511,112
Total investments	4,837,983
Total assets	4,999,647
Liabilities	
Investment fees payable	2,890
Due to broker for investments purchase	230,555
Benefits payable to retirees	59,231
Total liabilities	292,676
Net position restricted for pensions	$4,706,971

1. A note to the statement indicated that the plan net position was 75 percent of the North Orange (the employer) total pension liability. From this limited amount of information, can you tell how much North Orange would report as its net pension liability?
2. In light of your response to question #1, how do you explain that benefits payable to retirees are only $59,231?
3. Suppose the city reduced its discount rate from 7.75 to 7.50%. How would that reduction affect the pension plan's net position?
4. Suppose the city were to sell common stock for $1,500,000 that it had acquired for $1,000,000. How would such a sale affect the pension liability as reported on the balance sheet of North Orange?

P. 10-4

Some changes that reduce a reported pension liability are substantive; others are merely cosmetic.

A state government, concerned that one of its defined benefit pension plans is severely underfunded, is considering measures, some substantive, others merely cosmetic, that would enable it to reduce the reported pension liability and pension expense on its government-wide financial statements. For each, indicate the impact that the change would have on both the reported liability and expense. Also, indicate whether the change would substantively improve the government's fiscal condition (e.g., reduce retiree benefits or increase plan assets) or merely improve the look of the financial statements.

1. Reduce the percentage of final year's pay in the formula used to calculate benefits
2. Increase the discount rate

3. Increase the amount it contributes each year to the pension plan
4. Invest in higher yielding, but more risky, securities
5. Change the actuarial assumptions to decrease the estimated life expectancy of plan members
6. Delay paying benefits to retirees that are due the last day of the plan's fiscal year until the first day of the next fiscal year
7. Increase the age at which employees are eligible to receive benefits

P. 10-5

Accounting for OPEB is similar to that for pensions.

The following data were drawn from the required supplementary information section of the Modian School District's annual report (all dollar amounts in thousands).

	2020	2019
Total OPEB Liability		
Service Cost	$ 38,100	$ 36,389
Interest	60,544	55,768
Changes in benefit terms		(12,300)
Differences between expected and actual experience	18,690	8,654
Benefit payments	(15,600)	(15,480)
Net change in total OPEB Liability	101,734	73,031
Total OPEB liability—beginning	850,721	777,690
Total OPEB liability—ending	$952,455	$850,721
Plan Fiduciary Net Position		
Contributions—employer	$ 52,743	$ 50,211
Net investment income	64,621	82,000
Benefit payments	(15,600)	(15,480)
Administrative expense	(250)	(248)
Net change in plan fiduciary net position	101,514	116,483
Plan fiduciary net position—beginning	837,100	754,896
Plan fiduciary net position—ending	$938,614	$837,100
Net OPEB liability—ending	$ 13,841	$ 13,621

1. What is the amount that the district should report as its net OPEB obligation in its year-end 2020 government-wide financial statements?
2. Based on the data provided, can you tell the amount that the district should report as an expenditure on its *governmental fund* statement of revenues and expenditures?
3. What other information would you need to determine the amount that it should report as an expense on its *government-wide* statement of activities?
4. Why is it likely that the government will report "differences between expected and actual experience" in virtually every year but only occasionally (or rarely) report "change in benefit terms"?
5. What impact did the benefit payments of 2020 have on the amount that the district would report as its net OPEB liability?
6. The net OPEB liability increased in 2020 from what it was in 2019. In your opinion, based on the data provided, would you say that, on balance, the fiscal health of the district's OPEB plan improved or deteriorated in 2020? Explain.

P. 10-6

"New" GASB rules may have a major impact on cost-sharing employers.

The Westmont School District provides postemployment health care benefits through a cost-sharing plan administered through the State Teachers OPEB Plan (STOP). In its financial statements for its fiscal year ending June 30, 2018, STOP reported that the collective net liability of all member districts was $20,000,000 and the collective expense was $1,800,000 (all dollar amounts are in thousands). The district's share of contributions to the plan is 2 percent.

1. In its financial statements for its fiscal year-ending June 30, 2017, a year before it had to implement the "new" GASB standard relating to OPEB, the district's required contribution to the plan was $30,000. As it had in prior years, the district made its contribution in full and thereby did not have to report an OPEB liability. Suppose that in fiscal year ending 2018, when it had to implement the new standard, the district's percentage share of the required contributions remained the same.
   a. How much of an OPEB liability would the district now have to report?
   b. How much of an OPEB expense would it have to report?
2. The new GASB standard requires each member of the plan to indicate how the net OPEB liability would change if the health care cost rate increased and decreased by 1 percent. In general terms rather than specific numbers, how would an *increase* in the health care cost rate affect the net OPEB liability as reported by the Westmont School District?
3. Officials of the Westmont School District contend that, as was required by the "old" rules, as long as it makes its required contribution to the plan it should not have to report an OPEB liability. It notes that it has no control over the plan inasmuch as the OPEB benefits and other policies related to the plan are established by the state and that all investment decisions are made by the state. Therefore, it argues the plan is really that of the state and the state should have to report a liability for any unfunded amounts. Do you agree? What argument can you make in support of the new GASB standard?
4. Suppose that you are the chief financial officer of the district. A member of the board of trustees criticized the new GASB rules in the local newspaper, claiming that the new rules will increase district expenses and force it to either raise property taxes or make severe cuts to educational programs. How would you respond to the member?

P. 10-7

Fiduciary funds are accounted for on a full accrual basis

Upon the death of a police officer, Leff City establishes a trust fund to provide for the education of the officer's college-age children.

1. In what type of fund should the resources contributed to the fund be recorded?
2. Prepare journal entries to record the transactions that follow:
   a. City residents contribute a total of $500,000 in cash. Per the trust agreement, the funds are to be invested in high-quality securities until requested by the beneficiary children. They can then be disbursed to pay for tuition, room and board, and incidental expenses.
   b. The city invests the securities in stocks and bonds.
   c. The city earns interest and dividends of $35,000 and the fair value of the securities increases by $40,000.
   d. A beneficiary child requests that the city draw a check of $24,000 to Jackson College to cover her first semester's tuition.
   e. The city writes the check.
   f. As permitted by the trust agreement the city bills, and collects from the trust fund $600 to cover administrative costs.

3. Suppose that a fund were established by the city from tax dollars to provide scholarships for the children of any police officer. Moreover, city officials were responsible for determining eligibility requirements and determining the amounts that beneficiaries would receive. How, if at all, might your response to #1 differ?

P. 10-8

It is not always obvious what constitutes a fiduciary fund

For each of the following indicate the fund (or funds), if any, in which you think the activity should be accounted for and reported. If you think the fund should be a fiduciary fund, then indicate the type of fund; if a governmental or proprietary fund, then so state. Provide a brief explanation for your response.

1. The Jackson School District holds all funds of the foundation that supports the Jackson High School football team. The foundation is governed by a board of advisors, the members of which are selected by a committee of other advisors. The District performs no administrative functions other than depositing the funds in a checking account and writing checks as directed by the foundation.
2. Virginia State University requires that all cash collected by university-sponsored clubs be held in university maintained accounts and that all disbursements be approved by the Assistant Dean of Students, consistent with policies and procedures established by the university.
3. Using general revenues, Lawson City established and maintains an endowment fund, the income of which is to be used to provide financial assistance to the families of deceased fire fighters. The city will manage the investments of the fund, but all disbursement decisions will be made by a three-person committee of city employees.
4. The federal government's Department of Justice provides a grant to California that specifies that the resources provided are to be distributed to cities and towns that satisfy detailed Department of Justice criteria. The grant specifies that the particular recipients are to be selected by the state's governor and that it is the responsibility of the state to monitor compliance with the terms of the grant.
5. A state maintains an escheat fund for unclaimed property. Per the trust agreement establishing the fund, all property that is unclaimed after five years reverts to the state. In the past, approximately 60 percent of the property went unclaimed and hence reverted to the state.
6. Per a trust agreement, Green County maintains an investment pool to enable both the county itself and the various governments within the county to hold and invest liquid assets on a temporary basis. The aim of the fund is to enable the governments to maximize returns, minimize administrative costs and reap the benefits of professional asset management.
7. The City of Fairmont established a defined benefit plan for its employees. As required by GASB Statement No. 68, the city reports the unfunded liability of the plan on its balance sheet and discloses details of the plan in notes and RSI. The assets of the plan are held in various brokerage accounts and all investment decisions are made by a board of trustees elected by active and retired plan participants.

P. 10-9

Seemingly similar situations make be accounted for and reported in different fund types.

For each of the following, indicate the fund, if any in which the government would account for the resources described. If a fiduciary, rather than a governmental fund, indicate the type of fund. Briefly justify your response.

1. A government contributes to a pension fund maintained by a union representing some of its employees. The government determines all significant terms of the plan, most notably eligibility requirements and

retiree benefits. However, all investment decisions, including when to buy and sell securities are made by a committee composed of union officers.

2. A government holds the assets that its employees contribute to a defined contribution plan. It maintains the assets in separate trust funds for each employee and each employee can select among several mutual funds in which to invest the assets.
3. A high school requires its athletic booster association to deposit with the school any cash it may have collected from members or earned through its activities. The school does not monitor or control how the association spends its resources. Upon request of the association, the school writes a check either to the association itself or to a party designated by the association. Essentially, the school serves merely as the association's banker.
4. A high school requires its athletic booster association to deposit with the school any cash it may have collected from members or earned through its activities. All expenditures of the association must be approved by the school's athletic director to ensure that they conform to school policies.
5. A county maintains an investment pool to which towns within its jurisdiction can deposit their cash reserves. Investment pool policies specify that it can invest only a securities that have short-term maturities and satisfy other criteria that make them highly liquid. The pool is considered a trust and the assets are thereby protected from the claims of the government's creditors.
6. A county maintains an investment pool to which its various proprietary activities, such as its transportation service and its water utility can deposit their cash reserves. Investment pool policies specify that it can invest only in securities that have short-term maturities and satisfy other criteria that make them highly liquid.

P. 10-10

The major issue relating to custodial funds is when they should be established.

Consider each of the following situations. Indicate whether (and why or why not) you think that the government should account for the transactions and resources in a custodial fund, a governmental fund, or some other type of fiduciary fund. Not all the situations have been explicitly addressed in the text. Therefore, you may have to generalize from those that have been discussed.

1. A city extended sewer and water lines to a recently annexed community. Per agreement with the community, the improvements are to be paid for entirely by local residents. To finance the improvements, the city issued 10-year notes on behalf of the residents. It assessed the residents for the amount of the debt, plus interest. The city guaranteed the notes and agreed to collect the assessments from the residents and make appropriate payments to the note holders. However, the city's role is primarily one of an intermediary. The residents, not the city, are expected to service the debt.
2. A state receives a federal law-enforcement grant intended to assist local communities in hiring additional police officers. The federal granting agency selects the cities and counties that are to receive the awards and determines the amounts they are to receive. The federal government, not the state, is responsible for monitoring grant compliance. The state's only responsibility is to write the checks to the cities and counties.
3. A state receives a federal educational grant intended to assist local school districts in hiring additional teachers. The federal granting agency establishes general guidelines that the state is to use in determining the school districts to receive the awards and the amounts they are to receive. However, the state establishes the specific criteria and selects and monitors the recipients.
4. A county collects sales taxes that it distributes among itself and the towns within its jurisdiction. The taxes are levied by the county and are divided among the recipient governments in accordance with a formula set forth in the county legislation that authorized the tax.

P. 10-11

Permanent funds are typically related to the general fund or a special revenue fund

The McCracken County Humane Society (MCHS), a government agency that is part of a county's reporting entity, established a permanent fund to provide support for its pet neutering program. As of the start of the year, the fund had an endowment balance of $600,000, composed of both cash and marketable securities.

The program itself, which is accounted for in a special revenue fund, is funded by both direct contributions and the income from the permanent fund. At the start of the year, the special revenue fund had assets (all investments) of $26,000.

The following transactions and events occurred in a recent year.

1. The MCHS conducted a Walk Your Pet Day fundraising drive. The event raised $120,000, of which $20,000 was in pledges expected to be collected shortly after year-end. These contributions are intended to cover operating costs.
2. The society acquired food and medicine at a cost of $60,000 (cash). During the year, it used $30,000 of these supplies. The society accounts for supplies on a consumption basis. It incurred other operating costs (all paid in cash) of $85,000.
3. The society earned interest of $45,000 on investments accounted for in the permanent fund.
4. During the year, the market value of the investments held by the permanent fund increased by $30,000. Per the terms of the agreement establishing the endowment, all capital gains, both realized and unrealized, must be added to principal.
5. During the year, the value of investments held by the special revenue fund increased by $3,000.
6. The society transferred cash to the special revenue fund in the amount of the earnings (excluding capital gains) of the permanent fund.
   a. Prepare journal entries to record the events and transactions. Be sure you indicate the fund in which they would be recorded.
   b. How would the transfer from the permanent fund to the special revenue fund be reported in the government-wide statements?

QUESTIONS FOR RESEARCH, ANALYSIS, AND DISCUSSION

1. Sweetwater County Sheriff's Office maintains a fund to which it transfers the phone company commissions it earns on inmates' pay-phone calls. The monies collected are used to provide inmate "amenities"—books and magazines, writing paper, postage stamps, chewing gum, and so on. The resources of the fund are periodically transferred to the general fund, from which they are appropriated and expended. Should the fund be accounted for as a private-purpose trust fund (a fiduciary fund) or a governmental fund, such as a special revenue fund?
2. The City of Acton maintains a defined contribution pension plan for its employees. Employees contribute 6 percent of their salaries; the city contributes 8 percent. The city has a fiduciary duty for the plan, but certain management functions to a well-known private annuity company. The city makes all key investment decisions. The city deducts the employee contributions from paychecks and each month sends the annuity company a check representing the amounts deducted plus the city's match. The annuity company handles all correspondence with both employees and retirees and makes the benefit payments to the retirees. Each month it sends the city a report of transactions and balances. Should the plan be accounted for as a fiduciary fund, just as if the city managed the fund itself?

SOLUTION TO EXERCISE FOR REVIEW AND SELF-STUDY

1. The city should report as its pension liability its net pension liability, the difference between its total pension liability and the plan's net fiduciary net position— $935,400.

2. Impact on pension expense:

a. Service cost	$150,200
b. Interest	531,400
c. Net investment income	(210,000)
d. Excess of actual over projected net investment income. (Net Investment income above includes the actual income of $210,000. However, the excess earnings of $25,000 must be taken into account only over a five-year period—$5,000 per year. Hence, the investment income will be reduced by, and pension expense increased by, the $20,000 difference.)	20,000
e. Employer contributions (The other elements of pension expense and the employer contributions cannot both be counted; otherwise there would be double-counting.)	0
f. Benefit payments (No impact; they reduce both the total pension liability and the plan fiduciary net position.)	0
g. Changes in actuarial assumption (The $75,900 that increased the total pension liability will be amortized over the eight-year remaining service life of plan members; hence the changes will increase the expense by only $9,488.)	9,488
h. Increase in liability over what was expected based on actuarial assumptions (The $15,000 that increased the total pension liability over what was expected will also be amortized over the eight-year remaining service life of plan members; hence the difference will increase the expense by only $1,875.)	1,875
i. Change in benefit terms (The $48,000 that increased the total liability need not be amortized; it will increase the expense by the entire $48,000.)	48,000
j. Administration costs	4,900
Total expense	$ 555,863

Viewed from a different perspective:

Change in net pension liability	$435,400	
Add: Employer contributions	180,000	
Difference between excess of investment earnings over projected investment earnings ($25,000) and amount to be included in pension expense ($5,000)	20,000	$ 555,863
Subtract: Difference between impact of actuarial assumptions and actual experience ($15,000) and the amount to be included in pension expense ($1,875)	$ 13,125	
Difference between impact of changes in actuarial assumptions ($75,900) and amount to be included in pension expense ($9,488)	66,412	(79,537)
Total expense		$ 555,863

3. In its governmental funds, the city would report as an expenditure only the amount to be liquidated with expendable available financial resources; hence the employer contributions of $180,000.

4. An increase in the discount rate would cause the total pension liability (and hence the net pension liability) to decrease.

5. The pension plan would report as its assets its investments (stated at fair value). It would report as its liabilities mainly the amounts that are currently payable to retirees. It would not report as liabilities the actuarial value of the benefits earned by either current employees or retirees.

6. If the city maintained a defined contribution plan for its employees, its accounting would be rather simple. It would report as both an expense in its government-wide statements and an expenditure in its governmental fund statements only what it is required to contribute in a particular year. Insofar as it makes such contribution, it need not report a pension liability.

CHAPTER 11

Issues of Reporting, Disclosure, and Financial Analysis

LEARNING OBJECTIVES

After studying this chapter you should understand:

- How to convert fund statements to government-wide statements
- Why the makeup of a government's or not-for-profit's reporting entity is an issue
- The criteria that the Governmental Accounting Standards Board (GASB) have established to determine the units that constitute a government's reporting entity
- The various ways of reporting component units
- The reports of special-purpose entities
- The main elements of a government's comprehensive annual financial report (CAFR)
- The critical factors to be taken into account in assessing a government's financial condition

This chapter—the final chapter that deals mainly with external reporting by governments—presents an overview of the annual financial report. We have now discussed each of the major fund types maintained by governments. This chapter highlights how individual fund statements can be consolidated into government-wide statements—the first of the statements to be presented in a CAFR. The chapter then considers the issue of the reporting entity—which associated organizations a primary entity must incorporate into its financial reports. Thereafter it highlights the structure of the annual report and the need for statistical information to supplement the financial statements. It then addresses reporting issues faced by special-purpose governments. It concludes by presenting an approach to assessing a government's financial condition.

HOW CAN A GOVERNMENT PREPARE GOVERNMENT-WIDE STATEMENTS FROM FUND STATEMENTS?

In this text we have taken a conceptual, rather than a procedural, approach to the government-wide statements. That is, we illustrated, often with journal entries, how various transactions would be reflected in those statements. We noted, however, that governments do not typically prepare two sets of journal entries or maintain two sets of books—one for their fund statements and the other for their government-wide statements. Instead, they maintain only one set of accounts—that on a fund basis. At year-end they convert the fund statements to government-wide statements. Some governments do this manually, using an Excel-type worksheet. Others rely on their accounting software to automatically prepare both fund and government-wide statements. In this section, we present an overview of the key adjustments required to convert fund statements to government-wide statements. In keeping with the conceptual approach of the text, our aim is mainly to summarize the differences between the two statements, not to provide a how-to guide to make the worksheet adjustments.

A quick overview of the differences between the two sets of statements can be found in the statements themselves. As illustrated in the financial statements of Charlotte, North Carolina, included in Chapter 2, the governmental fund balance sheet contains a section that reconciles the total fund balances for governmental funds with the total net assets per the government-wide statement of net position (see Table 2-5). Similarly, the governmental statement of revenues, expenditures, and changes in fund balance incorporates a reconciliation of the net change in fund balances of the governmental funds with change in net position of governmental activities per the government-wide statement of activities (see Table 2-4).

In this section, we focus on the governmental funds, rather than on the enterprise funds, because the enterprise funds are already on a full accrual basis and hence present few problems of conversion.

The following presents the general approach to converting the governmental fund statements to the government-wide statements.

- *Start with a year-end trial balance that combines all the governmental funds.*
- *Eliminate interfund transactions.* During the period reported on in the statements, there were likely numerous transactions made among the governmental funds. These may include transfers—such as from the general fund to a debt service fund or payments for services, as when self-insurance activities are accounted for in a governmental fund. These transactions must be backed out because they have no impact on the government as a whole. Similarly, any interfund payables and receivables must be eliminated.
- *Adjust capital asset-related accounts.* Capital assets are reported on the government-wide statements but not on the fund statements. The beginning balance in the capital asset accounts (per the previous year's government-wide statements) must be added to the trial balance (offset by additions to net assets). Then, a series of entries must be made to eliminate the expenditures for new capital assets and add the amounts expended to the balance of the capital assets. To eliminate the proceeds from the sale of capital assets (from other financing sources), subtract the original cost of the assets sold from the balance of the capital assets and credit or charge any difference to a gain or loss on the sale of capital assets. Record a charge for depreciation.
- *Adjust long-term, debt-related accounts.* Long-term obligations are reported on the government-wide statement but not the fund statements. Accordingly, entries similar to those for capital assets must be made. The beginning balance in the long-term debt accounts must be added to the trial balance. Then, entries must be made to eliminate the proceeds from the issuance of bonds or other certificates of debt (from other financing sources). Add the bond proceeds to long-term liabilities. To eliminate the expenditures for the retirement of debt, subtract the "book value" of the retired debt from the long-term liabilities accounts and credit or charge any difference to a gain or loss on retirement of debt account. To adjust interest expenditure to interest expense, charge or credit the bond discount, bond premium, or prepaid or deferred interest as necessary.
- *Adjust for difference in basis of accounting.* Governmental funds are accounted for on a modified accrual basis; government-wide statements are prepared on a full accrual basis. Thus, there are revenue and expenditure/expense timing differences. Most notably, in the governmental fund statements, but not in the government-wide statements, revenues must satisfy the "available" criteria for recognition. Similarly, in governmental funds, inventories and prepaid items may be accounted for on a consumption or purchases basis; in the government-wide statements, only the consumption basis is acceptable. In governmental funds, compensated absences—such as vacation pay, pensions, and claims and judgments—are accounted for on what is, in essence, a pay-as-you-go basis; in the government-wide statements, they accounted for on an accrual basis. Therefore, to convert from the governmental fund to the government-wide

statements, the governmental revenues and expenditures must be recomputed so that they are on a full accrual basis. Correspondingly, an offsetting adjustment must be made to deferred revenues, prepaid expenses, long-term liabilities or assets.

- *Consolidate the internal service fund.* Although internal service funds are classified as proprietary funds, they provide services mainly to units that are accounted for in governmental funds. In the government-wide statements, their assets and liabilities are divided between governmental and business-type activities. Similarly any "profits" earned or "losses" incurred during the year are credited or charged back to the category of funds from which they originated. The required adjustments may necessitate a series of entries that are potentially extraordinarily complex and depend on the proportion of services used by units accounted for in governmental funds and those accounted for in enterprise funds.

Once a government-wide trial balance sheet is completed, the accounts must be divided first between the statement of net position and statement of activities and then among the various functional accounts (e.g., general government, public safety, health, and sanitation) and the various types of revenues (operating grants, capital grants, and general revenues). Suffice it to say that, in practice, the classification of revenues and expenses typically involves numerous intractable issues. Common among these are to what extent certain common administrative costs should be reported as general government expenses or allocated among the various functions.

WHY IS THE REPORTING ENTITY AN ISSUE FOR GOVERNMENTS?

The composition of the reporting entity has proven to be one of the most stubborn issues facing business, government, and not-for-profit standard setters. As has long been recognized in the business sector, an organization's legal entity may differ from its economic entity. If a company controls another company, then its economic entity comprises the company itself plus its subsidiaries. Recall, governments may operate certain activities through separate public authorities, or issue debt through a conduit; not-for-profits might segregate certain assets (especially property or endowments) into separate legal entities. Yet in light of today's complex organizational relationships, satisfactory definitions of control have proven elusive.

The reporting entity issue in the government sector is delineated in the example that follows and its subsequent variations.

Example

The Reporting Entity

A city operates an electricity generating facility that supplies power exclusively to its municipal subway system. The facility needs costly capital improvements, but owing to debt limitations the city is unable to borrow the required funds. To circumvent the limitations, the city forms a new unit of government—a public power authority—to which it transfers the generating facility. The facility is to be governed by a board of directors, the members of which will be the same officials that compose the city council. The authority will issue city-backed bonds, which it will repay from revenues earned from the sale of electricity to the city.

In this example, the power authority, although an independent legal entity, is within the economic and political control of the city, no less than if it were another city department. City council members govern the authority, and the city is obligated for its debt. The city is the sole beneficiary of its resources. Therefore, if the city's financial statements were to report on all its economic assets and liabilities, they would have to encompass the assets and liabilities of the authority.

Consider, however, a continuum of modifications to the example:

- The authority's governing board, rather than being composed of city council members, is appointed by the city's mayor.
- The authority's governing board is independently elected, but the city retains the right to approve the authority's budget.

- The governing board is independently elected, and the city has no right to approve the authority's budget.

In this sequence of variations, the city's ability to control the authority is gradually eroded and the economic borders between the city and the authority are made more pronounced. Consequently, with each variation the rationale for including the authority within the city's reporting entity is diminished. But where should standard-setters draw the line?

This sequence of variations oversimplifies the problem, however, in that it focuses exclusively on whether the city *controls* the authority. In fact, the extent to which entities are economically intertwined cannot be assessed on the single vector of control. Economic interdependence is also measured by whether one organization shares geographic boundaries with the other, is responsible for its debts, must fund its deficits, can benefit from its surpluses, and is a major source of its revenues. Rule-making authorities have had to develop a multidimensional framework of standards that is appropriate for the over 89,000 U.S. governments, all of which are tied to at least one other government.

The following are but a very small sample of common intergovernmental relationships in the United States:

- Housing authorities established by cities to provide low-cost financing for residents of the cities
- Turnpike commissions established by states to finance and operate toll roads
- Volunteer fire departments partially funded by counties or towns
- Universities that receive state funds but are controlled by independently elected boards of regents

WHAT CRITERIA HAVE BEEN ESTABLISHED FOR GOVERNMENT REPORTING ENTITIES?

GASB Statement No. 14, The Financial Reporting Entity, as amended in 2002 by GASB Statement No. 39, Determining Whether Certain Organizations Are Component Units, and in 2010 by GASB Statement No. 61, The Financial Reporting Entity: Omnibus—An Amendment of GASB Statements No. 14 and No. 34, sets forth the criteria for determining the units that should be included in a reporting entity and how they should be reported.

TYPES OF UNITS COMPOSING THE REPORTING ENTITY

Per Statement No. 14, a financial reporting entity should consist of a primary government (the larger, creating government) and its component units (the typically smaller, created government).

A **primary government** can be a state government, a general-purpose local government such as a municipality or a county, or a special-purpose state or local government. Statement No. 14 explicitly states that "a primary government is any state government or general-purpose local government (municipality or county)." Under the U.S. system of federalism, local governments are subunits of the states in which they are located and are subject to state control. Were the definition of a primary government not to include explicitly general-purpose local governments, then virtually all cities, towns, and counties would be component units of their states rather than primary governments.

Special-purpose governments include a vast array of authorities and districts, such as school districts, municipal utility districts, and transportation authorities. To qualify as a primary government, a special-purpose government must have a separately elected governing body, be legally separate from other primary governments, and be *fiscally independent* of other governments. Fiscal independence implies that the government has the authority, without approval from other governments, to:

- Determine its budget
- Levy taxes or set rates and charges
- Issue bonds

A *component unit* is a legally separate government for which the elected officials of the primary government are financially accountable. Governments create authorities, public benefit corporations, and other types of organizations, largely for the purpose of performing functions that are either not cost effective for, or prohibited by, primary governments. A component unit may also be an organization whose exclusion would cause a primary government's statements to be misleading or incomplete because of the nature and relationship between the two. Such a relationship would exist if the potential component unit were created solely to benefit the primary government. For example, to help New York City out of its financial difficulties in the mid-1970s, the State of New York established the Municipal Assistance Corporation (known as "Big MAC"). The function of the corporation was to supervise the city's fiscal affairs and to issue bonds on its behalf. Because the city was financially accountable to the corporation, not the other way around, the corporation would not qualify as a component unit were it not for this "misleading or incomplete" provision.

MEANING OF FINANCIALLY ACCOUNTABLE COMPONENT UNITS

Appoint a Majority of Board and Either Impose Will or There Is a Financial Benefit/Burden Relationship

The key criterion as to whether a primary government is financially accountable for another government—thus qualifying the other government as a component unit—is that the primary government is financially accountable if it appoints a voting majority of the organization's governing body ***and*** (1) it is able to impose its will on that organization ***or*** (2) there is a potential for the organization to provide specific financial benefits to, or impose specific financial burdens on, the primary government.

The primary government is able to *impose its will* on the potential component unit if it satisfies any one of the following criteria:

- It can remove appointed members of the potential component unit's governing board.
- It has the authority to modify or approve the unit's budget.
- It can approve or modify the unit's fee charges.
- It can veto, overrule, or modify decisions of the unit's governing board.
- It can appoint, hire, reassign, or dismiss the unit's managers responsible for day-to-day operations.

The component unit is able to provide specific financial benefits to, or impose specific financial burdens on, the primary government if

- The primary government is entitled to the potential component unit's financial resources, ***or***
- It is legally obligated for, or has assumed the obligation to finance, the unit's deficits or is otherwise obligated to support the unit's operations ***or***
- It is obligated "in some manner" for the unit's debt, whether that obligation is expressed or implied.

Example

Financially Accountable Component Units

The Jefferson Hospital District was established to furnish medical aid and hospital care to indigent persons residing in Jefferson County. The district is governed by a board of trustees that sets policy for the district and oversees its day-to-day operations. The district is located entirely within Jefferson County, and the county's commissioners' court appoints the members of the district's board of trustees. The commissioners' court has the authority to approve the hospital district's budget.

The hospital district is a component unit of the county. It satisfies the two criteria of financial accountability in that:

- The county appoints the voting majority of the district's governing board.
- The county's authority to approve the district's budget gives it the ability to impose its will on the district.

Fiscally Dependent and There Is a Financial Benefit/Burden Relationship

As a general rule, a potential component unit is fiscally accountable to a primary government *only* if the primary government controls the appointment of its governing board. However, the GASB Statements provide for an exception. Even if its board is independently elected and thereby outside the influence of the primary government, a potential component unit may be considered financially accountable to a primary government if the unit is **fiscally dependent** on the primary government. A unit is fiscally dependent on the primary government if it is unable to determine its own budget, levy taxes or set rates, or issue bonds without approval of the primary government and there is the potential for the unit to provide specific financial benefits to, or impose specific financial burdens on, the primary government.

Example

Fiscal Dependency

A school district has its own independently elected governing board. Nevertheless, the board of supervisors of the surrounding county must approve the district's budget and tax rates. Further, the county guarantees certain of the school district's outstanding bonds.

The school district is financially accountable to the county because it is financially dependent on the county (its budget is subject to county approval) and it imposes a potential financial burden on the county (the county guarantees its debts) Thus, even though the county has no control over the district's governing board, the district would nevertheless satisfy the criteria of a component unit.

WAYS OF REPORTING COMPONENT UNITS

Governments must report the component units in either of two ways:

- ***Discrete presentation:*** reporting one or more units in a single column, apart from the data of the primary government.
- ***Blending:*** combining the unit's transactions and balances as if they were part of the primary government, that is, reporting the unit's special revenue funds, capital projects funds, debt service funds, and permanent funds as if they were corresponding funds of the primary government.

Discrete presentation is the default means of reporting. **Blending** is appropriate only in the following three circumstances, each of which is intended to capture situations in which the primary government and the **component units** are, in economic substance, a single entity:

1. The component unit's governing body is substantively the same as the governing body of the primary government. This would be the case when, for example, the members of a city council also served as the component unit's board of directors. In addition, the primary government and the component unit must have a financial benefit or burden relationship, or management (below the level of the elected officials) of the primary government must have operational responsibility for the activities of the component unit (i.e., it manages the component unit in essentially the same manner as it manages its own activities).

2. The component unit provides services solely to the primary government. A common example of this type of relationship is when a financing authority issues debt and acquires property exclusively for lease to the primary government. This criterion is satisfied only when the component unit provides the services to the primary government itself, not to the same citizens who are served by the primary government.
3. Total debt outstanding is expected to be repaid entirely or almost entirely with resources of the primary government. This would be the situation when a city, perhaps because it faces legal debt limitations, establishes a financing authority that issues debt for the benefit of the city and such debt is backed exclusively by a revenue stream (such as lease payments) from the city.

Governments must report component units that satisfy the criteria for blending as if the component units were an integral part of the government. Moreover, the funds of a blended component unit must satisfy the same financial reporting requirements as those of the primary government. Thus, a primary government would incorporate a blended component unit into both its fund and its government-wide statements. By contrast, it would report all other component units (i.e., those that must be presented discretely) only in its government-wide statements, not in its fund statements. The rationale for this distinction is that, by the very criteria for blending, blended component units are as much a part of the government as the units that it accounts for in its own funds.

Example

Blended Component Units

New York State limits the amount of debt outstanding cities can have. In the 1990s, New York City was approaching its statutory debt limit, which would have meant the city could no longer issue bonds for its capital projects. In 1997, the New York State Legislature created the Transitional Finance Authority (TFA) so that the city could continue to issue debt. TFA debt is backed by collections of income and sales taxes. Although it is a separate legal entity, the TFA governing body comprises city appointments and is presented in the city's financials as a blended component unit.

Discrete Presentation

In their government-wide statements, governments should report those component units that must be presented discretely to the right of the "totals" columns of the primary government. However, they have several options:

- They may combine all the component units in a single column.
- They may report each component unit in a separate column.
- They may combine component units into any number of columns based on the characteristics of the component units (e.g., all power authorities into one column, and all housing authorities into another).

Thus, for example,

Total *Primary Government*	Component *Unit No. 1*	Component *Unit Nos. 2, 3, 4*

Blending

When a primary government blends one or more component units into its own financial statements, it reports the funds of the component units as if they were its own funds. Thus, it accounts for the component units' special revenue funds as if they were its own special revenue funds, its debt service funds as if they were its own debt service funds, and so on. However, owing to the significance of the primary government's general fund, there is an exception. A primary government should report only one general fund. It should report the general funds of its component units as if they were its own special revenue funds. In determining whether they are major or nonmajor special revenue funds, the government should apply the same criteria as it does to its own funds.

Required Disclosures

Irrespective of how it reports its component units, the primary government must disclose detailed information as to each *major* component unit. This information can be shown in one of three places:

- In the government-wide statements themselves (i.e., by presenting the component unit in a separate column)
- In notes to the financial statements
- In combining financial statements (one column for each major component unit) within the government's basic financial statements, presented in a section following the fiduciary funds

If the information is provided in notes, required disclosures include condensed statements of net assets and of activities, the elements of which should be drawn from the totals column of the component unit's own government-wide financial statements. The decision of whether a component unit is major or nonmajor is made by the government officials and is based on the significance of the unit's relationship to the primary government. Table 11-1 contains excerpts of Charlotte's note on its component units.

TABLE 11-1 City of Charlotte, North Carolina Note as to Reporting Entity June 30, 2016 (dollar amounts in thousands)

The City of Charlotte (City) is a municipal corporation governed by an elected mayor and eleven-member council. The accompanying financial statements present the activities of the City and its two component units, entities for which the City is financially accountable. The Charlotte Firefighters' Retirement System (System) is so intertwined with the City that it is, in substance, the same as the City. Accordingly, the System is blended and reported as a Fiduciary Fund as if it was part of the City. The Charlotte Regional Visitors Authority (Authority) is reported in a separate column in the government-wide financial statements to emphasize that it is legally separate from the City. The following table describes the City's component units:

Component Unit	Criteria for Inclusion	Reporting Method	Separate Financial Statements
Charlotte Firefighters' Retirement System	The System provides retirement, disability, and death benefits to civil service employees of the Charlotte Fire Department. These services are exclusively for the City.	Fiduciary Fund	Charlotte Firefighters' Retirement System 428 East Fourth Street, Suite 205 Charlotte, North Carolina 28202
Charlotte Regional Visitors Authority	A "special district" as defined by state statutes. The City Council appoints the governing board and the City pays outstanding general obligation bonded debt. Net operating proceeds are to be used to pay principal and interest on the bonded debt or as otherwise directed by City Council.	Discrete	Charlotte Regional Visitors Authority 501 South College Street Charlotte, North Carolina 28202

WAYS OF REPORTING OTHER TYPES OF UNITS

Joint Ventures

Governments sometimes enter into joint ventures with other governments. A **joint venture** is a contractual arrangement, whereby two or more participants agree to carry out a common activity, with each sharing in both its risks and rewards. For example, Dallas and Fort Worth have joined together to operate the Dallas-Fort Worth airport as a joint venture. Similarly the states of New York and New Jersey formed The Port Authority of New York and New Jersey as a joint venture to manage the bridges, tunnels, bus terminals, airports, and seaport that are critical to the trade and transportation capabilities of the two states.

If a government has invested in a joint venture and thereby has an equity interest in it (i.e., owns a share of it), then it should account for the investment as an asset. If it made the investment with proprietary fund resources, it would record the asset in a proprietary fund. It would account for gains and losses on the *equity* basis (just as a corporation accounts for unconsolidated subsidiaries in which it has a 20 percent or more interest).

If the government made the investment from a governmental fund, then it would report it as it does other long-lived assets. Because governmental funds are accounted for on a modified accrual basis, it would not report the investment in the fund itself, but only in its schedule of capital assets. Moreover, it would recognize revenue in the governmental fund based on the usual criteria for that fund. Generally, it would recognize revenue from the joint venture as the venture declares dividends that satisfy the "available" criterion. However, in its government-wide statements, the primary government would report its entire interest in the joint venture, measured on an equity basis, and would recognize revenue on a full accrual basis.

Related Organizations

Statement No. 14 defines a **related organization** as an entity that satisfies the criterion of financial accountability (i.e., the primary government appoints a voting majority of its governing board) but neither of the other two criteria (i.e., the primary government cannot impose its will on the organization and there is no potential for the organization to provide specific financial benefits to, or impose specific financial burdens upon, the primary government). For example, a transit authority would qualify as a city's related organization if the city council appoints a majority of the authority's governing board, but the governing board has the power, without approval of the city council or other city officials, to levy taxes, authorize the issue of debt, set fares, and adopt its own budget. Because a related organization does not qualify as a component unit, it therefore cannot be incorporated into the primary government's basic financial statements. Nevertheless, per Statement No. 14, the primary government should describe each organization to which it is related and indicate the nature of the relationship.

Other Organizations with Special Ties to the Reporting Entity

Governments may be closely tied to entities other than component units and related organizations. These entities may be distinguished from component units and related organizations in that the primary government does not appoint a majority of their governing boards and they are not fiscally dependent on the primary government. Many of these organizations qualify as tax-exempt, not-for-profit organizations under the Internal Revenue Code, Section 501(c)(3), and their purpose is to provide financial and other types of assistance to the government with which they are associated.

One example of an **affiliated organization** is a state university's development foundation, the main mission of which is to raise funds for the university. Although its officers might work closely with university administrators, the foundation would be governed by an independent board of trustees. The university would have no direct or indirect control over the foundation.

Other examples of entities that might be considered potential affiliated organizations include

- A state university's alumni association, football booster club, or research foundation
- A public school's parent–teacher association
- A government hospital's fundraising foundation

There can be a wide variety of relationships between governments and associated organizations. Consequently, the GASB has found it extraordinarily difficult to define precisely the types of organizations that governments should report on in their financial statements and to determine how governments should present information about them into their financial statements. Nevertheless, after many preliminary efforts, the GASB issued Statement No. 39, *Determining Whether Certain Organizations Are Component Units*.

In Statement No. 39, the GASB amended Statement No. 14 to require governments to report "certain organizations" as discretely presented component units if they are *legally separate* from the primary government, are *tax-exempt*, and meet *all three* of the following conditions:

- The economic resources received or held by the separate organization are entirely or almost entirely for the direct benefit of the primary government, its component units, or its constituents.
- The primary government, or its component units, is entitled to, or has the ability to otherwise access, a majority of the economic resources received or held by the separate organization.
- The economic resources received or held by an individual organization that the specific primary government, or its component units, is entitled to, or has the ability to otherwise access, are significant to that primary government.

The last provision is expected to exempt most small organizations, such as parent–teacher associations and booster clubs. If an organization does not meet the three criteria, governments should nevertheless report it in accord with Statement No. 14 if its exclusion would render the primary government's financial statements misleading or incomplete.[1]

Example

A Closely Affiliated Organization

A state university's cooperative bookstore is incorporated as a Section 501(c)(3) not-for-profit entity. The bookstore is governed by a nine-member board of directors.

Four members of the board are elected by university students, four are appointed by the university president, and one (the chair) is elected by the other eight members. The bookstore distributes a portion of its profits as sales rebates to students and faculty customers. It contributes

[1] The GASB has supplemented Statements No. 14 and No. 39 with detailed guidance in the form of questions and answers. Its *Comprehensive Implementation Guide* (2013–2014, Chapter 4) has over 100 questions and answers, a full glossary, 28 cases with variations, illustrative footnote disclosures, and a flowchart showing possibilities of disclosure and inclusion.

the balance, excluding amounts that it retains for expansion, capital replacement, and the like, to the university and to student organizations in support of specific programs and activities. In a recent year, it distributed $2 million to the university and the student organizations. The total university budget is $1 billion. In the event that the bookstore should be liquidated, its resources would revert to the university.

The bookstore is legally separate from the university, it is tax exempt, its resources (after rebates) are entirely for the benefit of the university, and the university is ultimately entitled to the bookstore's resources. However, the resources of the bookstore are not significant to the university, and therefore the university need not incorporate the bookstore into its reporting unit.

Example

Application of Current Standards

A legally separate financing authority was created to improve access to low- and moderate-income housing in a state by providing mortgage loans to homebuyers. The governing board of the authority is appointed by the governor. The authority determines its own budget, holds title to property in its own name, and controls its own day-to-day operations. Mortgage loans are made according to guidelines included in the authority's enabling legislation. The authority is permitted to issue debt, subject to a statutory limitation. All bonds issued to provide mortgage loans are secured by first mortgages on the related properties and are payable from the proceeds of mortgage repayments. In the event that the authority determines that funds will not be sufficient for the payment of the principal and interest on its bonds during the next succeeding state fiscal year, the chairman of the authority certifies to the governor the amount required to pay such principal and interest. The governor is obligated to include these amounts in the state budget. However, the legislature has no obligation to appropriate funds for the authority.[2]

The flowchart in Figure 11-1 can be used to assess whether and, if so, how the financing authority should be incorporated into the financial statements of the state:

- Is the financing authority legally separate? Yes.
- Does the state appoint a voting majority of its board? Yes.
- Is the state able to impose its will on the financing authority? There is no evidence that any one of the factors indicative of an ability to impose will are present.
- Is there a financial benefit/burden relationship? Yes, the state is obligated, in "some manner," for the authority's debt. It must include any required debt payments in its budget. Therefore, the agency qualifies as a component unit.
- Does the agency meet the blending criteria?
- Are the governing boards of the state and the authority the same? No. Does the authority provide services entirely or almost entirely to the state? No.
    - Is the total debt outstanding expected to be repaid entirely or almost entirely with the resources of the state? No.
    - Therefore, the state should report the authority as a component unit, using discrete presentation.

[2] Drawn from *GASB Implementation Guide, Q&A Statement 14, Appendix 1: Illustrative Examples, Case 16 (June 2014).*

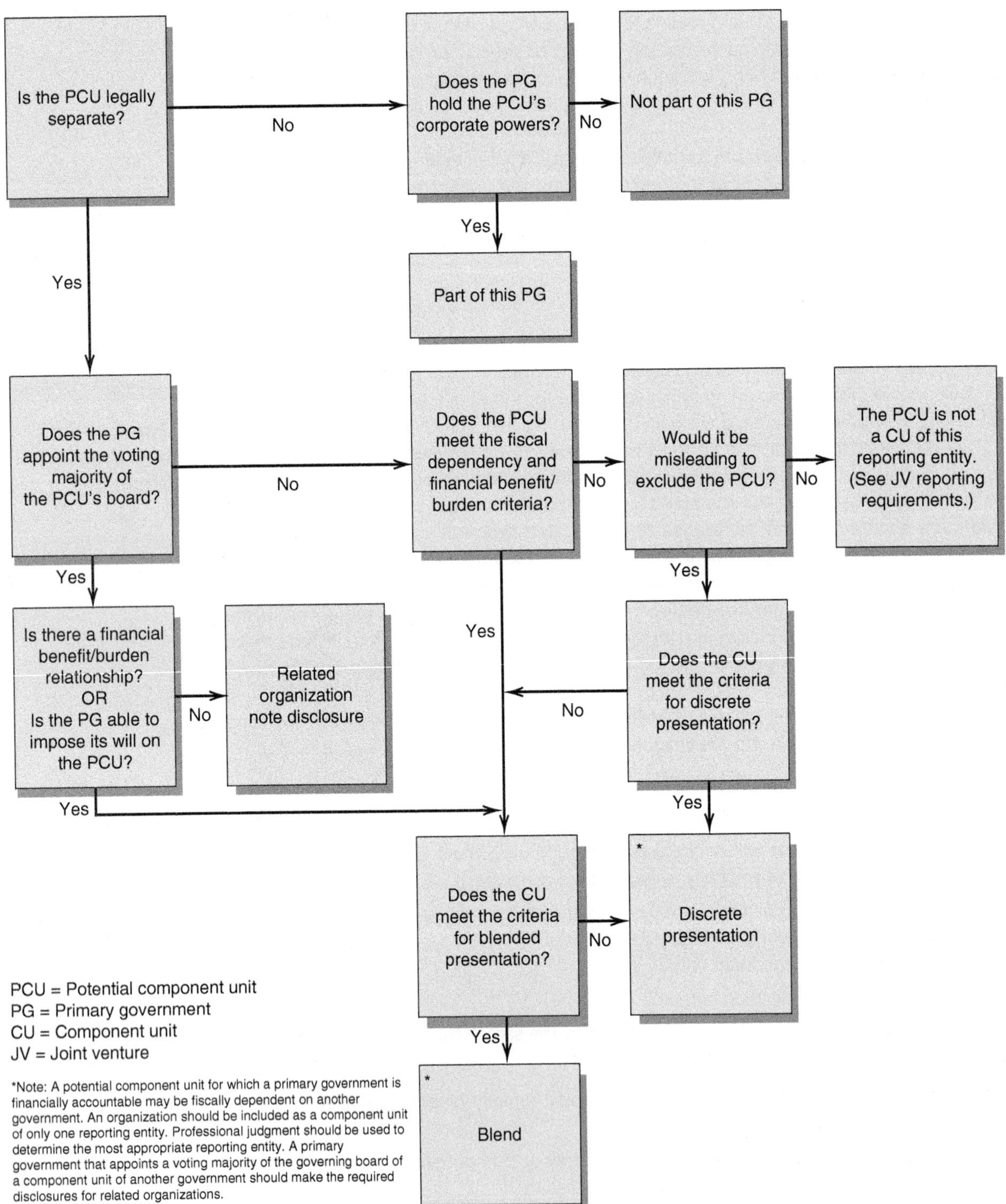

FIGURE 11-1 Flowchart for Evaluating and Presenting Component Units
Source: GASB Statement No. 61, The Financial Reporting Entity: Omnibus an Amendment of GASB Statements No. 14 and No. 34 (Norwalk, CT: GASB, November 2010).

WHAT OTHER ELEMENTS MAKE UP THE COMPREHENSIVE ANNUAL FINANCIAL REPORT?

In Chapter 2, we briefly summarized the main features of the comprehensive annual financial report (CAFR). In this chapter, we expand on the earlier discussion. A CAFR is the summation of all basic financial statements, with additional items included as introductory, statistical, or other supplementary information. The goal of a CAFR is to present a complete picture of the government for the fiscal year by way of comparative data for the immediate prior fiscal year and statistical information for several prior fiscal years.

As noted in Chapter 2, the CAFR is divided into three main sections:

- Introductory section
- Financial section
- Statistical section

SIGNIFICANT COMPONENTS OF THE INTRODUCTORY SECTION

The introductory section consists of:

- Cover and title page
- The table of contents
- A letter of transmittal
- Any other material deemed appropriate by management, such as the Government Finance Officers Association's certificate of achievement for excellence in financial reporting

Although governments must, per GASB Statement No. 34, incorporate into the required management discussion and analysis some of the information once included only in the letter of transmittal, the letter of transmittal remains one of the most informative sections of the CAFR. The letter of transmittal comprises four main sections:

- ***Formal transmittal of the CAFR.*** This section sets forth the legal requirements that the CAFR is intended to meet and indicates management's responsibility for the CAFR contents.
- ***Government profile.*** This section provides information on the jurisdiction area, population, organizational structure of the government, the activities in which it engages, the component units that are included in the financial statements, and the budget process.
- ***Information on economic conditions.*** This section, unquestionably the most edifying, addresses the key economic and financial issues facing the government. It describes the local economy and offers a prognosis of its future. It reviews any major fiscal-related initiatives that the government has undertaken in the past year and discusses its short- and long-term financial plans and policies.
- ***Awards and acknowledgments.*** This section reports on any honors that the government may have received for financial reporting excellence and acknowledges the individuals who made significant contributions to the preparation of the CAFR.[3]

The introductory section would generally contain a copy of the "certificate of achievement for excellence in financial reporting," if it had been awarded by the Government Finance Officers Association (GFOA) for the report of the previous year. The certificate of achievement is granted

[3] See Stephen J. Gautier, *Governmental Accounting, Auditing, and Financial Reporting* (Chicago: Government Finance Officers Association, 2012), 592.

to governments whose annual reports conform to GFOA standards. The GFOA does not, however, audit the government's books and records and therefore does not vouch for the accuracy of the underlying information. Subsequent to governments' investment losses or other fiscal failures, it is not unusual for reporters or other observers to question GFOA officials as to how, in light of the apparent fiscal mismanagement, they were given certificates of achievement. The officials have to explain that investment losses or other failures are by no means necessarily indicative of improper financial reporting, and that even if they were, the certificate of achievement is not an endorsement of the underlying data.

IMPORTANT PARTS OF THE FINANCIAL SECTION

The financial section consists of:

- The auditors' report
- The management's discussion and analysis (MD&A)
- The basic financial statements
- Required supplementary information other than the MD&A
- Combining statements, individual statements, and schedules

The Auditors' Report

The auditors' report serves the same general function in financial statements of governments as it does in business: It provides assurance that the statements are presented fairly and are in accordance with generally accepted accounting principles. However, as addressed in Chapter 16, audits of governments are considerably more comprehensive than those of businesses.

The typical audit is undertaken to express an opinion on the financial statements taken as a whole. It is not designed to cover all information included in the CAFR. Accordingly, auditors do not always subject statistical data, individual funds (if presented), and supplementary information to the same range of audit procedures as the basic financial statements.

The Management's Discussion and Analysis (MD&A)

The MD&A complements and supplements both of the basic financial statements. As noted in Chapter 1 and as reemphasized later in this chapter, basic financial statements, no matter how comprehensive and detailed, can never by themselves provide adequate information on a government's financial standing. In large part, this is because a government's fiscal health is as much dependent on the economic environment from which it draws its resources as on the resources already within its control. It is also because the financial statements fail to provide sufficient information on the nature and extent of services that the government will be expected to provide in the future. Governments have long been required to include in the statistical section of the CAFR extensive data on both demographic and economic trends. These data, however, are generally presented in tables. It was left to the statement users to interpret them and place them in perspective.

The MD&A contains a wealth of information and insights not previously available in the CAFR. Equally important, however, it provides government officials the opportunity to present the government's fiscal condition in a way that is understandable to the average citizen.

Table 11-2 highlights the main features of the MD&A as required by GASB Statement No. 34.

TABLE 11-2 Key Types of Information that Must Be Included in the MD&A

- A brief description of the required financial statements
- Condensed financial information derived from government-wide statements
- An analysis of the government's overall financial position and results of operations, including impact of important economic factors
- An analysis of balances and transactions of individual funds
- An analysis of differences between original and final budget amounts and between actual and budgeted amounts
- A description of changes in capital assets and long-term debt during the year
- A discussion of the condition of infrastructure assets
- A description of currently known facts, decisions, or conditions that have, or are expected to have, a material effect on financial position or results of operations

The Basic Financial Statements

The basic financial statements, as emphasized throughout this text, are of two main types: government-wide and fund. There are only two government-wide statements:

- The statement of net position (balance sheet)
- The statement of activities (statement of revenues and expenses)

Fund statements must be prepared for each of the three categories of funds—a total of seven statements:

- ***Governmental funds***
  - Balance sheet
  - Statement of revenues, expenditures, and changes in fund balances
- ***Proprietary funds***
  - Balance sheet
  - Statement of revenues, expenses, and changes in net assets
  - Statement of cash flows
- ***Fiduciary funds***
  - Statement of fiduciary net assets
  - Statement of changes in fiduciary net assets

The statements for the governmental and proprietary fund categories focus only on major funds. Nonmajor funds are aggregated into a single column. Major funds are those in which total assets (combined with deferred outflows of resources), liabilities (combined with deferred inflows of resources) revenues, or expenditures/expenses are at least 10 percent of those of the relevant fund category (i.e., total governmental or total enterprise) and 5 percent of the corresponding total for all governmental and enterprise funds combined. The concept of "major funds" does not apply to the fiduciary funds category. Instead, fiduciary fund statements should present all fiduciary funds aggregated into columns by each fund type: pension (and other employee benefit) trust funds, investment trust funds, private purpose trusts, and custodial funds.

As noted previously in the discussion of component units, governments may elect to provide detailed information about their major component units in the form of combining statements. If they choose this option, the combining statements (one column for each unit) should be included after the fund financial statements.

Like the statements themselves, notes are a required element of the financial section. Information incorporated into notes is considered to be "essential to a user's understanding" of the financial statements.[4] Similar to those of the financial statements of businesses, the notes describe significant accounting policies and disclose details of various accounts, commitments, and contingencies. Significantly, per the provisions of Statement No. 34, the notes must include the schedules of capital assets and long-term liabilities. These schedules reconcile, by type of asset and liability, beginning and ending balances and indicate the amount of depreciation allocated to each of the government's main functions. The notes also should include a summary reconciliation of the governmental fund statements to the government-wide statements unless this information is provided at the bottom of the fund statements.

Required Supplementary Information (RSI)

Required Supplementary Information is "essential for placing the basic financial statements and notes to the basic financial statements in an appropriate operational, economic, or historical context."[5] Examples include

- The budget-to-actual comparisons
- Information about infrastructure condition (for those governments that elect not to depreciate these types of assets)
- Details of pension actuarial valuations

Required supplementary information has much in common with the notes to the basic financial statements. In both sections governments present the GASB-mandated schedules and data. However, whereas the notes are considered part of the basic financial statements, the required supplementary information is not. As a consequence the RSI may be subject to a lower level of auditor scrutiny than the notes.

Combining Statements, Individual Statements, and Schedules

The combining statements support and supplement the basic statements. The basic fund statements for governmental and proprietary funds have columns for each of the major funds and a single column in which all the nonmajor funds are aggregated. The combining statements provide the details of the nonmajor funds, one column for each of the funds. The "totals" columns of the combining statements tie into the amounts reported in the "nonmajor funds" column of the fund statements. Except for fiduciary funds, GASB Statement No. 34 changed the emphasis of reporting from fund type (e.g., special revenue funds, capital projects funds) to major funds. Therefore, combining statements for nonmajor funds are *optional*, not required.

Internal service funds, as indicated in Chapter 9 on business-type activities, are presented in the proprietary fund statements in a single column that combines all of a government's funds of that type. Internal service funds do not have to be separately reported in the basic fund statements even if they would otherwise meet the criteria of major funds. Therefore, individual internal service funds would be reported on in the combining statements.

Governments may also include in this section statements of individual funds necessary to demonstrate compliance with legal and contractual provisions. For example, a government might present a statement of a nonmajor enterprise fund to show that it has made proper use of cash or other assets that secure outstanding revenue bonds. Similarly, it may incorporate in this section schedules that tie together data that are dispersed among several statements but that are nevertheless informative when presented together. Thus, a government might present a table that summarizes all its investments, irrespective of the funds in which they are held.

[4] GASB Concepts Statement No. 3, *Communication Methods in General Purpose External Financial Reports That Contain Basic Financial Statements* (2005), para. 36

[5] Ibid., para. 42.

NEED FOR AND KEY FEATURES OF THE STATISTICAL SECTION

Statistical data are a necessity because of key limitations of government financial reports. Governments have the power to tax. They can thereby command the resources of their constituents. The fiscal wherewithal of a government cannot be assessed merely by examining the resources actually within the government's control. The resources potentially within its control must also be taken into account.

Both Orange County, California, and Bridgeport, Connecticut, sought the protection of bankruptcy courts in the 1990s. The financial statements of both governments were equally dismal. Yet their overall fiscal conditions were dramatically different. Orange County was one of the wealthiest communities in the country, while Bridgeport was one of the poorest. If Orange County defaulted on its debts or reduced public services, it did so not because it lacked access to the necessary resources, but because it was limited by state law in its ability to increase tax revenues.

In addition, financial statements present key financial indicators, such as fund balances, revenues, and expenditures, for only a current year. Single-point data are, by themselves, not very useful in assessing a government's fiscal condition. Only by examining trends can an analyst make a reasonable assessment as to where a government has been and where it is heading in the future.

The statistical section supplements the financial statements. In May 2004, the GASB issued Statement No. 44, *Economic Condition Reporting: The Statistical Section*, an amendment of NCGA Statement 1. Per this pronouncement, a government that prepares a CAFR is required to present a statistical section that includes five categories of information:

- Financial trends that show how its financial position has changed over time
- Revenue capacity data that point to its ability to generate revenue from its own sources
- Debt capacity measures that reflect on its current debt burden and its ability to issue additional debt in the future
- Demographic and economic statistics that shed light on the socioeconomic environment in which it operates and facilitates comparisons with other governments
- Operating data that help give greater understanding to the dollar amounts reported in the basic financial statements

Table 11-3 provides specific examples of the data in each category required by GASB Statement No. 44.

WHAT ARE THE REPORTING REQUIREMENTS FOR SPECIAL-PURPOSE GOVERNMENTS?

GENERAL REQUIREMENTS

To this point, the text has focused mainly on "general-purpose" governments, such as towns, cities, countries, and states. Many (perhaps even most) government units serve only a single, well-defined, purpose. These include universities and special districts that provide utility, health, and educational services. These governments are legal entities in their own right, but may be component units of other governments. Nevertheless, they often are either required to, or elect to, issue their own financial statements.

Broadly speaking, GASB Statement No. 34's reporting guidelines direct that special-purpose governments that issue stand-alone financial statements should prepare the same types of statements as general-purpose governments unless they engage in such a narrow range of activities that a complete set of financial statements would be unwarranted. Thus, special-purpose governments that engage in more than one program or engage in both business- and governmental-type

TABLE 11-3 Examples of Statistical Information to Be Reported in the Statistical Section of the CAFR

(Generally this information will have to be presented for the most recent 10 years)

Financial trends

- The components of net position (invested in capital assets net of related debt, restricted, and unrestricted)
- Changes in net position, including expenses, general revenues, and programmatic revenues

Revenue capacity

- Revenue rates, including those for overlapping jurisdictions
- Revenue levies and collections
- Value of property by category (e.g., residential, commercial, tax exempt)
- Ten largest tax payers

Debt capacity

- Ratios of debt by category (general obligation, revenue, leases, loans, certificates of participation) such as debt per capital and debt to total personal income
- Amount of overlapping debt
- Details of debt limitations
- Details of debt that is backed by pledged revenues

Demographic and economic

- Population
- Total and per capita personal income
- Unemployment rate
- Largest employers including number of employees and percentage of total employment that each represents

Operating

- Number of employees by program or function
- Indicators of demand or level of service by function (for police activity these might include number of reported crimes, number of arrests, number of responses to 911 calls)
- Volume, usage, and nature of capital assets by function (for a motor vehicle pool this might include number of vehicles by type, mileage, and percentage of fleet in service)
- Data on pension and postemployment benefit plans

activities must prepare both government-wide and fund statements. They must adhere to the same reporting and disclosure requirements as general-purpose governments.

By contrast, special-purpose governments that engage in only a single governmental (as opposed to proprietary) program (e.g., a park or road district) have an option. First, they may combine their government-wide and fund statements into a single statement. That is, in one column they can present the government-wide full accrual data, and in one or more columns (one for each fund), they can present the fund, modified accrual, data. However, in another column, they must show the differences for each line item between the fund and the government-wide data. The differences (the amounts that reconcile the fund financial data to the government-wide data) must be described and explained either on the face of the financial statements or in an accompanying schedule.

As an alternative, special-purpose governments that engage in only a single governmental program may present separate government-wide and fund statements, but present the government-wide statement of activities in a simpler format than that required for general-purpose governments. Thus, for example, instead of the multicolumn statement (with revenues being deducted from expenses), they can show both revenues and expenses in two or more rows within a single column. However, unlike in the conventional income statements of businesses (and in keeping with the spirit of the statement of activities required of general-purpose governments), the program revenues must be deducted from the program expenses. The difference—the net expenses to be covered from other sources—should be followed by contributions to endowments, transfers, and extraordinary items.

Special-purpose governments engaged only in business-type activities need present only the statements required for enterprise funds—a balance sheet, statement of revenues and expenses, and a statement of cash flows. They must also, however, present the other key elements of the financial section of a CAFR—an MD&A, notes, and required supplementary information.

HOW CAN A GOVERNMENT'S FISCAL CONDITION BE ASSESSED?

Assessing a government's financial condition (i.e., its ability to finance its services and satisfy its obligations on a continuing basis) is a daunting task. Not only is a government's fiscal condition directly dependent on economic, political, social, and demographic factors within its jurisdiction, but also intertwined with those of other governments that provide financial aid or serve the same constituents.

Table 11-4 presents one approach to the task. Accountants are unquestionably as well trained as any other group of professionals to perform a comprehensive financial analysis of a government. Nevertheless, they must approach an analysis with humility. As the outline makes clear, financial statements are but one, albeit critical, source of information about governments. Nonfinancial considerations are at least as important as the financial factors, although they may be less subject to quantification as ratios or other numerical measures.

Assessing financial condition in government is especially challenging in light of recent economic conditions, the relatively few actual bankruptcy filings and debt defaults, large policy changes (such as health care and tax policy reforms) nationally, and the increased importance of complicated issues such as public pensions and retiree health care costs to future fiscal health. In the business sector, the ability of ratios and similar indicators to predict fiscal stress can be evaluated statistically by constructing regression or similar models in which the ratio and other indicators are associated with actual failures. In the public sector, owing to the small (albeit increasing) number of bankruptcies and defaults of general-purpose governments, considerably less evidence is available as to which indicators actually point to impending failure. Hence, even though the indicators presented in this section have not been statistically validated, they are widely accepted and are being used in research studies evaluating fiscal distress in governments.

The discussion that follows expands on the key elements of the outline, concentrating mainly on data that are reported in the CAFR. Although the outline is specific in some respects to cities, the general approach can readily be adapted as needed to special-purpose governments, such as school districts, as well as to not-for-profits.

The general approach described in the outline is to first assess the current economic, political, and social environment in which the government operates and then to identify the changes that are likely to occur in the future (e.g., the next five years). The accounting information can then be examined within the framework of the current and future available resources and claims upon those resources.

TABLE 11-4 A City's Fiscal Status: A Comprehensive Analysis

I. General approach

A. Review the current economic, political, and social environment in which the city operates

B. Identify and assess the impact of key factors likely to affect the city's economic, political, and social environment in the future (e.g., the next five years)

C. Assess the city's current status as revealed in its comprehensive annual financial report (taking into account the city's reporting practices and policies)

D. Forecast the city's fiscal status for the next five years, taking into account the previously identified environmental changes and the city's likely response to them

II. Current state of, and trends in, the government's operating environment

A. Population

1. Age of population
2. Income level
3. Educational and skill level
4. Other relevant demographic factors

B. Economic conditions

1. Wealth and income of citizenry (e.g., per capita net worth and income)
2. Major industries (and stability)
3. Unemployment rates
4. Value of property per capita
5. Sales tax base
6. Elasticity of revenues

C. Political climate

1. Formal structure of government
2. Extent of political competition
3. Competence of government officials
4. Overall citizen satisfaction with and expectations of government
5. "Liberal" or "conservative" citizen view as to role of government
6. Relations with state government and other local governments (e.g., those of surrounding and overlapping entities)

D. Social conditions

1. Crime rates
2. Other measures of social well-being

III. Changes likely to affect the government's operating environment and its finances

A. Demographics and geographical boundaries

1. Impact on infrastructure
   - **a.** Highways and streets
   - **b.** Utilities
2. Impact on operating revenues
3. Impact on operating expenses

B. Nature and scope of government services to be performed

C. Nature and scope of enterprise activities carried out (e.g., future of electric utility)

- **D.** Political climate (e.g., pro- or antigrowth; pro- or antibusiness)
- **E.** Form and organization of government (e.g., possibility of single-member election districts)
- **F.** Political attitudes and intergovernmental relationships
    - **1.** Changing views toward the role of government
    - **2.** Relations with legislature
    - **3.** Extent of state and federal assistance
    - **4.** Additional costs imposed by overlapping governments (e.g., school districts)
- **G.** Technological changes such as increased use of computers, and new means of transmitting electricity
- **H.** Social changes (e.g., changes in family structure resulting in need for more government facilities to provide care for elderly)
- **I.** Commerce and industry
    - **1.** Major employers (including stability and likelihood of relocating)
    - **2.** Impact on revenues (e.g., property taxes) and expenditures (e.g., infrastructure improvements)
- **J.** Wealth and income of population
- **K.** Other economic changes (e.g., those affecting the electric power and health care industries).

IV. Insight into city's financial condition as revealed by accounting and reporting practices

- **A.** Overall quality of disclosure
- **B.** Auditor's opinion
- **C.** GFOA certificate
- **D.** Letter of transmittal
- **E.** Key accounting policies
    - **1.** Reporting entity
    - **2.** Number, type, and character (purpose) of funds
    - **3.** Revenue and expenditure recognition
    - **4.** Accounting changes
- **F.** Budget- and accounting-related practices
    - **1.** "One-shot" additions to revenues or reductions in expenditures
    - **2.** Unusual budget-balancing transactions (e.g., interfund transfers)
    - **3.** Changes in budget-related practices (such as delaying payments or speeding up tax collections)
    - **4.** Use of "off the balance sheet" debt (e.g., leases, long-term contracts) and of revenue debt
    - **5.** Use of long-term debt to finance operating expenditures
    - **6.** Increased use of short-term debt to cover temporary cash shortages.

V. Calculation and interpretation of financial indicators

- **A.** Fiscal capacity and effort
    - **1.** Per capita revenues from own sources/median family income
    - **2.** Revenue from own sources/total appraised value of property
    - **3.** Total sales subject to tax/total retail sales
    - **4.** Sales and property tax rates
- **B.** Trends in fund balance
- **C.** Trends in mix of revenues and expenditures and reasons for trends
- **D.** Trends in adequacy and stability of revenues

(Continues)

TABLE 11-4 A City's Fiscal Status: A Comprehensive Analysis *(Continued)*

1. Total revenues/total expenditures
2. Intergovernmental revenues/total operating revenues
3. Property tax revenues/total operating revenues
4. Restricted revenues/total operating revenues
5. One-time revenues/total operating revenues
6. Uncollected property taxes

E. Trends in spending patterns

1. Number of employees per capita
2. Nondiscretionary expenditures/total expenditures
3. Percentage breakdown of total expenditures by function

F. Trends in liquidity

1. Adequacy of fund balance—unassigned fund balance/operating revenues
2. Adequacy of working capital—cash, short-term investments, and receivables/current liabilities

G. Trends in burden of debt

1. Debt margin
2. Debt service as a percentage of total general fund and debt service expenditures
3. Debt per capita
4. Debt as a percentage of taxable property
5. Maturity structure

H. Trends in pension and other postemployment benefits

1. Unfunded pension obligation
   - **a.** Pension assets compared to actuarial liabilities
   - **b.** Unfunded liabilities compared to values of property, annual payroll
2. Percent of annual pension costs actually contributed
3. Unfunded OPEB liability
   - **a.** OPEB assets compared to actuarial liabilities
   - **b.** Percent contributed annually
   - **c.** Trends in costs and liability
   - **d.** Flexibility in altering OPEB arrangements with current employees and/or retirees

I. Bond ratings

J. Trends in amounts of new borrowing

K. Overlapping debt

L. Trends in capital expenditures

1. By type
2. By geographic area
3. Reasons behind trends
4. Commitments and planned expenditures per capital improvement program

VI. Fiscal forecasts

A. Overview of how trends and exogenous variables will affect key fiscal indicators in the next five years (taking into account how city will likely respond to them)

B. Pro forma financial statements of general and other key funds

VII. Summary and conclusion

A. Will the city have the financial wherewithal to provide the services expected of it in the next years?

B. What are the key risks and uncertainties facing the city that might impair the ability of the city to provide these services?

1. How can the city best manage these risks?

2. What should be the key concerns of city managers, especially those directly concerned with finances?

THE CAFR AS AN IMPORTANT, BUT NOT EXCLUSIVE, SOURCE OF INFORMATION

The CAFR is probably the single richest source of data about a government's fiscal condition. But the data by themselves are little more than a collection of numbers. They provide a scant basis on which to assess past performance or make predictions as to the future. They are useful only when related to other data in the form of ratios, trends, and comparisons. Although the CAFR reports some of these relationships and trends, it is mainly a source of raw data. The burden of analysis and interpretation falls on individual users.

The CAFR is intended to provide information that is relevant to a wide range of decisions; it is not designed to be the sole source of information for any particular decision. Bond rating agencies, for example, require governments to supplement their CAFRs with additional documents, such as budgets, long-range forecasts and plans, biographical summaries of key officials, and economic reports. Diligent analysts are not bound by documents provided by government officials. They should also look to newspaper and magazine articles, economic reports and forecasts by government agencies, private research services, knowledgeable businesspeople, and community representatives.

In an effort to enhance the information content of the CAFR, the GASB, in 2011, issued a "preliminary views" document in which it proposed that governments provide information pertaining to five key components of fiscal sustainability (four projections and one narrative discussion):

- Total cash inflows and major individual cash inflows
- Total cash outflows and major individual cash outflows
- Total financial obligations and major individual financial obligations, including bonds, pensions, other postemployment benefits and long-term contracts
- Annual debt service payments (i.e., principal and interest)
- Major intergovernmental service dependencies (a narrative discussion regarding the nature of financial relationships with other levels of government)[6]

The projections would be based on current policy, informed by historical information and adjusted for known events and conditions and would be for a period of five years.

The information would be intended, in large part, to highlight the need for changes in current policies or practices. Thus, for example, the projections might indicate that over the following five years, consistent with current tax rates and service requirements, expenditures would greatly exceed revenues. If, however, the government were subject to a strict balanced budget requirement, it would be highly unlikely that the projections would be indicative of actual revenues and expenditures. The government would either have to increase revenues or decrease expenditure. For this reason the GASB makes it a point to emphasize that the projections are not intended to be predictions or forecasts.

[6] *Preliminary Views of the Governmental Accounting Standards Board on Major Issues Related to Economic Condition Reporting: Financial Projections* (November 2011).

As can be imagined, the GASB proposal was met with considerable opposition, mainly by organizations representing statement preparers. While not denying the value of the proposed information, they contended that it was outside the scope of traditional financial reporting, which is based mainly on historical transactions. In fact, the GASB placed the project on hold in 2013, where it still currently remains.

EVALUATING THE OPERATING ENVIRONMENT

The ultimate ability of a government to perform the services expected of it and to meet its obligations will be determined not by the resources currently on hand, but by those within the government's command. Thus, the demographic, economic, and social bases of the community that the government serves are of prime importance in assessing the government's financial condition.

Demographic Factors

Population size and composition have a major impact on a community's economic base. The composition of a population is as critical as its size. Factors that are of particular importance include

- Age (e.g., the elderly require extensive medical care; the young require education)
- Income distribution (e.g., the poor require more social services; the wealthy may demand more recreational and cultural services, as well as a higher level of basic services)
- Educational level (e.g., better educated populations make it easier to attract technologically oriented industries and are likely to demand higher-quality schools for their children)
- Native-born versus immigrant status (new arrivals to the country require different types of services than the native-born population)

Economic Conditions

The potential of an economy to generate tax and other revenues depends on the composition of its taxpayers. If the leading taxpayers are in a variety of industries rather than concentrated in just a few, the government's revenue stream is less likely to be adversely affected by recessions, technological developments or disruptions, changes in consumer tastes, or similar factors. In addition, some industries may be riding a wave of expansion, whereas others are caught in an undertow of decline. Some companies, perhaps because of high capital investments or historical ties, are likely to remain in a community. Others, maybe because their facilities are aging or they can reduce operating costs by relocating abroad, may be candidates for early departure. It is well known that textile and clothing manufacturing firms have transferred operations to other countries. In recent years, even "white-collar" activities such as insurance claim processing, the "back office" operations of banks and brokerage firms, and the telephone "tech support" functions of computer firms, and other service industries are being carried out overseas.

Political and Leadership Characteristics

The ability of a government to exercise decisive leadership both in planning for the future and in responding to crises adds strength to its fiscal condition. Bond rating agencies explicitly include analyses of leadership in their bond ratings. Ability can be influenced by several factors. These include:

- ***Formal structure of the government and the powers that are granted to key officials.*** In some governments, the chief executive officers have the authority to make major spending decisions on their own, without legislative approval. In others, even minor decisions are subject to lengthy administrative or legislative processes.

- ***Degree of political competition.*** In the absence of political competition, as might be evidenced by closely contested elections, the chief executive officer may be able to act swiftly and forcefully irrespective of requirements for formal legislative approval.
- ***Competence and integrity of government officials.*** Bright, experienced, and honest officials are a necessary, if not always a sufficient, condition for fiscal well-being.
- ***Relations with other governments.*** These are affected not only by the power of home rule (the authority to act without the approval of the state or some other government) but also by personal and political relationships among the officials of the various levels of government.
- ***Political climate.*** Politics and economics go hand-in-hand. Albeit a highly subjective factor, a favorable political climate makes it easier for a community to achieve its social, environmental, and educational goals while assuring that the costs are distributed equitably. Moreover, some elected officials may favor an expanded role for government and an increase in the range of services it provides; others may advocate a diminished role and a reduction of its activities.

In addition to these characteristics, evaluating a government's financial condition requires understanding limitations on the ability to raise revenues. The GASB now requires governments to report tax abatements—which are reductions of tax liabilities owed to the government for a specific period of time for some specific purpose deemed desirable by the government—usually for behavior or activity that is deemed beneficial to the public at large. For example, a city may offer property and corporate tax abatements for companies who locate or maintain presence in a municipality. Tax abatements are used primarily but not exclusively for economic development purposes.

GASB Statement No. 77, *Tax Abatement Disclosures*, requires disclosures about a government's tax abatement programs, as well as tax abatement programs of other governments that may reduce the reporting government's tax revenues in the future. The notes to the financial statements should include the names and purposes of tax abatement programs, the taxes abated by the programs, the authority under which the agreements were entered into, eligibility for the tax abatement, tax abatement mechanisms, any potential recapture of abated taxes, and the commitments of the recipients of the tax abatements. In addition to this descriptive information, the notes should disclose the reduction in tax revenues (measured on an accrual basis) during the year.

Social Considerations

Closely tied to demographic considerations are sociological factors such as crime rates, percentage of citizens requiring public assistance, and the percentage of residents owning their own homes. These factors affect the extent and level of services that the government will have to provide, as well as its ability to raise revenues.

ASSESSING CHANGES LIKELY TO OCCUR IN THE FUTURE

Analysts are concerned with both the past and the present mainly because they provide the basis for predicting the future. Although analysts are not seers, the essence of financial analysis is forecasting. Therefore, they must attempt to identify the changes that will likely affect the government's environment within the time horizon they are considering. The outline sets forth a few specific factors in addition to those presented in the previous section that must be considered.

Population

Increases in population are often associated with expanding economies and the creation of new businesses. Growth, however, may have its fiscal downside, especially in the short term. As new housing developments are constructed and families, often with young children, move into a community, the government may have to extend infrastructure, construct new schools, and augment social services.

Enterprises

Without question, the nature of services provided by governments is going to continue to change. Many governments are going to be under pressure to privatize (outsource) at least some of the functions they carry out today either to reduce operating costs or bring in one-shot revenues. One fiscally significant example of these changes is electric service. An electric utility may constitute the major portion of a city's revenues, expenses, assets, and liabilities. Until recently, electric utilities were the quintessential example of a regulated monopoly. The 1990s, however, witnessed a decided trend toward both competition and deregulation. More recently, governments have increasingly sought to privatize transportation projects. For example, the states of Indiana and Colorado have entered into contracts in which private operators maintain roads for the states and charge tolls to finance the projects; Chicago sold its revenue stream from parking meters for an immediate cash payment in 2008. Similar developments are also affecting other government activities. In response to economic and political uncertainty, many cities are considering selling to private companies not only their utilities or roads, but also their hospitals and sanitation facilities. Further, some governments are outsourcing clerical operations (such as processing welfare payments or payroll checks), internal audit functions, and repair and maintenance services.

Technology

"E-commerce" and related means of transmitting information electronically will almost certainly affect governments in much the same ways that they are transforming private businesses. Activities that some governments still carry out manually (e.g., reading electric and water meters and issuing purchase orders) are being performed electronically by other means. The increased use of electronic payments also has the potential to speed up cash management cycles at reduced costs—because municipal employees no longer need to remove paper checks from envelopes, process the payment internally, and deposit these checks in the bank. The shift to electronics may make governments more efficient and thereby reduce operating costs, especially in personnel. But it will also require enormous investments in computer hardware and software, as well as costs to maintain the infrastructure already in place.

Policy Changes

Subnational governments often must implement and finance policies from higher-level governments. Assessing potential policy changes can provide additional information on future fiscal health. For example, states and localities that levy income taxes frequently tie the definition of taxable income to the federal government's so that taxpayers can easily determine their state or local liability. Hence, any potential change in how income is defined by the federal government has the potential to influence revenues for states and localities as well. Further, expansions of programs such as Medicaid, which states and the federal government finance jointly, have the potential to affect the fiscal health of a government.

EXAMINING THE BUDGET AND FINANCIAL STATEMENTS

It goes without saying that the computation of ratio and statistical measures is central to financial analysis. However, key clues to the financial health of a government can be obtained as much from an organization's accounting and reporting practices as from its ratios or the underlying numbers.

The Budget

A government's plans are most explicitly revealed in future-oriented documents, such as its operating and capital budgets and long-term capital improvement plans. As indicated in Chapter 1, governments and not-for-profits are "governed" by their budgets (as opposed to the marketplace). Therefore, the budget is a detailed map of the fiscal path down which the government is proceeding.

Analysts must, of course, test the integrity of the budget by comparing previous budgets with actual results. In addition, they must assess whether the estimated revenues are attainable and the amounts budgeted for nondiscretionary expenditures are reasonable. Further, they must make certain that the budget provides for foreseeable changes in population and other changes in conditions as well as for contingencies and unanticipated events. Sound budgeting is characterized by conservative forecasting of revenues and expenditures, multiyear planning, and controls that ensure that governments do not exceed appropriations.

Budgets are generally on a cash or near-cash basis. Consequently, governments are able to engage in any number of measures to increase revenues or decrease expenditures even in the absence of substantive changes in economic resources. For example, as noted in previous chapters, they can delay payments to suppliers or employees, speed up collections from taxpayers, or transfer resources from one fund to another. These and other "one-shot" infusions to fund balance may provide compelling evidence of fiscal stress—that the government is unable to structurally balance its budget.

The Financial Statements

Financial statements must adhere to generally accepted accounting principles, which require a full or modified accrual basis. Therefore, governments have less opportunity to artificially manipulate their reported (i.e., actual) than they do their budgeted revenues and expenses. Nevertheless, as observed in previous chapters, they can influence values reported on their financial statements in numerous ways. To cite but a few, they can

- Account for certain transactions in internal service or proprietary funds rather than the general fund
- Finance capital acquisitions by incurring "off-the-balance-sheet" obligations (such as might be created by operating leases or service contracts) rather than general obligation debt
- Opt for "liberal" accounting practices and policies that recognize revenues sooner rather than later and delay the recognition of expenditures (e.g., lengthen the period after year-end during which cash receipts satisfy the "available" criterion for revenue recognition; reduce estimates of uncollectible taxes)
- Make "liberal" actuarial assumptions and estimates in determining the required contribution to pension plans
- Engage in discretionary transactions such as sales of capital assets and refunding of debt, which may provide no substantive economic benefit but result in reported financial statement gains

Analysts should take note of an entity's reporting practices for at least two reasons. First, and more important, certain reporting practices (like budget practices) may be a symptom of underlying financial deficiencies. If a government can produce a reported surplus only by stretching the limits of generally accepted accounting principles and taking advantage of available reporting loopholes, then it may be masking a true economic deficit. Second, insofar as analysts are comparing one government with another, they need to be sure that the governments are adhering to similar accounting principles.

IN PRACTICE BALANCED BUDGET REQUIREMENTS DON'T ALWAYS RESULT IN BALANCED BUDGETS

Illinois ended fiscal year 2016 with an unassigned fund balance deficit of $12.2 billion in its governmental funds and over $151 billion in unrestricted net position deficit in its government-wide financial statements. Yet, the state has a balanced budget requirement that reads: "*The budget shall set forth the estimated balance of funds available for appropriation at the beginning of the fiscal year, the estimated receipts and a plan for expenditures and obligations. Proposed expenditures shall not exceed funds estimated to be available for the fiscal year as shown in the budget*" [Article VIII, Section 2(a)]. The language of the constitutional requirement does not specify if "receipts" means revenues or borrowed money, and expenditures do not apply to items needing no cash outlay during the fiscal period.

Officials use these ambiguities when proposing budgets. The state was without a complete budget for fiscal years 2016 and 2017. The 2015 budget itself, however, included approximately $650 million in borrowing from special state funds (that is, sweeping funds from special funds to the general fund), $400 million in expenditure reductions from pushing bills into the next fiscal year (primarily for current workers' and retirees' health insurance), and using $650 million that was committed to paying down $5 billion in unpaid bills from prior years for current expenditures instead. Therefore, the balanced budget for Illinois for 2015 was actually out of balance by nearly $2 billion simply by these three budgetary sleights of hand.

The 2018 budget that was finally adopted projected a $360 million operating surplus. The budget assumes pension savings of $500 million in 2018 despite having no clear plan about to achieve this savings, does not include borrowing costs related to issuing $6 billion in bonds to pay down unpaid bills, and uses overly optimistic revenue projections that could leave a $300-$600 million hole in estimates. Taken together, these actions improved the Illinois budget's bottom line by more than $1.5 billion and resulted in a balanced budget.

CAVEATS REGARDING FINANCIAL INDICATORS

As with financial analysis in the business sector, individual numbers taken by themselves have virtually no significance. They acquire meaning only when related to other numbers, usually in the form of ratios. Ratios, however, must be interpreted with the utmost caution.

First, there are no reliable "rules of thumb" on what constitutes an acceptable or an out-of-line ratio. As noted previously, the over 89,000 governments in the United States carry out disparate functions. Even seemingly similar governments, such as cities that may be of similar size and within the same state, may engage in different types of activities. Thus, for example, the total per capita debt of a Texas city such as Austin, which operates an electric utility, should be expected to be significantly greater than that of Dallas, which does not. Nevertheless, both professional associations and government agencies make available extensive databases that enable analysts to make comparisons among similar government units. The Government Finance Officers Association, for example, maintains separate databases for cities, schools, and counties. The Texas Education Agency makes data available on its website so that users can analyze school districts with similar characteristics (e.g., size, ethnic composition, location) and evaluate them over a wide range of ratios and similar indicators.

Second, governments account for their operations in varying ways. One entity, for example, may account for a particular function in a governmental fund, and another in an internal service fund. Hence, ratios involving general-fund balances or expenditures may not be directly comparable.

Third, whether a higher or lower ratio is preferable is not always clear. Much depends on the issue that is being addressed and the perspective of the analyst. Consider, for example, a ratio of total general-fund revenues to total general-fund expenditures. Seemingly, a high ratio would be preferable to a low one because it would indicate that the government is having no difficulty meeting its expenditures and that the cost of providing services is being met by current, not future, taxpayers. That would definitely be true from the perspective of a bondholder who is concerned with the ability of the government to meet a forthcoming interest or principal payment or a creditor worried about receiving payment for goods or services that it provided.

On the other hand, a government's relatively high amount of revenues may be attributable to high taxes. Possibly, the government may face either legal or political barriers to additional increases in taxes. The government with the lower ratio might have greater capacity to raise taxes in the future and therefore be the more fiscally sound of the two over the long term. Thus, from the perspective of a long-term creditor, a low ratio (assuming it does not indicate ongoing deficits) might be preferable.

Fourth, cities can be expected to have higher or lower ratios depending on their stage of maturity. A high-growth city, for example, may have to expand rapidly its infrastructure, financing it with long-term debt. A mature city, by contrast, may have its infrastructure in place and may have repaid the associated debt years earlier. As a consequence, a city with high debt per capita may, in fact, have brighter long-term fiscal prospects than one with low debt per capita. Indeed, younger, fast-growing cities are more likely to have worse debt-related ratios than their older "rust belt" counterparts.

Fifth, ratios are no better than the underlying numbers. Throughout the text, we have emphasized the limitations of the current accounting model, some of which are inherent in any model that might be developed (e.g., it incorporates "subjective" estimates, allocations, and choices among competing accounting principles; it values most assets at historical, rather than current, costs). Moreover, the underlying accounting principles were developed for "general-purpose" financial statements, not for any particular decision on hand. These limitations do not disappear when the numbers are incorporated into ratios.

This is not to imply that ratios have no meaning. They are especially useful in identifying trends and raising pertinent questions. Analysts should never draw conclusions merely because the ratios of one government differ from those of others or have changed over time, no matter how great the difference or the change. But a significant difference or change should cry out for investigation. Only when analysts fully understand the reason behind the difference or change can they discern its implications.

DETERMINING THE SCOPE OF A RATIO

In calculating and interpreting financial indicators, analysts face an immediate issue—one for which there is no obvious resolution. Should ratios and other measures be based on (1) the government-wide statements, (2) the general fund only, or (3) some analyst-selected combination of funds?

Measures based on the government-wide statements capture the totality of the government's resources and do not show which specific assets are restricted and may therefore be used only for specified purposes. On the other hand, over the long term, all resources, whether restricted or not, benefit the government and can be used to provide government services or to satisfy its obligations.

Thus, the answer to the question must depend on why the measure is being calculated and how it will be interpreted. If analysts are interested in determining the total amount of government resources directed to specific functions (e.g., road repair), then it makes sense for them to include expenditures from all funds from which applicable expenditures can be made. Similarly, if they want to take a long-term perspective, then inasmuch as the government-wide statements include depreciation as an expense, they will likely give a more relevant measure of ongoing costs. By contrast, if the analysts are concerned with the ability of the government to meet its short-term obligations from a specific fund, such as the general fund or an enterprise fund, then they should probably take into account only the resources of that fund.

The issue of which funds to take into account in computing ratios is especially critical when comparing two or more governments. Suppose, for example, that one county imposes a gasoline sales tax that is restricted for road improvements and maintenance. It accounts for both the revenues and related expenditures in a special revenue fund. Another county pays for road improvements and repairs out of general property and sales tax revenues. It accounts for all road-related costs in its general fund. In this situation, even though the revenues of the first government are restricted, they are, in fact, used for a function common to most all counties. Therefore, for most analytical purposes it would be appropriate to combine the first county's general and special revenue funds.

ASSESSING FISCAL EFFORT

A government's **fiscal effort**—the extent to which it is taking advantage of its fiscal capacity—may be measured by comparing the revenues that it generates from its own sources (i.e., total revenues excluding grants from other governments) with either the wealth or the income of its taxpayers. Income can be captured by measures such as median family income; wealth can be represented by indicators such as total appraised (market) value of property. Thus, fiscal effort equals:

$$\frac{\text{Per capita revenue from own sources}}{\text{Median family income}}$$

or

$$\frac{\text{Revenue from own sources}}{\text{Total appraised value of property}}$$

These ratios increase as the government exerts greater fiscal effort and uses a greater portion of its fiscal capacity. The more it takes of its constituents' resources that are economically or politically available for taxation, the less it will be able to raise taxes in the future. Hence, lower ratios are generally preferable to higher.

ASSESSING THE SIGNIFICANCE OF OPERATING DEFICITS

Operating deficits should be to financial analysts what red flags are to bulls. They should draw attention, yet not distract focus away from other, more consequential, targets.

A widely used rule of thumb holds that two consecutive years of operating deficits connotes serious fiscal distress. But operating deficits as a measure of fiscal performance have inherent limitations and must be interpreted with considerable caution.

First, operating deficits (as well as all other accounting measures) result from the application of generally accepted accounting principles. These principles represent compromises among competing objectives and were not developed to facilitate any particular decisions. The resultant accounting revenues and expenditures may not necessarily have been determined on a basis that is most appropriate for the purpose at hand.

Second, operating deficits, whether government-wide or of individual funds, even if over a period of two or more years, do not necessarily signify a deteriorating financial condition. If a government has accumulated excessive surpluses in the past, it may elect, quite sensibly, to draw them down by running planned deficits over the following several years.

ANALYZING REVENUE AND EXPENDITURES TRENDS

In governments, more revenue is not necessarily preferable to less. Revenues need only, but at the same time must, be sufficient to cover expenditures. A key step in assessing the adequacy of revenues, therefore, is to associate trends in revenues with those in expenditures.

Both revenues and expenditures are closely correlated with size of the constituency. To compare the revenues and expenditures of the same government over time or of one government with another, it is necessary to take into account difference in population. For many analytical purposes, revenues and expenditures are best expressed per capita.

The adequacy of revenues is most obviously indicated by the extent to which revenues exceed expenditures—that is:

$$\frac{\text{Total revenues}}{\text{Total expenditures}}$$

In the short term, and from the perspective of bondholders or other creditors, the higher the ratio the better.

A stable revenue base is generally characterized by the presence of several diverse sources of revenues, so that a decline in one source will not necessarily be contemporaneous with declines in others. Moreover the revenues should be linked to population, so that costs of providing for a larger population are automatically offset by a broader revenue base. For example, a state government that generates its revenue from a mix of property taxes, income taxes, sales taxes, user fees, and intergovernmental aid is less likely to suffer from either a recession or a downturn in the price of a single commodity than one that relies primarily on taxes on the production of oil.

The following ratios spotlight the stability of a government's revenues:

- ***Intergovernmental revenues/Total operating revenues.*** Governments generally want to maximize the amount of resources received from other governments. Failure to take advantage of appropriate intergovernmental grants can rightfully be interpreted as a sign of poor management. But what a granting government gives, it can also take away. Therefore, a high or increasing ratio of intergovernmental revenues to total revenues is a sign of risk and hence is generally considered a negative fiscal characteristic.
- ***Restricted revenues/Total operating revenues.*** Restricted revenues decrease the flexibility of governments to respond to changing conditions and may lead to a misallocation of resources. State gasoline taxes, for example, may be dedicated to highway construction and thereby be unavailable to meet pressing needs for new schools. Therefore, lower percentages of restricted revenues are preferred to high percentages.
- ***One-time revenues/Total operating revenues.*** By definition, one-time revenues cannot be expected to be ongoing. As suggested earlier in the text, these revenues may result from substantive measures, such as sales of assets, or merely "one-shot" technical adjustments, such as changes in the due date of taxes or license fees. Some can be motivated by opportunities to enhance productivity; others by a need to artificially balance the budget. A high proportion of one-time revenues is generally viewed as a decidedly negative characteristic.
- ***Property tax revenues/Total operating revenues.*** Property tax revenues are considered a stable source of revenue; a high ratio of property tax revenues to other, less stable, revenues is a positive attribute.
- ***Uncollected property taxes/Total property taxes levied.*** A high rate of uncollected property taxes may signal an underlying weakness in the economy and hence be a warning of an impending reduction in revenues, not only from property taxes, but also from other sources as well.[7]

Expenditures are a measure of the cost of services provided. Changes in per capita expenditures can be the result of several factors, some positive, some negative, and some neutral. For example, increases in expenditures can be attributable to:

- Decreases in productivity or increases in prices (i.e., the government provides the same services but at greater cost)
- Changes in the number, quality, or mix of services owing to favorable economic conditions (e.g., new housing developments or new industries that require a city to enhance its infrastructure)

[7] These and several other ratios presented in this section have been adapted from Karl Nollenberger, Sanford M. Groves, and Maureen Godsey Valente, *Evaluating Financial Condition: A Handbook for Local Government,* 4th ed. (Washington, DC: International City/County Management Association, 2003).

- Changes in the number, quality, or mix of services owing to unfavorable economic factors (e.g., increases in unemployment that require a city to provide free medical care for a larger number of citizens)
- Factors beyond the control of the government, such as bad weather

Ratios that may be used to identify changes in spending patterns and thereby signal the need for an investigation into the cause of the change include the following:

- ***Number of employees/Population or payroll expenditures/Total expenditures.*** Without evidence of corresponding increases in the level or quality of services, increases in payroll costs may be a consequence of decreased productivity. On the other hand, government officials have been known to boast that they decreased the number of employees. However, they often accomplished this feat by outsourcing functions previously performed "in-house." They may have reduced payroll costs, but only by increasing the cost of consulting and other costs of purchasing services.
- ***Expenditures for specific functions/Total expenditures.*** Disproportionate increases in expenditures for specific functions (such as public safety, health and welfare, or recreation) may indicate new policies or circumstances that presage additional increases in the future.
- ***Nondiscretionary expenditures/Total expenditures.*** Governments typically have control over a limited percentage of their total costs. Many are dictated by contractual agreements (such as leases), debt commitments, and mandates from higher levels of government. The higher the percentage of nondiscretionary expenditures, the less flexibility the government has to reduce (or limit increases in) spending.

As in businesses, analysts can key in on a specific revenue or expenditure by comparing it to a related account. For example, the extent to which property taxes are being collected on a timely basis can be evaluated by dividing property taxes of a current year that were collected by the total property tax levy for the year. In the case of property taxes, governments are required to present this ratio in the statistical section of the CAFR.

ASSESSING ABILITY TO MEET SHORT-TERM COMMITMENTS

The balance sheets of governmental funds focus on short-term resources and claims against these resources. Therefore, they provide an indication of a government's near-term ability to perform the services expected of it to fulfill its obligations.

Of all the government-fund balance sheet accounts, fund balance typically draws the greatest attention. In large part, fund balance is so highly visible because it embodies all other balance sheet accounts and in governmental funds is indicative of net available financial resources.

Most governments try to maintain a positive fund balance so as to be better able to cope with unforeseen expenditures or revenue shortfalls. The adequacy of fund balance is often measured by the ratio of unassigned fund balance to operating revenues:

$$\frac{\text{Unassigned fund balance}}{\text{Total operating revenues}}$$

Rating agencies typically like to see governments maintain unassigned fund balances of 5–10 percent of annual operating revenues. Other factors being equal, a trend of decline in the ratio is seen as a sign of deteriorating financial condition. However, the significance of fund balance can easily be overstated. Fund balance is nothing more than the accumulation of annual surpluses and deficits and is therefore subject to the limitations ascribed earlier to operating deficits. If, as is common, the budgetary principles applicable to a particular government differ from the generally accepted accounting principles on which reported fund balance is based, the fund balance may not necessarily denote the resources legally available for expenditure.

Liquidity in governments can be measured just as in businesses—by comparing some or all current assets to current liabilities. Because a government's inventories are not usually for sale and will not be a source of cash, most analysts exclude them from their liquidity ratios. Thus, the current ratio includes only cash, short-term investments (i.e., near cash), and receivables:

$$\frac{\text{Cash, short-term investments, and receivables}}{\text{Current liabilities}}$$

A more rigorous form of the ratio also excludes receivables:

$$\frac{\text{Cash and short-term investments}}{\text{Current liabilities}}$$

This ratio can vary dramatically from month to month depending on the timing of revenue collections and spending patterns. Therefore, the analyst must be sure to examine trend data over a period of several years, comparing the ratio of particular dates with corresponding dates of earlier years.

ASSESSING ABILITY TO MEET LONG-TERM COMMITMENTS

In this text, key issues in assessing the burden of a government's long-term obligations and the adequacy of its long-term assets have already been addressed in the chapters dealing with general capital assets [Chapter 7) and long-term debt (Chapter 8). As noted in those chapters, an analyst must consider trends in debt per capita, debt as a percentage of taxable property, and debt service costs as a percentage of total general-fund and debt service expenditures. Also of special concern are debt margin, overlapping debt, and the ratings assigned to the government's bonds by independent rating services. Moreover, analysts must be wary of a build-up in unfunded pension obligations. This can be detected by examining trends in various pension ratios (e.g., plan fiduciary net position as a percentage of the total pension liability, and net pension liability as a percentage of covered-employee payroll). These are reported in the schedule of changes in net pension liability, which is included in the required supplementary information section of the CAFR.

Similarly, as noted in earlier chapters, no analysis of a government's fiscal condition can be meaningful if it fails to consider the condition of the entity's capital assets and especially its infrastructure. To be sure, both the government-wide statements and the schedule of changes in capital assets (included in notes to the financial statements) provide data on the historical cost of, and the accumulated depreciation applicable to, capital assets. As previously emphasized, however, these data tell the analyst nothing about the physical condition of assets and their adequacy for the future. Still, to gain insight into whether a government is properly maintaining its assets, analysts may be able to look to the note disclosures regarding the condition of infrastructure assets and comparison of actual to needed maintenance and preservation costs. These are required by governments that elect the "modified" as opposed to the "depreciation" approach to accounting for infrastructure assets.

Although GASB Statement No. 34 substantially improved disclosures regarding capital assets, analysts still cannot count on the CAFR for all relevant information. Analysts must therefore obtain from other sources information on the age, condition, and capacity of infrastructure and assess the demands that infrastructure maintenance and improvement will place on future-year revenues.

Table 11-5 illustrates key ratios based on the financial statements and supplementary information for the fiscal year 2016 of Charlotte, North Carolina. As noted previously, all of the ratios could have been computed differently, with equal justification, using either data from the government-wide statements or data from different combinations of funds.

TABLE 11-5 Selected Key Ratios Based on the 2016 Financial Statements and Supplementary Information of Charlotte, North Carolina

Ratio	Formula	Source	Interpretation
Fiscal Effort Revenue from own sources/Median family income	**Total governmental funds revenues less total intergovernmental revenues)/ Median Family Income** = (929,764,000 – 166,463,000)/68,564 = 11,133	Statement of Revenues, Expenditures and Changes in Fund Balances for Governmental Funds (Table 2-6) and Statistical Section[8]	Lower ratios are better. As the value increases, the government exerts greater fiscal effort and thereby uses a greater portion of its fiscal capacity. That means that it will have less ability to raise taxes in the future.
or			
Revenue from own sources/Total appraised value of property	**(Total governmental funds revenues less total intergovernmental revenues)/ Total appraised value of property** = (929,764,000 – 166,463,000)/ 91,200,098,000 = 0.008	Statistical Section[9]	
Adequacy of Revenues			
Total revenues/Total expenditures	**(Total governmental funds revenues less total intergovernmental revenues)/Total governmental funds expenditures** = (929,764,000 – 166,463,000)/975,406,000 = 0.783	Statement of Revenues, Expenditures and Changes in Fund Balances for Governmental Funds (Table 2-6) and Statistical Section	Higher ratios are better. A high value indicates that a government's own-source revenues are covering a larger share of expenditures.
Stability of Revenues			
Intergovernmental revenues/Total operating revenues	**(Intergovernmental revenues from General + Debt Service + Other Governmental Funds)[10]/ (Revenues from General + Debt Service + Other Governmental funds)** = 99,938,000 + 1,158,000 +55,942,000)/(624,129,000 + 107,321,000 + 147,045,000)=0.179	Statement of Revenues, Expenditures and Changes in Fund Balances for Governmental Funds (Table 6-6) and Statistical Section	This ratio indicates the proportion of revenues received from other governments. Insofar as the other governments may be able to arbitrarily cease to provide the revenues, an increase in the ratio may indicate increased risk and hence decreased fiscal strength. However, at the same time, a decrease in the ratio may point to the government's failure to take advantage of all the grants and other revenues available from other governments.
Restricted revenues/ Total operating revenues	**(Total governmental funds revenues less total General fund revenues)/ (Revenues from General + Debt Service + Other Governmental funds)** (929,764,000 – 624,129,000)/(624,129,000 + 107,321,000 +147,045,000) = 0.348	Statement of Revenues, Expenditures and Changes in Fund Balances for Governmental Funds (Table 2-6) and Statistical Section	Lower ratios are better. Restricted revenues decrease the flexibility of governments to respond to changing conditions and may lead to misallocation of resources.

Ratio	Formula	Source	Interpretation
Property tax revenues/Total operating revenues	**(Property tax revenues from General + Debt Service + Other Governmental Funds)**[11]**/(Revenues from General + Debt Service + Other Governmental funds)** = (348,988,000 + 86,539,000 + 4,883,000)/(624,129,000 + 107,321,000 + 147,045,000) = 0.501	Statement of Revenues, Expenditures and Changes in Fund Balances for Governmental Funds (Table 2-6) and Statistical Section	Higher ratios are better. Property tax revenues are considered a stable source of revenue.
Uncollected property taxes/Total property taxes levied	**(Total tax levy less Current tax collections)/Total tax levy** = (417,519,000 – 415,160,000)/ 417,519,000 =0.006	Statistical Section[12]	Lower ratios are better. A high rate of uncollected property taxes may signal an underlying weakness in the economy.
Spending Patterns			
Number of employees/ Population	7,237/827,097 = 0.0087	Statistical Section[13]	An increase may suggest that the government is operating less efficiently (a signal of fiscal weakness) or, on the other hand, may indicate that the government is able to increase the level of services that it is providing (a sign of fiscal strength).
Expenditure for specific functions/ Total expenditures	**Public Safety:** 359,187,000/ 975,406,000=0.368 **Sanitation:** 52,265,000/ 975,406,000=0.054 **General Administration** 40,294,000/975,406,000 =0.041 **Streets/Highways** 62,924,000/975,406,000=0.065 **Engineering and Property Management:** 20,973,000/975,406,000=0.022 **Support Services:** 29,728,000/975,406,000=0.030 **Community Planning/Development:** 49,813,000/975,406,000=0.051 **Culture and Recreation** 27,312,000/975,406,000 = 0.028	Statement of Revenues, Expenditures and Changes in Fund Balances for Governmental Funds (Table 2-6) and Statistical Section	An increase in expenditures for a specific function may indicate new policies or circumstances that presage additional increases in the future—perhaps a sign of deteriorating fiscal strength. Or, on the other hand, it could signal merely a change in priorities—a neutral development.

(Continues)

TABLE 11-5 **Selected Key Ratios Based on the 2016 Financial Statements and Supplementary Information of Charlotte, North Carolina** *(Continued)*

Ratio	Formula	Source	Interpretation
Adequacy of Fund Balance (Operating Position)			
Unassigned fund balance/Total operating revenues	**(Unassigned fund balance from General Fund/(Revenues from General Fund** = (101,590,000)/(624,129,000) = 0.163	Balance Sheet (Table 2-5); Statement of Revenues, Expenditures and Changes in Fund Balances for Governmental Funds (Table 2-6)	The higher the ratio, the greater the cushion against future deficits. An increase may be seen as a sign of fiscal strength. However, a larger reserve is not preferable per se. If the reserve is unnecessarily high, then the government may be either spending too little or taxing too much.
Liquidity Position			
Cash, short-term investments and receivables/Current liabilities	**(Cash and cash equivalent + Net receivables+ Due from other governmental agencies)/(Accounts payable + Deposits and retainage payable + Liabilities payable from restricted assets)** = (749,734,000 + 17,937,000 + 88,987,000)/(49,465,000 + 11,649,000 + 5,407,000) = 12.878	Balance Sheet (Table 2-5)	A high ratio indicates that the government is able to meet its short-term obligations as they come due—a sign of fiscal strength. However, inasmuch as the numerator encompasses receivables, an increase in the ratio as a result of a receivables build-up could be reflective of an inability to collect taxes or other revenues.
Debt Structure			
Debt service costs/Total general and debt service fund expenditures	**Debt service expenditures (interest + principal)/(Expenditures from General + Debt service fund)** = (112,033,000 + 66,557,000)/(552,949,000 + 178,590,000)= 0.244	Statement of Revenues, Expenditures and changes in Fund Balances for Governmental Funds (Table 2-6) and Statistical Section	Lower ratios are better. A low value suggests the entity is able to pay its debt service requirements when due.
Direct long-term debt/ Total population	**Total debt outstanding for governmental activities/Total population** = (1,629,400,000/ 827,097) = 1,965	MD&A[14]	Low ratios are better. That means that the government has the ability to repay its general long-term debt.

[8] Median Family Income for 2016 is determined based on the amount provided in the CAFR for Per Capita Personal Income ($26,575) and the average U.S. household size of 2.58 (as per the U.S. Census, 2010).

[9] Assessed and Actual Value of Taxable Property Last Ten Fiscal Years, Statistical Section, CAFR 2016.

[10] For consistency, capital projects fund revenues are excluded from the intergovernmental revenues because the denominator includes total operating revenues, which exclude capital project fund revenues.

[11] For consistency, capital projects fund revenues are excluded.

[12] Analysis of Current Tax Levy, Statistical Section, CAFR 2016.

[13] Full-Time Equivalent Employees by Function/Program Last Ten Fiscal Years, Statistical Section, CAFR 2016.

[14] Schedule of Outstanding Debt, MD&A, CAFR 2016.

DRAWING CONCLUSIONS

The goal of financial analysis is to draw conclusions regarding the ability of a government to provide the services expected of it in the future. One means of capturing the factors discussed so far is by preparing pro forma financial statements. Based on forecasts of revenues, expenditures, capital outlays, and proceeds from debt, analysts can prepare statements of revenues and expenditures, balance sheets, and statements of cash flow for each year covered by the projections. These will provide evidence of whether the revenues will be sufficient to cover expenditures and, even more important, whether cash inflows will be adequate to cover outflows. They will make apparent the need for increases in inflows or decreases in outflows that were not incorporated into initial projections.

Unless analysts are blessed with the power of prophecy, they are certain to be unable to foresee all events and circumstances that will affect the government in the future. Nevertheless, they must do their best to identify key risks and uncertainties and assess the ability of the government to cope with them. Indeed, one of the advantages of computer spreadsheets is that they enable analysts to examine any number of "what-if" situations. These should always include "bad-case" and even "worst-case" scenarios. Clearly, no government will have the resources to cover all potential calamities, but analysts should look for evidence that the entity is taking no imprudent risks.

SUMMARY

Governments do not typically maintain two sets of books to develop the two sets of required financial statements—the government-wide statements and the fund statements. Instead, they maintain their accounts on a fund basis. Then, at year-end, they convert the accounts from a fund (modified accrual) basis to a government-wide (consolidated, full accrual) basis. The major adjustments involve eliminating interfund transactions, adjusting capital asset and long-term debt accounts (and the related revenues and expenditures), adjusting other asset and liabilities to account for differences in basis (modified versus full accrual) and consolidating the internal service fund.

The United States is characterized by many types of governments and relationships among them. Therefore, rule-making authorities have had to develop a multidimensional framework for defining reporting entities.

According to the GASB, a primary government should include a potential component unit in its reporting entity if the unit is financially accountable to it. A potential component unit is financially accountable if the primary government can appoint a majority of its governing board and is either able to impose its will on the entity or the unit is able to provide specific financial benefits to, or impose specific financial burdens on, the primary government.

The most significant component of the introductory section of the comprehensive annual financial report (CAFR) is the letter of transmittal. This letter is analogous to a state-of-the-government address and reports on the overall fiscal health of the entity.

The financial section of the CAFR consists of the auditor's report, the management discussion and analysis (MD&A), the basic financial statements, required supplementary information, combining statements, individual statements, and schedules. The MD&A explains the basic financial statements, provides an analysis of key transactions and events, and presents information relevant to a government's financial health that is beyond the scope of the basic financial statements.

The basic financial statements consist of the two government-wide statements (the statement of net assets and statement of activities) and the fund statements for each of the three types of funds (governmental, proprietary, and fiduciary). They include also the notes to the financial statements. The governmental and proprietary fund statements present each major fund in a separate column. The fiduciary fund statements present all fiduciary funds aggregated by fund type. The nonmajor funds of each type are aggregated into a single column. The basic financial statements may also include combining statements of major component units.

Required supplementary information encompasses statistical data and information that supplements the basic financial statements. Examples include budget-to-actual comparisons, information about infrastructure condition (if the government elects not to depreciate infrastructure assets), and details of pension valuations.

Governments must present combining statements for all internal service funds because these funds do not have to be reported individually in the fund statements. They may also present combining statements for nonmajor funds that are aggregated in a single column in the fund statements as well as for nonmajor component units.

The statistical section is valuable because of its supplementary disclosures. The tables, which generally cover a period of 10 years, provide additional information or insights into the data reported in current or previous financial statements and report on economic conditions within the government's jurisdiction.

As a rule, special-purpose governments must prepare the same financial statements as general-purpose governments. However, those that engage in only a single activity have various options that permit them either to present the statements in a simpler format or to forgo the preparation of both government-wide and fund statements.

Governments have the power to tax and the obligation to provide services. Hence, the financial wherewithal of a government is tied directly to that of the citizens and businesses within its jurisdiction. The wealth of the community is a key determinant of the resources that can be commanded by the government as well as the services that are expected of it. Therefore, a comprehensive financial analysis of a government involves examining the government in the context of its economic, social, and political environment.

Analysts should first consider the current environment in which a government operates and then try to identify the critical changes that will affect the government. They should review the government's accounting and budgeting practices, looking especially for those that might have been used to obscure fiscal weaknesses. They should then calculate those financial ratios that are widely accepted as being indicative of fiscal health. These include ratios that indicate relationships not only between items reported on the basic financial statements but also between financial statement values and economic and demographic measures.

Ratios are of value mainly in that they highlight out-of-ordinary conditions and are especially useful in "benchmarking" one government against others. Nevertheless, financial analysis is very much an art rather than a mere mechanical process. Analysts must make subjective assessments of a wide range of factors, including competence of government officials, the political climate of the jurisdiction, and the nature of relations with other governments. Most important, they must be able to identify the risks faced by the government and its ability to respond to them.

KEY TERMS IN THIS CHAPTER

affiliated organization 474
blending 470
component units 470
discrete presentation 470
fiscal effort 494
fiscally dependent 470
joint venture 473
primary government 468
related organization 473

EXERCISE FOR REVIEW AND SELF-STUDY

The suburban town of Evansville experienced considerable growth in the five years between 2015 and 2020. Table 11-6 was drawn from the town's CAFR. Based on the limited information provided, you are to assess whether the town's fiscal condition has improved or deteriorated in that period. You may ignore the impact of inflation and assume that all significant revenues and expenditures are reported in the general fund.

1. Has the town's debt burden increased or decreased between 2016 and 2021?
2. Based on revenues from its own sources, has the government imposed a greater burden on its constituents? Assess the burden in terms of both population and wealth.
3. Is the town more liquid in 2021 than it was in 2016?
4. Does the town have a proportionately greater general-fund balance in 2021 than in 2016?
5. Has there been any change in the mix of revenues from more to less stable revenues?

TABLE 11-6 Selected Information from 2016 and 2021 CAFRs (All dollar amounts, including per capita amounts, in thousands)

	2016		2021	
	Actual	Per Capita	Actual	Per Capita
Population	73,706		95,818	
Total assessed value of property	$1,885,000	$25.57	$2,827,500	$29.51
Total property tax levy	21,560	0.29	32,340	0.34
General fund cash and investments	2,280	0.03	3,457	0.04
General fund total assets	18,201	0.25	19,307	0.20
General fund total liabilities	12,952	0.18	14,388	0.15
General fund nonspendable fund balance	510	0.01	307	0.00
General fund unassigned fund balance	4,739	0.06	4,612	0.05
General fund total tax revenues	36,764	0.50	56,617	0.64
General fund total expenditures	39,174	0.53	60,328	0.63
General fund debt service expenditures*	5,793	0.08	9,633	0.10
General fund revenue from own sources	38,600	0.52	56,550	0.59
General fund total revenues	40,063	0.54	61,697	0.64
General fund intergovernmental revenue	1,463	0.02	5,147	0.05
General fund public safety expenditures	13,654	0.19	24,301	0.25
General fund health and welfare expenditures	2,979	0.04	4,915	0.05
Direct debt	35,849	0.49	72,900	0.76
Overlapping debt	27,159	0.37	47,875	0.50

*Includes transfers to debt service fund

6. Has the annual burden of debt service increased?
7. Is there any evidence that the growth in population has forced a change in mix of services provided?
8. Propose at least five additional questions (the answers to which would not be obvious from the financial statements) you would raise before you would draw conclusions as to whether the fiscal condition of the town improved between 2016 and 2021.

QUESTIONS FOR REVIEW AND DISCUSSION

1. What typically are the two main adjustments required to convert the government fund balance sheet to the government-wide statement of net assets?
2. What typically are the main adjustments relating to capital assets and long-term obligations required to convert the government funds statement of revenues and expenditures to the government-wide statement of activities?
3. Per GASB standards, what is the key criterion as to whether a government should be included as a *component unit* in the reporting entity of another government?
4. How does *discrete presentation* differ from *blending*? When is each appropriate?
5. What is the primary deficiency of discrete presentation as it must be applied in government-wide statements?

6. What are the three main sections of the comprehensive annual financial report? What are the main components of the financial section?

7. What is meant by "combining statements"? Why is it especially appropriate to present combining statements for internal service funds?

8. Provide five examples of the type of information to be addressed by management in its discussion and analysis (MD&A).

9. A special-purpose government is established to operate parking garages. Will it have to prepare both government-wide and fund statements? Explain.

10. Suppose that a government has had several years of *general-fund* surpluses. Is this necessarily a sign of financial strength?

11. Notes to the financial statements and required supplementary information (RSI) must both be included in a government's CAFR. What, then, does it matter if information is provided in notes as opposed to RSI?

12. Why might analysts be concerned if a government has an unusually high ratio of intergovernmental revenues to total revenues relative to a comparable government? Why might they be concerned if the same ratio is unusually low?

13. What is meant by fiscal capacity and fiscal effort? Why are they of significance in assessing a government's financial condition?

14. Why do some analysts see the budget of a government as being of no less importance than its CAFR in assessing financial condition?

15. The GASB requires governments to identify their principal taxpayers in their CAFRs' statistical section. In what way does this information contribute to an analysis of financial condition?

16. Why are "one-shots" and other financial gimmicks of special concern to analysts?

EXERCISES

EX. 11-1

Select the *best* answer.

1. New York State has unlimited authority to control and regulate Yonkers as well as all other municipalities within its jurisdiction. Consistent with GASB standards:
   a. Both New York State and Yonkers could be considered primary governments.
   b. Only New York State could be considered a primary government.
   c. Yonkers could be considered a primary government only if the state has explicitly passed legislation ceding key fiscal controls to local governments such as Yonkers.
   d. Yonkers could be considered a primary government only if the state opts not to account for Yonkers as a component unit.

2. Which of the following is *not* a power that a municipality must have to be considered fiscally independent of other governments?
   a. To determine its budget
   b. To levy taxes and set rates
   c. To establish debt limitations
   d. To issue bonds

3. Carson City's council appoints a voting majority of the Carson City Housing Authority's governing board. Which of the following additional criteria would *not* be sufficient evidence that Carson City is financially accountable for the Carson City Housing Authority?
   a. The mayor of Carson City must approve the Housing Authority's budget.
   b. Two of the five members of the Housing Authority's governing board are also members of the Carson City council.

c. Carson City guarantees any debt incurred by the Housing Authority.
d. The Carson City council can appoint the managing director of the Housing Authority.

4. The Sierra Library District satisfies the criteria to be blended into the financial statements of Sierra County. Which of the following fund types of the two governments would *not* be combined in the blended statements?
   a. Pension trust funds
   b. General funds
   c. Permanent funds
   d. Proprietary funds

5. A primary government could "blend" its financial statements with those of a component unit as long as
   a. the governing boards of the two governments are substantively the same.
   b. there is a financial benefit/burden relationship between the two governments.
   c. the primary government provides services exclusively to the component unit.
   d. the two governments satisfy GASB Statement No. 14 criteria for "economic inseparability."

6. With respect to a *nonmajor* component unit, a government
   a. must disclose key financial data about the unit in either the financial statements themselves or in notes thereto.
   b. must, in its combining fund statements, present detailed financial statements of the unit in a separate column.
   c. may, in its government-wide statements, exclude data pertaining to the unit from its component units column.
   d. is not required to provide even summary financial data of the individual unit.

7. Which of the following is *incorrect* with respect to a joint venture?
   a. It must be reported as a component unit of each government that has an interest of 20 percent or more in the venture.
   b. It may be accounted for in a proprietary fund on the equity basis.
   c. It may be reported in a schedule of capital assets.
   d. It must be accounted for in government-wide statements on an equity basis.

8. A related organization
   a. must be reported in the combining statements of the government to which it is related, but must not be incorporated into the government-wide statements of that government.
   b. may be reported as a component unit of the reporting government to which it is related if the reporting government elects so.
   c. must be described in notes to the financial statements of the reporting government to which it is related but must not be incorporated into the financial statements of that government.
   d. may either be described in notes to the financial statements of the reporting government to which it is related or be incorporated into the financial statements of that government.

9. The James City school system, although not a separate legal entity, maintains its own set of financial records. It is administered by a board, the members of which are appointed by the James City mayor. The system receives 70 percent of its funds from city appropriations and the balance from state and federal grants. The James City council has the authority to approve the school system's budget and to veto any decisions of its administering board. James City
   a. Should account for the system as a component unit and blend its financial statements with its own
   b. Should account for the system as a component unit and report it "discretely"
   c. Should account for, and report, the system as it does other city departments
   d. Should account for the system as a component unit only if the system does not prepare its own stand-alone financial statements

10. If a primary government has several component units, none of which satisfies the criteria for blending, then in its government-wide statements it
    a. must report governmental component units in one column and business-type component units in another.
    b. must combine all component units into a single column.

c. must present each major component unit in a separate column but may combine all nonmajor component units into a single column.

d. must incorporate data of all component units, whether major or nonmajor, into one or more columns.

EX. 11-2

Select the *best* answer.

1. Which of the following should *not* be included in the introductory section of a city's CAFR?
   a. Management's discussion and analysis
   b. Letter of transmittal
   c. Government Finance Officers' certificate of achievement for excellence in financial reporting
   d. Photos of city officials

2. Which of the following should *not* be included in a city's management's discussion and analysis?
   a. Condensed financial information drawn from government-wide statements
   b. A 10-year forecast of sales tax revenues
   c. A discussion of the condition of the city's road system
   d. An explanation of the decrease during the past year in the unrestricted general-fund balance

3. A city's general-fund budget-to-actual comparisons should be included as part of a CAFR's
   a. introductory section.
   b. notes to the basic financial statements.
   c. required supplementary information.
   d. statistical section.

4. Internal service funds
   a. should be presented in the governmental fund statements in a single column.
   b. should be presented in the proprietary fund statements in a single column.
   c. should be presented in multiple columns (one for each major fund) in a separate set of fund statements.
   d. need not be reported in the fund statements.

5. Which of the following tables would be least likely to be found in the statistical section of a city's CAFR?
   a. General revenues by source—last 10 years
   b. Computation of overlapping debt
   c. Property values—last 10 years
   d. Salaries of key government officials—last 10 years

6. Which of the following would *not* be reported as required supplementary information?
   a. Management's discussion and analysis
   b. Details of pension actuarial valuations
   c. The condition of infrastructure
   d. The GFOA certificate of achievement (if earned)

7. Which of the following is least likely to be included in the CAFR of the New Bradford Water District, a public utility that reports as a business-type entity?
   a. Government-wide statement of activities
   b. Management's discussion and analysis
   c. Statement of cash flows
   d. Required supplementary information

8. A special-purpose government, such as an independent school district, that carries out multiple programs
   a. may opt to report as if it were a single-purpose government engaged in only governmental activities.
   b. may opt to report as if it were a single-purpose government engaged in only business-type activities.

c. must report as if it were a general-purpose government.
d. must report as if it were a general-purpose government, except that it need not prepare government-wide statements.

9. Silicon County is one of the fastest-growing counties in the state characterized by an influx of both industry and population. As a consequence it is likely to have a high
a. current ratio.
b. ratio of intergovernmental to total operating revenues.
c. unreserved fund balance.
d. long-term debt to total population.

10. A government's fiscal effort is best measured by the ratio of
a. revenue from own sources to total appraised value of property.
b. total revenues to total expenditures.
c. number of government employees to population.
d. intergovernmental revenues to total operating revenues.

EX. 11-3

Governments must apply the criteria of GASB Statement No. 14 in determining whether and how to include an associated entity in its reporting entity.

A city is considering whether and how it should include the following associated organizations in its reporting entity.

1. Its school system, although not a legally separate government, is managed by a school board elected by city residents. The system is financed with general tax revenues of the city, and its budget is incorporated into that of the city at large (and thereby is subject to the same approval and appropriation process as other city expenditures).
2. Its capital asset financing authority is a legally separate government that leases equipment to the city. To finance the equipment, the authority issues bonds that are guaranteed by the city and expected to be paid from the rents received from the city. The authority leases equipment exclusively to the city.
3. Its housing authority, which provides loans to low-income families within the city, is governed by a five-person board appointed by the city's mayor, and its debt is guaranteed by the city.
4. Its hospital is owned by the city but managed under contract by a private hospital management firm.
5. Its water purification plant is owned in equal shares by the city and two neighboring counties. The city's interest in the plant was acquired with resources from its water utility (enterprise) fund.
6. Its community college, a separate legal entity, is governed by a board of governors elected by city residents and has its own taxing and budgetary authority.

Based on the very limited information provided, indicate whether and how the city should report the associated entities.

EX. 11-4

Some component units are presented "discretely"; others are "blended."

A city's reporting entity includes the following component units:

1. A capital projects financing authority purchases capital assets and leases them exclusively to the city. It finances the acquisitions by issuing revenue bonds, which are payable out of the lease payments collected from the city.
2. A housing finance authority is governed by a board, the majority of whose members are appointed by the city council. The board purchases houses and leases them to low-income city residents. It finances the acquisitions by issuing revenue bonds, which are payable out of the lease payments collected from the residents.

3. A housing finance authority is governed by a board, the members of which are also members of the city council. The board purchases houses and leases them to low-income city residents. It finances the acquisitions by issuing revenue bonds, which are payable out of the lease payments collected from the residents.

4. A sanitation authority is governed by a board, the majority of whose members are appointed by the city council. The authority provides trash collection services exclusively to city residents. It finances its capital assets with bonds that are guaranteed by the city. It obtains all its revenues from user charges.
   a. Based on the limited information provided, indicate whether each of the component units described above should be presented discretely or should be blended. Justify your responses.
   b. Explain what is meant by "blending." How is the general fund of a component unit reported on the primary government's financial statements?

EX. 11-5

Ratios can help users assess fiscal condition.

The data that follow were taken from the CAFR of Chaseville, a midsized midwestern city with a population of 82,000. All dollar amounts are in thousands.

Total assessed value of property	$2,300,000
Total property tax levy	42,500
General-fund cash and investments	3,120
General-fund total assets	19,500
General-fund total liabilities	16,230
General-fund nonspendable fund balance	780
General-fund unassigned fund balance	5,789
General-fund total tax revenues	38,756
General-fund total expenditures	44,600
General-fund debt service expenditures	4,500
General-fund revenue from own sources	46,500
General-fund total revenues	48,865
General-fund intergovernmental revenue	2,003
General-fund public safety expenditures	9,321
General-fund health and welfare expenditures	4,567
Direct debt	70,000
Overlapping debt	46,486

Indicate and calculate the ratios that would best be used to compare Chaseville with similar cities as to whether

1. it is more dependent on revenues from other governments.
2. it is directing a greater share of its expenditures toward public safety.
3. it has the necessary liquid resources to be better able to meet its short-term obligations as they come due.
4. it has a greater available general-fund balance relative to revenues to meet future needs.
5. its citizens pay a higher tax rate.
6. its citizens pay more in taxes per person.
7. it is a wealthier city, in that its citizens own relatively more property.
8. it exerts greater fiscal effort.

EX. 11-6

The GASB flowchart can be used to guide decisions on whether and how to incorporate a potential component unit.

A town's library system is a legally constituted government entity. It is governed by a 10-person board. Six of the members are appointed by the town's council; the other four are selected by the other members of the board. The members serve staggered terms of three years. Once appointed, the members can be removed from office only for illegal activities.

The town provides 95 percent of the library system's resources and thereby can control the total amount spent by the system. However, the governing board adopts the system's budget, and the budget need not be approved by the town. The board also controls the day-to-day operations of the system.

Using the flowchart presented in the text, indicate whether and, if so, how the town should incorporate the library system into its own financial statements.

EX. 11-7

A government's comprehensive annual financial report (CAFR) is divided into three main sections.

The statements, schedules, tables, and other types of data that follow are found in the annual report of a typical municipality. For each of these items indicate whether it would be found in the:

- Introductory section
- Financial section
- Statistical section

If the item would be found in the financial section, then specify whether it would be included in:

- The management's discussion and analysis (MD&A)
- The basic financial statements
- Required supplementary information other than the MD&A
- Combining statements and schedules

1. A balance sheet of nonmajor special revenue funds
2. A certificate of achievement for excellence in financial reporting
3. Data on general revenues, by source, for the past 10 years
4. The letter of transmittal
5. The MD&A
6. A government-wide statement of activities
7. The total unfunded actuarial liability of its pension plan for the past three years
8. Data on property tax collections for the past 10 years
9. A statement of revenues, expenses, and changes in net assets for the city's utility fund (one of two major fund proprietary funds)
10. A statement comparing budgeted and actual revenues and expenditures for a special revenue fund
11. A statement of cash flows for a nonmajor enterprise fund

CONTINUING PROBLEM

1. Do the notes to the financial statements indicate the component units and other related entities that are included within the reporting entity? Do they indicate any units that are not included? Do they explain why these units are included or excluded?

2. How are the component units presented in the government-wide financial statements?

3. How are they presented in the fund statements?

4. Has the government entered into any joint ventures? If so, how are they reported?

5. What schedules or other information does the government report as "required supplementary information" (RSI)?

6. Does the report contain all of the statistical information presented in Table 11-3?

PROBLEMS

P. 11-1

Public housing authorities are typical of the associated entities toward which GASB Statement No. 14 is directed.

A city established a public housing authority to fund the construction of low-income residential homes within city limits. The authority is governed by a nine-person board of trustees. New trustees are nominated by the board itself, but are formally appointed by the city council. However, the city council has never rejected a board nominee. The trustees have complete responsibility for the day-to-day operations of the authority, but are required to obtain city council endorsement of the authority's annual budget and must submit audited annual financial statements to the council. The authority is permitted to issue its own debt, which is guaranteed by the federal government.

Approximately 90 percent of the authority's day-to-day operating costs are paid by the Housing and Urban Development Department (HUD, a federal agency) and 10 percent by the city.

The sources of the funds used by the authority to perform its functions are as follows:

- Authority-issued bonds (which will be repaid by tenant rents)—60 percent
- Direct federal subsidies—30 percent
- Direct city subsidies—10 percent

1. Should the city include the public housing authority in its reporting entity as a component unit per the provisions of GASB Statement No. 14? If so, how? Explain your response.

2. Suppose the same facts, except that the authority did not directly fund the construction of homes. Instead, it lent money to the city's housing department, which in turn lent the funds to home buyers. How, if at all, would your response differ?

3. Suppose, instead, that the city council also served as the authority's board of trustees. How, if at all, would your response differ? Explain.

P. 11-2

State governments face especially difficult issues of whether to incorporate their "independent" agencies in their reporting entity.

A state established the Mohansic River Power Authority to construct and operate dams and to provide electric power to rural areas. The authority, a state-owned corporation, is governed by an independent board of directors, the 10 members of which are appointed by the governor.

They can be removed only for criminal misconduct or comparable misdeeds. The board of directors has complete control over the authority's operations. The authority does not need approval to issue debt, to sign contracts, or to hire managers. Its debt is not guaranteed by the state. Per the authority's charter, any excess of revenues over expenditures is to be used for capital expansion or improvements or to offset future deficits.

Because the authority is a public utility, the rates that it charges its customers must be approved by the state's public utility commission. The public utility commission considers the authority's request for rate adjustments just as if the authority were a private utility.

1. Do you believe that the state should include the authority in its reporting entity? If so, how? Justify your response, with reference to the GASB criteria. (This problem is based on an actual situation; there is no clear-cut solution.)

2. Suppose, instead, that the governor could remove members of the board at will. Would your answer be the same? Explain.

3. Suppose the members can serve indefinitely on the board, subject to annual reappointment by the governor. Would your answer be the same? Explain.

P. 11-3

Discrete presentation, unlike blending, may combine two or more entities into a single column.

Hawkins Township has two component units that it is required to include in its reporting entity. The first, a housing authority, maintains two funds: a general fund and a special revenue fund. The second, a transportation authority, has but one fund: an enterprise fund. The township itself has only a general fund.

The fund balance sheets, in highly condensed form, of all three entities are shown here (in millions). Also presented, as appropriate, are capital assets and long-term obligations that are not recognized on the fund statements because the statements are on a modified accrual basis.

Hawkins Township

	General Fund	Capital Assets and Long-Term Obligations
Cash and investments	$800	
Capital assets		$140
Less: accumulated depreciation		(40)
Net capital assets		$100
Total assets	$800	$100
Long-term obligations		$ 30
Fund balance	$800	
Total long-term obligations and fund balances	$800	$ 30

Transportation Authority

Cash and investments	$ 50
Capital assets	800
Less: accumulated depreciation	200
Net capital assets	600
Total assets	$650
Long-term obligations	$200
Fund balance	$450
Total long-term obligations and fund balance	$650

Housing Authority

	General Fund	Special Revenue Fund	Capital Assets and Long-Term Obligations
Cash and investments	$10	$5	
Capital assets			$45
Less: accumulated depreciation			20
Net capital assets			$25
Total assets	$10	$5	$25
Long-term obligations			$ 5
Fund balance	$10	$5	
Total long-term obligations and fund balance	$10	$5	$ 5

1. Assume that both component units qualify for discrete presentation. On its government-wide statements, the township elects to combine the two units into a single column.
   a. Prepare a government-wide statement of net assets (on a full accrual basis) that presents both the township and its component units.
   b. Comment on the significance of the column in which the two component units are presented.

2. Suppose instead that the town is required to blend the two component units.
   a. Prepare a government-wide statement of net assets. Be sure to show the transportation authority as a business-type activity.
   b. If the township were to prepare fund statements, how would it report the housing authority's special revenue fund? How would it report its general fund?

P. 11-4

Citizens of wealthier cities may not only have a lighter tax burden, but also receive more intergovernmental assistance.

The following data were drawn from the CAFRs of two northern Virginia cities (all dollar amounts are in thousands):

	Fairfax	Manassas
Population	20,200	27,856
Value of taxable property	$1,933,472	$1,948,337
Property tax levy	$18,664	$24,534
Total general-fund revenues	$38,397	$36,092
General-fund tax revenues	$31,861	$29,706
Intergovernmental revenues	$5,050	$2,351

1. Based on the limited data provided, which city has the greater resources on which to draw?

2. Which city imposes the greater tax burden on its population based on
   a. Per capita total general-fund taxes?
   b. Per capita property taxes?
   c. Tax rate (i.e., property taxes as a percent of property value)?

3. Which city receives a greater amount of assistance from other governments
   a. As a percentage of its total general-fund revenues?
   b. Per capita?

P. 11-5

Environmental regulators see the financial forests, but not the trees.

The U.S. Environmental Protection Agency (EPA) requires owners of municipal solid waste landfills to demonstrate that they are financially capable of satisfying the costs of closing and subsequently caring for the landfills that they operate. Per EPA regulations, one way for a local government to demonstrate financial capability is by satisfying certain financial standards. In particular, a government must meet the following four ratio targets:

- Cash plus marketable securities to total expenditures must be greater than or equal to 0.05
- Annual debt service to total expenditures must be less than or equal to 0.20
- Long-term debt issued and outstanding to capital expenditures must be less than or equal to 2.00
- Current cost estimates for closure, postclosure, corrective action to total revenue must be less than or equal to 0.43

The regulations provide no interpretative guidance except to imply that the ratios are to be based on financial statements prepared in accordance with generally accepted accounting principles.

Suppose you are engaged as a consultant to a state agency that has to administer the regulations. In the course of examining the evidence of financial capability supplied by municipal landfill operators, state officials raised the following questions about how the ratios should be calculated:

1. Should the ratios be based only on a government's general fund, or should they encompass funds in addition to the general fund?

2. Assuming the ratios should not be based exclusively on the general fund, should they include proprietary funds (i.e., does use of the term *expenditures* imply that expenses should be excluded)?

3. Should the ratios incorporate restricted as well as unrestricted funds?

4. Should capital expenditures include only those for the year in question, or an average of several years?
   a. Propose answers to these questions that you believe are most consistent with the EPA's objective of ensuring financial capability. For each question, recommend an appropriate policy, justify it, and cite any potential limitations.
   b. Suggest at least three additional questions that you believe need to be addressed.

P. 11-6

Changes in mix of revenues and expenditures must be interpreted with care.

The data that follow were drawn from the city of Boulder, Colorado's CAFR. Dates have been changed. They are from two statistical-section schedules showing the mix of revenue and expenditures for a 10-year period. They include amounts only from the general fund, special revenue funds, and debt service funds.

	2020	2021
	(amounts in thousands)	
Revenues		
Sales and use taxes	$ 97,397	$104,136
General property taxes	29,474	29,434
Other taxes	20,278	21,184
Charges for services	27,030	22,670
Intergovernmental	16,420	13,348
Proceeds from bonds and notes	54,830	
Other	20,660	21,473
Total revenues	$266,089	$212,245
Expenditures		
General government and administration	$ 27,717	$ 30,185
Public safety	47,825	48,202
Public works	22,178	27,896
Housing and human services	13,384	20,226
Culture and recreation	25,677	28,089
Capital outlay	29,111	19,218
Debt service	13,574	16,375
Other	16,425	27,180
Total expenditures	$195,891	$217,371

1. As a consultant for a citizens' association, you have been asked to determine whether there have been significant changes in the way the city acquires and spends its resources. Prepare a schedule in which you compare the mix of revenues and of expenditures of 2020 with that of 2021. Note and comment on any items that might distort a straightforward comparison of revenues and expenditures.

2. Comment on any changes between the two years that you consider significant.
3. Expenditures for debt service increased significantly. What are the most likely reasons for the increase? Is it necessarily a sign of increased financial stress?

P. 11-7

Strong financial statements are not necessarily indicative of strong financial condition.

The following information was taken from the CAFRs of two cities of approximately the same size in the same state.

	Riverside	Lakeview
	(dollar amounts in thousands)	
Population	92,000	96,000
Number of employees	1,050	1,420
Total operating revenues	$120,000	$170,000
Property tax levy	83,000	102,000
Total operating expenditures	112,000	174,000
Cash, investments and receivables	27,000	15,000
Current liabilities	9,000	12,000
Unassigned general-fund balance	7,000	1,000
General obligation debt	21,000	32,000
Total appraised value of property	965,000	1,620,000

1. Compare the financial condition of the two cities based on the following indicators:
   a. Per capita operating expenditures
   b. Per capita general obligation debt
   c. Operating surplus (deficit)
   d. Liquid assets/current liabilities
   e. Unassigned general-fund balance/total operating revenues
   f. Per capita number of employees
2. Compare the financial condition of the two cities based on the following additional measures:
   a. Operating revenue/total appraised value of property
   b. Property taxes/total appraised value of property
   c. Per capita total appraised value of property
3. What conclusions can be drawn from the two sets of measures? Comment on the apparent discrepancy between them.

P. 11-8

Qualitative factors may be as important as quantitative factors in assessing a government's fiscal health.

You are a CPA in charge of auditing a midsize school district. You recognize that the risk of financial failure is dependent as much on factors not reported in the basic financial statements as on factors that are reported. Accordingly, you conduct a comprehensive analysis of the district. Some of your findings are summarized here. For each, indicate how it might affect the ability of the district to service its outstanding debt and provide the services that its constituents expect.

1. Owing to an influx of new high-tech firms into a nearby community (which is not within the jurisdiction of the school district), the population within the district is increasing by approximately 8 percent per year. Most of the new arrivals are young engineers and other professionals.
2. A developer is constructing a senior citizens' retirement village within the jurisdiction of the school district. The village is expected to increase both the district's population and its land value by approximately 4 percent.

3. During the year, the district changed the pay date of its employees. Previously employees were paid on the last day of the month; now they will be paid on the first day of the following month.

4. The district's largest taxpayer, representing 10 percent of its property tax revenues, manufactures blue jeans and other clothing made of denim.

5. The district's superintendent recently resigned in the wake of charges that he falsified student scores on state-wide achievement tests.

6. School district elections are hotly contested. The present school board is composed of three members who are committed to "traditional" educational methods and four who are considered "progressives." Board meetings are almost always contentious.

7. Voters of the county in which the school district is located recently approved the largest general obligation bond issue in the county's history.

8. One of two candidates for governor of the state in which the school district is located is a strong advocate of a school voucher plan. The plan would provide financial assistance to students who elect to attend private schools.

P. 11-9

One of the challenges of financial analysis in government is that it is not always obvious whether an increase in a financial ratio is a sign of increasing or decreasing fiscal strength.

Explain the significance of each of the following ratios. For each of the ratios indicate whether an increase can be interpreted as a sign of (1) increasing or (2) decreasing fiscal strength. Where appropriate, show how an increase in the ratio can be interpreted as a sign of either. Explain and justify your response.

1. Cash, short-term investments, and receivables/Current liabilities
2. Revenue from own sources/Median family income
3. Number of employees/Population
4. Property tax revenues/Total operating revenues
5. Nondiscretionary expenditures/Total expenditures
6. Unassigned general-fund balance/Total operating revenues
7. Intergovernmental revenues/Total operating revenues
8. Expenditures for public safety/Total expenditures

P. 11-10

Financial analysis of governments is not a static tool; rather, it changes as potential issues arise that may be of concern to analysts. Debt analysis, for example, traditionally focused on financial liabilities such as bonds and notes. More recently, other significant liabilities such as unfunded employee pensions and retiree health benefits are of increased concern.

Return to the data in P. 11-7 on Riverside and Lakeview. Suppose Riverside has unfunded pension liabilities of $15 million and another $15 million in retiree health care liabilities. By way of contrast, Lakeview has unfunded pension liabilities of $4 million, and $13 million in retiree health care liabilities. Incorporate this information into the cities' debt analyses.

1. How does including these liabilities alter your initial analysis?
2. What conclusions can you draw about the cities' unfunded pension and retiree health care liabilities?

QUESTIONS FOR RESEARCH, ANALYSIS, AND DISCUSSION

1. Many critics of GASB Statement No. 14 and its amendment, GASB Statement No. 39, believe that the standards cast too wide a net—that it requires governments to include in their reporting entity organizations over which the primary government has little control. For example, suppose that a city's mayor appoints the majority of the governing board of an authority but that the city has only minimal ability to influence the decisions of that board. As long as the city gets some financial benefit from the authority or has some burden of responsibility for it, it must include the authority in its reporting entity. Do you agree with the critics? Explain.

2. Owing to severe fiscal problems as well as a pattern of management incompetence and corruption, a city is placed under the control of a special authority established by the state. The authority has the power to impose its will on virtually all day-to-day management and fiscal decisions of the city. Should the city retain its status as a primary government, or should it be a component unit of the authority?

3. Newville City accounts for and reports on the Newville Housing Authority as a discretely presented component unit. It engages in numerous transactions with the housing authority (e.g., providing grants and occasionally buying or selling properties). How should the city account for these transactions (e.g., as it would with an outside entity or as intragovernmental transfers)?

4. The bylaws of the Wells City Downtown Development Authority state that of the seven members of its governing board, two must be members of the Wells City Council, one must be a member of the City Zoning Board, and one must be a member of the City Planning Commission. Does this provision imply that the city appoints a majority of the Development Authority's governing board?

SOLUTION TO EXERCISE FOR REVIEW AND SELF-STUDY

1. As measured by both per capita direct debt (discussed in Chapter 8) and percentage of total assessed value of property, the debt burden increased substantially. Per capita direct debt increased from $0.49 to $0.76 (all dollar amounts in thousands). Direct debt as a percentage of total assessed value of property increased from

	2016	2021
Direct debt	$ 35,849	$ 72,900
Total appraised value of property	1,885,000	2,827,500
Direct debt as a percentage of appraised value of property	1.90%	2.58%

Similarly, overlapping debt also increased both per capita and as a percentage of assessed value of property.

1. Based on population, the government is imposing a somewhat greater revenue burden on its constituents in 2021 than in 2016. Per capita revenue from own sources increased from $0.52 to $0.59. Relative to wealth (i.e., assessed value of property), however, it is imposing a slightly lighter burden

	2016	2021
Total revenue from own sources	$ 38,600	$ 56,550
Total appraised value of property	1,885,000	2,827,500
Revenue from own sources as a percentage of appraised value of property	2.05%	2.00%

2. Liquidity can be measured by the ratio of cash and investments to current liabilities. Based on liabilities of the general fund only (all of which can be assumed to be current), the town is more liquid in 2021 than it was in 2016. This ratio, however, tends to be volatile, so that more than two years of data need to be taken into account.

	2016	2021
General-fund cash and investments	$ 2,280	$ 3,457
General fund, total liabilities	12,952	14,388
Cash and investments as a percentage of general-fund liabilities	17.60%	24.03%

3. Based on a comparison of unassigned general-fund balance to total general-fund revenues, the town's reserves have been diminished:

	2016	2021
General-fund unassigned fund balance	$ 4,739	$ 4,612
General fund, total revenues	40,063	61,697
General-fund unassigned fund balance as a percentage of general-fund revenues	11.83%	7.48%

4. Property taxes are often considered a stable form of revenue. The percentage of revenue received from property taxes has remained approximately the same:

	2016	2021
Total property tax levy	$ 21,560	$ 32,340
General fund, total revenues	40,063	61,697
Property tax levy as a percentage of total general-fund revenues	53.82%	52.42%

However, intergovernmental revenues, generally considered more subject to risk, increased:

	2016	2021
General-fund intergovernmental revenue	$ 1,463	$ 5,147
General fund, total revenues	40,063	61,697
General-fund intergovernmental revenue as a percentage of total general-fund revenues	3.65%	8.34%

5. The per capita burden of debt service has increased from $0.08 to $0.10, but debt service as a percentage of general-fund expenditures has increased only slightly:

	2016	2021
Total debt service expenditures	$ 5,793	$ 9,633
Total general-fund expenditures	39,174	60,328
Debt service as a percentage of total general-fund expenditures	14.79%	15.97%

6. Between 2016 and 2021, expenditures for public safety increased substantially relative to other expenditures, whereas those for health and welfare increased slightly.

	2016	2021
Public safety expenditures	$ 13,654	$ 24,301
Total general-fund expenditures	39,174	60,328
Public safety expenditures as a percentage of total general-fund expenditures	34.85%	40.28%
Health and welfare expenditures	$ 2,979	$ 4,915
Total general-fund expenditures	39,174	60,328
Health and welfare expenditures as a percentage of total general-fund expenditures	7.60%	8.15%

7. Additional questions to be raised include the following:
   - **a.** Did the revenues or expenditures of either year include substantial "one-shot" transactions?
   - **b.** What changes were there in the mix of industries on which the town relies for its revenues?
   - **c.** What changes were there in the characteristics of the population (e.g., in age, income, and educational distribution)?
   - **d.** What changes were there in per capita income?
   - **e.** What is the condition of the town's infrastructure? Is it adequate for the future?
   - **f.** What are the town's forecasts of revenue and expenditures for the next five years?
   - **g.** How do the ratios and forecasts of this city compare with those of similar cities?

CHAPTER 12

Not-for-Profit Organizations

LEARNING OBJECTIVES

After studying this chapter you should understand:

- Which standard-setting authorities are responsible for not-for-profit organizations
- How and why the financial statements of not-for-profits divide all resources into two categories (without donor restrictions and with donor restrictions) based on donor stipulations
- What endowments are and how they are accounted for
- How not-for-profits report cash flows
- How contributions are distinguished from exchange transactions
- The general rules governing the recognition of contributions
- How pledges, both with and without donor restrictions, are accounted for
- When contributions of services should be recognized as revenue
- When collection items should be recognized as revenue
- The special issues pertaining to conditional promises to give
- How pass-through contributions are accounted for
- How and when gains and losses on investments should be recognized
- How capital assets should be depreciated and reported
- The special problems of determining the cost of fund-raising activities
- What factors should be taken into account in assessing the financial condition of not-for-profits

Governments and not-for-profit organizations confront similar accounting and reporting issues. However, they do not necessarily resolve them alike. Differences in standards can be partly explained—and indeed, justified—by differences in the entities' characteristics and resultant differences in constituents' information needs. For example, not-for-profits lack the authority of law to generate revenues, and they have greater flexibility in administering their budgets. Differences in standards may also be attributed to dissimilarities in the composition and perspectives of the standard-setting authorities. This chapter will address accounting and reporting issues that affect not-for-profits in general. The next two chapters will consider the issues facing two types of specialized entities—colleges and universities and hospitals and other health care institutions.

WHO'S IN CHARGE?

Whereas the Governmental Accounting Standards Board (GASB) has standard-setting jurisdiction over all state and local governments and other governmental entities, the Financial Accounting Standards Board (FASB) has jurisdiction over all other nonbusiness entities except the federal government. As a consequence, even similar types of organizations may fall within the province of different boards. A state university or city hospital would be under the authority of the GASB, whereas a private university or hospital would be under the jurisdiction of the FASB.

In addition, the American Institute of Certified Public Accountants (AICPA) has issued (and periodically updated) two "audit" guides[1] that summarize the FASB standards and provide guidance on issues not specifically addressed by those standards:

1. ***Health Care Entities*** covers hospitals, clinics, health maintenance organizations, nursing homes, and home health care organizations.
2. ***Not-for-profit Entities*** covers all other not-for-profits, including colleges and universities.

As will be evident in this chapter, the accounting practices of not-for-profits are more compatible with those of businesses than with those of governments. Like their GASB counterparts, the FASB and AICPA pronouncements emphasize the superiority of the accrual basis over the cash basis of accounting, although they are far less indulgent of modifications of and exceptions to the accrual basis.

External reporting is entirely on the full accrual basis. Irrespective of how not-for-profits maintain their records for purposes of internal management, the modified accrual basis has no place in their publicly issued statements. As a consequence, not-for-profits do not distinguish between expenses and expenditures. They have only expenses.

WHAT SHOULD BE THE FORM AND CONTENT OF FINANCIAL STATEMENTS?

As emphasized in Chapter 2, not-for-profits, like governments, may account for their resources in funds, each of which is a separate accounting entity. As in governments, most entities maintain an operating (or general) fund that includes resources not restricted by donors, as well as one or more restricted funds. Accordingly, most not-for-profits will make the journal entries illustrated in this chapter in the individual funds. In this chapter, we will make them only in a broad category of fund types.

The FASB is not concerned with the specific funds maintained by not-for-profits. Instead, it is interested in how entities report their overall financial position and results of operations. A key issue, therefore, is whether not-for-profits should display separately each of the funds, consolidate them into single-column presentation, or aggregate the funds in a way that would combine groups of funds. Although this chapter directs considerable attention to revenue and expense recognition, it will soon become apparent that how funds are combined affects how and when certain types of revenues and expenses are reported.

REPORTING ASSETS AND LIABILITIES

In 1993 the FASB issued Statement No. 117, *Financial Statements of Not-for-Profit Organizations*, which established standards for the form and content of financial statements.[2] The statement provides that not-for-profits must issue three primary financial statements:

- A statement of financial position (balance sheet)
- A statement of activities
- A statement of cash flows

[1] AICPA Audit and Accounting Guide, *Not-for-Profit Entities*, updated March 1, 2017, and AICPA Audit and Accounting Guide, *Health Care Entities, Organizations*, September 2017.
[2] FASB ASC 958-205-45.

Beginning after December 2017, FASB Accounting Standards Update (ASU) No. 2016-14 requires all not-for-profits to also report functional expenses, whereas only voluntary health and welfare organizations were required in the past. This information must be disclosed in one location, such as on the activity statement, in the notes to the financial statements as a separate schedule, or as a separate financial statement (a functional expense statement).

The new FASB standards also require not-for-profits to classify their net assets into two categories based on the existence or absence of *donor-imposed* restrictions:

- Net assets without donor restrictions
- Net assets with donor restrictions. Donor restricted resources may include those intended for specific purposes, in specific periods, when specified events have occurred, and endowments that must remain permanently intact with only earnings expended.

The focus is on donor-mandated restrictions because such restrictions impose special responsibilities on management to ensure that the resources are used in accordance with donor wishes. They are therefore of special relevance to a primary group of statement users. Not-for-profits may disclose additional information within these two categories of restrictiveness, such as those restricted to program or purpose and those restricted to endowment.

Donor restricted net assets can take several forms. Resources that must be used for research, for specific programs, or for acquisition of plant and equipment would be restricted as to *purpose* until they are expended. The resources would be released from the restriction when the organization incurred expenses that satisfied the donor's stipulations. A term endowment would be temporarily restricted as to *time*. A **term endowment** is a gift from which only the income (dividends, interest, or gains) is available for expenditure for a specified period of time. Once the period of time has expired, then the principal of the gift is also available for expenditure. Pledges that will not be received until future periods may also be seen as subject to time restrictions. They are unavailable for expenditure until then. An annuity would be restricted pending the occurrence of a *specified event*. An **annuity** is a gift that provides the donor with income until his or her death. Upon death, the balance of the gift reverts to the donee (i.e., the not-for-profit organization) and used as the donor intended (i.e., with restrictions or without).

Even assets classified as without donor restrictions are not necessarily free of all restrictions—only those imposed by *donors*. Restrictions imposed by the organization's members, by its own governing board, or by outside parties other than donors—such as bondholders and regulatory authorities—do not affect whether net assets should be classified as with restrictions or without restrictions.

ASU 2016-14 requires that not-for-profits present five totals on the statement of financial position: total assets, total liabilities, total net assets, total net assets without donor restrictions, and total net assets with donor restrictions. Individual funds are not shown on the statement of net position, but instead a consolidation of all funds a not-for-profit might use for internal control purposes. Information about the nature and amount of restrictions may be shown on the face of the statement of financial position, but must be disclosed in notes to the financial statements. If shown on the face of the statement of financial position, separate line items may be added to the two categories of restricted net assets (e.g., "restricted for acquisition of plant" or "restricted for scholarships"). As another (but not the only other) possibility, the two categories of assets may be presented in two separate columns, with specific resources as well as net assets assigned to each of the two categories.

The FASB update also sought to increase disclosures about a not-for-profit's liquidity for financial statement users. Specifically, ASU No. 2016-14 helps users by requiring disclosures about liquidity and the availability of restricted resources to fund an organization's "general expenditures." Not-for-profits must disclose quantitative information about the availability of their financial assets to meet cash needs for general expenditures over the next fiscal year. As per FASB ASC 958-210-50-1A, financial asset availability may be influenced by its nature, internal

IN PRACTICE

When a not-for-profit is offered a contribution that is restricted by a donor in some way, the board and management of the not-for-profit must decide if accepting the contribution is in the best interests of the organization. For example, if a donor offered money for a not-for-profit to construct or purchase a building, the not-for-profit might have concerns about future maintenance costs that would need to be funded out of future operating budgets. Sometimes, not-for-profits even require that contributions for fixed asset acquisitions also come with endowments (discussed later) to help cover these costs.

The Barry-Lawrence Library system in Missouri was seeking contributions to construct a new building to replace its aging and outdated existing one. An anonymous donor offered to contribute the acquisition cost to the library, but wanted the organization to move locations. After contemplating the donor's offer, the board turned down the multimillion dollar restricted gift because of concerns around moving the library's location.

Based on "Three Million? No Thank You! A Restricted Gift is Declined." By Ruth McCambridge. Nonprofit Quarterly. March 14, 2018.

limits placed on the asset by a governing board's decisions, or external limits imposed by a donor, contract, or law. In addition, not-for-profits are now required to disclose qualitative information about how the organization managed its liquidity to ensure general expenditures are met over the next fiscal year.

The improved liquidity disclosures include a reconciliation of a not-for-profit's financial assets as of the financial statement date with its financial assets available to meet cash needs for general expenditures within 12 months. The intent of this disclosure is to clarify that some financial assets listed on the statement of financial position may be unavailable for consumption during the year, either because of internal or external reasons. A disclosure might look like the following:

The following is an accounting of the organization's financial assets as of the date of the statement of financial position. The financial assets are adjusted because some are unavailable for general use owing to donor-imposed restrictions, board decisions, and contractual relationships.

Financial assets, at fiscal year end	$100,000
Less those unavailable for general expenditures within one year, due to:	
Donor-imposed restrictions:	
Restricted by donor with purpose restrictions	(10,000)
Board designations:	
Quasi-endowment fund	(20,000)
Liquidity reserve set aside account	(2,000)
Financial assets available to meet cash needs for general expenditures within one year	$ 68,000

As an alternative disclosure, a not-for-profit might simply list the assets that are cash, near cash, or expected to be converted into cash in the next fiscal year. Such a disclosure would look similar to the one above, but merely list the accounts and amounts.

For not-for-profits (unlike governments), there is little ambiguity as to what constitutes a current asset or liability: the definitions of business accounting dictate these. As per Chapter 3a of AICPA's *Accounting Research Bulletin* 43, current assets are resources reasonably expected to be realized in cash or sold or consumed during the normal operating cycle of the business. Current liabilities are obligations whose liquidation is expected to require the use of existing resources classified as current assets, or the creation of other current liabilities. Table 12-1 presents the statement of financial position of the American Health Association, a fictional voluntary health and welfare organization.

WHAT IS AN ENDOWMENT?

Some not-for-profits hold endowments, which are resources contributed by donors in which the principal is to be held in perpetuity to generate earnings that the not-for-profit may expend on operations or services. Some, however, referred to as term endowments, permit the principal to be expended after a specified number of years. Depending on the wishes of the donor, the income from an endowment may be either restricted for a specific purpose or without restriction. The following are but a few examples of endowments that are maintained by not-for-profits:

- University endowments may take the form of "chairs" or "professorships." Assigned to specific faculty members, they provide salary supplements and support teaching and research. Other types of endowments help to finance scholarships, teaching awards, research, or general operations.
- Private foundations such as the Ford and Carnegie Foundations are, in essence, endowment funds. With billions of dollars in assets, they promote a wide array of educational, social welfare, and scientific activities.
- Private primary and secondary schools sometimes maintain endowments to provide ongoing support for specific purposes, such as financial aid for needy students, or specific activities, such as extracurricular programs.
- Churches, synagogues, and comparable religious organizations maintain endowments to sponsor lectures, music programs, or youth activities.

Many not-for-profits used to simply expend interest, dividends, or other cash revenues generated from these endowments. As equity values surged during the 1990s and 2000s, however, many also consumed unrealized gains on the investments. Following the financial market retrenchments in 2007–2008, many not-for-profit endowments were below their original value of contributions (called "historic dollar value" (HDV)). As such, many not-for-profits that were endowed were unable to spend from their endowed resources because of this restriction on expending resources from "underwater endowments." The Uniform Prudent Management of Institutional Funds Act ("UPMIFA"), which was adopted by 49 states by 2012, changed endowment management guidance and permitted spending by underwater endowments as long as the rate of spending perserved the purchasing power of the endowments over time.

ASU No. 2016-14 requires that underwater endowments—those in which the fair-market values of the assets are less than the original contributed amount—show this accumulated deficit under net assets with donor restrictions; prior FASB standards required this accumulated deficit under unrestricted (without donor restrictions) net assets. In addition, not-for-profits must disclose aggregate amounts of original donor gifts required to be maintained, endowment spending policies, and discussion of any action taken resulting from the endowment being underwater.

REPORTING REVENUES AND EXPENSES

FASB adopted ASU No. 2014-09 which helped move US GAAP towards convergence with international accounting standards. Whereas not-for-profit revenue recognition had been based on transactions, the new standard which was implemented in 2017 uses a principles-based approach to revenue recognition. Importantly, contributions from donors are outside the scope of FASB ASC 606.[3] As such, contributions with donor restrictions attached do not alter the timing of revenue recognition.

[3] See *Revenue Recognition*, AICPA Audit & Accounting Guide, January 2018, Paragraph 8.7.01.

TABLE 12-1 Voluntary Health and Welfare Organization

American Health Association, Local Affiliate
Statement of Financial Position as of June 30, 2020

	Without Donor Restrictions	With Donor Restrictions	Total
Assets			
Current assets			
Cash and cash equivalents	$ 806,383	$ —	$ 806,383
Short-term investments	8,884,309	288,073	9,172,382
Accrued investment income	192,427	—	192,427
Accounts receivable			—
Federated and nonfederated	—	694,382	694,382
National center	20,382	—	20,382
Bequest receivable	—	286,000	286,000
Pledges	84,601	19,000	103,601
Other	70,719	—	70,719
Educational and campaign material inventory	250,670	—	250,670
Prepaid expenses	79,410	—	79,410
Total current assets	$10,388,901	$ 1,287,455	$11,676,356
Noncurrent assets			
Accounts receivable			
Pledges, net of discount of $1,000	$ —	$ 19,000	$ 19,000
Charitable gift annuity—national center	40,500	—	40,500
Long-term investments	6,622,538	2,715,315	9,337,853
Beneficial interest in perpetual trust	—	2,767,900	2,767,900
Contributions receivable from charitable remainder trust	—	4,963,216	4,963,216
Land, buildings, and equipment, at cost			—
Less accumulated depreciation of $2,344,393	3,921,690	—	3,921,690
Total noncurrent assets	$10,584,728	$10,465,431	$21,050,159
Total assets	$20,973,629	$11,752,886	$32,726,515
Liabilities and net assets			
Current liabilities			
Payable to the national center			
campaign share	$ 3,181,641	$ 414,241	$ 3,595,882
purchased material	137,781	—	137,781
Accounts payable and accrued expenses	585,896	—	585,896
Research awards payable within one year	3,315,845	—	3,315,845
Total current liabilities	$ 7,221,163	$ 414,241	$ 7,635,404

(Continues)

TABLE 12-1 **Voluntary Health and Welfare Organization** *(Continued)*

American Health Association, Local Affiliate
Statement of Financial Position as of June 30, 2020

	Without Donor Restrictions	With Donor Restrictions	Total
Noncurrent liabilities			
Payable to the national center campaign share		$ 1,240,804	$ 1,240,804
Annuity obligation	19,640	—	19,640
Research awards payable after one year, net of discount of $50,000	1,983,172	—	1,983,172
Post retirement benefit obligation	$ 932,246	—	$ 932,246
Total noncurrent liabilities	$ 2,935,058	$ 1,240,804	$ 4,175,862
Total liabilities	$10,156,221	$ 1,655,045	$11,811,266
Net assets			
Without donor restrictions			
Net investment in land, building, and equipment	$ 3,921,690	$ —	$ 3,921,690
Designated by the governing board for programs and operations for the ensuing fiscal year	6,697,513	—	6,697,513
Research designated to future years	177,345	—	177,345
Charitable gift annuity—national center	20,860	—	20,860
With donor restrictions			—
Land, buildings, and equipment		168,953	168,953
Research		232,759	232,759
Public health education		354,341	354,341
Community services		467,856	467,856
Charitable remainder trust		3,722,412	3,722,412
Endowment Funds		2,383,620	2,383,620
Beneficial interest in perpetual trust		2,767,900	2,767,900
Total net assets	10,817,408	10,097,841	20,915,249
Total liabilities and net assets	$20,973,629	$11,752,886	$32,726,515

Essentially, a revenue is recognized when a not-for-profit satisfies a performance obligation to a customer when transferring a promised good or service. Revenue recognition is based on five steps:

1. Identifying the contract with the customer. A contract is an agreement between at least two parties that creates enforceable rights and obligations.
2. Identify the performance obligation of the contract. A performance obligation is a contracted promise to transfer a good or service to the customer. For example, a college might have a performance obligation to an incoming student to provide housing for the upcoming academic year.

3. Determine the transaction price. This is the amount the not-for-profit expects to receive for transferring the good or service.
4. Allocate this price to the contract's performance obligation. If the performance obligation is multifaceted, the price must be allocated to each separately.
5. Recognize revenue when the not-for-profit meets a performance obligation. For example, a college would recognize revenues from fees paid by students for housing over the course of the academic year as the housing is used by the students. However, the college would recognize upon receipt a contribution without restrictions made by an alumna.

Revenues and expenses are reported in a **statement of activities**. Like the statement of financial position, the statement of activities should focus on the organization as a whole, rather than on individual funds. Further, it should report the changes in each of the two categories of net assets. The FASB specifies that the statement of activities must break out gains and losses recognized on investments and other assets from revenues and expenses, but otherwise leaves the form and content of the statement to the individual organization. Therefore, as in the statement of financial position, organizations can present the information with respect to the two categories of net assets in separate sections of the statement (several rows each for the different categories) or in two separate columns.

As would be expected, the statement instructs that revenues be reported as increases in one of the two categories of net assets, depending on donor-imposed restrictions. Similar to the balance sheet, individual not-for-profit organizations can report more details within these two categories (e.g., program restrictions separate from endowment under revenues with donor restrictions). However, in a controversial decision, the Board concluded that *all expenses should be reported as decreases in net assets without donor restrictions*. The Board reasoned that donors restrict only how the contributed resources may be used. They do not control expenses. "Expenses result from the decisions of an organization's managers about the activities to be carried out, and how and when particular resources are to be used," it explained. In other words, donors do not determine the activities in which an organization engages. Their control is limited to dictating the activities for which their contributions will be used to pay.

As a consequence of this requirement, a not-for-profit must make two sets of journal entries whenever it spends restricted resources. The first, in a restricted fund, records the decrease in cash or other assets and the release of the restrictions (a decrease in donor-restricted net assets); the second, in a fund without donor restrictions, records the expense and the release of the restriction. This entry has no effect on net assets without donor restrictions, inasmuch as it consists of an expense (a debit) offset by the bookkeeping equivalent of a transfer-in (a credit).

The Board permits an important exception to the requirement that all restricted contributions be classified on receipt as restricted. It gives not-for-profits the option of reporting restricted contributions as without restriction if the restriction is satisfied and the performance obligation is met in the same period as the contribution is made. Table 12-2 presents the statement of activities of the American Health Association.

To fulfill its stated goal, financial reporting should provide information on an organization's service efforts (see excerpts from the statement of objectives in Table 1-4 in Chapter 1). The FASB mandates that either the statement of activities or the accompanying notes report expenses by *function*—that is, by program services or supporting activities. As a result of this requirement, the statement indicates to users not only the activities on which the organization is spending its resources, but also more important, the proportion of

Example

Reporting Revenues and Expenses

The Professional Accountants' Association receives a $50,000 grant to promote "truth in budgeting" among state and local governments. In the following year it spends the funds for the stipulated purpose.

Inasmuch as the contribution is restricted as to purpose, it would be recorded in a fund with donor restrictions and recognized as revenue even with the accompanying restriction (recall that donor restrictions do not alter revenue recognition):

Cash	$50,000	
Revenue from contributions		$50,000

To record the receipt of a purpose-restricted contribution (donor-restricted fund)

When, in the following year, the association expends the resources for the stipulated purpose and meets the contract's performance obligation, it would account for the reduction in cash as "net assets released from restriction." Thus:

Net assets released from restriction	$50,000	
Cash		$50,000

To record the disbursement of cash in satisfaction of contributor restrictions (donor-restricted fund)

"Net assets released from restriction" is comparable to "other financing sources (or uses)," such as nonreciprocal transfers. It would be reported in the statement of activities as negative revenue (a negative revenue rather than an expense because, as indicated, restricted funds do not report expenses).

At the same time, a fund without donor restriction would recognize the expense and a corresponding increase in net assets:

Program expense	$50,000	
Net assets released from restriction		$50,000

To record an expense and the release of contributor restrictions (fund without donor restriction)

To be sure, the Board's approach adds complexity to the financial reporting process. However, it permits not-for-profits to report all expenses in a single column and thereby make clear the full cost of organizational operations.

resources being directed toward substantive—as opposed to administrative—undertakings. Not-for-profits must also now disclose how costs are allocated between programs and supporting activities.

In addition, all not-for-profits must also report expenses by "natural" (i.e., object) classification, such as salaries, rent, electricity, and interest. The dual classification should be presented in matrix form in a separate financial statement.

Table 12-3 illustrates the American Health Association's Statement of Functional Expenses. The Association, like almost all not-for-profits that present their expenses in both natural and functional classifications, had to allocate various natural expenses to the various programs (functions). Thus, for example, the association may have carried out all its programs in the same building and sometimes with common personnel. Therefore, it had to allocate on some reasonable and systematic basis "occupancy" expense, depreciation and amortization, and several other expenses, and describe this method in its notes.

TABLE 12-2 Voluntary Health and Welfare Organization

American Health Association, Local Affiliate Statement of Activities as of June 30, 2020			
	Without Donor Restrictions	**With Donor Restrictions**	**Total**
Revenue			
Public support			
Received directly			
Contributions	$ 2,603,328	$ 263,759	$ 2,867,087
Contributed services	85,160		85,160
Capital campaign		9,486	9,486
Special events	10,528,221	12,500	10,540,721
Special event incentives	(1,802,014)	–	(1,802,014)
Net special events	$ 8,726,207	$ 12,500	$ 8,738,707
Legacies and bequests	$ 1,327,126	$ 1,058,844	$ 2,385,970
Total received directly	$12,741,821	$ 1,344,589	$14,086,410
Received indirectly			
Allocated by federated fund-raising organizations		694,382	694,382
Allocated by unassociated and nonfederated fund-raising organizations	142,472		142,472
Total received indirectly	$ 142,472	$ 694,382	$ 836,854
Total public support	$12,884,293	$ 2,038,971	$14,923,264
Other revenue			
Grants from national center	$ 87,180	$ –	$ 87,180
Program fees	302,530		302,530
Sales of educational materials	1,106,074		1,106,074
Membership dues	68,103		68,103
Investment income	806,041	107,433	913,474
Perpetual trust revenue		64,732	64,732
Gains on sale of long-lived assets	6,468		6,468
Unrealized gain on perpetual trust contribution		308,100	308,100
Gains on investment transactions		103,544	103,544
Miscellaneous revenue	96,296	–	96,296
Total other revenue	$ 2,472,692	$ 583,809	$ 3,056,501
Net assets released from restrictions			
Satisfaction of research restrictions	$ 704,264	$ (704,264)	$ –
Satisfaction of program restrictions	118,256	(118,256)	–
Satisfaction of equipment acquisition restrictions	20,298	(20,298)	–
Satisfaction of geographic restrictions	266,000	(266,000)	–
Expiration of time restrictions	513,898	(513,898)	–
Total net assets released from restrictions	$ 1,622,716	$ (1,622,716)	$ –
Total public support and other revenue	$16,979,701	$ 1,000,064	$17,979,765

(Continues)

TABLE 12-2 Voluntary Health and Welfare Organization *(Continued)*

American Health Association, Local Affiliate Statement of Activities as of June 30, 2020

	Without Donor Restrictions	With Donor Restrictions	Total
Expenses			
Program services			
Research—to acquire new knowledge through biomedical investigation	$ 3,659,784	$ —	$ 3,659,784
Public health education—to inform the public about the prevention and treatment of cardiovascular diseases and stroke	3,565,704	—	3,565,704
Professional education and training—to improve the knowledge, skills, and techniques of health professionals	971,708	—	971,708
Community services—to provide organized training in emergency aid, blood pressure screening, and other community-wide activities	2,050,768	—	2,050,768
Total program services	10,247,964	—	10,247,964
Supporting services			
Management and general—providing executive direction, financial management, overall planning, and coordination of the association's activities	1,069,084	—	1,069,084
Fund-raising—activities to secure vital financial support from the public	2,487,090	—	2,487,090
Total supporting services	3,556,174	—	3,556,174
Total program and supporting services expenses	13,804,138	—	13,804,138
Allocation to the American Health Association, Inc. (national center) for national research and other activities	3,467,527	—	3,467,527
Total expenses and allocation to national center	17,271,665	—	17,271,665
Change in net assets before			
Cumulative effect of change in accounting principles	(291,964)	1,000,064	708,100
Cumulative effects of changes in accounting principles	(520,508)	6,304,638	5,784,130
Change in net assets	(812,472)	7,304,702	6,492,230
Net assets, beginning of year	11,629,880	2,793,139	14,423,019
Net assets, end of year	$10,817,408	$10,097,841	$20,915,249

As discussed in Chapter 9, pertaining to business-type activities, the GASB requires that governments report their cash flows in four categories:

1. Cash flows from operating activities
2. Cash flows from noncapital financing activities
3. Cash flows from capital and related financing activities
4. Cash flows from investing activities

TABLE 12-3 Voluntary Health and Welfare Organization

American Health Association, Local Affiliate, Statement of Functional Expenses for the Year Ended June 30, 2020

	Program Services						Supporting Services			
	Special Event Incentives	Research	Public Health Education	Professional Education and Training	Community Services	Sub Total	Management and General	Fund-Raising	Sub Total	Total
Salaries	$ —	$86,541	$1,600,091	$158,077	$951,992	$2,796,701	$366,639	$1,109,774	$1,476,413	$4,273,114
Payroll taxes	—	6,915	131,026	13,005	78,838	229,784	30,150	90,125	120,275	350,059
Employee benefits	—	9,169	283,924	26,003	171,947	491,043	65,398	194,719	260,117	751,160
Occupancy	—	4,501	146,862	12,827	84,405	248,595	36,220	103,152	139,372	387,967
Telephone	—	2,641	82,012	7,404	55,080	147,137	19,459	58,594	78,053	225,190
Supplies	—	1,015	76,404	5,343	30,400	113,162	20,832	24,382	45,214	158,376
Rental and maintenance of equipment	—	1,952	70,242	3,617	40,394	116,205	18,506	47,729	66,235	182,440
Printing and publication	—	3,900	587,178	549,617	338,437	1,479,132	26,616	338,334	364,950	1,844,082
Postage and shipping	—	4,092	188,810	27,479	64,285	284,666	26,826	194,228	221,054	505,720
Visual aids, films, and media	—	47	6,197	2,123	1,581	9,948	10,602	4,755	15,357	25,305
Conferences and meetings	—	24,681	77,137	106,291	55,776	263,885	137,827	44,357	182,184	446,069
Other travel	—	3,559	76,541	14,162	44,183	138,445	62,452	87,244	149,696	288,141
Professional fees	—	85,787	72,449	29,184	32,479	219,899	134,282	62,031	196,313	416,212

Awards and grants	—	3,419,771	—	—	—	3,419,771	—	—	—	3,419,771
Other expenses	—	503	20,979	3,218	12,642	37,342	79,495	27,639	107,134	144,476
Depreciation and amortization	—	4,710	145,852	13,358	88,329	252,249	33,780	100,027	133,807	386,056
Total expenses before allocation to national center	$ —	$3,659,784	$3,565,704	$971,708	$2,050,768	$10,247,964	$1,069,084	$2,487,090	$3,556,174	$13,804,138
Allocation to the national center	—	2,285,083	257,928	190,933	187,582	2,921,526	375,167	170,834	546,001	3,467,527
Total functional expenses and allocation to the national center	$ —	$5,944,867	$3,823,632	$1,162,641	$2,238,350	$13,169,490	$1,444,251	$2,657,924	$4,102,175	$17,271,665
Special event incentives	$1,802,014	$ —	$ —	$ —	$ —	$ —	$ —	$ —	$ —	$ 1,802,014
Total functional expenses, allocation to national center, and incentives	$1,802,014	$ 5,944,867	$3,823,632	$1,162,641	$ 2,238,350	$13,169,490	$1,444,251	$2,657,924	$4,102,175	$19,073,679

By contrast, the FASB in Statement No. 95, *Statement of Cash Flows*, directs that businesses classify their cash flows into three categories:

1. Cash flows from operating activities
2. Cash flows from financing activities
3. Cash flows from investing activities

In requiring a statement of cash flows for not-for-profits,[4] the FASB faced a dilemma. On the one hand, many experts, including a task force of the AICPA, asserted that with respect to cash flows, the operations of not-for-profits more closely parallel those of governments than those of businesses. Not-for-profits, like governments, draw the distinction between cash flows attributable to operations and those that are restricted to capital and comparable long-term purposes, such as permanent endowment funds. Accordingly, the experts contended, the FASB should adopt a four-way classification scheme similar to that established by the GASB. On the other hand, however, by requiring a four-way scheme, the FASB would be widening the gulf between business and not-for-profit reporting, thereby countering a trend, and apparent objective, of narrowing it.

Emphasizing the importance of comparability between businesses and not-for-profits, the FASB elected to apply the three-way scheme to not-for-profits. However, recognizing that not-for-profits engage in different types of transactions than businesses, the FASB (in Statement No. 117) modified Statement No. 95 so that it would be more germane to not-for-profits. For example, it stipulated that cash flows from financing activities should include both contributions restricted to long-term purposes and interest and dividends from investments restricted to long-term purposes. Other contributions and interest and dividends on investments not restricted to long-term purposes should be classified as operating cash flows. Table 12-4 sets forth the main types of cash flows included in each category, and Table 12-5 presents the Statement of Cash Flows of the American Health Association.

In another notable difference between the GASB and FASB approaches to cash flows, the GASB (per Statement No. 34) mandates that governments use only the direct, as opposed to the indirect, method to report their cash flows. Not-for-profits may choose to present the cash flow statement using either the direct or indirect method. In the past, organizations that use the direct method had to also report cash from operations using the indirect method. However, ASU No. 2016-14 encourages the use of the direct method and not-for-profits no longer must also report cash flows using the indirect method if it chooses the direct method.

WHAT ARE THE MAIN TYPES OF CONTRIBUTIONS, AND HOW SHOULD PLEDGES BE ACCOUNTED FOR?

Contributions, a mainstay means of support for many not-for-profits, encompass all *nonreciprocal* receipts of assets or services. A nonreciprocal receipt is one for which the recipient gives nothing in exchange. As defined by the FASB in its 1993 pronouncement *Accounting for Contributions Received and Contributions Made* (Statement No. 116), contributions include gifts of cash, marketable securities, property and equipment, utilities, supplies, intangible assets (such as patents and copyrights), and the services of professionals and skilled workers.[5] In 2016 the religion

[4] FASB ASC 958-230-05.

[5] Para. 5; also FASB ASC 958-605-25.

TABLE 12-4 Classification of Cash Receipts and Disbursements per FASB Statement No. 95, Statement of Cash Flows, as Modified by FASB Statement No. 117, Financial Statements of Not-for-Profit Organizations

Cash Flows from Operating Activities

Inflows

- Contributions that are either not restricted by donors or restricted to short-term purposes
- Sales of goods and services
- Interest and dividends not restricted to either long-term purposes, to acquisition of capital assets, or to additions to endowments

Outflows

- Payments to employees
- Payments for supplies
- Payments of interest
- Payments of taxes
- Grants to other organizations

Cash Flows from Investing Activities

Inflows

- Proceeds from sale of facilities
- Payments received on notes from sale of capital assets
- Receipts from the sale of stocks and bonds

Outflows

- Purchases of stocks and bonds
- Acquisitions of capital assets

Cash Flows from Financing Activities

Inflows

- Contributions restricted for long-term purposes
- Interest and dividends from investments restricted to long-term purposes
- Contributions restricted to the acquisition of capital assets
- Interest and dividends restricted to the acquisition of capital assets
- Contributions to endowments
- Proceeds of borrowing

Outflows

- Repayment of debt
- Lease payments under capital leases

TABLE 12-5 Statement of Cash Flows of a Not-for-Profit Organization

American Health Association, Local Affiliate, Inc.
Statement of Cash Flows
for the Year Ended June 30, 2020

Change in net assets	$ 6,492,230
Adjustments to reconcile change in net assets to net cash	
Provided by operating activities	
Depreciation and amortization	386,056
Unrealized gain on perpetual trust contributions	(308,100)
Gains on investment transactions	(103,544)
Gain on sale of long-lived assets	(6,468)
Contributions restricted to investment in property	(9,486)
Contributions to endowment funds	(270,000)
Increase in accrued investment income	(57,260)
Increase in federated and nonfederated receivable	(13,516)
Increase in national center receivable	(20,382)
Decrease in other receivable	116,532
Decrease in bequest receivable	314,000
Decrease in pledges receivable	2,812
Decrease in educational and campaign material inventory	78,454
Increase in other assets	(21,255)
Increase in perpetual trust	(2,459,800)
Increase in charitable gift annuity	(40,500)
Increase in charitable remainder trust	(4,963,216)
Increase in payable to national center	1,332,258
Increase in accounts payable and accrued expenses	808,360
Increase in research awards payable	225,508
Increase in annuity obligation	19,640
Decrease in deferred revenue and support	(413,959)
Net cash provided by operating activities	$(1,088,364)
Cash flows from investing activities	
Purchase of equipment	(724,492)
Proceeds from sale of equipment	200,217
Proceeds from maturities of investments	7,730,368
Purchase of investments	(8,216,079)
Net cash used in investing activities	$(1,009,986)
Cash flows from financing activities	
Contributions to endowment funds	270,000
Proceeds from contributions restricted to investment in property	9,486
Net cash provided by financing activities	$ 279,486
Net increase in cash and cash equivalents	357,864
Cash and cash equivalents (at beginning of year)	448,519
Cash and cash equivalents (at end of year)	$ 806,383
Supplemental data	
Noncash investing and financing activities—gifts of equipment	$ 30,000

not-for-profit subsector received the largest share of charitable contributions (32 percent). This was followed by education-related organizations (15 percent) and followed by human service organizations (12 percent).[6]

Contributions also include **unconditional promises**—that is, pledges—to give those items in the future. Thus, **pledges** are regarded as contributions, although they exclude **conditional promises** to give these items in the future. A conditional promise depends on a specified future and uncertain event to bind the donor. For example, a university alumnus may pledge funds to construct a new physics laboratory if the university is successful in obtaining a government research grant.

DISTINGUISHING A CONTRIBUTION FROM AN EXCHANGE TRANSACTION

Despite changes to how revenues are measured, contributions still must be distinguished from exchange transactions. A contribution is a transfer of assets in which the donor does not expect to receive equal value in return. An exchange transaction is a reciprocal transfer in which each party receives and gives up resources of commensurate value. For example, if a private corporation were to give a not-for-profit research foundation funds to study the cause of a disease with the expectation that the results would be published in a scientific journal, the transaction would be considered a contribution. If, on the other hand, it gave the funds with the contractual agreement that it would have the rights to resultant patents, then the transaction would be an exchange transaction.

The difference between the two is not always obvious. When people join the local Friends of the Library Association, do they do so to support the library's scholarly activities or to benefit from the right to attend member-only lectures? Do they join the American Automobile Association to promote auto safety and good roads or to obtain emergency road service and travel directions? Do they join the AARP (formerly known as the American Association of Retired Persons) to advance the interests of senior citizens or to take advantage of low-cost life and auto insurance offers?

Distinguishing between exchange transactions and contributions requires the exercise of judgment. Factors to be taken into account should include the recipient's intent in soliciting the resources, the party that establishes the amount of resources transferred (e.g., the transferor or the transferee), and the penalties assessed if either party fails to deliver what has been promised.

As previously discussed, the classification of resources into the two categories of restrictiveness is based on *donor* stipulation. Hence, only contributions can be so categorized. Exchange transactions are always classified as unrestricted when the performance obligation is met; by definition, the resources received are not subject to donor restrictions. They should be accounted for as ordinary commercial transactions and hence on a full accrual basis. Thus, if a not-for-profit organization agreed to perform research for the exclusive benefit of a drug company and received payment in advance, it would recognize revenue only as it either carried out or completed the project (i.e., on a percentage-of-completion or completed-contract basis) and fulfilled its performance obligation.

ACCOUNTING FOR PLEDGES

The recognition of gifts not restricted by donors of cash and other assets (that have not been preceded by a pledge) has never been a major issue. Not-for-profits, irrespective of type, have

[6] https://givingusa.org/see-the-numbers-giving-usa-2017-infographic/.

recognized gifts of cash and other assets as revenue on receipt. Gifts of assets other than cash have been measured at their fair (i.e., market) value.

But when should not-for-profits recognize pledges—promises to make donations of cash or other assets in the future? Organizations generally lack legally enforceable claims against fickle donors. Even if they do have legally enforceable claims, they may be reluctant to act on them because the likely benefit is exceeded by the costs in both goodwill and legal fees. Pledges may be legally enforceable when the organization has acted on a pledge and thereby incurred costs. Suppose, relying on a donor's promise to finance a new building, an organization engages an architect to draw up plans. The donor reneges. The organization may have a valid claim on the donor for its losses. The accompanying "In Practice" describes one not-for-profit's effort to enforce a claim against the estate of a deceased benefactor.

More important, pledges receivable, albeit assets, are not available for expenditure. They cannot be used to pay employees or suppliers. Recognition of pledges might give the unwarranted impression that the organization has excess spendable funds and thereby has less of a need for further fiscal assistance.

On the other hand, many organizations have sufficient experience to be able to estimate with reliability the percentage of pledges that will be uncollectible and, like merchants, can establish appropriate allowances for uncollectibles. Further, they can borrow against the pledges and spend the proceeds. Arguably, therefore, there is no more justification for a not-for-profit than for a merchant to delay revenue recognition until cash is in hand.

IN PRACTICE **EVEN THE VERY WEALTHY SOMETIMES RENEGE ON THEIR CONTRIBUTIONS**

Larry Ellison, the billionaire CEO of Oracle, wasn't too happy when Larry Summers, president of Harvard, resigned in the midst of a controversy over his management style. Unlike many Harvard alumni, faculty, and students who shared his views, Ellison was in a position to do more than merely write a letter of protest. He opted not to fulfill a $115 million pledge for a new health institute at Harvard.

Ellison is not the only high-profile donor to have second thoughts about fulfilling a pledge. Princeton University was also engaged in a legal battle with the Robertson Foundation over the appropriate use of the foundation's $600 million endowment. Established in 1961, by heirs to an A&P fortune, the foundation was intended to fund programs that would prepare students for careers in government service. Relatives of the foundation's original benefactors charge, however, that the university diverted resources for buildings and other projects and went to court seeking the right to redirect the foundation's income to institutions other than Princeton. A settlement agreement was reached on December 9, 2008, giving Princeton University full control of the endowment associated with Princeton.

Source: Based in part on "Big Donors Don't Always Follow Through," *USA Today*, June 20, 2006.

Example

Pledges

In November, a public broadcasting station conducts its annual pledge drive and receives telephone pledges of $700,000. By year-end December 31, it collects $400,000 of the pledges. In addition, it receives a pledge from a local foundation to contribute $100,000 at the end of each of the next three years. Based on previous experience, it estimates that $60,000 of the entire balance of pledges outstanding at year-end will be uncollectible.

FASB STANDARDS

The FASB, in Statement No. 116, over the vociferous objections of many of its constituent not-for-profit organizations, decided that pledges without donor restrictions should be reported as revenue in the period received; organizations need not wait until pledges are fulfilled. They should measure the pledges at "the present value of estimated future cash flows using a discount rate commensurate with the risks involved."[7] That is, they should take into account both anticipated bad debts and the time value of money. If they establish an allowance for uncollectibles, then they should use a risk-free discount. If not, then they should use a higher rate—one that takes into account the risk of being unable to collect the pledge. They should not both establish an allowance for uncollectibles and adjust the discount rate for risk. That would cause the default risk to be accounted for twice. Entities need not discount pledges to be collected within one year.

To avoid recognizing contributions as revenue before they are available for expenditure, not-for-profits should consider pledges of cash to be received in future periods as subject to time restrictions. The FASB concluded that by promising to make payments in the future, donors implicitly restricted the donated resources to support of future, not current, activities. Hence, the recipient organizations should classify them as restricted by donors (for a temporary time period). When the cash is received and available for expenditure, they should release resources from the restricted by donors category and transfer them to the not restricted by donors category.

The standard allows an option to recognize pledges that are restricted, either as to time or use, as not restricted if the restriction has been met in the same period as the donation is made.

[7] Para. 20; also FASB ASC 958-310-35.

Thus, in the example, the following entries—in both not restricted and restricted by donor funds—would summarize the results of the year's pledge drive:

Pledges receivable	$400,000	
Revenues from contributions		$400,000

To record the pledges of cash to be paid in the current year (in a fund not restricted by donors)

Cash	$400,000	
Pledges receivable		$400,000

To record the collection of cash (in a fund not restricted by donors)

These pledges need not be reported as being subject to time restrictions and thereby recorded in a restricted by donor fund. They fall under the exception that when time restrictions are satisfied within the same year, the revenue may be reported as unrestricted.

Pledges receivable	$300,000	
Pledges receivable—allowance for uncollectibles		$ 60,000
Revenues from contributions		240,000

To record the pledges expected to be collected in future periods (in a restricted by donor fund)

As the pledges are collected in subsequent years, the resources would be released from the restricted by donor category and added to the not restricted category. Thus, if $75,000 were collected:

Net assets released from restriction	$75,000	
Pledges receivable		$ 75,000

To release the resources from restriction upon collection of cash (restricted by donor fund)

Cash	$75,000	
Net assets released from restriction		$ 75,000

To record the collection of cash (not restricted fund)

Were the station to determine that 3 percent is an appropriate discount rate, then the present value of the annuity of $100,000 per year for three years would be $282,861. The present value of an annuity of $1 for three periods, discounted at a rate of 3 percent, is $2.8286. Hence, the present value of the annuity of $100,000 is $100,000 × 2.8286. The appropriate discount rate is the prevailing *risk-free* interest rate. The risk-free rate should be used because by establishing an allowance for uncollectibles the organization will have already factored in the risk of loss from bad debts.

Pledges receivable	$282,861	
Revenues from contributions		$282,861

To record a pledge of three annual payments of $100,000, the present value of which, discounted at 3 percent, is $282,861 (restricted by donors fund)

Each year, as the $100,000 is received, the station would recognize interest at a rate of 3 percent on the net balance of the pledge (the pledge receivable less the remaining discount) and record the excess as a reduction of the pledges receivable. Interest for the first year would be 3 percent of $282,861, or $8,486. In effect, the station received a contribution of only $282,861. The difference between that and the total payments of $300,000 represents interest. In the absence of donor stipulation, the interest would be unrestricted and therefore be recognized in a fund without donor restrictions. Thus when the first installment is received:

Net assets released from restriction	$91,514	
Pledges receivable		$ 91,514

To release the resources upon collection of cash in the first year (restricted by donor fund)—$100,000 cash received less interest at a rate of 3 percent on the pledge balance of $282,861

Cash	$100,000	
Contributions—interest revenue		$ 8,486
Net assets released from restriction		91,514

To record the first year's payment of $100,000 (not restricted by donor fund)

In the two subsequent years, as the balance in pledges receivable is reduced, greater proportions of the $100,000 would be assigned to principal and lesser proportions to interest. By the end of the third year the balance in the pledges receivable account would be reduced to zero. The interest should be reported as additional contributions.

WHEN SHOULD USE-RESTRICTED (PURPOSE-RESTRICTED) CONTRIBUTIONS BE RECOGNIZED?

In concept, a not-for-profit's *use-restricted (purpose-restricted) contributions* are equivalent to a government's restricted grants. Use-restricted contributions can be used only for donor-specified purposes. Before the FASB issued its pronouncement on contributions, most not-for-profits recognized revenue from restricted grants as they expended the funds for the specified purpose. In this way, they matched the revenues to the expenses to which they were related.

As a consequence of this practice, organizations failed to give timely recognition to transactions that, it could be argued, clearly enhanced their welfare. A restricted gift, no less than an unrestricted gift, provides an economic benefit; it helps the organization to carry out its mission.

Example

Use-Restricted Contributions

In 2020 the Lyric Opera Society receives a $150,000 contribution to fund a production of Gilbert and Sullivan's *H.M.S. Pinafore*, to be performed in 2021.

FASB STANDARDS

Based on FASB ASU No. 2016-14, revenue from donor-restricted contributions is accounted for on the same basis as that from contributions without donor restrictions. Restricted contributions, including pledges, are recognized as revenues in the period received, irrespective of when the resources will be expended.[8] As discussed previously, for reporting purposes, distinctions must be drawn among resources that are not restricted by donors and those that are restricted by donors.

[8] Paras. 14–16; also FASB ASC 958-605-45 (3–7); FASB ASC 958-360-50.

Thus, in the example, the Lyric Opera Society would report its gift in a donor-restricted fund:

Cash	$150,000	
Revenues from contributions		$150,000

To record a gift restricted by donor (in a donor-restricted fund)

When, in 2021, the Society expends the resources and meets its performance obligation, it would record the release of the funds in the restricted fund and the expenditure in its current operating fund:

Net assets released from restriction	$150,000	
Cash (or payables)		$150,000

To record the release of restrictions (in the donor-restricted fund)

Production expenses	$150,000	
Net assets released from restriction		$150,000

To record the expenditure of funds previously restricted (in a fund not restricted by donors)

The expenditure of the funds raises a related issue. Suppose the society budgeted an additional $150,000 or more of its own resources to finance the production. When it spent the first $150,000, was it spending its own resources or the donated resources?

As long as the organization incurs an expense for a purpose for which the donor-restricted resources are available, it should consider the restriction as having been released.[9] The only exception is that if the organization receives resources from two external donors, both of which restrict resources for the same purpose, then it cannot release the two restrictions with the expenditure of the same resources. Thus, if the opera society received $150,000 from Donor A and $150,000 from Donor B, it could not release both restrictions on spending the first $150,000.

The FASB approach is similar to that of the GASB in that pledges subject to use restrictions can be recognized as revenue on receipt of the pledge. Recall from Chapter 4 that GASB standards permit governments to give immediate recognition to grants or other revenues subject to purpose restrictions. The recipients should not delay recognition until they have satisfied the restrictions.

The accompanying "In Practice" raises still another issue regarding restricted gifts. It suggests that some gifts may not be as restricted as the donors may have been led to believe.

[9] Para. 17; also FASB ASC 958-205-45 (9–12).

IN PRACTICE **A GIFT WITH STRINGS ATTACHED**

Is it really possible to restrict a gift? Yes, but not as easily as it may appear. Resources are fungible and can readily be transferred from one account to another.

Suppose, for example, you contribute $100,000 to an agency in your community similar to the United Way, stipulating that the gift must be used to support the Boy Scouts. The agency had previously determined that the Scouts would receive 5 percent of total collections—an amount that would come to $150,000. On account of your gift, the agency gives only $50,000 to the Scouts—a total of $150,000 when combined with your contribution. As a consequence, your stipulation has in effect been nullified. To be sure, donors can add covenants to gift agreements that minimize the likelihood that their wishes will be circumvented. But these are difficult to enforce, and many organizations would be unwilling to accept unusual controls on their administrative prerogatives.

Only by limiting a gift to activities that the organization would not otherwise undertake can a donor be certain that the gift will support the intended activity.

SHOULD CONTRIBUTIONS OF SERVICES BE RECOGNIZED?

Not-for-profits benefit from the services of volunteers. In 2015, 62.8 million Americans volunteered 7.9 billion hours in local and national organizations, service which was valued at the equivalent of $184 billion of cash donations.[10] The services range from professional assistance that would otherwise have to be paid for at commercial rates to those that are part of the normal activities carried out by an organization's members. Consider some examples:

- An advertising agency develops a fund-raising campaign for a not-for-profit welfare agency.
- An attorney provides free legal counsel to a hospital.
- An attorney is a member of the board of directors of a performing arts association and is frequently called on for legal guidance.
- Nurses are paid considerably less than the prevailing wage by a hospital maintained by a religious order of which they are members.
- Community members perform odd jobs at a local hospital, such as carrying meals to patients, staffing the reception desk, and maintaining the hospital's library and recreation area.
- Church members paint the church facilities and construct a children's play center.

In each of these examples, the organization receives an economic benefit from the contributed services. Correspondingly, it incurs a cost in that it "consumes" the services provided. Yet it is not obvious whether the values of these contributed services can be reliably measured, and if they can be, whether they should be accorded financial statement recognition.

Example

Service Contributions

The Northern New Mexico Clinic, a not-for-profit health care provider, recruits a local contractor to repair its air conditioning unit. Had the contractor billed the clinic at standard rates, the cost would have been $12,000.

FASB STANDARDS

Recognizing the diverse nature of contributed services, the FASB in Statement No. 116 prescribes that they should be recognized only if they are of a professional nature and of the type that the *entity would ordinarily have had to pay for* had they not been donated. It establishes two

[10] http://www.nationalservice.gov/vcla/national.

conditions, either of which must be met, for recognition:

- The services create or enhance nonfinancial assets.
- The services require specialized skills, are provided by individuals possessing those skills, and would typically need to be purchased if not provided by donation. Services requiring specialized skills, according to the FASB, are those provided by accountants, architects, carpenters, doctors, electricians, lawyers, nurses, plumbers, teachers, and other professionals.[11]

[11] Para. 9; also FASB ASC 958-605-25-16.

The services received by the Northern New Mexico Clinic would ordinarily have had to have been purchased and were performed by a skilled professional. Hence, the clinic should recognize both, a revenue and a corresponding expense:

Repair and maintenance expense	$12,000	
Revenue from contributed services		$12,000
To recognize revenue and the related expense from contributed services		

To appreciate the required accounting for this transaction, suppose instead that the contractor had simply donated $12,000 of cash to the clinic. The clinic would have debited cash and credited donation revenue. Then when the clinic had the maintenance performed and paid the contractor, the clinic would debit the maintenance expense and credit cash. In other words, the clinic's final accounts would be the same in both cases. And this was the intent of the FASB standards.

SHOULD RECEIPTS OF COLLECTION ITEMS BE RECOGNIZED AS REVENUES?

In Chapter 7, pertaining to long-lived assets, we addressed the issue of whether governments should capitalize the "collectibles" that they hold in their museums, universities, libraries, and similar institutions. We noted that the GASB adopted the basic position of the FASB as set forth in FASB Statement No. 116. A notable difference between the FASB and GASB positions, however, is that the GASB requires that governments recognize the receipt of all collectibles as revenues. If they capitalize the collectibles, they would offset the revenues with a capital asset. If not, they would offset the revenues with an expense. The FASB, by contrast, does not permit not-for-profits to recognize as revenues the receipt of collectibles that they do not capitalize.

IN PRACTICE EXAMPLES OF CONTRIBUTED SERVICES

A veterans association conducts an annual fund-raising campaign to solicit contributions from members of the community. In prior years the association's own members made the phone calls. This year, a local telemarketing company agreed to contact the potential donors.

The association should not recognize the contributed services of the firm because neither of the two conditions is met. The services do not create nonfinancial assets. Moreover, they do not require specialized skills, and based on experience, the association would otherwise not have purchased the services.

A local welfare organization benefits from the services of two CPAs. One is its treasurer, a position that must be filled by a member of its board of directors, all of whom are unpaid. The second, who is not a member of the board, provides ongoing accounting services (e.g., making monthly journal entries, closing the books, and preparing annual financial statements). Were it not for the services of this CPA, the organization would have to engage a part-time bookkeeper or accountant.

The welfare organization should not recognize the services of the treasurer. Although the organization benefits from his professional advice, his services are offered as an unpaid board member, not as a professional accountant. Therefore, neither condition is satisfied.

The other CPA provides services that require special skills and would otherwise have to be purchased. Therefore, the second condition is satisfied, and the welfare organization should recognize his contributed services.

FASB STANDARDS

Statement No. 116 encourages not-for-profits to recognize contributions of collectibles as revenues and to capitalize their entire collections. However, it states that entities *need* not (note: not *cannot*) recognize contributions of collectibles as long as the items satisfy all of the following conditions:

- They are held for public exhibition, education, or research in furtherance of public service rather than financial gain.
- They are protected, kept unencumbered, cared for, and preserved.
- They are subject to an organizational policy requiring that proceeds from sales of collection items be used to acquire other items for collections.

If not-for-profits elect not to capitalize their collections, then they must disclose, in notes to the statements, the details of items both purchased and "deaccessed." If they capitalize their collections, they shall recognize contributions of collection items as revenues; if not, they should not recognize them as revenues.[12]

[12] Paras. 11–13; also FASB ASC 958-605-25-19, FASB ASC 958-360-25.

WHEN SHOULD CONDITIONAL PROMISES BE RECOGNIZED?

Donors may promise to contribute to a not-for-profit on condition that a specified event take place or that the entity take specified actions. Conditional promises to give must be distinguished from *restricted* contributions. A restricted gift is one that must be used for a particular purpose as specified by a donor. A conditional promise, by contrast, is one in which the donor will provide the resources *only if* the specified condition is satisfied. The resources to be provided may be either restricted or not restricted by the donor.

In practice, the distinction between a restricted gift and a conditional gift may be ambiguous. A donor may pledge resources that can be used only to support a particular activity, such as a conference. Although the promise is not explicitly conditioned on the entity holding the conference, the donor is not likely to provide the resources if the conference is not held. Such a restricted gift is not much different from a conditional gift—one in which the donor promises to provide resources to the organization if and when it holds the conference.

A conditional promise unquestionably is an economic benefit to a not-for-profit entity as long as there is a positive probability that the conditions can be met. Yet, if there is reasonable uncertainty that the conditions will be met, the entity may be premature in recognizing revenue until it has "earned" the right to the contribution by satisfying the conditions.

IN PRACTICE WHEN A CONTRIBUTION IS NOT A CONTRIBUTION

Not-for-profit organizations, no less than both businesses and governments may try to artificially boost their revenues or lower their expenses. Organizations try to appear promising and resourceful as they fight for contributions from potential donors. However, *Forbes India* (November 30, 2011) reports, "deworming medicine donations have made some non-profits seem bigger and stronger than they really are."

Deworming medicine are chewable pills that are highly effective in treating intestinal parasites in developing countries. The pills can be bought on world markets in Europe, China, and India for 2 cents each, according to *Forbes*, but they have been valued on some nonprofits' financial statements as non-cash gift-in-kind donations worth as much as $16.25 per pill. Thus, the most serious accusation against some not-for-profits on the annual *Forbes* list of the 200 largest U.S. charities is that they have exaggerated their contributions. Furthermore, some agents or brokers of the pills have been charged with masquerading as tax-exempt charities making donations.

Organizations have defended the practices by stating that the accounting rules are flexible and they have acted in good faith. Not to mention the concern that reflecting values closer to the lower market prices might discourage cash donors. Nevertheless, some charities have seen the accounting light and started using lower, more realistic, values. For example, Oklahoma City–based Feed the Children lowered their deworming valuation from $9.07 to 35 cents. This caused its 2009 yearly gifts in kind reported contributions to drop by $668 million—more than 55 percent of the prior-year amount.

Example

Conditional Promises

The City Symphony is conducting a campaign to provide financing for a new auditorium. In 2020 a private foundation agrees to match 50 percent of all other contributions up to $1 million (i.e., each $1 of its gift is conditioned on the symphony raising $2 from other sources). The following year, 2021, the symphony receives $500,000 in other donations.

FASB STANDARDS

Statement No. 116 stipulates that conditional promises to give shall be recognized when the conditions on which they depend are substantially met.[13]

[13] Para. 22; also FASB ASC 958-605-25 (11–13).

In 2018 the symphony in the example satisfied the conditions to receive $250,000 of the foundation's donation:

Pledges receivable	250,000	
Revenues from contributions		$250,000

To record the fulfillment of conditions necessary to receive the foundation's matching funds

It would delay recognition of any further contributions from the foundation until it raised additional funds from other parties.

Reimbursement grants generally fall within the category of conditional promises. Either implicitly or explicitly, the grantor (often a government agency) pledges to reimburse the grantee for allowable costs conditioned upon the grantee incurring those costs and providing suitable documentation of them.

HOW SHOULD "PASS-THROUGH" CONTRIBUTIONS BE ACCOUNTED FOR?

In Chapter 4, we raised the issue of how governments should account for "pass-through" grants. These are grants that a recipient is required to distribute to other parties—for example, when a state receives a federal grant that it must "pass through" to local governments. The position of the GASB is that the original recipient of the grant should recognize the grant as revenue (and the subsequent distribution as an expenditure) unless the original recipient is nothing more than a "cash conduit"—an entity that has no decision-making authority to select the ultimate beneficiaries.

Not-for-profits face similar issues with regard to contributions. Consider, for example, the following situations.

Example

A Federated Fund-Raising Organization

The United Campaign of Springfield is a **federated organization** that distributes all contributions received to numerous local, regional, and national organizations. These include entities as diverse as local food distribution centers and the Red Cross. Donors are given three choices of how their contributions may be used:

- They can give without restriction, in which case the distribution of their gifts is left to a committee composed of United Campaign board members.
- They can specify that their gifts be designated for one of several groups of organizations, each of which targets a specific community need (e.g., health care, youth activities, poverty, education, culture).
- They can designate a gift to one or more specific organizations.

Example

A Foundation That Transfers Assets to a Specified Organization

The Foundation for Classical Music, which is governed by an independent board of trustees, was established to benefit a local opera company. The charter of the foundation states that all contributions will be added to the foundation's permanent endowment. Income from the endowment will be transferred to the opera company, subject to the right of the foundation's trustees to redirect funds to other arts-related organizations without donor approvals if and when, in the judgment of the trustees, the opera company becomes self-supporting.

Example

A Foundation That Supports a Related Organization

The Friends of the Museum Foundation, which is governed by a board of trustees selected by the museum's board of governors, was established to stimulate private contributions from the community that would be used to acquire works of art and carry out various cultural activities. Although all funds collected by the foundation would eventually benefit the museum, the foundation's trustees can choose the timing of transfers from the foundation and the specific purposes for which they will be used.

FASB STANDARDS

In a 1999 pronouncement, *Transfers of Assets to a Not-for-Profit Organization or Charitable Trust that Raises or Holds Contributions for Others* (Statement No. 136),[14] the FASB took a position that is similar in spirit to, but slightly different in approach from, that of the GASB. The GASB, as noted in Chapter 4 in the section pertaining to pass-through grants, indicated that a contribution should be considered a pass-through grant (and hence reported in an agency fund) only when the government has no administrative involvement in the disposition of the cash received. The FASB held that when an organization accepts contributions from a donor and agrees to transfer the assets to, or use them on behalf of, a specific beneficiary, then it should not recognize the donation as revenue (or the subsequent distribution as an expense). Instead it should offset the assets received with a liability—a payable to the ultimate beneficiary. There are, however, two main exceptions:

1. If the donor has explicitly granted the organization **variance power**, then the organization must recognize the contribution as revenue. "Variance power" is the unilateral right to redirect the use of the assets received to another beneficiary. The rationale for this exception is that an organization that has variance power is not merely an agent but has substantive decision-making authority and discretion over how the donation may be used.
2. If the recipient organization and the beneficiary organizations are "financially interrelated," then the recipient organization must recognize the contribution as revenue. Correspondingly, the beneficiary organization must recognize an interest in the net assets of the recipient organization (an asset) and periodically adjust that interest for its share in the change in the net assets of the recipient organization. This type of accounting is similar to the equity method of accounting for an interest in a subsidiary. Organizations are considered to be "financially interrelated" when
3. one organization has the ability to influence the operating and financial decisions of the other (as when one organization has "considerable" representation on the governing board of the other) and
4. one organization has an ongoing economic interest in the net assets of the other characterized by "residual rights" (as when the beneficiary organization profits from the investment, fund-raising, or operating activities of the recipient organization).

[14] FASB ASC 958-605-15.

This exception is based on the premise that when two organizations have a close cooperative relationship with each other, the recipient organization is unlikely to have an obligation to transfer its assets to the beneficiary organization at any specific time. Instead, the beneficiary organization is content to leave the resources with the recipient organization, knowing that it will have access to the resources whenever it needs them. Typically, however, this exception may in fact be moot. If one of the entities is able to exercise control over the other, then the two are required to consolidate their financial statements per FASB Statement No. 164, *Not-for-Profit Entities: Mergers and Acquisitions*, discussed later in this chapter. Then, of course, the contribution would be recognized as revenue by the consolidated entity when received.

In the first of the pass-through examples, the United Campaign would recognize as revenue without donor restrictions the contributions in which the donors did not designate *specific* beneficiaries. The contributions that could be distributed by the board would be classified as without donor restrictions. Those donations designated for one of the several groups of organizations would be recorded as "with donor restrictions," because they must be used for specified purposes only. The United Campaign could not, however, recognize as revenue the contributions of the donors who designated specific organizations. The receipt of these contributions would have to be recorded as a liability to those organizations; the United Campaign does not have variance power, and it is not financially affiliated with the beneficiary organizations.

In the second example, the Foundation for Classical Music has been granted variance power; it can redirect endowment income to arts organizations other than the local opera company. Therefore, it can recognize contributions as revenue (restricted by the donor in perpetuity because they must be added to a permanent endowment) on receipt.

In the third example, the Friends of the Museum Foundation and the museum are related organizations. On receipt of contributions, the foundation can recognize contributions as revenue (restricted or not depending on the stipulations of the donors). In the same period, the museum would recognize an asset (e.g., "interest in net assets of museum foundation"), offset by a revenue (e.g., "increase in interest in net assets of museum"). However, assuming that the two entities are so tightly intertwined that they will have to prepare consolidated financial statements, the foundation's interest in the net assets of the museum (and the offsetting increase in the net assets) will be eliminated in the consolidation process.

WHEN SHOULD GAINS AND LOSSES ON INVESTMENTS BE RECOGNIZED?

FASB STANDARDS

As noted in Chapter 4, the FASB, in Statement No. 124, *Accounting for Certain Investments Held by Not-for-Profit Organizations*, prescribed that not-for-profits, like businesses, must report their investments at fair value and recognize the changes in fair value as they occur.[15] They should not, however, classify the investments into the three categories (trading, available-for-sale, and held-to maturity) as required of businesses. Therefore, even debt securities that are expected to be held to maturity must be stated at fair value. The only exempt securities are investments accounted for under the equity method, investments in consolidated subsidiaries, and investments for which the fair value is not readily determinable. The fair value of an equity security is generally considered to be "readily determinable" if the security is traded on a major exchange or over the counter.

As per Statement No. 124, interest, dividends, and gains and losses from changes in the fair

[15] FASB ASC 958-320-35.

value of securities should be reported on the statement of activities as increases or decreases in net assets without donor restrictions—unless their use is restricted (either temporarily or permanently) by explicit donor stipulation or by law. However, even investment income and gains from restricted assets may be recognized as increases in assets without donor restrictions if the restrictions are met in the same reporting period and the organization follows the same policy with respect to contributions received.

Example

Investment Gains

In June 2020, the Children's Welfare Association receives a grant of $100,000, which it classifies as restricted by donor. To earn a return until it needs the funds, the Association invests the proceeds in Treasury notes. As of December 31, 2020, the fair market value of the notes is $103,000. The following entry in a fund with no donor restrictions would be appropriate:

Investments	$3,000	
Investment earnings—appreciation in fair value		$3,000
To record the increase in fair value		

The investments would now be divided into the two fund categories:

Without donor restrictions	$ 3,000
With donor restrictions	100,000
Total	$103,000

If the securities were subsequently sold for $103,000, entries in both funds (with and without donor restrictions) would be needed:

Cash	$100,000	
Investments		$100,000
To record the sale of securities in a fund restricted by donors		

Cash	$3,000	
Investments		$3,000
To record the sale of securities in a fund without donor restrictions		

If instead, the $100,000 were not a grant but rather a contribution to an endowment fund, the same approach would be taken with respect to the gains. Unless the donor specified that investment gains should be added to principal, earnings from the endowment were restricted to a specified purpose, or the general rules of the FASB were trumped by legal provisions, then the $3,000 in unrealized investment gains would be recognized as having no donor restrictions. The FASB standards for not-for-profits are generally consistent with those of the GASB for governments. Both require that investments be marked-to-market.

SHOULD ENDOWMENT GAINS BE CONSIDERED NET ADDITIONS TO PRINCIPAL OR EXPENDABLE INCOME?

The primary accounting issue pertaining to endowments in both governments and not-for-profits relates to whether, in the absence of specific donor or legal stipulations, investment gains and losses—including unrealized appreciation—should be recognized as a component of expendable income or nonexpendable principal. The issue has economic consequences that reach far beyond the content of financial reports; it affects the amount of resources available for operations and is likely to influence the organization's investment policies.

POLICIES OF GOVERNMENTS AND NOT-FOR-PROFITS REGARDING ENDOWMENT GAINS

Whether gains on the sale of investments (capital gains) or gains from appreciation should be accounted for as income or as an adjustment to principal is undoubtedly one of the most provocative questions related to endowments. But it is as much a legal as an accounting question. If a particular policy is required either by donor stipulation or law, then that policy will dictate accounting practice.

Parties establishing endowments sometimes stipulate that gains from the sale of investments be added to the principal (the "corpus") of the endowment and not incorporated into income. Thus, the gains will not be expendable; they will be available only for reinvestment. However, in the absence of donor stipulations or other applicable legal provisions, the governing board of the recipient institution is generally free to appropriate investment gains for current use.

The practice of specifying that gains be added to endowment principal rather than to spendable income is grounded in the need to protect endowment principal from inflation. In the long term, owing to inflation, the market value of a corporation's common stock can be expected to increase, even in the absence of substantive changes in supply and demand relationships. Thus, when an endowment sells that stock, the gain may represent nothing more than a decrease in the purchasing power of a dollar.

Although it may protect an endowment from inflation, a policy of automatically assigning investment gains to principal rather than income may have the adverse consequence of encouraging institutions to adopt less than optimum investment strategies.

Example

Investment Gains

A university's policies require that all investment gains, both realized and unrealized, be added to endowment principal. The university has to choose between one of two stock portfolios as an investment for a $1 million endowment. The first portfolio contains the common stock of "high-tech" start-up companies that pay either no or very small, dividends. The returns will be almost entirely from appreciation. The second contains an extremely conservative mix of bonds, preferred stocks, and the common stocks of well-established industrial firms, all of which pay high dividends or interest. The endowment fund managers estimate that the first portfolio will provide a total return of 14 percent per year (almost all appreciation); the second only 6 percent per year (almost all interest and dividends).

Assuming that the university needs the income to be generated by the endowment, it has little choice but to select the second portfolio; the first provides no accessible resources. Yet the first provides the greater returns and—were the university to periodically liquidate a portion of the portfolio—the greater cash flows.

GASB STANDARDS

Current GASB pronouncements do not explicitly address the issue of whether investment gains should be added to endowment principal or should be made available for expenditure. Therefore, in the absence of specific donor or legal stipulations, the gains should be reported as unrestricted assets and, hence, considered expendable.

As emphasized previously, investments must be reported at fair value, and no distinction is made between realized and unrealized gains and losses. Therefore, unrealized gains, like realized gains, are also unrestricted, and hence expendable, absent donor or legal restrictions.

FASB STANDARDS

The FASB is more precise in prescribing how investment gains should be reported, but the resultant practices are the same as those of governments. GAAP for not-for-profit organizations require gains or losses be reported in the statement of activities as increases or decreases in net assets without donor restrictions, unless the gains or losses are restricted by donors (in which case they are reported as increases or decreases in net assets with donor restrictions.

Not-for-profits, like governments, must state their investments at fair value. Hence, gains from appreciation include those that are unrealized as well as those that are realized.

CURRENT DISCLOSURE REQUIREMENTS

The toughest investment decision for the managers of some not-for-profits is whether they should place their cash in a checking or a savings account. Others, however, must manage multibillion-dollar portfolios. The Ford Foundation, for example, had assets worth nearly $12 billion (for fiscal year 2016); the endowment portfolio of Harvard University was valued at approximately $33 billion (for fiscal year 2016). Many not-for-profits face the same pressures as governments and businesses to maximize their investment returns. As a result, they may place their funds in sophisticated financial instruments, such as derivatives, and engage in complex transactions, such as interest rate swaps. Financial reporting standards do not address the suitability of particular instruments. Rather, they ensure that reporting entities disclose information as to the value of their investments and the nature of the transactions in which they engage. The disclosure requirements have been set forth in FASB statements (Nos. 107, 155, 157, and 161)[16] that, although designed mainly for businesses, also apply to not-for-profits.

WHAT ARE SPLIT INTEREST AGREEMENTS, AND HOW SHOULD THEY BE ACCOUNTED FOR?

Split interest agreements are a specific type of giving arrangement in which the donor makes a gift to a not-for-profit organization but the organization is not the sole beneficiary. These agreements take many forms, they can be created through trusts or equivalent arrangements, and the accounting is governed by the specific rights and obligations of the recipient organization. Types of split interest agreements include charitable lead trusts, charitable remainder trusts, charitable annuity gifts, and life-interests in real estate. A donor establishes a trust fund, contributes assets to the fund, and appoints a recipient not-for-profit organization as the trustee. The trust agreement provides that as long as the donor or spouse is alive, a set percentage of the trust assets will be distributed to them. Any additional earnings will remain in the trust. Upon the death of both donor and spouse, the trust assets will revert to the not-for-profit organization.

As a general rule, the not-for-profit organization should recognize revenue from a split interest agreement on receipt of the assets. Thus, for example, in the case of the charitable remainder trust, the recipient organization should record the assets received at their fair market value. Correspondingly, however, it should recognize a liability to the other beneficiaries. This liability would be measured as the present value of the estimated future payments (based on actuarial tables) to be made to the donor and spouse. The difference between the assets and the liabilities would be recognized as contribution revenue.[17]

[16] FASB ASC 825-10-50; FASB ASC 815-15-25; FASB ASC 820-10-22; FASB ASC 815-15-65.

[17] For a comprehensive discussion of split interest agreements, see the AICPA Accounting & Auditing Guide, Not-for-Profit Entities (March 2017), Chapter 6 (FASB ASC 958-30).

HOW SHOULD DEPRECIATION BE REPORTED?

As emphasized in previous chapters, owing to their focus on budgets, governments do not currently charge depreciation in their governmental funds—only in their government-wide statements, and proprietary and fiduciary funds. Some not-for-profits, like governments, budget on a cash or near-cash basis, and governing boards, managers, and external constituents are vitally concerned with budget-to-actual comparisons. The major challenge faced by managers and governing boards of most not-for-profits is meeting day-to-day cash demands. Inasmuch as depreciation is not a cost that requires cash, they have little or no interest in it; it does not enter into their financial deliberations or decisions.

On the other hand, as important as the budget is to not-for-profits, it does not have the same force of law that it does for governments. Therefore, not-for-profit statement-users (particularly outsiders to whom general-purpose financial statements are directed) may place greater weight on reporting objectives calling for information on the cost of services than on budgetary compliance. Depreciation represents the cost of consuming assets; in any comparison of service efforts with accomplishments, it may be too significant to ignore.

Example

Depreciation

A not-for-profit job placement service acquires a personal computer for $3,000. It pays for the computer out of a fund restricted to the acquisition of equipment. Estimated useful life is three years.

FASB STANDARDS

The FASB, in its Statement No. 93, *Recognition of Depreciation by Not-for-Profit Organizations* (1987), mandates that not-for-profits "shall recognize the cost of using up the future economic benefits or service potentials of their long-lived tangible assets—depreciation." It requires that they disclose depreciation expense and accumulated depreciation for the period.

The FASB did not indicate the specific funds in which not-for-profits should account for long-lived assets and report depreciation. For purposes of internal control and reporting, some not-for-profits account for long-lived assets, and charge depreciation, in their current operating funds; others maintain special plant funds. However, owing to Statement No. 117, *Financial Statements of Not-for-Profit Organizations*, the fund in which the entity records depreciation has no reporting significance. As discussed previously, Statement No. 117 requires that all expenses be reported as decreases in net assets without donor restrictions. Thus, whether the depreciation is initially recorded in a current operating fund or in a plant fund, it would still be reported in the without donor restrictions column or section of the statement of activities.

In the example, the following entries would record the contribution of the funds to acquire the computer, the acquisition of the computer, and first-year depreciation:

Cash	$3,000	
Contribution revenue		$3,000

To record the contribution of funds restricted to the purchase of a computer (in a fund restricted by donors)

Net assets released from restriction	$3,000	
Cash		$3,000

To record the release of restricted assets to acquire the computer (in a fund restricted by donors)

Equipment	$3,000	
Net assets released from restriction		$3,000

To record the purchase of the computer (in a fund with no donor restrictions)

Depreciation expense	$1,000	
Accumulated depreciation		$1,000

To record first-year depreciation (in a fund without donor restrictions)

An organization may sometimes acquire property, plant, and equipment with funds received by a donor who specifies that the assets must be used for a set period of time. Alternatively, even in the absence of such donor restrictions, the organization may adopt a policy whereby if it acquires long-lived assets from restricted funds, it will impose a time restriction that expires over the life of the asset. In the past, not-for-profits were allowed to release the restricted net assets over time as the asset was depreciated, reflecting the use of the fixed assets over time. ASU No. 2016-14 removes this option for not-for-profits. Instead, not-for-profits are now required to use the placed-in-service approach in which the amounts are reclassified from those with donor restrictions to those without donor restrictions when the fixed asset is placed in service. As a result, not-for-profits will reclassify contributions as net assets without donor restrictions when the fixed asset is placed in service, and not-for-profits will no longer be able to match the depreciation expense from the fixed asset with the release of the restricted net assets.

WHAT ISSUES DOES A NOT-FOR-PROFIT FACE IN ESTABLISHING ITS REPORTING ENTITY?

Not-for-profits, no less than governments, can own or be integrally affiliated with either businesses or other not-for-profits. Indeed, these relationships among not-for-profits can be as varied as those among other types of entities. For the most part, however, the relationships manifest three basic (although overlapping) characteristics:

- ***Ownership.*** An organization may own all or part of another entity. For example, a hospital may own another hospital or a physicians' group practice; a college may own a research laboratory.
- ***Control.*** An organization may control another entity by having the power to appoint the majority of its governing board. For example, a health care organization may establish a fund-raising foundation, specifying that the foundation's governing board be composed of the organization's own officers. Alternatively, per affiliation agreements, a national fraternal organization may have the authority to establish operating policies and standards for its local chapters; a religious "judicatory," such as an archdiocese, presbytery, or synod, may have certain supervisory powers over local churches that are members of its denomination.
- ***Economic interest.*** An organization may have an economic interest in another entity because the entity holds or utilizes resources on its behalf, the entity produces income or provides services to it, or the organization guarantees the debt of the entity. For example, a professional association may provide 100 percent of the funding for a political action committee that lobbies on its behalf; a legally independent, self-governing, fund-raising foundation may support the activities of a university or hospital.

It would be misleading for a not-for-profit, just as for a business or government, to exclude certain affiliated organizations from its reporting entity. The primary source of guidance to date remains the AICPA's 1994 Statement of Position, *Reporting of Related Entities by Not-for-Profit Organizations* (94-3).[18] The overarching theme of that statement is that a not-for-profit should include a related organization in its own reporting entity when it can exercise significant influence over that organization. Its key provisions include the following:

- A not-for-profit organization should consolidate a related not-for-profit organization when it has a controlling financial interest through direct or indirect ownership of a majority voting interest.
- It should also consolidate a related not-for-profit organization when it is able to control that entity by having both a voting majority on its governing board and an "economic interest" (as previously discussed) in that entity. If it has either a voting majority or an economic interest (but not both), then only disclosure of the relationship is required.

[18] FASB ASC 958-810-15.

- It may consolidate another not-for-profit, but is not required to, when it is able to control the other entity by means other than majority ownership or voting interest, such as by means of a contract or affiliation agreement.

Owing to the myriad organizational relationships among not-for-profits, and the fact that sometimes a not-for-profit entity combines its activities with those of other entities, FASB issued Statement No. 164, *Not-for-Profit Entities: Mergers and Acquisitions—Including an Amendment of FASB Statement No. 142* in April 2009.[19] The statement provides guidance to determine whether the combination is a merger or an acquisition and the accounting principles to be followed.

FASB STANDARDS

In FASB Statement No. 164, *Not-for-Profit Entities: Mergers and Acquisitions—Including an Amendment of FASB Statement No. 142* (April 2009), the FASB distinguishes between (a) a merger, in which two or more not-for-profits establish a new not-for-profit entity and cede control of their former entities to the new entity, and (b) an acquisition, in which a not-for-profit obtains control of one or more not-for-profits or businesses and initially recognizes the assets and liabilities of the acquired entities in its own financial statements.

If the combination qualifies as a merger, the new not-for-profit should combine (add together) in its financial statements the amounts in the predecessor entities' financial statements as of the merger date. It should not recognize additional assets or liabilities as of the merger date or remeasure at fair value the assets and liabilities of the combining entities. By contrast, if the combination meets the criteria of an acquisition, the acquirer should recognize all identifiable assets and liabilities of the acquired entity and report them at their fair values at the acquisition date.

Comprehensive Example

Museum of American Culture

This example, which focuses on the fictional Museum of American Culture, synthesizes several of the principles presented so far. We start with the museum's statement of financial position as of December 31, 2020 (presented in Table 12-6), account for the transactions in which the museum engaged during 2021 (journalized in the body of the text), and prepare selected financial statements as of December 31, 2021 (presented in Table 12-7).

The museum engages in two main programs: curatorial and exhibits, and education. These are backed by two support functions: fund-raising and administration.

The key transactions in which the museum engaged during the year (in summary form) follow (in thousands).

Accrual of Wages and Salaries

Museum employees earned wages and salaries of $1,045. During the year the museum paid employees $1,039, including $8 from the previous year. At year-end, it owed employees $14, which was slated to be paid in early 2022. Hence, a provision must be made for the wages and salaries earned but not yet paid.

FASB ASU No. 2016-14, *Financial Statements of Not-for-Profit Organizations*, provides that the statement of activities shall set forth expenses by *function*. The museum allocated the wages and salaries to its functions as indicated in the following entry:

Wages and salaries—curatorial and exhibits	$780	
Wages and salaries—education	85	
Wages and salaries—fund-raising	50	
Wages and salaries—administration	130	
Cash		$1,039
Accrued wages and salaries payable		6

To record wages and salaries (in a fund without donor restrictions)

[19] FASB ASC 958-40-28.

TABLE 12-6 Museum of American Culture

Statement of Financial Position December 31, 2020
(in thousands)

Assets	
Current assets	
Cash	$ 120
Investments	4,210
Pledges receivable	165
Less: allowance for uncollectibles	(15)
	150
Supplies inventory	20
Prepaid expenses	50
Total current assets	4,550
Property, plant, and equipment	2,100
Less: accumulated depreciation	(540)
	1,560
Total assets	6,110
Liabilities	
Current liabilities	
Wages and salaries payable	$ 8
Accounts payable	250
Total liabilities	258
Net assets	
Without donor restrictions	$2,002
With donor restrictions	3,850
Total net assets	$5,852

Other Operating Expenses; Inventory

The museum incurred other operating expenses of $280 ($200 in curatorial and exhibit costs, $30 for education, $10 for fund-raising, and $40 for administration). The expenses are, of course, accounted for on an accrual basis and must also be allocated to the organization's functions.

Consistent with the accrual basis, the museum is required to account for both supplies inventory and prepaid items on the *consumption basis*. During the period, the museum purchased $5 more of supplies than it used, and as a consequence, inventory increased by the same amount. Moreover, it reduced its balances in accounts payable by $3 and in prepaid expenses by $7. It disbursed a total of $281 in cash relating to the operating expenses:

Other operating expenses—curatorial and exhibits	$200	
Other operating expenses—education	30	
Other operating expenses—fund-raising	10	
Other operating expenses—administration	40	
Accounts payable	3	
Inventory	5	
Cash		$281
Prepaid expenses		7

To record other operating expenses (in a fund without donor restrictions)

Acquisition of Long-lived Assets; Long-Term Debt

The museum acquired $20 of new furniture and fixtures in exchange for a long-term note of the same amount. Although for internal purposes many not-for-profits account for both their long-lived assets and related long-term debt in a plant fund (mentioned in Chapter 2), this museum accounts for them in its operating fund (a fund without donor restrictions). For reporting purposes, the results would be the same. The assets are reported in the funds without donor restrictions along with other resources that do not carry donor restrictions:

Property, plant, and equipment	$20	
Notes payable		$20
To record the acquisition of fixed assets (in a fund without donor restrictions)		

Unlike governments (in their governmental fund statements), not-for-profits must account for interest on the long-term note on the accrual basis.

Depreciation

The museum recognized depreciation of $210. Depreciation, like other expenses, is always recorded in a fund without donor restrictions:

Depreciation expense—curatorial and exhibits	$160	
Depreciation expense—education	15	
Depreciation expense—fund-raising	5	
Depreciation expense—administration	30	
Allowance for depreciation		$210
To record depreciation (in a fund without donor restrictions)		

Admissions and Memberships

The museum's main operating revenues are derived from admissions and membership fees. In 2021 they totaled $505:

Cash	$505	
Revenues—admissions and memberships		$505
To record revenues from admissions and members (in a fund without donor restrictions)		

Interest and Dividends

The museum earned $280 in interest and dividends on its investments, most of which are held in an endowment fund. For this particular museum, the endowment income does not have donor restrictions and thereby should be recorded in the operating fund and reported as income without donor restrictions. Were it restricted to a specific purpose, it would be recorded in a fund with donor restrictions and reported as income restricted by a donor. The endowment principal itself is also accounted for in the fund with donor restrictions and disclosed in the notes. For internal bookkeeping purposes, many not-for-profits initially account for endowment interest and dividends in the endowment fund and then transfer them to the beneficiary funds. For external reporting purposes, however, the investment income should be reported as revenue of the beneficiary fund:

Cash	$280	
Investment earnings—interest and dividends		$280
To record dividends and interest (in a fund without donor restrictions)		

Changes in Fair Values

During the year, the fair value of the museum's investments increased by $100. Assuming that there are no explicit legal or donor-imposed restrictions requiring that gains from the appreciation of the endowment portfolios be added to the principal of the endowment, the increase in fair value would be recognized as investment earnings without donor restrictions—the same as dividends and interest.

Investments	$100	
Investment earnings—appreciation in fair value		$100
To record appreciation in fair value (in a fund without donor restrictions)		

Revenues and Expenses of Auxiliary Enterprises

The museum operates a gift shop. In 2021 revenues and expenses totaled $470 and $350, respectively.

Governments account for their business-type activities in enterprise funds. These funds are accounted for on the full accrual basis and, for purposes of external reporting, are not combined with governmental funds.

Because not-for-profits account for their general operations on full accrual basis, there is less need to separate their business from their nonbusiness activities. Although it is usually convenient to account for "auxiliary" activities (i.e., business-type activities) in separate funds, for external purposes they are usually reported along with other operations and the resources classified as without donor restrictions. Many not-for-profits aggregate their auxiliary revenues on one line and their auxiliary expenses on another. Others break out the revenues and expenses by individual, or types of, enterprises. The following summary entry would capture the museum's 2021 auxiliary activities:

Expenses applicable to auxiliary activities	$350	
Cash	120	
Revenues from auxiliary activities		$470

To record the activities of auxiliary activities (in a fund without donor restrictions)

Insofar as the revenues and expenses affected accounts other than cash, such as inventory, prepaid expenses, and allowance for depreciation, then those statement of financial position accounts, rather than cash, would be debited or credited.

Pledges with and without Donor Restrictions

During the year, the museum conducted a fund-raising campaign. As of year-end it received cash of $338 and pledges for $180.

Contributions, including unconditional promises to pay, should generally be recognized as revenue on receipt. However, the pledges outstanding, inasmuch as they are unavailable for expenditures (and thereby subject to time restrictions), should be reflected as an increase in restricted resources, and disclosed in the notes.

Cash	$338	
Revenue from contributions without donor restrictions		$338

To record contributions without donor restrictions (in a fund without donor restrictions)

Pledges receivable (restricted by donor)	$180	
Revenue from contributions without donor restrictions		$180

To record pledges subject to time restrictions (in a fund with donor restrictions)

It is assumed that these pledges will be received with a few months of year-end and hence it is unnecessary to discount them to take into account the time value of money.

Of these (temporarily) restricted pledges, the museum estimates that $20 will be uncollectible.

Other operating expenses—fund-raising (uncollectible pledges—not restricted by donors)	$20	
Net assets released from restrictions (net assets without donor restrictions)		$20

To record the estimated bad debt expense (in a fund without donor restrictions)

Net assets released from restrictions (net assets with donor restrictions)	$20	
Allowance for uncollectible pledges (with donor restrictions)		$20

To add to the allowance for uncollectible pledges (in a fund with donor restrictions)

The latter two entries, although potentially confusing, are necessary because the pledges are being recorded as restricted by donors. Hence, the allowance for uncollectibles must also be recorded as restricted by donors. As emphasized previously, however, not-for-profits must recognize all expenses as not having donor restrictions. Hence, the expense for uncollectible pledges (herein aggregated with other operating expenses and allocated to fund-raising) must be recorded in a fund without donor restrictions. As is required when other restricted resources are used for their intended purposes, they must be released from their restrictions and, in effect, "transferred" from the restricted by donors to the without donor restriction categories.

During the year, the museum collected $145 of time-restricted pledges receivable outstanding from prior years and wrote off $10 as uncollectible:

Cash	$145	
Net assets released from restrictions		$145
To record cash collected on outstanding pledges (in a fund without donor restrictions)		
Net assets released from restriction	$145	
Allowance for uncollectible pledges	10	
Pledges receivable		$155
To release resources from time restrictions and to write-off uncollectible pledges (in a fund with donor restrictions)		

Use-Restricted Contributions

The museum received a $90 contribution from a patron who required that the gift be used to acquire additional works of art. During the year, the museum used the gift, along with $620 of resources that had previously been restricted by donors, to add to its collection.

Because the gift is restricted (and in this instance the museum did not expect to expend it in the current year), it should be disclosed in the notes as affecting the museum's liquidity:

Cash	$90	
Revenue from restricted contributions		$90
To record contributions restricted to acquisition of art (in a fund restricted by donors)		

This museum, like most others, elects *not* to capitalize its art collection (as long as it satisfies the FASB conditions that allow for this choice). Therefore, the costs to acquire the new art would be reported as an expense. However, because not-for-profits must report all expenses in a fund without donor restrictions, the resources must be released from the donor-restricted fund to the current fund:

Net assets released from restriction	$710	
Cash		$710
To record the release of restricted resources upon acquiring new art (in a fund restricted by donors)		
Acquisition of art—expense	$710	
Net assets released from restrictions		$710
To record the acquisition of art (in a fund without donor restrictions)		

To pay for the art, the museum sold $500 of investments without donor restrictions. There was no gain or loss on sale inasmuch as the museum carried the investments at fair value:

Cash	$500	
Investments		$500
To record the sale of investments (in a fund without donor restrictions)		

Volunteer Services

The museum benefits from the services provided by volunteer guides. Guides are essential to the operations of the museum, and were it not able to attract these volunteers, the museum would have to hire them. Nevertheless, the guides do not have to possess specialized abilities (those characteristic of skilled workers or professionals), and therefore the museum may not recognize the value of their services as either revenues or expenses. The museum might disclose the amount of volunteer hours in the notes to the financial statements.

Table 12-7 summarizes the museum's 2021 transactions in a statement of activity, a year-end statement of financial position, a schedule of program and support expenses, and a statement of cash flows.

TABLE 12-7 Museum of American Culture

Statement of Activities
For the Year Ending December 31, 2021 (in thousands)

	Without Donor Restrictions	With Donor Restrictions	Total
Support and revenues			
Admissions and memberships	$ 505		$ 505
Investments—dividends and interest	280		280
Investments—appreciation	100		100
Revenue from auxiliary enterprises	470		470
Unrestricted contributions, including pledges	338	$ 180	518
Restricted contributions		90	90
Net assets released from restrictions	875	(875)	
Total support and revenues	$2,568	$ (605)	$1,963
Expenses			
Program			
Curatorial and exhibits	$1,140		$1,140
Education	130		130
Support services			
Fund-raising	85		85
Administration	200		200
Acquisition of art	710		710
Expenses of auxiliary enterprises	350		350
Total expenses	$2,615		$2,615
Excess (deficiency) of support and revenue over expenses	$ (47)	$ (605)	$ (652)
Net (decrease) in fund balances	$ (47)	$ (605)	$ (652)
Net assets, beginning of period	2,002	3,850	5,852
Net assets, end of period	$1,955	$ 3,245	$5,200

Statement of Financial Position December 31, 2021 (in thousands)

Assets	
Current assets	
Cash	$ 68
Investments	3,810
Pledges receivable	190
Less: allowance for uncollectibles	(25)
	165
Supplies inventory	25
Prepaid expenses	43
Total current assets	$4,111
Property, plant, and equipment	$2,120
Less: accumulated depreciation	(750)
	$1,370
Total assets	$5,481

(Continues)

TABLE 12-7 Museum of American Culture *(Continued)*

Statement of Financial Position December 31, 2021 (in thousands)

Liabilities	
Current liabilities	
Wages and salaries payable	$ 14
Accounts payable	247
Total current liabilities	$ 261
Note payable	20
Total liabilities	$ 281
Net assets	
Without Donor Restrictions	$1,955
With Donor Restrictions	3,245
Total net assets	$5,200

Schedule of Program and Support Expenses For the Year Ending December 31, 2021 (in thousands)

	Curatorial & Exhibit	Education	Fund-Raising	Administration and Other	Total
Wages and salaries	$ 780	$ 85	$50	$ 130	$1,045
Other operating expenses	200	30	30	40	300
Depreciation	160	15	5	30	210
Acquisition of art				710	710
Auxiliary enterprise				350	350
Total	$1,140	$130	$85	$1,260	$2,615

Statement of Cash Flows For the Year Ending December 31, 2021

Cash flows from operating activities	
Contributions	$ 573
Admissions and memberships	505
Interest and dividends	280
Cash from auxiliary enterprises	120
Cash from sale of investments	500
Wages and salaries paid	(1,039)
Purchases of art	(710)
Payments for other operating expenses	(281)
Net cash provided by operating activities; net increase (decrease) in cash	$ (52)
Cash on hand, beginning of year	120
Supplemental data	$ 68
Supplemental data	
Noncash investing and financing activity—acquisition of property, plant, and equipment in exchange for a note payable	$ 20

HOW SHOULD THE COSTS OF FUND-RAISING ACTIVITIES BE DETERMINED?

Contributors, as well as other users of financial statements, want assurance that their donations are being used mainly to support substantive programs and activities rather than merely additional fund-raising or administrative efforts. To be sure, few individuals drop their coins into a charity's canister contingent on receiving financial statements. However, private foundations, umbrella agencies such the United Way, and major donors almost always demand detailed financial data prior to making a commitment of resources. Moreover, state and local government regulatory authorities established to deter fraud may require that organizations permitted to solicit funds in their jurisdictions furnish information on how they spend their resources.

Fund-raising activities are often carried out in conjunction with programmatic or administrative activities. Therefore, the costs of the fund-raising activities may not be easily distinguishable from those of the other activities.

Consider the following activities that are intended not only to advance an organization's main mission but also to solicit donations:

- The American Cancer Society takes out newspaper advertisements alerting readers to the seven danger signals of cancer. The ads include a plea for funds, accompanied by a coupon asking for the donor's name, address, and amount of contribution.
- Friends of the Environment conduct a door-to-door campaign seeking signatures on a petition urging a city council not to permit development in a wildlife habitat area. Each person spoken to is asked also to make a financial contribution to aid additional advocacy efforts.
- A hospital mails its annual report, which contains its financial statements and a report on its accomplishments, to trustees, employees, and previous donors. An accompanying letter suggests programs for which additional financial support is needed.
- An organization that seeks to prevent teenage drug abuse conducts a broad-based mail campaign to solicit funds. It includes in each mailing a pamphlet informing teens of ways in which they can "just say no" to their peers.

Each of these situations raises two related questions:

- Should the costs of the activity be apportioned between fund-raising and mission-related programs?
- If so, on what basis should they be apportioned?

In a 1998 Statement of Position (SOP 98-2), Accounting for Costs of Activities of Not-for-Profit Organizations and State and Local Governmental Entities that Include Fund-Raising,[20] the AICPA addressed both of these issues.

CRITERIA FOR ALLOCATING A PORTION OF COSTS TO PROGRAM OR MANAGEMENT FUNCTIONS

Left unchecked, many organizations would prefer to assign costs to programmatic rather than to fund-raising efforts. In that way, they would appear to be spending more of their funds fulfilling the purposes for which they were established.

The AICPA directs that not-for-profit organizations classify as fund-raising all costs of activities that include fund-raising as well as programmatic, management, or general functions unless the activities satisfy three broad criteria:

- Purpose
- Audience
- Content

[20] FASB ASC 958-720 (05, 45, 55)

That is, if an activity does satisfy *all* three criteria, then its costs may be allocated between fund-raising and the other applicable functions. If it does not, then *all* of its costs must be classified as fund-raising.

Purpose

The purpose criterion is met if the purpose of a joint activity includes accomplishing program or management and general functions. Factors that would indicate such a purpose include

- The activity calls for specific action by the audience that will help accomplish the entity's mission. For example, if the mission of an organization were to improve individuals' physical health, then an advertisement advising people on specific ways to stop smoking would satisfy the purpose criterion.
- The organization conducts a similar program or management activity separately and on a similar or greater scale. Suppose, for example, an environmental organization takes out a full-page newspaper ad appealing for donations and urging readers to recycle trash. The ad would be consistent with the purpose criterion if the organization ran similar full-page ads that promoted recycling but did not ask for donations.
- Other evidence—such as the measures used to assess the results and accomplishments of the joint activity, the qualifications of the parties carrying it out and organizational mission statements, minutes, or plans make it clear that the activity goes beyond fund-raising.

The purpose criterion is not met if a majority of compensation or fees paid to outside contractors—such as consultants—is based on contributions raised.

Audience

The audience criterion is met if the audience for the materials or activities is selected principally on its need for the program or for its ability to advance program goals in ways other than by financial support. Thus, in the examples presented earlier, the American Cancer Society would satisfy the criterion because its advertisement was directed to a broad segment of society, all the members of which are potential cancer victims. By contrast, the drug abuse organization would not (unless the mailing was specifically targeted at households with teenagers) because most of the recipients of the mailing would unlikely be of the age group toward which the informational pamphlet was aimed. Campaigns targeted exclusively at high-income individuals, selected mainly because of their ability to give, would seldom satisfy the criterion.

Content

The content criterion is met if the materials or activities call for specific actions that will help accomplish the entity's mission beyond providing financial support. For example, they might ask the recipients to take actions that would either improve the recipients' own physical, emotional, or spiritual well-being or address a societal need. If the materials or activities are in support of management or general functions, then they should fulfill one or more of the entity's management responsibilities—such as reporting on the organization's accomplishments or financial status.

Example

Allocating Charitable Costs

Facts. The Citizens for Educational Reform conducts a telephone campaign, both to solicit funds and to urge the persons called to write their legislators in favor of increased spending for education. The telephone list was purchased from a fund-raising concern and includes only households with incomes in the top 10 percent of the population.

Conclusion. In the absence of compelling evidence that persons in upper-income households are especially likely to contact their legislators in favor of increased spending for education, the campaign would not satisfy the audience criterion, and hence, all costs of the campaign should be reported as fund-raising costs.

Facts. The Protect our Children Society sends a brochure, along with a request for donations, to all citizens within selected areas of a city that have high crime rates. The brochures recommend ways in which parents can shield their children from criminal activity. The brochures were prepared by an outside consultant whose only compensation will be a percentage of the contributions received.

Conclusion. The mailing does not satisfy the purpose criterion, as the majority of compensation is based on amount of funds raised.

Facts. The Senior Citizens Coalition sends representatives to speak to senior citizens groups about the virtues of physical exercise. After a presentation, the coalition mails to each person that attended a request for a contribution, along with literature advising how to maintain a healthy lifestyle.

Conclusion. The mailing satisfies all three criteria, and its costs should be allocated between fund-raising and educational programs.

MEANS OF ALLOCATION

The statement of position allows organizations broad discretion in allocating joint costs between fund-raising and other activities. It specifies only that the method should be "rational and systematic," that it should result in an allocation that is reasonable, and that it should be applied consistently. It further emphasizes that costs need not be allocated when a fund-raising activity is only incidental to a substantive program or management activity (e.g., when a single line in an advertisement otherwise devoted entirely to a programmatic purpose provides an address to which contributions may be sent). The following three methods are among those that would be considered rational and systematic.

Physical Units Method

The joint costs are allocated on the basis of physical units—such as number of lines or square inches. Suppose an American Cancer Society newspaper ad costs $10,000. Based on square inches, 80 percent of the ad is directed to information about the disease and 20 percent to an appeal for funds. The organization would allocate $8,000 to its information program and $2,000 to fund-raising.

Relative Direct Costs Method

The joint costs are allocated to each of the component activities based on the identifiable direct costs. Suppose an organization mails to supporters an informational brochure, a flyer asking for a contribution, and a return envelope in which to mail the contribution. The mission-related brochures cost $90,000, whereas the fund-raising flyers and return envelopes cost $10,000. Direct costs thereby total $100,000, 90 percent of which are directed to informational activities and 10 percent to fund-raising. Common mailing costs, including postage and the outside envelope, cost $15,000. Based on the direct costs, the organization would allocate 90 percent ($13,500) of the common mailing costs to informational activities and 10 percent ($1,500) to fund-raising.

Stand-Alone Costs Method

The joint costs are allocated to each of the components based on what it would have cost to conduct each of the component activities independently. Suppose in the previous example, it would have cost a total of $100,000 to produce the brochures and mail them separately ($90,000 for the brochures and $10,000 for envelopes and postage). It would have cost $18,000 to send and mail the solicitation flyers and return envelopes ($10,000 for the flyers and $8,000 for the outside envelopes and postage). Hence, total costs would have been $118,000. Based on this amount the organization would allocate the $15,000 in common costs as follows:

Informational program	$100,000/118,000 × $15,000 = $12,712
Fund-raising	$18,000/118,000 × $15,000 = 2,288
Total common cost allocated	$15,000

HOW CAN A NOT-FOR-PROFIT'S FISCAL CONDITION BE ASSESSED?

In the previous chapter, we emphasized that the fiscal condition of a government can be assessed only by taking into account a wide range of economic, demographic, and social factors, many of which may not be incorporated into a complete CAFR, let alone in the basic financial statements. In a broad sense, the outline in Table 11-4, "A City's Fiscal Status: A Comprehensive Analysis," is as applicable to not-for-profits as it is to governments.

Every type of organization has unique characteristics, and an analysis must be custom-crafted to take them into account. Some not-for-profits are comparable to businesses, and hence the approach taken in a financial analysis of a business would generally be applicable to them. Thus, for example, insofar as not-for-profit hospitals rely mainly on patient billings for their revenues, the factors that affect the fiscal health of a not-for-profit hospital would generally be similar to those affecting a comparable for-profit institution. Indeed, most not-for-profit hospitals today are in direct competition with stockholder-owned facilities. Likewise, the fiscal dynamics of a not-for-profit country club are not very different from those of a for-profit club.

Other not-for-profits are more like governments in that their revenues are derived mainly from sources other than exchange transactions—grants and contributions. However, they lack at least two characteristics that may make it decidedly more difficult for an outsider to evaluate these not-for-profits. First, they lack the power to tax. To be sure, the tax revenues of governments may always be subject to the uncertainties of the economy and other factors. Nevertheless, within limits, governments can generally either increase taxes or reduce services to tide them over hard times. Not-for-profits, by contrast, may have no guaranteed revenue sources, and even mild perturbations in the overall economy or in the funding policies of grantors can have a profound impact on their fiscal wherewithal. Second, because not-for-profits are private rather than public institutions, their financial reports are not nearly as informative as those of governments, or even publicly traded corporations. For example, the reports are not required to include a management's discussion and analysis or a detailed statistical section comparable to those of governments.

Still other not-for-profits are hybrids, relying both on exchange and nonexchange revenues. Certain voluntary health and welfare organizations, such as those providing services for a designated group of citizens, may be funded by a mix of government contracts (exchange revenues) and contributions (nonexchange revenues).

TRADITIONAL FINANCIAL INDICATORS

Traditional financial indicators and ratios, most of which are similar to those applicable to both businesses and governments, are also germane to not-for-profits. These include, but are not limited to, those that assess:

- ***Liquidity:*** The quick ratio (cash, short-term investments, and current receivables to current liabilities) and the current ratio (current assets to current liabilities)

- ***Burden of debt:*** Total debt to total assets
- ***Adequacy of available resources:*** Net assets without donor restrictions (preferably excluding capital assets) divided by expenses (This ratio provides an indication of the extent to which the organization has "reserves" in case of a temporary imbalance between revenues and expenses)
- ***Current fiscal performance:*** The extent of operating surpluses or deficits
- ***Reliability of budgetary projections:*** Both the dollar and percentage variances between budgeted revenues and expenses and actual results

INDICATORS OF SPECIAL RELEVANCE TO NOT-FOR-PROFITS

Analysts of not-for-profits must go beyond the traditional financial indicators. Of unique concern is how a not-for-profit spends its money. First and foremost, an analyst needs to know how and what proportion of an organization's revenues are directed to its main mission as opposed to its administrative and fund-raising expenses. Organizations that exist mainly to pay the salaries of administrators and fund-raisers are unlikely to attract future contributions and be viable over the long-term. Accordingly, the following two ratios are central to any assessment of a not-for-profit entity:

- ***Fund-raising ratio:*** This ratio, which measures fund-raising expense as a percentage of total related revenues, can be expected to vary widely among not-for-profit organizations depending on their nature. Some organizations, especially those that derive most of their revenues from exchange transactions, incur no fund-raising costs. Others, however, including some that border on the fraudulent, spend almost all of their revenues on fund-raising (and salaries of administrators). Per the Better Business Bureau Wise Giving Alliance, this ratio should be no greater than 35 percent.
- ***Program ratio:*** Similar in concept to the fund-raising ratio, this ratio compares expenses devoted to mission-oriented programs to the total of fund-raising and administrative costs. The Better Business Bureau Wise Giving Alliance advises that program expenses should be at least 65 percent of *all* expenses (i.e., program, fund-raising, and administrative expenses).

Neither of these ratios measure "efficiency"—which examines outputs relative to inputs—even though they are frequently referred to as efficiency ratios. Also of interest to analysts of not-for-profit entities is how they obtain their revenues—in particular, the stability of their funding sources. The following two ratios are therefore of special relevance:

- ***Contributions and grants ratio:*** This ratio indicates revenues from contributions and grants as a percentage of total revenues and thereby encourages the analyst to consider the riskiness of the entity's revenue stream.
- ***Revenue from services ratio:*** Complementing the contributions and grants ratio, this ratio indicates revenues from fees and other charges for goods and services as a percentage of total revenues.

Generally but not always, contributions and grants are a less reliable source of revenue than user charges. Much more significant is the character of the revenues. Thus, for example, a theater company that relies on a few major grants from governments or private foundations, for which it must reapply each year, may face greater risks than one that derives its revenues mainly from ticket sales. On the other hand, if the theater company's ticket sales are dependent on a few major hits each season, then it too may face special threats to its fiscal stability.

Obviously there can be no universal guidelines as to what constitutes acceptable revenue ratios; all depends on the type of institution. Institutions that traditionally charge for their services,

IN PRACTICE NOT-FOR PROFITS, LIKE CORPORATIONS, TAINTED BY SCANDALS

Not-for-profit organizations, like their corporate counterparts, have been tainted by scandal. In 2004 and 2005 both the U.S. Senate Finance Committee and House of Representatives' Ways and Means Committee conducted hearings on the operations of not-for-profit organizations. In addition, the Internal Revenue Service reviewed tax abuses of charities and private foundations. As a consequence of their concerns, the Panel on the Nonprofit Sector was established in 2007. Composed mainly of the heads of leading foundations and charities, the panel undertook a thorough examination of the governance, transparency, and ethical standards of the not-for-profit sector, and issued principles of sound practice. These principles were updated in 2015 and contain 33 principles covering legal compliance and public disclosure, effective governance, strong financial oversight, and responsible fundraising.

The types of abuses the panel identified included

- The establishment of "donor-advised" entities in which donors contribute to a supposed charitable organization and obtain the resultant tax deductions. However, the donors retain control of the contributed funds and direct them so that they, rather than a legitimate charity or the public, are the ultimate beneficiaries.
- Credit counseling organizations that do more to enrich the individuals who established them than to provide assistance to the debtors who seek advice
- Individuals and corporations that take tax deductions for noncash gifts that greatly exceed the true value of the donated assets
- Excessive compensation of executives and board members
- Excessive expenditures for travel
- Poor board oversight as a result of board members' conflicts of interest and lack of training and expertise
- Failure of boards to establish an effective audit committee and to otherwise properly oversee financial matters
- Inadequate disclosure of both financial and performance data[21]

[21] The panel's report, Strengthening Transparency, Governance, and Accountability of Charitable Organizations: A Final Report to Congress and the Nonprofit Sector (June 2005), includes recommendations that address each of the listed abuses. It is available at the website of the Nonprofit Panel Report from the Independent Sector, www.nonprofitpanel.org/report/final/panel final report.pdf.

such as educational and health care organizations, can be expected to have very different ratios than those that rely primarily on donations.

Nevertheless, the ratios can be useful in comparing similar entities and in calling attention to changes in the mix of revenues within the same organization over time. The ratios must, however, be tailored to the specific type of organization being evaluated. Thus, for example, if one is assessing a medical research organization, the contributions and grants and the revenue from services ratios should be disaggregated for key specific sources of revenues, such as grants from the federal government, grants from private foundations, and gifts from individuals.

SOURCES OF INFORMATION ABOUT NOT-FOR-PROFITS

A wealth of information on not-for-profit organizations is readily available through the Internet. Philanthropic Research, Inc., whose mission is to collect and disseminate information on not-for-profit organizations, maintains an online database known as GuideStar (www.guidestar .org). The site contains extensive financial data on over 1.8 million IRS-recognized tax-exempt organizations and thousands of faith-based nonprofits not required to register with the IRS. Most of the digitized data are from the Internal Revenue Service (IRS) Form 990 filed by most organizations.[22] This is the informational tax form that most tax-exempt organizations must file annually to report on their finances to the federal government. This website provides millions of Form 990 images as well as information about the organization's mission, its classification based on the National Taxonomy of Exempt Entities (NTEE) system used by the IRS,[23] its officers and directors, and its goals and results.

[22] Some organizations, such as political organizations, churches and other religious organizations, are exempt from filing an annual Form 990.

[23] http://nccs.urban.org/classification/NTEE.cfm.

Form 990 contains a wealth of financial information about not-for-profit organizations. In addition to far more detailed data that would be found on the income statements and balance sheets of a typical not-for-profit organization, it includes a statement of "program service accomplishments," as well as information on the composition of the governing board, the compensation of management, the main beneficiaries of support to other organizations that it provided and the main sources of its own support. By collecting this information, the IRS wants to ensure that organizations continue to qualify for tax exemption after the status is granted.

The Better Business Bureau Wise Giving Alliance website (www.give.org), also provides fiscal and related information about hundreds of charitable organizations that solicit contributions. The alliance has established 20 standards that it expects charitable organizations to meet and reports whether each organization has met them. These standards pertain to governance and oversight, measuring effectiveness, finances, and fund-raising and informational materials. Another watchdog agency, Charity Navigator, also evaluates not-for-profit organizations, and these ratings are available on its website charitynavigator.org. As suggested by the accompanying "In Practice," whether one assesses a not-for-profit entity from the perspective of a donor, a creditor, or an analyst, a healthy skepticism is always in order.

SUMMARY

The Financial Accounting Standards Board (FASB) sets accounting standards for not-for-profits other than governments. As might be expected, therefore, not-for-profits, like businesses, are on a full accrual basis of accounting. However, inasmuch as not-for-profits typically derive a substantial portion of their revenues from contributions, many of which are restricted by donors, the form of their financial statements differs from those of businesses, and they must adhere to special guidelines as to revenue and expense recognition. Not-for-profits must disclose additional information about their liquidity, and also any information about endowments that may have fallen below their historic dollar value.

Per FASB pronouncements, not-for-profits should classify their resources into two categories: without donor restrictions and with donor restrictions. Whether or not resources are restricted is based solely on donor stipulations. Not-for-profits should report all expenses as changes in resources without donor restrictions. By contrast, governments can report expenses in both restricted and unrestricted funds.

Not-for-profits should recognize as revenue all unconditional contributions, including both pledges and restricted donations, when they are received. However, they should recognize conditional contributions only as the conditions are satisfied. Governments, on the other hand, account for their governmental funds on a modified accrual basis. Therefore, they recognize fund revenues, irrespective of source, only when they satisfy the "available" criterion. In their government-wide statements, similar to not-for-profits, they accrue contributions as soon as all eligibility requirements have been met.

Not-for-profits, according to the FASB, should recognize contributed services only if they are of a professional nature and are of the type that would have to be paid for if not donated. Similar to governments, they are also encouraged, but not required, to recognize and capitalize donations of art objects as long as they are held for public exhibition, are properly cared for, and will not be sold for purposes other than the acquisition of other collectibles. Unlike governments, they should not recognize contributions of collectibles as revenues when they do not capitalize them.

Not-for-profits, like governments, face special problems of accounting for pass-through grants and contributions. As a general rule, not-for-profits should not recognize as revenue contributions that they have agreed to transfer to other specific beneficiaries. They are permitted to recognize the contributions as revenue only if they have been granted variance power or are financially interrelated with the beneficiary organization. Not-for-profit organizations face the problem of how to allocate common costs of fund-raising and program and administrative activities. The AICPA's three general criteria for concluding that a bona fide program or management function has been conducted involve purpose, audience, and content.

The fiscal health of not-for-profits can be assessed using traditional financial ratios, such as those that measure liquidity and the burden of debt. Of additional concern to some analysts are those that indicate the percentage of contributions that support the main mission of the organizations as opposed to administrative and fund-raising activities. Ultimately, however, the fiscal wherewithal of not-for-profits, like that of governments, depends on a wide range of economic, social, and demographic factors. Therefore, although analysts should view the financial statements as a key source of information, they must also look to other sources.

KEY TERMS IN THIS CHAPTER

EXERCISE FOR REVIEW AND SELF-STUDY

The statement of financial position, the statement of activities, and the statement of cash flows for March of Dimes for 2016 are presented in Table 12-8. Note that these financial statements were changed to reflect the accounting standards discussed in this chapter. The March of Dimes carries out four programs to fight premature births and other infant health problems:

- **Research.** Partnering with universities and hospitals across the United States to discover the unknown causes of premature birth and translate these findings into practice.
- **Education.** Educating mothers and health care providers in best practices to eliminate medically unnecessary early deliveries.
- **Community Outreach.** Supporting local and hospital programming to improve maternal and child health within the community
- **Advocacy.** Through volunteers around the country, working for legislative wins in topics ranging from access to health care to funding for prematurity-related research

TABLE 12-8 **March of Dimes Foundation**

Balance Sheet
December 31, 2016, with comparative amounts as of December 31, 2015
(amounts in thousands)

Assets	2016	2015
Cash and cash equivalents	$18,633	$ 13,446
Sponsorships and other receivables	9,418	8,077
Inventory receivable	548	5,080
Inventory and other assets	4,706	5,534
Investments	43,317	61,709
Assets held in trust by others	10,382	10,250
Land, building and equipment—net	7,166	8,767
Total assets	$94,170	$112,863
Liabilities and Net Assets		
Accounts payable and accrued expenses	$ 14,905	$ 15,998
Line of credit	—	5,000
Grants and awards payable—net	19,746	22,646
Refundable advances and deferred revenue	3,943	2,249
Accrued pension and postretirement benefit obligation	68,479	53,555

(Continues)

TABLE 12-8 March of Dimes Foundation *(Continued)*

Balance Sheet
December 31, 2016, with comparative amounts as of December 31, 2015
(amounts in thousands)

Assets	2016	2015
Total liabilities	107,073	99,448
Commitments and contingencies (notes 8 and 9)		
Net assets (deficit)		
Unrestricted		
Operating	37,553	49,767
Accrued pension and postretirement benefit obligation	(68,479)	(53,555)
Total without donor restrictions	(30,926)	(3,788)
With donor restrictions	18,023	17,203
Total net assets (deficit)	(12,903)	13,415
Total liabilities and net assets	$ 94,170	$112,863

See accompanying notes to financial statements

March of Dimes Foundation
Statement of Activities Year ended
December 31, 2016, with summarized totals for the year ended December 31, 2015
(Amounts in thousands)

	Without donor restrictions	With donor restrictions	2016 Total	2015 Total
Operating activity				
Revenue				
Campaign contributions and sponsorships	$ 167,504	–	167,504	182,456
Less direct benefits to donors and sponsors	(13,880)	–	(13,880)	(14,886)
Net campaign contributions and sponsorships	153,624	–	153,624	167,570
Bequests	1,399	41	1,440	2,994
Government, foundation and corporate grants	2,852	867	3,719	3,901
Major gifts and other contributions	4,143	781	4,924	6,765
Contributed materials and services	1,370	–	1,370	2,143
Investment return appropriated for operations	2,762	338	3,100	5,750
Program service revenue	1,415	–	1,415	1,832
Other	2,395	–	2,395	1,151
Net assets released from restrictions	1,506	(1,506)	–	–
Total revenue	171,466	521	171,987	192,106
Expenses				
Program services				
Research and medical support	26,096	–	26,096	31,263

(Continues)

TABLE 12-8 **March of Dimes Foundation** *(Continued)*

Public and professional education	64,686	—	64,686	78,609
Community services	44,008	—	44,008	52,939
Total program services	134,790	—	134,790	162,811
Supporting services				
Management and general	19,451	—	19,451	23,137
Fund raising	25,167	—	25,167	29,780
Total supporting services	44,618	—	44,618	52,917
Total expenses	179,408	—	179,408	215,728
(Deficiency) excess of operating revenue over expenses	(7,942)	521	(7,421)	(23,622)
Nonoperating activity				
Investment return greater (less) than amount appropriated for operations	934	167	1,101	(6,152)
Net (decrease) increase in fair value of assets held in trust by others	—	132	132	(837)
Pension and postretirement (costs) credit other than net periodic benefit costs	(20,130)	—	(20,130)	19,409
Change in net assets	(27,138)	820	(26,318)	(11,202)
Net assets at beginning of year	(3,788)	17,203	13,415	24,617
Net assets (deficit) at end of year	($30,926)	18,023	(12,903)	13,415

See accompanying notes to financial statements.

March of Dimes Foundation
Statement of Cash Flows
Year ended December 31, 2016, with summarized totals for the year ended December 31, 2015
(Amounts in thousands)

	2016	2015
Cash flows from operating activities		
Change in net assets	($26,318)	(11,202)
Adjustments to reconcile change in net assets to net cash used in operating activities		
Depreciation	1,726	1,827
Net (appreciation) depreciation in fair value of investments	(3,118)	1,528
Net (increase) decrease in fair value of assets held in trust by others	(132)	837
Pension and postretirement charge other than net periodic benefit cost	20,130	(19,409)
Changes in operating assets and liabilities		
Sponsorships and other receivables	(1,341)	(736)
Assets held in trust by others	—	57
Inventory and other assets	828	316
Accounts payable and accrued expenses	(1,093)	6,092
Grants and awards payable	(2,900)	2,760
Refundable advances and deferred revenue	1,694	205
Accrued postretirement and pension benefit obligation	(5,206)	(5,561)
Net cash used in operating activities	(15,730)	(23,286)

(Continues)

TABLE 12-8 March of Dimes Foundation *(Continued)*

Cash flows from investing activities		
Purchase of fixed assets	(125)	(97)
Investment receivable	4,532	5,080
Purchase of investments	(15,800)	(2,574)
Proceeds from sale of investments	37,310	31,316
Net cash provided by investing activities	25,917	23,565
Cash flows from financing activities		
Proceeds from line of credit	10,000	15,000
Payments on line of credit	(15,000)	(15,000)
Net cash used in financing activities	(5,000)	–
Net increase in cash and cash equivalents	5,187	279
Cash and cash equivalents at beginning of year	13,446	13,167
Cash and cash equivalents at end of year	$ 18,633	13,446
Supplemental disclosures		
Interest paid	$ 103	106
Contributed materials and services	1,370	2,143

See accompanying notes to financial statements.

1. The March of Dimes was originally founded with the goal of eradicating polio in the United States. Why do you think their mission has changed?
2. What are the most likely reasons that some of the foundation's resources are restricted by donors?
3. Of the 2016 expenses, how much represents the use of net assets that were restricted to purpose or use by donors? Prepare appropriate summary entries to record the expenditure of these restricted assets.
4. Where does the March of Dimes classify its endowment?
5. A note to the financial statements indicates that the foundation recognized $1,370 of contributed services in 2016. The note also states that many other volunteers contributed services, but that these services are not recognized in the financial statements. Why would some volunteer services be recognized while others are not?

QUESTIONS FOR REVIEW AND DISCUSSION

1. Provide examples of resources that are restricted by donors as to: (a) purpose, (b) time, and (c) the occurrence of a specific event. Provide an example of resources that restricted by donors permanently.
2. A not-for-profit organization receives a restricted gift from a donor. When, and in which type of fund, should it recognize the revenue? When, and in which type of fund, should it recognize the related expense? What is the reason for the apparent inconsistency between the fund types in which the revenues and expenses are reported?
3. A foundation promises to donate $1 million to a local public broadcasting station (a not-for-profit organization) in one year. When, and in what amount, should the station recognize revenue? The station applies a discount rate of 10 percent to all pledges. Would your response be the same if the foundation pledged to donate the funds only if and when the station agreed to carry a particular program? Why do many not-for-profits object to the standards pertaining to revenue recognition of pledges?

4. Members of the National Accounting Association, a not-for-profit organization, are charged annual dues of $150. Of this amount, $50 is restricted, per association policy, for covering the cost of the association's journal, which every member receives. In what category of restrictiveness should the association report the portion of revenues associated with the journal assuming it has met its performance obligation? Explain.

5. In what significant way do not-for-profits account for investments differently from businesses?

6. In a recent month a CPA provided 10 hours of volunteer time to the Society for the Visually Impaired. He devoted 7 hours to maintaining the organization's financial records and 3 to recording tapes of newspapers and magazine articles. If volunteers had not provided these services, the organization would have had to hire paid personnel. Should the organization give accounting recognition to the CPA's services?

7. A museum received gifts of two valuable paintings. It recorded the value of one as an asset and recognized the corresponding revenue. It gave no accounting recognition to the other. What might be a legitimate explanation for such an apparent inconsistency?

8. How do not-for-profits differ from governments in the way they account for business-type activities, such as dining halls, gift shops, and admission fees?

9. What is meant by "variance power"? Suppose that a charitable foundation receives a gift that the donor specifies must be used to support the college education of a particular individual. What is the relevance of "variance power" in how the foundation accounts for the gift?

10. In what significant ways do the FASB standards differ from those of the GASB with respect to the statement of cash flows?

11. What special abuse does the AICPA address in its statement of position on the allocation of fund-raising costs? What general criteria does it establish as to when common costs of materials and activities that include a fund-raising appeal can be allocated to programmatic, rather than fund-raising, activities?

12. Why is the "fund-raising ratio" of key concern to both donors and financial analysts? What measures might be of more value to donors?

13. Suppose that you are the independent auditor for a local performing arts association (either government or not-for-profit) that recently received a sizable endowment. The association's president has asked whether gains, both realized and unrealized, from the appreciation of endowment investments should be accounted for as expendable or nonexpendable resources. What should be the primary factors that determine your response? How should GASB or FASB pronouncements influence your recommendation?

14. You are the sole contributor to a philanthropic foundation. You must specify whether investment gains should be expendable or nonexpendable. Present the key arguments in favor of, and against, permitting the gains to be expendable.

EXERCISES

EX. 12–1

Select the *best* answer.

1. A term endowment is a gift
   a. The principal of which must be returned to the donor after a specified period of time
   b. The principal of which is available for expenditure after a specified period of time
   c. The income from which must be expended within a specified period of time
   d. The income of which must be added to the principal for a specified period of time

2. A not-for-profit organization maintains an endowment of $1 million, the income from which must be used for research into substance abuse. In a particular year, the endowment had income of $60,000,

all of which was expended in accord with the donor's specifications. The expense should be reported as a decrease in

a. It is not recorded because it is not an expense
b. Net assets with donor restrictions
c. Net assets without donor restrictions
d. None of the above

3. A private think tank receives a gift of $100,000 that must be used to fund a symposium on federal accounting. When the institution conducts the symposium, which of the following accounts should be debited in a restricted by donor fund?

a. Program expense
b. Deferred revenue
c. Net assets released from restriction
d. Deferred program expense

4. The statement of cash flows of a not-for-profit should be divided into which of the following categories of cash flows?

a. Operating activities, noncapital financing activities, capital and related financing activities, investing activities
b. Operating activities, capital activities, investing activities
c. Operating activities, financing activities, capital activities
d. Operating activities, financing activities, investing activities

5. The Senior League, a not-for-profit welfare agency, redeemed a $100,000 bond that it had held as an investment of resources without donor restrictions. It also received an interest payment of $6,000. In its statement of cash flows, the league should report

a. $106,000 as a cash flow from investing activities
b. $106,000 as a cash flow from operating activities
c. $100,000 as a cash flow from investing activities and $6,000 as a cash flow from financing activities
d. $100,000 as a cash flow from investing activities and $6,000 as a cash flow from operating activities

6. Enrex Corporation gave a not-for-profit research foundation $500,000 to conduct research relating to the development of a new type of battery. Per the terms of the gift, Enrex owned the rights to any patents issued as a consequence of the research, and controlled when and where the research results would be published. At the time of receipt of the $500,000, the foundation should recognize

a. Revenue of $500,000 in a restricted by donor fund
b. Revenue of $500,000 in a fund not restricted by donor
c. Deferred revenue of $500,000 in a fund restricted by donor
d. Deferred revenue of $500,000 in afund not restricted by donor

7. Harley Safe Place, a not-for-profit organization, received a pledge from a donor without restrictions of $600,000. The donor promised to make payment within six months (which would be in the organization's next fiscal year). At the time of the pledge, the organization should recognize

a. Revenue of $600,000 in a fund restricted by donors
b. Revenue of $600,000 in a fund without donor restrictions
c. Deferred revenue of $600,000 in a fund restricted by donors
d. Deferred revenue of $600,000 in a fund without donor restrictions

8. Walden Institute, a not-for-profit, politically oriented association, was promised a $1 million endowment on condition that it establish a program in entrepreneurial studies and hire a leading scholar to lead it. Upon receiving the pledge the institute should recognize

a. Zero revenue
b. Revenue of $1 million in a fund restricted by a donor
c. Expense of $1 million in a fund restricted by a donor
d. Deferred revenue of $1 million in a fund restricted by a donor

9. Emerson Museum received a cash gift of $7 million. The board of trustees decided that the gift should be used to establish a permanent endowment, the income from which would be used to provide research grants to Impressionist art historians. The museum should report the gift as an increase in
   a. Resources without donor restrictions
   b. Resources with donor restrictions
   c. Deferred revenue
   d. Board-restricted resources

10. The Fellowship Church of America issues $10 million in bonds, the proceeds of which must be used to construct new facilities. Included in the bond indenture is a provision that the church must maintain $400,000 in a specially designated bank account to ensure timely payment of principal and interest. Upon receiving the $10 million in bond proceeds and placing the $400,000 in the designated bank account, the church should report
   a. Cash of $9.6 million in a fund without donor restrictions and $400,000 in a fund with donor restrictions
   b. Cash of $10 million in a fund without donor restrictions
   c. Cash of $10 million in a fund with donor restrictions

11. All costs of activities that have a fund-raising component must be classified as fund-raising costs unless it can be demonstrated that they satisfy the criteria dealing with all of the following except
   a. Purpose
   b. Audience
   c. Content
   d. Fiscal viability

12. In allocating joint costs between fund-raising and other activities, a not-for-profit could use all of the following methods *except*
   a. Physical units
   b. Relative direct cost
   c. Straight-line
   d. Stand-alone costs

EX 12-2

Select the *best* answer.

1. A local chapter of the Society for Protection of the Environment benefited from the voluntary services of two attorneys. One served as a member of the Society's board of directors, performing tasks comparable to other directors. During the year, he attended 20 hours of meetings. The other drew up a lease agreement with a tenant in a building owned by the Society. She spent five hours on the project. The billing rate of both attorneys is $200 per hour. In the year in which the services were provided, the Society should recognize revenues from contributed services of
   a. $0
   b. $1,000
   c. $4,000
   d. $5,000

2. The Museum of Contemporary Art received two valuable paintings. The museum has determined that one, with a market value of $7,000, is inappropriate for display and therefore will be sold and the proceeds will be used to acquire another painting that can be displayed. The other, with a market value of $10,000, will be placed on exhibit. The museum has a policy of not capitalizing works of art unless required to do so. In the year that it receives the two paintings, it should recognize contribution revenues of
   a. $0
   b. $7,000
   c. $10,000
   d. $17,000

3. The United Way of Lano County distributes all contributions to not-for-profit organizations within the area it serves. Donors have a choice: They can either designate the organization to which their contributions will be given, or permit the United Way to distribute their contributions as it deems appropriate. During the current year, the United Way received $1 million of specifically designated contributions and $6 million of undesignated contributions. It should recognize contribution revenue of
   a. $0
   b. $1 million
   c. $6 million
   d. $7 million

4. Variance power refers to the ability
   a. Of a not-for-profit organization to use property for commercial purposes even though it was zoned for residential purposes
   b. Of a charitable organization to unilaterally decide to direct the use of donated assets to a beneficiary other than that specified by the donor
   c. Of a donor to change the beneficiary of a gift from that which was initially specified
   d. Of a not-for-profit organization to alter the terms of any purpose restrictions associated with a contribution that it received

5. The Association for Educational Enrichment receives a contribution of $400,000 that must be used for student scholarships. Prior to granting any scholarships, the Association invests the funds received in marketable securities. During the year, the securities pay dividends of $10,000 and increase in market value to $440,000. The association should report
   a. Investment earnings without donor restrictions of $50,000
   b. Investment earnings with donor restrictions of $50,000
   c. Investment earnings without donor restrictions of $10,000 and investment earnings with donor restrictions of $40,000
   d. Investment earnings with donor restrictions of $10,000

6. Carter Research Center, a not-for-profit entity, acquires $50,000 of laboratory instruments with funds that were donated and restricted for the purchase of equipment. The instruments have a useful life of five years and no salvage value. During each of the five years of the instruments' useful life, the Center should recognize depreciation expense of
   a. $0
   b. $10,000 in a fund restricted by donors
   c. $10,000 in a fund not restricted by donors
   d. $10,000 in either a fund restricted by donors or a fund without donor restrictions, depending on which fund is used to account for the instruments

7. With respect to the statement of cash flows
   a. Both the FASB and the GASB encourage entities to use the direct method
   b. The GASB, but not the FASB, requires entities to use the direct method
   c. The FASB, but not the GASB, requires entities to use the direct method
   d. Both the FASB and the GASB require entities to use the direct method

8. The Friends of the Opera, a financially interrelated fund-raising support group for the City Opera Company, receives $100,000 in donations, all of which will eventually be transferred to the City Opera Company. When Friends of the Opera receives the gift
   a. Friends of the Opera should recognize revenue of $100,000, and the City Opera Company should make no journal entries.
   b. Friends of the Opera should recognize a liability of $100,000, and the City Opera Company should recognize a receivable.
   c. Friends of the Opera should recognize revenue of $100,000, and the City Opera Company should recognize an increase of $100,000 in its interest in the net assets of Friends of the Opera.
   d. Friends of the Opera should recognize a liability of $100,000, and the City Opera Company should make no entry.

9. At the start of the year, the permanent endowment fund of the State Performing Arts Festival Association reported net assets of $1 million. During the year, it earned $40,000 in interest and dividends, but its investments lost $60,000 in market value. The association spent the entire $40,000 of interest and dividends. At year-end the permanent endowment fund should report net assets of
   a. $1,000,000
   b. $980,000
   c. $960,000
   d. $940,000

10. The Mountain Research Institute began the year with net assets in its permanent endowment fund of $1 million. During the year it earned $70,000, and the market value of its investments increased by $20,000. However, the institute's policy, decided on by its board of directors, is to permit earnings to be spent only to the extent that they exceed an amount necessary to cover inflation. The inflation rate for the year was 3 percent. During the year, the institute spent none of the $70,000. At year-end, the permanent endowment fund should report net assets of
   a. $1,000,000
   b. $1,020,000
   c. $1,030,000
   d. $1,090,000

EX 12-3

Minor differences in the terms of a contribution may justify major differences in revenue recognition.

Upon meeting with the executive director of the Crime Victims Advocacy Group, the president of a private foundation agreed to contribute in the following year $100,000 in support of the group's proposed program to provide legal assistance to victims of violent crimes. Suppose that the foundation's formal letter describing its pledge was worded in three different ways:

1. "We are pleased to pledge $100,000 in support of your group's efforts to assist victims of violent crimes."
2. "We are pleased to pledge $100,000 in support of your group's efforts to develop a new program to provide legal assistance to victims of violent crimes."
3. "We are pleased to pledge $100,000 upon your developing a new program to provide legal assistance to victims of violent crimes."

For each of the three options:

a. Prepare the journal entries that should be made on receipt of the letter from the foundation. Assume that it was unlikely that the pledge would be fulfilled in the same period as it was made.
b. Prepare the journal entries that should be made to record the expenditure of $100,000 on activities related to the legal assistance program.
c. Prepare the journal entries that should be made on receipt of the $100,000 check, assuming that it was received shortly after the legal assistance program was established and the group spent the $100,000 on program related activities.
d. Comment on why minor differences in wording might justify major differences in accounting.

Be sure to indicate the type of fund in which your entries would be made.

EX 12-4

Some, but not all, contributions of goods and services are given accounting recognition.

In each of the following scenarios, an organization receives a contribution in-kind. Prepare journal entries, as necessary, to give them accounting recognition. For each, tell why you made an entry or why you did not.

1. A local not-for-profit art museum receives advertising for its yearly benefit from radio station WLOU. The airtime would have cost the museum $1,000.

2. Volunteers for "Breakfast on Bikes," a voluntary health and welfare organization, deliver hot meals to the elderly three times a week. Each of the ten volunteers works about six hours per week. All of the volunteers have permanent jobs with pay averaging $16.10 an hour.

3. Lynn Simms, a local CPA, maintains the books and records of her church. Although her normal billing rate is $60 per hour, she accepts no payment from the church. She works on church matters approximately four hours a week.

4. A construction company allows a not-for-profit community association to use its bulldozer at no cost to clear land for a new baseball park. If the association had to rent the bulldozer it would have incurred costs of $1,400.

EX 12-5

Investment gains and losses have to be recognized as they occur—and have to be assigned to the appropriate category of net assets.

During 2017 the Lung Association received a contribution of marketable securities that were to be placed in a permanent endowment fund. Neither donor stipulations nor applicable state law requires that capital gains or increases in value be added to the endowment principal. The income from the securities was to be restricted to research in pulmonary diseases. The following schedule indicates the value of the securities as of the date of receipt (labeled "cost"), the fair value at December 31, 2020, and the unrealized gains and losses of the year.

Endowment Portfolio as of December 31, 2020 (in thousands)

	Cost	Fair Value	Unrealized Gain (Loss)
Northwest Industries	$260	$275	$15
Campbell Corp.	317	304	(13)
St. Regis, Inc.	141	171	30
	$718	$750	$32

1. Prepare a journal entry to record the unrealized net gain during the year. Be sure to indicate the type of fund (with donor restriction or without donor restriction) in which the entry would be made. Assuming no other transactions and no other assets in the relevant funds, show how the investments would be reported on the hospital's year-end 2020 statement of financial position.

2. During 2021, the hospital sold Northwest Industries for $280. Prepare appropriate journal entries to record the sale. Credit the gain to the same account in which you credited the unrealized appreciation of 2020.

3. As of December 31, 2021, the market value of Campbell Corp. had increased to $320; that of St. Regis, Inc., to $180. Prepare a journal entry to record the unrealized gain during the year. Show how the association would report the investment portfolio on its December 31, 2021, statement of financial position. You may combine the cash and securities of each type of fund into a single account.

EX 12-6

Contributions of long-lived assets may affect more than one type of fund.

Discovery Barn, a not-for-profit science center for children, received a contribution of $30,000 explicitly designated for the acquisition of computers. During the year it acquired $21,000 of computers, which it estimated to have a useful life of three years. It is the policy of the organization to charge an entire year's depreciation in the year of acquisition.

Prepare all required journal entries, being certain to indicate the type of fund in which each entry would be made.

EX 12-7

Internet-based exercise

The objective of this exercise is to get you familiar with the audited financial statements and IRS Form 990 of a Nonprofit Entity, the American Cancer Society (www.cancer.org, click on "About Us," and click on "Financials and Governance") and obtain the audited financial statements for the fiscal year ended December 31, 2016 and Form 990 for 2016. Note that these financial statements reflect FASB standards in effect during 2016. Form 990 can also be obtained from www.Guidestar.org.

Answer the following questions:

1. What are the four broad mission areas of the organization? Where did you find this information?
2. Does ACS hold an endowment? What information is available and from where?
3. Does the American Cancer Society record any volunteer time as contributed service? How do you know?

EX 12-8

Investment losses may not affect the principal of not-for-profits' endowment funds.

In 2018, the Rubin Center for the Arts received a $2 million endowment, the income of which was to be used to support local artists. The center invested the proceeds in securities. In 2018, owing to interest, dividends, and changes in market prices, the value of the endowment increased by $120,000. Of this amount, the center spent $80,000 on programs that were consistent with the endowment's restrictions. In 2019, owing to a market downturn, the portfolio incurred net losses of $60,000. In 2020, it had net earnings of $70,000. In neither 2019 nor 2020 did the center use any endowment resources to support its programs.

In the absence of donor specifications and applicable statutes, what would be the balances, at the end of 2018, 2019, and 2020, in the center's endowment fund with donor restrictions? Indicate also any impact on funds without donor restrictions.

EX 12-9

Internet-based exercise

Analysis of a not-for-profit entity based on information in the annual report.

Based on Form 990 and the audited financial statements of the American Cancer Society obtained for fiscal year 2016

1. Identify the types of receivables presented in the statement of financial position. In addition, provide a simple explanation of how these items meet the definition of an asset and describe the journal entries that would be required to record these assets.
2. Calculate the program ratio (Total Program expenses/Total expenses) based on the financial statements and the 990. Do the ratios differ? Why and by how much?
3. The 990 Schedule A identifies the reason for the American Cancer Society's status as a public charity. What reason is identified?
4. What is the rating of this nonprofit by Charity Navigator or Better Business Bureau Wise Giving Alliance or other watchdog agencies? Explain what this means.

PROBLEMS

P. 12-1

This problem summarizes typical transactions engaged in by not-for-profit organizations.

The American Association for Freedom, a political think tank, was recently established. During its first year of operations it engaged in the following transactions and was affected by the following events (in summary form):

1. It received a $10,000,000 endowment contribution from a donor, all in stocks and bonds.

2. It received $3,000,000 in additional contributions, all restricted for its educational programs and $2,300,000 in contributions without donor restrictions.

3. It acquired $800,000 in furniture, fixtures, and equipment, all of which have an expected useful life of 10 years.

4. It recognized depreciation on the furniture, fixtures, and equipment, purchased earlier in the year.

5. It spent $2,400,000 on educational programs.

6. It earned $300,000 in interest and dividends on its endowment investments.

7. By year-end the value of its investments had appreciated by $600,000.

8. It incurred $1,300,000 in administrative expenses.

9. Near year-end it received a pledge of $4,500,000, to be fulfilled in three annual installments of $1,500,000 beginning in one year. The Association determined that a discount rate of 6 percent was appropriate.
   a. Prepare journal entries to record these events and transactions. Be sure to indicate the fund-type in which the entry would be made.
   b. Prepare a year-end statement of financial position and statement of activities.

P. 12-2

For purposes of external reporting, not-for-profits—unlike governments in their governmental funds—do not distinguish between plant and other types of resources.

In 2020, the Northwest Ballet Association (NBA), a not-for-profit performing arts organization, undertook a major capital campaign to fund a new theater, expected to cost $10 million. It was quickly able to raise $6 million, all of which was donor restricted. It borrowed the balance, issuing a five-year, 8-percent term note for $4 million.

During the year, the NBA broke ground on the project and incurred construction costs of $3.4 million. It earned $0.52 million in interest on investments. It incurred and paid $0.32 million in interest on the note. In addition, as required by the note, it placed $0.7 million in a reserve fund (a specially dedicated bank account) for the repayment of the debt.

1. To show how these transactions would be reflected on the NBA's financial statements, prepare a December 31, 2020, statement of financial position and statement of activities. Assume that these were the only transactions in which the organization engaged and that all available cash, except that in the reserve fund, had been invested in short-term marketable securities. Be sure to properly classify all resources as to whether they are restricted by donors or not.

2. Comment briefly on whether the contributions from donors and the proceeds from the bonds should be reported as restricted by donors or not.

3. Comment briefly on whether the $0.7 million in the reserve fund should be reported as restricted by donors or not.

P. 12-3

Should exchange transactions be accounted for differently than contributions?

In December 2020, the Consumer Association of America (CAA), a not-for-profit research organization, received a $6 million grant from the Sporting Goods Manufacturers Association (SGMA) to develop a football helmet that will provide better protection against head injuries. The grant was intended to cover $4 million of direct costs and $2 million of overhead costs. The grant contract stipulated that the SGMA would make its payment to the CAA upon receiving invoices from CAA for the actual direct costs incurred. It further required that the research results be reported only to the SGMA and not be made publicly available. Each reimbursement payment for direct costs incurred would also include an appropriate proportion of indirect costs (i.e., an additional $0.50 for each $1 of direct costs).

In 2021 the CAA carried out and completed the research for which it contracted. Direct costs were, as estimated, $4 million. It submitted the necessary invoices and received payment in full.

1. Prepare required journal entries for 2020 and 2021. Be sure to indicate whether each entry should be made to an restricted by donor fund or not restricted by donor fund. You need not, however, record the indirect costs themselves (inasmuch as, by their very nature, they are not tied directly to the grant).

2. Assume instead that in December 2020 the CAA received from the National Sports Association (NSA) a pledge of $6 million. The donation is for research relating to football helmets. The NSA is a not-for-profit agency, and the results of any research will be in the public domain. In January 2021, the CAA received the contribution. Throughout the remainder of 2021 it carried out its football-related research (incurring $4 million of direct costs). Prepare the required journal entries for 2020 and 2021 and indicate whether each entry should be made to a fund that is restricted by a donor or not.

3. Comment on any differences between the two awards that might justify differences in revenue recognition.

4. Suppose instead that the NSA promised to make its contribution only on receiving a report that the research had actually been completed. Would your approach have been different? Explain.

P. 12-4

The manner in which depreciation on capital assets acquired with donated funds depends on the terms of the donation.

Sea Life Aquarium, a not-for-profit entity, received a contribution of $500,000 that must be used to acquire plant and equipment. In the following year it applied the gift toward the purchase of various items of plant and equipment. Management estimates that the useful life will be 10 years (with no salvage value).

1. Prepare journal entries to record the contribution, the purchase of equipment, and first-year depreciation. Be sure to indicate the type of fund in which each entry would be made. Assume that the Aquarium adheres to current standard practice as to when resources are released from restriction.

2. Assume now that the donor specifies that the contributed resources be released from restriction by the not-for-profit over the life of the asset rather than follow current standard practice.
   a. Prepare journal entries to record the contribution, the purchase of equipment, and first-year depreciation.
   b. What would be the impact of the donor request on the financial statements and on availability for expenditure of cash or other organization assets?

P. 12-5

Contributions to be received in the future must take into account the time value of money as well as the likelihood that a portion of the contributions may be uncollectible.

1. Prepare journal entries to take into account the following events and transactions.
   a. In January 2020, the Wildlife Preservation Society received a grant from the Westwood Foundation of $6 million to be paid in three annual installments of $2 million starting on December 31, 2020. The grant may be used for any legitimate activity engaged in by the Society. The Society applies a discount rate of 6 percent to long-term receivables.
   b. During the year it also received $1 million in pledges from numerous individuals. The pledges must be used to support the Society's educational programs. The Society expects that 5 percent will be uncollectible. The balance will be fulfilled within several months of year-end.
   c. It collects $900,000 of the pledges and writes off $25,000 as uncollectible.
   d. The Society receives its three annual payments of $2 million from the Foundation.

2. Suppose instead that the Society received numerous grants that are spread over a period of several years and thereby has a basis for establishing an allowance for uncollectible grants. Would an interest rate of the same 6 percent still be appropriate for taking into account the time value of money? Explain.

P. 12-6

The distinction between contributed services that warrant financial statement recognition and those that do not is not always clear.

For each of the following situations, indicate whether the organization should recognize the described contributed services as revenue (offset by a corresponding expense). Briefly justify your response or identify key issues.

1. Nellie Wilson, the noted country-and-western singer, performs a benefit concert for the Save Our Farms Association, a political advocacy group. Wilson, who would normally charge $60,000 per concert, did not accept a fee.

2. Camp Chi-Wan-Da, a summer camp for disadvantaged youth, benefits from the services of four physicians, each of whom spends two weeks at the camp providing medical services to the campers. The doctors receive free room and board but no salary. Camp association standards require that a camp of Chi-Wan-Da's size either have a physician on premises or have a physician on call.

3. The Taconic Music Festival, a performing arts association, needed new practice facilities. The architecture firm of Lloyd Wright designed the facilities for the association without charge, and local merchants provided the building materials. All construction work was carried out by community volunteers, only a few of whom had professional experience in the building trades.

4. A neurologist serves on the board of trustees of the Neurological Disease Foundation, an organization that funds clinical research. He was asked to serve because of his expertise in neurological research, and he chairs the committee of the board that selects grant recipients.

5. Daughters of Charity Hospital draw its nursing staff from members of its religious order. The nurses are not paid a salary. Instead, they receive free room and board and a living allowance. The total cost to the hospital is approximately 60 percent of what it would have to pay in salary and benefits on the open market. In addition, the hospital benefits from the services of "candy stripers" and other volunteers who staff the hospital's gift shop, carry meals to patients, and perform a variety of other important functions. Were it not for these volunteers, the hospital would be required to hire additional personnel to carry out many of their duties.

P. 12-7

Pledges to be fulfilled in the future raise special issues of accounting.

The footnote in the financial statements of The Welfare Foundation contain the following note titled "Promises to Give":

Unconditional promises to give were as follows at December 31:

	2020	2019
Contributions due in less than one year	$2,293,775	$2,305,753
Contributions due in one to five years	5,454,320	6,272,198
Contributions due in more than five years	1,098,384	1,696,768
	8,846,479	10,274,719
Less allowance for bad debts	(166,972)	(398,723)
Less discount to net present value	(497,812)	(710,124)
	$8,181,695	$9,165,872

The discount rates used on long-term promises to give were 3 percent in 2020 and 2019.

1. Suppose that the foundation were to prepare a statement of financial position in columnar form, one column for net assets without donor restrictions, and another for net assets with donor restrictions. In which column would these receivables be reported? Explain.

2. Suppose that on December 31, 2020, the foundation collected $ 500,000 of the $1, 098,384 due over a five-year period. Prepare appropriate journal entries to record the collection of the $500,000 and to adjust the remaining balance in the receivables account. Be sure to recognize interest on the balance of the contributions due in over five years and one to five years (less the discount).

3. Another note to the statements indicates that the foundation has made grants to various other organizations. Some of these are payable over a five-year period. Accordingly it adjusted its grants payable account to take into account the time value of money and applied a discount rate of 3 percent. However per the note, the grants are classified as Level 3 in accordance with the fair value hierarchy and have been valued using an income approach. What are the different valuation techniques? What is level 3 classification? Explain this in simple words.

P. 12-8

The financial condition of a not-for-profit can be assessed, in part, with traditional financial ratios.

Review the financial statements of the March of Dimes for 2016 as presented in Table 12-8.

1. Comment as best you can (even in the absence of guidelines as to what constitutes norms for comparable foundations) on the fiscal strength of the organization as of December 31, 2016, with respect to:
   a. Liquidity
   b. Burden of debt relative to assets
   c. Adequacy of available resources to meet expenditures
   d. Current fiscal performance as indicated by surpluses or deficits
   e. Riskiness of revenue stream

2. Comparing 2016 versus 2015's results, do you see any changes that could be detrimental to the foundation's ability to achieve its mission?

P. 12-9

Not-for-profit organizations should be mindful of their fund-raising or administration expenses.

Refer to the financial statements of the March of Dimes for 2016 presented in Table 12-8.

1. Did the organization exert a greater fiscal effort on fund-raising in 2016 than it did in 2015?

2. Did it direct more of its revenues toward mission-oriented programs rather than to administrative or fund-raising activities?

3. Based on the guidelines set forth in this chapter, did the March of Dimes spend excessively on fund-raising or administration?

P. 12-10

When it comes to classifying costs, it's not only what you say, it's when you say it.

Parents Against Underage Drinking (PAUD) recently paid $50,000 to sponsor a series of commercials on a local television station. Each commercial is one minute in length.

In the first 45 seconds, sports stars plead with teenagers to avoid peer pressure to consume alcoholic beverages. In the remaining 15 seconds, a celebrity solicits funds for the organization and gives a telephone number to call and an address to which to send a contribution. The commercials are scheduled to run during *Real World*, a MTV program that is popular among teens and young adults.

1. How much of the cost of the commercials should PAUD allocate to mission-related programs and how much to fund-raising?
   a. Assume first that the allocation is to be based on physical units.
   b. Assume, alternatively, that the allocation is to be based on "stand-alone costs." The cost of a single 45-second commercial would be approximately $40,000; that of a 15-second commercial would be $20,000.

2. Suppose that the organization elected to run the same series of commercials on reruns of the Lawrence Welk Show, a musical variety program that features tunes of the 1950s and appeals primarily to the great-grandparents of those to whom Real World is targeted. The cost is the same $50,000. Would your response be the same? Explain.

P. 12-11

Extensive information about local charities can be obtained on the Internet.

Visit GuideStar at www.guidestar.org. Select two not-for-profit health and welfare organizations that have a similar mission and are of relatively similar size (e.g., the Parkinson's Disease Foundation and the American Parkinson Disease Association). Suppose that you are an analyst for a foundation, and you are concerned with the long-term fiscal viability of the two entities.

1. Compare the two as to:
   a. Proportion of resources directed to fund-raising
   b. Proportion of resources directed to program activities
   c. Percentage of revenues from contributions and grants
   d. Percentage of revenues from user charges and other sources
   e. Short-term liquidity
   f. Burden of debt
   g. Adequacy of fiscal resources
   h. Current fiscal performance
2. Comment on which appears to be the more fiscally sound.

SOLUTION TO EXERCISE FOR REVIEW AND SELF-STUDY

1. Through the work of the March of Dimes, polio was eradicated in the United States, thus allowing the organization to focus its efforts elsewhere.
2. The foundation's resources are restricted by donors because they must be used for a specific purpose or they are not yet available for expenditure (e.g., they include pledges that will be fulfilled in the future). They are permanently restricted because they are held in endowment funds.
3. As indicated in the statement of activities, $ 13,880 of net assets were released from restriction. This represents the amount of net assets with temporary donor restrictions that were expended. The following summary entries would record the expenses and the release from restriction:

Expenses	$13.880	
Net assets released from restriction		$13,880
To record the expenses (in a fund without donor restrictions)		
Net assets released from restriction	$13,880	
Cash		$13,880
To record the disbursement of cash and the release of the assets from restriction (in fund restricted by donors)		

4. In Note 4 of the Financial Statements, it is stated that the foundation classifies as net assets with donor restrictions (a) the original value of gifts to the permanent endowment, (b) the original value of subsequent gifts to the endowment, and (c) accumulations of investment returns on the permanent endowment as directed by the donor.
5. Volunteer services must meet one of the two key tests for recognition in order to be recognized as revenue:
   a. They enhance or create nonfinancial assets
   b. They require specialized skills, were provided by individuals possessing those skills, and would have been purchased if not provided by the donation

CHAPTER 13

Colleges and Universities

LEARNING OBJECTIVES

After studying this chapter you should understand:

- The unique issues faced by colleges and universities at large
- The different reporting options available to public (government) and private (other not-for-profit) colleges and universities
- The differences in form and content of reports between public and private colleges and universities
- How colleges and universities classify revenues and expenses
- How tuition and fees are accounted for
- How grants are accounted for
- How student loans are accounted for
- The special concerns related to auxiliary enterprises

In this chapter we address the special issues faced by colleges and universities. In addition, we will take note of the key differences between private (not-for-profit) and public (governmental) educational institutions. FASB's Accounting Standards Update (ASU) No. 2016-14 applies to not-for-profit colleges and universities no less than it does to other types of not-for-profit entities. Accordingly, there is little need to readdress the issues identified in Chapter 12.[1] We leave it to the reader to generalize from the discussion in that chapter and apply its principles to universities. For example, the accounting for exchange transactions, contributions and pledges, investment gains and losses, depreciation, split-interest agreements, and reporting entities are either not explicitly discussed in this chapter or are only briefly commented on.

WHAT UNIQUE ISSUES DO COLLEGES AND UNIVERSITIES FACE?

U.S. higher education is characterized by diversity unparalleled in other countries. In 2016, there were 1,623 public degree-granting institutions and 1,681 not-for-profit private institutions.[2] Not only is our system dichotomized between public and private institutions, but colleges and universities also range in size from small liberal arts colleges of several hundred students (often church-related) to multicampus systems of over a hundred thousand students (e.g., University System of Georgia with 30 campuses) and revenues in billions of dollars.[3] Figures 13-1 and 13-2 depict the sources of revenues for private and public colleges, respectively. As can be seen, public

[1] FASB ASC 958.

[2] *Source*: National Center for Education Statistics, https://nces.ed.gov/programs/digest/d17/tables/dt17_317.40.asp.

[3] Total operating revenues of the USG system for FY 2017 were $5.1 billion.

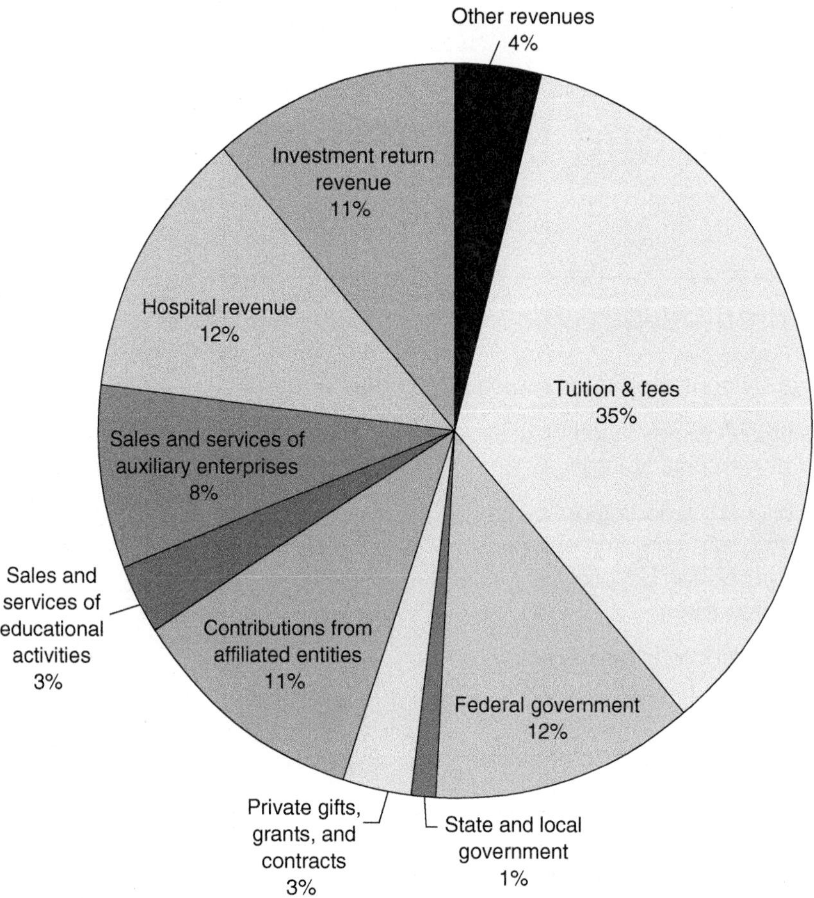

FIGURE 13-1 Sources of revenues for private colleges and universities for 2014–2015.
Source: U.S. Department of Education, National Center for Education Statistics, Integrated Postsecondary Education Data System (IPEDS), "Fall Enrollment Survey" (IPEDS-EF:99); Spring 2001 through Spring 2007, Enrollment component; Spring 2008 through Spring 2015, Fall Enrollment component; and Spring 2001 through Spring 2016, Finance component. https://nces.ed.gov/programs/digest/d16/tables/dt16_333.40.asp?current=yes.

institutions get a large share of their revenues from government **appropriations** and grants (from various levels), whereas private institutions are dependent to a large extent on student tuition, investments, and fees.

In addition, there are community colleges that are governmental entities that may have the power to levy a special tax on the residents for their source of revenue. There are also scores of proprietary (i.e., for-profit) colleges and universities (e.g., the University of Phoenix). These are accounted for as businesses and are beyond the scope of this text.

As a consequence of this diversity, standard setting has been beset by controversy, not only over specific accounting and reporting standards but even as to which bodies should have rule-making authority. When the GASB was being established, constituents of private colleges and universities contended that the FASB, not the GASB, should have jurisdiction over all colleges and universities, whereas those of public colleges and universities asserted that the GASB should have responsibility for government-operated institutions at a minimum. The issue was resolved by granting the FASB jurisdiction over all not-for-profit (private) colleges and universities and the GASB over all government (public) colleges and universities. Today, therefore, not-for-profit

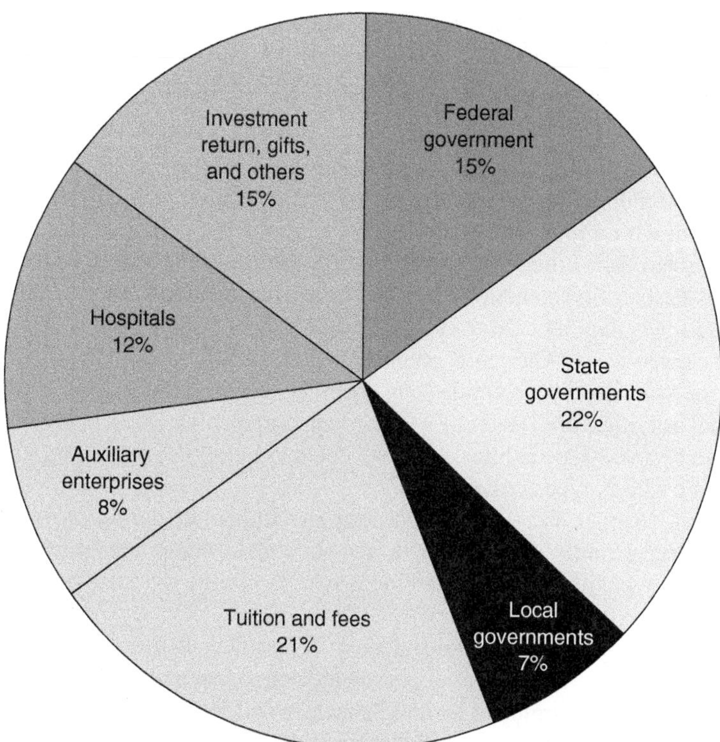

FIGURE 13-2 Total revenues of public degree-granting institutions, by source of funds: 2014–2015. *Source:* U.S. Department of Education, National Center for Education Statistics, Integrated Postsecondary Education Data System (IPEDS), Spring 2008 through Spring 2015, Fall Enrollment component; and Spring 2009 through Spring 2016, Finance component. https://nces.ed.gov/programs/digest/d16/tables/dt16_333.10.asp?current=yes.

colleges and universities follow the FASB pronouncements pertaining to not-for-profit organizations. Government colleges and universities must adhere to the GASB pronouncements, no differently than other types of governments. In light of the similarity between government and not-for-profit colleges and universities, this is hardly an ideal arrangement. However, it does represent a political compromise and has proven durable.

STANDARDS FOR PUBLIC COLLEGES AND UNIVERSITIES

Accounting and reporting by colleges and universities posed especially thorny issues to the GASB owing to several considerations, some of which are that:

1. Public colleges and universities have much in common with their private not-for-profit counterparts, so comparability is clearly desirable.
2. Most colleges and universities have a long tradition of using a distinctive accounting and reporting model that had been endorsed by the American Institute of Certified Public Accountants in an industry audit guide. However, some institutions, most notably community colleges, have used the standard government model.
3. Colleges and universities are unique institutions that differ from other governments in how they are funded and managed. For example, although colleges and universities have both donor-restricted funds and auxiliary enterprises, most do not budget by fund. Therefore,

statement users may have only limited interest in fund-by-fund information. **Auxiliary enterprises** are the units of a college or university that carry out business-type activities and are funded mainly by user charges. They typically include intercollegiate athletics, dormitories, food services, and bookstores.

With these considerations in mind (and after much debate), the GASB decided that colleges and universities should be subject to the same reporting requirements as other special-purpose governments—but with a loophole.[4] The loophole is that most public colleges and universities satisfy Statement No. 34's criteria of entities that engage exclusively in business-type activities. They qualify as business-type enterprises because (per the standards for enterprise fund reporting) "enterprise funds *may* be used to report any activity for which a fee is charged to external users for goods or services."[5] Therefore, public colleges and universities have a choice: They may elect to report as special-purpose entities engaging (1) only in business-type activities, (2) only in governmental activities, or (3) in both. Many colleges and universities lobbied the GASB to be able to report as business-type entities, and have opted to report as special-purpose governments engaged only in business-type activities.

As noted in Chapter 11, a special-purpose government engaging only in business-type activities need prepare only a statement of net position, a statement of revenues, expenses and changes in net position, and a statement of cash flows. It need not present detailed fund statements.

The statement of net position and statement of revenues and expenses would, of course, have to be prepared on a full accrual basis. These statements must include capital assets and depreciation. The University of Virginia's required statement of net position, statement of revenues, expenses, and changes in net position, and statement of cash flows are illustrated in Table 13-1.

Statement No. 34 requires all governments that use enterprise fund accounting to present segment information in notes to the financial statements. It defines a segment as any identifiable activity for which revenue bonds have been issued and which thereby has an identifiable revenue stream pledged in support of those bonds. For colleges and universities, segments are likely to include auxiliary enterprises such as dormitories, bookstores, and intercollegiate athletics. Required segment information includes key elements from the statement of net position, statement of activities, and statement of cash flows.[6]

The statement of revenues and expenses of a government that elects business-type reporting would usually be in object classification format. That is, its reported expenses would be items such as salaries, utilities, and supplies. To supplement this information the GASB encourages (but does not require) colleges and universities to present cost information about their various programs and activities.

STANDARDS FOR PRIVATE NOT-FOR-PROFIT COLLEGES AND UNIVERSITIES

Private not-for-profit colleges and universities are subject to the same FASB standards as are other not-for-profit entities. As pointed out in the previous section, most government colleges and universities exercise the GASB Statement No. 34 option that permits them to account for their activities in enterprise funds. Therefore, inasmuch as both government and not-for-profit colleges and universities account for their activities on a full accrual basis, the differences are likely to be less pronounced as they were when they used different models. Nevertheless, as will be discussed in Chapter 14 on health care providers, the FASB's reporting structure and

---

[4] GASB Statement No. 35, *Basic Financial Statements—and Management's Discussion and Analysis—for Public Colleges and Universities (An Amendment of GASB Statement No. 34)*, 1999.

[5] GASB Statement No. 34, *Basic Financial Statements—and Management's Discussion and Analysis—for State and Local Governments*, 1999, para. 67.

[6] Para. 122.

TABLE 13-1A University of Virginia Statement of Net Position (in thousands) as of June 30, 2017 (with comparative information as of June 30, 2016)

	2017	2016
Assets		
Current assets		
Cash and cash equivalents (Note 2)	$ 97,751	$ 129,683
Short-term investments (Note 2)	68	230,886
Appropriations available	4,380	5,320
Accounts receivable, net (Note 3a)	343,415	315,565
Prepaid expenses	28,707	28,907
Inventories	28,275	24,997
Notes receivable, net (Note 3b)	6,532	5,125
Total current assets	509,128	740,483
Noncurrent assets		
Cash and cash equivalents (Note 2)	13,237	11,680
Long-term investments (Note 2)	2,495,607	2,073,236
Endowment (Note 2)	4,444,091	4,084,301
Notes receivable, net (Note 3b)	62,865	67,820
Pledges and other receivables, net (Note 3c)	14,037	12,226
Derivative instruments (Note 6)	–	3,634
Capital assets—depreciable, net (Note 3d)	3,217,018	3,026,277
Capital assets—nondepreciable (Note 3d)	386,410	
Goodwill (Note 3e)	17,740	9,673
Total noncurrent assets	10,561,005	9,622,187
Deferred outflows of resources (Note 3f)	133,411	92,864
Total Assets and Deferred Outflows of Resources	$11,203,544	$10,455,534
Liabilities		
Current liabilities		
Accounts payable and accrued liabilities (Note 3g)	$ 310,267	$ 303,314
Unearned revenue (Note 3h)	105,726	100,271
Deposits held in custody for others	4,459	14,626
Commercial paper (Note 4)	86,295	153,045
Long-term debt—current portion (Note 5a)	10,333	6,558
Long-term liabilities—current portion (Note 5b)	85,413	78,284
Total current liabilities	602,493	656,098
Noncurrent liabilities		
Long-term debt (Note 5a)	1,507,280	1,352,333
Derivative instrument liability (Note 6)	31,620	43,042
Net pension liability (Note 11)	551,786	507,590
Other noncurrent liabilities (Note 5b)	217,559	199,932
Total noncurrent liabilities	2,308,245	2,102,897
Deferred inflows of resources (Note 3i)	87,389	111,711
Total Liabilities and Deferred Inflows of Resources	$ 2,998,127	$ 2,870,706
Net Position		
Net investment in capital assets	$ 1,921,181	$ 1,880,320
Restricted		
Nonexpendable	676,312	624,646
Expendable	2,987,365	2,819,180
Unrestricted	2,620,559	2,260,682
Total Net Position	$ 8,205,417	$ 7,584,828
Total Liabilities, Deferred Inflows of Resources, and Net Position	$11,203,544	$10,455,534

TABLE 13-1B University of Virginia Statement of Revenues, Expenses and Changes in Net Position (in thousands) for the year ended June 30, 2017 (with comparative information for the year ended June 30, 2016)

	2017	2016
Revenues		
Operating revenues		
Student tuition and fees, net of scholarship allowances of $113,061 and $115,705	$ 545,168	$ 511,063
Patient services, net of charity care of $3,658,619 and $3,470,187	1,545,404	1,501,746
Federal grants and contracts	256,145	241,568
State and local grants and contracts	7,072	6,150
Nongovernmental grants and contracts	58,689	54,065
Sales and services of educational departments	43,134	27,748
Auxiliary enterprises revenue, net of scholarship allowances of $19,355 and $19,284	137,057	132,583
Other operating revenues	60,423	53,728
Total Operating Revenues	2,653,092	2,528,651
Expenses		
Operating expenses (Note 9)		
Compensation and benefits	1,719,618	1,621,521
Supplies and other services	1,063,255	1,004,320
Student aid	92,691	75,808
Depreciation	225,247	219,683
Other	4,676	4,141
Total Operating Expenses	3,105,487	2,925,473
Operating Loss	(452,395)	(396,822)
Nonoperating Revenues (Expenses)		
State appropriations (Note 10)	168,664	159,757
Gifts	163,356	168,521
Investment income (loss)	728,658	(112,633)
Pell grants	12,485	12,489
Interest on capital asset-related debt	(69,062)	(70,808)
Build America Bonds rebate	8,151	8,133
Gains (losses) on capital assets	(3,566)	11,890
Other net nonoperating expenses	(28,959)	(23,304)
Net Nonoperating Revenues	979,727	154,045
Income (Loss) Before Other Revenues, Expenses, Gains, or Losses	527,332	(242,777)
Capital appropriations	15,691	32,555

(Continues)

(Continued)

Capital grants and gifts	30,603	24,187
Additions to permanent endowments	46,963	14,521
Total Other Revenues	93,257	71,263
Increase (Decrease) in Net Position	620,589	(171,514)
Net Position		
Net position—beginning of year	7,584,828	7,795,938
Net effect of prior period adjustments (Note 1)	-	(39,596)
Net Position—Beginning of Year as Restated	7,584,828	7,756,342
Net Position—End of Year	$8,205,417	$7,584,828

TABLE 13-1C University of Virginia Statement of Cash Flows (in thousands) for the Year Ended June 30, 2017 (with comparative information for the year ended June 30, 2016)

	2017	2016
Cash Flows from Operating Activities		
Tuition and fees	$ 547,718	$ 513,187
Grants and contracts	312,868	308,929
Patient services	1,551,066	1,442,817
Sales and services of educational activities	41,851	26,357
Sales and services of auxiliary enterprises	134,619	134,955
Payments to employees and fringe benefits	(1,725,883)	(1,616,893)
Payments to vendors and suppliers	(1,070,098)	(973,276)
Payments for scholarships and fellowships	(92,691)	(75,808)
Perkins and other loans issued to students	(62,984)	(17,609)
Collection of Perkins and other loans to students	61,862	18,277
Other receipts	63,598	60,364
Net Cash Used by Operating Activities	(238,074)	(178,700)
Cash Flows from Noncapital Financing Activities		
State appropriations	169,545	162,166
Additions to permanent endowments	46,963	14,521
Federal Direct Loan Program receipts	127,239	123,592
Federal Direct Loan Program payments	(127,239)	(123,592)
Pell grants	12,485	12,478
Deposits held in custody for others	(10,041)	8,499
Noncapital gifts and grants and endowments received	153,334	170,454
Repayments from noncapital debt	(25,000)	25,000
Other net nonoperating expenses	333	40,902
Net Cash Provided by Noncapital Financing Activities	347,619	434,020

(Continues)

(Continued)

Cash Flows from Capital and Related Financing Activities		
Capital appropriations	14,000	31,216
Capital gifts and grants received	30,468	24,321
Proceeds from capital debt	392,986	94,168
Proceeds from sale of capital assets	–	691
Acquisition and construction of capital assets	(368,289)	(393,406)
Principal paid on capital debt and leases	(265,412)	(45,176)
Interest paid on capital debt and leases	(74,211)	(61,821)
Net Cash Used by Capital and Related Financing Activities	(270,458)	(350,007)
Cash Flows from Investing Activities		
Proceeds from sales and maturities of investments	711,518	375,377
Interest on investments	21,116	2,442
Purchase of investments and related fees	(567,045)	(665,249)
Other investment activities	(35,051)	(61,864)
Net Cash Provided (Used) by Investing Activities	(130,538)	(354,178)
Net Decrease in Cash and Cash Equivalents	(30,375)	(448,865)
Cash and cash equivalents—beginning of year	141,363	590,228
Cash and Cash Equivalents—End of Year	$ 110,988	$ 141,363
Reconciliation of Operating Loss to Net Cash used by Operating Activities		
Operating loss	$ (452,395)	$ (396,811)
Adjustments to reconcile operating loss to net cash used by operating activities		
Depreciation expense	225,247	219,683
Provision for uncollectible loans and write-offs	1,786	699
Changes in assets and liabilities		
Receivables, net	3,941	(42,809)
Inventories	(1,942)	983
Prepaid expenses	1,136	1,832
Notes receivable, net	1,765	708
Capital assets, net	–	2,173
Deferred outflows of resources	(35,725)	(10,225)
Accounts payable and accrued liabilities	(19,383)	26,925
Unearned revenue	3,147	11,916
Accrual for compensated absences	6,922	6,662
Net pension liability	54,206	47,641
Deferred inflows of resources	(24,507)	(48,077)
Total Adjustments	214,321	218,111
Net Cash used by Operating Activities	$ (238,074)	$ (178,700)

(Continues)

(Continued)

University of Virginia Statement of Cash Flows, Continued (in thousands) for the year ended June 30, 2017 (with comparative information for the year ended June 30, 2016)

	2017	2016
Noncash Investing, Capital, and Financing Activities		
Assets acquired through assumption of a liability	$8,970	$365
Assets acquired through a gift	9,284	2,589
Change in fair value of investments	613,384	(99,481)
Increase in receivables related to nonoperating income	2,758	2,588
Gain (loss) on disposal of capital assets	1,004	11,890
Net loss on investments in affiliated companies	23,149	(2,319)
Goodwill reclassification	8,717	–
Change in non-controlling interest in subsidiary	1,260	–
VRS and VaLORS Special Revenue Allocation	13,576	–
Revaluation of investment	(5,968)	–
Amortization of bond premium	11,948	–

principles of revenue and expense recognition differ in significant ways from those of the GASB. Notably, for example, the FASB requires that revenues be classified into two categories of restrictiveness based on donor specification, whereas the GASB draws no distinction between resources restricted by donors and those restricted by other outside parties, such as bondholders.

Although the FASB pronouncements directed toward not-for-profits apply to colleges and universities, they do not address the unique accounting and reporting issues of these entities. For guidance on specific questions pertaining to colleges and universities, one can profitably look to the literature of the National Association of College and University Business Officers (NACUBO), which is the leading association of university accounting and financial managers, and to prevalent practice.

Prior to the issuance of FASB ASU No. 2016-14 and, before that, Statement No. 117 regarding the form and content of not-for-profit financial statements, universities based their accounting and reporting on what is widely referred to as the "AICPA model." This model establishes a fund structure, summarized in Table 13-2, that many colleges and universities continue to maintain for purposes of internal accounting and control. However, for purposes of external reporting, colleges and universities must now group their funds into the FASB's two categories of restrictiveness.

TABLE 13-2 **AICPA Model Funds Structure[7] (for Internal Accounting and Reporting Only)**

Unrestricted Current (or Unrestricted Operating or General) Funds

The current funds of a university are equivalent to a government's general fund and its special revenue funds. Like a government, a university maintains a single current operating fund plus as many current restricted funds as needed.

Restricted Current (or Restricted Operating or Specific-Purpose) Funds

The restricted funds are similar to the special revenue funds of a governmental entity. The funds are used to account for the activities of the educational institution that are supported by resources whose use is limited by external parties for specific purposes. The principal sources of restricted current funds are contributions from donors, contracts, grants, and appropriations.

Plant (or Land, Building, and Equipment) Funds

Universities divide their plant funds into four categories:

- ***Plant funds—unexpended.*** These are the university version of capital projects funds. They are maintained to account for resources reserved for the construction or purchase of plant and equipment. Universities finance the construction of capital projects by issuing bonds, by accepting gifts or grants, or by setting aside general operating revenues. To ensure that the resources are used only for their intended purposes, they are accounted for in specially-dedicated funds.
- ***Plant funds—renewals and replacements.*** These are, in essence, additional capital projects funds. The resources in these funds, however, are committed to the renewal and replacement of existing plant and equipment rather than the acquisition of new facilities.
- ***Plant funds—retirement of indebtedness.*** These funds correspond to a government's debt service funds. Their assets, mostly cash and investments, are held for the retirement of debt and the payment of interest.
- ***Plant funds—investment (or net investment) in plant.*** These funds report the university's long-term assets, including land, buildings, construction-in-progress, improvements other than buildings, equipment, and library books.

Plant funds report both assets and related debt. Thus, if proceeds from issuing bonds are initially reported in an unexpended plant fund, then the cash received would be recognized as an asset; the bonds payable as a liability. If the bond money were subsequently used to construct a building, then both the cash and the bonds payable would be removed from the unexpended plant fund. In the investment in plant fund, the new building would be reported as an asset; the related bonds payable as a liability. The excess of plant fund assets over liabilities in each of the categories is generally reported as either "fund balance" or "investment in plant."

Loan Funds

As implied by their title, loan funds account for resources dedicated for student loans. A type of restricted fund, the assets are principally loans receivable and investments. These funds do not typically have liabilities of consequence, except if the university itself has borrowed the funds that it lends. Fund balances are ordinarily increased by gifts and grants and by investment earnings. They are decreased by administrative costs and by provisions for bad debts.

Endowment Funds

Endowment funds are analogous to a government's permanent funds (i.e., nonexpendable trust funds). They are used most commonly to account for gifts that specify that the donated amount is to be invested and that only the income from the investments may be expended. The donors may either stipulate the purpose for which the income must be expended or leave it to the discretion of the university. There are three types of **endowments**: permanent endowments, term endowments, and quasi endowments or board designated funds that function as endowments. **Permanent endowments** refer to amounts that have been contributed with donor-specified restrictions that the principal be invested in perpetuity; income from those investments may also be restricted by donors. These amounts are reported under net assets with donor restrictions. **Term endowments** are similar to permanent endowments, except that the resources originally contributed become available to the entity at some future date or on the occurrence of a specified event for unrestricted or purpose restricted use. These amounts are also reported as net assets with donor restrictions. **Quasi endowments** refer to resources designated by an entity's governing board to be retained for a specific purpose and are reported as net assets without donor restrictions.

[7] Adapted from the *AICPA Audit and Accounting Guide, Not-for-Profit Entities* (March 2017), FASB ASC 958-10.

Annuity and Life-Income (Split-Interest) Funds

Annuity and life-income funds are special types of endowment funds. They are used to account for split-interest gifts[8] that provide a return to the donor (or a person designated by the donor) for a specified term or for the remainder of his or her life. Thereafter, what remains of the gift will revert to the university. For example, a donor may want to contribute his fortune to a university while he is alive, but still reap all or a portion of the earnings from it. He can accomplish this (and perhaps also be rewarded with advantageous tax treatment) by attaching to his gift the stipulation that he receive either a stated annual sum (an annuity) or a percentage of the investment earnings from his gift (life income) until his death.

Agency (or Custodian) Funds

The agency funds of a university are similar to those of a government's custodial funds. They are maintained to account for resources that the institution holds as a custodian or fiscal agent for "outsiders," such as student organizations and employees. The accounting for these funds is as straightforward as for governmental custodial funds; the funds have only assets and liabilities, no fund balances.

ACCOUNTING FOR REVENUES AND EXPENSES

CLASSIFICATION OF REVENUES AND EXPENSES

FASB standards do not specify how revenues should be classified. ASU No. 2016-14 does require that expenses be reported by function (either directly on the financial statements or in the notes). Most colleges and universities, both public (governmental) and private, classify revenues by source.

Common categories of revenues, which is also provided in the NACUBO chart of accounts, include

- Tuition and fees
- Government (federal, state, and local) grants and contracts
- Gifts and private grants (nongovernmental)
- Endowment (investment) income
- Sales and services of educational activities
- Revenues from auxiliary enterprises
- Other operating revenue
- Government (federal, state, and local) appropriations (nonoperating)
- Gains (or losses) on sales of investments (nonoperating)

Primary categories of functional expense classification include

- Education and general
  - Instruction and departmental research
  - Extension and public service

[8] GASB Statement No. 81, *Irrevocable Split-Interest Agreements* effective December 2016 is applicable to public colleges and universities.

- Academic support
- Student services
- Institutional support
- Scholarships and fellowships

- Sponsored research
- Operation and maintenance of plant
- General administration
- Expenses of auxiliary enterprises
- Depreciation
- Interest (nonoperating expense)
- Provision for uncollectible student loans

THE MEANING OF "OPERATING INCOME"—A CONTROVERSIAL ISSUE

Approximately 60 percent of not-for-profit colleges and universities distinguish between "operating" and "nonoperating" activities in their statement of activities. The remaining 40 percent do not. Moreover, among the institutions that do distinguish between the two, there is no uniformity as to the classification of the various activities. As a consequence, although the "bottom line" (net increase in net assets) is unaffected by how they report their revenues and expenses, some institutions may appear to be more efficient in their operations than others.

Among the items over which there is the greatest disparity of practice are contributions and bequests, gifts, investment gains and losses, and the change in value of split-interest agreements (including those that result from changes in actuarial assumptions).[9]

IN PRACTICE WHICH SET OF STANDARDS DO WE FOLLOW?

Most colleges and universities are clearly either public or private. Some, however, face an accounting and reporting identity crisis.

Cornell University, for example, consists of both public and private colleges. The public ("statutory") colleges include its School of Industrial and Labor Relations, College of Veterinary Medicine, and College of Agriculture and Life Sciences. The private ("endowed") colleges include its College of Arts and Sciences, School of Management, Law School, and Graduate School. The university has chosen to adhere to the FASB standards.

Even universities that are clearly considered to be public may, in key respects, be more private than public. Many major state universities receive less than 15 percent of their total budgets from state appropriations. The balance comes mainly from tuition, fees, and research grants. Of course, irrespective of the meagerness of their contributions, the states are able to exercise 100 percent control over their universities. This misalignment of control and contributions has led some universities to offer to trade state appropriations for enhanced operating and fiscal flexibility. For example, state universities in both Colorado and Texas have been granted the authority (within limits) to set their own tuition rates. In return, they not only had to forgo increases in state appropriations but also had to agree to be more accountable for outcomes—improved graduation and retention rates—as well. In fact, under a law that took effect July 1, 2005, Colorado became the first state to direct a substantial portion of higher education funds to undergraduate students, rather than universities, through the College Opportunity Fund, a voucher-like program. The state of Ohio and New York City followed suit and started the voucher program. However, in August 2014, the state of Colorado suspended this voucher program.

[9] See Mary Fischer, Teresa Gordon, Janet Greenlee, and Elizabeth Keating, "Measuring Operations: An Analysis of US Private Colleges and Universities' Financial Statements," *Financial Accountability & Management* 20 (May 2004), 129–151.

IN PRACTICE FROM PUBLIC TO PRIVATE

On June 7, 2012, the Academic Senate of UCLA (an unquestionably public university) voted to make its Anderson School of Management's MBA program entirely self-supporting—essentially to privatize it. The plan was first introduced in 2010 as a response to several years of severe cuts in state support of higher education. Under the proposed arrangement, the approximately $8.8 million in state funds that the school received would be shifted to other UCLA programs. The MBA program would make up for the lost revenue with philanthropic and tuition increases, but in return would be free from the many constraints that come with state monies. State legislatures provide only a minor proportion of university resources yet have control over most major university decisions.

After several years of public debate centered around concerns about educational quality, affordability for students, and the precedent for other schools in the system, UCLA's Anderson School did become a self-supporting entity within the public University of California system in 2014.

Sources: "UCLA's Business School Takes Step Away from Public Support," *Chronicle of Higher Education,* (June 7, 2012); "Public to Private MBA at UCLA," *Inside Higher Education* (June 30, 2014).

As noted earlier, public colleges are required by GASB Statement No. 34 to present separate subtotals for operating and nonoperating revenues and expenses. State appropriations must be classified as nonoperating revenues; they are intended to help cover an institution's operating expenses.[10]

RECOGNIZING TUITION AND FEE REVENUES AND RELATED EXPENSES

Not-for-profit colleges and universities recognize revenues using the new FASB standards in which organizations use the five-step model that all not-for-profit entities use. The AICPA Audit and Accounting guide, *Not-for-Profit Entities*, which applies to private colleges and universities, requires that tuition revenue be reported net of tuition discounts and **scholarships**; the revenue would be recognized over the semester as it fulfills its contract with students.[11] GASB requires that tuition revenues be shown net of any estimated uncollectible amounts. NACUBO indicates that colleges and universities should show tuition and fees net of any estimated uncollectible amounts and directly adjust the revenue account for the estimate, rather than treat uncollectible amounts as bad debt expense.[12]

According to NACUBO, scholarship allowances are the difference between the stated tuition charges and the actual amount billed to the student. If the tuition reduction is an employee

IN PRACTICE HOW SHOULD A UNIVERSITY CLASSIFY A GIFT THAT MAY NOT BE A GIFT?

When the University of Central Arkansas received a $700,000 "gift" from Aramark, the university food services vendor, the president and the board chairman of the university faced criticism and had to offer a public apology for failing to inform the Board of Trustees of conditions attached to the funds.

Aramark offered the money to the university as an "unrestricted grant." However, this was offered in exchange for a seven-year renewal of Aramark's contract with the university. Additional strings attached to the funds were the option for Aramark to amend the contract every year and increase fees to students per the consumer price index. The board was unaware of the contribution contingencies and had already planned to use the funds for renovations to the president's home.

The board chairman and the university president had to apologize repeatedly, as there was strong disapproval for the failure to properly inform the board that the stated "gift" related to the renewal of a vendor contract. The board called for a committee to interview under oath those involved with the misrepresentation. In light of the incident, a trustee of the university stressed that the board needs to be "100 percent transparent in everything that we do."

Source: "President of U. of Central Arkansas Apologizes over Handling of $700,000 'Gift'," *Chronicle of Higher Education* (September 1, 2011).

[10] GASB, *Comprehensive Implementation Guide, 2013–14* Section 7.73.4.

[11] AICPA, Audit and Accounting Guide: *Not-for-Profit Organizations* (March 2017); FASB ASC 958-10.

[12] NACUBO, Financial Accounting and Reporting Manual for Higher Education, Sec. 309.

benefit, the reduction is treated as compensation expense. For example, tuition waivers for work-study programs and graduate assistantships are expenses. However, scholarships that do not require service to the university or college, such as athletic or academic excellence scholarships, are allowances and treated as reductions in revenue.[13]

The issue of when tuition and fee revenue should be recognized has been a difficult one in the past because most colleges and universities end their fiscal year in the summer months, their "slow" season. Therefore, summer semesters or quarters may overlap fiscal years. Fall or spring terms, however, generally take place entirely within a single fiscal year.

Several events or transactions had been justified as a point of revenue recognition for tuition and fees:

- As students pay their tuition or fees (i.e., a cash collection basis)
- The start of a semester
- The last date at which refunds can be claimed
- The passage of time (i.e., if a semester overlaps two fiscal years, then the revenue could be allocated between the years based on the number of semester days in each year)

At the time of this book's writing, private colleges and universities are implementing FASB ASU No. 2014-09 about new revenue recognition standards. Revenue should be recognized for these organizations as the performance obligation is fulfilled. The new standard may better align some of these ambiguous areas for private schools.

Example

Tuition and Fee Revenues

The fiscal year of a college ends July 31. In May and June 2020 a college collects $120 million in tuition and fees for its summer semester that begins on June 1 and ends on August 15. It also collects $180 million for the following fall semester, which begins on September 5. Faculty salaries applicable to summer session courses are $10 million. Of this amount, $8 million are applicable to June and July and $2 million to August.

AICPA AND GASB GUIDANCE

The AICPA, in accordance with FASB standards, states that the college would recognize revenue over the course of the summer semester as it meets its performance obligation. However, the fall semester tuition has not yet met revenue recognition standards.[14] However, a GASB implementation guide says explicitly that tuition and fees for an academic semester that encompasses two fiscal years must be allocated between the two years.[15]

Following the AICPA guidance, the entire summer semester's tuition and fees, as well as the related faculty salaries, should be recognized in the year ending July 31, 2020 as it fulfills its performance obligation to students:

Cash	$120	
Revenue from tuition and fees		$120
To record revenue for the summer semester beginning June 1, 2020		
Faculty salaries relating to the summer semester—expense	$10	
Cash		$8
Deferred faculty salaries relating to the summer semester (liability)		2
To record the faculty salaries applicable to the summer semester beginning June 1, 2020		

[13] NACUBO. *Financial Accounting and Reporting Manual For Higher Education,* Section 360.41.
[14] See Chapter 8, *Revenue Recognition* (January 2018).
[15] *Comprehensive Implementation Guide, 2013–14* Section 7.72.13.

In this example it is assumed that faculty salaries, but not other operating costs, can be tied directly to summer courses (e.g., that faculty are paid on a "per course" basis). Therefore, the faculty salaries have been matched to the tuition revenues and fees. The other operating costs would be accounted for as "period" costs and expensed as incurred.

Following the GASB, instead of the AICPA, guidance, the revenue would be divided between the two semesters:

Cash	$120	
Revenue from tuition and fees		$96
Revenues from tuition and fees received in advance (a liability)		24

To recognize revenue for the summer semester beginning June 1, 2020, allocated to the year ending July 31, 2020 on the basis of number of days (60 of 75 semester days)

The faculty salaries would also be divided between the two semesters. No special allocation is necessary in this example inasmuch as the appropriate expense to be recognized in each year is equal to the amount earned by the faculty in that year:

Faculty salaries relating to the summer semester—expense	$8	
Cash		$8

To record the faculty salaries applicable to the summer semester beginning June 1, 2020

Under both FASB and GASB guidelines, the $180 million in tuition and fees applicable to the fall semester should be recognized as revenue in the year ending July 31, 2021, and should therefore be reported as revenue received in advance when received in June 2020:

Cash	$180	
Revenue received in advance—fall semester tuition and fees (a liability)		$180

To record tuition and fees applicable to the fall semester beginning September 5, 2020

Based on the AICPA guidance, tuition revenue paid in advance is deemed a "contract liability" which is similar to a deferred revenue. The cash that is debited to the college would be offset by a credit to the contract liability account. As the performance obligation is met, revenue would be credited, while the contract liability is debited.[16] The five-step revenue recognition model indicates that the college would fulfill its performance obligation to the students over the Fall semester. Therefore, over the upcoming Fall semester, the college would recognize $180 million in revenue ratably and reduce the contract liability equally.

ACCOUNTING AND REPORTING FOR GRANTS

OTHER ISSUES

For many colleges and universities, reimbursement grants for research and related activities are a mainstay of financial support. Grantors, especially the federal government, do not expect recipients to earn a "profit" from their grants; they expect the grants merely to cover the costs of the specified research or other activities. Nonetheless, almost all grants provide reimbursement for "indirect costs" or overhead, now known as facilities and administrative costs, and Office of Management and Budget rules detail how overhead allowances on federal grants should be computed.[17]

Two aspects are critical here. The first is whether the grant is a contribution or an exchange. An exchange means that the grantor expects the college or university to provide some goods or services for the money given, whereas no such expectation exists for a contribution. For a reimbursement grant, the performance obligation to expend resources in some particular manner is fulfilled, and so revenue would be recognized. The second is determining whether it is conditional

[16] See 8.6.69 of the AICPA *Audit and Accounting Guide: Revenue Recognition, 2018.*

[17] Office of Management and Budget Circular A-21, *Cost Principles for Educational Institutions* (revised May 2004).

or unconditional. Unconditional grants or contributions are recognized immediately, while conditional grants or contributions are not recognized immediately until a "barrier" (i.e., some agreement that must be overcome) is satisfied and assets are transferred to the organization.[18] The FASB continues to work on developing additional guidance on this topic.

Example

Grants

In 2020 a private university's accounting department received a $300,000 grant from a federal agency to carry out research in government budgeting. Of this amount, $180,000 was to reimburse the university for faculty salaries and $120,000 was to cover overhead. During 2020 the department began the research and paid faculty members $45,000. It was reimbursed by the federal government for $75,000 (the direct costs incurred plus a proportionate share of the overhead).

FASB STANDARDS

Per FASB ASU 2014-09, grants (excluding those that are exchange transactions in which the grantors expect to receive reciprocal value) are a form of contributions and should be accounted for as such.[19] Reimbursement grants are conditioned on the grantee's incurring qualifying costs. Therefore, they should be accounted for as conditional grants.[20] They should be recognized as revenue only as the grantee incurs qualifying costs.

In the example, the following entries would be appropriate in 2020:

Sponsored research—expense	$45,000	
Cash		$45,000

To record faculty salaries (in a fund without donor restrictions)

The overhead costs incurred are not broken out separately because by their very nature they cannot be. They are subsumed in categories such as maintenance, administration, and library costs.

Due from federal government	$75,000	
Government grants and contracts—direct reimbursement (revenue)		$45,000
Government grants and contracts—reimbursement for overhead (revenue)		30,000

To record the amount due from the federal government for reimbursement of direct and indirect costs (in a fund without donor restrictions)

Cash	$75,000	
Due from federal government		$75,000

To record the collection of cash from the federal government (in a fund without donor restrictions)

In this illustration, the resources received from the federal government are restricted to specified research. Nevertheless, the transactions are recorded entirely in the without donor restrictions category because it is assumed that the university will exercise its option to report restricted promises to give as not restricted if the restriction has been met in the same period as the donation is made.

[18] Contributions are discussed in 958-605 while exchanges are discussed in 958-606 under Update No. 2014-09.

[19] FASB 958-605-15-5A.

[20] 958-605-55-70B.

ACCOUNTING FOR STUDENT LOANS

Colleges and universities maintain loan funds to provide financial assistance to students. For internal purposes, loan transactions are accounted for in separate funds; for external reporting purposes, they present no unique problems.

Example

Student Loans

A college receives a contribution of $100,000 to be added to an existing fund restricted for student loans. Interest and dividends are to be added to the balance of the fund. In a particular year, the loan fund made loans of $900,000. Students repaid loans of $750,000 and paid $23,000 in interest. The fund earned $63,000 in interest and dividends.

The entries that follow would be appropriate. They would be recorded in a restricted fund. Loan funds can be accounted for as not restricted by a donor unless, of course, as in the example, the resources were donated with the stipulation that they be restricted.

Cash	$100,000	
Contributions		$100,000
To record the contributions		
Student loans receivable	$900,000	
Cash		$900,000
To record student loans		
Cash	$773,000	
Student loans receivable		$750,000
Interest revenue		23,000
To record the repayment of student loans along with interest on the loans		
Cash	$ 63,000	
Investment revenue		$ 63,000
To record investment earnings		

AUXILIARY ENTERPRISES

Colleges and universities engage in a variety of business-type activities. Most prominent of these, at least in major state and private universities, is intercollegiate athletics. However, they also include dormitories, dining halls, bookstores, and movie theaters. For purposes of internal reporting these "auxiliary enterprises" would almost always be accounted for as separate business-type entities. Thus, they would follow the five-step revenue recognition framework based on performance obligations outlined in the prior chapter, and also maintain their own set of books to prepare periodic "profit and loss" statements. For external reporting, however, their resources are accounted for no differently than other institutional resources. Thus, the revenues of auxiliary enterprises are ordinarily reported among operating revenues; the expenses are recorded as operating expenses. Often, the revenues of all auxiliary enterprises are combined into a single line, as are the expenses. Similarly, in not-for-profit universities the assets of auxiliary enterprises are categorized as to donor restriction. Thus, for example, donor funds that are restricted for athletic scholarships would be reported as assets with donor restrictions; an endowment that provides supplementary income to the football coach would also be reported as donor-restricted assets. In both cases, disclosures in the notes would provide additional details about the nature and purpose of restrictions.

FUND-RAISING FOUNDATIONS

Colleges and universities, particularly those that are public, are more likely than other not-for-profit organizations to be associated with fund-raising foundations that are separate legal entities. These organizations are generally governed by boards of trustees and collect funds on behalf of either the entire university or particular units, such as a law school. The funds that are collected are typically made available to the beneficiary university at the request of an appropriate university official. These types of foundations are especially popular in public institutions because they can be used to circumvent restrictions that are placed on resources that are in the universities' own (e.g., state-governed) accounts. For example, state regulations may allow a university to pay for a faculty recruit's dinner, but not an accompanying alcoholic beverage. The key reporting issues are whether and how these entities should be reported in the primary institution's financial statements.

IN PRACTICE HOW AUXILIARY ENTERPRISES CAN BE MISUSED

Go to any university that is a major football or basketball power, and its practice facilities, locker rooms, coaches' offices, and study halls for the athletes are likely to be opulent—far exceeding in luxury anything to be found elsewhere on campus. Similarly, the salary of the head football coach will almost certainly be many times that of the university president, to say nothing of the typical English professor.

On many campuses these differences may be blamed, in part, on a misunderstanding of accounting by university presidents and other administrators. The administrators will note that intercollegiate athletics are—and should be—accounted for as auxiliary enterprises. Therefore, they observe, the intercollegiate athletics department is—and should be—free to operate as an independent business, spending whatever revenues it earns as it sees fit. But that's where they go wrong. There's nothing in accounting literature or practice to suggest that merely because an activity is *accounted for* as an auxiliary enterprise it should be permitted to *operate as* an independent entity and apart from the rest of the institution. Thus, the revenues earned by intercollegiate athletics can just as properly be transferred to the university's general operating fund as left in the auxiliary enterprise fund. For purposes of budgeting, the need for a new training room can be weighed against that for a new chemistry lab.

The GASB provisions with regard to these types of affiliated organizations are discussed in Chapter 11, which addresses the reporting entity of governments in general and closely affiliated organizations in particular. In summary, they dictate that the government should report them as component units if: (1) the economic resources held by the separate organization are mainly for the direct benefit of the primary government; (2) the primary government is entitled to, or has the ability to, otherwise access a majority of the separate organization's economic resources; and (3) the resources of the separate organization are significant to the primary government.

The governing reporting standard for not-for-profit colleges and universities has been the AICPA pronouncement (adopted by the FASB), which suggests that these entities should do so when it: (1) has a controlling financial interest; or (2) is able to control that entity by having both a voting majority on its governing board and an economic interest in its resources.[21] However, as noted in the previous chapter, if a contribution to a university foundation is, in essence, a pass-through contribution to the university itself, then the university should recognize revenue as it is received by the foundation. In addition, as mentioned in Chapter 12, the FASB issued Statement No. 164, *Not-for-Profit Entities: Mergers and Acquisitions—including an Amendment of FASB Statement No. 142*, in April 2009. The statement addresses the issue of whether a combination is a merger or an acquisition and provides guidance as to the accounting principles to be followed.

The comprehensive example and exercise for review and self-study further illustrate the practices of nongovernment colleges and universities. See also Tables 2-11 and 2-12 in Chapter 2, which contains excerpts from the financial statements of Hamilton College.

[21] American Institute of Certified Public Accountants. Statement of Position 94-3, *Reporting of Related Entities by Not-for-Profit Organizations* (1994), para. 10. FASB ASC 958-810-05.

The illustrative example of Mars University, a private educational institution, summarizes the major transactions affecting colleges and universities. We start with the beginning trial balance for the fiscal year July 1, 2020–June 30, 2021 (presented in Table 13-3), journalize the major transactions the university entered into during the year, and present the statement of revenues, expenses and changes in net assets, and a statement of financial position.

Comprehensive Example

Mars University

TABLE 13-3 Mars University Trial Balance July 1, 2021

	Debits	Credits
Cash	$ 75,000	
Accounts receivable	2,817,000	
Allowance for uncollectible accounts		$ 245,000
Accrued interest receivable	76,000	
Contributions receivable	6,610,000	
Allowance for uncollectible contributions		225,000
Loans to students	630,000	
Long-term investments	18,425,000	
Property, plant, and equipment	17,600,000	
Accumulated depreciation		
Property, plant, and equipment		9,100,000
Accounts payable		749,000
Long-term debt—current installment		234,000
Long-term debt—noncurrent		9,874,000
Net assets—without donor restrictions, board designated		3,602,000
Net assets—without donor restrictions, undesignated		3,365,000
Net assets—with donor restrictions		18,839,000
Totals	$46,233,000	$46,233,000

Mars University, like most private not-for-profit colleges and universities (including Hamilton College) does not categorize its individual assets and liabilities by the two net assets categories (without donor restrictions and with donor restrictions). Instead, it categorizes only the net assets by this classification. By contrast, it does (as required by FASB ASU 2014-09) place each of the revenues and expenses in the appropriate column that designates these categories.

As of July 1, 2020, the trial balance for Mars University, a private institution, was as shown in Table 13-3.

During the fiscal year ended June 30, 2021, the university engaged in transactions that can be summarized as follows.

Tuition Revenue

It collected $35,892,000 in student tuition and fees, all applicable to the current year. The school provides the services as stipulated in its contracts with students.

Cash	$35,892,000	
Revenues—tuition and fees (without donor restrictions)		$ 35,892,000
To record revenue from tuition		

Collection of Receivables

It collected accounts receivable of $156,000 and accrued interest receivable of $76,000. In addition, it collected $6,328,000 in contributions receivable from its alumni and business partners.

Cash	$ 6,560,000	
Accounts receivable		$ 156,000
Accrued interest receivable		76,000
Contributions receivable		6,328,000
To record the collection of accounts, interest, and contributions receivable		

Auxiliary Enterprises

It had revenue of $17,250,000 (all in cash) from its two on-campus auxiliary enterprises, the bookstore and dining hall.

Cash	$17,250,000	
Revenues—unrestricted sales and services of auxiliary enterprises		$ 17,250,000
To record revenues from auxiliary enterprises		

Endowment Investments and Income

From its endowment investments, the university earned $1,530,000, none of which had a donor restriction.

Cash	$ 1,530,000	
Revenues—income without donor restrictions on endowment investments		$ 1,530,000
To record income without donor restrictions from endowments		

Scholarships

It awarded scholarships to graduate student accounts in the amount of $2,250,000. No services were required by the students on receipt of the scholarship.

Tuition deductions—student aid without donor restrictions	$ 2,250,000	
Accounts receivable		$ 2,250,000
To record scholarships (as deductions from revenue)		

Contributions

The university received contributions without donor restrictions of $3,260,000, and contributions with donor restrictions of $6,300,000. Of that amount, $2,000,000 was received in cash. Contributions receivable increased by $7,560,000.

Cash	$ 2,000,000	
Contributions receivable	7,560,000	
Revenues—contributions without donor restrictions		$ 3,260,000
Revenues—with donor restrictions		6,300,000
To record contributions		

Long-Term Debt

It paid $749,000 of its accounts payable and $234,000 for the current installment of its long-term debt.

Accounts payable	$ 749,000	
Long-term debt—current installment	234,000	
Cash		$ 983,000
To record payment of accounts and current portion of long-term debt		

Operating Expenses

The university incurred the following expenses during the year: instructional $12,389,000; research $16,750,000; student services $1,564,000; and auxiliary enterprises $9,200,000. Cash was paid in the amount of $38,000,000.

Instructional expense	$12,389,000	
Research expense	16,750,000	
Student services expense	1,564,000	
Auxiliary enterprises expense	9,200,000	
Cash		$38,000,000
Accounts payable		1,903,000
To record various expenses		

Investments

At year-end, the fair value of investments increased by $614,000. Of that amount, $400,000 increased net assets without donor restrictions and $214,000 increased net assets with donor restrictions.

Long-term investments	$ 614,000	
Gain on long-term investments—without donor restrictions		$ 400,000
Gain on long-term investments—with donor restrictions		214,000
To record gains on investments		

Closing Entries

Closing entries were prepared for net assets without donor restrictions, and net assets with donor restrictions.

Revenues—tuition and fees	$35,892,000	
Revenues—income without donor restrictions on endowment income	1,530,000	
Revenues—sales and services of auxiliary enterprises	17,250,000	
Revenues—contributions without donor restrictions	3,260,000	
Gain on long-term investments	400,000	
Tuition deduction—student aid		$ 2,250,000
Instructional expense		12,389,000
Research expense		16,750,000
Student services expense		1,564,000
Auxiliary enterprises expense		9,200,000
Net assets—without donor restrictions; undesignated		16,179,000
To close accounts to net assets without donor restrictions		

Revenues—contributions with donor restrictions	$ 6,300,000	
Gain on long-term investments, with donor restrictions	214,000	
Net assets—with donor restrictions	$ 6,514,000	
To close accounts to net assets with donor restrictions		

Table 13-4 presents the statement of revenues, expenses and changes in net assets, and the statement of financial position.

TABLE 13-4A Mars University Statement of Revenues, Expenses, and Changes in Net Assets for Year Ending June 30, 2021

	Without Donor Restrictions	With Donor Restrictions	Total
Revenues			
Net tuition and fees	$33,642,000		$33,642,000
Contributions	3,260,000	$ 6,300,000	9,560,000
Income on endowments without donor restrictions	1,530,000		1,530,000
Sales and services of auxiliary enterprises	17,250,000		17,250,000
Gain on long-term investments	400,000	214,000	614,000
Total Revenues	56,082,000	6,514,000	62,596,000
Expenses			
Instruction	12,389,000		12,389,000
Research	16,750,000		16,750,000
Student services	1,564,000		1,564,000
Total educational and general expenses	30,703,000		30,703,000
Auxiliary enterprises	9,200,000		9,200,000
Total expenses	39,903,000		39,903,000
Change in net assets	16,179,000	$ 6,514,000	$22,693,000
Net assets, July 1, 2020	$25,806,000		
Net assets, June 30, 2021	$48,499,000		

TABLE 13-4B Mars University Statement of Financial Position June 30, 2018

Assets	
Cash and cash equivalents	$ 24,324,000
Accounts receivable (net of allowance for doubtful accounts)	166,000
Accrued interest receivable	—
Contributions receivable (net of allowance for uncollectible contributions)	7,617,000
Loans to students	630,000
Long-term investments	19,039,000
Property, plant, and equipment (net of accumulated depreciation)	8,500,000
Total assets	$ 60,276,000
Liabilities and net assets	
Accounts payable	$ 1,903,000
Long-term debt	
Current Installment	—
Noncurrent	9,874,000
Total liabilities	11,777,000
Net assets	
Board designated	3,602,000

(*Continues*)

TABLE 13-4B Mars University Statement of Revenues, Expenses, and Changes in Net Assets for Year Ending June 30, 2021 *(Continued)*

Other without donor restrictions	19,544,000
Total without donor restrictions	23,146,000
With donor restrictions	25,353,000
Total net assets	48,499,000
Total liabilities and net assets	$60,276,000

EVALUATING THE FISCAL WHEREWITHAL OF COLLEGES AND UNIVERSITIES

Government colleges and universities are, of course, ultimately the fiscal responsibility of governments. Insofar as their bonds are backed by a government, the risk of a bond default is, in essence, that of the supporting government. Moreover, even if their bonds are backed by specific revenues, such as those from dormitory revenues, stadium ticket sales, or parking garages, the probability of the government allowing a default is generally considered low.

As suggested by the factors focused on by Standard & Poor's (see Table 13-5), assessing the fiscal health of a not-for-profit college or university is complex. To be sure, the traditional financial indicators, such as debt ratios and revenue and expenditure trends, must be taken into account. Moreover, to the extent that not-for-profit colleges typically rely on endowments as a significant source of revenues, both the size of and annual returns on the endowment are key factors to be reviewed— especially in light of financial markets volatilities. The total endowment funds in 2016 of the 120 colleges and universities with the largest endowments totaled over $547 billion.[22]

TABLE 13-5 Factors Focused on by Standard & Poor's in Evaluating the Revenue Bonds of Private Colleges and Universities

I. Student demand

- **A.** Enrollment trends, including the reasons for upward or downward cycles
- **B.** Flexibility in admissions and programs
  1. The acceptance rate (a college that accepts almost all applicants is more vulnerable to a decline in demand than one that is highly selective and admits only a small percentage)
  2. Geographic diversity (the wider the geographic diversity, the less likely that an economic downturn will affect enrollment)
  3. Student quality (strong student quality, as measured by high school class rank, standardized test scores, and other factors, enhances a school's ability to withstand a decline in enrollment)
  4. Faculty (the higher the percentage of tenured faculty, the less likely that the university's program offerings can change to reflect current demand)
  5. Program offerings (the more specialized the programs, the greater the risk of an enrollment decline owing to changes in the work force)
  6. Competition (schools that are the first choice of its students are less threatened by widespread enrollment declines than those that are their second or third selections)
  7. Attrition (high attrition may be a sign of student dissatisfaction and a precursor to declining demand)

(Continues)

[22] *Source*: U.S. Department of Education, National Center for Education Statistics. U.S. Department of Education, National Center for Education Statistics, Integrated Postsecondary Education Data System (IPEDS), Spring 2016, Finance component. https://nces.ed.gov/programs/digest/d16/tables/dt16_333.90.asp?current=yes.

TABLE 13-5 Factors Focused on by Standard & Poor's in Evaluating the Revenue Bonds of Private Colleges and Universities *(Continued)*

II. Finances

- **A.** Revenues
  - **1.** Diversification (a diverse revenue base, in which a substantial portion of revenue is from grants, endowment income, dormitories, and other sources in addition to tuition, tends to mitigate shortfalls in any single revenue stream)
  - **2.** Ability to raise revenues through tuition adjustments (low rates in comparison with competitors indicates room for increases)
- **B.** Expenditures
  - **1.** Ability to reduce expenditures (a high ratio of fixed to variable costs limits flexibility)
  - **2.** Amounts being retained to build up plant and endowment (large amounts of resources being transferred to plant and endowment funds signify the availability of resources that could be redirected to debt service)
- **C.** Operating results (modest surpluses convey that revenues are sufficient to meet expenditures, but one- or two-year deficits are not necessarily a problem)
- **D.** Endowment
  - **1.** Comparison with debt level
  - **2.** Amount per student
  - **3.** Proportion that is unrestricted (the greater the proportion, the greater the flexibility)
- **E.** Debt (a ratio of maximum annual debt service to unrestricted current fund expenditures; greater than 10 percent generally indicates an excessive debt burden)

III. Management

- **A.** Ability to foresee and plan for potential challenges
- **B.** Strategies and policies that appear realistic and attainable
- **C.** A track record indicative of an ability to deal with new situations and problems
- **D.** A history of management continuity

IV. Legal provisions

- **A.** Security pledges (debt secured by enterprise revenues, such as dormitory rentals, is seen as weaker than that backed by general revenues or tuition revenues)
- **B.** Covenants (provisions requiring the institution to set certain rates and fees at specified levels may enhance the security of the bonds)
- **C.** Debt service reserve policies (the existence of reserve funds enhances the security of the bonds, especially those that are backed strictly by enterprise revenues)
- **D.** Credit enhancements such as loan guarantees or bond insurance

Source: Drawn from *General Criteria: Methodology: Not-For-Profit Public and Private Colleges and Universities* (New York: Standard & Poor's, 2017).

To obtain a broader and longer-term perspective, the analysis must look to factors that are far afield from those associated with corporate financial analysis. Examples include admissions selectivity (selective schools are less vulnerable to sudden drops in enrollment than non-selective schools); the percentage of faculty that are tenured (the higher the percentage, the less readily the school can cut costs); and the nature of course offerings (a school that specializes in a particular area, such as aviation or computer training, may be susceptible to downturns in that industry). Wide geographic diversity of the student body is generally considered a fiscal strength as it reduces a school's exposure to regional economic downturns. At the same time, it can also be a weakness. Some U.S. schools that catered to overseas students, for example, found themselves particularly hard hit by the immigration restrictions imposed after 9/11. Recent changes in federal tax policy towards universities should also be considered. For example, universities with large endowments are now subject to excise taxes on these assets.

As a rule, schools that are the highest risk for economic failure are small regional private colleges (e.g., fewer than 3,000 students) that accept most of their applicants (e.g., 70 percent or more) and have relatively low total financial resources per student (tuition revenue and endowment earnings of less than $50,000).

The fiscal health of colleges and universities, both government and private, is sensitive to unfavorable national economic conditions—especially declines in the stock market. First, declines in the stock market reduce endowment returns. Second, they reduce the willingness and ability of donors to give. Third, they reduce the ability of students and their parents to pay tuition. Fourth, they increase the demands on university scholarship funds. Fifth, they cause state legislators to either reduce, or fail to increase, state appropriations. Sixth, they may result in tight federal budgets and hence in reductions in support of federally supported research.

SUMMARY

Government colleges and universities have the option of reporting similarly to "full-service" governments or to other governments that engage exclusively in business-type activities. Most choose the latter and, accordingly, use business-type accounting. Not-for-profit colleges and universities must report similarly to other not-for-profit organizations.

Government colleges and universities are required to distinguish between operating and nonoperating revenues and expenses. Most notably, they classify state appropriations as nonoperating revenues. By contrast, not-for-profit colleges and universities are not required to so distinguish, although the majority do. Still, there is diversity of practice on how various revenues such as contributions and investment gains should be classified.

Among the unique revenues and expenses of colleges and universities are

- Tuition and fees, especially as they apply to semesters that overlap two fiscal years. Government colleges and universities apportion the tuition between the two years; not-for-profit colleges and universities recognize them in the year in which the school fulfills its performance contract with the student.
- Grants. Most grants are reimbursement grants and should be accounted for as other conditional contributions—that is, recognized when the allowable costs are incurred.

Student loans are also unique to educational institutions, but they present no special accounting problems. Auxiliary enterprises are generally accounted for as businesses, but to the extent that their resources are not restricted by donors are reported along with general operating revenues and expenses (i.e., in funds without donor restrictions).

In a narrow sense the fiscal health of colleges and universities can be evaluated using analytical tools, such as financial ratios. Colleges and universities, however, are especially difficult to analyze because their future may be dependent on such a wide range of "nonfinancial" factors, such as academic standing, diversity of student body, percentage of faculty with tenure, and changes in public policies towards these institutions.

KEY TERMS IN THIS CHAPTER

appropriations 582
auxiliary enterprises 584
endowment 590
permanent endowments 590
quasi endowments 590
scholarships 593
term endowments 590

EXERCISE FOR REVIEW AND SELF-STUDY

The balance sheet and statement of activities of New Hampshire College (adapted from the financial statements of a well-known New England college) are presented in Table 13-6. The statements are as of June 30, 2020, and all amounts, both in the statements and in the text that follows, are in thousands.

In addition to the tuition and fees reported on the statement of activities (all of which were received in cash), the college received $4,000 in tuition applicable to the 2020 summer semester, which runs from June 15 to August 15.

TABLE 13-6 New Hampshire College

Statement of Financial Position as of June 30, 2020

	Without Donor Restrictions	With Donor Restrictions	Total
Assets			
Current			
Cash and temporary investments	$ 18,567	$ 65,920	$ 84,487
Grants and contracts receivable		30,200	30,200
Pledges receivable	4,000		4,000
Other receivables	14,772	838	15,610
Total current	$ $37,339	$ $96,958	$ $134,297
Noncurrent			
Student loans receivable		$ 36,954	$ 36,954
Inventories	$ 1,990		1,990
Deferred charges	5,628	6,867	12,495
Investments	24,940	806,641	831,581
Land, buildings, and equipment (net of $89,241 accumulated depreciation)	283,181		283,181
Other assets	15,475	6,879	22,354
Total noncurrent	$ 331,214	$ 857,341	$ 1,188,555
Total assets	$ 368,553	$ 954,299	$ 1,322,852
Liabilities			
Current			
Accounts payable	$23,024	$3,387	$26,411
Deferred revenue	12,672		12,672
Other current liabilities		1,399	1,399
Total current	$ 35,696	$ 4,786	$ 40,482
Noncurrent			
Notes and bonds payable	188,466	24,505	212,971
Other liabilities		23,000	23,000
Total noncurrent	$ 188,466	$ 47,505	$ 235,971
Total liabilities	$ 224,162	$ 52,291	$ 276,453
Net assets	$ 144,391	$ 902,008	$ 1,046,399

Statement of Activities For Year Ending June 30, 2020

	Without Donor Restrictions	With Donor Restrictions	Total
Revenues			
Tuition and fees	$ 110,568		$ 110,568
Grants and contracts		$ 38,914	38,914
Private gifts	16,503	54,264	70,767
Endowment income	12,382	18,548	30,930
Other investment income	1,593	3,619	5,212

(Continues)

TABLE 13-6 New Hampshire College *(Continued)*

Departmental sales and service	13,544		13,544
Athletic income	1,308		1,308
Income from museums and other programs	15,713		15,713
Auxiliary enterprises			
Student housing and dining	20,117		20,117
College inn	5,806		5,806
Rentals, recreational, and other facilities	11,871		11,871
Interest on student loans		1,856	1,856
Gains on investments		75,201	75,201
Total revenues	$ 209,405	$ 192,402	$ 401,807
Expenses			
Instruction and department research	$ 64,697		$64,697
Grants and contracts	47,661		47,661
Libraries, computers, and other academic support	37,406		37,406
Student services	15,677		15,677
General administration	13,326		13,326
Plant operation and maintenance	20,667		20,667
Financial aid	26,616		26,616
Athletics and physical education	6,207		
	6,207		
Auxiliary enterprises			
Student housing and dining	18,999		18,999
College inn	6,564		6,564
Rentals, recreational, and other facilities	11,079		11,079
Interest on debt	6,602		6,602
Depreciation expense	9,381		9,381
Other expenses	8,707		8,707
Total expenses	$293,589	$ 0	$ 293,589
Excess (deficiency) of revenues over expenses	($84,184)	$ 192,402	$108,218
Net assets released from restrictions	124,518	124,518	0
Change in net assets	$ 40,334	$ 67,884	$ 108,218

1. Prepare a summary journal entry to record the tuition and fees collected for the year ended June 30, 2020.

2. Prepare appropriate summary entries to record grant and contract revenues and expenses.

3. Among the college's funds with donor restrictions is a plant fund that accounts for resources reserved for the acquisition of facilities. During the year, the college used $24,000 of fund resources to acquire plant and equipment. Prepare appropriate journal entries to record the acquisition of the plant and equipment.

4. What was the college's "profit" on the inn that it operates? On its student housing and dining?

5. The college accounts for student loans in a restricted "student loans" fund. What is the amount owed to the college by students? How much interest on student loans did the college earn during the year? Is the interest on the loans available for general purposes, or is it restricted? Explain.

6. Why is endowment income not reported in the funds with donor restrictions? How much of the 2020 endowment income must be used for specific purposes? Why are gains on investments reported in the funds with donor restrictions?

7. During the year the college received the following pledges:
   a. $2,500 from an alumnus to construct a new wing to its science building.
   b. $4,500 to be used for general educational purposes.
   c. $5,000 to be used to acquire investment grade securities; only the earnings from these securities may be used to support teaching, research, and other routine activities of the college.
   d. Up to $1,000 to be used to match other expected contributions to a scholarship fund in honor of a recently retired faculty member. Indicate how each of the pledges would be accounted for.

8. Does the college distinguish between operating and nonoperating activities in its statement of activities?

QUESTIONS FOR REVIEW AND DISCUSSION

1. What key reporting options are available to government colleges and universities?

2. What are the key reporting options for private colleges and universities?

3. In what significant ways would each of the three major statements of a public university differ from those of a private university?

4. A public university receives approximately 20 percent of its revenue from state appropriations. In which category of revenues (operating or nonoperating) should it report the state appropriations and why?

5. Why are revenues presented on the financial statements net of scholarships and discounts?

6. What are auxiliary enterprises? How are they accounted for?

7. What are the three types of endowments? How are they presented on the financial statements of a public and a private college and university?

8. How are investments, investment income, and gains and losses on these investments accounted for? Is there a difference in treatment for public as opposed to private colleges and universities?

9. A not-for-profit technical college trains computer specialists, most of whom have, in the past, received offers for high-paying jobs in Silicon Valley. What special concerns might you have as to the ability of the college to repay its long-term debts?

10. Near the end of its fiscal year, a not-for-profit university was awarded a $2 million National Science Foundation grant to conduct biological research. Yet, consistent with GAAP, the college made no accounting entries with respect to the grant until the following year. How can you defend an accounting principle that permits an institution to avoid recording such a significant amount of revenue?

EXERCISES

EX. 13-1

Select the *best* answer.

1. For purposes of external reporting, private colleges and universities
   a. must adhere to all applicable FASB pronouncements.
   b. must adhere to all applicable GASB pronouncements.

c. can opt to follow either all applicable FASB or all applicable GASB pronouncements.
d. must follow all applicable NACUBO pronouncements.

2. For purposes of external reporting, a public college or university
   a. must report as if it were a general-purpose government.
   b. may report as if it were a comparable private college or university.
   c. may report as a special-purpose government engaged exclusively in business-type activities.
   d. may report in accordance with the AICPA college and university model if it had adhered to that model prior to the issuance of GASB Statement No. 35.

3. Public universities should report state appropriations as
   a. operating revenues.
   b. nonoperating revenues.
   c. noncapital revenues.
   d. special revenues.

4. Coleman College, a not-for-profit institution, issued $20 million in revenue bonds. Per the terms of the bond indenture, the college must maintain a cash reserve of $800,000—which is equal to six months of interest. The cash that is set aside should be classified as
   a. without donor restrictions.
   b. with donor restrictions.
   c. prepaid expense.
   d. either without donor restrictions or with donor restrictions depending on applicable state law.

5. For purposes of internal reporting Briggs College accounts for its bookstore as an auxiliary enterprise. The college should classify the store's inventory as
   a. assets without donor restrictions.
   b. assets with donor restrictions.
   c. auxiliary unit assets.
   d. component unit assets.

6. A government university receives a grant of $2,000,000 to improve its basketball arena. In its statement of cash flows the grant should be shown as a cash inflow from
   a. noncapital financing activities.
   b. capital financing activities.
   c. operating activities.
   d. investing activities.

7. A not-for-profit university receives a contribution without donor restrictions of $200,000. In its statement of cash flows, the contribution should be shown as a cash inflow from
   a. noncapital financing activities.
   b. capital financing activities.
   c. operating activities.
   d. investing activities.

8. Which of the following expenses would least likely be a line item on the statement of activities of a not-for-profit college?
   a. instruction
   b. salaries and wages
   c. auxiliary enterprises
   d. student services

9. A public college should most likely report its athletic foundation as which of the following in its financial statements under GASB 39:
   a. Student service
   b. Component unit
   c. Fund from external agency
   d. Affiliated organization

10. If a university receives a grant to test a product under a federal contract, but the government retains the patent to the product, the grant should be classified as a(n):
    a. nonexchange transaction.
    b. exchange transaction.
    c. contributed service.
    d. loan activity.

EX. 13-2

Select the *best* answer.

1. In June 2020, a public university bills and collects $30 million in tuition for the summer semester that runs from June 1 through July 15. In addition, in May and June it bills $200 million for the fall semester that runs from September 1 through December 15. Of this amount it collects only $80 million (expecting to collect the balance prior to September 1). In its statement of revenues and expenses for its year ending June 30, 2020 it should recognize as tuition revenue
   a. $20 million
   b. $30 million
   c. $100 million
   d. $110 million

2. In a particular year, a not-for-profit university receives $2 million in dividends and interest on an endowment, the income of which, per donor specification, must be used to provide scholarships to liberal arts students. During the year, it awards (and pays) scholarships of $1.9 million. In accord with a policy established by the university's board of trustees, it adds the $0.1 million balance to the endowment fund to offset the impact of inflation. For that year the university may recognize
   a. $1.9 million of revenue without donor restrictions and $0.1 million of revenue with donor restrictions.
   b. $2.0 million of revenue without donor restrictions.
   c. $1.9 million of revenue with donor restrictions and $0.1 of revenue without donor restrictions.
   d. $2.0 million of revenue with donor restrictions.

3. A not-for-profit university operates its college bookstore as an auxiliary enterprise. During the year the store has revenues of $20 million and expenses of $18 million. In its statement of activities the university should report
   a. operating revenues of $2 million.
   b. operating revenues of $20 million.
   c. nonoperating revenues of $2 million.
   d. nonoperating revenues of $20 million.

4. In 2020, a government university was awarded a federal reimbursement grant of $9 million to carry out research. Of this, $6 million was intended to cover direct costs and $3 million to cover overhead. In a particular year, the university incurred $2 million in allowable direct costs and received $1.7 million from the federal government. It expected to incur the remaining costs and collect the remaining balance in 2021. For 2020 it should recognize revenues from the grant of
   a. $1.7 million.
   b. $2.0 million.
   c. $3.0 million.
   d. $9.0 million.

5. A not-for-profit university maintained an endowment of $400,000, the income of which was restricted for an annual conference on international relations. In a particular year, the market value of the endowment increased by $40,000. The university held a conference on international relations at a cost of $43,000. The university should report
   a. no revenue and expenses without donor restrictions of $43,000.
   b. revenues without donor restrictions of $40,000 and expenses without donor restrictions of $43,000.

c. revenues with donor restrictions of $40,000, expenses with donor restrictions of $40,000 and expenses without donor restrictions of $3,000.
d. revenues with donor restrictions of $40,000 and expenses without donor restrictions of $43,000.

6. Other factors held constant, which of the following colleges is likely to present the least risk that it will default on its bonds?
   a. One that admits 98 percent of applicants
   b. One that draws the majority of its students from overseas
   c. One that prepares its students mainly for careers as automotive engineers
   d. One that draws its student body almost exclusively from the top 5 percent of high school graduating classes throughout the country

7. Scholarships for which no services are recorded should be recorded as ____________ and scholarships for which services are required should be recorded as ____________
   a. revenue deductions; expenses
   b. expenses; revenue deductions
   c. expenses; expenses
   d. revenue deductions; revenue deductions

8. A public university had tuition and fees for the year ended June 30, 2020, in the amount of $18,000,000. Scholarships, for which no services were required, amounted to $1,400,000. Graduate assistantships, for which services were required, amounted to $1,300,000. The amount to be reported by the university as net tuition and fee revenue would be
   a. $18,000,000
   b. $16,700,000
   c. $16,600,000
   d. $15,300,000

9. During the year, Griffin University's board of trustees established a $200,000 fund to be retained and invested for scholarship grants. The fund earned $12,000, which had not been distributed by December 31. What amount should Griffin report in a Board designated (quasi) endowment fund's net assets at December 31?
   a. $0
   b. $12,000
   c. $200,000
   d. $212,000

10. During the year, LeBlanc College received the following:
    - An unrestricted $70,000 pledge to be paid the following year
    - A $35,000 cash gift restricted by donors for study-abroad scholarships
    - A notice from a recent business school graduate that he has named the college as a beneficiary of $15,000 in his will

    What amount of contribution revenue should LeBlanc College report in its statement of activities?
    a. $35,000
    b. $50,000
    c. $105,000
    d. $120,000

EX. 13-3

Although universities may be characterized by transactions not typically engaged in by other types of entities, most can be accounted for within the framework applicable to not-for-profit organizations in general.

Windom College, a not-for-profit institution, engaged in the following transactions during its fiscal year ending June 30, 2020. Prepare appropriate journal entries, indicating the types of funds (by restrictiveness) in which they would be recorded.

1. The college collected $86,400,000 in student tuition. Of this amount $6,000,000 was applicable to the summer semester, which ran from June 1 to August 30, and $400,000 was applicable to the fall semester that began the following September.
2. It received a contribution of $1,000,000 in stocks and bonds to establish an endowed chair in chemistry. Income from the chair must be used to supplement the salary of a professor of chemistry.
3. During the year, the chemistry chair endowment earned interest and dividends of $50,000, all of which was used to supplement the salary of the chair holder.
4. The fair value of the investments of the chemistry chair endowment declined by $80,000.
5. Using funds restricted for this purpose, the college purchased $150,000 of equipment for intercollegiate athletics. Intercollegiate athletics is accounted for as an auxiliary enterprise. The college charged depreciation of $30,000.
6. The annual alumni campaign yielded $1,800,000 in pledges. The college estimated that 2 percent would be uncollectible. During the year the college collected $1,500,000 on the pledges.

EX. 13-4

University loan funds can readily be accounted for within the general framework applicable to not-for-profit organizations.

Bronxville College maintains a loan fund of approximately $1 million (including receivables). The funds are invested in stocks and bonds, and all investment income must be added to the balance in the fund. The fund, however, is not restricted inasmuch as it was established by the college itself, not by donors.

Prepare journal entries to record the following events and transactions that took place during the year.

1. The college directed an additional $75,000 of donor contributions to the loan fund.
2. The fund made new student loans of $200,000. It estimated that approximately 10 percent will be uncollectible.
3. It earned interest and dividends of $6,000. In addition, the market value of its investments increased by $3,000.
4. It collected $140,000 in loan repayments, plus an additional $40,000 in interest.
5. It wrote off $20,000 of loans as uncollectible.

EX. 13-5

Internet-based exercise

Please go to the Internet and obtain the financial report for the most recent year available of the following two (a public and a private) universities.

1. University of North Carolina at Chapel Hill
2. Duke University

Analyze the financial reporting differences between these two universities based on the following:

a. Balance Sheet (the equity section)
b. Statement of Activities and Statement of Revenues, Expenses and Changes in Net Position
c. Do both universities prepare a Statement of Cash Flows?

PROBLEMS

P. 13-1

A multifund balance sheet can readily be recast so that it conforms with FASB standards.

A balance sheet of Brown University, issued prior to the effective date of FASB Statement No. 117, is presented below.

Recast the fund balance (net asset) section of the balance sheet so that it presents the fund balances in the two categories required by ASU 2014-09. Show the balances in a single column, divided into two sections. Thus, for example, current undesignated funds should be reported in the without donor restrictions section; current restricted funds in the with donor restrictions section. Assume that the plant funds, other than the net investment in plant, are donor restricted, and make other appropriate assumptions as to the type of restriction that applies to each of the other fund balances.

Brown University Balance Sheet as of June 30 (in thousands)

	Total	Current Funds	Loan Funds	Endowment Funds	Plant Funds
Assets					
Cash	$110,922	$45,268	$590	$ 61,555	$ 3,509
Investments	507,503	9,042		456,126	42,335
Accounts receivable	15,070	14,499		426	145
Notes receivable	26,000		26,000		
Inventories and pre-paid expenses	5,047	5,047			
Land, buildings, and equipment (less accumulated depreciation)	196,897				196,897
Due from (to) other funds		11,338	(3,376)	3,323	(11,285)
Total assets	$861,439	$85,194	$23,640	$521,004	$231,601
Liabilities and fund balances					
Accounts payable—accrued liabilities	$ 29,788	$20,836	$ 6,597	$ 2,355	
Deferred revenues	5,424	5,424			
Agency accounts	10,375	10,375			
Bonds payable	88,399				88,399
Total liabilities	$133,986	$36,635		$ 6,597	$ 90,754
Fund balances					
Current funds					
Designated	$ 20,445	$20,445			
Restricted	28,114	28,114			
Student loan funds established by gift and grants	23,640		$23,640		
Endowment and similar funds					
Quasi-endowment funds	59,644			$ 59,644	
Restricted endowment funds	68,352			68,352	
Other endowment funds	369,399			369,399	
Life income funds	17,012			17,012	
Plant funds					
Unexpended	19,452				19,452
Retirement of indebtedness	6,306				6,306
Net investment in plant	115,089				115,089
Total fund balances	$727,453	$48,559	$23,640	$514,407	$140,847
Total liabilities and fund balances	$861,439	$85,194	$23,640	$521,004	$231,601

P. 13-2

University plant funds can readily be recast from an AICPA to a FASB presentation.

A university maintains several plant funds as shown in the condensed balance sheets presented below. The fund structure and presentation are consistent with the AICPA college and university reporting model. Although this model has been superseded by FASB ASU 2014-09, *Financial Statements of Not-for-Profit Organizations*, it is still used by many colleges and universities for internal purposes.

Plant Funds (in thousands)

Unexpended plant funds		
Assets		
Cash	$ 9,000	
Investments	27,000	
Total assets	$ 36,000	
Liabilities and fund balances		
Bonds payable	$ 24,000	
Fund balance		
Restricted by donors for specified projects	$ 4,000	
Not restricted by donors	8,000	12,000
Total liabilities and fund balances		$ 36,000
Funds for renewals and replacements		
Assets		
Cash		$ 4,500
Investments		85,100
Total assets		$ 89,600
Liabilities and fund balances		
Fund balance		$ 89,600
Funds for retirement of indebtedness		
Assets		
Cash		$ 21,600
Investments		25,600
Total assets		$ 47,200
Liabilities and fund balances		
Fund balance		$ 47,200
Investment in plant		
Assets		
Construction in process		$ 3,500
Equipment		39,300
Land		12,000
Buildings		127,800
Total plant		182,600
Less accumulated depreciation		(78,200)
Total investment in plant		$104,400
Liabilities and fund balances		
Notes payable		$ 20,000
Bonds payable		39,000
Capital lease obligations		8,500
Net investment in plant		36,900
Total investment in plant		$104,400

1. Recast the plant funds as they would appear in external reports in accord with ASU 2014-09. That is, show how each of the reported amounts would be shown in a balance sheet with one column each for without donor restrictions and another for with donor restrictions . Allocate the cash ($9,000) and investments ($27,000) of the unexpended plant funds to the donor-restricted category based on donor-restricted fund balance as a proportion of total liabilities and fund balances (e.g., $4,000/$36,000 to net assets with donor restrictions).

2. Comment briefly on the advantages and disadvantages of each presentation.

P. 13-3

The fund balance sheet of a public university can be recast so that it conforms with GAAP.

The fund balance sheet of Sundown State University, a public institution, is presented below. For purposes of external reporting, the university has opted to report as a special-purpose entity that engages in business type activities.

As best the data permit, recast the balance sheet into one that conforms to current generally accepted accounting principles.

Sundown State University, Fund Balance Sheet (in thousands)

	Current	Loan	Endowment	Plant	Total
Assets					
Cash and temporary investments	$18,567	$22,108	$29,611	$ 10,853	$ 81,139
Accounts receivable		2,736		45,974	48,710
Inventories	1,990				1,990
Loans to other funds	8,557		6,879		15,436
Land, buildings, and equipment, net of accumulated depreciation				283,181	283,181
Total assets	$29,114	$24,844	$36,490	$340,008	$430,456
Liabilities					
Accounts payable	$23,024			$ 1,704	$ 24,728
Loans from other funds		$ 32		15,404	15,436
Bonds payable		24,505		188,466	212,971
Total liabilities	$23,024	$24,537	$ 0	$205,574	$253,135
Net assets	$ 6,090	$ 307	$36,490	$134,434	$177,321
Fund balances					
Restricted by donors	$ 4,102		$20,346	$134,434	$158,882
Designated by the university	1,002		10,000		11,002
Without donor restrictions	986	$ 307	6,144	0	7,437
Total fund balance	$ 6,090	$ 307	$36,490	$134,434	$177,321

P. 13-4

Pledges must be distinguished by the extent to which they are restricted.

A private college receives the following pledges of support.

1. As part of its annual fund drive, alumni and friends of the college pledge $8 million. The college estimates that about 15 percent of the pledges will prove uncollectible.

2. A CPA firm promises to establish an endowed chair in the accounting department by donating $500,000. The chair agreement will provide that the funds be used to purchase investment grade securities and that the income from the securities be used to supplement the salary of the chair holder and support his or her academic activities.

3. A private foundation promises to donate $100,000 to be used to support a major revision of the college's accounting curriculum.

4. An alumnus pledges $25,000 to the college's loan fund, which is used to make loans to students requiring financial assistance.

5. The college is seeking support for construction of a new athletic fieldhouse. A local real estate investor promises to donate 10 acres of land on which a fieldhouse could be built if the college is able to raise the funds required to construct the building. The land has a market value of $1 million.

Indicate the category of net assets (with donor restrictions or without donor restrictions) in which each of the contributions should be recorded and the amount of revenue, if any, that should be recognized when the pledge was made. Briefly explain your response.

P. 13-5

A single contribution may affect both types of funds.

The following events and transactions relate to a single contribution.

1. A high-tech firm pledged to contribute $1 million in the company's common stock to a university's business school if the school would establish a new program in the management of information technology. The securities were to be placed in an endowment fund, and the annual dividend earnings were to be used to purchase computer hardware and software.
2. The business school established the program and thereby satisfied the conditions to receive the contribution.
3. The business school received the stock and placed it in an endowment fund.
4. In the first year after receiving the stock, the business school earned $30,000 in cash dividends. They were credited to an appropriate fund.
5. The business school purchased $20,000 of computer equipment.
6. The computer equipment was estimated to have a useful life of three years (no salvage). The school charged one year's depreciation.

Prepare journal entries, as necessary, to record these events and transactions. Be sure to indicate the type of fund (without donor restrictions or with donor restrictions) that would be affected by the entries.

P. 13-6

Is there a sound reason for accounting for contributions to a private not-for-profit university different from a public (government) university?

In January 2017, Kirkland University receives a pledge of $200,000 to be used exclusively to support research in a specialized area of communication disorders. The university's fiscal year ends on July 31.

In December 2017 (the following fiscal year), Kirkland receives the pledged contribution of $200,000 and spends $150,000 on qualifying research.

1. Prepare all required journal entries to reflect the transactions described. Indicate the type of fund in which the entries would be made.
   - **a.** Assume first that Kirkland is a private, not-for-profit university.
   - **b.** Assume instead that Kirkland is a public university and that it elects to be accounted for (i) as a government engaging exclusively in business-type activities and (ii) as a full-service government that accounts for the contribution in a governmental fund.
2. On what grounds, if any, can you justify different principles of accounting for the same transaction depending on type of institution (public or private) or assumption as to type of public institution?

P. 13-7

A review of the actual statements provides insight into the form and content of private not-for-profit college reporting practices.

Review the 2017 financial statements of Hamilton College in Chapter 2, and respond to the following questions:

1. What percentage of the college's total revenues (including nonoperating items and revenues of all funds) is attributable to tuition and fees (net of scholarship aid, because scholarships are, in effect, tuition discounts)? Do you think that, relative to other revenues, tuition is a fairly stable revenue? Explain.
2. A note to the financial statements indicates that the college's board of trustees designates only a portion of the college's cumulative investment return for support of current operations (both with and without

donor restrictions). How much was so designated in 2017? Taking into account that amount, what was the college's net income from investments for the year?

3. What are likely examples of "auxiliary enterprises"? Taken collectively, were they profitable in 2017?

4. How much funds with donor restrictions did the college receive during the year?

5. What percentage of the college's total assets is attributable to investments? Of the investments, approximately what percentage is most likely attributable to endowments?

6. A note to the financial statements reports that compensation costs were over $75 million. Why is that amount not reported on the statement of activities?

P. 13-8

Colleges and universities may report as if they engaged only in business-type activities.

Review the financial statements of the University of Virginia in Table 13-1 of the text.

1. For purposes of internal accounting, the university maintains several funds. Why must the university maintain so many funds? Provide examples of the funds most likely maintained by this (or for that matter any major public university).

2. What is the most likely distinction between the net assets classified as "expendable" and those as "non-expendable"?

3. Suppose that the university financed the construction of its dormitories by issuing bonds secured by revenues from student room fees. The dormitories are accounted for as an auxiliary enterprise. What information about the auxiliary enterprise would the university have to include in its CAFR? Why?

4. Suppose that the university elected to report as a special-purpose government engaged in both governmental and business-type activities. How would the financial statements differ from those presented? Which set of financial statements would provide more comprehensive information? Explain.

5. The university attributes some of its revenues to "auxiliary enterprises." What is the most likely distinction between auxiliary enterprises and other academic or service units of the university? Provide examples.

6. The university reports unrestricted net position of over $2.6 billion. Suppose that a faculty member complained in a letter to the university president that the institution is holding back resources that should properly be used to increase faculty salaries, acquire computers and library books, and improve classroom facilities. What might be an obvious response to the faculty member's complaint?

7. The university reports a significant ($452 million) operating loss. Why might you argue that such is misleading and, indeed, should be expected?

8. The university's reported operating loss exceeded its operating cash outflow. What was the primary reason for the difference?

9. Do the financial statements provide you with any reason to question whether the university is investing adequately in plant, equipment, and other capital assets?

P. 13-9

Financial statements of not-for-profit organizations may provide inadequate information to assess performance.

Review the Statement of Activities of Hamilton College for the year ended June 30, 2017, that is presented in Table 2-11. The statement indicates that during the year net assets increased by $96,746,000. Suppose that you are a member of the college's board of trustees.

1. From your perspective as a member of the college's board of trustees, does the increase in net assets indicate that the college was fiscally well managed during the year? That is, can it be said that the greater the increase in net assets the better the college was managed?

2. The "bottom line" (net income) of a comparable statement of change in net assets of a business is said to be consistent with the entity's primary goal—that is, to earn a profit. Can the same be said of a not-for-profit organization, such as a college? Explain.

3. The statement indicates that the college incurred instructional costs of $61,710,000. Suppose that such an amount were 5 percent greater than in the previous year but that the number of students enrolled in the college did not increase. Can you, as a trustee, make any determination as to whether the instructional money was well spent? If not, what other information would you need?

4. Suppose that as a trustee you had the authority to specify the types of financial (and related) reports that management prepares for you. Indicate in general terms the information that you would like to see in a statement that focuses on the costs incurred by the college.

5. The statements of not-for-profit organizations are directed mainly toward donors rather than members of governing boards. In your opinion do you think that donors might also benefit from the type of report you described in item 4 above? Explain.

SOLUTION TO EXERCISE FOR REVIEW AND SELF-STUDY

1. *Tuition and fees*

Cash	$114,568	
Tuition and fees		$110,568
Contract liability		4,000

To record tuition and fees (in a fund without donor restrictions)

The summer session tuition collected in the fiscal year ended June 30, 2020, would be recognized as revenue in the following fiscal year, because the school would not yet have fulfilled its obligations under the contract. If the college were a government institution, then per GASB guidelines, it would be apportioned between the two semesters.

2. *Grants and contracts*

Cash	$38,914	
Grants and contracts (revenue)		$38,914

To record revenue from grants and contracts (in a fund with donor restrictions)

Grants and contracts	$47,661	
Net assets released from restrictions		$47,661

To record expenses incurred to fulfill grants and contracts (in a fund without donor restrictions)

Net assets released from restrictions	$47,661	
Cash		$47,661

To record the payment of cash in connection with the grant and contract expenses (in a fund with donor restrictions)

Note that the net assets released from restriction exceeded the grants and contract revenue recognized during the year. However, the college may have had net assets restricted by donors for grants and contracts at the start of the year, from prior fiscal years.

3. *Acquisition of plant and equipment*

Land, buildings, and equipment	$24,000	
Net assets released from restrictions		$24,000

To record the acquisition of plant and equipment (in a fund not restricted by donors)

Net assets released from restrictions	$24,000	
Cash		$24,000

To record the payment of cash for the plant and equipment (in a plant fund with donor restrictions)

The resources were recorded initially in a donor-restricted fund, but as plant and equipment is acquired, it must be recorded in a fund without donor restrictions.

4. *Auxiliary enterprises*

	College Inn	Housing and Dining
Revenues	$5,806	$20,117
Expenses	6,564	18,999
Excess of revenues over expenses	($ 758)	$ 1,118

5. *Student loans* Per amounts reported in the funds with donor restrictions, the college is owed $36,954 in principal, and it earned $1,856 in interest. The interest is restricted, most probably for purposes related to student loans, which is probably why it is recorded with restrictions rather than without restrictions.

6. *Endowment income* The endowment income (unlike the endowment principal) is available for expenditure by the college and therefore must be reported as revenue of either unrestricted or temporarily restricted funds. The distribution depends on whether the income must be used for specific purposes or is available for general purposes. In 2020, $18,548 of the earnings were restricted, and the remaining balance was restricted not. The $75,201 of gains on investments is most likely reported in the restricted by donors funds because, by law or donor stipulation, they must be added to principal, not made available for expenditure.

7. *Pledges*
   - **a.** The pledge of $2,500 to construct the wing to the science building would be reported as revenue and a receivable in a fund with donor restrictions.
   - **b.** The pledge of $4,500 for general purposes would be reported as revenue and a receivable in a fund without donor restrictions if it were to be fulfilled in the same year as it were made; otherwise it would be reported in a fund with donor restrictions.
   - **c.** The pledge of $5,000 to purchase investment grade securities would be reported in an endowment fund (a fund with donor restrictions).
   - **d.** The pledge of $1,000 in matching funds is a *conditional contribution* and as such would *not* be reported as revenue and a receivable until the conditions on which the pledge is contingent (i.e., obtaining the other contributions) are satisfied.

8. *Statement of activities* No, the college does not distinguish between operating and nonoperating activities.

CHAPTER 14

Health-care Providers

LEARNING OBJECTIVES

After studying this chapter, you should understand:

- The unique issues faced by not-for-profit health-care providers
- The different reporting requirements of health-care providers
- The differences in financial statements of government and nongovernment health-care providers
- How health-care providers account for revenues and expenses
- How fee-for-service revenues are recognized
- What capitation revenues are and how are they recognized
- Why bad debts must be distinguished from charity care and how to account for them
- Why malpractice claims are of major concern to health-care providers and how they should be accounted for
- The accounting issues presented by "retrospective" insurance premiums
- How recent policy changes influence accounting of health-care entities

Chapter 12 provides an introduction and covers the accounting and financial reporting issues of not-for-profit organizations. Chapter 13 discusses the unique issues facing colleges and universities. In this chapter we address the special issues faced by health-care providers. Accounting and financial reporting for health-care organizations warrant separate coverage because of the importance and size of this sector not only in the United States but globally as well. The total national health-care expenditures in the United States grew from $35 billion in 1963 (about $261 billion in inflation-adjusted current prices) to $3.3 trillion in 2016 (which is equal to about $10,348 per person and 18 percent of the national economy) and are projected to reach in excess of $5.5 trillion by 2025 even with the Patient Protection and Affordable Care Act's (PPACA) cost savings provisions.[1] The amount spent on health-care in the United States on a per capita basis is the highest of any other nation in the world.[2] Between 1963 and 2017, the average growth in health-care spending in the United States exceeded 9 percent annually, compared with average GDP growth of about 6.6 percent.[3] Moreover, health-care is provided by entities in all three sectors of the economy. There are privately owned for-profit hospitals, nongovernmental not-for-profit hospitals, and government hospitals mainly owned by county and city governments. In addition, the

[1] Source: http://www.cms.gov/Research-Statistics-Data-and-Systems/Statistics-Trends-and-Reports/NationalHealthExpend-Data/NationalHealthAccountsProjected.html.

[2] *World Health Organization, World Health Statistics 2017: Global Health Indicators.*

[3] Calculated from http://www.bea.gov/national/index.htm#gdp.

federal government operates field hospitals as well as permanent hospitals (the Military Health System) to provide military-funded care to active military personnel. The federal Veterans Health Administration operates VA hospitals that provide medical care for both veterans and their families. The Indian Health Service operates facilities open to Native Americans from recognized tribes. With costs increasing faster than other public goods and services, budgetary pressures to reduce governments' funding for health-care (as seen in the "In Practice: Hospitals Face Economic Challenges While also Implementing Policy Changes"), and 22 million[4] people without health insurance despite significant reform efforts, health-care has also become the number one political issue of the twenty-first century.

IN PRACTICE — HOSPITALS FACE ECONOMIC CHALLENGES WHILE ALSO IMPLEMENTING POLICY CHANGES

As health-care costs continue to climb, states increasingly bear the fiscal consequences. Before the "Great Recession" nearly one-fifth of state spending was devoted to Medicaid, a state program funded in part by the federal government and in part by the states that provides medical coverage to eligible needy persons. After the fiscal downturn, Medicaid spending increased to nearly one-quarter of state spending. In fact, Medicaid spending surpassed state spending on K–12 education spending by 2009.[5] One of the key provisions of the PPACA was the expansion of Medicaid eligibility to citizens not eligible for Medicaid in the past. Although the initial expansion is largely financed by the federal government, states will be increasingly responsible for the financing of a growing population of Medicaid recipients. As of 2018, 32 states and the District of Columbia have expanded Medicaid eligibility, while 18 states have not.[6]

At the same time, another element of the PPACA is cost reduction. From the perspective of hospitals, these efforts are aimed at reducing their revenues. Some organizations have even reduced staff levels in anticipation of revenue losses—for example, the Cleveland Clinic announced in 2013 that it would cut its budget by 6 percent in anticipation of reduced revenues and lay off workers.[7] Moody's forecast is that operating cash flow for the not-for-profit health-care sector is expected to decline 2–4 percent between 2018 and 2019. Further, Moody's changed its outlook for the sector in 2018 to "negative" after it remained at stable since 2015.[8] The financial difficulties facing hospitals did not end when the economy began improving; rather, they now face a policy environment in which they are expected to do more with less.

Further, although Medicaid expansion is viewed as a positive for not-for-profit hospitals because it expands the amount of potential clients, Medicaid payments historically do not cover the costs of patients served. The same is true for Medicare—a federal program that provides health insurance coverage for U.S. citizens aged 65 and older; the rapidly expanding population of eligible baby boomers is expected to continue to financially strain the program. As a result, private pay insurers have significantly inflated payments relative to costs to subsidize these shortfalls.[9] As patients are increasingly insured by public payers such as Medicare and Medicaid, hospitals face an increasing number of clients whose payments are insufficient to maintain financial health without significant private payers. Further, increasing co-pays and deductibles for those with insurance are correlated with rising bad debts in the sector.

The current state of the PPACA remains in flux due to political concerns and differences. The uncertainty about the law's future adds an additional element of financial uncertainty to health-care providers.

[5] National Association of State Budget Officers (NASBO) State Expenditure Reports.

[6] From the Henry J. Kaiser Family Foundation at https://www.kff.org/health-reform/state-indicator/state-activity-around-expanding-medicaid-under-the-affordable-care-act/?currentTimeframe=0&sortModel=%7B%22colId%22:%22Location%22,%22sort%22:%22asc%22%7D.

[7] See, for example, Reuters "Cleveland Clinic Announces Job Cuts to Prepare for Obamacare," September 18, 2013.

[8] https://www.moodys.com/research/Moodys-US-not-for-profit-and-public-healthcare-outlook-changed--PR_376421.

[9] See http://www.aha.org/research/reports/tw/chartbook/index.shtml.

Because health-care is increasingly being offered by entities in the for-profit (investor owned), not-for-profit, and government sectors, the accounting distinctions among health-care providers in those three sectors are also becoming less significant. Nevertheless, there are some differences, and in this chapter we will take special note of those between

[4] In 2014, based on The Commonwealth Fund's Biennial Health Insurance Survey, 2016.

nongovernment not-for-profit and government entities. As discussed in Chapter 12 and also in Chapter 13, FASB's standards on not-for-profit entities[10] apply to all not-for-profit organizations. Thus the general issues pertaining to all not-for-profits are, as in Chapter 13, not explicitly discussed.

WHAT UNIQUE ISSUES DO HEALTH-CARE PROVIDERS FACE?

The accounting and reporting practices of health-care organizations have been strongly influenced by the Healthcare Financial Management Association and the American Hospital Association, both of which are industry associations, and the AICPA. The AICPA's current industry guide, *Health-Care Entities*, is the primary authoritative source for issues not addressed by the FASB, which oversees accounting standards for not-for-profit entities. Moreover, like other AICPA industry audit guides, it has been incorporated into the FASB's Accounting Standards Codification.[11]

Health-care may be provided by individual practitioners (including physicians, therapists, and counselors), hospitals, outpatient clinics, emergency departments, urgent care centers, medical service and retirement institutions, and a wide range of not-for-profit specialty organizations (such as surgicenters and screening clinics), support and counseling organizations (such as those dealing with hospice care, prenatal care, and family planning), and research institutes (such as the Howard Hughes Medical Institute and the National Institutes of Health). Most health-care organizations bill their patients (or **third-party payers**, such as insurance companies) for services actually rendered. **Health maintenance organizations (HMOs)** and related types of health plans provide services to members in return for fixed, periodic payments. These HMOs and health plans may subcontract with hospitals, physicians associations, or other medical groups to provide specialized services in exchange for **capitation (per person) fees**. The capitation fees are generally based on the number of persons covered and expected costs to be incurred rather than actual services provided. **Preferred provider organizations (PPOs)** are groups of doctors, hospitals, and other health-care providers that contract with employers or insurance companies to provide medical services to a specified group of potential patients. In contrast to HMOs, the services are neither prepaid nor fixed. However, the service providers do typically agree to charge set rates for specified services and procedures. PPOs generally offer the patient more choices of service providers than HMOs and, accordingly, are more costly. In 2016, nearly 92.4 million Americans were enrolled in HMOs nationally, up from 77 million in 2014.[12]

To a greater extent than most other not-for-profits, health-care organizations must be concerned with their costs. Many other not-for-profits focus mainly on fund-raising; they then adjust the level of services to available revenues. Health-care organizations charge for their services. Often, the amount of fees charged is limited by competition or preestablished reimbursement rates. Therefore, because they cannot control prices, health-care organizations must be vitally interested both in determining and controlling the cost of their services.

The PPACA sought to better join together physicians with other health-care entities and incentivize controlling the costs of treating patients. As a result, **accountable care organizations (ACOs)**, similar to other types of managed care networks, were created in which the ACO is responsible for the health outcomes of patients served and to reach cost and clinical quality goals set by the third-party payer. ACOs can penalize providers when targets are not missed and also provide incentives when targets are achieved or surpassed. Medicare, for example, shares a portion of cost savings that result from the ACO's effort.

[10] FASB ASC 958-10, *Not-for-Profit Entities.*

[11] FASB ASC 954-10, *Healthcare Organizations.*

[12] https://www.kff.org/other/state-indicator/total-hmo-enrollment/?activeTab=graph¤tTimeframe=0&startTimeframe=4&sortModel=%7B%22colId%22:%22Location%22,%22sort%22:%22asc%22%7D.

WHAT ARE THE KEY DIFFERENCES BETWEEN PRIVATE NOT-FOR-PROFIT AND GOVERNMENT HEALTH-CARE PROVIDERS?

Most, albeit not all, government hospitals and other providers of health-care services are operated as business-type activities. They are accounted for in enterprise funds if they are part of a larger government and, therefore, adhere to business-type accounting practices. If they are special-purpose governments that engage in only a single government program, then, as noted in Chapter 11, they need to present only the statements required for enterprise funds (a balance sheet, statement of revenues and expenses, and a statement of cash flows). In either case, their statements are on a full accrual basis and, therefore, similar to those of both not-for-profit and profit-oriented health-care providers.

Still, government entities are governed by GASB pronouncements, and not-for-profit organizations by FASB pronouncements. Thus, there are notable differences in their financial reports. Most significantly, not-for-profit health-care entities must provide information on the two categories of net asset *donor* restrictiveness, whereas governments do not. Hence, the not-for-profit statement of activities will likely have the line item "net assets released from restriction." Further, the not-for-profit statement of cash flows will report only three rather than four categories of inflows and outflows. The classification scheme for governments is indicated in Table 9-1 and for not-for-profits in Table 12-4. Other differences relate to how various accounts are classified and where on the financial statements they are included. The AICPA industry audit and accounting guide, *Health-Care Entities* (September 2017 edition), provides a useful summary of these differences.[13]

WHAT ARE THE BASIC FINANCIAL STATEMENTS?

The basic financial statements of not-for-profit health-care organizations are similar in major respects to those of the museum (illustrated in Chapter 12) and the private college and university (illustrated in Chapter 13). They include a statement of financial position (balance sheet), statement of operations, statement of cash flows, a statement of functional expenses, and statement of changes in net assets. The statement of financial position should distinguish between net assets with donor restrictions and without donor restrictions. The statement of operations should also classify the revenues as with or without donor restrictions but should report expenses only as decreases in resources without donor restrictions. Data on the change of both categories of net assets must also be presented. This information may be incorporated into the statement of operations (particularly if the statement is in the two-column format as illustrated in Chapter 12 in the museum example) or shown in a separate statement. The financial statements of a fictional assisted living facility are presented in Tables 14-1A through 14-1D.

For purposes of internal accounting, hospitals and health organizations typically maintain one or more operating funds that have no donor restrictions attached to it, as well as several funds with donor restrictions. The general operating funds report both financial resources and property, plant, and equipment. Funds with donor restrictions are established to account for donated resources received for particular purposes. These purposes include specified programs or services (e.g., geriatric care, research, community education) as well as replacement of, or additions to, plant and equipment.

In addition, funds with donor restrictions include term endowment funds, annuity funds, life income funds, and other split-interest agreements.

Two points regarding funds with donor restrictions warrant emphasis:

- Funds related to plant and equipment generally account only for *resources* restricted to the purchase or construction of plant and equipment. They do not usually account for the plant and equipment itself. Plant and equipment is typically reported in the general operating fund. (A notable exception involves plant and equipment acquired by gift. Accounting standards state that the expiration of donor-imposed restrictions should be recognized when the asset is placed in service and not as it is depreciated.[14])

[13] AICPA Audit and Accounting Guide, *Health-Care Entities* (September 2017), Para. 1.08 (FASB ASC 954-10-05-2).
[14] FASB ASC 954-205-45-9.

TABLE 14-1A Golden Springs Assisted Living Center Balance Sheet July 31, 2021 and 2020

	2021	2020
Assets		
Current assets:		
Cash	$ 286,875	$ 252,450
Short-term investments	202,725	130,050
Accounts receivable, net of allowance for doubtful accounts of $3,500 in 2015 and $4,000 in 2014	143,055	150,705
Inventories	30,600	16,065
Prepaid rent, insurance, and other items	87,975	55,845
Total current assets	751,230	605,115
Long-term investments	1,490,220	1,279,845
Property, plant, and equipment—net of accumulated depreciation	11,393,145	11,689,200
Total assets	$13,634,595	$13,574,160
Liabilities and net assets		
Liabilities:		
Current maturities of long-term debt	$ 68,850	$ 58,905
Accounts payable	137,700	133,110
Accrued expenses	139,995	166,770
Total current liabilities	346,545	358,785
Long-term debt, less current maturities	6,786,315	6,835,275
Deposits and refundable fees	45,135	110,160
Patient fees paid in advance	4,889,880	5,114,025
Total liabilities	12,067,875	12,418,245
Net assets:		
Without donor restrictions	983,790	637,245
With donor restrictions	582,930	518,670
Total net assets	1,566,720	1,155,915
Total liabilities and net assets	$13,634,595	$13,574,160

- An organization may opt to establish restricted funds to account for resources designated by its governing board for specific purposes (e.g., to replace plant and equipment). For purposes of external reporting, however, board-designated resources are *not* considered restricted and should therefore be reported along with other operating resources that are not with donor restrictions. They may, however, be classified within the fund without donor restrictions as "assets whose use is limited" (or some similar category).

As in other not-for-profits, funds restricted by donors in perpetuity encompass mainly ordinary endowments (funds the principal of which must remain intact and only the earnings are expendable).

Like other not-for-profits (as well as governments), health-care organizations may maintain numerous funds of each of the two categories. For reporting purposes, however, the funds should be combined by category.

TABLE 14-1B Golden Springs Assisted Living Center Statements of Operations Years Ended July 31, 2021 and 2020

	2021	2020
Operating revenues:		
Fees from residents	$3,018,690	$2,411,280
Fees from nonresidents	199,665	147,645
Net assets released from restrictions used for operations	18,360	38,250
Total operating revenues	3,236,715	2,597,175
Operating expenses:		
Salaries and benefits	1,306,620	956,250
Medical supplies and drugs	415,395	567,630
Insurance	222,615	237,915
Depreciation	345,780	341,955
Interest	739,755	730,575
Total operating expenses	3,030,165	2,834,325
Operating income (loss)	206,550	(237,150)
Contributions without donor restrictions	41,310	29,835
Investment income	22,185	22,950
Net assets released from restriction—purchase of equipment	19,125	34,425
Other	57,375	52,020
Increase (decrease) in net assets without donor restrictions	$ 346,545	$ (97,920)

TABLE 14-1C Golden Springs Assisted Living Center Statements of Changes in Net Assets Years Ended July 31, 2021 and 2020

	2021	2020
Net assets without donor restrictions:		
Operating income (loss)	$ 327,420	$ (132,345)
Net assets released from restriction—purchase of equipment	19,125	34,425
Increase (decrease) in net assets without donor restrictions	346,545	(97,920)
Net assets with donor restrictions:		
Contributions restricted to purpose	30,600	11,475
Contributions restricted in perpetuity	51,255	39,780
Net assets released from restrictions used for operations	(18,360)	(38,250)
Net assets released from restriction—purchase of equipment	(19,125)	(34,425)
Investment income	19,890	11,475
Increase in net assets restricted by donors	64,260	(9,945)
Increase (decrease) in net assets	410,805	(107,865)
Net assets, beginning of year	1,155,915	1,263,780
Net assets, end of year	$1,566,720	$1,155,915

TABLE 14-1D Golden Springs Assisted Living Center Statements of Cash Flows Years Ended July 31, 2021 and 2020

	2021	2020
Cash flows from operating activities:		
Cash received from residents and others	$2,487,780	$1,790,865
Advance fees received	500,310	655,605
Other receipts from operations	57,375	52,020
Investment income received	52,020	40,545
Contributions received	39,015	33,660
Cash paid to employees and suppliers	(1,970,640)	(1,560,600)
Interest paid	(726,750)	(722,925)
Net cash provided by operating activities	439,110	289,170
Cash flows from investing activities:		
Purchase of property and equipment	(49,745)	(16,065)
Cash flows from financing activities:		
Funds restricted by donor in perpetuity received	51,255	39,780
Refunds of deposits and refundable fees	(78,795)	(39,780)
Proceeds from issuance of long-term debt	19,890	
Principal payments of long-term debt	(347,310)	(234,855)
Net cash used in financing activities	(354,960)	(234,855)
Net increase in cash	34,425	38,250
Cash, beginning of year	252,450	214,200
Cash, end of year	$ 286,875	$ 252,450
Reconciliation of change in net assets to net cash provided by operating activities:		
Change in net assets	$ 410,805	$ (107,865)
Adjustments to reconcile change in net assets to net cash provided by operating activities:		
Advance fees received	500,310	655,605
Net assets restricted by donors received	(51,255)	(39,780)
Amortization of advance fees	(715,275)	(699,975)
Loss (gain) on obligation to provide future services	(9,180)	62,730
Depreciation	345,780	341,955
Amortization of deferred financing costs	5,355	26,010
Provision for bad debts	2,295	2,295
(Increase) decrease in:		
Accounts receivable	5,355	(25,245)
Other assets	(46,665)	(3,060)
Increase (decrease) in:		
Accounts payable and accrued expenses	(8,415)	76,500
Net cash provided by operating activities	$ 439,110	$ 289,170

The FASB requires not-for-profit hospitals to include on the statement of operations a "performance indicator"—essentially a measure that is analogous to income from continuing operations of a for-profit entity. This indicator should be clearly labeled so that it is obvious to the financial statement user; commonly used descriptions include revenues over expenses, earned income, performance earnings, and revenues and gains over expenses and losses.[15]

CLASSIFICATIONS OF REVENUES AND EXPENSES

The statement of operations of a health-care organization is relatively straightforward. Revenues are displayed by category: without donor restrictions and with donor restrictions. Often they are displayed in two columns side by side. Sometimes, as is illustrated in Table 14-1B, the statement of operations includes only revenues without donor restrictions; revenues restricted by donors are reported in the separate statement of changes in net assets (Table 14-1C). The revenues without donor restrictions are divided into at least two classifications (usually rows): patient care revenues and other revenues. Patient care revenues include:

- Routine services (such as room, board, and general nursing)
- Other nursing services (such as operating room services)
- Professional services (such as physicians' services, laboratories, and pharmacy)

Other revenues include:

- Contributions (that are not restricted by donors)
- Educational services
- Miscellaneous sources (such as rental of space, auxiliary enterprises, and fees charged for providing medical records)

Revenues from capitation fees should generally be shown apart from other types of revenues.

Expenses are reported exclusively within the category without donor restrictions. They may be classified either by function or by object. However, if the expenses are classified by object, then the functional classification must be presented in the notes.

The statement of operations must also indicate net assets released from restrictions and any transfers between funds. Likely functional and natural (object) classifications of expenses include the following:

Functional	Natural
Nursing services	Salaries and wages
Other professional services	Employee benefits
General services	Fees to individuals and organizations
Fiscal services	Supplies and other expense
Administrative services	Purchased services
Bad debts	Bad debts
Depreciation	Depreciation
Interest	Interest

[15] FASB ASC 954-225-45-4.

HOW ARE KEY REVENUES AND EXPENSES RECOGNIZED?

RECOGNIZING FEE-FOR-SERVICE PATIENT CARE REVENUES

Private and not-for-profit health-care organizations must follow the five-step model of FASB ASC 606 when recognizing revenues. The steps include identifying the contract with the customer, identifying the performance obligation in the contract, determining the transaction price, allocating the transaction price to the performance obligations in the contract, and then recognizing the revenue as the performance obligation is satisfied.

Health-care organizations may provide patient services over an extended period of time. Yet patients are often billed only at the conclusion of their stay at the facility. Consistent with the accrual basis, the revenues must be recognized as the organization provides the services (thereby satisfying a performance obligation) rather than when it prepares a bill.

In reality, most patients pay only a small portion of their bills themselves. Most health-care organizations derive the majority of their revenues from third parties, such as Medicare (a federal program), Medicaid (state programs), Blue Cross (a private insurer), and other private (for-profit and not-for-profit) insurance companies and health plans. These third parties pay the hospital or other health-care provider based on contractual or other predetermined reimbursement rates. For example, in most circumstances, Medicare reimburses hospitals based on the nature of patients' illnesses. Under its **prospective payment system**, it classifies patient care into **diagnosis-related groups (DRGs)** and allows a specified rate for each group. In some circumstances, however, it reimburses specified allowable costs. The amounts paid by the third-party payers are almost always less than the provider's "standard" billing rate that would be paid "out of pocket" by an uninsured patient.

At the time they provide patient care, hospitals and other health-care providers cannot always be certain as to the portion of their standard charges that they ultimately will be paid. Usually the amount is known for certain only when they receive payment. In fact, under some **"retrospective" payment** arrangements, payments are based on total costs incurred during a particular period. Although the third-party payer makes interim payments during the period, a final determination may not be reached until after the end of the period.

Inasmuch as many patients who are uninsured or purchase insurance plans with high deductibles requiring the patient to pay significant dollar amounts before insurance coverage begins cannot afford the costs of an extended hospital stay or expensive medical procedures, health-care providers may face high rates of bad debts. Moreover, unlike businesses, providers often serve patients who they know will be unable to pay the amounts billed. In these cases, the amount that the health-care entity would not expect to receive would be treated like an implicit price concession rather than a bad debt.

Example

Patient Care Revenues

During a particular week a hospital records $400,000 in patient charges. It estimates that 80 percent ($320,000) of the charges will be billed to third-party payers who have, on average, negotiated discounts from the invoiced amounts of 30 percent ($96,000). The remaining 20 percent ($80,000) of the hospital's charges will be billed to patients who are uninsured, and the hospital determines the patients have the ability to pay. However, of this 20 percent, 60 percent ($48,000) will be uncollectible.

AICPA/FASB GUIDANCE

According to the AICPA audit guide *Health-Care Entities*, revenue from health-care services is usually recorded "as services are rendered."[16] The primary issue of importance, however, is how the contract transaction price is determined. As stated, "The amount of consideration to which the entity will be entitled may be less than the price stated in the contract if the consideration

[16] Para. 10.31 (FASB ASC 954-605-25-3).

is variable because the entity may offer the customer a price concession."[17]

The AICPA guide further notes that:

> *[I]n general, gross service revenue is recorded in the accounting records on an accrual basis at the health-care entity's established rates, regardless of whether the health-care entity expects to collect that amount .... Any difference between the established rates for provided services and amounts agreed to under agreements with third parties is accounted for as a* ***contractual adjustment****. An estimate of the contractual adjustment is recorded in the same period that the services were provided. In addition, some health-care entities offer discounts (for example, a discount to uninsured patients that do not qualify for charity care of other courtesy, prompt pay, or employee discounts). The discount also is recorded in the same period that the services were provided. Thus, internal records will generally reflect the gross patient service revenues offset by the contractual adjustments and discounts* [emphasis added].[18]

Such treatment is consistent with new FASB revenue recognition standards. By extension, patient receivables should be reported at net realizable value to account for contractual adjustments, discounts, and an allowance for uncollectible accounts.[19] Patient bad debts that are not collected should be reported as a deduction from revenues and not as a separate expense.[20]

[17] FASB ASC 606-10-25-1e.

[18] Paras. 10.30 and 10.31 (FASB ASC 954-605-25-3).

[19] Para. 10.42 (FASB ASC 954-310-30-1).

[20] See Para. 10.21 for an illustration of estimating revenues.

In the example, the following entries would be consistent with these guidelines and standards:

Patient accounts receivable	$400,000	
Patient revenues		$400,000
To record one week's patient revenues		
Revenue from patient services—estimated contractual adjustments	$96,000	
Patient accounts receivable—allowance for contractual adjustments		$96,000
To establish an allowance for contractual adjustments (30 percent of the $320,000 that will be paid by third parties)		
Revenues from patient services—estimated bad debts	$48,000	
Patient accounts receivable—allowance for bad debts		$48,000
To establish an allowance for bad debts (60 percent of the $80,000 that will be paid directly by patients)		

The FASB aligned US GAAP with international standards in 2018 for bad debt reporting and community benefit reporting. Although not a required disclosure, many hospitals do report community benefits. In the past, some hospitals would report the difference between what they billed patients and what they were paid by these patients even if the hospital never expected to receive the payment as a community benefit. The new FASB standard can only report bad debt if something occurred to prevent the patient from being able to pay the expected amount.

RECOGNIZING CAPITATION FEE REVENUES

Health-care organizations receive capitation fees when they contract with an insurance company or other third-party payer to provide covered services to a specific population during a specified period of time. Typically an organization receives the per-member payments at the beginning of each month and is obligated to provide the services during that month. Sometimes the organization also assumes the risk of having to refer a patient to other organizations for diagnosis or treatment and to pay for those services.

Example

Capitation Fee Revenues

A physicians group receives $300,000 in capitation fees from the Hartford Insurance Company to provide comprehensive health-care to members of the company's health plan during that month. During the month it provides services for which it would bill, at standard rates, $240,000. In addition, it refers patients to hospitals and other health-care providers for which it expects to be billed $18,000.

AICPA/FASB GUIDANCE

Per the AICPA audit guide, revenues from capitation fees "are generated as a result of an agreement to provide health-care, rather than from the actual provision of services."[21]

Further, because the revenue is not earned from actual provision of services, it should be reported separately from patient service revenues.[22]

[21] Para. 10.37 (FASB ASC 954-605-05-6).

[22] Para. 10.40 (FASB ASC 954-605-45-3).

The physicians group in the example should recognize revenue in the period covered by the capitation fees. It fulfills its performance obligation through the passage of time. Correspondingly, it should establish a liability for any related costs for which it has not yet paid.

Thus:

Cash	$300,000	
Revenue from capitation fees		$300,000
To record capitation fees received		
Patient referrals (expense)	$18,000	
Obligations for patient referrals		$18,000
To record liability for patient referrals		

The amount for which it would have billed at standard rates is therefore irrelevant.

ACCOUNTING FOR AND REPORTING CHARITY CARE

Health-care organizations provide uncompensated patient care as a matter of both policy and law. The Hospital Survey and Construction Act of 1946 (Public Law 79–725, usually referred to as the Hill–Burton Act) stipulates that hospitals receiving federal construction funds must provide a certain amount of charitable care. This care does not result in cash inflows, and, consequently, it can be argued that it should not qualify for recognition either as revenue or as receivables. On the other hand, **charity care** is conceptually similar to patient care for which third parties will reimburse the hospital or other provider for less than full rates (in the case of charity care, at zero) or patient care for which substantial bad debts are anticipated.

AICPA/FASB GUIDANCE

The AICPA audit guide specifies that gross revenue should exclude charity care. However, it also makes clear that health-care organizations are obligated to disclose their policies for providing charity care and should indicate the amounts provided based on the provider's "direct and indirect costs of providing charity care services."[23]

The guide recognizes that distinguishing bad debt expense from charity care requires judgment, although this decision need not be made immediately at the time of admission or

[23] Paras. 10.26 and 10.28 (FASB ASC 954-605-25-10 and FASB ASC 954-605-50-3). ASU No. 2014-09 did not amend these standards.

registration. However, it notes that "charity care represents health-care services that are provided but are never expected to result in cash flows," whereas it defines bad debt expense as "the current period charge for actual or expected doubtful accounts resulting from the extension of credit."[24] The key distinction is that an entity provides charity care in the expectation that it will not receive compensation but incurs bad debts by providing service in the hope of at least partial payment.

[24] Glossary (FASB ASC 954-605-45-4).

Example

Charity Care

A hospital values care provided to indigent patients at $1,300,000, based on standard billing rates. However, it anticipates collecting for none of its services.

Thus, in the example, the hospital need not make an entry to record the value of the charity care. It should, however, explain its policies and report the total value of the care provided in notes to the financial statements.

If the hospital initially believed that the patients would pay, it would have recorded a revenue. When it determined that the initial determination was incorrect, it would record the provision of an implicit price concession that changed the price of the service (in this case to $0). The bad debt would be netted against the revenue recorded.[25]

ACCOUNTING FOR AND REPORTING MALPRACTICE COSTS AND CONTINGENCIES

Malpractice claims have become an accepted, if unwanted, concern of health-care organizations and a routine element of their financial reports. Potential losses arising from malpractice claims are obviously consequential, so most entities transfer a portion of their risk to independent insurers. However, even if all or a portion of the risk is insured, litigation costs can still be daunting. The key accounting and reporting issues relate to when and how much of a loss should be recognized owing to both unsettled claims and claims that have not yet been filed.

FASB STANDARDS

FASB standards for malpractice and other claims are drawn from FASB Statement No. 5, *Accounting for Contingencies*, and are therefore the same as for businesses.[26] They provide that a health-care organization should accrue an estimated loss by a charge to operations as soon as both of the following conditions are met:

- It is probable that an asset has been impaired or a liability has been incurred.
- The amount of the loss can be reasonably estimated.

If neither of these conditions is met but there is at least a *reasonable possibility* that a loss will be incurred, then the organization should disclose the nature of the contingency and estimate the possible loss or the range of the loss (or state that an estimate cannot be made).

Thus, the cost of a malpractice claim should be accrued when the incident giving rise to the claim occurs, as long as the eventual loss can be reasonably estimated. Obviously, health-care organizations face considerable practical difficulties in estimating the amounts for which claims will eventually be settled, particularly those that have not yet been asserted. Nevertheless, the organization can draw on both its own past experience and industry data. Moreover, it does not have to assess each incident individually. It can group together similar incidents and thereby take advantage of statistical relationships. The total accrued cost should take into account litigation fees but should be reduced by anticipated insurance recoveries.

[26] FASB ASC 954-450-25-2.

[25] *Revenue Recognition* (January 2018), page 285.

Example

Malpractice Claims

A hospital has been charged with negligence in the death of a patient. Although no claim has yet been filed, past experience indicates that the hospital is almost certain to be sued. In the example, the hospital would be required to charge an expense (a loss) in the period of the incident only if it were able to make a reasonable estimate of the amount. If it were unable to estimate the amount, then it would be required to disclose the details of the incident. Assuming that the hospital was, in fact, able to estimate reasonably that the loss would be $500,000 (after taking into account insurance recoveries), the following entry would be appropriate:

Anticipated legal claims (expense)	$500,000	
Commitments and contingencies (liability)		$500,000
To record the estimated cost of settling a potential malpractice claim		

If, by contrast, it was able only to estimate a range (e.g., between $300,000 and $800,000), then disclosure, as opposed to recognizing a loss, would be adequate.

REPORTING "RETROSPECTIVE INSURANCE PREMIUMS"

Another aspect of the question of when and how malpractice claims should be reported is that of reporting malpractice insurance expense. Many insurance policies make provisions for "retrospectively rated premiums." These policies require that at the expiration of the policy, the premium costs be adjusted to take into account actual loss experience. Thus, if claims during the period are greater than anticipated, the insured will have to pay an additional premium (a **retrospective insurance premium**); if claims are less, then it will receive a refund. As a consequence, the insured does not always know by year-end what that year's actual insurance costs will be. These types of policies do not provide true insurance coverage (except, perhaps, for claims above a specified amount), because the insured is being charged for all, or a portion, of actual losses.

Example

Retrospective Premiums

In June 2020 a not-for-profit physicians' practice plan entered into an insurance contract for the period July 1, 2020, through June 30, 2021. The basic premium was $120,000 for the year, which the physicians' group paid in June 2020. However, the policy also contained a complex formula for premium adjustments on the termination of the policy. Prior to preparing its financial statements for the year ended December 31, 2020, the practice plan estimated, based on both asserted and unasserted claims, that it would have to pay an additional $10,000 in premiums resulting from incidents in the last six months of 2020.

In the example, the following entry would summarize insurance activity for 2020 relating to the policy acquired in June:

Malpractice insurance expense (2020)	$70,000	
Prepaid insurance (basic premium for 2021)	60,000	
Cash		$120,000
Commitments and contingencies (liability to insurance company)		10,000
To record 2020 malpractice insurance expense (basic premium of $60,000 for six months plus anticipated claims adjustment of $10,000) and prepaid insurance for 2021 (basic premium of $60,000 for six months)		

AICPA/FASB GUIDANCE

The AICPA health-care audit guide indicates that the insured entity should charge the basic premium as an expense pro rata over the term of the policy. In addition, it should accrue additional premiums or refunds based on the FASB Statement No. 5 criteria for recognition of losses. If it is unable to estimate losses from claims, then it should disclose the contingencies in the notes.[27]

[27] Para. 8.23; also FASB ASC 450-20-50-3.

Comprehensive Example

Medical Center Hospital

This example is based on a hypothetical major urban not-for-profit hospital. It synthesizes several of the principles discussed in this chapter. We start with the hospital's statement of financial position as of December 31, 2019 (presented in Table 14-2), account for the main type of transactions that the hospital engaged in during 2020 (journalized in the body of the text), and prepare selected financial statements as of December 31, 2020 (all dollar amounts in thousands).

Patient Revenue

The hospital provided $705,943 in patient care at standard rates. On average, it expects to collect approximately 75 percent ($529,457) of this amount, owing mainly to discounts allowed to third-party payers. Further, it expects that 5 percent of the 75 percent ($26,473) will have to be written off as bad debts:

Receivables for patient care	$705,943	
Revenue from patient services—estimated contractual adjustments	176,486	
Revenue from patient services—estimated bad debts	26,473	
Patient care revenues		$705,943
Receivables for patient care—allowance for contractual adjustments		176,486
Patient accounts receivable—allowance for bad debts		26,473
To record patient service revenues (in a fund without donor restrictions)		

TABLE 14-2 Medical Center Hospital

Statement of Net Assets as of December 31, 2019

	Without Donor Restrictions	With Donor Restrictions
Assets		
Current assets		
Cash	$ 2,449	$ 255
Receivables for patient care ($110,465 less allowance for contractual adjustments and doubtful accounts of $45,755)	64,710	
Other receivables	13,059	11,343
Marketable securities	109,085	78,824
Other current assets	27,853	
Total current assets	$217,156	$90,962

(Continues)

TABLE 14-2 Medical Center Hospital *(Continued)*

Statement of Net Assets as of December 31, 2019

	Without Donor Restrictions	With Donor Restrictions
Noncurrent assets		
Property, plant, and equipment ($512,184 less accumulated depreciation of $223,259)	$288,925	
Other assets	11,522	
Total noncurrent assets	$300,447	
Total assets	$517,603	$90,962
Liabilities and net assets		
Current liabilities		
Accounts payable	$ 55,960	
Accrued wages and salaries	56,942	
Total current liabilities	$112,902	
Noncurrent liabilities		
Long-term debt	$292,370	
Deferred revenue and other noncurrent liabilities	96,609	$10,323
Total noncurrent liabilities	$388,979	$10,323
Total liabilities	$501,881	$10,323
Net assets	$ 15,722	$80,099
Total liabilities and net assets	$517,603	$90,422

This entry includes a contra asset, "Receivables for patient care—allowance for contractual adjustments." However, like the allowance for bad debts, for reporting purposes this account will be combined with "Receivables for patient care," inasmuch as it was similarly combined in the December 31, 2019, balance sheet. If the amount to be paid by the insurance companies and health plans is known in advance, then the receivable can be recorded at that amount, and the allowance for contractual adjustments would be unnecessary.

Receivables and Bad Debts

The hospital collected $480,125 in patient accounts, and it wrote off $50,000 of bad debts:

Cash	$480,125	
Receivables for patient care		$480,125
To record cash collections (in a fund without donor restrictions)		
Patient accounts receivable—allowance for bad debts	$50,000	
Receivables for patient care		$50,000
To write off bad debts (in a fund without donor restrictions)		

Charity Care

It also provided $52,000 in charity care that it never expected to collect.

No entry is required.

Charity care should not be included in patient care revenue as discussed earlier per AICPA/FASB guidance.

Investment Income

It earned $15,040 in investment income, of which $10,080 is unrestricted and $4,960 is temporarily restricted:

Cash (without donor restrictions)	$10,080	
Cash (with donor restrictions)	4,960	
Investment income (without donor restrictions)		$10,080
Investment income (with donor restrictions)		4,960
To record investment income (in the fund types indicated)		

Acquisition of Fixed Assets

It purchased plant and equipment of $242, all of which was paid for with donor-restricted resources:

Net assets released from restriction	$242	
Cash		$242
To record the release of restricted assets (in a fund with donor restrictions)		
Property, plant, and equipment	$242	
Net assets released from restriction		$242
To record the purchase of equipment (in a fund without donor restrictions)		

Depreciation Expense

It charged depreciation of $29,262:

Depreciation expense	$29,262	
Accumulated depreciation		$29,262
To record depreciation (in a fund without donor restrictions)		

Contributions

It received pledges without donor restrictions of $2,070 and pledges with donor restrictions of $120. It collected all of the pledges without donor restrictions and $100 of the pledges with donor restrictions:

Other receivables (without donor restrictions)	$2,070	
Other receivables (with donor restrictions)	120	
Revenue from contributions (without donor restrictions)		$2,070
Revenue from contributions (with donor restrictions)		120
To record pledges (in the fund types indicated)		
Cash (without donor restrictions)	$2,070	
Cash (with donor restrictions)	100	
Other receivables (without donor restrictions)		$2,070
Other receivables (with donor restrictions)		100
To record collections (in the fund types indicated)		

Other Revenues

It earned other operating revenues (including those from auxiliary enterprises) of $135,000:

Cash	$135,000	
Other operating revenues		$135,000
To record other operating revenues (in a fund without donor restrictions)		

Wages and Salaries

It incurred $430,650 in wages and salaries, of which it paid $425,000. The balance was accrued. It also incurred $200,000 in other operating expenses (including those of auxiliary enterprises), of which it paid $198,500. The balance was vouchered (and thereby credited to accounts payable):

Wages and salaries expense	$430,650	
Cash		$425,000
Accrued wages and salaries payable		5,650

To record wages and salaries (in a fund without donor restrictions)

Other operating expenses	$200,000	
Cash		$198,500
Accounts payable		1,500

To record other operating expenses (in a fund without donor restrictions)

Recall that all expenses are recorded in funds that do not have donor restrictions.

Contracts and Grants

It incurred and paid $210,200 in costs related to donor-restricted contracts and grants (amounts that were not included in any other expense category). It was reimbursed for $206,800 and expects to be reimbursed for the balance in the future. In addition, it received $3,000 in advances on other grants:

Net assets released from donor restrictions	$210,200	
Cash		$210,200

To record resources released from restrictions relating to contracts and grants (in a fund with donor restrictions)

Expenses related to grants and contracts	$210,200	
Net assets released from donor restrictions		$210,200

To record expenses related to contracts and grants (in a fund without donor restrictions)

Although the hospital's statement of activities combined grants and contracts in a single account, these entries assume that the amounts indicated were entirely for grants. If they were for contracts (exchange transactions), they would be reported in a fund without donor restrictions:

Cash	$209,800	
Other receivables	3,400	
Revenue from contracts and grants		$210,200
Deferred revenue and other noncurrent liabilities		3,000

To record reimbursements of, and advances for, grants and contracts (in a fund with donor restrictions)

Insurance Costs

The other operating expenses include insurance costs. However, under "retrospective" insurance policies, the hospital anticipates having to pay an additional $3,500 in premiums.

Insurance expense	$3,500	
Commitments and contingencies (insurance)		$3,500

To record the anticipated additional insurance premiums (in a fund without donor restrictions)

Based on these and other transactions, Table 14-3 presents a simplified hospital's statement of operations and statement of net assets for the year 2020.

TABLE 14-3 Medical Center Hospital Operating Statement for the Year Ending December 31, 2020

	Without Donor Restrictions	With Donor Restrictions
Revenues		
Revenue from patient services	$705,943	
Less: Estimated contractual adjustments	176,486	
Estimated bad debts	26,473	
Net patient care revenue	502,984	
Investment income	10,080	$ 4,960
Revenues from contributions	2,070	120
Revenue from contracts and grants		210,200
Other operating revenues	135,000	
Net assets released from donor restrictions	210,442	(210,442)
Total revenues	860,576	4,838
Expenses		
Wages and salaries expense	430,650	
Other operating expenses	200,000	
Expenses related to grants and contracts	210,200	
Insurance expense	3,500	
Depreciation	29,262	
Total expenses	873,612	
Net increase (decrease) in net assets	($ 13,036)	$ 4,838

Statement of Net Assets as of December 31, 2020

	Without Donor Restrictions	With Donor Restrictions
Assets		
Current assets		
Cash	$ 6,224	$ 4,673
Receivables for patient care ($286,283 less allowance for contractual adjustments and doubtful accounts of $198,714)	87,569	
Other receivables	13,059	14,763
Marketable securities	109,085	78,824
Other current assets	27,853	
Total current assets	$243,790	$98,260

(Continues)

TABLE 14-3 Medical Center Hospital Operating Statement for the Year Ending December 31, 2020 *(Continued)*

Statement of Net Assets as of December 31, 2020

	Without Donor Restrictions	With Donor Restrictions
Noncurrent assets		
Property, plant, and equipment ($512,426 less accumulated depreciation of $252,521)	259,905	
Other assets	11,522	
Total noncurrent assets	271,427	
Total assets	$515,217	$98,260
Liabilities and net assets		
Current liabilities		
Accounts payable	$ 57,460	
Accrued wages and salaries	62,592	
Total current liabilities	120,052	
Noncurrent liabilities		
Long-term debt	292,370	
Deferred revenues and other current liabilities	96,609	$13,323
Commitments and contingencies	3,500	
Total noncurrent liabilities	392,479	13,323
Total liabilities	512,531	13,323
Net assets	2,686	84,937
Total liabilities and net assets	$515,217	$98,260

HOW CAN THE FISCAL WHEREWITHAL OF HEALTH-CARE ORGANIZATIONS BE EVALUATED?

The fiscal wherewithal of health-care organizations, whether for-profit (investor owned), not-for-profit, or governmental, can be evaluated similar to most businesses. In the long run, the health of a hospital, nursing home, or related entity depends mainly on the demand for its services and the ability to meet that demand at a reasonable cost. In the short run, it depends on the ability of the entity to generate sufficient cash to meet its obligations. Table 14-4 sets forth the factors taken into account by a rating agency in assessing the bonds issued by health-care organizations.

Forecasting the fiscal prospects of health-care organizations is particularly difficult because the future of the industry is so highly dependent on both technology and government policy. In light of ongoing advances in areas such as genetics, stem cell research, and bioengineering, it is extremely difficult to predict the course that medical practice will take in the coming decades. Similarly, given the number of Americans who continue to lack health insurance, the increasing deficits faced by the federally sponsored Medicare program, increased market consolidation, and the rising costs of medical treatment, it is almost certain that there will be major changes in federal programs and the ways in which medical care is paid for.

TABLE 14-4 Factors Focused on by Moody's in Evaluating the Rating of Health-care Organizations

I. Market Position

- **A.** Scope of operations: measures the significance of the entity in a region. This is measured by operating revenue.
- **B.** Market demand: measures revenue growth potential. This is measured by the three-year operating revenue compound average growth rate, which measures hospital's ability to consistently increase revenue over long term.
- **C.** Market landscape: measured by population demographic factors, economic factors, and the presence or absence of industry regulation.

II. Operating Performance and Liquidity

- **A.** Performance: provides insight into management ability to control finances and policies. Operating cash flow margin measured as operating cash flow (operating income before depreciation, amortization, and income expense) relative to operating revenue. This ratio indicates a hospital's ability to generate cash from operations, which allows strategic and capital investments.
- **B.** Payor concentration: measures vulnerability to reimbursement fluctuations and related risks. Percent of gross revenue from combined Medicare and Medicaid.
- **C.** Financial reserves: measure of how long management could operate organizations with current available resources, measured by the days of cash on hand.
- **D.** Financial management and reinvestment: qualitative measures of governance and management.

III. Leverage

- **A.** Financial leverage: measured as the ratio of cash and investments without donor restrictions to total debt. This ratio provides a measure of financial flexibility.
- **B.** Debt affordability: measured as total debt to cash flow. This ratio measures how long operating cash flows would take to pay down debt (defined as including financial, contingent liabilities, and guarantees).

IV. Other Considerations

- **A.** Ownership model, because hospitals related to local governments or universities may enhance oversight and financial stability.
- **B.** Event risk responses, whether natural disasters or policy shifts.
- **C.** Multi-year trends to measure direction and momentum of credit trends.
- **D.** Liquidity quality, which examines the source and predictability of liquidity.
- **E.** Debt structure considerations, related to covenants and maturities.
- **F.** Pension, OPEB, and leases, to measure the extent that these long-term liabilities have on expenses and cash flows.

Source: Drawn from U.S. Public Finance, Moody's Investors Service, Not-for-Profit Healthcare Rating Methodology, November 1, 2017.

IN PRACTICE FINANCIAL PROBLEMS NOT CAUSED BY SINGLE ISSUE

The financial problems faced by two hospitals in New York City are illustrative of the varied reasons not-for-profit hospitals can become fiscally stressed. Long Island College Hospital (LICH), part of the State University of New York system, is located in the increasingly gentrified Brooklyn neighborhood of Cobble Hill, while Interfaith Medical Center (IMC) serves a poorer area near the neighborhood of Bedford-Stuyvesant. Even with wide differences between their communities' demographics, both hospitals attempted to enter bankruptcy in 2014. Despite a community that could afford medical services, LICH had to compete with hospital and medical providers in Manhattan and other parts of the city. Therefore, LICH faced competition from other health-care entities not physically proximate to it that resulted in LICH failing to generate volume that was sufficient for its financial viability. IMC, on the other hand, faced virtually no competition because no other hospital existed in the area. However, Medicare and Medicaid insured over 90 percent of patients, and virtually no patients had commercial insurance. Because these public insurance payers do not cover the full cost of services, IMC found itself with sufficient volume (unlike LICH) but insufficient revenues relative to its costs. IMC entered bankruptcy in 2014, while LICH closed entirely—but not without a public battle between politicians, other hospital networks seeking to potentially take over the hospital, and key community groups.

New York City's public hospital—Health + Hospital (H+H) system—itself faces financial problems. H+H operates with significant operating deficits (e.g., in 2016, H+H operated with an 18 percent operating deficit). The public hospital system accounts for one-half of all City uninsured admissions and 80% of uninsured clinic visits. While some of the City's not-for-profit hospitals report healthy profit margins, the public hospital system continues to face financial difficulties stemming from expense growth and revenue stagnation, requiring public subsidies to remain viable.[28]

[28] See "Hospitals face financial blow that could seriously weaken NYC health-care system" by Ginger Adams Otis (September 29, 2017), *New York Daily News*.

IMPACT OF THE PATIENT PROTECTION AND AFFORDABLE CARE ACT (PPACA) AND OTHER RECENT TRENDS

As the result of the PPACA, many states now cover more people through Medicaid because it became easier to qualify for benefits and federal subsidies increased. From the point of view of hospitals, these added patients may not only increase revenues but also costs. Given Medicaid's history of not covering costs, many hospitals continue to examine closely legislative and judicial changes to the PPACA and their impact on both costs and revenues.

In 2015, the Supreme Court reversed a lower court's decision allowing a state to challenge Medicaid's reimbursement rates. Hence, it is unlikely that Medicaid reimbursements will be increased to cover costs. PPACA-established individual insurance markets now exist in states across the country. However, some of these markets are unstable because of the small number of insurers in many of the markets and increases in premiums charged to customers. Further, although the number of uninsured has declined, many of the plans require significant out-of-pocket payments by the patient before the insurer begins making payments. As a result, hospitals increasingly find themselves in situations in which a patient has insurance but is unable to pay for services. Whether these patients might or might not qualify for charity care or other subsidies is an issue for hospitals to consider.

One important revenue stream affected by the PPACA is associated with the Disproportionate Share Hospital (DSH) program. Under the program, federal payments made to hospitals amounted to about $12 billion nationally in 2016. These payments are made almost exclusively to large urban hospitals, most of which serve large numbers of Medicaid and uninsured patients. As part of the PPACA, DSH payments were scheduled for reduction beginning in 2018 (after several years of congressionally approved delays) as hospitals were expected to provide less uncompensated care. PPACA scheduled $43 billion in cuts through 2025.[29] These cuts were delayed again as part of the February 2018 continuing resolution to avert a government shutdown. However, DSH payments will remain an important revenue source for many urban hospitals, even though it faces policy uncertainty. Importantly, DSH is only one of four supplemental Medicaid programs that face increasingly difficult financial futures.

In addition, mergers and acquisitions in the health-care sector continue. Since 2002, approximately 50 hospital mergers and acquisitions occurred annually; since 2010, the trend toward increased consolidation increased—to 100 in 2012 alone.[30] One study noted that between 2008 and 2014, there were more than 750 hospital acquisitions or mergers.[31] A merger is when the governing bodies of two or more not-for-profits cede control of those entities to create a new not-for-profit.[32] From an accounting perspective, the financial statements of the two entities are effectively combined. In contrast, an acquisition occurs when the "acquirer obtains control of one or more nonprofit activities or businesses and initially recognizes their assets and liabilities in the acquirer's financial statements."[33] Although these consolidations are driven at least in part by incentives to provide comprehensive health services to patients and reduce costs, reducing competition has the likely potential to have the opposite effect on costs.

SUMMARY

Government health-care organizations, especially hospitals, are accounted for as enterprises and, accordingly, are accounted for similar to businesses. Not-for-profit hospitals are also accounted for similar to businesses but, nevertheless, must adhere to the reporting standards that the FASB has established for not-for-profits in general. Hence, their statements must provide information on the two categories of restrictiveness.

Health-care organizations are distinguished from other types of organizations by several unique revenues and expenses. These include:

- ***Fee-for-service patient care revenues.*** These are usually established at the providers' standard rates. However, allowances must be made for anticipated bad debts and third-party payer discounts, both of which are often substantial.
- ***Capitation fee revenues.*** These are recognized over the period covered, rather than as services are provided.
- ***Charitable care.*** The value of charitable care should not be recognized as revenue.
- ***Malpractice claims.*** These should be reported per the provisions of FASB Statement No. 5, *Accounting for Contingencies*—that is, as other types of contingencies are accounted for.
- ***Retrospective insurance premiums.*** Anticipated additional insurance premiums should be recognized as expenses in the periods to which they are applicable.

In a narrow sense the fiscal health of both health-care organizations can be evaluated using analytical tools, such as financial ratios. Health-care organizations present special difficulties in that their future is so heavily dependent on technological advances and changes in government policy—both of which are so difficult to predict. Recent policy actions around health-care reimbursements and insurance will certainly continue to affect the financial performance of and the markets for health-care organizations.

[29] "Hospitals can expect $2B less in DSH payments in 2018," by Susan Morse, *Healthcare Finance* (July 28, 2017), available at http://www.healthcarefinancenews.com/news/hospitals-can-expect-2b-less-dsh-payments-2018.

[30] See American Hospital Association "Trends Affecting Hospitals and Health Systems."

[31] Deloitte Center for Health Solutions and the Healthcare Financial Management Association. "Hospital M&A: When done well, M&A can achieve valuable outcomes." Available at https://www.hfma.org/mergers/.

[32] Para. 12.95.

[33] Para. 12.97 (FASB ASC 958-805).

KEY TERMS IN THIS CHAPTER

EXERCISE FOR REVIEW AND SELF-STUDY

Doctors Hospital, a private, not-for-profit hospital, engaged in the following transactions. Answer the question pertaining to each transaction.

1. It provided patient services with a standard billing rate of $1,200,000 for which it invoiced third-party payers $900,000. Of the balance, $200,000 was billed to individual patients, and $100,000 was for charity care. The hospital estimates that third-party payers will, on average, pay only 80 percent of the invoiced amounts and that 40 percent of the amount billed to individual patients will be uncollectible.

   How much should the hospital report as net revenue?

2. Volunteer nurses provided services that were comparable with those provided by paid nurses. Were the volunteer services provided by the paid nurses, the hospital would have incurred $58,000 in additional compensation and benefit costs. Also, members of the Hospital Auxiliary staffed the reception desk, family waiting rooms, and the gift shop. If the hospital had to hire and pay employees to provide their services (all of which were essential to sound hospital operations), the cost would have been approximately $105,000.

   How much, relating to these services, should the hospital report as compensation? Explain.

3. The hospital received a $100,000 cash grant to fund, in part, a study of the efficacy of a certain patient care protocol. During the year, the hospital completed approximately 70 percent of the study, incurring total costs of $120,000.

   How much of the $100,000 grant should the hospital report as restricted by donor?

4. The hospital's malpractice insurance policy covers a period that coincides with its fiscal year. During the year the hospital paid premiums of $450,000. It received a retrospective premium adjustment for the prior year of $37,000 (which it was made aware of too late to be taken into income of the prior year). However, it estimates that it will have to pay an additional $25,000 as a retrospective adjustment for the current year.

   How much should it report as an insurance expense for the current year?

5. During the year, the hospital was sued by a patient for $5,600,000. Claims of this type are 80 percent covered by insurance. The hospital has denied culpability and expects that the suit will go to trial. It estimates that if it loses its case, the judgment will likely be between $1,000,000 and $3,000,000.

   How much should the hospital recognize as a loss (or expense) for the current year?

6. Suppose an insured patient is admitted to the hospital. The patient has an individual insurance plan that has a $20,000 deductible (i.e., the patient is responsible for paying the first $20,000 of his or her medical bills, and then the insurance company pays the rest). The final charge for services, including discounts negotiated with the insurance company, is $15,000. The patient is poor and does not have $15,000. How would the hospital account for this?

QUESTIONS FOR REVIEW AND DISCUSSION

1. In what significant ways would each of the three major statements of a government hospital differ from those of a private not-for-profit hospital?

2. What are the major categories of revenues and expenses for a health-care organization?

3. What are the differences between recording a hospital's expenses by natural classification than by function?
4. Why is the statement of functional expenses required for voluntary health and welfare organizations?
5. What are "capitation fees," and how should they be accounted for?
6. What is the difference between *restricted assets* and *assets limited as to use*?
7. Hospitals and other health-care organizations provide services knowing that they will collect from third-party payers, such as insurance companies, considerably less than their established billing rates. In addition, they provide services to uninsured patients and are aware that they will collect either none or only a small portion of the amounts to be billed. Comment on how these organizations distinguish between charity care, bad debts, and contractual adjustments, and indicate how each affects the amount of revenue from patient care that they should report.
8. What is meant by "retrospective" insurance premiums, and how should they be reported?
9. As the comptroller of a hospital, you were just informed that one of the surgeons failed to remove an instrument from a patient's innards. The hospital is certain to be sued. How should this information affect the hospital's financial statements?
10. Discuss the different kinds of information a user of a hospital's financial information can obtain from its financial statements. How would this information differ for a nongovernmental versus a governmental hospital?
11. Discuss the financial and nonfinancial measures that are important in evaluating the fiscal wherewithal of health-care organizations.

EXERCISES

EX. 14-1

Select the *best* answer.

1. A not-for-profit hospital pays $150,000 interest on its bonds outstanding. The bonds were issued to finance construction of a new hospital wing. In its statement of cash flow, the interest should be shown as a cash outflow from
   a. Noncapital financing activities
   b. Capital financing activities
   c. Operating activities
   d. Investing activities
2. A government hospital pays $150,000 in interest on its bonds outstanding. The bonds were issued to finance construction of a new hospital wing. In its statement of cash flows, the interest should be shown as a cash outflow attributable to
   a. Noncapital financing activities
   b. Capital financing activities
   c. Operating activities
   d. Investing activities
3. A not-for-profit voluntary health and welfare organization should report a contribution for the construction of a new building as cash flows for which of the following in the statement of cash flows?
   a. Capital financing activities
   b. Operating activities
   c. Financing activities
   d. Investing activities
4. During the current year, a voluntary health and welfare organization receives $400,000 in total pledges. Of this amount, $150,000 has been designated by donors for use next year to support operations in

the pharmacy. If 20 percent of the pledges without donor restrictions are expected to be uncollectible, what amount of support without donor restrictions should the organization recognize in its current-year financial statements?
a. $400,000
b. $350,000
c. $250,000
d. $200,000

5. Earnings without donor restrictions on specific-purpose fund investments that are part of a hospital's central operations are reported as
a. General fund revenues without donor restrictions
b. General fund deferred revenues
c. Specific-purpose fund revenues with donor restrictions
d. Specific-purpose fund revenues without donor restrictions

6. Percy's community hospital would ordinarily include proceeds from the sale of balloons in the gift shop in
a. Other revenues
b. Ancillary service revenues
c. Deductions from gift shop expenses
d. Patient service revenues

7. Hannah, an auditor, is performing a routine review of a not-for-profit hospital and noted the following account balances in the statement of operations for the fiscal year ending September 30, 2019:

Gross patient service revenue from all services at the hospital's established billing rate	$2,225,000
Bad debt expense	$45,000
Contractual adjustments	$210,000

Calculate the amount the hospital would report as net patient service revenue in its statement of operations for the fiscal year ending September 30, 2019.
a. $2,040,000
b. $2,070,000
c. $2,115,000
d. $1,970,000

8. Other revenue sources of a hospital would normally include which of the following?

Revenue from grants, specified by the donor for research	Revenue from a parking garage
a. No	No
b. No	Yes
c. Yes	No
d. Yes	Yes

9. Based on Saint Michael Hospital's established billing rate structure, the hospital would have earned patient service revenue of $8,500,000 for the year. However, Saint Michael does not expect to collect this amount because of charity care provided in the amount of $1,000,000 and contractual allowances to third-party payers of $750,000. How much should Saint Michael record as patient service gross revenue for the year?
a. $8,500,000
b. $7,750,000
c. $7,500,000
d. $6,750,000

10. The BSK Health-Care foundation donated $900,000 as an endowment to be held in perpetuity to a senior citizens health and welfare organization during the year. The foundation stipulated that the income and investment appreciation be used to maintain its preventive care center for the elderly. The following year, the endowment principal had an investment appreciation of $60,000 and investment income of $80,000. The organization spent $70,000 to maintain its preventive care center during the year. What is the amount of change in net assets with donor restrictions that the organization should report for the second year?
    a. $70,000
    b. $80,000
    c. $140,000
    d. $970,000

EX. 14-2

Select the *best* answer.

1. A not-for-profit hospital signs a contract with an insurance company in which the company agrees to pay it $6 million in capitation fees for the year July 1, 2020, through June 30, 2021. Between July 1, 2020, and December 31, 2021, the hospital provides services that, at its standard rates, would bill at $3.4 million. Between January 1, 2020, and June 30, 2021, it provides services that it would bill at $2.8 million. For the year ending December 31, 2020, the hospital should recognize capitation revenue of
    a. $0
    b. $3 million
    c. $3.4 million
    d. $6 million

2. During a particular year, a not-for-profit hospital provides services that at standard rates would be billed at $200 million. This amount includes $10 million of charity care. Of the remaining $190 million, it estimates that $120 million will be billed to third-party providers, which, per contractual agreements, will pay only 75 percent of the standards rate (i.e., $90 million). Of the $70 million to be billed to individuals, the hospital estimates that $40 million will have to be written off as bad debts. The hospital should recognize net patient care revenue of
    a. $120
    b. $160
    c. $190
    d. $200

3. A not-for-profit hospital received a donor-restricted contribution of $10 million, which is used to purchase new equipment. It estimates that the useful life of the equipment will be 10 years with no salvage value. In the year of the contribution, the hospital should recognize
    a. Depreciation of $1 million classified as an expense without donor restrictions
    b. A capital expense of $10 million classified as an expense without donor restrictions
    c. Depreciation of $1 million classified as an expense with donor restrictions
    d. Net assets released from donor restriction of $1 million

4. A government hospital determines that the death of a patient was the result of negligence on the part of its medical staff. As of the date its financial statements are to be released; no claims have been asserted against the hospital. Nevertheless, based on past experience, the hospital is reasonably certain that a lawsuit will be forthcoming and estimates it will likely result in a required cash payment of between $3 and $5 million after accounting for insurance recoveries. In its financial statements the hospital should
    a. Make no mention of the potential litigation and possible settlement
    b. Record an expense of $4 million
    c. Record an expense of $5 million
    d. Disclose the nature of the incident and indicate the likely range of the loss

5. Ms. Wiley's estate donated land with a fair market value of $600,000 and subject to a mortgage of $320,000 to Saint Joseph Hospital without any restriction. Which of the following entries should the St. Joseph Hospital make to record this donation?

a. Land	$600,000	
Mortgage payable		$320,000
Revenues without donor restrictions		280,000
b. Land	$600,000	
Mortgage payable		$320,000
Revenues with donor restrictions		280,000
c. Land	$280,000	
Revenues with donor restrictions		$280,000
d. Land	$600,000	
Net assets		$320,000
Contributions		280,000

6. A donor gave $100,000 to a not-for-profit hospital in 2019 with the restriction that it be used for the purchase of equipment. Although the cash was received in 2019, the equipment was purchased in 2020. The hospital would record the $100,000 as
   a. A revenue with donor restrictions in 2019 and the equipment as a fixed asset without donor restrictions in 2020
   b. A revenue with donor restrictions in 2019 and the equipment as a fixed asset with donor restrictions in 2020
   c. A revenue without donor restrictions in 2019 and the equipment as a fixed asset without donor restrictions in 2020
   d. Either a or b, depending on the choice of the hospital

7. The Gulf Coast Hospital, a not-for-profit health-care institute, issued $140 million in term bonds to finance the construction of a new cancer unit at its main hospital. Terms of the bond covenant stipulate that $10 million of the proceeds of the bond issue be invested in U.S. government securities and must be held until the maturity of the bonds. The $10 million will increase which class of net assets?
   a. Net assets without donor restrictions
   b. Net assets with donor restrictions
   c. No effect on net assets
   d. Either (a) or (b)

8. The Helping Hand Relief Hospital, a not-for-profit entity, received a pledge from a donor in support of a fund-raising effort by the hospital to finance construction of a new unit for pediatric neurology treatment. The donor promised to pay $1 million in equal annual installments of $100,000 over the next 10 years. The present value of the gift at the risk-free interest rate is $736,000.

   The amount of revenue without donor restrictions that should be recognized by the hospital in the year of the gift is
   a. $1 million
   b. $736,000
   c. $100,000
   d. $0

9. The Old-Fashioned Doc Clinic, a well-established health-care organization, received a $500,000 pledge in fiscal year 2021 that was restricted to cover operating expenses. The gift was received over two years, $200,000 in the first year and $300,000 in the second year. The following table reflects the funds received as well as the amount spent on operating the clinic.

	June 30, 2021	June 30, 2022
Gifts received	$200,000	$300,000
Clinic operating expenses	$180,000	$340,000

How much should The Old-Fashioned Doc Clinic report as *Support from Contributions* for the year ended June 30, 2022?

a. $0
b. $300,000
c. $340,000
d. $500,000

10. Using the same data as in question 9, what should the clinic report as *Net Assets Released from Restrictions* on the statement of operations for the fiscal year ended June 30, 2022?

a. $300,000
b. $320,000
c. $340,000
d. $500,000

EX. 14-3

The basis for recognizing patient care revenue is not always obvious.

In a particular month Northwest Medical Clinic reported the following:

1. It provided direct care services to patients, billing them $400,000. Of this amount it received $120,000 in cash, but as a consequence of bad debts, it expects to collect a total of only $330,000.
2. It provided direct care to patients covered by insurance and who are members of various group health plans for which, at standard rates, it would have billed $650,000. However, owing to contractual arrangements with the payers, it actually billed them for, and expects to collect, only $480,000.
3. It provided charity care for which it would have billed, at standard rates, $82,000.
4. It received capitation fees of $1,400,000 from health-care plans and provided services to members of those plans for which it would have billed, at standard rates, $1,600,000.

Prepare appropriate journal entries to recognize revenue.

EX. 14-4

The accounting principles applicable to not-for-profit organizations in general also apply to not-for-profit health-care facilities.

A not-for-profit residential assisted living center engaged in the following transactions during the year. Prepare appropriate journal entries.

1. It billed residents for $6,200,000. Of this amount it estimates that $3,000,000 will be paid by third-party providers at a rate of only 80 percent. Of the balance, it estimates that 2 percent will be uncollectible.
2. It collected $5,100,000.
3. It received a cash contribution of $100,000 to be used exclusively for residents' educational and cultural programs. Of this amount, it spent $80,000 on qualified activities during the year.
4. It earned interest and dividends of $40,000 (cash) on its endowment of $500,000. Income from the endowment is not restricted by donors. However, it is the policy of the center's board of trustees that only income greater than 2 percent of the principal balance will be available for expenditure. The balance will be retained in the endowment to compensate for inflation. Thus, only $30,000 of the income was made available for expenditure.
5. The market value of the endowment's investments increased by $10,000.
6. It recognized $250,000 of depreciation on its building and $80,000 on equipment.
7. It incurred other operating expenses of $5,300,000, of which $5,000,000 was paid in cash.

8. At year-end it received a pledge of $6,000,000 toward the center's new building campaign. It will be paid at the rate of $2,000,000 at the end of each of the following three years. The center uses a discount rate of 8 percent to value noncurrent pledges.

EX. 14-5

Patient revenues in a health-care organization are derived from multiple sources.

Prepare journal entries for the following transactions.

1. Mt. Helen Hospital billed the state Medicaid program $365,000 for services provided at its standard billing rate. The prospective payment system gives Medicaid a 38 percent discount from these rates.

2. The hospital has an arrangement with an HMO to provide hospital care to the HMO's members at a specific rate per member, per month. In April the HMO paid the hospital $425,000 per agreement for patients treated in March. Based on preestablished billing rates, the hospital would have billed the HMO $487,500.

3. The hospital provided services to patients under "charity care" that amounted to $1,315,000 for the year.

4. At its standard billing rates, Mt. Helen Hospital provided services to Amity Inc., a third-party payer, for $2,380,000. The retrospective billing arrangement with Amity Inc. stipulates that the hospital would receive payment at an interim rate of 85 percent of its established rates, subject to retrospective adjustment based on agreed-upon allowable costs. By the end of the fiscal year, Amity Inc. had paid all the billings. Before issuing its financial statements, the hospital estimated that it would need to refund $192,000 to Amity Inc. based on allowable costs.

EX. 14-6

Accounting for investments.

On June 30, 2021, a county (government) hospital bought 3,000 shares of stock for $94,000 intending to hold the investment for its proposed expansion of its trauma center. The market value of the stock on August 31, 2021, the hospital's fiscal year-end, was $102,000. When the trauma center expansion was approved by the county district in February 2022, the hospital liquidated the stock for $90,000.

1. Journalize all the transactions related to the investment.

2. Assuming instead that this was a private not-for-profit hospital, how would these journal entries differ?

EX. 14-7

Accounting for malpractice claims.

At the end of the year, O'Toole General Hospital, which carries no medical malpractice insurance, had the following list of malpractice claims:

1. Mr. Seymour Green, a heart patient, filed a claim for $600,000. Based on Mr. Green's medical records, the hospital's attorneys are not confident of winning the case if it goes to trial. If settled out of court, the settlement could range from $300,000 to $400,000.

2. Ms. Les Monet filed a claim for $750,000. The hospital's attorneys are 95 percent confident that the hospital will win this claim if it goes to trial. The hospital is awaiting trial and will not settle the claim for any amount.

3. The hospital has 30 smaller claims outstanding with an average claim of $15,000. Based on past history, management has estimated that the hospital will lose 70 percent of the claims, with an average loss of 40 percent on the amount claimed.

4. Three additional claims, averaging $15,000 relating to incidents occurring before the fiscal year-end, will probably be settled during the following year.

a. Under GAAP, compute the amount, if any, that the hospital should establish as a liability on its balance sheet for malpractice claims.
b. Under GAAP, discuss any note disclosures the hospital should make in its financial statements for the malpractice claims.

EX. 14-8 Internet-based exercise

Please go to www.Guidestar.org, and download the Form 990 of three health-care organizations for the most recent year available. Note that you will need to create a free account to access the forms:

1. Mental Health America of Greater Houston
2. Southern Illinois Hospital Services
3. Ronald McDonald House Charities of Southern California

Based on the data on Form 990, answer the following questions.

1. What is the National Taxonomy of Exempt Entities (NTEE) category classification for each organization? Do they differ from each other? Why?
2. What is the total amount of revenue and support for each organization? How much of this did each organization get from contributions and grants?
3. Which program does the organization spend the most on? How much of total expenses does this program use?
4. What is the amount of net assets without donor restrictions of the entity at the end of the year? What percentage of the net assets is without donor restrictions?
5. What is the amount of management and general expenses of each of these organizations? What is the percentage of management and general expenses to total expenses for each?
6. What is the amount of fund-raising expenses reported by each of the organizations?
7. How much revenue reported by each organization is donor restricted?

PROBLEMS

P. 14-1

Accounting for designated and restricted assets.

Rosewood Cancer Hospital, a county hospital, has the following assets:

1. $4 million restricted by third-party reimbursement agreements to be used to replace radiology equipment.
2. Cash and investments totaling $925,000 that the hospital board designated for the expansion of its oncology unit.
3. $2.6 million restricted by donors to be used to supplement the operating budget of the hospital's pediatric cancer center.
4. Investments of $3.8 million from a donation made specifically for the purpose of defraying part of the cost of constructing the hospital's new wing for chemotherapy.

Indicate the category of net assets these amounts should be reported in Rosewood Cancer Hospital's Statement of Net Assets.

P. 14-2

Hospitals and other health-care providers face several issues of accounting and reporting.

Mosby Memorial Hospital, a private, not-for-profit hospital, engaged in the following transactions:

1. At the beginning of the year, the hospital received a bequest in the form of equity securities. Mosby is required to hold the securities in perpetuity, but it can spend the income. The original cost of the

securities to the donor was $3.6 million, but their fair value had increased to $4.4 million on Mosby's receipt. During the year, the fair value of the securities fluctuated, with an average fair value of $4.0 million. When the hospital prepared its financial statements at year-end, the fair value of the securities was $4.1 million. At what amount should the hospital report the securities in its financial statements?

2. The American Sleep Apnea Association awarded a research grant of $160,000 to the hospital to fund a study on sleep apnea. During the year, the hospital's research team completed approximately 60 percent of the study, incurring total costs of $192,000. How much of the $160,000 grant should the hospital report as restricted by donors?

3. Radnor Nursing School provided volunteer nurses two days a week whose services were comparable with those provided by paid nurses. The hospital would have incurred $92,800 in additional compensation and benefit costs, if it had to pay for these services. Can the hospital report these services as contribution? Explain.

4. Members of the local high school's "Health Occupation Students of America" club staffed the gift shop and children's waiting rooms. If the hospital had to hire and pay employees to provide these services (all of which were needed for hospital operations), the estimated cost would have been approximately $168,000. How much should the hospital report as compensation expense? Explain.

5. It provided patient services amounting to $1,920,000 at its established billing rate for which it invoiced Medicare $1,440,000. Of the balance, $320,000 was billed to individual patients, and $160,000 was for charity care. The hospital estimates that Medicare will pay only 80 percent of the invoiced amounts. Mosby collected $192,000 from individual patients, and the remainder billed to individual patients will be uncollectible. How much should the hospital report as net revenue?

6. The hospital was sued by a patient for $8,960,000 during the year for a malpractice claim. Insurance covers 70 percent of medical malpractice claims. The hospital attorneys expect that the suit will go to trial and estimate that if they lose the case, the judgment will likely be between $1,600,000 and $4,800,000. How much should the hospital recognize as a loss (or expense) for the current year?

P. 14-3

The statement of cash flows for a government hospital would differ from that of a private not-for-profit hospital.

The following represent a hospital's inflows and outflows of cash:

- Patient service fees received
- Government grants for operating purposes
- Government grants for specific research programs
- Contribution restricted to construction of a new building
- Salaries and wages
- Supplies
- Interest paid on long-term debt
- Interest paid on short-term operating debt
- Acquisition of capital assets
- Purchases of marketable securities
- Proceeds from sale of marketable securities
- Interest received from investments
- Dividends received from investments
- Proceeds of long-term debt to finance a new building
- Proceeds of short-term borrowings for operating purposes

1. Categorize the cash inflows and outflows as they would be reported in a statement of cash flows, assuming that the hospital is government owned.

2. Do the same, this time assuming that the hospital is a not-for-profit.

3. Why did the GASB opt for a four-way classification, whereas the FASB retained for not-for-profits the three-way classification developed for businesses?

P. 14-4

This example, drawn from the actual financial statements of a major urban not-for-profit hospital, illustrates the main types of transactions (in summary form) in which hospitals engage.

The December 31, 2020, Statement of Net Assets of Mosholu Medical Center, a major urban hospital and research center, is presented.

Mosholu Medical Center Statement of Net Assets as of December 31, 2020

	Without Donor Restrictions	With Donor Restrictions
Assets		
Current assets		
Cash	$ 5,878	$ 612
Receivables for patient care ($265,116 less allowance for contractual adjustments and doubtful accounts of $109,812)	155,304	
Other receivables	31,342	27,223
Marketable securities	561,804	489,177
Other current assets	66,847	
Total current assets	$ 521,174	$517,012
Noncurrent assets		
Property, plant, and equipment ($1,229,242 less accumulated depreciation of $535,822)	$ 693,420	
Other assets	27,653	
Total noncurrent assets	$ 721,073	
Total assets	$1,242,247	$517,012
Liabilities and net assets		
Current liabilities		
Accounts payable	$ 134,304	
Accrued wages and salaries	136,661	
Total current liabilities	$ 270,965	
Noncurrent liabilities		
Long-term debt	$701,688	
Deferred revenue and other noncurrent liabilities	231,862	
Total noncurrent liabilities	$ 933,550	
Total liabilities	$1,204,514	
Net assets	$ 37,733	$517,012
Total liabilities and net assets	$1,242,247	$517,012

The following transactions and events occurred in 2021:

1. The hospital received pledges without donor restrictions of $372,600 and pledges with donor restrictions of $216,000. It collected all of the pledges without donor restrictions and $180,000 of the pledges with donor restrictions.

2. Cash gifts designated by donors for juvenile diabetes research amounted to $250,000 for the year. During the year, $200,000 was expended for juvenile diabetes research.

3. The total services provided by the hospital to all patients during the year amounted to $1,270,697 at the hospital's established billing rates. Based on the contracted rates with third-party payers, the hospital expects to collect approximately $889,488 (70 percent) of this amount. Due to current economic conditions, it expects that $133,423 (15 percent of the 70 percent) will have to be written off as bad debts.

4. It also provided $93,600 in charity care, which it never expected to collect.

5. It collected $864,225 in patient accounts recorded in question 3.

6. It earned and fully collected other operating revenues from its parking garage of $1,000,000, cafeteria of $820,000, and gift shop of $610,000.

7. It earned $27,072 in investment income, of which $18,144 is not restricted by donors and $8,928 is restricted.

8. The hospital sold marketable securities without donor restrictions to hire a well-known cancer researcher. It received $600,000 from investments that had a fair value of $550,000 at the end of the prior fiscal year.

9. It purchased equipment for its new gastroenterology unit of $435,600, all of which was paid for by liquidating marketable securities with donor restrictions.

10. It charged depreciation of $526,716.

11. Supplies were purchased in the amount of $800,000, all on account.

12. It incurred $1,775,170 in wages and salaries, of which it paid $1,765,000. The balance was accrued. It also incurred $860,000 in other operating expenses (including those of auxiliary enterprises), of which it paid $797,750. The balance was vouchered (and thereby credited to accounts payable).

13. Other operating expenses for the year include insurance costs. However, under "retrospective" insurance policies, the hospital anticipates having to pay an additional $6,300 in premiums.

14. It incurred and paid $378,360 in costs related to contracts (an exchange transaction). It was reimbursed for $372,240 and expects to be reimbursed for the balance in the future. In addition, it received $5,400 in advances on other contracts.
    - **a.** Prepare journal entries to record the transactions. Be sure to indicate whether each entry would affect fund types with or without donor restrictions.
    - **b.** Prepare a statement of operations for 2021 and a statement of financial position as of December 31, 2021.

P. 14-5

Seemingly similar contributions may have to be accounted for differently.

JMH (a not-for-profit) Rehabilitation Center engaged in the following transactions during its most recent fiscal year:

1. Michael Vincent donated $625,000 to the hospital to help pay for the purchase of new physical rehabilitation equipment.

2. Albert Olsen donated $250,000 to the center, stipulating that the resources be used only for the training of rehab care nurses. The center plans to conduct the training early next fiscal year.

3. The center received a $100,000 grant from the Orthopedic Association to determine the effects of three different kinds of physical therapy on female patients between the ages of 40 and 55.

   Prepare journal entries to record the transactions. Explain and justify any differences in your entries.

P. 14-6

Financial ratios are useful in comparing one not-for-profit to another.

The data below pertaining to two not-for-profit hospices were taken from GuideStar, an online database (www.guidestar.org) that provides information about not-for-profit organizations. Names and dates have been changed. The forms 990 that are included on the website indicate that Pleasant Valley and Ancient Falls had fund-raising expenses of $38,327 and $11,075, respectively. Because the data were taken from an Internal Revenue Service form, the statements are not in the format required by GAAP (e.g., they do not report net assets by degree of restrictiveness).

1. Which of the two is the more likely to be able to satisfy its current liabilities as measured by the quick ratio? Include only cash and receivables.
2. Which has the greater financial resources as measured by the ratio of total expenses to net assets (excluding property, plant, and equipment)?
3. Which spends the greater percentage of its revenues on fund-raising?
4. Which directs a greater portion of its revenues to program services?
5. Based on this limited amount of information, which of the two, in your opinion, is the more fiscally sound?

Statement of Operations for the Year Ending December 31, 20XX

	Hospice Pleasant Valley	Hospice Ancient Falls
Revenues		
Contributions	$ 841,162	$ 704,529
Government grants	94,830	—
Program services	1,555,450	2,331,263
Investments	3,455	146,318
Other	2,187	—
	$2,497,084	$3,182,110
Expenses		
Program services	$1,881,381	$2,521,516
Administration	444,853	403,425
Other	38,227	74,891
Total expenses	$2,364,461	$2,999,832
Excess of revenues over expenses	$ 132,623	$ 182,278

Statement of Financial Position as of December 31, 20XX

	Hospice Pleasant Valley	Hospice Ancient Falls
Assets		
Cash and equivalent	$ 215,999	$ 441,229
Accounts receivable	141,570	307,252
Pledges and grants receivable	70,135	6,331
Inventories for sale or use	—	14,250
Investments/securities	13,063	2,417,152

(Continues)

Statement of Financial Position as of December 31, 20XX *(Continued)*

	Hospice Pleasant Valley	Hospice Ancient Falls
Property, plant, and equipment	269,298	2,656,105
Other	1,295	78,801
Total assets	$ 711,360	$5,921,120
Liabilities		
Accounts payable	$ 165,809	$ 183,483
Noncurrent loans and notes	161,556	—
Other noncurrent obligations	5,319	—
Total liabilities	$ 332,684	$ 183,483
Net assets	$ 378,676	$5,737,637

P. 14-7

Not all health-care organizations are similar, complicating analysis.

Below are the abridged operating statements of two not-for-profit hospitals that serve similar populations.

Statement of Operations for the Year Ending December 31, 2021

	Hospital A	Hospital B
Operating revenues		
Net patient service revenue	$3,906,626	$2,678,248
Grants and contracts	177,360	4,789,169
Total operating revenue	$4,083,986	$7,467,417
Operating expenses		
Salaries and wages	$1,956,341	$3,359,110
Fringe benefits	689,542	1,312,890
Supplies	1,503,901	2,021,908
Depreciation and amortization	102,312	1,736,930
Interest	25,980	456,712
Total operating expenses	$4,278,076	$7,150,620
Income from operations	($194,090)	$ 316,797
Change in pension liabilities	135,670	(247,153)
Net assets released from restrictions	7,900	0
Increase/(decrease) in net assets without donor restrictions	($ 50,490)	$ 69,644

1. What is the performance indicator of the hospitals?
2. Using the performance indicator, which hospital reported better operations? Does anything else reported give you pause about this assessment?

3. Using just this data, what are some fundamental differences between these two entities that might be important for evaluating financial operations?

4. How much revenue do each earn from patient services? Do you think this difference between the two has any implications?

P. 14-8

Different accounting bases can lead to different accounting across organizations. This problem was written by Dave Mest of Seton Hall University.

The Dave Health-Care Center (DHCC) was created in 2020 to provide medical services to low-income residents of Dave Town. DHCC had the following transactions during the year:

1. Received a pledge from a donor for $20,000, payable in equal installments of $5,000 per year. The first payment of $5,000 was received in 2020. This pledge is to support general operations of DHCC (for purposes of this transaction, you may ignore time value of money).

2. Expenditures for the year included $2,000 for equipment and $2,500 for supplies. The equipment has a five-year expected life, with no salvage value. DHCC uses the straight-line depreciation method.

DHCC can be created using three different potential structures. These include:

A. Special revenue fund owned and operated by the government of Dave Town.
B. As an enterprise fund owned and operated by the government of Dave Town.
C. As a not-for-profit corporation owned and operated by the "Friends of Dave."

Show what amounts will be recorded as revenues and expenses/expenditures for 2020 under the three organizational structures listed. Then show how the differences between revenues and expenses/expenditures will be shown in the net position/net asset portion of the balance sheet.

SOLUTION TO EXERCISE FOR REVIEW AND SELF-STUDY

1. It should report as revenue $920,000:

Amounts billed to third parties	$900,000	
Less: 20 percent contractual discounts	(180,000)	720,000
Amounts billed to individuals		200,000
Total		$920,000

The hospital should recognize no revenue from charity care; the estimated uncollectible accounts from individual patients should be reported as an expense.

2. $58,000. Only the compensation to the nurses should be recognized as an expense (and as contribution revenue). The services provided by the nurses, unlike those provided by the others, require "specialized skills"—one of the essential conditions for revenues and expenses from contributed services to be recognized.

3. $0. Inasmuch as the hospital spent at least $100,000 on the donor-restricted activity, it can assume that the entire amount of the grant has been used for its intended purpose and can thereby be released from restriction.

4. $438,000. It should recognize the premium paid of $450,000 less the refund of $37,000 plus the required future payment of $25,000.

5. $0. The amount of loss cannot reasonably be estimated. The claim should be reported in notes to the financial statements.

6. Even though the patient is insured, the $15,000 would be handled as charity care. Hence, the hospital should disclose the total $15,000 in its notes, but it would not record an entry for the revenue.

CHAPTER 15

Auditing Governments and Not-for-Profit Organizations

LEARNING OBJECTIVES

After studying this chapter, you should understand:

- The primary differences between auditing in the government and not-for-profit sectors and in the business sector
- How the Yellow Book has influenced governmental and not-for-profit auditing
- The types of audits that governments conduct
- The standards to which government audits must comply
- The unique characteristics of performance audits
- The key elements of performance audits
- How the Single Audit Act and supporting regulations have influenced auditing
- The reports that auditors must prepare as part of a single audit
- The unique ethical issues facing governmental and not-for-profit accountants and auditors

The theme of the previous chapter is that government and not-for-profit organizations must be managed to achieve their objectives. By extension, therefore, their performance must also be evaluated as to whether they achieved these objectives. In this chapter, we consider how governments and not-for-profit organizations are audited—how their accomplishments are attested to and reported on.

Whereas in the development of financial auditing standards and practices the independent public accounting profession has played the leadership role, in the areas of reporting on compliance and assessing performance, the government and not-for-profit sectors have been at the forefront of progress. The advances in compliance and performance auditing can be attributed mainly to the federal government, especially to the leadership of the **Government Accountability Office** (GAO) and the requirements of the Single Audit Act. The federal government provides financial assistance, either directly or indirectly through the states, to almost all general-purpose local governments, most colleges and universities, and a substantial portion of not-for-profit entities. As a condition of awarding financial assistance, it requires that the entities submit financial statements that are audited in accord with federally specified standards. The federal government is thereby able to influence the auditing standards applicable to entities as disparate as major state governments and small-town soup kitchens. In addition, inasmuch as the internal audit departments of more progressive corporations began to focus on performance audits as early as the 1960s, the

Institute of Internal Auditors, the professional association of internal auditors, has also made substantial contributions to promoting performance auditing and to developing appropriate concepts and practices.

Auditing is a discipline in its own right, and therefore comprehensive coverage is well beyond the scope of this text.[1] The Institute of Internal Auditors refers to internal auditing as a "global, interdisciplinary knowledge profession" connected to, but not a subset of, the accounting profession. The objective of this chapter is to shed light on some of the unique features of government and not-for-profit auditing and to show how federal requirements have affected both state and local governments and not-for-profits. The chapter first discusses the distinctive elements of auditing in the government and not-for-profit sectors. It then addresses the two primary types of audits—financial audits and performance audits. A final section deals with ethical issues facing auditors and accountants—a topic only tangentially related to the main thrust of the chapter but nevertheless of special concern to government accountants and auditors.

HOW DO AUDITS OF GOVERNMENTS AND NOT-FOR-PROFITS DIFFER FROM THOSE OF BUSINESSES?

An **audit** is defined in general-purpose dictionaries as an examination of records or accounts to check their accuracy. Business-sector financial audits are characterized by the attest function. **Attest** means "to affirm, to be correct, true, or genuine; corroborate." The attest function adds credibility to the assertions of others—in the case of an independent financial audit, to an entity's financial data as presented by management.

In the government and not-for-profit sectors, auditing extends beyond the attest function. Auditors not only attest to the data reported in financial statements. They also make, and report on, their own independent evaluations as to whether auditees have complied with appropriate laws, regulations, and terms of grants. Further, they assess whether the auditees have achieved their objectives and carried out their missions efficiently and effectively.

HOW HAS THE YELLOW BOOK INFLUENCED GOVERNMENTAL AND NOT-FOR-PROFIT AUDITING?

In 1972, the GAO issued the first edition of *Government Auditing Standards (Standards for Audit of Governmental Organizations, Programs, Activities, and Functions)*, commonly referred to (because of the color of its cover) as the **Yellow Book**. The GAO is headed by the **Comptroller General of the United States**, who is appointed by the president, with the advice and consent of the Senate, for a term of 15 years. The GAO audits many, but not all, of the federal government's departments and agencies. Other departments and agencies are audited by independent Certified Public Accountant (CPA) firms.

Government Auditing Standards was issued to elevate the practice of auditing by both federal agencies and state and local governments. The GAO has no direct authority over state and local governments, but by publishing—and publicizing—the standards, it exerts its influence through the force of persuasion and example.

Federal legislation now requires that the **inspectors general** (the chief auditors) of all federal agencies apply the Yellow Book to their own audits. In addition, they must also ensure that all audits for which they are responsible, mainly those of entities to which their agencies provide funds, satisfy the GAO standards. Thus, if a federal department were to make an award to a state or local government or to a not-for-profit organization, then that organization's auditors, even if an independent CPA firm, must adhere to the GAO standards.

[1] See Raaum, Morgan and Waring, *Performance Auditing (3rd ed.)*, Internal Audit Foundation, 2016 for a comprehensive guide to performance auditing in government.

The GAO standards constitute "generally accepted government auditing standards," commonly referred to as GAGAS. GAGAS—that is, the Yellow Book—incorporates, by reference, many of the auditing standards applicable to financial audits established by the American Institute of Certified Public Accountants (AICPA). The GAO revises the Yellow Book every several years. The most recent version was issued in July 2018.[2] Whereas the original 1972 edition was a mere 54 pages, the current edition is 4½ times as long—far too long for this textbook to do anything more than highlight a few of its key features. Students can best get an overview of how the book is organized and the key issues that it addresses by skimming through it. It is available online at http://www.gao.gov/yellowbook.

Until 2002, the AICPA had primary responsibility for promulgating the audit standards that had to be followed by all CPAs. However, owing to accounting scandals involving Enron and numerous other major corporations, Congress (through the Sarbanes–Oxley bill) created the **Public Company Accounting Oversight Board (PCAOB)** to which it assigned the authority to establish auditing standards for *public corporations* (i.e., those corporations the shares of which are publicly traded).

The International Auditing and Assurance Standards Board (IAASB) also establishes auditing standards that have been adopted by many countries (although not the United States). Per the most recent edition of the Yellow Book, the standards of both the PCAOB and the IAASB may now be used "in conjunction with GAGAS."

The range of standards promulgated by the GAO and set forth in the Yellow Book is perhaps best summarized by the titles of its nine chapters. These are presented in Table 15-1.

TABLE 15-1 Chapter Headings of *Government Auditing Standards*

- Foundation and Principles for the Use and Application of Government Auditing Standards
- General Requirements for Complying with Government Auditing Standards
- Ethics, Independence, and Professional Judgment
- Competence and Continuing Professional Education
- Quality Control and Peer Review
- Standards for Financial Audits
- Standards for Attestation Engagements and Reviews of Financial Statements
- Fieldwork Standards for Performance Audits
- Reporting Standards for Performance Audits

WHAT TYPES OF AUDITS DO GOVERNMENTS CONDUCT?

The 2018 edition of *Government Auditing Standards* divides government audits into three categories: financial audits; attestation engagements and reviews of financial statements; and performance audits.

Financial audits determine whether an entity's financial statements are presented fairly in accordance with generally accepted accounting principles (GAAP). They typically provide users with an opinion on whether the entity's financial statements are fairly presented. They may also have related objectives, such as ensuring that the entity has complied with laws and regulations that may have a material effect on the financial statements, providing special reports on selected

[2] The 2018 revision is effective for financial audits, attestation engagements, and reviews of financial statements for periods ending on or after June 30, 2020 and for performance audits (which unlike the other types of engagement are not based on statements that bear specific beginning and ending dates) beginning on or after July 1, 2019. Early implementation is not permitted. The 2018 edition replaces a 2011 version.

accounts or items of a financial statement, issuing letters for underwriters or other parties, and reviewing internal control systems.

Attestation engagements cover a broad range of financial or nonfinancial objectives depending on the needs of the intended audience. Unlike financial statement audits which ensure that the statements are in accord with generally accepted accounting standards, attestation engagements measure or evaluate whether assertions adhere to suitable criteria. Attestation engagements include: "examinations"—engagements in which the level of assurance provided by the auditors is the same as that in a financial statement audit—as well as "reviews" and "agreed-upon procedures" in which the auditors provide lesser degrees of assurance. The subject matter of these engagements may include the following:

- Historical or projective financial information or specific performance measures
- Physical characteristics, such as square footage of facilities
- Analyses, such as break-even analyses
- Systems and processes, including internal controls
- Compliance with laws, regulations and policies

Performance audits, which in the private sector are often referred to as **operational audits**, may be intended to achieve a variety of different purposes. These include the following:

- Measuring the extent to which a program is achieving its goals and objectives and determining whether the entity is using its resources in the most effective and economical manner
- Determining whether an organization's internal controls are effective in relation to management's goals and objectives
- Verifying that the organization is complying with the terms of laws, grants, and contracts in that its programs are serving the appropriate population and delivering the intended services
- Analyzing assumptions about events that may occur in the future and identifying actions that may be taken in response to future events

WHAT LEVELS OF STANDARDS ARE APPLICABLE TO ALL ENGAGEMENTS?

Chapters 3, 4, and 5 of the Yellow Book set forth standards that are applicable to all three types of engagements.

ETHICS

With respect to ethics, the Yellow Book standards are generally comparable to those of the AICPA. Like those of the AICPA, they emphasize that the work of auditors must be guided by principles of public interest, integrity, objectivity, and professional behavior. They add, however, that the government auditor must also be concerned with the proper use of government information, resources, and positions. This principle implies that government auditors must be mindful that many government programs are subject to laws and regulations that limit disclosure of sensitive, classified, or similar types of information.

INDEPENDENCE

The Yellow Book is especially concerned with issues of independence that are unique to governments. Consistent with the AICPA standards, it underscores that auditors must be independent of the audited entity in both mind and in appearance. Going beyond the AICPA standards, it also establishes a conceptual framework as to how auditors should identify, evaluate, and apply safeguards to address threats to independence. Per the framework they should

- identify threats to independence;
- evaluate the significance of the threats identified, both individually and in the aggregate;
- apply safeguards to eliminate the threats or reduce them to an acceptable level.[3]

Threats to independence can take many forms. Like those facing auditors of businesses or not-for-profit organizations, they can be the result of the auditor having personal relationships with management, participating in managerial decisions, having financial interests in the outcome of the audit, or providing nonaudit services. But government auditors also face threats that are not typical of those facing business auditors.

In the private sector, auditors cannot be considered independent if employed by the entity they are to audit. However, most government audit agencies are part of the government that they have been established to audit. To ensure that a government audit agency is nevertheless viewed as being independent, the GAO requires it be from a different branch (e.g., legislative, executive) of the government than the particular units that it is to examine or from a different level of government (e.g., a federal auditor may audit a state program). Moreover, even when there are "structural" threats to independence, they may be mitigated by safeguards such as the auditor being directly elected by the jurisdiction's voters or by being elected or appointed by, and subject to removal by, a legislative body.

IN PRACTICE **TO WHOM SHOULD A CITY AUDITOR REPORT?**

As a general rule, auditors should not report to parties who are directly or even indirectly responsible for the departments and programs that they will audit. Thus, in a city headed by a city manager, the auditor should report not to the city manager but rather to the city council. In one such city, officials faced a dilemma. On the one hand, the city council appeared to be the natural body to which the auditor should report. On the other hand, the city council was headed by a mayor. Although the city manager was the CEO of the city and all department heads reported to him, the political culture dictated that the mayor be held responsible and accountable for all failings in the administration of the city. Thus, the mayor was exceedingly sensitive to any criticism of city activities by the city auditor. And the city auditor needed no reminder that it was the mayor and the council that determined his salary and the budget of his department.

CONTINUING PROFESSIONAL EDUCATION

Both the AICPA standards and GAGAS require that auditors be professionally competent. Per GAGAS, this means that they must be knowledgeable of government auditing standards and accounting principles in addition to those of general auditing standards and accounting principles. Auditors who perform government audits must complete at least 80 hours of continuing professional education (CPE) every two years, of which 24 hours must be related directly to the government environment and to government auditing. The requirement for 24 hours of specialized government education goes beyond the CPE standards of both the AICPA and state CPA licensing boards, which make no demands as to specific industry content. The good news for college and university students is that the standard does not apply to interns or other students temporarily employed as part of a college- or university-sponsored program. Also exempt are non supervisory auditors who charge less than 40 hours of time per year to government engagements.

[3] This framework is detailed in a flow chart that can be found on pages 61 and 62 of the Yellow Book.

QUALITY CONTROL

GAGAS requires that audit organizations establish policies and procedures to ensure that they maintain control over quality. The Yellow Book includes standards, backed by specific guidance, to make certain that its personnel satisfy all independence, ethical, and legal requirements, that they are competent to perform government audits, and that there is ongoing monitoring of quality.

Notably, the standards required each audit organization to obtain an external peer review to determine whether its quality control system is suitably designed and is being complied with. Audit organizations affiliated with certain specified organizations, such as the AICPA or the National State Auditors Association, can satisfy this requirement by meeting the standards of that organization. Thus, CPA firms can satisfy this requirement by adhering to the peer review standards of the AICPA. Organizations not already subject to some other peer review requirement must obtain an external review at least once every three years.

STANDARDS FOR FINANCIAL AUDITS

Waste and Abuse

The standards for financial audits and attest engagements supplement those of the AICPA. They incorporate, by reference, the AICPA standards and make clear that government auditors must adhere to those standards.

At the same time, however, they recognize that, owing to the nature of the transactions in which governments engage and the interest of their constituents, government auditors must take a broader view of accountability than do their private sector counterparts. Thus, the Yellow Book encourages auditors to expand the traditional boundaries of their reviews of internal control to encompass deficiencies that result in waste or abuse. While the standards do not require that auditors perform specific procedures to detect waste or abuse, they say that they *may* do so and "may consider whether and how to communicate such matters if they become aware of them."

The Yellow book defines waste as "the act of using or expending resources carelessly, extravagantly, or to no purpose," even if they do not necessarily involve a violation of law. Thus, making unnecessarily expensive travel arrangements might be considered an example of waste.

Abuse, by contrast, is "behavior that is deficient or improper when compared with behavior that a prudent person would consider reasonable and necessary business practices." Abuse would include practices such as creating unneeded overtime, requesting staff to perform personal services and misusing an official position for personal gain.

Compliance and Internal Controls

The standards relating to financial audits are generally more rigorous with respect to both compliance and internal control than those of the AICPA. Both the AICPA and the GAO standards require auditors to design their financial engagements to provide "reasonable assurance" of detecting fraud and material misstatements resulting from illegal acts or similar irregularities, such as intentional omissions or fabrications. But because governments and not-for-profits are typically more directly accountable than businesses to the parties from which they receive grants or have contracts, the GAO standards also require auditors to design their audits to provide reasonable assurance of detecting noncompliance with the terms of both grants and contracts.

The AICPA standards of reporting require that auditors evaluate internal controls and communicate in writing to management significant deficiencies and material weaknesses.[4] The GAO standards go further. In light of the importance governments place on both compliance and internal controls, the GAO stipulates that auditors must explicitly describe (either in their reports

[4] This is in contrast to the PCAOB standards, which require an explicit audit of, and report on, internal controls.

on the financial statements or in separate reports) the scope of their compliance and internal control testing. They must also indicate any irregularities, illegal acts, and other instances of material noncompliance that they found. To put the violations in perspective, the auditors should also indicate the number of infractions and their dollar amount.

The GAO has issued *Standards for Internal Control*, better known as the Green Book, that provides a framework for establishing and maintaining an effective internal control system. Figure 15-1, taken from the Green Book, summarizes its key features and intended uses.

Public Availability

As a general rule, government documents, unless explicitly excluded by legislation, are in the public domain. Hence, auditors must assume that their audit reports will be available for public inspection. Nevertheless, the GAO standards make it clear that certain circumstances, such as those associated with public safety, privacy, or security, justify omitting from a report certain items that would otherwise be included. Thus, detailed information relating to computer systems could undermine data security. In such instances, the auditor might omit such information from reports that would be widely distributed and include it only in those of officials that need to know. However, when auditors exclude information that they deem to be confidential, they should so note that they have done so.

WHAT ARE PERFORMANCE AUDITS?

Financial audits are intended to ensure that financial statements are fairly presented and that the organization has complied with applicable laws and regulations. Performance audits, by contrast, focus on organizational accomplishments. Inasmuch as the goals of a government or not-for-profit are seldom limited to profitability or other financial measures, the auditors may have to assess organizational performance on a wide range of nonfinancial dimensions, each of which relates to an entity's individual objectives.

Performance audits are most commonly carried out by "internal" audit departments—organizations that may be independent of the various agencies or departments that they examine, but not separate from the government or other entity at large. They are not typically required by creditors, regulatory agencies, or other outside parties. Therefore, the accounting profession, other than the GAO, has not developed a detailed set of standards for performance audits comparable to those for financial audits. However, the Yellow Book has provided auditors with fundamental guidance on how to carry out performance audits. It has also clarified the auditors' responsibility for reporting the views of responsible officials, for reporting on confidential and sensitive information, and for issuing and distributing reports.

The GAO standards for performance audits have had a substantial influence on practice mainly because audit departments have elected voluntarily to adhere to them. These standards are divided into two sections: field work and reporting. In addition, the general standards that apply to financial audits and attestation engagements also apply to performance audits.

KEY DIFFERENCES BETWEEN FINANCIAL AND PERFORMANCE AUDITS

Attest Function versus Independent Assessment

Performance audits differ conceptually from financial audits. In carrying out financial audits, the auditors *attest* to the fairness of the assertions of management. These assertions are incorporated in the entity's financial statements and for the most part relate to constructs, such as revenues, expenditures, assets, and liabilities, that are well defined and subject to accepted accounting standards of measurement.

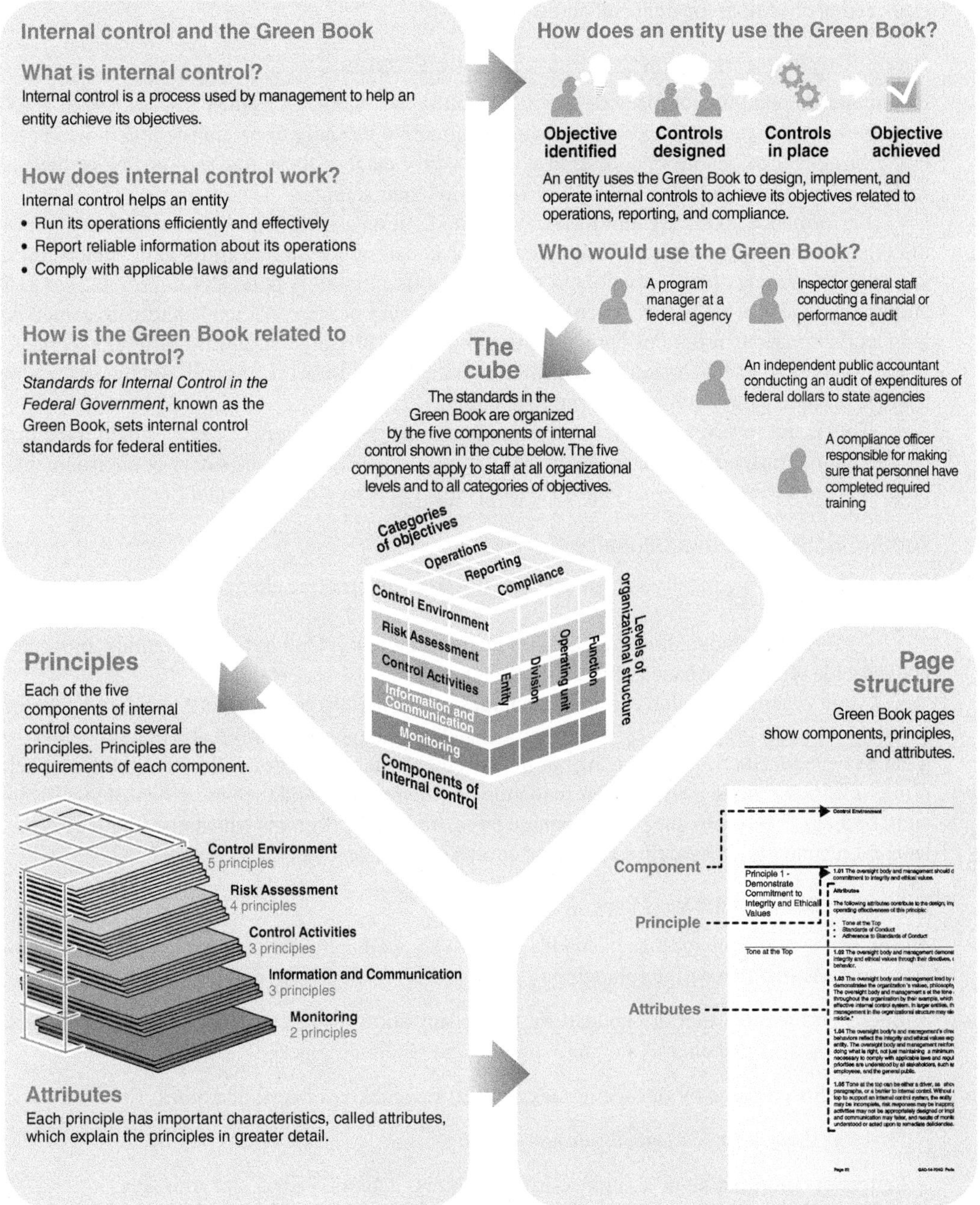

FIGURE 15-1 What is the Green Book and How is it Used.
Source: Standards for Internal Control in the Federal Government, (Government Accountability Office, September 2014).

In performance audits, the auditors make independent assessments on whether an entity is operating economically and efficiently and is achieving anticipated results. But the constructs to be measured and the standards of measurement, especially those relating to outcomes, are far less clear and precise than for financial audits.

Focus: Organization at Large versus Specific Programs

Financial statement audits focus on the organization as a whole. An entity's statement of activities (or income statement) and balance sheet summarize virtually every transaction in which the entity has engaged. Auditors do not, of course, verify each of these transactions. Nevertheless, each is within the population from which they draw their samples.

Performance audits are almost always carried out on a specific program or activity, not on the organization in its entirety. Unless the entity is extremely limited in its aims, determining whether the organization as a whole is carrying out its mission is generally infeasible. Imagine attempting to assess the performance of a major university or metropolitan health-care center. As long as their various programs have different objectives, are targeted toward different segments of the population, and are conducted by different employees, little is accomplished by performing a single, unified assessment of the complete entity.

This is not to say, however, that the particular program or activity cannot affect the entire organization. Thus, a performance audit can focus on organization-wide safety or environmental programs or on various internal control systems that cut across departmental lines.

Timing: Routine versus Occasional

Financial audits are typically conducted annually. They are routine elements of an organization's operating cycle.

Performance audits, however, are conducted irregularly. Unlike financial audits, they need not coincide with the issuance of the entity's annual financial statements.

Audit organizations have limited resources and generally cannot afford to expend them on audits of the same programs year after year. Instead, they target programs that will likely yield the greatest benefits (such as cost savings or improvements in results) per dollar of audit cost. Their prime selection criteria are the dollar magnitude of the program and the probability of significant audit findings. Therefore, they may examine large, high-risk programs with some frequency (perhaps even annually) but small, low-risk programs only occasionally.

Evidence: Well-Delineated versus Broad

The evidence examined in financial audits is relatively well delineated and limited to a few major categories. These include the following:

- Books and records that are created by the organization itself, such as journals and ledgers, schedules, canceled checks, purchase orders, and receiving reports
- Documents prepared by outside parties, such as invoices, contracts, and notes
- Physical assets, such as inventories and capital assets
- Letters of confirmation or assurance from creditors, debtors, banks, and attorneys

Performance audits are characterized by a broader range of evidence, much of which may be engagement specific. Depending on the objectives of a program, the auditors may have to review—in addition to financial data—economic and demographic statistics, engineering reports, and medical records.

Auditor Knowledge: Financial versus Program

Financial audits are performed mainly by specialists in accounting—CPAs or others with similar educational and experiential backgrounds. For some engagements, nonaccountants with expertise in areas such as computers, statistical sampling, or specific industries (e.g., jewelry appraisers or geologists) may be brought in as consultants to address certain phases of the examination. They generally play only supporting roles.

Owing to the wider range of evidence that must be examined, performance audits may require more program-specific knowledge and fewer traditional accounting skills. Thus, the GAO and many other government audit organizations have on their staff economists, engineers, health-care specialists, and statisticians. At the same time, however, "generalists"—those with MBA degrees or master's degrees in public administration or policy—make valuable additions to an audit team. Often, in fact, the contributions of accountants are not so much their knowledge of accounting per se, but rather their ability to define a problem and resolve it in a logical and orderly manner. As the inspector general of one federal agency put it, "We need broad-based skills, creative thinking, interpersonal skills, analytic ability, etc., if we're going to be effective in doing performance audits."[5]

MANNER OF CONDUCTING

In light of the dissimilarities among programs, each performance audit is unique. Consequently, no generic audit program can readily be tailored to specific engagements. Therefore, the following discussion is necessarily general and may not be applicable to all types of performance audits.

Selecting the Audit Target

Audit organizations target for examination the programs for which the potential for cost savings or impact on citizens is the greatest—those in which expenditures or risk of inefficiencies, ineffectiveness, or noncompliance is substantial. Thus, large programs are more likely to be selected than small ones; risky programs more likely than safe ones. The extent to which risk is substantial is a matter of auditor judgment. However, the following are examples of factors that add to a program's exposure to risk:

- Recently installed and untested computer systems
- Past inefficiencies as revealed in previous audits
- Ineffective administration or poor results as reflected in reports to supervisory agencies or higher levels of management
- Opportunities or incentives for illegal activities
- Adverse press reports or tips from employees or other knowledgeable parties
- Known deficiencies in financial or performance management systems

Some audit organizations are required either by law or political necessity to perform audits at the request of members of legislative or other governing bodies to which they are responsible. The GAO, for example, reports to Congress and therefore responds to requests, if reasonable, from its members. The audit departments of municipalities may be similarly responsive to suggestions from members of city councils.

Perhaps most important, audit organizations may have to rely on intangible factors to detect programs of high risk. Experienced auditors tend to develop long-term relations with personnel of the departments that they have examined in the past. Often, they become as knowledgeable of a department's operations as its most senior managers. Further, like streetwise detectives, they develop an intuitive sense as to where the entity hides its skeletons.

[5] "The Forward-Looking Inspector General," *Partnership for Public Service* Report by Grant Thornton (2017).

Establishing Scope and Purpose

Auditors must begin their engagement by establishing the scope and purpose of the audit. Because an organization's programs and objectives may be ill defined and overlap, the auditors must delineate specifically the activities and outcomes to be addressed.

Auditors can best establish the scope and purpose of an engagement by taking a preliminary survey, the aim of which is to gain an understanding of the entity's mission, personnel, history, and operating procedures. The survey might include

- Interviews with key executives on what they see as the mission of the program and its strengths and weaknesses
- A review of the legislation that established the program
- A review of other laws, governing board resolutions, contracts, and administrative regulations to which the organization is subject
- An examination of reports from previous audits. These audits may have been performed by the same or a different audit organization. The importance of these reports as a source of information cannot be overemphasized. Often, they spell out deficiencies that existed in the past and provide a map that marks out the entity's problem areas
- A review of the entity's financial statements, as well as related schedules that indicate the sources and uses of entity resources
- A search for literature (such as the GASB studies on service efforts and accomplishments) that sets forth potentially applicable performance measures and standards of economy and efficiency
- A review of management controls
- A search for newspaper articles, press reports, transcripts of legislative hearings, and other literature that might provide insight into the organization's strengths and weaknesses
- Explicit consideration of the organization's vulnerabilities to fraud and mismanagement and the "things that might go wrong"

IN PRACTICE TARGETING SEEMINGLY TRIVIAL ACTIVITIES

Internal audit organization may—and indeed should—select certain types of activities for examination even though they involve relatively small dollar amounts and are unlikely to reveal any sort of inefficiency or mismanagement. Rather, they are activities about which anything untoward is likely to wind up on the front page of local newspapers.

Consider, for example, the travel and entertainment expenses of the several college chancellors who head the component units of a major state university system. Relative to the multi-billion-dollar budgets of the system, their travel and entertainment expenses are almost certain to be trivial. Yet it is almost certain that any excessively lavish outlays for such purposes that come to the attention of a reporter (perhaps by way of a disgruntled employee) will draw media attention. A system auditor who failed to bring them to the attention of the system president before they appeared in the newspaper may not have a long tenure in his position.

In the same vein, a shrewd university internal auditor would opt to target the athletic department well before the English department, irrespective of the size of their budgets. The public has far less interest in the latter than the former.

Discerning the Objectives of the Programs

If the objectives of a program are clearly spelled out, are outcome oriented, and are both quantifiable and measurable, then the program is readily auditable. The auditors have either to measure the outcomes themselves or to verify the measurements of management or others.

In Chapter 15, we stressed that well-defined operational objectives are central to sound management. Yet auditors cannot always expect managers to have established a clear statement—written or even oral—as to the intended outcomes of their programs. The absence of clearly articulated objectives should itself be a reportable audit finding. Nevertheless, if a program is to be audited for performance, then the auditors may themselves have to discern its objectives. Auditors can take several steps to determine a program's objectives:

- Examine the legislation that created the program or authorized funds for it; governing bodies can greatly facilitate audits by explicitly incorporating program objectives into their authorization or appropriation measures, but often they do not.
- Study the "legislative history" of the program, including committee reports, various versions of the authorization bills as they passed through the legislative process, statements of the bills' sponsors, and transcripts of committee and floor debates.
- Review budgets, especially if they are in a program format.
- Read internal performance reports and memos.
- Interview program managers and other key personnel.

Scheduling Disbursements or Other Populations

As in a financial engagement, auditors will likely have to rely on sampling; they may not be able to review all activities within a program and seldom can test all transactions.

To determine which activities and transactions to test, the auditors must be aware of the nature and amount of disbursements. Therefore, they should schedule all outlays, summarizing them as appropriate.

However, depending on the objective of the audit, disbursements might not be the proper population from which to select a test sample. For example, to test whether participants in a job-training program satisfied admissions criteria, the auditors would want to obtain a list of either program participants or program applicants.

Assessing Management Controls

It is no less important for auditors to obtain an understanding of relevant internal controls as part of a performance audit than it is as part of a financial audit. Relevant controls are those that encompass the policies and procedures intended to ensure that

- Programs meet their objectives
- The data regarding the programs are valid and reliable
- The organization has complied with all laws, regulations, and contractual provisions
- Resources are properly safeguarded

The specific controls to be assessed and the means of reviewing them will depend on the objectives of the audit and the nature of the program. Controls that ensure that a program meets its objectives may be of a different type from those intended to safeguard assets or ensure compliance. In general, however, the procedures that auditors follow to gain an understanding of financial controls are equally applicable to the other types of controls. They include

- Making inquiries of employees
- Flowcharting appropriate systems
- Reviewing and inspecting policy manuals and other documents
- Preparing and administering questionnaires

Preparing a Written Audit Plan

To satisfy the standard that work be adequately planned, auditors must prepare a written plan (i.e., an audit program) that sets forth audit goals, procedures, staff assignments, and anticipated reports. Based on the preliminary survey, review of controls, and other beginning steps, the plan should always be seen as tentative, subject to change as additional insights into the entity are obtained during the evidence-gathering process.

Gathering Evidence

The overall objectives of performance audits are typically twofold: to provide information on the extent to which a program achieved its objectives and to explain the reasons for its successes or failures (in addition, of course, to making recommendations as to how the program can be improved).

In gathering evidence on program outcomes, auditors must either make their own observations and measurements or rely on those of others—that is, either the auditee or third parties. If they intend to rely on those of others, then they must either test the data or ensure their reliability by other means.

The specific evidence to be gathered stems directly from the program's objectives. For example, if the objective of a computer-training program were to obtain employment for participants, then the auditors would need to obtain appropriate placement data. If it were to improve high school graduation rates, then they would require data on the percentage of students graduating.

The reasons why a program failed to achieve its objectives can generally be attributed to one of three fundamental causes. Taken together, the three imply the auditors' approach to identifying a program's shortcomings:

- ***Shortcoming:*** The program's policies and procedures were poorly designed and, therefore, even if properly executed, would not lead to success.
  - ***Auditor approach:*** The auditors should examine the policies and procedures, including controls, noting any logical or conceptual flaws.
- ***Shortcoming:*** The program's policies and procedures (including those for supervision and review), although properly designed, were not properly executed.
  - ***Auditor approach:*** The auditors should test the policies and procedures to gauge the extent to which they were being followed.
- ***Shortcoming:*** The program was inherently flawed owing to incorrect assumptions or failure to take into account significant factors that would affect its success. For example, a computer-training program may have been based on the assumption that if participants learned certain skills, they would be able to find employment. In fact, there may be no demand for those skills in the community served. Hence, even if the policies and procedures were properly executed, the program was destined to be unsuccessful.
  - ***Auditor approach:*** The auditors should identify the conditions that would have been necessary for its success and assess whether they were satisfied.

The example below is illustrative of the auditors' approach to evidence gathering.

In obtaining and assessing evidence, auditors must document their procedures and findings. By the time the audit is completed, every assertion in the auditors' report should be backed by working papers setting forth the underlying evidence. Auditors should always assume that any unfavorable determinations will be challenged by the managers accountable for them. Therefore, they must be certain their working papers, when subjected to the most rigorous (and hostile) of analysis, can withstand assault.

Example

Evidence Gathering

A northwest city is becoming a center for the manufacture of silicon chips and other computer-related products. To encourage unemployed young adults (ages 20–30) to undertake technical training in skills needed by local businesses (as well as firms that it would like to attract), the city has established a $50 million revolving loan fund. The fund is used to make low-interest loans of up to $60,000 to eligible candidates so that they can enroll in suitable programs offered by local community colleges and proprietary schools. The loans are repayable over five years, starting when the candidate completes the program. The city makes approximately 150 loans per year. The loan program, which is administered by a specially created educational loan authority, is now in its sixth year of operation.

An audit team assigned to review the loan program has completed its preliminary survey and the other basic steps necessary to prepare an audit plan. It has determined that the program's operating policies and procedures (e.g., qualifications for loan recipients) are consistent with its objectives.

The following are examples of the audit procedures that the audit team should consider:

1. Obtain from the loan authority a schedule indicating all loans made during the period.
2. Select a sample of loans and obtain the recipient's loan file for each.
   a. Verify that the recipient met all specified qualifications and that all appropriate approval guidelines were followed.
   b. Verify that the file contains documents, such as school transcripts, showing that the candidate enrolled in an approved program and made required progress.
   c. Verify the loan recipient's payment history, ensuring that the authority properly pursued all delinquencies.
   d. Make certain that the file contains up-to-date records of the loan recipient's employment history subsequent to completing the training program. Confirm its accuracy by corresponding with the employers.
3. Obtain the authority's summary statistics and supporting schedules as to loans made, recipients successfully completing approved training programs, and participant employment experience.
   a. Reconcile the supporting schedules to the summary statistics.
   b. Test the accuracy of the supporting schedules by tracing a sample of the information on the schedule to the loan files of individual recipients.

Reporting the Results of the Audit

The GAO reporting standards specify that auditors should prepare timely written reports of each engagement. Auditors' reports on financial statement engagements generally constitute only a few standardized paragraphs in which the auditors explain the scope and nature of their engagement and attest to information included in the statements.[6] Those on performance audits, however, set forth data and findings as generated by the auditors, not merely the auditors' opinion on the assertions of others. Therefore, the auditors' reports are often 50–100 pages long.

Per the GAO standards, the reports should include:

- An explanation of the audit's objectives and of its scope and methodology.
- The significant auditing findings and the auditors' conclusions. The findings should relate to the objectives of the engagement. The report should indicate not only the quantitative measures of performance but also, if the program did not meet expectations, the reasons why. It should back any general assertions with specific examples. As noted by the GAO,

[6] If the audit falls within the jurisdiction of the PCAOB, the audit report must also include a description of "critical audit matters" that relate to accounts or disclosures that are material to the financial statements and that may involve especially challenging, subjective, or complex auditor judgments.

IN PRACTICE FINDINGS MUST RELATE TO PROGRAM OBJECTIVES

Upon auditing a federal housing program, the GAO reported that the agency in charge failed to fulfill the program's objectives. The purpose of the program, as established by Congress, was to prevent "middle-class" housing from deteriorating into slums. One aspect of the program required the agency to lend funds to homeowners so that they could improve their properties and ensure that they were in compliance with building codes. The GAO charged that the agency directed program funds to areas that were in far worse condition than permitted by the criteria specified in the enabling legislation.

A program official was critical of the GAO report. He claimed that the areas that his department focused on were in far greater need of assistance than those that satisfied the legislative criteria. "The auditors are just a bunch of bean counters," he said. "They know nothing about the realities of housing."

The GAO auditors rejected the program official's complaints. If the official thinks that the program was misguided and that resources could have been better spent otherwise, they said, he should take his complaint to Congress. "It's our job to inform the members of Congress that the program, as they established it, is not achieving its goals."

- Recommendations as to how to correct problems and improve operations. To be most useful, audits should be as much concerned with the future as with the past. They should be at least as constructive as they are critical.
- An indication of all significant instances of illegal acts or noncompliance with regulations and contractual provisions.
- A description of any significant deficiencies in management controls.

The GAO standards also require that the auditors include in the report the views of officials responsible for the program as to the auditors' conclusions and recommendations. To enable them to comment, the auditors should present the officials with a preliminary version of the report and solicit their written response as to why they agree or disagree with the report and what corrective measures, if any, they plan.

If the auditors agree that the objections of the officials are valid, then they can modify their report before issuing a final version. However, if the auditors do not believe that the officials' concerns are legitimate, they can include in their report their reasons why they believe they are invalid and, in effect, have the last word.

Per the GAO standards, reports on governmental performance audits, like those on governmental financial audits, should be made public, unless their distribution is limited by law or regulation. Some government agencies, such as the GAO, now promote wide distribution of their reports by making them available on the Internet.[7]

Although it is difficult to predict the future of accounting and auditing, it is almost certain that performance auditing will play an increasingly prominent role. As both governments and not-for-profits place greater emphasis on achieving their objectives, it is inevitable that increasing attention will be paid to reports as to the extent that they accomplished what was expected of them.

HOW HAVE THE SINGLE AUDIT ACT AND OTHER PRONOUNCEMENTS INFLUENCED AUDITING?

In the 1960s, the federal government greatly increased the number, funding, and complexity of its assistance programs. These programs, which were directed to a wide range of activities including education, health and welfare, job training, and transportation, were typically funded by the federal government but administered by the states. However, the federal agencies in charge of the programs were responsible for auditing them.

As a result of congressional disclosures of severe deficiencies in federal audit practices, the **Office of Management and Budget (OMB)** urged that federal agencies rely more on CPA

[7] The GAO's home page is at www.gao.gov/.

firms and other independent auditors than on their own "in-house" auditors. Nevertheless, federal agencies were interested mainly in whether grant recipients complied with the applicable laws, regulations, and grant provisions. Independent auditors, adhering to then-current standards, focused on financial statements and thereby did not provide the compliance assurances needed by the agencies. Hence, the agencies continued to perform their own audits.

Further, many grant recipients, especially local governments, received funds from several federal agencies and were subject to audits from each. Although each audit team directed its attention primarily to the grants from its own agency, they all had to review common books and records, accounting systems, and internal controls. The result was both costly duplication of audit effort and inadequate audit coverage of the entity as a whole.

In 1979, the OMB issued a directive calling for organization-wide **single audits** to be performed by CPAs or other independent auditors.[8] The directive did not preclude federal agencies from conducting their own examinations but instructed them to build on the independent audits.

To give legislative sanction to the directive, Congress enacted the **Single Audit Act of 1984**. Amended in 1996 to make it easier to administer and supplemented by periodic updates of OMB regulations, the act now applies to both direct and indirect recipients of federal assistance and requires that organizations expending more than $750,000 in federal assistance under more than one program be subject to a single audit.

The objectives of a single audit are to ensure that

- The financial statements of the entity as a whole can be relied on
- The entity is adhering to the common set of federal laws and regulations that apply to all recipients of federal aid
- The entity is satisfying the laws, regulations, and provisions that apply to each specific federal award

Whereas prior to the act a recipient of federal funds had to submit audit reports to each agency from which it received funds, now a recipient has to deal with only a single agency. That agency, referred to as the **cognizant agency**, is responsible for ensuring that all audit standards are met and for coordinating the special audit requirements of each of the individual agencies providing funds. The cognizant agency is typically the agency that provides the greatest portion of federal funds to the recipient.

The OMB is primarily responsible for administering the Single Audit Act. It issues circulars that provide detailed guidance on how the single audit is to be performed. Periodically updated, they address matters such as the nature and scope of internal control reviews, the extent of compliance testing, and the form and content of reports. The main circular that is of interest to auditors of both governments and not-for-profit entities receiving federal assistance is A-133, *Audits of States, Local Governments, and Non-Profit Organizations* (2003). A "Compliance Supplement" to A-133 (updated more frequently than A-133) provides even more detailed and specific rules and regulations.

The Single Audit Act specifies that single audits be conducted in accord with the GAO's *Government Auditing Standards*. However, it requires that federal recipients be subject only to financial audits, not to performance audits. Therefore, the sections of *Government Auditing Standards* on performance audits need not be applied.

To provide additional guidance on single and other government-related audits, the AICPA issued Statement on Auditing Standards (SAS) No. 74, *Compliance Auditing Considerations in Audits of Governmental Entities and Other Recipients of Governmental Financial Assistance*. By issuing this statement, the AICPA established that CPAs who conduct audits of financial assistance but fail to meet the federal audit requirements also fail to adhere to AICPA standards. More recently (2009), it issued SAS 117, *Compliance Audits*, as well as numerous practice aids.

[8] Attachment P, "Audit Requirements" to OMB Circular A-102, *Uniform Administrative Requirements for Grants-in-Aid to State and Local Governments*.

WHAT APPROACH DO AUDITORS TAKE IN PERFORMING SINGLE AUDITS?

A single audit has two main components:

- An audit of the financial statements conducted under GAGAS
- An audit of federal financial awards

Per Circular A-133, these two types of audits should culminate in at least four types of reports (which are commented on in greater detail in the following section):

- Opinions on whether the financial statements are fairly presented in accord with GAAP and on whether a schedule of expenditures of federal awards is fairly presented
- A report on compliance and on internal controls relating to the financial statements
- An opinion on whether the organization complied with the requirements of major programs
- A schedule of findings and questioned costs. **Questioned costs** are those that are not subject to federal reimbursement because they are in violation of laws or provisions pertaining to a grant, are not supported by adequate documentation, or appear to be unreasonable or imprudent

Although single audits incorporate a conventional financial audit, they are characterized by their focus on compliance with laws and requirements applicable to federally funded programs. Therefore, this section on single audits will focus mainly on the compliance component of single audits.

IDENTIFYING MAJOR PROGRAMS: A RISK-BASED APPROACH

The Single Audit Act distinguishes between major and nonmajor programs and requires a substantially higher level of auditing of major programs. Circular A-133 directs that in distinguishing between major and nonmajor programs, auditors focus on potential losses owing to noncompliance. As a general rule, major programs are those that make up a relatively large proportion of the total federal awards received by an entity and for which there is a high risk of noncompliance.

To determine whether a program is relatively large, the auditor must apply a sliding scale based on the percentage that federal funds received by the program bears to total federal funds received by the entire entity. If an entity receives less than $100 million in federal awards, then any program on which it expends more than 3 percent of the total would be considered large. On the other hand, if it receives more than $10 billion in federal awards, then only programs on which it expends more than 0.15 percent of the total would be considered large.

To determine whether a program is high risk, auditors must exercise professional judgment. Examples of factors that would point to a high risk of noncompliance include

- Weakness in internal controls over federal programs, taking into account competence and experience of personnel, systems for recording transactions, and effectiveness of management oversight
- Significant portions of federal funds being passed through to subrecipients without effective systems of monitoring whether subrecipients comply with applicable laws and grant requirements
- Newly installed computer systems that have not been adequately tested
- Absence of recent audits
- Complex compliance requirements
- Relatively new program

OMB Circular A-133 provides a detailed set of guidelines on how size and risk must be combined to establish whether a program is major and thereby subject to comprehensive auditing.

KEY PROCEDURES

Once the auditors have identified the major programs, their audit procedures follow a pattern similar in many respects to that of a financial engagement.

- ***Identify the applicable compliance requirements.*** **Compliance requirements** include those that are specific to the program itself and those that are applicable to all federal awards. The compliance supplement to OMB Circular A-133 as revised in 2018 describes 12 types of requirements that apply to all federal awards. These are presented in Table 15-2. Tests for compliance with these general requirements may seem far afield from conventional audit procedures. In practice, however, auditors are not expected to assume the role of detectives or law-enforcement investigators, and their tests may be comparable to those used to assess internal and administrative controls. For example, with regard to a proscribed activity such as political lobbying, auditors might examine personnel and payroll records to identify employees whose responsibilities or activities include partisan political activity. They would then review the accounts to make certain that neither the salaries of these employees

TABLE 15-2 General Compliance Requirements for Federal Programs

Activities allowed or unallowed. Federal funds must be used only for activities that are within the scope of the grant or contract; they must not be used for activities that are specifically prohibited by the grant, contract, or laws and regulations.

Allowable costs/cost principles. Entities that receive federal funds may be reimbursed only for certain allowable costs (e.g., those that are reasonable and necessary for the performance and administration of the award); they may not be reimbursed for certain explicitly proscribed costs (e.g., those for political activities). Moreover, in calculating allowable costs, federal funds recipients must follow accounting principles that are detailed in various Office of Management and Budget (OMB) circulars directed to cost accounting.

Cash management. Per the Federal Cash Management Improvement Act, recipients of federal funds must maintain systems that minimize the time between the receipt and the disbursements of cash.

Eligibility. Each federal program has its own unique requirements as to parties that are eligible to participate in the program or to receive program benefits.

Equipment and real property management. Entities that acquire equipment and real estate with federal funds must maintain proper inventory records, adequately maintain and safeguard the property, and properly sell or dispose of it.

Matching level of effort and earmarking. Under certain programs, participants must match federal funds received with their own funds or must provide a level of service specified in the grant or contract. Under others, a portion of the funds must be earmarked for (i.e., directed to) specified activities or subrecipients.

Period of availability of performance. Federal awards usually specify the time period during which the funds must be used. Only costs incurred during that period may be charged against the award.

Procurement, suspension, and debarment. Federal funds recipients must adhere to federal purchasing guidelines that are spelled out in various OMB circulars. Moreover, they are prohibited from procuring goods or services from vendors that have been suspended or debarred from contracting with the federal government.

Program income. Program income must be deducted from allowable costs or accounted for in other ways permitted by the federal government. Program income is revenue that an award recipient generates as a direct result of the grant. It would include, for example, fees or charges for services performed and rents received from property acquired with federal funds.

Reporting. Federal funds recipients must periodically report, using standard OMB-authorized forms, the status of funds received and disbursed.

Subrecipient monitoring. An award recipient that passes funds through to other entities may be responsible for monitoring the subrecipients to ensure that they adhere to applicable federal laws and regulations.

Special tests and provisions. Each program has unique provisions and thereby requires auditors to perform special audit procedures. These provisions and tests are found in the laws, regulations, and contract or grant agreements pertaining to the program.

Source: Adapted from OMB Circular A-133 *Compliance Supplement*, 2018.

nor related costs were improperly charged to a federally assisted program. The specific compliance requirements are set forth in the rules and regulations of each federal program or contract. In general, they relate to matters such as

- The individuals or groups that are eligible to participate in the program or to receive financial assistance
- The types of goods or services that may be acquired
- The percentage of its own funds that an entity must contribute to a program
- Any special reports that the organization must submit to the sponsoring agency

- ***Plan the engagement.*** The auditors must develop a strategy to understand the events, transactions, and practices that will have a significant impact on compliance and to ensure that their tests of transactions and other procedures are sufficient to detect material noncompliance. In planning their engagement, auditors must give paramount consideration to the various risks associated with an audit. These include
  - ***Inherent risk.*** The risk that material noncompliance could occur assuming that no internal controls have been established to prevent it
  - ***Control risk.*** The risk that material noncompliance that could occur would not be prevented by the entity's internal controls
  - ***Fraud risk.*** The risk that intentional material noncompliance could occur
  - ***Detection risk.*** The risk that the auditors will be unable to detect noncompliance that does occur

- ***Assess the internal control structure related to compliance requirements.*** Circular A-133 explicitly requires the auditor to assess, test, and report on the controls over compliance requirements. The auditor's tests of the controls should be adequate to ensure a low level of control risk (e.g., the risk that the internal controls fail to prevent noncompliance).

- ***Obtain sufficient evidence.*** Auditors must test transactions and perform other audit procedures to determine whether the entity has complied with relevant requirements. The compliance supplement suggests several audit procedures that can form the basis of an audit program. However, every entity is unique, and, therefore, the tests must be custom-tailored to the engagement at hand. Needless to say, auditors are not expected to test every transaction. They must rely on the same type of statistical sampling techniques that they do in conventional financial audits.

- ***Consider subsequent events.*** Auditors must take into account relevant information that comes to their attention after the end of the audit period but before they issue their report. This information is typically contained in reports of regulatory agencies or other auditors that identify instances of noncompliance.

- ***Evaluate and report on noncompliance.*** Having detected instances of noncompliance (referred to as "findings"), auditors must assess how (and to whom) they will report the violations and how the instances of noncompliance will influence the opinions that they must express. Compliance violations may require that the entity return funds to the granting agencies and may result in fines and other financial penalties. Hence, they are likely to have an impact on the auditors' opinion not only on compliance but also on the financial statements.

- ***Perform follow-up procedures.*** Circular A-133 requires auditors to follow up on findings and recommendations from both their current audit and previous audits (even if by other auditors). Correspondingly, it requires the auditee to develop a plan for appropriate corrective actions. To follow up on audit findings and recommendations, auditors should discuss with management the measures they have taken, review decisions of the federal agencies with respect to actions they have taken, and test transactions of the type that previously resulted in noncompliance.

These procedures are by no means discrete; they are intertwined. The auditors' study of the entity's internal controls, for example, strongly influences their assessment of risks and thereby affects the extent of testing. At the same time, however, the results of transaction tests bear heavily on the auditors' evaluation of internal controls.

WHAT REPORTS RESULT FROM SINGLE AUDITS?

As noted in the previous section, auditors are expected to produce four types of reports as part of their single audit.

OPINION ON THE FINANCIAL STATEMENTS AND ON THE SCHEDULE OF EXPENDITURES OF FEDERAL AWARDS

Auditors may combine in a single report their opinions on the basic financial statements and the schedule of expenditures of federal awards. The section of the report pertaining to the financial statements is that required for any audit conducted in accord with *Government Auditing Standards* (i.e., one that is not necessarily a single audit). It includes a brief description of the audit work and the standard opinion as to whether the information in the statements is fairly presented.

The **Schedule of Expenditures of Federal Awards** is a listing of total expenditures made by the organization under each federal program from which it received funding. Its main purpose is to enable the federal grantor agencies to coordinate their audit efforts and ensure adequate audit coverage. Per relevant OMB directives, the schedule must identify each program by its number as listed in the Catalog of Federal Domestic Assistance (CFDA). It must include expenditures to be reimbursed both directly from the federal government and indirectly through other governments (i.e., "pass-through" awards). The schedule should indicate whether programs are major or nonmajor and may include optional information as to matching contributions, the total amount of the program awards, and the time periods that are covered by them. Table 15-3 illustrates a Schedule of Expenditures of Federal Awards as might have been prepared by a not-for-profit organization that received assistance from three federal agencies.

TABLE 15-3 **Urban Assistance Federation**

Schedule of Expenditures of Federal Awards for Year Ended December 31, 2019

Grantor/Pass-Through Grantor/Program Title	Federal Catalog of Federal Domestic Assistance (CFDA) Number	Grant Award Number	Expenditures
U.S. Department of Housing and Urban Development			
Passed through City Housing Department			
Community Development Block Grant Programs Emergency Home Repair 11/07/19–10/31/20	15.649*	I C420.1	$487,198
U.S. Department of Labor			
Passed through the State Employment Commission	18.927*	1-027-70	152,188
Willard-Feyser 7(b) Program 1/1/19–2/28/20			
Passed through the County Private Industry Council	18.971*	II A36.98	38,899
Project Exceed (III-A) 5/1/19–9/30/20			
U.S. Department of Education			
Passed through the State Commission on Alcohol and Drug Abuse			
Drug Free Schools and Communities			
9/1/18–8/31/19	92.604*	12-016-841	87,625
9/1/19–8/31/20	92.604*	12-016-941	73,357
Total Federal Awards			$839,267

*Denotes a major program.

The auditors' responsibility for this schedule is to ensure that the information presented is materially complete and accurate and that the expenditures are properly categorized. In their report the auditors should express an opinion on whether the information in the schedule is fairly stated in relation to the basic statements taken as a whole.

REPORT ON COMPLIANCE AND ON INTERNAL CONTROL OVER FINANCIAL REPORTING

The report on compliance and on internal control over financial reporting, like the opinion on the financial statements, is directed toward the basic financial statements rather than the laws and provisions pertaining to federal awards. That is, it focuses on internal controls and on compliance with provisions of laws, regulations, contracts, or grant agreements that have a material effect on the financial statements. It is based on the audit requirements of *Government Auditing Standards* rather than those of Circular A-133.

Per *Government Auditing Standards*, the auditors must issue this report, on internal control and compliance regardless of whether or not they identify internal control deficiencies or instances of noncompliance. They should describe (either in the same report that they express an opinion on the financial statements or in one or more separate reports) the scope of their testing and should indicate whether the tests performed were sufficient to support opinions on the effectiveness of internal control and on compliance.

REPORT ON COMPLIANCE WITH REQUIREMENTS OF MAJOR PROGRAMS

The report on compliance with major program requirements, along with the schedule of findings and questioned costs, is the centerpiece of the Circular A-133 provisions. In this report the auditors should state that they have audited the entity's compliance with the requirements that are applicable to each of its major programs and explain briefly the nature of their examination. They should then express an opinion on whether the auditee complied "in all material respects" with those requirements. They should define what is meant by "significant deficiencies," and if the auditors detected any, they should indicate whether they were material. They should then refer the reader to the schedule of findings and questioned costs in which these deficiencies would be described.

SCHEDULE OF FINDINGS AND QUESTIONED COSTS

The schedule of findings and questioned costs is perhaps the most distinctive—and often the most informative—of the auditors' reports. In the first section of this report, the auditors should first summarize the results of their audit. They should indicate, for example, the type of opinions (e.g., qualified, adverse) they expressed on the financial statements and on compliance with major programs and whether the audit disclosed material weaknesses in internal control.

In the second section, the auditors should describe in detail any significant deficiencies relating to the *financial statements*. These would include weaknesses in internal controls, material violations of the provisions of contract or grant agreements, and instances of fraud and illegal acts. In presenting this information, however, the auditors must put it into perspective, noting, for example, the number of questioned transactions and their dollar value in relation to the entire universe of transactions.

In the third section, the auditors should set forth their findings pertaining to the major programs. These include

- Significant deficiencies in internal control
- Material noncompliance with provisions of laws, regulations, contracts, or grant agreements
- Known questioned costs that are above a specified amount (currently $25,000)
- The circumstances as to why the auditors' report on compliance is other than unqualified
- Instances of known fraud

The report should be forward-looking in that it should be in sufficient detail to allow the audited entity to prepare a plan of corrective action. It should also include the auditors' recommendations on how the violations could be prevented in the future.

WHAT UNIQUE ETHICAL ISSUES DO GOVERNMENTAL AND NOT-FOR-PROFIT ACCOUNTING AND AUDITING PRESENT?

Many, if not most, business schools require a course that focuses, at least in part, on professional ethics. Indeed most courses in auditing key on "ethics" as established by the AICPA's Code of Conduct. This section of the text is not intended to duplicate the materials ordinarily addressed in auditing courses—almost all of which are relevant to CPAs carrying out independent audits of governments and not-for-profit organizations. Neither is it intended to resolve any particular ethical issues. Instead, its purposes are to highlight the characteristics of governments that may justify a special perspective on ethical questions, to set forth an approach to resolving ethical dilemmas (one not unique to the governmental environment), and to illustrate how that approach can be applied to ethical dilemmas. The end-of-chapter material includes 10 mini-cases that are illustrative of "real-world" ethical predicaments faced by government as well as not-for-profit accountants and auditors.

DETERMINING RIGHT FROM WRONG

Discussions of ethics as they apply to accountants are often made more complex—as well as more controversial—by the difficulties of establishing what is right and wrong, what is ethical and unethical. In fact, many issues faced by government accountants and other finance managers are less questions of "ethics" than they are of "values." Values are the principles, standards, and qualities considered desirable or worthwhile and as such are the foundation of ethics. Whereas ethics is concerned with doing the right thing, values define what is the right thing. Inasmuch as values are often established by religion or culture, we typically are reluctant to make judgments regarding the values of others. Accordingly, we often take a legalistic view as to what constitutes unethical behavior, restricting it to violations of laws, policies, or accepted organizational practices or standards rather than extending it to infringements of our own individual systems of values. Consider a wealthy family that spends its fortune exclusively on material possessions. It never donates a dollar to charity. Few would accuse the family of acting unethically by choosing to spend its wealth as it sees fit. Yet few would respect such a family or hold its values in high regard. Similarly, and of more relevance to accountants, some believe it is perfectly legitimate to structure a transaction so that it is in accordance with either the letter of the law or GAAP even though it may be in violation of its spirit. Thus, they would be completely comfortable with configuring a borrowing transaction as a lease agreement if doing so would be a legally acceptable means of avoiding debt limitations or voter approvals. Others, by contrast, see the law as the starting, not the ending, point of virtue. They would not countenance the lease transaction as long as it is intended to circumvent what would otherwise be illegal.

CHARACTERISTICS OF GOVERNMENTS THAT JUSTIFY A UNIQUE PERSPECTIVE ON ETHICAL QUESTIONS

Governments (and to a lesser extent many not-for-profits) have characteristics that present their employees with ethical decisions different from those faced by employees of businesses. These include the following:

- ***Public expectations.*** The public holds employees of governments to a higher standard of conduct than those of businesses. Whereas it may accept that private companies—and hence, their employees—act in their own self-interest, it expects government employees to put the welfare of the public above that of themselves.

- ***Stewards of public funds.*** Government accountants are guardians of public funds and are accountable to the public on how they use them. Although corporate managers are accountable to stockholders, the public has far more rigorous standards than investors of what constitutes proper use of resources and is far less tolerant of frivolous expenditures. For example, investors may tolerate lavish entertainment, personal use of company jets, and palatial offices as acceptable management perks. The public, however, permits few government officials the same luxuries.
- ***Activities carried out in open view.*** Virtually all government activities are carried out in broad daylight. Public officials are answerable to the public for almost all their actions. Under federal and state "open records" and "freedom of information" statutes, relatively few types of documents, not even internal memos and correspondence, are immune from public scrutiny. "No comment—that's proprietary information," in response to a reporter's question may be acceptable from corporate executives, but it is seldom countenanced from government officials.
- ***Special powers.*** Governments have powers that businesses do not. For example, they may compel citizens to reveal to them personal information, such as earnings and holdings of personal property. Moreover, many citizens see as legitimate requests for data from government officials that they would view with suspicion if they came from private businesses. Therefore, government officials have a particular obligation to maintain the confidentiality of information that is not in the public domain and not to exceed the limits of their authority in their dealings with the public.
- ***Conflicting loyalties.*** Government workers are not only government employees but also citizens to whom the government is accountable. Government decisions may be made in a highly charged political atmosphere and may involve the most basic of human values. The government may be led by officials of a political party different from that of an individual employee. Hence, individual employees may be faced with a conflict between loyalty to their organization and their superiors and to their own political and moral values.

ANALYZING ETHICAL DILEMMAS

A *dilemma*, by definition, is a situation that requires a choice between two equally balanced alternatives—a predicament that seemingly defies a satisfactory solution. Few ethical dilemmas can be resolved without an individual selecting among, or compromising between, competing ethical values. There is almost never a single "correct" course of action. Nevertheless, by identifying and analyzing the factors relevant to the issue at hand, the individual can better develop available options and understand their consequences.

The following questions are indicative of an approach (merely one of several possibilities) that can be taken to resolve ethical dilemmas:

1. What are the relevant facts? (Although many situations are seemingly complex, there may be only a small number of facts that are genuinely germane.)
2. Who are the major parties affected, and what are their interests in how the dilemma is resolved?
3. What are the ethical values that are in question? How do they rank in importance?
   Examples of these values include
   - Honesty and integrity
   - Loyalty and obligations to colleagues
   - Responsibilities to family
   - Obligation to make full and fair disclosures to appropriate parties
   - Loyalty and other obligations to one's employer
   - Responsibilities as a citizen
   - Pursuit of excellence

4. What are the alternative courses of action?
5. What are the consequences of each course of action? Which values would have to be sacrificed or compromised?

The following example illustrates how these questions may be applied to a specific ethical dilemma.

Example

Ethical Dilemma

James Klavan is a city's assistant comptroller. Within the last year, the comptroller established an enterprise fund to account for the operation of the city's golf course. Previously, the course had been accounted for in the general fund. GAAP permits government flexibility as to the types of funds in which it may account for activities financed by user charges. There is no question that under those principles, golf course operations may be accounted for in either a governmental fund or an enterprise fund. The main reason for the change was to shift expenses out of the general fund and thereby help to eliminate a general fund deficit. Were it not for the accounting change, the general fund deficit would have to be offset by increased taxes or reductions in services. However, if the reasons for the change were made public, city officials would unquestionably be charged by political opponents with fiscal gimmickry.

The city comptroller was approached by a reporter covering the publication of the city's annual report. Owing to time constraints, the comptroller referred him to Klavan, his assistant. In the course of an interview, the reporter (who couldn't distinguish a debit from a credit) asked Klavan to explain the change and indicate its significance. Klavan is uncertain how to respond.

1. Relevant facts
   - **a.** The comptroller established an enterprise fund to reduce the reported general fund deficit.
   - **b.** Klavan is aware of the reason for the change and is asked by a reporter for an explanation of its significance.
   - **c.** Although the change is permissible under GAAP, it was made to eliminate a general fund deficit and thereby avert either increases in taxes or reductions in services.
   - **d.** Disclosure of the true reason for the change would embarrass both Klavan's immediate superior and the city administration.
2. Major parties affected (other than Klavan)
   - **a.** The comptroller, who stands to be embarrassed if the reason for the change were made public
   - **b.** The reporter, who presumably expects a full and fair explanation of the change
   - **c.** The citizenry, who might be misled by the change (yet might nevertheless support it if it would avert a tax increase or service reduction)
3. Ethical values in conflict
   - **a.** Loyalty to colleagues and employer (both the comptroller and the city administration)
   - **b.** Honesty (to reporter)
   - **c.** Obligation to make full and fair disclosures to appropriate parties
   - **d.** Responsibilities as a citizen (either to prevent the city from misleading its citizens or, by contrast, to facilitate a means of averting tax increases)
4. Possible courses of action available to Klavan
   - **a.** Explain the change to the reporter, but obfuscate the reason for it.
   - **b.** Explain the change and reveal the underlying reason for it.
   - **c.** Delay responding to the reporter, and tell the comptroller that he will not meet with the reporter unless the comptroller explicitly gives him permission to reveal the reason for the change.

5. Consequences of actions
   a. If Klavan explains the change to the reporter without revealing the reasons for it, he will not be providing full disclosure and will thereby be intentionally misleading. Moreover, he will be allowing his employer (both the comptroller and the city administration) to deceive the citizenry.
   b. If he explains the change and reveals the underlying reason for it, he will embarrass both the comptroller and the city (and thereby place his career with the city at risk).
   c. If he confronts the comptroller and indicates that he will meet with the reporter only if granted permission to reveal the underlying reason for the change, then he will place the comptroller in an uncomfortable position (by suggesting that the comptroller is being deceitful) and thereby jeopardize his relationship with the comptroller and consequently his career with the city.

To be sure, there may be other courses of action available to Klavan. Indeed, the key to resolving most ethical dilemmas is to develop options beyond those that are obvious. There are, unfortunately, no "textbook" solutions.

SUMMARY

In the area of government and not-for-profit auditing, the influence of the federal government has been paramount. It has had its impact mainly through the GAO's Yellow Book, *Government Auditing Standards*, and through the Single Audit Act.

The Yellow Book establishes generally accepted government auditing standards (GAGAS), which, owing to the Single Audit Act, must now be adhered to in virtually all audits of both governments and not-for-profit organizations that receive federal financial assistance. Although the standards cover both financial statement audits and performance audits, the Single Audit Act requires only financial audits.

The primary difference between financial audits as carried out in a government or not-for-profit entity, as opposed to a business, is the broader view of accountability that must be taken in government audits. Thus, government auditors are more concerned with compliance with laws, regulations, and contracts, with waste and abuse and with internal controls.

Performance audits differ in concept from financial audits in that the auditors do not merely *attest* to assertions of management. Rather, they make their own assessments as to the extent that an entity or program has achieved its objectives. The key to carrying out a performance audit (consistent with the theme of the previous chapter) is in identifying the operational objectives of the target program or activity. If these objectives are quantifiable and measurable, then the auditors have either to make the appropriate measurements or to verify those of others. Hence, performance audits can be as objective as traditional financial engagements.

As emphasized throughout this text, both governments and not-for-profits have objectives other than profit maximization. Accordingly, the conventional operating statements that highlight revenues and expenditures provide little indication of how well an entity is fulfilling its mission. These statements should be supplemented by reports on service efforts and accomplishments that focus on the entity's actual objectives. Correspondingly, audits that merely attest to the fairness of the conventional statements are of only limited value to the constituents of the entity. Performance audits are therefore an important supplement to conventional financial audits. They are unquestionably the wave of the future.

Legislative actions, now codified in the Single Audit Act, direct that recipients of federal aid be subject to a single independent financial audit even though they may receive funds from many agencies. Single audits comprise two elements: an audit of financial statements, conducted in accord with *Government Auditing Standards*, and an audit of federal financial awards that follows the provisions of OMB Circular A-133.

The Single Audit Act requires that in their audits of federal financial awards, the auditors take a risk-based approach by which they devote their audit effort mainly to major, as opposed to nonmajor, programs. Major programs are those that make up a relatively large proportion of the total federal awards received by the entity and for which there is a high risk of noncompliance. Moreover, in planning their engagement, the auditors must take into account the various audit risks that they face (i.e., inherent risk, control risk, fraud risk, and detection risk).

An audit of federal financial awards should ensure that the entity has complied not only with applicable laws and regulations but also with both general and program-specific provisions. The general requirements, of which there are 12, are common to all federal awards. These include provisions that promote effective cash management, ensure that entities are reimbursed only for allowable costs, and prohibit the use of federal funds to engage in political activity.

The program-specific provisions are typically directed to issues of eligibility, types of goods or services that may be acquired with federal funds, and the percentage of federal funds that the entity itself must match.

The single audit is expected to culminate in four reports: (1) an opinion on the financial statements and the schedule of expenditures of federal awards; (2) a report on compliance and on internal control over financial reporting; (3) a report on compliance with requirements of major programs; and (4) a schedule of findings and questioned costs.

Although government accountants and auditors face ethical dilemmas similar to those in the private sector, they must resolve them in face of the following unique characteristics of government employees: public expectations, status as guardians of public funds, the open environment in which they function, special powers they may have, and conflicting loyalties. Unfortunately, there are no textbook answers to ethical problems; the key to a satisfactory resolution is the development of options beyond the obvious.

KEY TERMS IN THIS CHAPTER

attest 657
attestation engagements 659
audit 657
cognizant agency 671
compliance requirements 673
Comptroller General of the United States 657
financial audits 658
Government Accountability Office (GAO) 656
Government Auditing Standards 657
generally accepted government auditing standards (GAGAS) 658
Green Book 662
inspectors general 657
Office of Management and Budget (OMB) 670
operational audits 659
performance audits 659
Public Company Accounting Oversight Board (PCAOB) 658
questioned costs 672
Schedule of Expenditures of Federal Awards 675
Single Audit Act of 1984 671
single audits 671
Yellow Book 657

EXERCISE FOR REVIEW AND SELF-STUDY

You are the partner of the CPA firm that has been engaged to perform the annual audit of the Euless School District. The district receives approximately $1.5 million per year in federal assistance. This includes $500,000 in annual grants to conduct an experimental high school science enrichment program. The program has now been in existence for three years.

1. You assign one of the firm's managers to be in charge of the audit's field work. The manager recently returned from a two-week professional education course in estate and gift taxation. She took the course to satisfy her state's biannual 80-hour CPE requirement. She took no other CPE courses in the past two years. Why might her appointment be in violation of Government Auditing Standards?

2. The audit manager who was eventually assigned to the engagement inquired as to whether the firm had on hand the most recent version of Circular A-133 and its Compliance Supplement. What are these documents, and why are they likely to be relevant to the financial audit of a local independent school district?

3. Soon after the audit staff began the engagement, the school district's chief financial officer called to complain that the auditors were making inquiries of the district's employees as to the political activities of district administrators. These matters, he asserted, were clearly beyond the scope of a financial engagement. How would you respond to his objection?

4. After your firm completed the financial audit of the district, the school board requested that it conduct a performance audit of the science enrichment program. In what critical way would the performance audit differ conceptually from the financial engagement?

5. Suppose the objectives of the program were not spelled out in the federal legislation that authorized the program. Moreover, the school district had never prepared a written "statement of objectives." What steps would you take to establish the program's objectives?

6. Suppose you are able to establish that a primary objective of the program is to encourage students to enter vocational fields related to science. The grant funds may be used to pay for teachers' training, curriculum development projects, equipment and texts, and extracurricular activities related to science.
   a. What would be the purpose of preparing a schedule showing how the grant funds were disbursed?
   b. How would you recommend the auditors gain an understanding of the internal controls over program expenditures?
   c. Inasmuch as the program has been in existence for only three years, how might you assess whether the program has fulfilled its objective?

QUESTIONS FOR REVIEW AND DISCUSSION

1. What is the Yellow Book, and why has it influenced audits both of state and local governments and of not-for-profit organizations?

2. In what significant way do financial audits in government and not-for-profit organizations differ from those carried on in businesses?

3. The State Auditor of Missouri is an elected official. In auditing the financial statements of the University of Missouri, what special problems relating to independence would he or she face that a private CPA firm would not? By conducting the audit, would he or she be in violation of the GAO standards? Explain, indicating how the GAO standards deal with the apparent conflicts of interest faced by state and local government audit departments.

4. In what way do the GAO standards impose more rigorous continuing professional education requirements than those of the AICPA?

5. In what way do the reporting standards of the GAO differ from those of the AICPA as tests of compliance and internal controls?

6. What is a single audit? What deficiencies in previous practice was the Single Audit Act intended to correct?

7. What are the two main components of a single audit?

8. What are "general" compliance requirements? Provide several examples.

9. What types of matters do "specific" requirements address?

10. It is sometimes said that performance audits are not "true" audits in that they are conceptually different from traditional financial audits. In what way are they conceptually different?

11. What are the four main types of reports required of a single audit?

12. In what ways can it be said that a single audit is "risk based"?

13. In what other significant ways do performance audits differ from financial audits?

14. What are the general criteria that audit organizations use in selecting programs and activities for performance audits?

15. What steps might auditors take to discern the objectives of a program or activity?

16. What are the key features of a performance audit report?

EXERCISES

Ex. 15-1

Select the *best* answer.

1. *Government Auditing Standards* must be adhered to in all financial audits of
   a. State and local governments
   b. Federal agencies
   c. Federally chartered banks
   d. All of the above

2. "Generally accepted government auditing standards" (GAGAS) refers to standards incorporated in
   a. The Yellow Book
   b. The Yellow Book and OMB Circular A-133
   c. The Yellow Book and the AICPA's Professional Standards
   d. The Yellow Book, OMB Circular A-133, and the AICPA's Professional Standards

3. *Government Auditing Standards* characterizes government engagements into which of the following three categories?
   a. Financial audits, compliance audits, and performance audits
   b. Financial audits, operational audits, and performance audits
   c. Financial audits, attest engagements, and performance audits
   d. Financial audits, efficiency and effectiveness audits, and compliance audits

4. The Yellow Book's general standards apply
   a. Only to financial audits
   b. Only to financial audits and other attest engagements
   c. To performance engagements as well as to the financial audits and attest engagements
   d. To all professional engagements relating to accounting

5. Which of the following is least likely to impair the independence of a county auditor
   a. He is appointed by the county manager and reports to the manager
   b. His responsibilities include preparing the county's CAFR
   c. He is elected by the citizenry
   d. He receives an annual bonus only in years in which the county has a surplus, not a deficit

6. Per the GAO standards, auditors
   a. Must design their audit to provide reasonable assurance of detecting noncompliance with the terms of contracts or grant agreements
   b. Are not responsible for detecting noncompliance with the terms of contracts or grant agreements but must report such noncompliance if they become aware of it
   c. Must design their audit so that "it is more likely than not" they will detect noncompliance with terms of contracts or grant agreements
   d. Are responsible for detecting noncompliance with the terms of contracts or grant agreements only insofar as such noncompliance will have a material impact on the financial statements

7. The GAO's *Green Book* deals with
   a. Environmental issues
   b. Federal investment policies
   c. Internal controls
   d. Waste, fraud, and abuse

8. Per the GAO standards, an auditor's report
   a. Must disclose instances of material inefficiencies
   b. Need not be made public if it contains information that would be harmful to national security
   c. Must be retained by the auditor for a period no less than ten years
   d. Must explicitly indicate that the individual auditors on the engagement have satisfied the standards' CPE requirements.

9. The GAO reporting standards differ from those of the AICPA in that the GAO standards require the auditors to explicitly comment on their testing of
   a. Financial transactions
   b. Compliance
   c. Efficiency and effectiveness
   d. Government-wide statements

10. An auditor has completed a draft of her report on a performance audit, which in several respects is critical of the program under review. The auditor should
   a. Refrain from discussing the findings with management until the final report is issued and made public
   b. Notify the federal agency that funded the program of the audit's findings
   c. Allow responsible officials to review the report, but only as a courtesy, not to suggest any changes
   d. Obtain and include in the final report the views of responsible officials concerning the findings

EX 15-2

Select the *best* answer.

1. A key determinant as to whether, under Circular A133, a program is considered major or nonmajor is
   a. The overall size of the program as measured by total revenues, regardless of source
   b. The overall size of the program as measured by total assets
   c. The amount of federal aid received
   d. Its score on the OMB risk assessment scale

2. "General" compliance requirements are set forth in
   a. The Yellow Book
   b. The Single Audit Act
   c. The compliance supplement to Circular A-133
   d. The AICPA's generally accepted auditing standards

3. Which of the following is not particularly indicative of a program's exposure to risk:
   a. Engagement of new independent auditors
   b. Recently installed and untested computer systems
   c. Past inefficiencies as revealed in previous audits
   d. Ineffective administration

4. Per OMB Circular A-133, the Schedule of Expenditures of Federal Awards
   a. Must be explicitly tested and reported on by the auditors
   b. Should serve to help auditors to determine the scope of their audit work but need not be explicitly tested
   c. Must be tested but need be reported on by the auditors only if the tests reveal material errors
   d. Must be explicitly tested and reported on by the auditors only if the total of federal awards is material relative to total expenditures

5. Which of the following would *not* be reported on in the *Schedule of Findings* and *Questioned Costs*?
   a. Significant deficiencies in internal control
   b. Material noncompliance with provisions of laws, regulations, contracts, or grant agreements
   c. Material examples of inefficiency and ineffectiveness in carrying out federally funded programs
   d. Federally reimbursed expenditures that are not adequately documented

6. The requirement for a report on the schedule of findings and questioned costs is set forth in the
   a. AICPA's Professional Standards
   b. GAO's Government Auditing Standards
   c. Single Audit Act
   d. OMB Circular A-133

7. The GAO standards pertaining to performance audits
   a. Mandate that programs be audited annually
   b. Mandate that programs be audited whenever information comes to the attention of the auditor indicating a need for a performance audit
   c. Mandate that a complete audit include both a financial audit and a performance audit
   d. Do not specify when and how often a program must be audited

8. Performance audits differ from financial audits in that
   a. The GAO's "general standards" do not apply to performance audits
   b. In conducting performance audits, the auditors do not necessarily attest to assertions of management
   c. The auditors need not issue a formal report setting forth their findings
   d. The main focus should be on activities that satisfy the criteria of Circular A-133 as "major programs"

9. In discerning the objectives of a program to be audited, the auditors should give the greatest credibility to
   a. The legislation creating the program
   b. The organization's program budget
   c. The organization's mission statement and strategic plan
   d. Comments by the midlevel employees who actually implement the program

10. In reporting the results of a performance audit, it would be inappropriate for the auditors to
    a. Conjecture as to the reasons for the program's failure to achieve desired results
    b. Include the auditors' response to management's objections to the auditors' findings
    c. Provide recommendations as to how the program can be improved
    d. Criticize management for failing to establish appropriate goals and objectives

Ex 15-3

Internet-based exercise

Access the website of the American Red Cross (www.redcross.com) and the American Diabetes Association (www.diabetes.org) and obtain the audited financial statements and Form 990 for the latest fiscal years available. If you have difficulty finding the financial reports, search for "consolidated financial statements." Form 990 can also be obtained from www.GuideStar.org. Answer the following questions for each organization.

1. What standards were applied in conducting the audit? Was the audit a single audit? How do you know? What reports result from single audit?
2. Identify the federal agencies (Hint: agencies are usually titled U.S. Department of...) that have extended grants to these organizations. Are these the agencies that you would expect? Why or why not?
3. Identify (1) any significant deficiencies or material weaknesses in the organization's internal controls over major programs, (2) any instances of noncompliance in major programs, and (3) any findings or questioned costs.

PROBLEMS

P. 15-1

The Yellow Book standards relating to financial audits apply to independent CPA firms as well as government audit departments.

The following descriptions relate to an independent CPA firm that includes among its audit clients municipalities, school districts, and not-for-profit organizations, all of which receive federal financial assistance. Each description presents a possible violation of *Government Auditing Standards.* For each description, indicate the standard at issue and tell why there might be a violation.

1. Each year the managing partner appoints a committee of three of its partners to evaluate the quality of the work performed by the firm. The firm is not otherwise reviewed by independent parties.

2. When the firm conducts a financial examination, its primary objective is to determine whether the auditee's financial system is properly designed, the system is operating as intended, and the resultant financial records can be relied on. Accordingly, the department does not test explicitly for fraud or other illegal activities.

3. The firm has a formal program of continuing professional education. To eliminate the need to pay for the staff to attend outside courses, it brings in outside experts to conduct 40 hours per year of training. Each year the training is directed to a specific area. This year's area was changes in the federal tax code; last year's was "how to market the firm."

4. The firm periodically assigns members of its staff on a temporary basis to government and not-for-profit audit clients. The staff members typically serve as financial consultants or as acting financial administrators.

5. The firm may not test compliance with certain federal grant provisions if the grant was examined by the client's internal auditors and no violations were detected.

6. In its single audit of a client's federally assisted program, the firm detected numerous instances of noncompliance with applicable federal regulations. Inasmuch as none of the violations was either serious or material, the firm reported them to the client in its "management letter" but did not mention them in its compliance report to federal officials.

7. As part of all financial audits of federal funds recipients, the auditors carefully assess the adequacy of internal controls. They do not, however, prepare a specific report on internal controls or address them in the standard audit report.

P. 15-2

Even programs involving relatively subjective judgments can readily be audited.

A Department of Housing and Urban Development (HUD) program is aimed at conserving and rehabilitating blighted but salvageable urban areas. One element of the program provides that HUD will make rehabilitation grants and low-interest loans to property owners to help them finance the repairs needed to bring their properties into compliance with housing codes.

When Congress authorized the program, it did not establish specific criteria as to what constitutes a "blighted but salvageable" area; it left that up to HUD.

A preliminary survey by the GAO has indicated that HUD is directing funds to areas that were far too deteriorated for conservation and rehabilitation to work.

Suppose that you are assigned to the engagement. Outline an approach that you would take to support (or reject) the findings of the preliminary survey.

P. 15-3

Compliance testing may require auditor ingenuity.

The CPA firm of which you are a manager has placed you in charge of the audit of the Thornburg School District. The district receives substantial financial support from the State Education Agency. The state requires aid recipients to have annual single audits conducted by independent CPA firms. The firms are responsible for verifying that recipients have complied with the provisions of all financial awards from the state.

From your preliminary survey, you learn that the district received an award of $3 million to provide free hot lunches to elementary schoolchildren of low-income families.

The award specifies that only children from families with incomes under $45,000 are eligible to participate in the program. The state requires districts to determine eligibility, but it provides no guidance on how they are to do so.

Based only on this limited information, it is obviously not possible to develop a specific audit program to ensure that the district has complied with the eligibility provisions. However, before you even meet with district officials to discuss the audit, you wish to have a preliminary strategy in mind.

1. As best you can from the limited amount of information provided, design a strategy to test compliance with the eligibility provisions.

2. Suppose that the audit was being conducted under the federal Single Audit Act and the auditors were required to adhere to all its reporting provisions. As part of your examination, you found that 25 students out of 350 in the program failed to meet the eligibility requirements. Assuming that the auditors consider the amounts involved as indicative of a weakness in internal controls, how, if at all, should that finding affect your report on the program?

P. 15-4

A performance audit of investment activities must ascertain whether commonsense controls (not explicitly discussed in this chapter) have been established.

The director of the internal audit department of a midsize city received a memo from a member of the city council that included the following:

> *I am certain that you have followed recent press reports of the losses incurred by city and state governments on their investment portfolios. Many of these losses can be attributed to pressures to boost investment returns. These pressures encouraged the investment officers to acquire derivatives and other high-risk securities, which are clearly inappropriate for governments. I am extremely concerned that our city might also be vulnerable to major losses.*
>
> *The city currently has investments (including those of our retirement funds, bond reserves, and endowments) totaling more than $800 million. These are managed by our Office of Investments (a subunit of the Treasury Department). The mission of the office as set forth in the enabling legislation is "to invest prudently the available resources of the city so as to maximize the return to the city."*
>
> *I note that whereas our independent CPAs have reviewed the city's investment portfolio as part of their annual financial audit, your department has never conducted a performance audit of the office. I urge, therefore, that you do so as soon as feasible. I think it is especially important that you report on the extent to which the office has in place the administrative controls, policies, and practices necessary to ensure that it is accomplishing its mission.*

1. In light of widely accepted criteria for selecting audit targets, do you find it surprising that the internal audit department has never conducted a performance audit of the Office of Investments? Explain, citing relevant criteria.

2. Suppose you are placed in charge of the engagement. Draft a memo to the head of the internal audit department in which you outline the approach you would take in carrying it out. Be as specific as possible, providing examples of the types of administrative controls that you would expect to find in place. Indicate how you would assess whether the Office of Investments is "maximizing the return to the city."

P. 15-5

The key to auditing the effectiveness of a social program is in establishing its objectives.

The Office of Economic Opportunity (OEO) designed "special impact programs" to reduce unemployment, dependency, and community tensions in urban areas with large concentrations of low-income residents and in rural areas having substantial migration to such urban areas. The purpose of these experimental programs, which combine business, community, and manpower development, is to offer low-income residents an opportunity to become self-supporting through the free enterprise system. The programs are intended to create training and job opportunities, improve the living environment, and encourage development of local entrepreneurial skills.

One area chosen to participate in several special impact programs was High Ridge. The High Ridge program was the first and largest such program to be sponsored by the federal government. It has received more than $960 million in federal funds from its inception through the current year. Another $250 million was obtained from private sources, such as the Ford Foundation and the Astor Foundation.

High Ridge is a five-square-mile area with a population of 350,000–400,000 in New York City's borough of Brooklyn. The area has serious problems of unemployment, underemployment, and inadequate housing.

High Ridge's problems are deep-seated and have resisted rapid solution. They stem primarily from the lack of jobs in the area and from the fact that local residents, to a considerable degree, lack the education and training required for the jobs available elsewhere in the city. Unemployment and underemployment, in turn, reduce buying power, which has a depressing effect on the area's economy.

The magnitude of High Ridge's problems is indicated by the following data disclosed by the U.S. Census Bureau:

- Of the total civilian labor force, 8.9 percent are unemployed, compared with unemployment rates of 4.1 percent for New York City and 3.8 percent for the New York Standard Metropolitan Statistical Area (SMSA).
- Per capita income is 66 percent that of New York City and 51 percent that of the SMSA.
- Families below the poverty level make up 24.8 percent of the population, compared with 11.4 percent in New York City and 9.2 percent in the SMSA.
- Families receiving public assistance make up 25.4 percent of the population, compared with 9.6 percent in New York City and 7.5 percent in the SMSA.

A number of factors aggravate the area's economic problems and make them more difficult to solve. Some of these are:

- A reluctance of some companies to move into New York City because of traffic congestion
- A net outflow of manufacturing industry from New York City
- High city taxes and a perception of a high crime rate
- A dearth of local residents possessing business managerial experience

The area's housing problems result from the widespread deterioration of existing housing and are, in part, a by-product of below-average income levels resulting from unemployment and underemployment. They are aggravated by a shortage of mortgage capital for residential housing associated with a lack of confidence in the area on the part of financial institutions.

One of the special impact programs that High Ridge participates in is intended to stimulate the private economy by providing funds to local businesses, both new and existing. Under this program, begun five years ago, the sponsors propose to create jobs and stimulate business ownership by local residents. At first, investments in local businesses were made only in the form of loans. Later, the sponsors adopted a policy of making equity investments in selected companies to obtain for the sponsors a voice in management. Equity investments totaling about $2.5 million were made in four companies.

Loans are to be repaid in installments over periods of up to 10 years, usually with a moratorium on repayment for six months or longer. Repayment is to be made in cash or by applying subsidies allowed by the sponsors for providing on-the-job training to unskilled workers. Loans made during the first two years of the program were interest-free. Later, the sponsors revised the policy to one of charging below-market interest rates. Rates charged are now from 3 to 6.5 percent. This policy change was made to (1) emphasize to borrowers their obligations to repay the loans and (2) help the sponsors monitor borrowers' progress toward profitability.

Prospective borrowers learn of the program through information disseminated at neighborhood centers, advertisements on radio and television and in a local newspaper, and word of mouth. Those who wish to apply for loans are required to complete application forms providing information relating to their education, business and work experience, and personal financial condition and references. The sponsors set up a management assistance division that employed consultants to supplement its internal marketing assistance efforts and to provide management, accounting, marketing, legal, and other help to borrowers.

The sponsors proposed to create at least 1,700 jobs during the first four years of the loan program by making loans to 73 new and existing businesses.

Required

Put yourself in the position of the GAO manager in charge of all audits pertaining to the Office of Economic Opportunity. Your staff has undertaken a preliminary survey of the High Ridge program, and the preceding information was extracted from its report on the survey.

The New York City field office has been assigned the job of conducting the detailed performance audit of the special impact program just described. Prepare a memo to the New York City field office in which you indicate, in as great detail as is possible from the information provided, the specific steps its staff should perform in conducting an evaluation of the effectiveness of the program.

P. 15-6

Performance audits are often far removed from financial audits, but even seemingly unauditable programs can be evaluated.

The president of a major state university has a problem. A group of alumni are complaining that the university's athletic program is an embarrassment to the university and are demanding that the athletic director be fired. In response, the president has promised an intensive "audit" of all aspects of the department's performance.

The university has never explicitly established formal goals for the athletic department. Nevertheless, five years prior to this "crisis," at the press conference announcing his appointment, the athletic director (with characteristic exuberance and hyperbole) made the following statements:

1. We intend to compete in national championships in all major sports.
2. Every one of our athletes will be graduated in five years.
3. The student body will once again be proud of its teams, showing its support by attending our games.
4. We will be "number one" as measured by TV appearances and revenues.

Although these comments are obviously visions, rather than operational objectives, they do imply performance indicators that can be objectively assessed.

Suppose that you are placed in charge of the president's promised audit of the athletic department. For each of the four visions, propose objective indicators that could be used to assess the department's performance. Recognizing that you will be unable to make definitive judgments as to whether the department's performance was satisfactory or not, tell what information you would want to provide the president and the university's board of trustees so that they can make an informed judgment about the quality of the department's performance.

P. 15-7

Assessment of the procurement process may be a central element in an operations audit.

The chairman of a state legislature's finance committee has charged that the Division of Taxation's computer systems are in chaos and, as a consequence, the state is failing to collect hundreds of millions in income taxes to which it is entitled. According to the chairman, the system was improperly designed, and many of its component computers, software programs, and peripheral items of equipment have failed to perform as promised.

The overall system had been designed three years earlier by an outside consulting firm. The component computers, software programs, and peripheral items of equipment were purchased by the state from numerous different vendors.

The chairman has charged that the new system, costing $50 million, was a fiscal disaster and demanded that the State Auditor determine the reasons for the failure.

Suppose that you are a senior-level auditor in the State Auditor's Office. You are asked by the State Auditor to head a team to assess whether, in fact, the systems are not working as intended and, if not, why not and who is responsible.

1. Indicate in general terms how you might determine what was intended of the system.
2. Assume that you concluded that the system was not operating as intended. Indicate your general approach to discerning the reason for the failures and to pinpointing responsibility.

P. 15-8

Even when objectives are clearly stated, the reasons they have not been met may not be easy to discern.

The City on the Lake Convention Center was constructed at a cost of $250 million with the aim of attracting visitors to the area. Taxpayers were assured that the convention center would be self-supporting and that convention center revenue would be sufficient to cover all expenses, including debt service. Yet in its first five years of operation, the center consistently reported operating deficits.

In a recent report to the city council, the convention center manager attributed the deficits to the center's inability to attract sufficient conventions and other events. Whereas convention planners had projected that the center would have events scheduled for at least 250 days during the year, it has so far averaged only 180 days—far fewer than the break-even point.

As the city auditor, you have been requested by the city council to conduct a performance audit to learn why the center has been unable to attract the projected number of conventions and other events and to make recommendations for appropriate changes so that the projections can be met.

Required

Propose, in general terms, an approach to fulfilling the mandate of the city council.

CASES IN ETHICS

C. 15-1: Conflicting Responsibilities

Kevin Watkins is a manager of a CPA firm. At the recommendation of the partner-in-charge, he applied, and was accepted, for membership on the Accounting Standards Committee of the Government Finance Officers Association. Committee members are selected on their individual qualifications. In appointing members the association tries to ensure that they are drawn from all major constituent groups, but members do not represent their employers.

The committee has under consideration a resolution urging municipalities to develop measures of service efforts and accomplishment and to report on them in their annual reports. It is divided on the resolution, but Watkins is convinced of its merits. The partner in charge of Watkins's CPA firm, however, is strongly opposed to it, noting that obtaining the required information would impose a substantial net cost upon the firm.

A voice vote on the resolution is scheduled for the next meeting.

C. 15-2: Audit Failure

In a management letter following its year-end audit of the North Country Hospital, the not-for-profit hospital's independent audit firm questioned the adequacy of the hospital's accounts receivable allowance for contractual adjustments. It noted that owing to contractual changes, the discounts given to insurance companies and HMOs were increasing, and it urged that the hospital carefully review the collectability of its receivables. It asserted that audit tests revealed numerous required adjustments and as a consequence the hospital reduced its receivable balance by 7 percent. Nevertheless, the firm warned that additional write-downs would likely be required in the future. The firm had issued an unqualified opinion on the financial statements.

Several months following the audit, the hospital announced that operating losses for the then-current year would far exceed expectations, owing to a 30 percent write-down of accounts receivable. The required write-down was greatly in excess of the allowance for contractual adjustments.

The partner in charge of the engagement was asked by a reporter, who was unaware of the management letter, why the audit of the previous year failed to detect the overstatement of receivables.

C. 15-3: Charity Begins with the Auditor

In June 2020, Jason King completed his audit of a 2019 grant that a city made to Field of Dreams, a private, not-for-profit organization that sponsors recreational programs for disadvantaged teens. In the course of his testing, King discovered that material disbursements that were made in 2020 were charged as 2019 expenditures. The program director acknowledged the 2019 overcharges, pointing out that the organization faced a temporary cash shortage in that year. By charging the 2020 disbursements as 2019 expenditures, he was able to obtain early reimbursement and thereby avoid a fiscal crisis. He assured King that no dishonesty was intended; he was simply shifting funds from one year to another. Indeed, King was able to verify that the organization did not request reimbursement for the same charges in 2020.

The Field of Dreams grant was a pass-through grant in that the federal government provided the funds to the city. Were this discrepancy set forth as a finding in King's single audit report, it is almost certain that the organization would be ineligible for federal awards in the future.

Over the course of several years, King has become familiar with the organization's programs and considers them to be of uncommon value to the community.

C. 15-4: Undisclosed Losses

The Office of the Treasurer maintains an investment pool for several quasi-independent governments, such as housing authorities and development boards, affiliated with a city. Michelle Ruiz, a senior manager in the treasurer's office, recently became aware that the treasurer has been investing pool funds in risky derivatives and has been leveraging the funds by financing the purchase of long-term securities with short-term loans. Because of a sustained rise in interest rates over the past year, the market value of the portfolio is considerably below the contributions of pool participants. If the pool participants were to learn of the losses, it is virtually certain that some would withdraw from the fund immediately, thereby prompting an overall run on the pool.

As long as the losses are kept quiet, it is more than probable that the interest rates will soon decline and that the portfolio will recover its value. Indeed, within the last week the Federal Reserve Board announced a reduction in interest rates, and the value of the portfolio rebounded slightly. By contrast, a run on the pool would ensure that virtually all participants incur substantial losses.

Shortly after Ruiz learns of the losses, she is making a presentation to the media as to the operations of the pool. During a question-and-answer session, she is asked how the pool has performed over the last several years. She explains (truthfully) that over the long term, investment returns have been well above average. She is uncertain, however, as to whether she should add anything as to its short-term results.

C. 15-5: Politically Uncomfortable Conclusion

In verifying the capital asset records of the electric utility department, Jean Hanson, staff auditor of a city's internal audit department, noted that several trucks and pieces of equipment were out of service and apparently unrepairable. Therefore, they should have been written off. She described and documented her conclusions in her working papers.

When she discussed her findings with the manager in charge of the engagement, the manager indicated that she was aware of the problem because it had been raised in previous years. Moreover, she had already discussed it with the head of the internal audit department, and both had agreed that this was not the year to make the required write-off. A large write-off would cause considerable embarrassment to the city manager, the mayor, and members of the city council, all of whom had recently defended the electric utility department against charges that it was mismanaged. Further, the budget of the internal audit department was coming up for consideration before the city council.

Jean Hanson had reason to believe that the working paper in which she described her findings was removed from the audit binder.

C. 15-6: Managing Earnings

Henry Green is the assistant to a county's comptroller. During the year he becomes aware of several accounting and budgeting practices that, taken together, clearly establish a pattern that the county is attempting to turn both budget and reporting deficits into surpluses. Green takes his concerns to the comptroller, who informs him that (1) although the practices may be considered by many to be "aggressive," they are, in fact, in accord with GAAP and have been approved by the county's independent auditors and (2) they have been discussed with and approved by the county executive. Indeed, the county executive has encouraged the comptroller to do everything that is both legal and in accord with GAAP to enhance revenues and reduce expenditures.

C. 15-7: Split Bids

As business officer of a school district, Charles Bidright is required to sign off on all purchase orders over $1,000. Under state law and district policy, all orders over $5,000 must be put out for bid. Government agencies are required to accept the low bid unless there are specific and compelling reasons not to.

Bidright recently received five purchase orders totaling $19,500 for computer components. Each was for under $5,000. All had been approved by the district superintendent. It was clear to Bidright, however, that the components were part of a single system and therefore should have been combined into a single purchase order and put out for bid.

Bidright contacted the superintendent and explained to him the state law and district policy. The superintendent indicated that he understood the policy but that in this instance he wanted to purchase the equipment from a particular merchant because he knew from past experience that the benefits of the high quality of service provided by this merchant far outweighed any additional merchandise cost that the district was likely to incur. Bidright had no doubt that the superintendent's explanation was legitimate and that the superintendent had no business or personal relationship with the merchant from whom he wanted to purchase the equipment. At the same time, the district superintendent's reason for rejecting the low bid would not have met the legal criteria for so doing.

C. 15-8: Opulent Convention

Five (of 10) members of a town council returned from the three-day national convention of town council members in Las Vegas and submitted their expenses for reimbursement. The bills they presented indicated that they had stayed in luxurious suites, had lavish dinners with extraordinarily expensive wines, and spent freely in nightclubs. Although the town has no specific policy on allowable travel costs, William Hamilton, business officer, knew illegitimate expenses when he saw them, and these were clearly beyond the bounds of propriety. He expressed his concerns to the town manager (to whom he reports and who is appointed by the council), who advised, "Forget it. I have bigger battles that I want to fight with the council."

C. 15-9: Balancing the Budget the Easy Way

State law requires that school district budgets be balanced. After having worked for weeks to reduce expenditures to the minimum that would be educationally acceptable and politically feasible, the school board and the superintendent found the budget still $3 million short of balance. Facing the deadline as to when the budget must be approved, the superintendent (with the school board president at his side) said to Henry Wilson, business officer, "You know, I just took another look at those attendance estimates and I now believe that they were a bit too conservative. Go ahead and increase the estimates by another 600 students and that should just about give us the $3 million additional state aid that we need to get that budget in balance." State aid is based on actual, not estimated, student attendance. Wilson, who has to prepare the budget, is unaware of any evidence that would support a modification of the estimates he had been working with for the past several weeks.

C. 15-10: Pay to Play

Merrill Sachs is an accountant with the treasurer's office of a midsize city. The city is about to issue $50 million in general obligation bonds to construct a new office complex. The treasurer has recommended that the city negotiate the sale of the bonds with a single investment banking firm rather than opening the offering for bids. He cites several advantages to the negotiated sale, all of which have been validated to some extent by reputable experts.

Sachs has evidence that for an offering of the size contemplated by the city and by a government with the characteristics of the city, an auctioned sale would be preferable. More significantly, she is convinced (although she cannot prove) that the treasurer selected the investment banking firm under pressure from the mayor and city council members. This firm was by far the largest contributor to their election campaigns.

SOLUTION TO EXERCISE FOR REVIEW AND SELF-STUDY

1. The appointment of the manager would be in violation of *Government Auditing Standards* because she has not completed the requisite 24 hours of CPE in areas directly related to the governmental environment.

2. The school district receives federal financial assistance and thereby would likely be subject to a single audit. Circular A-133, *Audits of States, Local Governments, and Non-Profit Organizations*, and its "Compliance Supplement" both provide detailed guidance as to how audits of government organizations, including school districts, should be performed and to specific requirements that must be complied with.

3. The auditors were correct in making inquiries as to political activities. As part of a single audit, the auditors must test for violations of general compliance requirements, one of which prohibits federal funds from being used to promote political activity.

4. A performance audit is conceptually different from a financial audit in that in a financial audit the auditors attest to the assertions of management as set forth in management-prepared financial statements. In performance audits, the auditors make, and report upon, their own, independent assessments of organizational performance.

5. The steps the auditors might undertake to discern the objectives of the program might include the following:

   - Review the legislative history of the program.
   - Review the district's budgets, especially those related directly to the program.
   - Examine school board minutes.
   - Review internal memos.
   - Interview school board members and district administrators and teachers.

6. **a.** By scheduling the disbursements, the auditors would have a starting point from which to determine whether the outlays were in compliance with the terms of the program and whether they were for purposes consistent with its objectives.

   b. The auditors can gain an understanding of the internal controls by interviewing personnel involved in the program, preparing and administering internal control questionnaires, flowcharting relevant systems, and reviewing applicable policies.

   c. If the program has been in existence only three years, then it would clearly be impossible to make definitive judgments as to its success in encouraging students to enter science-related fields. Nevertheless, the auditors can first determine the number of students participating in the program (i.e., taking extra science classes or engaging in science-related extracurricular activities). If this number is small, then it is unlikely that the program is achieving its objective. Similarly, they can identify any curriculum changes as a consequence of the program. The absence of significant improvements would suggest that the program is having only limited impact. Further, they can establish the percentage of students that are enrolled in university science-related programs and compare this percentage with those of past years or with those of control groups—students possessing similar characteristics (academic, economic, cultural) who have not participated in the program.

CHAPTER 16

Federal Government Accounting

LEARNING OBJECTIVES

After studying this chapter, you should understand:

- The unique characteristics of the federal government that necessitate special accounting and reporting practices
- The roles of the main agencies responsible for federal accounting and reporting
- The key objectives of federal financial reporting
- The concept of a unified budget
- The types of accounts maintained by the federal government
- What constitutes a federal reporting entity
- The form and content of government-wide financial reports
- The form and content of agency financial reports
- The main accounting issues addressed by the Federal Accounting Standards Advisory Board (FASAB)
- The significance of tax expenditures
- The recent efforts by the federal government to improve its fiscal management
- Recent trends in international accounting

Thomas Jefferson stated that every American "should be able to comprehend [the nation's finances], to investigate abuses, and consequently to control them." Reflecting that view, the U.S. Constitution mandates that the federal government periodically issues financial reports. Article I, Section IX states:

> *No money shall be drawn from the Treasury, but in consequence of appropriations made by law; and a regular statement and account of the receipts and expenditures of all public money shall be published from time to time.*

Although the founding fathers demonstrated uncommon wisdom in setting forth this mandate, it is hard to believe that they had any idea how difficult it would be for the government, two centuries later, to abide by it. The federal government is unique among U.S. institutions—and so, also, are its accounting and reporting concerns. Although obviously distinguishable by its size (dollar amounts in financial statements are typically shown in "billions"), it also is differentiated by:

- The range of its activities (e.g., defense, Social Security and Medicare, and managing the money supply)
- The diversity of its resources (e.g., national parks and monuments, stores of gold bullion, and military hardware)

- The nature of its obligations (e.g., Social Security and Medicare benefits, loan guarantees, and commitments to carry out social programs)
- The extent of its powers (e.g., to tax, to print currency, and to regulate commerce)

In this chapter, we provide an overview of the federal accounting structure and the special accounting and reporting issues that it faces. First, we consider the roles played by the key agencies responsible for establishing and administering the federal accounting and reporting system. We follow by describing the federal budget and its relationship to federal accounts and reports. We then present the key features of the accounting and reporting model specified by the Federal Accounting Standards Advisory Board (FASAB). We set forth selected accounting issues addressed by the FASAB and indicate how they have been resolved. We also describe federal initiatives to supplement the agency financial statements with reports on service efforts and accomplishments as well as detailed information on financial assistance and federal contracts with outside parties. We conclude by addressing recent trends in the international arena.

Federal accounting is often said to be an oxymoron, with critics claiming that if the federal government were a publicly traded corporation, its financial statements would never be accepted by the Securities and Exchange Commission. Although there may be an element of truth to this charge, it is also a gross mischaracterization. In fact, as shall be highlighted in this chapter, the federal government as a whole, as well as each of its component entities, issues annual reports that are on a full accrual basis, are founded on principles that for the most part are at least as rigorous as those applicable to the private sector, and incorporate disclosures that are far more forthright than can be found in any corporate financial statements. Moreover, in significant ways the federal government's financial statements are considerably more progressive—and most definitely more candid—than those of both private-sector entities and lower-level governments. Notably, for example, the financial report of the federal government as a whole, the *Financial Report of the United States Government*, incorporates a managements discussion and analysis that includes a detailed discussion of the government's current net position as well as long-term trends. Accompanied by numerous charts and graphs that project revenues and expenditures as well as key ratios for up to 75 years, the most recent statements contain explicit warnings that current federal policies are not fiscally sustainable. One chart (see **Figure 16-1**) indicates that if present trends continue, by 2091, federal spending will increase to approximately 38 percent of gross domestic product, while another (not shown) points to a 2091 federal debt of over 250 percent (from a current 10 percent) an obviously untenable amount. How many corporate reports are so forthright?

Readers are strongly urged to view the government's entire annual report. It can readily be obtained at the website of the Treasury Department (http://fms.treas.gov/fr/index.html).

The financial statements of the government agencies, as opposed to the federal government as a whole, are also progressive in that they include information on service efforts and accomplishments—the very type of information that the GASB has been promoting for three decades but, owing to opposition from certain user groups has been unable to mandate. **Figure 16-2** illustrates a table included in the Department of Homeland Security's management's discussion and analysis.

Nevertheless, there is still room for improvement. The federal government's financial statements are subject to annual audit, but as of 2017, its auditor, the Government

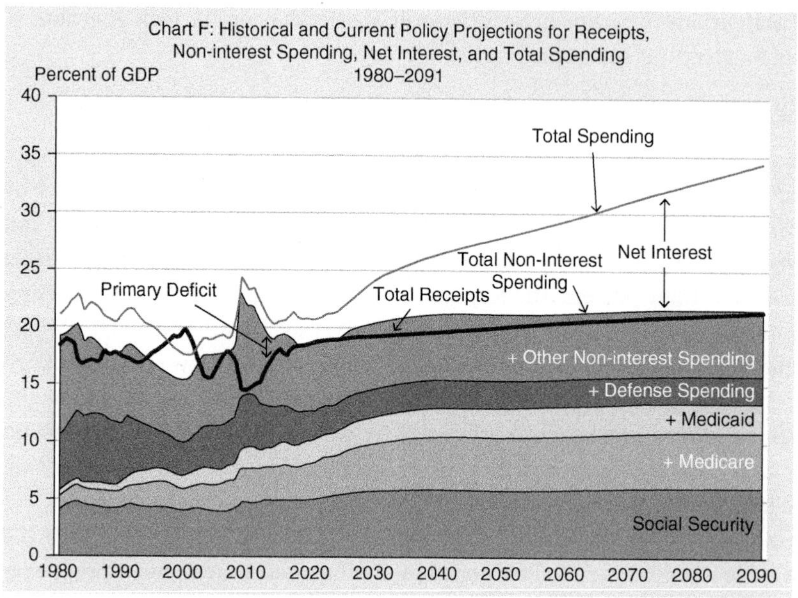

FIGURE 16-1 Illustrative Graph from of Federal Annual Report's Projections
Source: Financial Report of the United States Government for Fiscal Year 2016, p. 23.

Percent of customers satisfied with the citizenship and immigration-related support received from the National Customer Service Center (USCIS)

FY12 Result	FY13 Result	FY14 Result	FY15 Result	FY16 Target	FY16 Result
93%	87%	86%	88%	85%	85%

This measure gauges the overall rating of the immigration process and is based on the results from the following areas: 1) accuracy of information, 2) responsiveness to customer inquiries, 3) accessibility to information, and 4) customer satisfaction. The FY 2016 result for this measure, 85 percent, is consistent with the results for the past four years and is indicative of the attention USCIS has given to the customer service approach. In addition, these results continue to exceed industry customer satisfaction averages. Throughout the year, USCIS has met the target by constantly listening to customer feedback and taking deliberate steps to improve the level of service provided to its customers.

FIGURE 16-2 Illustrative Chart of Department of Homeland Security's Performance Measures
Source: Department of Homeland Security's Agency Financial Report, Fiscal Year 2016, Management's Discussion and Analysis, p. 22.

Accountability Office (GAO), has still been unable to issue an unqualified opinion on them. In part, that is because of the complexity of coordinating and consolidating the separate accounting systems of over 150 federal departments and agencies. Most notably, the Defense Department, which accounts for approximately 16 percent of all federal outlays, was unable to earn an unqualified opinion on its own financial statements, mainly because of problems of managing the separate accounting systems of the army, navy, air force, and various other component units.

WHICH AGENCIES ARE RESPONSIBLE FOR FEDERAL ACCOUNTING AND REPORTING?

Federal accounting has historically been decentralized among the government's various agencies and departments, with each agency and department having its own accounting system and preparing its own reports. Currently, however, the three federal agencies with oversight responsibility for financial management—the Department of the Treasury, the Office of Management and Budget (OMB), and the GAO—as well as the FASAB (the board that issues accounting standards) are taking major strides toward coordinating the accounting systems and reporting practices of the individual agencies.

DEPARTMENT OF THE TREASURY

Per the United States Code (31 U.S.C. §321), the Department of the Treasury is responsible for a broad range of financial functions. These include managing the public debt, collecting receipts and making disbursements, minting coins and printing currency, managing the government's gold supply, and regulating the nation's banking system. The department's divisions include the Internal Revenue Service (IRS), the Alcohol and Tobacco Tax and Trade Bureau, the U.S. Mint, and the Office of the Comptroller of the Currency.

Another of its units, the Bureau of Fiscal Service, is the government's central collection and disbursement agent. As such, it is responsible for taking in revenue from the IRS, Customs, and other agencies, writing most of the government's checks, and borrowing the money needed to operate the government. It is also in charge of the government's main accounting functions, such as overseeing the central accounting and reporting systems, keeping track of monetary assets and liabilities, and issuing financial reports. The Bureau also works with the individual federal agencies to bring greater uniformity to their accounting and reporting practices.

OFFICE OF MANAGEMENT AND BUDGET

The OMB assists the president in preparing the federal budget and supervises the executive branch agencies in implementing it. Because it has the authority to make budgetary recommendations to the president, the OMB is one of the most powerful agencies in the federal government. The OMB not only recommends overall funding priorities and assesses competing demands for resources, but it also reviews each federal agency's spending plans and evaluates the effectiveness of its programs.

In addition, the OMB oversees and coordinates the administration's procurement, financial management, information, and regulatory policies. It has the authority to prescribe the form and content of financial statements and other administrative reports, a power that it exercises by issuing bulletins and circulars that establish reporting, cost accounting, auditing, and procurement standards (but not specific accounting standards).

The OMB has the further responsibility of apportioning federal appropriations. First, Congress (either with the approval of the president or by overriding a veto) appropriates the total amount that can be spent by each agency. Then, OMB grants the agency its apportionments. **Apportionments** are shares of the total appropriation that are available to be spent. The total appropriation is most commonly apportioned by specific time periods (such as quarters) but alternatively by programs, activities, or projects. The apportionment process helps to ensure that an agency does not dissipate its resources prior to year-end, and it gives the executive branch added control over its spending.

The OMB's responsibilities for fiscal management were substantially expanded by the Chief Financial Officers Act of 1990 (31 U.S.C. §501). Asserting that billions of dollars were lost each year because of fiscal ineptitude, the bill aimed to build a modern fiscal management structure. To this end, it established both the position of **Chief Financial Officer (CFO) of the United States** and corresponding CFO positions within each federal agency and department. Officially designated as "Deputy Director for Management" and reporting to the head of the OMB, the CFO of the United States is responsible for overseeing a wide range of federal agencies internal budgeting, accounting, and other fiscally related activities.

The CFO Act also mandated that federal agencies submit their annual reports for independent audit. These audits may be carried out either by their own inspectors general or by independent external auditors. Further, it required the OMB to prepare an annual report setting forth its accomplishments in the area of fiscal management and, as appropriate, recommending improvements.

GOVERNMENT ACCOUNTABILITY OFFICE

The **Government Accountability Office (GAO)** was created in 1921 (during the administration of President Harding) by the Budget and Accounting Act (31 U.S.C.S. §702). Until then, all federal audit and accounting functions were within the domain of the Treasury Department. The act specified that the GAO was to be "independent of the executive departments and under the control and direction of the Comptroller General of the United States." Subsequently, the Reorganization Act of 1945 made clear that the GAO was part of the legislative branch.[1]

The GAO (the watchdog of Congress) is most closely identified with its role as the government's auditor, conducting both financial and performance examinations of federal organizations and programs. In fulfilling this role, and as discussed in the previous chapter, it prescribes standards for auditing and evaluating government programs, and participates with the OMB and the Treasury in being a sponsoring member of the FASAB.

Many of the GAO's engagements that one may think of as audits are, in fact, more in the order of investigations or research projects than audits. Thus, in recent years it has studied the reasons behind high textbook prices, the adequacy of the nation's retirement systems, the costs and benefits of the mandatory auditor rotation, and the success of U.S. efforts in Iraq and Afghanistan.

The GAO also has a wide variety of responsibilities that are considerably removed from accounting and auditing. These include, but are by no means limited to, adjudicating claims against the U.S. government and assisting Congress in drafting legislation.[2]

FEDERAL ACCOUNTING STANDARDS ADVISORY BOARD

Established in 1990, the FASAB is responsible for promulgating federal accounting standards. In 1999 the American Institute of CPAs, in accordance with **Rule 203** of its Code of Ethics, granted the FASAB exclusive authority to establish generally accepted accounting principles (GAAP) for federal entities, thereby giving it status comparable with that of the Governmental Accounting Standards Board (GASB) and the Financial Accounting Standards Board (FASB).

The FASAB is titled "advisory" because technically both the OMB and the GAO have the authority to dictate accounting practices for federal agencies. Although in practice the FASAB may be as independent as the FASB or the GASB, it must nevertheless submit for review each proposed standard to the Treasury, the GAO, and the OMB—three principal agencies through whose combined effort the board was established. If either the GAO or the OMB objects, then the standard is returned to the board for reconsideration.

The FASAB is composed of nine members:

- One from the legislative branch of the federal government (the GAO)
- Two from the executive branch (one each from the OMB and the Treasury)
- Six, including the chair, who are "public members" (i.e., not employees of the federal government)

[1] For a comprehensive history of the early days of the GAO see Frederick C. Mosher, *The GAO: The Quest for Accountability in American Government* (Boulder, CO: Westview Press, 1979).

[2] Primary source: The GAO's website, www.gao.gov.

The mission of the FASAB is to establish accounting standards "after considering the financial and budgetary information needs of congressional oversight groups, executive agencies, and the needs of other users of federal financial information."[3] Hence, its constituents encompass parties both within and outside the federal government. Unlike the GASB or the FASB, the FASAB is not concerned primarily with accounting reports that will be used by capital market participants to assess stocks and bonds (although increasingly the financial health of the federal government is being assessed by investors, especially from other countries, in U.S. Treasury bonds). Also unlike those two boards, the general area of "managerial cost accounting" is within its purview (although another federal board, the Cost Accounting Standards Board, located within the OMB establishes detailed cost accounting rules that must be adhered to by government contractors).

Standard setting for the federal government is especially challenging because key users have sharply contrasting information requirements. For example, economists request statistics on national income and product accounts to obtain a "macro" view of the economy. Budget analysts, however, need data on the various federal appropriation, apportionment, and cash flow accounts so that they can monitor the budgetary process. Oversight agencies want information on financial positions, results of operations, and costs of services. Moreover, as will be discussed in a section to follow, the federal budget can include different combinations of costs and revenues depending on the purpose for which it is to be used. Upon its establishment, the FASAB set out to develop, from the ground up, a fundamental model of accounting for both the federal government as a whole and its separate components. By the mid-1990s, it had largely accomplished that objective, having recommended standards that encompass a wide range of resources, obligations, and transactions. Since then it has not only been fine-tuning its basic model but also adding major components to it. By 2018 it had issued 56 standards, plus eight statements of concepts and several technical bulletins. Moreover, as this text goes to press, it has underway a project that will consider major enhancements to the model, such as linking an agency's costs to its performance measures.

As one of its early projects (following the precedent of both the FASB and the GASB), the FASAB established a set of financial reporting objectives, which were intended to lay the foundation for resolving specific accounting issues. These objectives call for federal reporting to provide information that facilitates and promotes:

- Budgetary integrity
- Sound operating performance
- Effective stewardship over government resources
- Adequate financial management systems and controls[4]

WHAT CONSTITUTES THE FEDERAL BUDGET?

MEANING OF THE TERM "BUDGET"

Upon seeing or hearing mention of the federal budget, a knowledgeable observer may rightfully ask, "What constitutes the federal budget?" In fact, the federal government does not actually either prepare or pass a budget that is comparable with that of state and local governments. Most commonly, in the federal government the term "budget" refers to a document submitted by the president to Congress. This "budget" represents the president's requests for budget authority and estimates of revenues and outlays for the coming year. Congress then takes the president's proposals under consideration and passes a series of appropriation measures (currently 11 or 12

[3] Mission statement as approved by the Board and the Secretary of the Treasury, the Director of the OMB, and the Comptroller General of the United States.

[4] See Statement of Federal Financial Accounting Concepts No. 1, *Objectives of Federal Financial Reporting* for the complete set of objectives.

regular measures plus possible supplementary measures) that authorize "obligations" (the ability to incur expenditures) for the budget year and, in some cases, for future years as well. Taken collectively, these appropriation bills provide the funding for the various federal agencies and their individual programs. Congress does not, however, pass a single budget document, as might a state legislature or city council, that encompasses all revenues and expenditures.

Alternatively, however, the term "budget" is sometimes also used to refer to actual revenues and expenditures rather than those that are proposed. Thus, when mention is made of the "budget deficit," it is often to actual results rather than to projections. To add further confusion, at the agency level, the term "budget" may refer either to budget requests to the OMB or plans for spending previously appropriated funds. Notably, the federal budget is near-cash based.[5] Accordingly, it is subject to the types of manipulations that were discussed earlier in the text with respect to state and local governments (e.g., delaying the payment of certain liabilities and speeding up the collection of revenues). By contrast, the *Financial Report of the United States* that will be discussed later is on a full accrual basis.

THE FOUR TYPES OF FEDERAL FUNDS

Federal operations are accounted for in four types of funds: a general fund, special funds, trust funds, and revolving funds. Because federal operations are so vast and information requirements of users so varied, the OMB tabulates receipts and outlays in different ways, some of which may include only selected fund types.

Like its counterpart in municipalities, the federal government's **general fund** accounts for the resources, mainly from income taxes, that are not restricted for specific purposes. These resources are used to pay for national defense, interest on the public debt, and most social programs (excluding large-dollar programs such as Social Security, Medicare, and unemployment compensation, which are accounted for in trust funds). The general fund includes both capital and operating expenditures. However, the federal budget distinguishes between the two in that the capital expenditures are concentrated in particular budget accounts or identified separately in accounts that include both types of expenditures.

Special funds, like the special revenue funds of municipalities, are maintained to account for resources that are designated for specific programs or activities. Typically financed by dedicated fees, these include the Crime Victims Fund and the Land and Water Conservation Fund.

Trust funds are also used to account for resources restricted for specific purposes. The largest of the trust funds are the Old-Age and Survivors Insurance Fund (which along with the Disability Insurance Trust Fund constitutes the Social Security program), the Supplementary Medical Insurance Fund and the Hospital Insurance Trust Fund (which constitute Medicare), and various government employee retirement funds. Trust funds are conceptually different in the federal government than in other governments or not-for-profits. In the federal sector, they are simply any funds that are designated by law as trust funds and have dedicated receipts. Like special funds, they are similar to special revenue funds. They are *not* funds in which only the income, not the principal, can be expended.

Revolving funds, comparable with a municipality's enterprise funds, account for the federal government's business-type activities. The most significant of these is the U.S. Postal Service. The activities accounted for in revolving funds generate their own receipts, and therefore the sponsoring agencies are authorized by law to expend their resources without annual congressional appropriation.

THE UNIFIED BUDGET

In 1968 (for fiscal year 1969), the government adopted the practice of preparing a **unified federal budget** that encompasses all four types of funds. The objective was to capture, in a single

[5] Significant exceptions to the cash bases include payments and receipts related to direct loans, to interest on such loans, and to loan guarantees.

tabulation, the impact of federal activities on the national economy. In addition, the unified budget was intended to provide a comprehensive measure of the cost of the government's programs that officials could use in establishing spending priorities.

Mentions of the unified federal budget almost always refer to actual revenues and expenditures rather than those that are projected or that must be voted upon by Congress. Unlike, for example, the property taxes of a local government, most federal revenues do not have to be levied or otherwise voted upon each year. Similarly, many outlays are appropriated for a period extending beyond a year. Others are considered entitlements attributable to programs, such as Social Security and Medicare, that, once authorized, no periodic appropriations are necessary.

Ironically, through a series of laws enacted in 1983, 1985, and 1990, Congress excluded Social Security receipts and disbursements from the "official" calculation of the budget and accorded them special "off-budget" standing. The aim of Congress was to remove Social Security from the constraints to which on-budget expenditures are subject. Accordingly, when the various mandatory spending caps are applied, Social Security receipts and outlays are not taken into account.

The treatment of Social Security is one of the most confusing aspects of the federal budget. Social Security represents nearly one-fifth of federal expenditures and is therefore of critical importance in assessing the federal budget's economic effect. As a consequence, budget policy makers tend to emphasize aggregate budget data, including Social Security, and most references to the federal budget are to the unified budget rather than to the official budget and hence incorporate the off-budget Social Security accounts. Thus, the budget deficits or surpluses that are most commonly referred to incorporate Social Security receipts and disbursements.

Until 2011, cash receipts to the Social Security fund have exceeded cash disbursements, thereby increasing aggregate budget surpluses or decreasing aggregate budget deficits. This excess of receipts over disbursements has now been reversed. As baby boomers retire and begin to draw benefits, in the absence of changes to the structure of contributions or benefits, Social Security will have a significantly negative impact on budgetary surpluses or deficits.

Postal Service receipts and outlays are accounted for similar to those of Social Security, mainly to accord the service the flexibility to manage its operations more like a business than a traditional government agency. Hence, although officially part of the unified budget, they too are considered "off budget" with respect to certain spending limitations.

WHAT CONSTITUTES THE FEDERAL GOVERNMENT REPORTING ENTITY?

The federal government consists of the legislative, executive, and judicial branches of government. Within the executive branch are:

- The offices of the president and vice-president as well as various other offices, such as the Council of Economic Advisers, the National Security Council, and the Office of Management and Budget
- The 15 cabinet-level departments
- Approximately 130 additional entities. Of these, many, such as the Postal Service, the Securities and Exchange Commission, and the Social Security Administration, have names that are widely recognized. Others, such as the Delta Regional Authority, the State Justice Institute, and the Marine Mammal Commission, are undoubtedly unknown to most readers of this text.

It might appear that the federal reporting entity is simply all these entities. But such is not the case. It is not easy to define what, in fact, is a federal entity. Some entities are only partially in the federal domain. The Holocaust Memorial Museum, for example, was chartered by a vote of Congress, receives funding from both federal and private sources, and is governed by a board of trustees composed mainly of private citizens. Others, such as the Federal National Mortgage Association (better known as Fannie Mae), which purchases mortgages on residential properties, are government-sponsored enterprises designed to be stockholder owned and governed and operated like most publicly held corporations. Still other entities have been taken over temporarily by federal regulatory agencies and placed in receivership owing to financial difficulties. Many failed banks were in this category, as were General Motors and the giant insurance company AIG for a time. In addition, other organizations are explicitly appropriated funds by the federal government, but by virtually all other criteria would not be considered part of the federal government (e.g., Gallaudet University).

The most problematic entity of all is the Federal Reserve System. The Federal Reserve System is the nation's central bank and thereby controls the nation's monetary policy. Although ultimately responsible to Congress, it was nevertheless granted relative operating independence to shield it from political influence. Historically, therefore, it was not considered part of the federal government for purposes of financial reporting. As a result of the fiscal crises of 2008, however, the relationship between the Fed and the federal government changed significantly. In an effort to provide assistance to various financial institutions and to prevent the economy from falling into an abyss, the Federal Reserve System closely coordinated its policies with those of the Treasury Department. The fiction that the Federal Reserve System was still not an agency of the federal government became more difficult to sustain.

Largely as a result of the changing relationship between the Fed and the rest of the federal government, the FASAB revisited previous pronouncements that defined the federal reporting entity and in 2014 issued Statement No. 47, *Reporting Entity*, which made it clear that the Fed should be considered part of the federal government for purposes of financial reporting.

Per Statement No. 47, the federal government-wide reporting entity should include all organizations:

- Budgeted for by elected officials of the federal government
- Owned by the federal government
- Controlled by the federal government with risk of loss or expectation of benefits

The statement then distinguishes between entities that should be consolidated in the government-wide statements and those about which information should merely be disclosed in notes. Per the statement, the following characteristics, no one of which is determinative, should be taken into account in determining whether the entity should be a consolidation rather than a disclosure entity:

- It is financed with taxes or other nonexchange revenue.
- It is governed by Congress and/or the president.
- It imposes, or may impose, risks and rewards on the federal government.
- It provides goods or services on a nonmarket basis.

Although the statement is silent on whether any particular entity should be a consolidation as opposed to a disclosure entity, based on its criteria, it is likely that beginning in 2018 and going forward, the Federal Reserve System will be reported only by way of disclosure, not consolidation.[6]

WHAT ARE THE FORM AND CONTENT OF GOVERNMENT-WIDE FEDERAL STATEMENTS?

Each year the federal government issues an "official" comprehensive financial report that covers all its activities and was subjected to audit. This report, the *Financial Report of the United States Government*, must be distinguished from the *United States Government Annual Report*. The *Financial Report* features statements that are on a full accrual basis. The *Annual Report*, by

[6] The statement does, however, specify that irrespective of whether the Federal Reserve System is consolidated, owing to its importance, the federal government-wide statements must include certain specified note disclosures in addition to those required of other entities.

contrast, presents budgetary results (receipts and disbursements) and thereby focuses on cash, other monetary assets, and monetary liabilities.

As required by the FASAB, the federal government's annual *Financial Report* should be divided into six main sections:

1. A brief letter of transmittal and management's discussion and analysis (MD&A). The MD&A is similar in form and content to that required of municipalities by GASB Statement No. 34, though it is more expansive. The FASAB standards invite the preparer to include performance and forward-looking information. The information should include separate segments that address:
   a. Mission and organizational structure
   b. Performance goals, objectives, and results
   c. Financial statements
   d. Systems, controls, and legal compliance

   In fact, however, the MD&A does more than that. It also provides a lengthy discourse on the state of the U.S. economy and the federal government's long-term fiscal outlook.
2. The report of the auditors (the GAO)
3. Eight basic financial statements:
   a. ***Statement of net cost.*** Perhaps the easiest of statements to understand, this statement presents the full cost of operations for all federal entities, miscellaneous earned revenue (usually from providing services to the public at a price), and gains or losses from changes in long-term assumptions used to measure liabilities such as pensions and comparable benefits.
   b. ***Statement of operations and changes in net position.*** This statement shows the total revenues (in separate columns for general revenues and for those classified as "funds from dedicated collections" that are set aside for specific purposes, such as for social insurance). It also shows the total net cost of government operations (drawn from the statement of net cost) as well as miscellaneous items such as intragovernmental interest and transfers between funds from dedicated collections and other governmental funds (both of which are eliminated in the consolidation process) and "unmatched transactions and balances" (required adjustments that result mainly from imperfections in the government's accounting system).
   c. ***Reconciliation of net operating cost and unified budget surplus or deficit.*** This statement identifies the differences between the accrual-based net operating cost (per the statement of operations and changes in net position) and the budget deficit that is on a near-cash basis.
   d. ***Statement of changes in cash balance from the unified budget and other activities.*** This statement reconciles the change in the government's budget deficit with the change in its balance of cash and other monetary assets.[7] Even though the focus of the budget is said to be on a near-cash basis, certain key transactions are nevertheless accounted for on an accrual basis. These (the reconciling items in the statement) are primarily borrowings and repayments of debt and the payment of interest on the debt.
   e. ***Balance sheet.*** The balance sheet takes the form of a corporate balance sheet. It set forth the government's assets, liabilities, and the difference between the two—its net position. For reasons discussed later in the chapter, the government's obligations for social insurance programs are not recognized as liabilities until they are due and payable. Hence, they are not reported on the balance sheet, and to the consternation of critics, they do not enter into the computation of the government's negative net position. The amounts are not trivial. Whereas in 2017, the net negative position of the government was $17.7 trillion, the obligations for social insurance were either $41.9 trillion or $56.7 trillion, depending on certain assumptions. However, counter to the charges often made by the critics that by excluding the social insurance obligations from the balance sheet, the government is trying to obfuscate the severity of its fiscal position, it should be noted that the social

[7] Other monetary assets are mainly holdings with the International Monetary Fund, gold and silver, and foreign currency.

insurance obligations are highlighted and detailed in a required statement that is presented on a page immediately following the balance sheet. Hence, anyone who believes that the obligation should be recognized as a liability and who can add can readily adjust the reported liabilities and resultant net position to his or her liking.

f. ***Statement of social insurance***. This statement provides key actuarial information pertaining to social insurance program obligations, mainly Social Security and Medicare (including hospital insurance, other medical insurance, and drug benefits). It presents the **present value**, over a period of 75 years, of the expected benefit payments net of the expected contributions of plan participants.

g. ***Statement of changes in social insurance amounts.*** This statement indicates the reasons for changes in the social insurance obligations during the year. The major changes pertain to the number of participants entering or leaving the program, in the law or policies, and various economic and other health-care assumptions.

h. ***Statement of long-term fiscal projections.*** This statement displays the present value of projected receipts and non-interest spending under current policy in terms of both present value dollars and present value dollars as a percent of the present value of the gross domestic product. It also indicates the change from the prior year. Like the statement of social insurance, its time horizon is 75 years. This statement of projections is unlike anything required by either the FASB or the GASB and is unquestionably controversial. It is intended to fulfill a key objective of financial reporting—to show whether future budgetary resources will likely be sufficient to sustain public services and to meet obligations as they come due. Critics, however, fear that the projections are not only inherently subjective but that they may, for political reasons, be intentionally biased.

4. Notes to the financial statements, including a summary of significant accounting policies and details and explanations of amounts reported in the basic financial statements. Notes also provide information on "stewardship assets" (federal land holdings and assets that have historical, cultural, and artistic value).

5. Required Supplementary Information (RSI). Subject only to limited auditing procedures, this section includes extensive discussions of the sustainability of current fiscal policies, detailed data on social insurance programs, as well as estimates of deferred maintenance and repairs, oil and gas reserves, and unpaid tax assessments.

6. Other Accompanying Information (OAI). Similar to RSI, but no item of which is explicitly required by FASAB, this section might include information on technical matters, such as unexpended balances of budget authority, as well as effective tax rates, and the "tax gap" (the difference between what taxpayer should pay and what they actually pay).

7. Required Supplementary Stewardship Information (RSSI). This section is unaudited and provides information on "stewardship investments"—expenditures for **human capital** (such as education and training programs) and research and development activities and nonfederal physical property (such as bridges and roads that the federal government finances but not own). These investments are recorded as expenses as incurred but, like capital assets, provide a long-term benefit.

Tables 16-1A–H display the 2016 basic government-wide statements. Owing to deficiencies in the federal financial management systems, the GAO auditors were unable to express an opinion on these statements (just as they were not in each of the years since they began to audit the government's financial statements).[8]

[8] The annual report of the U.S. government can be found on the website of the GAO, gao.gov. Search for "Financial Report of the U.S. Government" and indicate year. The report itself includes explanations of the basic financial statements. It also includes a "Citizen's Guide" that summarizes the key data reported in the statements.

TABLE 16-1A

United States Government Statement of Net Cost for the Year Ended September 30, 2016

(In billions of dollars)	Gross Cost	Earned Revenue	Subtotal	(Gain)/Loss from Changes in Assumptions	Net Cost
Department of Health and Human Services	1,170.0	96.1	1,073.9	0.4	1,074.3
Social Security Administration	982.1	0.3	981.8	–	981.8
Department of Veterans Affairs	276.5	4.9	271.6	377.5	649.1
Department of Defense	721.9	55.1	666.8	(57.6)	609.2
Interest on Treasury Securities Held by the Public	273.0	–	273.0	–	273.0
Department of Agriculture	142.1	8.5	133.6	–	133.6
Department of the Treasury	148.7	19.4	129.3	–	129.3
Department of Transportation	80.7	0.9	79.8	–	79.8
Department of Education	103.1	29.9	73.2	–	73.2
Department of Energy	68.6	4.3	64.3	–	64.3
Department of Homeland Security	66.5	13.1	53.4	0.2	53.6
Department of Labor	46.4	–	46.4	–	46.4
Department of Justice	38.7	1.6	37.1	–	37.1
Defense Security Cooperation Agency	36.0	–	36.0	–	36.0
Department of Housing and Urban Development	31.2	1.7	29.5	–	29.5
Department of State	32.6	4.7	27.9	(0.1)	27.8
National Aeronautics and Space Administration	20.0	0.2	19.8	–	19.8
Department of the Interior	19.2	2.5	16.7	–	16.7
U.S. Agency for International Development	12.6	–	12.6	–	12.6
Railroad Retirement Board	15.3	3.9	11.4	–	11.4
Federal Communications Commission	10.4	0.5	9.9	–	9.9
Department of Commerce	12.5	3.3	9.2	–	9.2
Environmental Protection Agency	9.0	0.4	8.6	–	8.6
National Science Foundation	7.0	–	7.0	–	7.0
U.S. Postal Service	77.2	70.4	6.8	–	6.8
Pension Benefit Guaranty Corporation	11.4	6.7	4.7	–	4.7
Smithsonian Institution	0.8	–	0.8	–	0.8
Millennium Challenge Corporation	0.6	–	0.6	–	0.6
Small Business Administration	0.5	0.3	0.2	–	0.2
U.S. Nuclear Regulatory Commission	0.9	0.8	0.1	–	0.1
General Services Administration	0.6	0.7	(0.1)	–	(0.1)
Overseas Private Investment Corporation	–	0.1	(0.1)	–	(0.1)
Securities and Exchange Commission	1.7	2.0	(0.3)	–	(0.3)
Farm Credit System Insurance Corporation	–	0.3	(0.3)	–	(0.3)
National Credit Union Administration	(0.7)	0.1	(0.8)	–	(0.8)
Tennessee Valley Authority	9.3	10.6	(1.3)	–	(1.3)
Export–Import Bank of the United States	(0.2)	1.2	(1.4)	–	(1.4)
Office of Personnel Management	60.2	21.3	38.9	(47.1)	(8.2)
Federal Deposit Insurance Corporation	0.2	9.5	(9.3)	–	(9.3)
All other entities	21.1	1.3	19.8	–	19.8
Total	4,507.7	376.6	4,131.1	273.3	4,404.4

TABLE 16-1B

United States Government Statement of Operations and Changes in Net Position for the Year Ended September 30, 2016

(In billions of dollars)	Funds Other than those from Dedicated Collections (Combined)	Funds from Dedicated Collections (Note 20) (Combined)	Elimination	Consolidated
		2016		
Revenue (Note 17):				
Individual income tax and tax withholdings	1,525.5	1,077.7	–	2,603.2
Corporation income taxes	294.3	–	–	294.3
Excise taxes	42.1	58.3	–	100.4
Unemployment taxes	–	46.9	–	46.9
Customs duties	33.3	–	–	33.3
Estate and gift taxes	21.0	–	–	21.0
Other taxes and receipts	185.1	42.9	–	228.0
Miscellaneous earned revenues	15.3	2.9	–	18.2
Intragovernmental interest	–	102.8	(102.8)	–
Total revenue	2,116.6	1,331.5	(102.8)	3,345.3
Net cost of government operations:				
Net cost	2,798.7	1,605.7	–	4,404.4
Intragovernmental net cost	(8.7)	8.7	–	–
Intragovernmental interest	102.8	–	(102.8)	–
Total net cost	2,892.8	1,614.4	(102.8)	4,404.4
Intragovernmental transfers	(409.5)	409.5	–	–
Unmatched transactions and balances (Note 1.S)	11.7	–	–	11.7
Net operating (cost)/revenue	(1,174.0)	126.6	–	(1,047.4)
Net position, beginning of period	(21,491.3)	3,247.7	–	(18,243.6
Prior period adjustments—changes in accounting principles (Note 1.T)	(1.4)	–	–	(1.4)
Net operating (cost)/revenue	(1,174.0)	126.6	–	(1,047.40)
Net position, end of period	(22,666.7)	3,374.3	–	(19,292.40)

TABLE 16-1C

United States Government Reconciliations of Net Operating Cost and Unified Budget Deficit for the Years Ended September 30, 2016, and 2015

(In billions of dollars)	2016	Restated 2015
Net operating cost	(1,047.4)	(514.2)
Components of net operating cost not part of the budget deficit		
Excess of accrual-basis expenses over budget outlays		
* Federal employee and veteran benefits payable		
Pensions and accrued benefits	(106.9)	37.9
Veterans compensation and burial benefits	477.7	11.5
Post-retirement health and accrued benefits	56.8	(2.1)
Other benefits	9.4	52.5
Subtotal – federal employee and veteran benefits payable	437.0	99.8
Insurance and guarantee program liabilities	9.9	2.1
* Environmental and disposal liabilities	35.0	42.5
Other liabilities	9.8	45.8
* Accounts payable	(5.9)	(0.7)
* Benefits due and payable	4.3	22.3
Subtotal – excess of accrual-basis expenses over budget outlays	490.1	211.8
Amortized expenses not included in budget outlays		
Property, plant, and equipment depreciation expense	52.2	54.5
Other expenses that are not reported as budget outlays		
Property, plant, and equipment disposals and revaluations	(24.9)	(47.0)
Agencies year-end credit reform subsidy re-estimates	10.4	(2.3)
Excess of accrual-basis revenue over budget receipts		
* Accounts receivable, net	(7.4)	(12.5)
* Taxes receivable, net	(8.1)	(1.3)
Other revenue and gains that are not budget receipts		
* Investments in government-sponsored enterprises	(2.3)	(10.5)
Deposit fund balances	(0.7)	(19.1)
Subtotal – components of net operating cost not part of budget deficit	509.3	173.6
Components of the budget deficit that are not part of net operating cost		
Budget receipts not included in net operating cost		
Credit reform and other loan activities	9.5	4.8
Budget outlays not included in net operating cost		
Acquisition of capital assets	(81.5)	(54.5)
Debt and equity securities	0.5	11.0
* Other assets	21.3	(2.9)
* Inventories and related property	6.3	(2.2)
Effect of prior year agencies credit reform subsidy re-estimates	2.3	(24.5)
Subtotal – components of the budget deficit that are not part of net operating cost	(41.6)	(68.3)
Other		
All other reconciling items	(7.7)	(30.0)
Unified budget deficit	(587.4)	(438.9)

*The amounts represent the year over year net change in the Balance Sheet line items.

TABLE 16-1D

United States Government Statements of Changes in Cash Balance from Unified Budget and Other Activities for the Years Ended September 30, 2016, and 2015

(In billions of dollars)	2016	Reclass 2015
Cash flow from unified budget activities		
Total unified budgetary receipts	3,266.7	3,248.7
Total unified budgetary outlays	(3,854.1)	(3,687.6)
Unified budget deficit	(587.4)	(438.9)
Adjustments for non-cash outlays included in the unified budget		
Interest accrued on Treasury securities held by the public	264.1	245.4
Agencies year-end credit reform subsidy re-estimates	(12.7)	26.8
Subsidy expense accrued under direct loan & guarantee programs	11.8	(22.0)
Subtotal – adjustments for non-cash transactions in unified budget	263.2	250.2
Cash flow from activities not included in unified budget		
Cash flow from non-budget activities		
Interest paid on Treasury securities held by the public	(262.7)	(243.5)
Other direct loan transactions	(80.3)	(119.9)
Repayment of principal on direct loans	(11.6)	17.4
Other guaranteed loan transactions	(10.2)	9.8
Miscellaneous liabilities	1.6	(0.3)
Deposit fund liability balances	(0.7)	20.5
Seignorage	0.6	0.6
Subtotal – cash flow from non-budget activities	(363.3)	(315.4)
Cash flow from monetary transactions		
Loans to the IMF	0.9	3.0
Other monetary assets	1.9	0.6
Special drawing rights	(0.3)	(2.9)
Subtotal – cash flow from monetary transactions	2.5	0.7
Cash flow from financing		
Borrowing from the public	8,390.4	7,037.5
Repayment of debt held by the public	(7,343.3)	(6,700.6)
Effect of uninvested principal from the Thrift Savings Plan (TSP) G Fund	(203.2)	203.2
Agency securities	0.1	0.1
Subtotal – cash flow from financing	844.0	540.2
Other	0.5	3.4
Change in cash balance	159.5	40.2
Beginning cash balance	305.1	264.9
Ending cash balance	464.6	305.1

The accompanying notes are an integral part of these financial statements.

TABLE 16-1E

United States Government Balance Sheets as of September 30, 2016, and 2015		
(In billions of dollars)	**2016**	**Restated 2015**
Assets:		
Cash and other monetary assets (Note 2)	464.6	305.1
Accounts and taxes receivable, net (Note 3)	133.3	117.8
Loans receivable, net (Note 4)	1,277.6	1,216.0
Inventories and related property, net (Note 5)	314.3	320.6
Property, plant and equipment, net (Note 6)	979.5	925.3
Debt and equity securities (Note 7)	48.2	104.4
Investments in government-sponsored enterprises (Note 8)	108.6	106.3
Other assets (Note 9)	144.4	165.7
Total assets	3,470.5	3,261.2
Stewardship land and heritage assets (Note 24)		
Liabilities:		
Accounts payable (Note 10)	62.4	68.3
Federal debt securities held by the public and accrued interest (Note 11)	14,221.1	13,172.5
Federal employee and veteran benefits payable (Note 12)	7,209.4	6,772.4
Environmental and disposal liabilities (Note 13)	446.6	411.6
Benefits due and payable (Note 14)	218.2	213.9
Insurance and guarantee program liabilities (Note 15)	122.3	170.3
Loan guarantee liabilities (Note 4)	18.2	36.3
Other liabilities (Note 16)	464.7	659.5
Total liabilities	22,762.9	21,504.8
Contingencies (Note 18) and Commitments (Note 19)		
Net Position:		
Funds from Dedicated Collections (Note 20)	3,374.3	3,247.7
Funds other than those from Dedicated Collections	(22,666.7)	(21,491.3)
Total net position	(19,292.4)	(18,243.6)
Total liabilities and net position	3,470.5	3,261.2

TABLE 16-1F

United States Government Statements of Long-Term Fiscal Projections (Note 23)
Present Value of 75 Year Projections as of September 30, 2016 and 2015[1]

	Dollars in Trillions			Percent of GDP[2]		
	2016	**2015**	**Change**	**2016**	**2015**	**Change**
Receipts:						
Social Security Payroll Taxes	56.3	52.4	3.9	4.3	4.4	(0.1)
Medicare Payroll Taxes	18.8	17.4	1.4	1.4	1.5	–
Individual Income Taxes	139.0	127.8	11.2	10.7	10.7	–
Other Receipts	47.5	43.5	3.9	3.6	3.6	–
Total Receipts	261.6	241.2	20.4	20.1	20.2	(0.1)
Non-interest Spending:						
Social Security	75.6	70.0	5.6	5.8	5.9	–
Medicare Part A[3]	26.5	24.0	2.5	2.0	2.0	–
Medicare Parts B & D[4]	31.3	28.7	2.6	2.4	2.4	–
Medicaid	31.7	27.3	4.4	2.4	2.3	0.1
Other Mandatory	41.6	36.8	4.8	3.2	3.1	0.1
Defense Discretionary	32.0	28.6	3.4	2.5	2.4	0.1
Non-defense Discretionary	33.6	30.0	3.7	2.6	2.5	0.1
Total Non-interest Spending	272.2	245.3	26.9	20.9	20.5	0.4
Non-interest Spending less Receipts	10.6	4.1	6.5	0.8	0.3	0.5

[1] 75-year present value projections for 2016 are as of 9/30/2016 for the period FY 2017-2091; projections for 2015 are as of 09/30/2015 for the period FY 2016-2090.

[2] The 75-year present value of nominal Gross Domestic Product (GDP), which drives the calculations above is $1,302.8 trillion starting in FY 2017, and was $1,196.3 trillion starting in FY 2016.

[3] Represents portions of Medicare supported by payroll taxes.

[4] Represents portions of Medicare supported by general revenues. Consistent with the President's Budget, outlays for Parts B & D are presented net of premiums. Totals may not equal the sum of components due to rounding.

TABLE 16-1G

United States Government Statements of Social Insurance (Note 22), Present Value of Long-Range (75 Years, except Black Lung) Actuarial Projections: (Summary Only)

(In trillions of dollars)	2016	2015	2014	2013	2012
Social Insurance Summary					
Participants who have attained eligibility age:					
Revenue (e.g., contributions and dedicated taxes)	3.1	2.8	2.3	2.1	2.0
Expenditures for scheduled future benefits	(22.9)	(21.3)	(19.4)	(18.2)	(16.7)
Present value of future expenditures in excess of future revenue	(19.8)	(18.5)	(17.1)	(16.1)	(14.7)
Participants who have not attained eligibility age:					
Revenue (e.g., contributions and dedicated taxes)	47.1	43.4	40.0	38.4	36.0
Expenditures for scheduled future benefits	(92.2)	(83.1)	(79.6)	(76.3)	(72.9)
Present value of future expenditures in excess of future revenue	(45.1)	(39.7)	(39.6)	(37.9)	(36.9)
Closed-group—Total present value of future expenditures in excess of future revenue	(64.9)	(58.2)	(56.7)	(54.0)	(51.6)
Future participants:					
Revenue (e.g., contributions and dedicated taxes)	41.9	36.8	34.3	32.9	30.6
Expenditures for scheduled future benefits	(23.7)	(20.1)	(19.6)	(18.6)	(17.6)
Present value of future revenue in excess of future expenditure	18.2	16.8	14.8	14.3	13.1
Open-group—Total present value of future expenditures in excess of future revenue	(46.7)	(41.5)	(41.9)	(39.7)	(38.6)

TABLE 16-1H

United States Government Statement of Changes in Social Insurance Amounts for the Year Ended September 30, 2016 (Note 22)

(in trillions of dollars)	Social security[1]	Medicare HI[1]	Medicare SMI[1]	Other[2]	Total
Net present value (NPV) of future revenue less future expenditures for current and future participants (the "open group") over the next 75 years, beginning of the year	(13.4)	(3.2)	(24.8)	(0.1)	(41.5)
Reasons for changes in tne NPV during the year:					
Changes in valuation period	(0.5)	(0.1)	(1.1)	–	(1.7)
Changes in demographic data, assumptions, and methods	0.6	0.2	0.3	–	1.1
Changes in economic data, assumptions, and methods	(0.9)	–	–	–	(0.9)
Changes in law or policy	0.1	–	0.2	–	0.3
Changes in methodology and programmatic data	–	–	–	–	–
Changes in economic and other health care assumptions	–	(0.4)	(3.0)	–	(3.4)
Change in projection base	–	(0.3)	(0.3)	–	(0.6)
Net change in open group measure	(0.7)	(0.6)	(3.9)	–	(5.2)
Open group measure, end of year	(14.1)	(3.8)	(28.7)	(0.1)	(46.7)

[1] Amounts represent changes between valuation dates 1/1/2015 and 1/1/2016.
[2] Includes Railroad Retirement changes between valuation dates 1/1/2015 and 10/1/2015 and Black Lung changes between 9/30/2015 and 9/30/2016.

Totals may not equal the sum of components due to rounding.

WHAT TYPES OF ACCOUNTS ARE MAINTAINED BY FEDERAL ENTITIES?

Federal departments, bureaus, agencies, and other types of units maintain dual systems of accounts:

- Budget accounts ensure that the entity complies with budgetary mandates, does not overspend its appropriations, and is able to fulfill uniform budgetary reporting requirements.
- Proprietary accounts provide the information for the financial statements based on FASAB standards and are intended to provide an economic, rather than a budgetary, measure of operations and resources. (The term proprietary does not, however, imply business activities, as when used in a municipal context.)

The budget accounts are comparable to both the budgetary accounts and the encumbrance accounts established by municipalities. Entries are made to record apportionments, allotments (a part of an apportionment that an agency is permitted to expend during a specified time period), commitments (reservations of funds prior to an order), and obligations (encumbrances).

The proprietary accounts are similar to conventional revenue, expense, asset, liability, and equity accounts. The accounts that are unique to the federal government are mainly in the equity (referred to as "net position") section of the balance sheet. Thus, for example, "unexpended appropriations" represent the portion of net assets made available by Congress, but not yet expended. "Cumulative results of operations" (the equivalent of retained earnings) indicate the net assets from operations in both the current and previous years. Proprietary accounting is mainly on a full accrual basis.

WHAT STATEMENTS ARE REQUIRED OF FEDERAL AGENCIES?

The FASAB reporting model for individual federal agencies is similar to that of the federal government at large. Like the financial report of the government at large, agency statements should contain a discussion and analysis by management, the auditor's report, the basic financial statements, information on stewardship assets, investments and responsibilities, notes to the financial statements, and other RSI.

The 2016 statements of the Department of Labor are illustrated in Table 16-2A–G. The number of basic financial statements of agencies varies with the type of agency. Agencies that collect funds for other agencies or that are responsible for social insurance programs must present certain additional statements not required of agencies that do not.

BALANCE SHEET (OR STATEMENT OF FINANCIAL POSITION)

The balance sheet shows the entity's assets, liabilities, and net position. The assets would include the entity's fund balance with the Treasury. This balance can be used only for the purposes for which the funds were appropriated. Net position is the residual difference between assets and liabilities. It generally comprises unexpended appropriations (amounts not yet obligated or expended) plus the cumulative difference, over the years, between the entity's revenues and other sources of funding and its expenses.

Conspicuously missing from the balance sheet of the Department of Labor is a cash balance. Most federal agencies do not have substantial cash accounts. What would otherwise be a cash balance is subsumed within the fund balance with the Treasury.

The balance sheet is on a full accrual basis and accordingly reports long-lived assets. However, as is discussed in the following section, owing to their special nature, certain types of long-lived assets are not given balance sheet recognition. These include parklands, historic sites, and national monuments. Such assets are considered **stewardship assets** and are reported in a section of the report that supplements the basic financial statements.

TABLE 16-2A **United States Department of Labor**

CONSOLIDATED BALANCE SHEETS
As of September 30, 2016 and 2015

(Dollars in Thousands)	2016	2015
ASSETS		
Intra-governmental		
Funds with U.S. Treasury (Note 1-C and 2)	$ 11,960,730	$ 11,568,982
Investments (Note 1-D and 3)	54,098,358	44,644,478
Accounts receivable (Note 1-E and 4)	5,534,674	5,616,399
Advances (Note 1-G and 6)	3,409	11,831
Total intra-governmental	71,597,171	61,841,690
Accounts receivable, net of allowance (Note 1-E and 4)	1,379,029	1,747,211
General Property, plant and equipment, net (Note 1-F and 5)	1,264,080	1,294,528
Advances (Note 1-G and 6)	1,105,972	1,343,733
Total assets	$ 75,346,252	$ 66,227,162
LIABILITIES AND NET POSITION		
Liabilities (Note 1-I and 12)		
Intra-governmental		
Accounts payable	$ 15,865	$ 22,324
Debt (Note 1-J and 8)	14,264,915	18,527,186
Other liabilities (Note 9)	249,811	348,713
Total intra-governmental	14,530,591	18,898,223
Accounts payable	325,041	259,334
Accrued benefits (Note 1-K and 10)	1,642,495	1,301,844
Future workers' compensation benefits (Note 1-L and 11)	1,917,478	1,479,265
Energy employees occupational illness compensation benefits (Note 1-M)	15,373,336	14,832,013
Accrued leave (Note 1-N)	128,045	115,177
Other liabilities (Note 9)	836,870	850,517
Total liabilities	34,753,856	37,736,373
Contingencies (Note 13)		
Net position (Note 1-R)		
Funds from dedicated collections		
Cumulative results of operations (Note 21)	40,442,362	27,153,317
All other funds		
Unexpended appropriations	7,919,543	7,991,121
Cumulative results of operations	(7,769,509)	(6,653,849)
Total net position - all other funds	150,034	1,337,472
Total net position	40,592,396	28,490,789
Total liabilities and net position	$ 75,346,252	$ 66,227,162

STATEMENT OF NET COST

The **statement of net cost**, probably the most significant of the six statements, reports on program operating costs and revenues. Similar to the government-wide statement of activities required by GASB Statement No. 34, it presents earned revenues (i.e., those from exchange transactions) as a deduction from costs, thereby highlighting the amount that must be paid from taxes and other financing sources. By focusing on the net cost to the government of individual programs, it provides decision-makers a basis on which to compare program inputs with results and thereby assess agency performance. Like the balance sheet, the statement is on a full accrual basis. Hence, the reported expenses capture the full cost of operating a program, including depreciation, not merely the cash disbursements of a particular year.

TABLE 16-2B United States Department of Labor

CONSOLIDATED STATEMENTS OF NET COST
For the Years Ended September 30, 2016 and 2015

(Dollars in Thousands)	2016	2015
NET COST OF OPERATIONS (Note 1-S and 15)		
CROSSCUTTING PROGRAMS		
Income maintenance		
Gross Cost	$ 43,314,156	$ 41,384,332
Less Earned Revenue	(3,546,200)	(3,757,686)
Net Program Cost	39,767,956	37,626,646
Employment and training		
Gross Cost	6,301,715	6,245,765
Less Earned Revenue	(10,045)	(13,496)
Net Program Cost	6,291,670	6,232,269
Labor, employment and pension standards		
Gross Cost	912,018	864,880
Less Earned Revenue	(19,277)	(11,834)
Net Program Cost	892,741	853,046
Worker safety and health		
Gross Cost	1,072,944	1,055,674
Less Earned Revenue	(7,678)	(4,432)
Net Program Cost	1,065,266	1,051,242
OTHER PROGRAMS		
Statistics		
Gross Cost	660,604	645,560
Less Earned Revenue	(32,165)	(28,823)
Net Program Cost	628,439	616,737
COSTS NOT ASSIGNED TO PROGRAMS		
Gross Cost	18,505	17,825
Less Earned Revenue not attributed to programs	(9,680)	(572)
Net Cost not assigned to programs	8,825	17,253
Net cost of operations	$ 48,654,897	$ 46,397,193

TABLE 16-2C United States Department of Labor

CONSOLIDATED STATEMENTS OF CHANGES IN NET POSITION
For the Years Ended September 30, 2016 and 2015

(Dollars in Thousands)	2016 Consolidated			2015 Consolidated		
	Funds from Dedicated Collections	All Other Funds	Total	Funds from Dedicated Collections	All Other Funds	Total
Cumulative results of operations, beginning	$ 27,153,317	$ (6,653,649)	$ 20,499,668	$ 11,304,501	$ (7,461,467)	$ 3,843,034
Budgetary financing sources (Note 1-T)						
Appropriations used	–	10,277,935	10,277,935	–	9,964,324	9,964,324
Non-exchange revenue (Note 16)						
Employer taxes	47,370,792	–	47,370,792	49,628,888	–	49,628,888
Interest	1,219,327	25	1,219,352	1,194,863	–	1,194,863
Reimbursement of unemployment benefits and other	1,596,876	536	1,597,412	1,902,743	7,389	1,910,132
Total non-exchange revenue	50,186,995	561	50,187,556	52,726,494	7,389	52,733,883
Transfers without reimbursement (Note 17)	(3,635,425)	3,885,853	250,428	(3,682,768)	3,925,290	242,522
Other financing sources (Note 1-U)						
Imputed financing from costs absorbed by others	2,734	104,743	107,477	2,868	105,537	108,405
Transfers without reimbursement (Note 17)	–	4,930	4,930	–	4,544	4,544
Other	–	(244)	(244)	–	149	149
Total financing sources	46,554,304	14,273,778	60,828,082	49,046,594	14,007,233	63,053,827
Net cost of operations	(33,265,259)	(15,389,638)	(48,654,897)	(33,197,778)	(13,199,415)	(46,397,193)
Net change	13,289,045	(1,115,860)	12,173,185	15,848,816	807,818	16,656,634
Cumulative results of operations, end of period	40,442,362	(7,769,509)	32,672,853	27,153,317	(6,653,649)	20,499,668
Unexpended appropriations, beginning	–	7,991,121	7,991,121	–	9,272,731	9,272,731
Budgetary financing sources (Note 1-T)						
Appropriations received (Note 18-F)	–	10,761,084	10,761,084	–	10,450,010	10,450,010
Appropriations used	–	(10,277,935)	(10,277,935)	–	(9,964,324)	(9,964,324)
Appropriations transferred	–	(1,000)	(1,000)	–	(294)	(294)
Other adjustments	–	(553,727)	(553,727)	–	(1,767,002)	(1,767,002)
Total Budgetary Financing Sources	–	(71,578)	(71,578)	–	(1,281,610)	(1,281,610)
Unexpended appropriations, end of period	–	7,919,543	7,919,543	–	7,991,121	7,991,121
Net position	$ 40,442,362	$ 150,034	$ 40,592,396	$ 27,153,317	$ 1,337,472	$ 28,490,789

TABLE 16-2D United States Department of Labor

CONSOLIDATED STATEMENTS OF CHANGES IN NET POSITION
For the Years Ended September 30, 2016 and 2015

(Dollars in Thousands)	2016 Consolidated			2015 Consolidated		
	Funds from Dedicated Collections	All Other Funds	Total	Funds from Dedicated Collections	All Other Funds	Total
Cumulative results of operations, beginning	$ 27,153,317	$ (6,653,649)	$ 20,499,668	$ 11,304,501	$ (7,461,467)	$ 3,843,034
Budgetary financing sources (Note 1-T)						
Appropriations used	–	10,277,935	10,277,935	–	9,964,324	9,964,324
Non-exchange revenue (Note 16)						
Employer taxes	47,370,792	–	47,370,792	49,628,888	–	49,628,888
Interest	1,219,327	25	1,219,352	1,194,863	–	1,194,863
Reimbursement of unemployment benefits and other	1,596,876	536	1,597,412	1,902,743	7,389	1,910,132
Total non-exchange revenue	50,186,995	561	50,187,556	52,726,494	7,389	52,733,883
Transfers without reimbursement (Note 17)	(3,635,425)	3,885,853	250,428	(3,682,768)	3,925,290	242,522
Other financing sources (Note 1-U)						
Imputed financing from costs absorbed by others	2,734	104,743	107,477	2,868	105,537	108,405
Transfers without reimbursement (Note 17)	–	4,930	4,930	–	4,544	4,544
Other	–	(244)	(244)	–	149	149
Total financing sources	46,554,304	14,273,778	60,828,082	49,046,594	14,007,233	63,053,827
Net cost of operations	(33,265,259)	(15,389,638)	(48,654,897)	(33,197,778)	(13,199,415)	(46,397,193)
Net change	13,289,045	(1,115,860)	12,173,185	15,848,816	807,818	16,656,634
Cumulative results of operations, end of period	40,442,362	(7,769,509)	32,672,853	27,153,317	(6,653,649)	20,499,668
Unexpended appropriations, beginning	–	7,991,121	7,991,121	–	9,272,731	9,272,731
Budgetary financing sources (Note 1-T)						
Appropriations received (Note 18-F)	–	10,761,084	10,761,084	–	10,450,010	10,450,010
Appropriations used	–	(10,277,935)	(10,277,935)	–	(9,964,324)	(9,964,324)
Appropriations transferred	–	(1,000)	(1,000)	–	(294)	(294)
Other adjustments	–	(553,727)	(553,727)	–	(1,767,002)	(1,767,002)
Total Budgetary Financing Sources	–	(71,578)	(71,578)	–	(1,281,610)	(1,281,610)
Unexpended appropriations, end of period	–	7,919,543	7,919,543	–	7,991,121	7,991,121
Net position	$ 40,442,362	$ 150,034	$ 40,592,396	$ 27,153,317	$ 1,337,472	$ 28,490,789

TABLE 16-2E **United States Department of Labor**

COMBINED STATEMENTS OF BUDGETARY RESOURCES
For the Years Ended September 30, 2016 and 2015

(Dollars in Thousands)	2016	2015
Note 1-Z and 18		
BUDGETARY RESOURCES		
Unobligated balance brought forward, October 1	$ 3,447,458	$ 4,611,740
Recoveries of prior year unpaid obligations	603,674	564,577
Other changes in unobligated balance	(228,293)	(1,216,674)
Unobligated balance from prior year budget authority, net	3,822,839	3,959,643
Appropriations (discretionary and mandatory)	47,611,750	46,890,818
Spending authority from offsetting collections (discretionary and mandatory)	7,410,865	7,286,090
Total budgetary resources	$ 58,845,454	$ 58,136,551
STATUS OF BUDGETARY RESOURCES		
New obligations and upward adjustments (Total)	$ 54,889,189	$ 54,689,093
Unobligated balance, end of year		
Apportioned, unexpired account	3,083,935	2,767,119
Exempt from apportionment, unexpired accounts	37,251	41,804
Unapportioned, unexpired accounts	73,288	100,030
Unexpired unobligated balance, end of year	3,194,474	2,908,953
Expired unobligated balance, end of year	761,791	538,505
Total unobligated balance, end of year	$ 3,956,265	$ 3,447,458
Total budgetary resources	$ 58,845,454	$ 58,136,551
CHANGE IN OBLIGATED BALANCE		
Unpaid Obligations:		
Unpaid obligations, brought forward, October 1	$ 13,200,831	$ 14,053,217
New obligations and upward adjustments	54,889,189	54,689,093
Less: outlays (gross)	(54,606,695)	(54,976,902)
Less: recoveries of prior year unpaid obligations	(603,674)	(564,577)
Unpaid obligations, end of year	$ 12,879,651	$ 13,200,831
Uncollected Payments:		
Uncollected payments, Federal sources, brought forward, October 1	(1,697,626)	(2,017,703)
Change in uncollected payments, Federal sources	(50,551)	320,077
Uncollected payments, Federal sources, end of year	(1,748,177)	(1,697,626)
Obligated balance, start of year	$ 11,503,205	$ 12,035,514
Obligated balance, end of year	$ 11,131,474	$ 11,503,205
BUDGET AUTHORITY AND OUTLAYS, NET		
Budget authority, gross (discretionary and mandatory)	$ 55,022,615	$ 54,176,908
Actual offsetting collections (discretionary and mandatory)	(7,389,858)	(7,762,559)
Change in uncollected customer payments from Federal sources (discretionary and mandatory)	(50,551)	320,077
Recoveries of prior year paid obligations (discretionary and mandatory)	29,544	156,392
Budgetary authority, net (discretionary and mandatory)	$ 47,611,750	$ 46,890,818
Outlays, gross (discretionary and mandatory)	$ 54,606,695	$ 54,976,902
Actual offsetting collections (discretionary and mandatory)	(7,389,858)	(7,762,559)
Outlays, net (discretionary and mandatory)	47,216,837	47,214,343
Distributed offsetting receipts	(740,914)	(1,058,051)
Agency outlays, net (discretionary and mandatory)	$ 46,475,923	$ 46,156,292

TABLE 16-2F **United States Department of Labor**

STATEMENTS OF SOCIAL INSURANCE
As of September 30, 2016, 2015, 2014, 2013, and 2012
For the Projection Period Ending September 30, 2040

(Dollars in Thousands)	Unaudited 2016	2015	2014	2013	2012
BLACK LUNG DISABILITY BENEFIT PROGRAM (Note 1-W and 1-Y)					
Current participants (closed group)					
Present value of estimated future excise tax Income during the projection period	$ 2,906,046	$ 4,738,572	$ 7,301,416	$ 7,494,800	$ 7,804,178
Less the present value of estimated future administrative costs during the projection period	953,474	1,242,920	942,107	920,740	963,995
Less the actuarial present value of future benefit payments to disabled coal miners and dependent survivors during the projection period	1,359,109	1,898,939	1,876,522	1,953,763	2,181,654
Excess of present value of estimated future excise tax income over present value of estimated future administrative costs and actuarial present value of future benefit payments during the projection period (closed group measure)	593,463	1,596,713	4,482,787	4,620,297	4,658,529
New participants					
Present value of estimated future excise tax income during the projection period	1,452,086	-	-	-	-
Less the present value of estimated future administrative costs during the projection period	476,429	-	-	-	-
Less the actuarial present value of future benefit payments to disabled coal miners and dependent survivors during the projection period	679,116	-	-	-	-
Excess of present value of estimated future excise tax income over present value of estimated future administrative costs and actuarial present value of future benefit payments during the projection period	296,541	-	-	-	-

(Continues)

TABLE 16-2F **United States Department of Labor** *(Continued)*

STATEMENTS OF SOCIAL INSURANCE
As of September 30, 2016, 2015, 2014, 2013, and 2012
For the Projection Period Ending September 30, 2040

(Dollars in Thousands)	Unaudited 2016	2015	2014	2013	2012
Current and new participants (open group)					
Present value of estimated future excise tax income during the projection period	4,358,132	4,738,572	7,301,416	7,494,800	7,804,178
Less the present value of estimated future administrative costs during the projection period	1,429,903	1,242,920	942,107	920,740	963,995
Less the actuarial present value of future benefit payments to disabled coal miners and dependent survivors during the projection period	2,038,225	1,898,939	1,876,522	1,953,763	2,181,654
Excess of present value of estimated future excise tax income over present value of estimated future administrative costs and actuarial present value of future benefit payments during the projection period (open group measure)	$ 890,004	$ 1,596,713	$ 4,482,787	$ 4,620,297	$ 4,658,529
Trust fund net position deficit at start of projection period (Note 1-W and 21)	$ (5,604,460)	$ (5,644.208)	$ (5,755,352)	$ (5,894,222)	$ (5,977,619)
Summary Section					
Closed group measure	$ 593,463	$ 1,596,713	$ 4,482,787	$ 4,620,297	$ 4,658,529
Add: Funds with U.S. Treasury and receivables from benefit overpayments (Note 21)	113,856	54,859	129,376	145,794	102,498
Total of closed group measure plus fund assets (Note 1-W)	$ 707,319	$ 1,651,572	$ 4,612,163	$ 4,766,091	$ 4,761,027
Open group measure	$ 890,004	$ 1,596,713	$ 4,482,787	$ 4,620,297	$ 4,658,529
Add: Funds with U.S. Treasury and receivables from benefit overpayments (Note 21)	113,856	54,859	129,376	145,794	102,498
Total of open group measure plus fund assets (Note 1-W)	$ 1,003,860	$ 1,651,572	$ 4,612,163	$ 4,766,091	$ 4,761,027

Table 16-2G **United States Department of Labor**

STATEMENT OF CHANGES IN SOCIAL INSURANCE AMOUNTS
For the Years Ended September 30, 2016 and 2015

BLACK LUNG DISABILITY BENEFIT PROGRAM (Note 1-W and 1-Y)
Open Group Measure

(Dollars in Thousands)	Unaudited 2016	2015
The excess of present value of estimated future excise tax income over present value of estimated future administrative costs and actuarial present value of future benefit payments to disabled coal miners and dependent survivors in the open group during the projection period (open group measure), beginning of year	$ 1,596,713	$ 4,482,787
Changes in the assumptions about beneficiaries, including costs, number, type, age and life expectancy	(22,732)	25,406
Changes in assumptions about coal excise tax revenues	(652,225)	(2,726,804)
Changes in assumptions about Federal civilian pay raises for income benefits	9,653	4,431
Changes in assumptions about medical cost inflation for medical benefits	(8,373)	(1,652)
Changes in assumptions about administrative costs	(95,670)	(253,365)
Changes in assumptions about interest rates	62,638	65,910
Net change in open group measure	(706,709)	(2,886,074)
Open group measure, end of year	$ 890,004	$ 1,596,713

STATEMENT OF CHANGES IN NET POSITION

The **statement of changes in net position** summarizes all entity transactions in addition to net cost of operations that affect net position. It explains how the entity financed its net costs. It includes prior period adjustments and amounts received from appropriations, dedicated taxes, borrowings, and other financing sources. It also reports "imputed financing"—costs incurred by the federal agency that are paid for by another federal entity. In the case of the Department of Labor, these imputed costs are pensions and other postemployment benefits. The column marked "Funds from Dedicated Collections" indicates funds, such as the Unemployment Trust Fund and the Black Lung Disability Trust Fund, that are restricted for specified purposes.

As shown in Table 16-2, the statement of changes in net position links the statement of net costs to the balance sheet. "Net Cost of Operations" ($48,654,897) per the middle of the Consolidated Statement of Changes in Net Position (Table 16-2C) is also the bottom line of the Consolidated Statement of Net Cost (Table 16-2B). Net position, the bottom line of the Consolidated Statement of Changes in Net Position ($40,592,396), also ties into "Total net position" on the Consolidated Balance Sheet (Table 16-2A).

STATEMENT OF BUDGETARY RESOURCES

The **statement of budgetary resources**, which is prepared on a budgetary rather than an accrual basis, reports on the amounts available from both current and prior year appropriations and the entity's cash outlays, newly incurred obligations (the federal equivalent of encumbrances), and obligations of prior years that have been liquidated. The amounts in this report are incorporated in the Treasury's cash-oriented *Annual Report*. As shown in Table 16-2E, the first part of the statement shows the source of budgetary resources (the spending authorized by the federal budget, unobligated balances from prior years, and miscellaneous transfers and collections—a total of $58,845,454). The second shows the status of those resources (those obligated during the year, and those not obligated and thus available for future expenditure—also a total of $58,845,454). Note that the unobligated balance brought forward from 2015 ($3,447,458) is the total unobligated balance, end of year in the column of 2015. The Department of Labor has an unobligated balance from 2016 ($3,956,265) that is available for obligation in 2017.

The third part of the statement reconciles the beginning and ending obligated balances. The agency began the year having a balance of unpaid obligations, carried forward from the previous year, of $13.200,831. As shown in the second part of the statement, during the year it obligated an additional $54,889,189 and liquidated $54,606,695 of those obligations. Thus, after taking account various miscellaneous payments and recoveries and unpaid amounts from the prior year, it had year-end obligated balances of $11,131,474.

The fourth part of the statement indicates the agency's budget authority and outlays. Budget authority is granted mainly through the appropriation process, but it includes other types of spending approval as well—for example, the authority to spend from offsetting collections and from borrowing.

STATEMENT OF RECONCILIATION OF NET COST OF OPERATIONS TO BUDGET (STATEMENT OF FINANCING)

The 2016 annual report of the Department of Labor contains an additional required report, one that reconciles the net cost of operations per the budget to the net cost of operations as reported in the Consolidated Statement of Net Cost. It is referred to most commonly as a **Statement of Financing**. The main difference between the net cost of operations per the Consolidated Statement of Net Cost (Table16-2B) and the total budget resources (indicated in the Combined Statements of Budgetary Resources (Table 16-2E) is the amounts that are included in one of the two statements but not the other. For example, depreciation is included as a component of net cost, in that the statement of net cost is on a full accrual basis. However, it is not considered a use of net budgetary resources in as much the Statement of Budgetary Resources is on a near-cash basis. By contrast, the purchase of a capital asset is a budgetary outlay but is not included as a cost of operations.

The Statement of Financing as currently prepared is exceedingly confusing, filled with line items that only an expert could interpret. For that reason, the FASAB, in 2017, issued Statement of Federal Financial Accounting Standards 53, *Budget and Accrual Reconciliation.* This standard prescribes a reconciliation statement that is far easier to understand. However, that statement will not appear in the financial reports of federal agencies until fiscal year-end 2019. Rather than illustrate a statement that will be out of date, we include a pro forma example, one using a fictitious agency and fictitious numbers (Table 16-3).

STATEMENT OF CUSTODIAL ACTIVITIES

The **statement of custodial activities**, similar to that of a custodial fund, is required only of an entity, such as the IRS or Homeland Security, which through its Customs Service has a main

TABLE 16-3 Budget and Accrual Reconciliation

Department of XXX

For the Year Ending 201X

(In thousands of dollars)	
NET COST	374,911,504
Intra agency eliminations	598,824
Agency Combined	**374,312,680**
Components of Net Cost That Are Not Part of Net Outlays	
Property, plant and equipment depreciation	(508,925)
Property, plant, and equipment disposal & reevaluation	5,044
Unrealized valuation Gain/(Loss) on investments	10,460,000
	9,956,119
(Increase)/decrease in assets	
Accounts receivable	(1,268,551)
Loan receivable	(2,469,301)
Other assets	(901,591)
	15,272,795
Increase/(decrease) in liabilities	
Accounts payable	808,234
Salaries and benefits	(34,326)
Insurance and guarantee program liabilities	519
Other liabilities (Unfunded Leave, Unfunded FECA, Actuarial FECA)	1,758,180
	2,532,607
Other financing sources	
Federal employee retirement benefit costs paid by other agencies and imputed to this agency	(1,264,887)
Transfers out (in) without reimbursement	533,457
Other imputed financing	(292)
	(731,722)
Total Components of Net Cost That Are Not Part of Net Outlays	**27,029,799**
Components of Net Outlays That Are Not Part of Net Cost	
Acquisition of capital assets	224,335
Acquisition of inventory	2,886,686
Acquisition of other assets	1,093
Other	4,949,372
Total Components of Net Outlays That Are Not Part of Net Cost	**8,061,486**
Other Temporary Timing Differences	**(136)**
NET OUTLAYS	**409,403,829**

Budgetary and financial accounting information differ. Budgetary accounting is used for planning and control purposes and relates to both the receipts and use of cash, as well as reporting the federal deficit. Financial accounting is intended to provide a picture of the government's financial operations and financial position, so it presents information on an accrual basis. The accrual basis includes information about costs arising from the consumption of assets and the incurrence of liabilities. The reconciliation of net outlays, presented on a budgetary basis, and the net cost, presented on an accrual basis, provides an explanation of the relationship between budgetary and financial accounting information. The reconciliation serves not only to identify costs paid for in the past and those that will be paid in the future but also to assure integrity between budgetary and financial accounting. The analysis above illustrates this reconciliation by listing the key differences between net cost and net outlays. Unrealized valuation loss on investment in the reconciliation is related to the write down of security investments due to recent market volatility, which did not result in an outlay but did result in a cost.

mission of collecting funds to be turned over to the Treasury or other departments. It shows the resources collected and their disposition (i.e., the amounts transferred to other agencies and the amounts not yet transferred). As a consequence, its bottom line should always be zero. The Department of Labor is not required to prepare the statement of custodial activities, and therefore it is not included in Table 16-2.

STATEMENTS OF SOCIAL INSURANCE AND CHANGES IN SOCIAL INSURANCE

The statement of social insurance presented in Table 16-2F is required only of the relatively few agencies that are charged with administering the government's major social insurance programs. These include not only the Department of Labor, which administers the Black Lung Disability Program, but also the Social Security Administration, the Railroad Retirement Board (railroad retirement benefits), and the Department of Health and Human Services (Medicare). The Department of Labor's statement shows the actuarial present value of the benefit payments that it will have to pay out to the eligible victims of coal mine dust exposure as well as expected receipts.[9] Notably, agencies must also present a statement that indicates the reasons for the changes in the value of the benefit payments (see Table 16-2G).[10]

WHAT ARE OTHER KEY FEATURES OF THE FASAB MODEL?

Not surprisingly, many of the issues being dealt with by the FASAB are similar to those being addressed by the GASB and, in a broad sense, the FASB. They deal with the recognition of revenue and expenses and, correspondingly, with the valuation of assets and liabilities.

BASIS FOR RECOGNIZING REVENUES

The FASAB distinguishes between two types of revenues:

- **Exchange (or earned) revenues** arise from sales transactions in which each party receives benefits and incurs costs.
- **Nonexchange revenues** materialize when the government commands resources but gives nothing in exchange (at least not directly). Nonexchange revenues include taxes, duties, fines, and penalties.[11]

Exchange revenues, the FASAB asserts, should be recognized similar to conventional business-type principles—that is, when goods or services are provided to the public or to another governmental entity. Thus, for example:

- Revenues from services should be recognized as an agency performs the services and meets some obligations.
- Revenues from long-term contracts should be recognized on a percentage of completion basis. If a contract is expected to result in a loss, the loss should be spread over the contract in proportion to the share of estimated total costs incurred in each period. This provision is

[9] Because the Black Lung Program was established in 1978 to compensate exposures prior to 1970, the projection period extends only to 2040. By that time, it is assumed, all the disabled miners as well as their widows and adult children who were entitled to benefits would be diseased. By contrast, the Social Security Administration and Health and Human Services project benefits for Social Security and Medicare over a 75-year period.

[10] The statement of changes in social insurance is required by Statement of Federal Financial Accounting Standards No. 37, *Social Insurance: Additional Requirements for Management's Discussion and Analysis and Basic Financial Statements* (April 2010).

[11] Statement of Federal Financial Accounting Standards No. 7, *Accounting for Revenues and Other Financing Sources* (April 1996).

contrary to the principles of both the FASB and the GASB (as articulated in the FASB's Statement No. 5 and adopted by the GASB) that losses should be recognized when it is probable that an asset has been impaired or a liability incurred and the amount of the loss can be reasonably estimated.

- Revenues from goods sold should be recognized on delivery of the goods to the customer.

According to the FASAB, a federal entity should accrue nonexchange revenues "when a specifically identifiable, legally enforceable claim to resources arises, to the extent that collection is probable and the amount is measurable." Thus, for example:

- *Income taxes* should be recognized when assessed by the taxpayer (as indicated by a cash payment or a filed tax return) or by the result of audits, investigations, or litigation. The government should not recognize as revenues amounts that it estimates it will receive as the result of audits to be conducted in the future.
- *Fines and penalties* may be accrued (1) upon the expiration of the period during which the offender may contest a court summons, (2) when the offender pays the fine before a court date, or (3) when the court imposes a fine.
- *Donations* (as to a federal museum, presidential library, or memorial) should be recognized when the entity has a legally enforceable claim to the donated resources, collection is "more likely than not," and the amount is measurable.

ACCOUNTING FOR PLANT AND EQUIPMENT

The federal government controls over a trillion dollars in long-lived assets, some of which are unlike assets owned by businesses or other levels of government. They include military weapons, national parks and monuments (that produce little or no revenue but are in constant need of maintenance and repair), and conventional assets, such as office buildings and equipment. Recognizing that their diversity necessitates different approaches to accounting and reporting, the FASAB groups the assets into two broad categories: general and stewardship. Stewardship assets are then further divided into two subcategories: land and heritage assets.

General Assets

General assets are comparable to those of a business and include land, buildings, and equipment. Accordingly, the FASAB recommends that they be accounted for similarly. That is, they should be capitalized and (with the exception of land) depreciated over their useful lives. This category consists of assets that:

- Are used to produce goods or services or to support the mission of the entity and can be used for alternative purposes (that is, by other federal programs, state or local governments, or nongovernmental entities)
- Are used in business-type activities
- Are used by entities in activities whose costs can be compared to other entities (e.g., costs of federal hospitals that can be compared to nonfederal hospitals)[12]

Military Assets Military assets, such as aircraft, ships, vehicles, tanks, and extraordinarily complex and costly weapons systems, pose special accounting issues. In times of peace these assets have useful lives that are as estimable as those of general assets. However, when used for

[12] Statement of Federal Financial Accounting Standards No. 6, *Accounting for Property, Plant and Equipment* (June 1996).

the purpose for which they were designed—to fight wars—their anticipated useful lives become considerably shorter and less certain.

Prior to May 2003, recognizing the special characteristics of military hardware, the FASAB directed that what it referred to as "national defense property, plant, and equipment" had to be accounted for as "other stewardship assets." That is, acquisition costs had to be expensed as incurred, not capitalized. In 2003, however, the board took a different tack. Focusing on the need to provide information to facilitate annual performance assessment, the board stipulated that the cost of military assets should be capitalized and depreciated over their expected useful lives. That is, they should be accounted for like general assets.[13]

The board recognized that its general directive to capitalize and depreciate military assets leaves several thorny implementation issues unresolved. For example, it is not clear to what extent the various cost elements of research, testing, development, and evaluation of complex weapons systems should be expensed, rather than capitalized. Accordingly in 2009 it issued its Statement No. 35, *Estimating the Historical Cost of General Property, Plant, and Equipment*, to provide additional accounting guidance.

Space Assets Assets used in the government's space program have characteristics similar to traditional military assets. Nevertheless, even prior to its decision mandating capitalization of military assets, the FASAB prescribed that these assets be accounted for as general assets. Space assets continue to be capitalized and depreciated.[14]

Stewardship Assets

Heritage Assets Heritage assets have value because of their historical, natural, cultural, educational, architectural, or artistic significance. They include museums, monuments, and historical sites; they are expected to be preserved indefinitely.

Some heritage assets may have the characteristics of both operational and true heritage assets. The government holds some heritage assets, such as the Washington Monument, purely for their cultural, architectural, or aesthetic qualities. It holds others, such as the White House and the Eisenhower Executive Office Building in Washington, D.C. (an operating administrative complex), for both their historical and functional attributes. To reduce the subjectivity that would be required in having agencies either allocate a portion of an asset's cost to one category or another or in having them determine whether an asset was primarily operational or heritage, the FASAB stipulated that all multiuse heritage assets be capitalized as general property, plant, and equipment and depreciated over their useful lives.

The cost of acquiring heritage assets that have only historical, artistic, or cultural significance should be expensed as incurred. That is, entities should report them in their statement of net cost. The assets should be referenced on the balance sheet, but no dollar value should be assigned. Instead, information such as the following should be disclosed in notes to basic financial statements:

- A brief statement explaining how the assets relate to the entity's mission
- The goals and principles the entity established to acquire and maintain the assets
- A brief description of the types of assets that the entity holds
- The physical quantities of assets in each of its major heritage asset categories

---

[13] Statement of Federal Financial Accounting Standards No. 23, *Eliminating the Category National Defense Property, Plant and Equipment* (May 2003).

[14] Statement of Federal Financial Accounting Standards No. 11, *Amendments to Accounting for Property, Plant and Equipment: Definitional Changes* (October 1998).

Entities should also report on the condition of its heritage assets; this information may be included in notes to the basic statements or as "required supplementary information." RSI is deemed to be of lesser significance than the information included in notes and is subject to a lesser degree of auditor scrutiny.

Land The federal government owns approximately 640 million acres, which is about 28 percent of all of the land in the United States. Most of this is managed for purposes related to preservation, recreation, and development of natural resources. It includes national parks, national forests, and nature preserves—the vast seemingly uninhabited terrain that one observes when flying from the midwest to the far west. It also includes more than 4,800 defense installations as well as land on which post offices and other federal buildings stand.

In that it is neither used in government operations nor held for sale; stewardship land need not be capitalized and therefore should not be reported on an entity's balance sheet. Instead, like heritage assets it should be expensed as acquired. In periods subsequent to acquisition, the entity should provide, in a note to the financial statements, salient information relating to the land. This should include the relationship of the land to the mission of the entity, the entity's policies relating to the land, the amount of land in physical units, and a description of each major category of land. In addition, in a separate note included in the RSI, the entity should report on the condition of the land.[15]

As this text goes to press, the category of stewardship land encompasses land other than that in the general category. It includes mainly national forests, national parks, and the federal government's vast holdings of undeveloped acreage, but it excludes land that is used for operational purposes. Thus, it excludes the land on which post offices and most other federal buildings are situated as well as that of military installations. That land is capitalized at cost and accorded balance sheet recognition. The FASAB, however, has proposed that all government land, including that in the general category, be accounted for similarly to stewardship land. This proposal is motivated mainly by the inconsistency inherent in requiring some land to be capitalized and other land to be expensed as acquired, as well as research that indicated that financial statement users see little value in the historical cost of any land, irrespective of how it is being used.

Deferred Maintenance In contrast to those of both the FASB and the GASB, the standards of the FASAB mandate extensive RSI disclosures pertaining to deferred maintenance and repairs. Deferred maintenance and repairs "is maintenance and repair activity that was not performed when it should have been or was scheduled to be and which is put off or delayed to a future period."[16] Per the FASAB Statement No. 6, *Accounting for Property, Plant, and Equipment* (November 1995), and amended by Statement No. 42, *Deferred Maintenance and Repairs* (April 2012), government organizations are required to measure their deferred maintenance either by performing a condition assessment or using "life-cycle costing" techniques.[17] Then they must provide detailed information, for each of its asset classes, of the dollar cost of the deferred maintenance and how they arrived at that cost.

[15] The discussion of stewardship assets is based on Federal Financial Accounting Standards No. 29, *Heritage Assets and Stewardship Land* (July 2005). This standard revised previous standards that required entities to issue a "stewardship report" that was to be part of required supplementary information. In effect, it elevated much of the information that was included in the report from required supplementary information to notes that are considered an inherent part of the financial report and are subject to the same degree of auditing as the basic quantitative statements.

[16] Statement of Federal Financial Accounting Standards No. 40, *Definitional Changes Related to Deferred Maintenance and Repairs: Amending Statement of Federal Financial Accounting Standards 6, Accounting for Property, Plant, and Equipment* (May 2011).

[17] Per Statement No. 42, "*Condition assessment* surveys are periodic visual (i.e., physical) inspections of property, plant and equipment (PP&E) to determine their current condition and estimated cost to correct any deficiencies." "*Life-cycle costing* is an acquisition or procurement technique which considers operating, maintenance, and other costs in addition to the acquisition cost of assets. Since it results in a forecast of maintenance and repairs expense, these forecasts may serve as a basis against which to compare actual maintenance and repairs expense and estimate deferred maintenance and repairs."

ACCOUNTING FOR HUMAN CAPITAL

One of the most intriguing questions facing the federal government is whether investments in human capital should be accorded the same accounting recognition as those in physical capital. As defined by the FASAB, investments in human capital are the outlays for the education and training of the public (excluding federal civilian and military employees) intended to increase the nation's productive capacity.

Government agencies undertake educational and training programs to benefit the future, not the present. Arguably, therefore, consistent with the concepts of both matching and interperiod equity, the costs of these programs should be capitalized as incurred and subsequently amortized over the periods to be benefited. Moreover, accounting principles permitting agencies to capitalize outlays for physical assets, but not human "assets," might bias allocation decisions in favor of the physical assets. The reported expenses for the physical assets would be reported over the life of the assets; those for the human assets would have to be recognized as the costs were incurred.

On the other hand, the long-term benefits of educational and training programs are far less identifiable and measurable than those of physical assets. Determinations of the length of the benefit period would necessarily require arbitrary assumptions.

Faced with obvious practical difficulties, the FASAB (like both the FASB and the GASB) rejects the notion of capitalizing investments in human capital. Instead (unlike both the FASB and the GASB) it mandates disclosure as *required supplementary stewardship information* (RSSI) in the financial report. Minimal reporting, it says, should include the annual investment made for the past five years and a narrative description of the major human capital programs.[18] Nevertheless, as this text goes to press, with an eye toward streamlining both the federal government-wide statements and those of its component entities, the FASAB is likely to propose the elimination of the RSSI category and thus no longer require entities to report on their investments in human capital. Per the proposal entities may, however, elect to identify such investments either in their basic financial statements or in the Required Supplementary Information (RSI) category.

RECOGNIZING LIABILITIES AND RELATED EXPENSES

Of all the accounting and reporting issues facing the federal government, those pertaining to liabilities are probably the least tractable and the most controversial.[19] As explained by the FASAB, government liabilities are attributable to *events*. "Events" encompass both "transactions" and other "happenings of consequence" involving the government.

Transactions can be of two types:

- **Exchange transactions**, in which each party gives and receives something of value (e.g., when the government purchases goods or services).
- **Nonexchange transactions**, in which the government provides something of value without directly receiving something of value in return—for example, when the government incurs an obligation under a grant or entitlement program. An entitlement program is one that provides benefits to parties if they satisfy certain conditions (such as being unemployed or having an income below a specified amount). Once the program is authorized, no further congressional action is needed to appropriate the funds to sustain it. Thus, the cost to the government is never certain; it depends on the number of parties satisfying the conditions.

---

[18] Statement of Federal Financial Accounting Standards No. 8, *Supplementary Stewardship Reporting* (May 1996).

[19] This discussion is based on Statement of Federal Financial Accounting Standards No. 5, *Accounting for Liabilities of the Federal Government* (September 1995).

Happenings of consequence can also be classified into two categories:

- **Government-related events** represent mainly accidents for which the government is responsible and required by law to reimburse the injured parties for damages.
- **Government-acknowledged events** are occurrences for which the government is not responsible but elects, as a matter of policy, to provide relief to the victims. They include primarily natural disasters, such as hurricanes and earthquakes.

Neither exchange transactions nor government-related events pose issues unique to governments. Therefore, consistent with the principles of accrual accounting, the FASAB prescribes that federal entities recognize both a liability and a related expense resulting from an exchange transaction when an exchange takes place (e.g., when the government receives the contracted-for goods or services). They should recognize a liability and a related expense for a government-related event as soon as the event occurs and the anticipated outflows of resources are both probable and measurable.

Nonexchange transactions and government-acknowledged events raise the difficult question of recognition because they stem from the government's use of its sovereign power and there may be no well-defined event or transaction that establishes the obligation. For example, Congress authorizes financial assistance to parties satisfying specified conditions. It thereby commits the federal government to a future outflow of resources. Yet, until the parties demonstrate that they have met the specified conditions, the government does not have an obligation either of an established amount or to identifiable parties. The commitment may extend over an unspecified number of years, and the ultimate amount to be paid may depend on economic and social conditions well into the future. Further, the government can unilaterally cancel or change the program at any time.

To help ensure consistency among a broad spectrum of events and transactions, the FASAB directs that federal entities recognize liabilities for:

- *Nonexchange transactions when due.* Thus, government agencies need recognize liabilities for grants and entitlements only as payments are due.
- *Government-acknowledged events* when the government formally *acknowledges* financial responsibility for the event and an amount is *due and payable* as a result. Thus, the government need recognize liabilities for disaster relief only when it has authorized specific grants to specific individuals, or contractors have actually provided their goods or services.

REPORTING THE OBLIGATIONS FOR SOCIAL INSURANCE PROGRAMS

The liabilities that the FASAB had to address that were far and away the most contentious were those stemming from social insurance programs in general and Social Security and Medicare in particular. These programs have no direct counterpart in either the private or municipal government sectors of our economy.

The accounting controversy over social insurance programs stems largely from the different ways in which these programs can be interpreted. Social Security, for example, can be seen as either a government-sponsored pension plan (involving mainly exchange transactions) or a government-managed income redistribution program (involving mainly nonexchange transactions). It is a pension program in that both employees and employers contribute to a fund over the course of the employees' working lives in anticipation of the employees receiving a lifetime stipend on retirement. It is an income redistribution program in that the government taxes both employees and employers, dedicating the tax to program beneficiaries. The tax rate is not calculated on any generally accepted actuarial basis, and the payments that beneficiaries receive on retirement are not actuarially tied to the taxes that they or their employers paid.

In its Statement No. 17, *Accounting for Social Insurance* (1999), the FASAB specified that both the federal government at large and the individual agencies that administer social insurance programs should account for social insurance costs as if they were nonexchange transactions. That is, the reporting entities need recognize a liability (and related expenditure) for payments to beneficiaries or service providers only when the payments are actually due. Therefore, they need not record on their balance sheet the actuarial value of the benefits earned by program participants.

The FASAB acknowledges that of prime interest to anyone concerned with social insurance programs are their long-term sustainability and their impact on the overall fiscal condition of the federal government. Indeed, these have been a focal point of ongoing political and economic discourse. Consequently, the FASAB requires extensive disclosure of information such as the following:

- Long-range cash flow projections in nominal dollars and as a percentage of both the payroll that is subject to the tax dedicated for the program and the gross domestic product
- Long-range projection of the ratio of contributors to beneficiaries (commonly called the "dependency ratio")
- Statements presenting the actuarial present values of future benefits, contributions, and tax income and changes in such values

Well into the twenty-first century, the debate continued over when social insurance obligations should be reported as balance sheet liabilities or merely disclosed in notes and RSI as required by Statement No 17 (and subsequent amendments). Unable to reach consensus among its members, the FASAB issued a compromise statement, *Social Insurance: Additional Requirements for Management's Discussion and Analysis and Basic Financial Statements* (No. 37, April 2010). This statement retained the provisions of Statement No. 17, which did not require the government to show the obligations as a liability until they were actually due and payable. However, it mandates that the government-wide entity (as well as entities that are responsible for social insurance programs) add a section to the statement of social insurance that summarizes the net present values of the anticipated cash flows, present a statement that indicates the reasons for the changes in net present value during the year, and include in management's discussion and analysis information about commitments, projections, assets, and other key fiscal measures.

Closely tied to the issue of the amounts to be recorded as liabilities and expenditures is that of how the required disclosures should be calculated. In a nutshell, the questions the FASAB faced were: (1) which participants should be taken into account in making projections and measuring the actuarial benefits and obligations, and (2) over how long a period should the projections be made and the actuarial present value calculated?

Private employers report as their actuarial liability the amount that their current employees and retirees have earned but have not yet been paid. For the federal government, a similar approach—that is, reporting what current participants in the insurance programs and retirees have earned—may not be entirely adequate. Social Security and Medicare are not voluntary programs; everyone must join, and everyone can expect to receive benefits. Therefore, the federal government's obligation for benefits extends not only to current participants or even current U.S. citizens but also to the unborn children of both U.S. citizens and future immigrants to the United States.

After considerable debate, the FASAB stipulated that the Statement of Social Insurance should focus primarily on the present value of cash flows related to a "closed group" population—those persons who as of the valuation date are current beneficiaries, covered workers, or payers of dedicated taxes. However, extensive disclosures pertaining to an "open group" measure—which includes future as well as current participants—are also required.[20] The FASAB does not specify the length of the projection period; however, for Social Security and Medicare, it has been 75 years.

RECOGNIZING THE COST OF SUBSIDIZED DIRECT LOANS AND LOAN GUARANTEES

As part of their social, educational, and commercial programs, federal entities make low-interest direct loans and guarantee loans made by banks and other institutions. The low-interest loans provide a direct benefit to the borrowers by providing funds at less than the rate they would

[20] For an in-depth discussion of the characteristics and decision-utility of the two methods see the Basis for Conclusion of FASAB Statement No. 37.

otherwise have to pay. The guarantees virtually eliminate credit risks to the lenders and thereby enable them to provide funds to the borrowers at reduced interest rates. The targeted beneficiaries of these loan programs include farmers, veterans, students, and small businesses.

Prior to the Federal Credit Reform Act of 1990, agencies were not required to recognize explicitly the costs of making the low-interest loans. Instead, they simply reported less-interest revenue than they would have had they charged prevailing interest rates. Correspondingly, they recognized the costs of the loan guarantees only as they reimbursed the lenders upon borrower defaults.

The Federal Credit Reform Act of 1990 requires that the president's budget reflect the long-term costs in the year in which the direct loans and the guarantees are made. To enhance conformity between budgeting and accounting practices, the FASAB directed that the same principles apply to annual financial reports.[21] According to the FASAB, when a government makes a subsidized direct loan, it should recognize as an asset the present value of its estimated net cash receipts, including both interest and repayment of principal. It should report an expense equal to the difference between the face value of the loan and the present value of the estimated net cash receipts.

Per current standards, present value should be based on the interest rate of marketable Treasury securities with similar terms to maturity as the cash flows. Some critics, however, contend that such is too low. It thereby overstates the value of the anticipated cash receipts and understates the value of the subsidy. They assert that the government should use a rate that reflects what a borrower would have add to pay on loans from a private-sector bank or comparable lender.

Example

Subsidized Loan

A government agency makes a three-year, two percent, direct loan of $1,000 at a time when prevailing Treasury rates on short- and intermediate-term securities are four percent. The loan is to be repaid in three annual installments of $347 (the amount required to amortize a $1,000, two percent loan over three years—$1,000 divided by 2.88388, the present value of an annuity of $1 for three periods).

Inasmuch as the present value of three payments of $347, discounted at four percent, is only $963 ($347 times 2.77509, the present value of an annuity of $1 for three periods), the agency should recognize an expense of $37 (the difference between the loan's $1,000 face value and the $963 present value of the payments). The following entry would therefore be appropriate when the loan is made:

Loan receivable	$963	
Loan subsidy (expense)	37	
Cash		$1,000
To record a direct loan		

In subsequent periods, the agency should recognize revenue of 4 percent of the balance of the loan receivable and correspondingly reduce the balance of the loan receivable by the difference between the revenue recognized and the cash received. Thus, in the first year:

Cash	$347	
Loan receivable		$308
Interest revenue (four percent of $963)		39
To record the first payment from the borrower[22]		

Each year the agency should reestimate the present value of its anticipated cash flows (taking into account updated information on both potential defaults and changes in the prevailing interest rate) and adjust its accounts to reflect the new calculations.

[21] Statement of Federal Financial Accounting Standards No. 2, *Accounting for Direct Loans and Loan Guarantees* (July 1993), as modified by Standard No. 18, *Amendments to Accounting Standards for Direct Loans and Loan Guarantees in Statement of Federal Financial Accounting Standards No. 2* (May 2000), and Standard No. 19, *Technical Amendments to Accounting Standards for Direct Loans and Loan Guarantees in Statement of Federal Financial Accounting Standards No. 2* (March 2002).

[22] The entries recommended by the FASAB are somewhat more complex, requiring various contra accounts. However, the reported loan subsidy expense, interest revenue, and the next loan receivable would be the same.

When a government *guarantees* loans (as opposed to making them directly), it should also recognize both an expense and an obligation in the amount of the present value of its anticipated payments to the lender. Then, each year the government should reassess the present value of the anticipated payments and recognize the change in value as either an increase or a decrease in its loan guarantee liability, offset by either a debit or credit to loan guarantee expense.

Example

Loan Guarantees

At the start of year 1, an agency guarantees $100 million of student loans. The following schedule indicates the agency's estimates of the payments (all at year-end) that it will have to make to lenders owing to defaults and the present value of those payments. The agency applies a discount rate of eight percent.

End of Present Net Present Year Amount Value of $1 Value

End of Year	Amount	Present Value of $1	Net Present Value
1	$2,100,000	0.92593	$1,944,453
2	1,500,000	0.85734	1,286,010
3	1,000,000	0.79383	793,830
Total			$4,024,293

Upon guaranteeing the loans, the agency would make the following entry:

Interest expense	$4,024,293	
Liability for loan guarantees		$4,024,293

To record expense of guaranteeing loans (which, per the FASAB, should be classified as "interest expense")

Suppose that during the first year the agency pays lenders $2.1 million, as estimated, to fulfill its guarantees. Its new estimate of the present value of the anticipated payments, measured as of the end of year 1, is now as follows:

End of Year	Amount	Present Value of $1	Net Present Value
2	$1,500,000	0.92593	$1,388,895
3	1,000,000	0.85734	857,340
Total			$2,246,235

The following entry would be appropriate to record the cash payment of $2.1 million and the adjustment of the liability:

Liability for loan guarantees	$1,778,058	
Interest expense	321,942	
Cash		$2,100,000

To record payment of $2,100,000 and adjust the balance on the remaining liability for the difference between $4,024,293 and $2,246,235 (the interest expense represents 8 percent of the beginning of year balance of $4,024,293)

If the agency revises its estimate of the second- or third-year payments, then to compute the loan guarantee expense in year 1 and the liability at year-end, it would incorporate the net present value of the addition (or reduction) in expected payments. Thus, if the agency estimates that the year 3 payment would now be $1.3 million, then it would substitute $1.3 million for $1 million in this computation. If interest rates decreased to six percent, it would use that rate in discounting the cash flows.

ACKNOWLEDGING TAX EXPENDITURES

Governments can subsidize activities in one of two ways. They can offer direct payments to parties that engage in targeted activities, or they can provide tax credits, deductions, or similar tax benefits to those parties. Thus, for example, the federal government can subsidize farmers by paying them cash if their revenue per acre falls below a benchmark or guaranteed level. Alternatively, it could give them tax credits—an allowable reduction of their tax liability—in the same amount. The economic impact on the government's surplus or deficit would be the same, and the benefit to the farmers would also be virtually identical. However, if the government paid the farmers directly, the outlay would be reported as an expense in both its budget and its financial statements. By contrast if it provided the tax credit, it would not be reported as an expense and would not be given any explicit budgetary or accounting recognition. The government would incur what is known as a **tax expenditure.**

Tax expenditures are revenue losses attributable to provisions of the tax code that allow taxpayers special exclusions, exemptions, credits, or deductions, usually to achieve identified policy objectives. Although tax expenditures are often thought of as tax "loopholes," they are, in fact, far broader than that. They range from provisions that affect only well-targeted taxpayers and activities to those that benefit wide segments of society. They include, for example, provisions in the tax code that permit natural gas companies to take accelerated depreciation on their pipelines as well as those that permit employees to exclude from taxable income the value of health insurance provided by their employers. The revenue "lost" to the Treasury of these special provisions is by no means small. It is estimated, for example, that the exclusions of employer-paid medical insurance alone will cost the Treasury $236 billion in revenue in 2018.[23]

Consistent with its reporting objectives of providing information to statement users as to the federal government's budgetary integrity, operating performance, and fiscal stewardship, the FASAB, in 2017, issued its Statement No. 52, *Tax Expenditures.* This statement requires that the federal government, in its consolidated financial report:

- include narrative disclosures that inform readers as to the definition of tax expenditures, their general purpose, how they are treated within the federal budget process, and their impact on the government's financial position
- alert readers as to the availability of published estimates of tax expenditures, such as those published annually by the Department of the Treasury's Office of Tax Policy

While such note disclosures are no substitute for incorporating the tax expenditures into the government's statement of net cost—an impractical requirement in light of definitional and measurement issues—it does serve to warn statement users that targeted tax benefits, even when virtuous, can be as expensive as direct appropriations.

WHAT ELSE CONSTITUTES THE FEDERAL GOVERNMENT'S REPORTING SYSTEM

The reporting system of the federal government is far broader than the annual reports of the government as a whole and its individual agencies and departments. When viewed holistically, the federal government is far more transparent regarding its finances than either private-sector corporations or state and local governments.

Recognizing the limitations of traditional accounting systems that focus exclusively on financial metrics, Congress enacted the Government Performance and Results Act of 1993, which requires federal agencies to develop strategic plans, operational objectives, and measures of performance and to report on the extent to which it met its objectives.

[23] U.S. Department of the Treasury, *Tax Expenditures*, Resource Center, Tax Policy, https://home.treasury.gov/policy-issues/tax-policy/tax-expenditures (accessed September 30, 2018).

As detailed in the act, as part of its annual budget request to the OMB, each agency must prepare and submit a performance plan that includes:

- Objective, quantifiable, and measurable goals that define the agency's anticipated level of performance
- A description of the operational processes, skills, technology, and "human capital" required to meet the performance goals
- A basis for comparing actual results to the goals
- The means of verifying and validating actual performance

In addition it must also submit a report that:

- Reviews success in achieving the performance goals of the previous fiscal year
- Evaluates the performance plan for the current fiscal year relative to the previous year's results
- Explains any deviations from its goals, indicating why a goal was not met, describing plans for achieving the goal, and, if the goals were impractical or infeasible, spelling out why and recommending corrective steps

The act also requires agencies to develop "strategic plans" that cover five-year period. The plans should set forth the agencies' missions, goals, and objectives and the means to achieve them.

In 2010 Congress updated the Government Performance and Results Act with the passage of the Government Performance and Results Modernization Act. Based on the experience with the initial act, the new measure is intended to ensure that agency goals better align with the broader goals of the federal government, provide a tighter link between their performance goals and their strategic plans, and mandate quarterly reviews and progress assessment of priority goals.

In another measure, albeit only indirectly related to accounting, Congress in 2006 enacted the Federal Funding Accountability and Transparency Act (FFATA) (P.L. 109-282). Intended to reduce wasteful spending, the legislation makes available on a searchable website (www.USASpending.gov) detailed information on federal awards and contracts. This act was subsequently amended in 2014 by the Digital Accountability and Transparency Act (DATA Act) (P.L. 113-101) both to require full disclosure of virtually all federal agency expenditures and to ensure that such information is compiled and collected in a standardized format. As a result of these acts, one can go to USASpending.gov and with a few clicks learn the details of almost every contract entered into by the federal government.

Since 1990, the GAO has been publishing an annual list of "high-risk areas"—government programs and operations that are especially vulnerable to fraud, waste, and mismanagement, as well as areas in need of broad reform. Each year it reviews its list, adding new programs and deleting others. Among areas that are perennially on the list are certain Department of Defense activities, tax collection operations, Medicare, and NASA contract management.[24]

WHAT ARE THE KEY INTERNATIONAL TRENDS IN GOVERNMENTAL ACCOUNTING?

Over the last several decades, accounting practitioners as well as students have directed considerable attention to the "international" aspects of business accounting. Initially, owing to the prevalence of international trade and cross-border investment, their concerns were mainly with understanding the accounting and reporting systems of other countries. More recently, however, they have focused efforts on "harmonizing"—making uniform—business accounting standards throughout the world.

[24] See https://www.gao.gov/products/GAO-18-645T (accessed September 30, 2018).

By contrast, far less attention has been paid to the international aspects of governmental accounting. In large measure, governmental accounting standards have been strongly influenced by the institutional characteristics of individual countries. Accordingly, the practices of one country have not been as readily transferable to others. Further, governments—particularly local governments—have typically generated their resources within their own country, so there has been less need for them to present financial statements to outsiders. In addition, even though national governments may have sought funds from sources beyond their borders, the lenders apparently have been willing to base their credit analyses mainly on broad economic, social, and political indicators rather than on financial statements prepared in accordance with GAAP.

This, however, is now changing. Governments themselves increasingly engage in international exchanges. At both the national and local levels, they use nondomestic contractors to construct major infrastructure projects, they purchase goods and services from international corporations, and they sell securities in the international credit markets. In the 1960s, for example, foreign holdings of the U.S. federal debt held by the public were less than five percent. By 2017, they had soared to over 42 percent—$6.2 trillion. Moreover, owing perhaps to major defaults by national governments and losses on projects that they financed, lenders are demanding more and better fiscal data.

Credit rating agencies, such as Moody's, Standard & Poor's, and Fitch, have responded to the demand for improved information by rating the bonds of governments, both national and local, outside the United States just as they do those within. Indeed, the factors that they take into account are similar to those they use domestically. Hence, they assess factors that are generally reported on in financial statements as well as those that bear only indirectly on the entity's fiscal condition. Examples include:

- The diversity, performance, and prospects of each member state's national economy
- Intergovernmental fiscal and financial arrangements
- Trends in fiscal balances
- Debt burdens, pension obligations, and contingent liabilities
- Tax competitiveness within a regional and worldwide context, along with tax-raising flexibility
- Liquidity and debt management

As might be expected, no standard-setting organization has the authority to establish accounting standards for governments other than those within its own country. Nevertheless, the International Public Sector Accounting Standards Board (IPSASB) of the International Federation of Accountants (IFAC) is responsible for developing a set of standards intended to improve both the quality and comparability of financial reports.

AN INTERNATIONAL STANDARD-SETTING AGENCY

As of November 2017, IPSASB has issued more than 40 standards (in addition to studies, implementation guides, and occasional papers). Many of its standards address issues similar to those dealt with by the GASB. A key part of its strategy is to converge its standards with those of the International Accounting Standards Board (IASB), the board that sets standards for businesses. Not surprisingly, therefore, in its pronouncements, the IPSASB makes clear that regardless of historical tradition, public-sector accounting should be on a full accrual, not a cash, basis. This position is manifest in all its pronouncements. Thus, for example, per the standards:

- Property, plant, and equipment, including infrastructure (but excluding heritage assets) should be capitalized and depreciated.
- Revenue from exchange transactions should be recognized when the revenue can be measured reliably, it is probable that the entity will realize an economic benefit, and both the stage of completion of the transaction and the costs incurred can be measured reliably.

- Inventories intended for sale should be recognized as an expense in the period in which related revenues are recognized. If there is no related revenue, then the expense should be recognized when the goods are distributed or a related service is rendered (i.e., on a consumption rather than a purchases basis).
- Borrowing costs should be recognized as an expense as "incurred" (i.e., not necessarily when cash is disbursed).

The IPSASB cannot require individual countries to adopt its standards; it can merely encourage them to do so. According to the IPSASB, the GASB is considered a standard setter with full accrual accounting standards that are "broadly consistent" with IPSAS requirements. The public-sector standards for Australia, Canada, New Zealand, and the United Kingdom are also considered broadly consistent.

SUMMARY

The U.S. Constitution left it to Congress and the executive branch to determine the form and content of financial reports and to implement and administer the underlying accounting systems of the government. The federal government in the last several years has made significant improvements in its accounting and reporting systems. In fact, contrary to conventional wisdom, federal accounting standards are at least as rigorous as those in the private and state and local government sectors, and the federal annual report is considerably more transparent.

The three federal agencies with oversight responsibility for financial management are making major strides in coordinating the accounting systems and reporting practices of individual agencies. The Department of the Treasury has a broad range of functions, including managing the public debt and acting as a central collection and disbursement agent. The OMB, a part of the executive branch and one of the most powerful agencies in the federal government, helps prepare and supervise the federal budget and reviews and evaluates agency programs. The GAO, a part of the legislative branch, performs an array of functions but is most closely identified with its role as the government's auditor—the watchdog of Congress.

FASAB, which was established in 1990, is responsible for promulgating accounting standards for the government as a whole as well as its separate components. Since its inception it has developed a comprehensive accounting model as well as detailed standards that address specific types of transactions.

The federal government's unified budget is intended to show the impact of federal activities on the national economy. It encompasses four types of funds—the general fund, special funds, trust funds, and revolving funds. Ironically, the receipts and disbursements of both Social Security and the U.S. Postal Service, despite their major impact on the fiscal welfare of both the government and the nation at large, are excluded from unified budget calculations relating to spending caps. Nevertheless, they are included in receipts and outlays that are commonly at the center of most political and economic discussions.

Budget accounts ensure that a federal entity complies with budgetary mandates, does not overspend appropriations, and is able to fulfill reporting requirements. Proprietary accounts, which are based on FASAB standards, provide an economic rather than a budgetary measure of the government's operations and resources. The FASAB established three criteria for a component to be considered a reporting entity: it is budgeted for by elected officials of the federal government, it is owned by the federal government, or it is controlled by the federal government with risk of loss or expectation of benefits. In addition, it has set forth several other criteria to determine whether the entity should be consolidated in the annual report or merely disclosed in notes.

The FASAB's comprehensive reporting model helps ensure that the financial statements of the government at large, as well as its component units, focus on all economic resources and are on a full accrual basis. Key requirements of the FASAB include the following:

- Exchange revenues should be recognized when goods or services are provided to the public or to another governmental agency. Nonexchange revenues should be recognized on both an accrual and a cash basis. That is, an entity should report the actual cash collections and add or subtract from them an "accrual adjustment," representing the difference between amounts accrued and amounts collected. Revenues should be accrued when the government has a legal claim on the resources and collection of cash is both probable and measurable.

- General property, plant, and equipment, multiuse heritage assets, and military assets should be capitalized and depreciated. By contrast, stewardship assets and "pure" heritage assets should be expensed as acquired and described in notes to the financial statements..
- Liabilities for nonexchange transactions should be recognized when due; those for government-acknowledged events should be recognized when the government formally acknowledges financial responsibility and an amount is due and payable.
- Liabilities, and related expenses, for both loan guarantees and subsidized loans, should be recognized at the time the loans are made.

The Government Performance and Results Act of 1993 (and updated in 2010) further improved federal accounting and fiscal management. It requires that agencies establish specific goals and objectives and report annually on the extent to which they achieve them. Moreover, owing to recent legislation, information on most individual government contract is available at USASpending.gov.

Recent years have witnessed increased interest in harmonizing international standards and enhancing their quality. These efforts are being spearheaded by the IPSASB. This board has issued standards for governments at all levels that, consistent with trends in the United States, are full accrual based.

KEY TERMS IN THIS CHAPTER

Apportionments 697
Chief Financial Officer (CFO) of the United States 697
general fund 700
Government Accountability Office (GAO) 698
human capital 704
Rule 203 698
statement of budgetary resources 722
statement of changes in net position 720
statement of custodial activities 721
Statement of Financing 721
statement of net cost 714
Statement of social insurance 704
stewardship assets 712
Tax expenditures 732
unified federal budget 700

EXERCISE FOR REVIEW AND SELF-STUDY

Congress established the Wilderness Lands Preservation Commission (a fictional entity). Its main function is to encourage farmers, ranchers, and similar types of landowners to take specified conservation measures. To help the landowners finance these measures, the commission makes subsidized loans. It is also empowered to regulate certain land-usage practices and to impose financial penalties on landowners who violate them.

1. The Commission is governed by a seven-person board, the members of which are appointed by the president, subject to the approval of Congress. The commission is funded through the normal appropriation process—i.e., with tax dollars. Should the commission be considered a federal reporting entity, and if so should it be a "consolidation" entity or merely a "disclosure" entity?

2. The entity maintains both budget accounts and proprietary accounts. What is the distinction between the two types of accounts?

3. Employees of the commission participate in the Social Security system. How will the federal government's obligation to provide benefits to them be reported on the government's consolidated financial statements (i.e., will it be included among its liabilities)? If not, why not?

4. In a recent year, the Commission received an appropriation of $100 million. Of this amount, it spent only $80 million. Assuming that the appropriation does not lapse, how would the unspent $20 million be reported on the *Commission's* year-end balance sheet?

5. To educate the public on the importance of wildlife preservation, the Commission received a legally binding pledge of $2 million from a private foundation. Of this amount, only $0.5 million was received during the year. The balance is expected to be received in the following year. How much of the pledge should be recognized as revenue in the year it was made?

6. To assist landowners in covering their conservation-related costs, the Commission lends them the required funds at below market rates. During its first year of operations, the Commission lent one landowner $400,000. The landowner was required to repay the loan in three annual payments of $144,139, an amount that reflects an interest rate of four percent. At the time of the loan, the prevailing rate on three-year Treasury securities was eight percent. How should the Commission account for the cost of the loan?

7. In the course of the year, the Commission acquired the following assets:
   a. Buildings for $5 million (to provide office space)
   b. Land for $40 million (acquired as a wildlife refuge)
   How should each of these assets be accounted for?

8. Per regulations established by the Commission, landowners in specified areas near designated wildlife refuges are not permitted to kill or trap animals of prey. In return, the Commission reimburses landowners for the value of any livestock killed by the animals. Toward the end of the year, one farmer submitted a claim to the Commission for $12,000. As of year-end, the Commission had not yet authorized payment. What journal entry, if any, should the Commission make to record the claim?

QUESTIONS FOR REVIEW AND DISCUSSION

1. What is the primary role of the Treasury Department's Bureau of Fiscal Service?
2. The Office of Management and Budget is responsible for granting agencies apportionments. What are apportionments?
3. Why is the FASAB named an advisory board? What is the relationship between the FASAB and the GAO, the Treasury Department, and the OMB?
4. What are the four main objectives of federal financial reporting as established by the FASAB?
5. What is meant by the unified budget? Why are Social Security receipts and disbursements said to be "off budget?"
6. Why may it be unclear whether a particular program or subunit of an agency or department is an appropriate independent reporting entity?
7. What are the key criteria of whether an entity should be included in the Financial Report of the U.S. Government?
8. What are the key criteria of whether an entity should be accounted for as a "consolidation" entity or a "disclosure" entity?
9. What are the basic statements that an agency may have to prepare to be in compliance with FASAB standards?
10. Into what two categories does the FASAB divide government assets? How are each of the two accounted for?
11. Why does it matter whether Social Security is considered a pension plan or an entitlement program? How does the FASAB direct that Social Security be reported? What unique issue does the federal government face in calculating the actuarial value of its Social Security obligation that a private corporation would not face in calculating the corresponding obligation of its pension plan?
12. If an agency makes a loan at a below market rate, what would be the nature of any expense recognized at the time of the loan? If it guaranteed a loan made by others, what would be the nature of any expense recognized at the time of the guarantee?
13. What are tax expenditures, and how must they be reported upon in the federal government's consolidated financial report?

EXERCISES

EX. 16-1

Select the *best* answer

1. The federal government's annual financial statements are issued by
   a. The Department of the Treasury
   b. The Office of Management and Budget
   c. The Department of Commerce
   d. The Government Accountability Office

2. The Government Accountability Office is part of which of the following branches of government?
   a. The executive branch
   b. The legislative branch
   c. The judicial branch
   d. None of the above; it is an independent agency

3. The Chief Financial Officer of the United States reports directly to
   a. The comptroller general
   b. The president
   c. The majority leader
   d. The head of the OMB

4. The "budget" as adopted by Congress
   a. Includes receipts and disbursement of both Social Security and U.S. Postal Service accounts
   b. Is similar to those of state and local governments in that it includes estimates of all revenues and expenditures
   c. Coverage is on a full accrual basis
   d. Is essentially a series of 11 or 12 appropriation measures

5. Which of the following is *not* a required element of federal government-wide statements?
   a. Management's discussion and analysis
   b. Descriptions of stewardship assets
   c. A schedule comparing actual with anticipated nonmonetary performance measures
   d. A statement that shows, by major department or agency, the net cost of operations

6. Per the FASAB, a federal entity should be considered a reporting entity and thereby must issue annual reports if it
   a. Is listed in the OMB's Catalog of Federal Agencies
   b. Has been designated as a reporting entity by Congress
   c. Is controlled by the federal government with risk of loss or expectation of benefits
   d. Meets OMB minimum revenue requirements

7. In the federal government, "proprietary accounts" are those that
   a. Provide the data required to prepare accrual-basis financial statements
   b. Provide the data required to prepare budget-basis financial statements
   c. Are used to account for business-type activities
   d. Are used to account for classified information that cannot be made public for security reasons

8. Which of the following statements would report net cost of operations, appropriations, transfers, and revenues?
   a. Statement of net cost
   b. Statement of financing
   c. Statement of changes in financial position
   d. Statement of budgetary resources

9. Which of the following is an example of an "exchange" revenue?
   a. Proceeds from the sale of goods or services
   b. Transfers from another agency
   c. An increase in an OMB allotment
   d. Collections of taxes on liquor sales

10. The federal government should recognize revenue from income taxes
    a. As taxpayers earn their income
    b. As taxpayers report on their tax returns the amount of their tax or make periodic cash payments
    c. As soon as it is able to make a reasonable estimate of the amount that it will collect
    d. On the date the taxes are due

EX. 16-2

Select the *best* answer.

1. Military hardware should be accounted for as
    a. Stewardship assets
    b. Heritage assets
    c. National defense assets
    d. General assets
2. The Executive Office Building has historical significance yet is also used as functioning office space. The cost of the building should be
    a. Depreciated, like that of other general assets
    b. Not accorded balance sheet recognition
    c. Allocated between general assets and heritage assets
    d. Reported on the balance sheet but not depreciated
3. The cost of constructing and renovating the Washington Monument should be
    a. Reported on the balance sheet and depreciated
    b. Not accorded balance sheet recognition
    c. Reported on the balance sheet at a symbolic amount (e.g., $1)
    d. Reported on the balance sheet but not depreciated
4. In a particular year, Congress establishes a program that entitles all senior citizens to reimbursements for eye examinations.
    a. The estimated actuarial cost of the program for a period of 75 years should be reported as a liability and corresponding expenditure in the year Congress authorized the program
    b. The cost of the program should be reported as a liability and corresponding expense as the payments are due to the senior citizens
    c. The cost of the program should be reported as an expense as the payments are made to the senior citizens
    d. The cost of the program should be reported as a liability and corresponding expense as the OMB issues an allotment authorizing the agency to make the required disbursements
5. A hurricane strikes the Florida coast, and, as required by law, the federal government provides financial assistance to parties who suffer property losses. The federal government should recognize the assistance payments as expenditures in the period in which
    a. The hurricane occurred
    b. The department in charge of the program authorizes the payments and the amount is due and payable
    c. The Treasury Department issues the checks
    d. The department in charge of the program acknowledges that it is responsible for providing assistance to hurricane victims
6. The actuarial liability for Social Security that the federal government discloses in its financial statements is based on a projection of
    a. One year
    b. 10 years
    c. 75 years
    d. A perpetuity
7. The federal government should recognize the expenses associated with a subsidized loan program
    a. In the period in which it establishes the program
    b. In the periods that it makes the loans
    c. In the periods in which the loan recipients disburse the funds that they borrow
    d. Over the periods the loans are outstanding

8. In the period in which it guarantees a loan, the federal government should recognize a liability in the amount of
   a. Zero, assuming that there are no defaults in that period
   b. The total amount of the loans that it guarantees
   c. The amount that it expects to pay owing to borrower defaults
   d. The present value of the amount that it expects to pay owing to borrower defaults

9. The Government Performance and Results Act of 1993 (and updated in 2010) mandates that
   a. Each federal agency submit a performance plan to OMB
   b. All federal funds recipients be subject to an annual performance audit
   c. Each federal agency be subject to an annual performance audit
   d. Each federal agency prepare its budget using zero-base budgeting or a comparable form of performance budgeting

10. The accounting standards established by the International Public Sector Accounting Standards Board (IPSASB)
   a. Must be adhered to by all national governments the debt of which is traded in international markets
   b. Must be adhered to by all national governments that are signatories to the United Nations International Commerce Treaty
   c. Must be adhered to by members of the European Economic Community
   d. Represent recommended "best practices" and are for guidance only

EX. 16-3

The financial statements of the federal government are unique.

The left-hand column of the following table describes each of seven financial statements that the FASAB recommends agencies prepare. The right-hand column indicates the names of the seven statements. Match the description in the left-hand column with the correct title in the right-hand column.

a. Summarizes all entity transactions, such as earned revenues and expenses and net cost of operations; explains how the entity financed its net costs; includes amounts received from appropriations, dedicated taxes, borrowings, and other financing sources.	1. Statement of budgetary resources
b. Shows the resources collected and disbursed; required only of entities, such as the Internal Revenue Service and Customs that collect funds to be turned over to the Treasury or other organizations.	2. Statement of custodial activities
c. Shows the entity's assets, liabilities, and net position, including fund balance with the Treasury.	3. Statement of financing
d. In essence an operating statement; shows operating costs and earned revenues.	4. Statement of changes in net position
e. Reconciles the statement of budgetary resources to the statement of net cost.	5. Statement of net costs
f. Prepared on a budget basis; shows amount available for appropriations, cash outlays, and newly incurred obligations.	6. Balance sheet
g. Required only of selected agencies, it presents actuarial data pertaining to various entitlement programs.	7. Statement of social insurance

EX. 16-4

Nonexchange, as opposed to exchange, revenues present the more difficult issues of accounting recognition.

The federal government, through its various government agencies, engaged in the following transactions involving revenues.

1. In the middle of its fiscal year, it rented land to a tenant. It signed a one-year lease requiring monthly payments of $2,000. In the year in which the lease was signed, the tenant occupied the land for six months but paid an entire year's rent (i.e., $24,000).

2. It signed two contracts to provide engineering services to a foreign government; each contract was for $50 million. During the year, the federal agency completed 100 percent of one contract and 60 percent of the other. It collected the entire $100 million in cash.
3. It assessed fines of $100,000 each on two firms for polluting waterways. One offender paid the fine; the other notified the government that it would contest the fine in court.
4. It accepted from a private foundation a pledge of $120,000 to fund an exhibit in a government museum. During the year the foundation paid $40,000 of its pledge, promising to pay the balance in the following year. The pledge does not constitute an enforceable legal agreement.
5. As the result of an audit, it assessed a company $250,000 in income taxes for a previous year, the entire amount of which was certain to be collected. In their audit report, the auditors estimated that audits of subsequent years would yield an additional $150,000.

Prepare journal entries to record the transactions. For each entry comment briefly on the amount of revenue recognized.

EX. 16-5

Low-interest loans constitute a subsidy and hence an expense.

The Business Development Corporation (BDC), a federal agency (fictitious), makes loans to high-tech companies that satisfy specified criteria. The loans are intended to encourage research and development and are made at rates substantially below market.

The BDC made a loan of $100,000 to Interface Networks, Inc. The interest rate was six percent, and the loan was payable over a three-year period in equal installments of $37,411. At the time of the loan, prevailing Treasury interest rates for loans of comparable maturities were 10 percent.

1. What was the amount of the loan subsidy?
2. How and when should the agency recognize the value of the subsidy? Explain.
3. Prepare a journal entry to record the loan and recognize the subsidy.

EX. 16-6

Different types of assets are accounted for in different ways. The government purchased or constructed the following assets.

1. A monument to honor the sailors who served in the U.S. Coast Guard.
2. Land to be incorporated into a national forest.
3. A train station that will serve as both an operating office building and a historical monument.
4. An office building for the Government Accountability Office.
5. Land on which will be built an office building.
6. Operating room equipment for a Veterans Administration hospital.
7. A navy fighter plane.
8. A historical building that is being used—and will continue to be used—to house federal offices. For each, indicate whether it should be:
   a. Capitalized and depreciated (or amortized) over its useful life
   b. Capitalized but not depreciated (or amortized)
   c. Expensed as acquired and described in notes
   d. Reported either at historical cost (based on either the FIFO or the weighted average methods) or at latest acquisition cost
   e. Reported only at historical cost

PROBLEMS

P. 16-1

It is a matter of professional judgment whether and how certain entities should be included in the Financial Report of the U.S. Government.

Based on the criteria set forth in this chapter and the limited facts presented, indicate which of the following apocryphal entities you believe should be incorporated into the Financial Report of the U.S. Government. For those that you think should be included, tell whether you think it should be a consolidation entity or a disclosure entity.

1. The Entrepreneurial Business Administration was established by Congress to promote investment in innovative small businesses. The agency is financed with congressionally appropriated funds and is considered a unit of the Department of Commerce.
2. Electronics, Inc. is a major Defense Department contractor and, in fact, receives all of its revenue from military contracts. Accordingly, it is completely dependent on the U.S. government for its survival. Although the revenues of Electronics, Inc. are not directly appropriated by Congress, funds to support the weapons systems on which Electronics, Inc. works are.
3. Congress and the president established Delta Corporation as a not-for-profit organization to promote the export of U.S. robotics technology. The corporation is governed by a five-person board of directors, two of whom are appointed by the Secretary of Commerce and two of whom are named by the Robotics Industry Association. The corporation is funded from fees assessed to members of the association. The Corporation is audited by the Government Accountability Office and must submit an annual report to the Senate and House Commerce Committees.
4. Congress and the president chartered Mt. Vernon Technical College to engage in sophisticated research in nanotechnology. Most of its funding comes from contracts with suppliers and from private donations. However, Congress explicitly appropriates approximately 15 percent of the college's budget under a Department of Education program. Although the appropriations provide general guidance on how the resources may be used, the college nevertheless has broad discretion over specific activities and projects to which it can allocate the funds.
5. The Energy Industry Accounting Standards Board was established by major oil and gas companies as a not-for-profit corporation with the mission, as its name implies, of establishing accounting standards for energy firms. It is governed by a 10-member board of trustees appointed by the firms that established it. The board is financed by a tax on shares of energy companies that are traded either on major exchanges or in over-the-counter markets. The Securities and Exchange Commission determines the tax rate and collects the tax. However, it has no administrative responsibility for the taxes collected other than to pass them through to the board. Further, although it unquestionably influences the decisions of the board, it has no direct control over them.

P. 16-2

The impact of consolidating the Fed may not be obvious.

Among the most contentious of federal accounting issues is how the Federal Reserve System should be accounted for in the Financial Report of the U.S. Government.

1. Review a recent balance sheet of the Federal Reserve System ("Federal Reserve Banks Combined Statements of Condition"). The financial statements of the Federal Reserve System can be found on the system web page (for 2016: https://www.federalreserve.gov/aboutthefed/files/combinedfinstmt2016_508.pdf).

   In reviewing the balance sheet, be sure to examine that of the Federal Reserve System Banks Combined, not that of the Board of Governors.

   a. What is the single largest asset of the Federal Reserve System; what is the single largest liability?

   b. Suppose that the government were to consolidate the financial statements of the Fed with its other assets and liabilities. How would the largest asset and liability of the Fed affect the government's reported assets and liabilities? Would consolidation of those items increase or decrease the net financial position of the government? Explain.

2. What arguments can you make both for and against consolidating the Fed?

P. 16-3

Accounting for social insurance remains controversial.

Because only the summary of the Statement of Social Insurance is presented in the text, obtain the most recent complete Consolidated Financial Report. It is available on the website of the Bureau of the Fiscal Service of the Department of the Treasury (try https://www.fiscal.treasury.gov/fsreports/rpt/finrep/fr/fr_index.htm).

Review the Statement of Social Insurance, the related notes, and the discussion of social insurance that is included as "required supplementary information."

1. In terms of both revenues and expenditures, which is the largest of the social insurance programs?
2. Assuming no change in current law, which of the programs is likely to impose the greatest financial burden on the government's general fund? Explain.
3. What are the three main components of Medicare? How do they differ?
4. The Social Insurance Summary presents the total present value of future expenditures in excess of revenues for both a "closed group" and an "open group." What is the difference between the two (see the related notes for an explanation)? Why would the excess be greater for the closed group than for the open group?
5. The federal government has been criticized for not including the obligations for social insurance as balance sheet liabilities.
   a. What is the rationale for not including them?
   b. Do you think federal spending policies would be more conservative (i.e., there would be less spending) if such obligations were included as liabilities? Explain.

P. 16-4

Federal agency financial statements were illustrated but not discussed in detail in this chapter. Nevertheless, despite some unusual terminology, they are readily understandable.

Examine the following financial statements, which are condensed versions of those of a federal agency responsible for collecting taxes and duties and transferring them to the Treasury.

Statement of Custodial Activity for Year Ended September 30 (in millions)	
Tax revenues for others	
Collections	$ 4,900
Increase in taxes receivable	200
Total revenues for others	$5,100
Disposition of revenues	
Amounts transferred to the treasury	$4,800
Increase in amounts to be transferred	300
Total disposition of revenues	$5,100
Net custodial activity	$ 0

Statement of Net Cost for Year Ended September 30 (in millions)	
Personnel costs	$ 300
Other costs	500
Net cost of operations	$ 800

Statement of Net Changes in Net Position for Year Ended September 30 (in millions)	
Financing sources—appropriations used	$ 775
Less: net cost of operations	800
Net results of operations	$ (25)
Increase in unexpended appropriations	125
Increase in net position	$ 100
Net position, beginning of year	450
Net position, end of year	$ 550

Balance Sheet as of September 30 (in millions)

Assets	
Fund balance with treasury	$ 125
Taxes receivable	615
Plant, equipment, and other assets (net of accumulated depreciation)	285
Total assets	$1,025
Liabilities	
Custodial liability	$450
Other liabilities	25
Total liabilities	$ 475
Net position	
Unexpended appropriations	$ 125
Cumulative results of operations	425
Total net position	$ 550
Total liabilities and net position	$1,025

Statement of Budgetary Resources for Year Ended September 30 (in millions)

Budgetary resources made available	
Current appropriations	$ 900
Status of budgetary resources	
Obligations incurred	$ 775
Unobligated balance not available (expired allotments)	125
Total, status of budgetary resources	$ 900
Outlays	
Obligations incurred	$ 775
Add: obligated fund balance and accounts payable, beginning of year	70
Deduct: obligated fund balance and accounts payable, end of year	(60)
Total outlays	$ 785

Statement of Financing for Year Ended September 30 (in millions)

Obligations and nonbudgetary resources	
Obligations incurred	$ 775
Increase in goods and services ordered but not yet received	(5)
Costs capitalized on the balance sheet and not expensed	
Acquisition of capital assets	(10)
Expenses that do not require budgetary resources	
Depreciation	40
Net cost of operations	$ 800

1. How much did the agency actually collect in taxes? How much did it submit to the Treasury? How much did it owe the Treasury at year-end for both taxes collected and taxes receivable (i.e., its custodial liability per the balance sheet)? How much did it owe at the beginning of the year?

2. How much did it cost the agency to carry out its activities during the year?

3. Of its operating costs, how much was financed by federally appropriated funds?

4. What was the total amount that the agency was appropriated during the year? What was the balance that was not used? Is this amount available for immediate use by the agency? If not, why not? Did the agency have a balance in unexpended appropriations at the start of the year? How can you tell?

5. What was the total amount of goods and services ordered by the agency during the year? How much of goods or services was received (including amounts ordered in the previous year but received in the current year)? How much was paid for?

6. Per the statement of financing, the agency ordered $775 of goods and services (obligations incurred), but the net cost of operations per both the statement of financing and the statement of net cost is $800. How can the net cost of operations exceed the amount of goods and services ordered? Explain and account for the differences.

P. 16-5

Veterans benefits (not discussed in this chapter) present especially challenging issues of accounting.

The financial statements of the Department of Veterans Affairs (VA) contained the following excerpt from a note entitled "Veteran Benefits:

> *Certain Veterans, who die or are disabled from military service-related causes as well as their dependents, receive compensation benefits. Also, Veterans are provided with burial flags, headstones/markers, and grave liners for burial in a VA national cemetery or are provided a burial flag, headstone/marker and a plot allowance for burial in a private cemetery. These benefits are provided under Title 38, Part 2, Chapter 23 in recognition of a Veteran's military service and are recorded as a liability on the balance sheet in the period the requirements are met.*

The note also indicates that the actuarial value of these benefits as of year-end was $1.975 trillion. In addition, the VA offers medical benefits to veterans. These are provided through VA hospitals but only to the extent that required facilities are available (except for veterans with service-connected disabilities, who are automatically entitled to medical services). The government makes no guarantees as to level of care, and Congress decides annually how adequately the facilities will be funded.

Although this chapter did not address veterans' benefits, it did raise the related question of whether the government should report a liability for the actuarial value of anticipated Social Security benefits and correspondingly recognize an expense for the benefits as they are "earned" by the beneficiaries.

Suppose that you are the auditor of the VA. Do you think that the VA should recognize a liability (and a corresponding expense) for each of the following benefits during the years in which the veterans perform their military service (or are injured or die)? Or alternatively, do you think that the liability (and related expense) for the benefits should be recognized only when the payments are actually due or the medical services are actually provided?

1. Payments to be made to veterans or their families as a consequence of disability or death from service-connected causes.

2. Pension benefits attributable to non-service-connected causes. (The actual amount of the benefits is tied mainly to need, rather than to length of service, compensation, or rank. These benefits are in addition to the traditional pension benefits available to career military personnel.)

3. Medical benefits to be provided at VA facilities. (The VA makes no promises to veterans as to the availability or level of care. Congress decides annually on the level of funding.)
   Be sure to present your response in the context of FASAB-established principles as discussed in the text.

P. 16-6

The primary statements of a federal agency can be constructed from the proprietary and budget accounts.

The following balances, in trial balance form, were drawn from the year-end ledgers of the Federal Lending Agency (a fictitious entity) following the agency's first year of operations. Some of the accounts are aggregations of those that would typically be maintained by a federal entity. Budgetary (as opposed to proprietary) accounts are marked with an asterisk.

	Debit (in millions)	Credit
Various expenses	$ 219	
Miscellaneous revenues		$ 93
Appropriations used		412
Fund balance with the treasury	1,140	
Loans receivable	126	

	Debit (in millions)	Credit
Equipment	80	
Allowance for depreciation		16
Accounts payable and other liabilities		256
Unexpended appropriations		788
Cumulative results of operation, beginning of year	0	
Current appropriations	1,200*	
Borrowing authority	160*	
Obligations incurred		640*
Funds available for commitment		720*
	$2,925	$ 2,925

1. Following the formats illustrated in the text, prepare the following statements:
   a. A statement of net cost
   b. A statement of changes in net position
   c. A balance sheet
   d. A statement of budgetary resources (omitting the section on outlays)

2. Review the amounts on the financial statements.
   a. Do the cumulative results of operations per the balance sheet agree with the cumulative results of operations per the statement of changes in net position?
   b. Are the unexpended appropriations per the balance sheet equal to the appropriations received per the statement of budgetary resources less the appropriations used per the statement of changes in net position?

P. 16-7

Federal revenues may be accounted for and reported in an unusual manner.

A federal environmental agency engaged in the following transactions during a particular year.

1. It billed corporations for which it provided services $160 million. Of this, it collected $140 million.

2. It levied $150 million in fines and penalties against corporations. Of this, $90 million was collected in cash. Of the balance, the protest period has expired on $35 million, which the agency expects to collect in the following year. The remaining $25 million is in dispute, and court dates have not yet been set.

3. It collected an additional $20 million in fines and penalties that had been assessed by federal courts in the previous period.

4. It received cash donations of $3 million and pledges of an additional $2 million. The agency's counsel advises that the pledges are not legally enforceable.
   a. Prepare journal entries to record the revenues and collections.
   b. Show how the revenues and related receivables would be reported on the agency's statement of net cost (i.e., an operating statement) and balance sheet.

P. 16-8

Loan guarantee costs should be reported mainly in the year the guarantees are made.

To help middle-income students finance the cost of their university educations, the Student Loan Authority guarantees student loans made by private banks. By guaranteeing the loans, the agency enables the banks to make the loans at rates far lower than they would without the guarantees.

In 2017 the agency guaranteed $120 million of loans. It estimates that, owing to student defaults, it will have to fulfill its guarantees as follows (in millions):

Year	Amount
2018	$0.5
2019	1.2
2020	2.0
2021	1.8

1. Prepare the entry that the agency should make in 2017, the year it guarantees the loans. The agency applies a discount rate of six percent. It assumes that all guarantee payments will be made at the end of the indicated years.

2. Prepare the entries that it should make at the end of 2018, assuming that it fulfills its guarantees, as estimated, of $0.5 million.

P. 16-9

When should the costs of subsidized loan programs be recognized?

In 2020, Congress established a small business direct loan program. The program provides that qualifying businesses can obtain loans at a rate five percent below that prevailing on Treasury securities of comparable maturity. The program was to be in effect for a period of 12 years. Its total cost was estimated at $1.3 billion.

In 2021, the Small Business Administration, which administers the program, loaned the S & D Produce Company $100,000 for 10 years at a rate of five percent. At the time, the prevailing Treasury rate was 10 percent. The loan was to be repaid in 10 annual installments of $12,950.

1. What journal entry, if any, should the Small Business Administration make in 2020 when Congress authorized the program? Explain and justify your response.

2. What journal entry should it make in 2021 when it loaned the S&D Produce Company $100,000? Explain and justify your response.

3. What journal entries should it make in 2022 and 2023 on collection of the first two loan repayments?

P. 16-10

Federal expenditures raise unique issues of recognition.

In a particular year, the federal government was affected by the following transactions and events. For each, indicate the amount that it should recognize as an expense during that year. Cite the FASAB principle on which you rely.

1. The government ordered 10 military aircraft from a manufacturer at a cost of $100 million each. During the year it received five and paid for two. Their expected useful life is 10 years.

2. In response to extraordinary floods, Congress appropriated $24 billion in disaster relief. Some of the aid was targeted for infrastructure repair. During the year, the government contracted with a construction firm to repair a bridge at an agreed-upon price of $12 million. The contractor completed a portion of the job, billing the government for $6,000,000.

3. As part of the same flood relief program, the government authorized direct grants to individuals and businesses. During the year, it approved grants totaling $400 million, of which it actually paid $240 million. It expected to pay the balance, which is due and payable, in the following year.

4. To assist workers laid off as the result of a recently passed free-trade agreement, Congress approved an employee relief act. The act provides that eligible employees would receive direct payments of $1,500 per month for up to 12 months. The cost of the program over its lifetime is expected to be $680 million. During the year, 25,000 laid-off workers applied and were certified as eligible for benefits. They were paid a total of $150 million.

5. During the year, the employees of one government agency earned pension benefits having an actuarial present value of $30 million. The government made actual payments of $23 million to employees who had previously retired from that agency.

P. 16-11

Federal long-lived assets have unique characteristics justifying unique accounting practices.

For each of the following assets acquired by federal departments and agencies, indicate how the government should report the asset. If it is to be reported on the government's balance sheets, then state whether it should be amortized or depreciated. Justify your response by specifying the category into which the asset would fall.

1. The U.S. Coast Guard purchases, for $3 million, a mainframe computer to be used to enhance nonmilitary navigation systems.
2. The Department of Defense purchases a mainframe computer for $6 million. The computer is specially designed to be used onboard a guided-missile cruiser to target missiles.
3. The Department of Interior constructs a monument, at a cost of $7 million, honoring the military personnel who served in the Gulf War.
4. The Department of Interior purchases land in Bethesda, Maryland, for $6 million. It expects to construct an office complex on the land.
5. The Department of the Interior purchases land in East Glacier, Montana, for $130 million. The land will be incorporated into Glacier National Park.
6. NASA incurs $24 million to improve facilities at its Johnson Space Center. The facilities are to be used both as a training center for astronauts and other personnel and as a museum for visitors.

P. 16-12

Federal statements may understate both assets and liabilities.

Review the government-wide statements as presented in **Tables** 16-1A–G of the text.

1. What was the amount of the government's deficit for the year? What was the amount of its net position?
2. What three departments incurred the largest amount of expenses (net)?
3. What was the government's main source of revenues?
4. The government's balance sheet excludes a significant amount of both assets and liabilities. What government-owned assets are omitted from the balance sheet? What liabilities are omitted?
5. Suppose that the federal government would change the paydays of certain employees from the last day of each month to the first day of the next (a classic means of decreasing budgetary expenditures for a particular year). Would that gimmick reduce the net cost of operations as reported in the statement of net cost?
6. The statement of net cost indicates the gross cost of the Social Security program, but it does not include under "earned revenue" the amounts that the program collects as payroll deductions. Where in the financial statements would such amounts be reported? What justification is there for not reporting these revenues as earned revenues of the Social Security program?

P. 16-13

Although not tied to "conventional" accounting reports, detailed information on individual government contracts, grants, and loan guarantees is readily available to the public.

Go to www.USAspending.gov.

1. In the latest year for which data are available, which state was the beneficiary of the greatest amount of total federal assistance. How much did it receive?
2. Of that amount, how much was provided by the Department of Education?
3. Of the amount provided by the Department of Education, how much was received by the University of California System (i.e., Regents of the University of California)?

SOLUTION TO EXERCISE FOR REVIEW AND SELF-STUDY

1. The Commission is budgeted for by elected officials of the federal government. That, by itself, qualifies it as a reporting entity. In addition, however, it is also controlled by the federal government insofar as the board members are appointed by the president and approved by Congress. Moreover, because it is financed with tax revenues, accountable to Congress and the president, imposes financial risks to the government through its lending programs, and provides goods and services on a nonmarket basis, it is clearly a consolidation entity.

2. Budget accounts ensure compliance with budgetary mandates and hence are generally on a budgetary (i.e., cash or near-cash) basis. Proprietary accounts, based on FASAB standards, are intended to provide an economic, rather than a budgetary, perspective and are generally on a full accrual basis.

3. The obligation for Social Security benefits will not be reported on the federal government's balance sheet as a liability. It will be reported instead on a separate statement of social insurance. Social Security, unlike a traditional pension plan, is considered to be an entitlement program. Taxes paid by participants in the program are not calculated on an actuarial basis, and benefits are not tied directly to taxes paid. Therefore, the government recognizes a benefit expense only as the benefits are due and payable and does not record a liability until then.

4. The unexpended appropriation would be shown on the Commission's balance sheet as "Fund Balance with the Treasury." It would also be included in the equity (net position) account "Unexpended Appropriations."

5. Donations should be recognized on the receipt of a legally binding pledge. Hence, the entire $2 million should be recognized as revenue.

6. The cost of subsidizing the loan is the difference between the loan's face value ($400,000) and the present value of the anticipated receipts (three payments of $144,139 discounted at eight percent). The present value of the three payments is $371,461 ($144,139 times 2.5771, the present value of annuity of $1 for three periods discounted at eight percent). The difference is $28,539. The Commission should recognize this amount as an expense of the period in which it makes the loan.

7. The assets should be accounted for as follows:
   a. Buildings are general assets and should be capitalized and depreciated over their useful lives.
   b. The land to be used as a wildlife refuge is a stewardship asset. It should be expensed when acquired and in that year and subsequent years described in notes to the financial statements.

8. The Commission's obligation is the consequence of a "government-acknowledged event"—an occurrence for which the government is not responsible but elects, as a matter of policy, to provide relief to the victims. The government should recognize a liability and corresponding expense for such an event when it formally acknowledges financial responsibility and an amount is due and payable. Thus, the Commission need not recognize any liability or expense for the damages until an amount is due and payable.

Glossary

2a7-like investment pool A government external investment pool that operates similarly to investment companies subject to the Security and Exchange Commission's Rule 2a7 of the Investment Company Act of 1940. These companies invest in securities, such as Treasury bills, notes, and certificates of deposit, that are both safe and have short-maturities— typically 60 days or less—and hence are not subject to major price swings.

A

ABC See activity-based costing.

accountability The cornerstone of financial reporting; requires governments to answer to its citizens and provide a "right to know" for public information.

account group An accounting entity with a set of accounts that is self-balancing and is used to account for a government's general fixed assets or general long-term obligations. Account groups are distinguished from funds in that they are not used to account for sources, uses, and balances of expendable available financial resources. Account groups were an integral part of the "old" accounting model; they are no longer needed under the model prescribed by GASB Statement No. 34.

accrual basis A method of accounting that recognizes revenues when a performance obligation is met and expenses when incurred regardless of when cash is received or paid.

accrued expenses Expenses that have been incurred and recorded, but have not yet been paid.

accrued revenue Revenue that has been earned and recorded, but not yet received.

activity A line of work contributing to a function or program.

activity-based costing (ABC) A method of costing where overhead costs are collected in cost pools and distributed to particular products or services using cost drivers. **See cost driver**.

actuarial accrued liability A government's pension obligation as determined by an appropriate actuarial cost method.

actuarial cost method A means of allocating the total cost of expected pension benefits over the total years of employee service.

ad valorem property taxes Property taxes based on the value of the property.

advance refunding Issuance of debt to retire outstanding bonds or other debt instruments prior to their maturity or call date.

affiliated organization A legally independent entity directly tied to a primary government. May be distinguished from both a component unit and a related organization (as defined in GASB Statement No. 14, *The Financial Reporting Entity*, and its amendment in 2002, GASB Statement No. 39, *Determining Whether Certain Organizations Are Component Units*) in that the primary government does not appoint a majority of its governing board, and it is not fiscally dependent on the primary government.

agent A party that acts on behalf of another. For example, a government that collects taxes for another government.

agent multiple-employer plan A pension plan in which many government employers pool investments together, yet maintain separate accounts for calculating liabilities.

allocated costs Costs that cannot be associated directly with specific products or services, but are assigned to them according to a predetermined formula or algorithm.

allot To divide a budgetary appropriation into amounts that may be encumbered or expended during an allotment period (e.g., a government may choose to allot its annual budget to 12 monthly periods), or for specified programs or activities.

allotments Periodic allocations of funds to departments or agencies to ensure that an entire year's appropriation is not expended early in the period covered by the budget or expended for certain programs or activities to the detriment of others.

American Institute of Certified Public Accountants (AICPA) A professional organization for certified public accountants (CPAs) that is responsible for establishing auditing and related professional standards.

amortization (1) The process of allocating the cost of an intangible asset over its useful life. (2) The reduction of debt by regular payments of principal and interest sufficient to retire the debt by maturity.

annual report The financial report of a business, government, or not-for-profit entity. Typically consists of a balance sheet, operating statement, statement of changes in equity, a statement of cash flows, and other supplementary information.

annuity A series of equal payments over a specified number of equal time periods.

annuity fund An endowment fund to account for gifts that provide fixed payments to the donor (or a person designated by the donor) for a specified term or for the remainder of his or her life. Thereafter, what remains of the gift will typically revert to the recipient organization.

apportionment The shares of a total federal appropriation that the Office of Management and Budget permits an agency to spend within a particular time period (such as a quarter) or for designated programs, activities, or projects.

appropriation An amount authorized by a legislative body for a department or to make expenditures and incur liabilities for a specified purpose.

appropriations budget The legislatively approved budget that grants expenditure authority to departments and other governmental units in accordance with applicable laws.

arbitrage The concurrent purchase and sale of the same or an equivalent security in order to profit from differences in interest rates. Generally, as it relates to state and local governments, the issuance of debt at relatively low, tax-exempt, rates of interest and the investment of the proceeds in taxable securities yielding a higher rate of return.

assess To value property for the purpose of property taxes.

assets limited as to use The resources designated by the organization's governing board for specific purposes (e.g., to replace plant and equipment). For purposes of external reporting, however, board-designated resources are *not* considered restricted and thus are reported along with other operating resources without donor restrictions. They may, however, be classified within the fund without donor restrictions as assets limited as to use.

asset retirement obligation A legal obligation related to retiring a tangible long-lived asset.

assigned fund balance The net position (assets minus liabilities) of a fund the government intends to use for a specific purpose.

attest To affirm to be correct, true, or genuine; corroborate. The attest function (i.e., an audit) adds credibility to the assertions of others; in the case of a financial audit, credibility is added to an entity's financial data as presented by management.

attestation engagements Services provided by audit organizations that cover a broader scope than financial statements audits. They involve performing agreed-upon procedures as to various types of management assertions or types of transactions or processes that do not necessarily have a direct impact on the financial statements. These might include an entity's internal accounting or administrative controls; compliance with rules, regulations, or terms of contracts; prospective or pro forma financial statements; and costs of contracts.

audit A systematic investigation or review to corroborate the assertions of others or to determine whether operations have conformed to prescribed criteria or standards. An examination of records to check their accuracy.

auxiliary enterprises Units of colleges, universities, or other not-for-profit entities that charge for the services they provide and whose activities are conducted on a business-type basis. Examples include intercollegiate athletics, bookstores, and dining facilities.

B

basis of accounting The means of determining the timing of revenue and expenditure recognition. **See also cash basis** and **accrual basis**.

benefit-cost analysis A generic term for any form of expenditure analysis that identifies and quantifies the benefits of a proposal and compares them to its costs.

bequest To give property by will.

betterment An addition or modification to a capital asset that either enhances its useful life or increases its productivity. Contrasted with maintenance.

blending One of two methods of reporting components units required by GASB Statement No. 14, *The Financial Reporting Entity* (**see discrete presentation** for a description of the other method). This method combines a component unit's transactions and balances with the data of the primary government as if the component unit were a part of that government.

bond A written promise to pay a specified sum of money (its face value) at one or more specified times in the future along with periodic interest. Bonds are a form of notes payable but are characterized by longer periods of maturity and more formal documentation.

bond anticipation notes (BANs) Short-term interest bearing notes issued by a lender in the expectation that they will soon be replaced by long-term bonds.

bond discount At issue date, the excess of a bond's stated (par) value over the bond's initial sales (issue) price. Bonds are issued at a discount so that the return to investors will be equal to the prevailing market interest rate, even though the prevailing market interest rate may be higher than the interest rate stated on the bond (the coupon rate). At later dates, bond discount is the excess of a bond's stated value over the bond's initial price plus the portion of the discount already amortized.

bond premium The same as bond discount except that the bond's initial sales price exceeds the bond's stated (par) value.

bond rating agencies Companies, the leading ones being Standard & Poor's (S&P), Moody's Investors Service, and Fitch Ratings, that evaluate bonds or other securities based on the likelihood that the issuer will not default on payments of principal or interest.

bond refunding The issuance of new bonds to replace bonds already outstanding, usually with the intent of reducing debt service costs.

book value The value of an asset or liability as reported on financial statements; distinguished from market value.

budget A plan of financial operations embodying an estimate of proposed expenditures for a given period and the proposed means of financing them.

budgetary accounts Accounts used to enter a formally adopted annual operating budget into the general ledger to enhance management control over revenues and expenditures.

budgetary control The control or management of a government or enterprise in accordance with an approved budget to keep expenditures within the limitations of available appropriations and available revenues.

business-type activities Activities engaged in by a government or not-for-profit entity that are similar in nature to those carried out by businesses; activities that are financed in whole or in part by fees charged to external parties for goods or services.

C

CAFR See Comprehensive Annual Financial Report.

call price A predetermined price at which the issuer of bonds may redeem (call) the bonds irrespective of the current market price.

callable bond A bond that permits the issuer to redeem the obligation at a specified price before the stated maturity date.

capital assets Long-term assets, such as buildings, equipment, and infrastructure, intended to be held or used in operations; sometimes referred to as "fixed" assets.

capital budget A plan of proposed capital outlays, such as for infrastructure, buildings, equipment and other longlived assets, and of the means of financing them.

capital debt Long-term debt issued to finance capital assets.

capital expenditures Expenditures to acquire or construct capital assets.

capital improvement program (CIP) A plan for the acquisition of capital assets over several (typically five) years.

capital projects fund A fund to account for financial resources set aside for the acquisition or construction of major capital facilities.

capitation fee A fee, paid by an insurance company or other third-party payor to a health care organization, that is based on number of persons covered rather than on actual services provided.

cash basis A method of accounting in which revenues and expenses are recognized and recorded when received, not necessarily when earned.

cash equivalents Short-term, highly liquid investments that can readily be converted into fixed amounts of cash.

cash flow statement A financial statement that details the inflows and outflows of cash.

certificate of participation (COP) A long-term debt instrument that, although similar in economic substance to a bond, is secured by a long-term capital lease.

charity care Health care services that are provided to patients and for which no compensation is expected.

Chief Financial Officer of the United States The Deputy Director for Management, a position created by the Chief Financial Officers Act of 1990. He or she is responsible for providing overall direction and leadership in the establishment of sound federal financial practices.

Codification of the Government Accounting Standards Board *Governmental Accounting and Financial Reporting Standards*, a compendium of GASB promulgated accounting principles, including those adopted from predecessor standard-setting organizations.

cognizant agency Under the Single Audit Act, a federal agency responsible for coordinating the special requirements of each federal agency that provides funds to the auditee and ensuring that all audit standards are met; typically the federal agency providing the greatest amount of funds to the auditee.

collateral Assets pledged to secure deposits, investments, or loans.

collateralized debt obligation An asset-backed security whose value and payments are derived from a portfolio of fixed-income underlying assets; such as a pool of subprime mortgages.

collectibles Works of art, rare books, and historical artifacts.

combined statements The five basic statements that constitute General Purpose Financial Statements (GPFS) under the "old" model. They include the (1) combined balance sheet of all fund types and account groups; (2) combined statement of revenues, expenditures, and changes in fund balances—all governmental fund types; (3) combined statement of revenues, expenditures, and changes in fund balances—budget and actual for general and special revenues funds (and other governmental fund types for which annual budgets have been legally adopted); (4) combined statement of revenues, expenses, and changes in retained earnings—all proprietary funds; and (5) combined statement of changes in financial position—all proprietary fund types.

combining statements Financial statements that provide the details of individual funds (e.g., nonmajor funds or internal service funds) that might be combined in higher level statements. A statement in which each fund is displayed in a separate column and in which a "totals" column ties into amounts reported in another statement.

committed fund balance The net assets (assets minus liabilities) of a fund that can be used only for the specific purposes determined by the government's highest level of decision-making authority.

Common Rule See Uniform Administrative Requirements for Grants and Cooperative Agreements to State and Local Governments.

compensated absences Absences, such as vacations, illness, and holidays, for which it is expected employees will be paid. The term does not encompass severance or termination pay, postretirement benefits, deferred compensation, or other long-term fringe benefits, such as group insurance and long-term disability pay.

compliance audit An audit designed to provide reasonable assurance that an auditee has complied with applicable laws, regulations, and contractual agreements.

compliance requirements A set of fourteen requirements that involve policies and practices to which all federal funds recipients must adhere. Examples are those pertaining to cash management, allowable costs, eligibility, and subrecipient monitoring.

component unit Per GASB Statement No. 14, *The Financial Reporting Entity*, as amended in 2002 by GASB Statement No. 39, *Determining Whether Certain Organizations Are Component Units*, and in 2010 by GASB Statement No. 61, *The Financial Reporting Entity: Omnibus—An Amendment of GASB Statements No. 14 and No. 34*, is a legally separate government for which the elected officials of the primary government are financially accountable, appoints a voting majority of the organization's governing body ***and*** (1) it is able to impose its will on that organization ***or*** (2) there is a potential for the organization to provide specific financial benefits to, or impose specific financial burdens on, the primary government.

Comprehensive Annual Financial Report (CAFR) The official annual report of a state or local government. It includes introductory materials (such as a letter of transmittal and auditors report), financial statements (and supporting notes and supplementary schedules), and statistical data.

Comptroller General of the United States The head of the Government Accountability Office (GAO).

conditional promise A promise to donate an asset or provide a service in the future that is contingent on a specified future event.

conduit debt Obligations issued in the name of a government on behalf of a nongovernmental entity. The debt is expected to be serviced entirely by the nongovernmental unit.

consolidated statements Statements in which two or more funds are combined so that they are reported as if they were a single economic entity.

constant dollar cost The cost of goods or services in dollars that have been adjusted to take into account changes in the general level of prices (i.e., inflation).

consumption method A method of accounting for inventories and prepaid costs, such as ret, in which goods or services are recorded as expenditures or expenses when used rather than when purchased; differentiated from the purchases method.

contingent grants Grants contingent on a specified occurrence or action on the part of the recipient (e.g., the ability of the recipient to raise resources from other parties).

contingent liability An obligation that must be paid only if certain events occur (such as when a government guarantees the debt of another party and that party defaults on the guaranteed obligation).

contracting out Engaging an outside, private-sector firm to provide services that have previously been performed in house; also known as outsourcing or privatizing.

contractual adjustment The difference between established billing rates and third-party-payer payments.

contributed capital The permanent capital of a proprietary fund, generally resulting from transfers from other funds, or from grants or customer fees restricted to capital acquisition or construction. Per GASB Statement No. 34, contributed capital is no longer reported separately from other net assets.

control account An account in the general ledger in which is recorded the aggregate of debit and credit postings to a number of related accounts called subsidiary accounts.

cost accounting The method of accounting that provides for the assembling and recording of all the elements of cost incurred to accomplish a purpose, to carry on an activity or operation, or to complete a unit of work or a specific job.

cost-benefit analysis See benefit-cost analysis.

cost driver A basis for allocating overhead to particular products or services that is conceptually similar to an overhead charging rate. However, whereas in practice an overhead charging rate is based on broadly representative factors (such as direct labor dollars, direct labor hours, or direct materials) that influence the amount of overhead costs incurred, a cost driver is more specifically indicative of the factors affecting overhead. Examples include materials requisitions, machine hours, and maintenance costs.

cost-sharing multiple-employer plan A pension plan in which multiple government employers pool assets and liabilities. Contributions are made at a common rate by all employer participants.

coupon rate The stated interest rate on the face of a bond; a bond's nominal interest rate.

credit risk The risk that a party to a contract, such as a borrower, will be unable to make its contractually required payments.

current assets In business and not-for-profit accounting, cash and other resources that are expected to be converted into cash during the normal operating cycle of the entity or within one year, whichever is longer. In government accounting, the assets that are available to meet the cost of operations or satisfy liabilities of the current year.

current financial resources In government accounting, the cash or other assets that will be converted into cash soon enough thereafter to satisfy the obligations of the current period.

current fund The general or main operating fund of a not-for-profit organization.

current liabilities In business and not-for-profit accounting, financial obligations that are reasonably expected to be paid using current assets or by creating other current liabilities within one year or the entity's operating cycle, whichever is longer. In governmental accounting, obligations that are expected to be met from funds appropriated for the current period.

custodial fund These funds are used to account for resources not held in trust by governments, but instead are held temporarily by one government for another.

custodial risk The risk that if a financial institution fails a depositor will be unable to recover its deposit in, or securities held by, that institution. Also, the risk that an investor or lender will be unable to recover collateral held by an outside party.

D

debt forgiveness A partial or total pardon of debt.

debt limit The maximum amount of debt that an entity is permitted to incur by constitutional provision or statute.

debt margin The difference between the amount of debt outstanding computed according to applicable legal provisions and the maximum amount of debt that can legally be issued.

debt refunding See bond refunding.

debt service fund A fund to account for financial resources set aside for the payment of interest and principal on long-term debt; a sinking fund.

decision package The key element of a zero-based budget in which the entity indicates the objectives of the activity for which funding is proposed, alternative means of accomplishing the same objectives; consequences of not performing the activity, and inputs, outputs, and outcomes at various levels of funding.

defeasance A transaction that annuls or voids a liability or other contractual arrangement. **See in-substance defeasance**.

deferred inflow of resources The acquisition of net position by the government that is applicable to a future reporting period.

deferred maintenance costs The costs that an entity avoided in a current year or past years by failing to perform required routine maintenance and repairs, but that will have to be incurred in the future.

deferred outflow of resources The consumption of net position by the government that is applicable to a future reporting period.

deferred revenue Receipts of cash or other assets for which asset recognition criteria have been met, but for which revenue recognition criteria have not been met.

deficit (1) The excess of liabilities and reserved equity of a fund over its assets. (2) The excess of expenditures over revenues during an accounting period; or in the case of proprietary funds, the excess of expenses over revenues.

defined benefit pension plan A pension plan that specifies the pension benefits to be paid to retirees, usually as a function of factors such as age, years of service, and compensation.

defined contribution pension plan A pension plan that specifies the amount of contributions to an individual's retirement account instead of the amount of benefits the individual is to receive. Under a defined contribution pension plan, the benefits a participant will receive depend on the amount contributed to the participant's account and the returns earned on investments of those contributions.

demand bonds Long-term debt instruments with demand ("put") provisions that require the issuer to repurchase the bonds, upon notice from the bondholder, at a specified price that is usually equal to the principal plus accrued interest. To ensure their ability to redeem the bonds, issuers of demand bonds frequently enter into standby liquidity agreements ("takeout" agreements) with banks or other financial institutions.

depreciation The systematic and rational allocation of the cost of tangible noncurrent operating assets over the periods benefited by the use of the assets.

derivative A financial asset whose value is derived from the shift in the price of an underlying asset, such as a bond, or an index of asset values, such as the Standard & Poors' index of 500 stocks, or an index of interest rates.

derived tax revenues Tax revenues that are based on exchange transactions between parties other than the taxing government. Examples include sales taxes and income taxes.

diagnosis-related groups (DRGs) Under Medicare, a classification scheme of patient conditions used for purposes of reimbursement. Hospitals or other health-care providers receive fixed amounts based on the diagnosis of patients' conditions rather than on the amounts they actually spend to treat the patients.

direct costs Costs such as for labor and materials, directly associated with specific products or activities of an organization. Distinguished from indirect (overhead) costs.

direct debt Debt of a government unit itself, as opposed to that of governments with overlapping boundaries.

discrete presentation One of two methods of reporting component units required by GASB StatementNo. 14, *The Financial Reporting Entity* (**see blending** for description of the other method). This method reports the component unit in a single column separate from the data of the primary government (as if the unit were another fund). For example, a state government might report its state-owned power authorities in a single column.

donated assets Assets, other than cash, donated to an organization.

donated services Services provided for no charge to an organization by individual volunteers or businesses.

donor-imposed restriction A stipulation by one who contributes to a not-for-profit organization that a contribution must be used for a purpose more specific than indicated by the organization's general goals.

donors People or organizations that give something voluntarily; as opposed to management, board of governors, or creditors.

due from (to) other funds An asset (liability) account used to indicate amounts owed to (by) one fund by (to) another.

E

economic cost The full cost of goods or services, as opposed to that which might be recognized for financial accounting. For example, the full amount of compensation to be paid by a government, including that of pensions and compensated absences, rather than merely the amount paid to the employees in a current period.

economic gain (loss) In the context of an advance refunding, the difference between the present value of the old debt service requirements and the present value of the new debt service requirements, discounted at the effective interest rate and adjusted for additional cash paid.

encumbrances Commitments to purchase goods or services.

endowment A sum of cash, investments, or other assets, generally received as gift, of which only the income, not the principal, may be expended.

enterprise fund A proprietary fund established to account for operations financed and operated in a manner similar to a private business (e.g., water, gas and electric utilities; airports; parking garages; and transit systems). Per GASB Statement No. 34, an enterprise fund may be used to account for any activity for which a fee is charged to external users for goods or services. It must be used to account for an activity financed with revenue debt, when laws or regulations require that an activity's costs be recovered with fees and charges or when pricing policies dictate that fees and charges be established to cover the activity's costs.

entitlements Payments, usually from a higher-level government, to which a state or local government or an individual is entitled as a matter of law in an amount determined by a specified formula.

equity transfer See residual equity transfer.

escheat property Private property that has reverted to a government owing to lack of heirs or claimants or because of a breach of a condition.

escheat trust fund A fiduciary fund used to account for escheat property.

exchange revenues Revenues that arise from sales transactions in which each party receives benefits and incurs costs.

exchange transaction A sales-type transaction in which goods and services are exchanged for consideration of approximately equal value.

exchange-like transaction See quasi-external transactions.

expendable funds Governmental funds whose resources are received from taxes, fees, or other sources and may be expended ("spent"); the governmental as opposed to the proprietary funds of a government.

expendable trust funds Funds used to account for assets over which the entity acts as a trustee; distinguished from nonexpendable trust funds in that both principal and income may be spent.

expenditures Decreases in net financial resources under the modified accrual basis of accounting.

expenses Decreases in overall net assets from delivering services or producing goods under the full accrual basis.

exposure draft A preliminary version of a standard-setting authority's official pronouncement, issued as means of obtaining public comment.

external report A report issued for use by parties outside the reporting entity, such as citizens, investors, and creditors, as opposed to inside parties, such as managers.

external subsidy An amount of money, generally a grant, received by a governmental entity from a nongovernmental source.

extraordinary items Transactions or other events that are both unusual in nature and infrequent in occurrence. Per GASB Statement No. 34, these items, unlike *special items*, are outside the control of management. **See *also* special items**.

F

face value As applied to securities, the amount indicated on the face of a bond that will have to be paid at maturity.

FASAB See Federal Accounting Standards Advisory Board.

FASB See Financial Accounting Standards Board.

Federal Accounting Standards Advisory Board (FASAB) The federal board charged with establishing federal accounting standards.

federal funds The federal government's general fund, special funds and most revolving funds.

federated organization A group of charitable organizations established to provide common administrative, fund-raising, and management services to its members.

fiduciary activities Per GASB Statement No. 34, a government's activities for which the government acts as a trustee or agent for individuals, external organizations, or other governments.

fiduciary funds The trust and agency funds used to account for assets held by a government unit in a trustee capacity or as an agent for individuals, private organizations, other government units, or other funds.

finance Lease A lease that is essentially an installment purchase and meets the criteria of FASB Statement No. 13, *Accounting for Leases*. The lessee ("purchaser") records the acquired property as an asset and correspondingly recognizes the present value of the agreed-upon lease payments as a liability.

Financial Accounting Standards Board (FASB) The organization responsible for establishing external accounting and reporting standards for all nongovernmental entities, including not-for-profit organizations.

financial audit An examination or review made to determine whether financial statements or related financial reports conform to generally accepted accounting principles or other prescribed criteria.

financial related audits In the context of federal auditing, these determine whether financial reports, including those on specific funds or accounts, are either fairly presented or presented in accordance with stated criteria, and whether the entity has complied with specific financial-related requirements, such as those set forth in laws and regulations, grants, and contracts.

financial resources Cash, investments and receivables, and other assets that can be expected to be transformed into cash in the normal course of operations. Financial resources minus the current claims against them equals net financial resources.

financial statement audits Examinations that determine whether an entity's financial statements are presented fairly in accordance with generally accepted accounting principles and whether the entity has complied with laws and regulations that may have a material effect on the financial statements.

fiscal capacity The economic base that the government can draw on for the resources necessary to provide the goods or services expected of it.

fiscal compliance One of the three subobjectives of government accountability; financial reporting should demonstrate compliance with other finance-related legal or contractual requirements.

fiscal dependence A unit is fiscally dependent on the primary government if it is unable to determine its own budget, levy taxes or set rates, or issue bonds without approval of the primary government.

fiscal effort The extent to which a government is taking advantage of its fiscal capacity. Generally measured by comparing the revenues that the government generates from its own sources (i.e., total revenue excluding grants from other governments) with either the wealth or income of its taxpayers.

fiscal funding clause A clause in a lease agreement providing that the lease is cancelable if the legislature or other funding authority does not appropriate the funds necessary for the government unit to fulfill its obligations under the lease agreement.

fiscal period (year) Any period at the end of which a government determines its financial position and the results of its operations; also accounting period.

fixed assets Long-lived tangible assets, such as buildings, equipment, improvements other than buildings, and land.

fixed assets account group See general fixed assets account group.

fixed budget A budget in which costs and revenues are fixed—that is, not subject to change as a result of increases or decreases in the volume of goods or services to be provided.

fixed costs Costs of goods or services that do not vary with the volume of goods or services provided (e.g., rent, interest, executive salaries, and air-conditioning costs).

flexible budget A budget in which dollar amounts vary according to the volume of goods or services to be provided.

full accrual basis A method of accounting that recognizes revenues when a performance obligation is met and expenses when incurred regardless of when is received or paid.

full cost The cost of goods or services that includes both direct and indirect (overhead) costs.

full faith and credit A government's pledge, usually incorporated into bond indentures, to back a bond issue with its full taxing authority.

functional classification Expenditures that are grouped according to the purpose for which they are made, such as public safety, general administration, or recreation.

fund A fiscal and accounting entity with a self-balancing set of accounts used to account for resources, and claims against them, that are segregated in accord with legal or contractual restrictions or to carry out specific activities.

fund accounting An accounting system in which an entity's resources are divided among two or more accounting entities known as funds.

fund balance The net assets (assets minus liabilities) of a fund.

fund financial statements Financial statements of a government required by GASB Statement No. 34 that report on one or more funds. Governmental fund statements are on a modified accrual basis; business-type fund statements are on a full accrual basis.

funded pension plan A pension plan in which contributions are made and assets are accumulated to pay benefits to potential recipients before cash payments to recipients actually are required, as opposed to a pay-as-you-go plan.

funded ratio The ratio, associated with pension plans, of the actuarial value of assets to the actuarially accrued liabilities.

funded status The ratio of a pension plan's total assets to total pension obligations.

fund type A fund category. In government accounting, any one of several categories into which all funds are classified. These include general, special revenue, debt service, capital projects, permanent, enterprise, internal service, and agency.

G

GASB See Governmental Accounting Standards Board.

general capital assets Capital assets that are not assets of any particular fund, but of the government unit as a whole. Most often these assets arise from the expenditure of the financial resources of governmental (as opposed to proprietary or fiduciary) funds.

general fund A fund used to account for resources that are not restricted. The fund that accounts for all resources that are not required to be accounted for in other funds.

general journal A journal in which all entries are recorded, excluding those recorded in special journals.

general ledger A record containing the accounts needed to reflect an entity's financial position and results of operations.

generally accepted accounting principles (GAAP) Uniform minimum standards and guidelines for financial accounting and reporting that govern the form and content of financial statements. They encompass the conventions, rules, and procedures necessary to define accepted accounting practice at a particular time.

generally accepted auditing standards (GAAS) Standards established by the AICPA for the conduct and reporting of financial audits.

generally accepted government auditing standards (GAGAS) Standards established by the GAO in its publication *Standards for Audit of Governmental Organizations, Programs, Activities and Functions* (the Yellow Book) for the conduct and reporting of both financial and performance audits.

general obligation debt Debt that is secured by the full faith and credit of the issuing body.

general property, plant, and equipment A classification of assets in the federal government that represents property, plant, and equipment used for general purposes; distinguished from stewardship assets.

Government Accountability Office (GAO) The congressional agency responsible for conducting financial and performance audits of federal agencies, programs, and activities and for carrying out other accounting and financerelated activities of the federal government.

Government Auditing Standards (Standards for Audit of Government Organizations, Programs, Activities and Functions) The auditing standards of the GAO; the Yellow Book.

government-acknowledged events In federal accounting, occurrences for which the government is not responsible but elects, as a matter of policy, to provide relief to the victims. They include primarily natural disasters, such as hurricanes and earthquakes.

government-assessed taxes Taxes, such as property taxes, assessed by the government in which the government determines the amount owed. Distinguished from taxpayer-assessed taxes, such as income taxes, in which the parties other than the government determine the amount owed.

Government Auditing Standards (GAS) See generally accepted government auditing standards (GAGAS).

Government FinanceOfficers Association (GFOA) An association of state and local governments and officials and other individuals interested in state and local government finance.

government-mandated nonexchange transactions Transactions that occur when a government at one level (e.g., the federal or a state government) provides resources to a government at another level (e.g., a local government or school district) and requires that the recipient use the resources for a specific purpose. For example, a state may grant funds to a county stipulating that the resources be used for road improvements. Acceptance and use of the resources are mandatory.

government-related events In federal accounting, mainly accidents for which the federal government is responsible and required by law to reimburse the injured parties for damages.

government-wide statements Statements required by GASB Statement No. 34 that report on all of a government's activities (both governmental and business-type) and are on full accrual basis. These statements are distinguished from *fund* financial statements.

governmental accounting The composite activity of analyzing, recording, summarizing, reporting, and interpreting the financial transactions of governments.

Governmental Accounting Standards Board (GASB) The authoritative accounting and financial reporting standard-setting body for government entities.

governmental activities Activities of a government that are financed predominantly through taxes and intergovernmental grants; distinguished from business-type activities.

governmental funds Funds used to account for the acquisition, use, and balances of expendable financial resources and the related current liabilities, except those accounted for in proprietary funds and fiduciary funds; the five governmental fund types are general, special revenue, debt service, capital projects, and permanent.

grant A contribution from one party to another to be used or expended for a specified purpose, activity, or facility; ordinarily distinguished from an exchange transaction in that the grantor does not receive compensation in return for the resources contributed.

H

Health Maintenance Organization (HMO) An organization that provides health care on a prepaid basis (i.e., patients or their employers pay a fixed annual fee regardless of actual services rendered by the organization).

heritage assets As defined by the Federal Accounting Standards Advisory Board, assets that have value because of their historical, cultural, educational, or artistic significance.

historical cost The purchase price or construction cost plus any additional costs incurred in placing an asset in its intended location, condition, and purpose, less accumulated depreciation or amortization.

human capital As defined by the FASAB, outlays for education and training of the public intended to increase the nation's productive capacity.

I

impact fees Fees charged to developers by a governmental entity for costs of anticipated improvements, such as sidewalks and parks, that will be necessary as a result of a development.

impaired asset A capital asset whose service utility has declined significantly and unexpectedly as a consequence of physical damage, technological obsolescence, changes in the laws, or financial reversals and whose book value may thereby have to be reduced.

imposed nonexchange revenues Assessments imposed on individuals and business entities, the most prominent of which are property taxes and fines.

income The excess of an enterprise's revenue over its expenses.

incremental receipts (disbursements) Receipts (disbursements) that differ if one alternative course of action were chosen over another.

independent sector The sector of the economy that is composed of not-for-profit organizations (as opposed to governmental and business entities).

indirect costs Costs that are related to an activity or object but cannot be directly traced to that activity; overhead costs; distinguished from direct costs.

industrial development bonds Bonds issued by governmental units at low interest rates to encourage private development in their area. Repayment of the debt is expected to be the responsibility of the beneficiary of the bond.

infrastructure assets Public domain fixed assets such as roads, bridges, curbs, gutters, streets and sidewalks, drainage systems, lighting systems, and similar assets that are immovable and of value only to the government unit.

inputs The resources applied to a service, such as dollar cost, number of labor hours, and amount of material.

insolvent The condition of being unable to meet debts or discharge liabilities owing to a deficiency of available financial resources.

inspectors general The heads of the internal audit departments of federal agencies.

in-substance defeasance An advance refunding (retirement of bonds) in which the government places sufficient resources in a trust account to cover all required principal and interest payments on the defeased debt. Although the government is not legally released from being the primary obligor on the refunded bonds, the possibility of it having to make additional payments is considered remote.

intangible asset An asset that has a future benefit, but cannot be physically seen—for example, a patent or copyright.

interest rate risk The risk that a change in interest rates will adversely affect the value of an investment.

interfund transfers See reciprocal interfund activity and nonreciprocal interfund activity.

intergenerational equity See interperiod equity.

internal service funds Funds used to account for business-type activities in which the customers are other government departments or agencies.

internal subsidies An amount of money, such as a transfer from the general fund, received by a government entity from another governmental source.

interperiod equity The extent to which current-year revenues are sufficient to pay for current-year services (as opposed to whether the costs of current-year services are being shifted to future years or were paid in past years).

investment in plant fund A fund (no longer reported on financial statements) maintained mainly by colleges and universities and other not-for-profits to account for the entity's fixed assets and the liabilities incurred to acquire those assets; comparable to a government's "old model" general fixed assets and general long-term debt account groups.

investment pools Fiscal entities established to invest the resources of two or more funds or independent entities; comparable to a mutual fund.

investment trust funds Funds maintained by a government to account for investment pools maintained for other governments.

issue costs Costs incurred to issue bonds, such as amounts paid to underwriters, attorneys, accountants, and printers.

J

joint venture A contractual arrangement whereby two or more participants agree to carry out a common activity, with each sharing in both risks and rewards.

journal A book of original entry in which transactions or events are recorded.

L

lessee The entity that rents an asset from the asset's owner, the lessor.

lessor The owner of rental property who transfers the right to use the property for a specified fee and for a specified period of time, to the user, the lessee.

levy To impose or collect a tax.

lien A claim that a government has on property, most commonly owing to a failure of the owner to pay property taxes.

life income fund An endowment fund to account for gifts that provide a return to the donor (or a person designated by the donor) for the remainder of his or her life. Thereafter, what remains of the gift will typically revert to the recipient entity.

liquidity The ability of an entity to meet its financial obligations as they come due.

loan fund A fund used to account for resources that will provide loans to a designated class of beneficiaries, such as students or small businesses.

long-term debt In government, obligations that are not expected to be paid with currently available financial resources. In not-for-profits, obligations that are not expected to be paid in cash or other operating assets within one year or the entity's normal operating cycle.

M

maintenance The upkeep of a capital asset to preserve its expected useful life or level of productivity. Contrasted with a betterment, which increases expected useful life or enhances productivity.

major fund In the context of GASB standards, a fund whose revenues, expenditures/expenses, assets, or liabilities (excluding extraordinary items) are at least 10 percent of corresponding totals for all governmental or enterprise funds and at least 5 percent of the aggregate amount for all governmental and enterprise funds. Also may be any other fund that the government considers to be of particular importance to statement users.

malpractice claims Claim caused by professional negligence by a health care provider and causes injury or death of the patient.

management's discussion and analysis A component of an annual report in which management provides an analysis of the entity's financial activities.

matching concept The principle that expenses or expenditures should be recognized in the same accounting period as related revenues.

measurement focus The accounting convention that determines which assets and liabilities are included on an entity's balance sheet and which will thereby affect the determination of revenues and expenses (or expenditures) to be reported on the entity's operating statement. Measurement focus determines what is being measured—for example, net profits or flows of financial resources.

modified accrual basis The accrual basis of accounting adapted to the governmental fund-type measurement focus. Revenues are recognized in the period in which they become available and measurable. Some expenditures are recognized on a accrual basis; others on a cash basis.

moral obligation debt Bonds or notes issued by one entity (usually a state agency), but backed by the implied (not legally binding) promise of another entity (usually the state itself) to make up any debt service deficiencies.

municipal bond A bond issued by a municipality.

municipality A city or town or other area incorporated for self-government. Also, in its broadest sense, any state or local government, including states, counties, cities, towns, and special districts.

N

National Association of College and University Business officers (NACUBO) An association that specifically represents chief business and financial officers through advocacy efforts, community service, and professional development activities. The association's mission is to advance the economic viability and business practices of higher education institutions in fulfillment of their academic missions.

National Council on Governmental Accounting (NCGA) The governmental accounting standard setting authority that preceded the GASB.

natural classification Expenditures that are grouped according to an object, such as salaries and wages.

net assets The residual of assets minus liabilities in a not-for-profit organization.

net pension liability The reported difference between total pension liability and net plan position. Reported as a liability on the Statement of Net Position as per GASB Statement No. 68.

net plan position The total assets of a pension plan less any plan liabilities (amounts currently due to plan members as well as accrued investments and administrative expenses).

net position The residual of all other elements presented in a statement of financial position; that is the assets and deferred outflows less the liabilities and deferred inflows.

nominal interest rate The contractual interest rate shown on the face of a bond and used to compute the amount of interest to be paid; in contrast to the effective interest rate.

nonappropriation budget A financial plan for an organization, program, activity, or function approved in a manner authorized by constitution, charter, statute, or ordinance but not subject to appropriation and, therefore, outside the boundaries of an appropriated budget.

nonappropriation clause See fiscal funding clause.

noncommitment debt See conduit debt.

nonexchange revenues Revenues that materialize when a government commands resources but gives nothing in exchange (at least not directly). Examples include taxes, duties, fines, and penalties.

nonexchange transaction A transaction in which one party provides resources to another without getting consideration of approximately equal value in return; includes voluntary nonexchange transactions, such as contributions and grants and imposed nonexchange transactions, such as taxes, duties, and fines.

nonexpendable funds Proprietary funds that "pay their own way" through customer charges. Contrasted with expendable funds, the resources of which are provided by taxes, fees, or other revenues and are expected to be spent each year.

nonexpendable trust funds Endowment funds, the principal of which must be maintained intact; only the income of which can be expended.

nonmajor fund In the context of GASB standards, any fund that is not considered a major fund. **See major fund.**

nonoperating expenditures/expenses Expenditures/ expenses not related directly to a fund's or entity's primary activities.

nonoperating revenues Revenues not directly related to a fund's or entity's primary activities.

nonreciprocal interfund activity (transfers) Per GASB Statement No. 34, the internal equivalent of nonexchange transactions; transfers of cash for which goods or services of equivalent value have not been received, such as when the general fund transfers cash to a debt service fund for payment of principal or interest on long-term debt or when the general fund transfers cash to a newly established internal service fund for start-up capital.

nonreciprocal receipt A contribution for which the recipient gives nothing in exchange. Per FASB 116, *Accounting for Contributions Received and Contributions Made*, contributions may be made in cash, marketable securities, property and equipment, utilities, supplies, intangible assets, and the services of professionals and craftsmen.

nonspendable fund balance The net assets (assets minus liabilities) of a fund that are not in spendable form or are required to be maintained intact.

nonsubstitution clause A provision often incorporated into governments' capital lease agreements that prohibits the leasee (the government) from replacing the leased property with similar property in the event that it cancels the lease.

normal cost With respect to pensions, the portion of the present value of pension plan benefits that is allocated to a particular year by an appropriate actuarial cost method. See service cost.

not-for-profit (Nonprofit, NFP, NPO) Organization An entity that conducts operations for the benefit of its users without a profit motive and has absence of ownership interests.

note disclosures Information disclosed in the notes to the financial statements.

O

object An item in an expenditure classification that relates to the type of goods or services obtained rather than to the purpose of the expenditure or the nature of the activity that it supports. Examples include wages and salaries, supplies, and contractual services.

object classification budget A budget that details revenues and expenditures by object, rather than, for example, program or nature of activity.

off-balance-sheet financing Obligations, such as those from operating leases, that do not satisfy the accounting criteria of reportable liabilities and are therefore not disclosed on an entity's balance sheet.

Office of Management and Budget (OMB) The executive branch agency of the federal government that assists the president in preparing the federal budget and supervises the executive branch agencies in implementing it. It also oversees and coordinates federal procurement, financial management, information and regulatory policies. It further has authority to prescribe the form and content of federal agency financial statements and related reports and to establish requirements pertaining to single audits.

on-behalf payments Payments made by one government for the benefit of another. For example, pension contributions paid by a state for employees of a school district.

OPEB See Postemployment Benefits Other than Pensions

operating debt Debt issued to cover general operating, as opposed to capital, expenditures.

operating expenditures/expenses Expenditures/ expenses related directly to a fund's or entity's primary activities.

operating lease A rental agreement permitting an entity to use an asset for a specified period of time, but does not meet the criteria, set forth in FASB Statement No. 13, *Accounting for Leases*, of a capital lease.

operating revenues Revenues related directly to a fund's or entity's primary activities.

operating statement A statement that shows an entity's revenues, expenditures/expenses and transfers over a specified period of time. **See also statement of activities**.

operational audit See performance auditing.

operational objectives Specific sought-after results of a program or activity. The objectives should be quantifiable, measurable, and distinguishable from broad, nonspecific statements of purpose.

opportunity cost The economic gains that are forgone by choosing one course of action over an alternative.

other financing sources/uses An operating statement classification presenting financial inflows and outflows other than revenues and expenditures. Examples include transfers in/out and proceeds of long-term debt.

outcomes The results (accomplishments) of a service, generally measured so as to take into account the quality of performance.

outputs The quantity, or units of service, provided by an activity.

overhead Indirect costs; those elements of cost necessary in the production of a good or service that are not directly traceable to the product or service.

overlapping debt The proportionate share that property within the reporting government must bear of the debts of all other governments located wholly or in part within its geographic boundaries.

P

pass-through grants Grants that a government must transfer to, or spend on behalf of, a secondary recipient. For example, a federal education grant that a state must distribute to local school districts.

pay-as-you-go-basis In the context of pension accounting and risk management, the failure to finance retirement obligations or anticipated losses on a current basis using an acceptable actuarial funding method.

payments in lieu of taxes Amounts paid by government or not-for-profit in place of property taxes they are not required to pay. Generally occurs when a jurisdiction contains a substantial amount of facilities of other governments or not-for-profits; for example, when the federal government makes payments to a local school district in lieu of property taxes it would be required to pay on a military base within the district if federal property were not tax-exempt.

PCAOB See Public Company Accounting Oversight Board.

pension Sums of money paid periodically (usually monthly) to a retired or disabled employee (or a surviving spouse) owing to his or her years of employment.

pension contribution The amount paid into a pension plan by an employer (or employee), pursuant to the terms of the plan, state law, actuarial calculations, or some other basis for determination.

pension expense The annual change in the net pension liability. In general, this annual change will equal the service cost plus interest on the total pension obligations less earnings on plan assets, and then adjusted for differences from actuarial assumptions.

pension obligation The portion of the actuarial present value of total projected benefits estimated to be payable in the future as a result of employee service to date.

pension and other employee benefit trust funds Trust funds used to account for the assets accumulated by a pension or other employee benefit plan. Pension and other employee benefit trust funds, like nonexpendable trust funds, are accounted for on an accrual basis.

per capita debt The amount of a government's debt divided by its population.

performance auditing A systematic process of objectively obtaining and evaluating evidence regarding the performance of an organization, program, function, or activity in terms of its economy and efficiency of operations and its effectiveness in achieving desired results.

performance budget A budget that focuses on measurable units of efforts and accomplishments and associates dollar expenditures directly with anticipated units of outputs or outcomes.

permanent endowment A sum of cash, investments, or other assets, generally received as gift, of which only the income, not the principal, may be expended.

permanent funds Per GASB Statement No. 34, trust funds in which the beneficiary is the government itself rather than outside parties. Permanent funds are categorized and accounted for as governmental funds.

PERS **See Public Employee Retirement System**.

plant fund A fund, generally maintained by colleges and universities and other not-for-profit organizations (but no longer explicitly reported on their external financial statements), to account for fixed assets and the resources set aside to acquire or replace fixed assets. As used by colleges and universities, plant funds may be of four types: unexpended plant fund, renewal and replacement fund, retirement of indebtedness fund, and investment in plant fund.

pledge A promise by a donor to make a donation of cash or assets in the future.

postemployment benefits other than pensions Benefits commonly offered by employers to retirees. These frequently include continued health care benefits, life insurance, disability insurance, among others.

preferred provider organization Groups of doctors, hospitals, and other health care providers that contract with employers or insurance companies to provide medical services to a specified group of patients.

present value The amount that a buyer is willing to pay for one or a series of payments to be received in the future. Computed by discounting the future cash flows at an appropriate rate of interest and for an appropriate period of time.

primary government Per GASB Statement No. 14, *The Financial Reporting Entity*, a state government, a generalpurpose local government, such as a municipality or a county, or a special-purpose government, such as a school district, that has a separately elected governing body, is legally separate from other primary governments and is fiscally independent of other governments.

private purpose trust fund A fund maintained by a government to account for assets held for the benefit of outside parties—for example, individuals, private organizations, or other governments.

privatization **See contracting out**.

pro forma statements Projected financial statements of an organization for future periods.

program A series of related activities intended to fulfill a common objective.

program audit An audit to determine the extent to which an organization is achieving desired results or benefits and whether the entity has complied with significant laws and regulations applicable to its programs. **See also performance auditing**.

program budget A budget in which resources and results are identified with programs rather than traditional organizational units. **See also performance budget**.

proprietary accounts In the context of federal accounting, the accounts that provide the information necessary to prepare financial statements based on FASAB standards rather than to demonstrate budgetary compliance.

proprietary fund Income determination funds that are used to account for a government's business-type activities; enterprise and internal service funds that are accounted for on a business-type basis.

prospective payment system Medicare payment system that reimburses hospitals based on the nature of patients' illnesses.

Public Company Accounting Oversight Board (PCAOB) A private-sector, nonprofit corporation, created by the Sarbanes–Oxley Act of 2002, to oversee the audits of public companies in order to protect the interests of investors and further the public interest in the preparation of informative, fair, and independent audit reports.

Public Employee Retirement System (PERS) A pension plan maintained for government employees.

purchases method A method of accounting for inventories and prepaid costs, such as rent, in which goods or services are recorded as expenses or expenditures when purchased, rather than when consumed. Differentiated from the consumption method.

purpose restrictions Stipulations, usually as part of a grant, as to the purpose for which the resources must be used.

put bonds **See demand bonds**.

Q

qualified opinion An audit opinion stating that "except for" the effect of the matter to which the qualification relates, the financial statements present fairly the financial position, results of operations and (when applicable), changes in financial position in conformity with GAAP. Generally expressed when auditors cannot obtain adequate information to express an unqualified opinion, there are significant uncertainties as to the value of assets or liabilities, or there are material departures from generally accepted accounting principles.

quasi-endowment fund A fund maintained to account for assets to be retained and invested as if they were contractually required endowments—for example, earnings (and only the earnings) from investments acquired with the resources are to be used for a specified purpose.

quasi-external transactions Interfund transactions that would be treated as revenues, expenditures, or expenses if they involved organizations external to the government unit (e.g., payments in lieu of taxes from an enterprise fund to the general fund; internal service fund billings to departments; routine employer contributions to a pension trust fund; and routine service charges for inspection, engineering, utilities, or similar services). These transactions should be accounted for as revenues, expenditures, or expenses in the funds involved. Under the new GASB model, these transactions are referred to as "exchange-like" transactions.

questioned costs Costs identified by auditors of federal assistance programs that appear to be in violation of laws, regulations, or contractual provisions and are thereby ineligible for reimbursement.

R

reciprocal interfund activity Per GASB Statement No. 34, the internal equivalent of exchange transactions (those in which the parties receive and surrender consideration of approximately equal value). Examples include payments for the purchase of goods and services, and loans and repayments of loans.

redemption value In the context of investment pools and mutual funds, the amount that the pool or fund will pay per share to an investor electing to withdraw its funds. Generally based on the current market value of the underlying securities.

refinance To replace existing debt with new debt, generally to take advantage of lower interest rates, or to shorten or lengthen the debt payout period.

refundings **See bond refunding**.

related organization Per GASB Statement No. 14, *The Financial Reporting Entity*, an entity that satisfies the criteria of financial accountability, but not other necessary criteria and therefore does not qualify as a component unit.

relevant range The range of output that is relevant for the particular decision at hand. The span of output in which the behavior of fixed and variable costs is assumed to remain constant.

renewal and replacement fund A plant fund used mainly by colleges and universities and other not-for-profit entities to account (internally) for resources set aside to restore and replace existing buildings, equipment, and other fixed assets.

replacement cost The cost of acquiring or constructing an asset today that is identical to or has the same service potential as an asset already owned. An indicator of an asset's current value.

reporting entity The organizational unit covered by a set of financial statements. In government, the oversight unit and all of its component units, if any, that are combined in the financial statements per the requirements of GASB Statement No. 14, *The Financial Reporting Entity*, or FASAB Concepts Statement No. 4, *Entity and Display*.

repurchase agreement ("repo") An investment instrument in which an investor (buyer-lender) transfers cash to a broker-dealer or financial institution (seller-borrower). The broker-dealer or financial institution transfers securities to the investor and promises to repay the cash plus interest in exchange for the same securities or for different securities. Contrast with a reverse repurchase agreement.

required supplementary information (RSI) Statements, schedules, statistical data, or other information not included in, but required to supplement, the basic financial statements. Per GASB Statement No. 34 it includes management's discussion and analysis, budget to actual comparisons, information about infrastructure, and details of actuarial pension valuations.

reserve for encumbrances A segregation of fund equity in the amount of encumbrances (commitments to purchase goods or services).

reserved fund balance That portion of fund balance that either represents resources that are not of a type that can be appropriated (e.g., reserves for inventory) or that are legally segregated for a specific future use (reserves for encumbrances).

residual equity transfers Under the "old" model, nonrecurring or nonroutine transfers of equity between funds (e.g., the contribution of capital by the general fund to an enterprise fund or internal service fund, and the subsequent return of all or part of such contributions to the general fund).

restricted fund balance The net position (assets minus liabilities) of a fund that are constrained to specific purposes by their providers, constitutional provisions, or by enabling legislation.

restricted grants Payments intended for specified purposes, projects, or activities.

retirement of indebtedness fund A fund maintained by colleges and universities and other not-for-profits (but not explicitly reported on their financial statements) that is comparable to a debt service fund and used to account for resources set aside for the retirement of indebtedness.

retrospective insurance premium Same as retrospective payments.

retrospective payments Insurance policy that requires at the expiration of the policy for premium costs to be adjusted to actual loss experienced.

revenue The inflow of net resources owing to the production and delivery of goods or services or from transactions (e.g., taxes, contributions) involving an entity's primary activities.

revenue anticipation notes (RANS) Short-term notes, issued in anticipation of the collection of revenues, that will not be converted into long-term instruments.

revenue debt Bonds and other obligations whose principal and interest are payable exclusively from earnings of a specific enterprise, such as an electric utility, toll road, or dormitory, and are thereby not backed by the full faith and credit of the issuer. Contrast with general obligation debt.

reverse repurchase agreement ("reverse repo") A borrowing instrument by which a borrower (seller) receives cash from a broker-dealer or financial institution (buyer-lender); in exchange the borrower (seller) transfers securities to the broker-dealer or financial institution and promises to repay the cash plus interest in exchange for the same or different securities. Contrast with a repurchase agreement.

revolving funds Funds used to account for business-type enterprises; **See also expendable funds**.

Rule 203 (of the American Institute of Certified Public Accountants' Code of Professional Conduct) The provision that auditors should not express an unqualified opinion on financial statements that are in violation of the standards established by organizations designated by the AICPA's Council.

S

Schedule of Expenditures of Federal Awards A listing made by an organization of total expenditures under each federal program from which it receives funding.

scholarships A financial aid award for a student to further education; can be awarded based on criteria that reflect the values and purposes of the donor.

SEA See service efforts and accomplishments indicators.

self-insurance The retention of a risk by an entity, as opposed to the transfer of the risk to an independent third party through the purchase of an insurance policy.

serial bonds Bonds that mature in a series of installments at future dates—e.g., a portion of a bond issue matures in five years, a portion in six, a portion in seven, and so on.

service assessments Special assessments for operating activities, such as street cleaning or fire protection, as opposed to capital assets and infrastructure.

service concession arrangements Long-term arrangements in which a government contracts with a private-sector entity or another government to operate a major capital asset, such as a toll road, hospital, or student housing, in return for the right to collect fees from the asset users.

service cost Actuarial present value of pension benefits earned by employees during the current accounting period. See normal cost.

service efforts and accomplishments (SEA) indicators Measures of an entity's inputs, outputs, outcomes, and efficiency in carrying out its activities.

shared revenues Revenues levied by one government, such as a state, but shared on a predetermined basis with other governments, such as cities.

short-term debt Obligations that are expected to be paid within one year or the entity's operating cycle.

single audit An audit by a single audit organization intended to meet the needs of more than one regulatory agency or funds provider; an audit performed in accordance with the Single Audit Act and supporting Office of Management and Budget (OMB) circulars.

Single Audit Act of 1984 A federal act mandating that recipients of federal financial assistance meeting specified criteria be subject to organization-wide single audits.

single employer plan A pension plan established by a single employer covering only that employer's employees. Also called a sole employer plan.

sinking fund A fund to account for financial resources set aside for the payment of interest and principal on long-term debt.

special assessment A compulsory levy on certain properties to defray all or part of the cost of a specific capital improvement or service deemed to benefit primarily those properties or their owners.

special assessment bonds Bonds payable from the proceeds of special assessments.

special items Transactions or other events within the control of management that are significant and either unusual in nature or infrequent in occurrence. **See also extraordinary items**.

special-purpose governments Governments that serve only a single, well-defined purpose, such as universities, utility districts, and library districts.

special revenue fund A fund used to account for the proceeds of specific revenue sources that are legally restricted to expenditure for specific purposes.

special termination benefit Improvement to a pension plan or other incentive provided by employers to encourage employees to retire early.

statement of activities One of the two government-wide statements required by GASB Statement No. 34 (the other being the statement of net position). An operating statement that consolidates separately the revenues, expenses and other items of a government's governmental and business-activities.

statement of budgetary resources In federal accounting, an operating statement prepared on a budgetary basis.

statement of cash flows The statement that provides information about the cash inflows (receipts) and outflows (payments) of an entity during a period of time.

statement of changes in fiduciary net position As per GASB Statement No. 67, a financial statement that shows the inflows and outflows of a pension plan.

statement of changes in net position In federal accounting, a statement summarizing all agency transactions other than those reported in the statement of net cost.

statement of custodial activities In federal accounting, a statement showing resources collected and disbursed. Required only of agencies such as the Internal Revenue Service and Customs Service, that collect funds to be turned over to the Treasury or other agencies.

statement of fiduciary net position As per GASB Statement No. 67, a balance sheet of the pension plan.

statement of financial position A balance sheet.

statement of financing (also known as statement of reconciliation of net cost of operations to budget) In federal accounting, a statement that reconciles the statement of budgetary resources to the statement of net cost.

statement of net position One of the two government-wide statements required by GASB Statement No. 34 (the other being the statement of activities). In essence a balance sheet that displays the consolidated assets, liabilities and net position of governmental and business-type activities (separate by type).

statement of net cost In federal accounting, an operating statement that shows an agency's operating costs and revenues and highlights the net costs that must be paid from taxes or other financing sources.

statement of revenues and expenditures The operating statement of a governmental fund that presents increases (revenues and other financing sources) and decreases (expenditures and other financing uses) in net current financial resources.

statement of social insurance In federal accounting, a statement that presents projected and actuarial data for the government's major social insurance programs. Required only of agencies such as the Social Security Administration, the Railroad Retirement Board, the Centers for Medicare and Medicaid, and the Department of Labor.

stewardship assets In federal accounting, assets that the federal government owns but does not use to produce goods or services and which are not accorded balance sheet recognition. Includes, for example, national parks and forests, undeveloped acreage, and heritage assets.

student-aid Money intended to help pay educational expenses at a college or university, such as tuition and fees, room and board, and books and supplies.

sunk costs Costs that have already been incurred and cannot be recovered.

suspense account An account carrying charges or credits temporarily pending the determination of the proper account or accounts to which they are to be posted.

T

take-out agreement An agreement between an issuer of demand bonds and a financial institution per which the financial institution will provide funding for the issuer in the event that bondholders demand redemption of their bonds.

tangible asset An asset used in the normal operations of an organization that can be physically seen.

tap fees Fees charged by a governmental utility to new customers to hook up to its system.

tax abatement Reduction of tax liability owed to a government for a specific period of time for some specific purpose deemed desirable by the government.

tax anticipation notes (TANs) Short-term notes, not expected to be converted into long-term debts, issued in anticipation of future collection of taxes.

tax lien See lien.

taxpayer-assessed taxes Taxes, such as sales and income taxes determined by parties other than the government. Distinguished from government-assessed taxes, such as property taxes.

term bonds Bonds that mature in one lump sum at a specified future date.

term endowment An endowment (trust) in which the principal may be expended after a specified number of years.

third-party payor With respect to health care, the insurance company or party other than the patient that pays for services.

time requirements Stipulations, usually as part of a grant, as to the time period in which resources must be used or when use may begin.

total pension liability Projection of future benefit payments for current and prior employees discounted to a present value, and allocated to current, past, or future time periods.

transfers See reciprocal interfund activity and **nonreciprocal interfund activity**.

trustee A party that administers property for a beneficiary.

trust funds Funds used to account for assets over which the entity acts as a trustee or that must be invested and the income only, not the principal, may be expended. In federal accounting the term refers to any fund that is designated by law as a trust fund and has earmarked receipts.

U

unassigned fund balance The net position (assets minus liabilities) of a fund available for any purpose; reported only in the general fund.

unconditional promise A pledge or promise to give an asset or provide a service in the future that is not dependent on a certain event occurring.

unearned income See deferred revenue.

unfunded actuarial accrued liability The excess of a pension plan's actuarial accrued liability over the actuarial value of its assets.

unified federal budget The budget that encompasses all programs and transactions and is intended to capture the impact of all federal activities on the national economy.

Uniform Administrative Requirements for Grants and Cooperative Agreements to State and Local Governments (the Common Rule) A detailed compendium of administrative rules and regulations that supplements the Single Audit Act and related circulars.

unqualified opinion An auditor's opinion stating that the financial statements present fairly the financial position, results of operations, and (when applicable) changes in financial position in conformity with GAAP.

unrestricted grants Grants that are not restricted by donors as to purpose, project, or activity.

user charge A charge for the use of a service, such as for parking or trash collections, as opposed to a tax that is unrelated to services received.

V

variable costs Costs that change in direct proportion to volume.

variance power The right of a not-for-profit organization to unilaterally redirect contributed assets to a beneficiary other than that specified by the donor.

vested benefit A benefit for which an employer has an obligation to make payment even if an employee is terminated.

Thus, the benefit is not contingent on an employee's future service.

voluntary health and welfare organization A not-for-profit organization formed to provide services to a community, rather than to its own members. Examples include the United Way, the American Heart Association, and most social service agencies.

voluntary nonexchange transactions Transactions that result from legislative or contractual agreements entered into willingly by two or more parties. They include grants given by one government to another and contributions from individuals (e.g., gifts to public universities).

voucher A written document that supports a payment and provides evidence of its propriety.

W

with donor restrictions Net assets or revenues that must be held in perpetuity, for a specified purpose, or when specified events have occurred because of donors.

without donor restrictions Net assets or revenues that are not restricted by donors.

Y

Yellow Book See Government Accounting Standards (Standards for Audit of Government Organizations, Programs, Activities, and Functions).

yield rate The actual (effective), as distinguished from the nominal (coupon or stated), rate of return on a bond or other investment.

Z

zero-based budgeting A form of program budgeting characterized by its requirement that all activities, both existing and proposed, be evaluated and ranked.

zero coupon bond A bond with a stated annual interest rate of zero. It provides a return to investors in that it is issued at a price considerably less than the bond's face value and sufficiently low so that the difference between face value and issue price will equal a return comparable to that on conventional bonds.

Value Tables

TABLE I Future Value of $1 (Future Value of a Single Sum)

$$FV_{n,i} = (1+i)^n$$

(n) Periods	2%	2½%	3%	4%	5%	6%
1	1.02000	1.02500	1.03000	1.04000	1.05000	1.06000
2	1.04040	1.05063	1.06090	1.08160	1.10250	1.12360
3	1.06121	1.07689	1.09273	1.12486	1.15763	1.19102
4	1.08243	1.10381	1.12551	1.16986	1.21551	1.26248
5	1.10408	1.13141	1.15927	1.21665	1.27628	1.33823
6	1.12616	1.15969	1.19405	1.26532	1.34010	1.41852
7	1.14869	1.18869	1.22987	1.31593	1.40710	1.50363
8	1.17166	1.21840	1.26677	1.36857	1.47746	1.59385
9	1.19509	1.24886	1.30477	1.42331	1.55133	1.68948
10	1.21899	1.28008	1.34392	1.48024	1.62889	1.79085
11	1.24337	1.31209	1.38423	1.53945	1.71034	1.89830
12	1.26824	1.34489	1.42576	1.60103	1.79586	2.01220
13	1.29361	1.37851	1.46853	1.66507	1.88565	2.13293
14	1.31948	1.41297	1.51259	1.73168	1.97993	2.26090
15	1.34587	1.44830	1.55797	1.80094	2.07893	2.39656
16	1.37279	1.48451	1.60471	1.87298	2.18287	2.54035
17	1.40024	1.52162	1.65285	1.94790	2.29202	2.69277
18	1.42825	1.55966	1.70243	2.02582	2.40662	2.85434
19	1.45681	1.59865	1.75351	2.10685	2.52695	3.02560
20	1.48595	1.63862	1.80611	2.19112	2.65330	3.20714
21	1.51567	1.67958	1.86029	2.27877	2.78596	3.39956
22	1.54598	1.72157	1.91610	2.36992	2.92526	3.60354
23	1.57690	1.76461	1.97359	2.46472	3.07152	3.81975
24	1.60844	1.80873	2.03279	2.56330	3.22510	4.04893
25	1.64061	1.85394	2.09378	2.66584	3.38635	4.29187
26	1.67342	1.90029	2.15659	2.77247	3.55567	4.54938
27	1.70689	1.94780	2.22129	2.88337	3.73346	4.82235
28	1.74102	1.99650	2.28793	2.99870	3.92013	5.11169
29	1.77584	2.04641	2.35657	3.11865	4.11614	5.41839
30	1.81136	2.09757	2.42726	3.24340	4.32194	5.74349
31	1.84759	2.15001	2.50008	3.37313	4.53804	6.08810
32	1.88454	2.20376	2.57508	3.50806	4.76494	6.45339
33	1.92223	2.25885	2.65234	3.64838	5.00319	6.84059
34	1.96068	2.31532	2.73191	3.79432	5.25335	7.25103
35	1.99989	2.37321	2.81386	3.94609	5.51602	7.68609
36	2.03989	2.43254	2.89828	4.10393	5.79182	8.14725
37	2.08069	2.49335	2.98523	4.26809	6.08141	8.63609
38	2.12230	2.55568	3.07478	4.43881	6.38548	9.15425
39	2.16474	2.61957	3.16703	4.61637	6.70475	9.70351
40	2.20804	2.68506	3.26204	4.80102	7.03999	10.28572

(Continues)

TABLE I Future Value of $1 (Future Value of a Single Sum) (*Continued*)

$$FV_{n,i} = (1+i)^n$$

8%	9%	10%	11%	12%	15%	(n) Periods
1.08000	1.09000	1.10000	1.11000	1.12000	1.15000	1
1.16640	1.18810	1.21000	1.23210	1.25440	1.32250	2
1.25971	1.29503	1.33100	1.36763	1.40493	1.52088	3
1.36049	1.41158	1.46410	1.51807	1.57352	1.74901	4
1.46933	1.53862	1.61051	1.68506	1.76234	2.01136	5
1.58687	1.67710	1.77156	1.87041	1.97382	2.31306	6
1.71382	1.82804	1.94872	2.07616	2.21068	2.66002	7
1.85093	1.99256	2.14359	2.30454	2.47596	3.05902	8
1.99900	2.17189	2.35795	2.55803	2.77308	3.51788	9
2.15892	2.36736	2.59374	2.83942	3.10585	4.04556	10
2.33164	2.58043	2.85312	3.15176	3.47855	4.65239	11
2.51817	2.81267	3.13843	3.49845	3.89598	5.35025	12
2.71962	3.06581	3.45227	3.88328	4.36349	6.15279	13
2.93719	3.34173	3.79750	4.31044	4.88711	7.07571	14
3.17217	3.64248	4.17725	4.78459	5.47357	8.13706	15
3.42594	3.97031	4.59497	5.31089	6.13039	9.35762	16
3.70002	4.32763	5.05447	5.89509	6.86604	10.76126	17
3.99602	4.71712	5.55992	6.54355	7.68997	12.37545	18
4.31570	5.14166	6.11591	7.26334	8.61276	14.23177	19
4.66096	5.60441	6.72750	8.06231	9.64629	16.36654	20
5.03383	6.10881	7.40025	8.94917	10.80385	18.82152	21
5.43654	6.65860	8.14028	9.93357	12.10031	21.64475	22
5.87146	7.25787	8.95430	11.02627	13.55235	24.89146	23
6.34118	7.91108	9.84973	12.23916	15.17863	28.62518	24
6.84847	8.62308	10.83471	13.58546	17.00000	32.91895	25
7.39635	9.39916	11.91818	15.07986	19.04007	37.85680	26
7.98806	10.24508	13.10999	16.73865	21.32488	43.53532	27
8.62711	11.16714	14.42099	18.57990	23.88387	50.06561	28
9.31727	12.17218	15.86309	20.62369	26.74993	57.57545	29
10.06266	13.26768	17.44940	22.89230	29.95992	66.21177	30
10.86767	14.46177	19.19434	25.41045	33.55511	76.14354	31
11.73708	15.76333	21.11378	28.20560	37.58173	87.56507	32
12.67605	17.18203	23.22515	31.30821	42.09153	100.69983	33
13.69013	18.72841	25.54767	34.75212	47.14252	115.80480	34
14.78534	20.41397	28.10244	38.57485	52.79962	133.17552	35
15.96817	22.25123	30.91268	42.81808	59.13557	153.15185	36
17.24563	24.25384	34.00395	47.52807	66.23184	176.12463	37
18.62528	26.43668	37.40434	52.75616	74.17966	202.54332	38
20.11530	28.81598	41.14479	58.55934	83.08122	232.92482	39
21.72452	31.40942	45.25926	65.00087	93.05097	267.86355	40

TABLE II Present Value of $1 (Present Value of a Single Sum)

$$PV = \frac{1}{(1+i)^n} = (1+i)^{-n}$$

(n) Periods	2%	2½%	3%	4%	5%	6%
1	.98039	.97561	.97087	.96154	.95238	.94340
2	.96117	.95181	.94260	.92456	.90703	.89000
3	.94232	.92860	.91514	.88900	.86384	.83962
4	.92385	.90595	.88849	.85480	.82270	.79209
5	.90573	.88385	.86261	.82193	.78353	.74726
6	.88797	.86230	.83748	.79031	.74622	.70496
7	.87056	.84127	.81309	.75992	.71068	.66506
8	.85349	.82075	.78941	.73069	.67684	.62741
9	.83676	.80073	.76642	.70259	.64461	.59190
10	.82035	.78120	.74409	.67556	.61391	.55839
11	.80426	.76214	.72242	.64958	.58468	.52679
12	.78849	.74356	.70138	.62460	.55684	.49697
13	.77303	.72542	.68095	.60057	.53032	.46884
14	.75788	.70773	.66112	.57748	.50507	.44230
15	.74301	.69047	.64186	.55526	.48102	.41727
16	.72845	.67362	.62317	.53391	.45811	.39365
17	.71416	.65720	.60502	.51337	.43630	.37136
18	.70016	.64117	.58739	.49363	.41552	.35034
19	.68643	.62553	.57029	.47464	.39573	.33051
20	.67297	.61027	.55368	.45639	.37689	.31180
21	.65978	.59539	.53755	.43883	.35894	.29416
22	.64684	.58086	.52189	.42196	.34185	.27751
23	.63416	.56670	.50669	.40573	.32557	.26180
24	.62172	.55288	.49193	.39012	.31007	.24698
25	.60953	.53939	.47761	.37512	.29530	.23300
26	.59758	.52623	.46369	.36069	.28124	.21981
27	.58586	.51340	.45019	.34682	.26785	.20737
28	.57437	.50088	.43708	.33348	.25509	.19563
29	.56311	.48866	.42435	.32065	.24295	.18456
30	.55207	.47674	.41199	.30832	.23138	.17411
31	.54125	.46511	.39999	.29646	.22036	.16425
32	.53063	.45377	.38834	.28506	.20987	.15496
33	.52023	.44270	.37703	.27409	.19987	.14619
34	.51003	.43191	.36604	.26355	.19035	.13791
35	.50003	.42137	.35538	.25342	.18129	.13011
36	.49022	.41109	.34503	.24367	.17266	.12274
37	.48061	.40107	.33498	.23430	.16444	.11579
38	.47119	.39128	.32523	.22529	.15661	.10924
39	.46195	.38174	.31575	.21662	.14915	.10306
40	.45289	.37243	.30656	.20829	.14205	.09722

(Continues)

TABLE II Present Value of $1 (Present Value of a Single Sum) (*Continued*)

$$PV = \frac{1}{(1+i)^n} = (1+i)^{-n}$$

8%	9%	10%	11%	12%	15%	(n) Periods
.92593	.91743	.90909	.90090	.89286	.86957	1
.85734	.84168	.82645	.81162	.79719	.75614	2
.79383	.77218	.75132	.73119	.71178	.65752	3
.73503	.70843	.68301	.65873	.63552	.57175	4
.68058	.64993	.62092	.59345	.56743	.49718	5
.63017	.59627	.56447	.53464	.50663	.43233	6
.58349	.54703	.51316	.48166	.45235	.37594	7
.54027	.50187	.46651	.43393	.40388	.32690	8
.50025	.46043	.42410	.39092	.36061	.28426	9
.46319	.42241	.38554	.35218	.32197	.24719	10
.42888	.38753	.35049	.31728	.28748	.21494	11
.39711	.35554	.31863	.28584	.25668	.18691	12
.36770	.32618	.28966	.25751	.22917	.16253	13
.34046	.29925	.26333	.23199	.20462	.14133	14
.31524	.27454	.23939	.20900	.18270	.12289	15
.29189	.25187	.21763	.18829	.16312	.10687	16
.27027	.23107	.19785	.16963	.14564	.09293	17
.25025	.21199	.17986	.15282	.13004	.08081	18
.23171	.19449	.16351	.13768	.11611	.07027	19
.21455	.17843	.14864	.12403	.10367	.06110	20
.19866	.16370	.13513	.11174	.09256	.05313	21
.18394	.15018	.12285	.10067	.08264	.04620	22
.17032	.13778	.11168	.09069	.07379	.04017	23
.15770	.12641	.10153	.08170	.06588	.03493	24
.14602	.11597	.09230	.07361	.05882	.03038	25
.13520	.10639	.08391	.06631	.05252	.02642	26
.12519	.09761	.07628	.05974	.04689	.02297	27
.11591	.08955	.06934	.05382	.04187	.01997	28
.10733	.08216	.06304	.04849	.03738	.01737	29
.09938	.07537	.05731	.04368	.03338	.01510	30
.09202	.06915	.05210	.03935	.02980	.01313	31
.08520	.06344	.04736	.03545	.02661	.01142	32
.07889	.05820	.04306	.03194	.02376	.00993	33
.07305	.05340	.03914	.02878	.02121	.00864	34
.06763	.04899	.03558	.02592	.01894	.00751	35
.06262	.04494	.03235	.02335	.01691	.00653	36
.05799	.04123	.02941	.02104	.01510	.00568	37
.05369	.03783	.02674	.01896	.01348	.00494	38
.04971	.03470	.02430	.01708	.01204	.00429	39
.04603	.03184	.02210	.01538	.01075	.00373	40

TABLE III Future Value of an Ordinary Annuity of $1

$$FV, OA_{n,i} = \frac{(1+i)^n - 1}{i}$$

(n) Periods	2%	2½%	3%	4%	5%	6%
1	1.00000	1.00000	1.00000	1.00000	1.00000	1.00000
2	2.02000	2.02500	2.03000	2.04000	2.05000	2.06000
3	3.06040	3.07563	3.09090	3.12160	3.15250	3.18360
4	4.12161	4.15252	4.18363	4.24646	4.31013	4.37462
5	5.20404	5.25633	5.30914	5.41632	5.52563	5.63709
6	6.30812	6.38774	6.46841	6.63298	6.80191	6.97532
7	7.43428	7.54743	7.66246	7.89829	8.14201	8.39384
8	8.58297	8.73612	8.89234	9.21423	9.54911	9.89747
9	9.75463	9.95452	10.15911	10.58280	10.02656	11.49132
10	10.94972	11.20338	11.46338	12.00611	12.57789	13.18079
11	12.16872	12.48347	12.80780	13.48635	14.20679	14.97164
12	13.41209	13.79555	14.19203	15.02581	15.91713	16.86994
13	14.68033	15.14044	15.61779	16.62684	17.71298	18.88214
14	15.97394	16.51895	17.08632	18.29191	19.59863	21.01507
15	17.29342	17.93193	18.59891	20.02359	21.57856	23.27597
16	18.63929	19.38022	20.15688	21.82453	23.65749	25.67253
17	20.01207	20.86473	21.76159	23.69751	25.84037	28.21288
18	21.41231	22.38635	23.41444	25.64541	28.13238	30.90565
19	22.84056	23.94601	25.11687	27.67123	30.53900	33.75999
20	24.29737	25.54466	26.87037	29.77808	33.06595	36.78559
21	25.78332	27.18327	28.67649	31.96920	35.71925	39.99273
22	27.29898	28.86286	30.53678	34.24797	38.50521	43.39229
23	28.84496	30.58443	32.45288	36.61789	41.43048	46.99583
24	30.42186	32.34904	34.42647	39.08260	44.50200	50.81558
25	32.03030	34.15776	36.45926	41.64591	47.72710	54.86451
26	33.67091	36.01171	38.55304	44.31174	51.11345	59.15638
27	35.34432	37.91200	40.70963	47.08421	54.66913	63.70577
28	37.05121	39.85980	42.93092	49.96758	58.40258	68.52811
29	38.79223	41.85630	45.21885	52.96629	62.32271	73.63980
30	40.56808	43.90270	47.57542	56.08494	66.43885	79.05819
31	42.37944	46.00027	50.00268	59.32834	70.76079	84.80168
32	44.22703	48.15028	52.50276	62.70147	75.29883	90.88978
33	46.11157	50.35403	55.07784	66.20953	80.06377	97.34316
34	48.03380	52.61289	57.73018	69.85791	85.06696	104.18376
35	49.99448	54.92821	60.46208	73.65222	90.32031	111.43478
36	51.99437	57.30141	63.27594	77.59831	95.53632	119.12087
37	54.03425	59.73395	66.17422	81.70225	101.62814	127.26812
38	56.11494	62.22730	69.15945	85.97034	107.70955	135.90421
39	58.23724	64.78298	72.23423	90.40915	114.09502	145.05846
40	60.40198	67.40255	75.40126	95.02552	120.79977	154.76197

(*Continues*)

TABLE III Future Value of an Ordinary Annuity of $1 (*Continued*)

$$FV, OA_{n,i} = \frac{(1+i)^n - 1}{i}$$

8%	9%	10%	11%	12%	15%	(n) Periods
1.00000	1.00000	1.00000	1.00000	1.00000	1.00000	1
2.08000	2.09000	2.10000	2.11000	2.12000	2.15000	2
3.24640	3.27810	3.31000	3.34210	3.37440	3.47250	3
4.50611	4.57313	4.64100	4.70973	4.77933	4.99338	4
5.86660	5.98471	6.10510	6.22780	6.35285	6.74238	5
7.33592	7.52334	7.71561	7.91286	8.11519	8.75374	6
8.92280	9.20044	9.48717	9.78327	10.08901	11.06680	7
10.63663	11.02847	11.43589	11.85943	12.29969	13.72682	8
12.48756	13.02104	13.57948	14.16397	14.77566	16.78584	9
14.48656	15.19293	15.93743	16.72201	17.54874	20.30372	10
16.64549	17.56029	18.53117	19.56143	20.65458	24.34928	11
18.97713	20.14072	21.38428	22.71319	24.13313	29.00167	12
21.49530	22.95339	24.52271	26.21164	28.02911	34.35192	13
24.21492	26.01919	27.97498	30.09492	32.39260	40.50471	14
27.15211	29.36092	31.77248	34.40536	37.27972	47.58041	15
30.32428	33.00340	35.94973	39.18995	42.75328	55.71747	16
33.75023	36.97371	40.54470	44.50084	48.88367	65.07509	17
37.45024	41.30134	45.59917	50.39593	55.74972	75.83636	18
41.44026	46.01846	51.15909	56.93949	63.43968	88.21181	19
45.76196	51.16012	57.27500	64.20283	72.05244	102.44358	20
50.42292	56.76453	64.00250	72.26514	81.69874	118.81012	21
55.45676	62.87334	71.40275	81.21431	92.50258	137.63164	22
60.89330	69.53194	79.54302	91.14788	104.60289	159.27638	23
66.76476	76.78981	88.49733	102.17415	118.15524	184.16784	24
73.10594	84.70090	98.34706	114.41331	133.33387	212.79302	25
79.95442	93.32398	109.18177	127.99877	150.33393	245.71197	26
87.35077	102.72314	121.09994	143.07864	169.37401	283.56877	27
95.33883	112.96822	134.20994	159.81729	190.37401	327.10408	28
103.96594	124.13536	148.63093	178.39719	214.58275	377.16969	29
113.28321	136.30754	164.49402	199.02088	241.33268	434.74515	30
123.34587	149.57522	181.94343	221.9137	271.29261	500.95692	31
134.21354	164.03699	201.13777	247.32362	304.84772	577.10046	32
145.95062	179.80032	222.25154	275.52922	342.42945	644.66553	33
158.62667	196.98234	245.47670	306.83744	384.52098	765.36535	34
172.31680	215.71076	271.02437	341.58955	431.66350	881.17016	35
187.10215	236.12472	299.12681	380.16441	484.46312	1014.34568	36
203.07032	258.37595	330.03949	422.98249	543.59869	1167.49753	37
220.31595	282.62978	364.04343	470.51056	609.83053	1343.62216	38
238.94122	309.06646	401.44778	523.26673	684.01020	1546.16549	39
259.05652	337.88245	442.59256	581.82607	767.09142	1779.09031	40

TABLE IV Present Value of an Ordinary Annuity of $1

$$PV, OA_{n,i} = \frac{1 - \frac{1}{(1+i)^n}}{i}$$

(n) Periods	2%	2½%	3%	4%	5%	6%
1	.98039	.97561	.97087	.96154	.95238	.94340
2	1.94156	1.92742	1.91347	1.88609	1.85941	1.83339
3	2.88388	2.85602	2.82861	2.77509	2.72325	2.67301
4	3.80773	3.76197	3.71710	3.62990	3.54595	3.46511
5	4.71346	4.64583	4.57971	4.45182	4.32948	4.21236
6	5.60143	5.50813	5.41719	5.24214	5.07569	4.91732
7	6.47199	6.34939	6.23028	6.00205	5.78637	5.58238
8	7.32548	7.17014	7.01969	6.73274	6.46321	6.20979
9	8.16224	7.97087	7.78611	7.43533	7.10782	6.80169
10	8.98259	8.75206	8.53020	8.11090	7.72173	7.36009
11	9.78685	9.51421	9.25262	8.76048	8.30641	7.88687
12	10.57534	10.25776	9.95400	9.38507	8.86325	8.38384
13	11.34837	10.98319	10.63496	9.98565	9.39357	8.85268
14	12.10625	11.69091	11.29607	10.56312	9.89864	9.29498
15	12.84926	12.38138	11.93794	11.11839	10.379966	9.71225
16	13.57771	13.05500	12.56110	11.65230	10.83777	10.10590
17	14.29187	13.71220	13.16612	12.16567	11.27407	10.47726
18	14.99203	14.35336	13.75351	12.65930	11.68959	10.82760
19	15.67846	14.97889	14.32380	13.13394	12.08532	11.15812
20	16.35143	15.58916	14.87747	13.59033	12.46221	11.46992
21	17.01121	16.18455	15.41502	14.02916	12.82115	11.76408
22	17.65805	16.76541	15.93692	14.45112	13.16300	12.04158
23	18.29220	17.33211	16.44361	14.85684	13.48857	12.30338
24	18.91393	17.88499	16.93554	15.24696	13.79864	12.55036
25	19.52346	18.42438	17.41315	15.62208	14.09394	12.78336
26	20.12104	18.95061	17.87684	15.98277	14.37519	13.00317
27	20.70690	19.46401	18.32703	16.32959	14.64303	13.21053
28	21.28127	19.96489	18.76411	16.66306	14.89813	13.40618
29	21.84438	20.45355	19.18845	16.98371	15.14107	13.59072
30	22.39646	20.93029	19.60044	17.29203	15.37245	13.76483
31	22.93770	21.39541	20.00043	17.58849	15.59281	13.92909
32	23.46833	21.84918	20.38877	17.87355	15.80268	14.08404
33	23.98856	22.29188	20.76579	18.14765	16.00255	14.23023
34	24.49859	22.72379	21.13184	18.41120	16.19290	14.36814
35	24.99862	23.14516	21.48722	18.66461	16.37419	14.49825
36	25.48884	23.55625	21.83225	18.90828	16.54685	14.62099
37	25.96945	23.95732	22.16724	19.14258	16.71129	14.73678
38	26.44064	24.34860	22.49246	19.36786	16.86789	14.84602
39	26.90259	24.73034	22.80822	19.58448	17.01704	14.94907
40	27.35548	25.10278	23.11477	19.79277	17.15909	15.04630

(Continues)

TABLE IV Present Value of an Ordinary Annuity of $1 (*Continued*)

$$PV, OA_{n,i} = \frac{1 - \frac{1}{(1+i)^n}}{i}$$

8%	9%	10%	11%	12%	15%	(n) Periods
.92593	.91743	.90909	.90090	.89286	.86957	1
1.78326	1.75911	1.73554	1.71252	1.69005	1.62571	2
2.57710	2.53130	2.48685	2.44371	2.40183	2.28323	3
3.31213	3.23972	3.16986	3.10245	3.03735	2.85498	4
3.99271	3.88965	3.79079	3.69590	3.60478	3.35216	5
4.62288	4.48592	4.35526	4.23054	4.11141	3.78448	6
5.20637	5.03295	4.86842	4.71220	4.56376	4.16042	7
5.74664	5.53482	5.33493	5.14612	4.96764	4.48732	8
6.24689	5.99525	5.75902	5.53705	5.32825	4.77158	9
6.71008	6.41766	6.14457	5.88923	5.65022	5.01877	10
7.13896	6.80519	6.49506	6.20652	5.93770	5.23371	11
7.53608	7.16073	6.81369	6.49236	6.19437	5.42962	12
7.90378	7.48690	7.10336	6.74987	6.42355	5.58315	13
8.24424	7.78615	7.36669	6.98187	6.62817	5.72448	14
8.55948	8.06069	7.60608	7.19087	6.81086	5.84737	15
8.85137	8.31256	7.82371	7.37916	6.97399	5.95424	16
9.12164	8.54363	8.02155	7.54879	7.11963	6.04716	17
9.37189	8.75563	8.20141	7.70162	7.24967	6.12797	18
9.60360	8.95012	8.36492	7.83929	7.36578	6.19823	19
9.81815	9.12855	8.51356	7.96333	7.46944	6.25933	20
10.01680	9.29224	8.64869	8.07507	7.56200	6.31246	21
10.20074	9.44243	8.77154	8.17574	7.64465	6.35866	22
10.37106	9.58021	8.88322	8.26643	7.71843	6.39884	23
10.52876	9.70661	8.98474	8.34814	7.78432	6.43377	24
10.67478	9.82258	9.07704	8.42174	7.84314	6.46415	25
10.80998	9.92897	9.16095	8.48806	7.89566	6.49056	26
10.93516	10.02658	9.23722	8.54780	7.94255	6.51353	27
11.05108	10.11613	9.30657	8.60162	7.98442	6.53351	28
11.15841	10.19828	9.36961	8.65011	8.02181	6.55088	29
11.25778	10.27365	9.42691	8.69379	8.05518	6.56598	30
11.34980	10.34280	9.47901	8.73315	8.08499	6.57911	31
11.43500	10.40624	9.52638	8.76860	8.11159	6.59053	32
11.51389	10.46444	9.56943	8.80054	8.13535	6.60046	33
11.58693	10.51784	9.60858	8.82932	8.15656	6.60910	34
11.65457	10.56682	9.64416	8.85524	8.17550	6.61661	35
11.71719	10.61176	9.67651	8.87859	8.19241	6.62314	36
11.75518	10.65299	9.70592	8.89963	8.20751	6.62882	37
11.82887	10.69082	9.73265	8.91859	8.22099	6.63375	38
11.87858	10.72552	9.75697	8.93567	8.23303	6.63805	39
11.92461	10.75736	9.77905	8.95105	8.24378	6.64178	40

Index

S